STREET ATLAS

Gloucestershire

South Gloucestershire and Bristol

www.philips-maps.co.uk

First published in 2001 by

Philip's, a division of
Octopus Publishing Group Ltd
www.octopusbooks.co.uk
2-4 Heron Quays, London E14 4JP
An Hachette Livre UK Company

Second edition 2005
Third impression 2008
GLOBB

ISBN-10 0-540-08760-2 (spiral)
ISBN-13 978-0-540-08760-0 (spiral)

Printed by Toppan, China

Contents

III **Key to map symbols**

IV **Key to map pages**

VI **Route planning**

X **Administrative and Postcode boundaries**

1 **Street maps** at 3½ inches to 1 mile

140 **Street maps** at 1¾ inches to 1 mile

190 **Street maps** at 3½ inches to 1 mile

193 **Street maps of centres of Cheltenham, Bristol and Gloucester** at 7 inches to 1 mile

197 **Index** of towns and villages

201 **Index** of streets, hospitals, industrial estates, railway stations, schools, shopping centres, universities and places of interest

Digital Data

The exceptionally high-quality mapping found in this atlas is available as digital data in TIFF format, which is easily convertible to other bitmapped (raster) image formats.

The index is also available in digital form as a standard database table. It contains all the details found in the printed index together with the National Grid reference for the map square in which each entry is named.

For further information and to discuss your requirements, please contact james.mann@philips-maps.co.uk

Key to map symbols

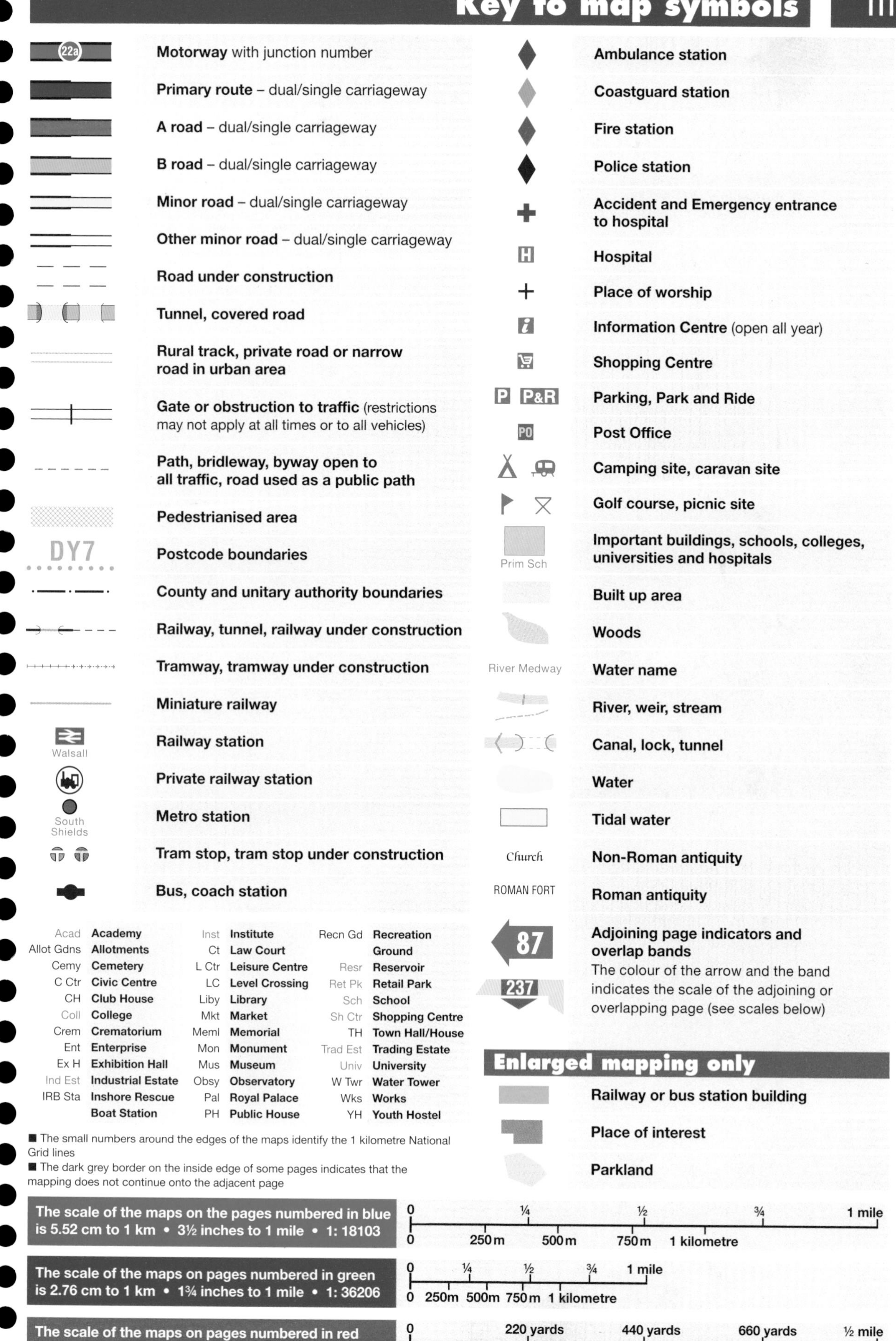

Acad	Academy	Inst	Institute	Recn Gd	Recreation Ground
Allot Gdns	Allotments	Ct	Law Court	Resr	Reservoir
Cemy	Cemetery	L Ctr	Leisure Centre	Ret Pk	Retail Park
C Ctr	Civic Centre	LC	Level Crossing	Sch	School
CH	Club House	Liby	Library	Sh Ctr	Shopping Centre
Coll	College	Mkt	Market	TH	Town Hall/House
Crem	Crematorium	Meml	Memorial	Trad Est	Trading Estate
Ent	Enterprise	Mon	Monument	Univ	University
Ex H	Exhibition Hall	Mus	Museum	W Twr	Water Tower
Ind Est	Industrial Estate	Obsy	Observatory	Wks	Works
IRB Sta	Inshore Rescue Boat Station	Pal	Royal Palace	YH	Youth Hostel
		PH	Public House		

■ The small numbers around the edges of the maps identify the 1 kilometre National Grid lines

■ The dark grey border on the inside edge of some pages indicates that the mapping does not continue onto the adjacent page

Enlarged mapping only

Railway or bus station building

Place of interest

Parkland

The scale of the maps on the pages numbered in blue is 5.52 cm to 1 km • 3½ inches to 1 mile • 1: 18103

The scale of the maps on pages numbered in green is 2.76 cm to 1 km • 1¾ inches to 1 mile • 1: 36206

The scale of the maps on pages numbered in red is 11.04 cm to 1 km • 7 inches to 1 mile • 1: 9051

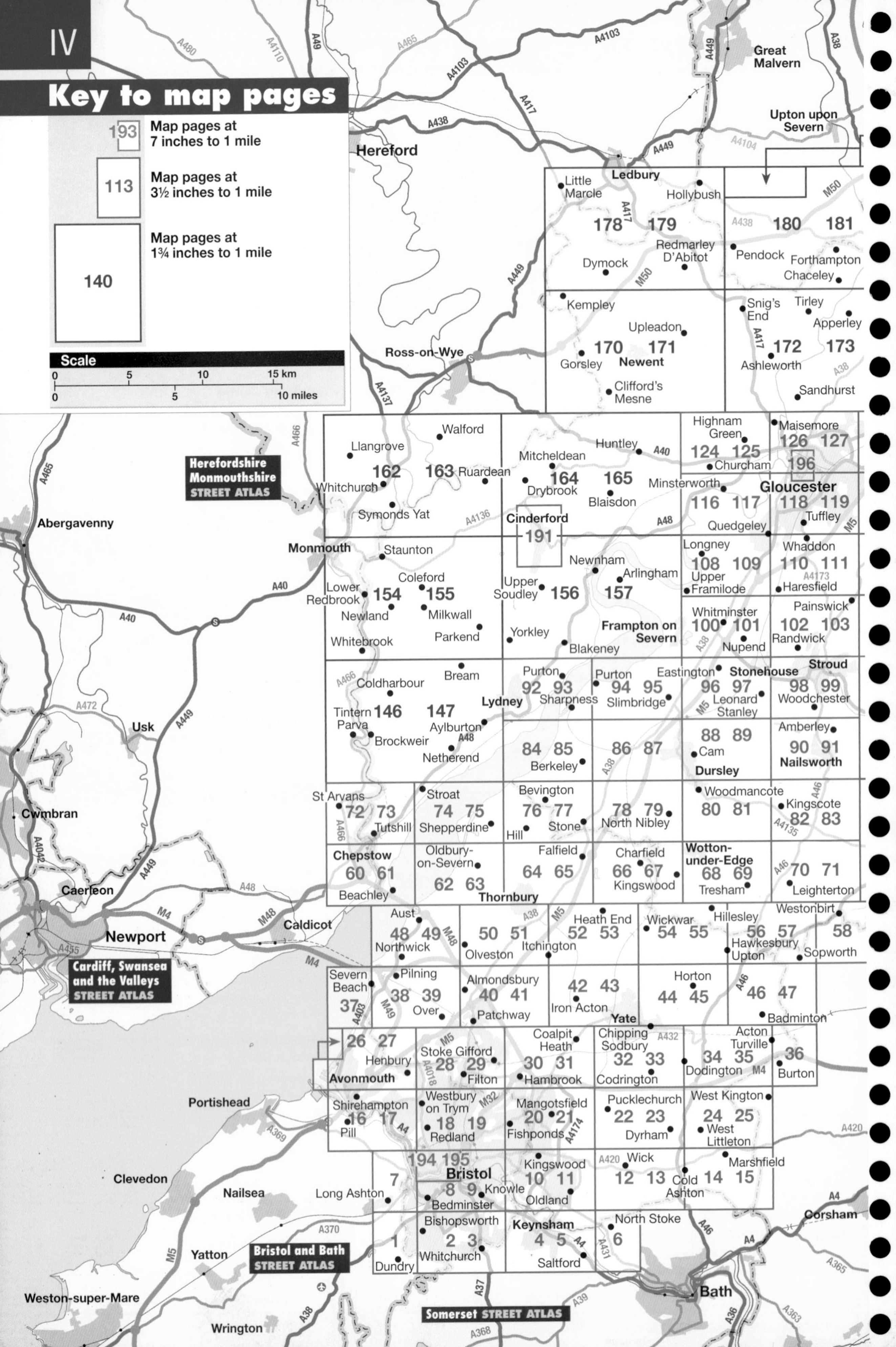
IV
Key to map pages
193 Map pages at 7 inches to 1 mile
113 Map pages at 3½ inches to 1 mile
140 Map pages at 1¾ inches to 1 mile
Scale
0 5 10 15 km
0 5 10 miles
Herefordshire Monmouthshire STREET ATLAS
Cardiff, Swansea and the Valleys STREET ATLAS
Bristol and Bath STREET ATLAS
Somerset STREET ATLAS
Hereford
Great Malvern
Upton upon Severn
Ledbury
Little Marcle
Hollybush
178 179 180 181
Redmarley D'Abitot
Pendock
Forthampton
Chaceley
Dymock
Kempley
Upleadon
Snig's End
Tirley
Apperley
170 171 172 173
Gorsley
Newent
Ashleworth
Clifford's Mesne
Sandhurst
Ross-on-Wye
Walford
Llangrove
Mitcheldean
Huntley
Highnam Green
Maisemore
162 163 164 165 124 125 126 127
Ruardean
Churcham
196
Whitchurch
Drybrook
Blaisdon
Minsterworth
Gloucester
116 117 118 119
Symonds Yat
Cinderford
191
Quedgeley
Tuffley
Abergavenny
Monmouth
Staunton
Newnham
Longney
Whaddon
108 109 110 111
Coleford
Arlingham
Upper Framilode
Haresfield
Lower Redbrook
154 155 156 157
Upper Soudley
Newland
Milkwall
Whitminster
Painswick
100 101 102 103
Parkend
Yorkley
Frampton on Severn
Whitebrook
Blakeney
Nupend
Randwick
Coldharbour
Bream
Purton
Eastington
Stonehouse
Stroud
92 93 94 95 96 97 98 99
Sharpness
Slimbridge
Leonard Stanley
Woodchester
Lydney
Tintern Parva
146 147
Aylburton
Brockweir
Usk
88 89
Amberley
84 85 86 87
Cam
90 91
Netherend
Berkeley
Dursley
Nailsworth
St Arvans
Stroat
Bevington
Woodmancote
Kingscote
72 73 74 75 76 77 78 79 80 81 82 83
Cwmbran
Tutshill
Shepperdine
Hill
Stone
North Nibley
Chepstow
Oldbury-on-Severn
Falfield
Charfield
Wotton-under-Edge
60 61 62 63 64 65 66 67 68 69 70 71
Kingswood
Tresham
Leighterton
Caerleon
Beachley
Thornbury
Newport
Caldicot
Aust
Heath End
Wickwar
Hillesley
Westonbirt
48 49 50 51 52 53 54 55 56 57 58
Northwick
Olveston
Itchington
Hawkesbury Upton
Sopworth
Severn Beach
Pilning
Almondsbury
Horton
38 39 40 41 42 43 44 45 46 47
37
Over
Patchway
Iron Acton
Yate
Badminton
Coalpit Heath
Chipping Sodbury
Acton Turville
26 27 28 29 30 31 32 33 34 35 36
Henbury
Stoke Gifford
Avonmouth
Filton
Hambrook
Codrington
Dodington
Burton
Portishead
Westbury on Trym
Mangotsfield
Pucklechurch
West Kington
Shirehampton
16 17 18 19 20 21 22 23 24 25
Pill
Redland
Fishponds
Dyrham
West Littleton
194 195
Kingswood
Wick
Marshfield
Clevedon
Bristol
7 8 9 10 11 12 13 14 15
Nailsea
Long Ashton
Knowle
Oldland
Cold Ashton
Bedminster
Corsham
Bishopsworth
Keynsham
North Stoke
1 2 3 4 5 6
Yatton
Whitchurch
Saltford
Dundry
Bath
Weston-super-Mare
Wrington

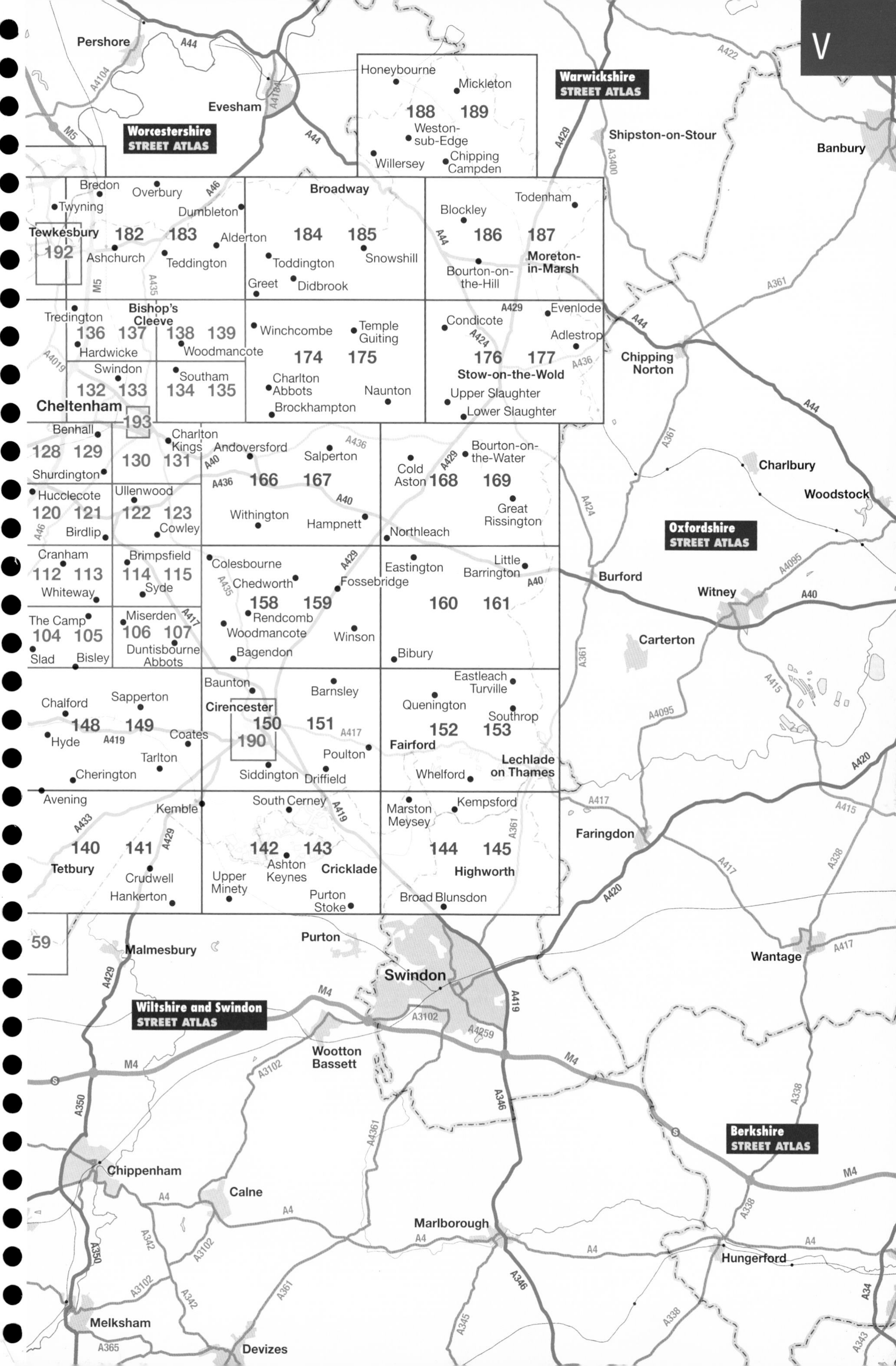
Worcestershire STREET ATLAS
Warwickshire STREET ATLAS
Oxfordshire STREET ATLAS
Wiltshire and Swindon STREET ATLAS
Berkshire STREET ATLAS
Pershore
Evesham
Honeybourne
Mickleton
188 189
Weston-sub-Edge
Willersey
Chipping Campden
Shipston-on-Stour
Banbury
Bredon
Overbury
Twyning
Dumbleton
Broadway
Todenham
Blockley
Tewkesbury
192
182 183
Alderton
184 185
186 187
Ashchurch
Teddington
Toddington
Snowshill
Bourton-on-the-Hill
Moreton-in-Marsh
Greet
Didbrook
Tredington
Bishop's Cleeve
Condicote
Evenlode
136 137
138 139
Winchcombe
Temple Guiting
Adlestrop
Hardwicke
Woodmancote
174 175
176 177
Chipping Norton
Swindon
Southam
Charlton Abbots
Stow-on-the-Wold
132 133
134 135
Naunton
Upper Slaughter
Cheltenham
193
Brockhampton
Lower Slaughter
Benhall
Charlton Kings
Andoversford
Salperton
Bourton-on-the-Water
128 129
130 131
Cold Aston
168 169
Charlbury
Shurdington
166 167
Woodstock
Hucclecote
Ullenwood
Withington
Great Rissington
120 121
122 123
Hampnett
Birdlip
Cowley
Northleach
Cranham
Brimpsfield
Colesbourne
Eastington
Little Barrington
112 113
114 115
Chedworth
Fossebridge
Burford
Witney
Whiteway
Syde
158 159
160 161
Miserden
Rendcomb
The Camp
104 105
106 107
Woodmancote
Winson
Carterton
Slad
Bisley
Duntisbourne Abbots
Bagendon
Bibury
Baunton
Barnsley
Eastleach Turville
Chalford
Sapperton
Cirencester
Quenington
148 149
150 151
Southrop
Hyde
Coates
190
152 153
Tarlton
Poulton
Fairford
Lechlade on Thames
Cherington
Siddington
Driffield
Whelford
Avening
Kemble
South Cerney
Marston Meysey
Kempsford
Faringdon
140 141
142 143
144 145
Tetbury
Ashton Keynes
Cricklade
Highworth
Crudwell
Upper Minety
Hankerton
Purton Stoke
Broad Blunsdon
59
Purton
Malmesbury
Swindon
Wantage
Wootton Bassett
Chippenham
Calne
Marlborough
Hungerford
Melksham
Devizes
M5
M4
A44
A4104
A4184
A46
A435
A4019
A40
A436
A429
A424
A417
A419
A433
A361
A4095
A415
A420
A338
A422
A3400
A3102
A4259
A346
A4361
A350
A4
A342
A345
A34
A343
A365

Route planning

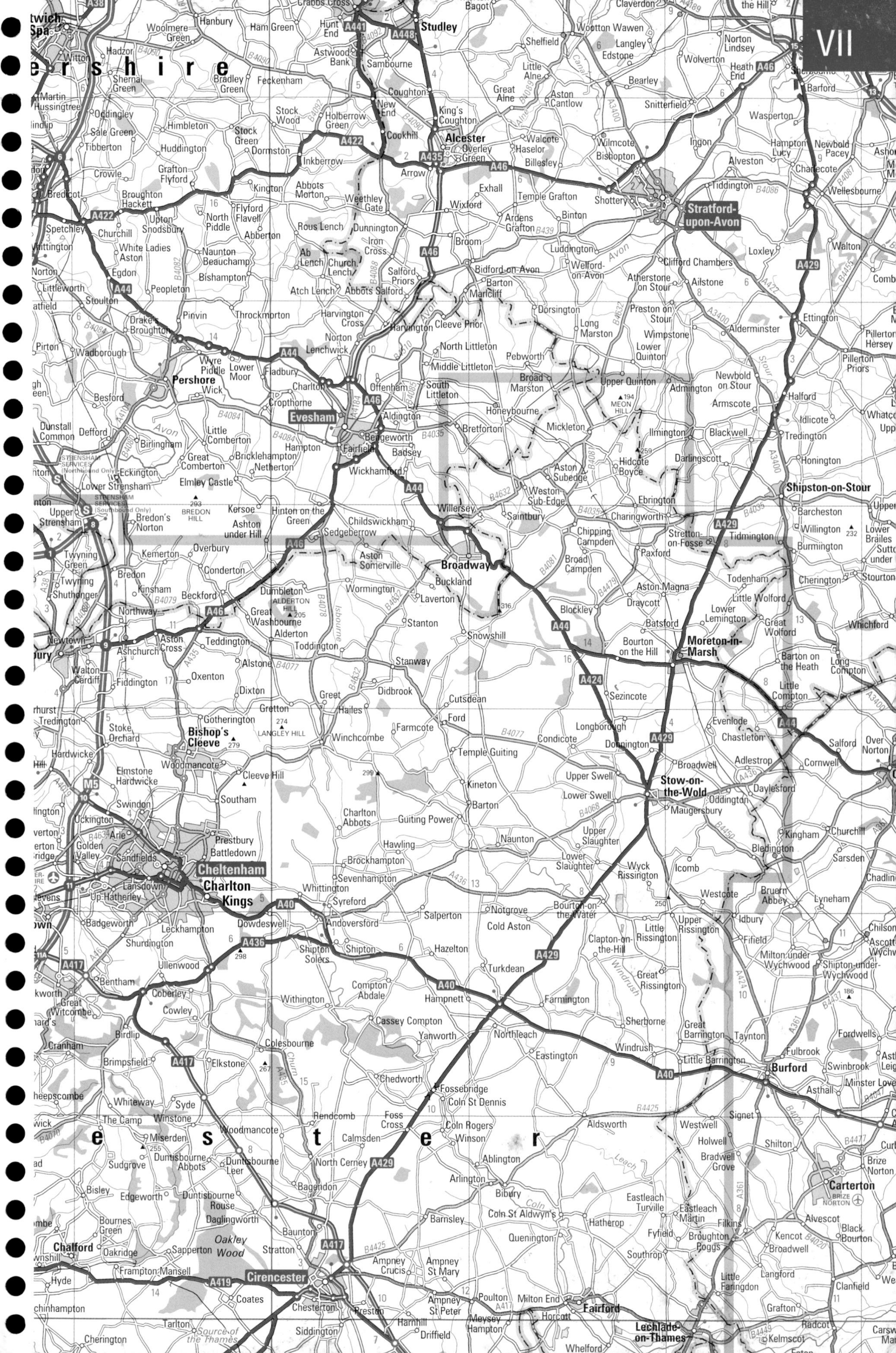
VII
ershire
Gloucester
Crabbs Cross
Studley
Mappleborough Green
Claverdon
Hanbury
Woolmere Green
Ham Green
Hunt End
Wootton Wawen
Shelfield
Langley
Edstone
Norton Lindsey
Wolverton
Heath End
Barford
Hadzor
Astwood Bank
Sambourne
Little Alne
Bearley
Sherrifs Green
Bradley Green
Feckenham
Coughton
Great Alne
Aston Cantlow
Snitterfield
Martin Hussingtree
Oddingley
Himbleton
Stock Wood
Holberrow Green
New End
King's Coughton
Wasperton
Sale Green
Stock Green
Cookhill
Alcester
Walcote
Wilmcote
Ingon
Hampton Lucy
Newbold Pacey
Tibberton
Huddington
Dormston
Inkberrow
Arrow
Oversley Green
Haselor
Billesley
Bishopton
Alveston
Charlecote
Crowle
Grafton Flyford
Kington
Abbots Morton
Exhall
Temple Grafton
Shottery
Tiddington
Wellesbourne
Bredicot
Broughton Hackett
Flyford Flavell
Weethley Gate
Wixford
Ardens Grafton
Binton
Stratford-upon-Avon
Spetchley
Churchill
Upton Snodsbury
North Piddle
Abberton
Rous Lench
Dunnington
Iron Cross
Broom
Luddington
Loxley
Walton
White Ladies Aston
Naunton Beauchamp
Ab Lench
Church Lench
Salford Priors
Bidford-on-Avon
Welford-on-Avon
Clifford Chambers
Norton
Egdon
Bishampton
Atherstone on Stour
Ailstone
Littleworth
Stoulton
Peopleton
Atch Lench
Abbots Salford
Barton
Marlcliff
Dorsington
Preston on Stour
Ettington
Pinvin
Throckmorton
Harvington Cross
Harvington
Cleeve Prior
Long Marston
Wimpstone
Alderminster
Drake's Broughton
Pirton
Wadborough
Wyre Piddle
Lower Moor
Norton
Lenchwick
North Littleton
Pebworth
Lower Quinton
Pillerton Hersey
Pillerton Priors
Pershore
Fladbury
Middle Littleton
Broad Marston
Upper Quinton
Newbold on Stour
Admington
Wick
Charlton
Offenham
South Littleton
Besford
Cropthorne
Evesham
Aldington
Honeybourne
Meon Hill
Armscote
Halford
Idlicote
Dunstall Common
Defford
Birlingham
Little Comberton
Hampton
Bengeworth
Bretforton
Mickleton
Ilmington
Blackwell
Tredington
Great Comberton
Bricklehampton
Netherton
Fairfield
Badsey
Aston Subedge
Hidcote Boyce
Darlingscott
Honington
Strensham Services (Northbound Only)
Eckington
Lower Strensham
Elmley Castle
Wickhamford
Weston-Sub-Edge
Ebrington
Shipston-on-Stour
Strensham Services (Southbound Only)
Upper Strensham
Bredon Hill
Bredon's Norton
Kersoe
Ashton under Hill
Hinton on the Green
Childswickham
Sedgeberrow
Willersey
Saintbury
Chipping Campden
Charingworth
Barcheston
Willington
Stretton-on-Fosse
Tidmington
Burmington
Lower Brailes
Sutton under Brailes
Twyning Green
Twyning
Kemerton
Overbury
Conderton
Aston Somerville
Broadway
Broad Campden
Paxford
Todenham
Cherington
Stourton
Bredon
Shuthonger
Kinsham
Beckford
Dumbleton
Wormington
Buckland
Laverton
Aston Magna
Draycott
Little Wolford
Northway
Great Washbourne
Alderton Hill
Alderton
Stanton
Blockley
Batsford
Lower Lemington
Great Wolford
Whichford
Newtown
Ashchurch
Aston Cross
Teddington
Toddington
Snowshill
Bourton on the Hill
Moreton-in-Marsh
Barton on the Heath
Long Compton
Walton Cardiff
Fiddington
Oxenton
Alstone
Stanway
Dixton
Didbrook
Sezincote
Little Compton
Tredington
Gretton
Greet
Hailes
Cutsdean
Ford
Stoke Orchard
Gotherington
Langley Hill
Winchcombe
Farmcote
Condicote
Longborough
Evenlode
Chastleton
Salford
Over Norton
Bishop's Cleeve
Temple Guiting
Donnington
Adlestrop
Cornwell
Hardwicke
Woodmancote
Elmstone Hardwicke
Cleeve Hill
Kineton
Upper Swell
Broadwell
Stow-on-the-Wold
Daylesford
Swindon
Southam
Barton
Lower Swell
Oddington
Maugersbury
Uckington
Arle
Golden Valley
Prestbury
Battledown
Charlton Abbots
Guiting Power
Naunton
Upper Slaughter
Kingham
Churchill
Sarsden
Sandfields
Cheltenham
Hawling
Brockhampton
Lower Slaughter
Wyck Rissington
Icomb
Bledington
Lansdown
Up Hatherley
Charlton Kings
Sevenhampton
Whittington
Syreford
Westcote
Bruern Abbey
Lyneham
Chadlington
Badgeworth
Leckhampton
Dowdeswell
Andoversford
Salperton
Notgrove
Cold Aston
Bourton-on-the-Water
Little Rissington
Upper Rissington
Idbury
Fifield
Chilson
Shurdington
Shipton Solers
Shipton
Hazelton
Clapton-on-the-Hill
Milton under Wychwood
Shipton-under-Wychwood
Ascott-under-Wychwood
Bentham
Ullenwood
Compton Abdale
Turkdean
Great Rissington
Great Witcombe
Coberley
Cowley
Withington
Hampnett
Farmington
Birdlip
Cassey Compton
Yanworth
Northleach
Sherborne
Great Barrington
Taynton
Fordwells
Cranham
Colesbourne
Windrush
Fulbrook
Brimpsfield
Elkstone
Eastington
Little Barrington
Burford
Swinbrook
Minster Lovell
Asthall
Chedworth
Fossebridge
Coln St Dennis
Sheepscombe
Whiteway
Syde
Signet
The Camp
Winstone
Rendcomb
Foss Cross
Coln Rogers
Aldsworth
Westwell
Miserden
Woodmancote
Calmsden
Winson
Holwell
Shilton
Duntisbourne Abbots
Duntisbourne Leer
North Cerney
Ablington
Bradwell Grove
Brize Norton
Sudgrove
Bisley
Edgeworth
Duntisbourne Rouse
Bagendon
Arlington
Bibury
Carterton
Brize Norton
Daglingworth
Eastleach Turville
Eastleach Martin
Bournes Green
Oakley Wood
Barnsley
Coln St Aldwyn's
Hatherop
Filkins
Alvescot
Black Bourton
Chalford
Oakridge
Sapperton
Baunton
Stratton
Quenington
Fyfield
Broughton Poggs
Kencot
Broadwell
Frampton Mansell
Cirencester
Ampney Crucis
Ampney St Mary
Southrop
Hyde
Coates
Langford
Little Faringdon
Clanfield
Chesterton
Preston
Ampney St Peter
Poulton
Milton End
Fairford
Grafton
Tarlton
Source of the Thames
Siddington
Harnhill
Driffield
Meysey Hampton
Horcott
Lechlade-on-Thames
Radcot
Kelmscot
Cherington
Whelford
Eaton
Avon
Isbourne
Windrush
Coln
Leach
Churn
Stour
A38
A441
A448
A422
A435
A46
A44
A4184
A429
A424
A40
A436
A435
A417
A419
A361
A3400
M5
B4090
B4092
B4089
B4086
B4088
B4084
B4035
B4632
B4081
B4479
B4077
B4078
B4068
B4450
B4425
B4437
B4020
B4477
B4449
B4070

St Briavels
Llandogo
Coldharbour
Hewelsfield
Lydney
Newerne
Aylburton
Purton
Sharpness
Halmore
Newtown
Wanswell
Breadstone
Slimbridge
Moorend
Gossington
Cambridge
Leonard Stanley
Frocester
King's Stanley
Rodborough
Thrupp
Brimscombe
Eastcombe
Woodchester
Littleworth
Amberley
Minchinhampton
Coaley
Nympsfield
Windsoredge
Nailsworth
Box
Whiteway
Avening
Tetbury
Tintern Parva
Brockweir
Netherend
Alvington
New Inn
Devauden
Chapel Hill
Woolaston
Brookend
Berkeley
The Quarry
Lower Cam
Cam
Stinchcombe
Dursley
Uley
Woodmancote
Horsley
Kilgwrrwg Common
Chepstow Park Wood
Itton Common
Newchurch
St Arvans
Wibdon
Stroat
Boughspring
Tidenham
Woodcroft
Tutshill
Ham
Bevington
Woodford
Stone
Nibley Green
North Nibley
Kingscote
Michaelwood Services
Shepperdine
Hill
Mynydd-bach
Shirenewton
Mounton
Pwll-Meyric
Sedbury
Chepstow (Cas-gwent)
Rockhampton
Oldbury-on-Severn
Falfield
Tortworth
Charfield
Kingswood
Wotton-under-Edge
Beverston
Whitfield
Tresham
Beachley
Mathern
Severn Road Bridge
Pont Hafren
Severn View Services
Littleton-on-Severn
Morton
Milbury Heath
Cromhall
Cromhall Common
Churchend
Alderley
Leighterton
Caerwent
Grick
Highmoor Hill
Thornbury
Elberton
Aust
Hillesley
Oldbury on the Hill
Westonbirt
Rogiet
Caldicot
Portskewett
Sudbrook
Ingst
Alveston
Tytherington
Wickwar
Hawkesbury Upton
Hawkesbury
Didmarton
Sopworth
Sherston
Second Severn Crossing
Redwick
Northwick
Olveston
Rudgeway
Tockington
Itchington
Rangeworthy
South Gloucestershire
Pilning
Awkley
Severn Beach
Almondsbury
Latteridge
Iron Acton
Engine Common
Horton
Little Sodbury
Norton
Luckington
Little Badminton
Badminton
Alderton
Hullavington
Over
Easter Compton
Frampton Cotterell
Nibley
Yate
Old Sodbury
Chipping Sodbury
Watley's End
Patchway
Hallen
Filton
Catbrain
Stoke Gifford
Winterbourne
Coalpit Heath
Winterbourne Down
Westerleigh
Wapley
Dodington
Acton Turville
Littleton Drew
Grittleton
Leigh Delamere
Tormarton
Burton
Avonmouth
Henbury
Horfield
Hambrook
Frenchay
Downend
Blackhorse
Codrington
Nettleton
West Kington
Castle Combe
Yatton Keynell
Shirehampton
Westbury on Trym
Mangotsfield
Hinton
Pucklechurch
West Littleton
North Wraxall
Ford
Gordano Services
Sheepway
Ham Green
Pill
Easton-in-Gordano
Portbury
Stapleton
Fishponds
Redland
Eastville
Soundwell
Kingswood
Siston
Abson
Dyrham
Clapton-in-Gordano
Abbots Leigh
Clifton
Warmley
Bridge Yate
Doynton
Marshfield
Slaughterford
Biddestone
Leigh Woods
Bristol
Hanham
Wick
Cold Ashton
Thickwood
Stone-edge Batch
Wraxall
Warmley Tower
Colerne
Corsham
Nailsea
Failand
Long Ashton
Knowle
Brislington
Oldland
Upton Cheyney
St Catherine
Alcombe
Bedminster
Willsbridge
Bitton
North Stoke
Langridge
Woolley
Swainswick
Northend
Batheaston
Hawthorn
East End
Farleigh
Flax Bourton
Backwell
Bishopsworth
Keynsham
Box
Neston
Chelvey
Brockley
West Town
Barrow Gurney
Dundry Hill
Dundry
Whitchurch
Saltford
Kelston
Weston
Charlcombe
Bath
Bathford
Atworth
Whitley
Cleeve
Lulsgate Bottom
Upper Town
North Wick
Norton Malreward
Queen Charlton
Chewton Keynsham
Corston
Bathampton
Monkton Farleigh
Norrington Common
Bristol International
Felton
Winford
Norton Hawkfield
Burnett
Newton St Loe
Twerton
Claverton
South Wraxall
Broughton Common
Broughton Gifford
Chew Magna
Pensford
Compton Dando
Stanton Prior
The Oval
Odd Down
Combe Down
Bradford Leigh
Wrington
Redhill
Ridgehill
Stanton Drew
Bath and N.E. Somerset
Englishcombe
Monkton Combe
Bradford-on-Avon
Holt
Lye Cross
Butcombe
Chew Stoke
Stanton Wick
Chelwood
Hunstrete
Marksbury
Inglesbatch
Lower Langford
Nempnett Thrubwell
Priston
Southstoke
Combe Hay
Limpley Stoke
Winsley
Turleigh
Staverton
Chew Valley Lake
Bishop Sutton
Clutton
Farmborough
Dunkerton
Freshford
Hilperton
Burrington
Blagdon Lake
Blagdon
Ubley
Timsbury
Carlingcott
Twinhoe
Trowle Common
Westwood
Sutton Wick
Temple Cloud
High Littleton
Wellow
Hinton Charterhouse
Farleigh Hungerford
Trowbridge
South Widcombe
Hinton Blewett
Hallatrow
Camerton
Peasedown St John
Compton Martin
West Harptree
Paulton
Clandown
Shoscombe
Norton St Philip
Tellisford
Wingfield
Southwick
Charterhouse
East Harptree
Farrington Gurney
Radstock
Midsomer Norton
Writhlington
Faulkland
Woolverton
North Bradley
Yarnbrook
Heywood
Cheddar
Litton
Chewton Mendip
Ston Easton
Kilmersdon
Hemington
Hardington
Laverton
Rode
Hawkeridge
Chilcompton
Charlton
Lullington
Beckington
Rudge
Westbury
Draycott
Priddy
Emborough
Stratton on the Fosse
Buckland Dinham
Oldford
Westbury Leigh
Rodney Stoke
Green Ore
Binegar
Gurney Slade
Ashwick
Holcombe
Highbury
Mells
Great Elm
Clink
Berkley
Dilton Marsh
Upton Scudamore
Westbury-sub-Mendip
West Horrington
Nettlebridge
Coleford
Vobster
Little Green
Whatley
Frome
Chapmanslade
Corsley
Warminster Services
Latcham
Easton
Wookey Hole
East Horrington
Oakhill
Leigh upon Mendip
Stoke St Michael
Chantry
The Butts
Theale
Wookey
Wells
Downhead
Nunney
Corsley Heath
Henton
Dinder
Croscombe
Downside
Heale
Tytherington
West Woodlands
Bugley
Bishopstrow
Mudgley
Coxley
Dulcote
Dean
East Cranmore
Leighton
Trudoxhill
Shepton Mallet
West Cranmore
Crockerton
Polsham
Worminster
Doulting
Godney
Southway
West Compton
East Compton
Horningsham
Shear Cross
North Wootton
Pilton
Cannard's Grave
Prestleigh
Chesterblade
Wanstrow
Witham Friary
Longbridge Deverill
Whitelake
Glastonbury
Stoney Stratton
Westcombe
Upton Noble
Bruton Forest
Gare Hill
Maiden Bradley
Brixton
Batcombe

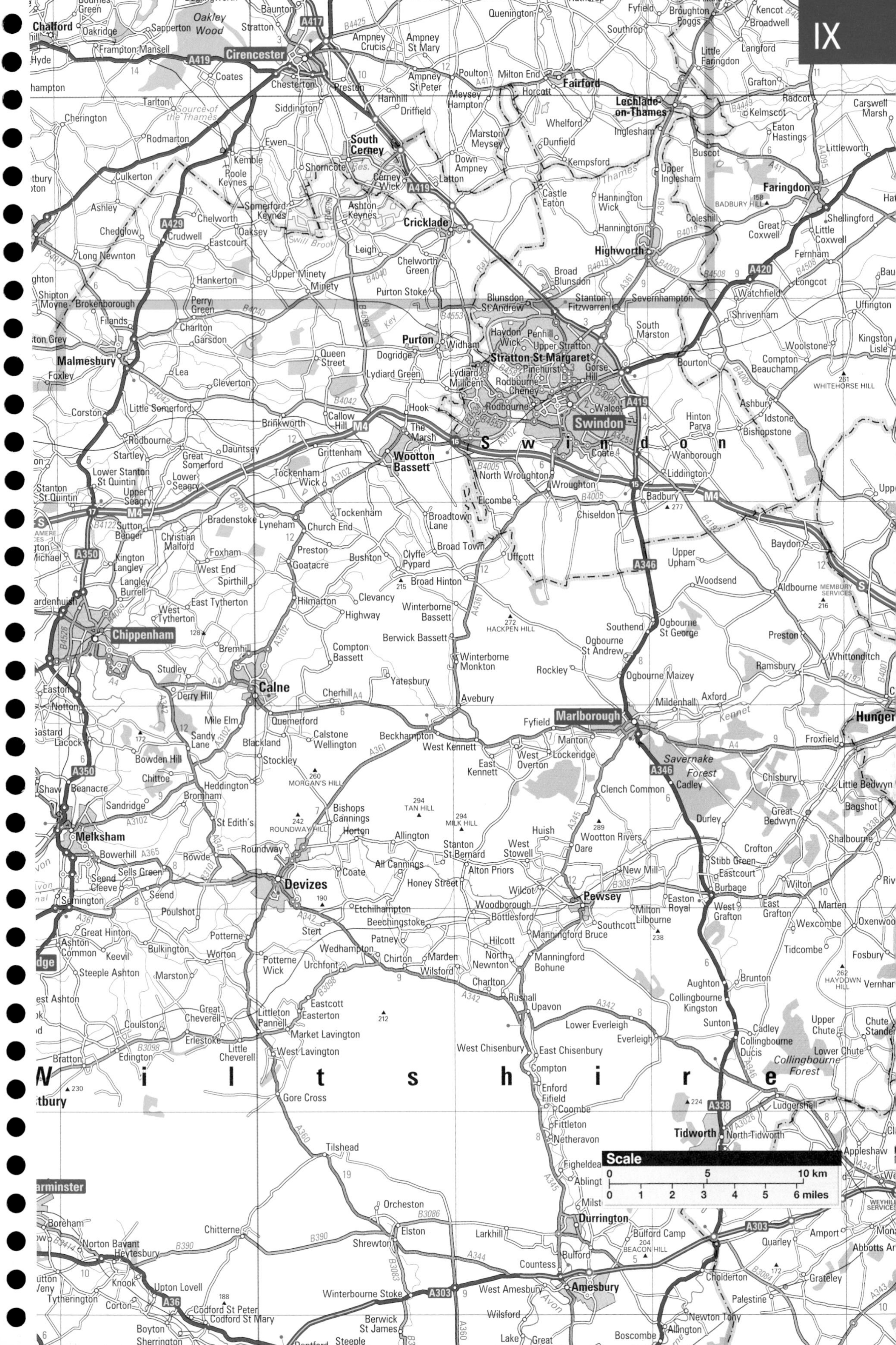
Bournes Green
Daglingworth
Oakley Wood
Baunton
Barnsley
Hatherop
Fyfield
Filkins
Kencot
Chalford
Oakridge
Sapperton
Stratton
A417
Ampney Crucis
Ampney St Mary
Quenington
Broughton Poggs
Southrop
Broadwell
Frampton Mansell
Cirencester
A419
Little Faringdon
Langford
Hyde
Coates
Chesterton
Preston
Ampney St Peter
Poulton
Milton End
Fairford
Horcott
Grafton
hampton
Tarlton
Source of the Thames
Siddington
Harnhill
Driffield
Meysey Hampton
Lechlade-on-Thames
Radcot
Kelmscot
Carswell Marsh
Cherington
Whelford
Inglesham
Eaton Hastings
Rodmarton
Ewen
South Cerney
Marston Meysey
Dunfield
Buscot
Littleworth
Kemble
Down Ampney
Kempsford
Thames
Culkerton
Poole Keynes
Shorncote
Cerney Wick
Latton
Upper Inglesham
Faringdon
Ashley
Somerford Keynes
Ashton Keynes
Castle Eaton
Hannington Wick
Badbury Hill
Chelworth
Cricklade
Coleshill
Shellingford
Chedglow
A429
Crudwell
Oaksey
Swill Brook
Hannington
Great Coxwell
Little Coxwell
Long Newnton
Eastcourt
Leigh
Highworth
Fernham
Chelworth Green
Broad Blunsdon
A420
Longcot
Hankerton
Upper Minety
Minety
Shipton Moyne
Brokenborough
Perry Green
Purton Stoke
Blunsdon St Andrew
Stanton Fitzwarren
Sevenhampton
Watchfield
Uffington
Filands
Charlton
Haydon Wick
Penhill
Shrivenham
South Marston
Garsdon
Purton
Widham
Upper Stratton
Woolstone
Kingston Lisle
Malmesbury
Queen Street
Dogridge
Stratton St Margaret
Bourton
Compton Beauchamp
Foxley
Lea
Lydiard Green
Lydiard Millicent
Pinehurst
Gorse Hill
Rodbourne Cheney
Whitehorse Hill
Cleverton
Corston
Little Somerford
Callow Hill
Hook
Rodbourne
Walcot
Ashbury
Idstone
Brinkworth
M4
The Marsh
Swindon
Hinton Parva
Bishopstone
Rodbourne
Startley
Dauntsey
Great Somerford
Grittenham
Wootton Bassett
Coate
Wanborough
Lower Stanton St Quintin
Lower Seagry
Tockenham Wick
North Wroughton
Liddington
Stanton St Quintin
Upper Seagry
Wroughton
Badbury
Elcombe
Sutton Benger
Bradenstoke
Lyneham
Tockenham
Church End
Broadtown Lane
Chiseldon
Baydon
Christian Malford
A350
Kington Langley
Foxham
Preston
Bushton
Clyffe Pypard
Broad Town
Uffcott
Upper Upham
West End
Goatacre
Spirthill
Broad Hinton
Langley Burrell
Woodsend
Aldbourne
Membury Services
East Tytherton
Hilmarton
Clevancy
Winterborne Bassett
West Tytherton
Highway
Hackpen Hill
Southend
Ogbourne St George
Chippenham
Berwick Bassett
Ogbourne St Andrew
Preston
Bremhill
Compton Bassett
Winterborne Monkton
Whittonditch
Studley
Rockley
Ramsbury
Calne
Yatesbury
Ogbourne Maizey
Easton
Notton
Derry Hill
Cherhill
Avebury
Mildenhall
Axford
Mile Elm
Quemerford
Fyfield
Marlborough
Kennet
Hungerford
Gastard
Lacock
Sandy Lane
Blackland
Calstone Wellington
Beckhampton
West Kennett
Manton
Lockeridge
West Overton
Froxfield
Bowden Hill
Stockley
East Kennett
Savernake Forest
A346
Cadley
Chisbury
Shaw
Beanacre
Chittoe
Heddington
Morgan's Hill
Clench Common
Little Bedwyn
Sandridge
Bromham
Bishops Cannings
Tan Hill
Milk Hill
Great Bedwyn
Bagshot
Melksham
St Edith's
Roundway Hill
Horton
Allington
Huish
Wootton Rivers
Durley
Shalbourne
Bowerhill
Roundway
Rowde
Stanton St Bernard
West Stowell
Oare
Crofton
Seend Cleeve
Sells Green
Devizes
Coate
All Cannings
Alton Priors
New Mill
Stibb Green
Eastcourt
Seend
Honey Street
Wilcot
Pewsey
Burbage
Wilton
Semington
Poulshot
Etchilhampton
Woodborough
Easton Royal
West Grafton
East Grafton
Marten
Beechingstoke
Bottlesford
Milton Lilbourne
Oxenwood
Great Hinton
Stert
Potterne
Southcott
Wexcombe
Ashton Common
Bulkington
Worton
Wedhampton
Patney
Hilcott
Manningford Bruce
Tidcombe
Fosbury
Keevil
Potterne Wick
Urchfont
Chirton
Marden
North Newnton
Manningford Bohune
Steeple Ashton
Marston
Wilsford
Charlton
Haydown Hill
Vernham
Brunton
Aughton
Rushall
West Ashton
Eastcott
Easterton
Collingbourne Kingston
Upavon
Great Cheverell
Littleton Pannell
Lower Everleigh
Upper Chute
Chute Standen
Coulston
Sunton
Cadley
Market Lavington
Everleigh
Erlestoke
Little Cheverell
West Chisenbury
East Chisenbury
Collingbourne Ducis
Lower Chute
Bratton
Edington
West Lavington
Collingbourne Forest
Compton
Wiltshire
Enford
Fifield
Gore Cross
Ludgershall
Coombe
Tidworth
North Tidworth
Fittleton
Netheravon
Tilshead
Appleshaw
Figheldean
Ablington
Warminster
Orchestон
Durrington
Boreham
Chitterne
Elston
Larkhill
Bulford Camp
Norton Bavant
Heytesbury
Shrewton
Beacon Hill
Quarley
Amport
Abbotts Ann
Bulford
Knook
Countess
Cholderton
Grateley
Upton Lovell
Winterborne Stoke
West Amesbury
Amesbury
Tytherington
Corton
Codford St Peter
Codford St Mary
Palestine
Boyton
Sherrington
Berwick St James
Wilsford
Newton Tony
Lake
Great Durnford
Boscombe
Allington
Steeple
Deptford
Scale
0 5 10 km
0 1 2 3 4 5 6 miles

Major administrative and Postcode boundaries

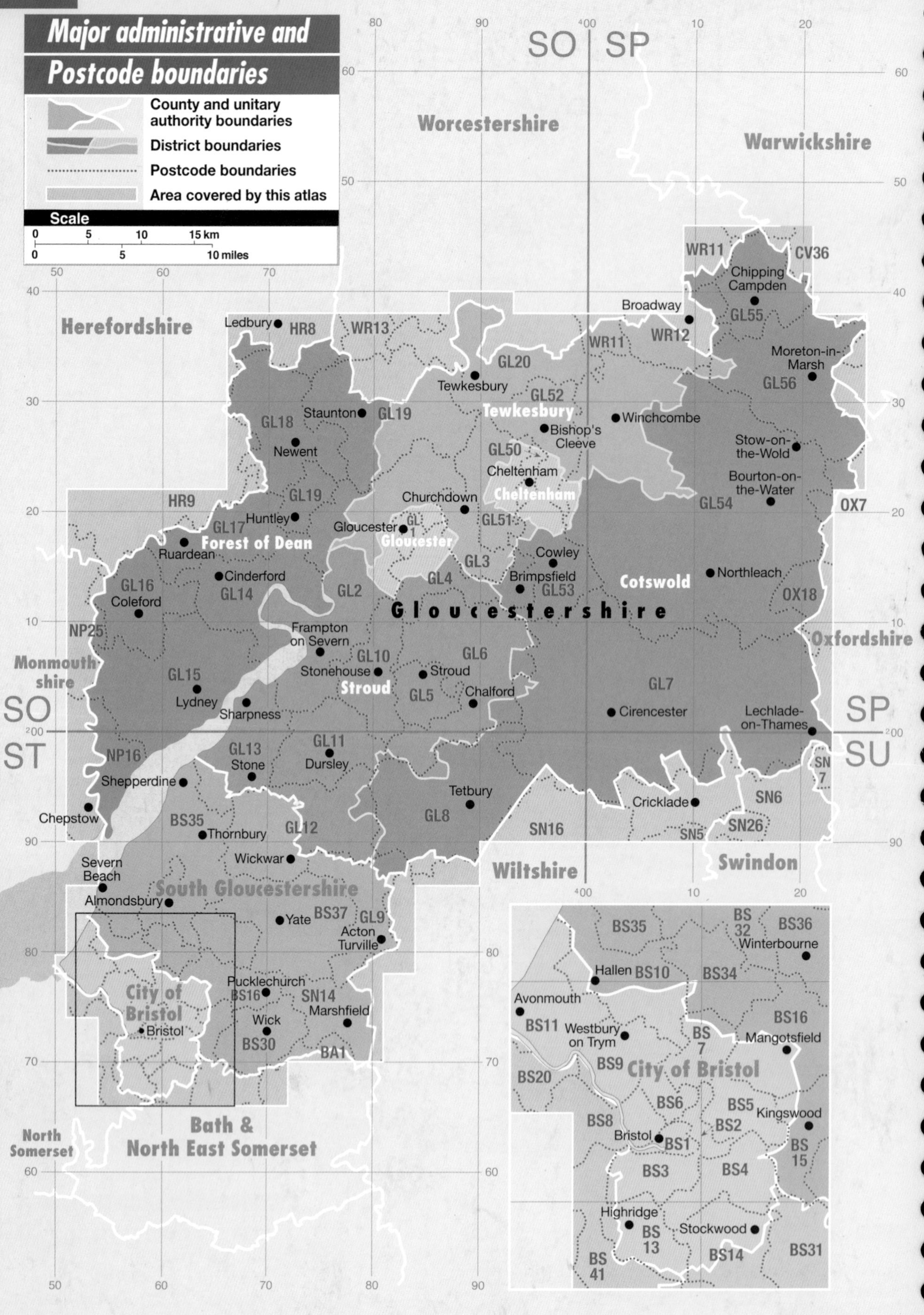

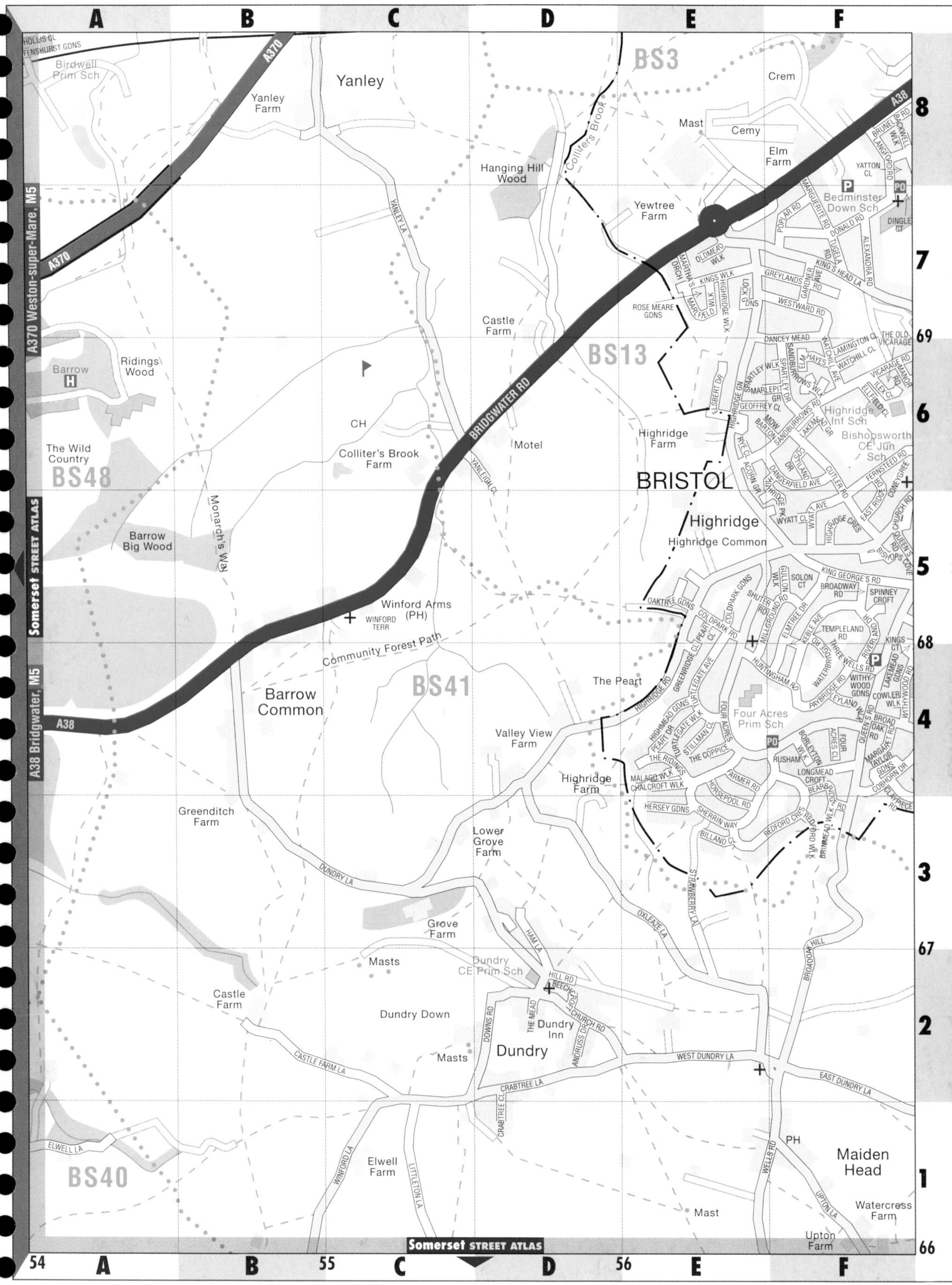
A B C D E F
BS3
Birdwell Prim Sch
Yanley
Yanley Farm
Crem
Mast
Cemy
Elm Farm
Hanging Hill Wood
Colliters Brook
Yewtree Farm
Bedminster Down Sch
A370
A38
A370 Weston-super-Mare, M5
Castle Farm
BS13
Ridings Wood
Barrow
BRIDGWATER RD
CH
Motel
Highridge Farm
The Wild Country
BS48
Colliter's Brook Farm
BRISTOL
Highridge Inf Sch
Bishopsworth CE Jun Sch
Highridge
Highridge Common
Barrow Big Wood
Monarch's Way
Somerset STREET ATLAS
Winford Arms (PH)
WINFORD TERR
Community Forest Path
BS41
The Peart
Barrow Common
Four Acres Prim Sch
Valley View Farm
A38 Bridgwater, M5
Highridge Farm
Greenditch Farm
Lower Grove Farm
DUNDRY LA
Grove Farm
Masts
Dundry CE Prim Sch
Castle Farm
Dundry Down
Dundry Inn
Dundry
Masts
CASTLE FARM LA
CRABTREE LA
WEST DUNDRY LA
EAST DUNDRY LA
ELWELL LA
PH
BS40
Elwell Farm
WINFORD LA
LITTLETON LA
WELLS RD
Maiden Head
Mast
Watercress Farm
Upton Farm
UPTON LA
8 7 69 6 5 68 4 3 67 2 1 66
54 55 56

A B C D E F
8
7
69
6
5
68
4
3
67
2
1
66
57
58
59
Bedminster Down
BS3
Novers Park
Filwood Park
Courtlands Unit
The Florence Brown Com Sch
Novers Lane Inf Sch
Novers Lane Jun Sch
BS4
Playing Fields
Kenn Court Bsns Pk
Denvale Trad Pk
Headley Park
Headley Park Prim Sch
Bakers Park
BS13
Crox Bottom
Imperial Pk
Hengrove L Pk
BRISTOL
Hengrove Park
Recn Gd
BS14
Bishopsworth
St Pius X RC Prim Sch
The Gatehouse Ctr
Withywood Com Sch
Whitehouse Ctr
Hawkfield Bsns Pk
Works
Whitchurch Sports Ctr
Gay Elms Prim Sch
Withywood
Hartcliffe
Fulford Ctr
City of Bristol Coll Hartcliffe Ctr
Hartcliffe Engineering Com Coll
Teyfant Com Sch
Hareclive Prim Sch
Wandsdyke Prim Sch
The Business Park
Hill Farm
Dundry Hill
Meadow Lane
Mast
North Hill Farm
BS41
Community Forest Path
Spring Farm
Walnut Farm
East Dundry
BS39
Maes Knoll
A38
A4174
HARTCLIFFE WAY
HENGROVE WAY
AIRPORT RD
WHITCHURCH LA
EAST DUNDRY RD
Pigeonhouse Stream
The Malago
Liby
Somerset STREET ATLAS

9
4

A B C D E F

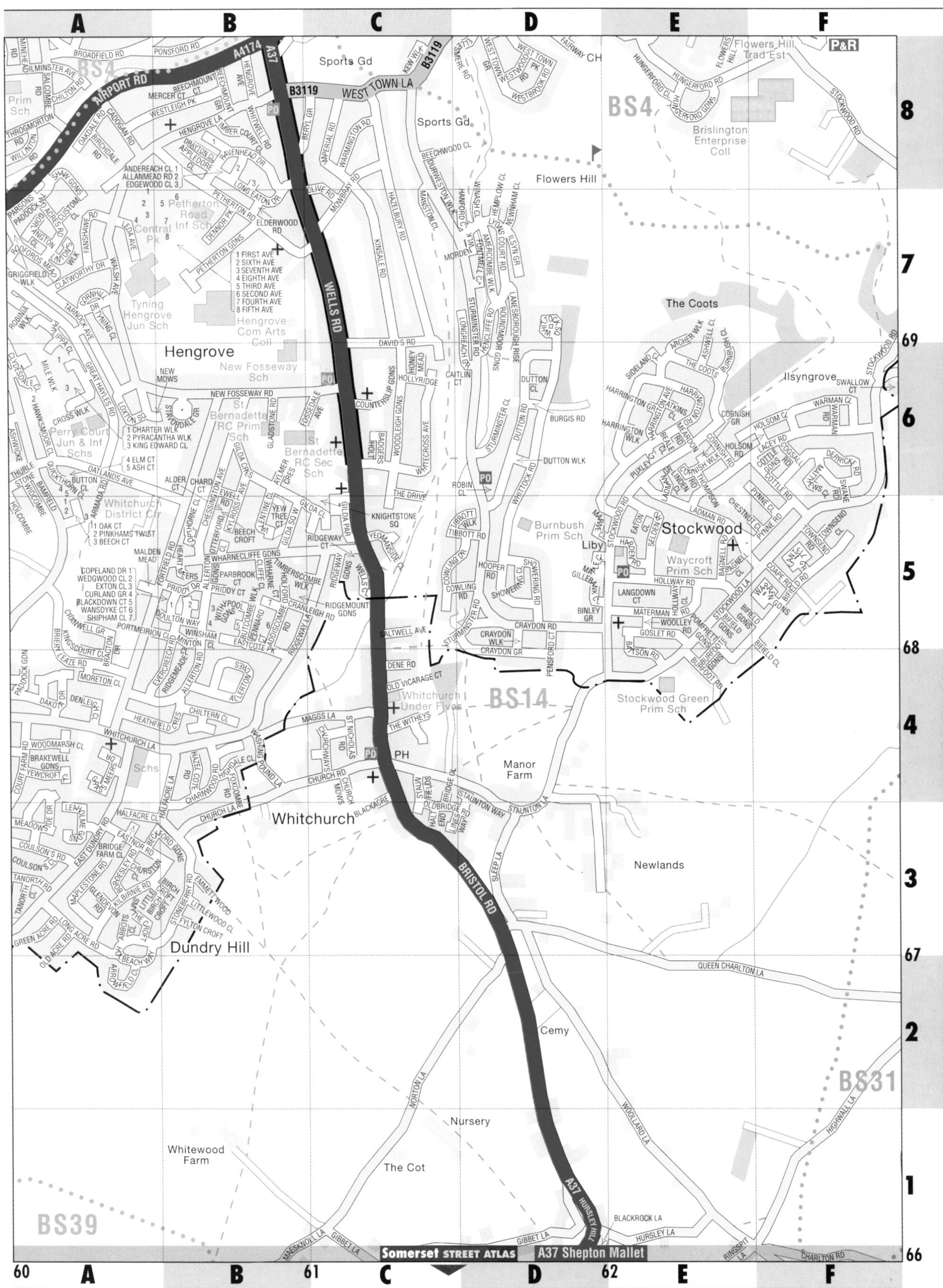

8
7
69
6
5
68
4
3
67
2
1
66

60 A B 61 C D 62 E F

4

3
10

Hicks Gate
BS4
BS15
BS30
BS14
BS31
Keysham Hams
Factory
Somerdale
Recn Gd
Durleypark
Cemy
Oaklease Farm
Stockwood Vale
Wood Covert
Broadlands Sch
Broadlands House
Keynsham Prim Sch
St John's CE Prim Sch
Temple Jun Sch
Temple Hill Inf Sch
Castle Prim Sch
Lays Farm Bsns Ctr
Lays Farm Trad Est
Lays Farm
KEYNSHAM
Queen Charlton
Manor Farm
Parkhouse Farm
Wellfield House
Poplars Cottage
Chewton Place
Chewton Keynsham
Warners Farm
Harvey's Ditch
Charlton Field
Scotland Bottom
Charlton Bottom
Parkhouse Lane
River Avon
River Chew
Avon Walkway
Community Forest Path
BATH RD
BRISTOL RD
STATION RD
KEYNSHAM BY-PASS
KEYNSHAM RD
DURLEY HILL
WELLSWAY
B3116 HIGH ST
Somerset STREET ATLAS

3

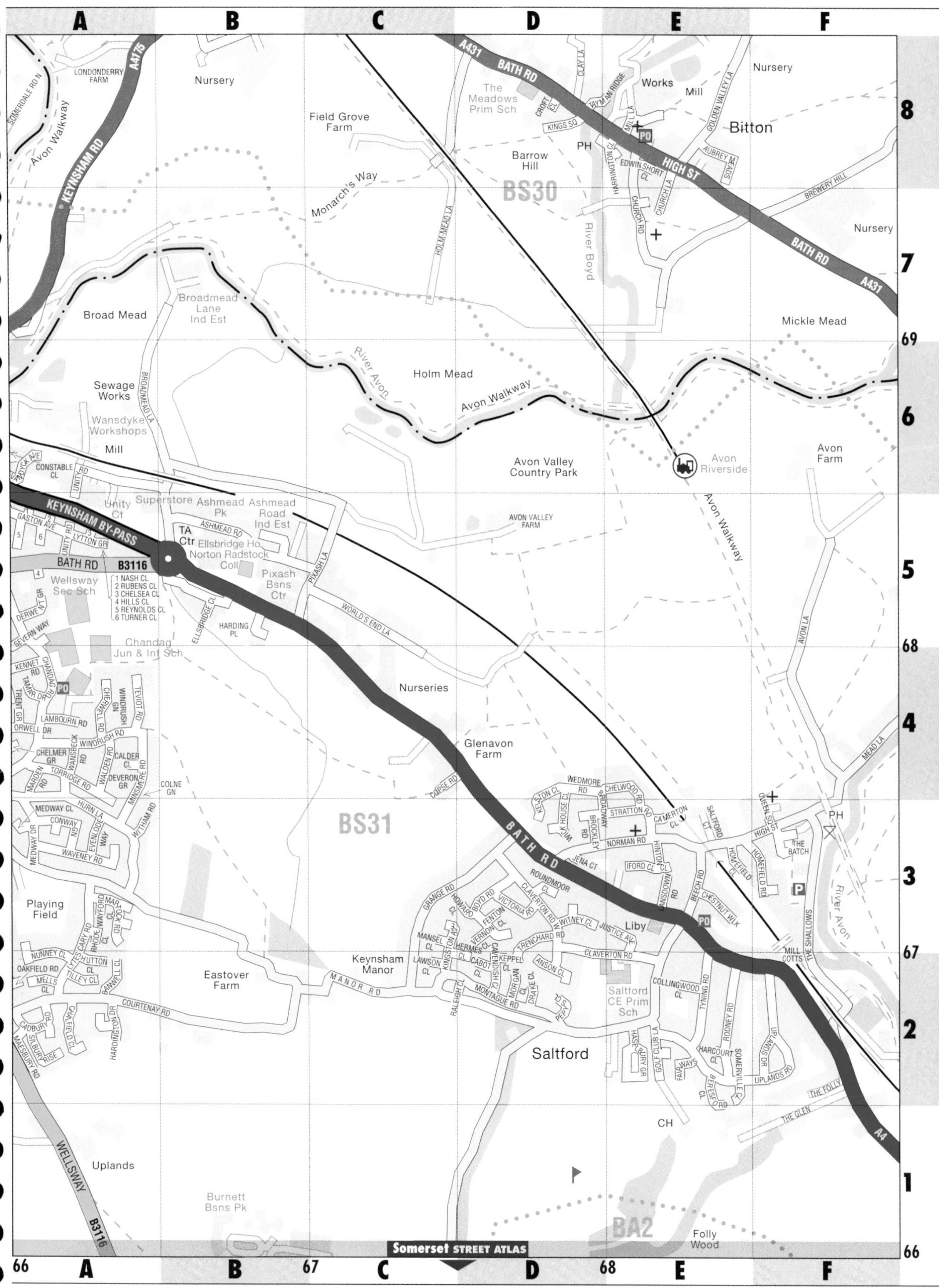
A
B
C
D
E
F
8
7
69
6
5
68
4
3
67
2
1
66
LONDONDERRY FARM
Nursery
Field Grove Farm
The Meadows Prim Sch
Barrow Hill
BS30
Works
Mill
Bitton
Nursery
Avon Walkway
KEYNSHAM RD
A4175
A431
BATH RD
HIGH ST
Monarch's Way
River Boyd
Broad Mead
Broadmead Lane Ind Est
Mickle Mead
Sewage Works
River Avon
Holm Mead
Avon Walkway
Wansdyke Workshops
Mill
Avon Valley Country Park
Avon Riverside
Avon Farm
KEYNSHAM BY-PASS
Superstore
Ashmead Pk
Ashmead Road Ind Est
TA Ctr
Ellsbridge Ho
Norton Radstock Coll
AVON VALLEY FARM
BATH RD
B3116
Wellsway Sec Sch
1 NASH CL
2 RUBENS CL
3 CHELSEA CL
4 HILLS CL
5 REYNOLDS CL
6 TURNER CL
Pixash Bsns Ctr
WORLD'S END LA
Chandag Jun & Inf Sch
Nurseries
Glenavon Farm
BS31
BATH RD
Playing Field
Keynsham Manor
Eastover Farm
MANOR RD
Saltford CE Prim Sch
Saltford
Liby
CH
Uplands
Burnett Bsns Pk
BA2
Folly Wood
WELLSWAY
B3116
A4
River Avon
THE SHALLOWS
MILL COTTS
66
67
68

5
12

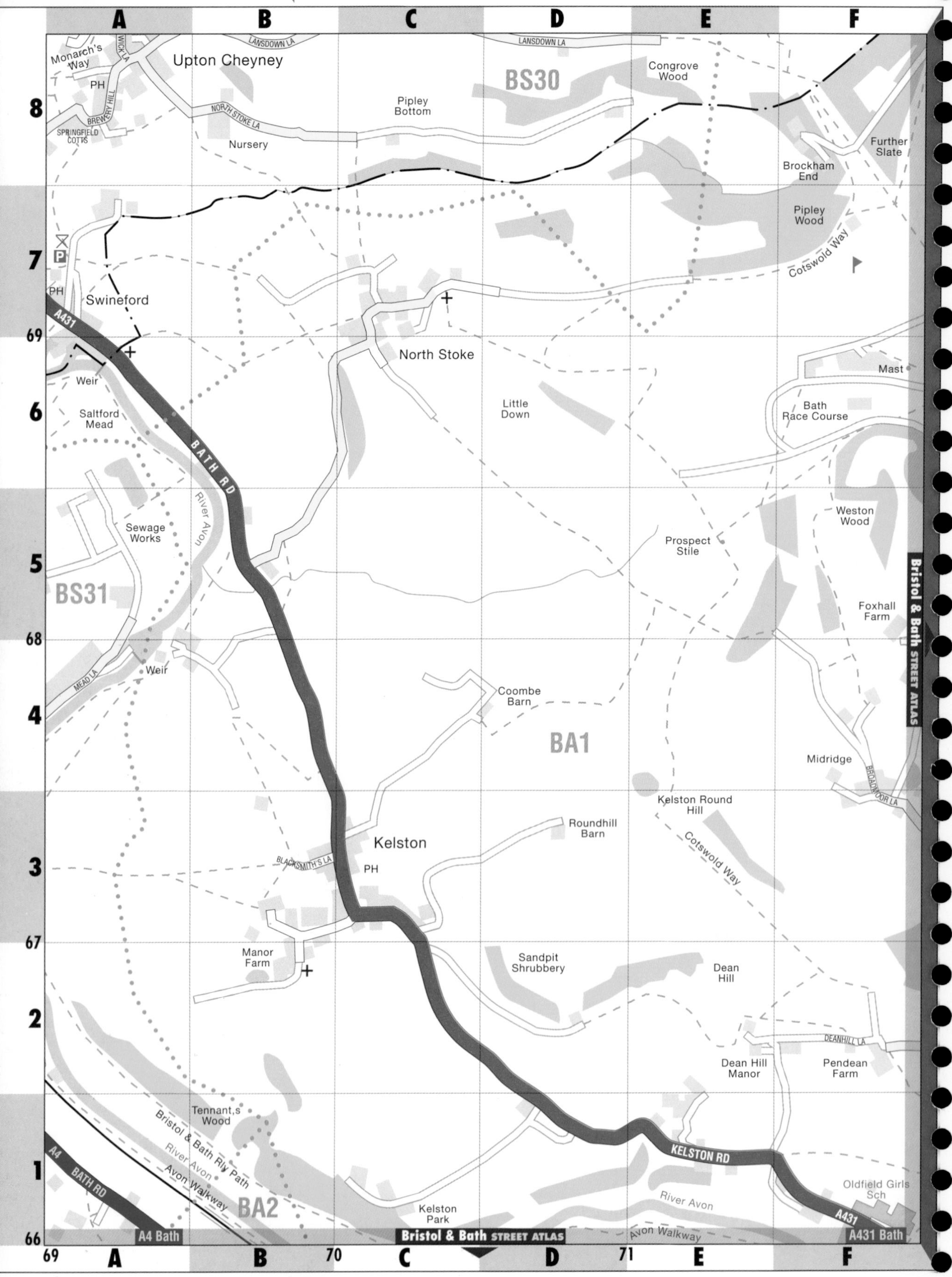
A
B
C
D
E
F
8
7
69
6
5
68
4
3
67
2
1
66
69
70
71
Monarch's Way
Upton Cheyney
PH
WICK LA
BREWERY HILL
SPRINGFIELD COTTS
LANSDOWN LA
NORTH STOKE LA
Nursery
Pipley Bottom
BS30
Congrove Wood
Brockham End
Further Slate
Pipley Wood
Cotswold Way
Swineford
A431
North Stoke
Weir
Saltford Mead
Little Down
Mast
Bath Race Course
BATH RD
River Avon
Sewage Works
BS31
Prospect Stile
Weston Wood
Foxhall Farm
MEAD LA
Coombe Barn
BA1
Midridge
BROADMOOR LA
Kelston Round Hill
Roundhill Barn
Kelston
BLACKSMITH'S LA
PH
Manor Farm
Sandpit Shrubbery
Dean Hill
DEANHILL LA
Dean Hill Manor
Pendean Farm
Tennant,s Wood
Bristol & Bath Rly Path
River Avon
Avon Walkway
BA2
A4
BATH RD
KELSTON RD
River Avon
Oldfield Girls Sch
Kelston Park
Avon Walkway
A4 Bath
A431 Bath
Bristol & Bath STREET ATLAS

5

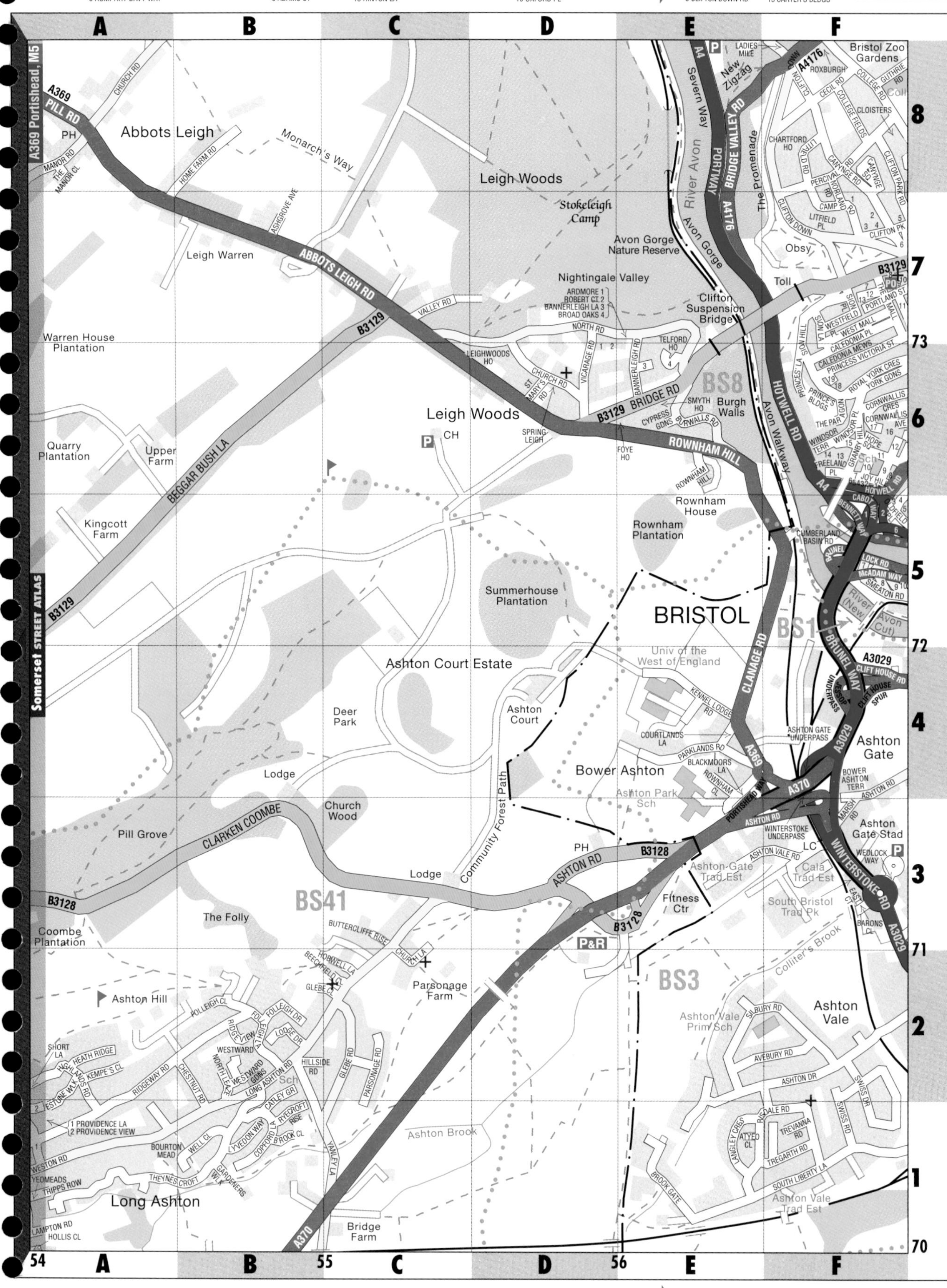

A
B
C
D
E
F
Somerset STREET ATLAS
A369 Portishead, M5
A369
PILL RD
Abbots Leigh
Monarch's Way
Leigh Woods
Stokeleigh Camp
Avon Gorge Nature Reserve
Leigh Warren
ABBOTS LEIGH RD
B3129
VALLEY RD
Nightingale Valley
Clifton Suspension Bridge
Warren House Plantation
Quarry Plantation
Upper Farm
Kingcott Farm
BEGGAR BUSH LA
BS8
B3129 BRIDGE RD
Burgh Walls
ROWNHAM HILL
Rownham House
Rownham Plantation
Summerhouse Plantation
BRISTOL
BS1
Univ of the West of England
Ashton Court Estate
Deer Park
Ashton Court
Bower Ashton
Ashton Park Sch
Lodge
Church Wood
Pill Grove
CLARKEN COOMBE
Community Forest Path
ASHTON RD
B3128
BS41
The Folly
Coombe Plantation
Fitness Ctr
P&R
BS3
Ashton Hill
Parsonage Farm
Ashton Brook
Long Ashton
Bridge Farm
A370
Ashton Vale
Ashton Vale Prim Sch
Ashton Gate
Ashton Gate Stad
South Bristol Trad Pk
Ashton Vale Trad Est
Bristol Zoo Gardens
Clifton
River Avon
Avon Gorge
PORTWAY
BRIDGE VALLEY RD
HOTWELL RD
CLANAGE RD
WINTERSTOKE RD
BRUNEL WAY
Avon Walkway
Severn Way
54
55
56
70
71
72
73
8
7
6
5
4
3
2
1

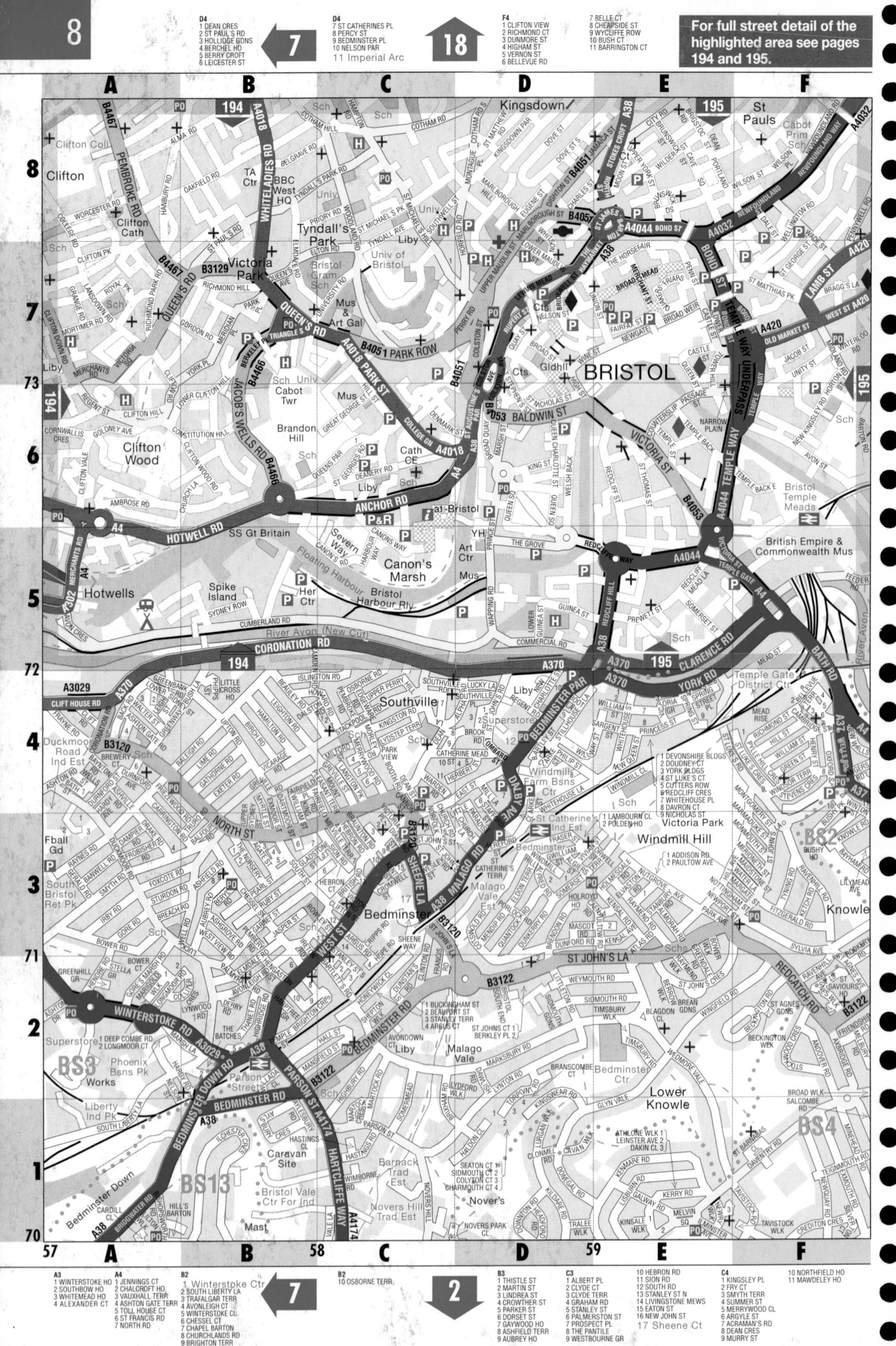

8
D4
1 DEAN CRES
2 ST PAUL'S RD
3 HOLLIDGE GDNS
4 BERCHEL HO
5 BERRY CROFT
6 LEICESTER ST
7
D4
7 ST CATHERINES PL
8 PERCY ST
9 BEDMINSTER PL
10 NELSON PAR
11 Imperial Arc
18
F4
1 CLIFTON VIEW
2 RICHMOND CT
3 DUNMORE ST
4 HIGHAM ST
5 VERNON ST
6 BELLEVUE RD
7 BELLE CT
8 CHEAPSIDE ST
9 WYCLIFFE ROW
10 BUSH CT
11 BARRINGTON CT
For full street detail of the highlighted area see pages 194 and 195.
A B C D E F
8 7 73 6 5 72 4 3 71 2 1 70
194
195
Kingsdown
Clifton
Clifton Coll
Clifton Cath
TA Ctr
BBC West HQ
Tyndall's Park
Univ of Bristol
Victoria Park
Bristol Gram Sch
Mus & Art Gal
PARK ROW
St Pauls
Cabot Prim Sch
BRISTOL
Cabot Twr
Brandon Hill
Clifton Wood
Cath CE
SS Gt Britain
HOTWELL RD
ANCHOR RD
Canon's Marsh
Floating Harbour
Bristol Harbour Rly
Spike Island
Hotwells
River Avon (New Cut)
CORONATION RD
Bristol Temple Meads
British Empire & Commonwealth Mus
TEMPLE WAY UNDERPASS
VICTORIA ST
BALDWIN ST
Southville
Duckmoor Road Ind Est
Fball Gd
South Bristol Ret Pk
Bedminster
Windmill Farm Bsns Ctr
St Catherine's Ind Est
Victoria Park
Windmill Hill
BS2
Knowle
Temple Gate District Ctr
Malago Vale Est
Malago Vale
WINTERSTOKE RD
BS3
Phoenix Bsns Pk
Works
Liberty Ind Pk
Parson Street
BEDMINSTER RD
BS13
Caravan Site
Bristol Vale Ctr For Ind
Barnack Trad Est
Novers Hill Trad Est
Nover's
Bedminster Down
Bedminster Ctr
Lower Knowle
BS4
Mast
57 A B 58 C D 59 E F
A3
1 WINTERSTOKE HO
2 SOUTHBOW HO
3 WHITEMEAD HO
4 ALEXANDER CT
A4
1 JENNINGS CT
2 CHALCROFT HO
3 VAUXHALL TERR
4 ASHTON GATE TERR
5 TOLL HOUSE CT
6 ST FRANCIS RD
7 NORTH RD
B2
1 Winterstoke Ctr
2 SOUTH LIBERTY LA
3 TRAFALGAR TERR
4 AVONLEIGH CT
5 WINTERSTOKE CL
6 CHESSEL CT
7 CHAPEL BARTON
8 CHURCHLANDS RD
9 BRIGHTON TERR
7
B2
10 OSBORNE TERR
2
B3
1 THISTLE ST
2 MARTIN ST
3 LINDREA ST
4 CROWTHER ST
5 PARKER ST
6 DORSET ST
7 GAYWOOD HO
8 ASHFIELD TERR
9 AUBREY HO
C3
1 ALBERT PL
2 CLYDE CT
3 CLYDE TERR
4 GRAHAM RD
5 STANLEY ST
6 PALMERSTON ST
7 PROSPECT PL
8 THE PANTILE
9 WESTBOURNE GR
10 HEBRON RD
11 SION RD
12 SOUTH RD
13 STANLEY ST N
14 LIVINGSTONE MEWS
15 EATON ST
16 NEW JOHN ST
17 Sheene Ct
C4
1 KINGSLEY PL
2 FRY CT
3 SMYTH TERR
4 SUMMER ST
5 MERRYWOOD CL
6 ARGYLE ST
7 ACRAMAN'S RD
8 DEAN CRES
9 MURRY ST
10 NORTHFIELD HO
11 MAWDELEY HO

A6
1 KINGSLAND CL
2 UNION RD
3 KINGSLAND ROAD BRIDGE
4 DINGS WLK
5 BIRKIN ST
6 BARTON VALE

A8
1 HARLESTON ST
2 WINSFORD ST
3 PENNYWELL CT
4 BEAUFORT ST
5 TWINNELL HO
6 BEAUMONT TERR
7 RAWNSLEY HO

B7
1 THE ARCHES
2 BAYNTON HO
3 KINGSMARSH HO
4 HEMMINGS PAR
5 BRENTRY AVE
6 Ducie Rd Bsns Pk
7 CATTYBROOK ST
8 THOMAS ST
9 CASHMORE HO
10 ROWAN CT
11 STRAWBRIDGE RD
12 BEAUFORT HO
13 ST LUKE ST
14 HARWOOD HO
15 ERNEST BARKER CL
16 ROBERT ST
17 CHARLTON ST
18 ATCHLEY ST
19 WILLIAM MASON CL

19

10

F6
1 BARTON CL
2 RIVERSIDE CT
3 BUTLERS WLK
4 QUAYSIDE LA
5 PORT SIDE CL
6 RIVERSIDE WLK
7 ST ANNES CL
8 PARFITT'S HILL
9 CORKER'S HILL
10 ST GEORGES AVE
11 DE LA WARRE CT
12 ELIZABETHS MEWS

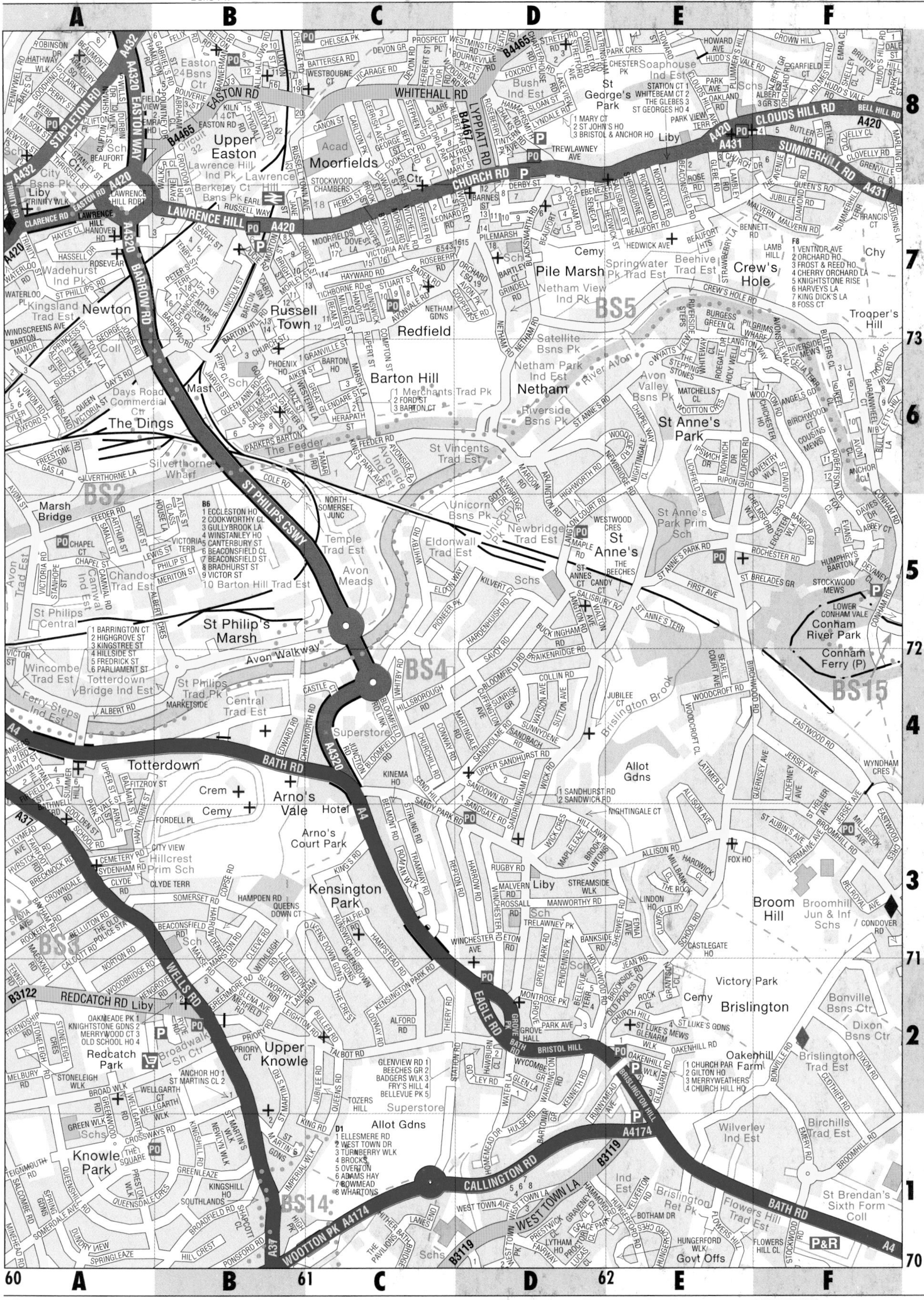

A B C D E F

60 A B 61 C D 62 E F

B8
1 CROYDON HO
2 LANSDOWNE CT
3 SHAW CL
4 VINING WLK
5 HILTON CT
6 LANSDOWN RD
7 THOMSON RD
8 WESTBOURNE RD
9 EASTBOURNE RD
10 ELMGROVE AVE
11 ALL HALLOWS CT
12 ADELAIDE PL
13 COMBFACTORY LA
14 Lawnwood Ind Units
15 LAWNWOOD RD
16 BRIGHTON PK
17 KILBURN CT
18 OWEN ST
19 KILBURN ST
20 WINDSOR GR
21 CLAYTON ST
22 BRIXTON ROAD MEWS
23 CATTYBROOK ST
24 St Gabriel's Bsns Pk

C7
1 MILTON PK
2 WEIGHT RD
3 DRAPER CT
4 CHESTER CT
5 BARKER CT
6 ADRYAN CT
7 OXFORD ST
8 CAMBRIDGE ST
9 YORK ST
10 LANCASTER ST
11 CORBETT HO
12 ASHMEAD HO
13 LONGLANDS HO
14 GARVEY HO
15 OSPREY RD
16 HOWETT RD
17 MATTHEW'S RD
18 Russell Town Ind Pk

3

C8
1 JOHNSONS RD
2 IDA RD
3 SAMUEL ST
4 Whitehall Trad Est
5 LILLIAN ST
6 ALBION ST
7 ARTHUR ST
8 WILLIAM ST
9 LYNTON PL

10

D7
1 SENECA PL
2 HANDEL AVE
3 PARKFIELD AVE
4 WESTON AVE
5 SPEEDWELL AVE
6 BLACKSWARTH HO
7 PADMORE CT
8 SHAFTESBURY TERR
9 LEWIN ST
10 CLAREMONT TERR
11 GEORGE & DRAGON LA
12 ST GEORGE'S HTS
13 GLADSTONE ST
14 TERRELL GDNS
15 GIBBS CT
16 FRAMPTON CT
17 EDWARDS CT
18 DILLON CT
19 ORCHARD CT

A7
1 AIR BALLOON CT
2 MONTREAUX HO
3 WIDCOMBE CL
4 PARSLOW BARTON
5 MOUNTAIN MEWS

A8
1 WHITEWAY CT
2 MALDOWERS LA
3 KENSINGTON RD
4 GINGELL'S GN
5 KENSINGTON HO

9

B5
1 MAYPOLE CT
2 CODY CT
3 BENCE CT
4 BAYNHAM CT
5 VENTON CT
6 POLLY BARNES CL

20

B5
7 GILLINGHAM HILL
8 PLOWRIGHT HO

C8
1 GRANTHAM CT

D8
1 CICIL RD
2 WEST ST
3 MACDONALD WLK
4 MORAVIAN CT
5 BOULTON'S RD
6 BOULTON'S LA

D8
7 WHITFIELD HO
8 EXCHANGE CT

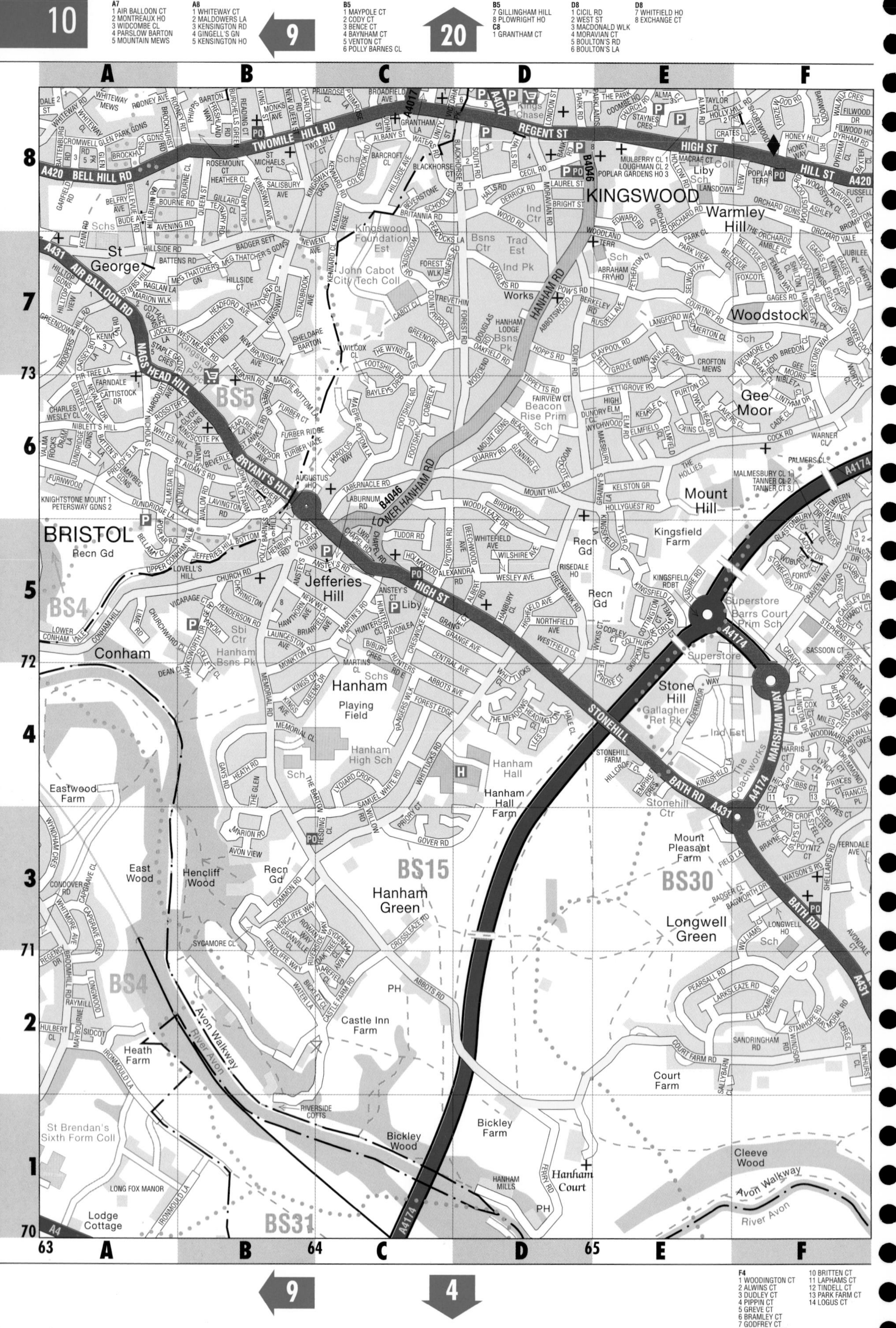

9

4

F4
1 WOODINGTON CT
2 ALWINS CT
3 DUDLEY CT
4 PIPPIN CT
5 GREVE CT
6 BRAMLEY CT
7 GODFREY CT
8 FRAMPTON CT
9 TURNERS CT
10 BRITTEN CT
11 LAPHAMS CT
12 TINDELL CT
13 PARK FARM CT
14 LOGUS CT

A5
1 HENRY WILLIAMSON CT
2 BETJEMAN CT
3 LAURIE LEE CT
4 DYLAN THOMAS CT

A8
1 FILWOOD DR
2 DYRHAM RD
3 LYNTON
4 CHARFIELD

C6
1 ASHBOURNE CL
2 CHARGROVE
3 HIGHCROFT

21
12

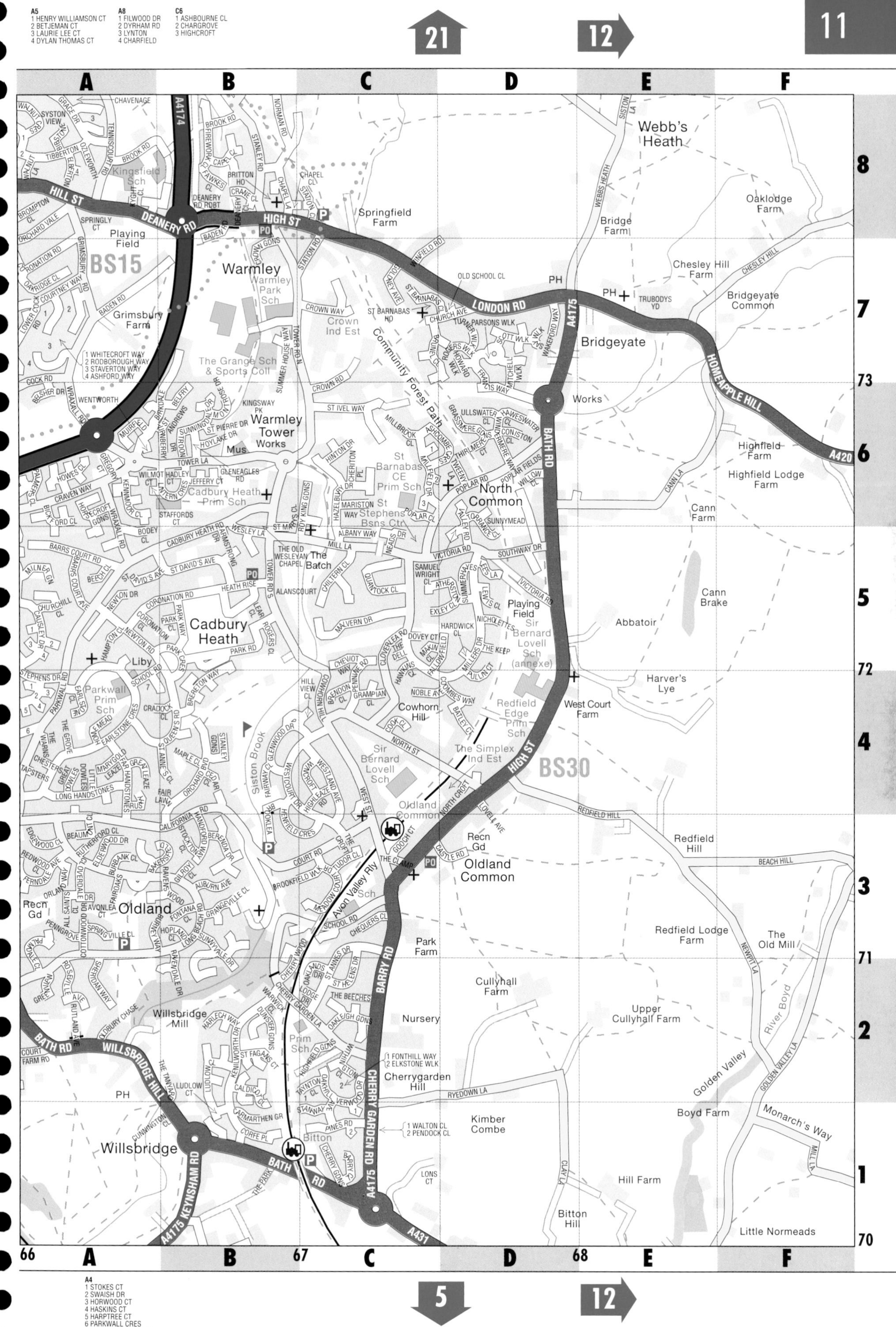

5
12

A4
1 STOKES CT
2 SWAISH DR
3 HORWOOD CT
4 HASKINS CT
5 HARPTREE CT
6 PARKWALL CRES
7 ALFRED LOVELL GDNS

11
22

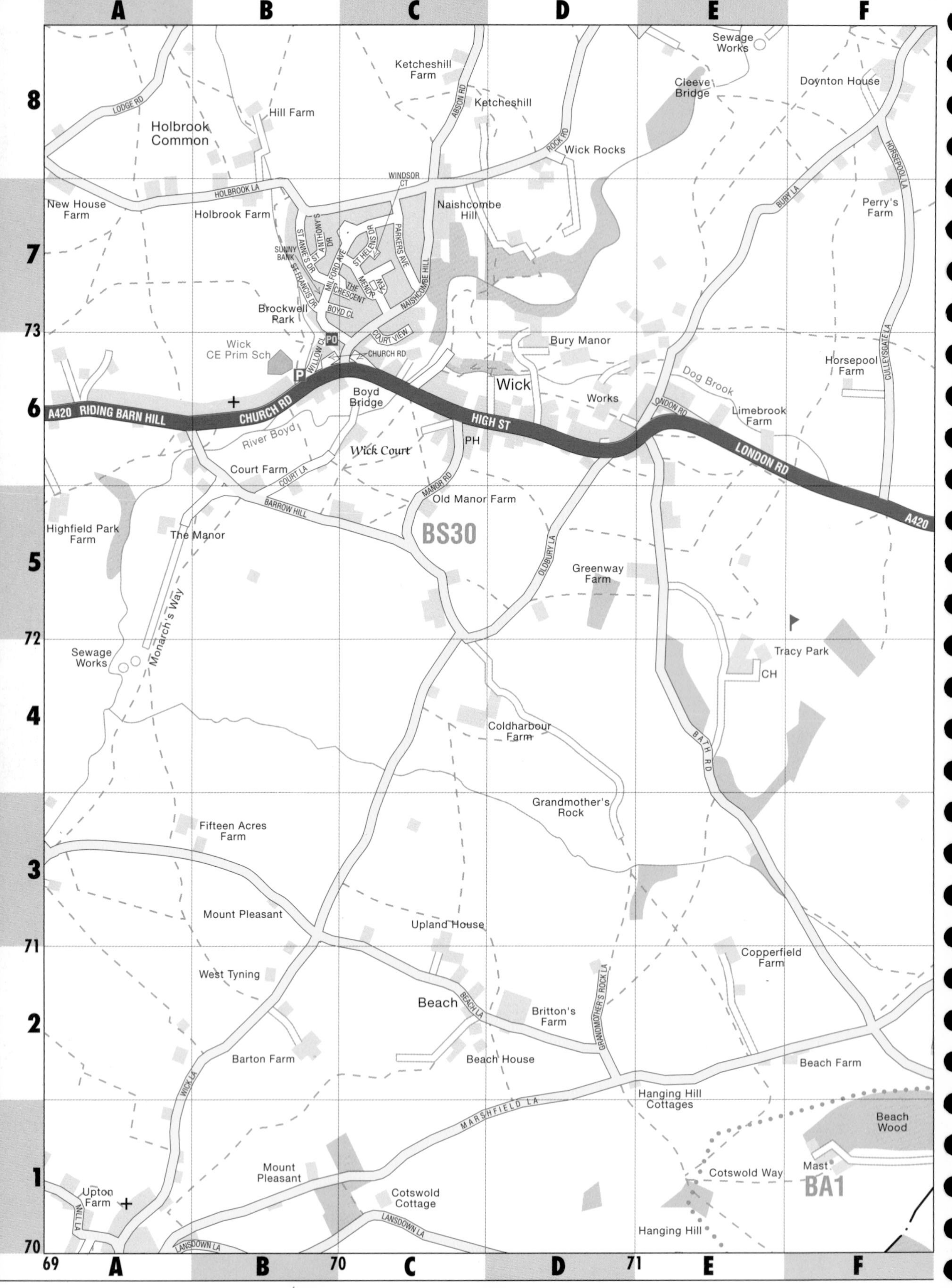
A
B
C
D
E
F
8
7
73
6
5
72
4
3
71
2
1
70
69
70
71
Holbrook Common
Hill Farm
Ketcheshill Farm
Ketcheshill
Sewage Works
Cleeve Bridge
Doynton House
Wick Rocks
New House Farm
Holbrook Farm
Naishcombe Hill
Perry's Farm
Brockwell Park
Wick CE Prim Sch
Bury Manor
Horsepool Farm
Wick
Works
Dog Brook
Limebrook Farm
Boyd Bridge
River Boyd
Wick Court
PH
Court Farm
Old Manor Farm
Highfield Park Farm
The Manor
BS30
Greenway Farm
Monarch's Way
Sewage Works
Tracy Park
CH
Coldharbour Farm
Grandmother's Rock
Fifteen Acres Farm
Mount Pleasant
Upland House
West Tyning
Copperfield Farm
Beach
Britton's Farm
Barton Farm
Beach House
Beach Farm
Hanging Hill Cottages
Beach Wood
Mount Pleasant
Cotswold Way
Mast
BA1
Upton Farm
Cotswold Cottage
Hanging Hill
A420 RIDING BARN HILL
CHURCH RD
HIGH ST
LONDON RD
A420
LODGE RD
HOLBROOK LA
ABSON RD
ROCK RD
WINDSOR CT
ST ANTHONYS DR
ST ANNE'S DR
SUNNY BANK
ST FRANCIS DR
MILFORD AVE
ST HELENS DR
PARKERS AVE
THE CRESCENT
MENDIP VW
NAISHCOMBE HILL
BOYD CL
COURT VIEW
CHURCH RD
WILLOW CL
PO
P
BURY LA
HORSEPOOL LA
CULLEYSGATE LA
LONDON RD
COURT LA
BARROW HILL
MANOR RD
OLDBURY LA
BATH RD
BEACH LA
GRANDMOTHER'S ROCK LA
WICK LA
MARSHFIELD LA
LANSDOWN LA
LANSDOWN LA
MILL LA

11
6

23
14

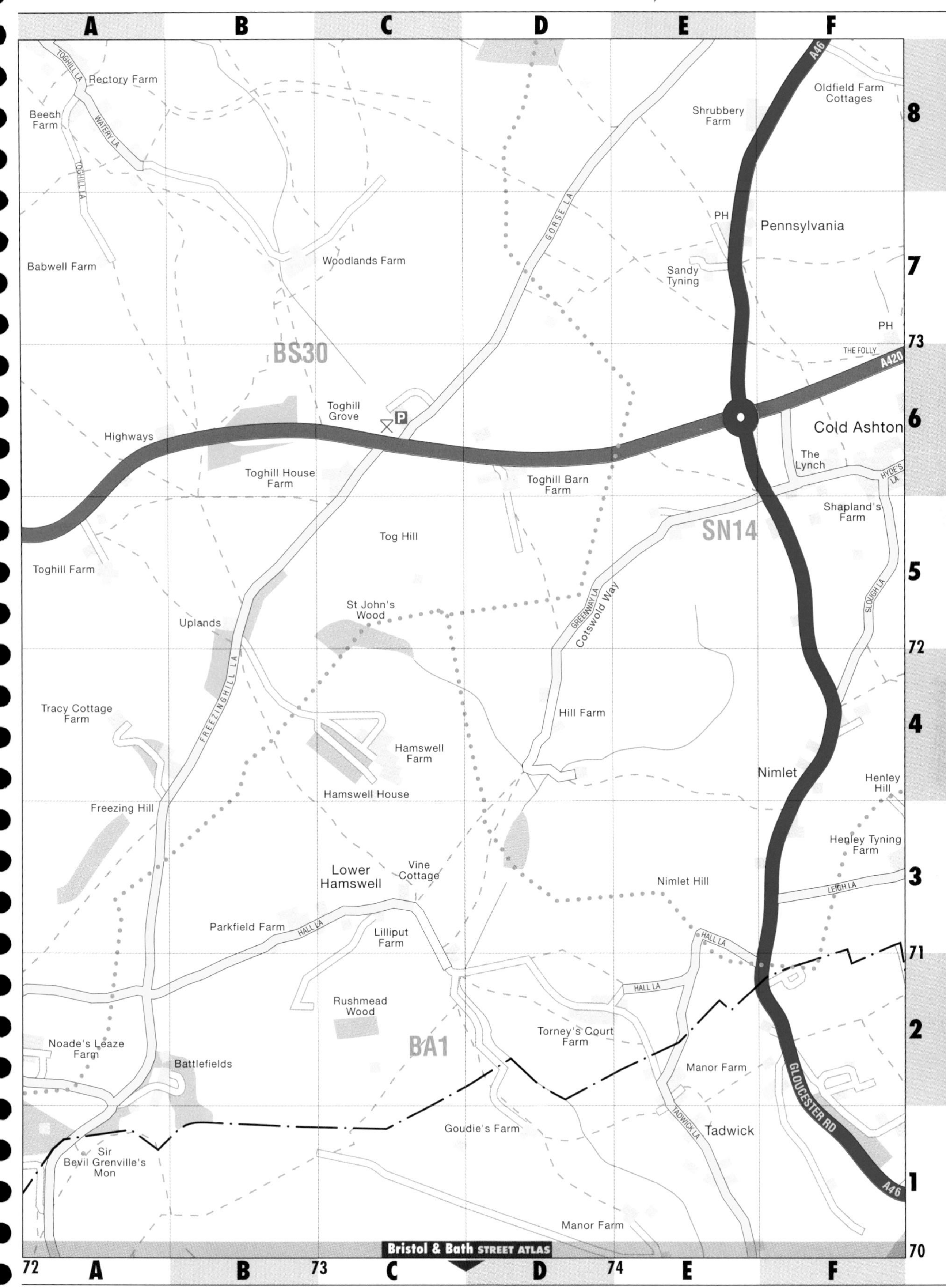
Rectory Farm
Beech Farm
Babwell Farm
Woodlands Farm
BS30
Toghill Grove
Highways
Toghill House Farm
Toghill Farm
Tog Hill
Uplands
St John's Wood
Tracy Cottage Farm
Hamswell Farm
Hamswell House
Freezing Hill
Lower Hamswell
Vine Cottage
Parkfield Farm
Lilliput Farm
Rushmead Wood
BA1
Noade's Leaze Farm
Battlefields
Sir Bevil Grenville's Mon
Goudie's Farm
Manor Farm
Torney's Court Farm
Manor Farm
Tadwick
Nimlet Hill
Nimlet
Hill Farm
Cotswold Way
Toghill Barn Farm
SN14
Shapland's Farm
The Lynch
Cold Ashton
Pennsylvania
Sandy Tyning
PH
Shrubbery Farm
Oldfield Farm Cottages
Henley Hill
Henley Tyning Farm
GORSE LA
FREEZINGHILL LA
HALL LA
LEIGH LA
SLOUGH LA
HYDE'S LA
THE FOLLY
A46
A420
GLOUCESTER RD
TOGHILL LA
WATERY LA
GREENWAY LA
TADWICK LA
Bristol & Bath STREET ATLAS
A B C D E F
8 7 6 5 4 3 2 1
72 73 74
70 71 72 73

14

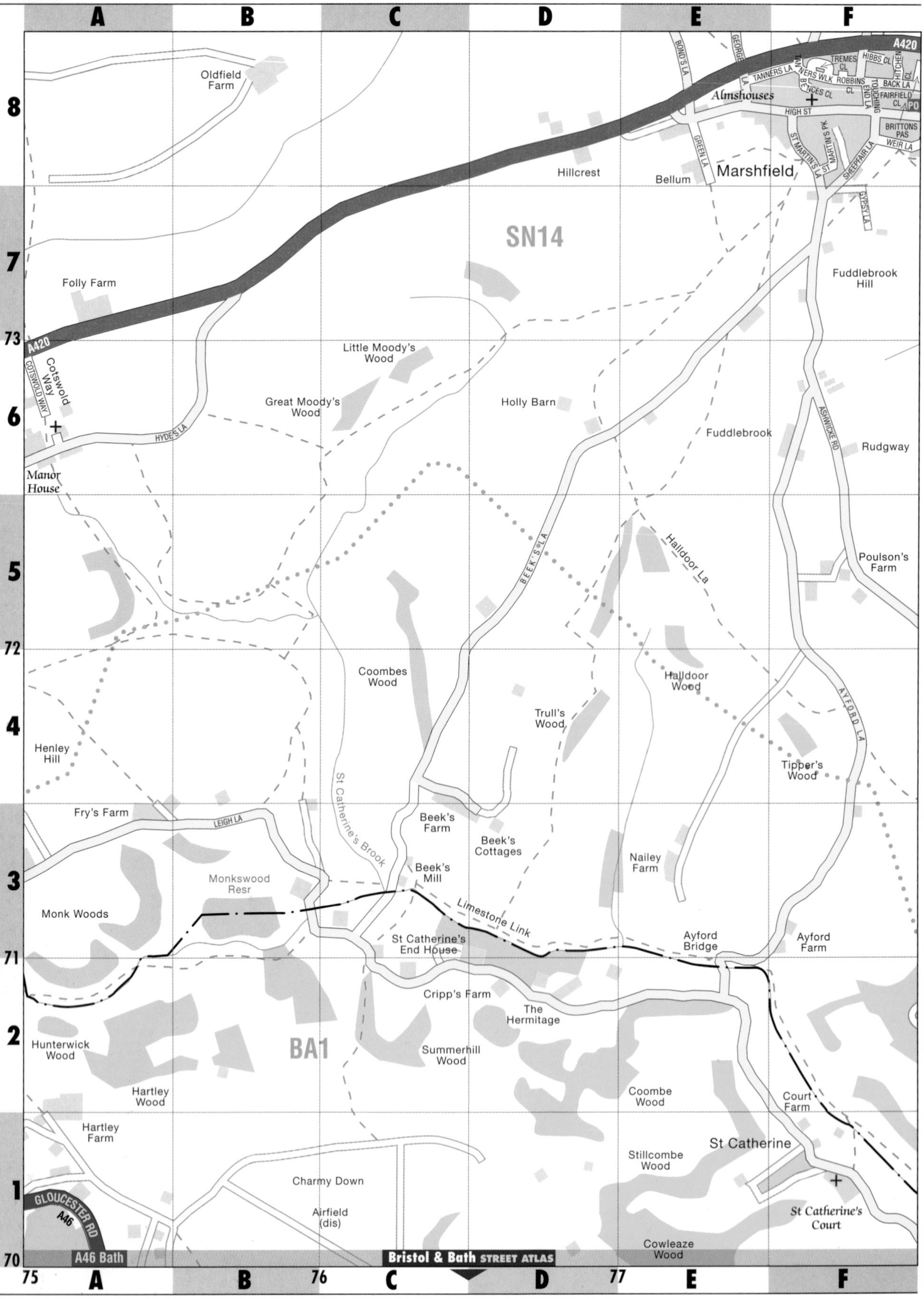

A B C D E F

8 7 73 6 5 72 4 3 71 2 1 70

A420
Oldfield Farm
BOND'S LA
GEORGE LA
TANNERS LA
TANNERS WLK
ROBBINS CL
TREMES CL
HIBBS CL
KITCHEN CL
BACK LA
FAIRFIELD CL
TOUCHING END LA
BENCES CL
Almshouses
PO
HIGH ST
BRITTONS PAS
WEIR LA
ST MARTIN'S PK
ST MARTIN'S LA
SHEEPFAIR LA
GREEN LA
Hillcrest
Bellum
Marshfield
GYPSY LA
SN14
Folly Farm
Fuddlebrook Hill
A420
Cotswold Way
COTSWOLD WAY
Little Moody's Wood
Great Moody's Wood
Holly Barn
HYDE'S LA
Manor House
Fuddlebrook
ASHWICKE RD
Rudgway
BEEK'S LA
Halldoor La
Poulson's Farm
Coombes Wood
Halldoor Wood
Trull's Wood
AYFORD LA
Henley Hill
Tipper's Wood
St Catherine's Brook
Fry's Farm
LEIGH LA
Beek's Farm
Beek's Cottages
Monkswood Resr
Beek's Mill
Nailey Farm
Monk Woods
Limestone Link
St Catherine's End House
Ayford Bridge
Ayford Farm
Cripp's Farm
The Hermitage
Hunterwick Wood
BA1
Summerhill Wood
Hartley Wood
Coombe Wood
Court Farm
Hartley Farm
St Catherine
Stillcombe Wood
Charmy Down
GLOUCESTER RD
A46
Airfield (dis)
St Catherine's Court
Cowleaze Wood
A46 Bath

25

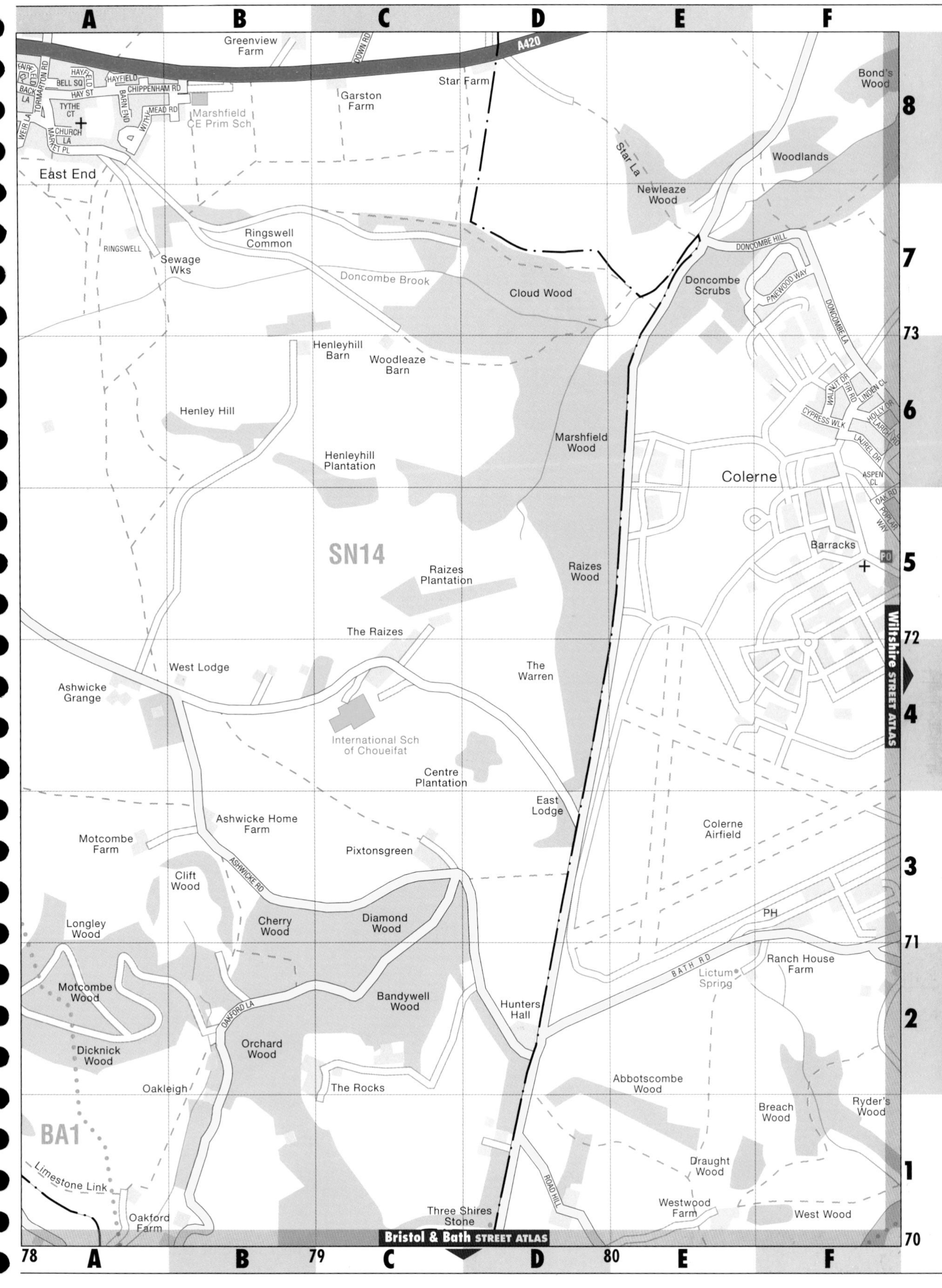

A
B
C
D
E
F
Greenview Farm
A420
Star Farm
Garston Farm
Bond's Wood
Marshfield CE Prim Sch
East End
Star La
Woodlands
Newleaze Wood
Ringswell Common
RINGSWELL
Sewage Wks
Doncombe Brook
Cloud Wood
DONCOMBE HILL
Doncombe Scrubs
PINEWOOD WAY
DONCOMBE LA
Henleyhill Barn
Woodleaze Barn
Henley Hill
Marshfield Wood
Henleyhill Plantation
Colerne
Barracks
SN14
Raizes Plantation
Raizes Wood
The Raizes
West Lodge
The Warren
Ashwicke Grange
International Sch of Choueifat
Centre Plantation
East Lodge
Ashwicke Home Farm
Colerne Airfield
Motcombe Farm
Pixtonsgreen
ASHWICKE RD
Clift Wood
PH
Cherry Wood
Diamond Wood
Longley Wood
BATH RD
Ranch House Farm
Lictum Spring
Motcombe Wood
Bandywell Wood
OAKFORD LA
Hunters Hall
Orchard Wood
Dicknick Wood
Oakleigh
The Rocks
Abbotscombe Wood
Ryder's Wood
Breach Wood
BA1
Draught Wood
Limestone Link
ROAD HILL
Westwood Farm
West Wood
Oakford Farm
Three Shires Stone
Wiltshire STREET ATLAS
Bristol & Bath STREET ATLAS
8
7
73
6
5
72
4
3
71
2
1
70
78
79
80

26

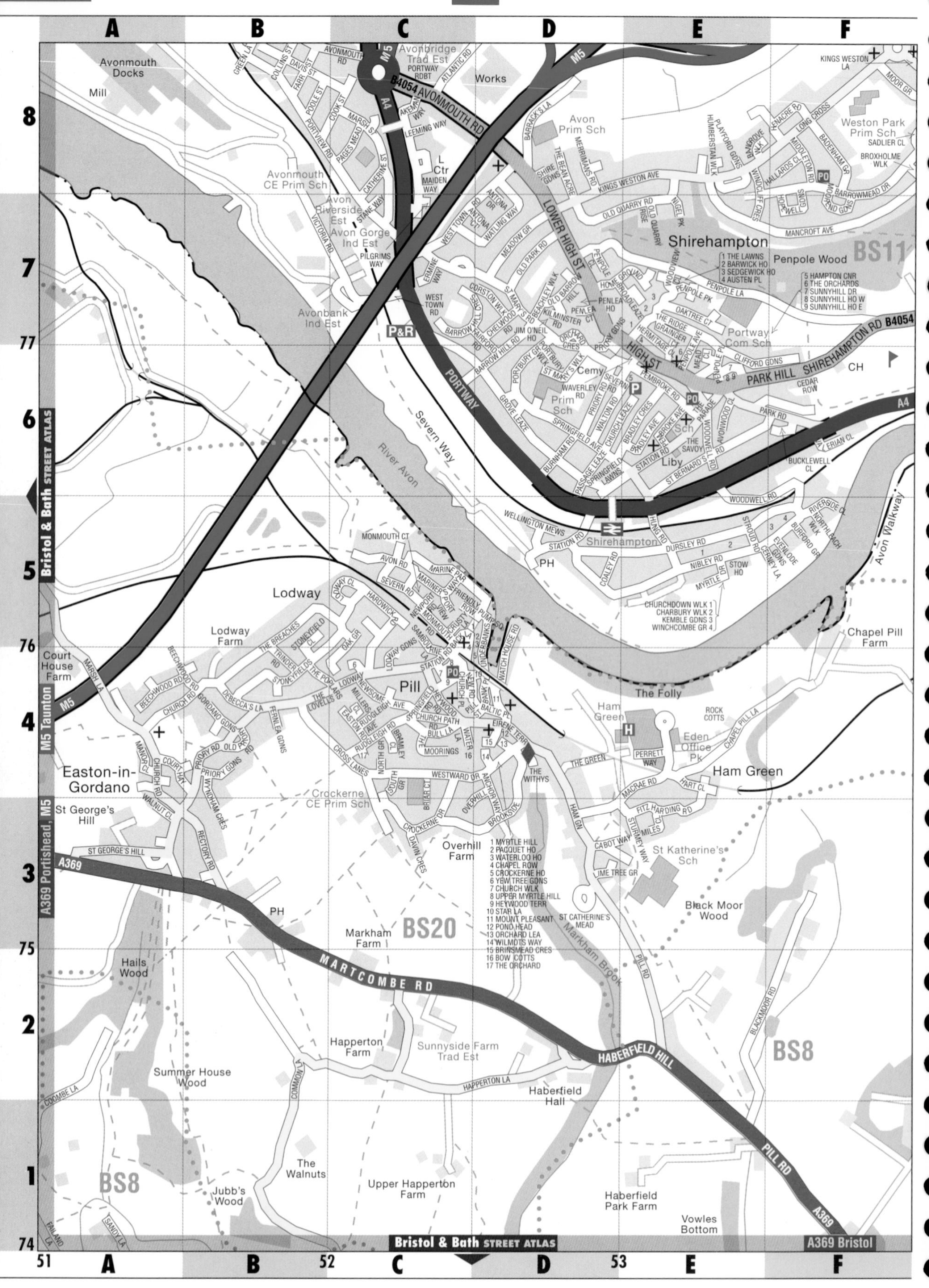

Bristol & Bath STREET ATLAS

27 18

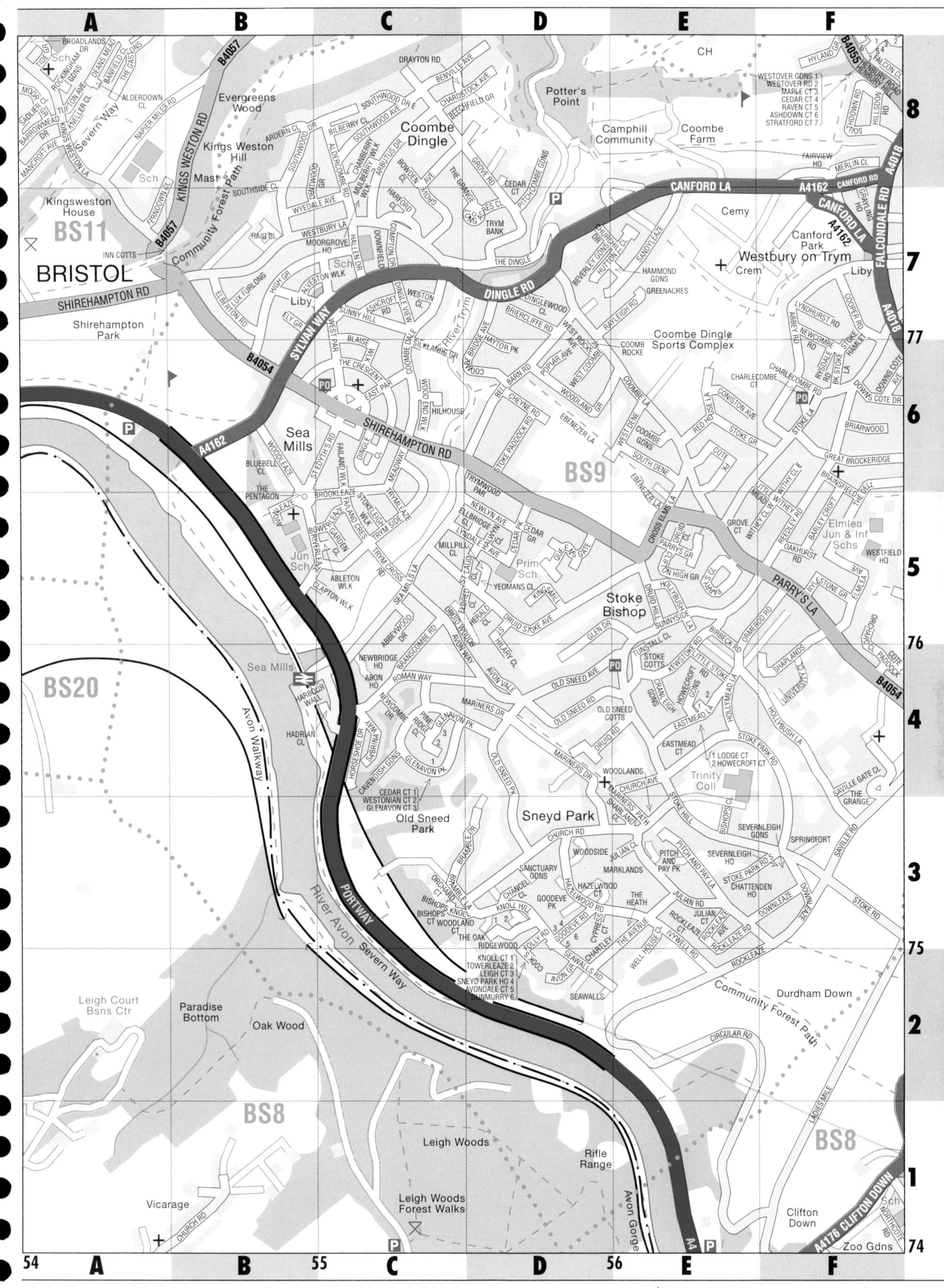

7 18

A7
1 WESTMINSTER CL
2 CARLTON HO
3 CARLTON CT
4 IVY LODGE
5 BELLEVUE COTTS
6 WESTBURY MEWS

B6
1 CRANFORD CT
2 BLANDFORD CL
3 ST PETER'S WLK

F1
1 ASHLEY CT
2 CARY CT

17

F1
3 CARR HO
4 WINKWORTH PL
5 COREY CL
6 LANGSDOWN HO
7 DAVEY TERR
8 NEWFOUNDLAND RD

28

F1
9 FRANKLYN LA
10 DERMOT ST
11 CAIRNS' CRES
12 LOWER ASHLEY RD
13 GORDON RD
14 MARY CARPENTER PL

F2
1 SOMMERVILLE RD S
2 ASHLEY COURT RD
3 BALMORAL MANS
4 FALKLAND RD
5 CUMBERLAND GR
6Ashley Trad Est
7 ASHLEY GROVE RD
8 Minto Road Ind Ctr
9 MINTO RD
10 Parkway Trad Est
11 LYNMOUTH RD

F4
1 CARLTON CT
2 COULSON HO
3 ATHENA CT

A B C D E F

8 7 77 6 5 76 4 3 75 2 1 74

BS10 BS9 BS7 BS6 BS8

Eastfield · Holmwood · Henleaze · Golden Hill · Horfield · Horfield Common · Southmead · Westbury Park · Durdham Down · Bishopston · Ashley Down · Redland · Montpelier · Cotham · Woolcott Park

57 A B 58 C D 59 E F

A2
1 ST VINCENT'S HILL
2 YORK ST
3 HIGHLAND CRES
4 HIGHLAND SQ
5 BELGRAVE HILL
6 RICHMOND DALE
7 RICHMOND CT
8 QUARRY STEPS
9 SUTHERLAND PL
10 WORRALL MEWS
11 WORRALL PL
12 HAYDON CT
13 HIGHLAND PL
14 MORNINGTON RD
15 ANGLESEA PL
16 NORMANTON RD

B1
1 KING'S PARADE AVE
2 GROSVENOR CT
3 COMPTON LODGE
4 COLLINGWOOD RD
5 PLIMSOLL HO
6 OAKLAND RD
7 TYNDALE CT
8 IMPERIAL RD
9 WHATLEY CT
10 CLIFTON METRO
11 Clifton Down Sh Ctr
12 GEORGE CT

17

13 HOPKINS CT
14 BHIRRAFF CT
15 COTHAM GDNS
16 PITVILLE PL
17 HAMPTON LA

B2
1 FERNLEIGH CT
2 LOWER REDLAND MEWS
3 EAST SHRUBBERY
4 SHRUBBERY COTTS

8

5 WEST SHRUBBERY
6 SOUTH TERR
7 FITZROY TERR
8 REDLAND TERR
9 BURLINGTON CT
10 GREENWAY HO

C2
1 ERMLEET RD
2 FERNBANK CT
3 CLYDE MEWS

D1
1 ELMGROVE PK
2 CHELTENHAM CRES
3 LLANARTH VILLAS
4 ARLEY COTTS
5 HILLSIDE HO
6 VICTORIA CT
7 VICTORIA GDNS
8 FREMANTLE LA
9 THORPE LODGE

D1
10 ST MATTHEW'S AVE
11 PRIOR'S HILL
12 THOMAS ST N

D2
1 PROSPECT PL
2 BROOKFIELD LA
3 BROOKFIELD RD
4 GILLHAM HO
5 ELTON MANS

E1
1 MONTPELIER CENTRAL
2 THE MONT
3 MILLBROOK CT
4 ARMIDALE AVE
5 ARMIDALE COTTS
6 PICTON MEWS
7 WOODMANCOTE RD
8 NORRISVILLE RD
9 BARNABAS ST
10 DALRYMPLE RD
11 WELLINGTON CT
12 BRIGHTON ST
13 HEPBURN RD
14 CATHERINE CT
15 SYDENHAM PL
16 NINE TREE HILL
17 DOVE ST
18 ARMADA HO
19 ARMADA PL

A1
1 ASHLEY GROVE RD
2 CONDUIT PL
3 SUMMERS TERR
4 SUMMERS RD
5 BYRON ST
6 NEWFOUNDLAND RD
7 GABLE RD
8 WAVERLEY ST
9 MILLPOND ST
10 MILL HO
11 BEAN ST
12 KENSINGTON PK
13 RAWNSLEY HO

A2
1 RYLAND PL
2 BOUCHER PL
3 LYNMOUTH RD
4 SEDDON RD
5 TREEFIELD PL
6 WEEDON CL
7 TRENTHAM CL
8 Minto Road Ind Ctr
9 DORSET GR
10 DURHAM RD
11 TEWKESBURY RD
12 MERSTHAM RD

29

B1
1 ST MARK'S AVE
2 CHAPEL RD
3 CHURCH AVE
4 ST MARKS CHURCH HO
5 HENRIETTA ST
6 MANOR HO
7 WARWICK AVE

20

B1
8 ST MARK'S GR
9 MANOR CT
10 ST NICHOLAS PK
11 ST MARK'S TERR
12 RENE RD
13 ST MARKS HO
14 OXFORD PL
15 ROSHNI GAR W
16 ROSHNI GAR E
17 MOORHILL ST
18 NORTHCOTE ST
19 BELTON RD
20 NORMANBY RD
21 GRAHAM RD

A B C D E F

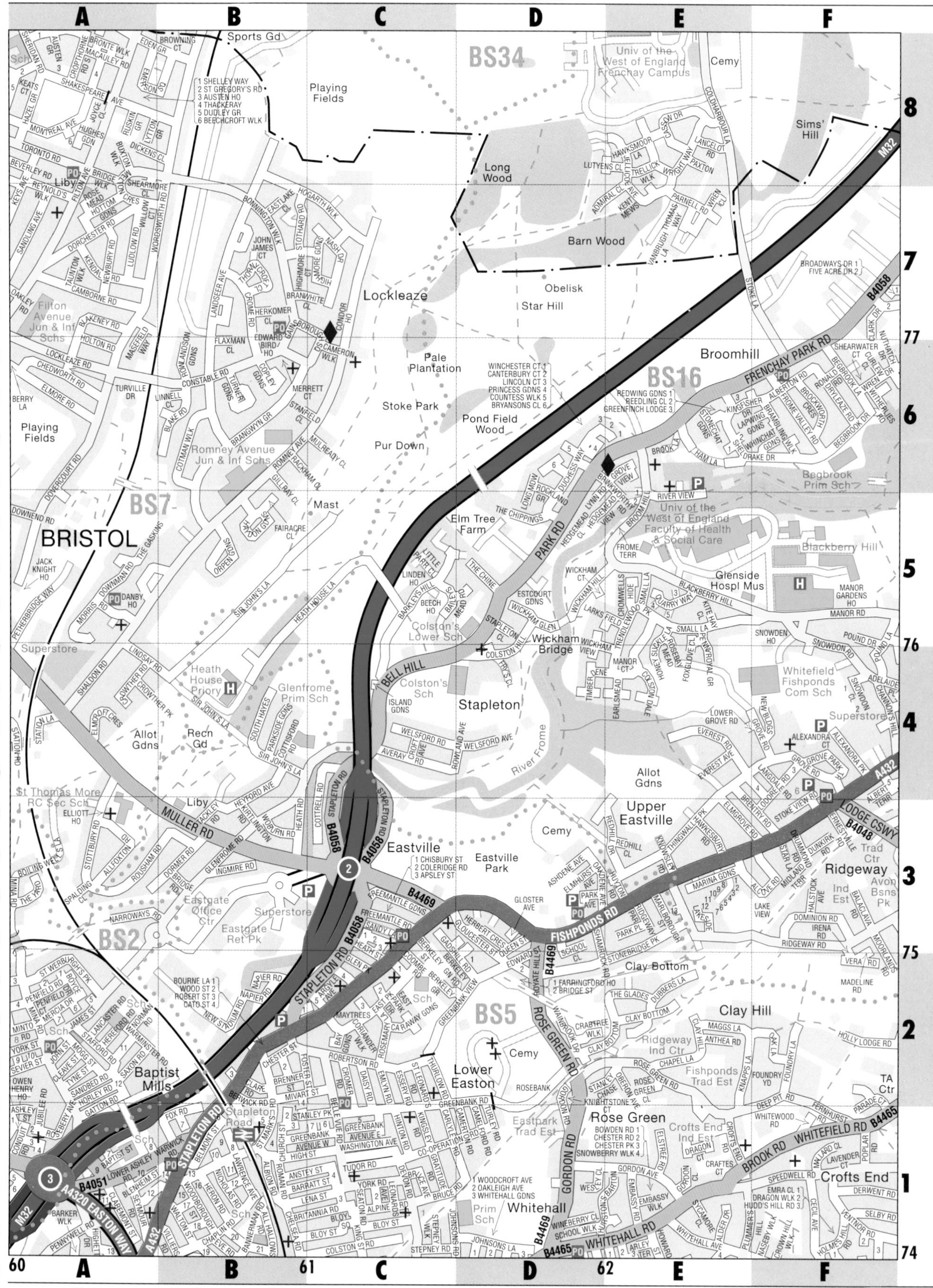

60 A B 61 C D 62 E F 74

C1
1 Devon Road Trad Est
2 COLWYN RD
3 LENA AVE
4 LITTLETON ST
5 GREENHAVEN
6 CARTLEDGE RD
7 PRUDHAM ST

C2
1 FREELAND BLDGS
2 JUNIPER CT
3 FOUNTAINE CT
4 BOSWELL ST
5 ARGYLE ST

E3
1 ASHMAN CT
2 BURTON CT
3 COLSTONE CT
4 DAINES CT
5 ELLYOTT CT
6 FRANKLYN CT
7 GOLDNEY CT
8 HAYTHORNE CT
9 JEFFREYS CT
10 KYNGSTONE CT
11 LANGTON CT
12 MARTIN CT
13 MARLBOROUGH AVE

9

20

E5
1 FROME PL
2 SCHOOL LA
3 GLENSIDE PK
4 SPIRES VIEW
5 BLACKBERRY AVE

F4
1 MARSHALL HO
2 COLLARD HO
3 GROVE AVE
4 FEATHERSTONE RD
5 WHARF RD
6 Stoke View Bsns Pk

19

30

D5
1 BRITANNIA CT
2 OVERNHURST CT
3 GARTON HO
4 PLEASANT HO
5 PENDENNIS HO
6 SHRUBBERY CT
7 BERKELEY HO
8 NELSON HO
9 JOHN WESLEY CT
10 ORCHARD COTTS
11 VICARAGE COTTS

C6
1 URFORDS DR
2 SHIMSEY CL
3 BRIDGES DR
4 GRANGEWOOD CL
5 HORNBEAM HO
6 SYCAMORE HO
7 WHITEBEAM HO

BRISTOL
BS16
Frenchay
Downend
Bromley Heath
Oldbury Court Estate
Fishponds
Mangotsfield
Staple Hill
Page Park
Hillfields
Upper Soundwell
Lower Soundwell
Mayfield Park
Chester Park
Speedwell
BS5
Whiteway
Burchells Green
Two Mile Hill
Hopewell Hill
BS15
New Cheltenham

A1
1 THOMAS PRING WLK
2 MALDOWERS LA

A4
1 ADELAIDE TERR
2 ANNIE SCOTT CL
3 STATION AVE
4 ELMDALE GDNS
5 STATION AVENUE S
6 LOWER STATION RD
7 WAYLAND CT

B4
1 CHASEFIELD LA
2 BRIDGES CT
3 MAYWOOD AVE
4 PARKHURST AVE

C1
1 HIGH POINT HO
2 HILL VIEW HO
3 HANDEL COSSHAM CT
4 TANNERS CT

19

C2
1 WILLOW GR
2 WENTFORTH DR

C4
1 ECLIPSE CT
2 Eclipse Office Pk

D1
1 MORLEY TERR
2 GLADSTONE RD
3 KENNINGTON AVE
4 ALSOP RD
5 MAPLE CT
6 Oatley Trad Est
7 PARK RD
8 HICKING CT

D3
1 Hayward Ind Est
2 VINCENT CT
3 BEVERLY CT
4 THE GARDENS
5 BEAZER CL
6 ST CLEMENTS CT
7 WESLEY CL
8 WHITEFIELD CL
9 CHURCH CT
10 MONTREAUX CT
11 MULBERRY GDNS

D4
1 PRATTEN'S LA
2 HAYNES HO
3 NELSON RD
4 ACACIA MEWS
5 BROOKRIDGE CT
6 KENSINGTON RD
7 CHESTNUT HO

A7
1 WAKEFORD RD
2 WESTBOURNE CL

31 22

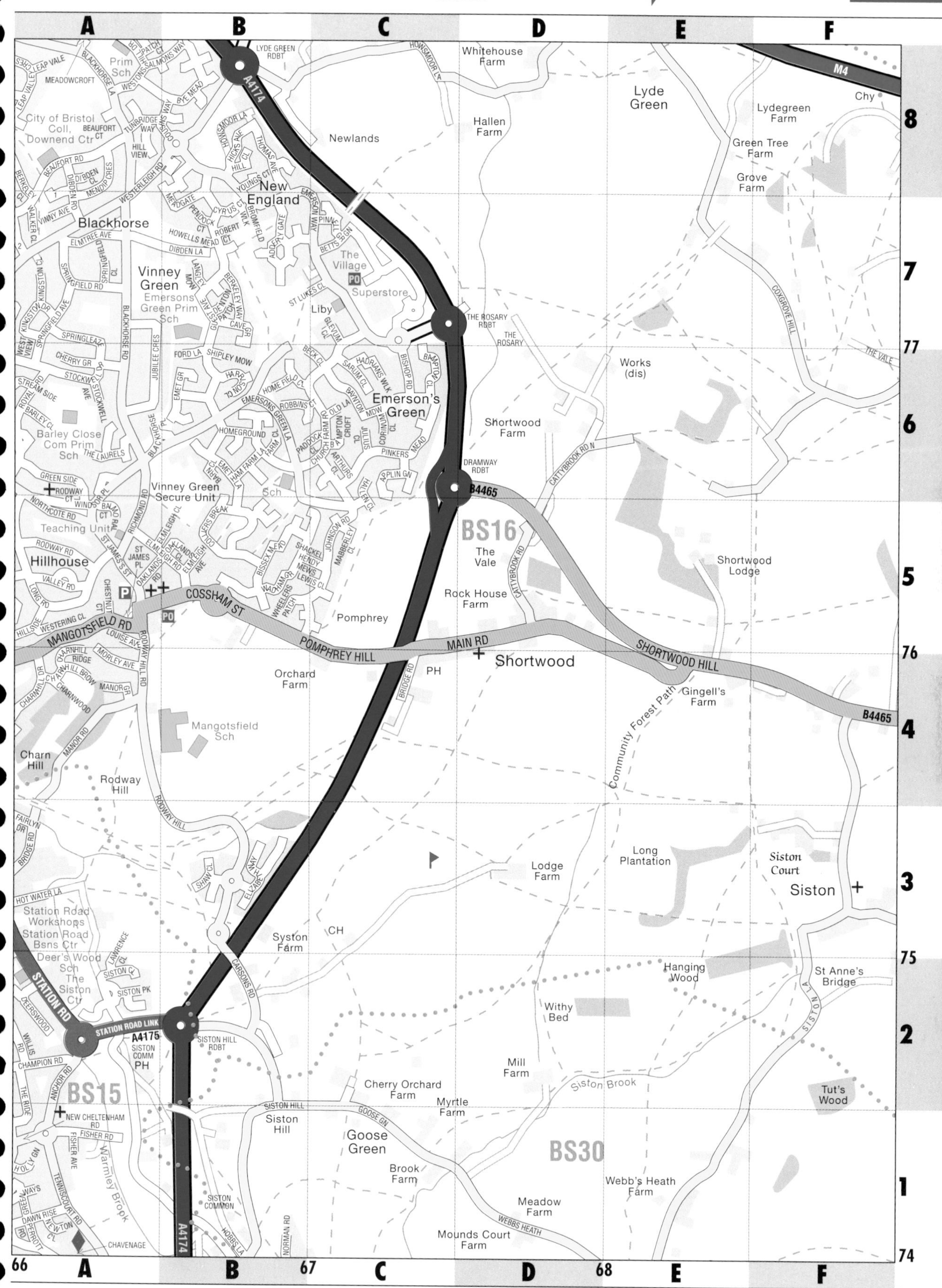

11 22

21 32

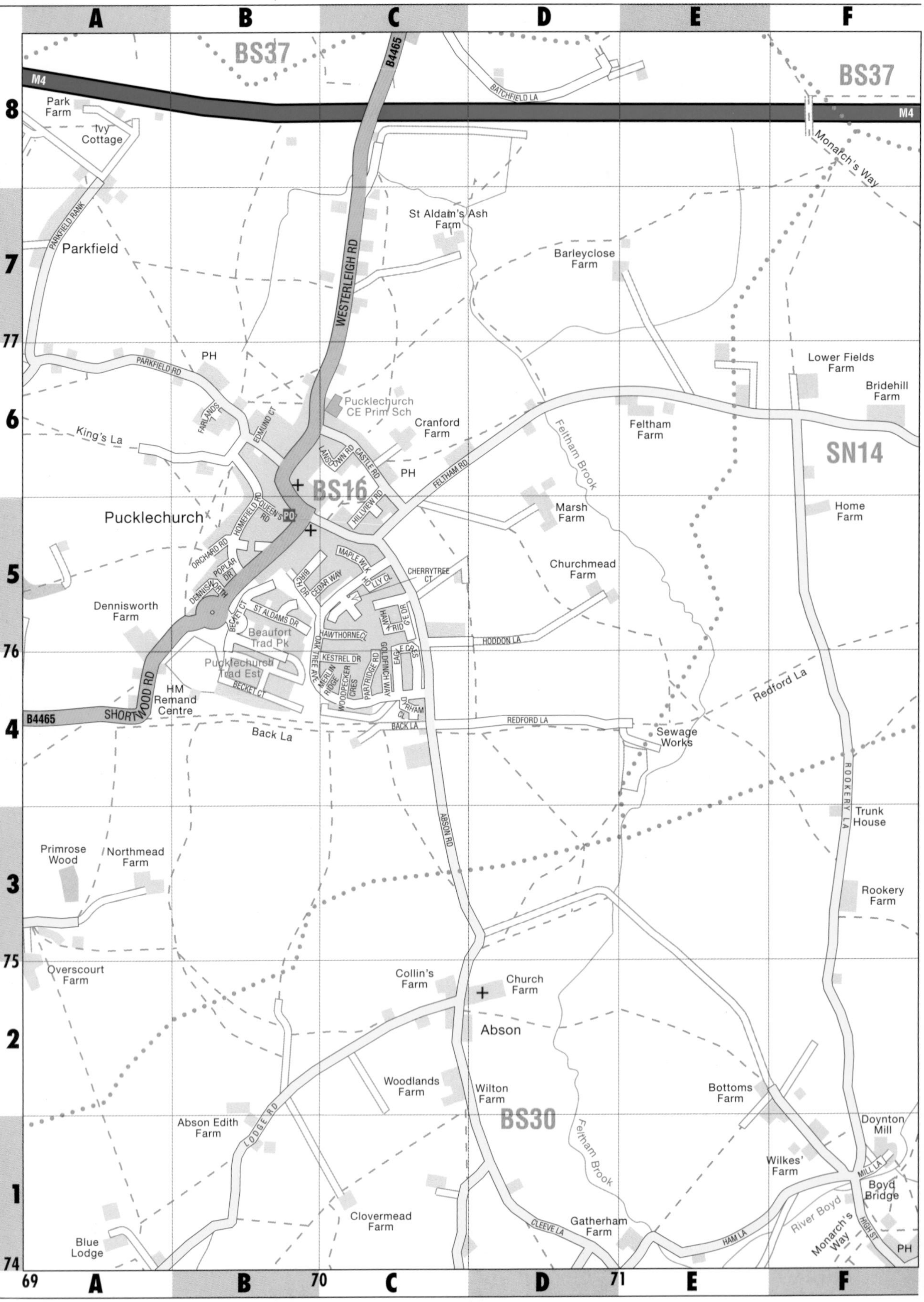

A B C D E F
8 7 77 6 5 76 4 3 75 2 1 74
BS37
M4
B4465
BATCHFIELD LA
Park Farm
Ivy Cottage
Monarch's Way
St Aldam's Ash Farm
PARKFIELD RANK
Parkfield
WESTERLEIGH RD
Barleyclose Farm
Lower Fields Farm
Bridehill Farm
PH
PARKFIELD RD
Pucklechurch CE Prim Sch
Cranford Farm
King's La
FARLANDS
EDMUND CT
LANSDOWN RD
CASTLE RD
Feltham Farm
SN14
PH
FELTHAM RD
Feltham Brook
BS16
HILLVIEW RD
Marsh Farm
Home Farm
Pucklechurch
HOMEFIELD RD
QUEEN'S RD
PO
ORCHARD RD
POPLAR DR
MAPLE WLK
CHERRYTREE CT
Churchmead Farm
HOLLY CL
BIRCH DR
CEDAR WAY
DENNISWORTH
Dennisworth Farm
BECKET CT
ST ALDAMS DR
HAWTHORNE CL
HAWTHORN RIDGE DR
HODDON LA
Beaufort Trad Pk
Pucklechurch Trad Est
KESTREL DR
EAGLE CRES
OAK TREE AVE
MERLIN RIDGE
WOODPECKER CRES
PARTRIDGE RD
GOLDFINCH WAY
Redford La
BECKET CT
HM Remand Centre
DYRHAM CL
B4465
SHORTWOOD RD
REDFORD LA
BACK LA
Back La
Sewage Works
ROOKERY LA
ABSON RD
Trunk House
Primrose Wood
Northmead Farm
Rookery Farm
Overscourt Farm
Collin's Farm
Church Farm
Abson
Woodlands Farm
Wilton Farm
Bottoms Farm
BS30
Abson Edith Farm
LODGE RD
Feltham Brook
Doynton Mill
Wilkes' Farm
MILL LA
Boyd Bridge
Clovermead Farm
Gatherham Farm
CLEEVE LA
River Boyd
HAM LA
Monarch's Way
HIGH ST
Blue Lodge
PH
69 A B 70 C D 71 E F

21 12

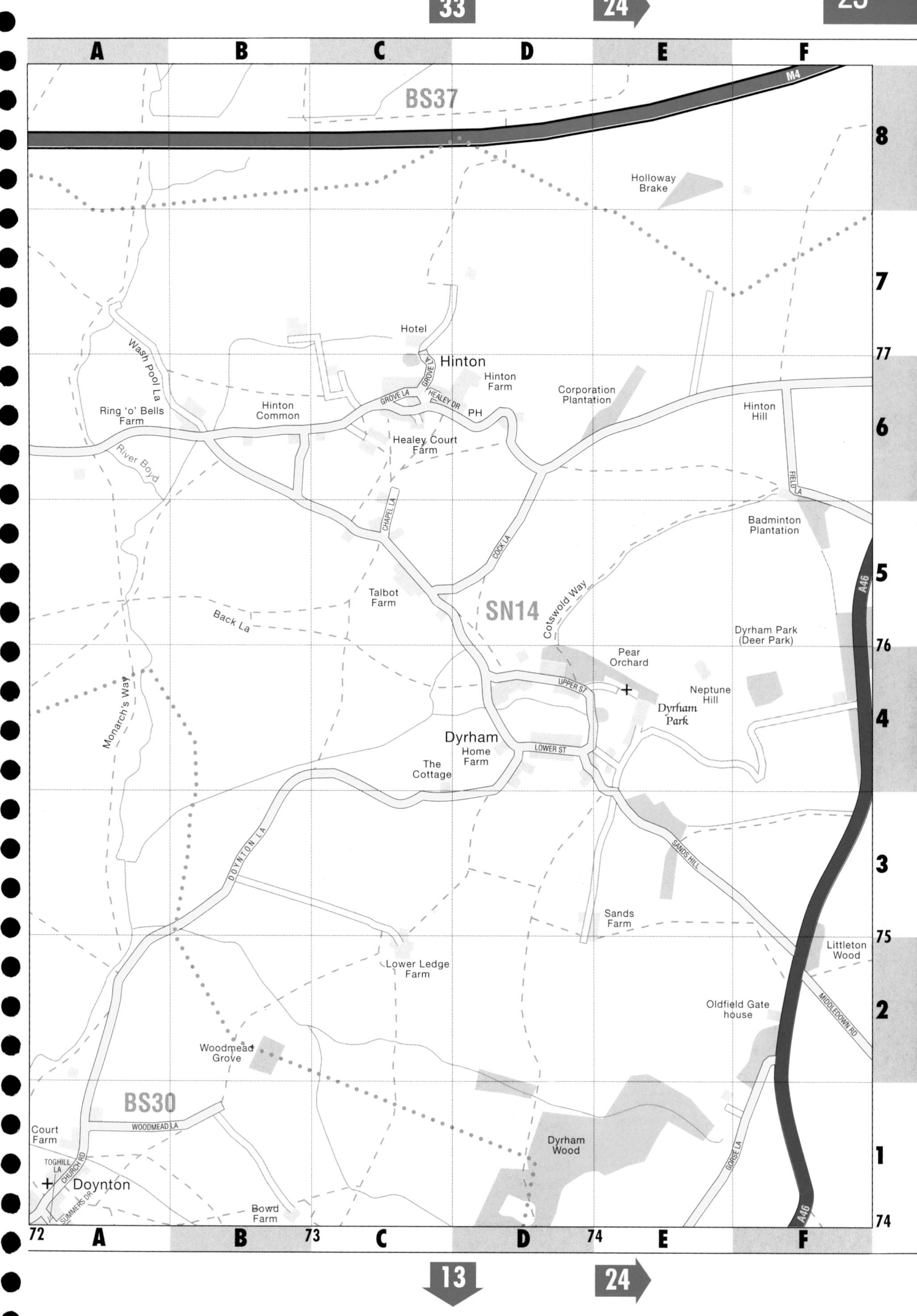

33
24
A
B
C
D
E
F
BS37
M4
8
Holloway Brake
7
Hotel
77
Hinton
Hinton Farm
Corporation Plantation
Wash Pool La
GROVE LA
HEALEY DR
PH
Ring 'o' Bells Farm
Hinton Common
Hinton Hill
6
Healey Court Farm
River Boyd
FIELD LA
CHAPEL LA
Badminton Plantation
COCK LA
5
A46
Talbot Farm
SN14
Cotswold Way
Back La
Dyrham Park (Deer Park)
76
Pear Orchard
UPPER ST
Neptune Hill
Dyrham Park
Monarch's Way
4
Dyrham
Home Farm
LOWER ST
The Cottage
DOYNTON LA
SANDS HILL
3
Sands Farm
75
Littleton Wood
Lower Ledge Farm
Oldfield Gate house
2
MIDDLEDOWN RD
Woodmead Grove
BS30
WOODMEAD LA
Court Farm
Dyrham Wood
1
TOGHILL LA
CHURCH RD
Doynton
SUMMERS DR
GORSE LA
Bowd Farm
A46
74
72
73
74
13
24

23
34

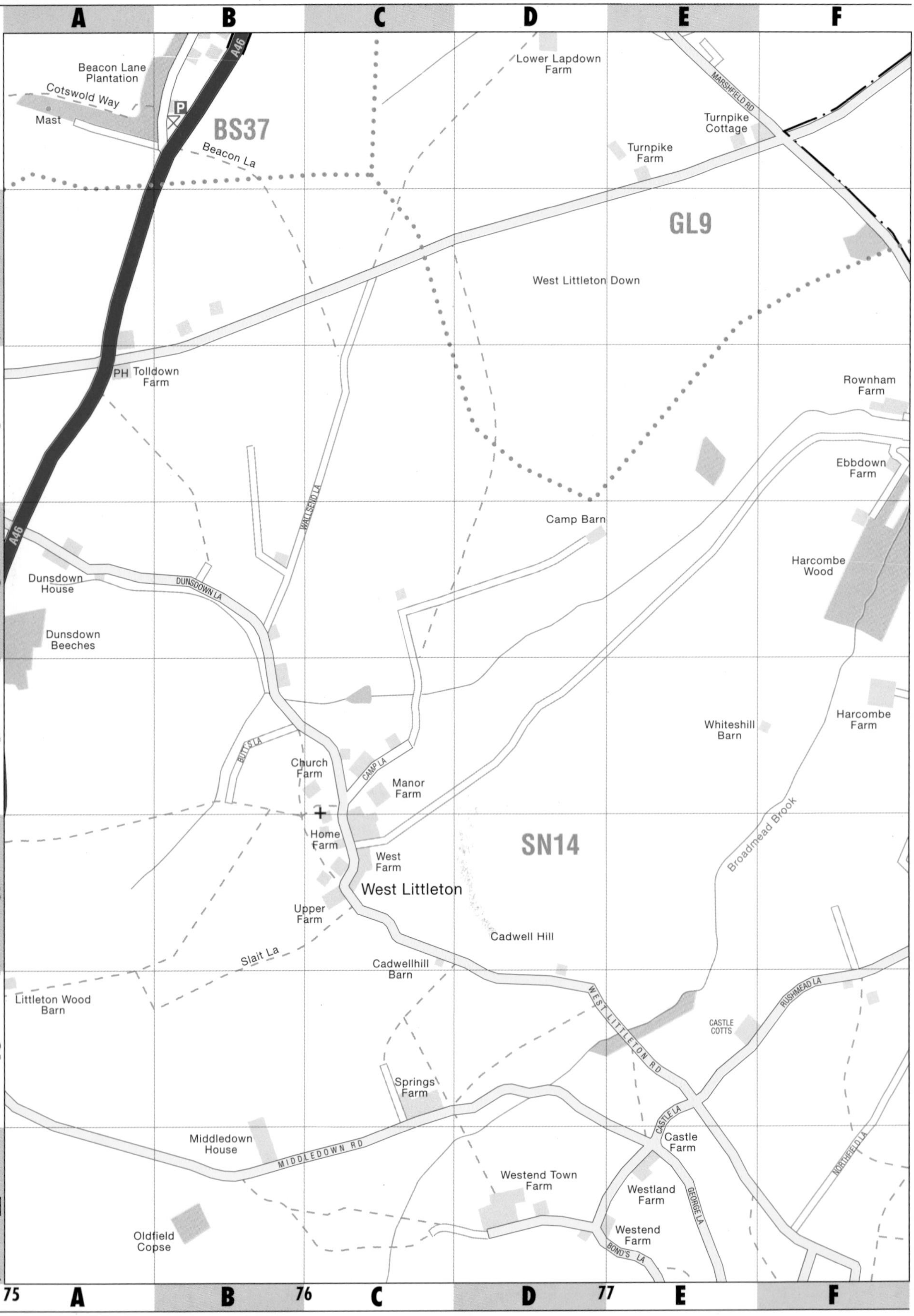

A B C D E F
8 7 77 6 5 76 4 3 75 2 1 74
Beacon Lane Plantation
Cotswold Way
Mast
A46
BS37
Beacon La
Lower Lapdown Farm
MARSHFIELD RD
Turnpike Cottage
Turnpike Farm
GL9
West Littleton Down
PH Tolldown Farm
Rownham Farm
Ebbdown Farm
WALLSEND LA
Camp Barn
Dunsdown House
DUNSDOWN LA
Harcombe Wood
Dunsdown Beeches
Whiteshill Barn
Harcombe Farm
BUTTS LA
Church Farm
CAMP LA
Manor Farm
Home Farm
SN14
Broadmead Brook
West Farm
West Littleton
Upper Farm
Cadwell Hill
Slait La
Cadwellhill Barn
WEST LITTLETON RD
RUSHMEAD LA
Littleton Wood Barn
CASTLE COTTS
Springs Farm
CASTLE LA
Middledown House
MIDDLEDOWN RD
Castle Farm
NORTHFIELD LA
Westend Town Farm
Westland Farm
GEORGE LA
Oldfield Copse
Westend Farm
BOND'S LA
75 A B 76 C D 77 E F

23
14

35

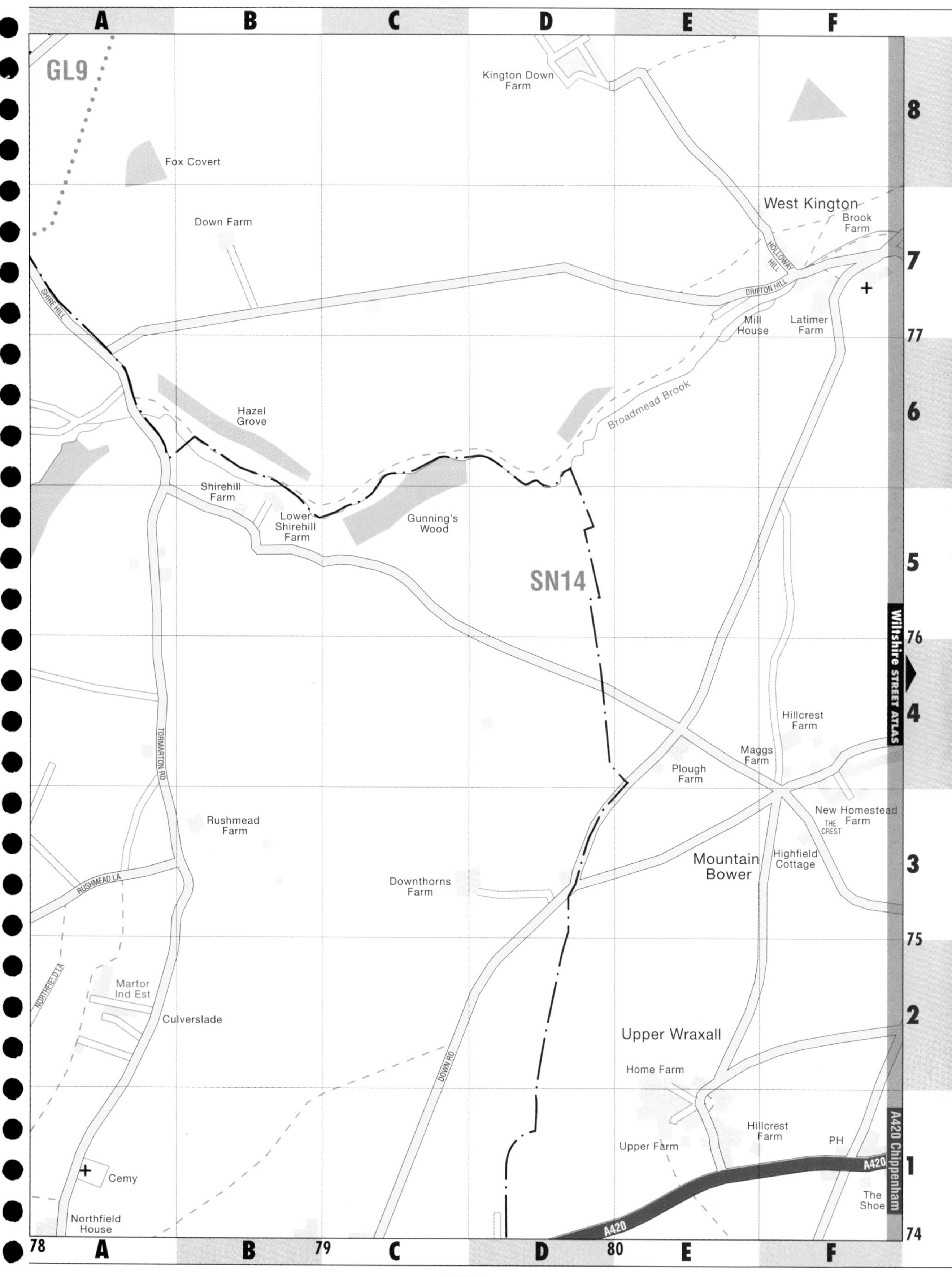

GL9
Kington Down Farm
Fox Covert
Down Farm
West Kington
Brook Farm
HOLLOWAY HILL
DRIFTON HILL
SHIRE HILL
Mill House
Latimer Farm
Hazel Grove
Broadmead Brook
Shirehill Farm
Lower Shirehill Farm
Gunning's Wood
SN14
TORMARTON RD
Hillcrest Farm
Maggs Farm
Plough Farm
New Homestead Farm
THE CREST
Rushmead Farm
RUSHMEAD LA
Mountain Bower
Highfield Cottage
Downthorns Farm
NORTHFIELD LA
Martor Ind Est
Culverslade
Upper Wraxall
Home Farm
DOWN RD
Hillcrest Farm
Upper Farm
PH
A420
Cemy
The Shoe
Northfield House
A420 Chippenham
Wiltshire STREET ATLAS
A B C D E F
8 7 77 6 5 76 4 3 75 2 1 74
78 79 80

15

37

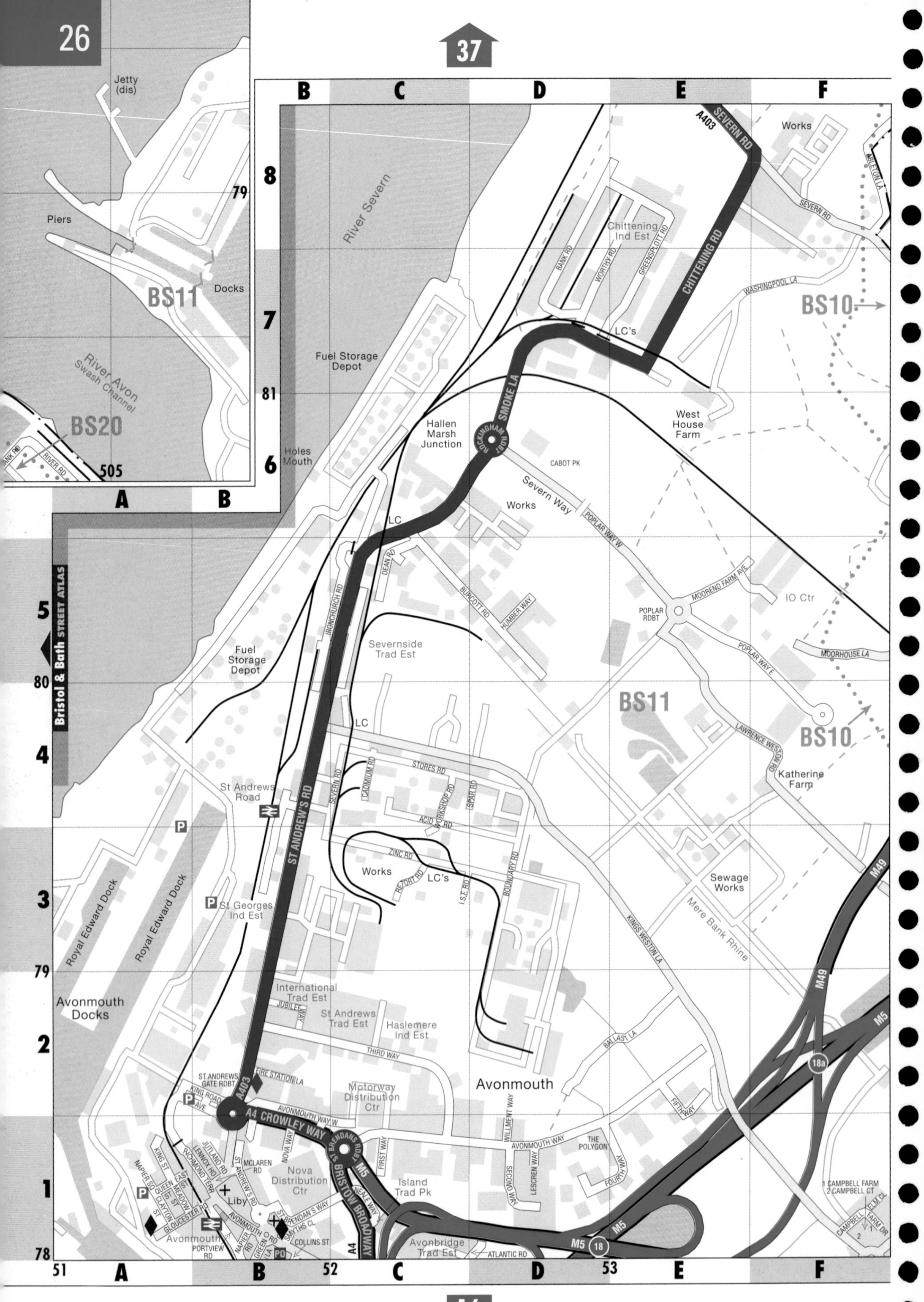
Jetty (dis)
Piers
Docks
BS11
River Avon Swash Channel
BS20
River Severn
Fuel Storage Depot
Holes Mouth
Hallen Marsh Junction
SMOKE LA
ROCKINGHAM RDBT
SEVERN RD
A403
CHITTENING RD
Chittening Ind Est
BANK RD
WORTHY RD
GREENSPLOTT RD
LC's
Works
SEVERN RD
WASHINGPOOL LA
BS10
West House Farm
CABOT PK
Severn Way
Works
POPLAR WAY W
LC
DEAN RD
BURCOTT RD
HUMBER WAY
MOOREND FARM AVE
IO Ctr
POPLAR RDBT
MOORHOUSE LA
POPLAR WAY E
Fuel Storage Depot
IRONCHURCH RD
Severnside Trad Est
BS11
LAWRENCE WESTON RD
BS10
Katherine Farm
LC
STORES RD
SEVERN RD
CADMIUM RD
WORKSHOP RD
SPAR RD
ACID RD
St Andrews Road
ST ANDREW'S RD
ZINC RD
Works
RETORT RD
LC's
I.S.F. RD
BOUNDARY RD
Sewage Works
Mere Bank Rhine
KINGS WESTON LA
M49
Royal Edward Dock
Royal Edward Dock
St Georges Ind Est
Avonmouth Docks
International Trad Est
JUBILEE WAY
St Andrews Trad Est
Haslemere Ind Est
BALLAST LA
M5
18a
THIRD WAY
ST ANDREWS GATE RDBT
FIRE STATION LA
KING ROAD AVE
A403
Motorway Distribution Ctr
Avonmouth
FIFTH WAY
A4 CROWLEY WAY
AVONMOUTH WAY W
ST BRENDANS RDBT
BRISTOW BROADWAY
M5
AVONMOUTH WAY
THE POLYGON
WILLMENT WAY
MOVA WAY
FIRST WAY
Nova Distribution Ctr
Island Trad Pk
SECOND WAY
LESCREN WAY
FOURTH WAY
JUTLAND RD
LENNOX RD
MCLAREN RD
ST ANDREW'S RD
KING ST
NAPIER SQ
QUEEN ST
EAST ST
MEADOW ST
CLAYTON ST
RICHMOND TERR
GLOUCESTER RD
Liby
ST BRENDAN'S WAY
SMYTHS CL
NEALE WAY
1 CAMPBELL FARM
2 CAMPBELL CT
ELM CL
CAMPBELL FARM DR
AVONMOUTH RD
Avonmouth
PORTVIEW RD
NAPIER RD
GREEN LA
COLLINS ST
A4
Avonbridge Trad Est
ATLANTIC RD
M5
18
Bristol & Bath STREET ATLAS
A B C D E F
8 7 6 5 4 3 2 1
79 81 505 80 79 78
51 52 53

16

38
28

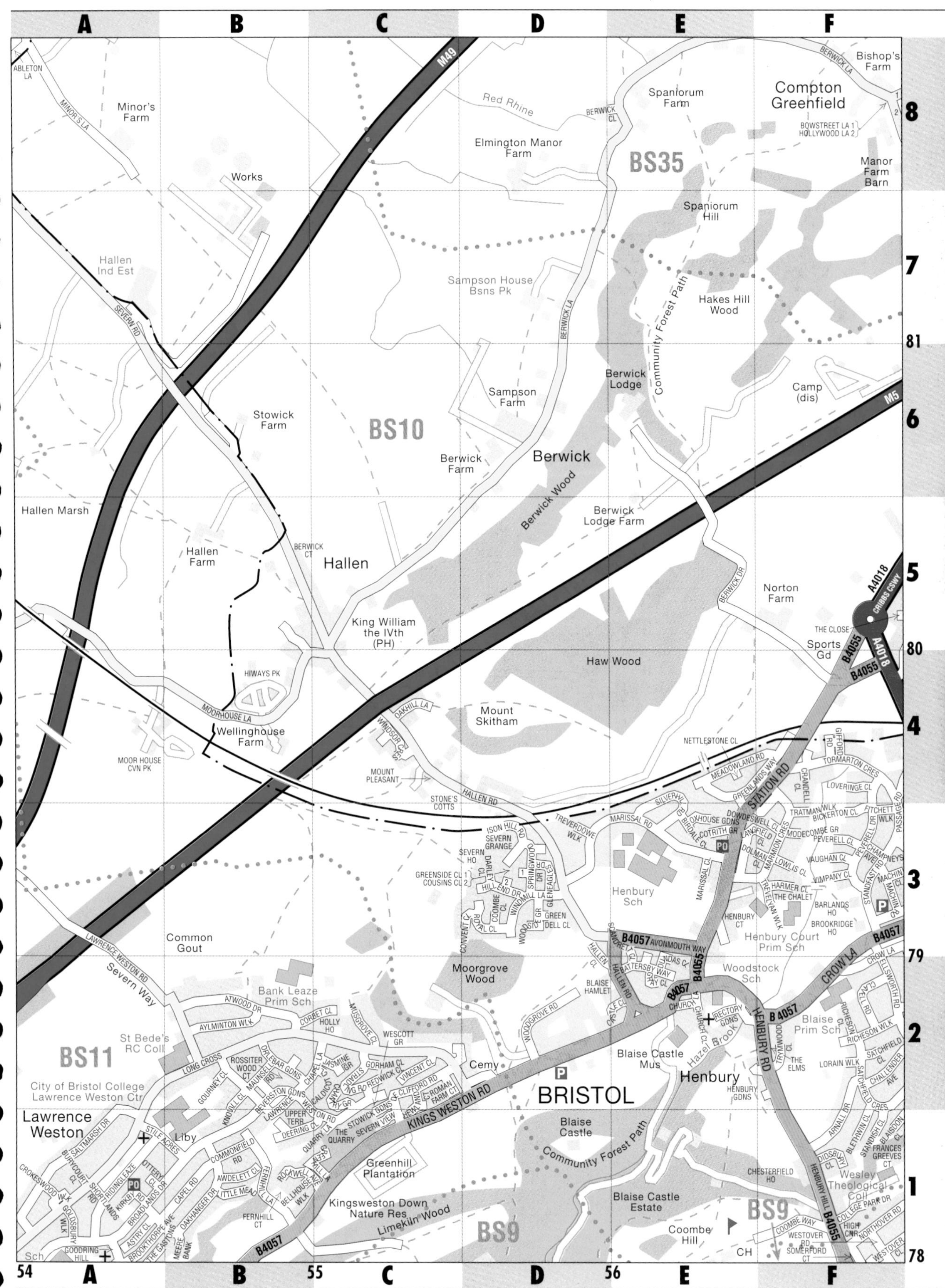

A B C D E F
8 7 81 6 5 80 4 3 79 2 1 78
54 55 56
M49
M5
Minor's Farm
Works
Hallen Ind Est
Hallen Marsh
Hallen Farm
Stowick Farm
BS10
Hallen
King William the IVth (PH)
Wellinghouse Farm
MOOR HOUSE CVN PK
Red Rhine
Elmington Manor Farm
Sampson House Bsns Pk
Sampson Farm
Berwick Farm
Berwick
Berwick Wood
Berwick Lodge
Berwick Lodge Farm
Spaniorum Farm
BS35
Spaniorum Hill
Hakes Hill Wood
Community Forest Path
Compton Greenfield
Bishop's Farm
Manor Farm Barn
Camp (dis)
Norton Farm
Sports Gd
Haw Wood
Mount Skitham
MOUNT PLEASANT
STONE'S COTTS
Henbury Sch
Henbury Court Prim Sch
Woodstock Sch
Blaise Prim Sch
Common Gout
Severn Way
Bank Leaze Prim Sch
St Bede's RC Coll
BS11
City of Bristol College Lawrence Weston Ctr
Lawrence Weston
Liby
Moorgrove Wood
Cemy
BRISTOL
Blaise Castle Mus
Henbury
Blaise Castle
Blaise Castle Estate
Greenhill Plantation
Kingsweston Down Nature Res
Limekiln Wood
BS9
Coombe Hill
Wesley Theological Coll
KINGS WESTON RD
HENBURY RD
STATION RD
CROW LA
B4057
B4055
A4018
CRIBBS CSWY

17
28

27
39

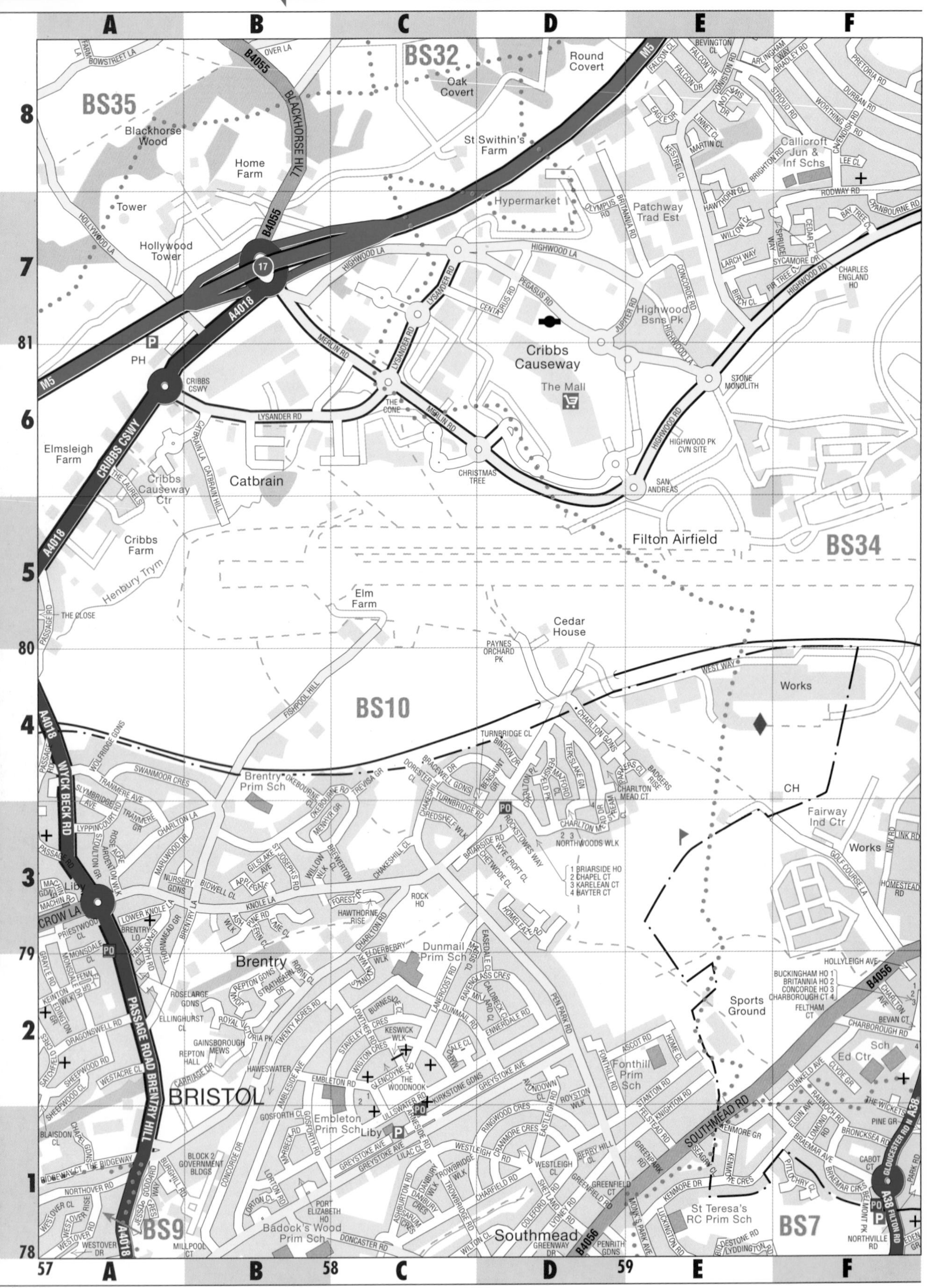

C2
1 GLENCOYNE CT
2 ST STEPHENS CL

27
18

40 30

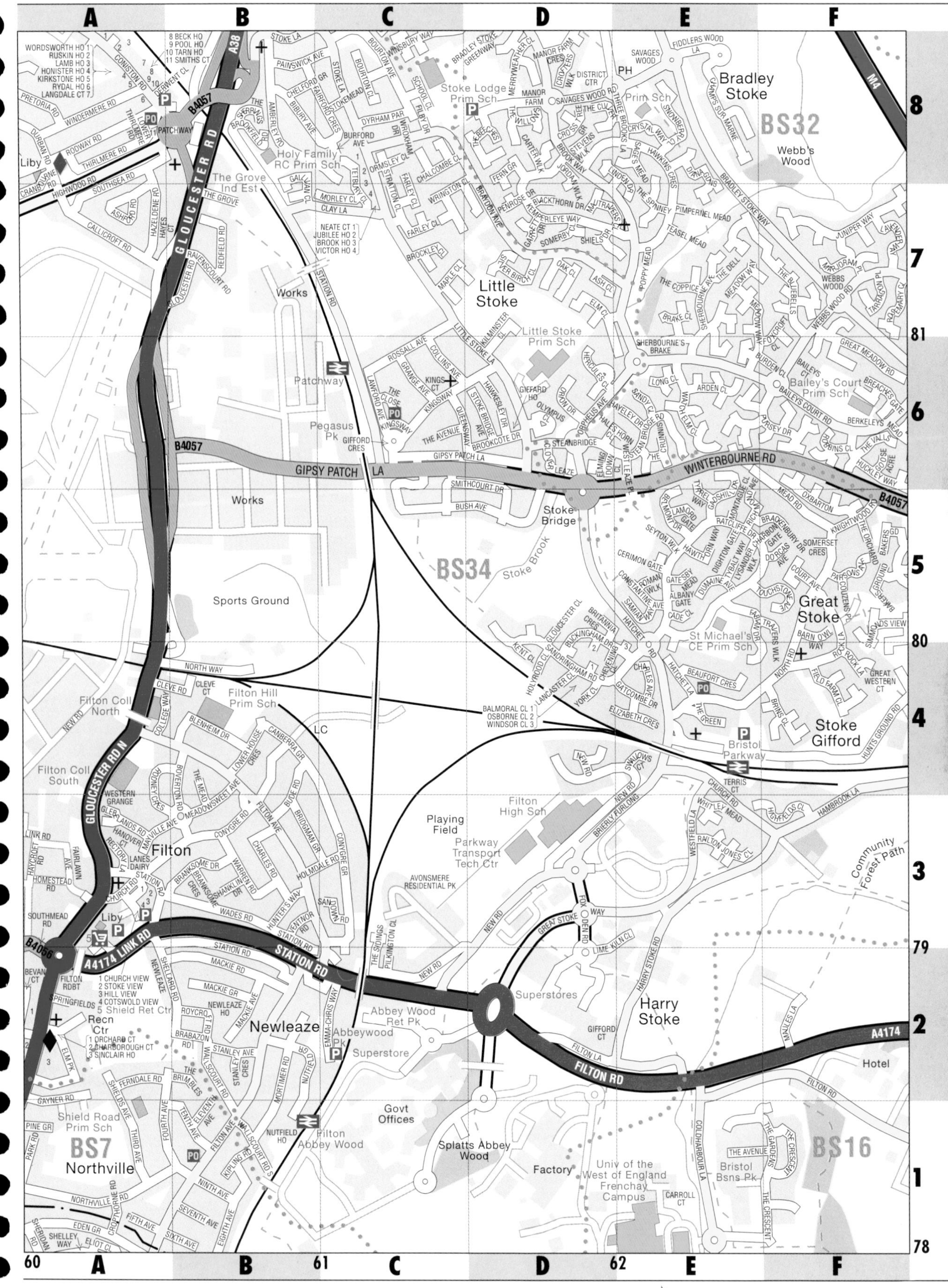

19 30

29 41

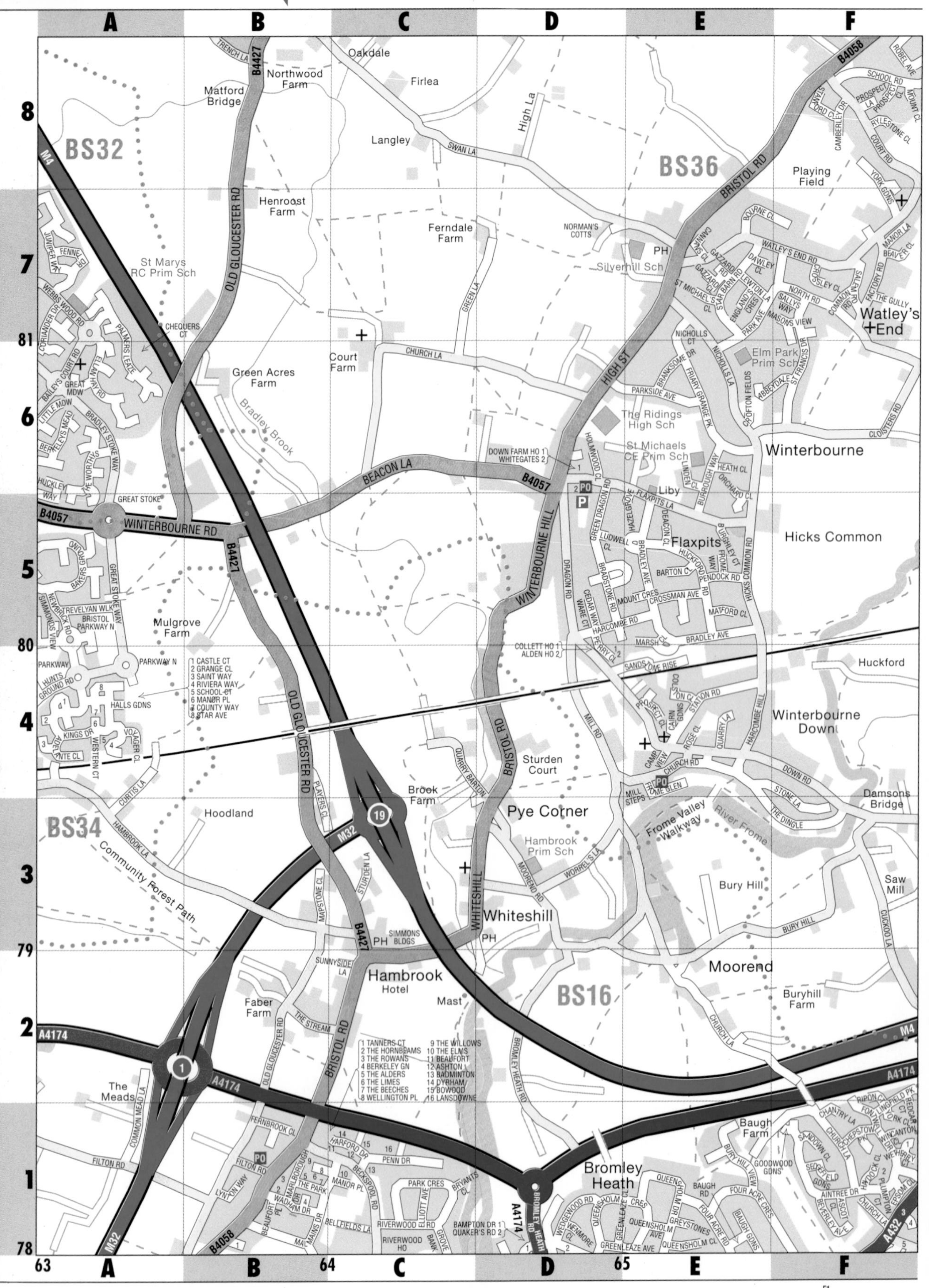

29 20

F1
1 WETHERBY GR
2 KEMPTON CL
3 BADMINTON RD
4 BRITANNIA CL
5 BLACKHORSE LA

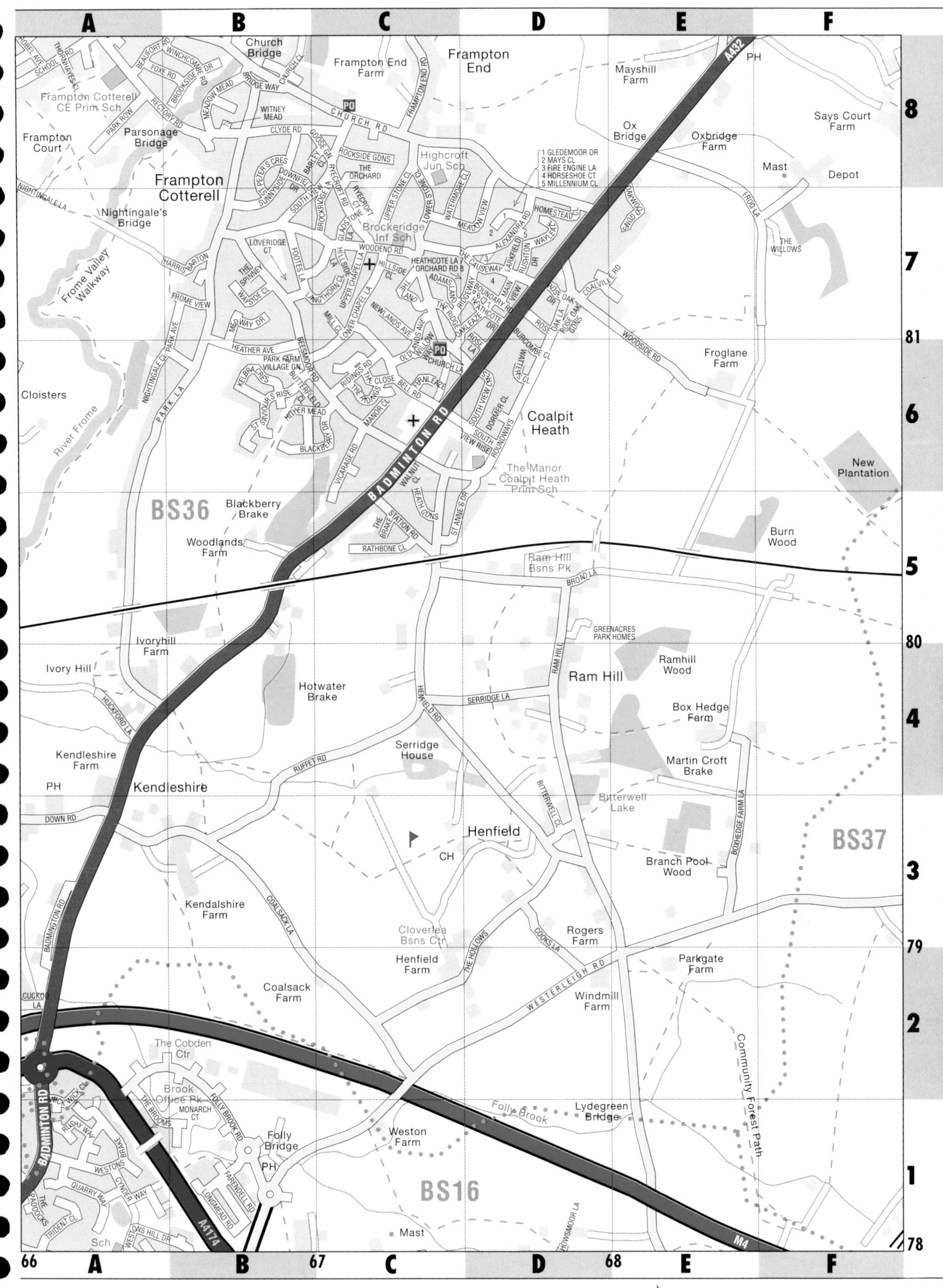
42
32
21
32
Frampton Cotterell
Frampton End
Frampton End Farm
Church Bridge
Frampton Cotterell CE Prim Sch
Frampton Court
Parsonage Bridge
Nightingale's Bridge
Frome Valley Walkway
Highcroft Jun Sch
Brockeridge Inf Sch
Mayshill Farm
Ox Bridge
Oxbridge Farm
Says Court Farm
Mast
Depot
The Willows
Froglane Farm
Cloisters
River Frome
Coalpit Heath
The Manor Coalpit Heath Prim Sch
New Plantation
BS36
Blackberry Brake
Woodlands Farm
Burn Wood
Ram Hill Bsns Pk
Greenacres Park Homes
Ivoryhill Farm
Ivory Hill
Hotwater Brake
Ram Hill
Ramhill Wood
Box Hedge Farm
Kendleshire Farm
Kendleshire
PH
Serridge House
Martin Croft Brake
Bitterwell Lake
Henfield
CH
BS37
Branch Pool Wood
Kendalshire Farm
Cloverlea Bsns Ctr
Henfield Farm
Rogers Farm
Parkgate Farm
Coalsack Farm
Windmill Farm
The Cobden Ctr
Brook Office Pk
Folly Bridge
Folly Brook
Lydegreen Bridge
Weston Farm
Community Forest Path
BS16
Mast
Sch
Badminton Rd
Westerleigh Rd
Ruffet Rd
Serridge La
Coalsack La
Huckford La
Down Rd
Park La
Woodside Rd
Boxhedge Farm La
Broad La
Church Rd
A432
A4174
M4
1 Gledemoor Dr
2 Mays Cl
3 Fire Engine La
4 Horseshoe Ct
5 Millennium Cl
A B C D E F
8 7 81 6 5 80 4 3 79 2 1 78
66 67 68

31
43

D7
1 MINSTER CT
2 FOUNTAIN CT
3 MONKS HO
4 FRIARS HO
5 ABBEY HO
6 PRINKNASH CT

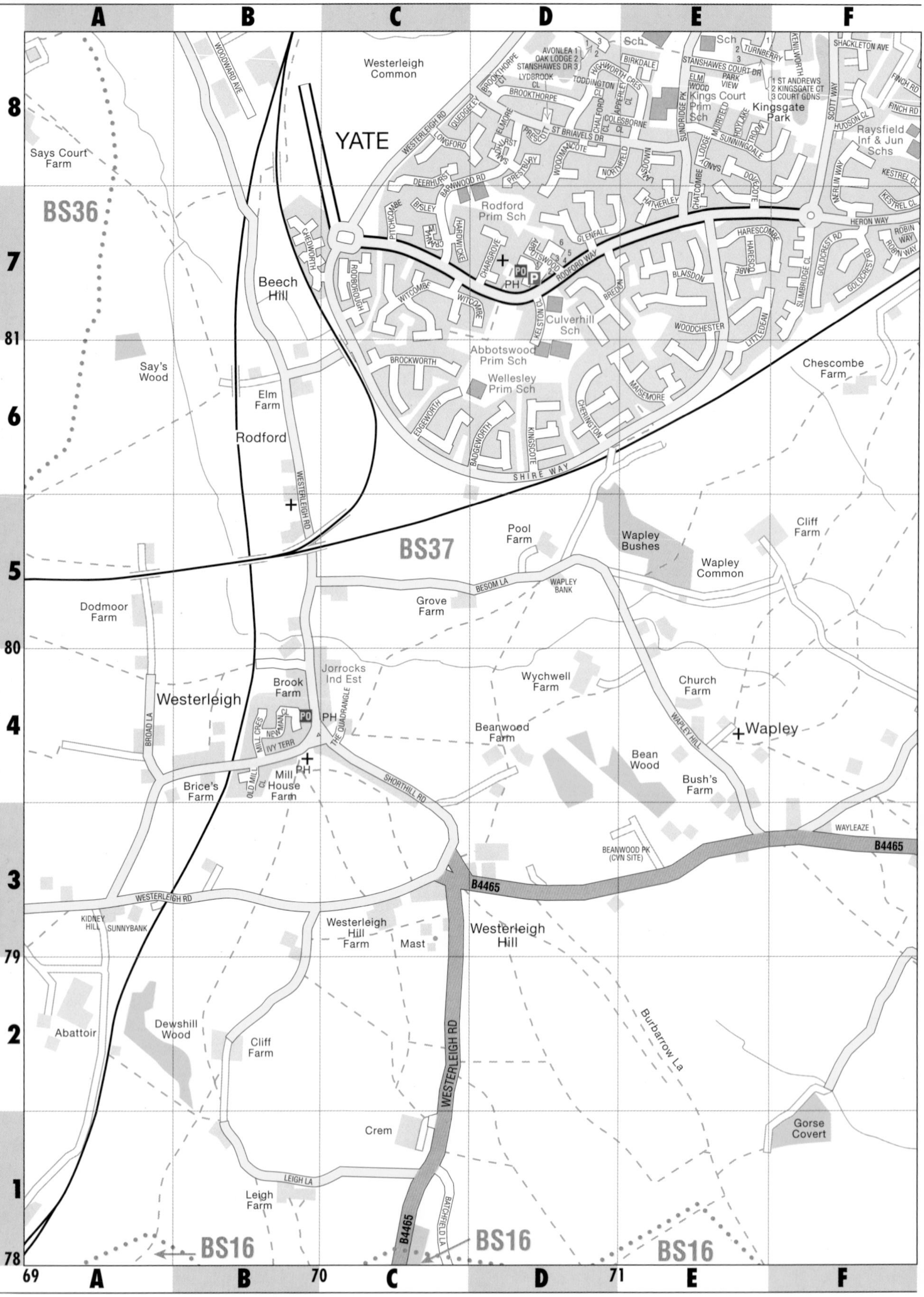

Westerleigh Common
YATE
Says Court Farm
BS36
Beech Hill
Rodford Prim Sch
Culverhill Sch
Abbotswood Prim Sch
Wellesley Prim Sch
Kings Court Prim Sch
Kingsgate Park
Raysfield Inf & Jun Schs
Say's Wood
Elm Farm
Rodford
Chescombe Farm
Pool Farm
BS37
Wapley Bushes
Wapley Common
Cliff Farm
Dodmoor Farm
Grove Farm
Jorrocks Ind Est
Brook Farm
Westerleigh
Wychwell Farm
Church Farm
Beanwood Farm
Wapley
Bean Wood
Bush's Farm
Brice's Farm
Mill House Farm
Westerleigh Hill Farm
Mast
Westerleigh Hill
Dewshill Wood
Abattoir
Cliff Farm
Burbarrow La
Crem
Gorse Covert
Leigh Farm
BS16
BS16
BS16

31
22

44
34

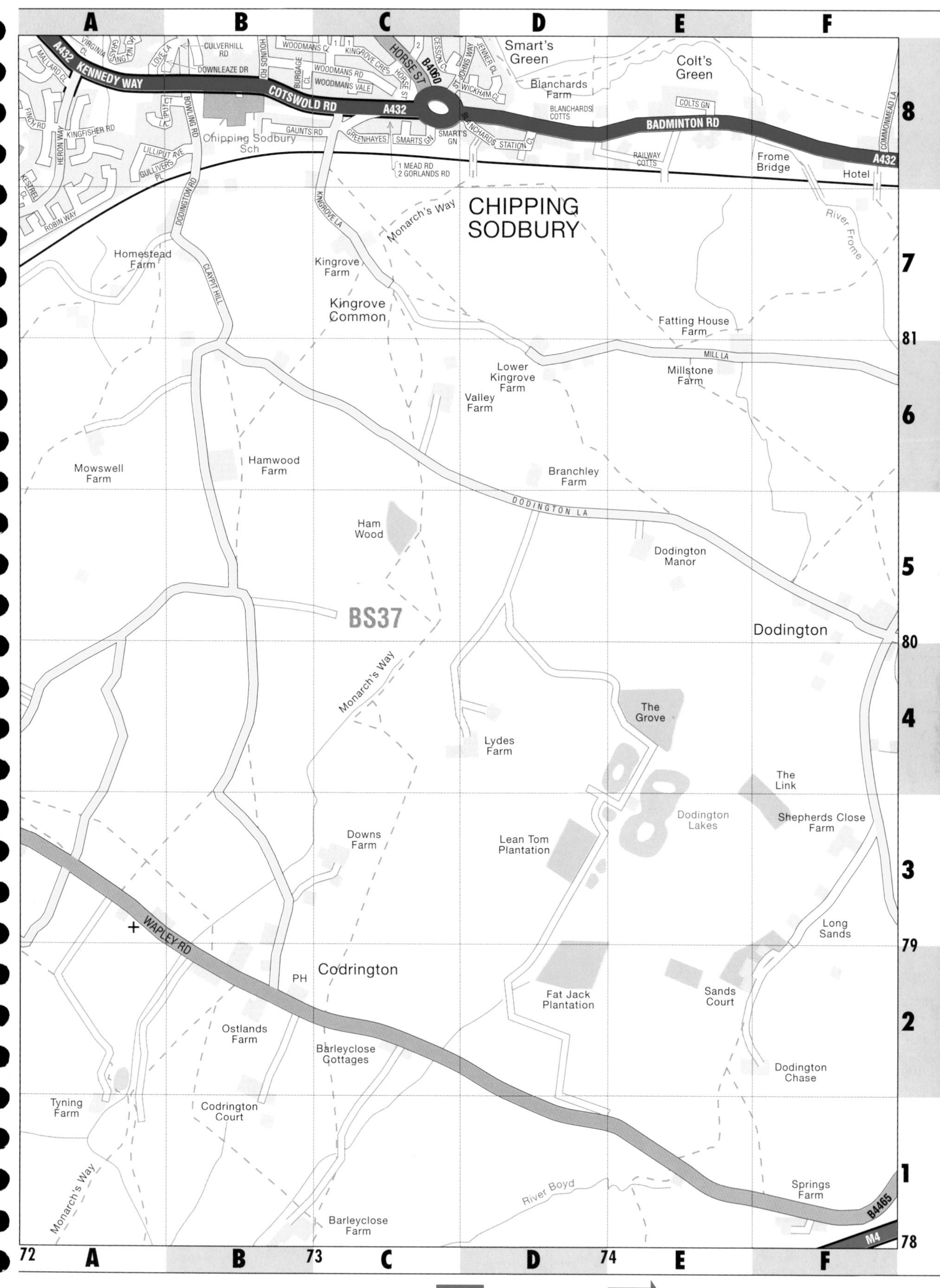
A
B
C
D
E
F
A432
KENNEDY WAY
COTSWOLD RD
A432
BADMINTON RD
A432
HORSE ST
B4060
CHIPPING
SODBURY
Smart's Green
Colt's Green
Blanchards Farm
Chipping Sodbury Sch
Frome Bridge
Hotel
River Frome
Monarch's Way
Homestead Farm
Kingrove Farm
Kingrove Common
Fatting House Farm
MILL LA
Millstone Farm
Lower Kingrove Farm
Valley Farm
Mowswell Farm
Hamwood Farm
Branchley Farm
DODINGTON LA
Ham Wood
Dodington Manor
BS37
Dodington
The Grove
Lydes Farm
The Link
Dodington Lakes
Shepherds Close Farm
Downs Farm
Lean Tom Plantation
Long Sands
WAPLEY RD
Codrington
PH
Fat Jack Plantation
Sands Court
Ostlands Farm
Barleyclose Cottages
Dodington Chase
Tyning Farm
Codrington Court
Monarch's Way
River Boyd
Springs Farm
B4465
M4
Barleyclose Farm
8
7
81
6
5
80
4
3
79
2
1
78
72
73
74

23
34

33
45

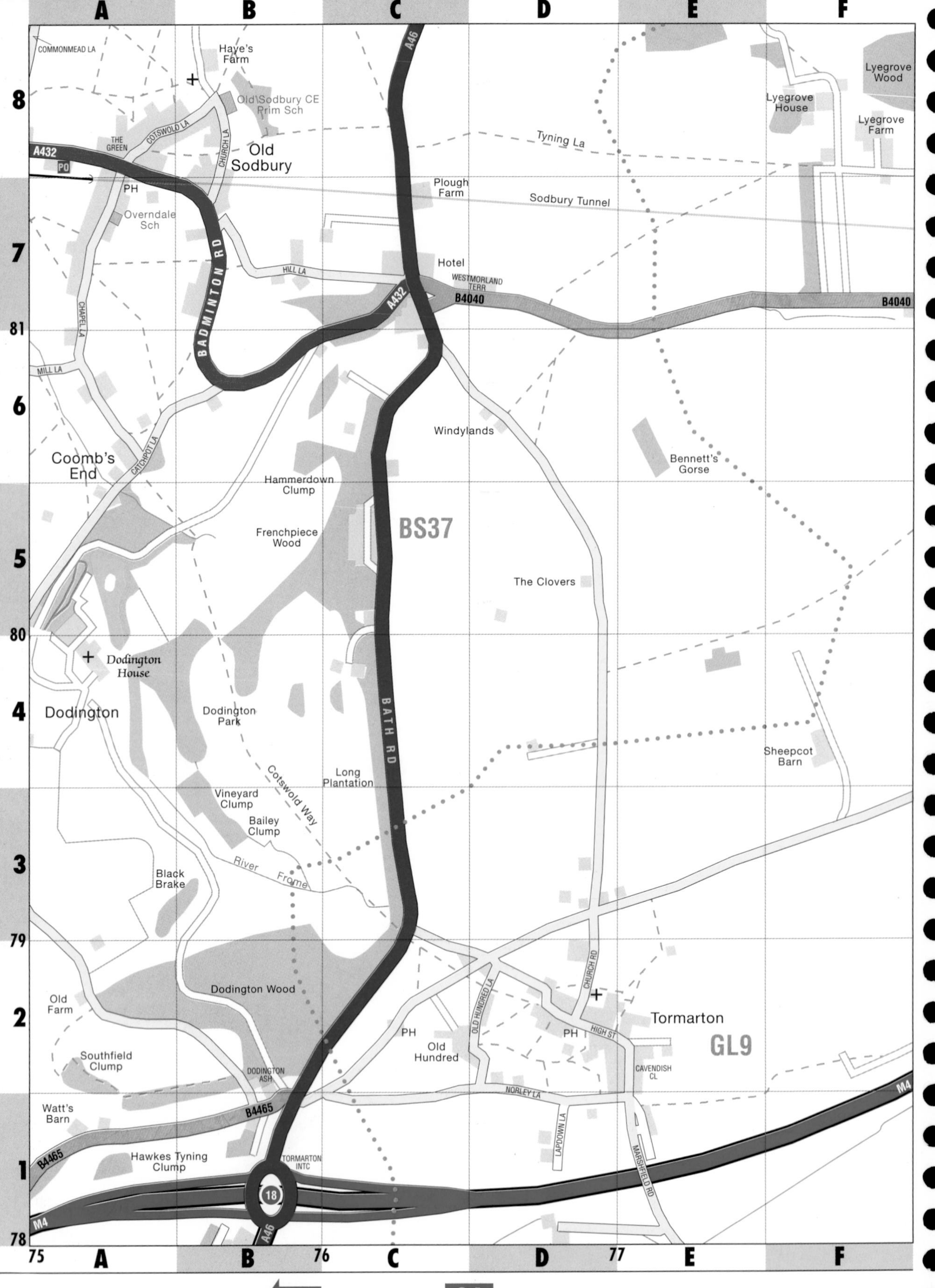
A
B
C
D
E
F
8
7
81
6
5
80
4
3
79
2
1
78
75
76
77
COMMONMEAD LA
Haye's Farm
Old Sodbury CE Prim Sch
Old Sodbury
THE GREEN
COTSWOLD LA
CHURCH LA
A432
PO
PH
Overndale Sch
BADMINTON RD
HILL LA
A46
Plough Farm
Sodbury Tunnel
Tyning La
Hotel
WESTMORLAND TERR
B4040
Lyegrove Wood
Lyegrove House
Lyegrove Farm
CHAPEL LA
MILL LA
CATCHPOT LA
Coomb's End
Windylands
Hammerdown Clump
Frenchpiece Wood
BS37
Bennett's Gorse
The Clovers
Dodington House
Dodington
Dodington Park
BATH RD
Sheepcot Barn
Long Plantation
Cotswold Way
Vineyard Clump
Bailey Clump
River Frome
Black Brake
Dodington Wood
Old Farm
Southfield Clump
OLD HUNDRED LA
CHURCH RD
HIGH ST
Tormarton
GL9
Old Hundred
CAVENDISH CL
NORLEY LA
DODINGTON ASH
B4465
Watt's Barn
Hawkes Tyning Clump
TORMARTON INTC
18
LAPDOWN LA
MARSHFIELD RD
M4

33
24

46
36

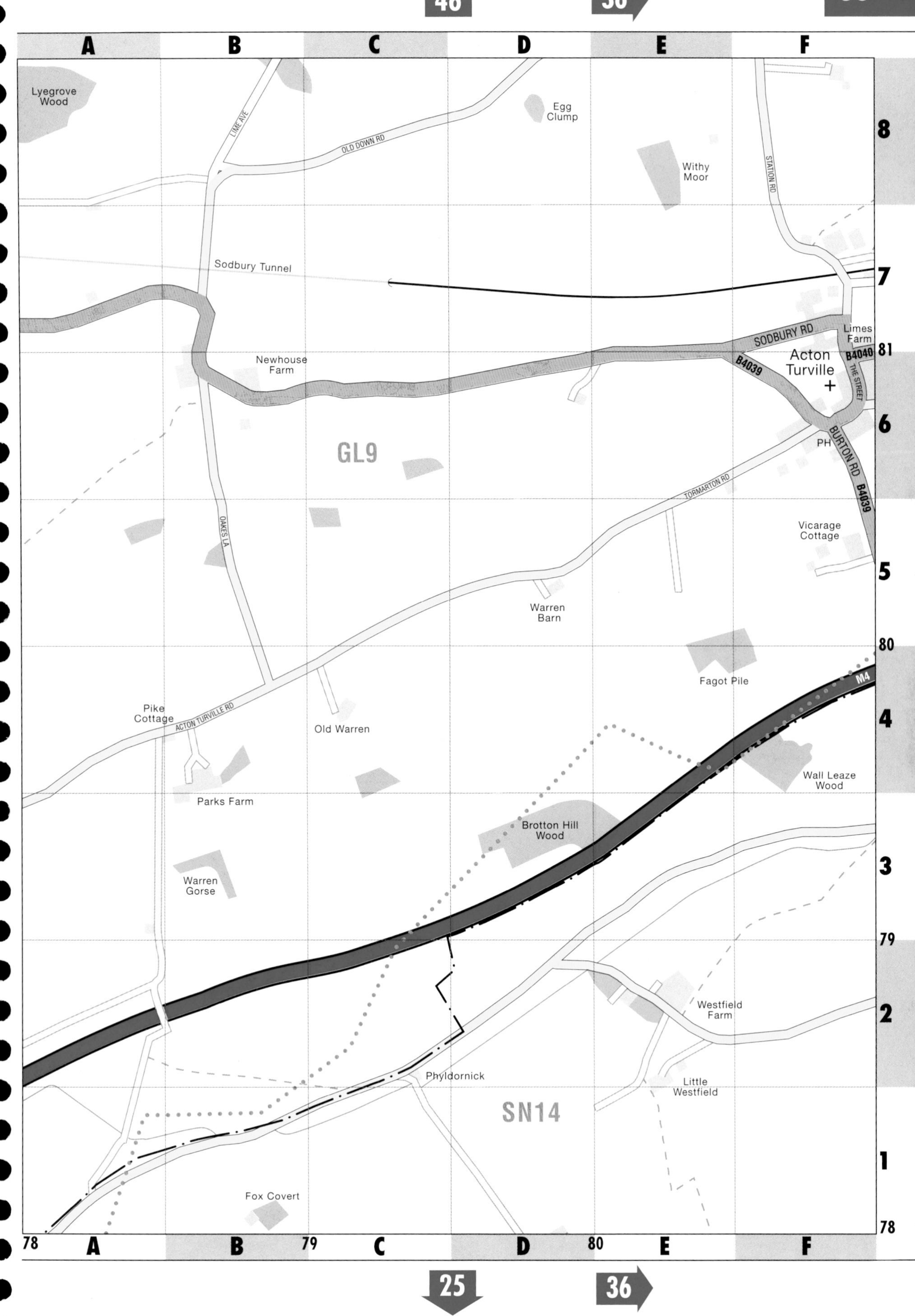
A
B
C
D
E
F
Lyegrove Wood
LIME AVE
OLD DOWN RD
Egg Clump
Withy Moor
STATION RD
Sodbury Tunnel
SODBURY RD
Limes Farm
B4040
Acton Turville
B4039
THE STREET
Newhouse Farm
GL9
PH
BURTON RD
B4039
TORMARTON RD
OAKES LA
Vicarage Cottage
Warren Barn
Fagot Pile
M4
Pike Cottage
ACTON TURVILLE RD
Old Warren
Wall Leaze Wood
Parks Farm
Brotton Hill Wood
Warren Gorse
Westfield Farm
Phyldornick
Little Westfield
SN14
Fox Covert
8
7
81
6
5
80
4
3
79
2
1
78
78
79
80

25
36

35
47

A
B
C
D
E
F
8
7
81
6
5
80
4
3
79
2
1
78
81
82
83
Centre Walk Brake
B4040
Cranhill Wood
Alderton Grove Farm
Macmillan Way
Alderton Grove
B4040
CHAPEL LA
1 CHESTNUT CL
2 LITTLETON DREW LA
3 HOLLYBUSH CL
GL9
Goulter's Gorse
ALDERTON RD
Hollybush Farm
Trinity CE Prim Sch
VIMER'S LA
Ivy Leaze
Manor Farm
Littleton Drew
B4039
Withy Beds
Townsend Farm
M4
Mast
Wiltshire STREET ATLAS
MARSH LA
HILLSIDE
New House Farm
PH
THE STREET
New Town
TOLL DOWN WAY
FREDERICKS WAY
CHURCH HILL
BURTON FARM CL
THE MEADS
Burton
SN14
Horsedown
M4
M4 Swindon
The Gibb
EDGECORNER LA
The Piggeries
Littleworth Plantation
Step Hill Plantation
SUMMER LA
PH
Goulter's Hill Farm
NETTLETON RD
Fosse Bridge
B4039
Macmillan Way
Green Farm
Priory Farm
Lugbury Longbarrow
Mill
Gatcombe Plantation
Gatcombe Hill
Nettleton Green
PO
Gatcombe Wood
Manor Farm
Hanger Wood
Elm Tree Farm
Garrick Wood
LONG LEASE
Square Plantation
Wiltshire STREET ATLAS

35

38

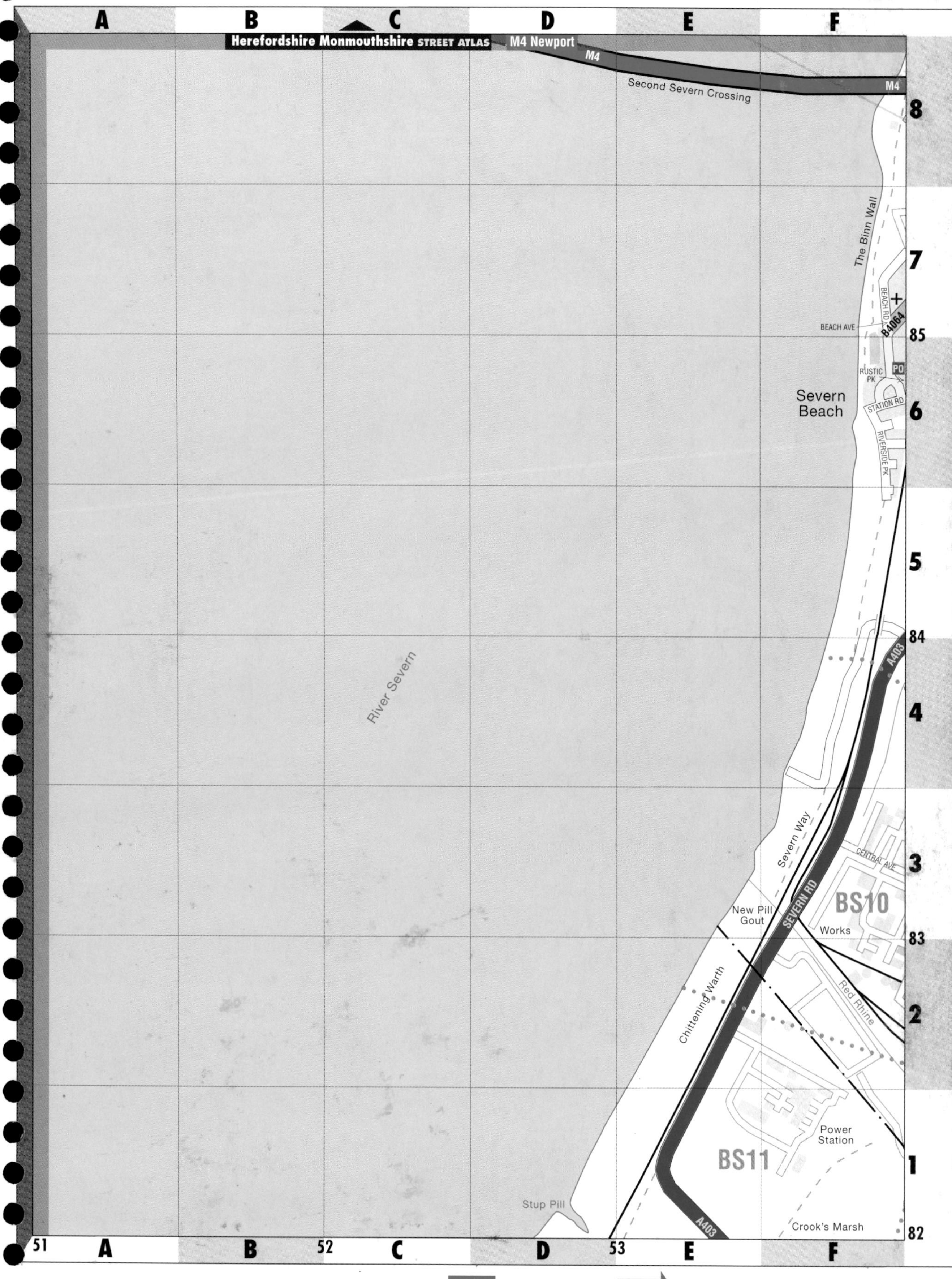

A
B
C
D
E
F
Herefordshire Monmouthshire STREET ATLAS
M4 Newport
M4
Second Severn Crossing
8
The Binn Wall
7
BEACH RD
B4064
BEACH AVE
85
RUSTIC PK
PO
Severn Beach
STATION RD
6
RIVERSIDE PK
5
84
A403
4
River Severn
Severn Way
CENTRAL AVE
3
BS10
SEVERN RD
New Pill Gout
Works
83
Chittening Warth
Red Rhine
2
Power Station
BS11
1
Stup Pill
A403
Crook's Marsh
82
51
52
53

26

38

37 48

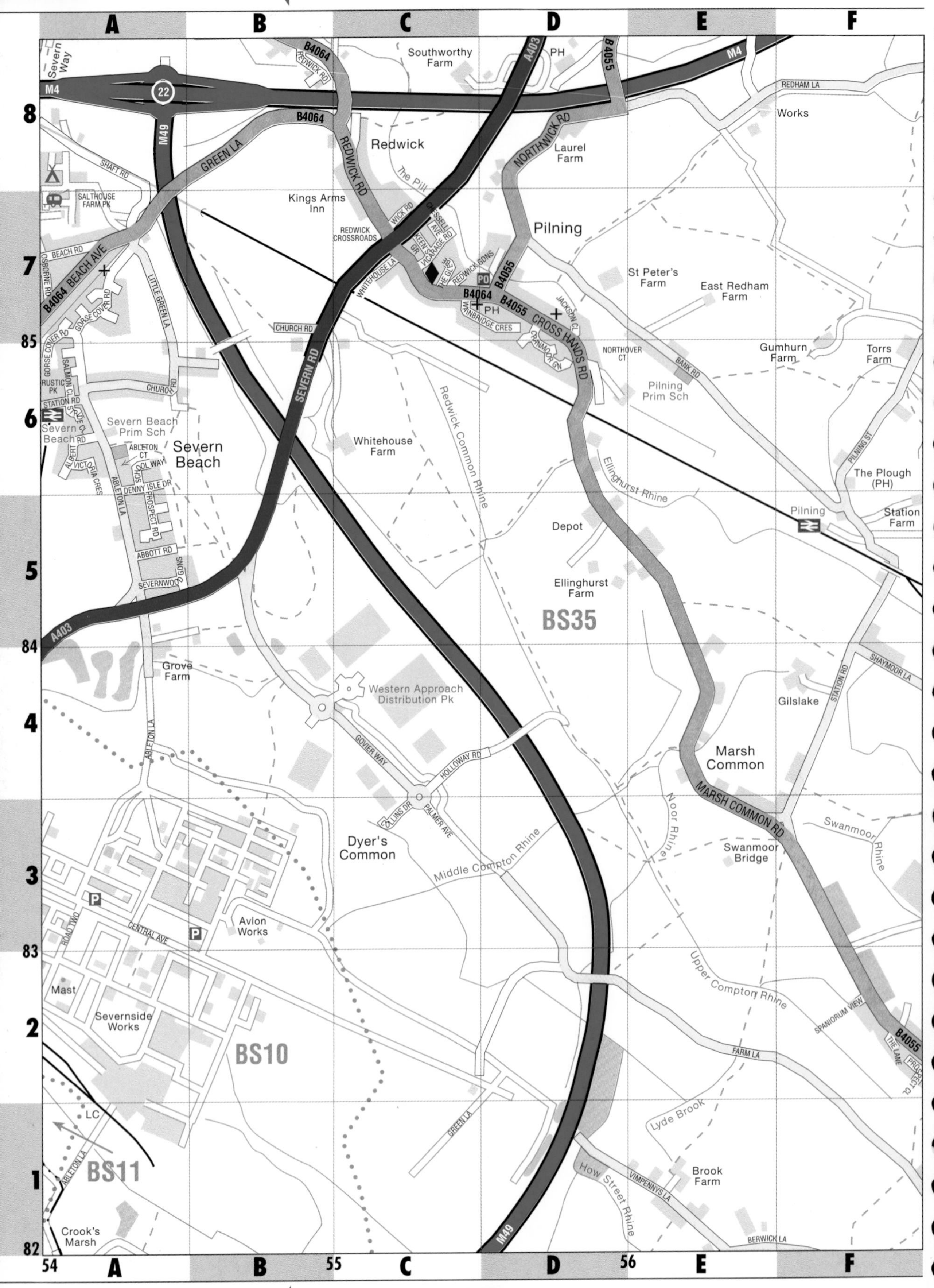
A B C D E F
8 7 85 6 5 84 4 3 83 2 1 82
54 55 56
M4
22
M49
A403
B4064
B4055
Southworthy Farm
PH
Works
Redwick
Laurel Farm
REDWICK RD
GREEN LA
SHAFT RD
SALTHOUSE FARM PK
Kings Arms Inn
REDWICK CROSSROADS
The Pill
Pilning
NORTHWICK RD
REDHAM LA
BEACH RD
BEACH AVE
OSBORNE RD
LITTLE GREEN LA
St Peter's Farm
East Redham Farm
REDWICK GDNS
WHITEHOUSE LA
WAINBRIDGE CRES
CROSS HANDS RD
JACKSON CL
CHURCH RD
NORTHOVER CT
Gumhurn Farm
Torrs Farm
BANK RD
Pilning Prim Sch
SEVERN RD
Redwick Common Rhine
Whitehouse Farm
Severn Beach Prim Sch
Severn Beach
STATION RD
ABLETON LA
DENNY ISLE DR
PROSPECT RD
ABBOTT RD
SEVERNWOOD GDNS
Ellinghurst Rhine
Depot
Pilning
The Plough (PH)
Station Farm
PILNING ST
Ellinghurst Farm
BS35
Grove Farm
Western Approach Distribution Pk
GOVIER WAY
HOLLOWAY RD
SHAYMOOR LA
STATION RD
Gilslake
Marsh Common
MARSH COMMON RD
Noor Rhine
Swanmoor Rhine
Swanmoor Bridge
Dyer's Common
COLLINS DR
PALMER AVE
Middle Compton Rhine
Avlon Works
CENTRAL AVE
ROAD TWO
P
Mast
Severnside Works
BS10
Upper Compton Rhine
SPANIORUM VIEW
FARM LA
THE LANE
Lyde Brook
LC
GREEN LA
BS11
ABLETON LA
How Street Rhine
VIMPENNYS LA
Brook Farm
Crook's Marsh
BERWICK LA

37 27

49
40

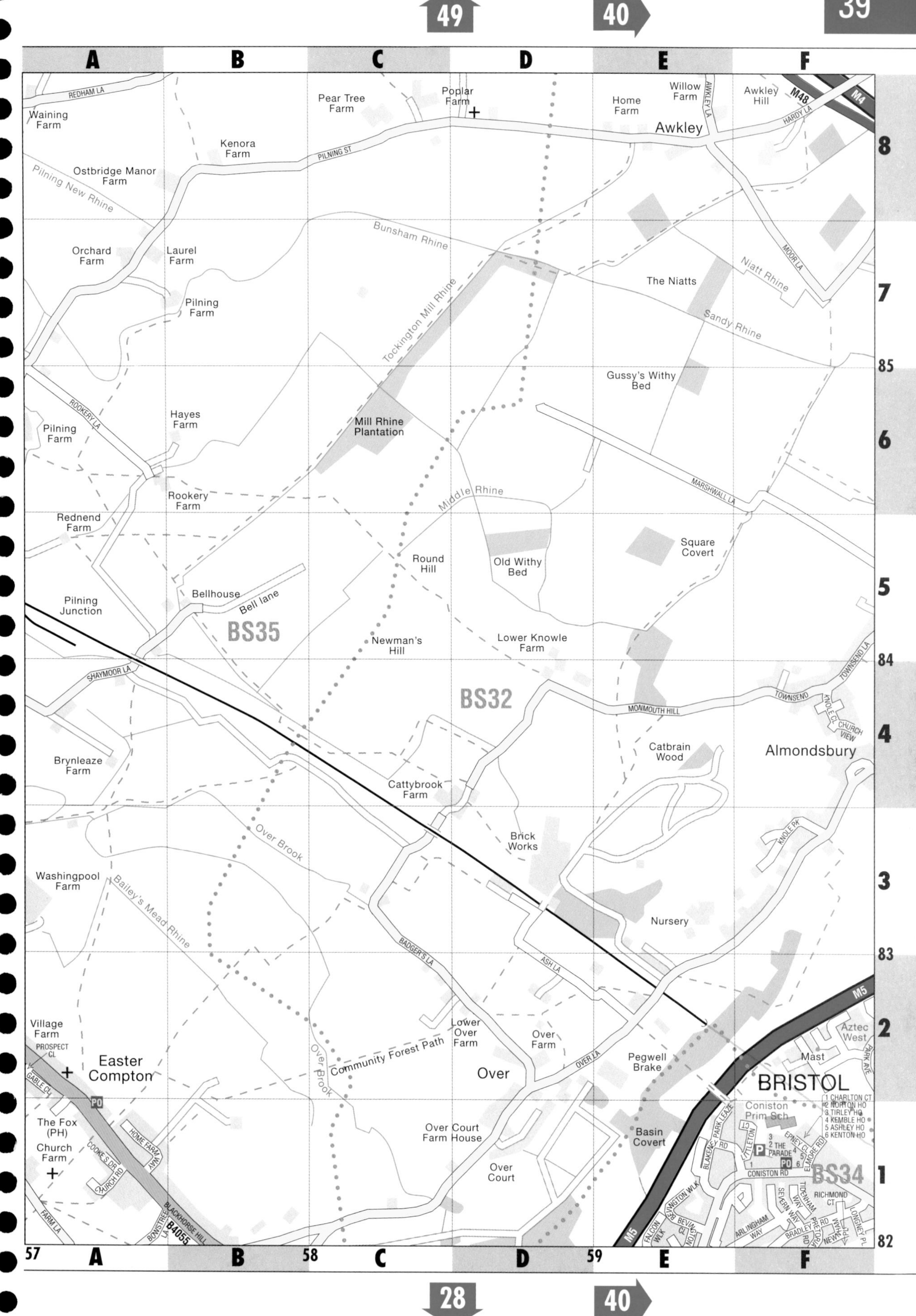
A
B
C
D
E
F
Waining Farm
REDHAM LA
Pear Tree Farm
Poplar Farm
Home Farm
Willow Farm
AWKLEY LA
Awkley Hill
M48
M4
Awkley
HARDY LA
Kenora Farm
PILNING ST
Ostbridge Manor Farm
Pilning New Rhine
Bunsham Rhine
Orchard Farm
Laurel Farm
Pilning Farm
Tockington Mill Rhine
The Niatts
Niatt Rhine
MOOR LA
Sandy Rhine
Gussy's Withy Bed
ROOKERY LA
Pilning Farm
Hayes Farm
Mill Rhine Plantation
Rookery Farm
Middle Rhine
MARSHWALL LA
Rednend Farm
Round Hill
Old Withy Bed
Square Covert
Bellhouse
Bell lane
Pilning Junction
BS35
Newman's Hill
Lower Knowle Farm
SHAYMOOR LA
BS32
MONMOUTH HILL
TOWNSEND
TOWNSEND LA
KNOLE CL
CHURCH VIEW
Brynleaze Farm
Catbrain Wood
Almondsbury
Cattybrook Farm
Over Brook
Brick Works
KNOLE PK
Washingpool Farm
Bailey's Mead Rhine
Nursery
BADGER'S LA
ASH LA
M5
Village Farm
PROSPECT CL
Lower Over Farm
Over Farm
Aztec West
Easter Compton
GABLE CL
Community Forest Path
Over Brook
Over
OVER LA
Pegwell Brake
Mast
PARK AVE
BRISTOL
PO
The Fox (PH)
Church Farm
HOME FARM WAY
COOKE'S DR
CHURCH RD
Over Court Farm House
Coniston Prim Sch
Basin Covert
1 CHARLTON CT
2 NORTON HO
3 TIRLEY HO
4 KEMBLE HO
5 ASHLEY HO
6 KENTON HO
BLAKENEY RD
PARK LEAZE
LYTTLETON
EPNEY CL
ELMORE RD
THE PARADE
Over Court
CONISTON RD
BS34
RICHMOND CT
BLACKHORSE HILL
BOWSTREET LA
B4055
FARM LA
M5
FALCON WLK
BEVINGTON WLK
BEVINGTON CL
ARLINGHAM WAY
SEVERN WAY
TIDENHAM WAY
BRADLEY RD
PRETORIA RD
NEWNHAM PL
LONGNEY PL
8
7
85
6
5
84
4
3
83
2
1
82
57
58
59

28
40

39
50

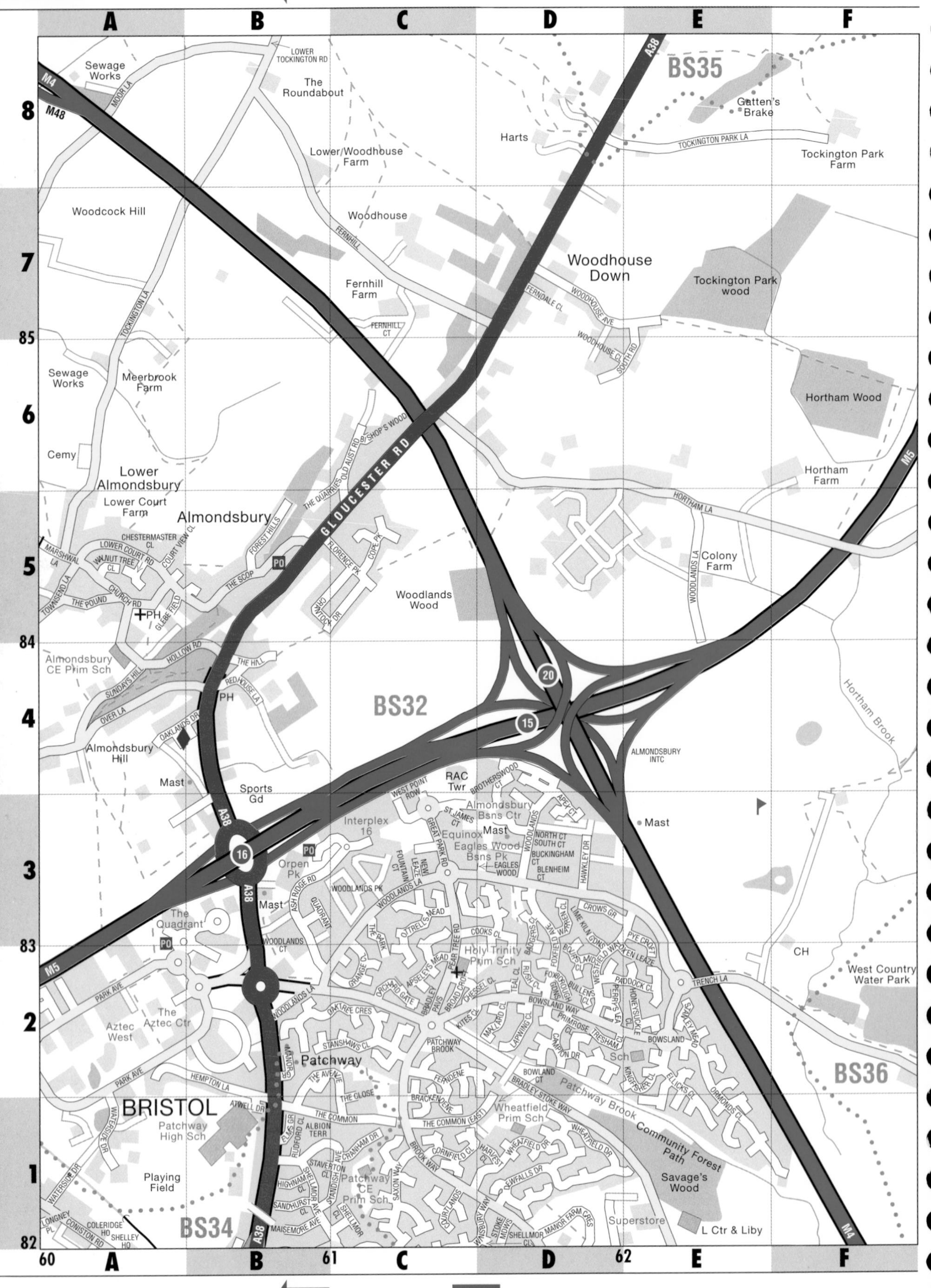
A
B
C
D
E
F
8
7
85
6
5
84
4
3
83
2
1
82
60
61
62
BS35
BS32
BS36
BS34
Sewage Works
Moor La
M4
M48
Lower Tockington Rd
The Roundabout
Harts
Gatten's Brake
Tockington Park La
Tockington Park Farm
Lower Woodhouse Farm
Woodcock Hill
Woodhouse
Fernhill
Woodhouse Down
Tockington Park wood
Fernhill Farm
Fernhill Ct
Ferndale Cl
Woodhouse Ave
Woodhouse Cl
South Rd
Tockington La
Sewage Works
Meerbrook Farm
Hortham Wood
Bishop's Wood
Old Aust Rd
Gloucester Rd
Cemy
Hortham Farm
Lower Almondsbury
M5
Lower Court Farm
Almondsbury
The Quarries
Forest Hills
Hortham La
Chestermaster Cl
Court View Cl
Florence Pk
Cope Pk
Colony Farm
Marshwal La
Lower Court Rd
Walnut Tree Cl
The Scop
PO
Woodlands La
Townsend La
The Pound
Church Rd
Glebe Field
Woodlands Wood
Cherrytock Dr
PH
Almondsbury CE Prim Sch
Hollow Rd
The Hill
Sundays Hill
Red House La
PH
20
Hortham Brook
Over La
Oaklands Dr
15
Almondsbury Hill
Almondsbury Intc
Mast
Sports Gd
RAC Twr
Brotherswood Ct
West Point Row
Almondsbury Bsns Ctr
Apex Ct
A38
Interplex 16
St James Ct
Mast
Mast
16
Equinox
Eagles Wood Bsns Pk
North Ct
South Ct
Buckingham Ct
Blenheim Ct
Hawkley Dr
PO
Orpen Pk
Great Park Rd
New Leaze
Fountain Ct
Eagles Wood
Ash Ridge Rd
Woodlands Pk
Woodlands La
A38
Mast
Quadrant
Crows Gr
Pye Croft
The Quadrant
Trelks Mead
Cooks Cl
Woodlands Ct
Holy Trinity Prim Sch
PO
CH
West Country Water Park
Trench La
Park Ave
Paddock Cl
Apsleys Mead
Pear Tree Rd
Badgers Cl
Teal Cl
Rush Cl
Foxglove Cl
Bullens Cl
Honeysuckle Cl
Perrys Lea
The Aztec Ctr
Aztec West
Woodlands La
Oaktree Cres
Bradley Pavs
Broad Croft
Chessel Cl
Kites Cl
Mallard Cl
Lapwing Cl
Bowsland Way
Primrose Cl
Tresham Cl
Bowsland
Stanshaws Cl
Patchway Brook
Campion Dr
Sch
Park Ave
Patchway
The Avenue
Ferndene
Bowland Ct
Hempton La
The Close
Brackendene
Bradley Stoke Way
Patchway Brook
BRISTOL
Atwell Dr
The Common
Wheatfield Prim Sch
Community Forest Path
Patchway High Sch
Waterside Dr
Albion Terr
Rudford Cl
The Common (East)
Cranham Dr
Cornfield Cl
Harvest Cl
Wheatfield Dr
Playing Field
Staverton Cl
Shellmor Ave
Standish Ave
Patchway CE Prim Sch
Saxon Way
Brook Way
Dewfalls Dr
Savage's Wood
Highnam Cl
Sandhurst Cl
Courtlands
Stoke Mdws
Manor Farm Cres
Superstore
Waterside Dr
Longney Pl
Coniston Rd
Coleridge Ho
Shelley Ho
Maisemore Ave
Shellmor Cl
L Ctr & Liby
M4
A38

39
29

51
42

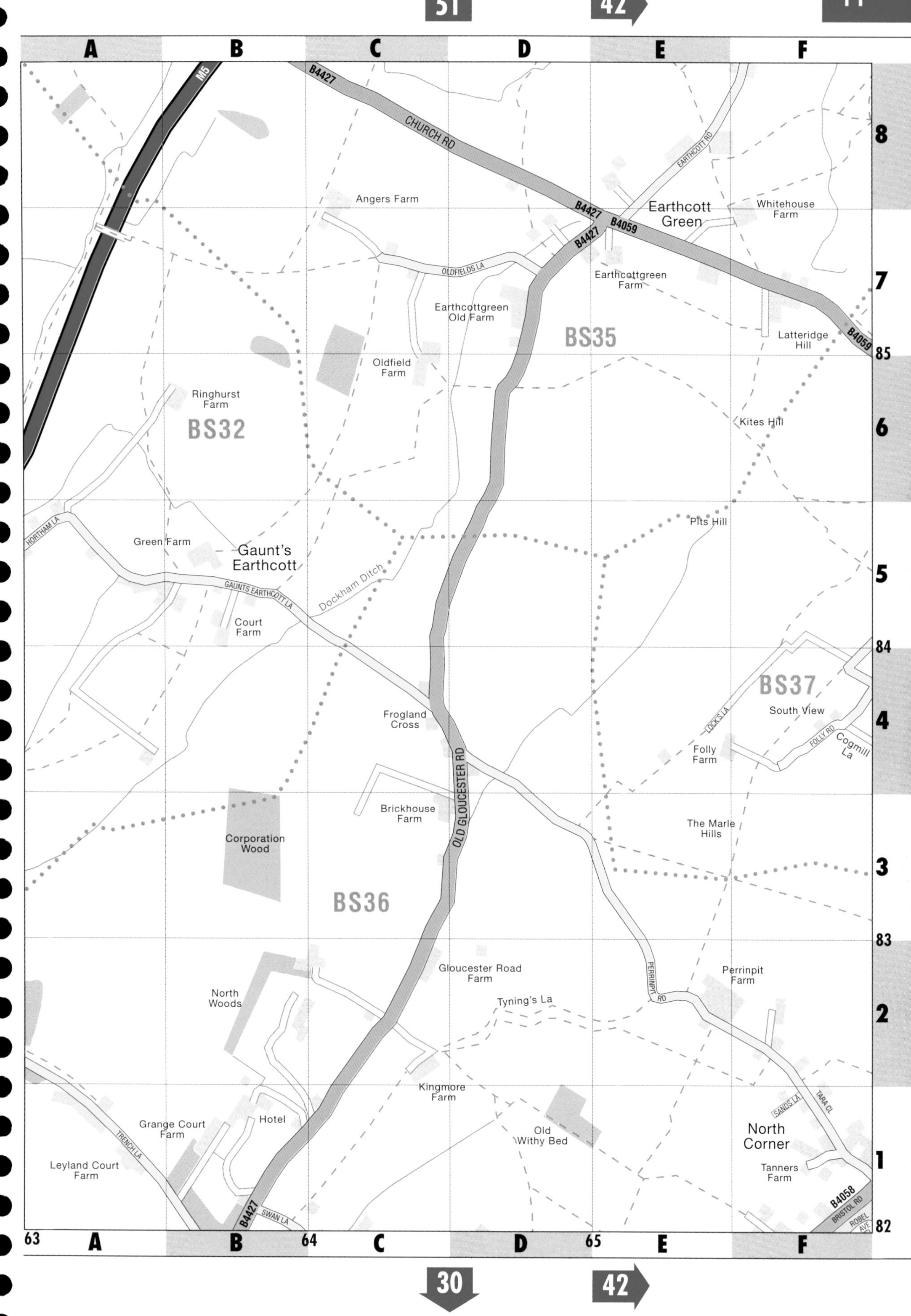
A
B
C
D
E
F
M5
B4427
CHURCH RD
EARTHCOTT RD
Angers Farm
Earthcott
Green
Whitehouse
Farm
B4427
B4059
OLDFIELDS LA
Earthcottgreen
Farm
Earthcottgreen
Old Farm
BS35
Latteridge
Hill
B4059
Oldfield
Farm
Ringhurst
Farm
BS32
Kites Hill
HORTHAM LA
Green Farm
Gaunt's
Earthcott
Pits Hill
GAUNTS EARTHCOTT LA
Dockham Ditch
Court
Farm
BS37
South View
Frogland
Cross
LOCKS LA
Folly
Farm
FOLLY RD
Cogmill
La
OLD GLOUCESTER RD
Brickhouse
Farm
The Marle
Hills
Corporation
Wood
BS36
Gloucester Road
Farm
Perrinpit
Farm
PERRINPIT
RD
North
Woods
Tyning's La
Kingmore
Farm
SANDS LA
TARA CL
Grange Court
Farm
Hotel
TRENCH LA
Old
Withy Bed
North
Corner
Leyland Court
Farm
Tanners
Farm
B4058
BRISTOL RD
ROBEL
AVE
B4427
SWAN LA
8
7
85
6
5
84
4
3
83
2
1
82
63
64
65

30
42

41
52

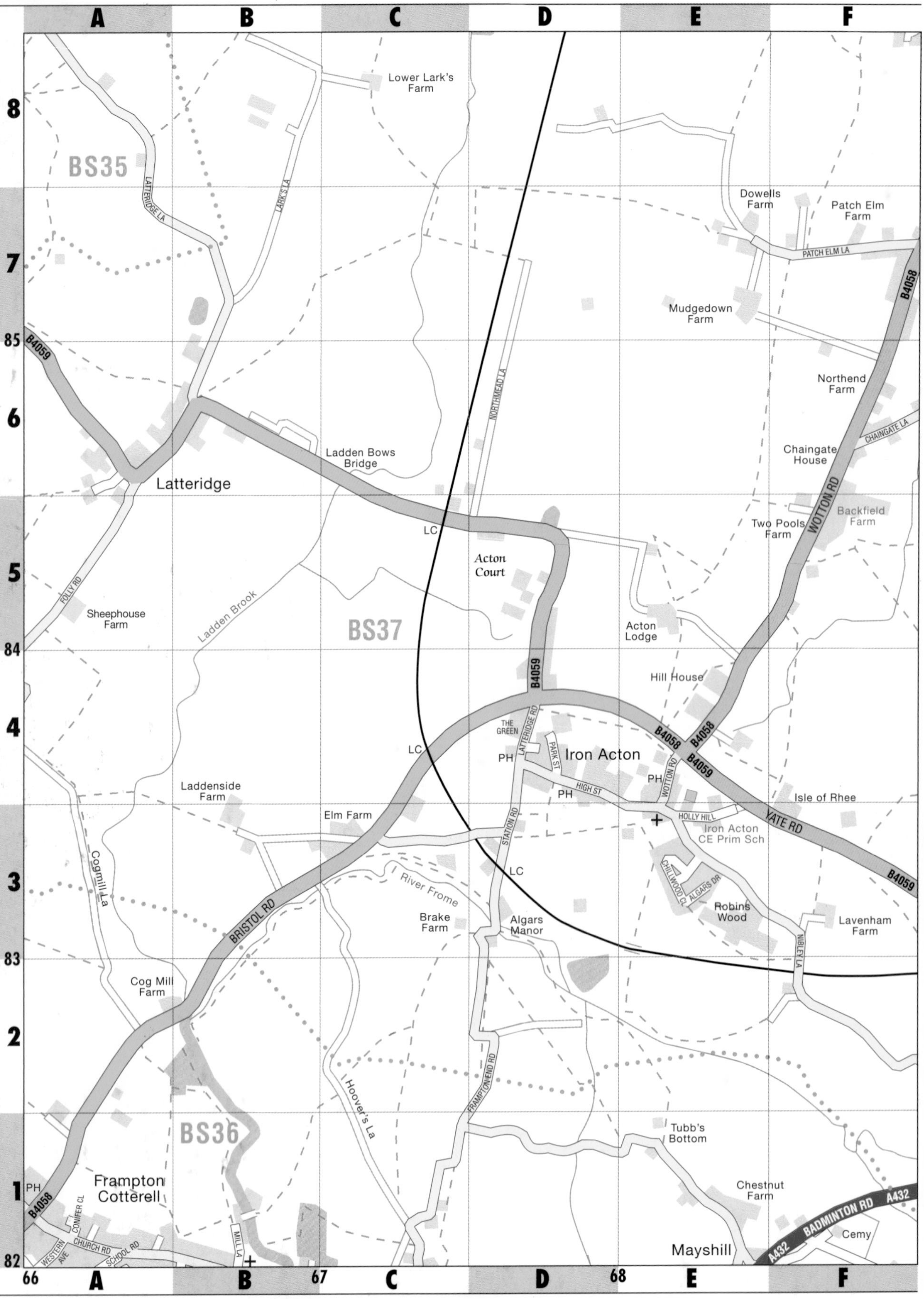

A B C D E F

8 7 85 6 5 84 4 3 83 2 1 82

BS35
BS37
BS36

Lower Lark's Farm
Dowells Farm
Patch Elm Farm
PATCH ELM LA
Mudgedown Farm
Northend Farm
Chaingate House
CHAINGATE LA
Backfield Farm
Two Pools Farm
WOTTON RD
B4058
B4059
LATTERIDGE LA
LARK'S LA
NORTHMEAD LA
Ladden Bows Bridge
Latteridge
LC
Acton Court
Acton Lodge
Hill House
FOLLY RD
Sheephouse Farm
Ladden Brook
THE GREEN
LATTERIDGE RD
PARK ST
Iron Acton
PH
HIGH ST
WOTTON RD
HOLLY HILL
Iron Acton CE Prim Sch
YATE RD
Isle of Rhee
Laddenside Farm
Elm Farm
STATION RD
Cognmill La
River Frome
BRISTOL RD
CHILLWOOD CL
ALGARS DR
Robins Wood
Lavenham Farm
NIBLEY LA
Brake Farm
Algars Manor
Cog Mill Farm
FRAMPTON END RD
Hoover's La
Tubb's Bottom
Chestnut Farm
Frampton Cotterell
CONIFER CL
WESTERN AVE
CHURCH RD
SCHOOL RD
MILL LA
Mayshill
A432
BADMINTON RD
Cemy

66 67 68

41
31

53
44

A B C D E F

8
7
85
6
5
84
4
3
83
2
1
82

Rangeworthy
Southwood Farm
Yate Court
Yate Court (remains of)
Mill
Leechpool
Tan House Farm
Hartstrow
Ladden Brook
Yate Rocks
Ford Farm
Old Wood Colliery (dis)
The Barton Farm
Greenlane Farm
Sunnyside Farm
Engine Common
BS37
Outdoor Sports Complex
Brimsham Green Sch
Stone Mill
Brimsham Park Sh Ctr
PH
THE BRITISH
North Road Com Prim Sch
PO
1 Oakland Bsns Pk
2 ORCHARD CT
Pool Farm
The Alpha Ctr
Goose Green
Inf Sch
Great Western Bsns Pk
Northavon Bsns Ctr
Frome bank Jun Sch
Northridge Bsns Ctr
Beeches Ind Est
Stover Trad Est
The Laurels
St Mary's CE Prim Sch
Yate Her Ctr
Schs
Yate
Superstore
Nibley
Badminton Road Trad Est
L Ctr
Liby
Sh Ctr
Westerleigh Bsns Pk
Factory
Westerleigh Common
1 BADMINTON CT
2 The Badminton Ctr
YATE
King Edmund Com Sch
BS36
CORBETT CL 1
PARTRIDGE CL 2
HAMPSHIRE WAY 3
GREENWAYS RD 4

B4058
WOTTON RD
GIFFORD CL
AUDLEY CL
NEW RD
THE GROVE
THE MEAD
BERROWS MEAD
WICKWAR RD
PATCH LA
MANOR RD
CHAINGATE LA
OLDWOOD LA
BULLY LA
LIMEKILN RD
TANHOUSE LA
BURY HILL LA
YATE ROCKS
ENGINE COMMON LA
NORTH RD
DYER'S LA
MISSION RD
BROAD LA
LODGE RD
IRON ACTON WAY
B4059
YATE RD
WADE RD
CHURCHWARD RD
ARMSTRONG WAY
HAWKESWORTH RD
ARMSTRONG CT
ROWAN CT
DEAN CT
COLLETT WAY
DEAN RD
FALCONS GATE
RIVER MEAD
RAINBOW CT
LAVENHAM RD
WAVERLEY RD
LAWRENCE DR
CHAPEL ORCH
BRUNEL CT
BRIDGE RD
HOPE RD
STOVER RD
MILLBROOK RD
WELLINGTON DR
NIBLEY LA
BADMINTON RD
SOUTH AVE
CULVERT AVE
TURNER DR
GOODRICH CL
WOODWARD AVE
EASTER CT
PEAR TREE HEY
SKYLEAZE
MEADOW MEAD
LEECHPOOL WAY
THE BRAKE
LONG MEAD
CLAYFIELD
THE KNAPP
COOPERS DR
EASTFIELD DR
SUMMERS MEAD
LOWER MOOR RD
TYLERS WAY
BARKERS MEAD
HARTS CROFT
PEG HILL
B4060
LIME CROFT
THE DINGLE
TYLERS FARM
HESTER WOOD
GRAVE HILL RD
CARMARTHEN CL
LARK RISE
LONG CROFT
RANDOLPH AVE
HAYLEAZE
GOOSE GREEN WAY
HAMPDEN CL
STIRLING CL
YORK CL
SUTHERLAND AVE
HALIFAX RD
STURMER CL
ARGYLE DR
GOOSE GN
OAK CL
ASH CL
BADER CL
WAVELL CL
WELLINGTON RD
HOMEFIELD
RECTORY CL
CORNWALL CRES
KENT AVE
CELESTINE RD
BLENHEIM DR
MOUNTBATTEN CL
CAMBRIAN DR
LANCASTER RD
PIPER RD
ULLSWATER CL
CHURCH RD
CHICHESTER WAY
CHESHIRE CL
WARREN WAY
CROWTHERS AVE
GREENWAYS RD
CANTERBURY CL
CHURCHILL CL
SOMERSET AVE
WHITLEY CL
WINDSOR DR
CRANLEIGH COURT RD
TYNDALE AVE
MADISON CL
BEAUFORT AVE
BEAUFORT RD
SHARE RD
BIRCH RD
TEMPLAR RD
ELMGROVE DR
ORCHARD CL
ST MARY'S WAY
MELROSE AVE
MERCIER CL
HIGHGROVE CRES
PLOVER CL
LONGS DR
RANNAL CRES
THE WILLOWS
FOX AVE
GATHORNE CRES
STAPLES RD
MILTON RD
BIRCH CT
HOME ORCH
THE GLEN
SCHOOL WLK
TYNING
TURNPIKE CL
LAWNS RD
TREE LEAZE
SWAN FIELD
RIDGEWAY
NEWLYN WAY
HIGHWAY
BROADWAY
FOLLY BRIDGE CL
MILTON CL
POOLE COURT DR
THE LEAZE
B4060
STATION RD
WEST WLK
NORTH PAR
EAST WLK
NORTH WLK
FOUR SEASONS SQ
SOUTH WLK
SOUTH PAR
LINK RD
B4059
ANDREW MILLMAN CT
WESTLEIGH CL
WESTLEIGH CT
SUNNYSIDE LA
MOORPARK AVE
MOORLAND RD
MOORDELL CL
THE AVENUE
CHATTERTON RD
MAYBANK RD
EGGSHILL LA
WELLSTEAD AVE
THORN CL
CRANTOCK DR
LYNDALE RD
VILLAGE CL
TOBIAS GDNS
WESTERLEIGH RD
STANSHAWES DR
BLAKENEY MILLS
PRIORS LEA
THORNS FARM
STANSHAWE CRES
CLEEVE RD
NAILSWORTH AVE
PAINSWICK DR
KENNEDY WAY
STINCHCOMBE
DURSLEY CL
SUNDRIDGE PK
WENTWORTH
GLENEAGLES
ST ANDREWS
KENNEDY HO
ESTORIL
WALTON HEATH
KENILWORTH
FAIRHAVEN
FERNDOWN
SCOTT WAY
CABOT CL
SHACKLETON AVE
BENNETTS CT
A432

69 70 71
A B C D E F

32
44

43 54

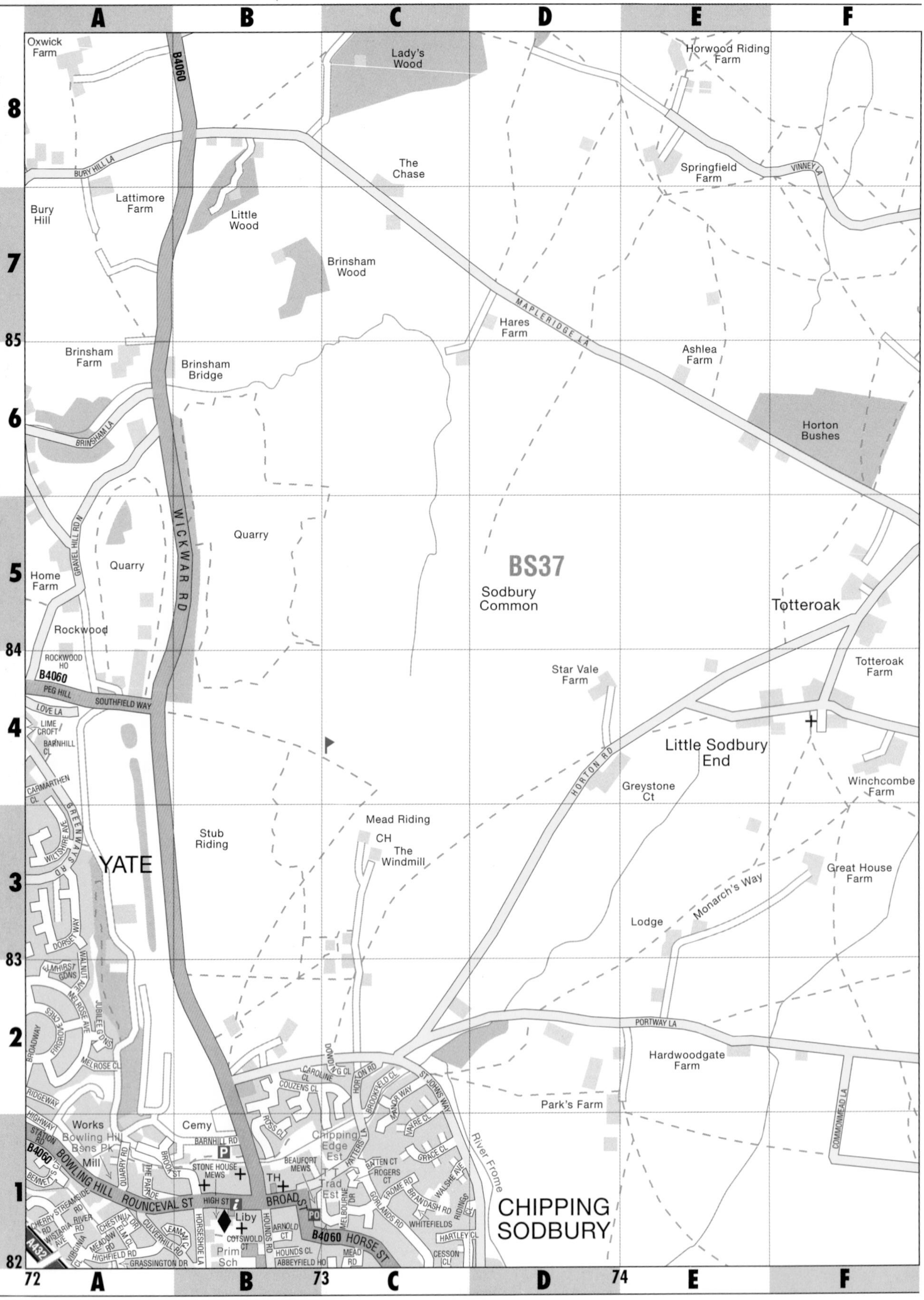

Oxwick Farm
Lady's Wood
Horwood Riding Farm
B4060
Bury Hill La
Bury Hill
Lattimore Farm
Little Wood
The Chase
Springfield Farm
Vinney La
Brinsham Wood
Mapleridge La
Hares Farm
Brinsham Farm
Brinsham Bridge
Ashlea Farm
Brinsham La
Horton Bushes
Gravel Hill Rd
Quarry
Wickwar Rd
BS37
Sodbury Common
Home Farm
Totteroak
Rockwood
Rockwood Ho
Star Vale Farm
Totteroak Farm
Peg Hill
Southfield Way
Love La
Lime Croft
Barnhill Cl
Little Sodbury End
Horton Rd
Carmarthen Cl
Greenways Rd
Greystone Ct
Winchcombe Farm
Wiltshire Ave
Mead Riding
CH
The Windmill
Stub Riding
YATE
Great House Farm
Monarch's Way
Dorset Way
Lodge
Walnut La
Lyndhurst Gdns
Melrose Ave
Jubilee Gdns
Firgrove Cres
Broadway
Portway La
Melrose Cl
Caroline Cl
Dowding Cl
Horton Rd
Brookfield Cl
St Johns Way
Hardwoodgate Farm
Couzens Cl
Manor Way
Ridgeway
Ross Cl
Vayre Cl
Park's Farm
Highway
Station Rd
Works
Bowling Hill Bsns Pk
Mill
Cemy
Barnhill Rd
P
Chipping Edge Est
Hatters La
Grace Cl
River Frome
Commonmead La
Bennett
Quarry Rd
The Parade
Brook St
Stone House Mews
Beaufort Mews
Batten Ct
Rogers Ct
Walshe Ave
Bowling Hill
Rounceval St
TH
Trad Est
Frome Rd
Brandash Rd
Ridings Cl
High St
Broad St
Melbourne Dr
Gorlands Rd
Cherry Rd
Streamside
River Rd
Wistaria Ave
Chestnut Dr
Elm Cl
Culverhill Rd
Leaman Cl
Liby
Cotswold Ct
Arnold Ct
Hounds Rd
PO
B4060 Horse St
Whitefields
Hartley Cl
CHIPPING SODBURY
Virginia Cl
Meadow Rd
Highfield Rd
Grassington Dr
Horseshoe La
Prim Sch
Hounds Cl
Abbeyfield Ho
Mead Rd
Cesson Cl
A432

A B C D E F

8 7 85 6 5 84 4 3 83 2 1 82

72 73 74

43 33

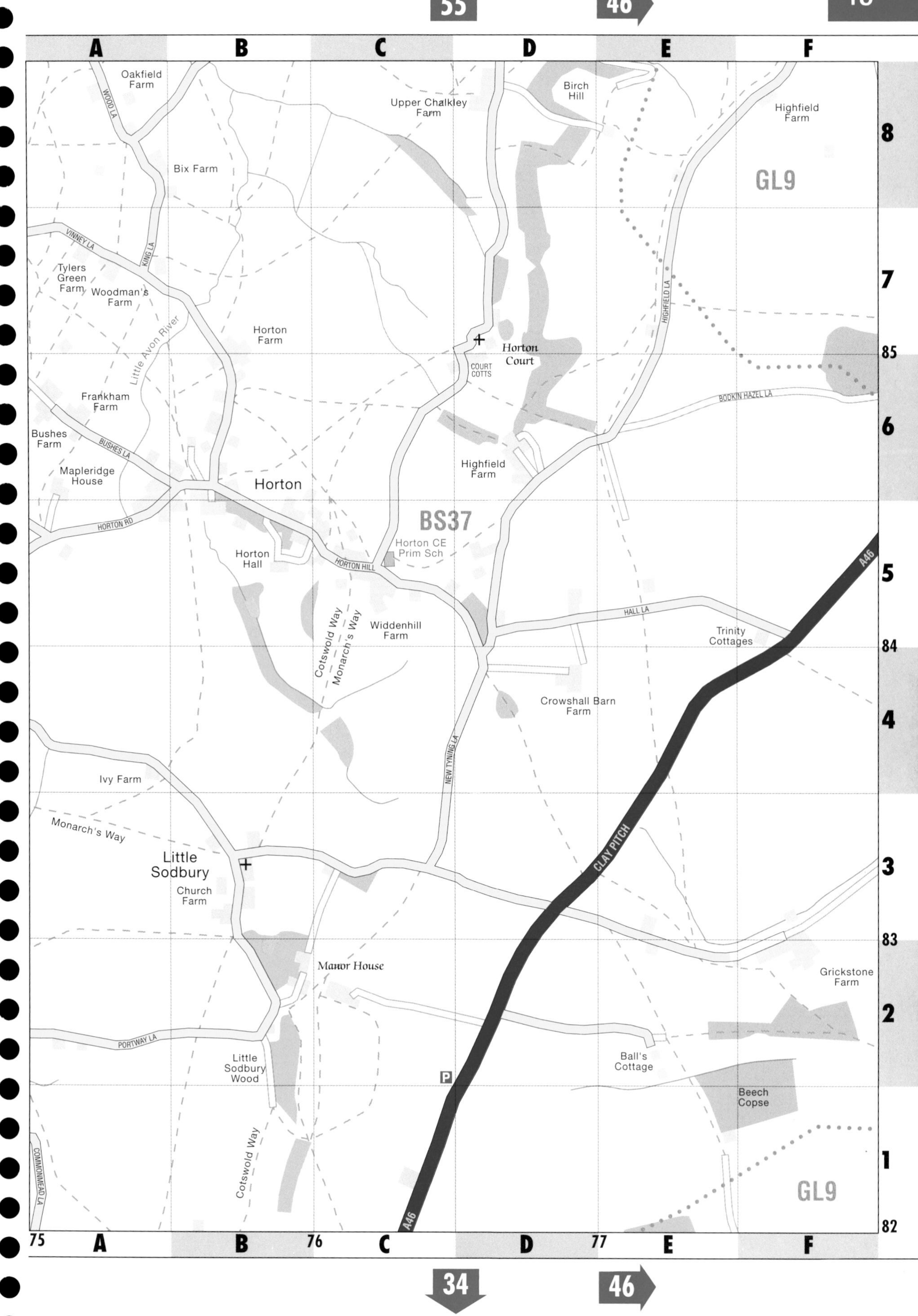
55
46
A
B
C
D
E
F
Oakfield Farm
WOOD LA
Upper Chalkley Farm
Birch Hill
Highfield Farm
8
Bix Farm
GL9
VINNEY LA
KING LA
Tylers Green Farm
Woodman's Farm
7
HIGHFIELD LA
Little Avon River
Horton Farm
Horton Court
COURT COTTS
85
Frankham Farm
BODKIN HAZEL LA
Bushes Farm
BUSHES LA
6
Highfield Farm
Mapleridge House
Horton
BS37
HORTON RD
Horton CE Prim Sch
Horton Hall
HORTON HILL
A46
5
Cotswold Way
Monarch's Way
Widdenhill Farm
HALL LA
Trinity Cottages
84
Crowshall Barn Farm
4
NEW TYNING LA
Ivy Farm
Monarch's Way
CLAY PITCH
Little Sodbury
3
Church Farm
83
Manor House
Grickstone Farm
2
PORTWAY LA
Little Sodbury Wood
Ball's Cottage
P
Beech Copse
1
Cotswold Way
COMMONMEAD LA
GL9
A46
82
75
76
77
34
46

45
56

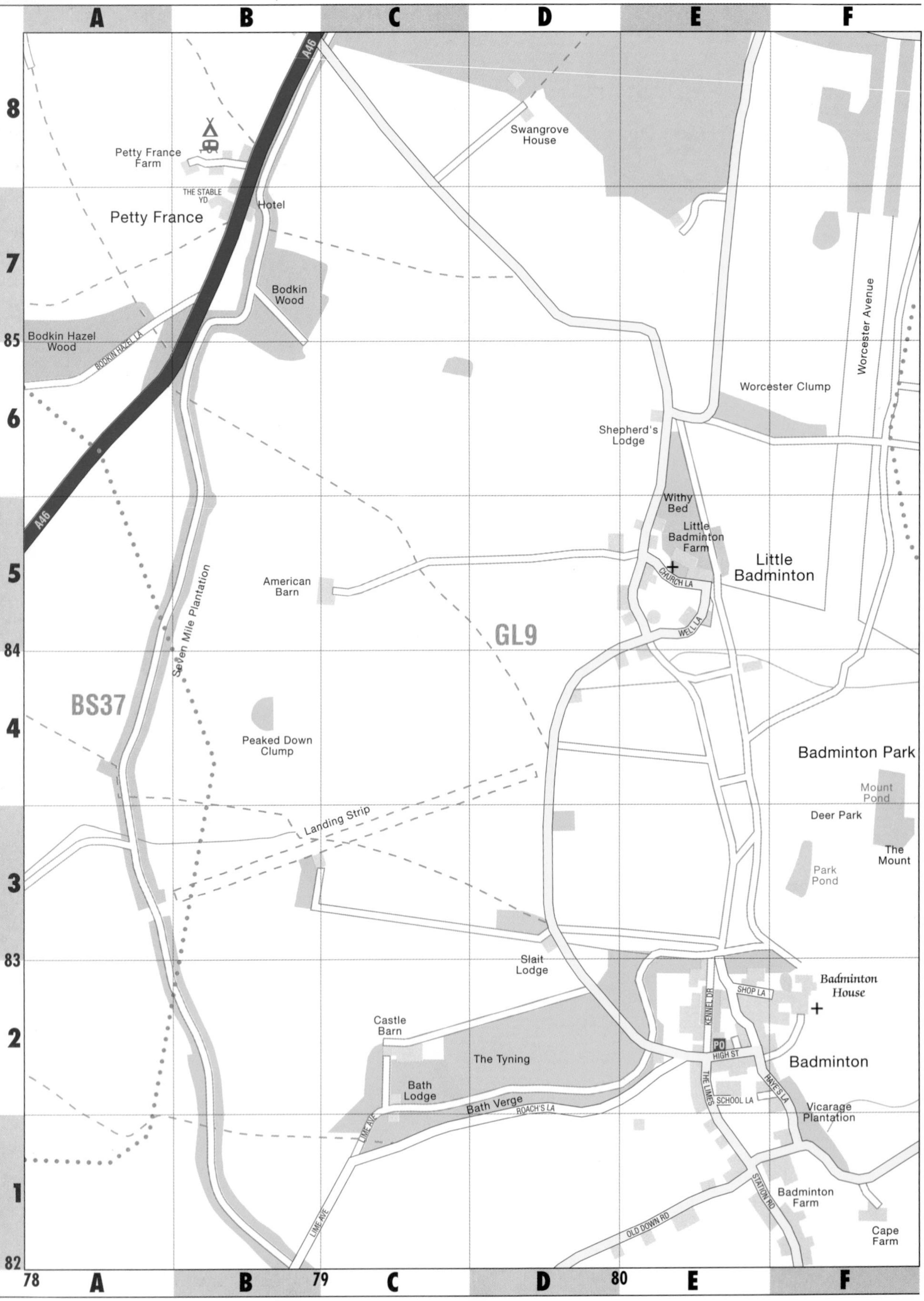

A B C D E F
8 7 85 6 5 84 4 3 83 2 1 82
78 79 80
Petty France Farm
THE STABLE YD
Petty France
Hotel
A46
Swangrove House
Bodkin Wood
Bodkin Hazel Wood
BODKIN HAZEL LA
Worcester Avenue
Worcester Clump
Shepherd's Lodge
Withy Bed
Little Badminton Farm
CHURCH LA
Little Badminton
American Barn
Seven Mile Plantation
GL9
WELL LA
BS37
Peaked Down Clump
Badminton Park
Mount Pond
Deer Park
The Mount
Park Pond
Landing Strip
Slait Lodge
Badminton House
KENNEL DR
SHOP LA
Castle Barn
PO
HIGH ST
The Tyning
Badminton
Bath Lodge
THE LIMES
SCHOOL LA
HAYE'S LA
Bath Verge
ROACH'S LA
Vicarage Plantation
LIME AVE
STATION RD
Badminton Farm
OLD DOWN RD
Cape Farm

45
35

57

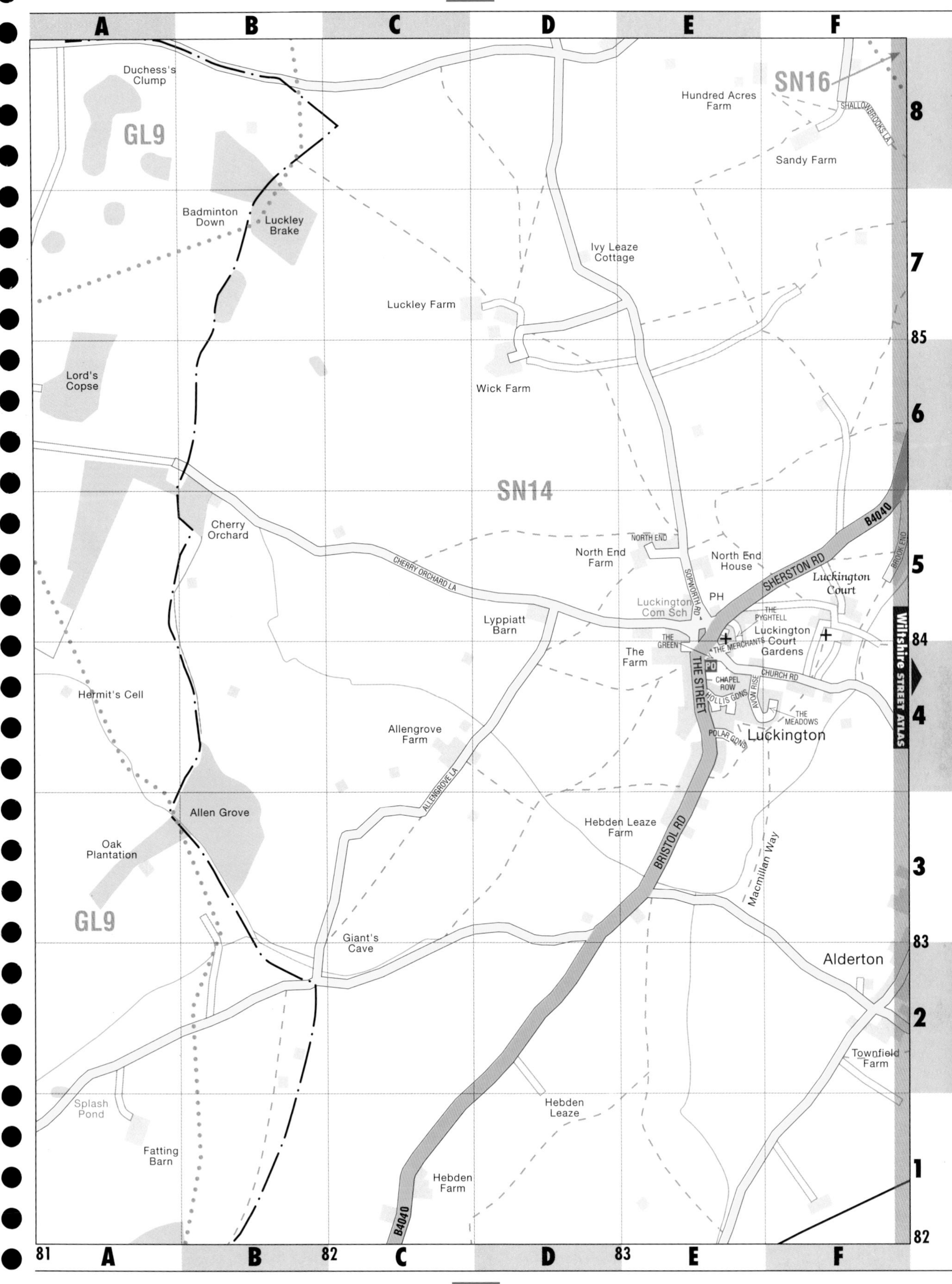
A
B
C
D
E
F
Duchess's Clump
GL9
Badminton Down
Luckley Brake
SN16
Hundred Acres Farm
SHALLOWBROOKS LA
Sandy Farm
8
Ivy Leaze Cottage
7
Luckley Farm
85
Lord's Copse
Wick Farm
6
SN14
Cherry Orchard
CHERRY ORCHARD LA
NORTH END
North End Farm
North End House
B4040
SHERSTON RD
Luckington Court
BROOK END
5
SOPWORTH RD
PH
Luckington Com Sch
Lyppiatt Barn
THE PYGHTELL
Luckington Court Gardens
THE GREEN
THE MERCHANTS
84
The Farm
PO
THE STREET
CHAPEL ROW
CHURCH RD
HOLLIS GDNS
AVON RISE
Wiltshire STREET ATLAS
Hermit's Cell
THE MEADOWS
4
Allengrove Farm
POLAR GDNS
Luckington
ALLENGROVE LA
Allen Grove
Hebden Leaze Farm
Oak Plantation
BRISTOL RD
Macmillan Way
3
GL9
Giant's Cave
83
Alderton
2
Townfield Farm
Splash Pond
Hebden Leaze
Fatting Barn
Hebden Farm
1
B4040
82
81
82
83

36

61

A B C D E F
8
7
89
6
5
88
4
3
87
2
1
86
54
55
56
M48
Footpath/Cycle Way
Severn Road Bridge
Mast
Toll
Severn Way
Aust Cliff
PASSAGE RD
New House Farm
Old Passage
Old Passage House
River Severn
Aust Warth
A403
Foss Ditch
Cake Pill
Cake Pill Gout
Northwick Oaze
Severn Way
Asnum Copse
Lords Rhine
Bilsham Rhine
Northwick Pig Farm
BS35
Bilsham Farm
WARTH LA
AUST RD
Laural Farm
Church Farm
Northwick
B4055
Redwick & Northwick CE Prim Sch
Mill Farm
BILSHAM LA
Manor Farm
DANGER AREA
Red Lodge
Rifle Range
North Worthy Farm
SEVERN RD
NORTHWICK RD
Holm Rhine
REDWICK
Severn Lodge Farm
REDWICK RD
BLANDS ROW
B4064
New Passage
M4
Herefordshire Monmouthshire STREET ATLAS

38

62
50

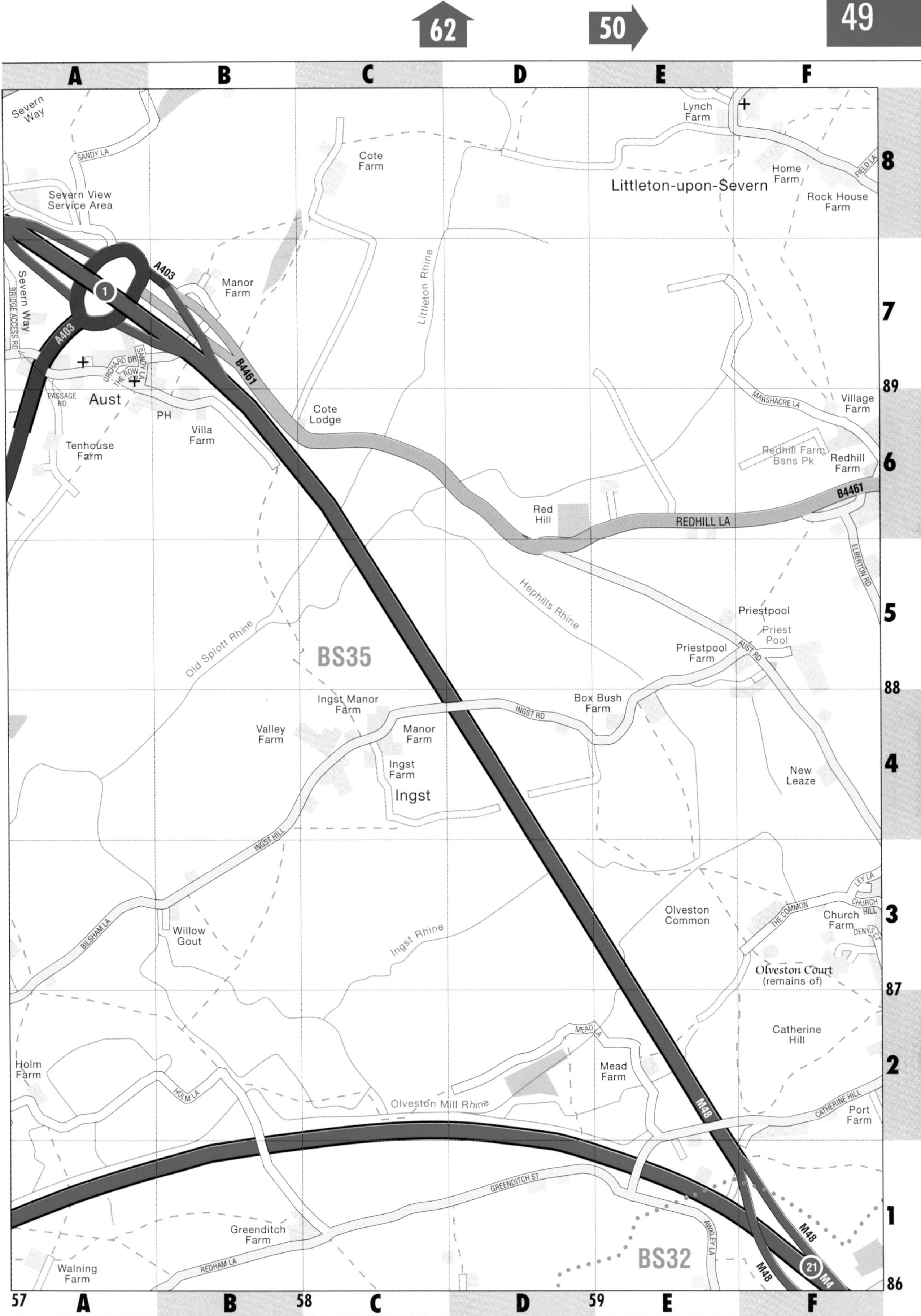
Severn Way
SANDY LA
Severn View Service Area
Severn Way
BRIDGE ACCESS RD
A403
A403
1
Manor Farm
B4461
ORCHARD DR
THE ROW
SANDY LA
PASSAGE RD
Aust
PH
Villa Farm
Tenhouse Farm
Cote Farm
Cote Lodge
Littleton Rhine
Lynch Farm
Littleton-upon-Severn
Home Farm
FIELD LA
Rock House Farm
MARSHACRE LA
Village Farm
Redhill Farm Bsns Pk
Redhill Farm
B4461
Red Hill
REDHILL LA
ELBERTON RD
Hephills Rhine
Old Splott Rhine
BS35
Priestpool
Priest Pool
Priestpool Farm
AUST RD
Box Bush Farm
INGST RD
Ingst Manor Farm
Valley Farm
Manor Farm
Ingst Farm
Ingst
New Leaze
INGST HILL
BILSHAM LA
Willow Gout
Ingst Rhine
Olveston Common
LEY LA
THE COMMON
CHURCH HILL
Church Farm
DENYS CT
Olveston Court (remains of)
Catherine Hill
MEAD LA
Mead Farm
Holm Farm
HOLM LA
Olveston Mill Rhine
M48
CATHERINE HILL
Port Farm
GREENDITCH ST
Greenditch Farm
AWKLEY LA
BS32
M48
M48
21
M4
Walning Farm
REDHAM LA
A B C D E F
8 7 89 6 5 88 4 3 87 2 1 86
57 58 59

39
50

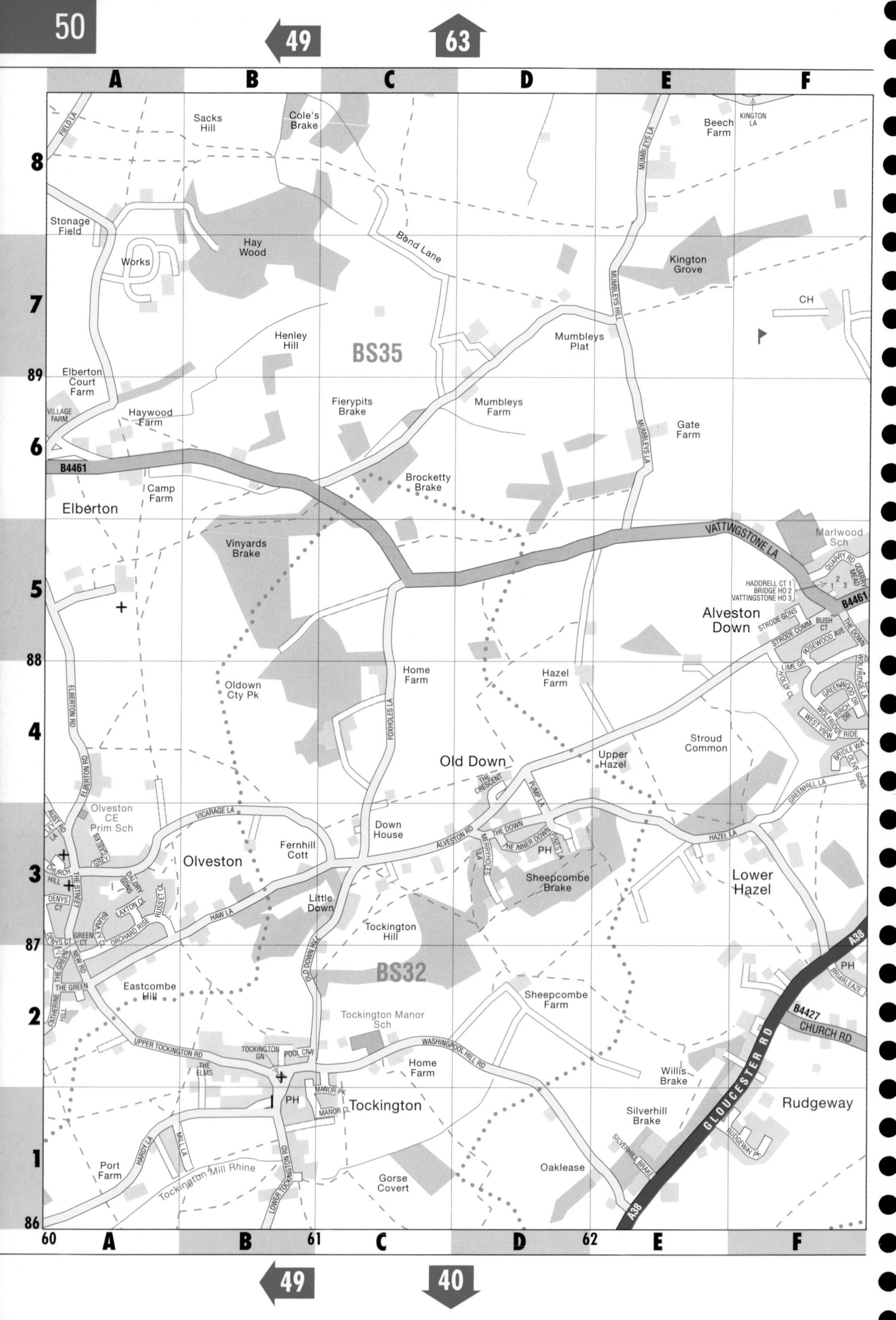

49
63
Sacks Hill
Cole's Brake
Beech Farm
KINGTON LA
FIELD LA
MUMBLEYS LA
Stonage Field
Hay Wood
Works
Bond Lane
Kington Grove
MUMBLEYS HILL
CH
Henley Hill
BS35
Mumbleys Plat
Elberton Court Farm
VILLAGE FARM
Haywood Farm
Fierypits Brake
Mumbleys Farm
MUMBLEYS LA
Gate Farm
B4461
Brocketty Brake
Camp Farm
Elberton
Vinyards Brake
VATTINGSTONE LA
Marlwood Sch
QUARRY RD
QUARRY MEAD
HADDRELL CT 1
BRIDGE HO 2
VATTINGSTONE HO 3
B4461
Alveston Down
STRODE GDNS
STRODE COMM
BUSH CT
ROSEWOOD AVE
THE DOWN
LIME GR
HOLLY CL
Home Farm
Hazel Farm
Oldown Cty Pk
ELBERTON RD
FOXHOLES LA
GREENWOOD DR
WOLFRIDGE LA
BIRCH DR
WOLFRIDGE RIDE
WEST VIEW
Stroud Common
Upper Hazel
Old Down
BRIDLE WAY
OLIVE GDNS
THE CRESCENT
PUMP LA
GREENHILL LA
ELBERTON RD
AUST RD
Olveston CE Prim Sch
VICARAGE LA
Down House
ALVESTON RD
THE DOWN
THE INNER DOWN
MERRYHOLES LA
FIRS LA
PH
HAZEL LA
Fernhill Cott
Olveston
Sheepcombe Brake
Lower Hazel
CHURCH HILL
THE STREET
DALDRY GDNS
DENYS CT
LAXTON CL
RUSSET CL
HAW LA
Little Down
Tockington Hill
GREEN CT
BRAMLEY CT
ORCHARD RISE
DENYS CT
THE GREEN
NEW RD
OLD DOWN HILL
BS32
A38
PH
BRIARLEAZE
THE GREEN
Eastcombe Hill
Sheepcombe Farm
CATHERINE HILL
Tockington Manor Sch
B4427
CHURCH RD
UPPER TOCKINGTON RD
TOCKINGTON GN
POOL CNR
WASHINGPOOL HILL RD
Home Farm
GLOUCESTER RD
THE ELMS
Willis Brake
PH
MANOR PK
MANOR CL
Tockington
Rudgeway
Silverhill Brake
RUDGEWAY PK
SILVERHILL BRAKE
HARDY LA
MILL LA
LOWER TOCKINGTON RD
Port Farm
Tockington Mill Rhine
Gorse Covert
Oaklease
A38
A B C D E F
8 7 6 5 4 3 2 1
89 88 87 86
60 61 62
49
40

A5
1 DOWNFIELD CL
2 DOWN LEAZE
3 DOWNS CL
4 BODYCE RD
5 GREENHILL PAR
6 ORCHARD LEA

C8
1 THE BATHINGS
2 SPRING HO
3 BROOK HO
4 AXE CT
5 USK CT
6 CABOT HO
7 CLYDE HO
8 TYNE HO
9 THAMES HO

D8
1 SPRINGFIELD
2 MEADOWSIDE
3 SIBLAND CL
4 KENNET WAY
5 HILLBROOK RD

64
52

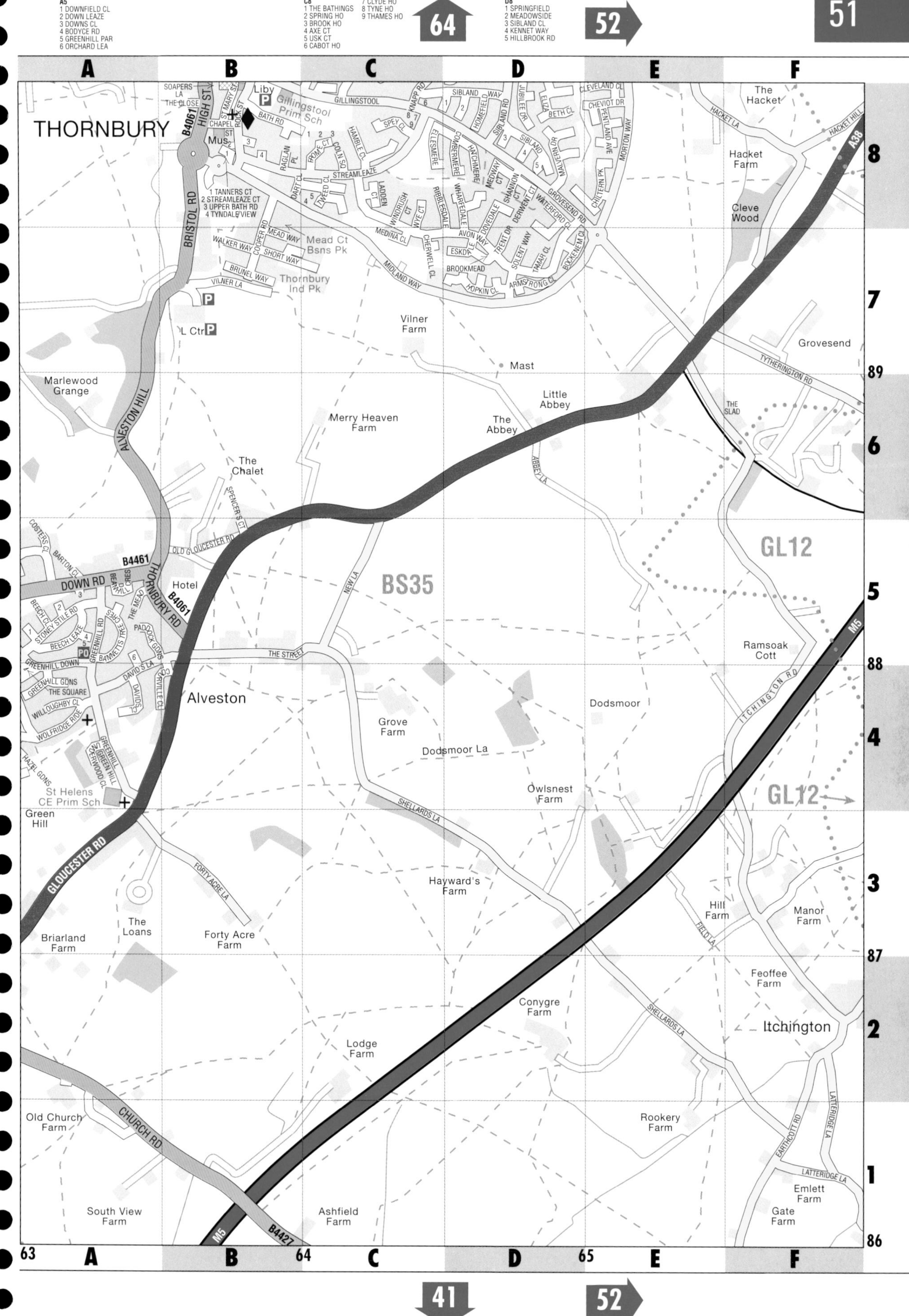

41
52

51
65

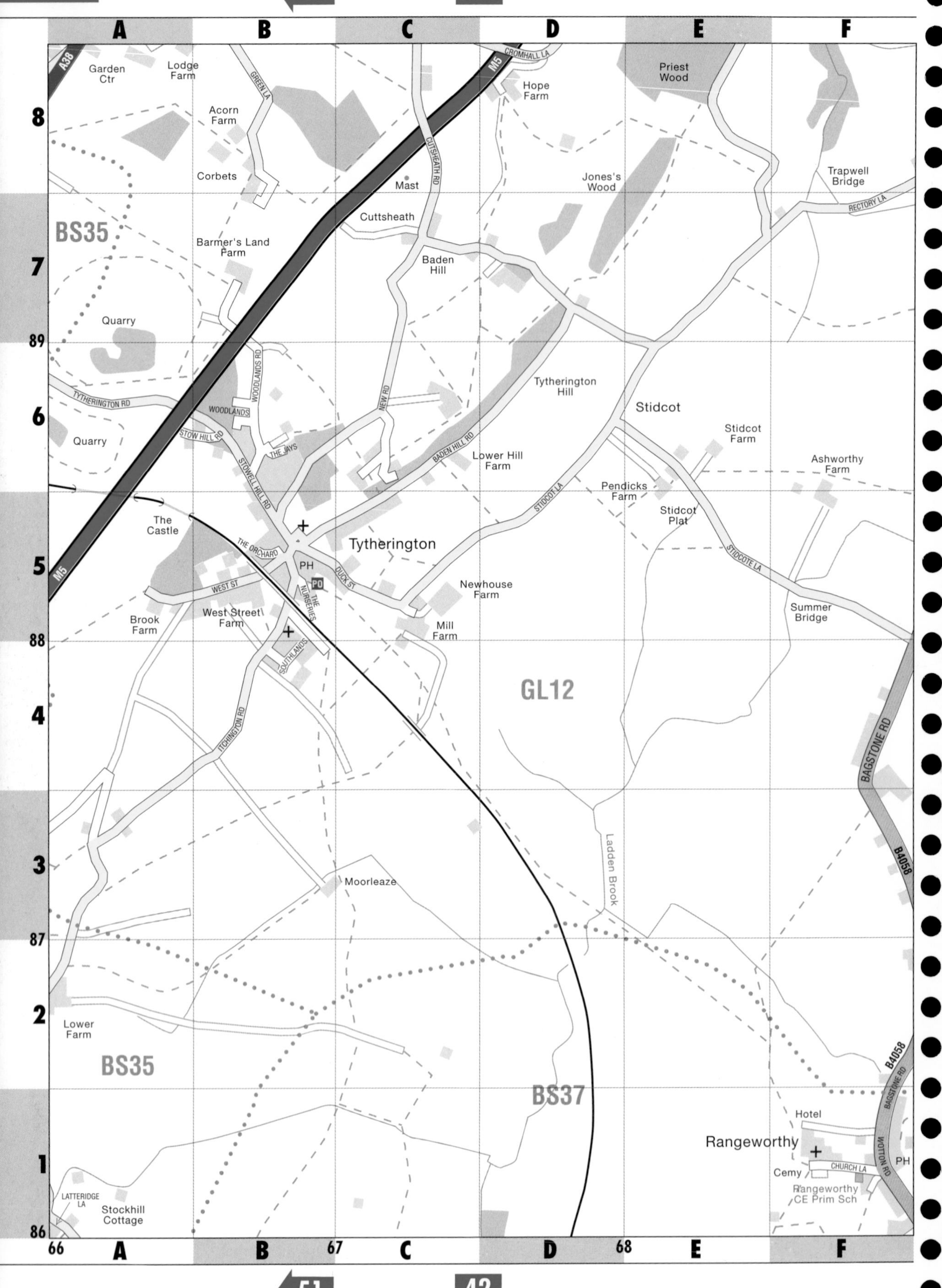
A
B
C
D
E
F
8
7
89
6
5
88
4
3
87
2
1
86
66
67
68
A38
M5
Garden Ctr
Lodge Farm
GREEN LA
Acorn Farm
Corbets
CROMHALL LA
Hope Farm
Priest Wood
Mast
CUTTSHEATH RD
Jones's Wood
Trapwell Bridge
RECTORY LA
BS35
Cuttsheath
Barmer's Land Farm
Baden Hill
Quarry
WOODLANDS RD
TYTHERINGTON RD
WOODLANDS
NEW RD
Tytherington Hill
Stidcot
Quarry
STOW HILL RD
THE JAYS
STOWELL HILL RD
BADEN HILL RD
Lower Hill Farm
Stidcot Farm
Ashworthy Farm
Pendicks Farm
STIDCOT LA
The Castle
Stidcot Plat
Tytherington
THE ORCHARD
PH
DUCK ST
STIDCOTE LA
WEST ST
PO
THE NURSERIES
Newhouse Farm
Brook Farm
West Street Farm
Mill Farm
Summer Bridge
SOUTHLANDS
GL12
ITCHINGTON RD
BAGSTONE RD
B4058
Ladden Brook
Moorleaze
Lower Farm
BS35
B4058
BS37
BAGSTONE RD
Hotel
Rangeworthy
WOTTON RD
CHURCH LA
PH
Cemy
Rangeworthy CE Prim Sch
LATTERIDGE LA
Stockhill Cottage

51
42

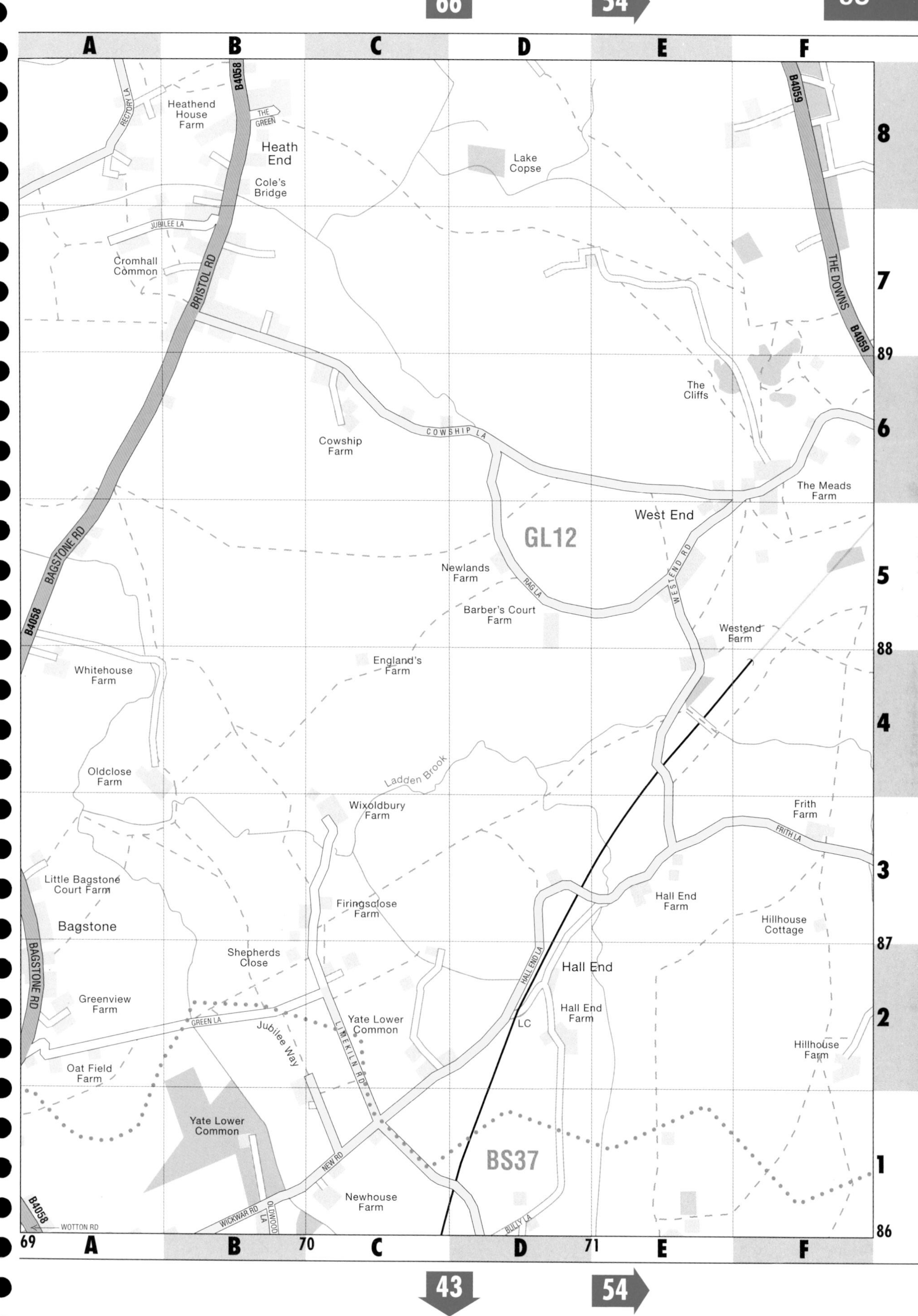
66
54
A
B
C
D
E
F
8
7
89
6
5
88
4
3
87
2
1
86
69
70
71
43
54
B4058
RECTORY LA
Heathend
House
Farm
THE GREEN
Heath
End
Cole's
Bridge
Lake
Copse
B4059
JUBILEE LA
Cromhall
Common
BRISTOL RD
THE DOWNS
The
Cliffs
Cowship
Farm
COWSHIP LA
The Meads
Farm
West End
GL12
BAGSTONE RD
Newlands
Farm
RAG LA
WESTEND RD
Barber's Court
Farm
Westend
Farm
England's
Farm
Whitehouse
Farm
Oldclose
Farm
Ladden Brook
Wixoldbury
Farm
Frith
Farm
FRITH LA
Little Bagstone
Court Farm
Bagstone
Firingsclose
Farm
Hall End
Farm
Hillhouse
Cottage
Shepherds
Close
Hall End
HALL END LA
Greenview
Farm
GREEN LA
Jubilee Way
Yate Lower
Common
LIMEKILN RD
Hall End
Farm
LC
Hillhouse
Farm
Oat Field
Farm
Yate Lower
Common
BS37
NEW RD
Newhouse
Farm
WICKWAR RD
OLDWOOD LA
BULLY LA
WOTTON RD

53
67

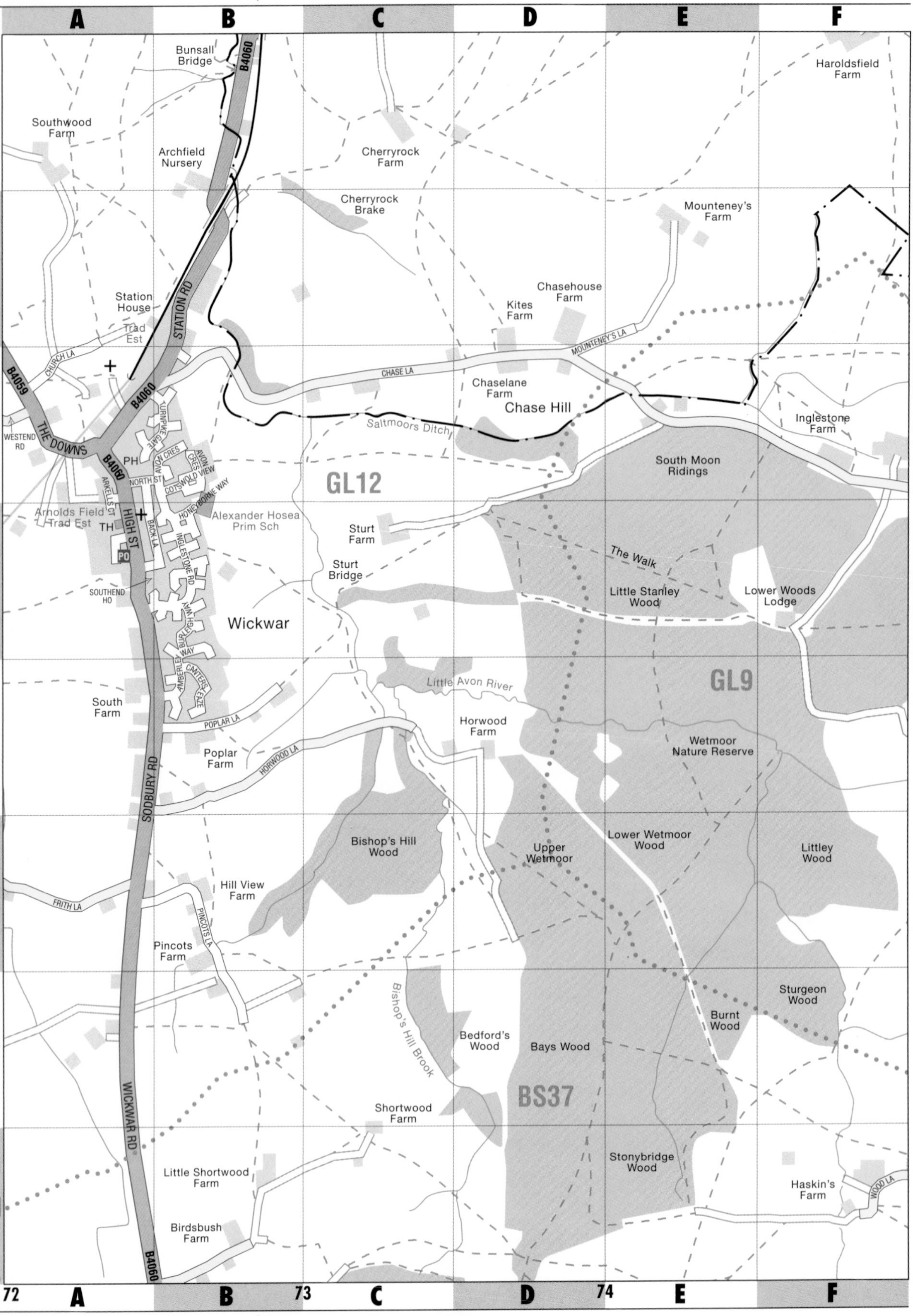

A B C D E F

8
7
89
6
5
88
4
3
87
2
1
86

Bunsall Bridge
B4060
Haroldsfield Farm
Southwood Farm
Archfield Nursery
Cherryrock Farm
Cherryrock Brake
Mounteney's Farm
Station House
STATION RD
Chasehouse Farm
Kites Farm
Trad Est
MOUNTENEY'S LA
B4059
CHURCH LA
CHASE LA
Chaselane Farm
Chase Hill
B4060
TURNPIKE GATE
WESTEND RD
THE DOWNS
Saltmoors Ditch
Inglestone Farm
PH
AVON CRES
AVON CRES
COTSWOLD VIEW
B4060
NORTH ST
South Moon Ridings
GL12
HONEYBORNE WAY
ARKELLS CT
Arnolds Field Trad Est
HIGH ST
Alexander Hosea Prim Sch
TH
BACK LA
Sturt Farm
PO
INGLESTONE RD
The Walk
Sturt Bridge
Little Stanley Wood
Lower Woods Lodge
SOUTHEND HO
AVON WAY
BURLEIGH WAY
Wickwar
GL9
AMBERLEY
CANTERS LEAZE
Little Avon River
South Farm
Horwood Farm
POPLAR LA
Wetmoor Nature Reserve
Poplar Farm
HORWOOD LA
SODBURY RD
Bishop's Hill Wood
Lower Wetmoor Wood
Upper Wetmoor
Littley Wood
Hill View Farm
FRITH LA
PINCOTS LA
Pincots Farm
Sturgeon Wood
Bishop's Hill Brook
Burnt Wood
Bedford's Wood
Bays Wood
BS37
WICKWAR RD
Shortwood Farm
Stonybridge Wood
Little Shortwood Farm
Haskin's Farm
WOOD LA
Birdsbush Farm
B4060

72 A B 73 C D 74 E F

53
44

A B C D E F

Lower Witheymore Farm
Hareley Common
Day House La
Kingswood Rd
Farmcote
Alderley Rd
School Cl
New Mills La
Hillesley CE Prim Sch
Vicarage Cl
Church View
PH
Killcott Rd
Chapel La
High St
St Giles Barton
Day House Farm
Hillesley
Withymore Wood
GL12
Reed's Row
Assley Common
Withymore Farm
Mear's Plantation
Raven's Coombe
Splatt's Barn
The Barton
Lovetts Wood Farm
Hawkesbury Rd
Splatt's Wood
Long Coombe
Frith Wood
Lance Coppice
Oxleaze Farm
Spoil Coppice
Inglestone Common
Monarch's Way
Cotswold Way
Clay Hill
Orange End
Oakhall Cottage
Monument Farm
Mon
Bucklesbury Farm
GL9
Newhouse Farm
Hawkesbury Knoll
Home Farm
Coombe Farm
The Barton
The Barton
Court Farm
High St
Fox Cl
Hawkesbury Common
Pound Farm
Hawkesbury CE Prim Sch
PH
Hawkesbury
Highfields
Church Hill
Birgage Rd
Bath La
Sandpits La
Cat Cottage
Little Avon River
Mill Farm
Broad Hill
Wood La
Lower Chalkley Farm
Monarch's Way
Cotswold Way
Stevens' Farm
King La
BS37
Highfield La

8 7 89 6 5 88 4 3 87 2 1 86

75 A B 76 C D 77 E F

55
69

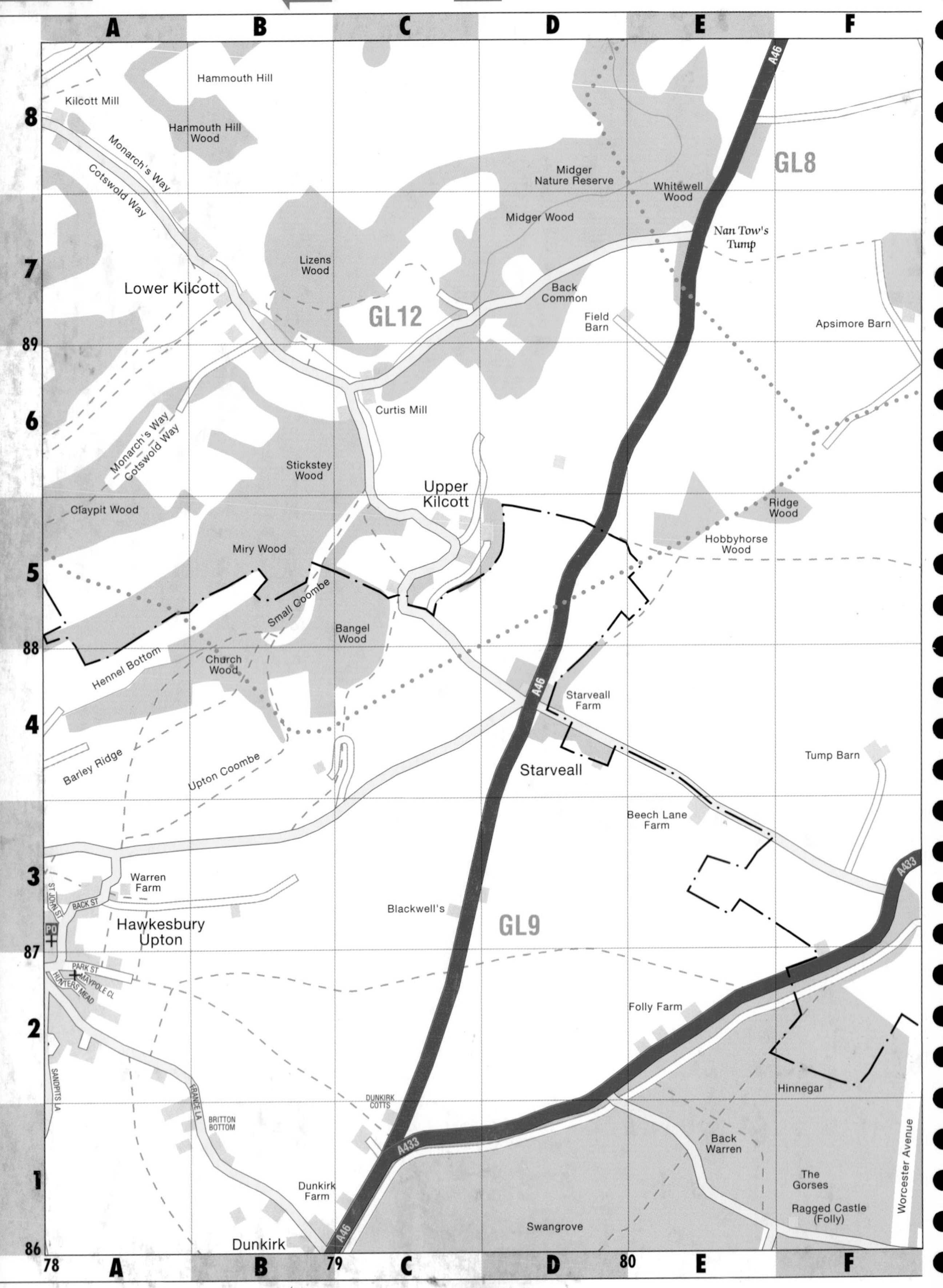
A
B
C
D
E
F
Hammouth Hill
Kilcott Mill
Hanmouth Hill Wood
Monarch's Way
Cotswold Way
Midger Nature Reserve
Whitewell Wood
GL8
Midger Wood
Nan Tow's Tump
Lizens Wood
Lower Kilcott
Back Common
GL12
Field Barn
Apsimore Barn
Curtis Mill
Monarch's Way
Cotswold Way
Stickstey Wood
Upper Kilcott
Claypit Wood
Ridge Wood
Hobbyhorse Wood
Miry Wood
Small Coombe
Bangel Wood
Church Wood
Hennel Bottom
A46
Starveall Farm
Barley Ridge
Upton Coombe
Starveall
Tump Barn
Beech Lane Farm
Warren Farm
ST JOHN'S
BACK ST
Hawkesbury Upton
PO
Blackwell's
GL9
A433
PARK ST
MAYPOLE CL
HUNTERS MEAD
Folly Farm
SANDPITS LA
FRANCE LA
BRITTON BOTTOM
DUNKIRK COTTS
A433
Hinnegar
Back Warren
Worcester Avenue
The Gorses
Ragged Castle (Folly)
Dunkirk Farm
Swangrove
A46
Dunkirk
8
7
89
6
5
88
4
3
87
2
1
86
78
79
80

55
46

70
58

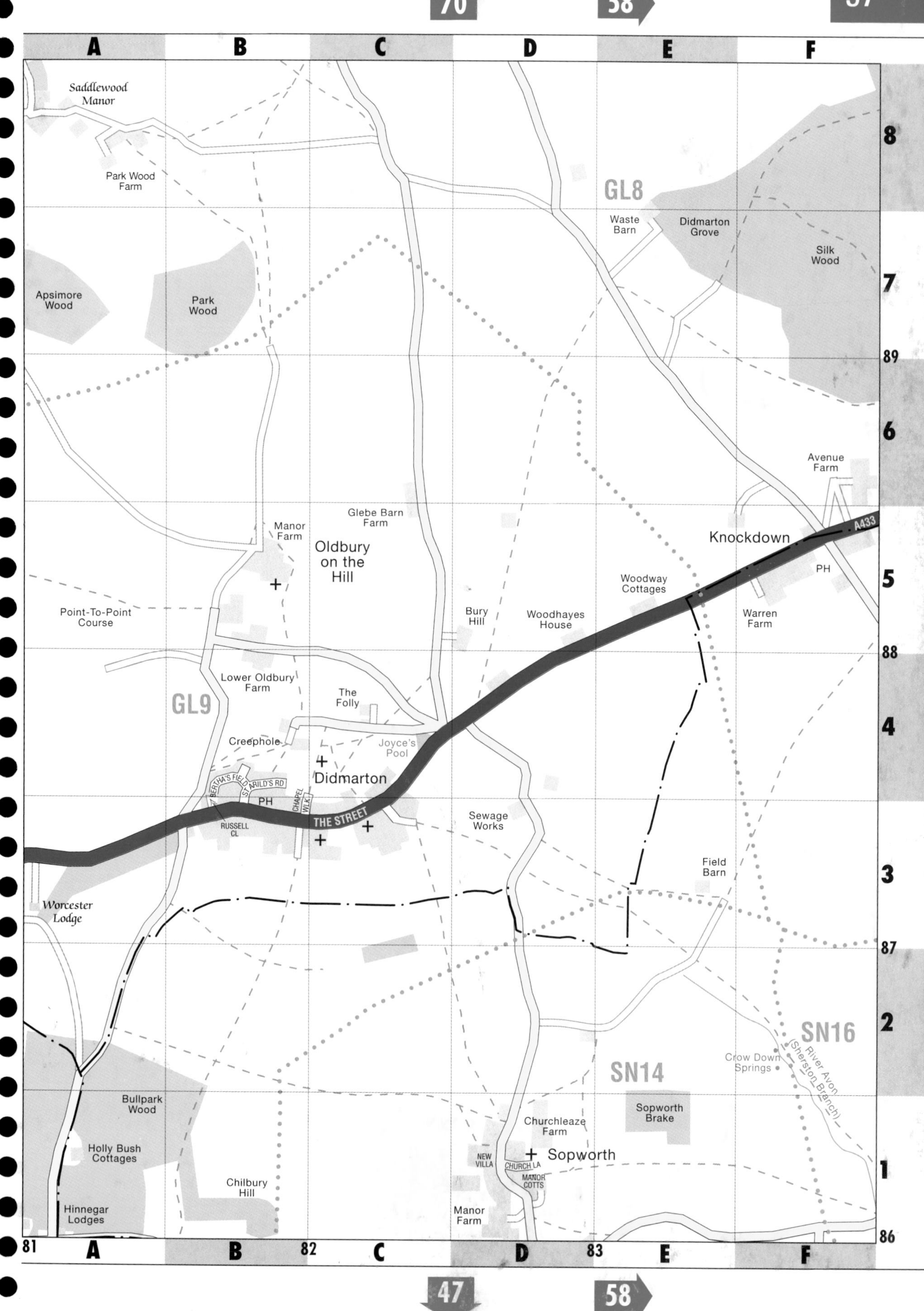
A
B
C
D
E
F
Saddlewood Manor
Park Wood Farm
GL8
Waste Barn
Didmarton Grove
Silk Wood
Apsimore Wood
Park Wood
Avenue Farm
Glebe Barn Farm
Manor Farm
Oldbury on the Hill
Knockdown
A433
PH
Woodway Cottages
Point-To-Point Course
Bury Hill
Woodhayes House
Warren Farm
Lower Oldbury Farm
The Folly
GL9
Creephole
Joyce's Pool
Didmarton
BERTHA'S FIELD
ST ARILD'S RD
PH
CHAPEL WLK
THE STREET
RUSSELL CL
Sewage Works
Field Barn
Worcester Lodge
SN16
Crow Down Springs
River Avon (Sherston Branch)
SN14
Bullpark Wood
Sopworth Brake
Churchleaze Farm
Holly Bush Cottages
NEW VILLA
CHURCH LA
Sopworth
MANOR COTTS
Chilbury Hill
Hinnegar Lodges
Manor Farm
8
7
89
6
5
88
4
3
87
2
1
86
81
82
83

47
58

57
71

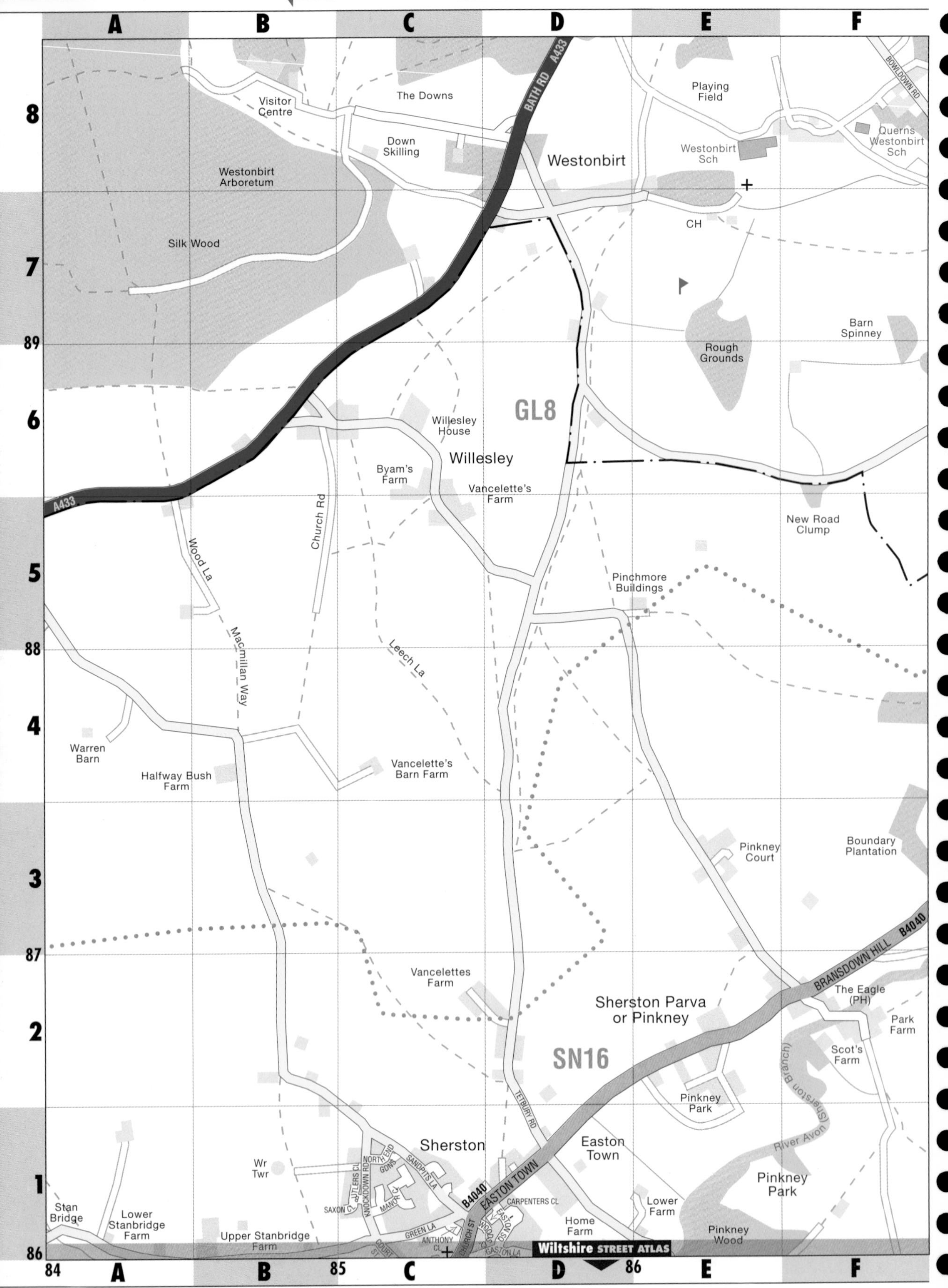
A
B
C
D
E
F
8
7
89
6
5
88
4
3
87
2
1
86
84
85
86
Visitor Centre
The Downs
Playing Field
BOWLDOWN RD
Down Skilling
BATH RD
A433
Westonbirt
Westonbirt Sch
Querns Westonbirt Sch
Westonbirt Arboretum
CH
Silk Wood
Barn Spinney
Rough Grounds
GL8
Willesley House
Willesley
Byam's Farm
Vancelette's Farm
New Road Clump
Wood La
Church Rd
Pinchmore Buildings
Macmillan Way
Leech La
Warren Barn
Halfway Bush Farm
Vancelette's Barn Farm
Pinkney Court
Boundary Plantation
Vancelettes Farm
Sherston Parva or Pinkney
BRANSDOWN HILL
B4040
The Eagle (PH)
Park Farm
Scot's Farm
SN16
Pinkney Park
River Avon
(Sherston Branch)
Sherston
Easton Town
Wr Twr
TETBURY RD
EASTON TOWN
Pinkney Park
Stan Bridge
Lower Stanbridge Farm
Upper Stanbridge Farm
Home Farm
Lower Farm
Pinkney Wood
CARPENTERS CL
GREEN LA
ANTHONY CL
CHURCH ST
EASTON LA
COURT ST
SAXON CL
CUTLERS CL
KNOCKDOWN RD
NORTH END GDNS
SANDPITS LA
MANOR CL
Wiltshire STREET ATLAS

57

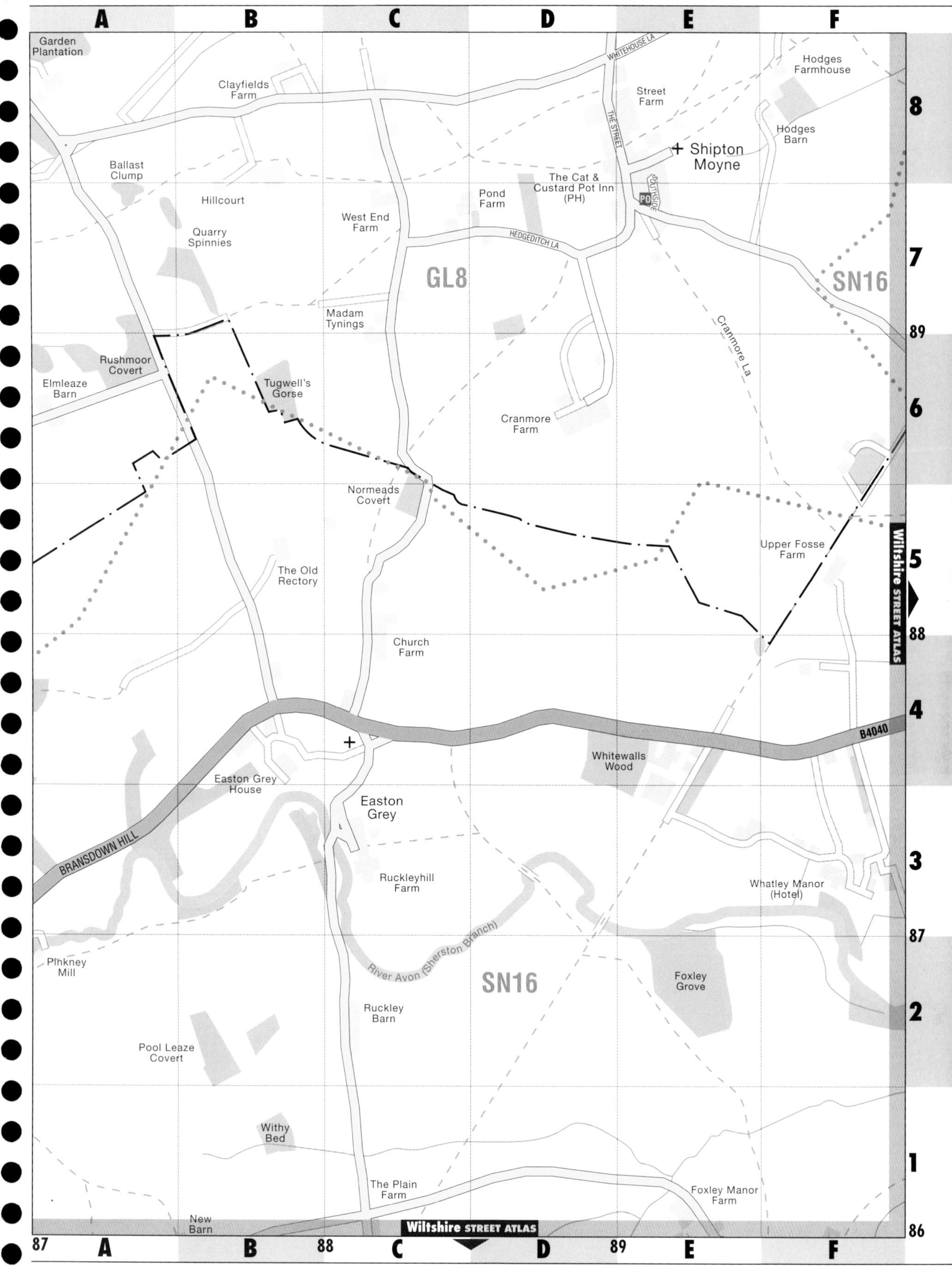

Wiltshire STREET ATLAS
Wiltshire STREET ATLAS

72

E8
1 ALBION SQ
2 LIBRARY PL
3 OLD BELL CHAMBERS
4 HOCKER HILL ST
5 BEAUFORT SQ
6 BANK SQ
7 MIDDLE ST
8 ST MARY ST
9 ST MARY STREET ARC
10 OXFORD ST
11 RESTWAY WALL
12 GARDEN CITY WAY
13 School Hill Ind Est
14 EXEMOUTH PL

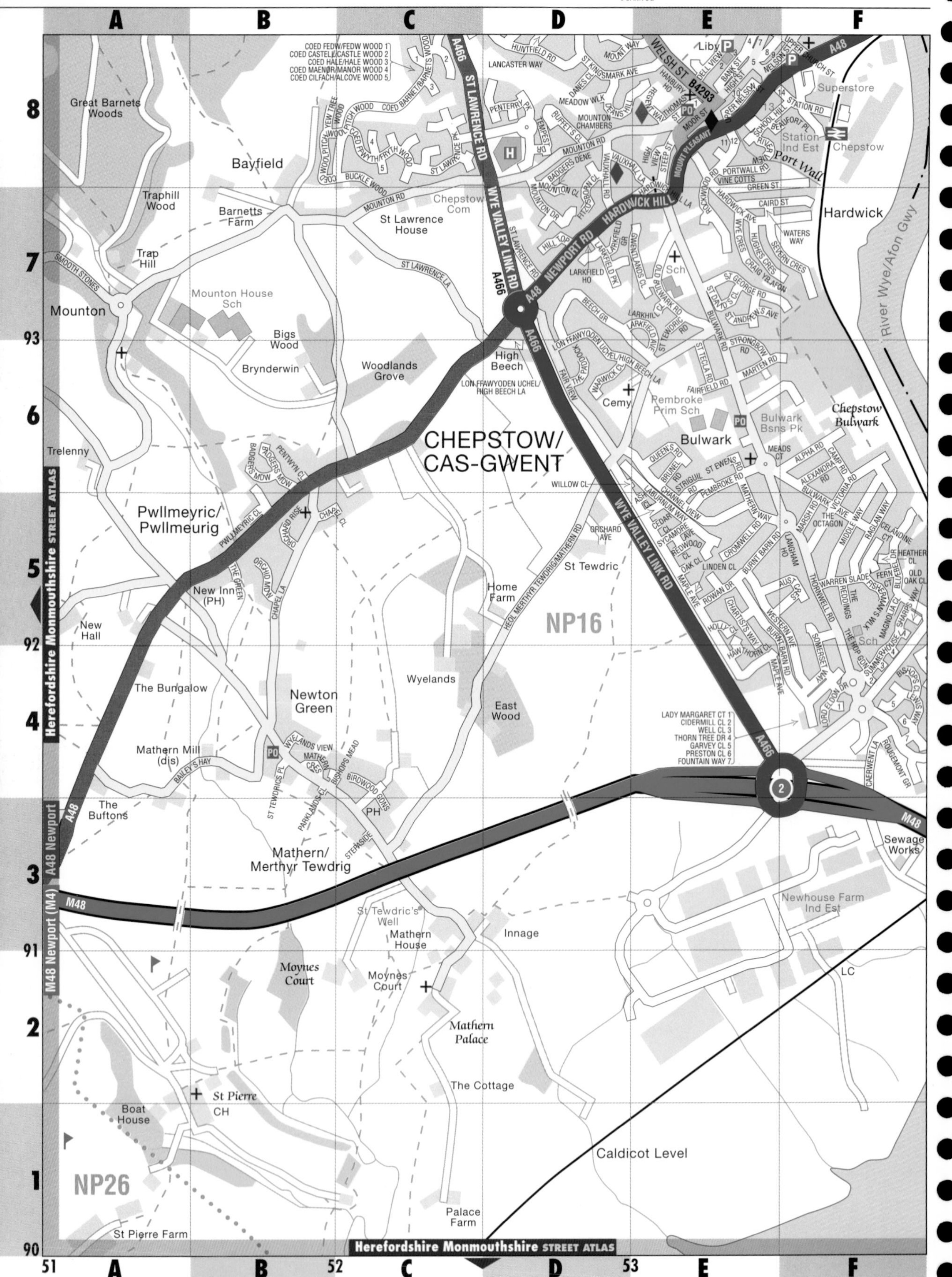

A B C D E F

8
Mast
EDMOND RD
GRAHAMSTOWN RD
GRAHAMSTOWN GR
Sedbury Bsns Pk
Badams Court
Baker's Wood
Hitchen's Grove
Sch
THE HAYES
Offa's Dyke Path
WYEBANK CRES
HENDRICK DR
WYEBANK RD
WYEBANK CL
HANOVER CT
WYEBANK RISE
BEACHLEY RD
TYLERS WAY
PARK V
ARLINGTON CT
PH
PO
Sedbury
WYEBANK VIEW
WYEBANK PL
TALLARD'S PL
WYNTOUR HO
BUTTINGTON RD
KING ALFRED'S RD
PENDA PL
MADOCKE RD
ORMEROD RD
THE YETTS
THE BELFRY
WYEBANK WAY
Sewage Works
NOXYS PL
DENMARK DR
NORSE WAY
WYNDECLIFFE HO
WYE VIEW HO
OFFA'S CL
DANES HILL
BUTTINGTON HILL
Sedbury Park
MERCIAN WAY
7
BRIDGET DR
ORCHARD FARM CL
CLIFF VIEW
Sedbury Cliffs
Pennsylvania Farm
Offa's Dyke Path
The Combe
Buttington Trump
BUTTINGTON TERR
93
Buttington Farm
NP16
6
INNER LOOP RD
LOOP RD
Warren Slade
5
Park Redding
Works
Slime Road
River Severn
SEVERN BRIDGE PK
DENBIGH DR
COLLINGWOOD CL
CROMWELL CL
ST GEORGES WAY
GIBRALTAR WAY
FERRY WAY
TIDE END
BEACHLEY RD
92
VALENTINE CL
MARINERS REACH
GRASMERE WAY
River Wye (Afon Gwy)
APPRENTICE CL
POTTERS CROFT
HITCHEN HOLLOW
4
1 PHOENIX DR
2 CLARENDON CL
3 ALMA DR
4 BRITON CL
THE HEADLAND
3
Beachley
Beachley Barracks
LC
OLD COACH RD
OLD COACH CL
91
Hunger Pill
PAVILION RD
The Old Ferry Hotel
2
IRB Sta
Sports Gd
WYVERN RD
Footpath/Cycleway
Severn Road Bridge
1
Beachley Point
M48
90

54 A B 55 C D 56 E F

61
74

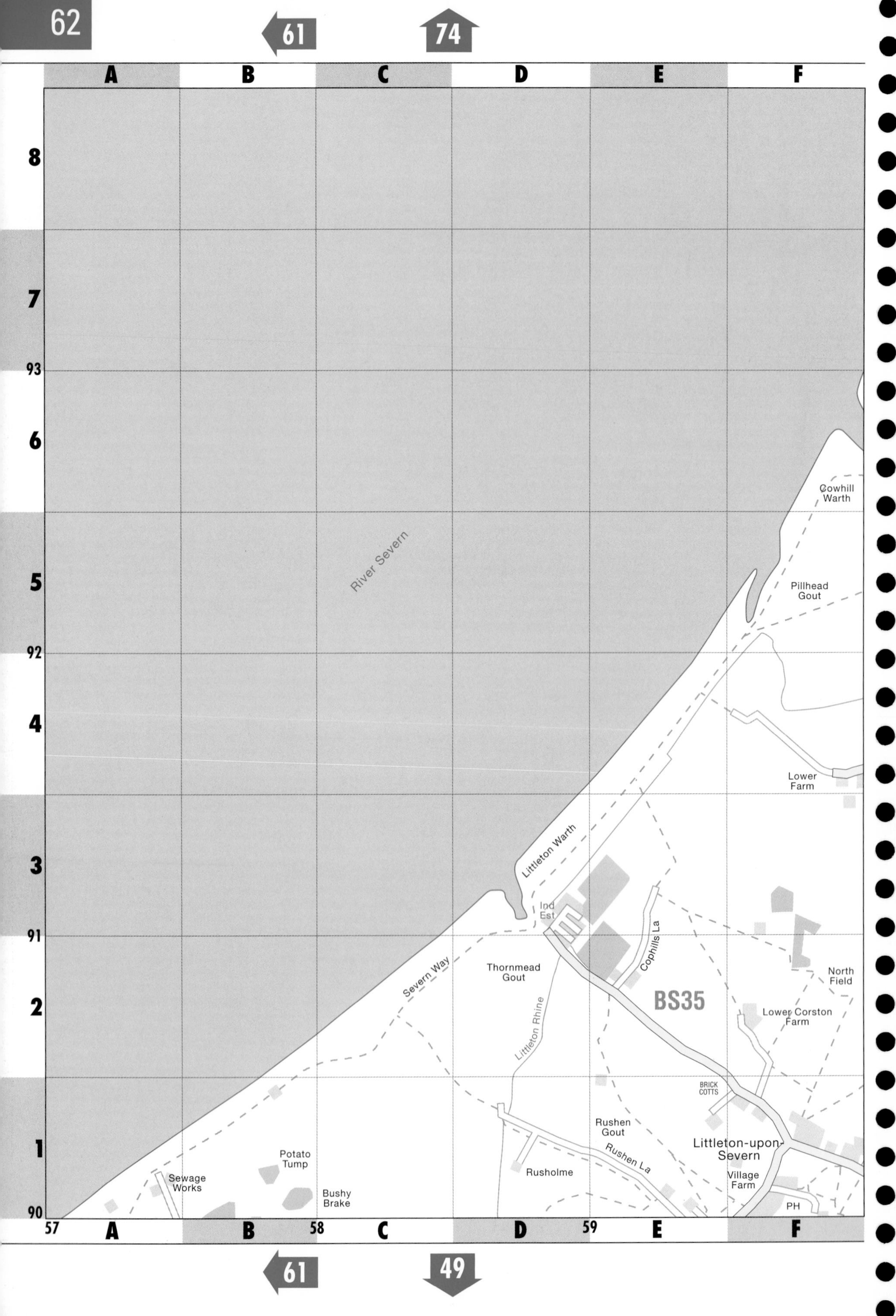
A
B
C
D
E
F
8
7
93
6
5
92
4
3
91
2
1
90
57
58
59
River Severn
Cowhill Warth
Pillhead Gout
Lower Farm
Littleton Warth
Ind Est
Cophills La
Thornmead Gout
Severn Way
North Field
BS35
Lower Corston Farm
Littleton Rhine
BRICK COTTS
Rushen Gout
Littleton-upon-Severn
Rushen La
Potato Tump
Sewage Works
Rusholme
Village Farm
Bushy Brake
PH

61
49

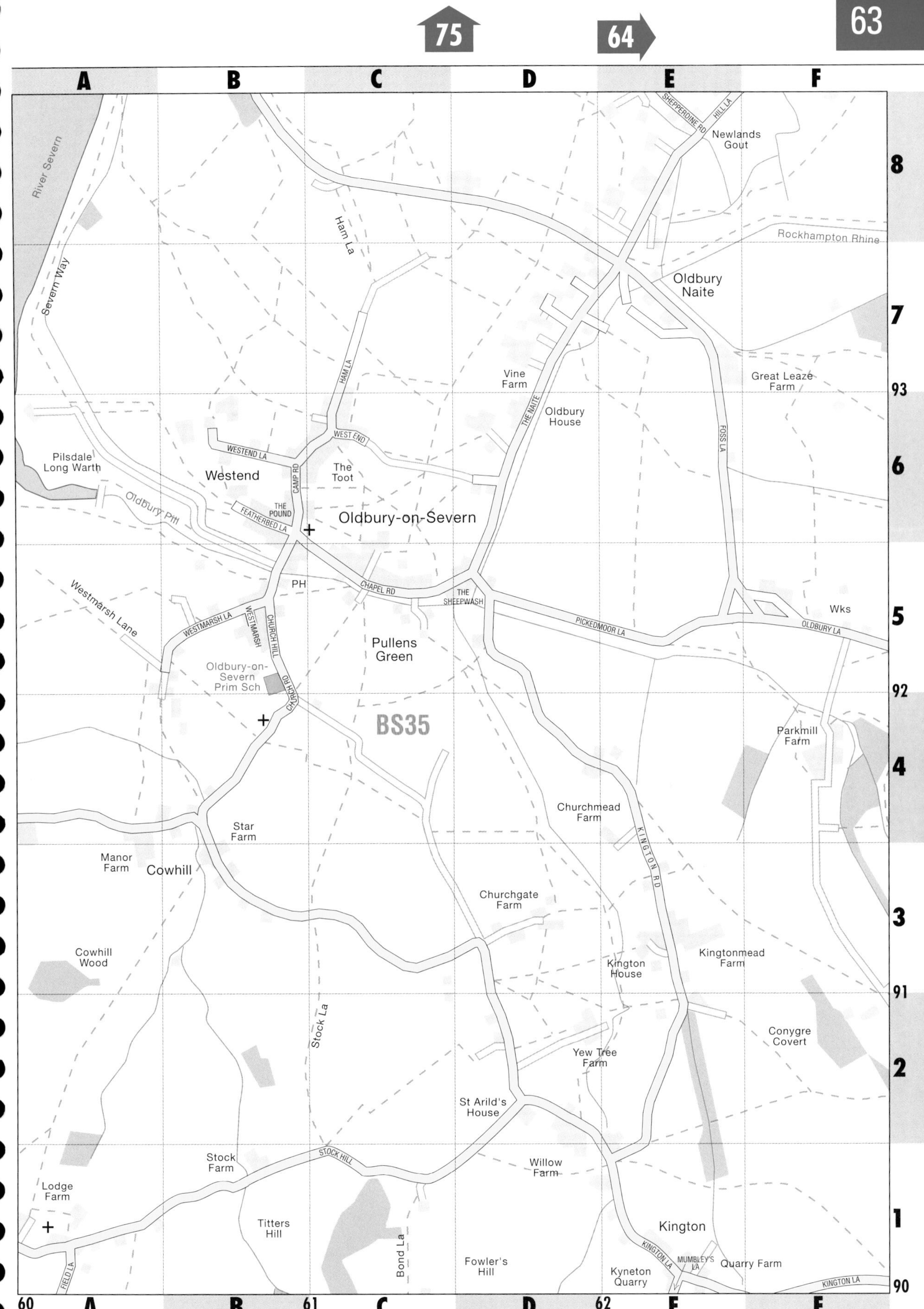
75
64
A
B
C
D
E
F
River Severn
Severn Way
SHEPPERDINE RD
HILL LA
Newlands
Gout
Ham La
Rockhampton Rhine
Oldbury
Naite
Vine
Farm
Great Leaze
Farm
HAM LA
THE NAITE
Oldbury
House
FOSS LA
WEST END
WESTEND LA
Pilsdale
Long Warth
Westend
The
Toot
CAMP RD
THE
POUND
FEATHERBED LA
Oldbury Pill
Oldbury-on-Severn
PH
CHAPEL RD
THE
SHEEPWASH
Westmarsh Lane
WESTMARSH LA
WESTMARSH
CHURCH HILL
Pullens
Green
PICKEDMOOR LA
Wks
OLDBURY LA
Oldbury-on-
Severn
Prim Sch
CHURCH RD
BS35
Parkmill
Farm
Churchmead
Farm
Star
Farm
Manor
Farm
Cowhill
KINGTON RD
Churchgate
Farm
Cowhill
Wood
Kington
House
Kingtonmead
Farm
Stock La
Conygre
Covert
Yew Tree
Farm
St Arild's
House
Stock
Farm
STOCK HILL
Willow
Farm
Lodge
Farm
Titters
Hill
Bond La
Kington
FIELD LA
Fowler's
Hill
KINGTON LA
MUMBLEY'S
LA
Quarry Farm
Kyneton
Quarry
KINGTON LA
8
7
93
6
5
92
4
3
91
2
1
90
60
61
62
50
64

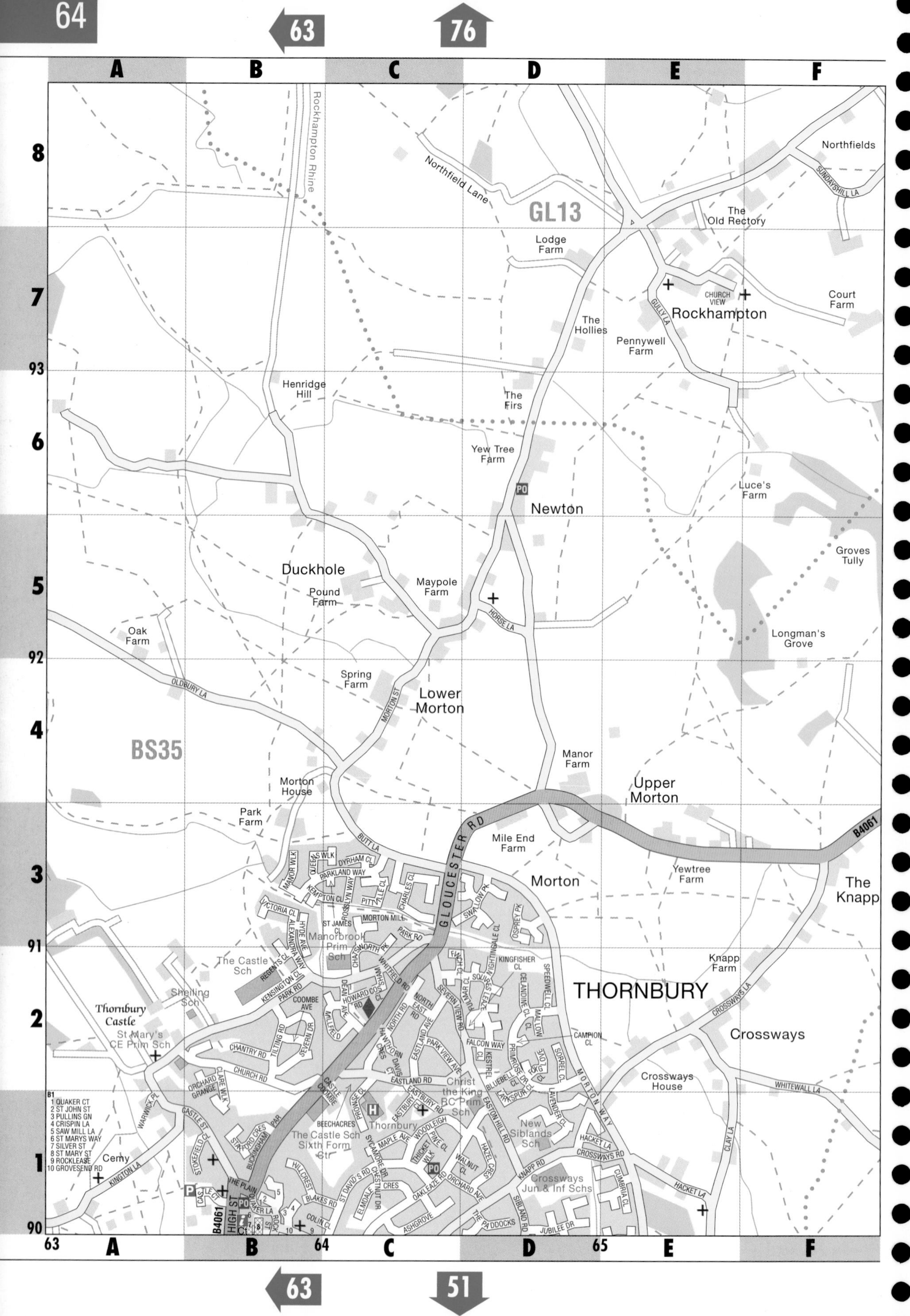
63
76
Northfields
Northfield Lane
GL13
The Old Rectory
Lodge Farm
Court Farm
Rockhampton
CHURCH VIEW
GULLY LA
The Hollies
Pennywell Farm
Henridge Hill
The Firs
Yew Tree Farm
Rockhampton Rhine
SUNDAYSHILL LA
Newton
Luce's Farm
Duckhole
Pound Farm
Maypole Farm
HORSE LA
Groves Tully
Oak Farm
Longman's Grove
OLDBURY LA
Spring Farm
Lower Morton
MORTON ST
BS35
Manor Farm
Morton House
Upper Morton
Park Farm
Mile End Farm
GLOUCESTER RD
B4061
BUTT LA
Yewtree Farm
Morton
The Knapp
THORNBURY
Knapp Farm
Thornbury Castle
St Mary's CE Prim Sch
The Castle Sch
Shelling Sch
Manorbrook Prim Sch
Crossways
CROSSWAYS LA
Christ the King RC Prim Sch
Thornbury
Crossways House
WHITEWALL LA
The Castle Sch Sixth Form Ctr
New Siblands Sch
Crossways Jun & Inf Schs
Cemy
KINGTON LA
HACKET LA
CLAY LA
B1
1 QUAKER CT
2 ST JOHN ST
3 PULLINS GN
4 CRISPIN LA
5 SAW MILL LA
6 ST MARYS WAY
7 SILVER ST
8 ST MARY ST
9 ROCKLEASE
10 GROVESEND RD
HIGH ST
THE PLAIN
MORTON WAY
KNAPP RD
SIBLAND RD
JUBILEE DR
THE PADDOCKS
ASHGROVE
63
51

77
66

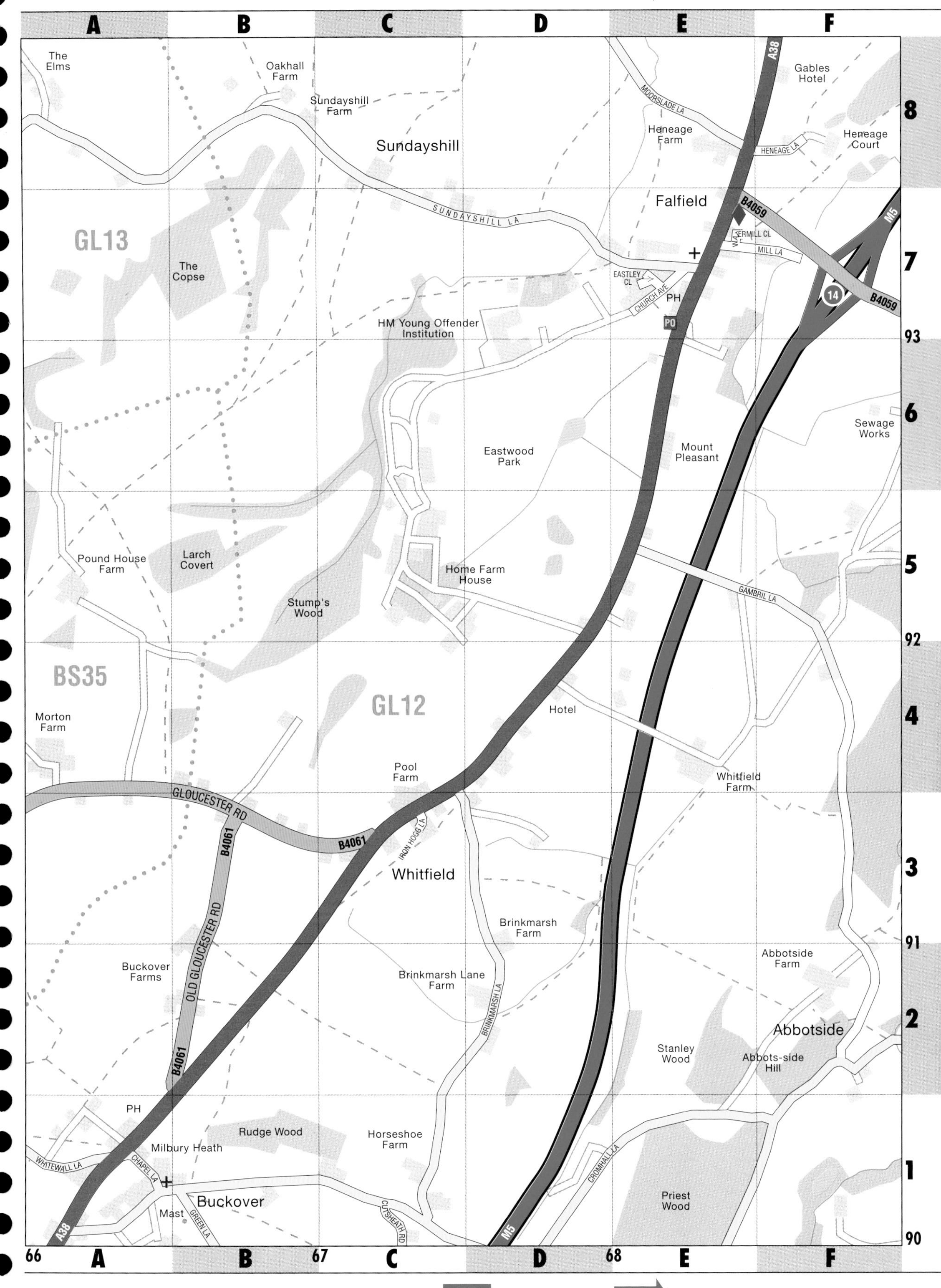
A B C D E F
8 7 93 6 5 92 4 3 91 2 1 90
66 67 68
The Elms
Oakhall Farm
Sundayshill Farm
Sundayshill
SUNDAYSHILL LA
GL13
The Copse
HM Young Offender Institution
Gables Hotel
MOORSLADE LA
Heneage Farm
HENEAGE LA
Heneage Court
Falfield
B4059
MILL LA
EASTLEY CL
CHURCH AVE
PH
PO
A38
M5
14
Eastwood Park
Mount Pleasant
Sewage Works
Pound House Farm
Larch Covert
Home Farm House
Stump's Wood
GAMBRIL LA
BS35
GL12
Hotel
Morton Farm
Pool Farm
Whitfield Farm
GLOUCESTER RD
B4061
IRON HOGG LA
Whitfield
OLD GLOUCESTER RD
Brinkmarsh Farm
Buckover Farms
Brinkmarsh Lane Farm
BRINKMARSH LA
Abbotside Farm
Abbotside
Stanley Wood
Abbots-side Hill
PH
Rudge Wood
Horseshoe Farm
Milbury Heath
WHITEWALL LA
CHAPEL LA
CROMHALL LA
Priest Wood
Buckover
Mast
GREEN LA
CUTSHEATH RD

52
66

65
78

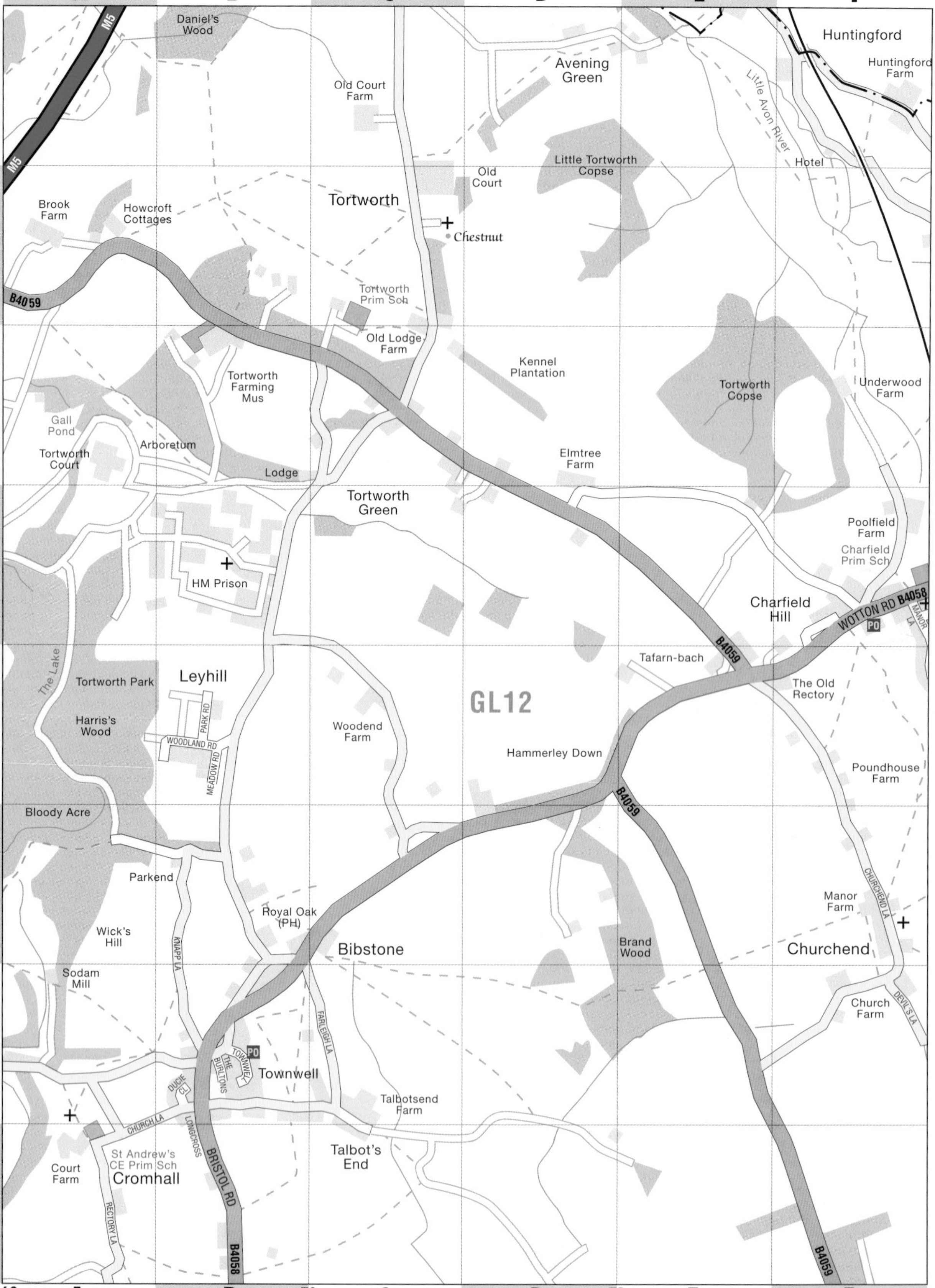

A B C D E F
8
7
93
6
5
92
4
3
91
2
1
90
69 A B 70 C D 71 E F
M5
Daniel's Wood
Old Court Farm
Avening Green
Huntingford
Huntingford Farm
Little Avon River
Hotel
Old Court
Little Tortworth Copse
Brook Farm
Howcroft Cottages
Tortworth
Chestnut
B4059
Tortworth Prim Sch
Old Lodge Farm
Kennel Plantation
Tortworth Copse
Underwood Farm
Tortworth Farming Mus
Gall Pond
Tortworth Court
Arboretum
Lodge
Elmtree Farm
Tortworth Green
Poolfield Farm
Charfield Prim Sch
HM Prison
Charfield Hill
WOTTON RD B4058
MANOR LA
PO
Tafarn-bach
The Old Rectory
The Lake
Tortworth Park
Leyhill
GL12
Harris's Wood
PARK RD
WOODLAND RD
MEADOW RD
Woodend Farm
Hammerley Down
Poundhouse Farm
Bloody Acre
Parkend
Manor Farm
CHURCHEND LA
Royal Oak (PH)
Wick's Hill
KNAPP LA
Bibstone
Brand Wood
Churchend
Sodam Mill
Church Farm
DEVIL'S LA
FARLEIGH LA
TOWNWELL
THE BURLTONS
DUCIE CL
Townwell
Talbotsend Farm
CHURCH LA
LONGCROSS
St Andrew's CE Prim Sch
Court Farm
Cromhall
Talbot's End
BRISTOL RD
RECTORY LA
B4058

65
53

79
68

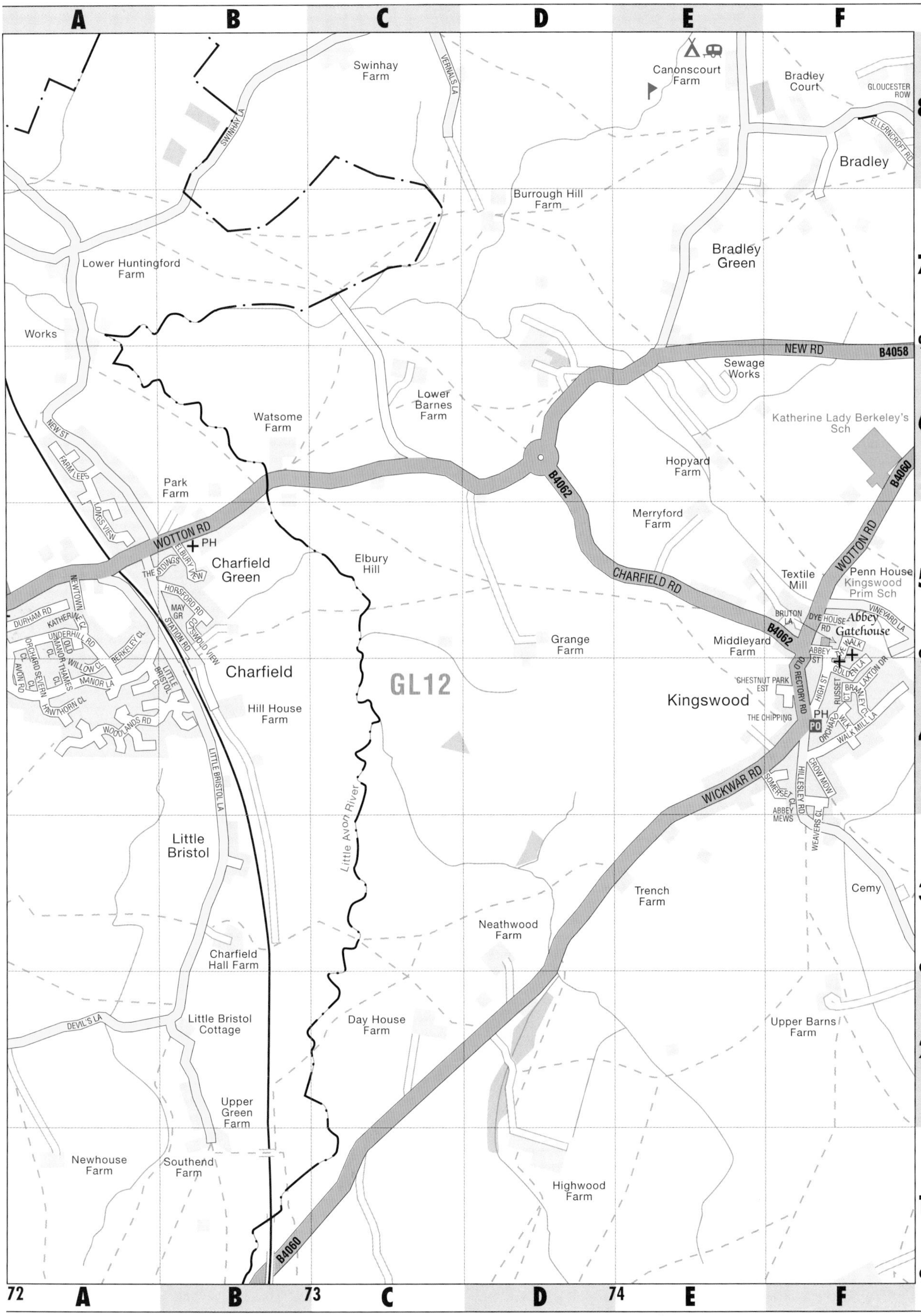

Swinhay Farm
Canonscourt Farm
Bradley Court
Bradley
Burrough Hill Farm
Bradley Green
Lower Huntingford Farm
Works
Sewage Works
Lower Barnes Farm
Watsome Farm
Katherine Lady Berkeley's Sch
Hopyard Farm
Park Farm
Merryford Farm
WOTTON RD
Charfield Green
Elbury Hill
Textile Mill
Penn House
Kingswood Prim Sch
Abbey Gatehouse
Grange Farm
Middleyard Farm
Charfield
GL12
Kingswood
Hill House Farm
WICKWAR RD
CHARFIELD RD
NEW RD
B4058
B4062
B4060
Little Bristol
Little Avon River
Trench Farm
Cemy
Neathwood Farm
Charfield Hall Farm
Little Bristol Cottage
Day House Farm
Upper Barns Farm
Upper Green Farm
Newhouse Farm
Southend Farm
Highwood Farm
DEVIL'S LA
LITTLE BRISTOL LA
A B C D E F
72 73 74
90 91 92 93
1 2 3 4 5 6 7 8

B7
1 ALMSHOUSES
2 CLARENCE CT
3 ROPE WLK
4 BEAUMONT SQ
5 BEAUMONT ROW
6 CHIPPING GDNS

67
80

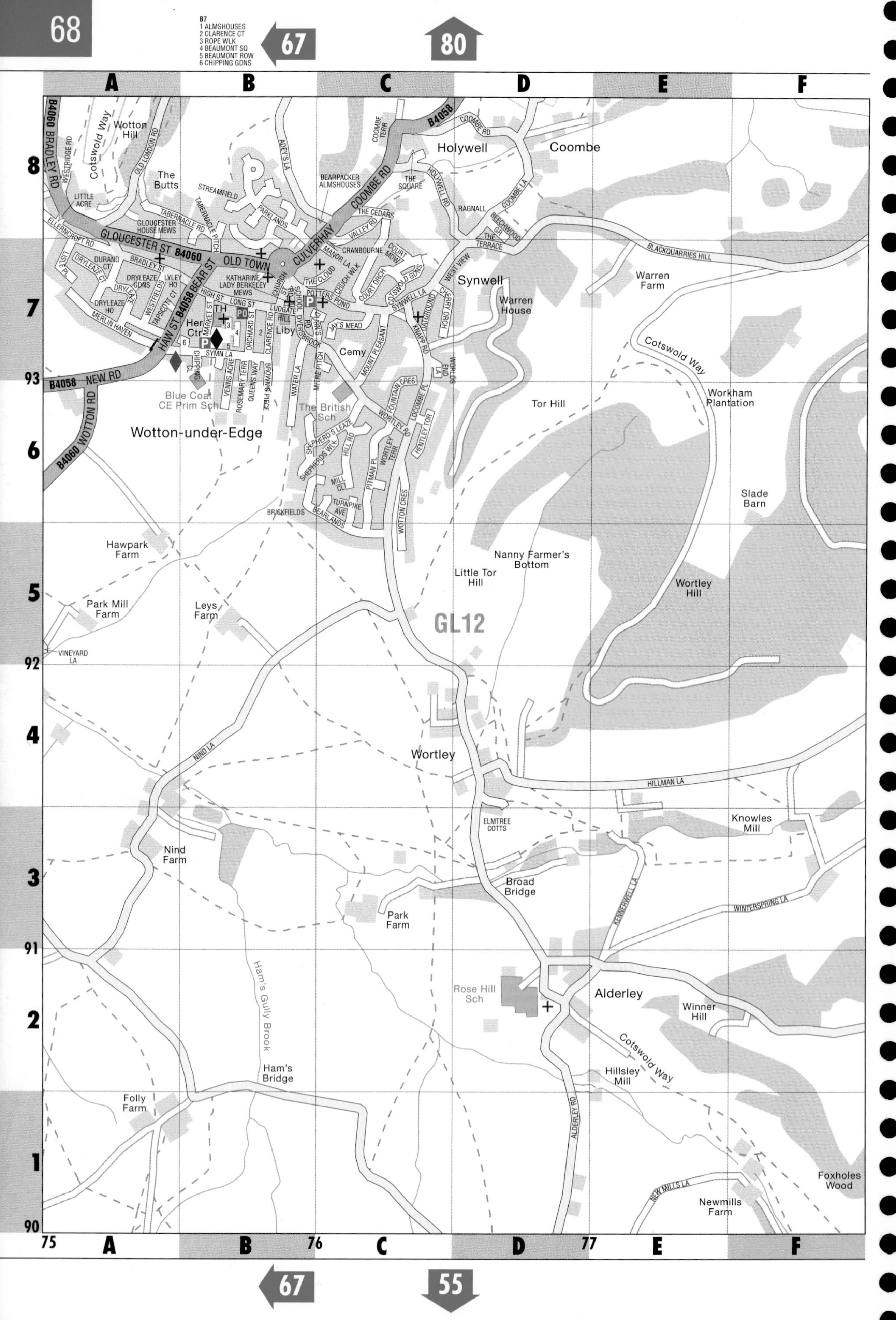

67
55

81
70

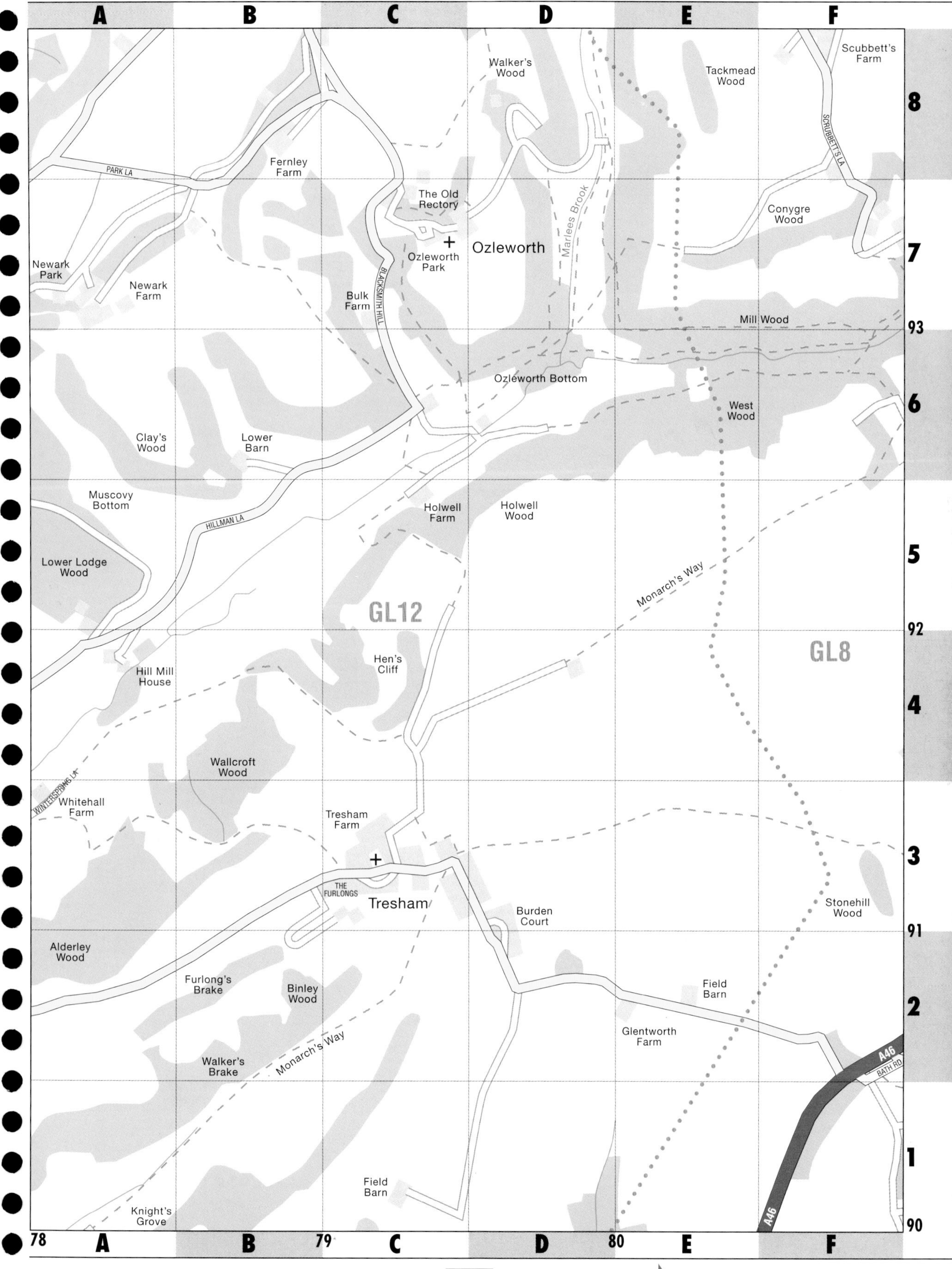
A
B
C
D
E
F
Walker's Wood
Tackmead Wood
Scubbett's Farm
SCUBBETT'S LA
PARK LA
Fernley Farm
The Old Rectory
Ozleworth
Ozleworth Park
Marlees Brook
Conygre Wood
Newark Park
Newark Farm
Bulk Farm
BLACKSMITH HILL
Mill Wood
Ozleworth Bottom
West Wood
Clay's Wood
Lower Barn
Muscovy Bottom
HILLMAN LA
Holwell Farm
Holwell Wood
Lower Lodge Wood
Monarch's Way
GL12
Hen's Cliff
GL8
Hill Mill House
Wallcroft Wood
WINTERSPRING LA
Whitehall Farm
Tresham Farm
THE FURLONGS
Tresham
Burden Court
Stonehill Wood
Alderley Wood
Furlong's Brake
Binley Wood
Field Barn
Glentworth Farm
Walker's Brake
Monarch's Way
A46
BATH RD
Field Barn
Knight's Grove
A46
8
7
93
6
5
92
4
3
91
2
1
90
78
79
80

56
70

69
82

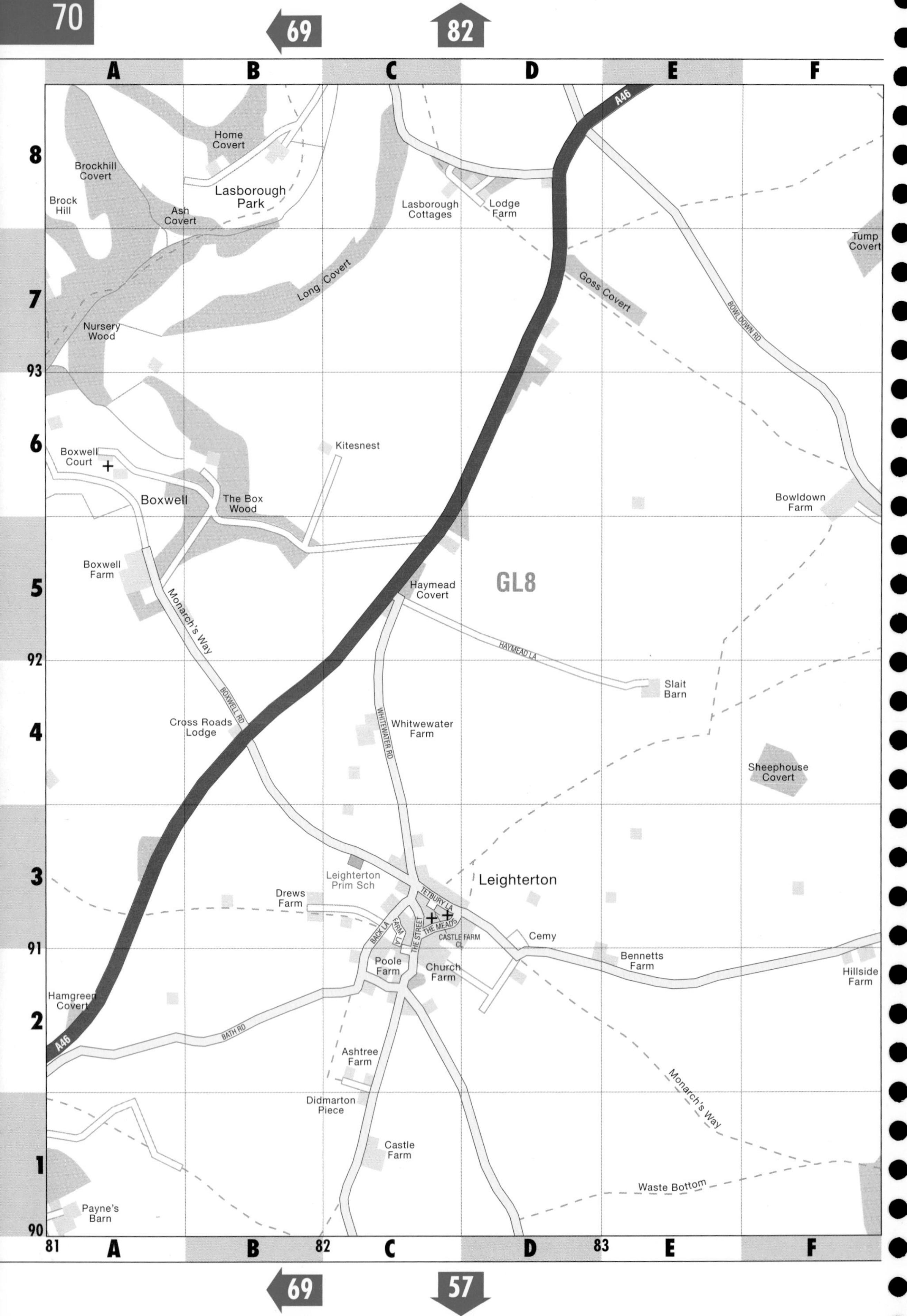
A
B
C
D
E
F
8
7
93
6
5
92
4
3
91
2
1
90
81
82
83
Home Covert
Brockhill Covert
Brock Hill
Lasborough Park
Ash Covert
Lasborough Cottages
Lodge Farm
A46
Tump Covert
Long Covert
Goss Covert
Nursery Wood
BOWLDOWN RD
Kitesnest
Boxwell Court
Boxwell
The Box Wood
Bowldown Farm
Boxwell Farm
Haymead Covert
GL8
Monarch's Way
HAYMEAD LA
Slait Barn
BOXWELL RD
Cross Roads Lodge
WHITEWATER RD
Whitwewater Farm
Sheephouse Covert
Leighterton Prim Sch
Leighterton
Drews Farm
TETBURY LA
THE MEADS
BACK LA
FARM LA
THE STREET
CASTLE FARM CL
Cemy
Poole Farm
Church Farm
Bennetts Farm
Hillside Farm
Hamgreen Covert
BATH RD
Ashtree Farm
Monarch's Way
Didmarton Piece
Castle Farm
Waste Bottom
Payne's Barn

69
57

83
140

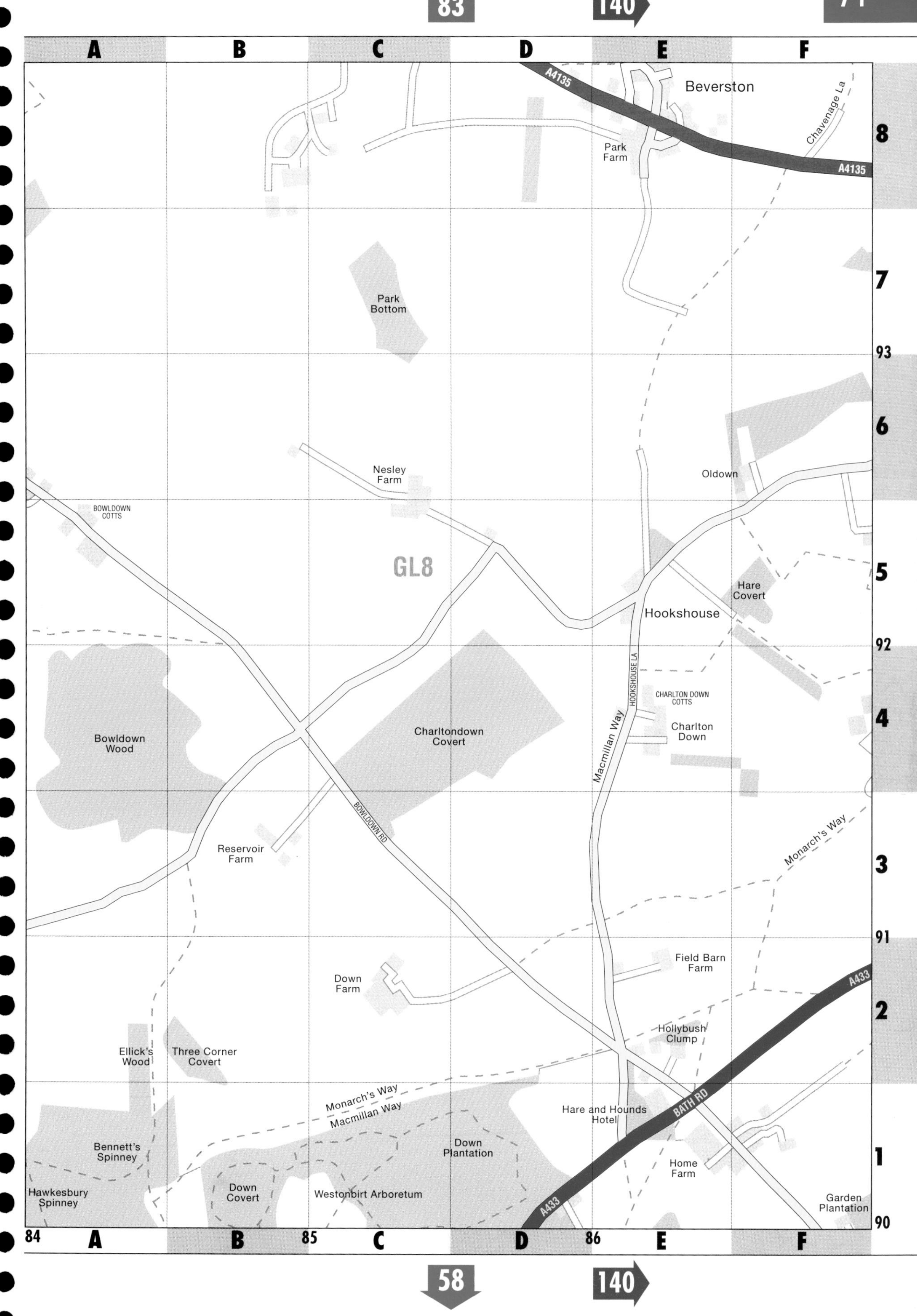
A
B
C
D
E
F
A4135
Beverston
Chavenage La
Park Farm
Park Bottom
Nesley Farm
Oldown
BOWLDOWN COTTS
GL8
Hare Covert
Hookshouse
HOOKSHOUSE LA
CHARLTON DOWN COTTS
Charlton Down
Bowldown Wood
Charltondown Covert
Macmillan Way
BOWLDOWN RD
Reservoir Farm
Monarch's Way
Field Barn Farm
Down Farm
A433
Hollybush Clump
Ellick's Wood
Three Corner Covert
Monarch's Way
Macmillan Way
BATH RD
Hare and Hounds Hotel
Down Plantation
Bennett's Spinney
Home Farm
Hawkesbury Spinney
Down Covert
Westonbirt Arboretum
Garden Plantation
8
7
93
6
5
92
4
3
91
2
1
90
84
85
86

58
140

146

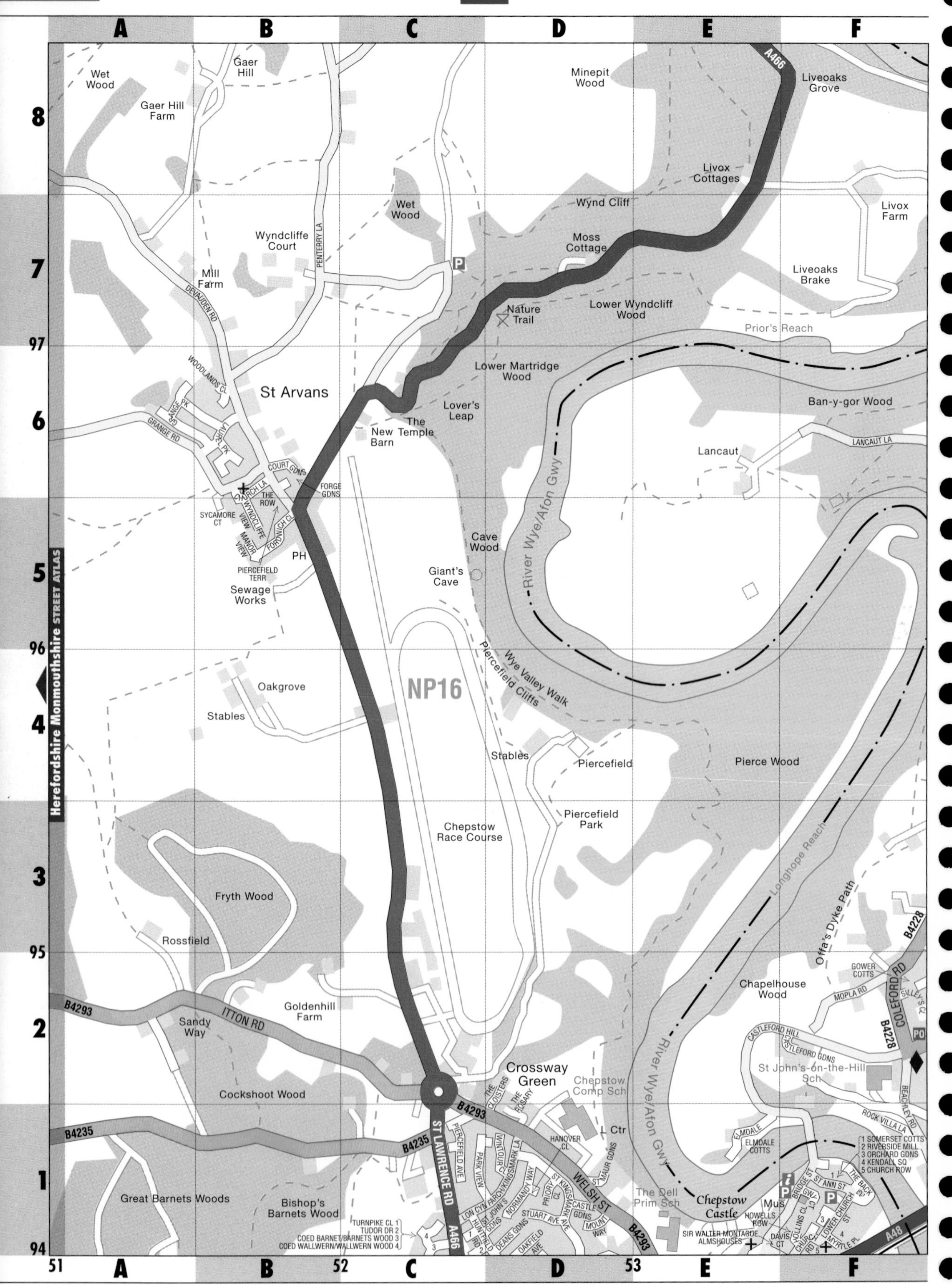

A
B
C
D
E
F
Wet Wood
Gaer Hill
Gaer Hill Farm
Minepit Wood
Liveoaks Grove
A466
Livox Cottages
Wet Wood
Wynd Cliff
Livox Farm
Wyndcliffe Court
PENTERRY LA
Moss Cottage
Mill Farm
DEVAUDEN RD
Liveoaks Brake
Nature Trail
Lower Wyndcliff Wood
Prior's Reach
Lower Martridge Wood
WOODLANDS CL
St Arvans
Ban-y-gor Wood
Lover's Leap
The New Temple
New Barn
GRANGE RD
LANCAUT LA
Lancaut
COURT GDNS
CHURCH LA
THE ROW
FORGE GDNS
SYCAMORE CT
WYNDCLIFFE VIEW
FORDWICH CL
MANOR VIEW
River Wye/Afon Gwy
Cave Wood
PH
Giant's Cave
PIERCEFIELD TERR
Sewage Works
Oakgrove
Stables
NP16
Wye Valley Walk
Piercefield Cliffs
Stables
Piercefield
Pierce Wood
Herefordshire Monmouthshire STREET ATLAS
Piercefield Park
Chepstow Race Course
Longhope Reach
Fryth Wood
Offa's Dyke Path
Rossfield
B4228
GOWER COTTS
Chapelhouse Wood
COLEFORD RD
MOPLA RD
B4293
ITTON RD
Sandy Way
Goldenhill Farm
CASTLEFORD HILL
CASTLEFORD GDNS
St John's-on-the-Hill Sch
Crossway Green
Chepstow Comp Sch
THE CLOISTERS
THE ROSARY
Cockshoot Wood
B4293
River Wye/Afon Gwy
ROCK VILLA LA
BEACHLEY RD
B4235
B4235
ST LAWRENCE RD
PIERCEFIELD AVE
HANOVER CL
Ctr
ELMDALE
ELMDALE COTTS
1 SOMERSET COTTS
2 RIVERSIDE MILL
3 ORCHARD GDNS
4 KENDALL SQ
5 CHURCH ROW
WELSH ST
ST MAUR GDNS
NORMANDY WAY
PRIORY CL
Great Barnets Woods
Bishop's Barnets Wood
The Dell Prim Sch
Chepstow Castle
Mus
BRIDGE ST
ST ANN ST
THE BACK
TURNPIKE CL 1
TUDOR DR 2
COED BARNET/BARNETS WOOD 3
COED WALLWERN/WALLWERN WOOD 4
A466
STUART AVE
OAKFIELD AVE
CASTLE GDNS
MOUNT WAY
B4293
HOWELLS ROW
SIR WALTER MONTAGUE ALMSHOUSES
DAVIS CT
LOWER CHURCH ST
MYRTLE PL
A48
8
7
97
6
5
96
4
3
95
2
1
94
51
52
53

60

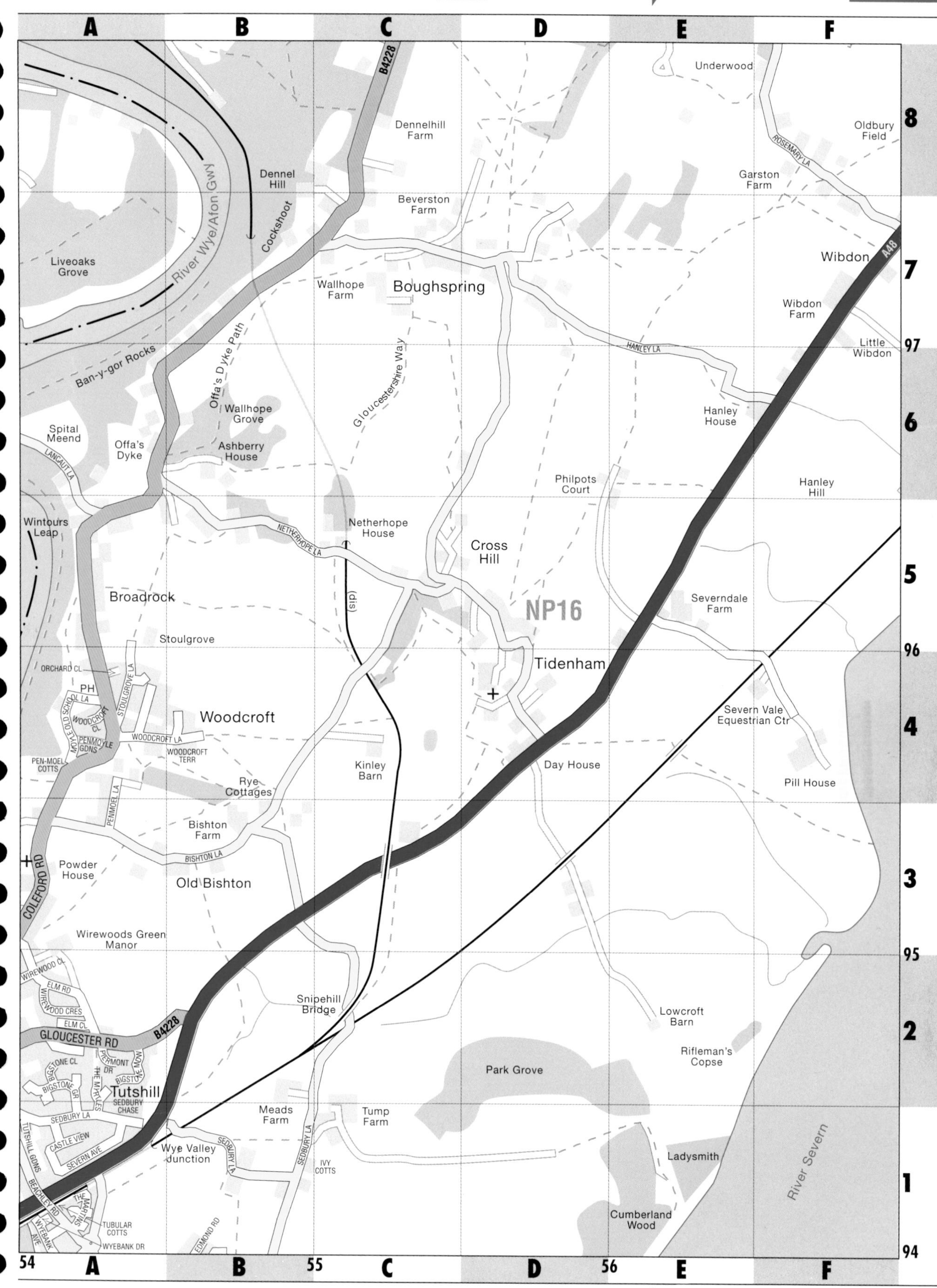
A
B
C
D
E
F
Underwood
Dennelhill Farm
Oldbury Field
Dennel Hill
Beverston Farm
Garston Farm
ROSEMARY LA
River Wye/Afon Gwy
Cockshoot
B4228
Liveoaks Grove
Wallhope Farm
Boughspring
Wibdon
A48
Wibdon Farm
Little Wibdon
Ban-y-gor Rocks
Offa's Dyke Path
Gloucestershire Way
HANLEY LA
Wallhope Grove
Hanley House
Spital Meend
Offa's Dyke
Ashberry House
LANCAUT LA
Philpots Court
Hanley Hill
Wintours Leap
Netherhope House
NETHERHOPE LA
Cross Hill
Broadrock
(dis)
NP16
Severndale Farm
Stoulgrove
ORCHARD CL
Tidenham
PH
STOULGROVE LA
OLD SCHOOL LA
WOODCROFT CL
Woodcroft
Severn Vale Equestrian Ctr
PENMOYLE GDNS
WOODCROFT LA
WOODCROFT TERR
PEN-MOEL COTTS
Kinley Barn
Day House
Rye Cottages
Pill House
PENMOEL LA
Bishton Farm
BISHTON LA
Powder House
COLEFORD RD
Old Bishton
Wirewoods Green Manor
WIREWOOD CL
ELM RD
WIREWOOD CRES
ELM CL
Snipehill Bridge
Lowcroft Barn
GLOUCESTER RD
B4228
Rifleman's Copse
Park Grove
BIGSTONE CL
PIERMONT DR
BIGSTONE GR
THE MYRTLES
Tutshill
SEDBURY CHASE
Meads Farm
Tump Farm
SEDBURY LA
CASTLE VIEW
SEVERN AVE
TUTSHILL GDNS
Wye Valley Junction
SEDBURY LA
IVY COTTS
Ladysmith
River Severn
BEACHLEY RD
THE MARTINS
TUBULAR COTTS
WYEBANK AVE
WYEBANK DR
EDMOND RD
Cumberland Wood
8
7
97
6
5
96
4
3
95
2
1
94
54
55
56

73
147

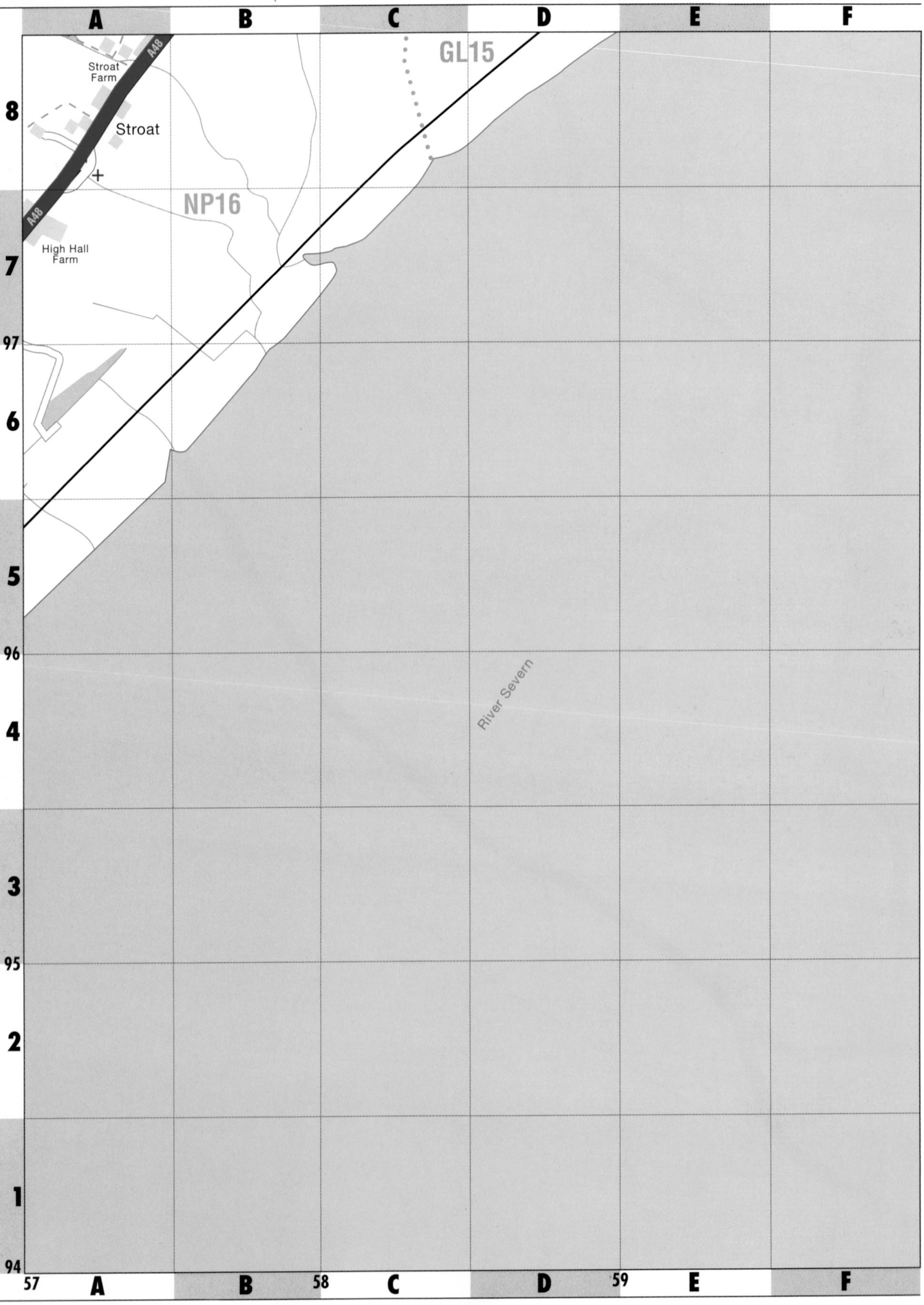

A B C D E F

A B C D E F

73
62

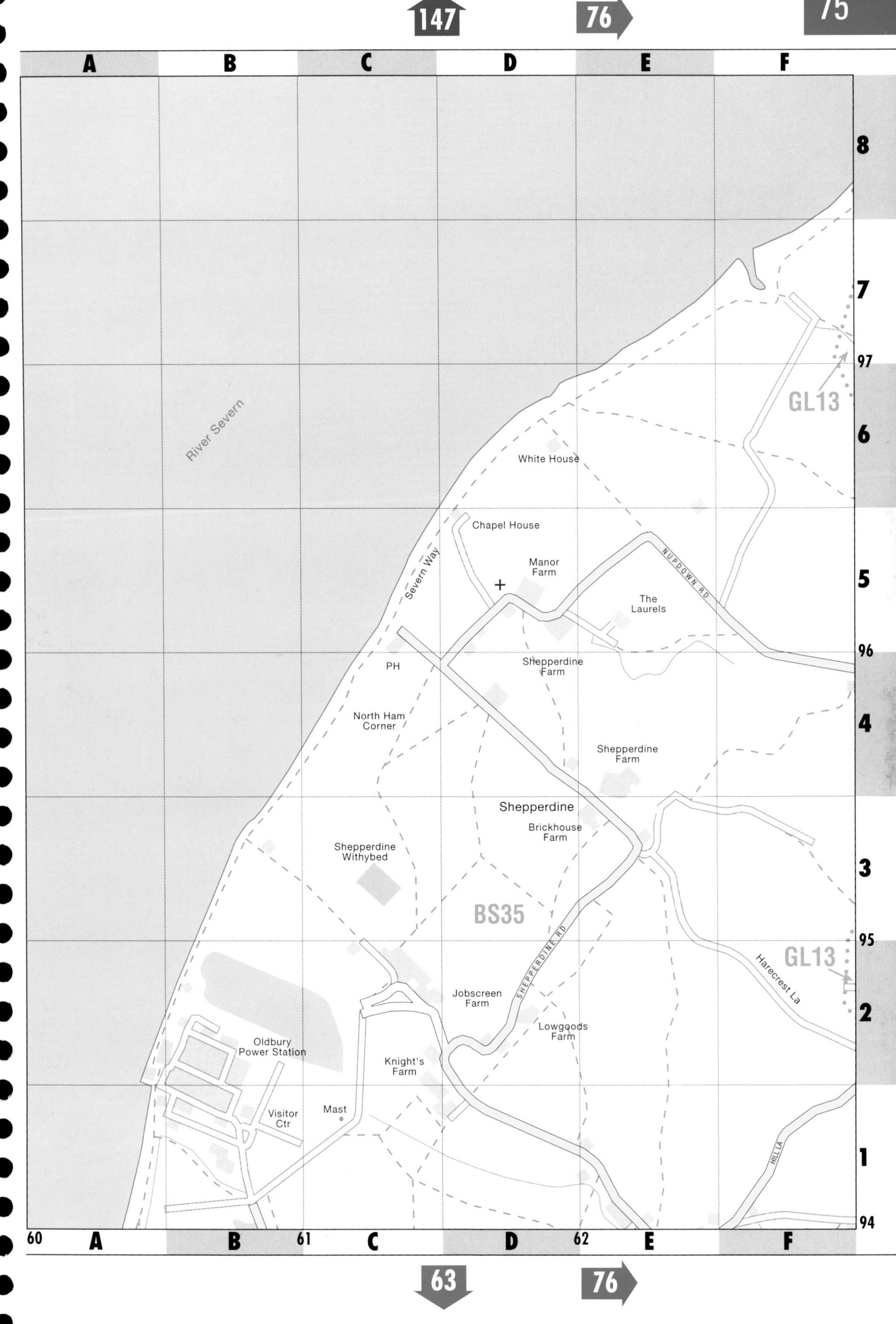
147
76
A
B
C
D
E
F
8
7
97
6
5
96
4
3
95
2
1
94
60
61
62
River Severn
GL13
White House
Chapel House
Manor
Farm
NUPDOWN RD
The
Laurels
Severn Way
PH
Shepperdine
Farm
North Ham
Corner
Shepperdine
Farm
Shepperdine
Brickhouse
Farm
Shepperdine
Withybed
BS35
SHEPPERDINE RD
GL13
Harecrest La
Jobscreen
Farm
Lowgoods
Farm
Oldbury
Power Station
Knight's
Farm
Visitor
Ctr
Mast
HILL LA
63
76

75
84

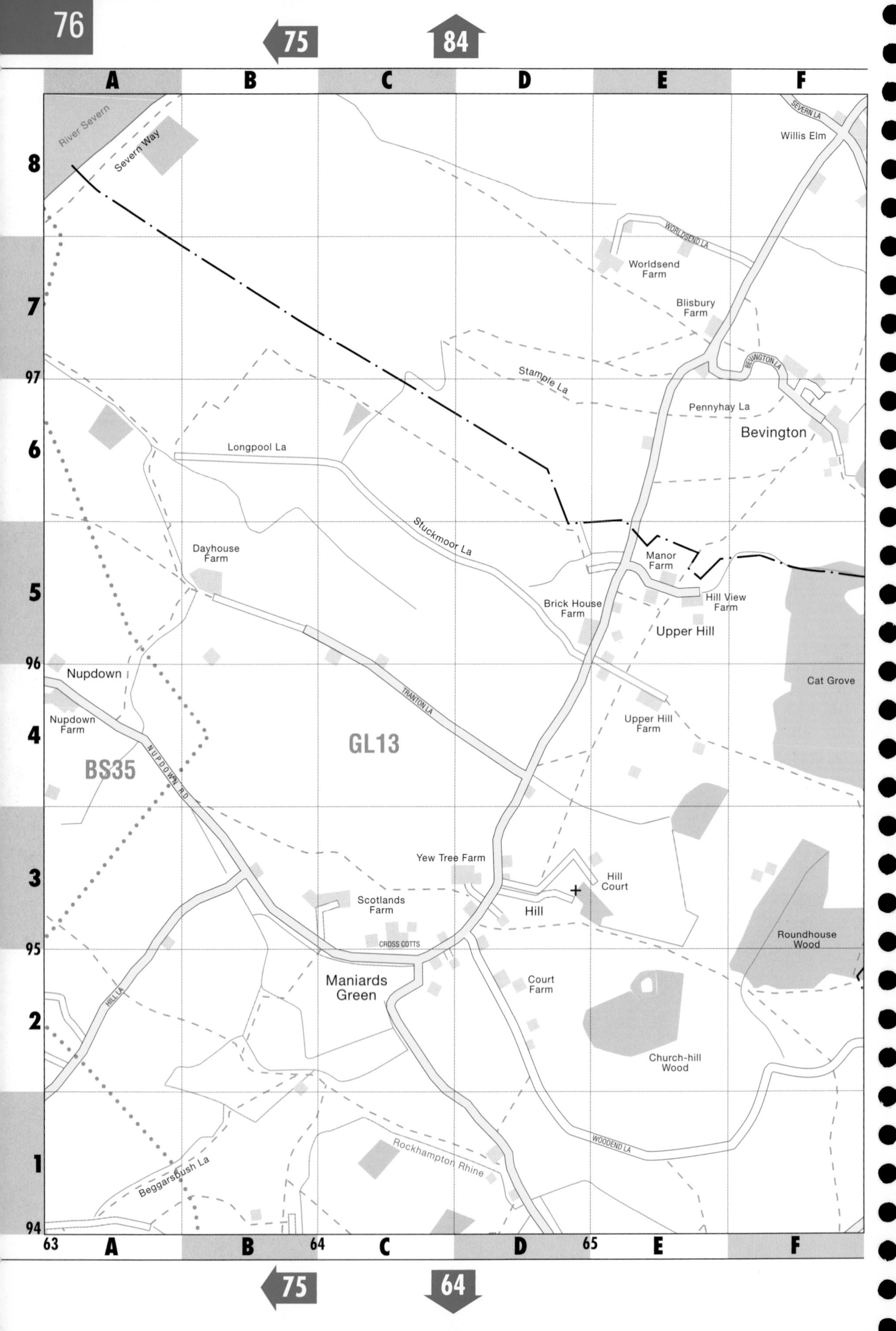
A
B
C
D
E
F
8
7
97
6
5
96
4
3
95
2
1
94
63
64
65
River Severn
Severn Way
SEVERN LA
Willis Elm
WORLDSEND LA
Worldsend Farm
Blisbury Farm
BEVINGTON LA
Stample La
Pennyhay La
Bevington
Longpool La
Stuckmoor La
Dayhouse Farm
Manor Farm
Brick House Farm
Hill View Farm
Upper Hill
Nupdown
Nupdown Farm
TRANTON LA
Cat Grove
Upper Hill Farm
GL13
BS35
NUPDOWN RD
Yew Tree Farm
Hill Court
Scotlands Farm
Hill
CROSS COTTS
Roundhouse Wood
Maniards Green
Court Farm
HILL LA
Church-hill Wood
WOODEND LA
Rockhampton Rhine
Beggarsbush La

75
64

85
78

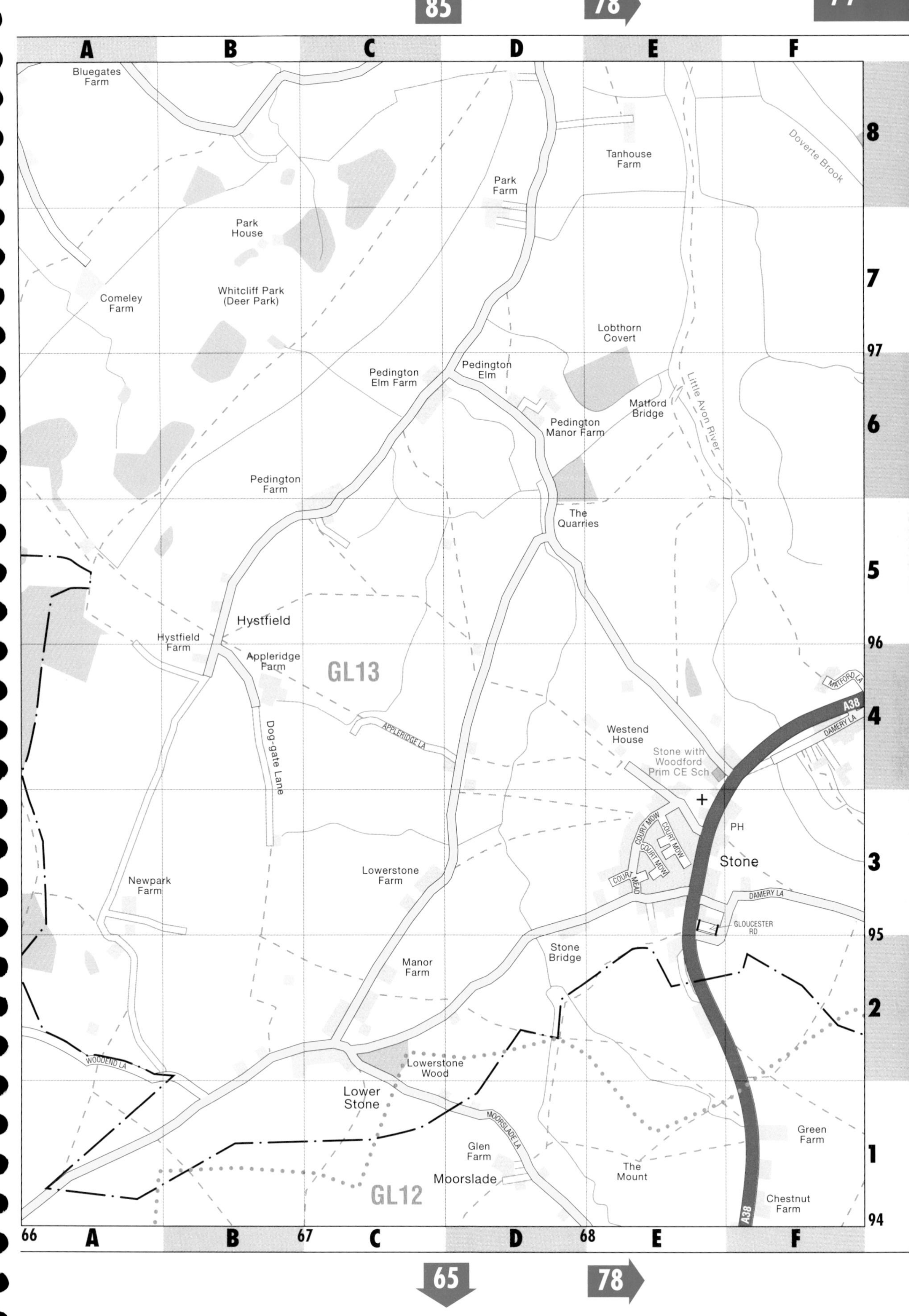
A
B
C
D
E
F
Bluegates Farm
Tanhouse Farm
Doverte Brook
Park Farm
Park House
Whitcliff Park (Deer Park)
Comeley Farm
Lobthorn Covert
Pedington Elm Farm
Pedington Elm
Matford Bridge
Little Avon River
Pedington Manor Farm
Pedington Farm
The Quarries
Hystfield
Hystfield Farm
Appleridge Farm
GL13
Dog-gate Lane
APPLERIDGE LA
Westend House
Stone with Woodford Prim CE Sch
MATFORD LA
A38
DAMERY LA
PH
Stone
COURT MDW
COURT MEAD
Newpark Farm
Lowerstone Farm
GLOUCESTER RD
Manor Farm
Stone Bridge
WOODEND LA
Lowerstone Wood
Lower Stone
MOORSLADE LA
Glen Farm
Moorslade
The Mount
Green Farm
Chestnut Farm
GL12
8
7
97
6
5
96
4
3
95
2
1
94
66
67
68

65
78

77 86

A
B
C
D
E
F
8
7
97
6
5
96
4
3
95
2
1
94
69
70
71
Newport
PH
Hotel
A38
CHURCH VIEW
CHAPEL HILL
Greenways
Goldwick Farm
CROSSWAYS
Baynhamcourt Farm
Hogsdown Farm
Oakleaze Farm
Doverte Brook
M5
Lower Wick
GL13
GL11
HAYCROFT LA
Manor Farm
Swanley Farm
Lowerwick Farm
SWANLEY LA
Swanley
Middle Wick
Woodfordgreen Farm
Whitehall Farm
Middlewick Farm
PH
Woodford
Wick Bridge
Michaelwood Farm
DAMERY LA
Harold's Brake
Damery Wks
Woodford Farm
MULE ST
Michaelwood Service Area
Sweetbrier Brake
Middle Mill Farm
DAMERY LA
Furzeground Wood
Michaelwood Lodge Farm
Micheal Wood
DAMERY LA
Little Avon River
GL12
Crockley's Farm
Damery
Damery Bridge
Iron Mill Grove
Daniel's Wood

77 66

87
80

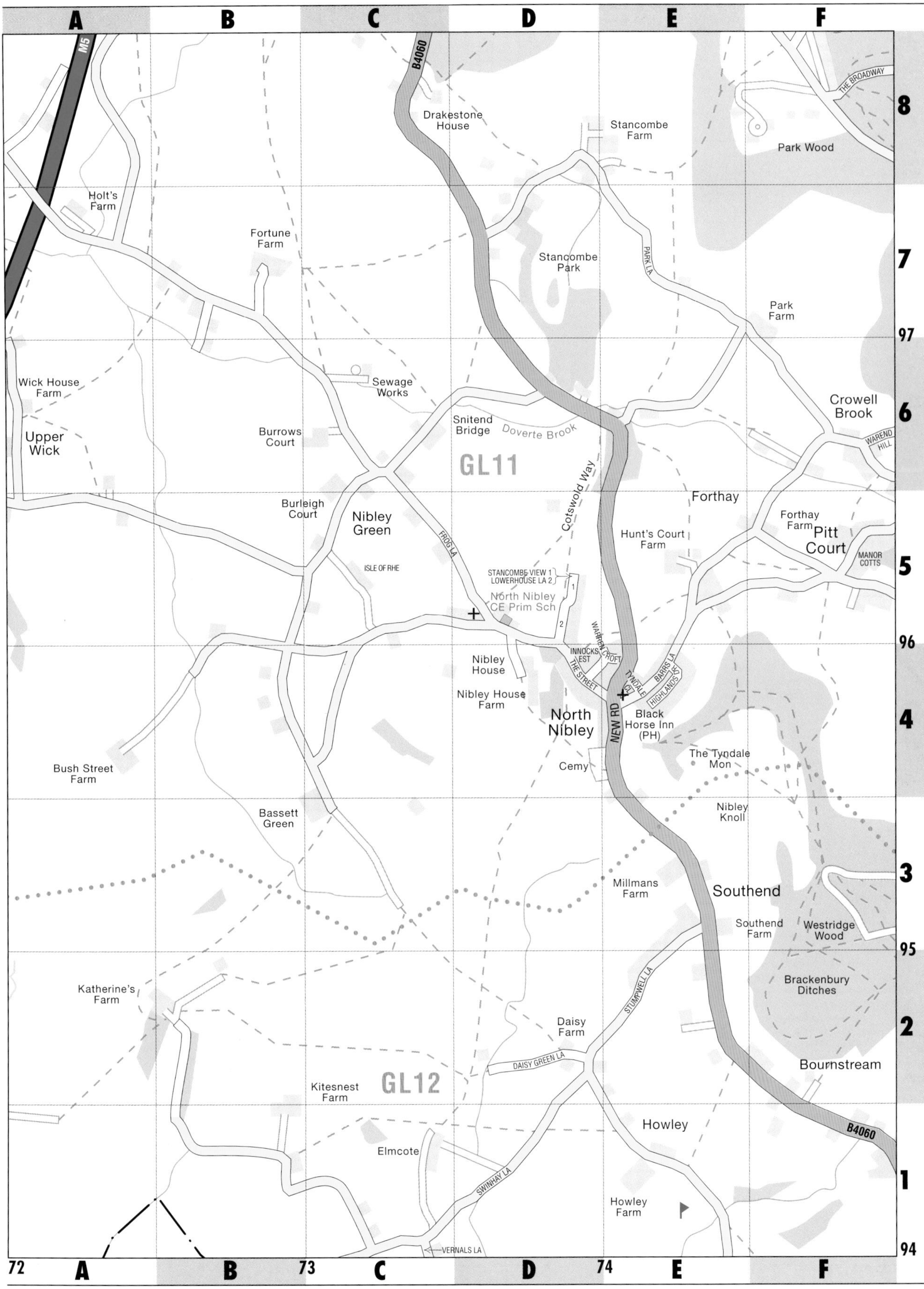

A B C D E F

8
7
97
6
5
96
4
3
95
2
1
94

72 A B 73 C D 74 E F

67
80

79 88

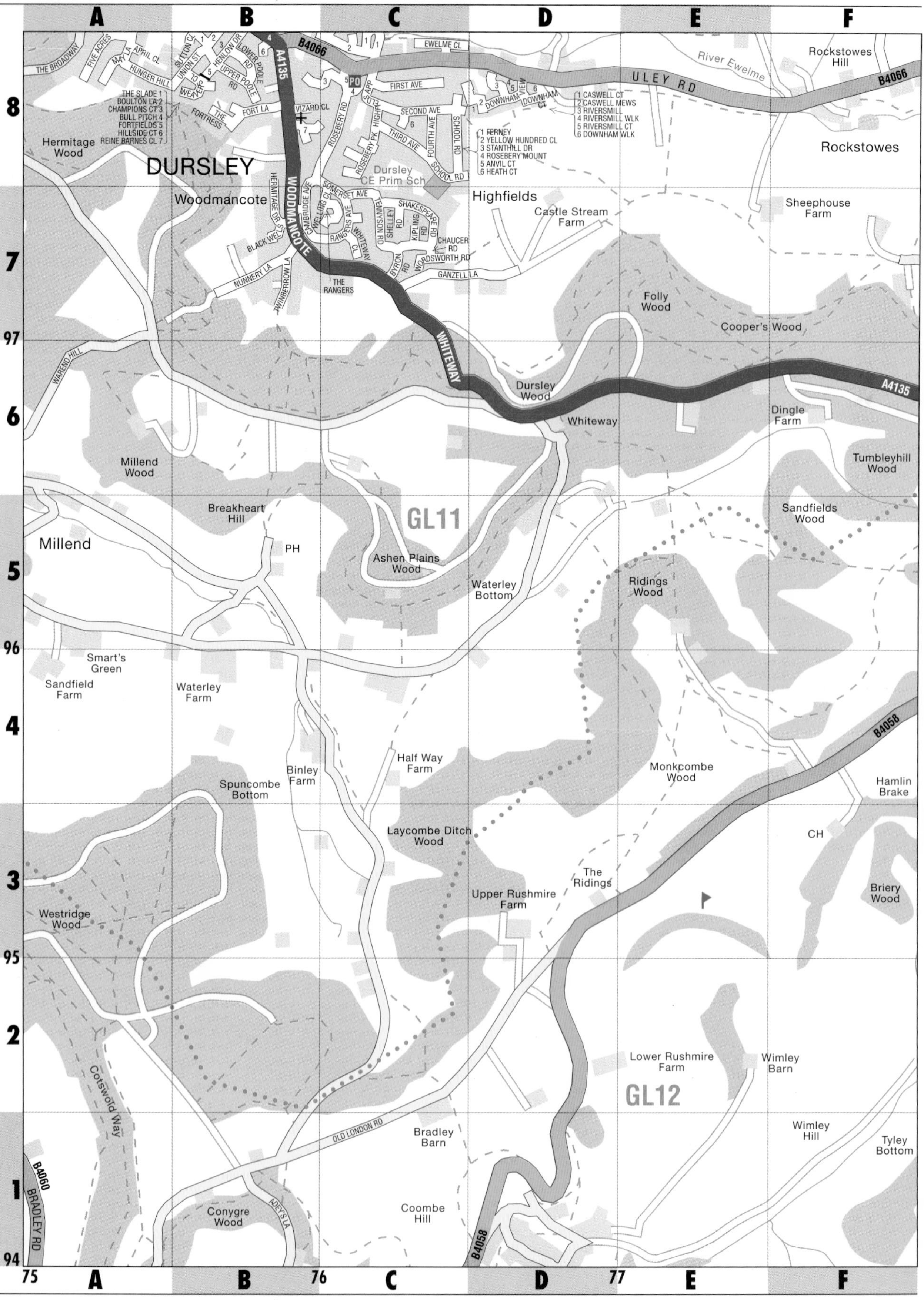

DURSLEY
Woodmancote
Highfields
Hermitage Wood
Castle Stream Farm
Dursley CE Prim Sch
Rockstowes Hill
Rockstowes
Sheephouse Farm
River Ewelme
ULEY RD
B4066
A4135
WOODMANCOTE
WHITEWAY
THE SLADE 1
BOULTON LA 2
CHAMPIONS CT 3
BULL PITCH 4
FORTFIELDS 5
HILLSIDE CT 6
REINE BARNES CL 7
1 FERNEY
2 YELLOW HUNDRED CL
3 STANTHILL DR
4 ROSEBERY MOUNT
5 ANVIL CT
6 HEATH CT
1 CASWELL CT
2 CASWELL MEWS
3 RIVERSMILL
4 RIVERSMILL WLK
5 RIVERSMILL CT
6 DOWNHAM WLK
THE BROADWAY
FIVE ACRES
APRIL CL
HUNGER HILL
SUTTON CL
UNION ST
HENLOW DR
LOWER POOLE RD
UPPER POOLE RD
FORT LA
FORTRESS
VIZARD CL
EWELME CL
FIRST AVE
SECOND AVE
THIRD AVE
FOURTH AVE
SCHOOL RD
ROSEBERY RD
ROSEBERY PK
DOWNHAM VIEW
DOWNHAM CT
SOMERSET AVE
CAMBRIDGE AVE
HERMITAGE DR
BLACK WELL
NUNNERY LA
WINBERROW LA
RANGERS AVE
WHITEWAY CL
TENNYSON RD
SHELLEY RD
SHAKESPEARE RD
KIPLING RD
CHAUCER RD
BYRON RD
WORDSWORTH RD
GANZELL LA
THE RANGERS
Folly Wood
Cooper's Wood
Dursley Wood
Whiteway
Dingle Farm
Tumbleyhill Wood
WAREND HILL
Millend Wood
Breakheart Hill
GL11
Sandfields Wood
Millend
PH
Ashen Plains Wood
Ridings Wood
Waterley Bottom
Smart's Green
Sandfield Farm
Waterley Farm
B4058
Half Way Farm
Binley Farm
Spuncombe Bottom
Monkcombe Wood
Hamlin Brake
Laycombe Ditch Wood
CH
The Ridings
Westridge Wood
Upper Rushmire Farm
Briery Wood
Cotswold Way
Lower Rushmire Farm
Wimley Barn
GL12
OLD LONDON RD
Bradley Barn
Wimley Hill
Tyley Bottom
B4060
BRADLEY RD
Conygre Wood
ADEYS LA
Coombe Hill
A B C D E F
8 7 97 6 5 96 4 3 95 2 1 94
75 76 77

79 68

89
82

A B C D E F
8
7
97
6
5
96
4
3
95
2
1
94
78 79 80
ULEY RD
B4066
THE STREET
FOR ST
WINDSOR LA
SHADWELL
ELCOMBE
Elcombe Farm
Stouts Hill
Lye Farm
Bencombe
Luggershall Farm
Whitley Wood
Oldleaze Wood
South Lodge
B4058
GL11
Lampern House
Twopence Covert
Groomes Grove Farm
Rook Wood
Bowcote Knoll Wood
Virgin's Corner Wood
Bowcott Farm
Dingle Wood
Symonds' Hall Firs
WINDMILL LA
Mast
A4135
Home Farm
The Ridge
Symonds' Hall Farm
Field Cottages
GL8
Westfield Brake
GL12
Barnhill Wood
Barnhill Farm
Golden Knoll Wood
Hollowley Covert
ASHCROFT RD
Ashcroft House
Bagpath
Tyley Long Wood
Common Hill
Scubbett's Farm
Radio Twr
Radio Station
Sawcombe Farm
Goose Green
Marlees Brook
SCUBBETT'S LA
Field Barn

69
82

81 90

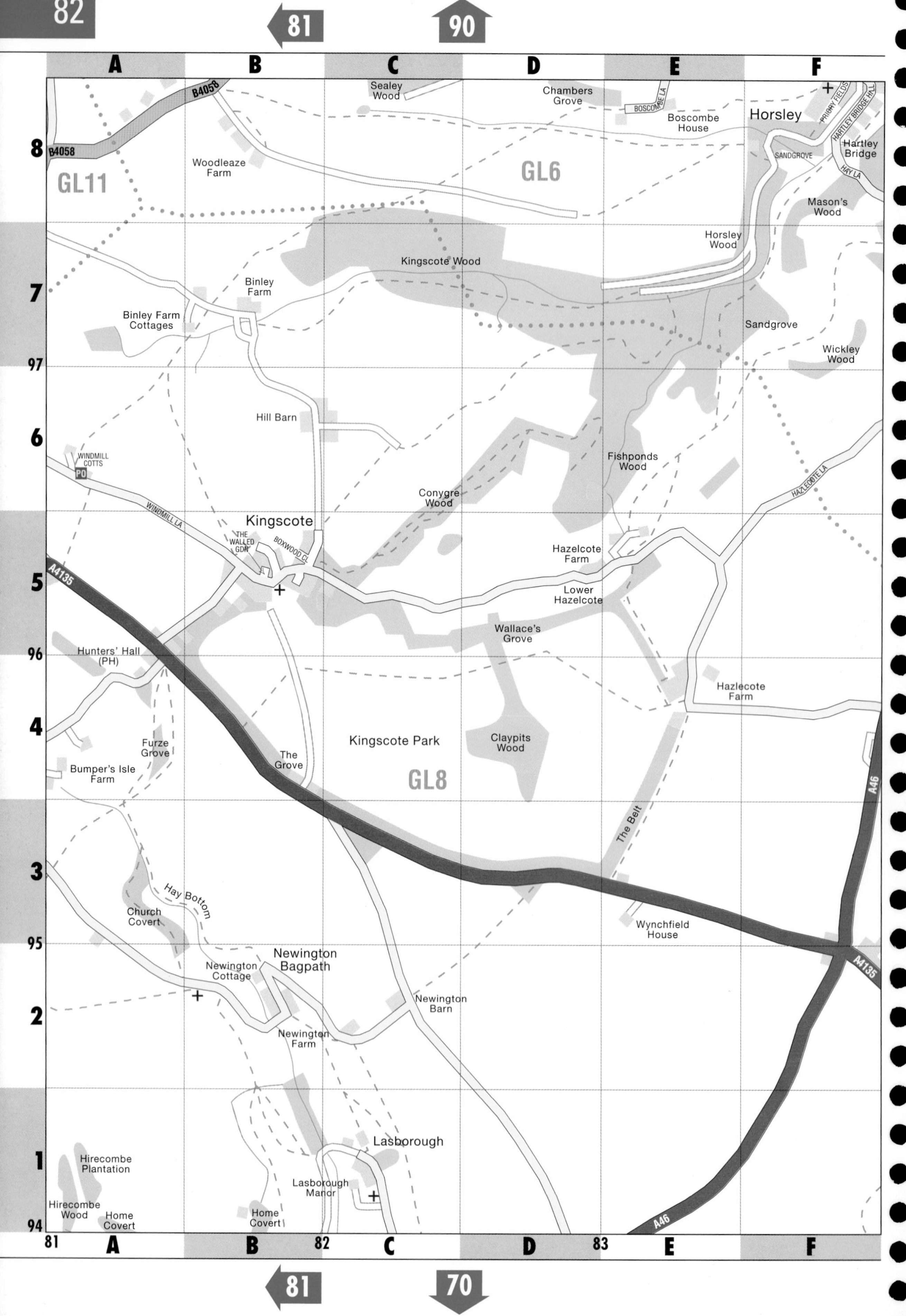

A B C D E F
8 7 97 6 5 96 4 3 95 2 1 94
81 82 83
B4058
GL11
GL6
GL8
Sealey Wood
Chambers Grove
BOSCOMBE LA
Boscombe House
Horsley
PRIORY FIELDS
HARTLEY BRIDGE HILL
Hartley Bridge
SANDGROVE
HAY LA
Woodleaze Farm
Mason's Wood
Horsley Wood
Kingscote Wood
Binley Farm
Binley Farm Cottages
Sandgrove
Wickley Wood
Hill Barn
WINDMILL COTTS
PO
Fishponds Wood
Conygre Wood
HAZLECOTE LA
WINDMILL LA
Kingscote
THE WALLED GDN
BOXWOOD CL
Hazelcote Farm
A4135
Lower Hazelcote
Wallace's Grove
Hunters' Hall (PH)
Hazlecote Farm
Furze Grove
Kingscote Park
Claypits Wood
Bumper's Isle Farm
The Grove
The Belt
A46
Hay Bottom
Church Covert
Wynchfield House
Newington Bagpath
Newington Cottage
Newington Barn
Newington Farm
Lasborough
Hirecombe Plantation
Lasborough Manor
Hirecombe Wood
Home Covert
Home Covert

81 70

91
140

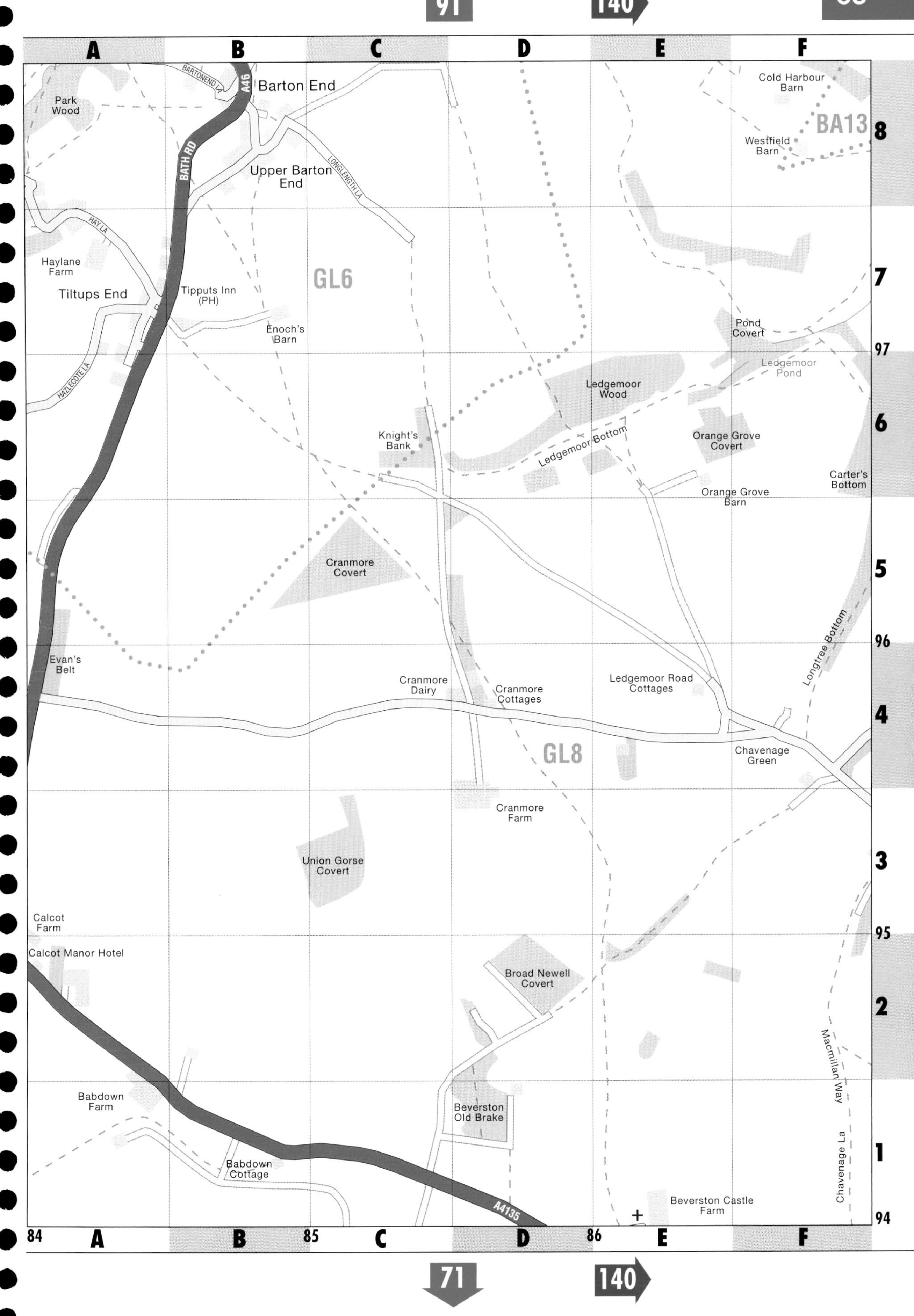
A
B
C
D
E
F
Barton End
Park Wood
BARTONEND LA
A46
BATH RD
Upper Barton End
LONGLENGTH LA
Cold Harbour Barn
Westfield Barn
BA13
8
HAY LA
Haylane Farm
Tiltups End
Tipputs Inn (PH)
GL6
Enoch's Barn
7
Pond Covert
97
Ledgemoor Pond
HAZLECOTE LA
Ledgemoor Wood
Knight's Bank
Ledgemoor Bottom
Orange Grove Covert
6
Carter's Bottom
Orange Grove Barn
Cranmore Covert
5
Longtree Bottom
96
Evan's Belt
Cranmore Dairy
Cranmore Cottages
Ledgemoor Road Cottages
4
GL8
Chavenage Green
Cranmore Farm
Union Gorse Covert
3
Calcot Farm
95
Calcot Manor Hotel
Broad Newell Covert
2
Macmillan Way
Babdown Farm
Beverston Old Brake
1
Chavenage La
Babdown Cottage
Beverston Castle Farm
A4135
94
84
85
86

71
140

147
92

A B C D E F
8
7
01
6
5
00
4
3
99
2
1
98
Lydney
COOKSON TERR
STATION RD
MEAD LA
Ward Ind Est
LC
RAILWAY TERR
THE MARINA
GL15
HARBOUR RD
Lydney Ind Est
Naas House
Lydney Harbour
Lydney Marsh
HARBOUR RD
New Grounds
River Severn
Severn Way
GL13
Severn House Farm
SEVERN LA
63 A B 64 C D 65 E F

147
76

93
86
A
B
C
D
E
F
8
7
01
6
5
00
4
3
99
2
1
98
66
67
68
77
86
Newtown
Sharpness Prim Sch
Saniger Farm
Panthurst Farm
Severn Way
Oakhunger Farm
Westfield Brake
GL13
The Paddock
Rookery Farm
Wanswell
Berkeley Vale Com Sch
Hertsgrove Farm
Sugar-loaf Villa
Hainses
Butler's Farm
Pitbrook
Penny Grove
Abwell
Abwell Farm
Tintock Wood
The Fishers
Wickselm
Severn Way
Berkeley Pill
Berkeley Power Station
Lynch Road Ind Est
Hook Street
Oakhunger
Lynch
Cemy
Berkeley
Berkeley Prim Sch
Berkeley
Long Bridge
Edward Jenner Mus
Berkeley Castle
Butterfly House
Hamfield Farm
Parham Brake
Berkeley Pill
Floodgates Farm
Kennels
Woodlands Farm
Ham
Salutation Inn (PH)
Fowler's Plantation
Brownsmill Farm
Parham La
Blackhall
Bluegates Farm
B4066
B4066
SAWIGER LA
SAWIGER LA
STATION RD
HAMFIELD LA
OAKHUNGER LA
LYNCH RD
WOODLANDS LA
HALMORE LA
ROOKERY LA
STAMBOURNE VILLAS
STAMBOURNE LA
VINECROFT
GLOUCESTER RD
BAYS HILL
HAMFALLOW CT
SEVERN VIEW PAR
LEWISHAM TERR
BAYLANDS
THE CRESCENT
LYCH VALE CVN PK
BERKELEY VALE PARK
FIELDVIEW 1
WATTS CL 2
BEVANS HILL
FORREST VIEW RD
FISHERS RD
HOWMEAD
CANON PK
BERRYCROFT
FITZHARDINGE WAY
SEVERN DR
GILBERT HILL
THE BRAMBLES
THE LEYS
HILLCREST
LOWER BERRY CROFT
1 TREVISA CRES
2 MASON CT
3 SCHOOL LA
JAMES ORCH
LEAZE CL
MARYBROOK ST
SALTER ST
MKT PL
CANONBURY ST
OLD WHITE HART
PARK VIEW RD
STOCK LA
JENNER CT
COACH CL
LANTERN CL
JUMPERS LA
HIGH ST
CHURCH LA
PH
PO
TH
Liby

85 94

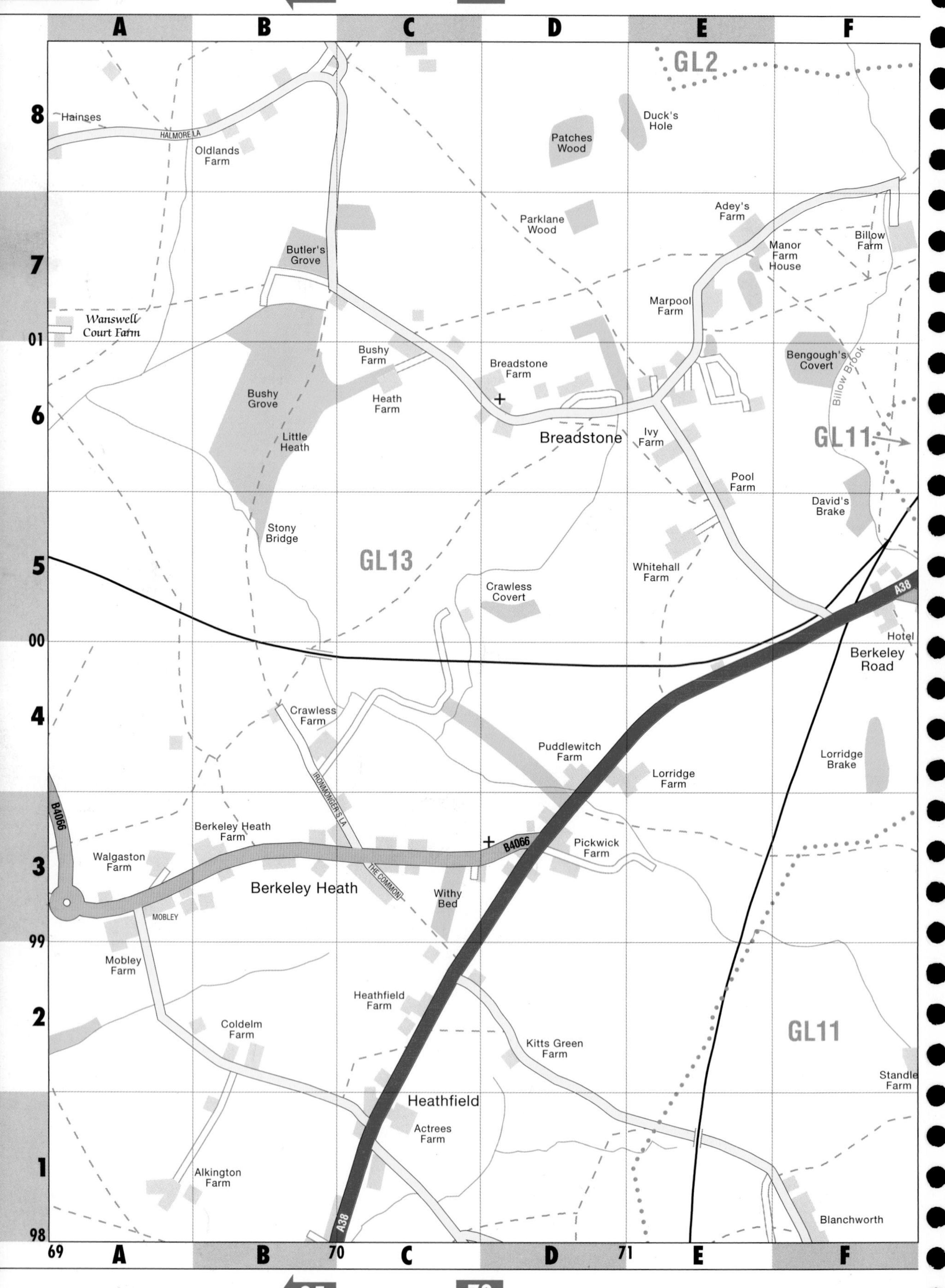

A B C D E F
8 7 01 6 5 00 4 3 99 2 1 98
69 70 71
GL2
Hainses
HALMORE LA
Oldlands Farm
Duck's Hole
Patches Wood
Parklane Wood
Adey's Farm
Manor Farm House
Billow Farm
Butler's Grove
Wanswell Court Farm
Marpool Farm
Bushy Farm
Breadstone Farm
Bengough's Covert
Billow Brook
Bushy Grove
Heath Farm
Little Heath
Breadstone
Ivy Farm
GL11
Pool Farm
David's Brake
Stony Bridge
GL13
Whitehall Farm
Crawless Covert
A38
Hotel
Berkeley Road
Crawless Farm
Puddlewitch Farm
Lorridge Brake
Lorridge Farm
IRONMONGER'S LA
B4066
Berkeley Heath Farm
Walgaston Farm
Pickwick Farm
THE COMMON
Berkeley Heath
Withy Bed
MOBLEY
Mobley Farm
Heathfield Farm
Coldelm Farm
Kitts Green Farm
GL11
Standle Farm
Heathfield
Actrees Farm
Alkington Farm
Blanchworth

85 78

95
88

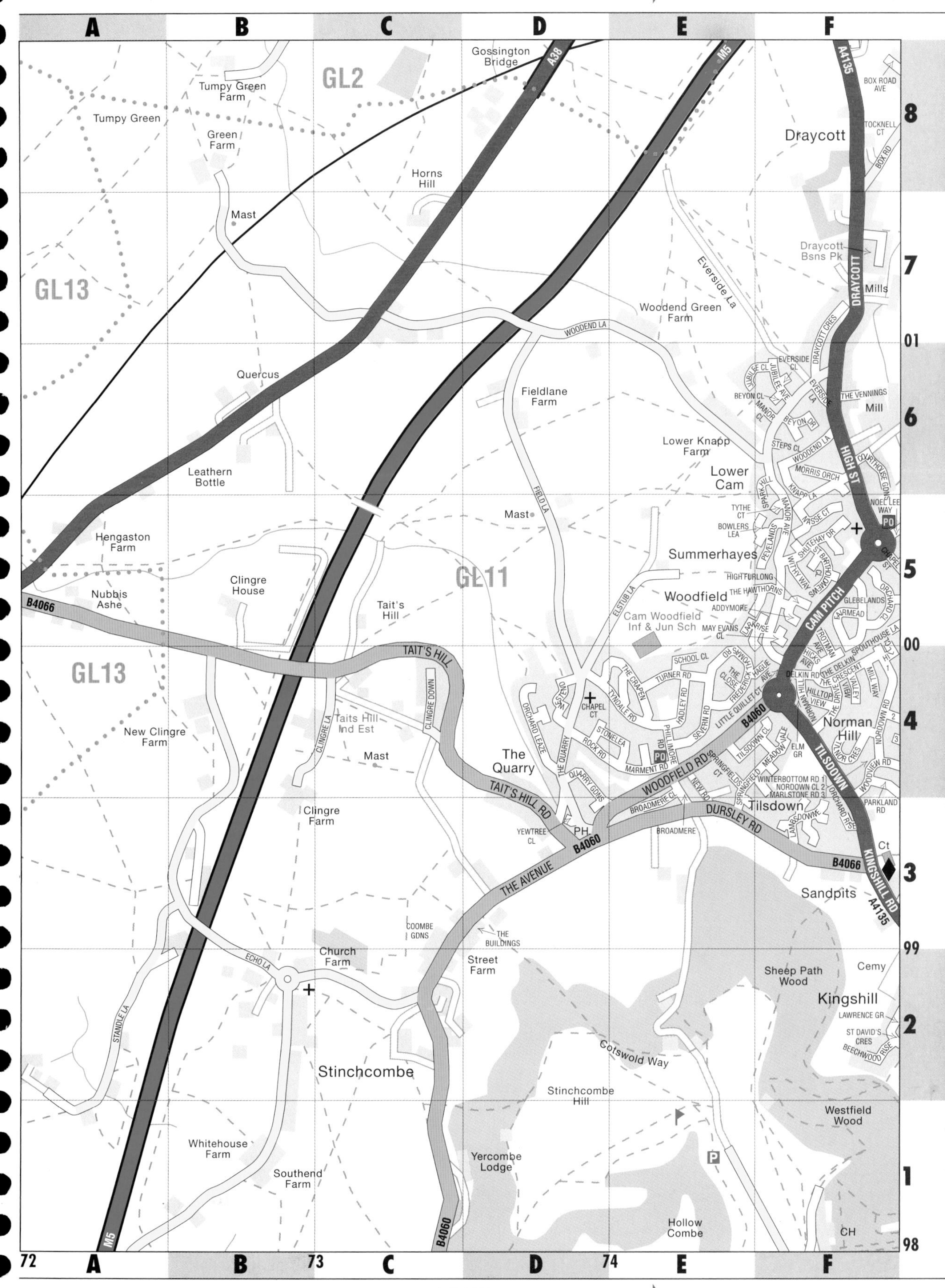
A
B
C
D
E
F
8
7
01
6
5
00
4
3
99
2
1
98
72
73
74
Gossington Bridge
A38
M5
A4135
GL2
Tumpy Green Farm
Tumpy Green
Green Farm
Horns Hill
Mast
Draycott
BOX ROAD AVE
TOCKNELL CT
BOX RD
Draycott Bsns Pk
DRAYCOTT
Mills
Eversíde La
GL13
Woodend Green Farm
WOODEND LA
Quercus
Fieldlane Farm
EVERSIDE CL
JUBILEE CL
BEYON CL
MANOR CL
THE VENNINGS
Mill
Leathern Bottle
Lower Knapp Farm
Lower Cam
STEPS CL
WOODEND LA
MORRIS ORCH
HIGH ST
COURTHOUSE GDNS
FIELD LA
Mast
Hengaston Farm
TYTHE CT
BOWLERS LEA
NOEL LEE WAY
PO
Summerhayes
GL11
Clingre House
Nubbis Ashe
HIGH FURLONG
THE HAWTHORNS
ADDYMORE
Woodfield
Cam Woodfield Inf & Jun Sch
MAY EVANS CL
CAM PITCH
GLEBELANDS
FAIRMEAD
SOUTHOUSE LA
B4066
Tait's Hill
TAIT'S HILL
GL13
CLINGRE DOWN
SCHOOL CL
TURNER RD
THE CRAPEN
TYNDALE RD
CHAPEL CT
Taits Hill Ind Est
CLINGRE LA
New Clingre Farm
Mast
ORCHARD LEAZE
The Quarry
STONELEA
ROCK RD
PHILLIMORE RD
YADLEY RD
SEVERN RD
LITTLE QUILLET CT
FREDERICK THOMAS RD
Norman Hill
NORDOWN RD
TILSDOWN
TAIT'S HILL RD
QUARRY GDNS
MARMENT RD
WOODFIELD RD
B4060
TILSDOWN CL
MEADOW VALE
ELM GR
WINTERBOTTOM RD
NORDOWN CL
MARLSTONE RD
Tilsdown
PARKLAND RD
Clingre Farm
YEWTREE CL
PH
BROADMERE CL
BROADMERE
DURSLEY RD
LAMBSDOWNE
Ct
B4066
KINGSHILL RD
THE AVENUE
B4060
Sandpits
A4135
COOMBE GDNS
THE BUILDINGS
Street Farm
Church Farm
ECHO LA
Sheep Path Wood
Cemy
Kingshill
LAWRENCE GR
ST DAVID'S CRES
BEECHWOOD RISE
STANDLE LA
Cotswold Way
Stinchcombe
Stinchcombe Hill
Westfield Wood
Whitehouse Farm
Yercombe Lodge
P
Southend Farm
Hollow Combe
CH
B4060
M5

79
88

87
96

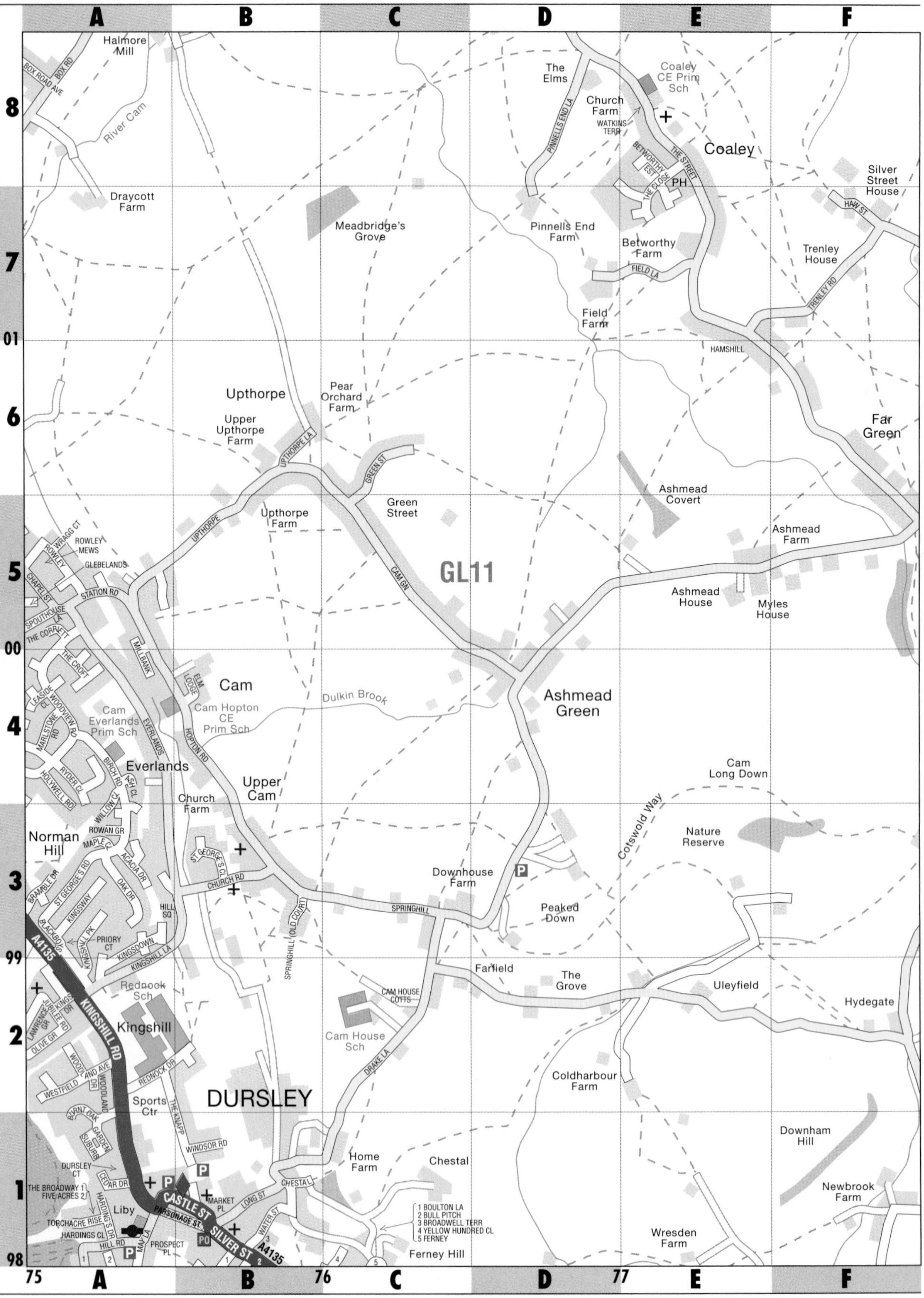

A B C D E F
8 7 01 6 5 00 4 3 99 2 1 98
Halmore Mill
River Cam
Draycott Farm
Meadbridge's Grove
The Elms
Church Farm
Coaley CE Prim Sch
Coaley
Silver Street House
Pinnells End Farm
Betworthy Farm
Trenley House
Field Farm
HAMSHILL
Upthorpe
Pear Orchard Farm
Upper Upthorpe Farm
Far Green
Upthorpe Farm
Green Street
Ashmead Covert
Ashmead Farm
GL11
Ashmead House
Myles House
Cam
Cam Hopton CE Prim Sch
Dulkin Brook
Ashmead Green
Cam Everlands Prim Sch
Everlands
Cam Long Down
Upper Cam
Church Farm
Norman Hill
Nature Reserve
Cotswold Way
Downhouse Farm
Peaked Down
Farfield
The Grove
Uleyfield
Hydegate
Rednock Sch
Kingshill
Cam House Sch
Coldharbour Farm
DURSLEY
Sports Ctr
Home Farm
Chestal
Downham Hill
Newbrook Farm
Liby
Wresden Farm
Ferney Hill
1 BOULTON LA
2 BULL PITCH
3 BROADWELL TERR
4 YELLOW HUNDRED CL
5 FERNEY
THE BROADWAY 1
FIVE ACRES 2
DURSLEY CT
A4135
KINGSHILL RD
CASTLE ST
SILVER ST
PARSONAGE ST
MARKET PL
LONG ST
WATER ST
CHESTAL
DRAKE LA
SPRINGHILL
SPRINGHILL (OLD COURT)
CAM HOUSE COTTS
CHURCH RD
HOPTON RD
EVERLANDS
MILLBANK
STATION RD
UPTHORPE
UPTHORPE LA
GREEN ST
CAM GN
PINNELLS END LA
WATKINS TERR
BETWORTHY EST
THE CLOSE
THE STREET
FIELD LA
HAW ST
TRENLEY RD
BOX ROAD AVE
BOX RD
WRAGG CT
ROWLEY
ROWLEY MEWS
GLEBELANDS
CHAPEL ST
SPOUTHOUSE LA
THE CORRIETT
THE CROFT
LEASIDE CL
WOODVIEW RD
MARLSTONE RD
HOLYWELL RD
RYDER CL
BIRCH RD
ASH CL
WILLOW CL
ROWAN GR
MAPLE CL
ACACIA DR
OAK DR
ST GEORGE'S RD
ST GEORGE'S CL
BRAMBLE DR
KINGSWAY
BLACKBOY
KINGSHILL PK
PRIORY CT
KINGSDOWN
KINGSHILL LA
HILL SQ
ELM LODGE
LAWRENCE GR
JUBILEE RD
KINGS DR
OLIVE GR
WOODLAND AVE
WOODLAND DR
WESTFIELD
REDNOCK DR
THE KNAPP
WINDSOR RD
BURNT OAK
GARDEN SUBURB
CEDAR DR
HARDING'S DR
TORCHACRE RISE
HARDINGS CL
HILL RD
MAY LA
PROSPECT PL
PH
PO

87
80

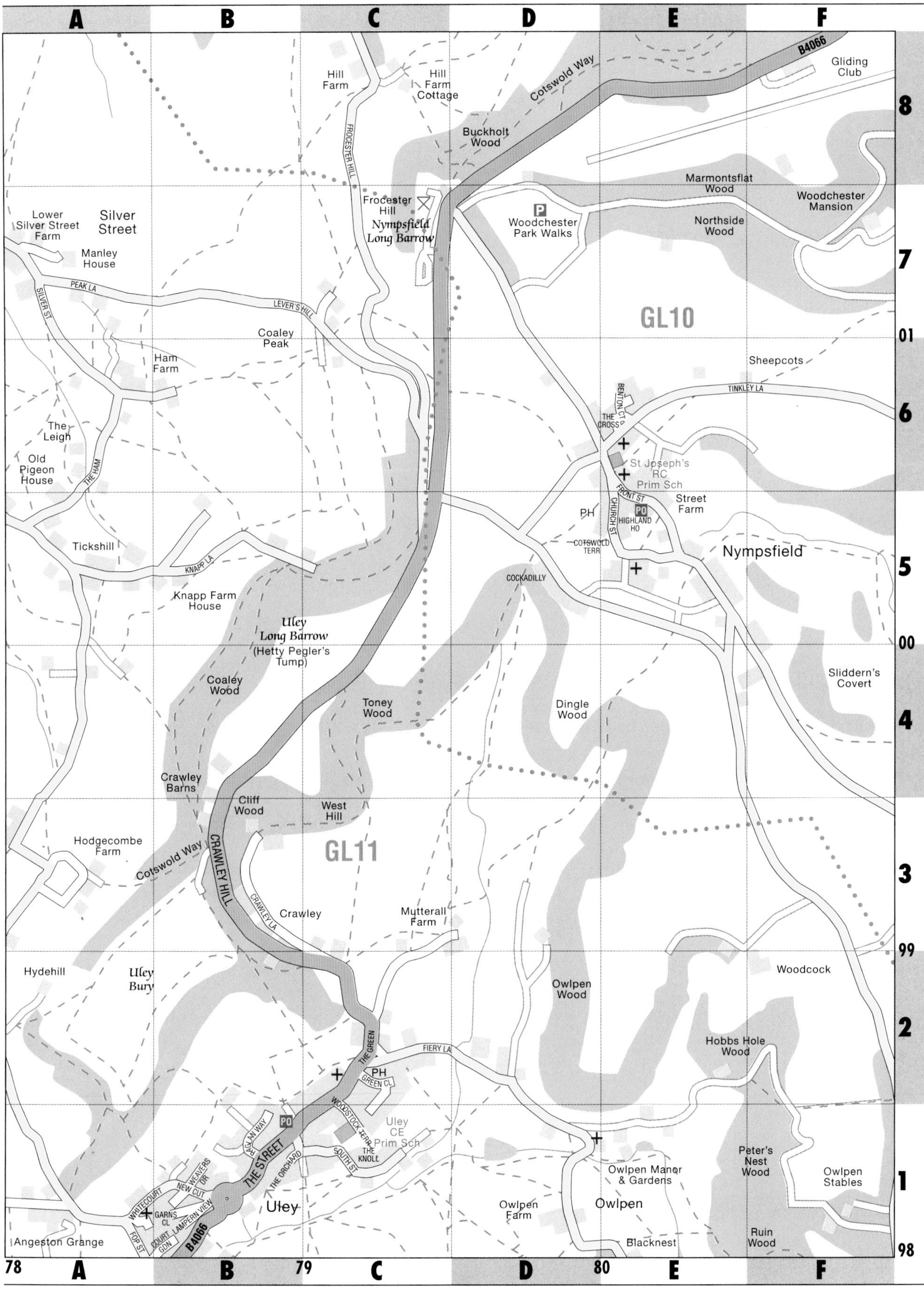

A B C D E F

8
7
01
6
5
00
4
3
99
2
1
98

B4066
Gliding Club
Cotswold Way
Hill Farm
Hill Farm Cottage
FROCESTER HILL
Buckholt Wood
Marmontsflat Wood
Woodchester Mansion
Frocester Hill
Nympsfield Long Barrow
Woodchester Park Walks
Northside Wood
Lower Silver Street Farm
Silver Street
Manley House
PEAK LA
SILVER ST
LEVER'S HILL
GL10
Coaley Peak
Ham Farm
Sheepcots
BENTON CT
TINKLEY LA
THE CROSS
The Leigh
Old Pigeon House
THE HAM
St Joseph's RC Prim Sch
FRONT ST
CHURCH ST
PH
HIGHLAND HO
Street Farm
Tickshill
KNAPP LA
COTSWOLD TERR
Nympsfield
COCKADILLY
Knapp Farm House
Uley Long Barrow
(Hetty Pegler's Tump)
Coaley Wood
Toney Wood
Dingle Wood
Sliddern's Covert
Crawley Barns
Cliff Wood
West Hill
Hodgecombe Farm
Cotswold Way
CRAWLEY HILL
GL11
CRAWLEY LA
Crawley
Mutterall Farm
Hydehill
Uley Bury
Owlpen Wood
Woodcock
THE GREEN
FIERY LA
PH
GREEN CL
Hobbs Hole Wood
WOODSTOCK TERR
RAGLAN WAY
Uley CE Prim Sch
THE KNOLL
SOUTH ST
THE STREET
THE ORCHARD
WEAVERS DR
NEW CUT
WHITECOURT
GARNS CL
LAMPERN VIEW
COURT GDN
FOP ST
B4066
Uley
Owlpen Manor & Gardens
Peter's Nest Wood
Owlpen Stables
Owlpen Farm
Owlpen
Angeston Grange
Blacknest
Ruin Wood

78 A B 79 C D 80 E F

89
98

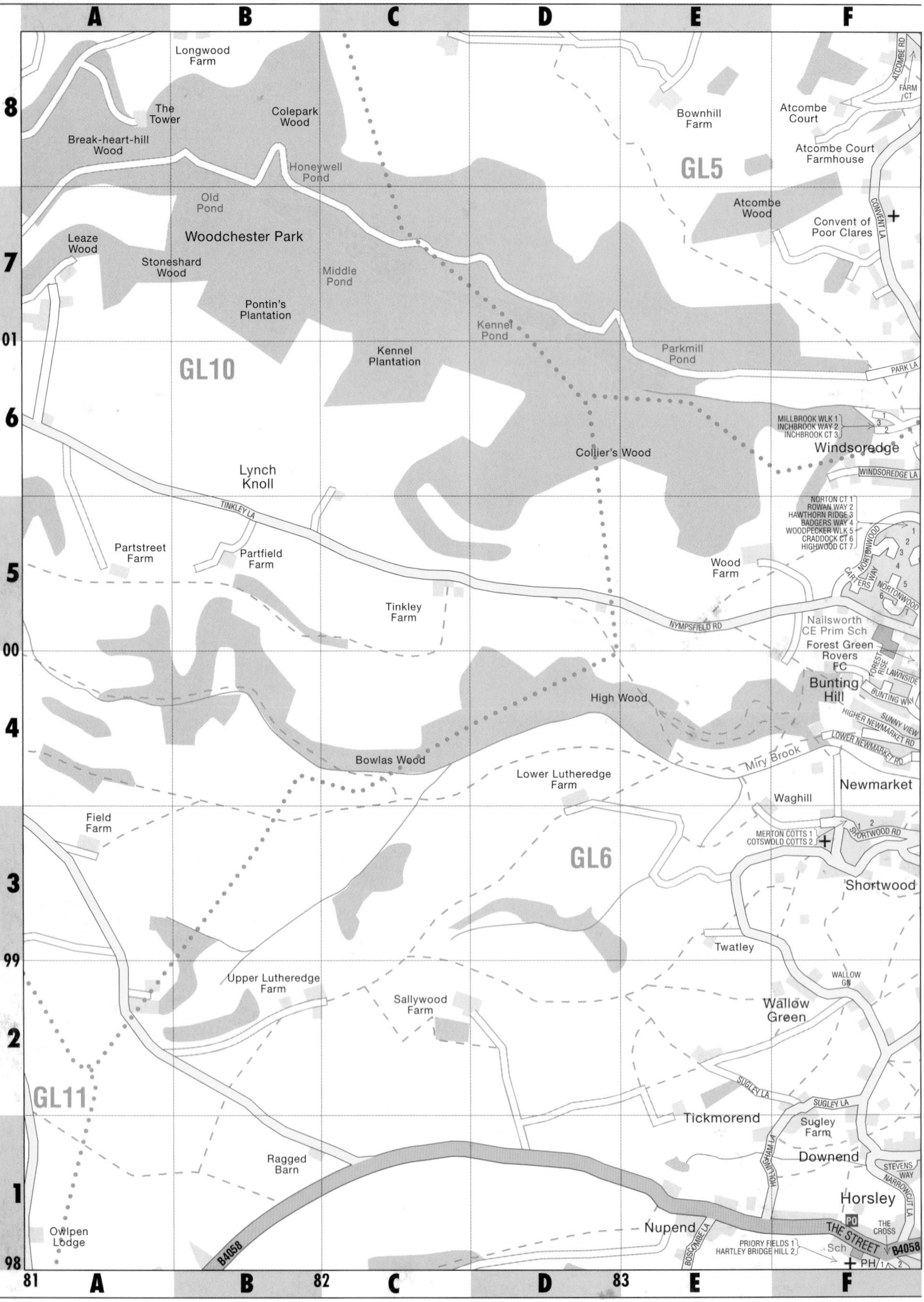

A B C D E F
8 7 01 6 5 00 4 3 99 2 1 98
Longwood Farm
The Tower
Colepark Wood
Break-heart-hill Wood
Honeywell Pond
Old Pond
Woodchester Park
Leaze Wood
Stoneshard Wood
Middle Pond
Pontin's Plantation
Kennel Pond
Kennel Plantation
GL10
Bownhill Farm
Atcombe Court
Atcombe Court Farmhouse
GL5
Atcombe Wood
Convent of Poor Clares
ATCOMBE RD
FARM CT
CONVENT LA
Parkmill Pond
PARK LA
MILLBROOK WLK 1
INCHBROOK WAY 2
INCHBROOK CT 3
Windsoredge
WINDSOREDGE LA
Collier's Wood
Lynch Knoll
TINKLEY LA
NORTON CT 1
ROWAN WAY 2
HAWTHORN RIDGE 3
BADGERS WAY 4
WOODPECKER WLK 5
CRADDOCK CT 6
HIGHWOOD CT 7
NORTONWOOD
CARTERS WAY
Partstreet Farm
Partfield Farm
Wood Farm
Tinkley Farm
NYMPSFIELD RD
Nailsworth CE Prim Sch
Forest Green Rovers FC
FOREST RISE
LAWNSIDE
Bunting Hill
BUNTING WAY
SUNNY VIEW
HIGHER NEWMARKET RD
LOWER NEWMARKET RD
High Wood
Bowlas Wood
Lower Lutheredge Farm
Miry Brook
Newmarket
Waghill
Field Farm
MERTON COTTS 1
COTSWOLD COTTS 2
SHORTWOOD RD
GL6
Shortwood
Twatley
Upper Lutheredge Farm
Sallywood Farm
WALLOW GN
Wallow Green
GL11
SUGLEY LA
Tickmorend
Sugley Farm
HOLLINGHAM LA
Downend
STEVENS WAY
NARROWCUT LA
Ragged Barn
Horsley
Owlpen Lodge
B4058
Nupend
BOSCOMBE LA
PO
THE CROSS
THE STREET
PRIORY FIELDS 1
HARTLEY BRIDGE HILL 2
Sch
PH
81 82 83

89
82

99
148

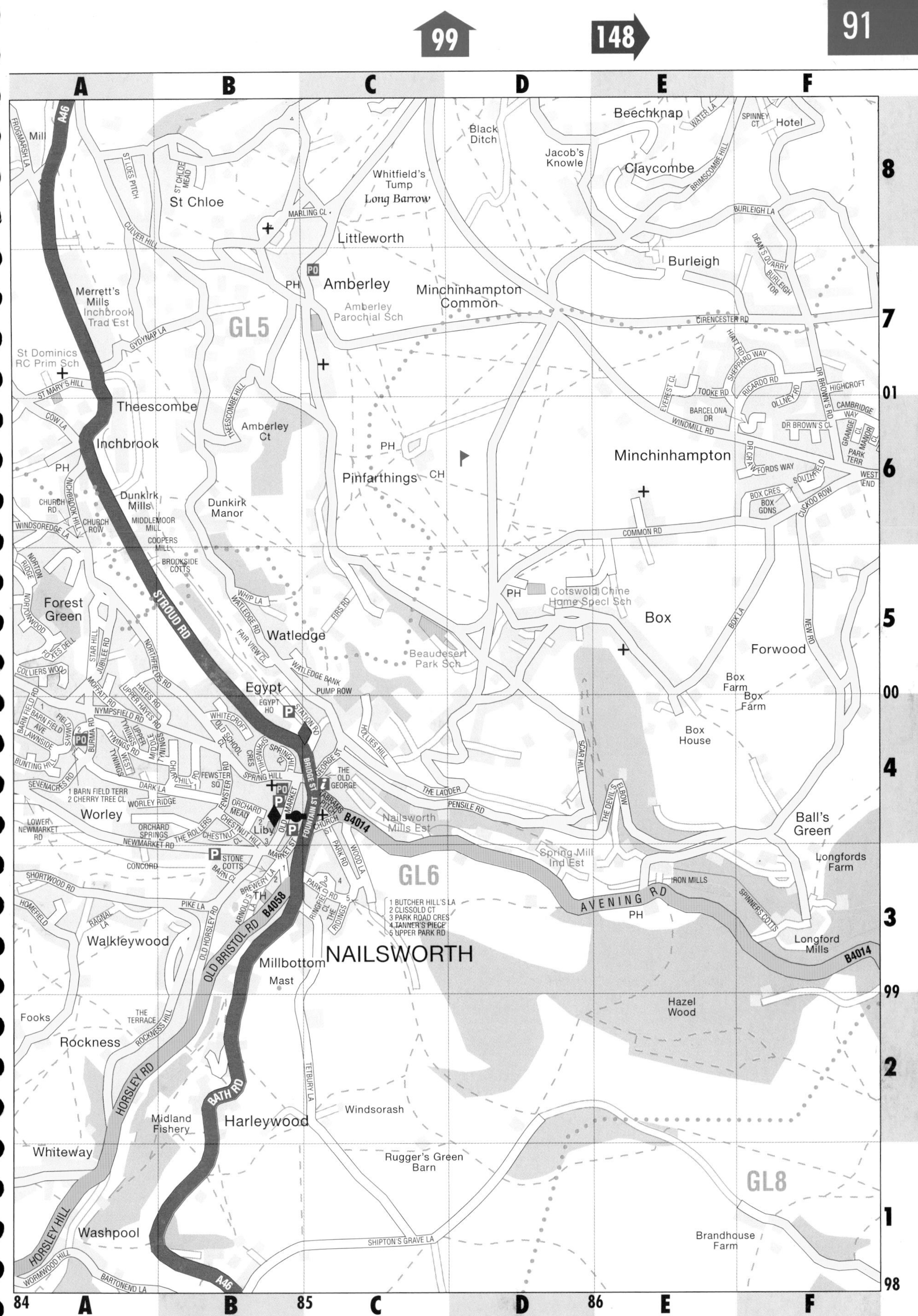

B4
1 CHURCHILL CL
2 HANOVER GDNS
3 WHEELWRIGHTS CNR

83
148

147
156

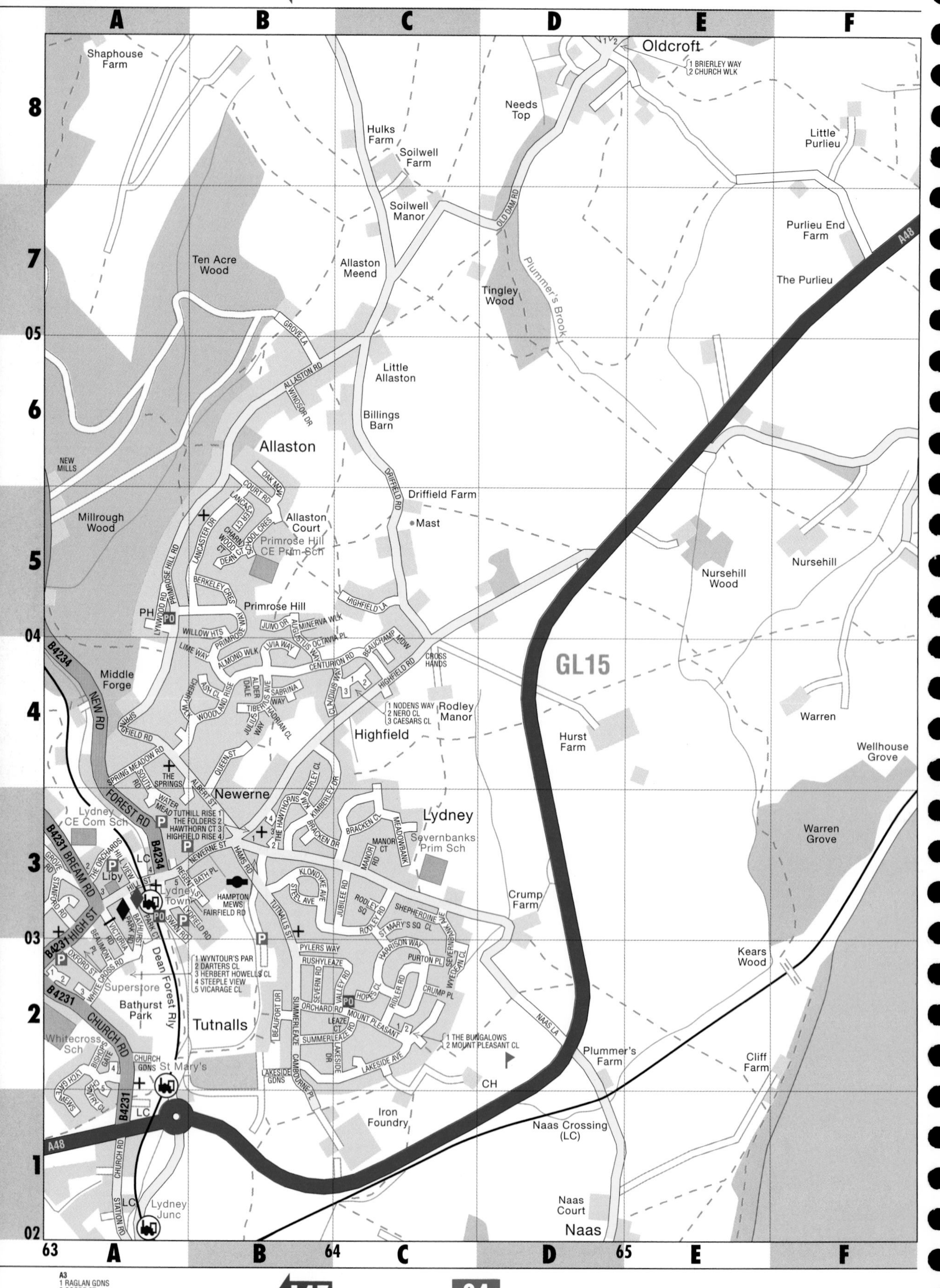

A3
1 RAGLAN GDNS
2 GOODE CT
3 CAVENDISH BLDGS
4 FOREST PAR
5 REGENTS WLK

147
84

156
94

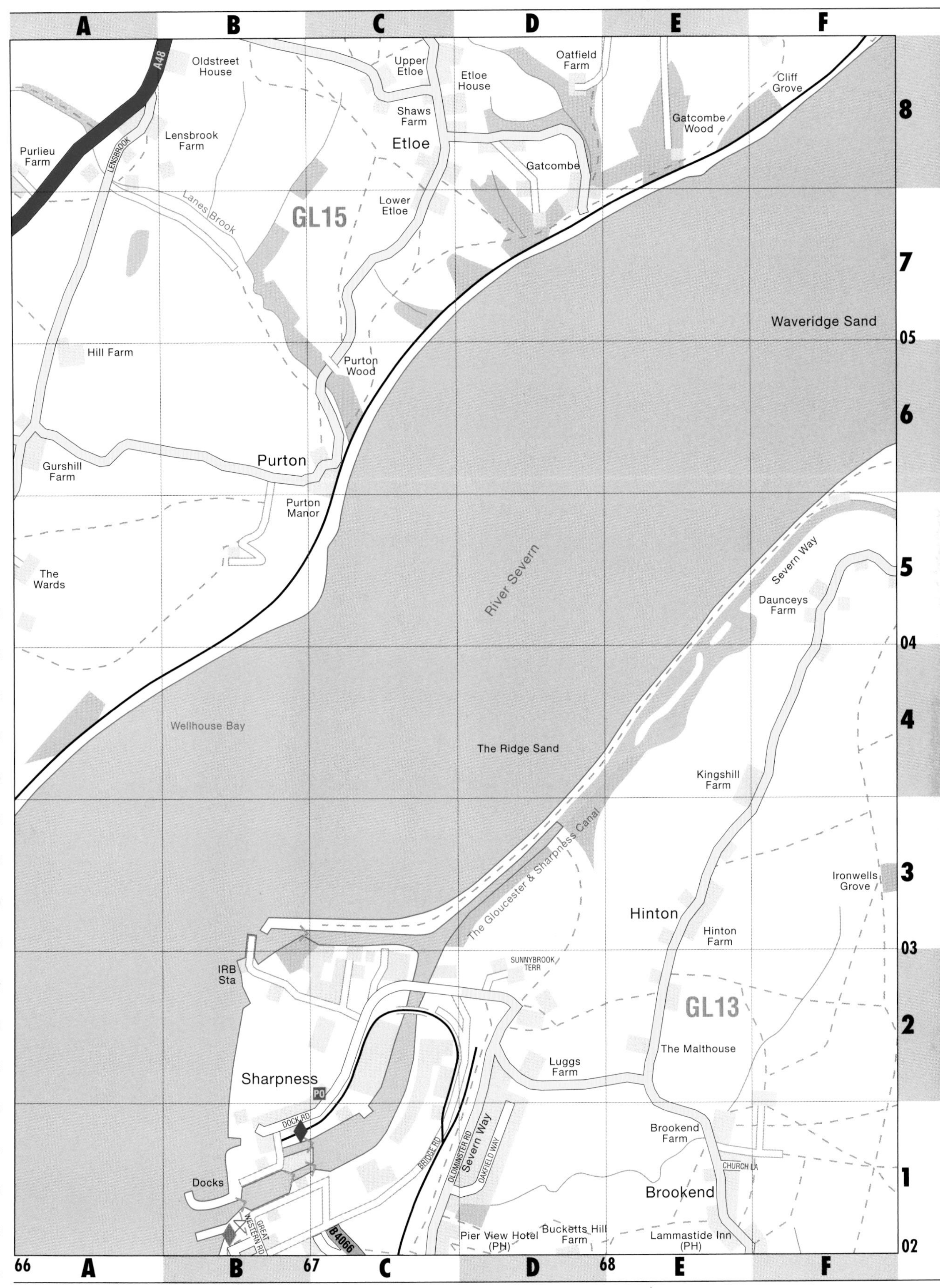
A
B
C
D
E
F
A48
Oldstreet House
Upper Etloe
Etloe House
Oatfield Farm
Cliff Grove
Shaws Farm
Gatcombe Wood
Purlieu Farm
LENSBROOK
Lensbrook Farm
Etloe
Gatcombe
Lanes Brook
GL15
Lower Etloe
8
7
Waveridge Sand
05
Hill Farm
Purton Wood
6
Gurshill Farm
Purton
Purton Manor
River Severn
5
The Wards
Severn Way
Dauncey Farm
04
4
Wellhouse Bay
The Ridge Sand
Kingshill Farm
The Gloucester & Sharpness Canal
3
Ironwells Grove
Hinton
Hinton Farm
03
IRB Sta
SUNNYBROOK TERR
GL13
2
The Malthouse
Luggs Farm
Sharpness
PO
DOCK RD
Brookend Farm
CHURCH LA
BRIDGE RD
OLDMINSTER RD
Severn Way
OAKFIELD WAY
1
Docks
Brookend
GREAT WESTERN RD
B4066
Pier View Hotel (PH)
Bucketts Hill Farm
Lammastide Inn (PH)
02
66
67
68

85
94

93
157

A B C D E F

8 Middle Point
River Severn
7 Frampton Sand
05 Twr
6 Tites Point
The Dumbles
The Trumps
PH
Twr
PH
Swing Bridge
The Royal Drift
Purton
5 Oldmoor Cliff
Swing Bridge
Severn Way
04 The Gloucester and Sharpness Canal
Decoy Pool
Pockington Farm
4 Decoy Pool House
Water Treatment Works
GL2
RIDDLE ST
Gilgal Brook
3
Ironwells New Covert
GL13
Red Wood
03
Halmore Farm
2 The Plantation
Priorswood Farm
Hurst Farm
Pool Farm
Halmore
PH
SLIMBRIDGE LA
Gilgal Bridge
TYNDALE RD
Wards Grove
Oxenbrook
1 Howes's Grove
Acton Hall
02

69 A B 70 C D 71 E F

93
86

157
96

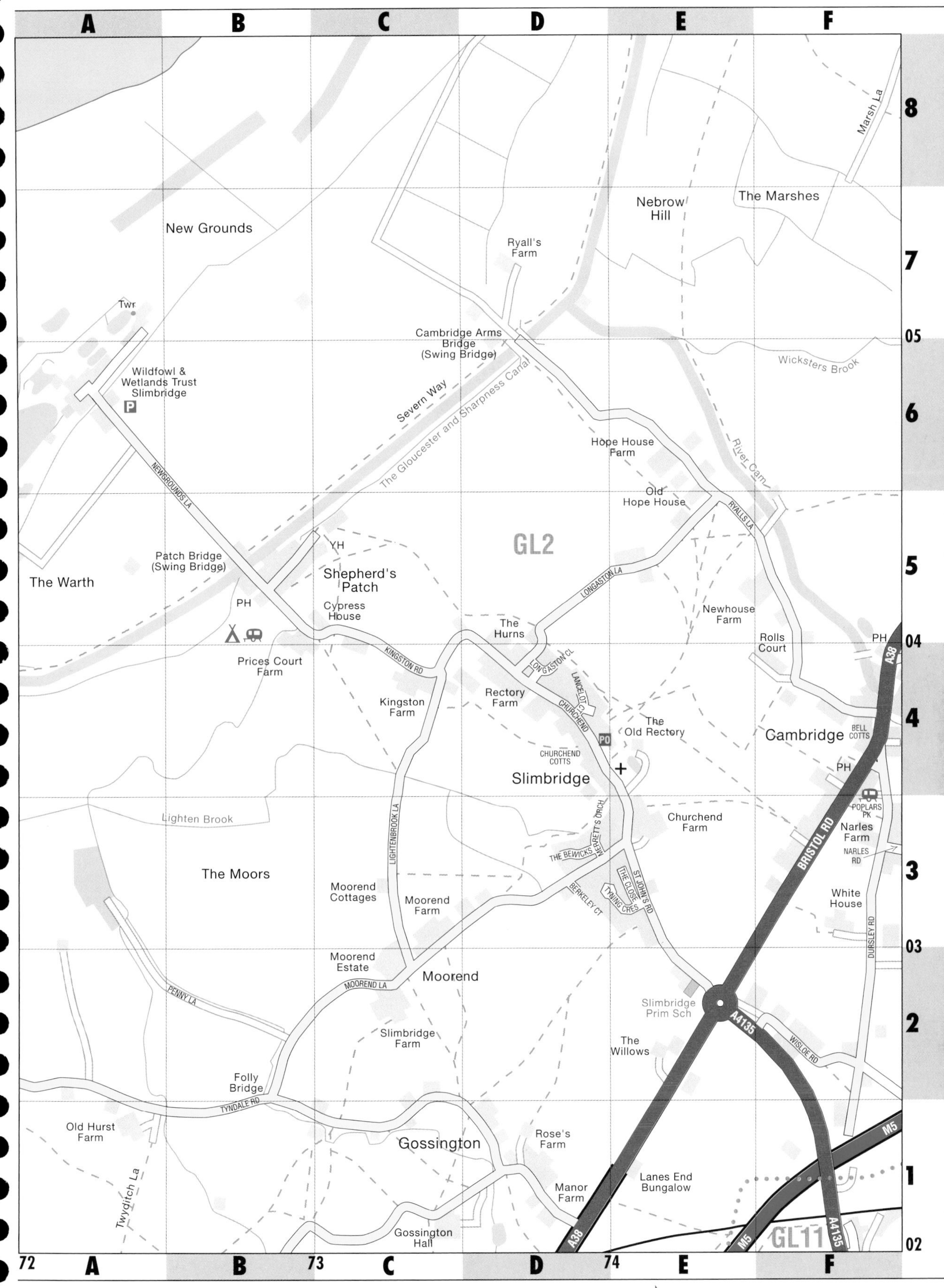
A
B
C
D
E
F
8
7
05
6
5
04
4
3
03
2
1
02
72
73
74
New Grounds
Nebrow Hill
The Marshes
Marsh La
Ryall's Farm
Twr
Cambridge Arms Bridge (Swing Bridge)
Wicksters Brook
Wildfowl & Wetlands Trust Slimbridge
Severn Way
The Gloucester and Sharpness Canal
Hope House Farm
River Cam
NEWGROUNDS LA
Old Hope House
RYALLS LA
GL2
YH
Patch Bridge (Swing Bridge)
Shepherd's Patch
The Warth
LONGASTON LA
Newhouse Farm
PH
Cypress House
The Hurns
Rolls Court
PH
A38
KINGSTON RD
LONGASTON CL
Prices Court Farm
Rectory Farm
LANCELOT CL
Kingston Farm
CHURCHEND
The Old Rectory
Cambridge
BELL COTTS
PO
CHURCHEND COTTS
Slimbridge
PH
LIGHTENBROOK LA
POPLARS PK
Lighten Brook
MERRETT'S ORCH
Churchend Farm
Narles Farm
NARLES RD
THE BEWICKS
BRISTOL RD
The Moors
THE CLOSE
ST JOHN'S RD
Moorend Cottages
Moorend Farm
BERKELEY CT
TYNING CRES
White House
DURSLEY RD
Moorend Estate
Moorend
MOOREND LA
PENNY LA
Slimbridge Prim Sch
A4135
Slimbridge Farm
WISLOE RD
The Willows
Folly Bridge
TYNDALE RD
Old Hurst Farm
Gossington
Rose's Farm
M5
Twyditch La
Manor Farm
Lanes End Bungalow
A38
Gossington Hall
M5
GL11
A4135
A
B
C
D
E
F

87
96

95
100

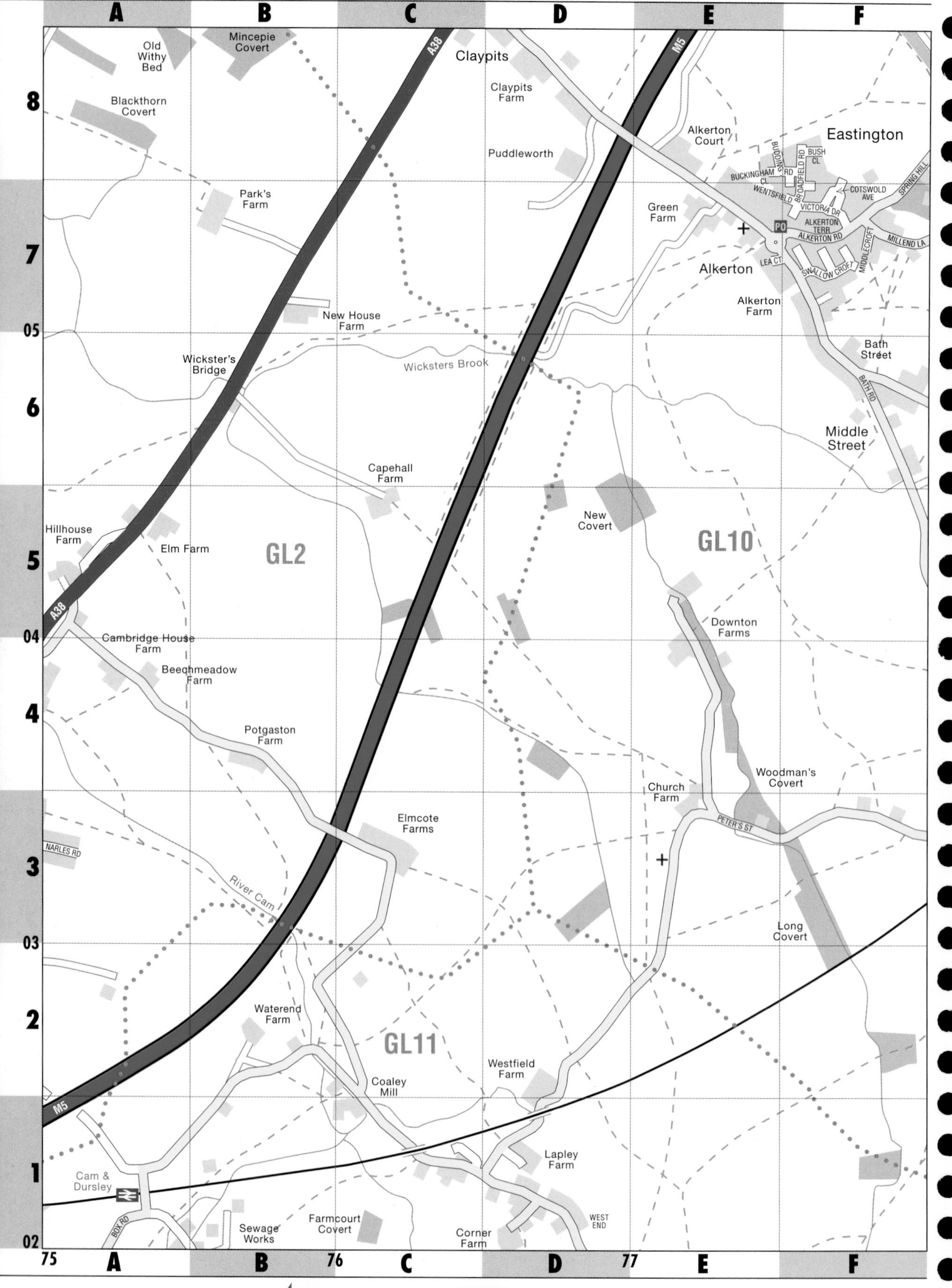
A
B
C
D
E
F
Old Withy Bed
Mincepie Covert
Claypits
Claypits Farm
Blackthorn Covert
Alkerton Court
Eastington
Puddleworth
Park's Farm
Green Farm
Alkerton
Alkerton Farm
New House Farm
Wickster's Bridge
Wicksters Brook
Bath Street
Middle Street
Capehall Farm
New Covert
Hillhouse Farm
Elm Farm
GL2
GL10
Downton Farms
Cambridge House Farm
Beechmeadow Farm
Potgaston Farm
Church Farm
Woodman's Covert
Elmcote Farms
River Cam
Long Covert
Waterend Farm
GL11
Westfield Farm
Coaley Mill
Lapley Farm
Cam & Dursley
Sewage Works
Farmcourt Covert
Corner Farm
WEST END
A38
M5
BUCKINGHAM CL
BUDDING RD
BROADFIELD RD
BUSH CL
WENTSFIELD
VICTORIA DR
COTSWOLD AVE
SPRING HILL
ALKERTON TERR
ALKERTON RD
MILLEND LA
MIDDLECROFT
LEA CT
SWALLOW CROFT
BATH RD
PETER'S ST
NARLES RD
BOX RD
PO
8
7
05
6
5
04
4
3
03
2
1
02
75
76
77

95
88

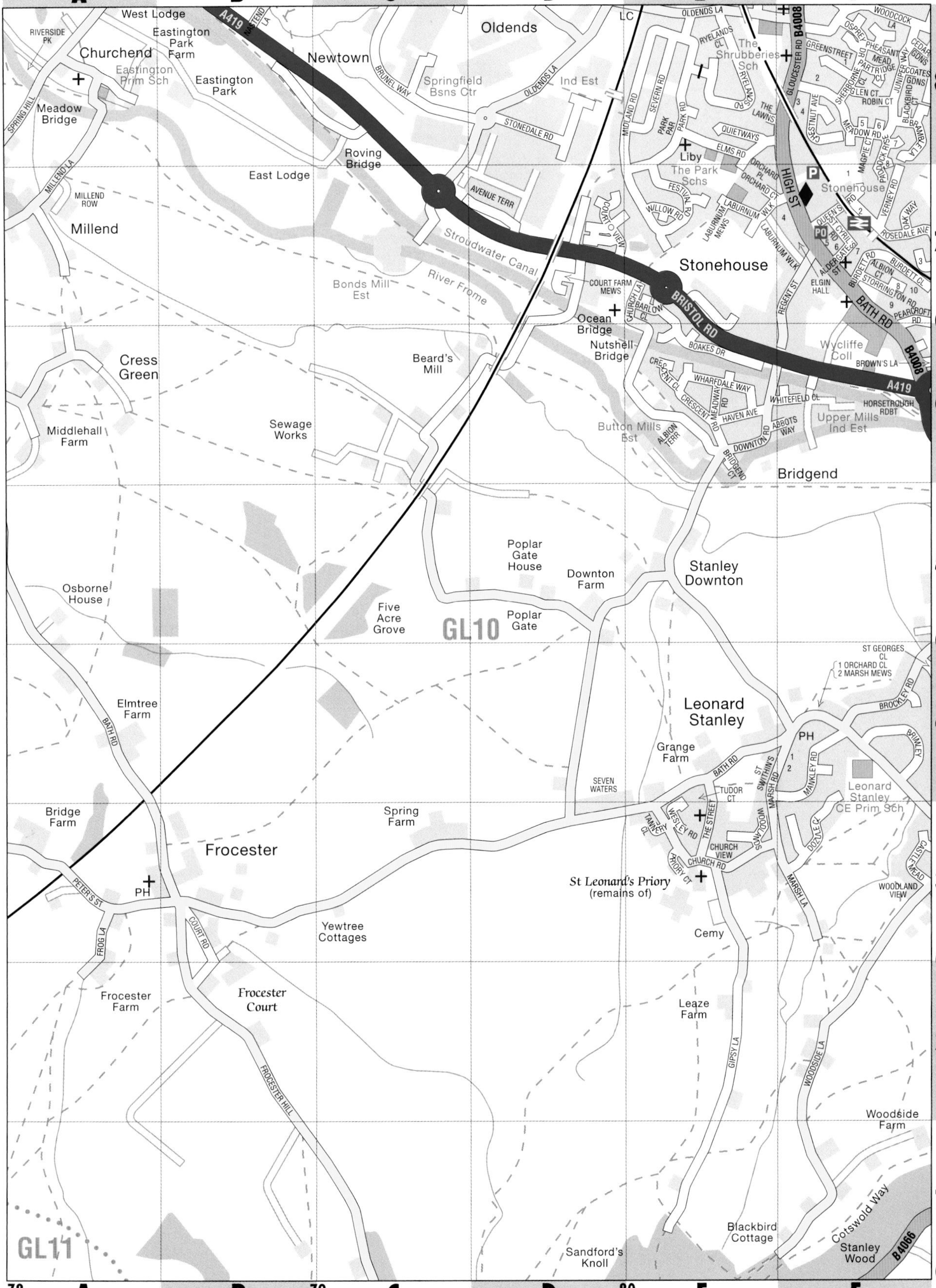

A B C D E F

8 7 05 6 5 04 4 3 03 2 1 02

West Lodge
Eastington Park Farm
Churchend
Riverside Pk
Eastington Prim Sch
Eastington Park
Meadow Bridge
Spring Hill
Millend La
Millend Row
Millend
East Lodge
Newtown
A419
Nastend La
Brunel Way
Springfield Bsns Ctr
Oldends
Oldends La
Ind Est
LC
Stonedale Rd
Roving Bridge
Avenue Terr
Stroudwater Canal
River Frome
Bonds Mill Est
Cress Green
Middlehall Farm
Beard's Mill
Sewage Works
Court Farm Mews
Ocean Bridge
Nutshell Bridge
Bristol Rd
Church La
Barlow Cl
Boakes Dr
Crescent Cl
Crescent
Wharfdale Way
Meadway Rd
Haven Ave
Abbots Way
Albion Terr
Downton Rd
Bridgend Ct
Button Mills Est
Bridgend
Whitefield Cl
Upper Mills Ind Est
Horsetrough Rdbt
Brown's La
Wycliffe Coll
B4008
Oldends La
Ryelands Cl
Ryelands Rd
The Shrubberies Sch
Midland Rd
Severn Rd
Park Par
Park Rd
Quietways
Liby
Elms Rd
The Park Schs
Festival Rd
Willow Rd
Orchard Pl
Orchard Ct
Laburnum Mews
Laburnum Wlk
The Lawns
Gloucester Rd
High St
Stonehouse
Regent St
Elgin Hall
Queen's Rd
St Cyril's Rd
Aldergate St
Bath Rd
Burdett Rd
Albion Ct
Storrington Rd
Burdett Cl
Pearcroft Rd
Rosedale Ave
Oak Way
Verney Rd
Magpie Ct
Paddock Rise
Meadow Rd
Chestnut Ave
Robin Ct
Glen Ct
Sherborne Cl
Partridge Cl
Mead Cl
Pheasant Way
Greenstreet
Osprey Dr
Woodcock La
Cedar Gdns
Coates Gdns
Juniper Way
Blackbird Ct
Bramble La
Poplar Gate House
Downton Farm
Stanley Downton
Osborne House
Five Acre Grove
Poplar Gate
GL10
St Georges Cl
1 Orchard Cl
2 Marsh Mews
Brockley Rd
Leonard Stanley
Elmtree Farm
Grange Farm
PH
Brimley
Seven Waters
Bath Rd
St Swithin's Rd
Marsh Rd
Mankley Rd
Leonard Stanley CE Prim Sch
Tudor Ct
The Street
Woodcock Rd
Tannery Cl
Wesley Rd
Church View
Church Rd
Priory Ct
Dozule Cl
Castle Mead
Woodland View
Bridge Farm
Spring Farm
Frocester
St Leonard's Priory (remains of)
Peter's St
PH
Court Rd
Frog La
Yewtree Cottages
Cemy
Marsh La
Frocester Farm
Frocester Court
Leaze Farm
Frocester Hill
Gipsy La
Woodside La
Woodside Farm
Cotswold Way
Stanley Wood
B4066
Blackbird Cottage
Sandford's Knoll
GL11

78 A B 79 C D 80 E F

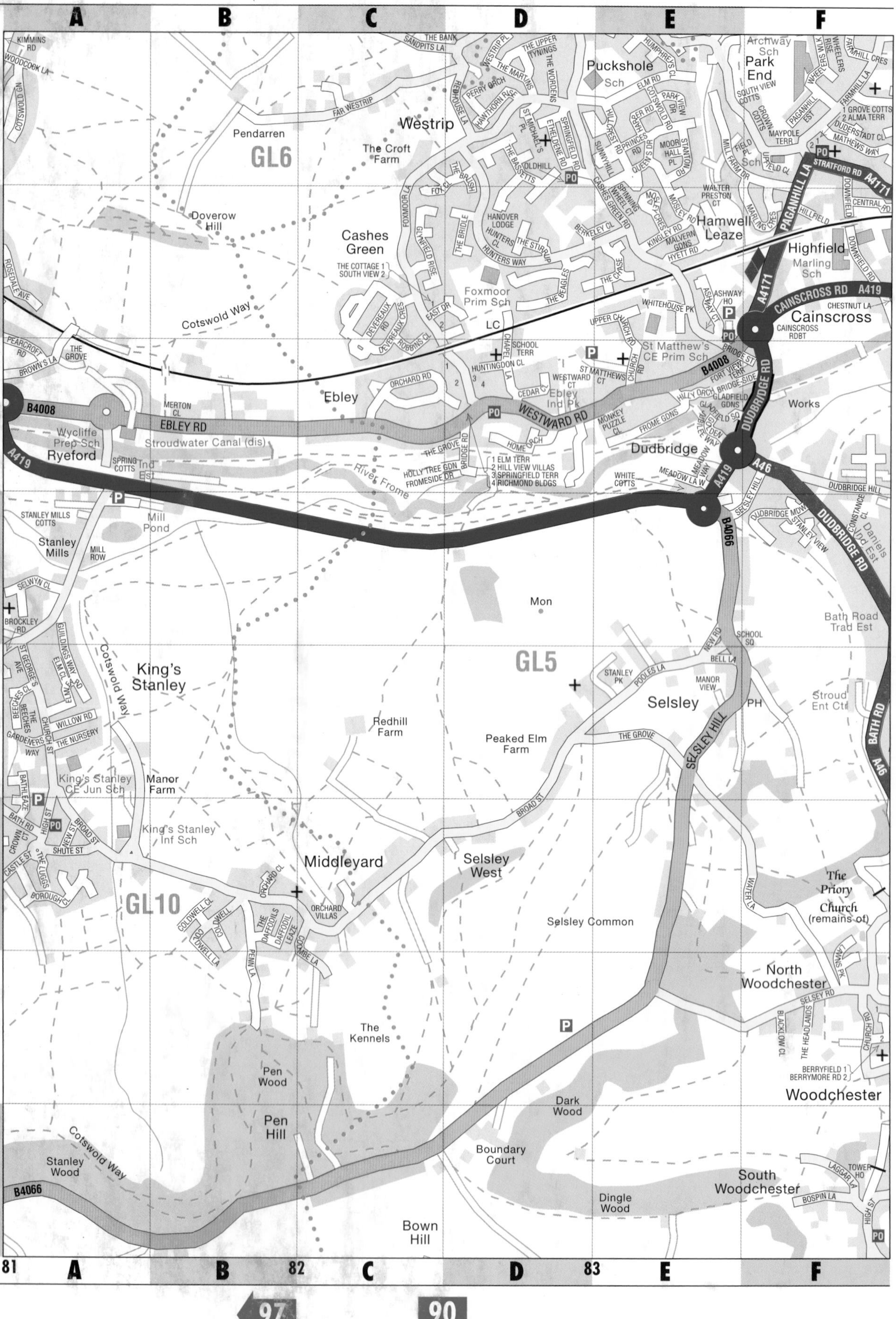

A B C D E F

8 7 05 6 5 04 4 3 03 2 1 02

Puckshole
Park End
Westrip
Pendarren
GL6
The Croft Farm
Doverow Hill
Cashes Green
Hamwell Leaze
Highfield
Marling Sch
Foxmoor Prim Sch
Cainscross
Cotswold Way
St Matthew's CE Prim Sch
Ebley
EBLEY RD
WESTWARD RD
B4008
A419
A4171
A46
B4066
Wycliffe Prep Sch
Ryeford
Stroudwater Canal (dis)
River Frome
Dudbridge
Works
Stanley Mills
Mill Pond
Mon
GL5
King's Stanley
Selsley
Bath Road Trad Est
Stroud Ent Ctr
Redhill Farm
Peaked Elm Farm
King's Stanley CE Jun Sch
Manor Farm
King's Stanley Inf Sch
Middleyard
Selsley West
GL10
The Priory Church (remains of)
Selsley Common
North Woodchester
The Kennels
Pen Wood
Pen Hill
Woodchester
Dark Wood
Stanley Wood
Boundary Court
South Woodchester
Dingle Wood
Bown Hill

81 A B 82 C D 83 E F

C7
1 Merrywalks Sh Ctr
2 GLOUCESTER ST
3 LOCKING HILL
4 KING STREET PAR
5 GEORGE ST
6 CLARENDON CT
7 FAWKES PL
8 BEDFORD ST
9 KENDRICK ST
10 THREADNEEDLE ST
11 KENDRICK LA
12 THE SHAMBLES
13 SWAN LA
14 HIGH VEW LODGE
15 SPINNERS HO
16 WESLEY CT
17 WEAVERS HO
18 BLACKBOY
19 CASTLE VILLAS
20 CASTLE CT

103 148

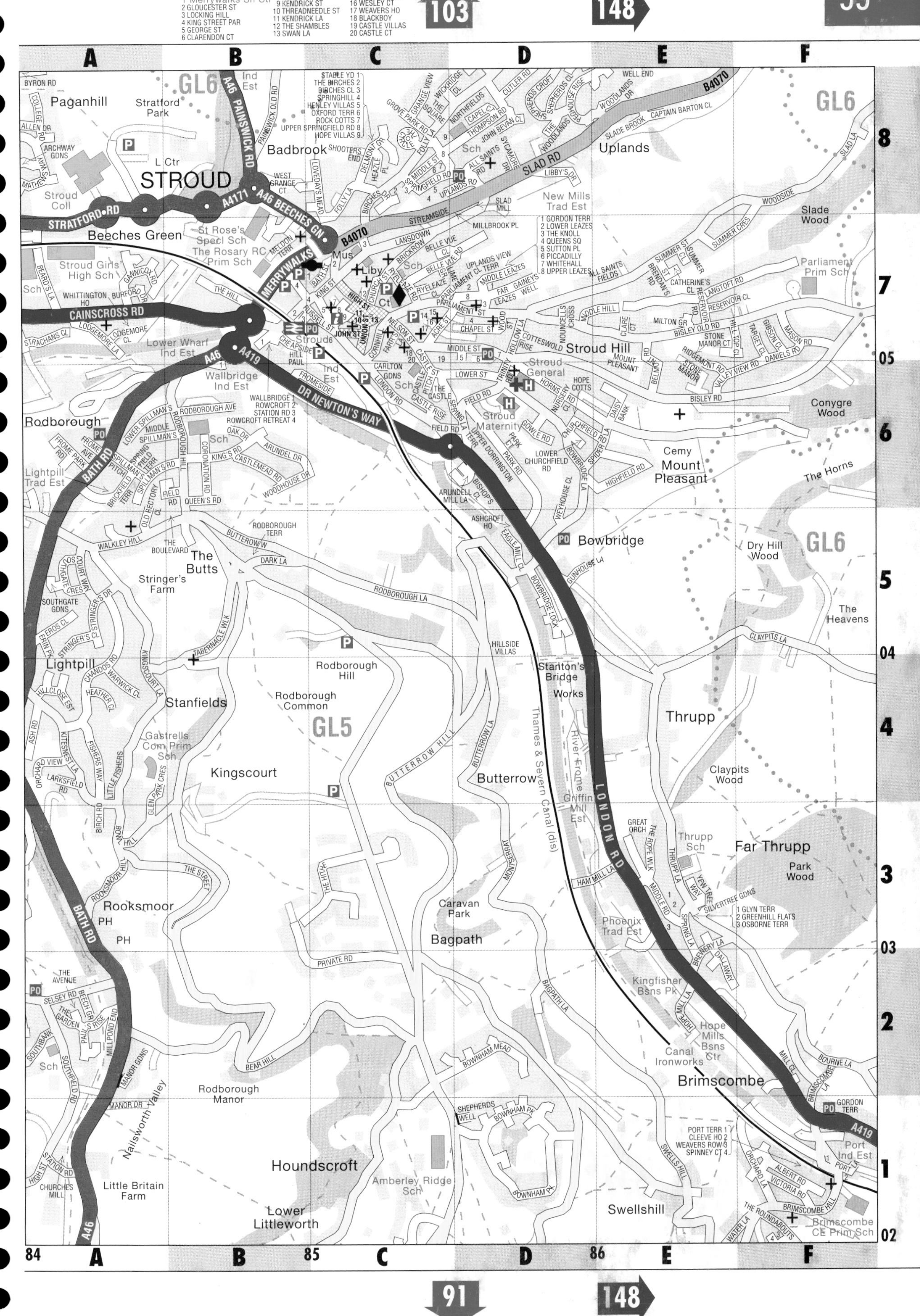

91 148

157 108

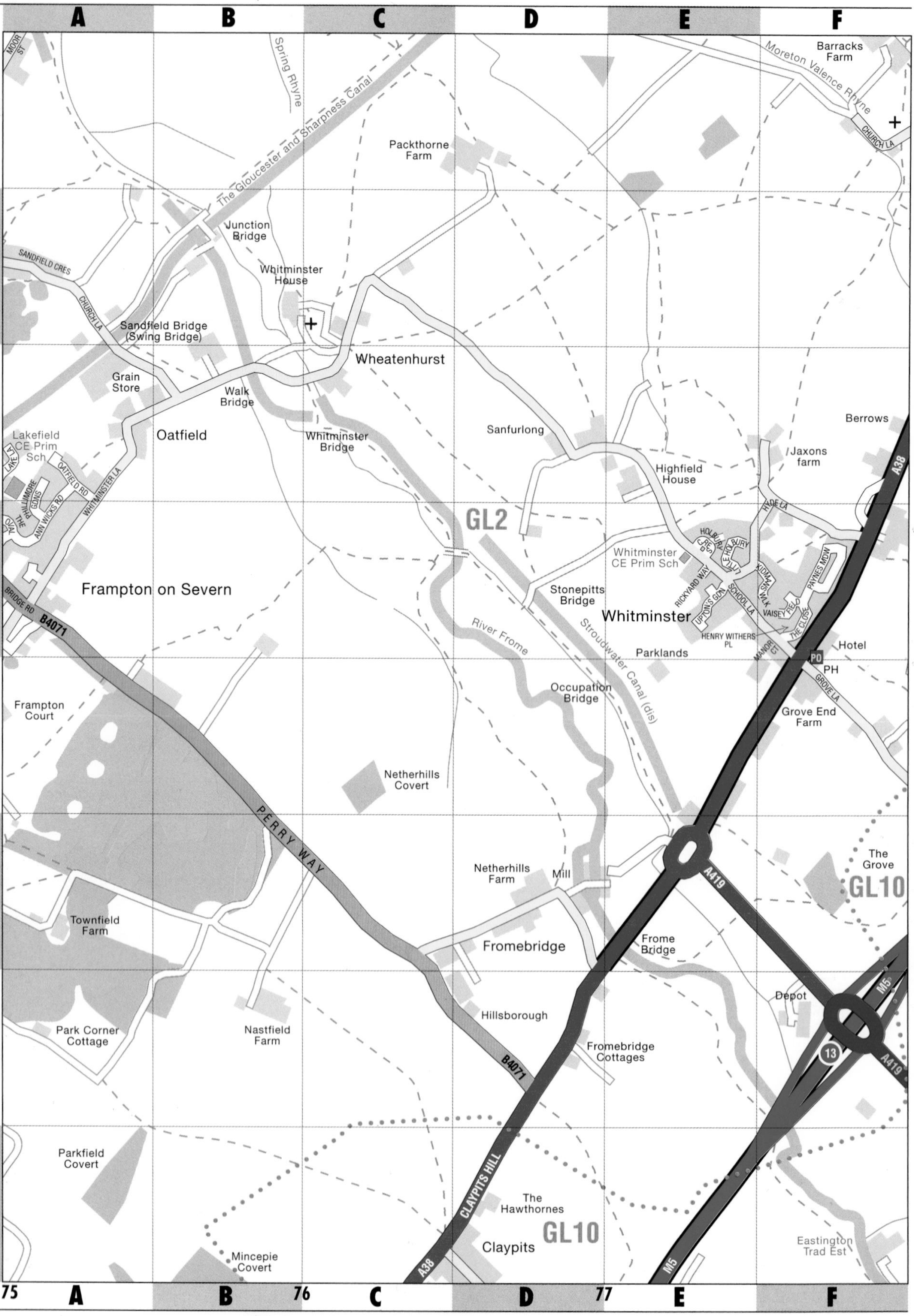

157 96

109
102 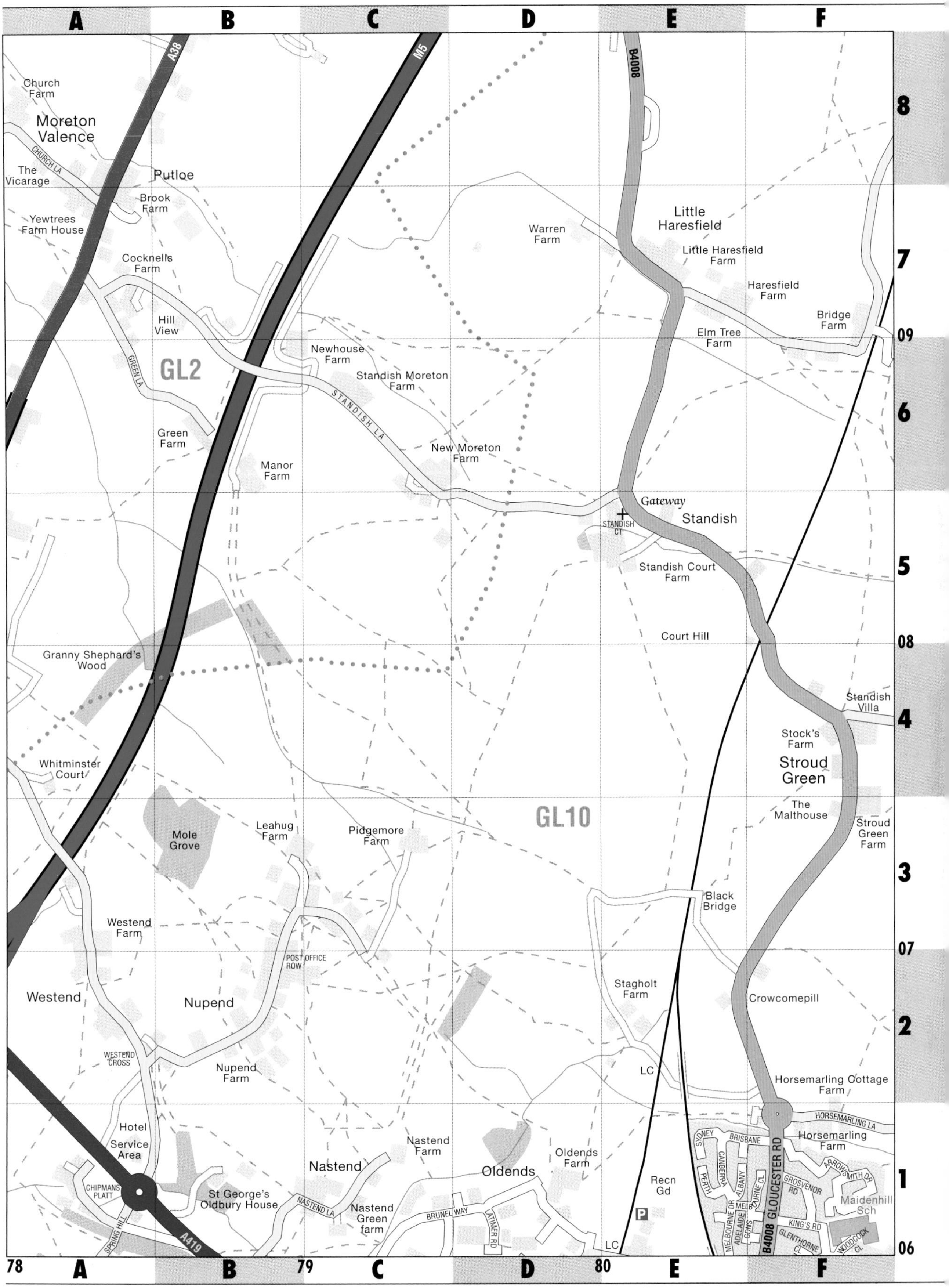
A B C D E F
8 7 09 6 5 08 4 3 07 2 1 06
78 79 80
Church Farm
Moreton Valence
CHURCH LA
The Vicarage
Putloe
Brook Farm
Yewtrees Farm House
Cocknells Farm
Hill View
GREEN LA
GL2
Green Farm
A38
M5
Newhouse Farm
Standish Moreton Farm
STANDISH LA
Manor Farm
New Moreton Farm
Warren Farm
B4008
Little Haresfield
Little Haresfield Farm
Haresfield Farm
Bridge Farm
Elm Tree Farm
Gateway
Standish
STANDISH CT
Standish Court Farm
Court Hill
Granny Shephard's Wood
Whitminster Court
Standish Villa
Stock's Farm
Stroud Green
The Malthouse
Stroud Green Farm
GL10
Mole Grove
Leahug Farm
Pidgemore Farm
Black Bridge
Westend Farm
POST OFFICE ROW
Westend
Nupend
Stagholt Farm
Crowcomepill
WESTEND CROSS
Nupend Farm
LC
Horsemarling Cottage Farm
HORSEMARLING LA
Horsemarling Farm
Hotel
Service Area
Nastend Farm
Nastend
Oldends
Oldends Farm
Recn Gd
CHIPMANS PLATT
St George's Oldbury House
NASTEND LA
Nastend Green farm
BRUNEL WAY
LATIMER RD
SPRING HILL
A419
LC
SYDNEY
BRISBANE
CANBERRA
PERTH
ALBANY
MELBOURNE CL
MELBOURNE DR
ADELAIDE GDNS
B4008 GLOUCESTER RD
GROSVENOR RD
ARROWSMITH DR
Maidenhill Sch
KING'S RD
GLENTHORNE CL
WOODCOCK CL
97
102

101
110

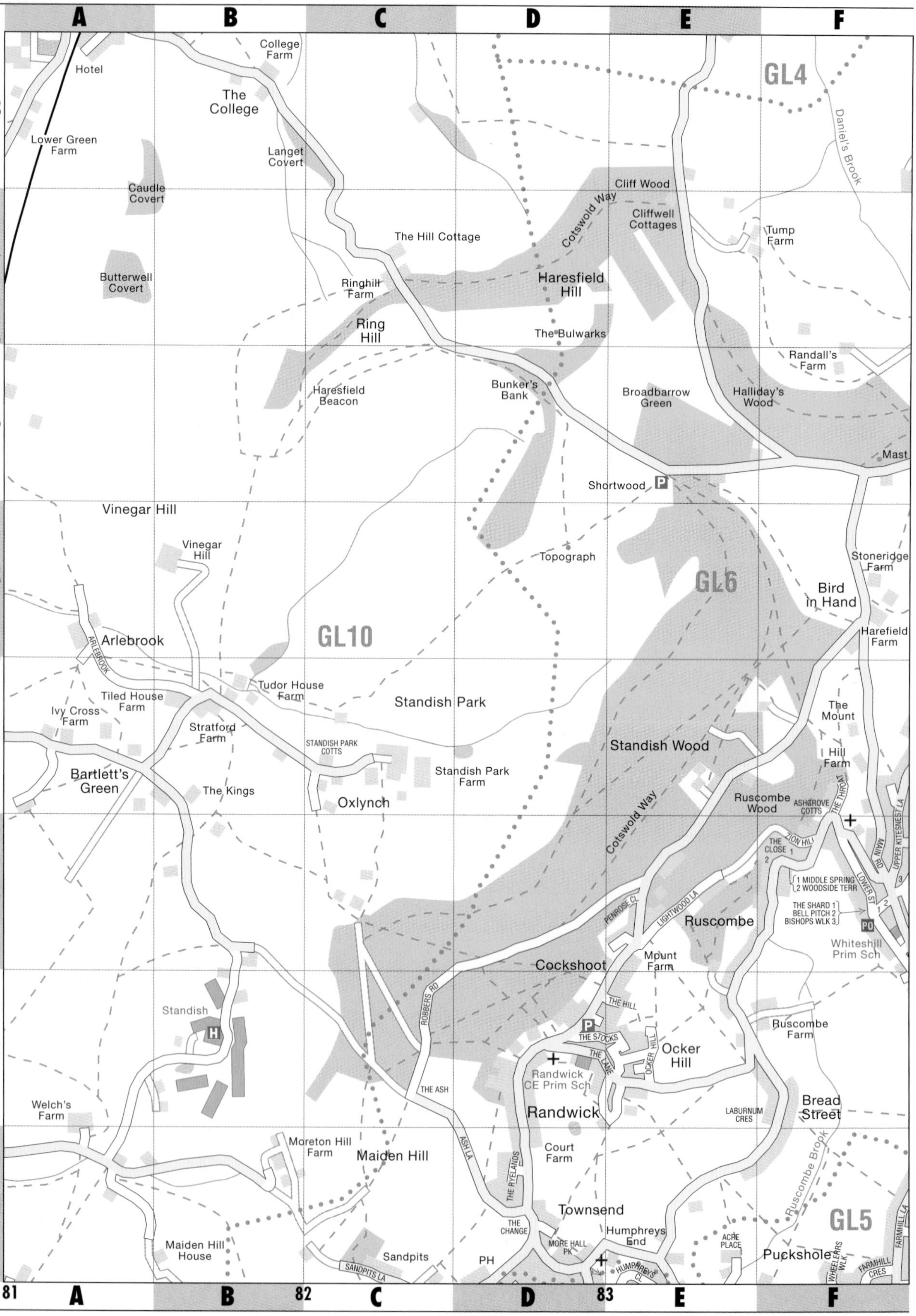

101
98

111
104

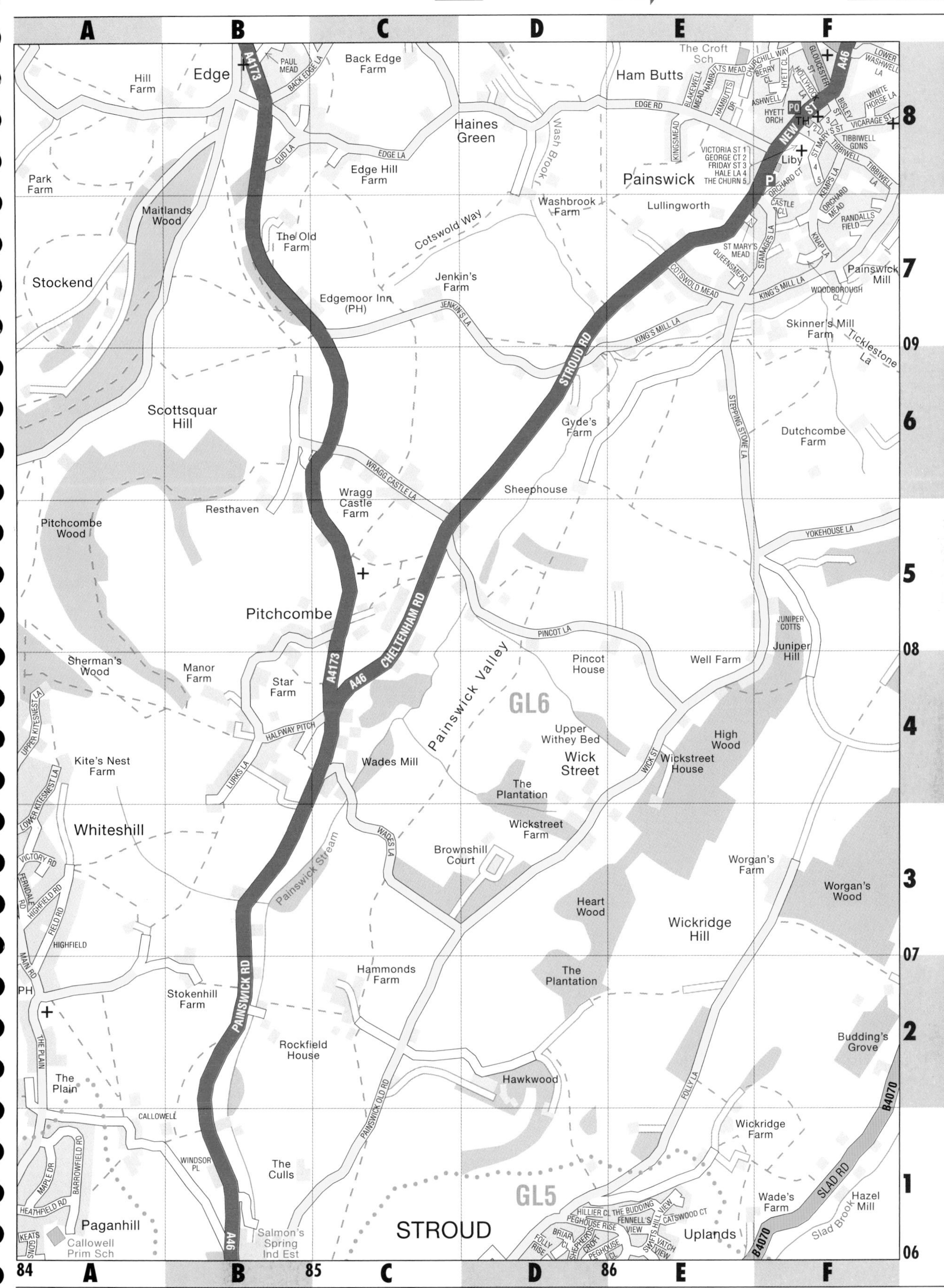

99
104

103
112

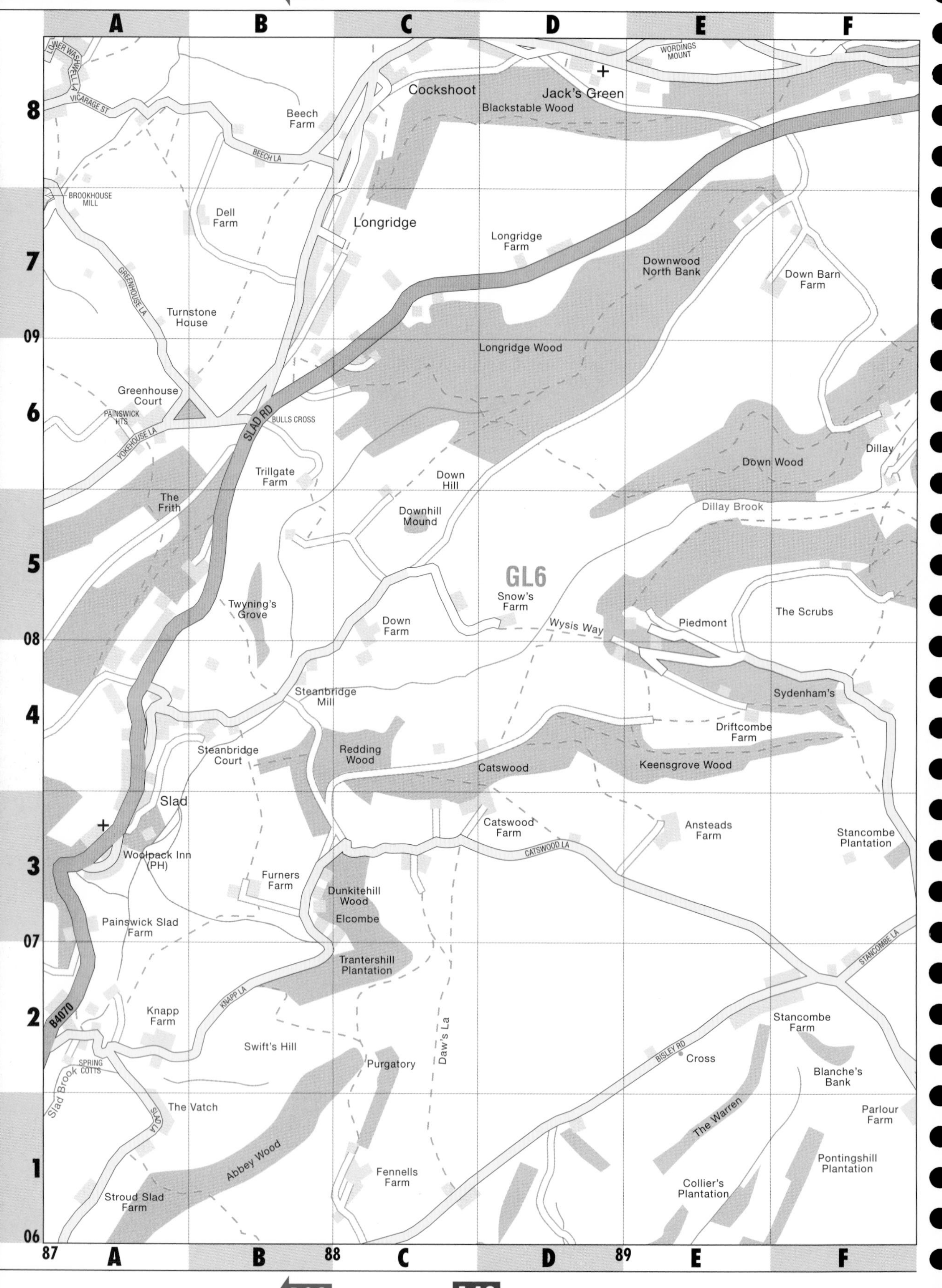

103
148

113
106

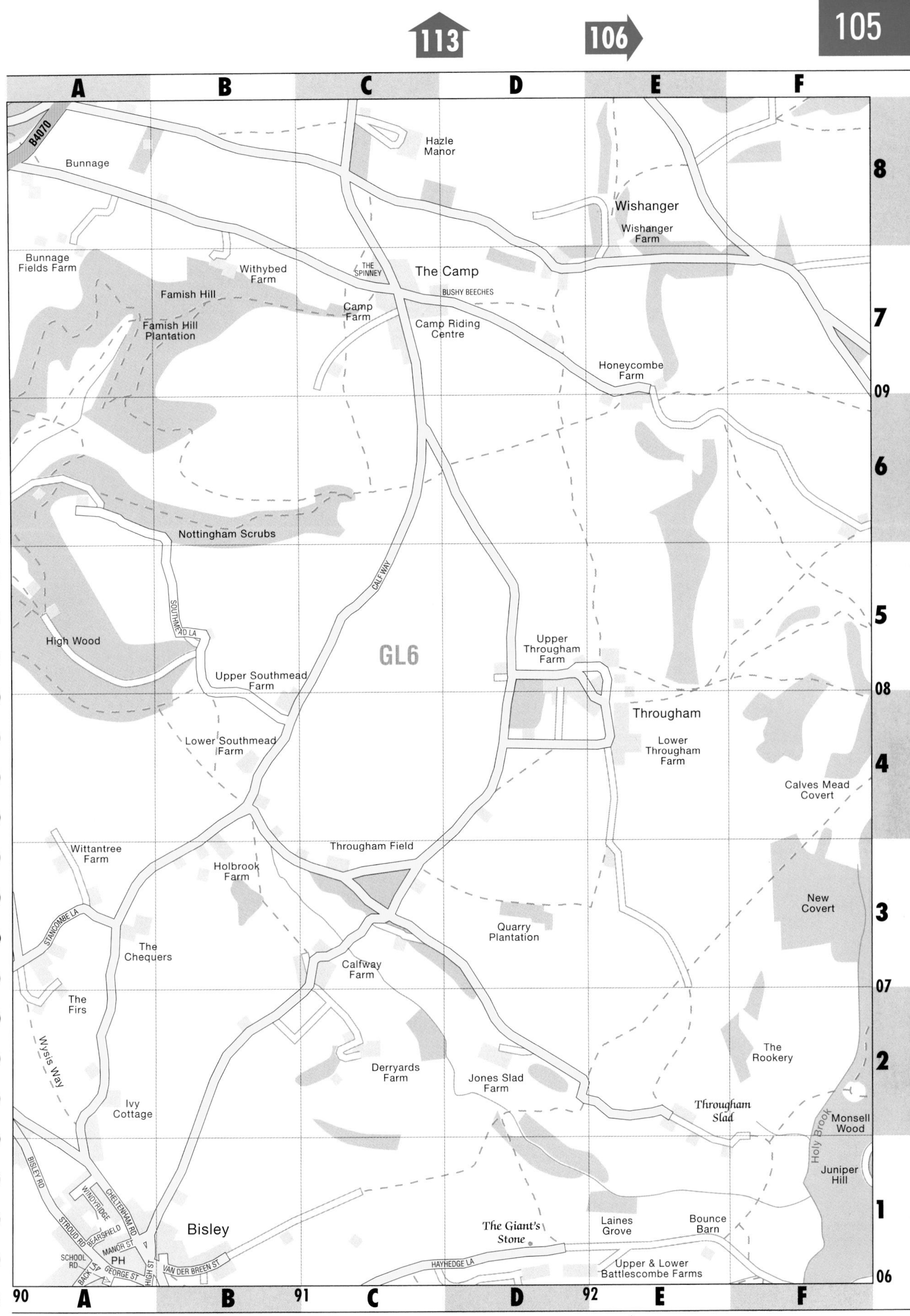

148
106

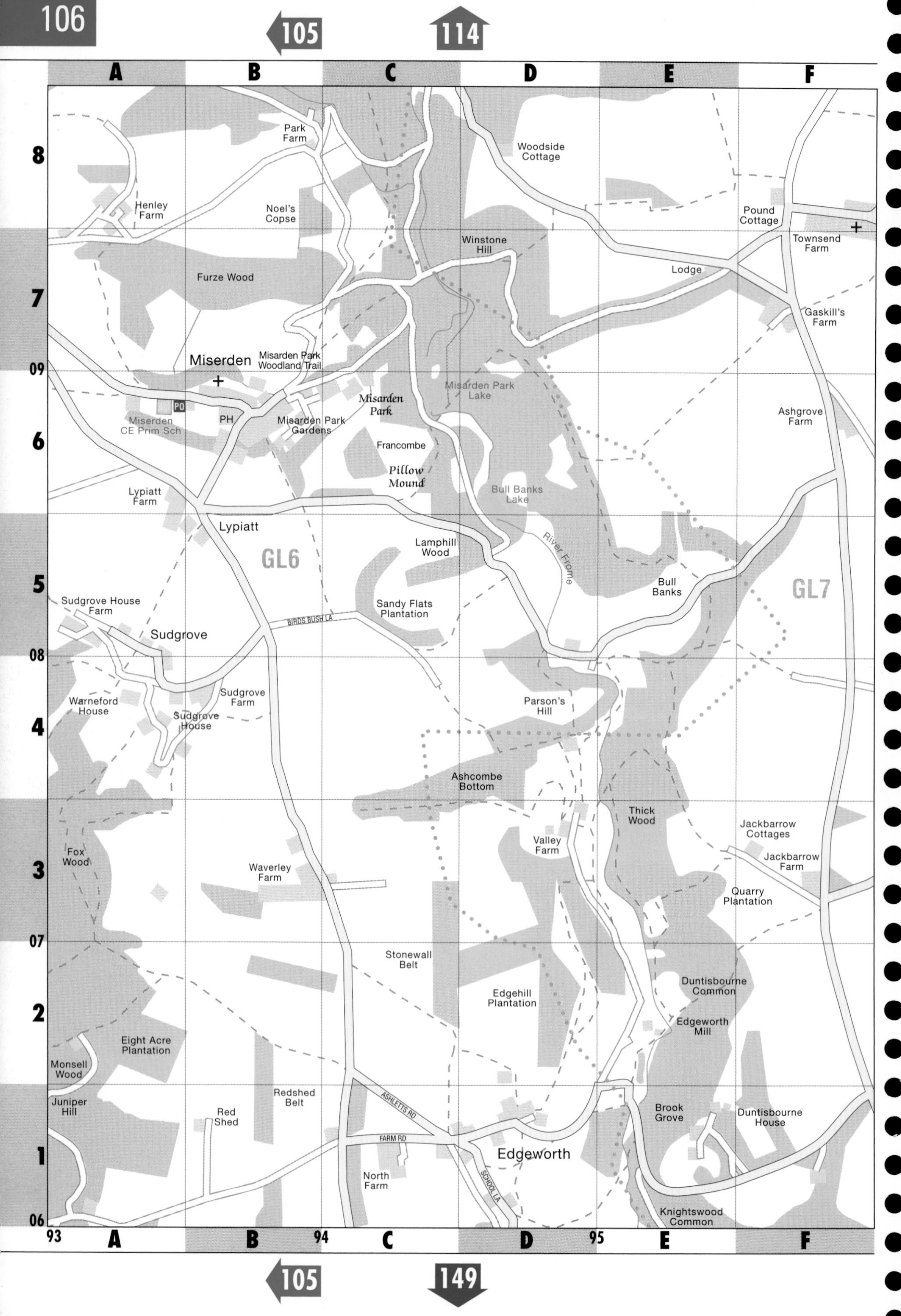

105
114
A
B
C
D
E
F
8
7
09
6
5
08
4
3
07
2
1
06
93
94
95
Park Farm
Woodside Cottage
Henley Farm
Noel's Copse
Pound Cottage
Townsend Farm
Winstone Hill
Lodge
Furze Wood
Gaskill's Farm
Miserden
Misarden Park Woodland Trail
Misarden Park Lake
PO
Misarden Park
Miserden CE Prim Sch
PH
Misarden Park Gardens
Ashgrove Farm
Francombe
Pillow Mound
Lypiatt Farm
Bull Banks Lake
Lypiatt
Lamphill Wood
River Frome
GL6
Bull Banks
GL7
Sudgrove House Farm
Sandy Flats Plantation
BIRDS BUSH LA
Sudgrove
Sudgrove Farm
Warneford House
Sudgrove House
Parson's Hill
Ashcombe Bottom
Thick Wood
Jackbarrow Cottages
Valley Farm
Fox Wood
Waverley Farm
Jackbarrow Farm
Quarry Plantation
Stonewall Belt
Edgehill Plantation
Duntisbourne Common
Edgeworth Mill
Eight Acre Plantation
Monsell Wood
Redshed Belt
Juniper Hill
Red Shed
ASHLETTS RD
Brook Grove
Duntisbourne House
FARM RD
Edgeworth
SCHOOL LA
North Farm
Knightswood Common
105
149

115
158

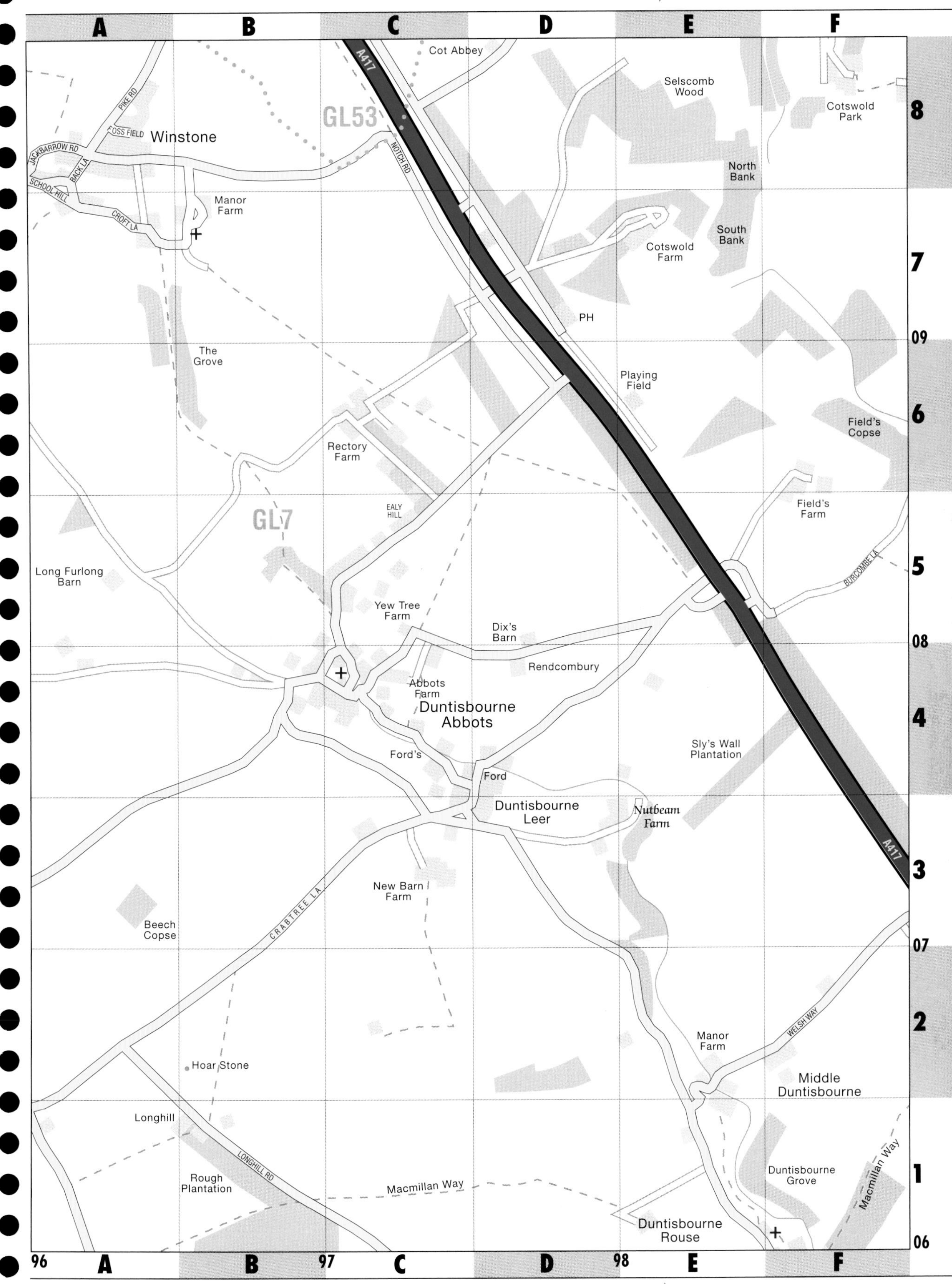

149
158

157
116

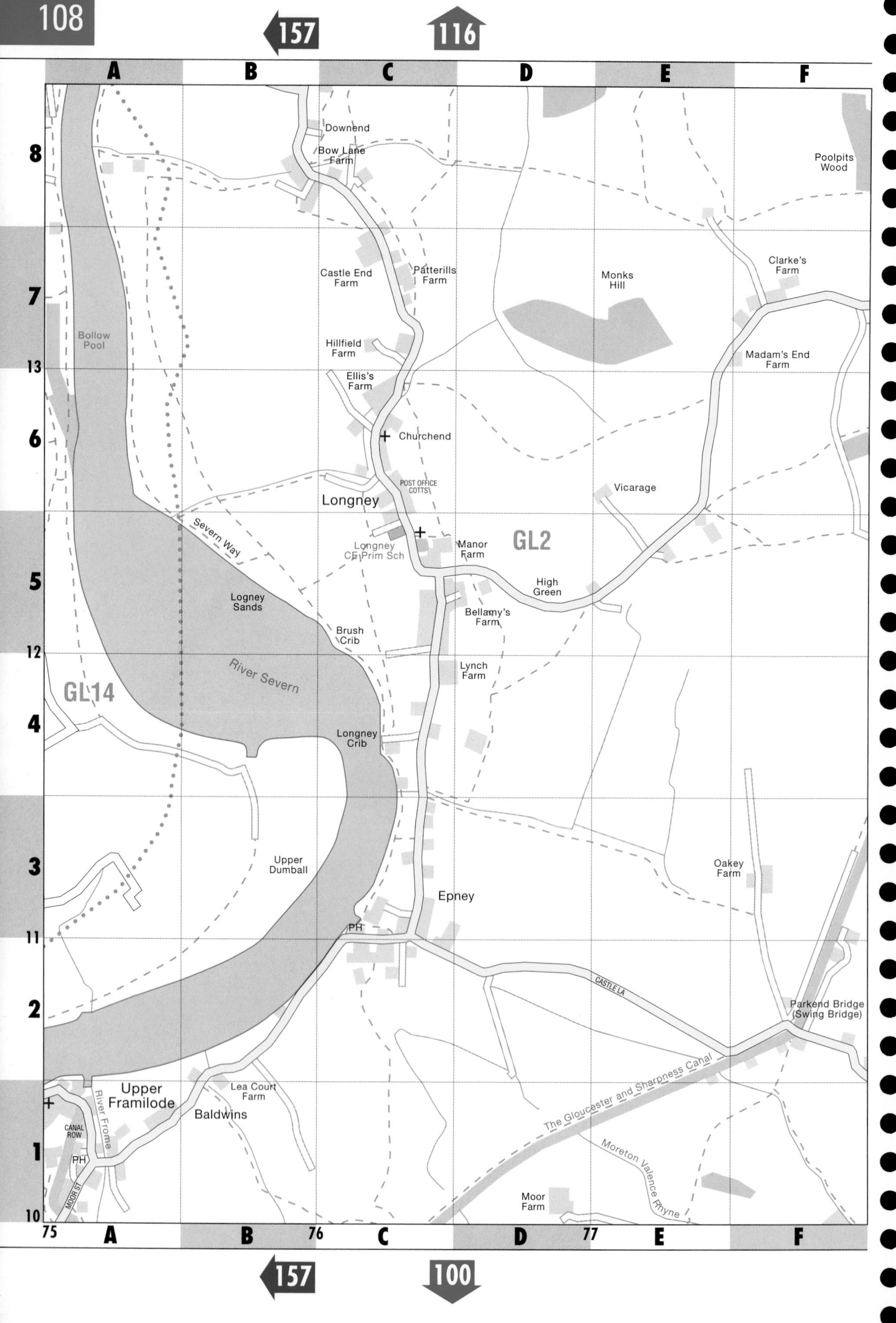

157
100

117
110

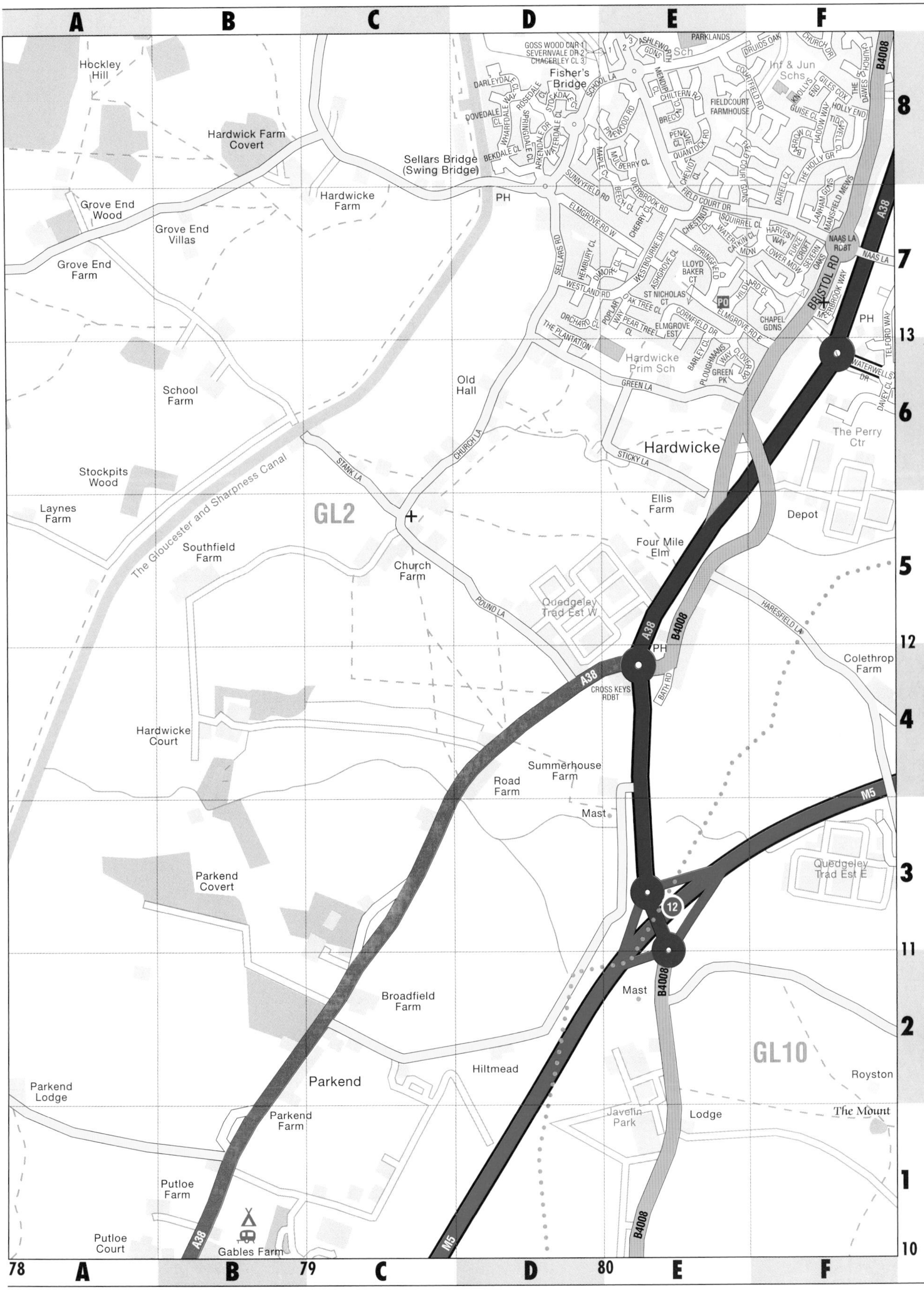

A B C D E F
Hockley Hill
Hardwick Farm Covert
Sellars Bridge (Swing Bridge)
Fisher's Bridge
Hardwicke Farm
Grove End Wood
Grove End Villas
Grove End Farm
PH
School Farm
Old Hall
Stockpits Wood
Laynes Farm
The Gloucester and Sharpness Canal
GL2
Southfield Farm
Church Farm
Hardwicke
Hardwicke Prim Sch
Ellis Farm
Four Mile Elm
Quedgeley Trad Est W
Depot
The Perry Ctr
Colethrop Farm
CROSS KEYS RDBT
Hardwicke Court
Summerhouse Farm
Road Farm
Mast
Parkend Covert
Quedgeley Trad Est E
Broadfield Farm
GL10
Royston
Parkend Lodge
Parkend
Hiltmead
Parkend Farm
Javelin Park
Lodge
The Mount
Putloe Farm
Putloe Court
Gables Farm
A38
M5
B4008
BRISTOL RD
NAAS LA RDBT
Inf & Jun Schs
FIELDCOURT FARMHOUSE
PARKLANDS
Sch
PO
8 7 6 5 4 3 2 1
13 12 11 10
78 79 80

109
118

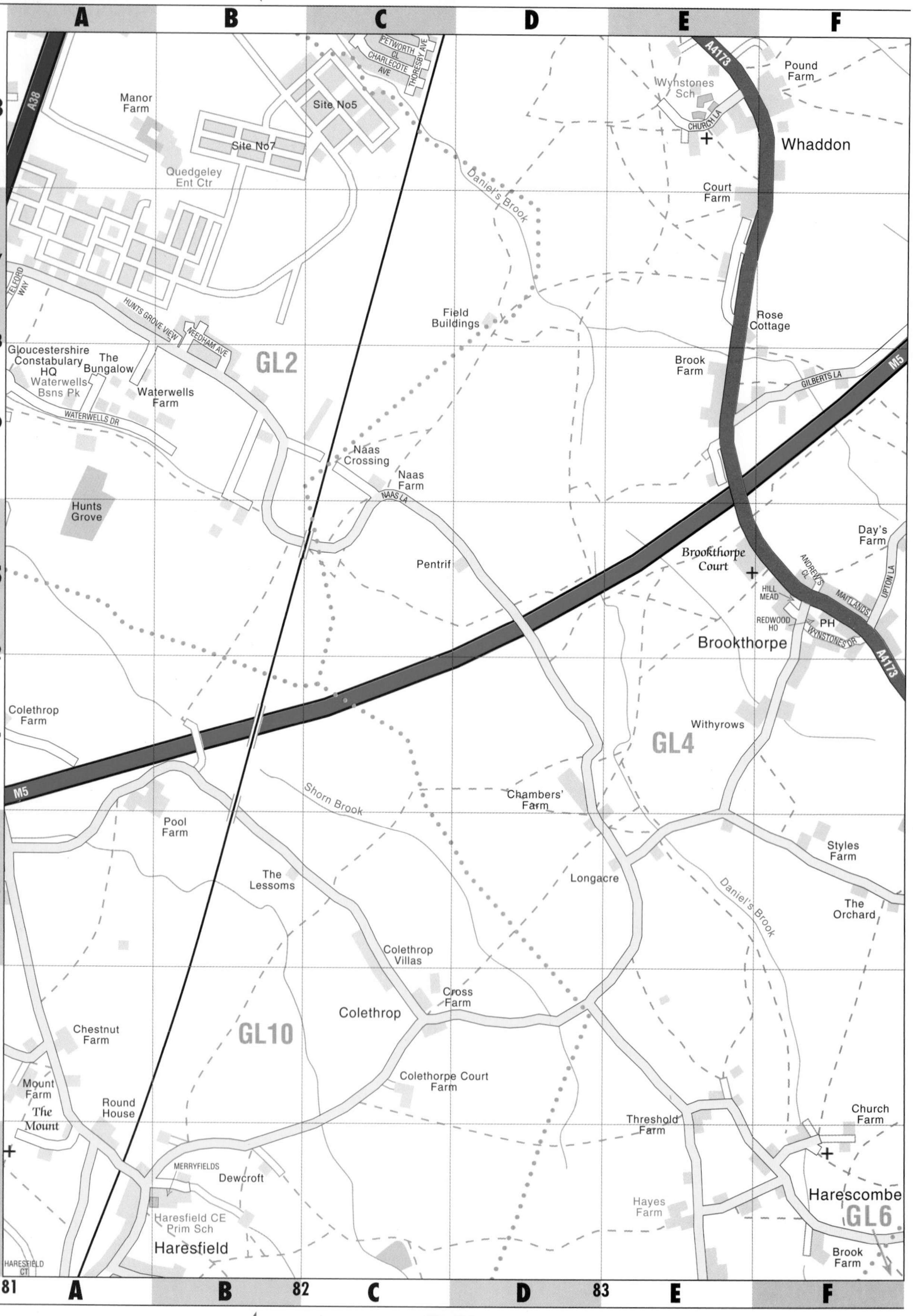

109
102

119
112

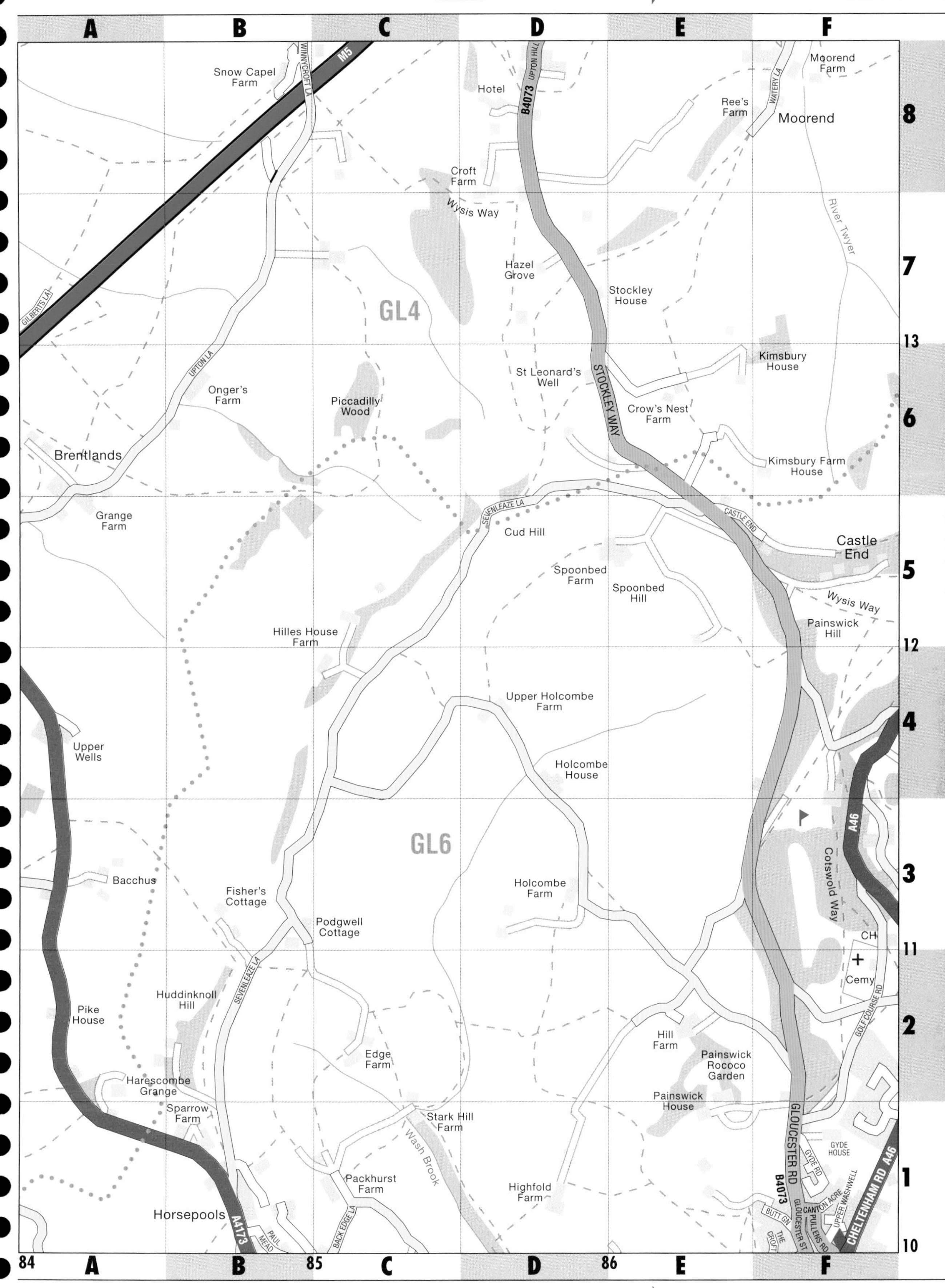

103
112

111
120

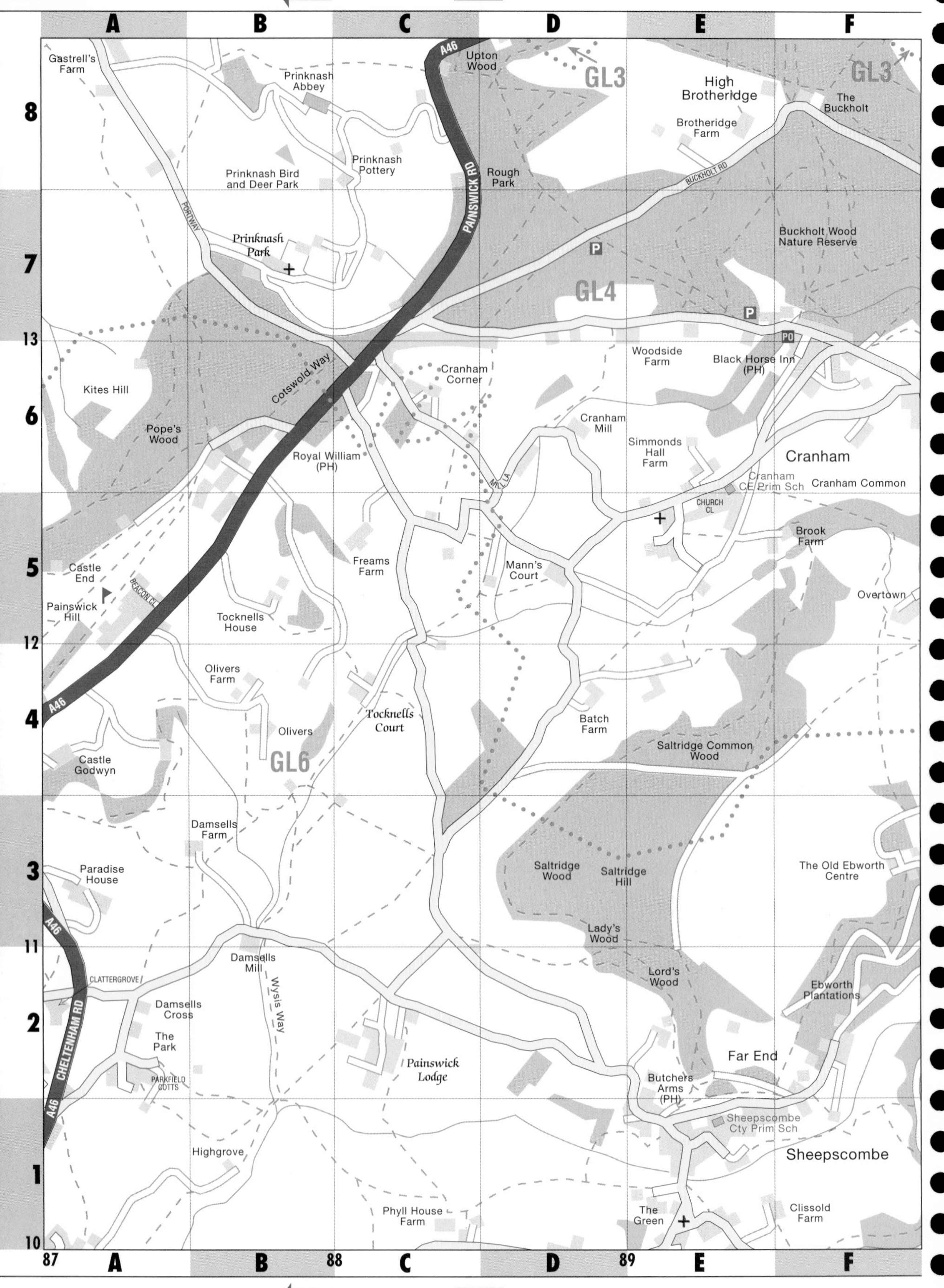

111
104

121
114

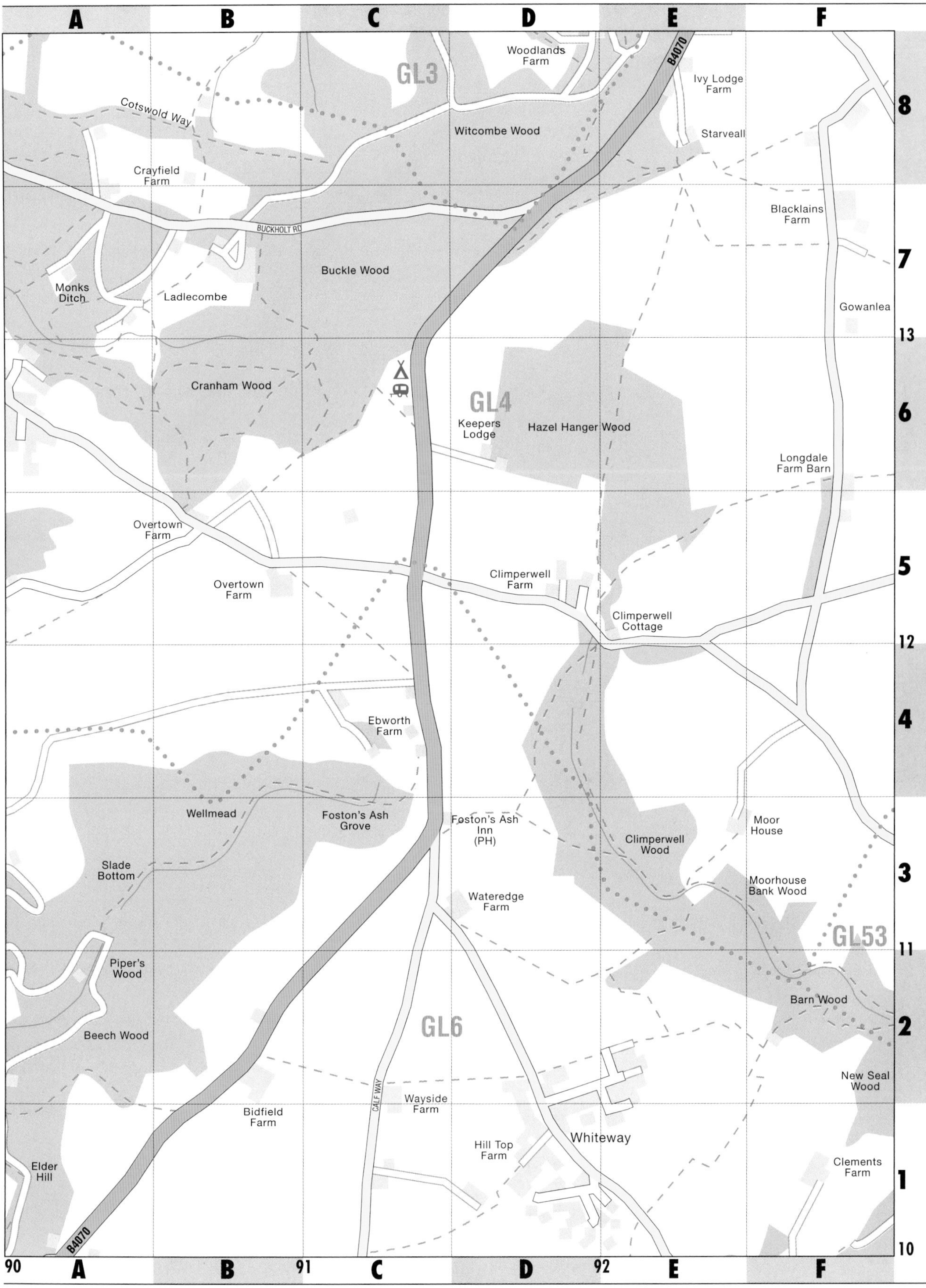

A
B
C
D
E
F
Woodlands Farm
GL3
B4070
Ivy Lodge Farm
Cotswold Way
Witcombe Wood
Starveall
Crayfield Farm
BUCKHOLT RD
Blacklains Farm
Buckle Wood
Monks Ditch
Ladlecombe
Gowanlea
Cranham Wood
GL4
Keepers Lodge
Hazel Hanger Wood
Longdale Farm Barn
Overtown Farm
Overtown Farm
Climperwell Farm
Climperwell Cottage
Ebworth Farm
Wellmead
Foston's Ash Grove
Foston's Ash Inn (PH)
Moor House
Climperwell Wood
Slade Bottom
Wateredge Farm
Moorhouse Bank Wood
GL53
Piper's Wood
Barn Wood
GL6
Beech Wood
New Seal Wood
CALF WAY
Wayside Farm
Bidfield Farm
Whiteway
Hill Top Farm
Elder Hill
Clements Farm
B4070
8
7
13
6
5
12
4
3
11
2
1
10
90
91
92
A
B
C
D
E
F

113 122

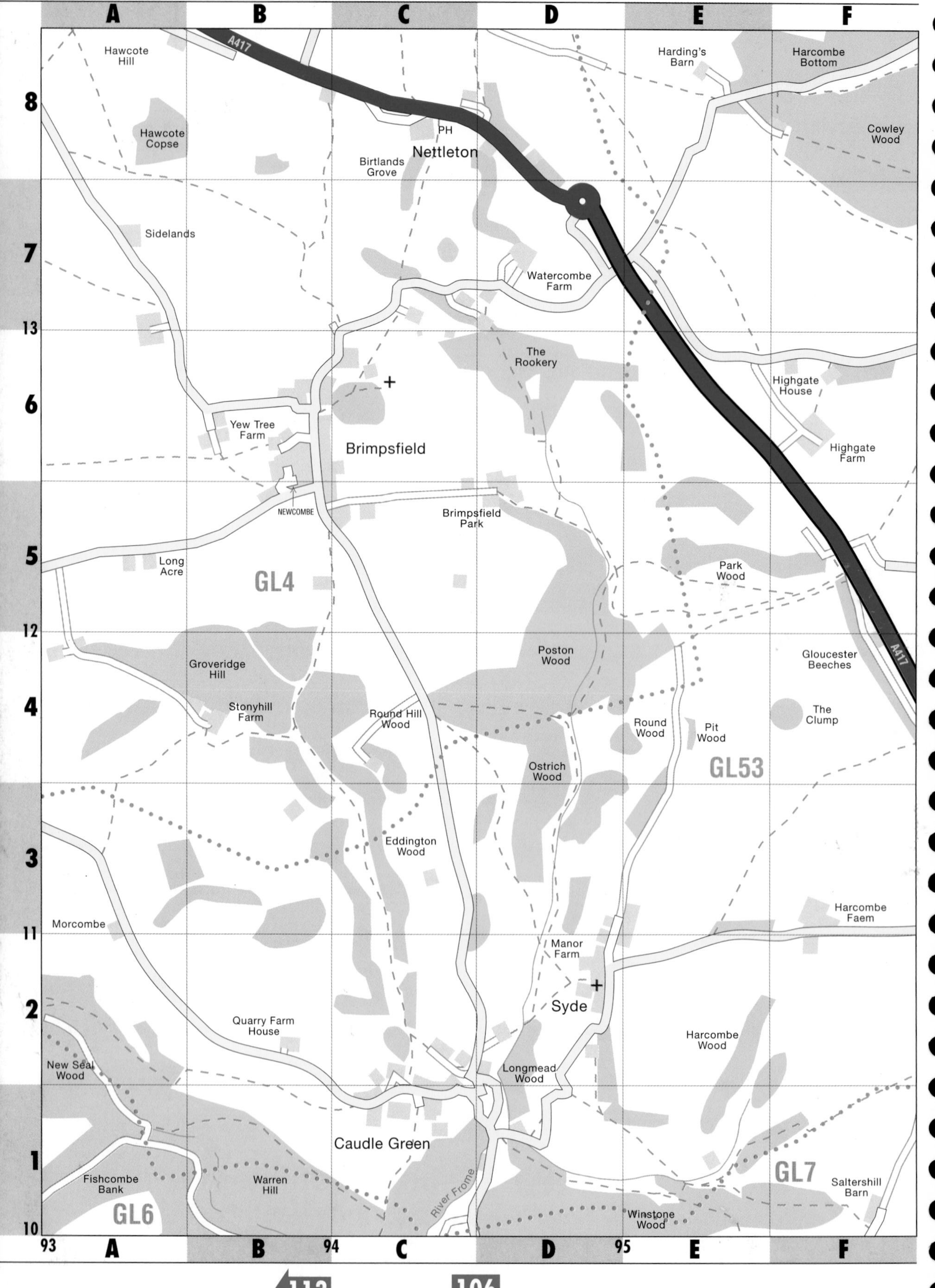

113 106

123
158

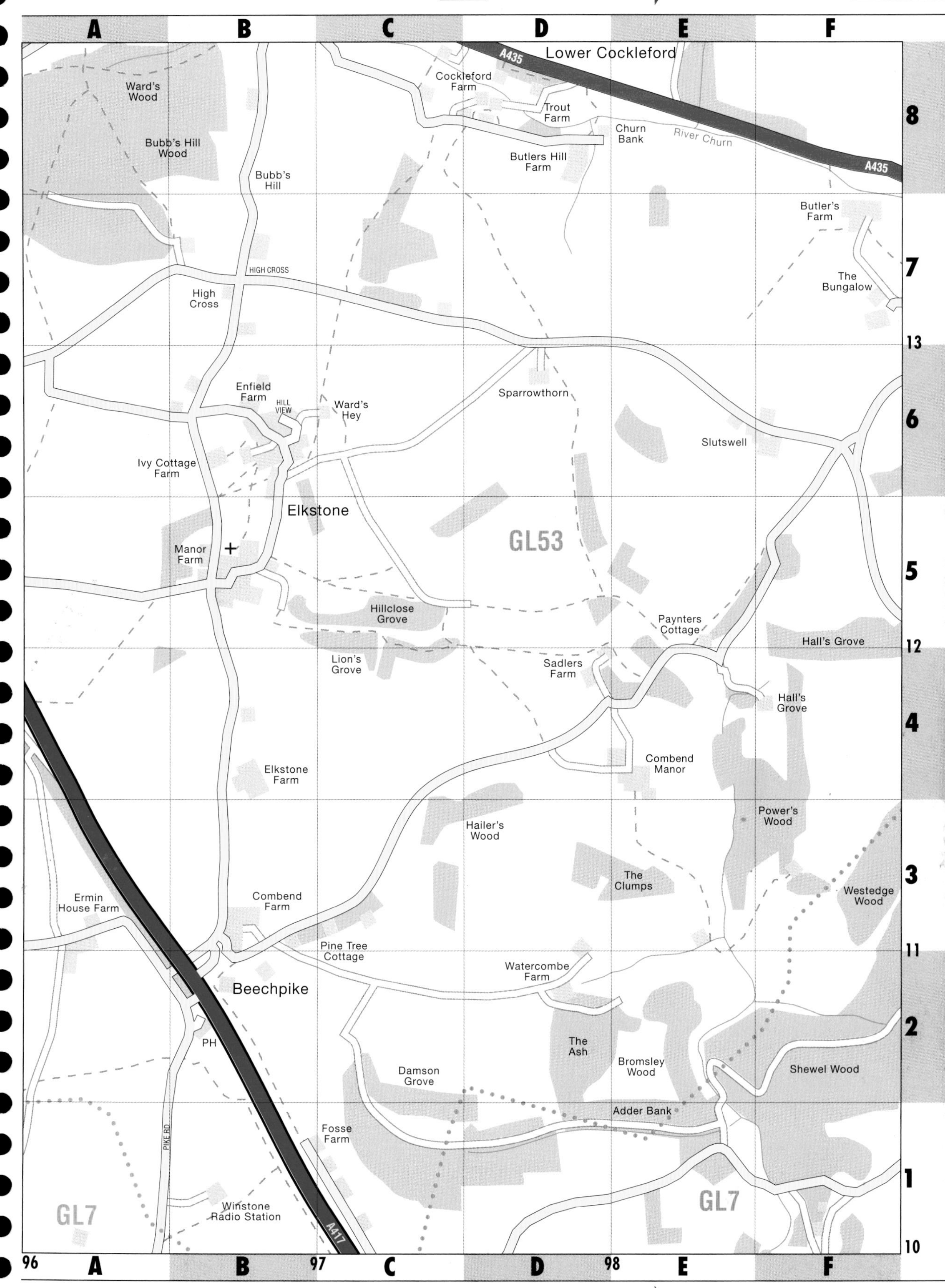

107
158

165 124

A B C D E F

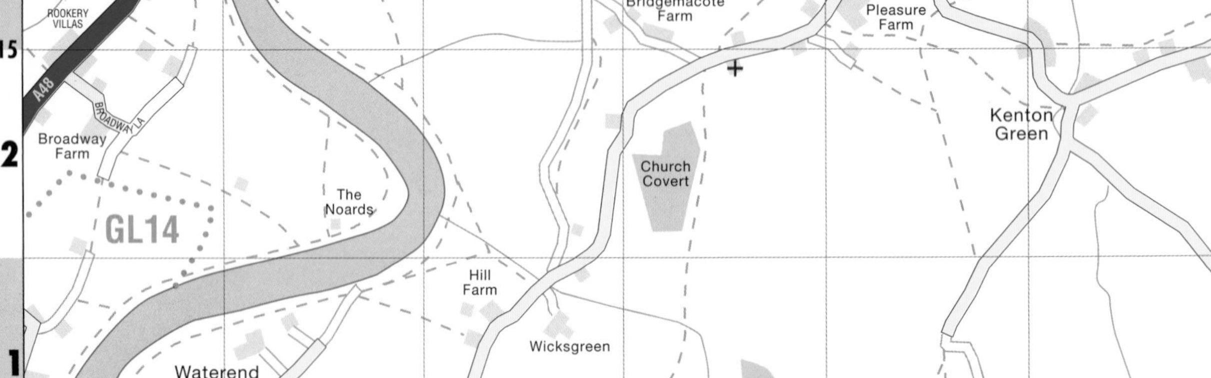

A B C D E F

165 108

125
118

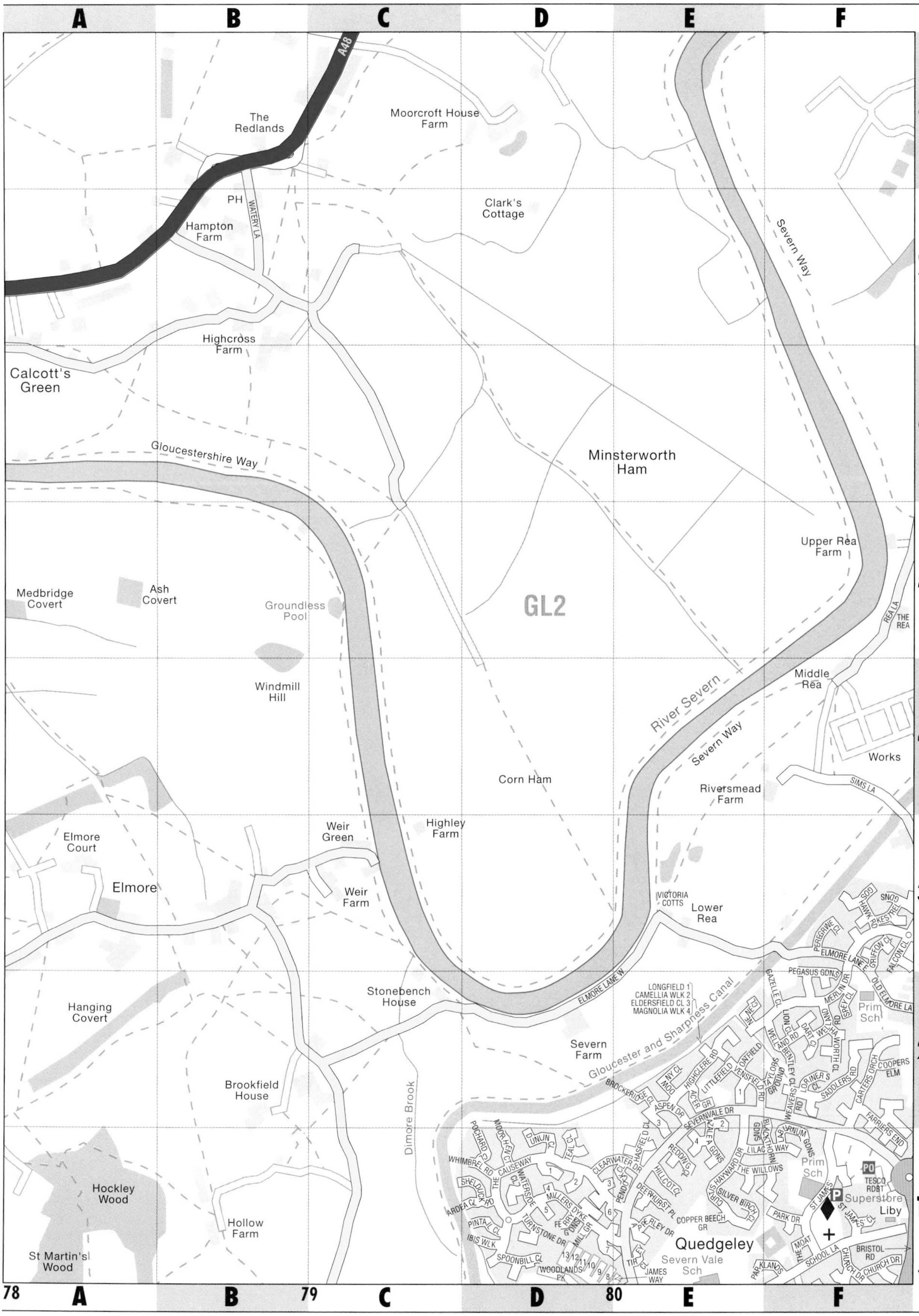

A
B
C
D
E
F
8
7
17
6
5
16
4
3
15
2
1
14
78
79
80
A48
The Redlands
Moorcroft House Farm
PH
WATERY LA
Hampton Farm
Clark's Cottage
Severn Way
Highcross Farm
Calcott's Green
Gloucestershire Way
Minsterworth Ham
Upper Rea Farm
Medbridge Covert
Ash Covert
Groundless Pool
GL2
REA LA
THE REA
Windmill Hill
Middle Rea
River Severn
Severn Way
Works
Corn Ham
Riversmead Farm
SIMS LA
Weir Green
Highley Farm
Elmore Court
Elmore
Weir Farm
VICTORIA COTTS
Lower Rea
ELMORE LANE
PEGASUS GDNS
Stonebench House
ELMORE LANE W
LONGFIELD 1
CAMELLIA WLK 2
ELDERSFIELD CL 3
MAGNOLIA WLK 4
Hanging Covert
Gloucester and Sharpness Canal
Severn Farm
Prim Sch
Brookfield House
Dimore Brook
Hockley Wood
Hollow Farm
St Martin's Wood
Quedgeley
Severn Vale Sch
Superstore
Liby
PO
TESCO RDBT
BRISTOL RD
CHURCH DR
SCHOOL LA
PARK DR
JAMES WAY
WOODLANDS PK
SPOONBILL CL
A
B
C
D
E
F

109

D1
1 MALLARD CL
2 SANDPIPER CL
3 THE CAUSEWAY
4 WATERMANS CT
5 MERCHANTS MEAD
6 KINGFISHER RISE

118

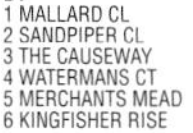

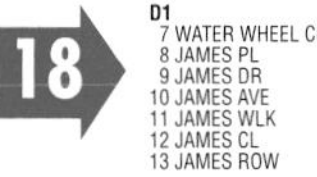

D1
7 WATER WHEEL CL
8 JAMES PL
9 JAMES DR
10 JAMES AVE
11 JAMES WLK
12 JAMES CL
13 JAMES ROW

117
126
For full street detail of the highlighted area see page 196.

F7
1 LLANDILO ST
2 CARMARTHEN ST
3 GLYNBRIDGE CT
4 FARADAY CL
5 MASSEY PAR
6 DORA WLK
7 TARRINGTON RD

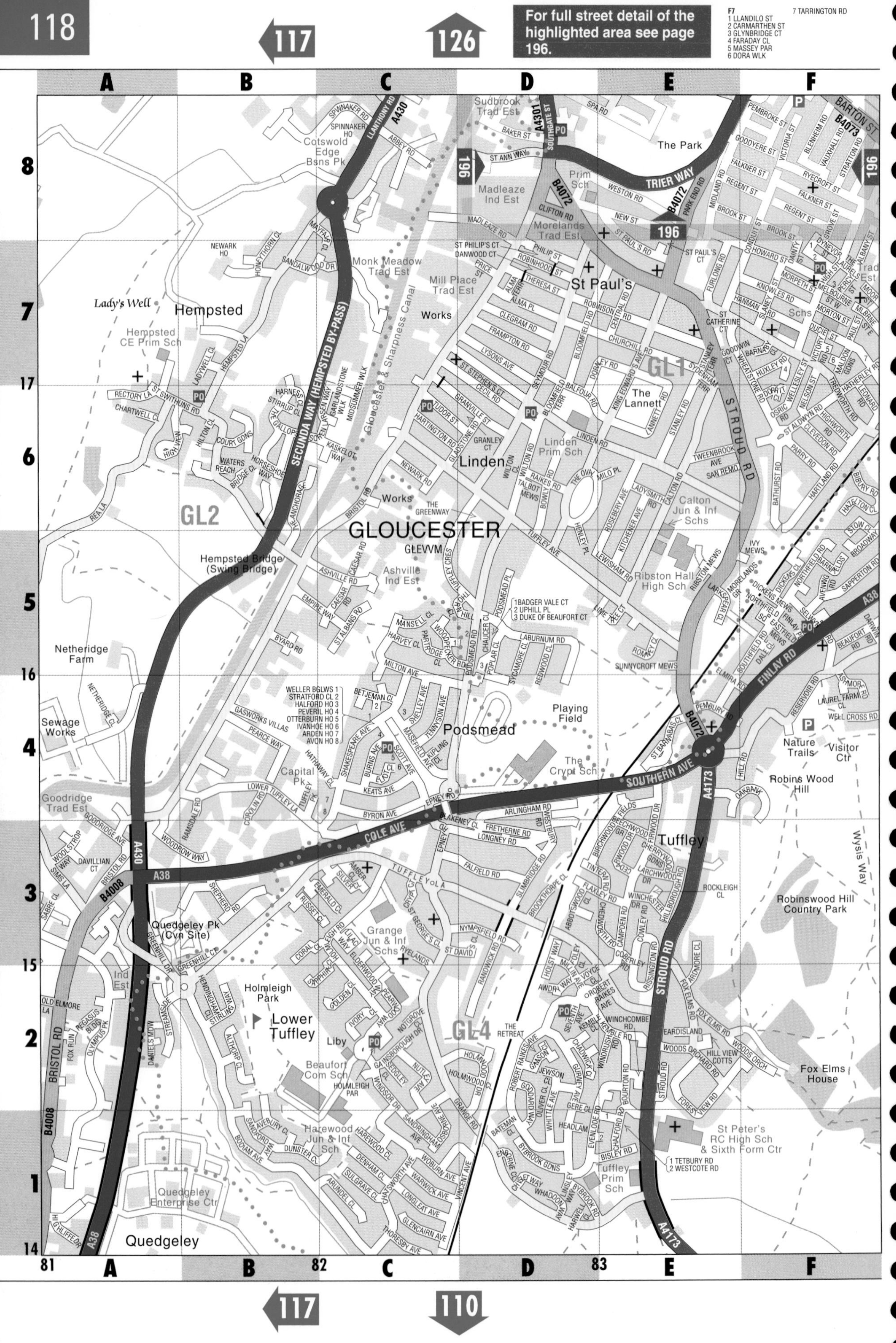

117
110

A8
1 SALISBURY HO
2 RED LION CT
3 ST JAMES MEWS
4 St James Trad Est
5 Francis Woodcock Trad Est

127

120

E6
1 CENTURION CL
2 SPARTAN CL
3 BENSON CL
4 PILGRIM CL
5 WIGMORE CL

F5
1 HOWGATE CL
2 MARJORAM CL
3 CAMOMILE CL
4 VIBURNUM VIEW
5 BILBERRY CL

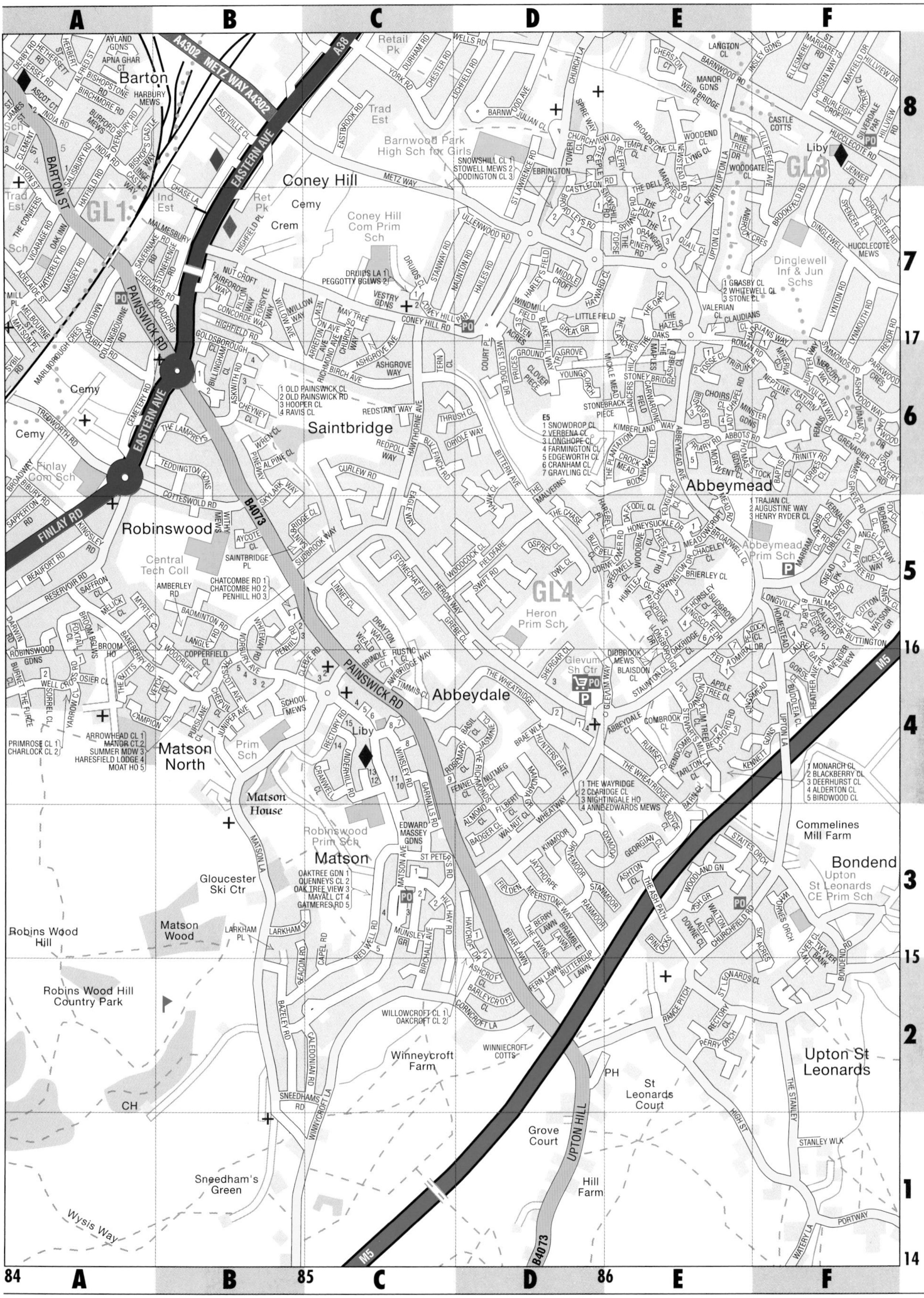

A B C D E F

8 7 17 6 5 16 4 3 15 2 1 14

84 A B 85 C D 86 E F

C4
1 DRAYTON CL
2 PAINSWICK LODGE
3 SEVERN LODGE
4 PARK VIEW
5 GEORGE WHITEFIELD CL
6 ABBEY VIEW
7 PRINKNASH CL
8 PRINKNASH RD
9 ACORN CT
10 WINSLEY CT
11 ROBINSWOOD PL
12 UNDERHILL CT
13 MATSON LODGE
14 CHERRY TREE CT
15 FAIRFIELD CT

111

120

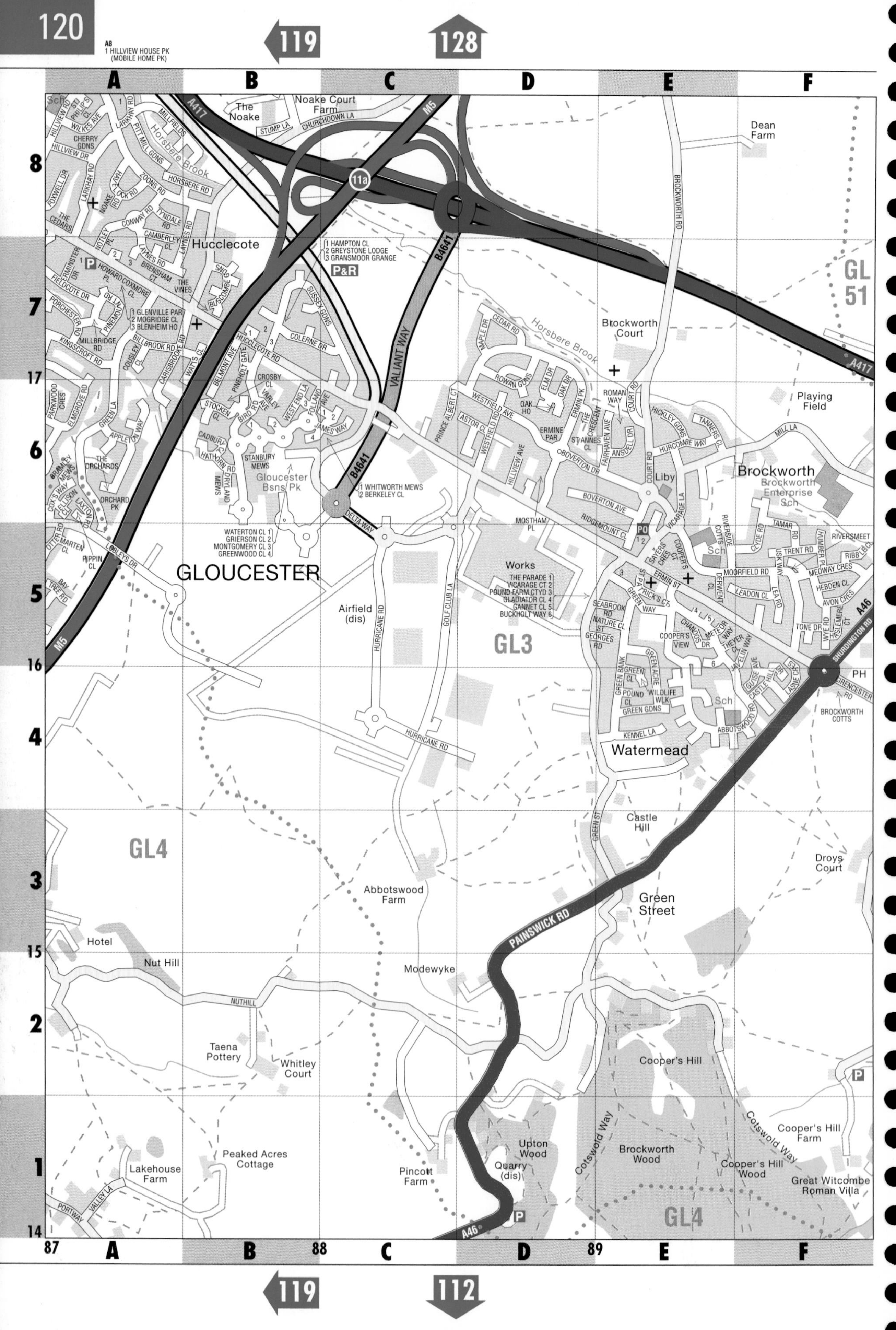
A8
1 HILLVIEW HOUSE PK
(MOBILE HOME PK)
119
128
A B C D E F
8
7
17
6
5
16
4
3
15
2
1
14
87
88
89
The Noake
Noake Court Farm
STUMP LA
CHURCHDOWN LA
Dean Farm
A417
M5
11a
B4641
BROCKWORTH RD
Hucclecote
1 HAMPTON CL
2 GREYSTONE LODGE
3 GRANSMOOR GRANGE
P&R
GL 51
VALIANT WAY
SUSSEX GDNS
COLERNE DR
HUCCLECOTE RD
1 GLENVILLE PAR
2 MOGRIDGE CL
3 BLENHEIM HO
Brockworth Court
Horsbere Brook
CEDAR RD
MAPLE DR
ROWAN GDNS
ELM DR
OAK DR
OAK HO
ERMINE PAR
WESTFIELD AVE
PRINCE ALBERT CT
ASTOR CL
HILLVIEW AVE
BOVERTON DR
BOVERTON AVE
RIDGEMOUNT CL
Playing Field
MILL LA
HURCOMBE WAY
TANNERS CL
HICKLEY GDNS
Brockworth
Brockworth Enterprise Sch
Liby
PO
VICARAGE LA
COURT RD
RIVERSMEET
RIVERSIDE COTTS
TAMAR RD
TRENT RD
MOORFIELD RD
LEADON CL
MEDWAY CRES
HEBDEN CL
AVON CRES
TONE DR
Sch
1 WHITWORTH MEWS
2 BERKELEY CL
DELTA WAY
Gloucester Bsns Pk
STANBURY MEWS
JAMES WAY
WATERTON CL 1
GRIERSON CL 2
MONTGOMERY CL 3
GREENWOOD CL 4
MOSTHAM PL
Works
THE PARADE 1
VICARAGE CT 2
POUND FARM CTYD 3
GLADIATOR CL 4
GANNET CL 5
BUCKHOLT WAY 6
ERMIN ST
GLOUCESTER
LOBLEYS DR
Airfield (dis)
HURRICANE RD
GOLF CLUB LA
GL3
SEABROOK RD
NATURE CL
ST GEORGES RD
COOPER'S VIEW
CHANDOS DR
METEOR WAY
JAVELIN WAY
GREEN BANK
GREEN CL
POUND CL
GREEN GDNS
WILDLIFE WLK
KENNEL LA
ABBOTSWOOD RD
A46
SHURDINGTON RD
PH
CIRENCESTER RD
BROCKWORTH COTTS
Watermead
Castle Hill
GREEN ST
GL4
Droys Court
Abbotswood Farm
Green Street
PAINSWICK RD
Hotel
Nut Hill
Modewyke
NUTHILL
Taena Pottery
Whitley Court
Cooper's Hill
Cooper's Hill Farm
Cotswold Way
Upton Wood
Quarry (dis)
Brockworth Wood
Cooper's Hill Wood
Great Witcombe Roman Villa
Peaked Acres Cottage
Lakehouse Farm
Pincott Farm
PORTWAY
VALLEY LA
119
112

A B C D E F

8
Syringa Farm
A46
WHITELANDS LA
Orchard Farm
Hotel
GREENWAY LA
Brook Villa Farm
Hunt Court Farm
SANDY PLUCK LA
WHITELANDS LA
Greenway Farm
The Plantation
Norman's Brook
Little Shurdington

7
GL51
Primrose Vale Farm
Yew Tree Farm
Gloucestershire Way
GL53
SHURDINGTON RD
Windy Farm

17
Dryhill Farm
Greenfield Farm
Henley Bank Farm
Bentham

6
MILL LA
Orchard Farm
DOG LA
Country Club
Oakland Farm
Cold Slad
Henley
GL4
Grickley Hill Country Park Visitor Centre

5
Hotel
Middle Pig Farm

16
PILLCROFT RD
PILLCROFT CL
BRYERLAND RD
BOUNDARY COTTS
ASTRIDGE RD
PO
CIRENCESTER RD
Court Farm
Little Witcombe
A417

4
PH
Crickley Hill Farm
Grove Farm
LITTLE WITCOMBE CT
GL3
GREEN LA
Droys Court
Willow Farm
The Peak

3
Witcombe Farm
Hill Farm
Cuckoo Pen

15
Witcombe Reservoirs
Church Farm
Upper Farm
Great Witcombe
Birdlip Hill
B4070

2
Birdlip
PH
Cotswold Way
BIRDLIP FARM
Birdlip Prim Sch
Witcombe Park
IVY LODGE BARNS
Green Farm
GL4
GL4

1
SPRINGFIELD PL
B4070
Woodlands Farm

14

90 A B 91 C D 92 E F

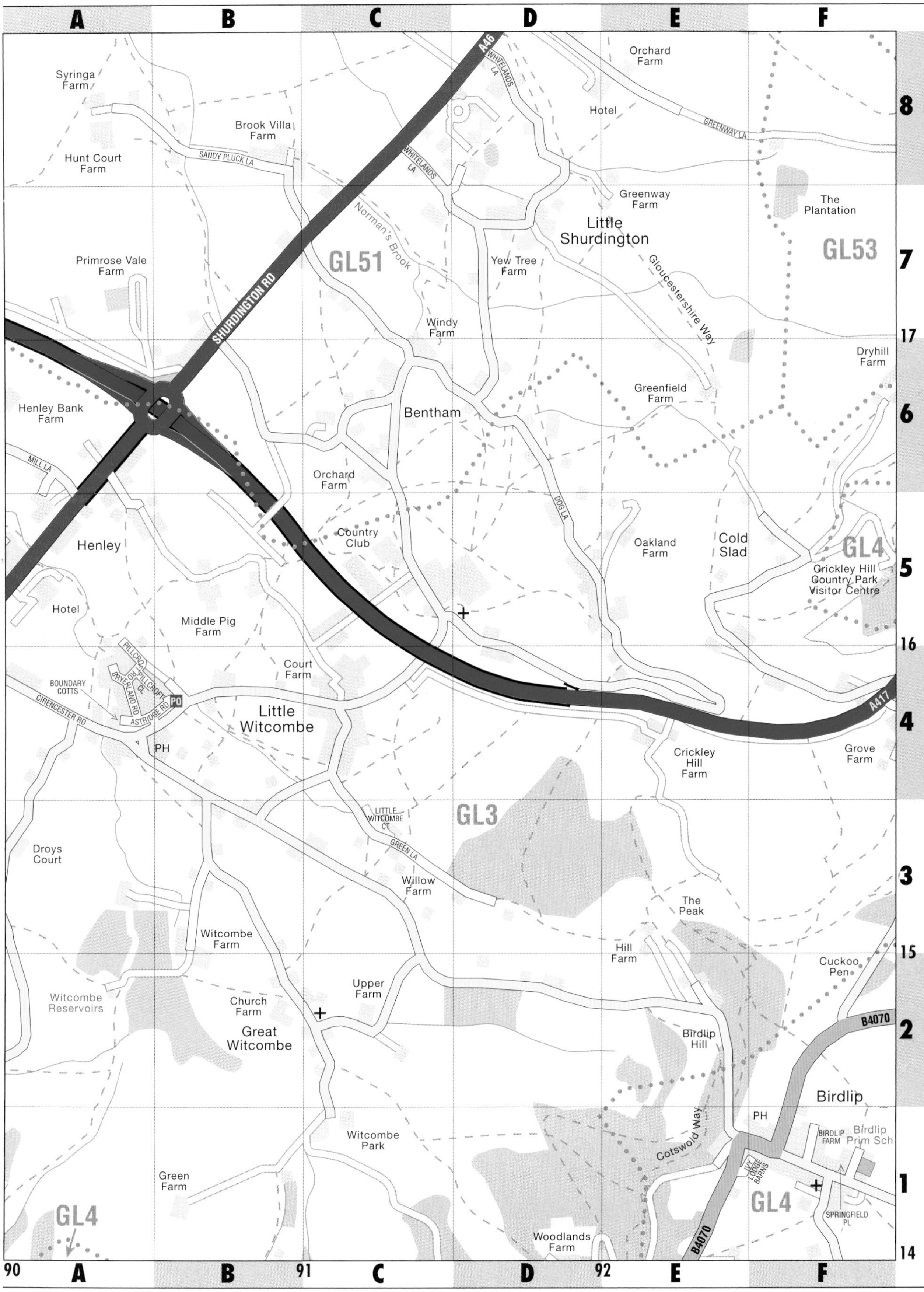

113
122

121
130

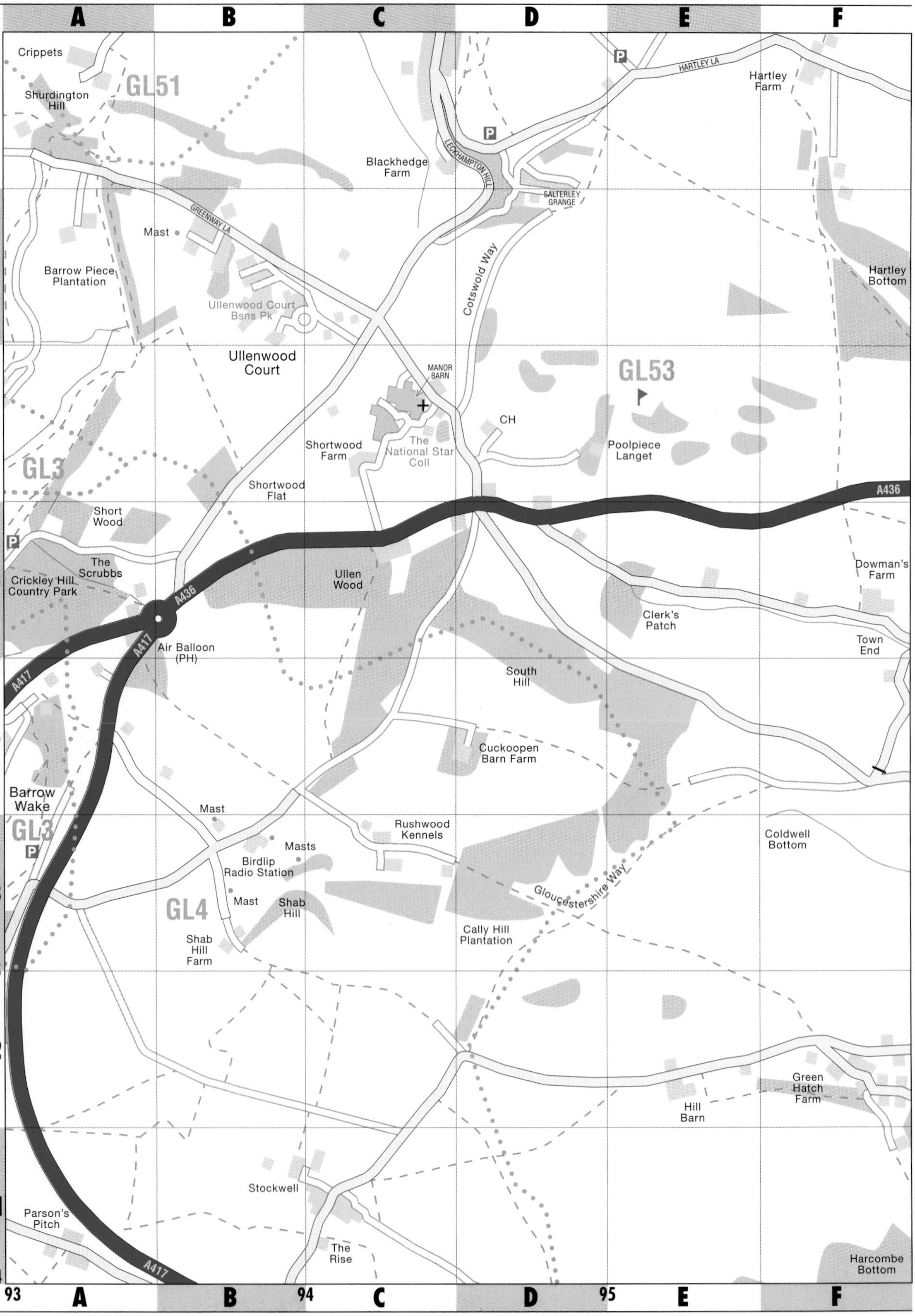

121
114

131
166 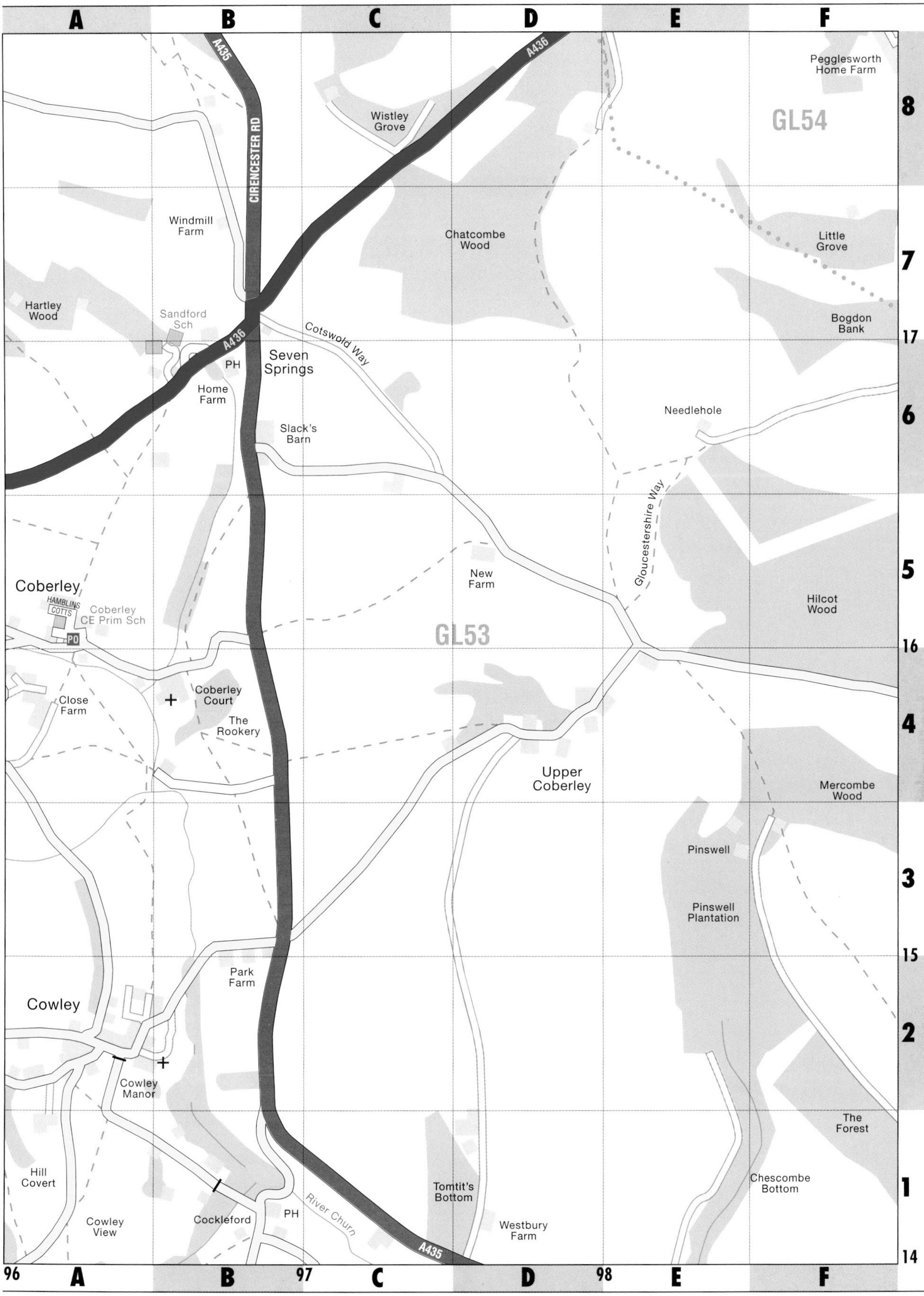
A B C D E F
A435
A436
CIRENCESTER RD
Pegglesworth Home Farm
GL54
Wistley Grove
Windmill Farm
Chatcombe Wood
Little Grove
Hartley Wood
Sandford Sch
Bogdon Bank
A436
PH
Seven Springs
Cotswold Way
Home Farm
Needlehole
Slack's Barn
Gloucestershire Way
New Farm
Coberley
HAMBLINS COTTS
Coberley CE Prim Sch
PO
Hilcot Wood
GL53
Coberley Court
Close Farm
The Rookery
Upper Coberley
Mercombe Wood
Pinswell
Pinswell Plantation
Park Farm
Cowley
Cowley Manor
The Forest
Hill Covert
Tomtit's Bottom
Chescombe Bottom
PH
River Churn
Cowley View
Cockleford
Westbury Farm
A435
8 7 17 6 5 16 4 3 15 2 1 14
96 97 98
115
166

165
171

165
116

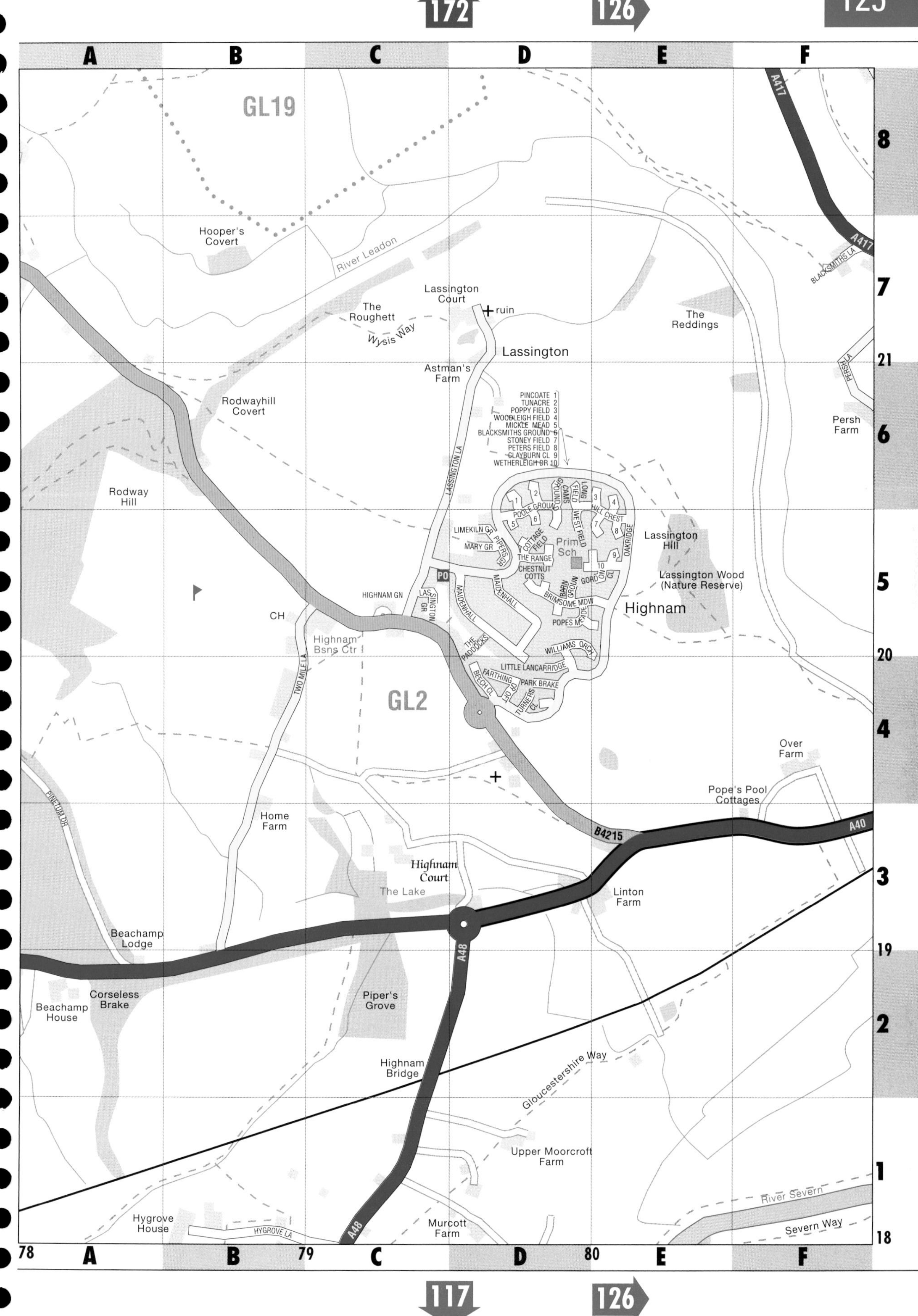
172
126
A
B
C
D
E
F
GL19
Hooper's Covert
River Leadon
Lassington Court
ruin
The Roughett
Wysis Way
Lassington
The Reddings
Astman's Farm
Rodwayhill Covert
PINCOATE 1
TUNACRE 2
POPPY FIELD 3
WOODLEIGH FIELD 4
MICKLE MEAD 5
BLACKSMITHS GROUND 6
STONEY FIELD 7
PETERS FIELD 8
CLAYBURN CL 9
WETHERLEIGH DR 10
Rodway Hill
LASSINGTON LA
Prim Sch
Lassington Hill
Lassington Wood (Nature Reserve)
Highnam
HIGHNAM GN
PO
CH
Highnam Bsns Ctr
TWO MILE LA
GL2
Over Farm
Pope's Pool Cottages
Home Farm
B4215
A40
A417
BLACKSMITHS LA
PERSH LA
Persh Farm
Highnam Court
The Lake
Linton Farm
Beachamp Lodge
PINETUM DR
Corseless Brake
Beachamp House
A48
Piper's Grove
Highnam Bridge
Gloucestershire Way
Upper Moorcroft Farm
River Severn
Severn Way
Hygrove House
HYGROVE LA
Murcott Farm
8
7
21
6
5
20
4
3
19
2
1
18
78
79
80
117
126

125
172

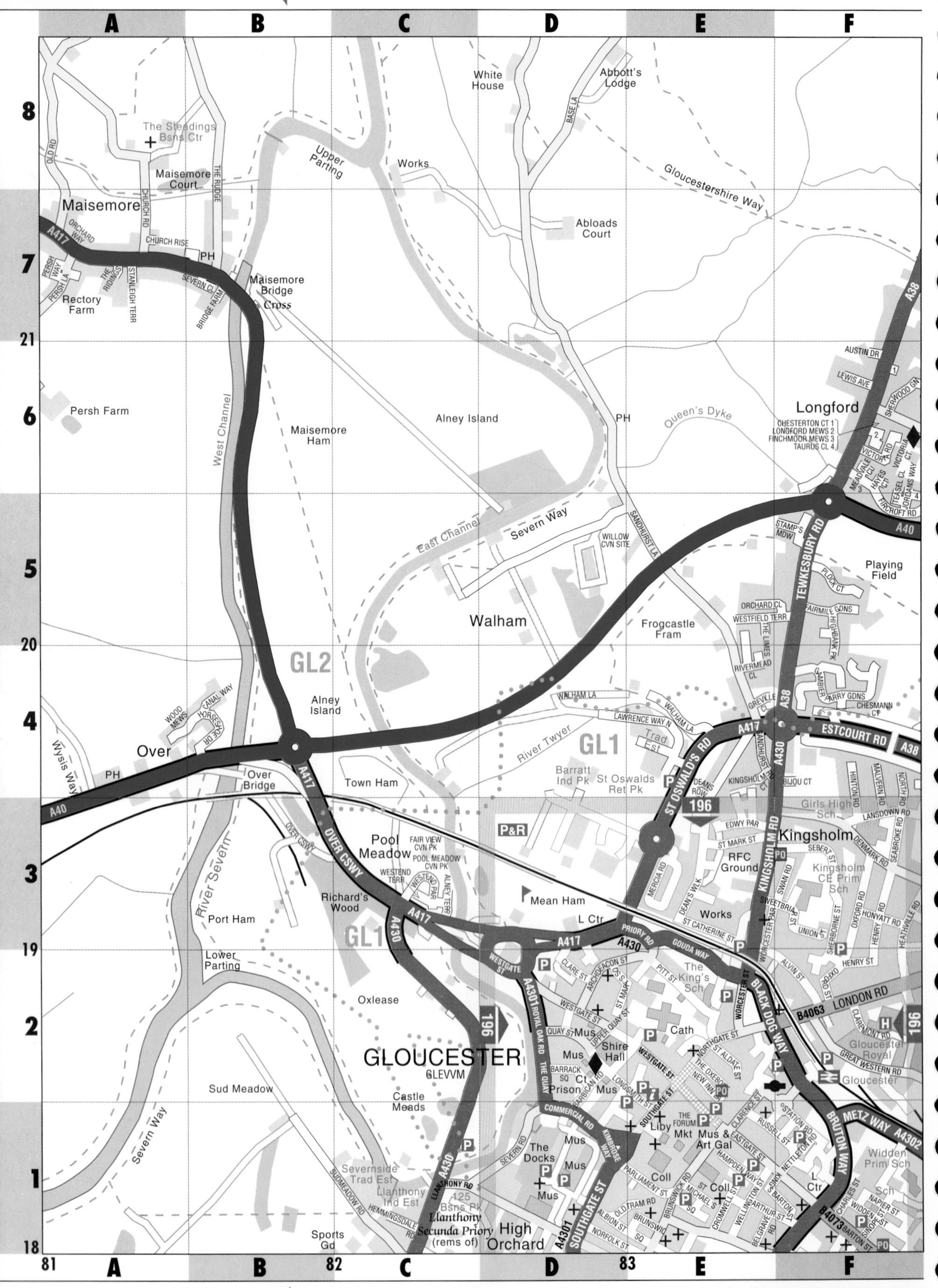

For full street detail of the highlighted area see page 196.

173
128

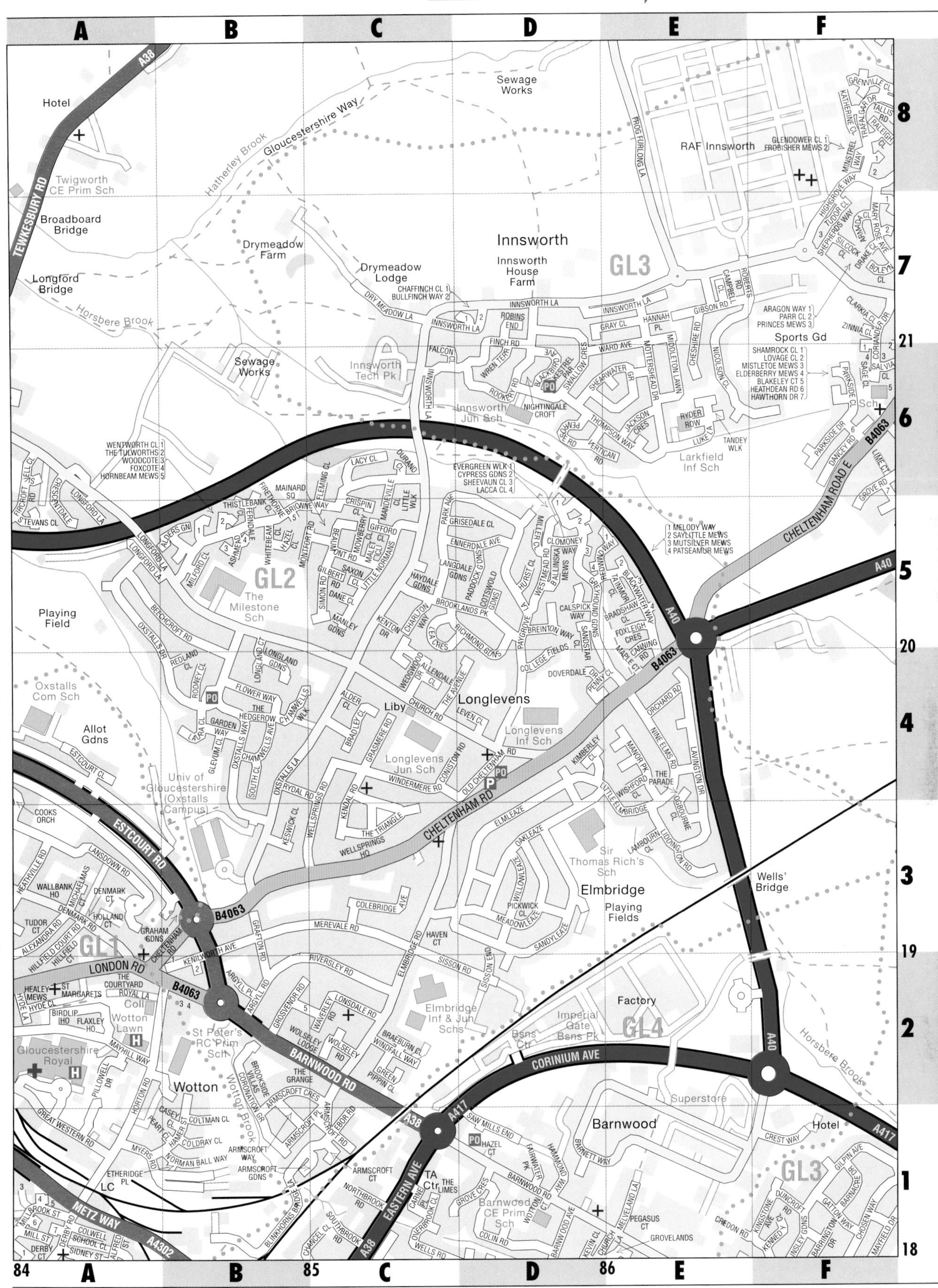

A1
1 MAGDALA RD
2 BECKSIDE CT
3 GREAT WESTERN CT
4 LOBB CT
5 COUNTY CRES
6 MILLBROOK CL
7 ALINGTON CL

B2
1 ALDERNEY FLATS
2 KENCOURT CL
3 WESTMINSTER CT
4 WOTTON ELMS CT
5 BRADFORD RD

119
128

127
173

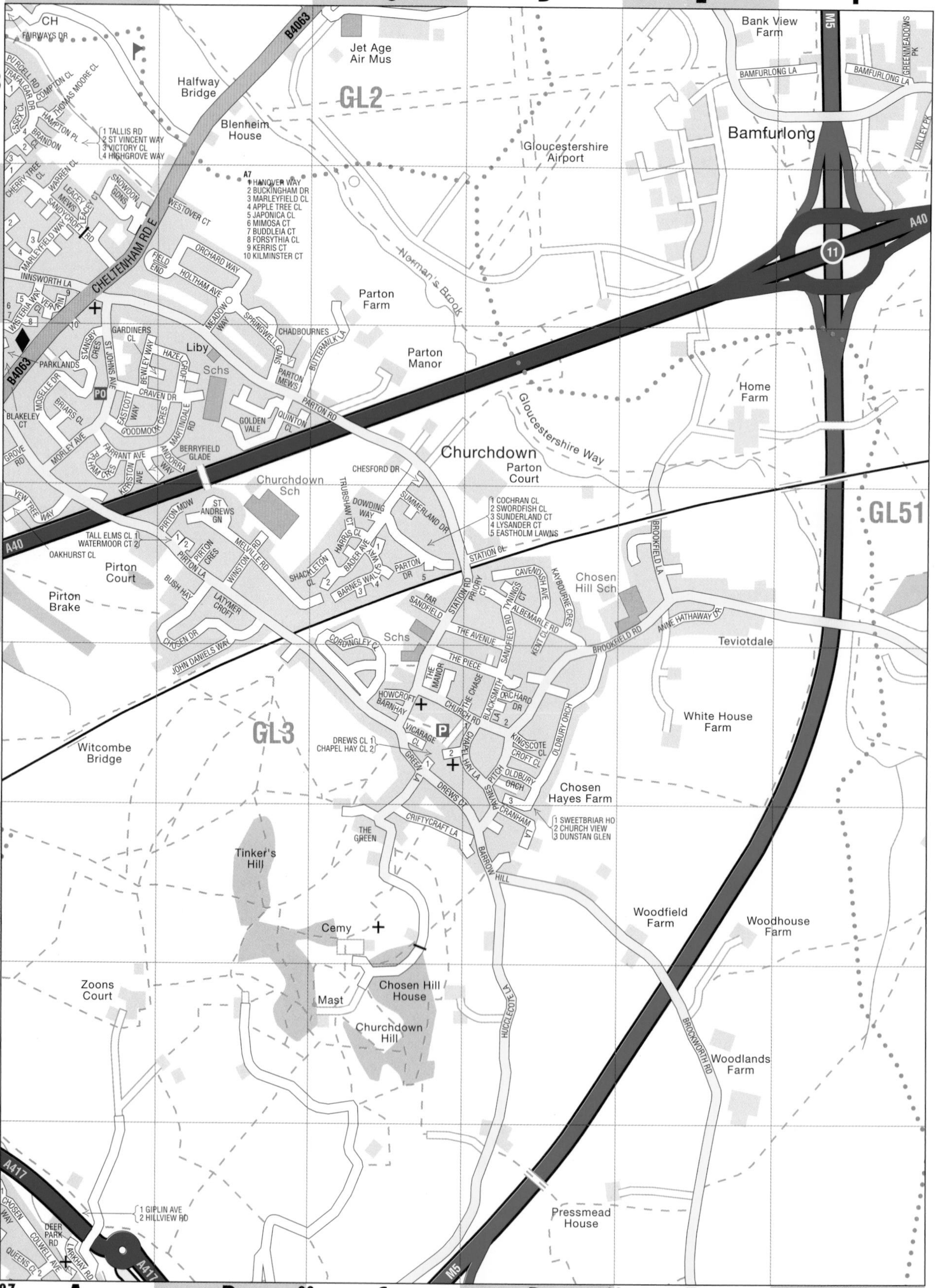

127
120

F7
1 DERWENT WLK
2 BRONTE CL
3 DEANS CT
4 MANSE GDNS
5 BELWORTH CT
6 BELWORTH DR
7 MORRIS CT
8 BROOK HO

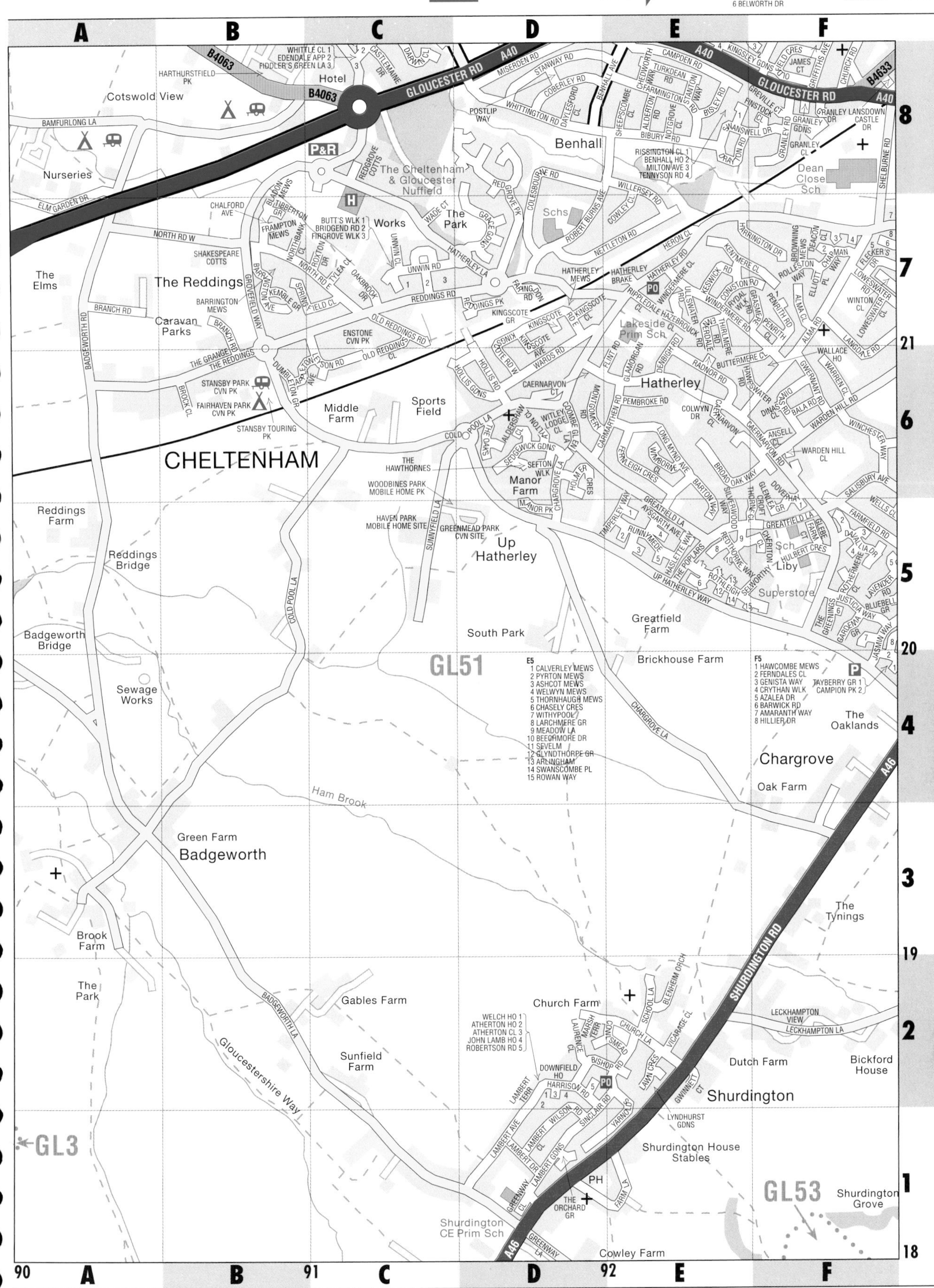

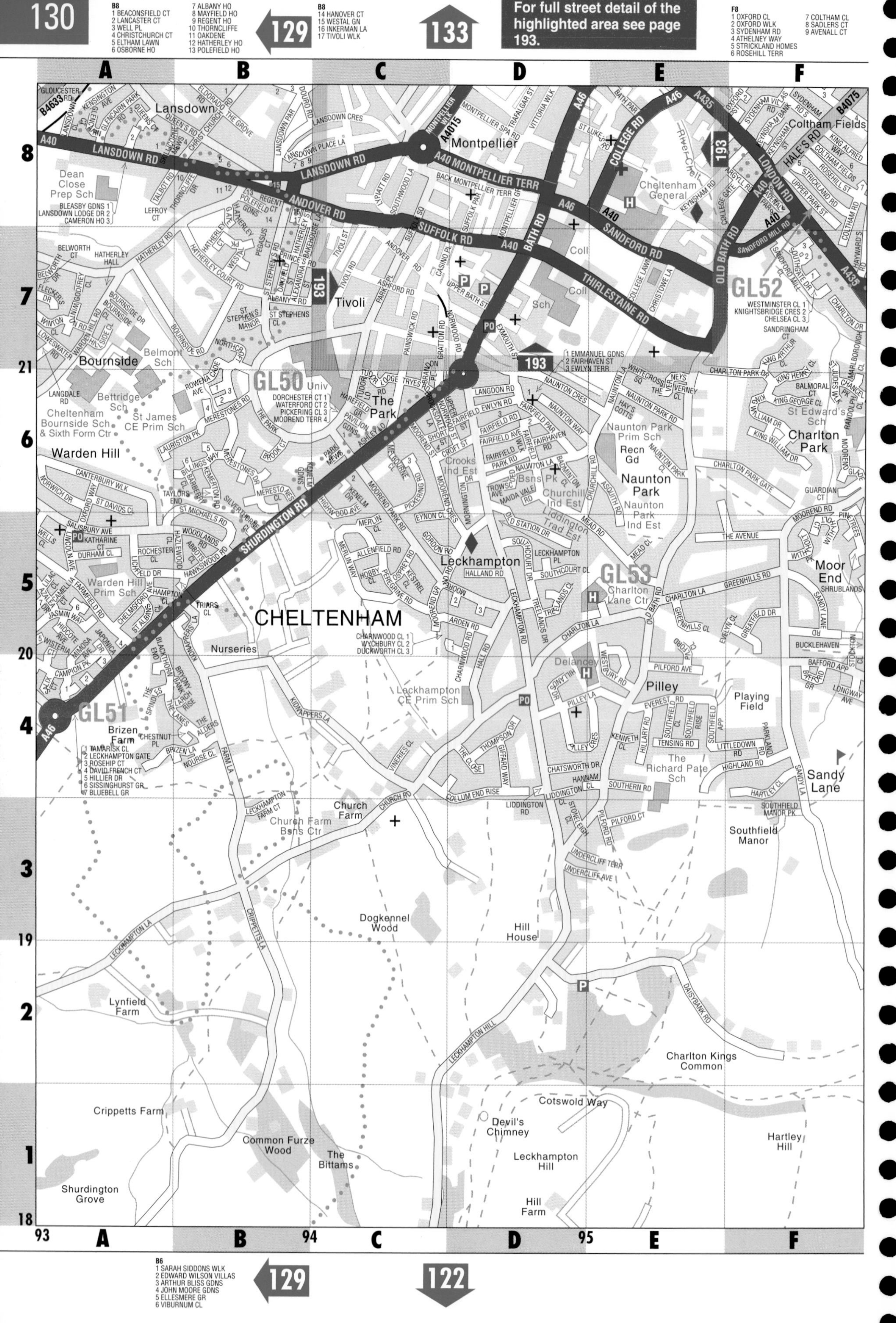
130
B8
1 BEACONSFIELD CT
2 LANCASTER CT
3 WELL PL
4 CHRISTCHURCH CT
5 ELTHAM LAWN
6 OSBORNE HO
7 ALBANY HO
8 MAYFIELD HO
9 REGENT HO
10 THORNCLIFFE
11 OAKDENE
12 HATHERLEY HO
13 POLEFIELD HO
129
B8
14 HANOVER CT
15 WESTAL GN
16 INKERMAN LA
17 TIVOLI WLK
133
For full street detail of the highlighted area see page 193.
F8
1 OXFORD CL
2 OXFORD WLK
3 SYDENHAM RD
4 ATHELNEY WAY
5 STRICKLAND HOMES
6 ROSEHILL TERR
7 COLTHAM CL
8 SADLERS CT
9 AVENALL CT
A
B
C
D
E
F
8
7
21
6
5
20
4
3
19
2
1
18
93
94
95
Lansdown
LANSDOWN RD
Montpellier
MONTPELLIER TERR
Dean Close Prep Sch
Cheltenham General
COLLEGE RD
LONDON RD
HALE'S RD
Coltham Fields
ANDOVER RD
SUFFOLK RD
BATH RD
SANDFORD RD
THIRLESTAINE RD
OLD BATH RD
Tivoli
Coll
Sch
GL52
GL50
GL51
GL53
Bournside
Belmont Sch
Bettridge Sch
Cheltenham Bournside Sch & Sixth Form Ctr
St James CE Prim Sch
Warden Hill
Warden Hill Prim Sch
The Park
Univ
SHURDINGTON RD
Naunton Park Prim Sch
Recn Gd
Naunton Park
Naunton Park Ind Est
St Edward's Sch
Charlton Park
Crooks Ind Est
Bsns Pk
Churchill Ind Est
Liddington Trad Est
Leckhampton
CHELTENHAM
Charlton Lane Ctr
CHARLTON LA
Moor End
Nurseries
Delancey
Pilley
Playing Field
Leckhampton CE Prim Sch
Brizen Farm
The Richard Pate Sch
Sandy Lane
Southfield Manor
Church Farm
Church Farm Bsns Ctr
Dogkennel Wood
Hill House
Lynfield Farm
Charlton Kings Common
Cotswold Way
Devil's Chimney
Leckhampton Hill
Hartley Hill
Crippetts Farm
Common Furze Wood
The Bittams
Shurdington Grove
Hill Farm
LECKHAMPTON RD
LECKHAMPTON HILL
DAISYBANK RD
CRIPPETTS LA
LECKHAMPTON LA
B6
1 SARAH SIDDONS WLK
2 EDWARD WILSON VILLAS
3 ARTHUR BLISS GDNS
4 JOHN MOORE GDNS
5 ELLESMERE GR
6 VIBURNUM CL
129
122

B6
1 GROVELANDS CL
2 PORTURET WAY
3 SCHOOL ROAD FLATS
4 THE OLD SCHOOL MEWS
5 REABURN CL
6 COURTFIELD DR

134
166

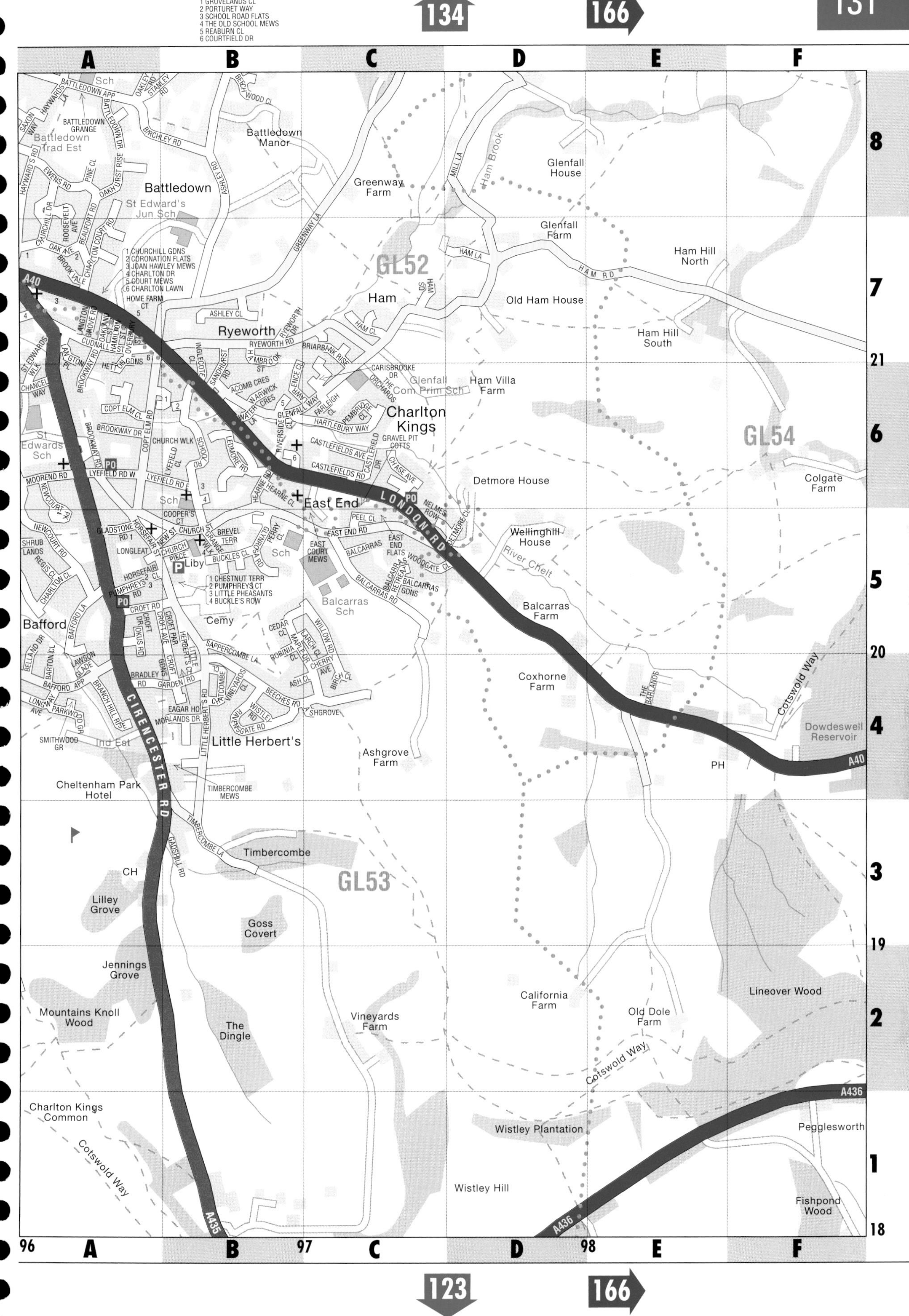

123
166

173 136

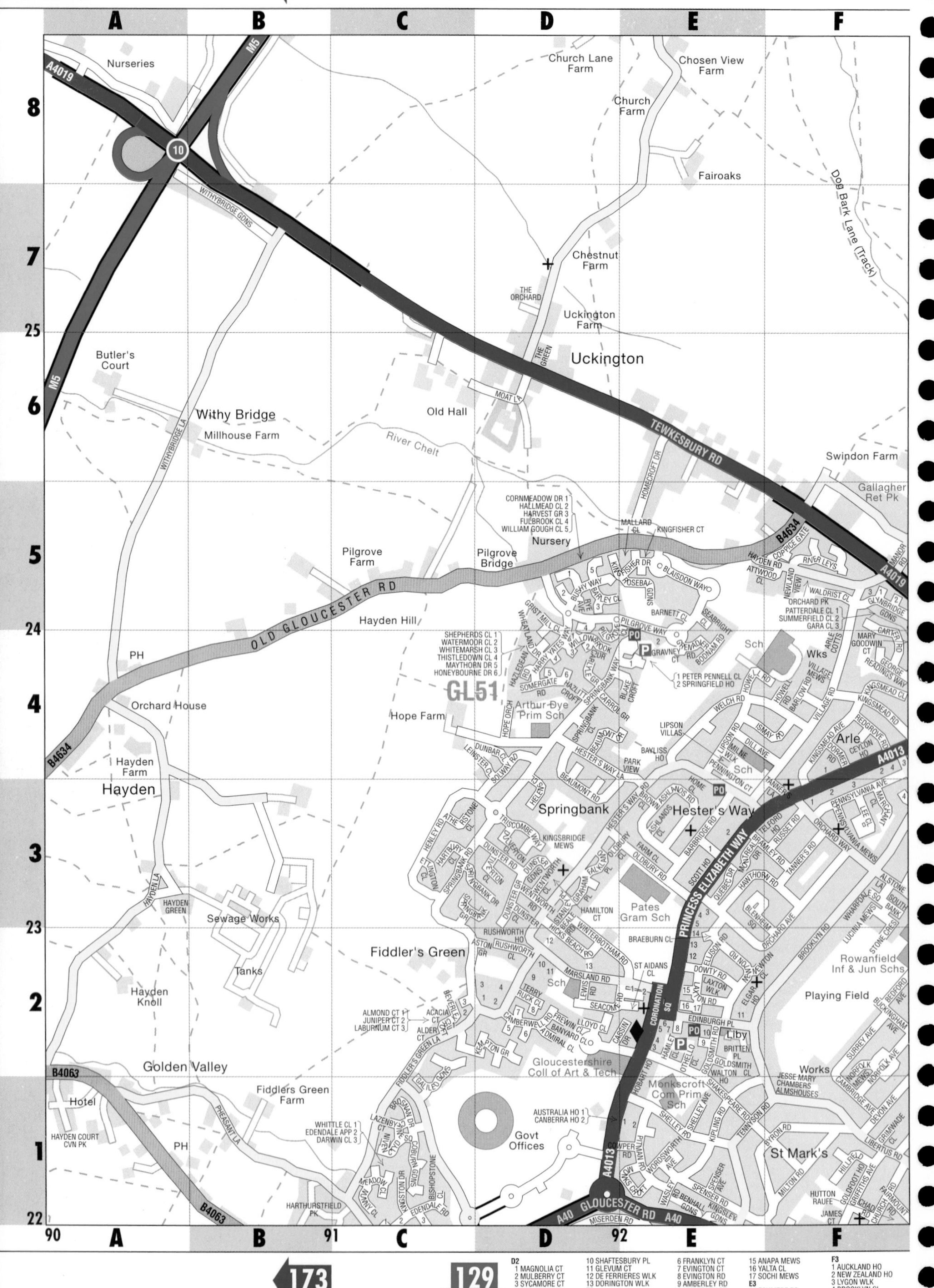

D2
1 MAGNOLIA CT
2 MULBERRY CT
3 SYCAMORE CT
4 REDWOOD CT
5 PEACOCK CL
6 SWALLOWTAIL CL
7 EMPEROR CL
8 HEAPEY CL
9 ROYAL CT
10 SHAFTESBURY PL
11 GLEVUM CT
12 DE FERRIERES WLK
13 DORINGTON WLK

E2
1 PAKISTAN HO
2 INDIA HO
3 TYLER CT
4 TASMANIA HO
5 GRESHAM CT
6 FRANKLYN CT
7 EVINGTON CT
8 EVINGTON RD
9 AMBERLEY RD
10 AMBERLEY CT
11 COATES HO
12 ARUNDEL HO
13 CHEPSTOW HO
14 EASTNOR HO
15 ANAPA MEWS
16 YALTA CL
17 SOCHI MEWS

E3
1 LECHMERE RD
2 EDWARD WILSON HO
3 KENILWORTH HO
4 BERKELEY HO
5 SUDELEY HO

F3
1 AUCKLAND HO
2 NEW ZEALAND HO
3 LYGON WLK
4 BROOKLYN CL

F4
1 RHODESIA HO
2 SOUTH AFRICA HO
3 GREVIL RD
4 DURBAN HO

173 129

For full street detail of the highlighted area see page 193.

137

134

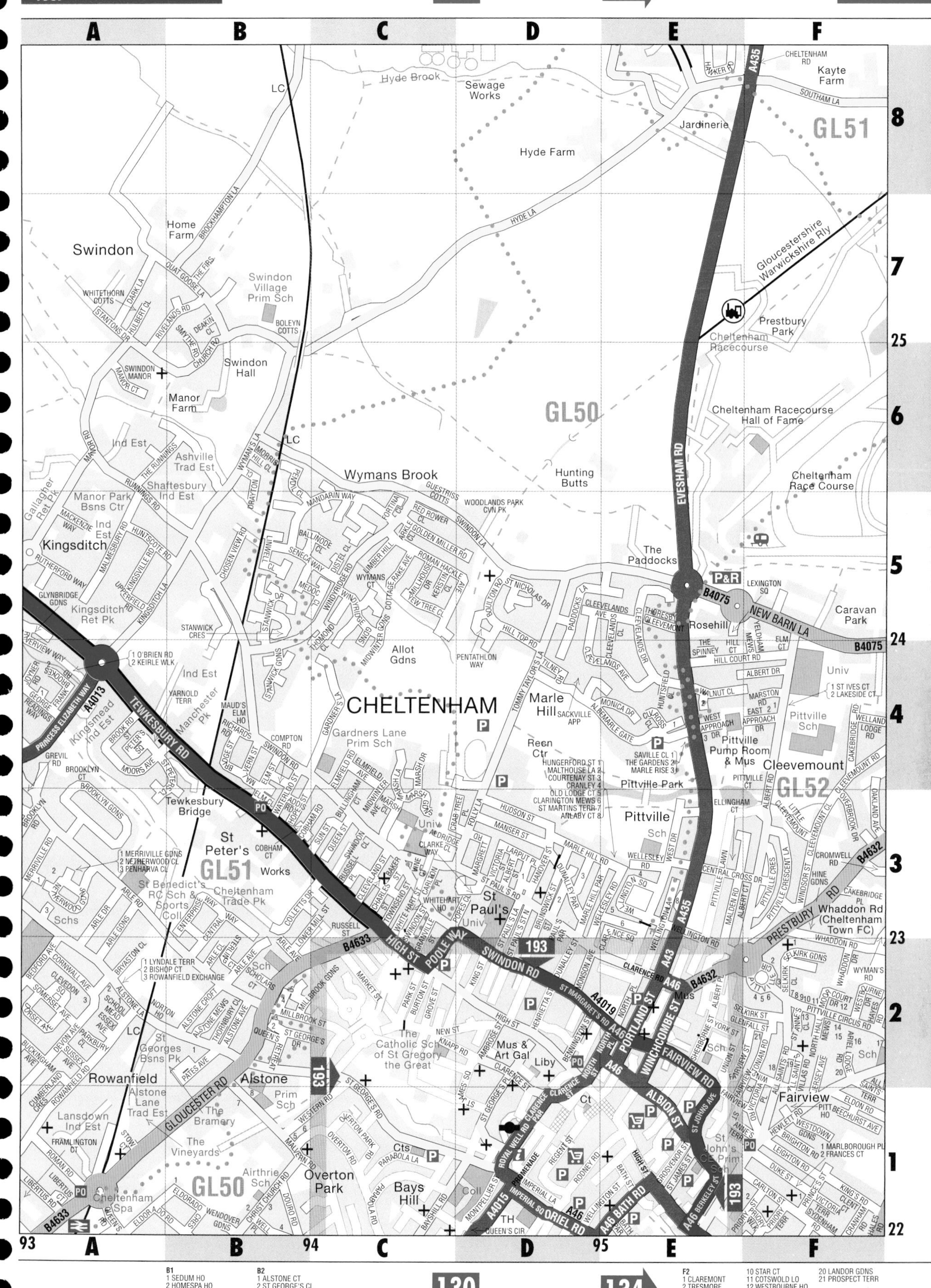

B1
1 SEDUM HO
2 HOMESPA HO
3 CHARLOTTE ROSE HO
4 RUTLAND CT
5 WINCHESTER HO
6 WESTERN CT
7 CHRIST CHURCH VILLAS
8 CHRIST CHURCH TERR

B2
1 ALSTONE CT
2 ST GEORGE'S CL
3 ST JOHN'S CT
4 OLD MILLBROOK TERR
5 GLOUCESTER COTTS

130

134

F2
1 CLAREMONT
2 TRESMORE
3 SELKIRK CT
4 TERHILL
5 PRIORS LO
6 HEATH LO
7 BERKELEY HO
8 ASKHAM CT
9 FAIRHAVENS CT
10 STAR CT
11 COTSWOLD LO
12 WESTBOURNE HO
13 ST ANNE'S
14 IRVING HO
15 GODWIN CL
16 THE GRYPHONS
17 BYRON CT
18 CADOGAN HO
19 ALL SAINT'S CT
20 LANDOR GDNS
21 PROSPECT TERR

133
138

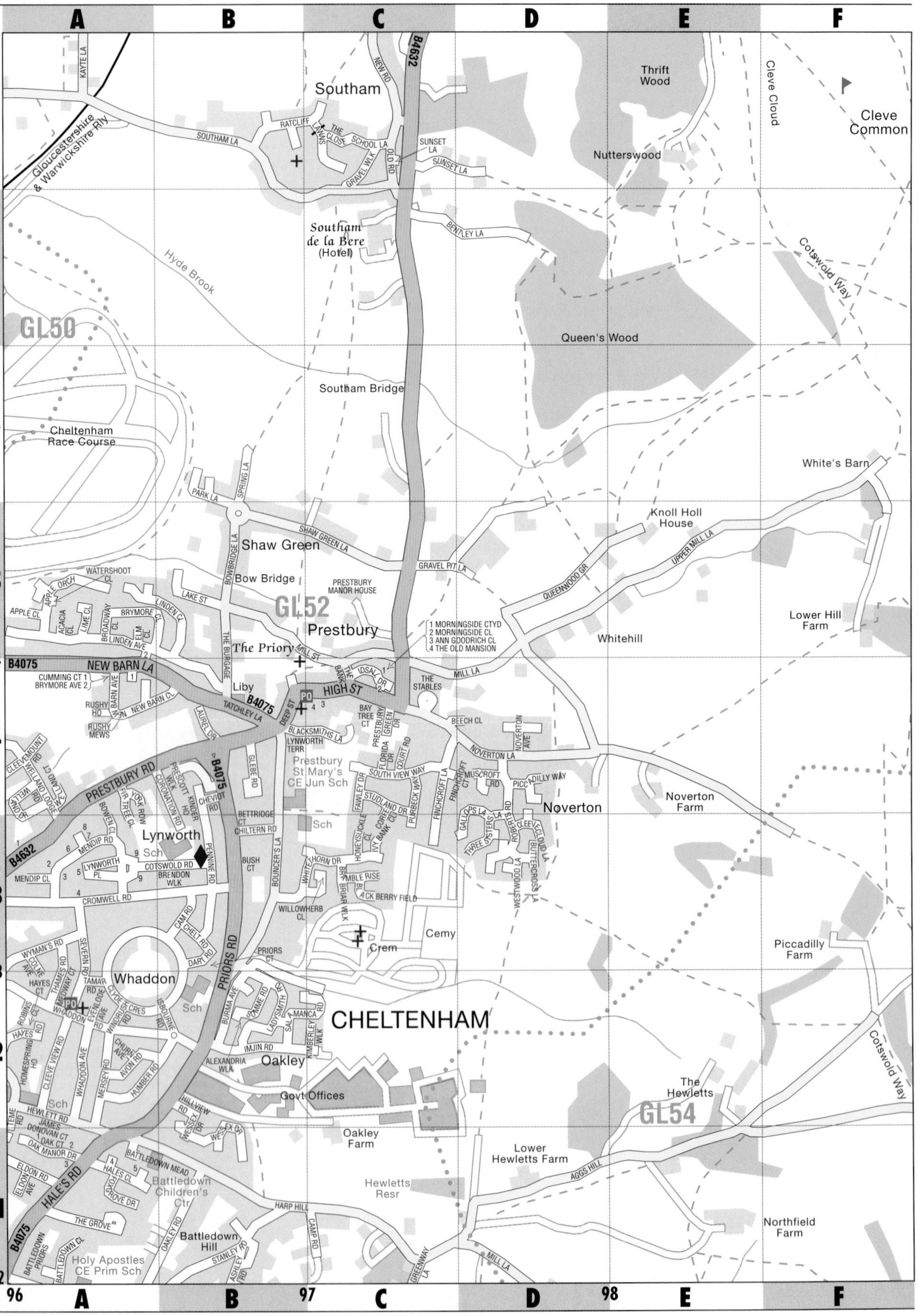

A B C D E F

8
Southam
Thrift Wood
Cleve Cloud
Cleve Common
KAYTE LA
NEW RD
B4632
RATCLIFF
LAWNS
THE CLOSE
SCHOOL LA
SOUTHAM LA
Gloucestershire & Warwickshire Rly
SUNSET LA
OLD RD
GRAVEL WLK
Nutterswood

7
Southam de la Bere (Hotel)
BENTLEY LA
Hyde Brook
Cotswold Way
GL50
Queen's Wood

25
Southam Bridge

6
Cheltenham Race Course
White's Barn
PARK LA
SPRING LA
Knoll Holl House
SHAW GREEN LA
Shaw Green
UPPER MILL LA
GRAVEL PIT LA
QUEENWOOD GR

5
WATERSHOOT CL
APPLE ORCH
Bow Bridge
PRESTBURY MANOR HOUSE
APPLE CL
ACACIA CL
LIME CL
BROADWAY
BRYMORE CL
ELM CL
LINDEN CL
LAKE ST
BOWBRIDGE LA
GL52
Prestbury
LINDEN AVE
Lower Hill Farm
1 MORNINGSIDE CTYD
2 MORNINGSIDE CL
3 ANN GOODRICH CL
4 THE OLD MANSION
Whitehill
The Priory
MILL ST
THE BURGAGE

24
B4075
NEW BARN LA
CUMMING CT 1
BRYMORE AVE 2
MILL LA
THE BANK
LINDSAY DR
THE STABLES
Liby
HIGH ST
RUSHY HO
RUSHY MEWS
NEW BARN CL
TATCHLEY LA
DEEP ST
PO
BAY TREE CT
PRESTBURY GREEN DR
BEECH CL
NOVERTON AVE

4
LAUREL DR
BLACKSMITHS LA
LYNWORTH TERR
NOVERTON LA
CLEEVEMOUNT
WELLAND LODGE
WELLAND CT
PRESTBURY RD
B4075
GLEBE RD
Prestbury St Mary's CE Jun Sch
FLORIDA DR
COURT RD
SOUTH VIEW WAY
FINCHCROFT LA
FINCHCROFT CT
MUSCROFT RD
PICCADILLY WAY
Noverton Farm
PRESCOTT WLK
CORONATION RD
KINDER HO
CHEVIOT RD
YORK ROW
FIR TREE CL
BOWEN CL
FAWLEY DR
STUDLAND DR
PURBECK WAY
Noverton
BETTRIDGE CT
CHILTERN RD
HONEYSUCKLE CL
CORFE CL
IVY BANK CL
GALLOPS LA
ROBERTS RD
CLEEVECLOUD LA
Sch
THREE SISTERS LA
Lynworth
Sch
MENDIP RD
PENNINE RD
B4632
LYNWORTH PL
COTSWOLD RD
BRENDON WLK
BUSH CT
WHITETHORN DR
BRAMBLE RISE
BRIAR WLK
BLACKBERRY FIELD
WESTWOOD LA
BUTTERCROSS LA
MENDIP CL

3
CROMWELL RD
BOUNCER'S LA
WILLOWHERB CL
CAM RD
CHELT RD
Cemy
Crem
Piccadilly Farm
WYMAN'S RD
COLNE AVE
SEVERN RD
PRIORS CT
DART RD
PRIORS RD

23
Whaddon
THAMES RD
MEDWAY CT
HAYES CT
TAMAR RD
CLYDE CRES
WINDRUSH CRES
ISBOURNE RD
Sch
BURMA AVE
SOMME RD
LADYSMITH RD
SALAMANCA RD
KIMBERLEY WLK
CHELTENHAM
ROBINS CL
PO
WHADDON RD
EVENLODE AVE
HAYES RD
CHURN AVE
AVON RD
IMJIN RD

2
HOMESPRING HO
CLEEVE VIEW RD
WHADDON AVE
MERSEY RD
HUMBER RD
ALEXANDRIA WLK
Oakley
Cotswold Way
Sch
Govt Offices
The Hewletts
HEWLETT RD
HILLVIEW RD
WESSEX DR
WESSEX DR
GL54
JAMES DONOVAN CT
OAK CT
OAK MANOR DR
Oakley Farm
BATTLEDOWN MEAD
Lower Hewletts Farm
HALES CL
AGGS HILL
ELDON RD
ELDON AVE
HALE'S RD
Battledown Children's Ctr
OXFORD GROVE DR
Hewletts Resr

1
B4075
THE GROVE
HARP HILL
CAMP RD
Northfield Farm
BATTLEDOWN PRIORS
BATTLEDOWN CL
OAKLEY RD
Battledown Hill
Holy Apostles CE Prim Sch
STANLEY RD
ASHLEY RD
GREENWAY LA
MILL LA

22

96 A B 97 C D 98 E F

A1
1 HOPWOOD GR
2 OAKDENE
3 OAK MANOR
4 RICHMOND DR
5 BARN FIELD

A3
1 CHELBURY MEWS
2 THE CONIFERS
3 FOSTER CT
4 NASEBY HO
5 LYNWORTH CT
6 GEORGE NAISEY HO
7 MENDIP HO
8 HANNAH BOOTE HO
9 LYNWORTH EXCHANGE

133
131

139
174

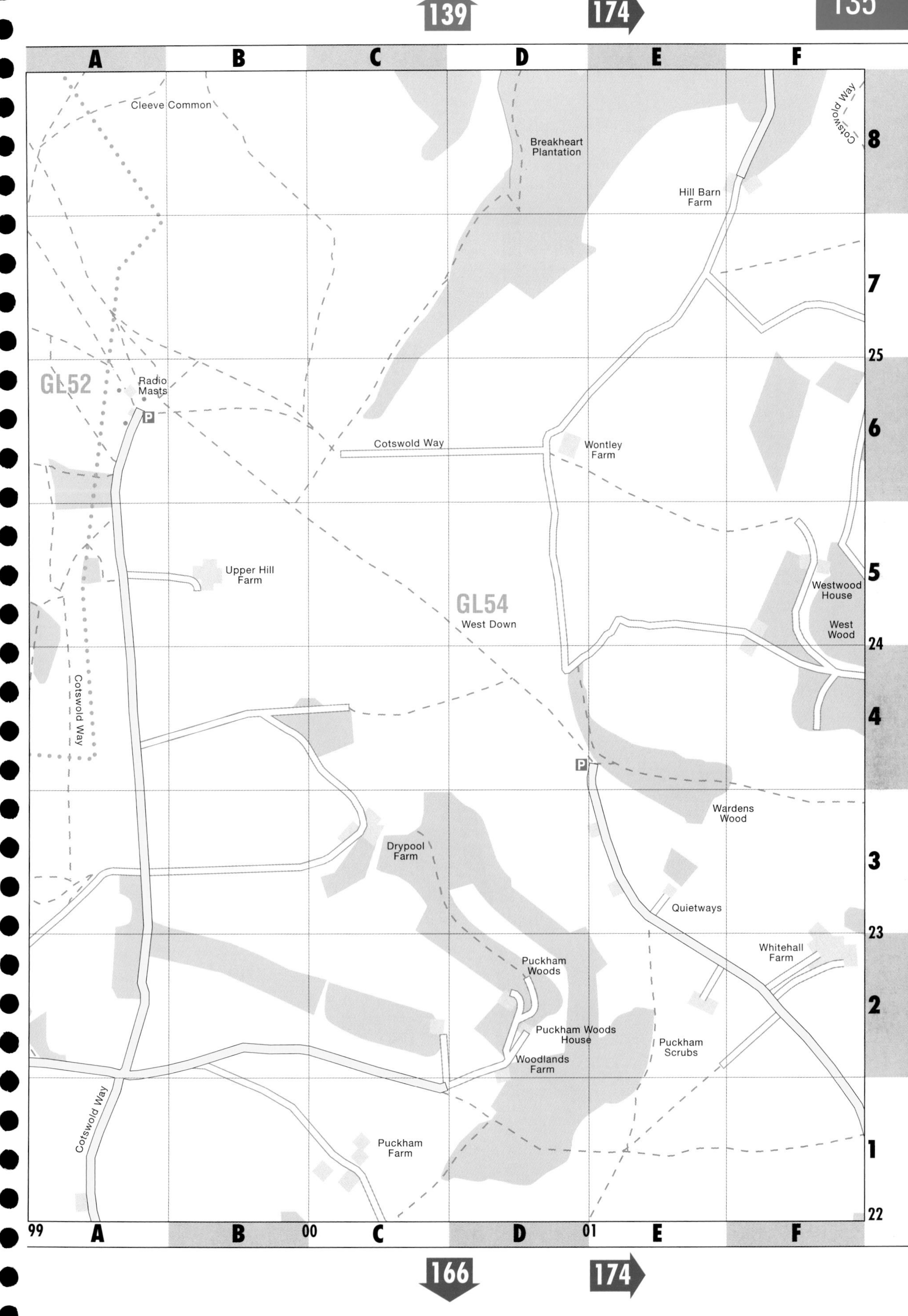

166
174

173
182

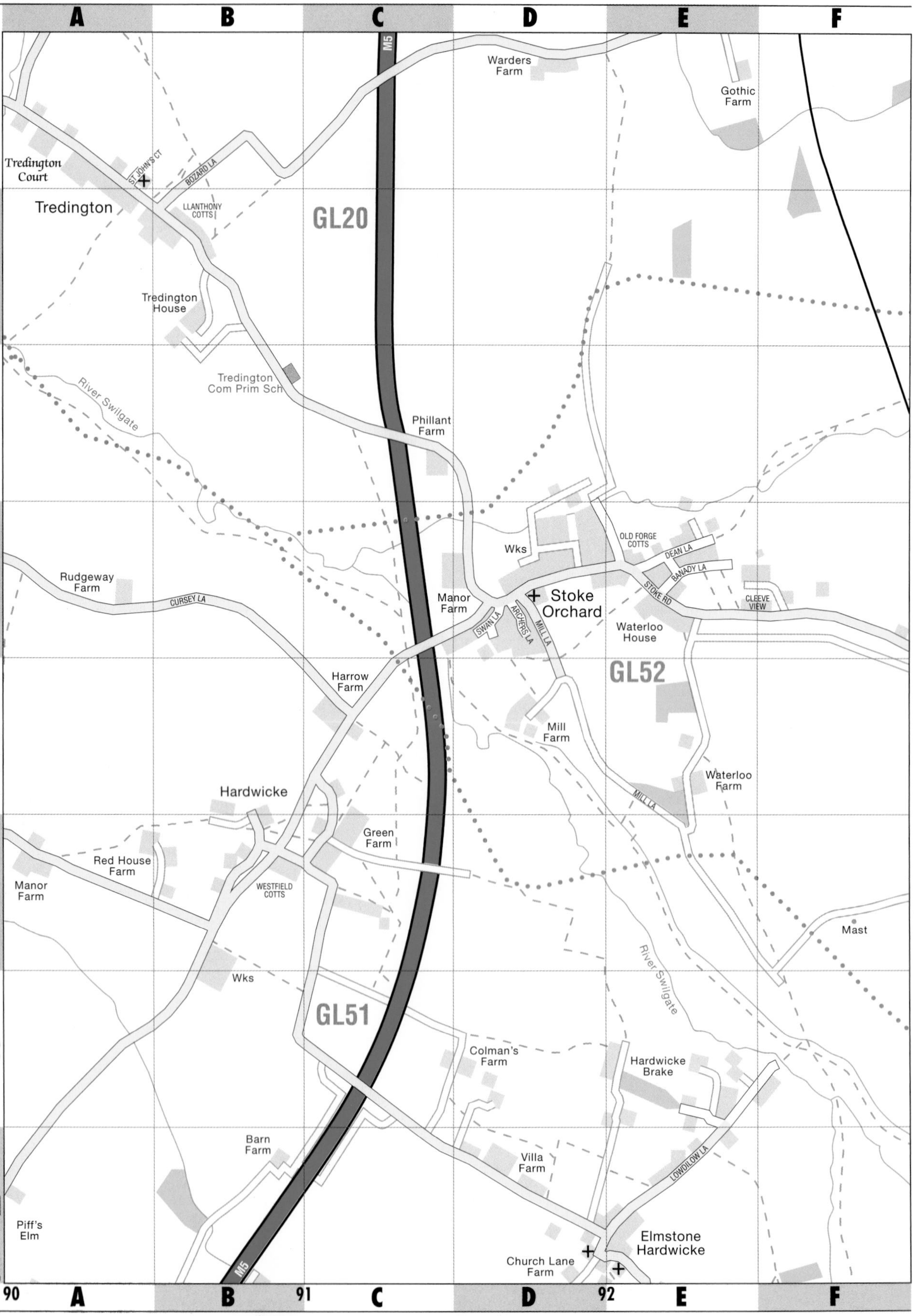

173
132

182
138

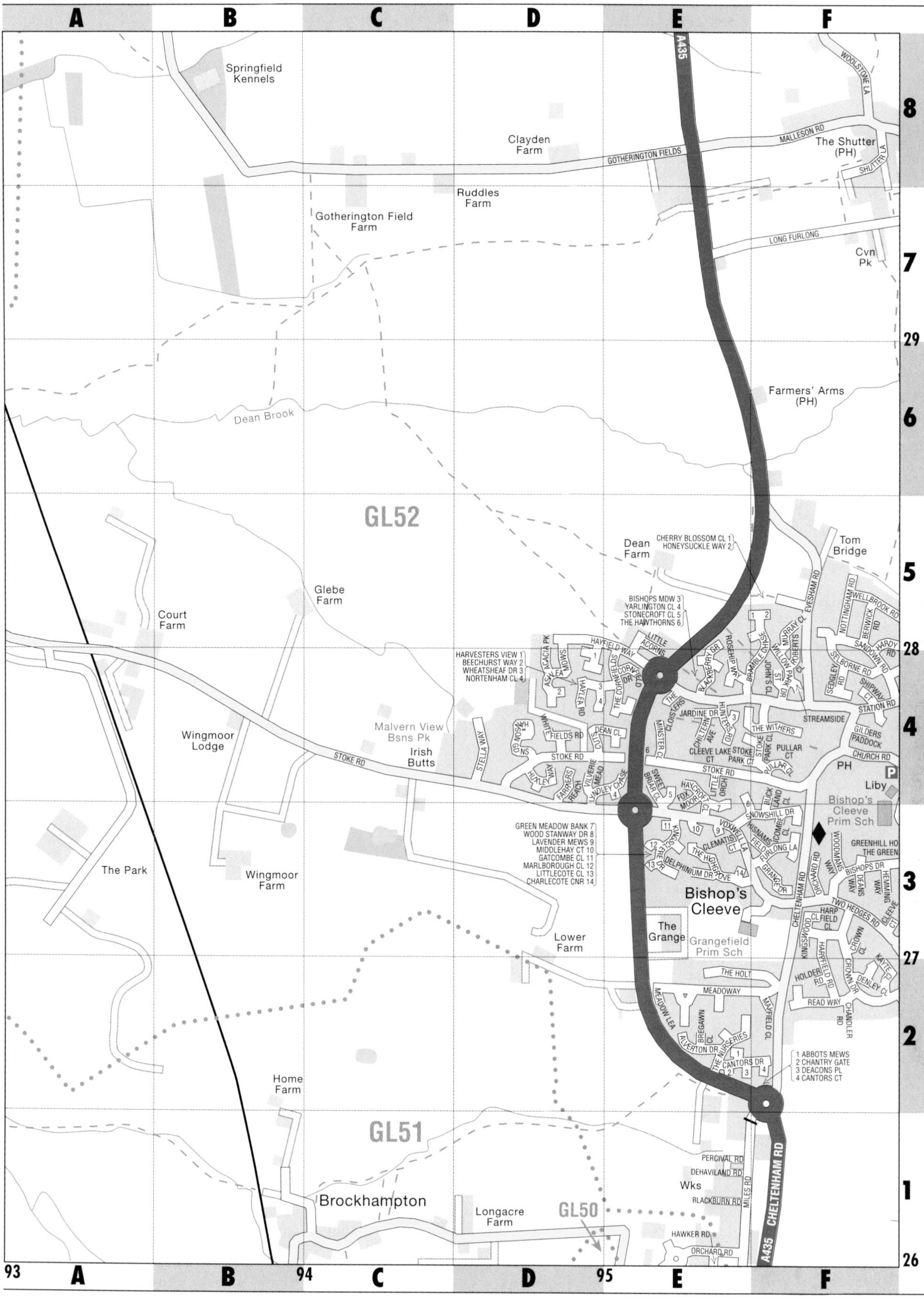
A
B
C
D
E
F
8
7
29
6
5
28
4
3
27
2
1
26
93
94
95
A435
Springfield Kennels
WOOLSTONE LA
Clayden Farm
MALLESON RD
The Shutter (PH)
GOTHERINGTON FIELDS
SHUTTER LA
Ruddles Farm
Gotherington Field Farm
LONG FURLONG
Cvn Pk
Farmers' Arms (PH)
Dean Brook
GL52
Dean Farm
CHERRY BLOSSOM CL 1
HONEYSUCKLE WAY 2
Tom Bridge
EVESHAM RD
NOTTINGHAM RD
WELLBROOK RD
Glebe Farm
Court Farm
BISHOPS MDW 3
YARLINGTON CL 4
STONECROFT CL 5
THE HAWTHORNS 6
HARVESTERS VIEW 1
BEECHURST WAY 2
WHEATSHEAF DR 3
NORTENHAM CL 4
HAYFIELD WAY
LITTLE ACORNS
ACACIA PK
HAYLEA RD
THE CORNFIELDS
CORNFIELD DR
ROSEHIP WAY
BLACKBERRY GR
BRAMBLE CHASE
JOHN'S CL
WILLOW PARK DR
MURRAY CL
ROBERTS CL
BERWICK RD
HARDY RD
SANDOWN RD
SELBORNE RD
SEDGLEY RD
SHIPWAY CT
STATION RD
Wingmoor Lodge
Malvern View Bsns Pk
Irish Butts
STOKE RD
STELLA WAY
FIELDS RD
DEAN CL
THE CLOISTERS
MINSTER CL
JARDINE DR
HUNTERS RD
CHILTERN AVE
CLEEVE LAKE CT
STOKE PARK CT
THE WITHERS
STREAMSIDE
GILDERS PADDOCK
CHURCH RD
PULLAR CT
PULLAR CL
PH
Liby
P
HUXLEY WAY
FARRIERS REACH
VILVERIE MEAD
LYNDLEY CHASE
SWEET BRIAR CL
HAYCROFT DR
FOX MOOR
LITTLE ORCH
BUCKLAND CL
SNOWSHILL DR
Bishop's Cleeve Prim Sch
GREEN MEADOW BANK 7
WOOD STANWAY DR 8
LAVENDER MEWS 9
MIDDLEHAY CT 10
GATCOMBE CL 11
MARLBOROUGH CL 12
LITTLECOTE CL 13
CHARLECOTE CNR 14
CLEMATIS CT
THE HIGHGROVE
DELPHINIUM DR
FURLONG LA
GRANGE DR
ORCHARD RD
WOODMANS WAY
GREENHILL HO
THE GREEN
BISHOPS DR
DEANS WAY
HEMMING WAY
The Park
Wingmoor Farm
Bishop's Cleeve
CHELTENHAM RD
TWO HEDGES RD
HARP CL
FIELD CL
KINGSWOOD CL
CROWN CL
The Grange
Grangefield Prim Sch
Lower Farm
THE HOLT
HOLDER RD
HARFIELD RD
CROMWELL DR
DENLEY CL
MEADOWAY
MEADOW LEA
BREGAWN CL
MAYFIELD CL
READ WAY
CHANDLER RD
ALVERTON DR
THE NURSERIES
CANTORS DR
1 ABBOTS MEWS
2 CHANTRY GATE
3 DEACONS PL
4 CANTORS CT
Home Farm
GL51
PERCIVAL RD
DEHAVILAND RD
Wks
MILES RD
BLACKBURN RD
Brockhampton
Longacre Farm
GL50
HAWKER RD
ORCHARD RD
CHELTENHAM RD

133
138

A B C D E F

8
7
29
6
5
28
4
3
27
2
1
26

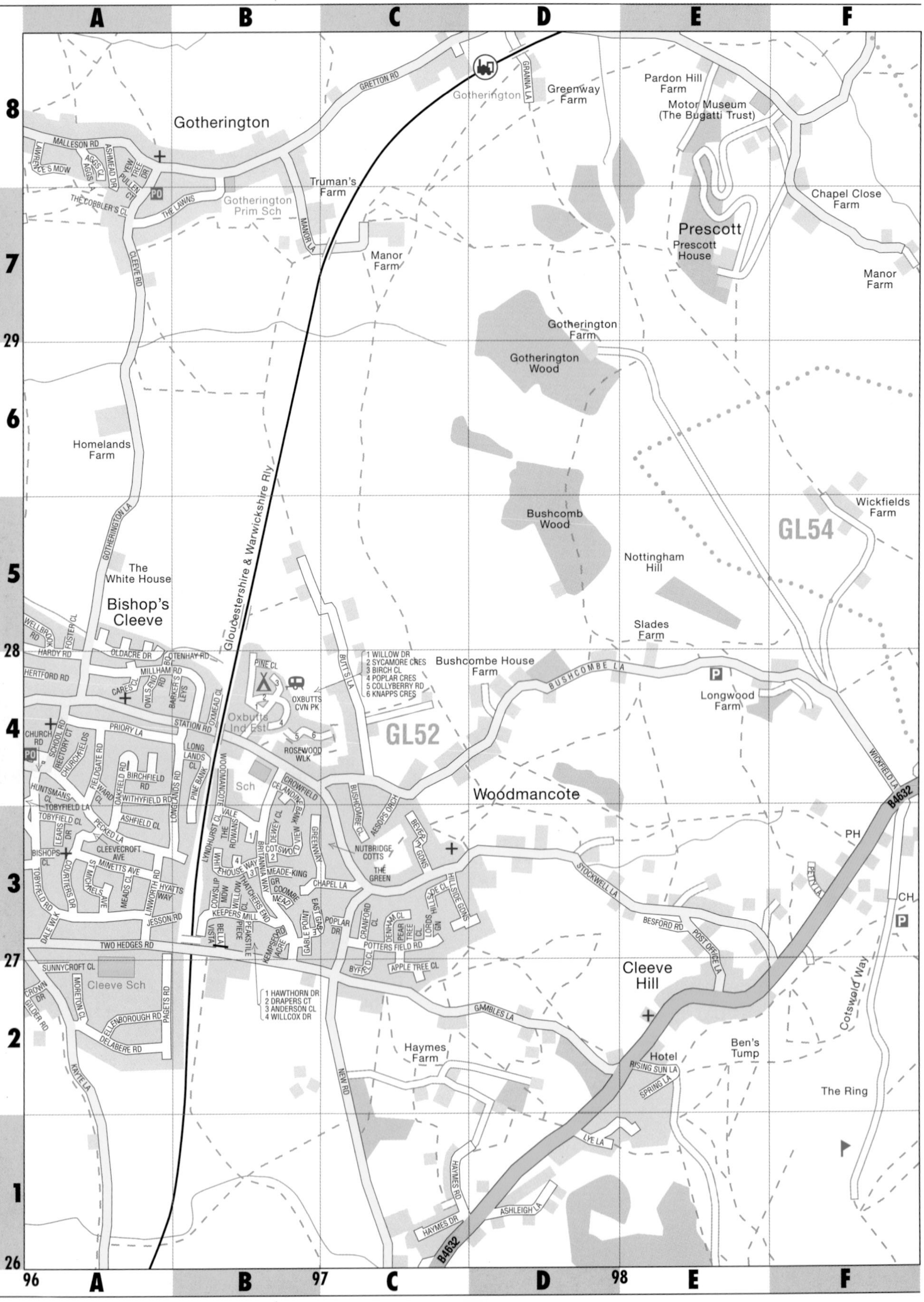

Gotherington
Gotherington
Greenway Farm
Pardon Hill Farm
Motor Museum (The Bugatti Trust)
GRETTON RD
GRANNA LA
MALLESON RD
LAWRENCE'S MDW
AGGS CL
AGGS LA
ASHMEAD DR
YEW TREE DR
PULLEN CT
PO
THE LAWNS
THE COBBLER'S CL
Gotherington Prim Sch
Truman's Farm
MANOR LA
Manor Farm
Prescott
Prescott House
Chapel Close Farm
Manor Farm
CLEEVE RD
Gotherington Farm
Gotherington Wood
Homelands Farm
Bushcomb Wood
Wickfields Farm
GL54
Nottingham Hill
GOTHERINGTON LA
Gloucestershire & Warwickshire Rly
The White House
Bishop's Cleeve
Slades Farm
WELLBROOK RD
FOSTER CL
HARDY RD
OLDACRE DR
OTENHAY RD
HERTFORD RD
MILLHAM RD
CARES CL
OWLSEND RD
BARKER'S LEYS
OXMEAD CL
STATION RD
PINE CL
OXBUTTS CVN PK
Oxbutts Ind Est
BUTT'S LA
1 WILLOW DR
2 SYCAMORE CRES
3 BIRCH CL
4 POPLAR CRES
5 COLLYBERRY RD
6 KNAPPS CRES
Bushcombe House Farm
BUSHCOMBE LA
P
Longwood Farm
GL52
CHURCH RD
SCHOOL RD
RECTORY CT
CHURCHFIELDS
PRIORY LA
LONG LANDS CL
ROSEWOOD WLK
PO
FIELDGATE RD
BIRCHFIELD RD
OAKFIELD RD
WITHYFIELD RD
LONGLANDS RD
PINE BANK
WOODMANCOTE VALE
Sch
CROWFIELD
CELANDINE BANK
BUSHCOMBE CL
AESOPS ORCH
WICKFIELD LA
B4632
Woodmancote
HUNTSMANS CL
TOBYFIELD LA
TOBYFIELD CL
LEARS DR
WARD
PECKED LA
ASHFIELD CL
LYNDHURST CL
THE ROWANS
DEWEY CL
COTSWOLD VIEW
GREENWAY
BELVEDERE GDNS
PH
BISHOPS CL
CLEEVECROFT AVE
MINETTS AVE
ST MICHAELS AVE
MEADS CL
LINWORTH RD
HYATTS WAY
WHITEHOUSE WAY
BRITANNIA WAY
MEADE-KING GR
COOMBE MEAD
NUTBRIDGE COTTS
THE GREEN
CHAPEL LA
STOCKWELL LA
COURTIERS DR
TOBYFIELD RD
COWSLIP MDW
KEEPERS MILL
WILLOW CL
THATCHERS END
PEAKSTILE PIECE
EAST GABLE
GABLE POINT
POPLAR DR
CRANFORD CL
DENHAM CL
PEAR TREE CL
LORDS GN
HILLSIDE GDNS
BESFORD RD
POST OFFICE LA
CH
P
DALE WLK
JESSON RD
BELLA VISTA
KEMPSFORD ACRE
POTTERS FIELD RD
TWO HEDGES RD
BYFFORD CL
APPLE TREE CL
Cleeve Hill
SUNNYCROFT CL
Cleeve Sch
CROWN DR
MORETON CL
PAGETS RD
1 HAWTHORN DR
2 DRAPERS CT
3 ANDERSON CL
4 WILLCOX DR
GAMBLES LA
Cotswold Way
GILDER RD
ELLENBOROUGH RD
DELABERE RD
Haymes Farm
Hotel
RISING SUN LA
SPRING LA
Ben's Tump
KAYTE LA
NEW RD
The Ring
LYE LA
HAYMES RD
ASHLEIGH LA
HAYMES DR
B4632

96 A B 97 C D 98 E F

183
174

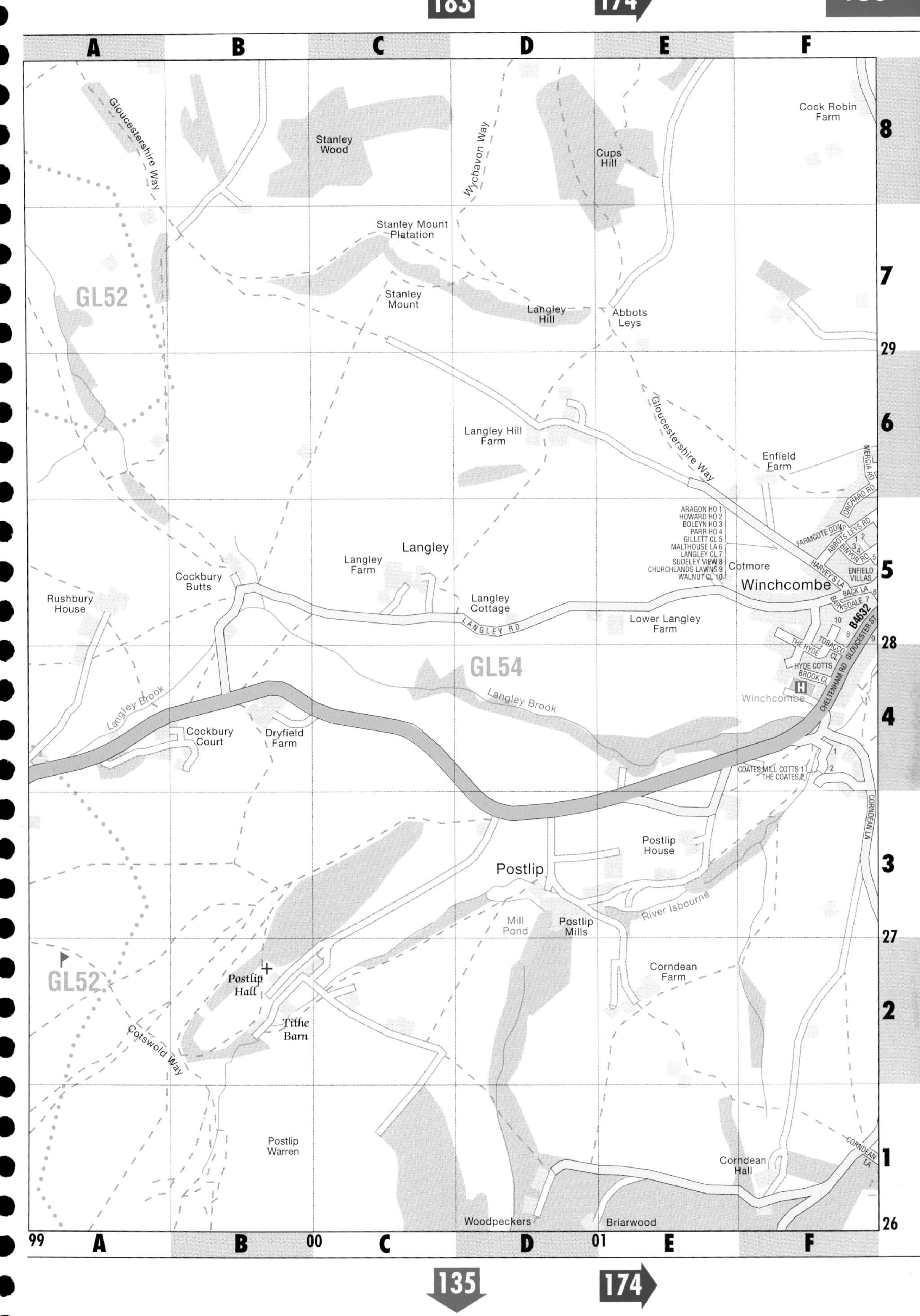

135
174

83

148

C5
1 CHEVIOT CL
2 SUFFOLK CL
3 SHEPHERDS MEAD
4 JACOBS CL
5 COTSWOLD CL
6 TALBOY'S WLK
7 BERKELEY WAY

Scale: 1¾ inches to 1 mile
0 ¼ ½ mile
0 250m 500m 750m 1 km

A B C D E F

Avening
ORCHARD FIELD
PO
HIGH ST
HAMPTON
FARM HILL
B4014
MAYS LA
Avening Court
WEST END
Avening Park
Mast
TETBURY HILL
STAR LA
1 NEW INN LA
2 POINT RD
3 POUND HILL
4 THE GROVE
5 MILL LA
BA13
GL7
8
97
Macmillan Way
Longtree Barn
Star Farm
RIDGE'S LA
Grove Farm
Wickfield Wood
Trull House
TRULL COTTS
7
A433
96
Troublehouse Covert
Summerwell Farm
Warren Farm
Holt Farm
OXLEAZE RD
CULKERTON
Colly Farm
PH
Purley Covert
6
Wr Twr
Tetbury Upton
Lodge Farm
Lowfield Farm
Chavenage House
95
Upton Grove
UPTON GDNS 1
GROVE GDNS 2
CORONATION RD 3
HIGHFIELD RD 4
BLIND LA
Broadfield Farm
5
Hermit's Cave
Highfield Farm
Sch
LONGTREE CL
WOODWARD CL
LOWFIELD RD
NORTHLANDS WAY
RYLAND CL
LONDON RD
ILSOM COTTS
NEWNTON HILL
WEBB RD
ROMNEY
CONYGAR RD
ST MARY'S RD
Ind Est
BRAYBROOKE CL
94
Great Larkhill Farm
HAMPTON ST
CHAVENAGE LA
Sch
NORTHFIELD RD
NORTHLEAZE
CIRENCESTER RD
Northfield
A4135
NEWLEAZE GDNS
QUAIL MDWS
Ind Est
SPRINGFIELDS
4
GL8
Charlton House
LINFOOT RD
SHERWOOD RD
Mus
HERD LA
COMBE HO
Addy's Firs
LONG ST
KING ST
CHANTRY CT
CHARLTON RD
NEW CHURCH ST
TETBURY
Monarch's Way
Boldridge Farm
93
COTTON'S LA 1
BLACK HORSE HILL 2
THE BERRELLS 3
BERRELLS RD 4
SOUTHFIELD 5
CUTWELL
WEST ST
CHURCH ST
PO
Tetbury
H
FOX HILL
NEWNTON RD
The Folly Farm
Church Farm
HOOKSHOUSE LA
THE GREEN
Ind Est
CRUDWELL LA
Ring & Bailey
3
GRANGE LA
Long Newnton
LONG FURLONG LA
Slads Farm
GRANGE COTTS
The Priory
92
PUMP LA
POWELLS WAY
THE DRIVE
Newnton Farm
Elmestree House
Close Farm
BATH RD
Highgrove
Oak Covert
2
HIGHGROVE COTTS
Manor House
Thorn Covert
Doughton
MEMORIAL COTTS
Shipton Wood
Merchants Farm
91
BARBER LA
A433
Estcourt House
Gilboa Farm
SN16
1
Manor Farm
Bell Farm
Eagle Lodge
Tanner's
WHITEHOUSE LA
B4014
90

Wiltshire STREET ATLAS

87 A 88 B 89 C 90 D 91 E 92 F

71

59

B4
1 WISTARIA RD
2 WHEAT HILL
3 WINDSOR RD
4 OXLEAZE CL
5 ELIZABETH GDNS
6 CHESTNUT CL
7 OXLEAZE RD
8 FIVE TREES CL
9 MALTHOUSE WLK
10 ALEXANDER GDNS
11 COURT FIELD
12 PRINCE CT
13 HOLDER CL
14 CLOSE GDNS
15 WARNS CT
16 OLD BREWERY LA
17 PRINCE OF WALES ROW
18 THE OLD SCHOOL CT

C4
1 CLARRIE RD
2 COOKSPOOL
3 BARTLEY CROFT
4 THE RETREAT
5 BEECH TREE GDNS
6 CHERRY ORCHARD RD
7 PRIORY WAY
8 PARK CL
9 THE DAMSELLS
10 LONDON RD
11 ECCLES CT
12 CHIPPING CT
13 GUMSTOOL HILL
14 MARKET PL
15 SILVER ST

Scale: 1¾ inches to 1 mile

149
142

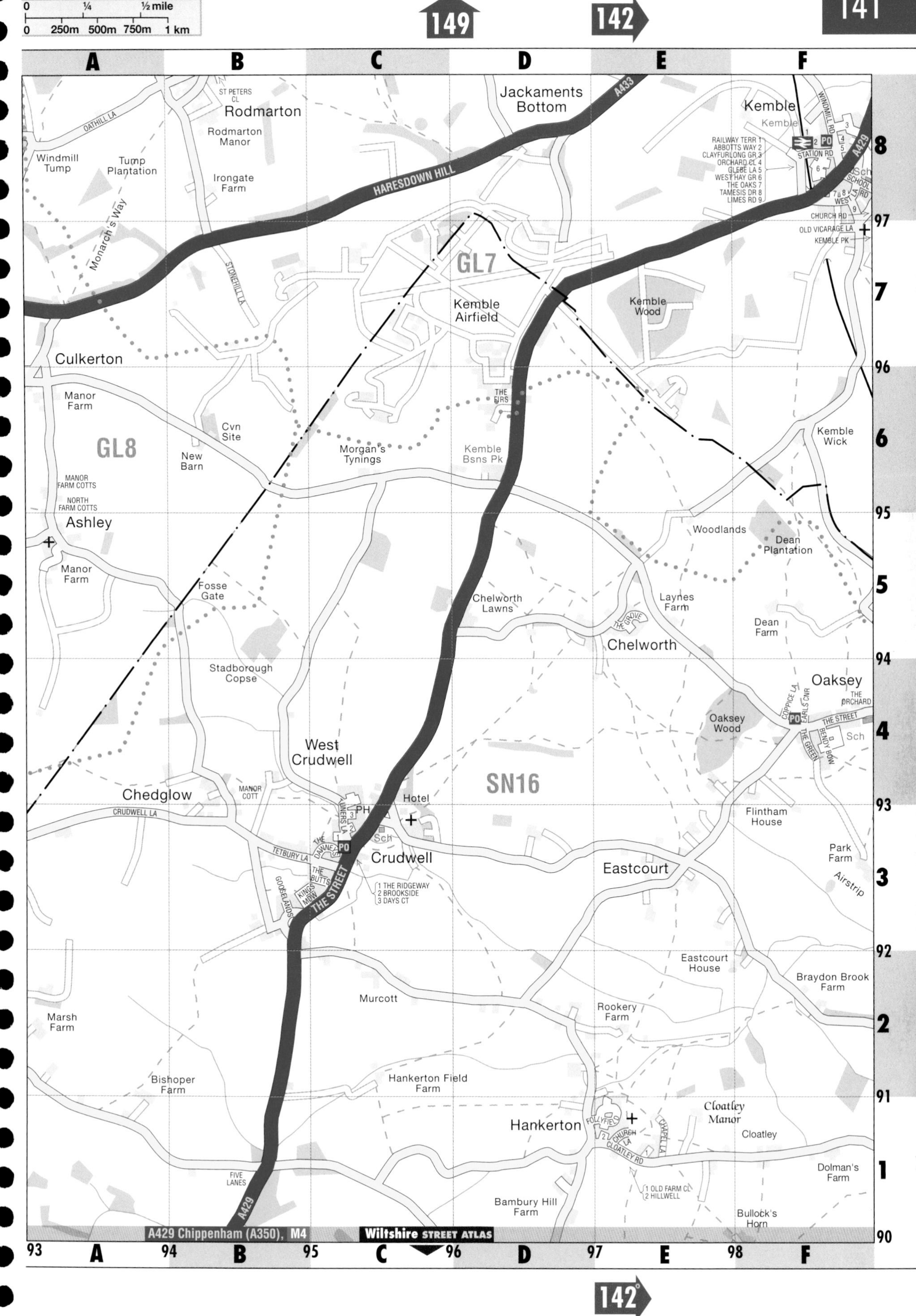

141 150

Scale: 1¾ inches to 1 mile
0 ¼ ½ mile
0 250m 500m 750m 1 km

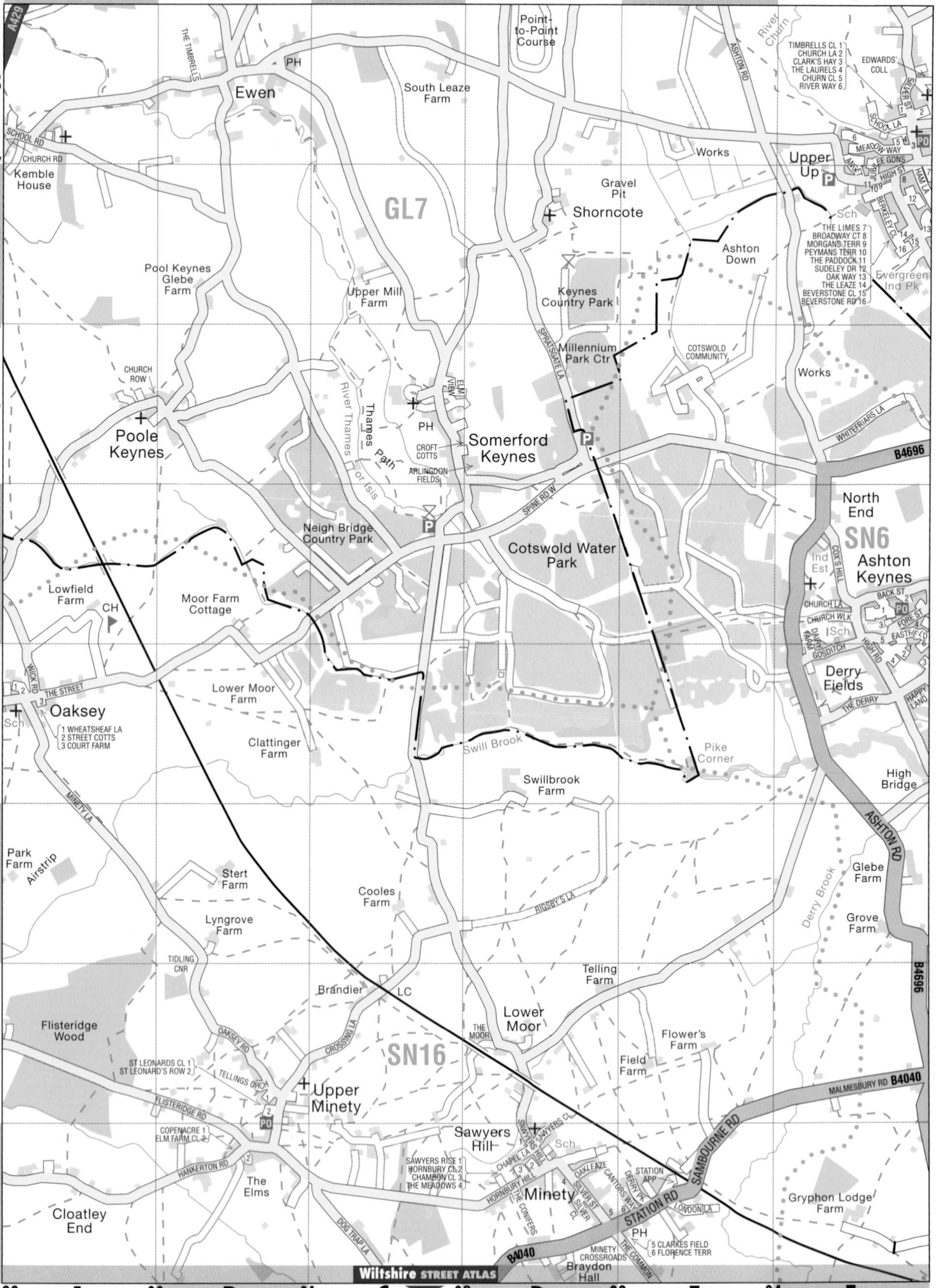

A B C D E F

Ewen
Point-to-Point Course
South Leaze Farm
Kemble House
School Rd
Church Rd
The Timbrells
GL7
Shorncote
Gravel Pit
Works
Upper Up
Ashton Down
Pool Keynes Glebe Farm
Upper Mill Farm
Keynes Country Park
Millennium Park Ctr
Cotswold Community
Church Row
Poole Keynes
Somerford Keynes
Thames Path
River Thames or Isis
Croft Cotts
Arlingdon Fields
Elm View
Spratsgate La
Spine Rd W
Whitefriars La
Works
Evergreen Ind Pk
North End
SN6
Ashton Keynes
Neigh Bridge Country Park
Cotswold Water Park
Lowfield Farm
CH
Moor Farm Cottage
Lower Moor Farm
Oaksey
The Street
Wick Rd
1 Wheatsheaf La
2 Street Cotts
3 Court Farm
Clattinger Farm
Swill Brook
Pike Corner
Swillbrook Farm
Derry Fields
The Derry
Happy Land
High Bridge
Church La
Church Wlk
Back St
Fore St
Gosditch
High Rd
Dairy Farm
Minety La
Park Farm
Airstrip
Stert Farm
Lyngrove Farm
Cooles Farm
Rigsby's La
Glebe Farm
Grove Farm
Derry Brook
Ashton Rd
B4696
Tidling Cnr
Flisteridge Wood
Brandier
LC
Telling Farm
Lower Moor
The Moor
SN16
Oaksey Rd
Crossing La
Flower's Farm
Field Farm
St Leonards Cl 1
St Leonard's Row 2
Tellings Orch
Upper Minety
Flisteridge Rd
Malmesbury Rd B4040
Copenacre 1
Elm Farm Cl 2
Hankerton Rd
The Elms
Sawyers Hill
Sawyers Rise 1
Hornbury Cl 2
Chambon Cl 3
The Meadows 4
Chapel La
Hornbury Hill
The Conifers
Minety
Silver St
Silver Cl
Oakleaze
Cantors Way
Derry Pk
Station App
Sambourne Rd
Station Rd
London La
Gryphon Lodge Farm
Cloatley End
Dog Trap La
B4040
Minety Crossroads
Braydon Hall
The Common
PH
5 Clarkes Field
6 Florence Terr

Timbrells Cl 1
Church La 2
Clark's Hay 3
The Laurels 4
Churn Cl 5
River Way 6
Edwards' Coll
School La
Meadow Way
High St
Berkeley Cl
The Limes 7
Broadway Ct 8
Morgans Terr 9
Peymans Terr 10
The Paddock 11
Sudeley Dr 12
Oak Way 13
The Leaze 14
Beverstone Ct 15
Beverstone Rd 16
River Churn
Ashton Rd

97 96 95 94 93 92 91 90
99 00 01 02 03 04

141

F5
1 Richmond Ct
2 The Leaze
3 Cove House Gdns
4 Sadlers Field
5 Park Pl
6 The Lotts

F4
1 Park End
2 Thames View
3 The Mead
4 Birch Glade

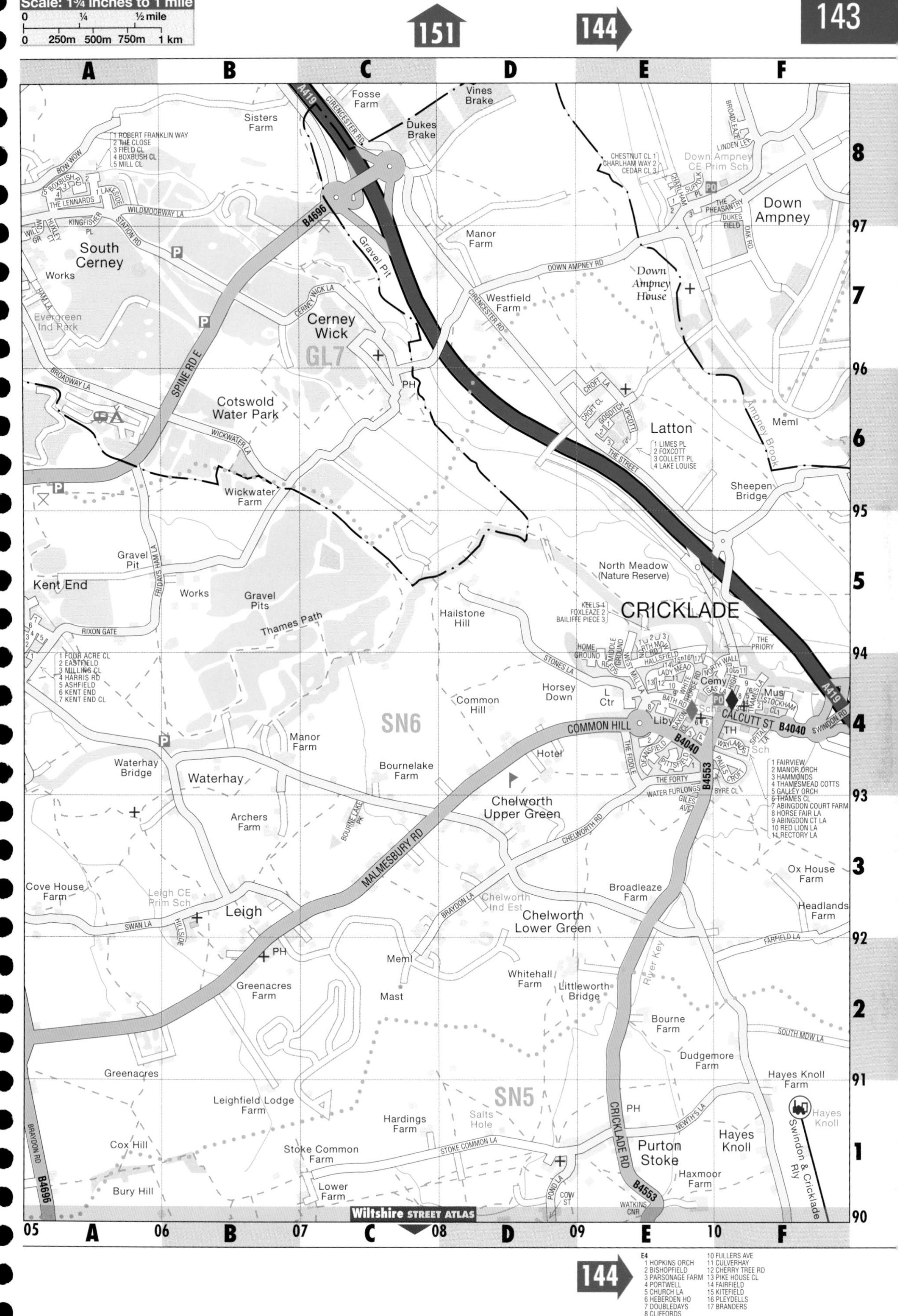
Scale: 1¾ inches to 1 mile
0 ¼ ½ mile
0 250m 500m 750m 1 km
151
144
A B C D E F
8
97
7
96
6
95
5
94
4
93
3
92
2
91
1
90
Fosse Farm
Vines Brake
Sisters Farm
Dukes Brake
CIRENCESTER RD
A419
1 ROBERT FRANKLIN WAY
2 THE CLOSE
3 FIELD CL
4 BOXBUSH CL
5 MILL CL
BOW WOW
BOXBUSH RD
THE LENNARDS
LAKESIDE
WILDMOORWAY LA
KINGFISHER PL
STATION RD
HUXLEY CT
South Cerney
Works
Evergreen Ind Park
B4696
Gravel Pit
Manor Farm
DOWN AMPNEY RD
Westfield Farm
CERNEY WICK LA
Cerney Wick
GL7
BROADWAY LA
SPINE RD E
Cotswold Water Park
WICKWATER LA
PH
CHESTNUT CL 1
CHARLHAM WAY 2
CEDAR CL 3
Down Ampney CE Prim Sch
BROADLEAZE
LINDEN LEA
SUFFOLK
THE PHEASANTRY
DUKES FIELD
OAK RD
Down Ampney
Down Ampney House
CROFT LA
CROFT CL
GOSDITCH
UPCOTT
Latton
1 LIMES PL
2 FOXCOTT
3 COLLETT PL
4 LAKE LOUISE
THE STREET
Meml
Ampney Brook
Sheepen Bridge
Wickwater Farm
Gravel Pit
FRIDAYS HAM LA
Kent End
Works
Gravel Pits
Thames Path
RIXON GATE
Hailstone Hill
North Meadow (Nature Reserve)
KEELS 1
FOXLEAZE 2
BAILIFFE PIECE 3
CRICKLADE
HOME GROUND
MIDDLE GROUND
WEST MILL LA
NORTH WALL
HALLSFIELD
LADY MEAD
THE PRIORY
1 FOUR ACRE CL
2 EASTFIELD
3 MILLING CL
4 HARRIS RD
5 ASHFIELD
6 KENT END
7 KENT END CL
STONES LA
Horsey Down
L Ctr
Common Hill
SN6
Manor Farm
COMMON HILL
Liby
BATH RD
WHITE RD
HORSE FAIR
SAXON
GAS LA
HIGH ST
Cemy
Sch
TH
Mus
STOCKHAM CL
CALCUTT ST
B4040
SWINDON RD
SPITAL LA
WAYLANDS
Sch
B4553
DEANSFIELD
PITTSFIELD
PAULS CROFT
THE FIDDLE
THE FORTY
WATER FURLONGS
GILES AVE
BYRE CL
Hotel
Waterhay Bridge
Waterhay
Bournelake Farm
1 FAIRVIEW
2 MANOR ORCH
3 HAMMONDS
4 THAMESMEAD COTTS
5 GALLEY ORCH
6 THAMES CL
7 ABINGDON COURT FARM
8 HORSE FAIR LA
9 ABINGDON CT LA
10 RED LION LA
11 RECTORY LA
Archers Farm
BOURNE LAKE PK
Chelworth Upper Green
CHELWORTH RD
MALMESBURY RD
Cove House Farm
Leigh CE Prim Sch
Ox House Farm
Broadleaze Farm
Headlands Farm
BRAYDON LA
Chelworth Ind Est
Chelworth Lower Green
SWAN LA
HILLSIDE
Leigh
FARFIELD LA
PH
Meml
Whitehall Farm
Littleworth Bridge
River Key
Greenacres Farm
Mast
Bourne Farm
SOUTH MDW LA
Dudgemore Farm
Greenacres
Hayes Knoll Farm
Leighfield Lodge Farm
Hardings Farm
SN5
Salts Hole
PH
NEWTH'S LA
Hayes Knoll
CRICKLADE RD
Hayes Knoll
Swindon & Cricklade Rly
Cox Hill
Stoke Common Farm
STOKE COMMON LA
Purton Stoke
BRAYDON RD
B4696
Bury Hill
Lower Farm
POND LA
COW ST
Haxmoor Farm
B4553
WATKINS CNR
Wiltshire STREET ATLAS
05 06 07 08 09 10
144
E4
1 HOPKINS ORCH
2 BISHOPFIELD
3 PARSONAGE FARM
4 PORTWELL
5 CHURCH LA
6 HEBERDEN HO
7 DOUBLEDAYS
8 CLIFFORDS
9 VALE CT
10 FULLERS AVE
11 CULVERHAY
12 CHERRY TREE RD
13 PIKE HOUSE CL
14 FAIRFIELD
15 KITEFIELD
16 PLEYDELLS
17 BRANDERS

143
152

Scale: 1¾ inches to 1 mile
0 ¼ ½ mile
0 250m 500m 750m 1 km

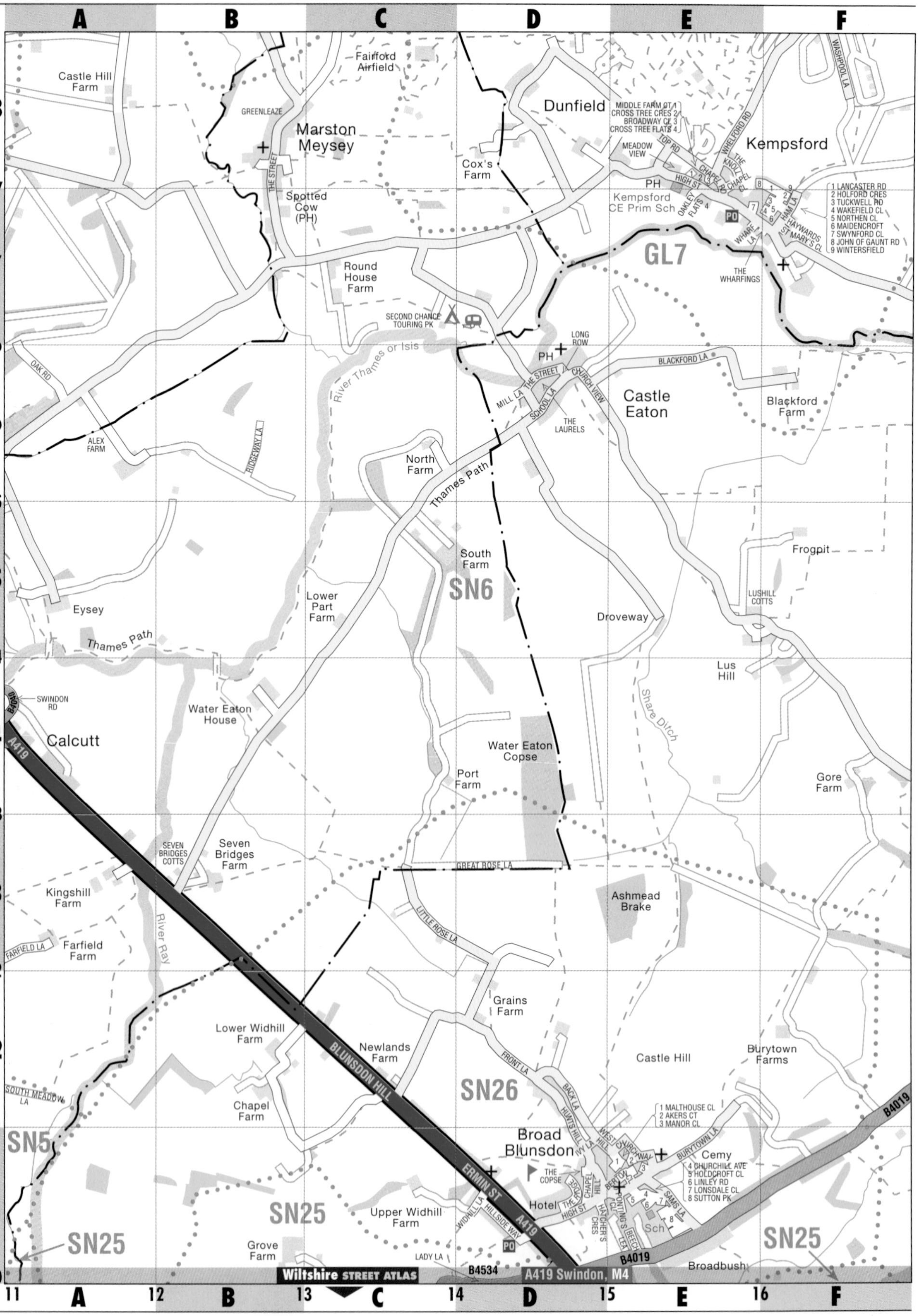

143

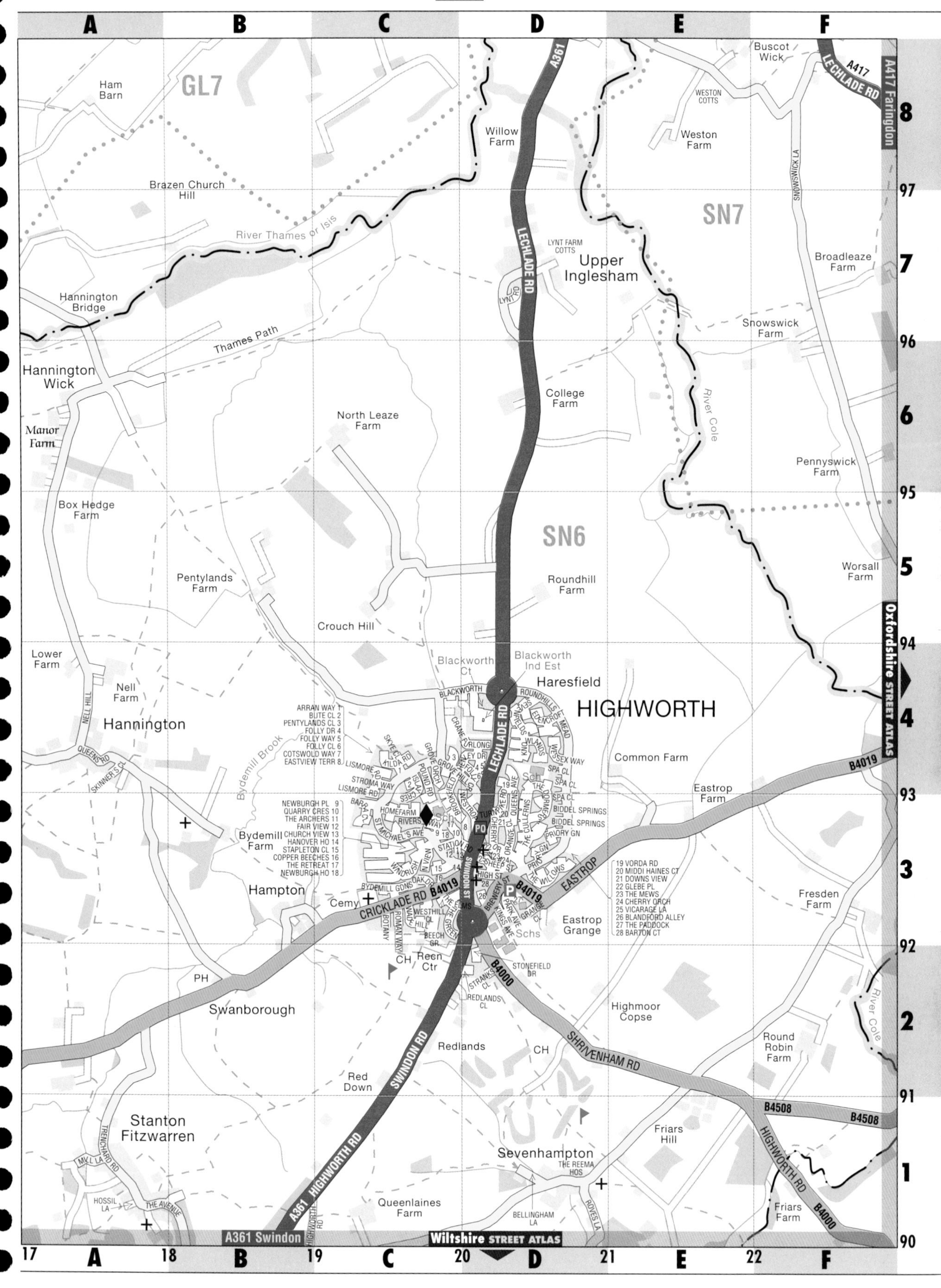
Scale: 1¾ inches to 1 mile
153
GL7
SN7
SN6
Ham Barn
Brazen Church Hill
River Thames or Isis
Hannington Bridge
Thames Path
Hannington Wick
Manor Farm
Willow Farm
Weston Farm
Buscot Wick
LECHLADE RD
A417 Faringdon
Upper Inglesham
Broadleaze Farm
Snowswick Farm
College Farm
North Leaze Farm
River Cole
Pennyswick Farm
Box Hedge Farm
Pentylands Farm
Roundhill Farm
Worsall Farm
Crouch Hill
Lower Farm
Nell Farm
Blackworth Ind Est
Haresfield
HIGHWORTH
Hannington
Oxfordshire STREET ATLAS
Common Farm
Eastrop Farm
Bydemill Brook
Bydemill Farm
Hampton
Cemy
CRICKLADE RD
EASTROP
Eastrop Grange
Fresden Farm
Swanborough
Recn Ctr
Highmoor Copse
SWINDON RD
Redlands
SHRIVENHAM RD
Round Robin Farm
Red Down
Stanton Fitzwarren
Friars Hill
Sevenhampton
HIGHWORTH RD
Queenlaines Farm
Friars Farm
A361 Swindon
Wiltshire STREET ATLAS

154

Scale: 1¾ inches to 1 mile

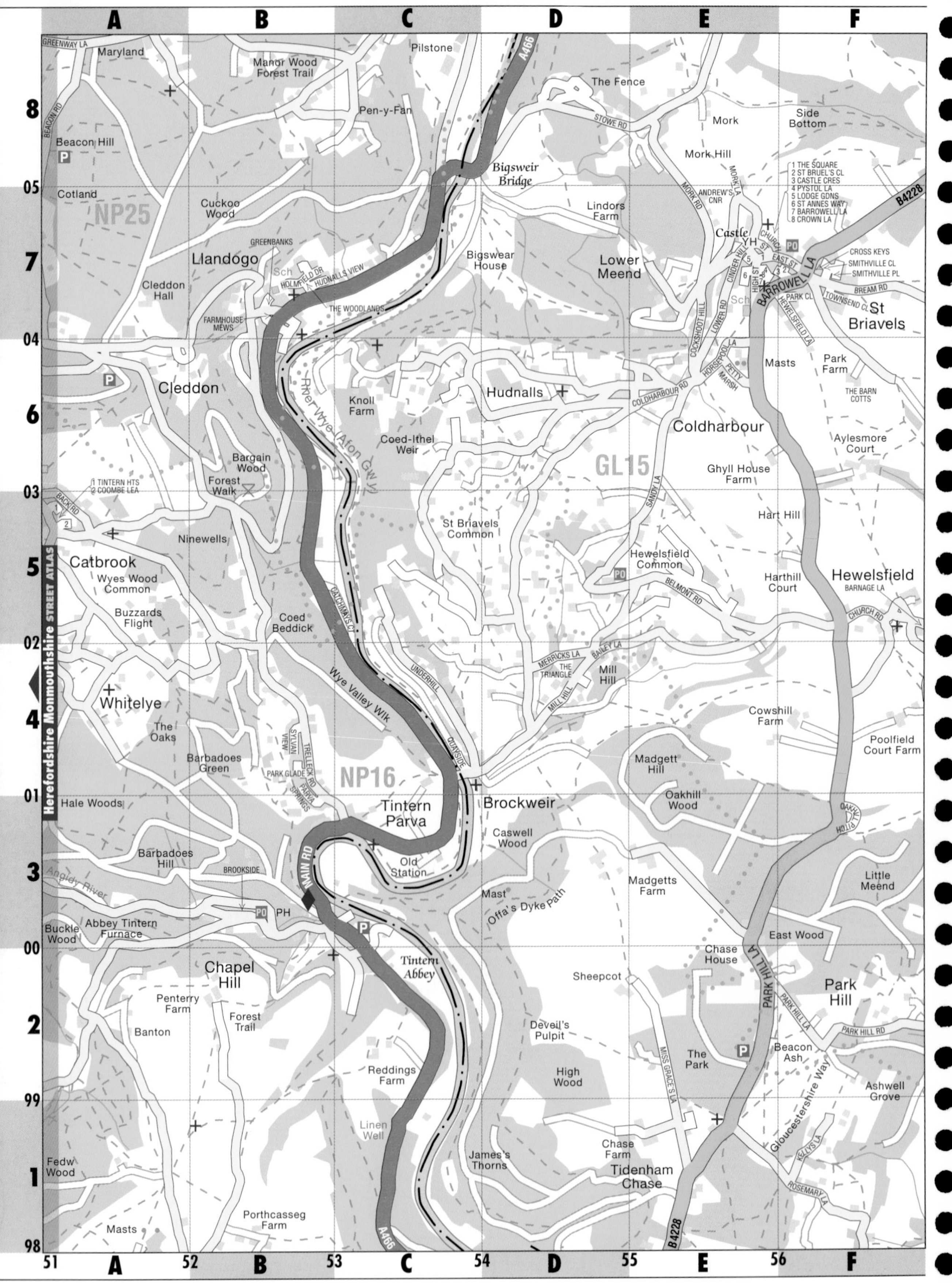

72

73

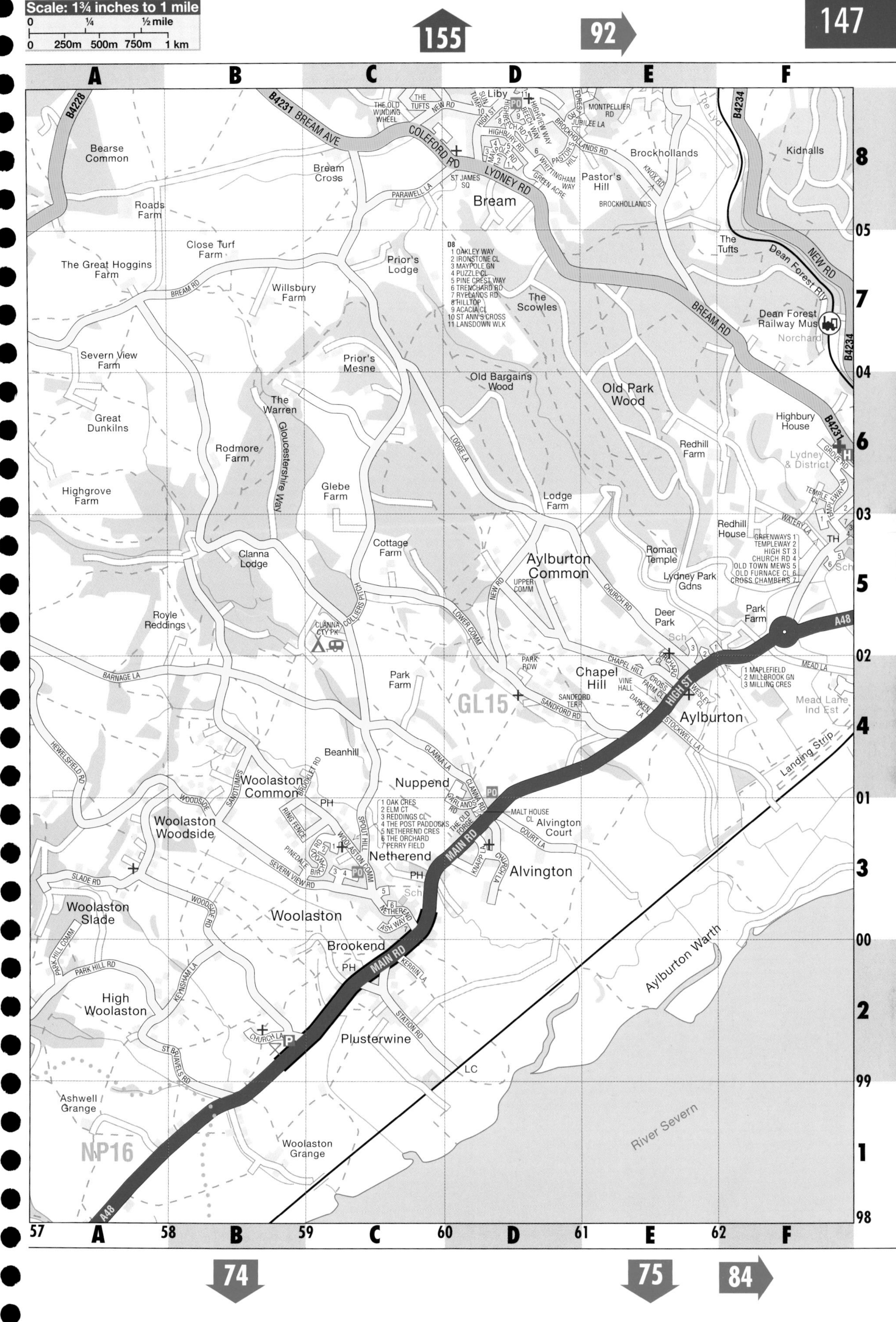
Scale: 1¾ inches to 1 mile
0 ¼ ½ mile
0 250m 500m 750m 1 km
155
92
A B C D E F
B4228
B4231 BREAM AVE
COLEFORD RD
LYDNEY RD
Bearse Common
Roads Farm
Bream Cross
Bream
Liby
Brockhollands
Kidnalls
Pastor's Hill
BROCKHOLLANDS
MONTPELLIER RD
JUBILEE LA
BROCKHOLLANDS RD
KNOX RD
WHITTINGHAM WAY
GREEN ACRE
HIGHVIEW WAY
ST JAMES SQ
PARAWELL LA
THE OLD WINDING WHEEL
THE TUFTS
NEW RD
B4234
The Lyd
8
05
The Tufts
Dean Forest Rly
NEW RD
Close Turf Farm
The Great Hoggins Farm
BREAM RD
Willsbury Farm
Prior's Lodge
D8
1 OAKLEY WAY
2 IRONSTONE CL
3 MAYPOLE GN
4 PUZZLE CL
5 PINE CREST WAY
6 TRENCHARD RD
7 RYELANDS RD
8 HILLTOP
9 ACACIA CL
10 ST ANN'S CROSS
11 LANSDOWN WLK
The Scowles
BREAM RD
Dean Forest Railway Mus
Norchard
7
Severn View Farm
Prior's Mesne
Old Bargains Wood
Old Park Wood
04
B4234
The Warren
Great Dunkilns
Gloucestershire Way
Highbury House
B4231
Rodmore Farm
Redhill Farm
LODGE LA
6
Lydney & District
GROVE RD
Highgrove Farm
Glebe Farm
Lodge Farm
TEMPLE CL
TEMPLEWAY W
WATERY LA
03
Redhill House
GREENWAYS 1
TEMPLEWAY 2
HIGH ST 3
CHURCH RD 4
OLD TOWN MEWS 5
OLD FURNACE CL 6
CROSS CHAMBERS 7
TH
Clanna Lodge
Cottage Farm
Aylburton Common
Roman Temple
Lydney Park Gdns
Sch
UPPER COMM
NEW RD
CHURCH RD
COLLIERS PITCH
5
Royle Reddings
Deer Park
Park Farm
CLANNA CTY PK
LOWER COMM
A48
Sch
02
BARNAGE LA
PARK ROW
CHAPEL HILL
Chapel Hill
ORCHARD CL
MEAD LA
1 MAPLEFIELD
2 MILLBROOK GN
3 MILLING CRES
Park Farm
VINE HALL
CROSS FARM CL
HIGH ST
WESLEY CL
Mead Lane Ind Est
GL15
SANDFORD TERR
SANDFORD RD
DARKENT LA
Aylburton
STOCKWELL LA
4
HEWELSFIELD RD
Beanhill
Landing Strip
CLANNA LA
Woolaston Common
Nuppend
BROOKLET RD
SANDTUMPS
WOODSIDE
01
PH
1 OAK CRES
2 ELM CT
3 REDDINGS CL
4 THE POST PADDOCKS
5 NETHEREND CRES
6 THE ORCHARD
7 PERRY FIELD
CLANNA RD
PARKLANDS RD
MALT HOUSE CL
Alvington Court
Woolaston Woodside
RING FENCE
THE OLD FORGE
MAIN RD
COURT LA
WOOLASTON COMM
SPOUT HILL
Netherend
KNAPP LA
Alvington
CHURCH LA
SLADE RD
PINEDALE
SEVERN VIEW RD
PH
3
Sch
Woolaston Slade
WOODSIDE RD
Woolaston
NETHEREND
ASH WAY
00
PARK HILL COMM
Brookend
Aylburton Warth
PARK HILL RD
KEYNSHAM LA
PH
MAIN RD
KERRIN LA
2
High Woolaston
STATION RD
CHURCH LA
Plusterwine
ST BRIAVELS RD
LC
99
Ashwell Grange
River Severn
NP16
Woolaston Grange
1
A48
98
57 A 58 B 59 C 60 D 61 E 62 F
74
75
84

99
104
105

B6
1 VELHURST DR
2 ASHLEY DR
3 CHASEWOOD CNR
4 BEECHWOOD DR
5 GREYS CL
6 DORINGTON CT
7 BURLEIGH VIEW
8 MUNDAY CL
9 FERRIS COURT VIEW
10 YEW TREE COTT

C6
1 SPARROW CL
2 ROBIN CL
3 PADIN CL
4 CUCKOO CL
5 HAWK CL
6 FOXES CL
7 ALDER WAY
8 STONECOTE RIDGE
9 FARRIERS CROFT
10 LAPWING CT
11 WELCOMYN

Scale: 1¾ inches to 1 mile
0 ¼ ½ mile
0 250m 500m 750m 1 km

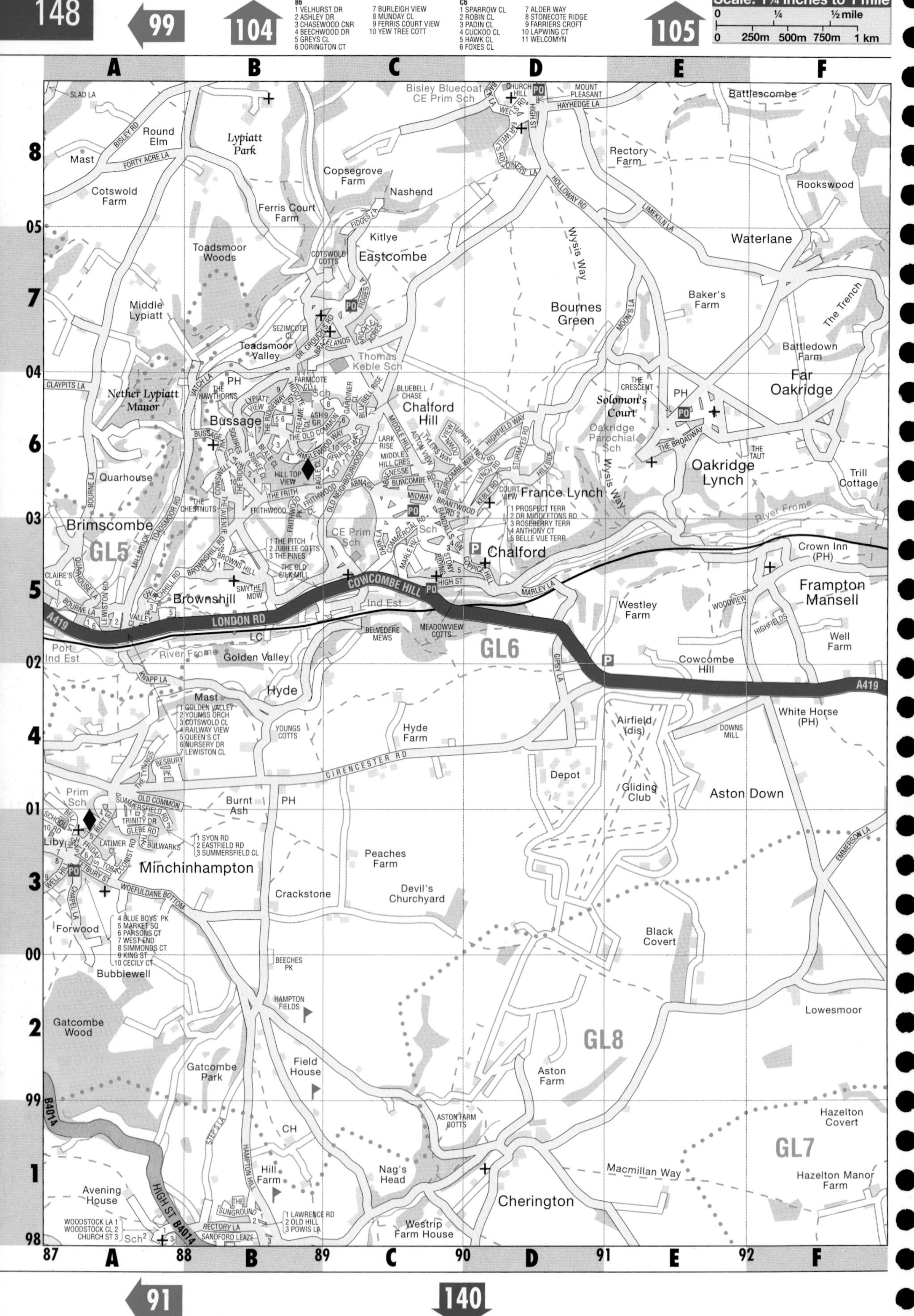

91
140

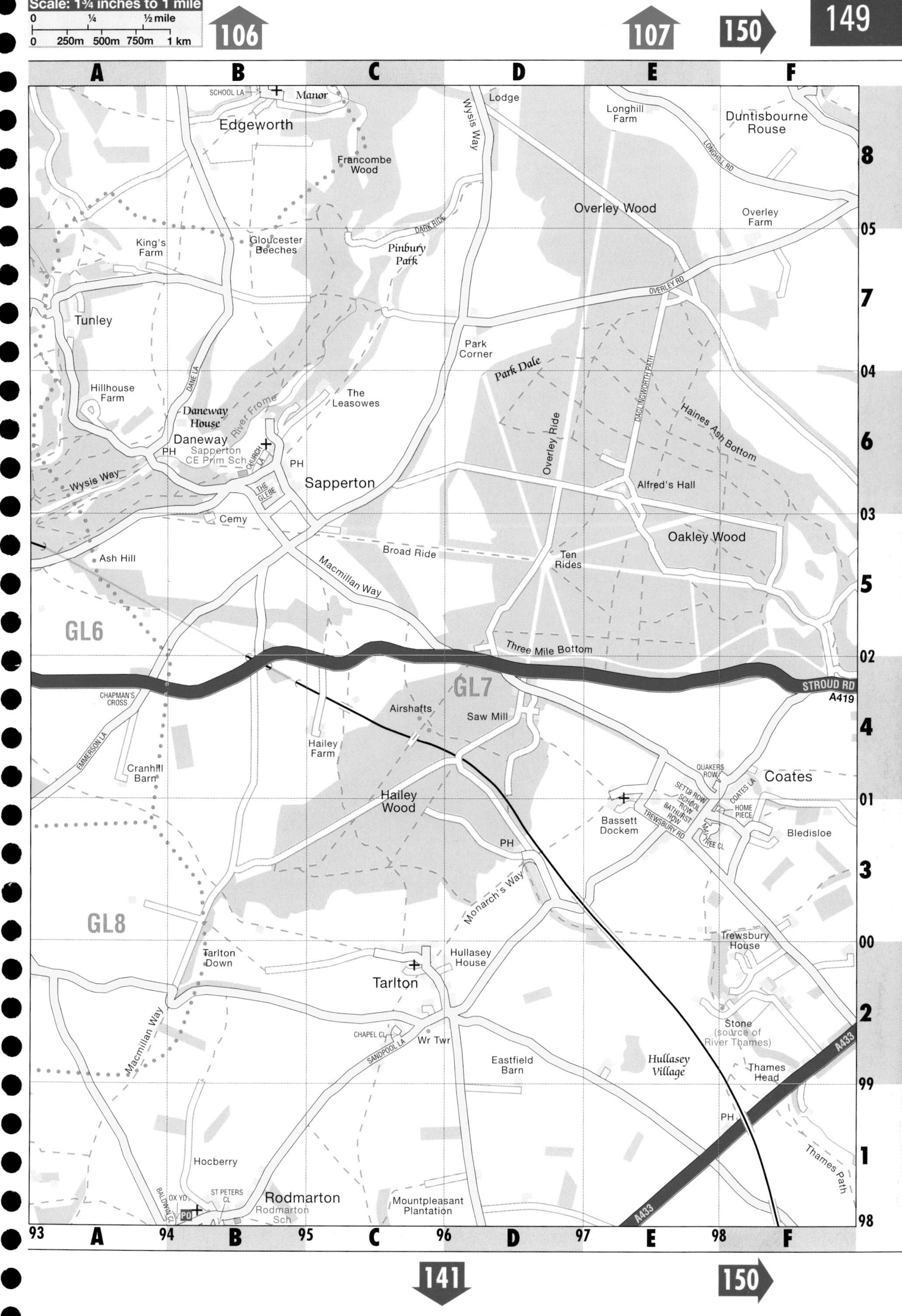

Scale: 1¾ inches to 1 mile
0 ¼ ½ mile
0 250m 500m 750m 1 km
106
107
150
A B C D E F
Edgeworth
Manor
SCHOOL LA
Francombe Wood
Lodge
Wysis Way
Longhill Farm
Duntisbourne Rouse
LONGHILL RD
Overley Wood
Overley Farm
King's Farm
Gloucester Beeches
DARK RIDE
Pinbury Park
OVERLEY RD
Tunley
Park Corner
Park Dale
Hillhouse Farm
The Leasowes
DANE LA
DAGLINGWORTH PATH
Daneway House
River Frome
Haines Ash Bottom
Overley Ride
Daneway
PH
Sapperton CE Prim Sch
CHURCH LA
PH
Sapperton
Alfred's Hall
Wysis Way
THE GLEBE
Cemy
Oakley Wood
Ash Hill
Broad Ride
Ten Rides
Macmillan Way
GL6
Three Mile Bottom
GL7
CHAPMAN'S CROSS
STROUD RD
A419
Airshafts
Saw Mill
EMMERSON LA
Hailey Farm
Cranhill Barn
QUAKERS ROW
Coates
Hailey Wood
SETTS ROW
SCHOOL ROW
BATHURST ROW
COATES LA
HOME PIECE
TREWSBURY RD
Bassett Dockem
Bledisloe
PH
Monarch's Way
GL8
Trewsbury House
Tarlton Down
Hullasey House
Tarlton
Stone (source of River Thames)
Macmillan Way
CHAPEL CL
SANDPOOL LA
Wr Twr
Eastfield Barn
Hullasey Village
Thames Head
A433
PH
Thames Path
Hocberry
BALDWIN CL
OX YD
ST PETERS CL
PO
Rodmarton
Rodmarton Sch
Mountpleasant Plantation
A433
8
05
7
04
6
03
5
02
4
01
3
00
2
99
1
98
93 94 95 96 97 98
141
150

149
158

Scale: 1¾ inches to 1 mile
0 ¼ ½ mile
0 250m 500m 750m 1 km

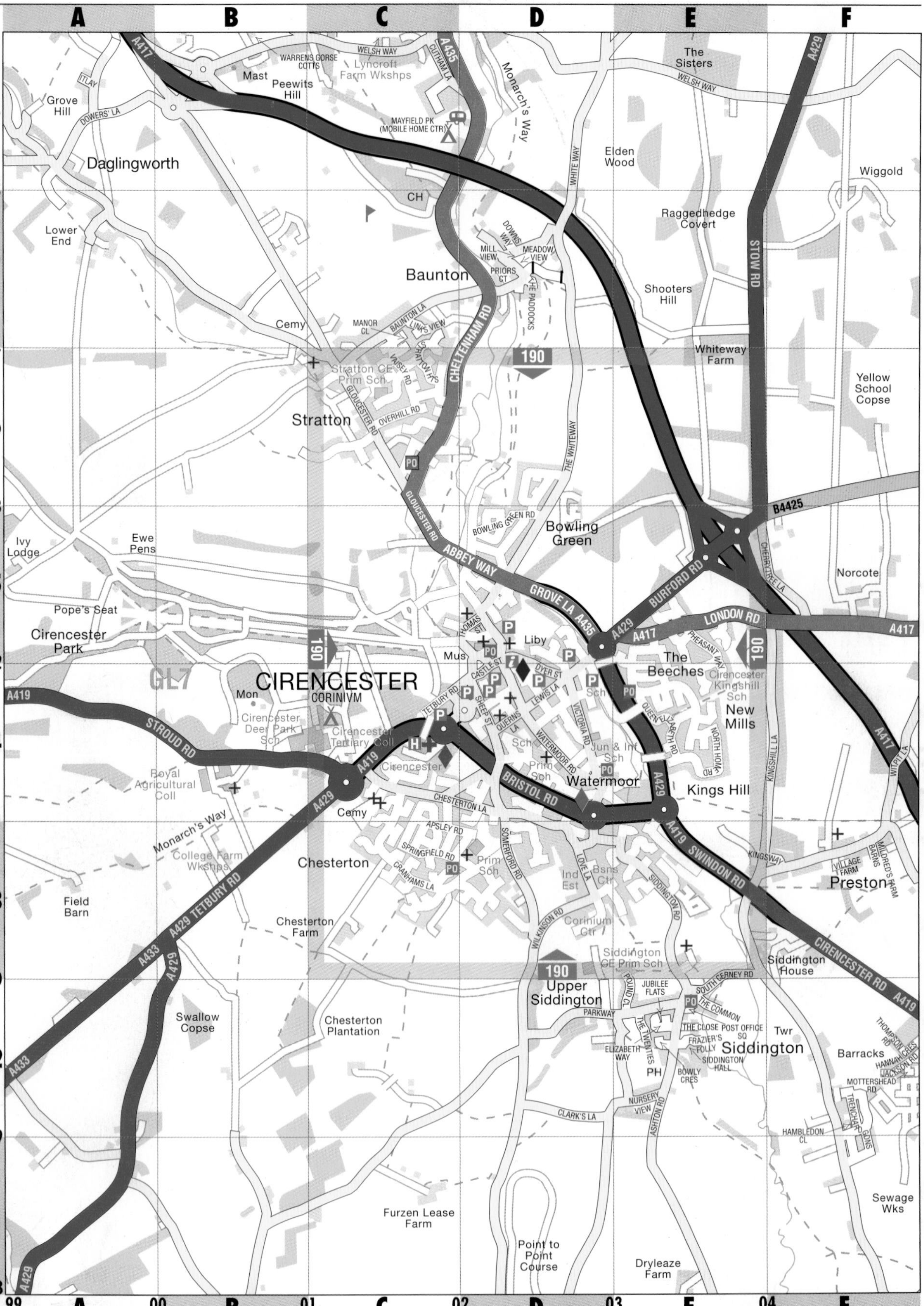

A B C D E F

8
05
7
04
6
03
5
02
4
01
3
00
2
99
1
98

A417
WARRENS GORSE COTTS
WELSH WAY
Lyncroft Farm Wkshps
CUTHAM LA
A435
Mast
Peewits Hill
ITLAY
Grove Hill
DOWERS' LA
MAYFIELD PK (MOBILE HOME CTR)
Monarch's Way
The Sisters
WELSH WAY
A429
Daglingworth
Elden Wood
WHITE WAY
Wiggold
CH
Lower End
DOWNS WAY
MILL VIEW
MEADOW VIEW
Raggedhedge Covert
PRIORS CT
THE PADDOCKS
Baunton
STOW RD
Shooters Hill
Cemy
MANOR CL
BAUNTON LA
LINKS VIEW
CHELTENHAM RD
Whiteway Farm
Stratton CE Prim Sch
VAISEY RD
STRATTON HTS
Yellow School Copse
GLOUCESTER RD
OVERHILL RD
Stratton
THE WHITEWAY
PO
GLOUCESTER RD
BOWLING GREEN RD
Bowling Green
B4425
Ivy Lodge
Ewe Pens
ABBEY WAY
BURFORD RD
CHERRYTREE LA
Norcote
GROVE LA
A435
A429
LONDON RD
A417
Pope's Seat
THOMAS ST
Liby
A417
Cirencester Park
PHEASANT WAY
Mus
CASTLE ST
DYER ST
The Beeches
Cirencester Kingshill Sch
GL7
CIRENCESTER
CORINIVM
LEWIS LA
Sch
PO
A419
Mon
TETBURY RD
SHEEP ST
QUERNS LA
QUEEN ELIZABETH RD
New Mills
Cirencester Deer Park Sch
Cirencester Tertiary Coll
VICTORIA RD
STROUD RD
Sch
Jun & Inf Sch
NORTH HOME RD
H
A419
WATERMOOR RD
Prim Sch
A417
Royal Agricultural Coll
Cirencester
BRISTOL RD
Watermoor
A429
Kings Hill
WITPIT LA
KINGSHILL LA
A429
Cemy
CHESTERTON LA
Monarch's Way
APSLEY RD
SPRINGFIELD RD
A419 SWINDON RD
KINGSWAY
College Farm Wkshps
Chesterton
GRANHAMS LA
PO
Prim Sch
SOMERFORD RD
Ind Est
LOVE LA
Bsns Ctr
VILLAGE FARM
BARNS
MILDRED'S FARM
Preston
Field Barn
A429 TETBURY RD
SIDDINGTON RD
Chesterton Farm
WILKINSON RD
Corinium Ctr
CIRENCESTER RD
A433
A429
Siddington CE Prim Sch
Siddington House
SOUTH CERNEY RD
A419
Upper Siddington
POUND CL
JUBILEE FLATS
PO
THE COMMON
Swallow Copse
Chesterton Plantation
PARKWAY
THE TWENTIES
THE CLOSE
POST OFFICE SQ
Twr
THOMPSON RD
FRAZIER'S FOLLY
Siddington
Barracks
HANNAH CRES
JACKSON RD
A433
ELIZABETH WAY
SIDDINGTON HALL
PH
BOWLY CRES
MOTTERSHEAD RD
TRENCHARD GDNS
NURSERY VIEW
CLARK'S LA
ASHTON RD
HAMBLEDON CL
Sewage Wks
Furzen Lease Farm
Point to Point Course
Dryleaze Farm
A429

190
190
190
190

99 A 00 B 01 C 02 D 03 E 04 F

149
142
For full street detail of the highlighted area see page 190.

Scale: 1¾ inches to 1 mile

159
152

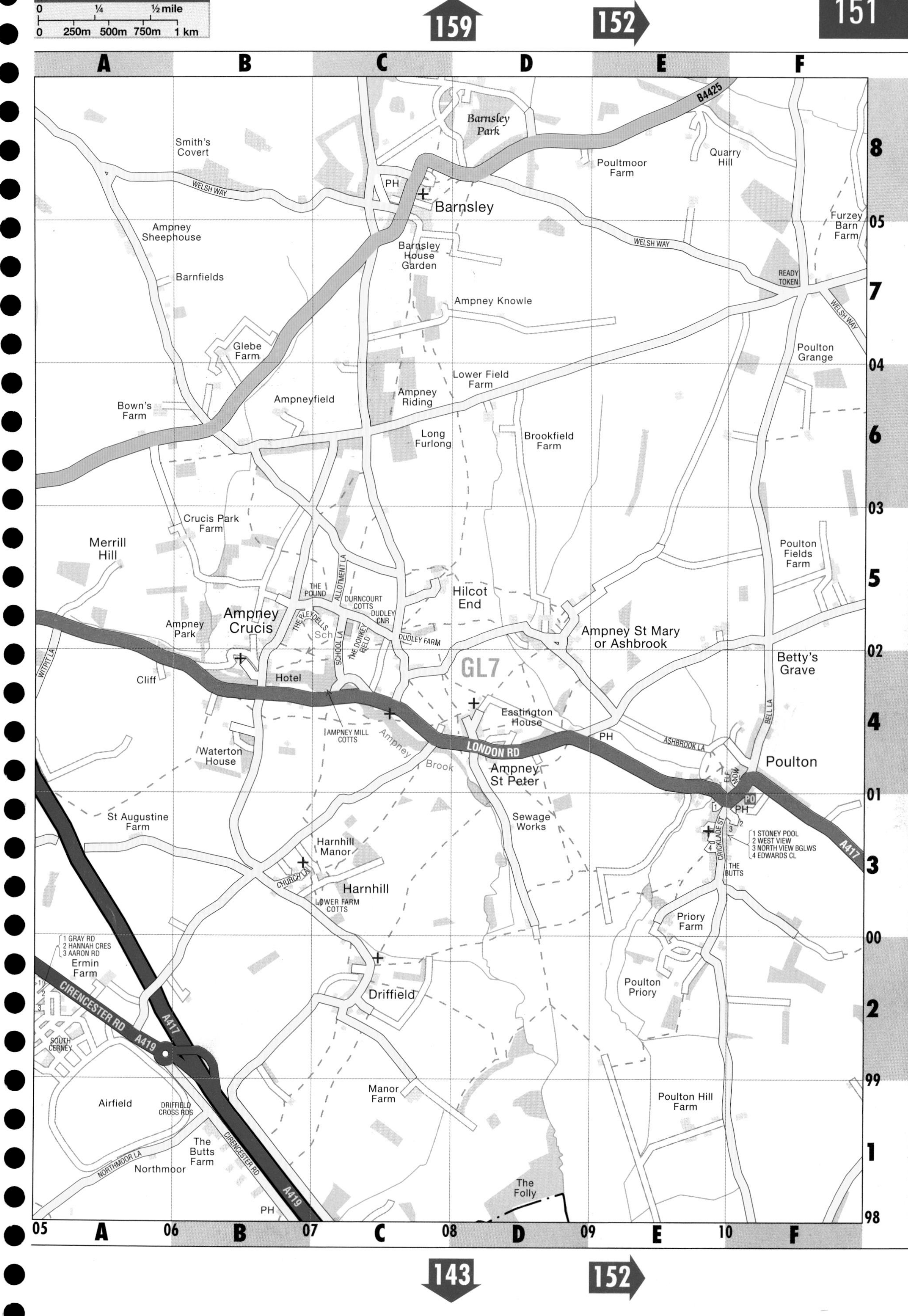

143
152

151
160

Scale: 1¾ inches to 1 mile
0 ¼ ½ mile
0 250m 500m 750m 1 km

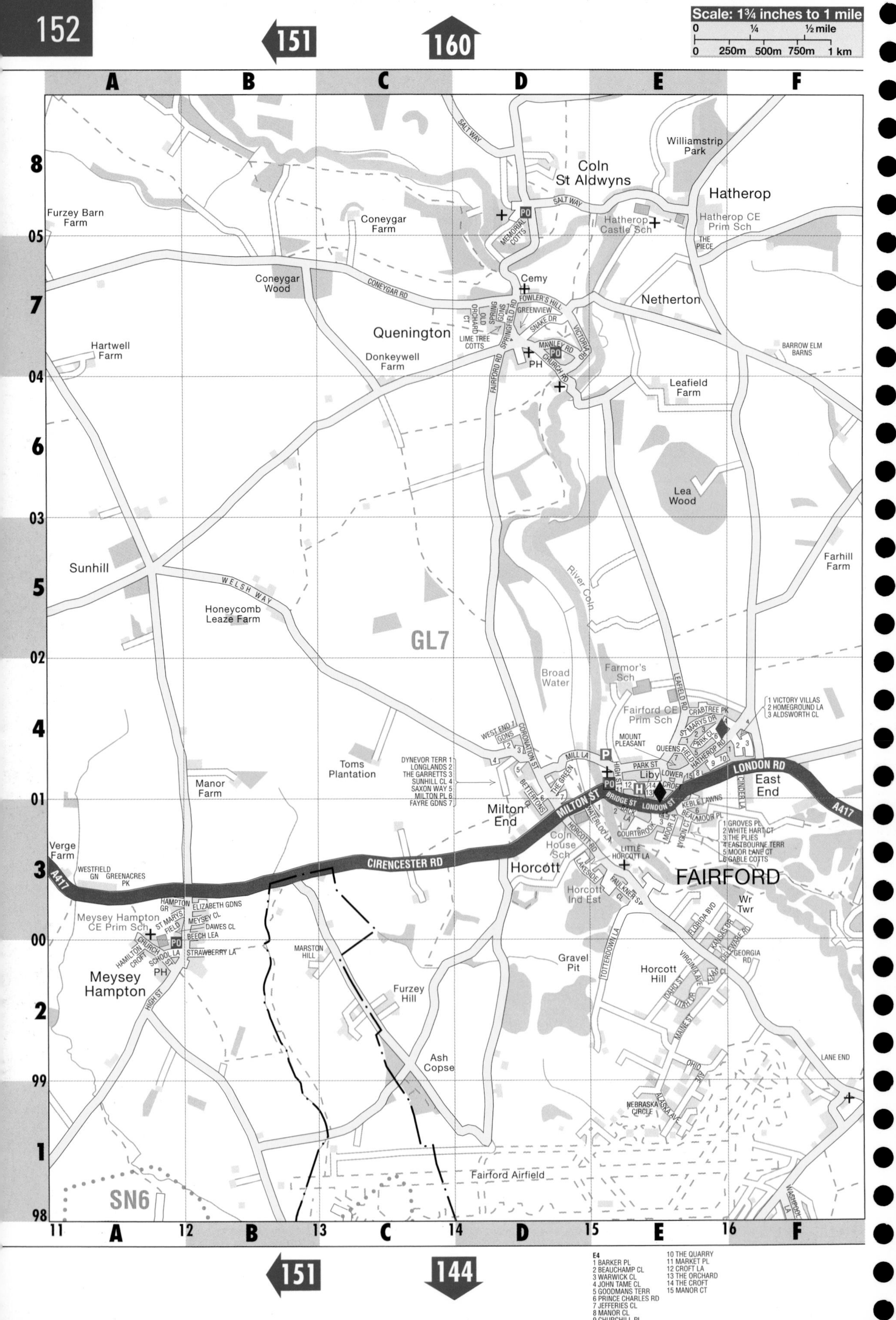

151
144

E4
1 BARKER PL
2 BEAUCHAMP CL
3 WARWICK CL
4 JOHN TAME CL
5 GOODMANS TERR
6 PRINCE CHARLES RD
7 JEFFERIES CL
8 MANOR CL
9 CHURCHILL PL
10 THE QUARRY
11 MARKET PL
12 CROFT LA
13 THE ORCHARD
14 THE CROFT
15 MANOR CT

Scale: 1¾ inches to 1 mile

0 ¼ ½ mile

0 250m 500m 750m 1 km

161

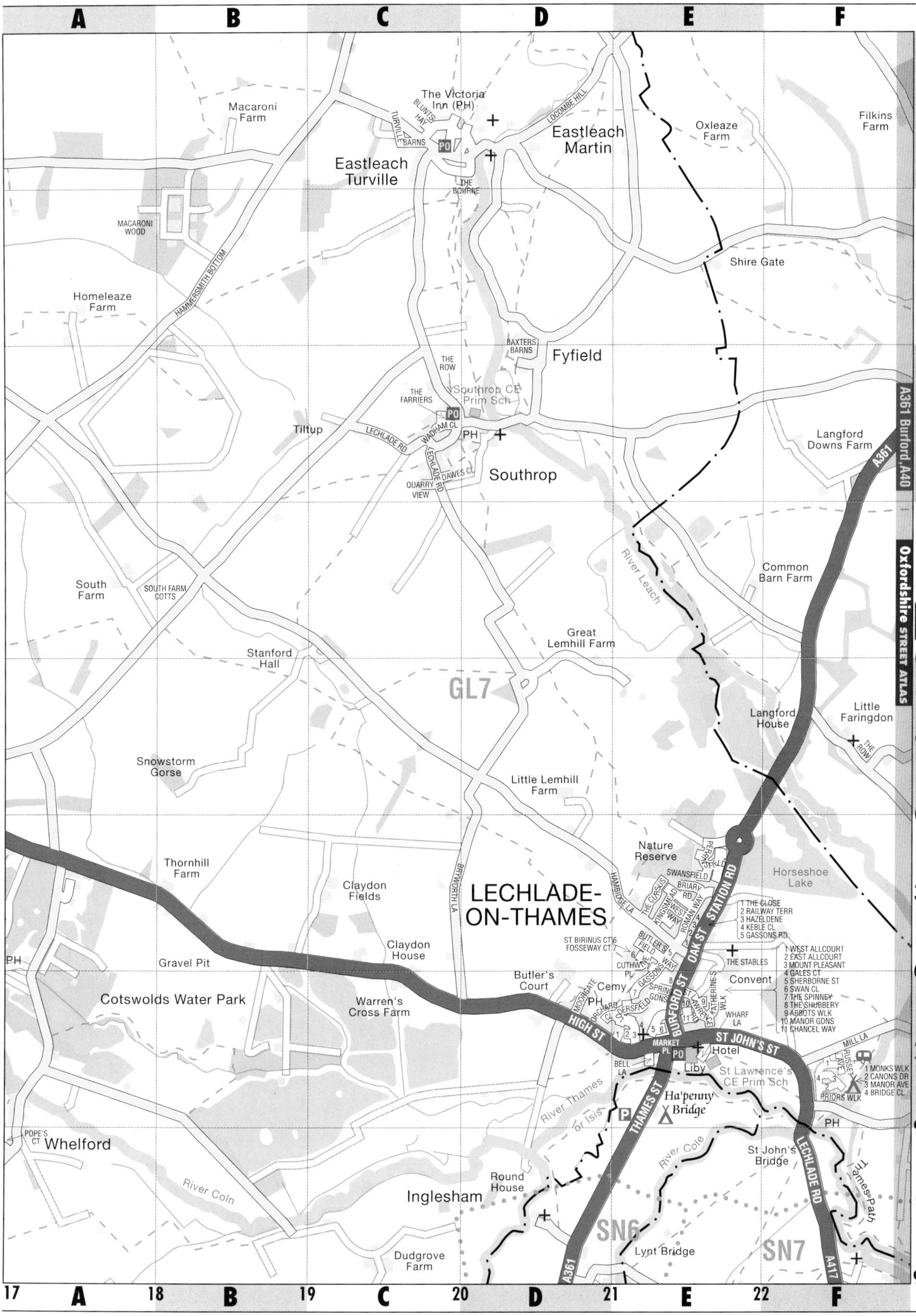

145

A8
1 MONKSWELL RD
2 MONKSWELL CL
3 JONES HO
4 BURGAGE
5 Hadnock Rd Ind Est

A7
1 NEWLAND WAY
2 CHURCH FARM
3 ORCHARD CT
4 RHODFA WYESHAM/WYESHAM AVE
5 CLAYPATCH RD
6 Y PADDGAU/ THE PADDOCKS
7 CHESTNUT TERR
8 CILGANT DEFIW/OAK CRES
9 LIMETREE AVE
10 CHESTNUT CT
11 HEATH ST
12 READE ST
13 BLAKE ST

162

A7
14 THE DOWNHAMS
15 HILLCREST CL
16 GREENLANDS CL
17 WYEBRIDGE ST
18 ST JAMES' ST
19 WHITECROSS ST
20 ST JAMES' SQ
21 GRANVILLE ST
22 YR HEN HEOL/THE OLD RD
23 RIVERSIDE PK
24 Mayhill Ind Est
25 Wyeside Com Ctr

Scale: 1¾ inches to 1 mile
0 ¼ ½ mile
0 250m 500m 750m 1 km

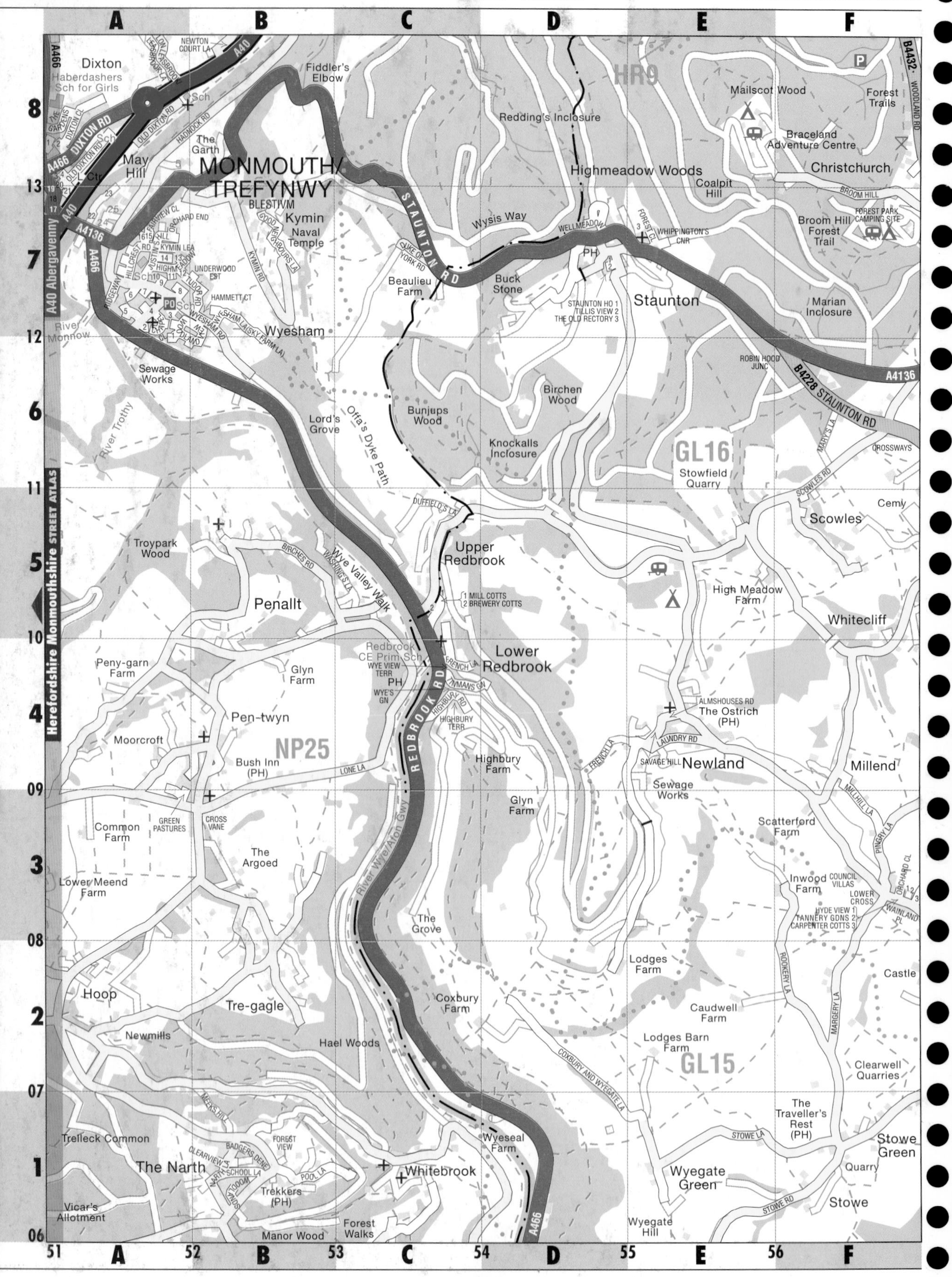

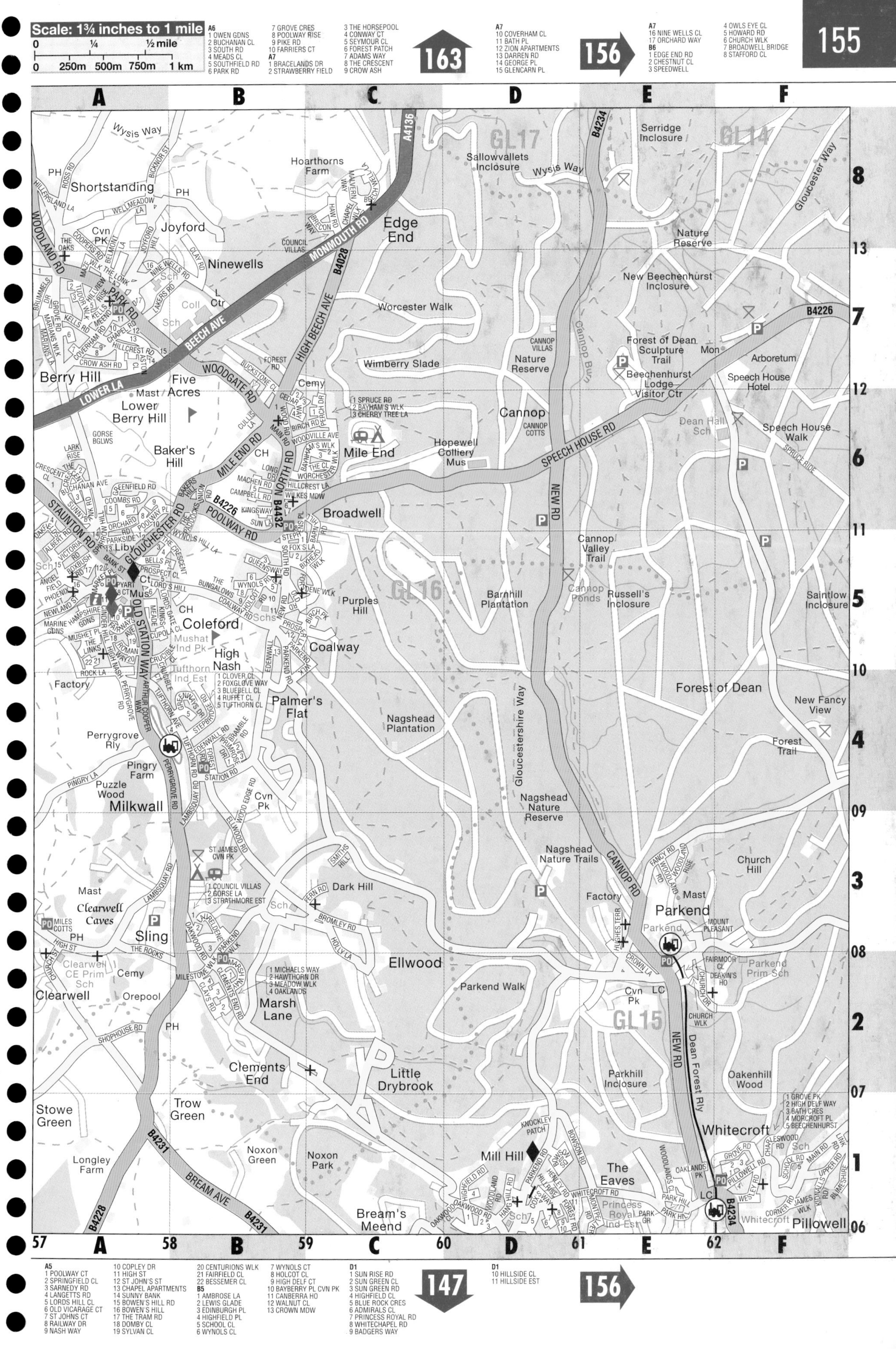

155
Scale: 1¾ inches to 1 mile
0 ¼ ½ mile
0 250m 500m 750m 1 km
A6
1 OWEN GDNS
2 BUCHANAN CL
3 SOUTH RD
4 MEADS CL
5 SOUTHFIELD RD
6 PARK RD
7 GROVE CRES
8 POOLWAY RISE
9 PIKE RD
10 FARRIERS CT
A7
1 BRACELANDS DR
2 STRAWBERRY FIELD
3 THE HORSEPOOL
4 CONWAY CT
5 SEYMOUR CL
6 FOREST PATCH
7 ADAMS WAY
8 THE CRESCENT
9 CROW ASH
163
A7
10 COVERHAM CL
11 BATH PL
12 ZION APARTMENTS
13 DARREN RD
14 GEORGE PL
15 GLENCARN PL
156
A7
16 NINE WELLS CL
17 ORCHARD WAY
B6
1 EDGE END RD
2 CHESTNUT CL
3 SPEEDWELL
4 OWLS EYE CL
5 HOWARD RD
6 CHURCH WLK
7 BROADWELL BRIDGE
8 STAFFORD CL
A B C D E F
8 13 7 12 6 11 5 10 4 09 3 08 2 07 1 06
57 58 59 60 61 62
Wysis Way
Shortstanding
Joyford
Ninewells
Hoarthorns Farm
Edge End
MONMOUTH RD
BEECH AVE
HIGH BEECH AVE
B4028
A4136
B4234
GL17
Sallowvallets Inclosure
Serridge Inclosure
GL14
Gloucester Way
Nature Reserve
New Beechenhurst Inclosure
Worcester Walk
Wimberry Slade
Cannop Villas
Cannop Brook
Forest of Dean Sculpture Trail
Beechenhurst Lodge Visitor Ctr
Arboretum
Speech House Hotel
B4226
Berry Hill
Five Acres
Lower Berry Hill
LOWER LA
WOODGATE RD
Cemy
Mile End
Cannop
Hopewell Colliery Mus
Dean Hall Sch
Speech House Walk
SPEECH HOUSE RD
Baker's Hill
MILE END RD
NORTH RD
B4432
Broadwell
POOLWAY RD
STAUNTON RD
GLOUCESTER RD
NEW RD
Cannop Valley Trail
Cannop Ponds
Russell's Inclosure
Saintlow Inclosure
Barnhill Plantation
Purples Hill
GL16
Coleford
Mushat Ind Pk
High Nash
Tufthorn Ind Est
Coalway
Factory
Forest of Dean
New Fancy View
Palmer's Flat
Nagshead Plantation
Gloucestershire Way
Forest Trail
Perrygrove Rly
Pingry Farm
Puzzle Wood
Milkwall
Cvn Pk
Nagshead Nature Reserve
Nagshead Nature Trails
CANNOP RD
Church Hill
St James Cvn Pk
Dark Hill
Mast
Clearwell Caves
Sling
Parkend
Factory
Clearwell CE Prim Sch
Cemy
Clearwell
Orepool
Ellwood
Parkend Walk
Marsh Lane
GL15
Parkend Prim Sch
Clements End
Little Drybrook
Parkhill Inclosure
Oakenhill Wood
Dean Forest Rly
Stowe Green
Trow Green
Whitecroft
Longley Farm
Noxon Green
Noxon Park
Mill Hill
The Eaves
Princess Royal Ind Est
Bream's Meend
B4231
BREAM AVE
B4228
Pillowell
A5
1 POOLWAY CT
2 SPRINGFIELD CL
3 SARNEDY RD
4 LANGETTS RD
5 LORDS HILL CL
6 OLD VICARAGE CT
7 ST JOHNS CT
8 RAILWAY DR
9 NASH WAY
10 COPLEY DR
11 HIGH ST
12 ST JOHN'S ST
13 CHAPEL APARTMENTS
14 SUNNY BANK
15 BOWEN'S HILL RD
16 BOWEN'S HILL
17 THE TRAM RD
18 DOMBY CL
19 SYLVAN CL
20 CENTURIONS WLK
21 FAIRFIELD CL
22 BESSEMER CL
B5
1 AMBROSE LA
2 LEWIS GLADE
3 EDINBURGH PL
4 HIGHFIELD PL
5 SCHOOL CL
6 WYNOLS CL
7 WYNOLS CT
8 HOLCOT CL
9 HIGH DELF CT
10 BAYBERRY PL CVN PK
11 CANBERRA HO
12 WALNUT CL
13 CROWN MDW
D1
1 SUN RISE RD
2 SUN GREEN CL
3 SUN GREEN RD
4 HIGHFIELD CL
5 BLUE ROCK CRES
6 ADMIRALS CL
7 PRINCESS ROYAL RD
8 WHITECHAPEL RD
9 BADGERS WAY
147
D1
10 HILLSIDE CL
11 HILLSIDE EST
156

155
164

Scale: 1¾ inches to 1 mile
0 ¼ ½ mile
0 250m 500m 750m 1 km

155
92
For full street detail of the highlighted area see page 191.
93

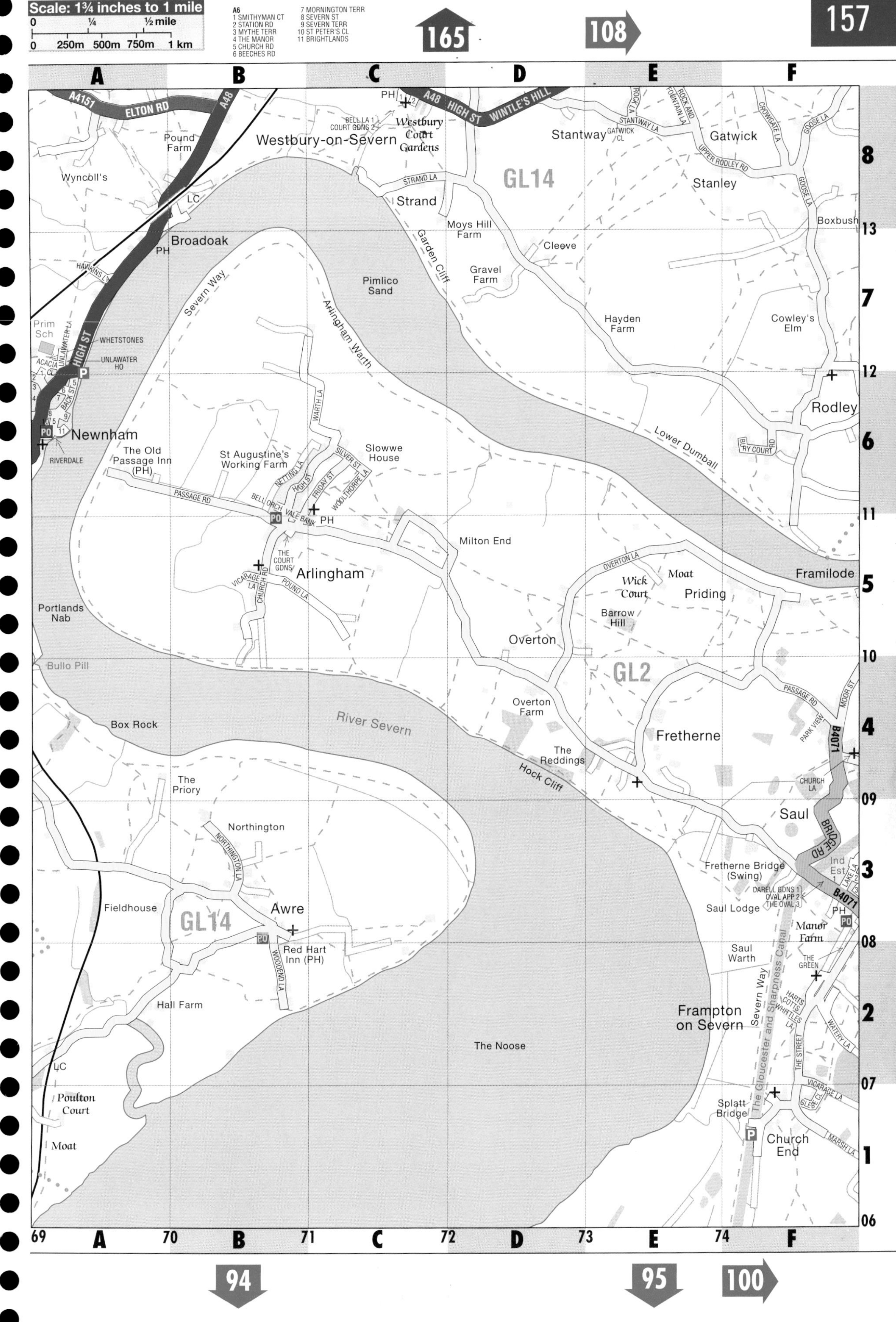
Scale: 1¾ inches to 1 mile
0 ¼ ½ mile
0 250m 500m 750m 1 km
A6
1 SMITHYMAN CT
2 STATION RD
3 MYTHE TERR
4 THE MANOR
5 CHURCH RD
6 BEECHES RD
7 MORNINGTON TERR
8 SEVERN ST
9 SEVERN TERR
10 ST PETER'S CL
11 BRIGHTLANDS
165
108
94
95
100
Westbury-on-Severn
Westbury Court Gardens
Stantway
Gatwick
Stanley
Strand
Pound Farm
Wyncoll's
Broadoak
Moys Hill Farm
Cleeve
Boxbush
Gravel Farm
Pimlico Sand
Garden Cliff
Severn Way
Arlingham Warth
Hayden Farm
Cowley's Elm
Rodley
Lower Dumball
Newnham
The Old Passage Inn (PH)
St Augustine's Working Farm
Slowwe House
Milton End
Arlingham
Framilode
Wick Court
Moat
Priding
Barrow Hill
Overton
Portlands Nab
Bullo Pill
GL14
GL2
Overton Farm
Box Rock
River Severn
Fretherne
The Reddings
Hock Cliff
The Priory
Saul
Northington
Fretherne Bridge (Swing)
Fieldhouse
Awre
Saul Lodge
Manor Farm
Red Hart Inn (PH)
Saul Warth
Hall Farm
Frampton on Severn
The Gloucester and Sharpness Canal
The Noose
Poulton Court
Moat
Splatt Bridge
Church End
ELTON RD
A4151
A48
HIGH ST
WINTLE'S HILL
B4071
BRIDGE RD
PASSAGE RD
OVERTON LA
WARTH LA
POUND LA
CHURCH RD
VICARAGE LA
NORTHINGTON LA
WOODEND LA
THE STREET
MARSH LA
VICARAGE LA
WATERY LA
MOOR ST
PARK VIEW
CHURCH LA
STRAND LA
GOOSE LA
UPPER RODLEY RD
STANTWAY LA
HAWKINS LA
UNLAWATER LA
WHETSTONES
UNLAWATER HO
RIVERDALE
BACK ST
DARELL GDNS
OVAL APP
THE OVAL
THE GREEN
HARTS COTTS
WHITTLES LA
A B C D E F
69 70 71 72 73 74
8 7 6 5 4 3 2 1
13 12 11 10 09 08 07 06

115
166

Scale: 1¾ inches to 1 mile
0 ¼ ½ mile
0 250m 500m 750m 1 km

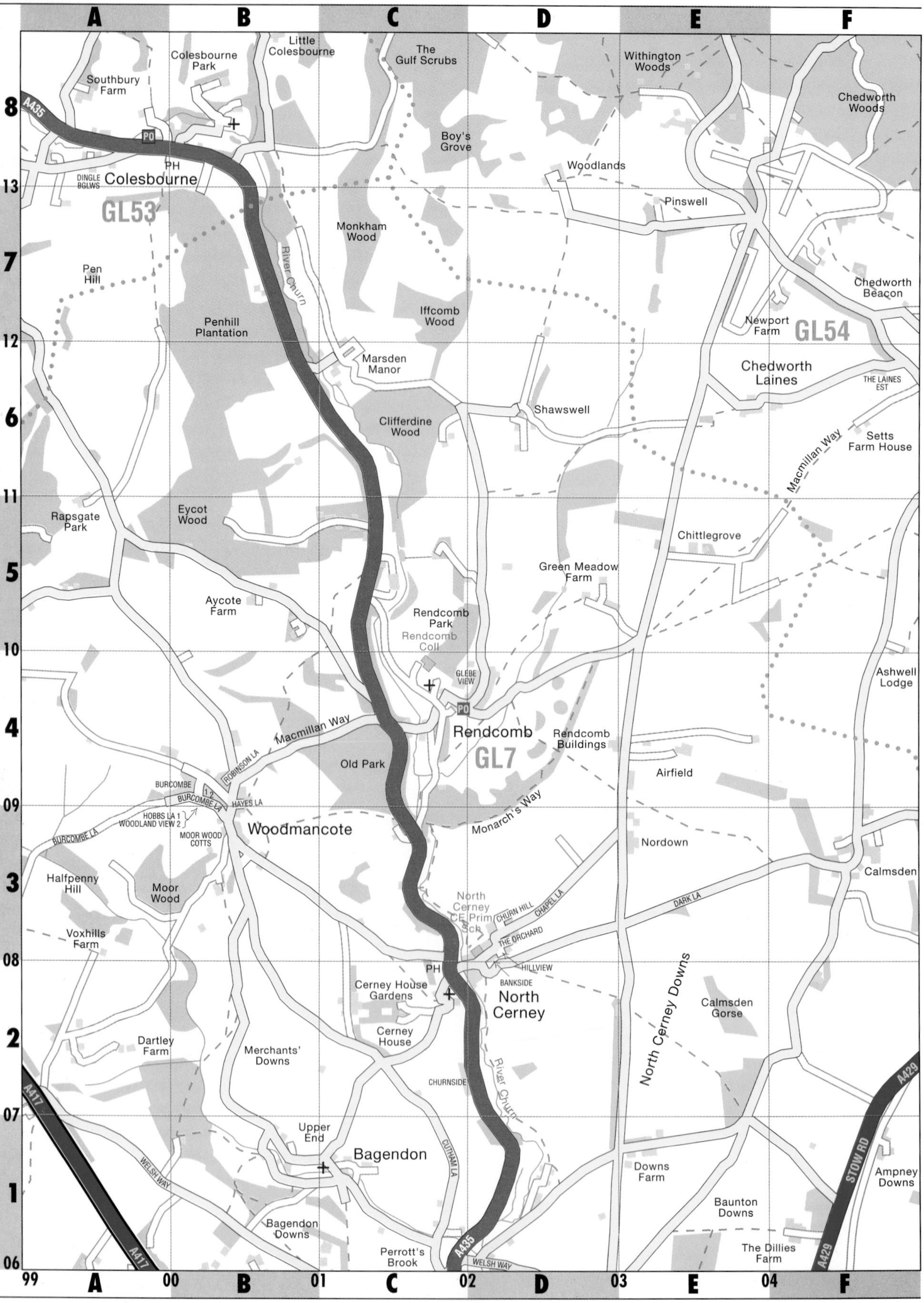

A B C D E F

Little Colesbourne
Colesbourne Park
Southbury Farm
The Gulf Scrubs
Withington Woods
Chedworth Woods
A435
PO
PH
Boy's Grove
Woodlands
DINGLE BGLWS
Colesbourne
GL53
Pinswell
Monkham Wood
River Churn
Pen Hill
Iffcomb Wood
Chedworth Beacon
Newport Farm
GL54
Penhill Plantation
Marsden Manor
Chedworth Laines
THE LAINES EST
Shawswell
Clifferdine Wood
Setts Farm House
Macmillan Way
Eycot Wood
Rapsgate Park
Chittlegrove
Green Meadow Farm
Aycote Farm
Rendcomb Park
Rendcomb Coll
GLEBE VIEW
Ashwell Lodge
PO
Rendcomb
Rendcomb Buildings
Macmillan Way
GL7
ROBINSON LA
Old Park
Airfield
BURCOMBE
BURCOMBE LA
HAYES LA
HOBBS LA 1
WOODLAND VIEW 2
Monarch's Way
BURCOMBE LA
MOOR WOOD COTTS
Woodmancote
Nordown
Halfpenny Hill
Moor Wood
North Cerney CE Prim Sch
CHURN HILL
CHAPEL LA
DARK LA
Calmsden
Voxhills Farm
THE ORCHARD
PH
HILLVIEW
BANKSIDE
Cerney House Gardens
North Cerney
Calmsden Gorse
North Cerney Downs
Dartley Farm
Cerney House
Merchants' Downs
CHURNSIDE
River Churn
A417
A429
Upper End
Bagendon
CUTHAM LA
WELSH WAY
STOW RD
Downs Farm
Ampney Downs
Baunton Downs
Bagendon Downs
A435
Perrott's Brook
WELSH WAY
The Dillies Farm
A417
A429

8 13 7 12 6 11 5 10 4 09 3 08 2 07 1 06

99 A 00 B 01 C 02 D 03 E 04 F

107
150

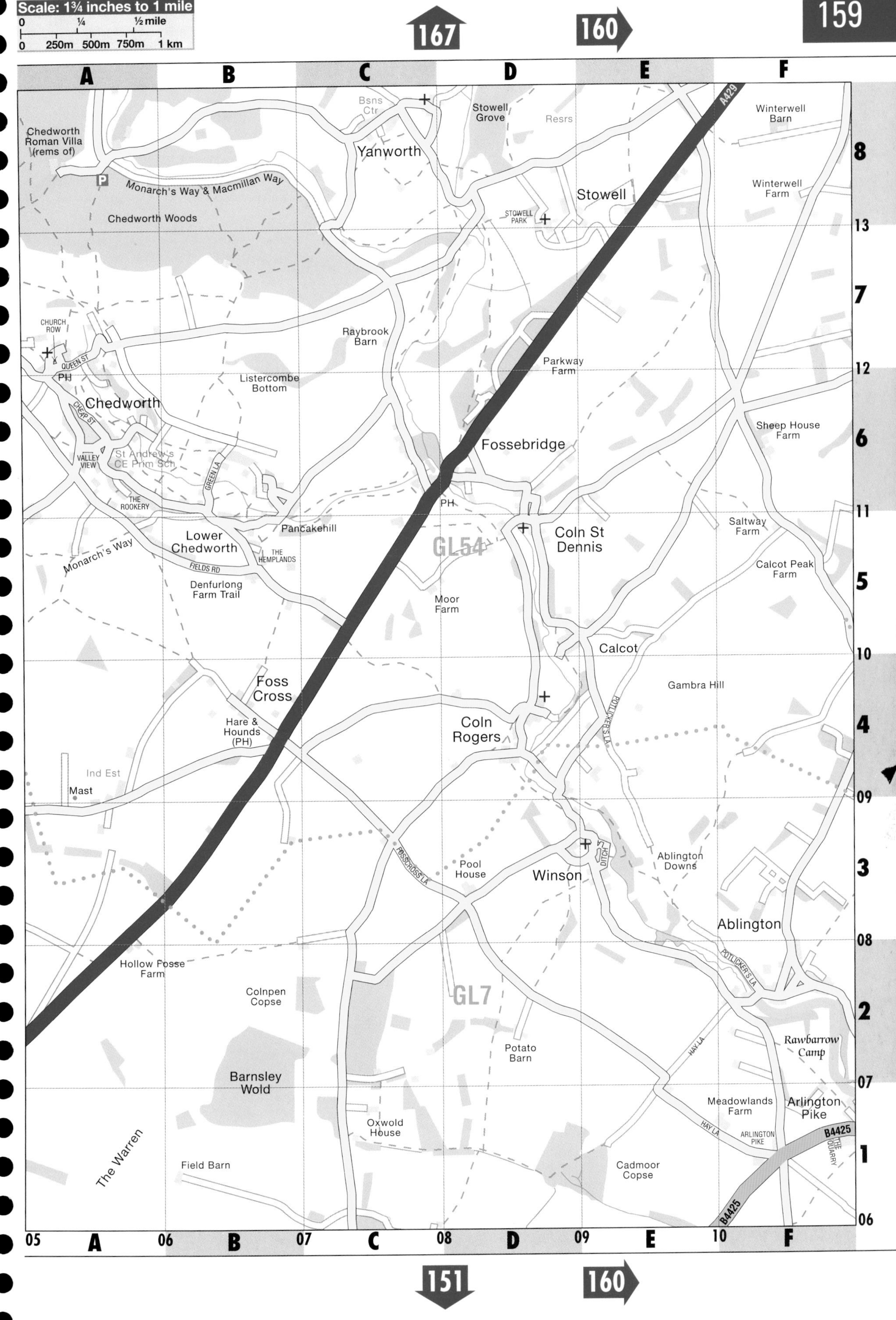

Scale: 1¾ inches to 1 mile
0 ¼ ½ mile
0 250m 500m 750m 1 km
167
160
A B C D E F
Chedworth Roman Villa (rems of)
P
Monarch's Way & Macmillan Way
Chedworth Woods
Bsns Ctr
Yanworth
Stowell Grove
Resrs
A429
Winterwell Barn
8
Winterwell Farm
Stowell
STOWELL PARK
13
7
CHURCH ROW
QUEEN ST
PH
Raybrook Barn
Parkway Farm
12
Listercombe Bottom
Chedworth
CHEAP ST
Sheep House Farm
Fossebridge
6
VALLEY VIEW
St Andrew's CE Prim Sch
GREEN LA
THE ROOKERY
PH
11
Pancakehill
Saltway Farm
Lower Chedworth
GL54
Coln St Dennis
Monarch's Way
THE HEMPLANDS
FIELDS RD
Calcot Peak Farm
Denfurlong Farm Trail
5
Moor Farm
Calcot
10
Foss Cross
Gambra Hill
Hare & Hounds (PH)
Coln Rogers
POTLICKER'S LA
4
Ind Est
Mast
09
FOSSCROSS LA
Pool House
Winson
DITCH'S
Ablington Downs
3
Ablington
08
Hollow Fosse Farm
POTLICKER'S LA
Colnpen Copse
GL7
2
Rawbarrow Camp
Potato Barn
HAY LA
Barnsley Wold
07
Meadowlands Farm
Arlington Pike
Oxwold House
HAY LA
ARLINGTON PIKE
B4425
THE QUARRY
1
The Warren
Field Barn
Cadmoor Copse
B4425
06
05 A 06 B 07 C 08 D 09 E 10 F
151
160

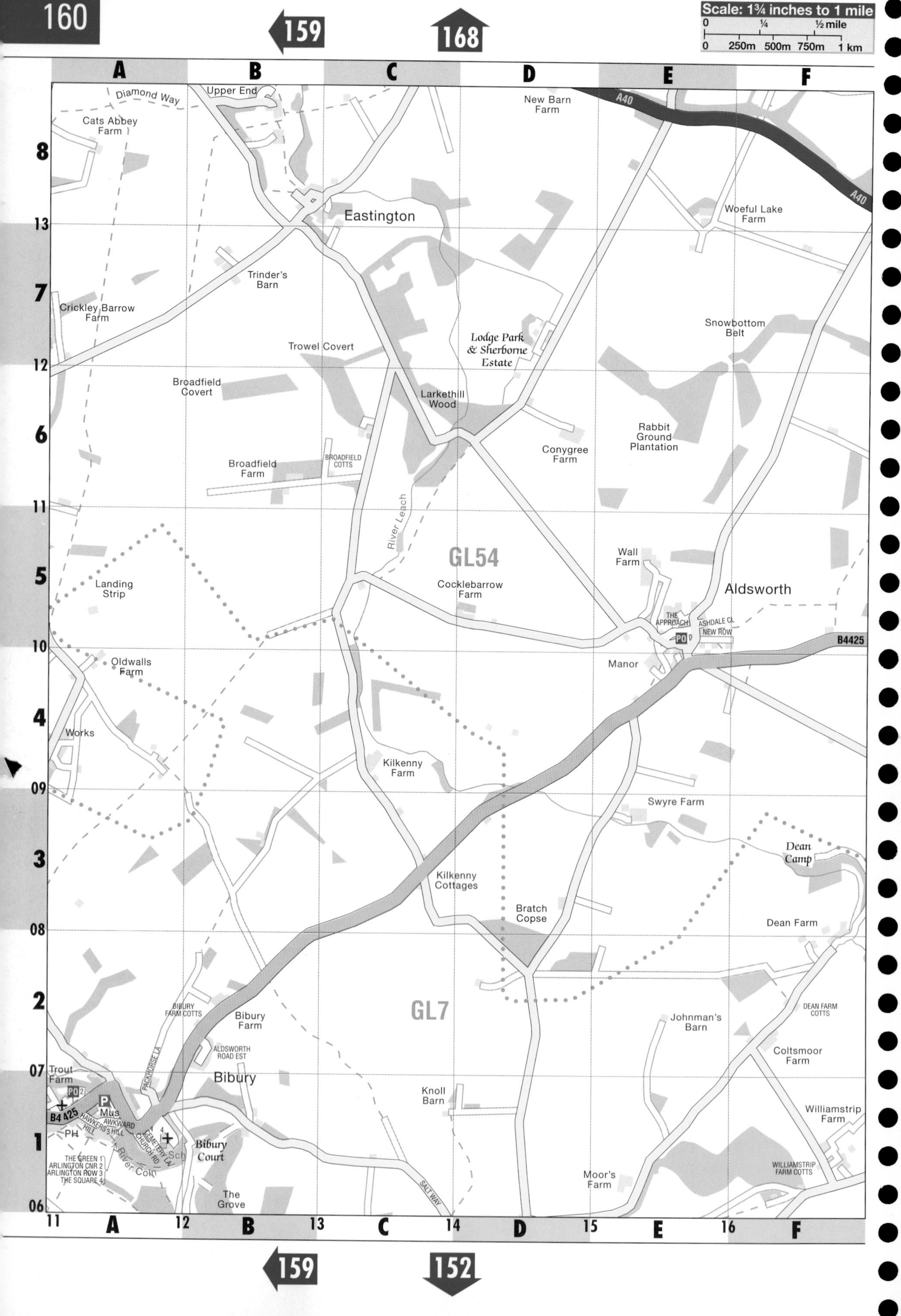
159
168
Scale: 1¾ inches to 1 mile
0 ¼ ½ mile
0 250m 500m 750m 1 km
A B C D E F
8 13 7 12 6 11 5 10 4 09 3 08 2 07 1 06
Diamond Way
Upper End
Cats Abbey Farm
New Barn Farm
A40
Woeful Lake Farm
Eastington
Trinder's Barn
Crickley Barrow Farm
Trowel Covert
Lodge Park & Sherborne Estate
Snowbottom Belt
Broadfield Covert
Larkethill Wood
Rabbit Ground Plantation
Conygree Farm
Broadfield Farm
BROADFIELD COTTS
River Leach
GL54
Wall Farm
Aldsworth
Landing Strip
Cocklebarrow Farm
THE APPROACH
ASHDALE CL
NEW ROW
PO
B4425
Manor
Oldwalls Farm
Works
Kilkenny Farm
Swyre Farm
Dean Camp
Kilkenny Cottages
Bratch Copse
Dean Farm
GL7
BIBURY FARM COTTS
Bibury Farm
DEAN FARM COTTS
Johnman's Barn
ALDSWORTH ROAD EST
Coltsmoor Farm
Trout Farm
Bibury
PACKHORSE LA
Knoll Barn
Williamstrip Farm
B4425
Mus
AWKWARD HILL
HAWKERS HILL
CEMETERY LA
CHURCH RD
PH
Sch
River Coln
Bibury Court
THE GREEN 1
ARLINGTON CNR 2
ARLINGTON ROW 3
THE SQUARE 4
SALT WAY
Moor's Farm
WILLIAMSTRIP FARM COTTS
The Grove
11 A 12 B 13 C 14 D 15 E 16 F
159
152

Scale: 1¾ inches to 1 mile
0 ¼ ½ mile
0 250m 500m 750m 1 km

169

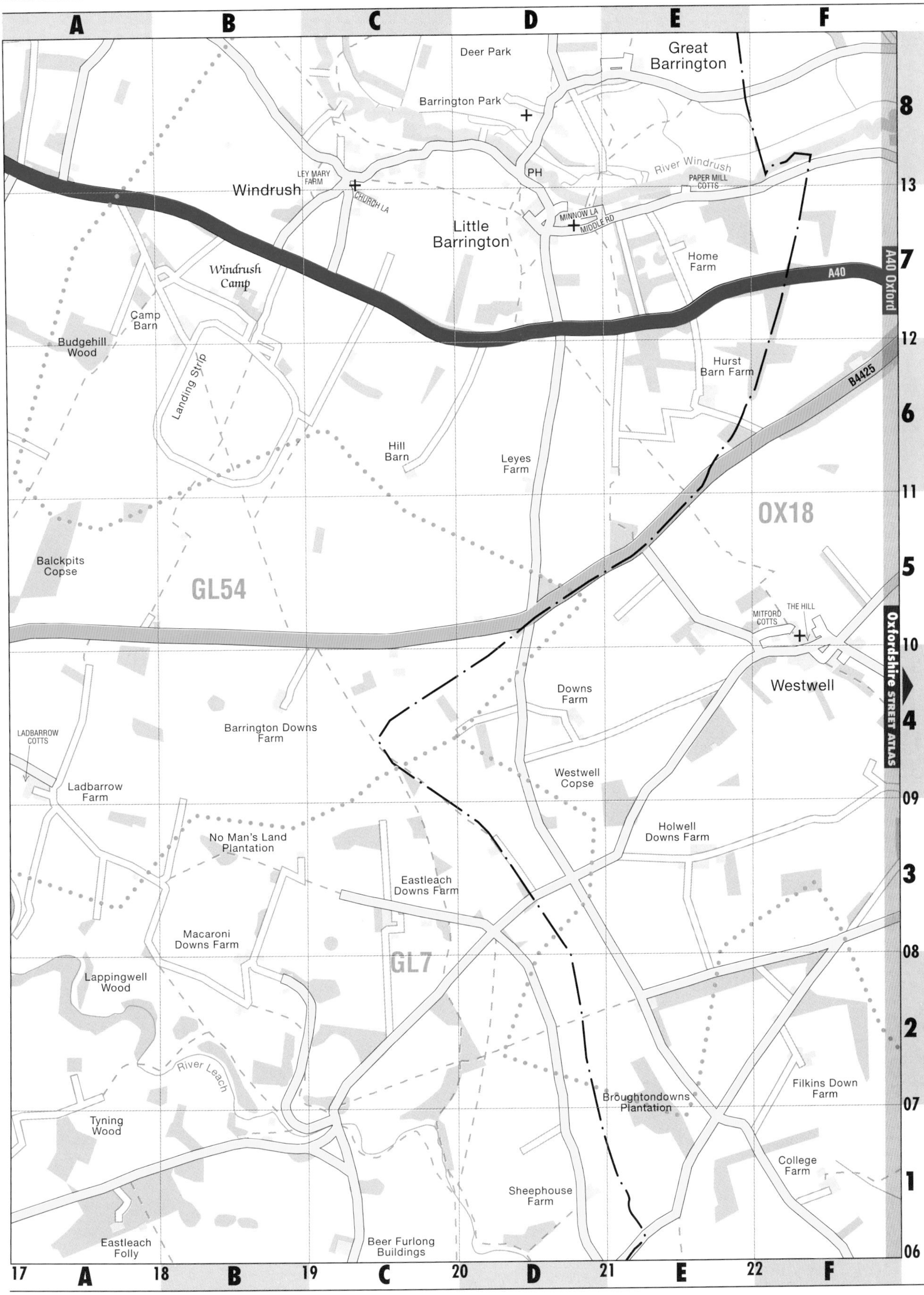

153

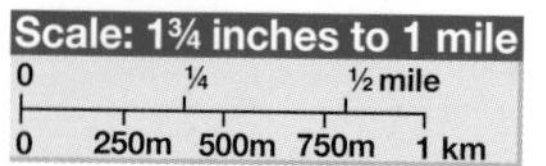

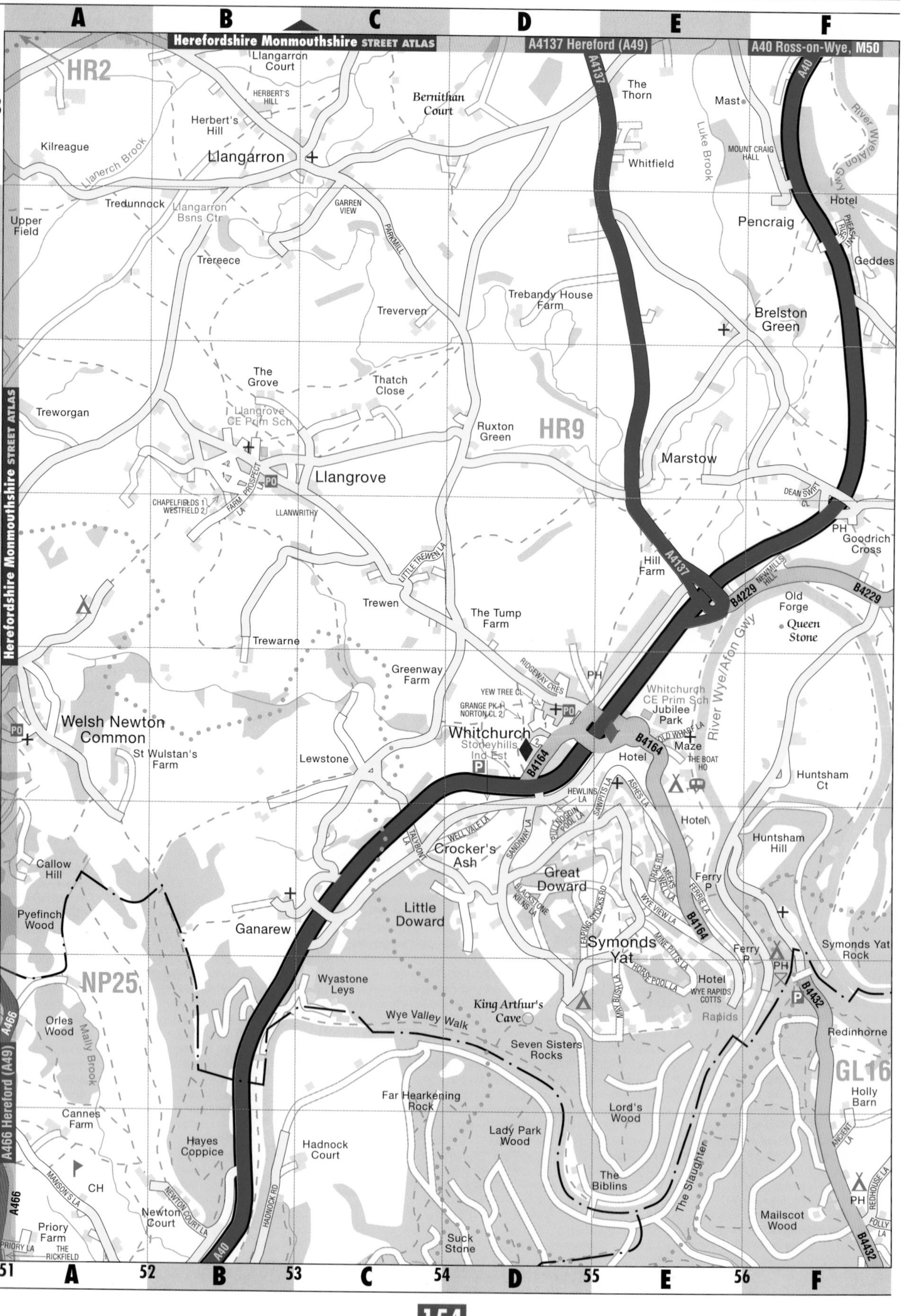

Scale: 1¾ inches to 1 mile
Herefordshire Monmouthshire STREET ATLAS
A4137 Hereford (A49)
A40 Ross-on-Wye, M50
HR2
Llangarron Court
Bernithan Court
The Thorn
Mast
Herbert's Hill
Kilreague
Llangarron
Whitfield
Mount Craig Hall
Luke Brook
River Wye/Afon Gwy
Llanerch Brook
Tredunnock
Llangarron Bsns Ctr
Garren View
Upper Field
Parkmill
Hotel
Pencraig
Geddes
Trereece
Trebandy House Farm
Treverven
Brelston Green
The Grove
Thatch Close
Treworgan
Llangrove CE Prim Sch
Ruxton Green
HR9
Marstow
Llangrove
Chapelfields 1
Westfield 2
Farm Prospect La
Llanwrithy
Dean Swift Cl
PH
Goodrich Cross
Little Trewen La
Hill Farm
A4137
B4229
Newmills Hill
Old Forge
Queen Stone
Trewen
The Tump Farm
Trewarne
Greenway Farm
Ridgeway Cres
Yew Tree Cl
Grange Pk 1
Norton Cl 2
Whitchurch CE Prim Sch
Jubilee Park
Old Wharf La
Maze
Welsh Newton Common
St Wulstan's Farm
Whitchurch
Stoneyhills Ind Est
Lewstone
B4164
Hotel
The Boat Ho
Huntsham Ct
Hewlins La
Sawpits La
Ashes La
Pullnoggin Pool La
Sandway La
Well Vale La
Talybont La
Crocker's Ash
Huntsham Hill
Callow Hill
Great Doward
Blackstone Kilns La
Leaping Stocks Rd
Crag Rd
Mierscourt La
Ferrie La
Wye View La
Ferry P
Pyefinch Wood
Ganarew
Little Doward
Symonds Yat
Mine Pitts La
Symonds Yat Rock
NP25
Wyastone Leys
Horse Pool La
Hotel
Wye Rapids Cotts
May Bush La
King Arthur's Cave
Rapids
B4432
Orles Wood
Wye Valley Walk
Redinhorne
Mally Brook
Seven Sisters Rocks
GL16
A466 Hereford (A49)
Far Hearkening Rock
Lord's Wood
Holly Barn
Cannes Farm
Lady Park Wood
Hayes Coppice
Hadnock Court
Ancient La
Redhouse La
CH
The Biblins
The Slaughter
Manson's La
Newton Court La
Hadnock Rd
Newton Court
Mailscot Wood
Folly La
A466
Priory Farm
Priory La
The Rickfield
Suck Stone
A40
A B C D E F
51 52 53 54 55 56
8 21 7 20 6 19 5 18 4 17 3 16 2 15 1 14

154

Scale: 1¾ inches to 1 mile
0 ¼ ½ mile
0 250m 500m 750m 1 km

164

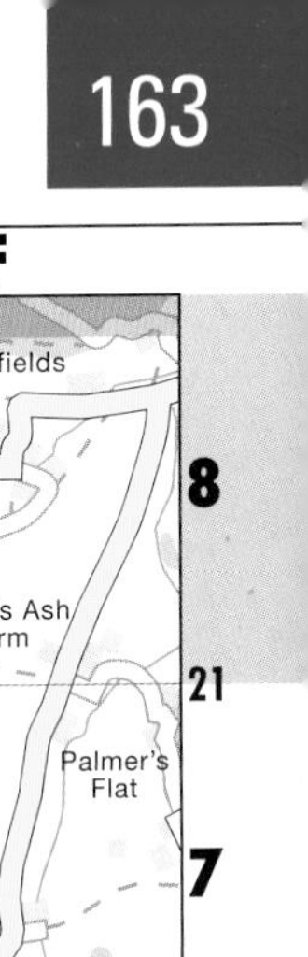

A B C D E F

8
21
7
20
6
19
5
18
4
17
3
16
2
15
1
14

Hill Court
Old Hill Court
Bollin Farm
B4234
Chase Wood
Wye Valley Walk
Coleraine Farm
Parkfields
Cobrey Park
COUGHTON PL
PRIORY LEA HO
PRIORY LEA
CEDAR GR
Coughton
NORRLAND PL
FOWBRIDGE GDNS
ALDER CL
Hope's Ash Farm
The Callow
Walford Prim Sch
Upper Wythall
Howle Hill
PH
Palmer's Flat
Walford Court
HR9
SHARMAN PITCH
Bull's Hill
Deep Dean
Walford
NELSONS CL
PH
GREEN COLLEY CL
Great Howle Farm
Kiln Green
Goodrich Castle
Leys Hill
STAR BEECH HILL
The Dam
Hope Mansell
KNAPP CL
THE SQUARE
CASTLE LA
PH
Flanesford Priory
PH
Bishop's Wood
Cruse
PO
B4229
THE DEAN
Cowles House
Goodrich CE Prim Sch
Kerne Bridge
Goodrich
Home Farm
HAZELHURST BGLWS
River Wye/Afon Gwy
PO
WYESIDE PK
Drybrook House
Rocklands Farm
Vain Farm
Great Marstow Farm
Thomas Wood
Welsh Bicknor
Ruardean
THE SQUARE 1
CAUDLE CL 2
CAUDLE LA 3
SPRING PL 4
PERRY'S COURT LA 5
CASH HILL
ST JOHN'S RD
ST MARGARET'S RD
Crooked End
VARNISTER RD
Baynhams
WYELANDS PK
CINDERHILL WAY
HIGH ST
SCHOOL RD
HIGHFIELD RD
YH
Mainoaks
Works
Stowfield
Pottery
WEST END
TOWNSEND
PO
PH
1 HART LA
2 NORMAN WAY
3 SCHOOL LA
4 KINGSWAY LA
5 MOUNTAIN VIEW
6 BOX TREE CL
7 BELLE VUE RD
8 PARK VIEW
9 CROOKED END PL
10 VARNISTER LA
Coppet Hill
UPPER STOWFIELD RD
STOWFIELD RD
Courtfield
THE MALTINGS
PETTYCROFT
WALKERS LA
1 HILLSIDE TERR
2 ORCHARD RD
3 SCHOOL CRES
4 WEST VIEW
5 WOODLAND VIEW
Ruardean CE Prim Sch
Turner's Tump
MEENDS LA
Wye Valley Walk
The Green
P
Lower Lydbrook
VENTION LA
Joy's Green
Ruardean Woodside
BAKERS PIECE RD
THE PATCHES
FARM RD
Smithers Cross
RUARDEAN RD
FOREST RD
DENEHURST
PROBERTSBARN LA
COPPICE RD
PH
ROCKS RD
SCHOOL RD
PO
Sch
Readings
EDENS LA
GL17
BRIERLEY RD
MILL ROW 1
THE FORGE 2
HIGH ROW 3
Meredith Ind Est
GREENFIELD RD
FORGE HILL
GREENFIELD CL
EDWARDS CL
HORSE LA
HIGHBEECH RD
ASH DENE RD
Woodside Prim Sch
WEBLEY RD 1
MARFELLS WAY 2
ROEBUCK MDWS 3
DUTTONS LA 4
Common Grove
THE ANCHORAGE
JOYS GREEN RD
PH
PLUDDS COURT RD
HIGH ST
ROYAL OAK RD
ASTON BRIDGE RD
English Bicknor CE Prim Sch
PO
Upper Lydbrook
The Pludds
Bicknor Court
LUCY CT
Coldwell Rocks
CHURCH HILL CL
1 UPHILL RD
2 MERTHYR TERR
3 SCHOOL RD
4 CHURCH RD
5 CHURCH HILL
ORCHARD CL
CROSS BARN
FOREST RISE
Brierley
BRIERLEY BANKS
PH
HOLBROOK
A4136
REDHOUSE LA
English Bicknor
ROBINSON LA
Sch
BRIERLEY COUNCIL HOS
HIGH ST
MURRELLS RD
SMITHY CL
Eastbach Court
CAMOMILE GN
HANGERBERRY NEW RD
Waterloo Bsns Pk
Serridge Green
COUNCIL VILLAS
VALLEY RD
GL16
Dryslade Farm
Worrall Hill
HATTON CL
RIDGE PL
CHAPEL HILL
BICKNOR ST
NEW RD
B4234
P
Carterspiece
Wysis Way
FOLLY LA
A4136
P
GL14

57 A 58 B 59 C 60 D 61 E 62 F

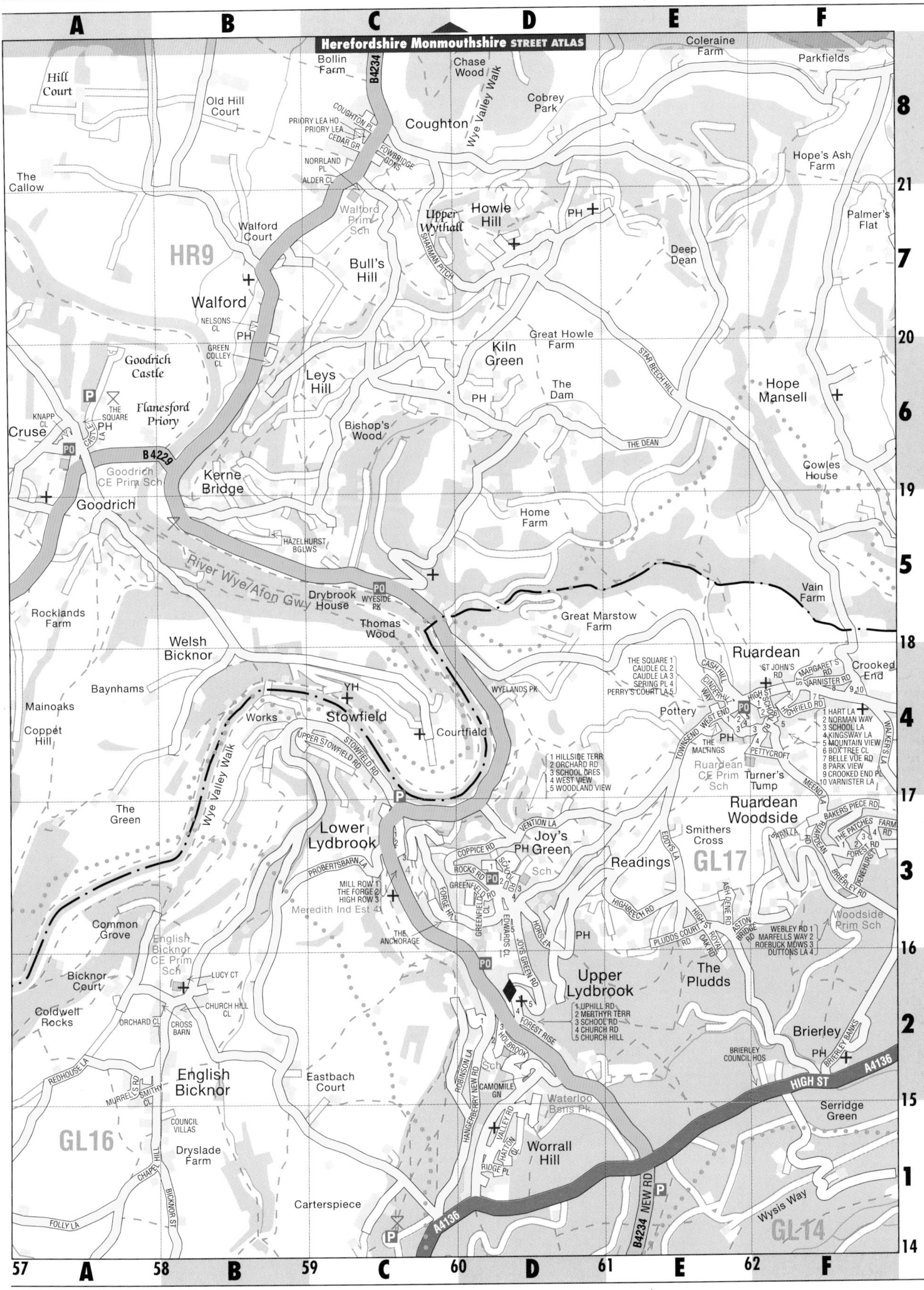

155
164

163

170

Scale: 1¾ inches to 1 mile

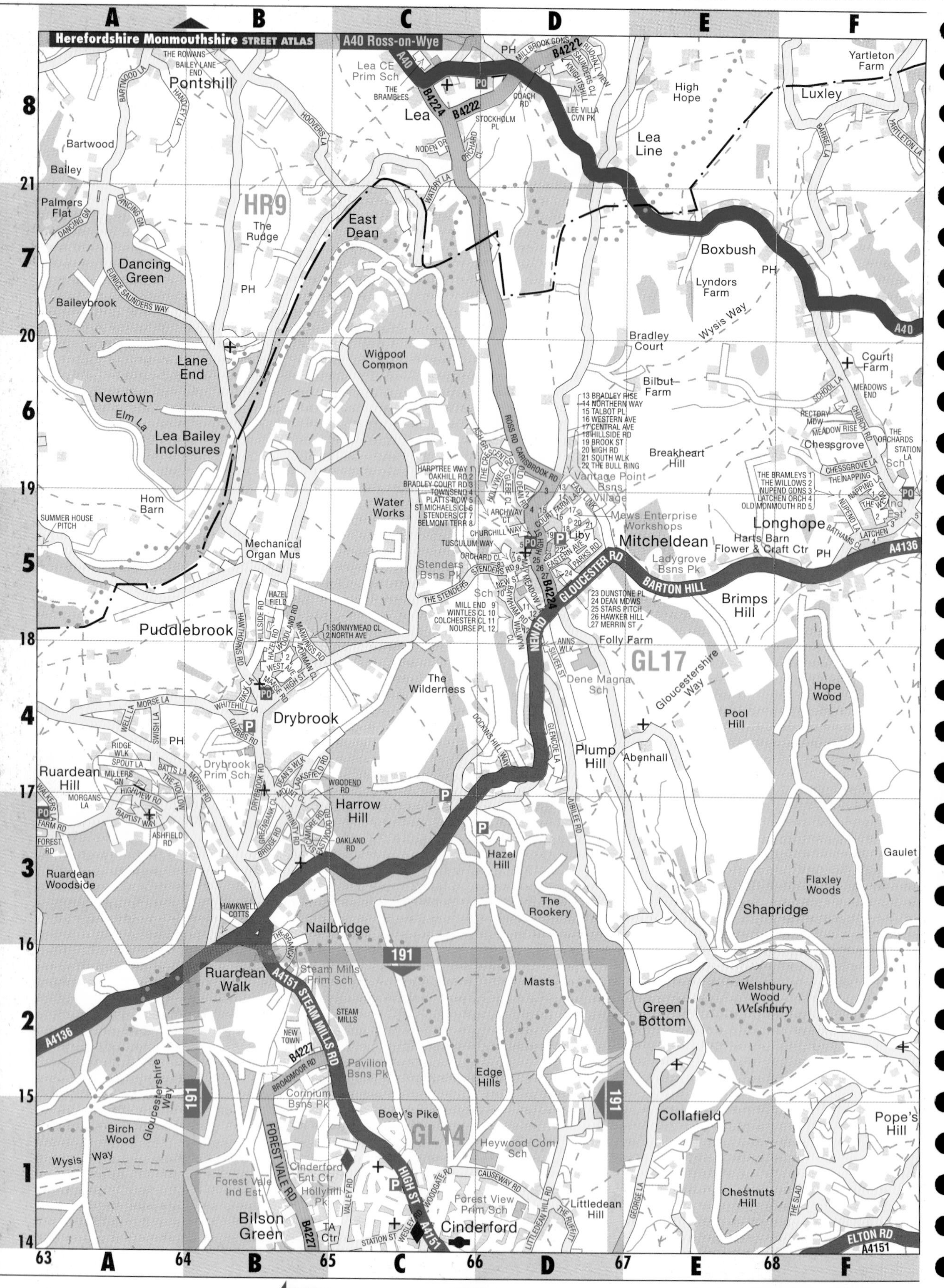

163

156

For full street detail of the highlighted area see page 191.

170 171 124

Scale: 1¾ inches to 1 mile

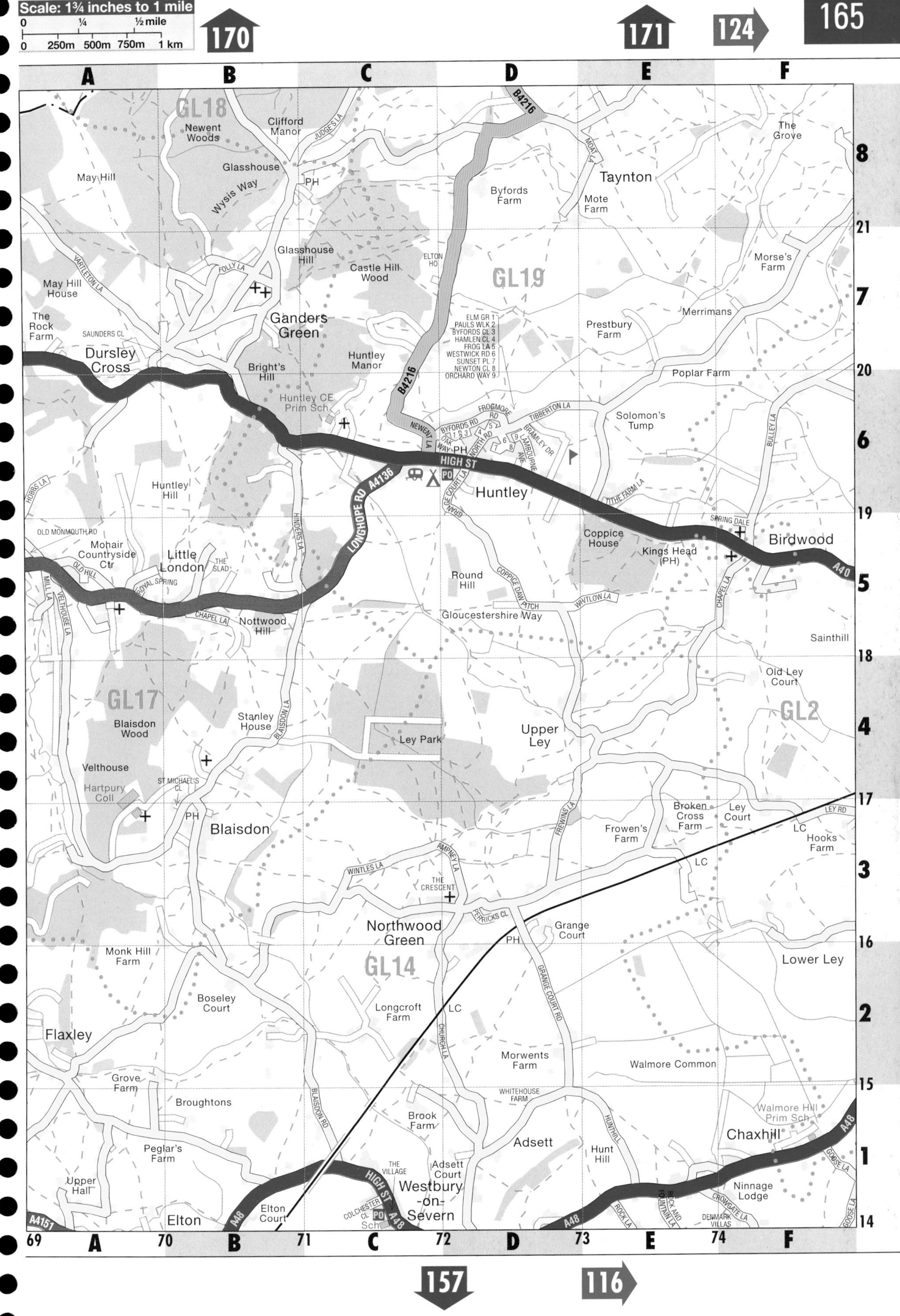

157 116

131 135 174

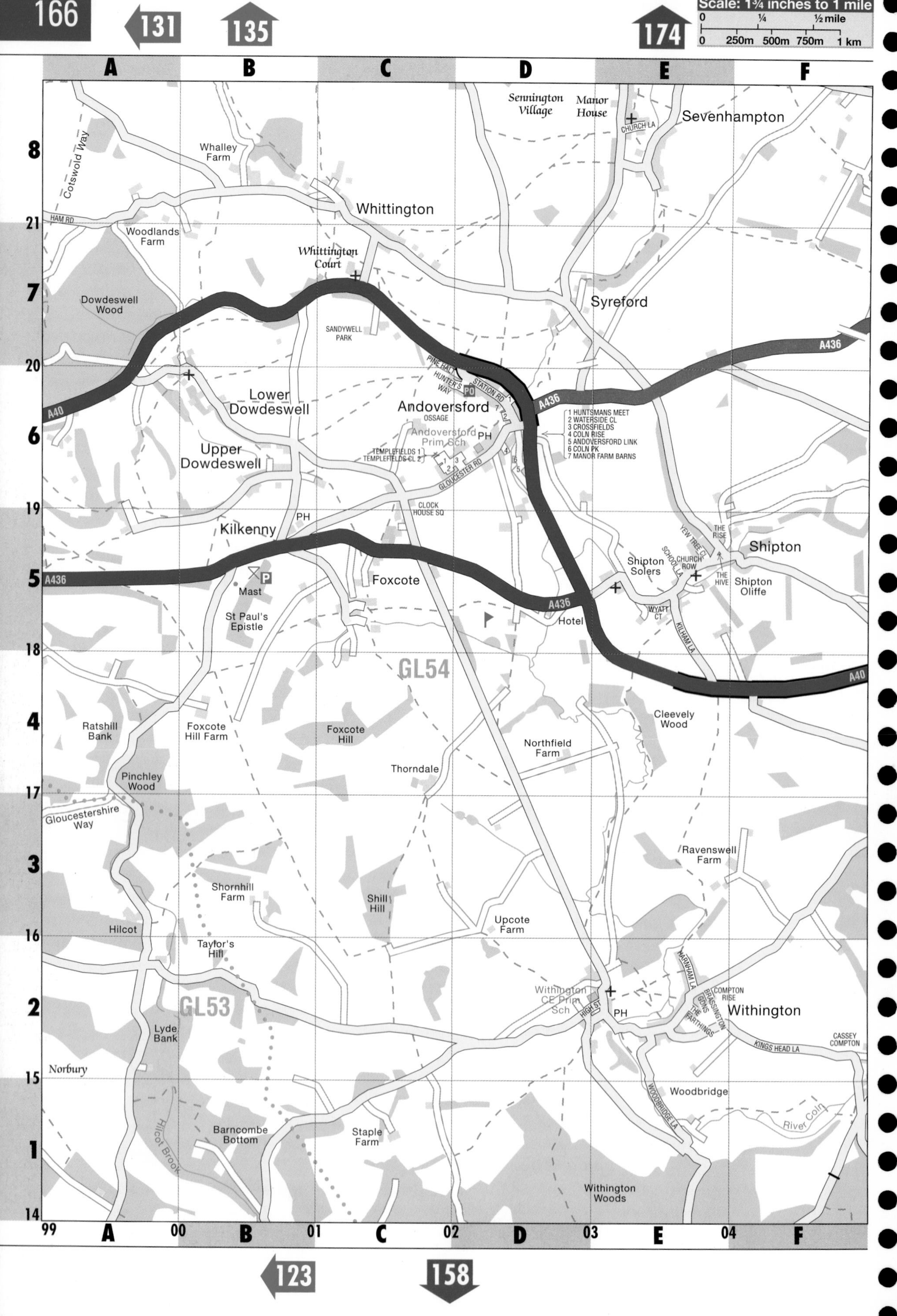

123 158

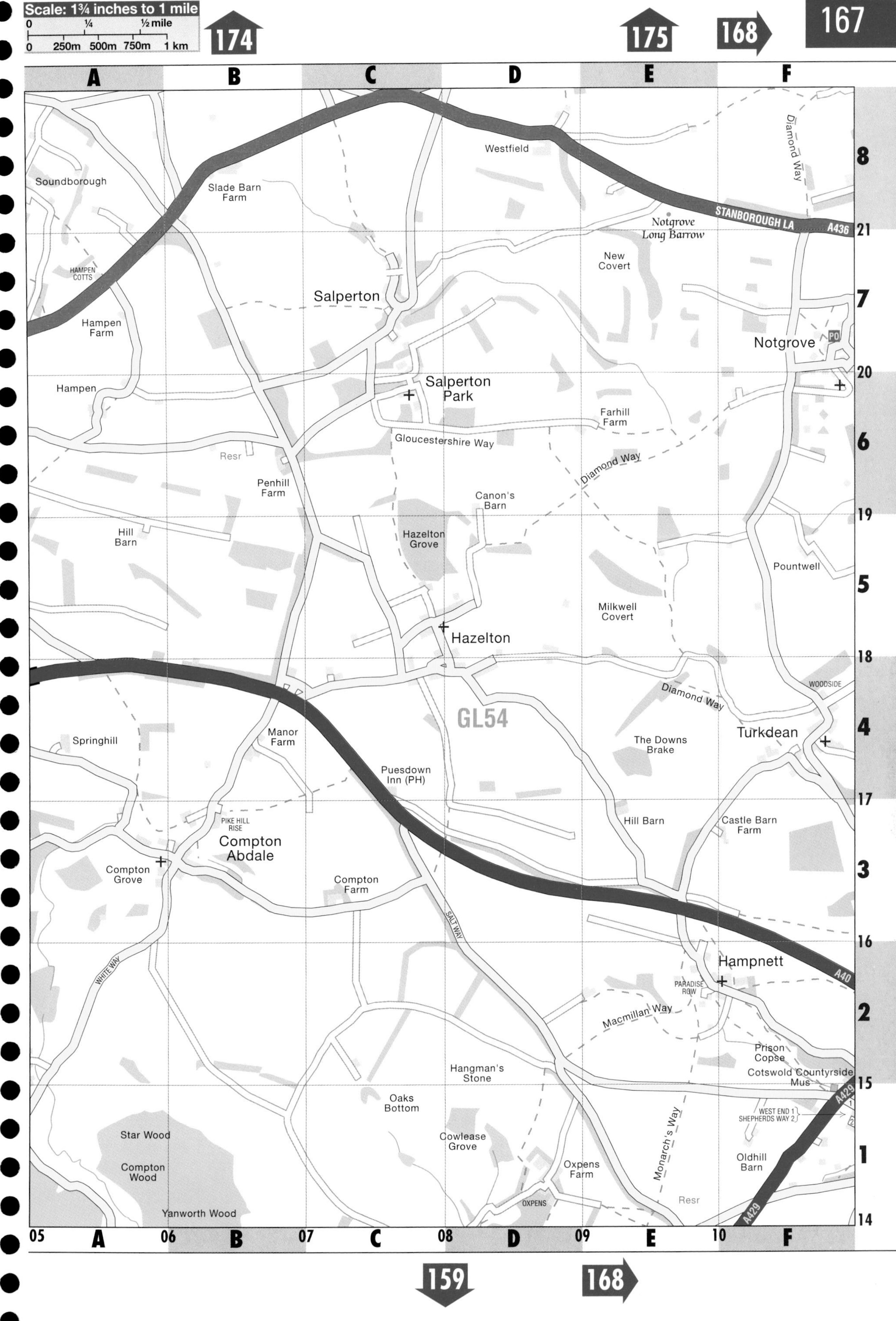

Scale: 1¾ inches to 1 mile
0 ¼ ½ mile
0 250m 500m 750m 1 km
174
175
168
A B C D E F
Westfield
Diamond Way
Soundborough
Slade Barn Farm
STANBOROUGH LA
A436
Notgrove Long Barrow
HAMPEN COTTS
New Covert
Salperton
Hampen Farm
Notgrove
PO
Hampen
Salperton Park
Farhill Farm
Gloucestershire Way
Resr
Diamond Way
Penhill Farm
Canon's Barn
Hill Barn
Hazelton Grove
Pountwell
Milkwell Covert
Hazelton
Diamond Way
WOODSIDE
GL54
Turkdean
Springhill
Manor Farm
The Downs Brake
Puesdown Inn (PH)
PIKE HILL RISE
Hill Barn
Castle Barn Farm
Compton Abdale
Compton Grove
Compton Farm
SALT WAY
WHITE WAY
Hampnett
A40
PARADISE ROW
Macmillan Way
Prison Copse
Hangman's Stone
Cotswold Countryside Mus
Oaks Bottom
A429
WEST END 1
SHEPHERDS WAY 2
Star Wood
Monarch's Way
Cowlease Grove
Compton Wood
Oxpens Farm
Oldhill Barn
OXPENS
Resr
Yanworth Wood
A429
8 21 7 20 6 19 5 18 4 17 3 16 2 15 1 14
05 06 07 08 09 10
159
168

F7
1 PERRYFIELD CT
2 COLLETTS CT
3 FOXES CL
4 SHERBORNE TERR
5 BOW LA
6 VICTORIA ST
7 CHARDWAR GDNS
8 CLAPTON ROW
9 VICTORIA TERR
10 LETCH LA
11 BAINES CL

Scale: 1¾ inches to 1 mile

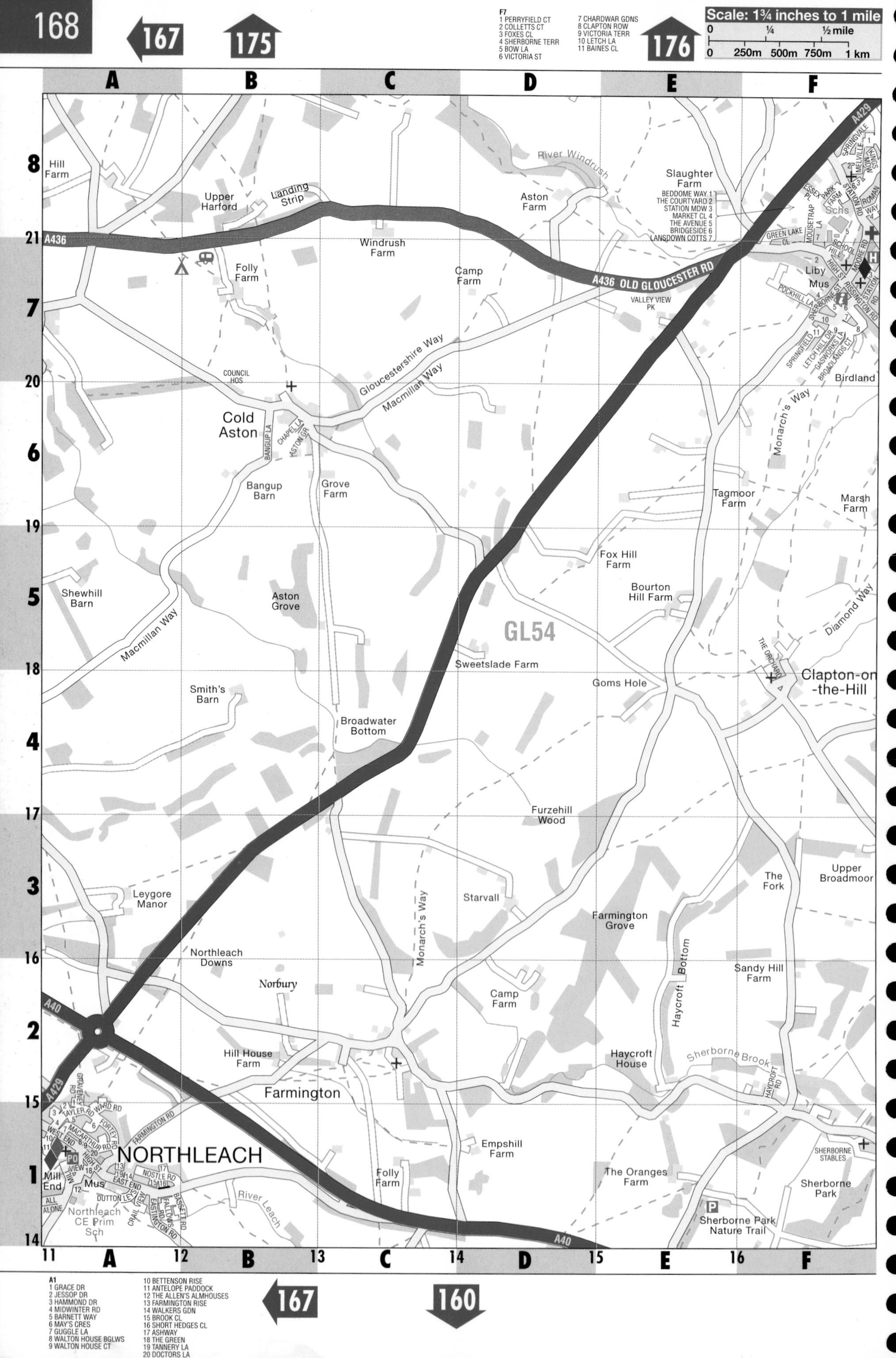

A1
1 GRACE DR
2 JESSOP DR
3 HAMMOND DR
4 MIDWINTER RD
5 BARNETT WAY
6 MAY'S CRES
7 GUGGLE LA
8 WALTON HOUSE BGLWS
9 WALTON HOUSE CT
10 BETTENSON RISE
11 ANTELOPE PADDOCK
12 THE ALLEN'S ALMSHOUSES
13 FARMINGTON RISE
14 WALKERS GDN
15 BROOK CL
16 SHORT HEDGES CL
17 ASHWAY
18 THE GREEN
19 TANNERY LA
20 DOCTORS LA

Scale: 1¾ inches to 1 mile

176
177

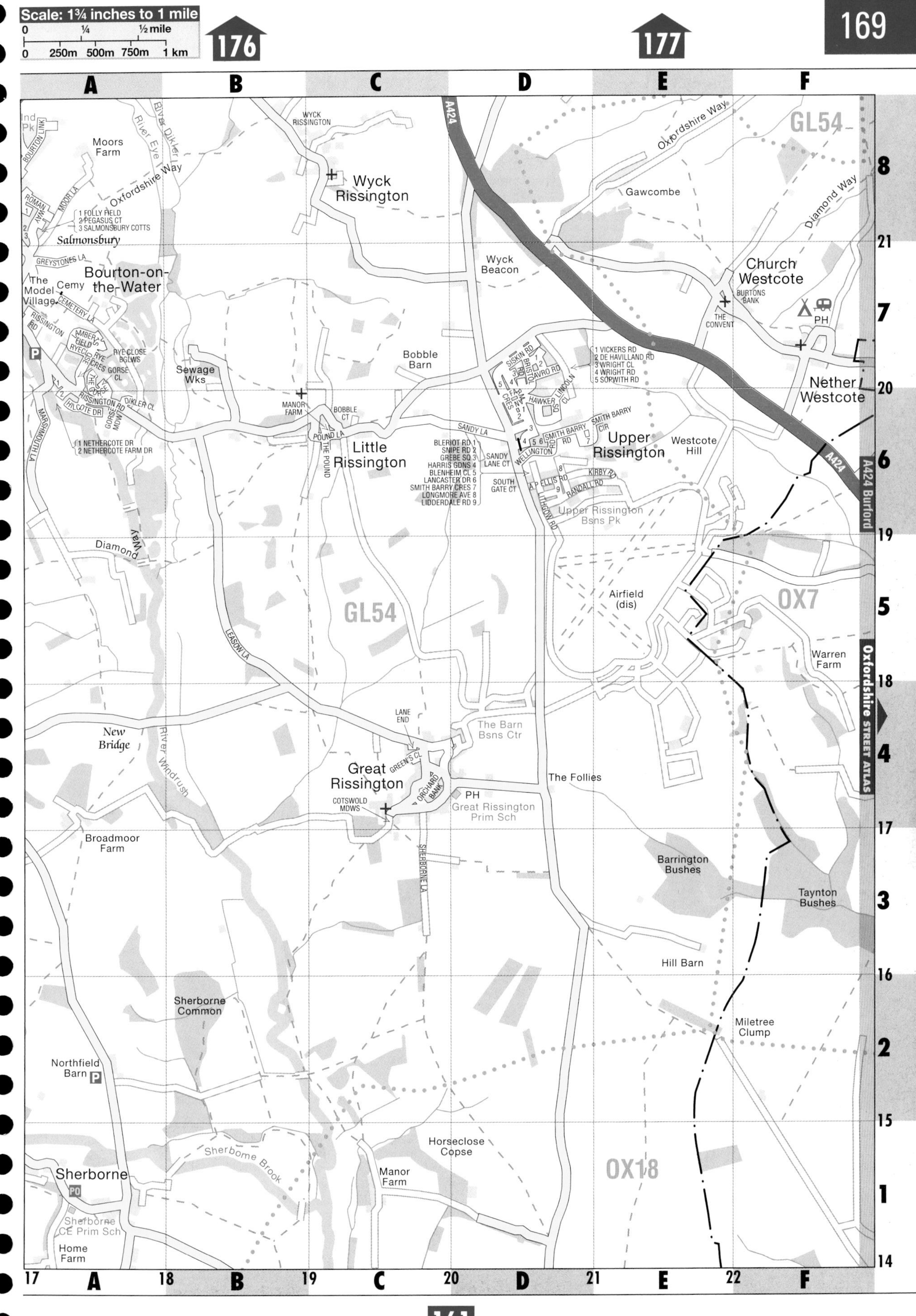

161

178

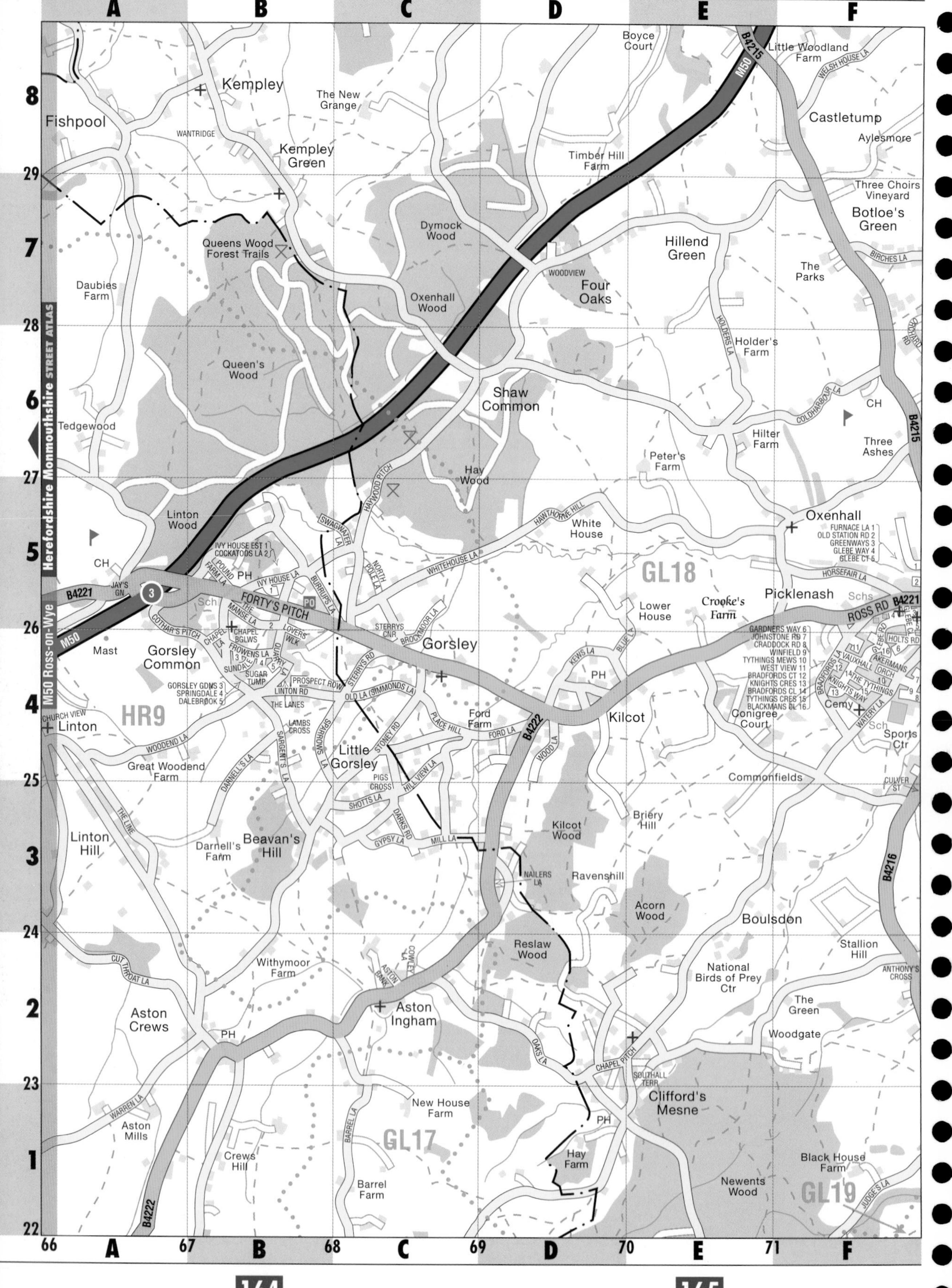

Scale: 1¾ inches to 1 mile
0 ¼ ½ mile
0 250m 500m 750m 1 km
A B C D E F
8 29 7 28 6 27 5 26 4 25 3 24 2 23 1 22
66 67 68 69 70 71
Herefordshire Monmouthshire STREET ATLAS
M50 Ross-on-Wye
Kempley
Fishpool
The New Grange
Boyce Court
Little Woodland Farm
Castletump
Aylesmore
Kempley Green
Timber Hill Farm
Three Choirs Vineyard
Botloe's Green
Dymock Wood
Hillend Green
Queens Wood Forest Trails
The Parks
Daubies Farm
Oxenhall Wood
Four Oaks
Holder's Farm
Queen's Wood
Shaw Common
CH
Tedgewood
Hilter Farm
Three Ashes
Peter's Farm
Hay Wood
Linton Wood
White House
Oxenhall
GL18
Picklenash
Lower House
Crooke's Farm
Gorsley
Gorsley Common
Mast
Kilcot
Ford Farm
HR9
Linton
Conigree Court
Great Woodend Farm
Little Gorsley
Commonfields
Linton Hill
Darnell's Farm
Beavan's Hill
Kilcot Wood
Briery Hill
Ravenshill
Acorn Wood
Boulsdon
Withymoor Farm
Reslaw Wood
Stallion Hill
National Birds of Prey Ctr
Aston Crews
Aston Ingham
The Green
Woodgate
Clifford's Mesne
Aston Mills
New House Farm
GL17
Crews Hill
Barrel Farm
Hay Farm
Black House Farm
Newents Wood
GL19
M50
B4215
B4221
B4222
B4216
FORTY'S PITCH
ROSS RD
WANTRIDGE
WOODVIEW
HAWTHORNE HILL
WHITEHOUSE LA
HAYWOOD PITCH
SWAGWATER LA
NORTH POLE LA
BURRUPS LA
IVY HOUSE LA
IVY HOUSE EST 1
COCKATOOS LA 2
POUND FARM LA
JAY'S GN
COTHAR'S PITCH
CHAPEL LA
CHAPEL BGLWS
MANSE LA
LOVERS WLK
FROWENS LA
QUARRY
SUNDAL
SUGAR TUMP
GORSLEY GDNS 3
SPRINGDALE 4
DALEBROOK 5
PROSPECT ROW
LINTON RD
THE LANES
STERRYS CNR
STERRYS RD
BROCKMOOR LA
OLD LA (SIMMONDS LA)
LAMBS CROSS
SPARROWS LA
SARGENT'S LA
STONEY RD
PLACE HILL
FORD LA
WOOD LA
KEWS LA
BLUE LA
PIGS CROSS
HILL VIEW LA
SHOTTS LA
DARKS RD
GYPSY LA
MILL LA
NAILERS LA
DARNELL'S LA
WOODEND LA
THE LINE
CHURCH VIEW
CUT THROAT LA
COWLEY LA
ASTON BANK
OAKS LA
CHAPEL PITCH
SOUTHALL TERR
BARREL LA
WARREN LA
HOLDERS LA
COLDHARBOUR LA
BIRCHES LA
WELSH HOUSE LA
ORCHARD RD
FURNACE LA 1
OLD STATION RD 2
GREENWAYS 3
GLEBE WAY 4
GLEBE CT 5
HORSEFAIR LA
GARDNERS WAY 6
JOHNSTONE RD 7
CRADDOCK RD 8
WINFIELD 9
TYTHINGS MEWS 10
WEST VIEW 11
BRADFORDS CT 12
KNIGHTS CRES 13
BRADFORDS CL 14
TYTHINGS CRES 15
BLACKMANS CL 16
BRADFORDS LA
VAUXHALL
AKERMANS ORCH
THE TYTHINGS
KNIGHTS WAY
WATERY LA
HOLTS RD
Cemy
Sch
Schs
Sports Ctr
CULVER ST
ANTHONY'S CROSS
JUDGE'S LA
PH
PO

164

165

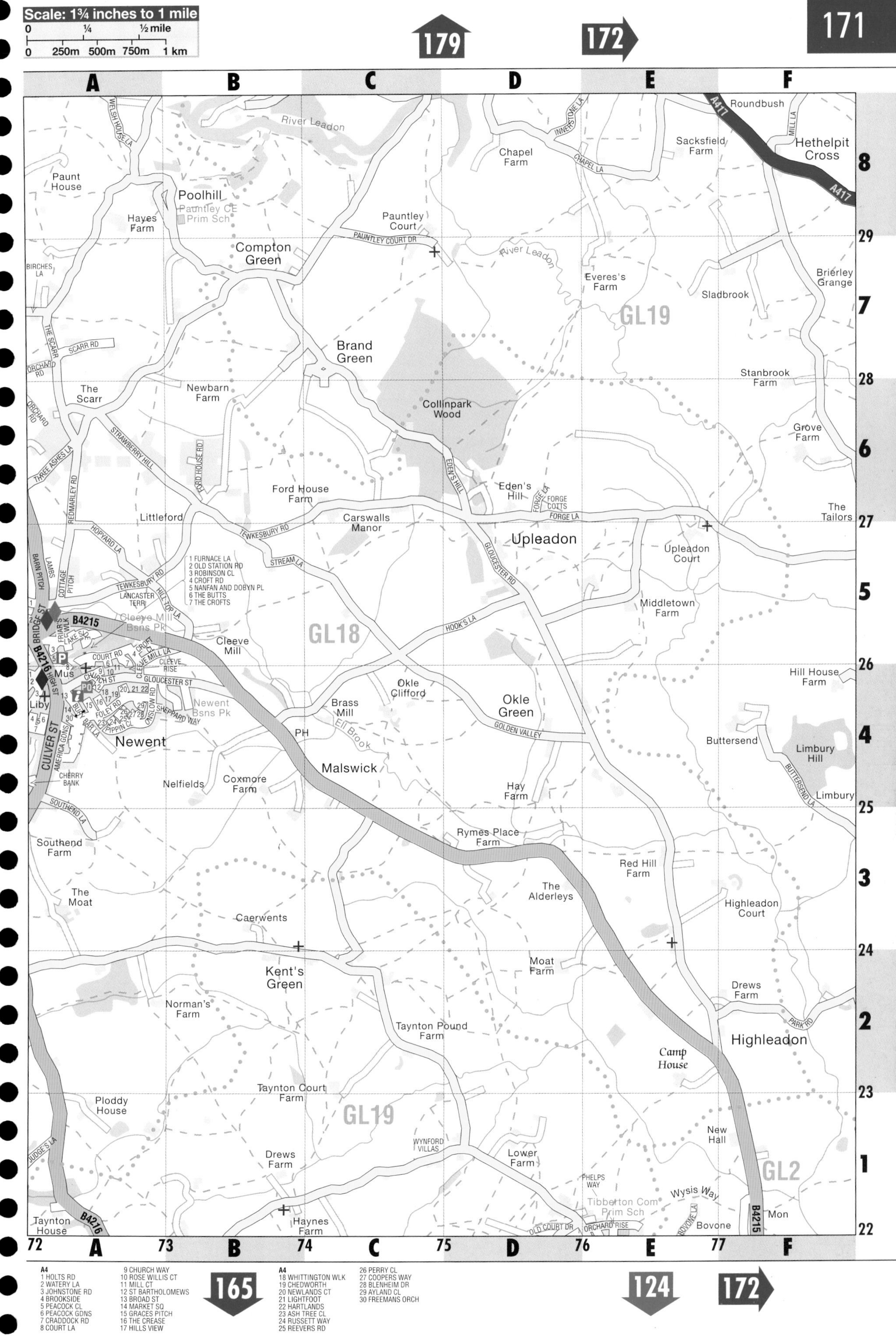

A4
1 HOLTS RD
2 WATERY LA
3 JOHNSTONE RD
4 BROOKSIDE
5 PEACOCK CL
6 PEACOCK GDNS
7 CRADDOCK RD
8 COURT LA
9 CHURCH WAY
10 ROSE WILLIS CT
11 MILL CT
12 ST BARTHOLOMEWS
13 BROAD ST
14 MARKET SQ
15 GRACES PITCH
16 THE CREASE
17 HILLS VIEW

A4
18 WHITTINGTON WLK
19 CHEDWORTH
20 NEWLANDS CT
21 LIGHTFOOT
22 HARTLANDS
23 ASH TREE CL
24 RUSSETT WAY
25 REEVERS RD
26 PERRY CL
27 COOPERS WAY
28 BLENHEIM DR
29 AYLAND CL
30 FREEMANS ORCH

165 124 172

171
180

Scale: 1¾ inches to 1 mile
0 ¼ ½ mile
0 250m 500m 750m 1 km

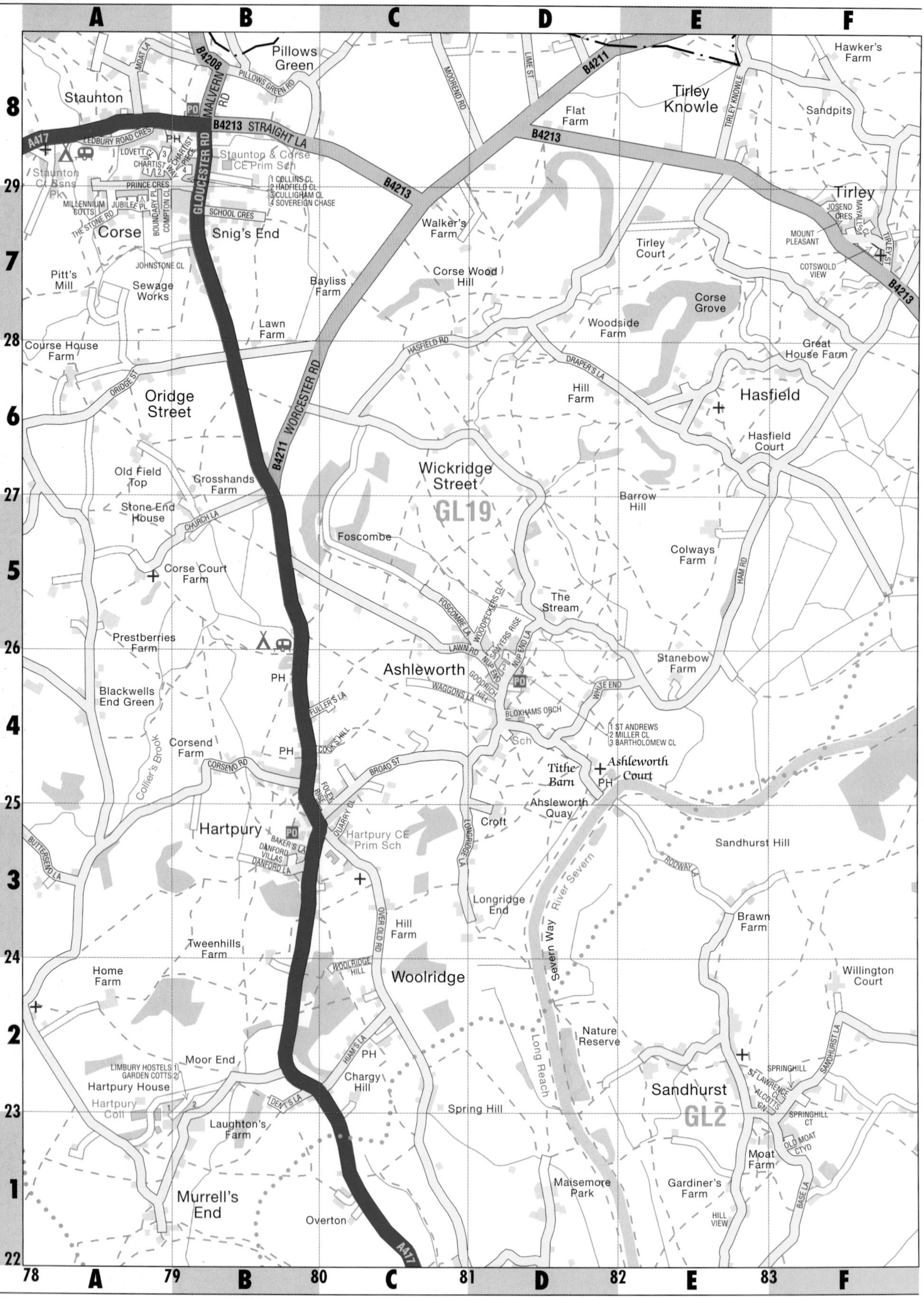

171
125
126

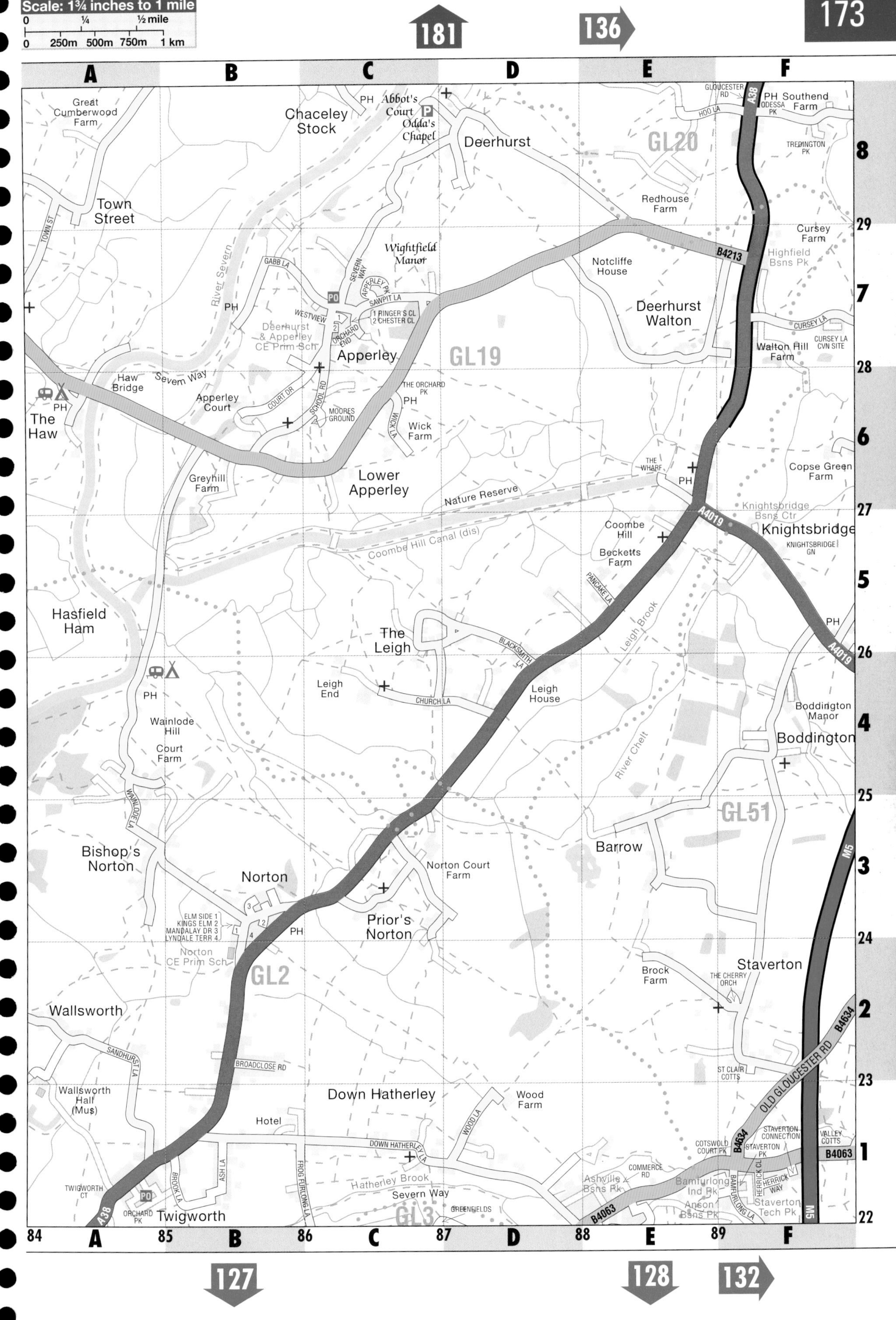
Scale: 1¾ inches to 1 mile
181
136
A B C D E F
Great Cumberwood Farm
Town Street
Chaceley Stock
Abbot's Court
Odda's Chapel
Deerhurst
GL20
PH Southend Farm
Redhouse Farm
Wightfield Manor
Notcliffe House
B4213
Cursey Farm
Highfield Bsns Pk
Deerhurst Walton
River Severn
Deerhurst & Apperley CE Prim Sch
Apperley
GL19
Walton Hill Farm
Haw Bridge
Severn Way
Apperley Court
The Haw
Wick Farm
Greyhill Farm
Lower Apperley
Nature Reserve
Copse Green Farm
Coombe Hill Canal (dis)
Coombe Hill
Becketts Farm
Knightsbridge
Knightsbridge Bsns Ctr
A4019
Hasfield Ham
The Leigh
Leigh End
Leigh House
Leigh Brook
Wainlode Hill
Court Farm
River Chelt
Boddington Manor
Boddington
GL51
Barrow
Bishop's Norton
Norton
Norton Court Farm
Prior's Norton
Norton CE Prim Sch
GL2
Staverton
Brock Farm
Wallsworth
Wallsworth Hall (Mus)
Down Hatherley
Wood Farm
Hotel
Hatherley Brook
Severn Way
Ashville Bsns Pk
Bamfurlong Ind Pk
Anson Bsns Pk
Staverton Tech Pk
Twigworth
GL3
A38
M5
B4063
B4634
OLD GLOUCESTER RD
84 85 86 87 88 89
22 23 24 25 26 27 28 29
1 2 3 4 5 6 7 8
127
128
132

A7
1 CRISPIN CL
2 RATHMORE CL
3 BASSETT CL
4 CEDAR GR
5 SPITTLE LEYS
6 ORCHARD RD
7 MERCIA RD
8 BARNMEADOW RD
9 ABBOTS LEYS RD
10 SEYMOUR PL
11 BINYON RD
12 ST PETERS WAY
13 SUMMERS RD

139

A7
14 BLENHEIM CT
15 ABBEY VIEW
16 ENFIELD VILLAS
17 MALTHOUSE LA
18 ODDFELLOWS TERR
19 TYTHE TERR

184

A7
20 ABBEY CT
21 QUEENS SQ
22 CHANDOS ALMSHOUSES
23 ABBEY TERR
24 DENT'S TERR
25 STANCOMBE VIEW
26 CHANDOS ST
27 BULL LA
28 HAILES ST
29 KENULF RD
30 BICKS LA
31 SILK MILL CT
32 PEAR TREE CL

Scale: 1¾ inches to 1 mile

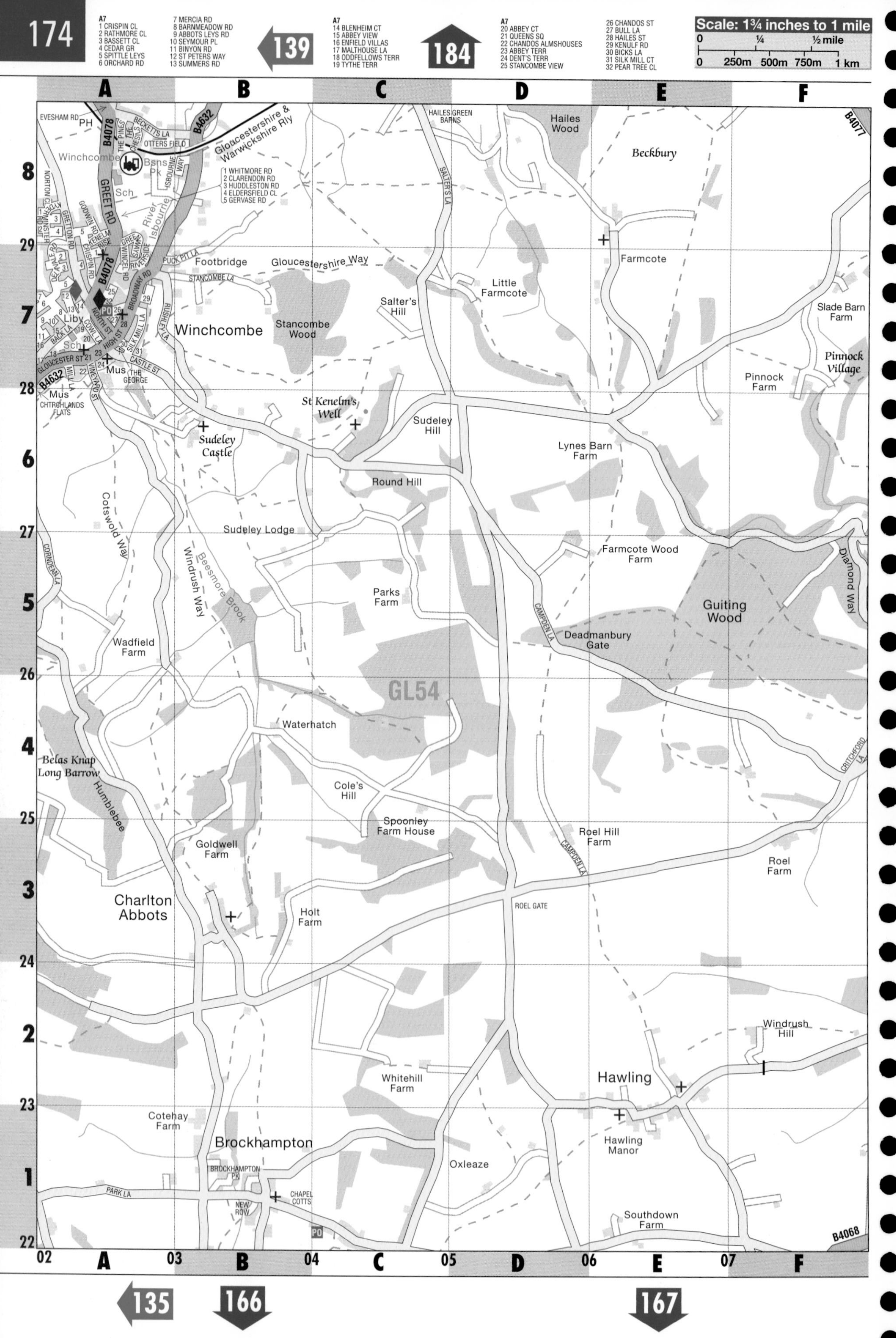

135 166 167

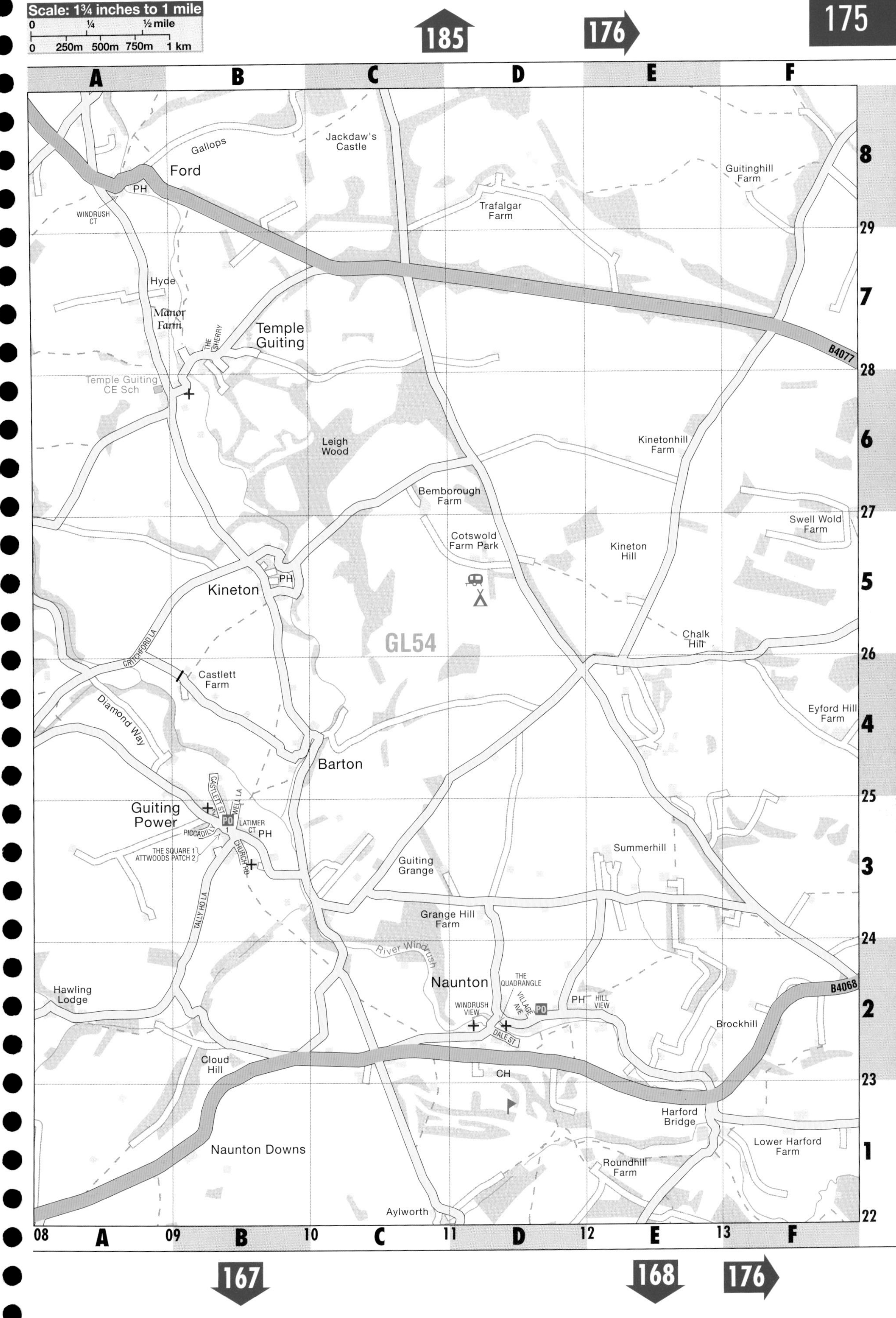
Scale: 1¾ inches to 1 mile
0 ¼ ½ mile
0 250m 500m 750m 1 km
185
176
A B C D E F
Gallops
Ford
Jackdaw's Castle
Guitinghill Farm
PH
WINDRUSH CT
Trafalgar Farm
Hyde
Manor Farm
THE SHERRY
Temple Guiting
B4077
Temple Guiting CE Sch
Leigh Wood
Kinetonhill Farm
Bemborough Farm
Swell Wold Farm
Cotswold Farm Park
Kineton Hill
PH
Kineton
CRITCHFORD LA
GL54
Chalk Hill
Castlett Farm
Diamond Way
Eyford Hill Farm
Barton
CASTLETT ST
WELL LA
Guiting Power
PO
LATIMER CT
PH
PICCADILLY
CHURCH RD
THE SQUARE 1
ATTWOODS PATCH 2
Guiting Grange
Summerhill
TALLY HO LA
Grange Hill Farm
River Windrush
Hawling Lodge
Naunton
THE QUADRANGLE
VILLAGE AVE
WINDRUSH VIEW
PO
PH
HILL VIEW
B4068
Brockhill
DALE ST
Cloud Hill
CH
Harford Bridge
Lower Harford Farm
Naunton Downs
Roundhill Farm
Aylworth
8
29
7
28
6
27
5
26
4
25
3
24
2
23
1
22
08 A 09 B 10 C 11 D 12 E 13 F
167
168
176

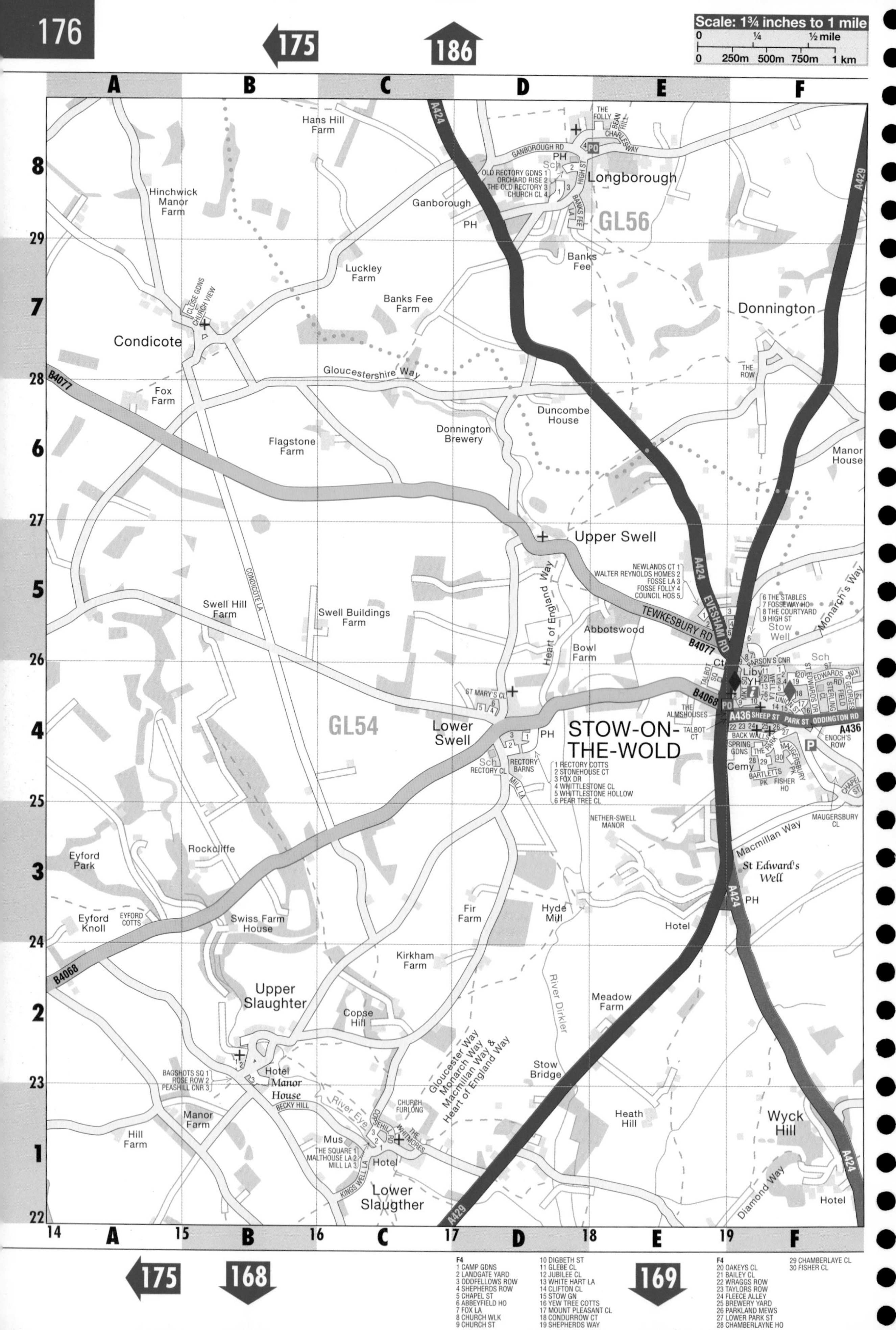
176
175
186
Scale: 1¾ inches to 1 mile
0 ¼ ½ mile
0 250m 500m 750m 1 km
A
B
C
D
E
F
8
29
7
28
6
27
5
26
4
25
3
24
2
23
1
22
14
15
16
17
18
19
Hans Hill Farm
THE FOLLY
BEAN HILL
CHARLESWAY
GANBOROUGH RD
PO
PH
HIGH ST
Sch
OLD RECTORY GDNS 1
ORCHARD RISE 2
THE OLD RECTORY 3
CHURCH CL 4
Longborough
BANKS FEE LA
Ganborough
PH
GL56
Hinchwick Manor Farm
Banks Fee
Luckley Farm
Banks Fee Farm
CLOSE GDNS
CHURCH VIEW
Condicote
Donnington
Gloucestershire Way
B4077
THE ROW
Fox Farm
Duncombe House
Donnington Brewery
Flagstone Farm
Manor House
Upper Swell
NEWLANDS CT 1
WALTER REYNOLDS HOMES 2
FOSSE LA 3
FOSSE FOLLY 4
COUNCIL HOS 5
A424
EVESHAM RD
CONDICOTE LA
Heart of England Way
6 THE STABLES
7 FOSSEWAY HO
8 THE COURTYARD
9 HIGH ST
Stow Well
Monarch's Way
Swell Hill Farm
Swell Buildings Farm
TEWKESBURY RD
B4077
Abbotswood
Bowl Farm
PARSON'S CNR
Sch
TALBOT SQ
Ct
Liby
YH
EDWARDS
B4068
ST MARY'S CL
THE ALMSHOUSES
A436
SHEEP ST
PARK ST
ODDINGTON RD
A436
GL54
Lower Swell
PH
STOW-ON-THE-WOLD
TALBOT CT
BACK WALLS
THE PARK
MAUGERSBURY PK
ENOCH'S ROW
SPRING GDNS
Sch
RECTORY CL
RECTORY BARNS
1 RECTORY COTTS
2 STONEHOUSE CT
3 FOX DR
4 WHITTLESTONE CL
5 WHITTLESTONE HOLLOW
6 PEAR TREE CL
Cemy
BARTLETTS PK
FISHER HO
CHAPEL ST
MILL LA
NETHER-SWELL MANOR
MAUGERSBURY CL
Macmillan Way
Eyford Park
Rockcliffe
St Edward's Well
A424
PH
Fir Farm
Hyde Mill
Eyford Knoll
EYFORD COTTS
Swiss Farm House
Hotel
B4068
Kirkham Farm
Upper Slaughter
River Dikler
Meadow Farm
Copse Hill
Gloucester Way
Monarch's Way
Macmillan Way & Heart of England Way
Stow Bridge
BAGSHOTS SQ 1
ROSE ROW 2
PEASHILL CNR 3
Hotel
Manor House
BECKY HILL
River Eye
CHURCH FURLONG
THE WHITMORES
Manor Farm
Heath Hill
Wyck Hill
Hill Farm
Mus
THE SQUARE 1
MALTHOUSE LA 2
MILL LA 3
Hotel
KINGS WELL LA
Lower Slaughter
A429
A429
Diamond Way
A424
Hotel
175
168
169
F4
1 CAMP GDNS
2 LANDGATE YARD
3 ODDFELLOWS ROW
4 SHEPHERDS ROW
5 CHAPEL ST
6 ABBEYFIELD HO
7 FOX LA
8 CHURCH WLK
9 CHURCH ST
10 DIGBETH ST
11 GLEBE CL
12 JUBILEE CL
13 WHITE HART LA
14 CLIFTON CL
15 STOW GN
16 YEW TREE COTTS
17 MOUNT PLEASANT CL
18 CONDURROW CT
19 SHEPHERDS WAY
F4
20 OAKEYS CL
21 BAILEY CL
22 WRAGGS ROW
23 TAYLORS ROW
24 FLEECE ALLEY
25 BREWERY YARD
26 PARKLAND MEWS
27 LOWER PARK ST
28 CHAMBERLAYNE HO
29 CHAMBERLAYE CL
30 FISHER CL

Scale: 1¾ inches to 1 mile

187

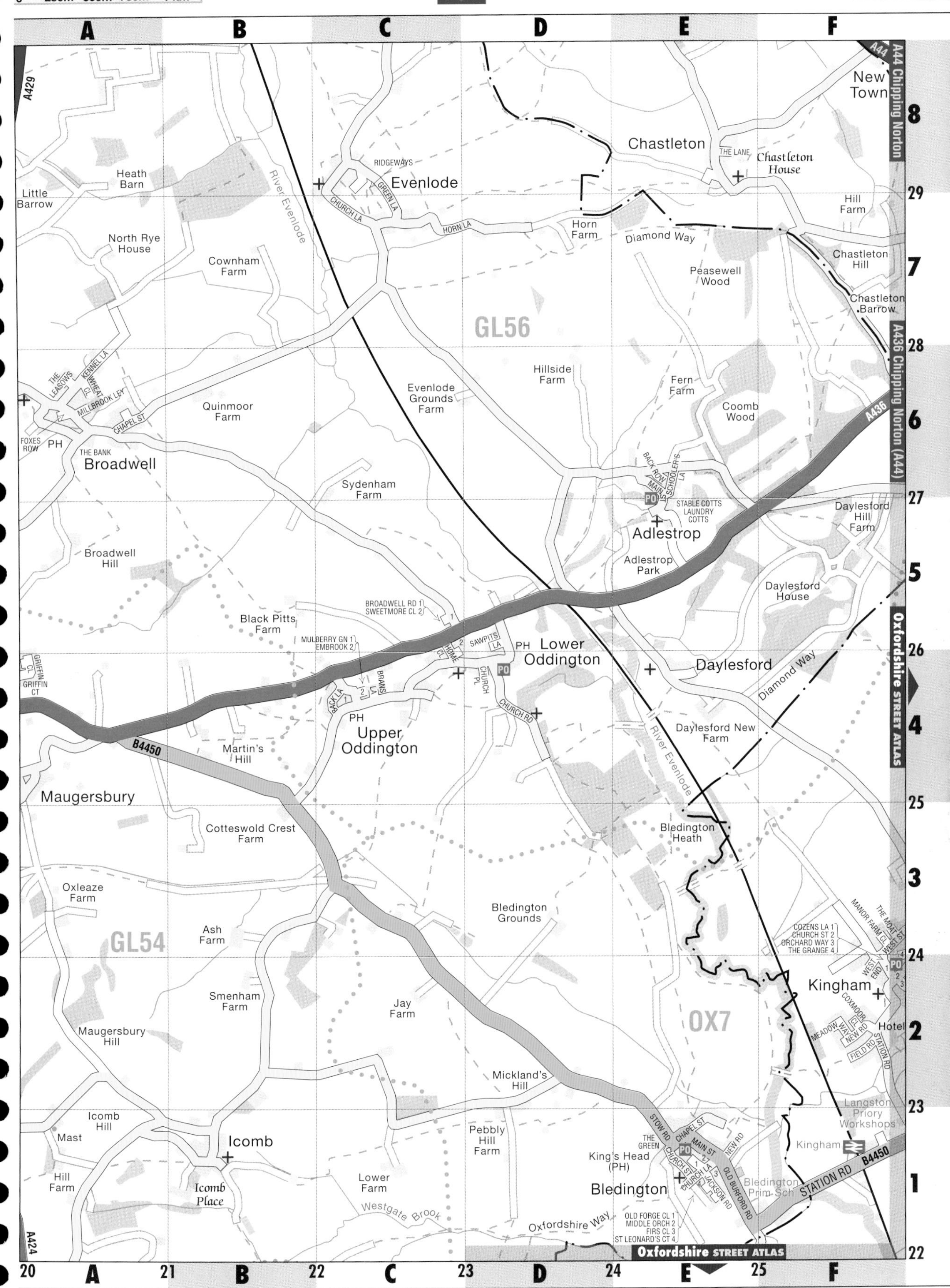

169

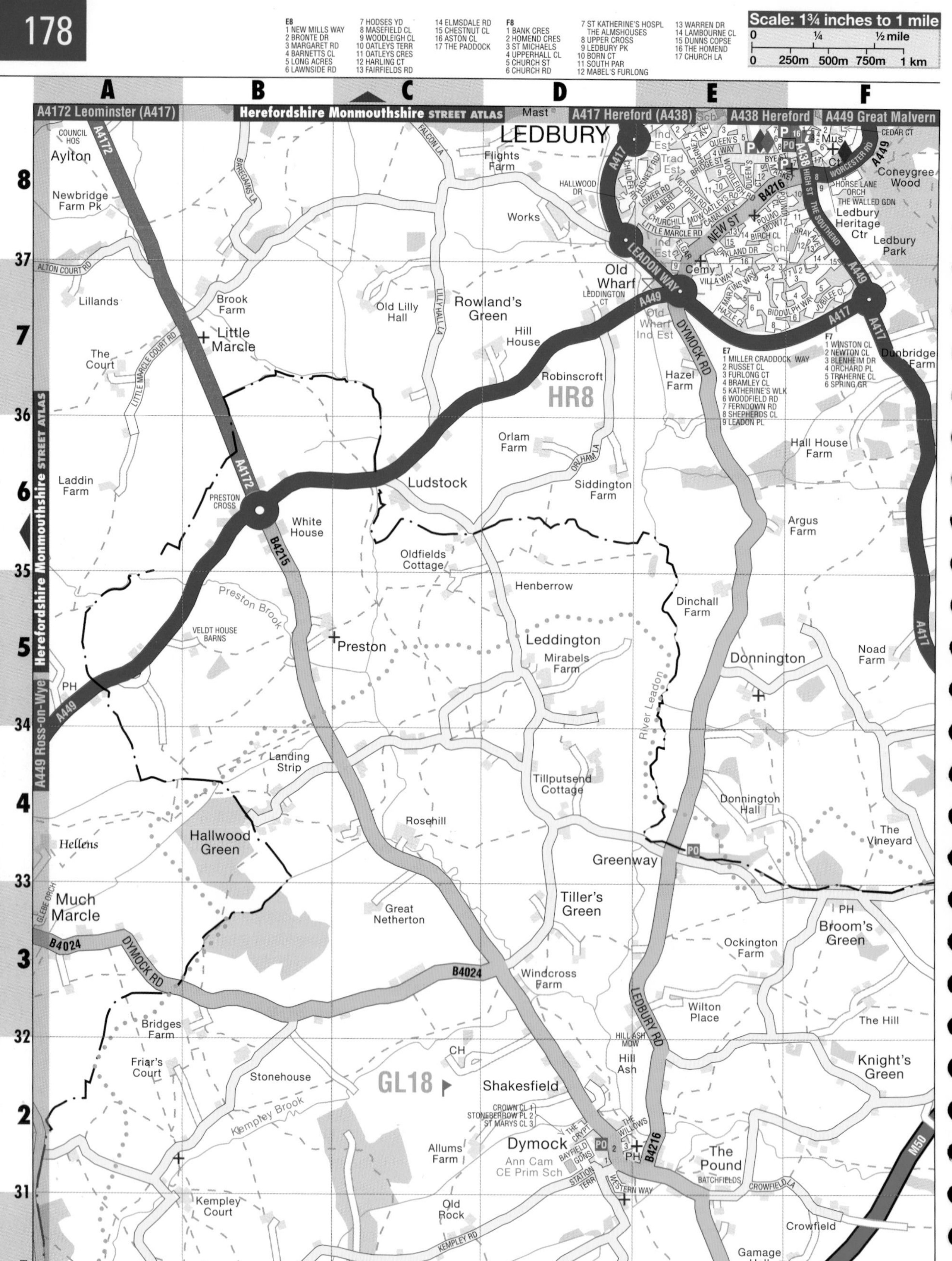
E8
1 NEW MILLS WAY
2 BRONTE DR
3 MARGARET RD
4 BARNETTS CL
5 LONG ACRES
6 LAWNSIDE RD
7 HODSES YD
8 MASEFIELD CL
9 WOODLEIGH CL
10 OATLEYS TERR
11 OATLEYS CRES
12 HARLING CT
13 FAIRFIELDS RD
14 ELMSDALE RD
15 CHESTNUT CL
16 ASTON CL
17 THE PADDOCK
F8
1 BANK CRES
2 HOMEND CRES
3 ST MICHAELS
4 UPPERHALL CL
5 CHURCH ST
6 CHURCH RD
7 ST KATHERINE'S HOSPL THE ALMSHOUSES
8 UPPER CROSS
9 LEDBURY PK
10 BORN CT
11 SOUTH PAR
12 MABEL'S FURLONG
13 WARREN DR
14 LAMBOURNE CL
15 DUNNS COPSE
16 THE HOMEND
17 CHURCH LA
Scale: 1¾ inches to 1 mile
0 ¼ ½ mile
0 250m 500m 750m 1 km
A4172 Leominster (A417)
Herefordshire Monmouthshire STREET ATLAS
A417 Hereford (A438)
A438 Hereford
A449 Great Malvern
A449 Ross-on-Wye
LEDBURY
Aylton
Newbridge Farm Pk
Flights Farm
Works
Coneygree Wood
Ledbury Heritage Ctr
Ledbury Park
Lillands
Brook Farm
Little Marcle
The Court
Old Lilly Hall
Rowland's Green
Hill House
Old Wharf
Robinscroft
HR8
Hazel Farm
Dunbridge Farm
E7
1 MILLER CRADDOCK WAY
2 RUSSET CL
3 FURLONG CT
4 BRAMLEY CL
5 KATHERINE'S WLK
6 WOODFIELD RD
7 FERNDOWN RD
8 SHEPHERDS CL
9 LEADON PL
F7
1 WINSTON CL
2 NEWTON CL
3 BLENHEIM DR
4 ORCHARD PL
5 TRAHERNE CL
6 SPRING GR
Laddin Farm
Orlam Farm
Ludstock
Siddington Farm
Hall House Farm
Preston Cross
White House
Oldfields Cottage
Argus Farm
Henberrow
Dinchall Farm
Preston Brook
Veldt House Barns
Preston
Leddington
Mirabels Farm
Donnington
Noad Farm
River Leadon
Landing Strip
Tillputsend Cottage
Donnington Hall
Hellens
Hallwood Green
Rosehill
Greenway
The Vineyard
Much Marcle
Great Netherton
Tiller's Green
Broom's Green
Ockington Farm
Windcross Farm
Bridges Farm
Wilton Place
The Hill
Friar's Court
Stonehouse
GL18
Shakesfield
Hill Ash
Knight's Green
Kempley Brook
Allums Farm
Dymock
Ann Cam CE Prim Sch
The Pound
Kempley Court
Old Rock
Crowfield
Gamage Hall
Brookland
New Rock
Haind Park Wood
Normans Land Farm
B4215
B4024
B4216
A449
A4172
A417
M50
DYMOCK RD
LEDBURY RD
KEMPLEY RD
LEADON WAY

170

Scale: 1¾ inches to 1 mile
0 ¼ ½ mile
0 250m 500m 750m 1 km

180

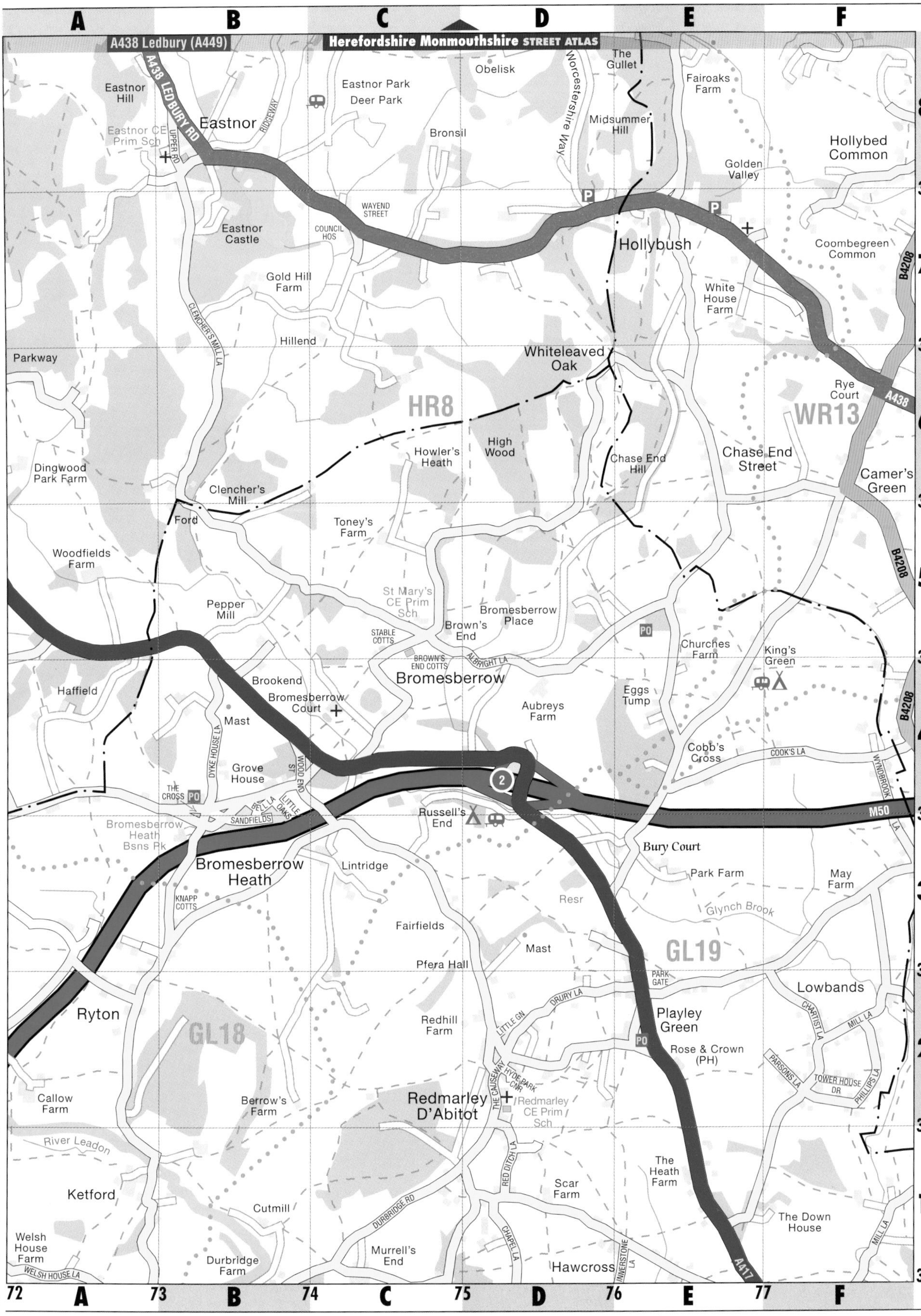

A B C D E F

A438 Ledbury (A449)
Herefordshire Monmouthshire STREET ATLAS

The Gullet
Obelisk
Fairoaks Farm
Eastnor Hill
Eastnor Park Deer Park
A438 LEDBURY RD
RIDGEWAY
Eastnor
Eastnor CE Prim Sch
UPPER RD
Bronsil
Worcestershire Way
Midsummer Hill
Hollybed Common
Golden Valley
8
37
WAYEND STREET
COUNCIL HOS
Eastnor Castle
Hollybush
Coombegreen Common
B4208
7
Gold Hill Farm
White House Farm
CLENCHER'S MILL LA
Hillend
36
Parkway
Whiteleaved Oak
Rye Court
A438
HR8
WR13
6
Howler's Heath
High Wood
Chase End Hill
Chase End Street
Dingwood Park Farm
Camer's Green
Clencher's Mill
35
Ford
Toney's Farm
Woodfields Farm
B4208
5
St Mary's CE Prim Sch
Pepper Mill
Bromesberrow Place
Brown's End
STABLE COTTS
PO
Churches Farm
King's Green
34
BROWN'S END COTTS
ALBRIGHT LA
Bromesberrow
Haffield
Brookend
Bromesberrow Court
Eggs Tump
Aubreys Farm
B4208
Mast
DYKE HOUSE LA
4
Grove House
WOOD END ST
Cobb's Cross
COOK'S LA
2
WYNDBROOK LA
THE CROSS
PO
BELL LA
LITTLE OAKS
SANDFIELDS
Russell's End
M50
33
Bromesberrow Heath Bsns Pk
Bury Court
Bromesberrow Heath
Lintridge
Park Farm
May Farm
KNAPP COTTS
Resr
Glynch Brook
3
Fairfields
Mast
GL19
Pfera Hall
PARK GATE
Lowbands
32
DRURY LA
Ryton
GL18
Redhill Farm
LITTLE GN
Playley Green
CHARTIST LA
MILL LA
PO
Rose & Crown (PH)
2
PARSONS LA
HYDE PARK CNR
TOWER HOUSE DR
PHILLIPS LA
THE CAUSEWAY
Callow Farm
Berrow's Farm
Redmarley D'Abitot
Redmarley CE Prim Sch
31
River Leadon
RED DITCH LA
The Heath Farm
Ketford
Scar Farm
1
Cutmill
DURBRIDGE RD
The Down House
Welsh House Farm
CHAPEL LA
MILL LA
Durbridge Farm
Murrell's End
Hawcross
INNERSTONE LA
A417
WELSH HOUSE LA
30

72 A 73 B 74 C 75 D 76 E 77 F

171 180

179

Scale: 1¾ inches to 1 mile

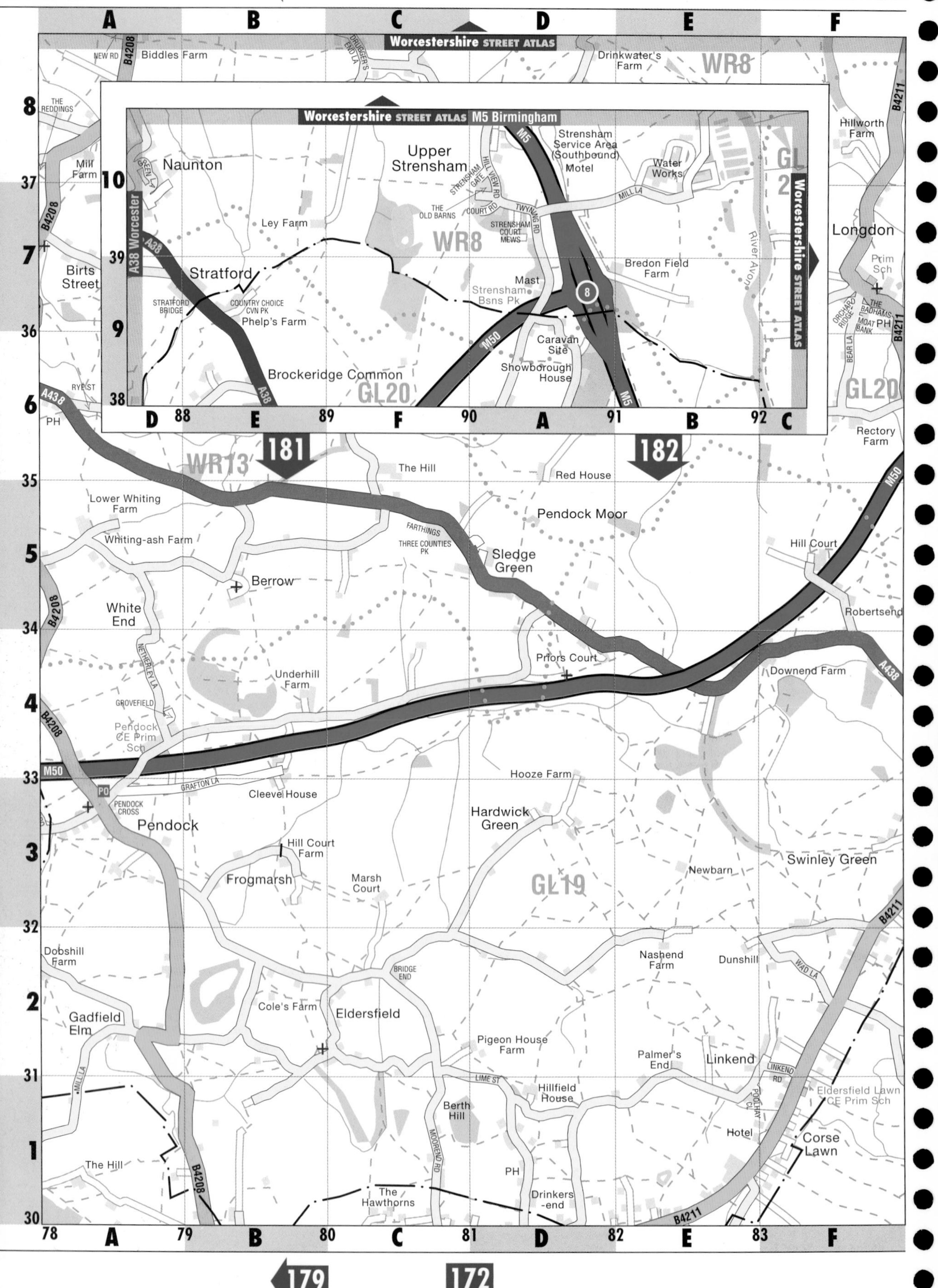

181

182

179

172

Scale: 1¾ inches to 1 mile
0 ¼ ½ mile
0 250m 500m 750m 1 km

182 180

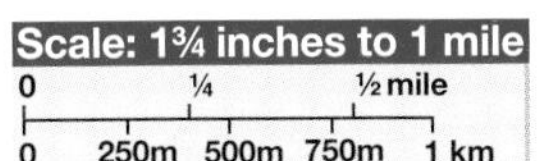

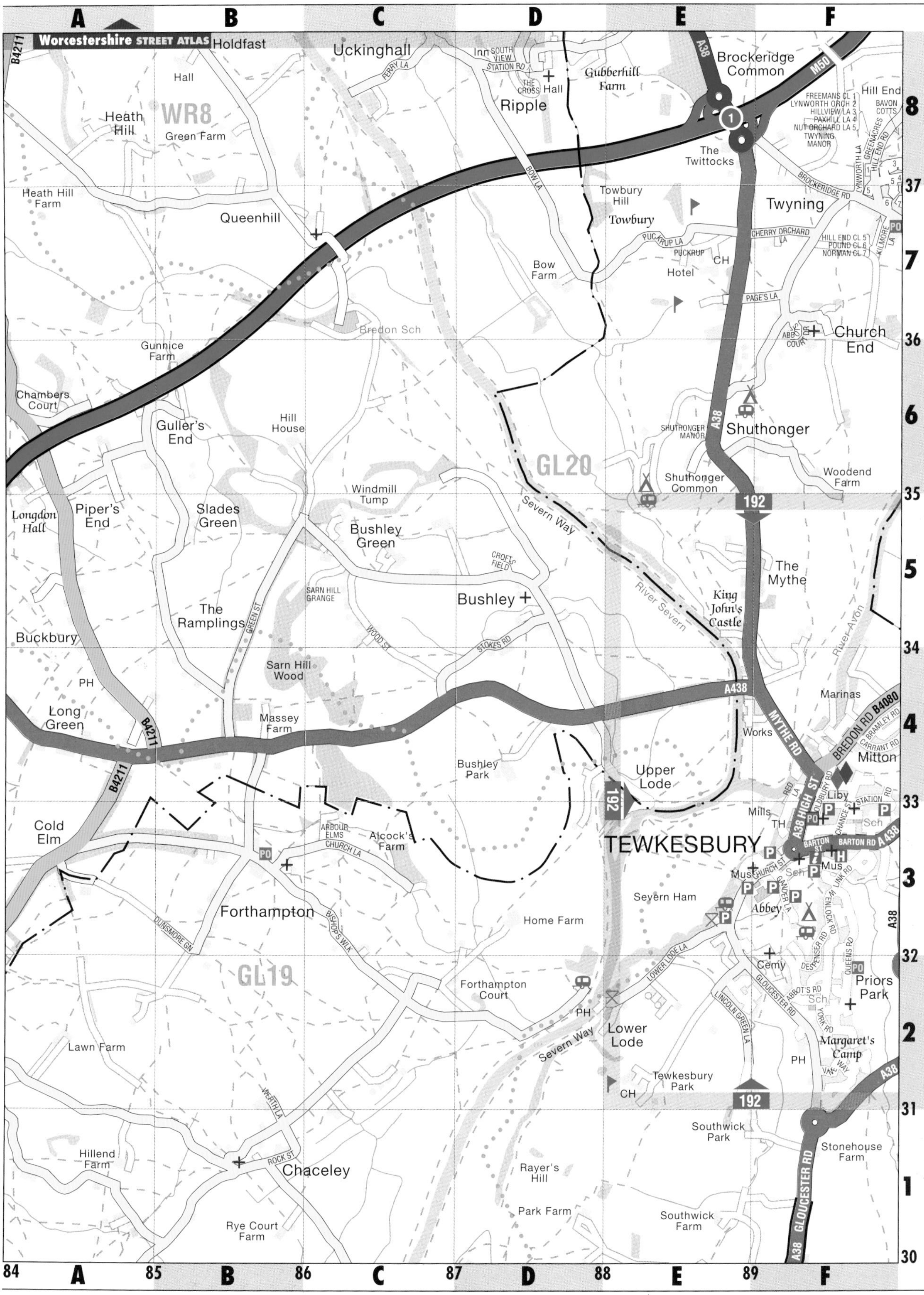

A B C D E F
Worcestershire STREET ATLAS
B4211
Holdfast
Uckinghall
FERRY LA
Inn
SOUTH VIEW
STATION RD
THE CROSS
Hall
Ripple
Gubberhill Farm
A38
Brockeridge Common
M50
Hill End
1
FREEMANS CL 1
LYNWORTH ORCH 2
HILLVIEW LA 3
PAXHILL LA 4
NUT ORCHARD LA 5
TWYNING MANOR
BAVON COTTS
GREENACRES
HILL END RD
8
Hall
Heath Hill
WR8
Green Farm
The Twittocks
BOW LA
BROCKERIDGE RD
LYNWORTH LA
37
Heath Hill Farm
Queenhill
Towbury Hill
Towbury
Twyning
PUCKRUP LA
PUCKRUP
CH
Hotel
CHERRY ORCHARD LA
HILL END CL 5
POUND CL 6
NORMAN CL 7
KILMORE LA
PO
7
Bow Farm
PAGE'S LA
Bredon Sch
Gunnice Farm
Church End
36
Chambers Court
Hill House
Guller's End
SHUTHONGER MANOR
A38
Shuthonger
6
GL20
Shuthonger Common
Woodend Farm
Windmill Tump
Severn Way
192
35
Longdon Hall
Piper's End
Slades Green
Bushley Green
CROFTS FIELD
The Mythe
5
SARN HILL GRANGE
River Severn
King John's Castle
Bushley
The Ramplings
GREEN ST
WOOD ST
STOKES RD
River Avon
Buckbury
34
Sarn Hill Wood
A438
Marinas
PH
Long Green
Massey Farm
B4211
MYTHE RD
Works
BREDON RD B4080
BRAMLEY RD
CARRANT RD
4
Mitton
Bushley Park
Upper Lode
B4211
192
RED LA
A38 HIGH ST
OLDBURY RD
Liby
STATION RD
Cold Elm
ARBOUR ELMS
Alcock's Farm
Mills
TH
PO
CHANCE ST
Sch
33
A438
CHURCH LA
PO
TEWKESBURY
BARTON ST
BARTON RD
Mus
H
Mus
CHURCH ST
Sch
LINK RD
3
DUNSMORE GN
Forthampton
BISHOP'S WLK
Severn Ham
GANDER LA
Abbey
ENLOCK RD
Home Farm
A38
SPENSER RD
QUEENS RD
GL19
Cemy
DESPENSER RD
PO
32
LOWER LODE LA
ABBOT'S RD
Forthampton Court
Priors Park
GLOUCESTER RD
LINCOLN GREEN LA
Sch
YORK RD
PH
Lower Lode
Severn Way
Margaret's Camp
2
Lawn Farm
PH
VALE WAY
Tewkesbury Park
CH
192
A38
31
WORTH LA
Southwick Park
Hillend Farm
ROCK ST
Chaceley
Rayer's Hill
Stonehouse Farm
GLOUCESTER RD
1
Park Farm
Rye Court Farm
Southwick Farm
A38
30
84 A 85 B 86 C 87 D 88 E 89 F

173 182

For full street detail of the highlighted area see page 192.

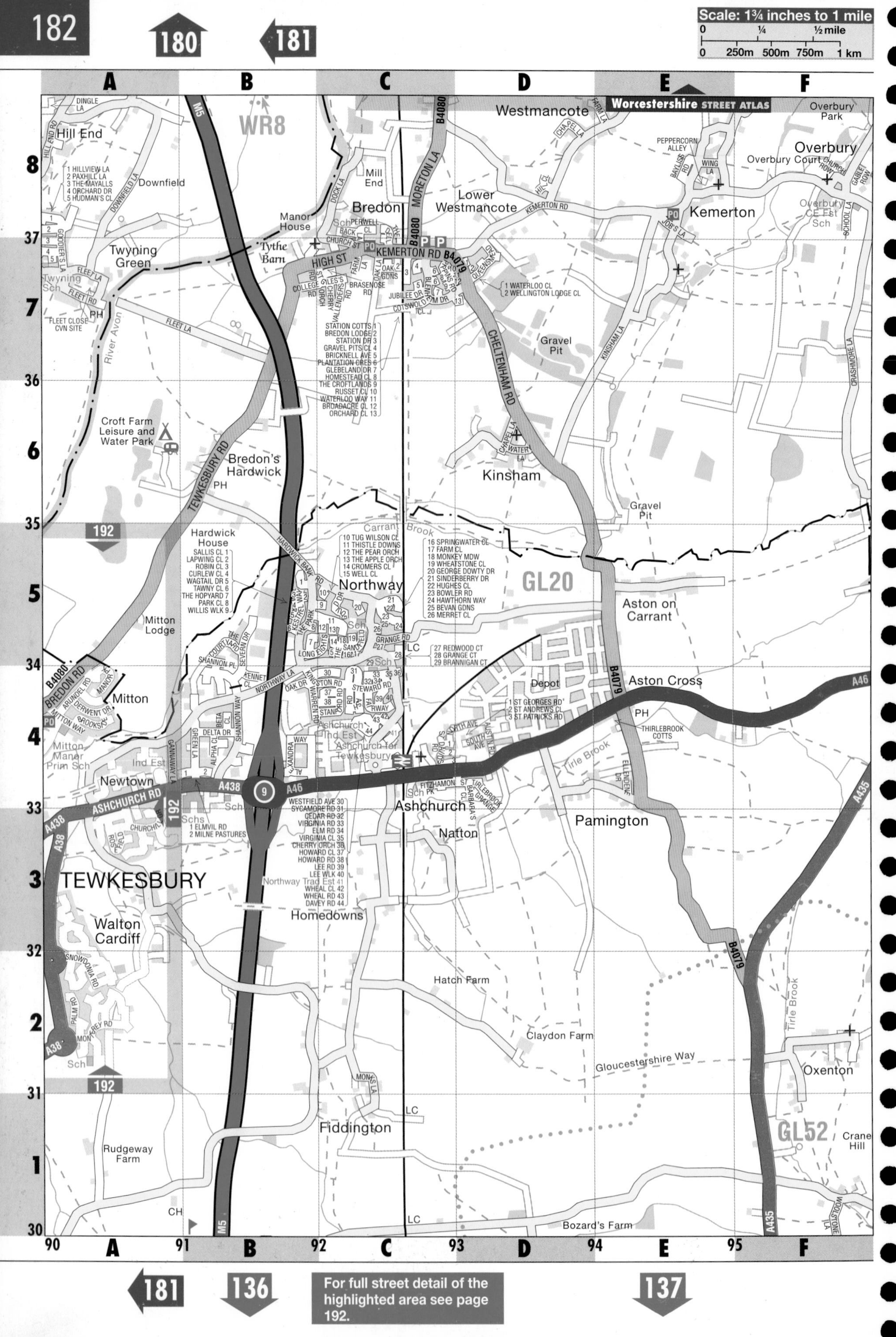

For full street detail of the highlighted area see page 192.

Scale: 1¾ inches to 1 mile

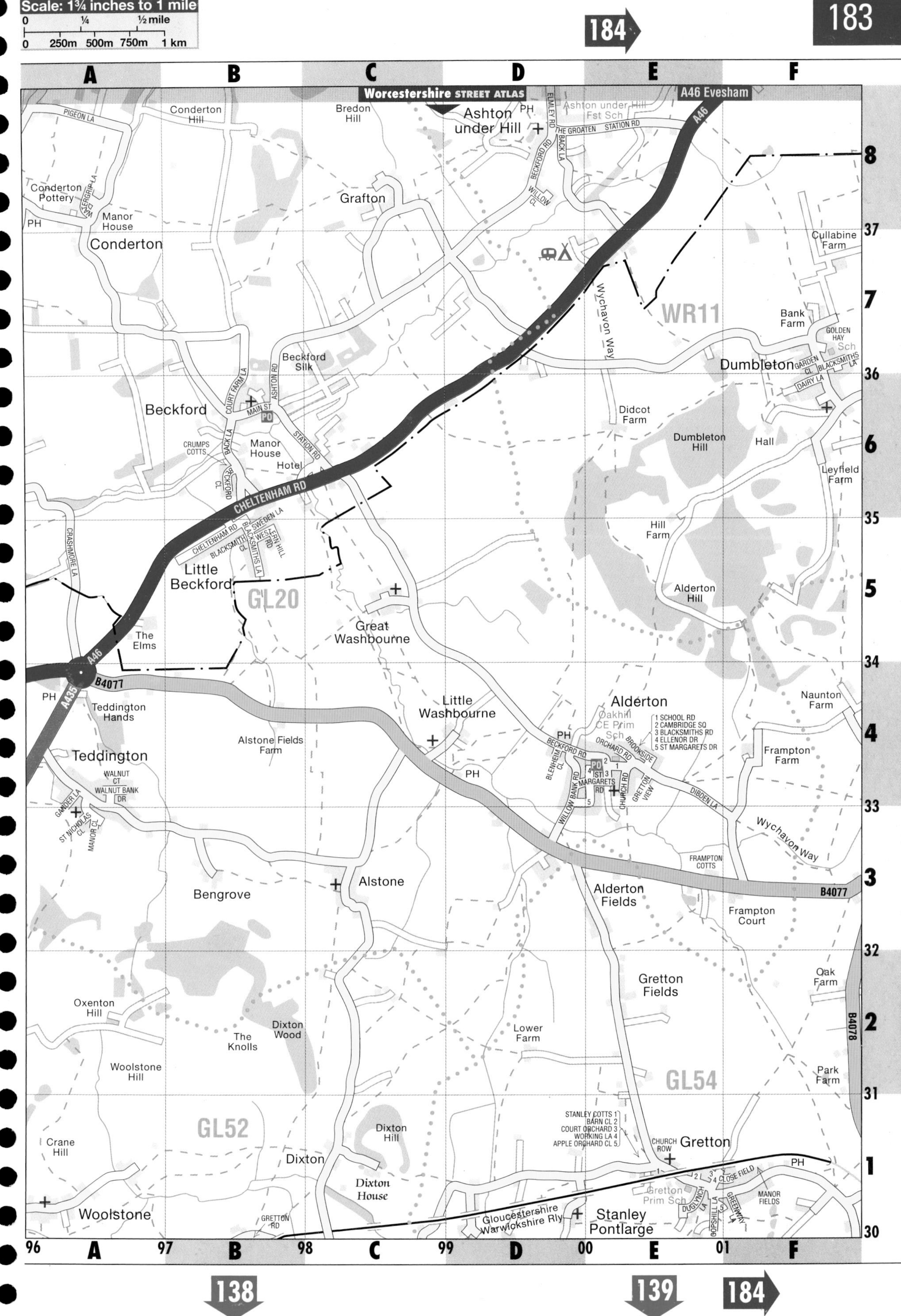

138
139
184

183

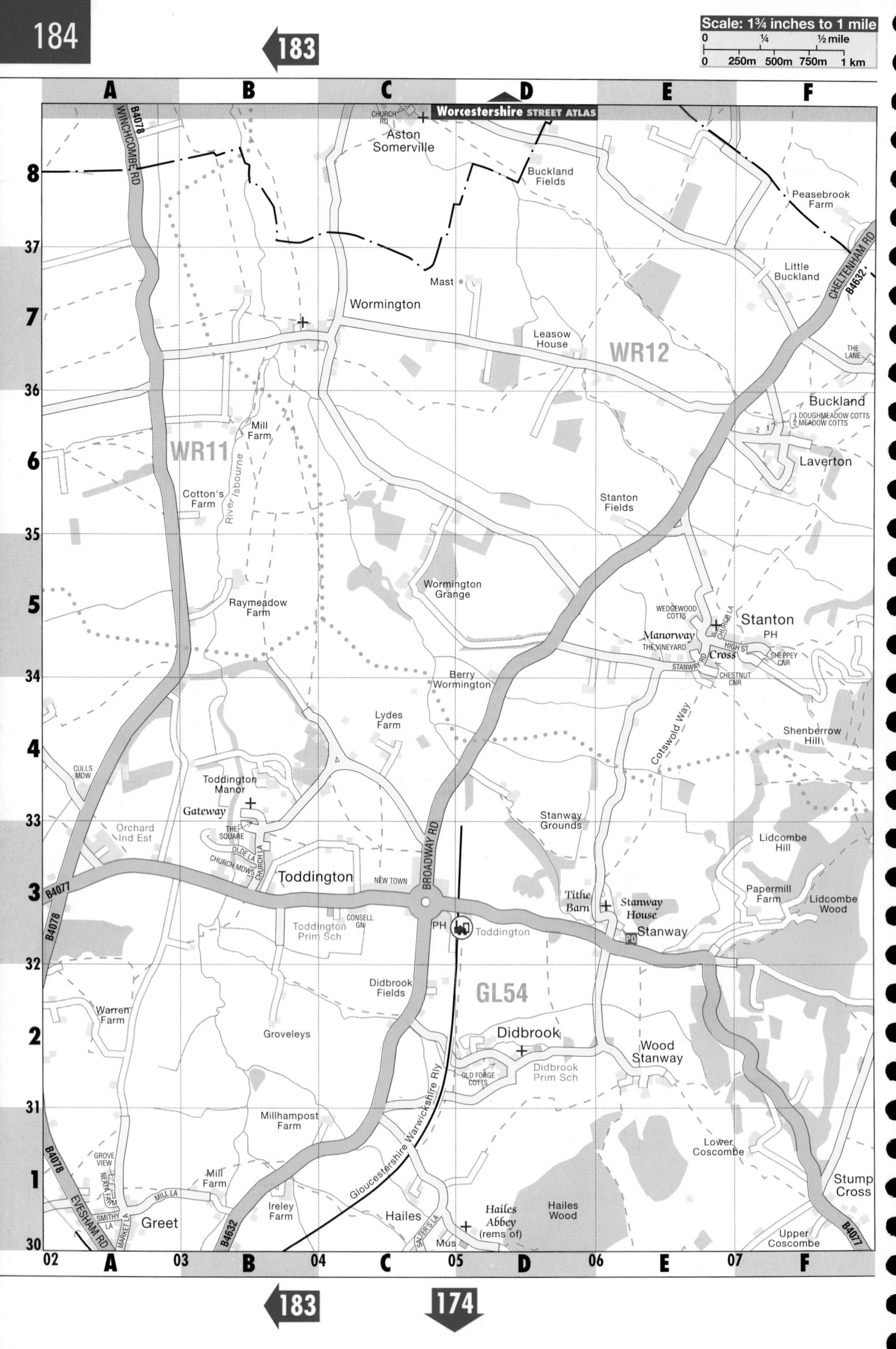
Scale: 1¾ inches to 1 mile
0 ¼ ½ mile
0 250m 500m 750m 1 km
A B C D E F
Worcestershire STREET ATLAS
B4078
WINCHCOMBE RD
CHURCH RD
Aston Somerville
Buckland Fields
Peasebrook Farm
Little Buckland
CHELTENHAM RD
B4632
Mast
Wormington
Leasow House
WR12
THE LANE
Buckland
1 DOUGHMEADOW COTTS
2 MEADOW COTTS
Laverton
Mill Farm
WR11
River Isbourne
Cotton's Farm
Stanton Fields
Wormington Grange
Raymeadow Farm
WEDGEWOOD COTTS
CHURCH LA
Stanton
PH
Manorway
THE VINEYARD
HIGH ST
Cross
SHEPPEY CNR
STANWAY RD
CHESTNUT CNR
Berry Wormington
Lydes Farm
Cotswold Way
Shenberrow Hill
CULLS MDW
Toddington Manor
Gateway
THE SQUARE
OLDE LA
CHURCH MDWS
CHURCH LA
Orchard Ind Est
Stanway Grounds
Lidcombe Hill
BROADWAY RD
Toddington
NEW TOWN
B4077
Tithe Barn
Stanway House
Papermill Farm
Lidcombe Wood
B4078
Toddington Prim Sch
CONSELL GN
PH
Toddington
Stanway
PO
Didbrook Fields
GL54
Warren Farm
Groveleys
Didbrook
Wood Stanway
OLD FORGE COTTS
Didbrook Prim Sch
Gloucestershire Warwickshire Rly
Millhampost Farm
Lower Coscombe
GROVE VIEW
NEATA FARM
Mill Farm
MILL LA
SMITHY LA
MARKET LA
EVESHAM RD
Greet
B4632
Ireley Farm
Hailes
SALTER'S LA
Mus
Hailes Abbey (rems of)
Hailes Wood
Stump Cross
Upper Coscombe
B4077
8 37 7 36 6 35 5 34 4 33 3 32 2 31 1 30
02 03 04 05 06 07

183
174

Scale: 1¾ inches to 1 mile
0 ¼ ½ mile
0 250m 500m 750m 1 km

B8
1 PARKER PL
2 MILLS CL
3 THE RETREAT
4 MEADOW ORCH
5 KEIL CL
6 THE GREEN
7 THE HUNTINGS
8 CROFT GDNS
9 BUTCHERS ROW
10 KENNEL LA
11 THE SANDS
12 PEGASUS CT

C8
1 SANDS CROFT AVE
2 DASTON CL
3 LIME TREE AVE
4 BIBSWORTH AVE
5 WELLS GDNS
6 COLLETTS GDNS

C8
7 SHEAR HO
8 YEW TREE CT

188
186

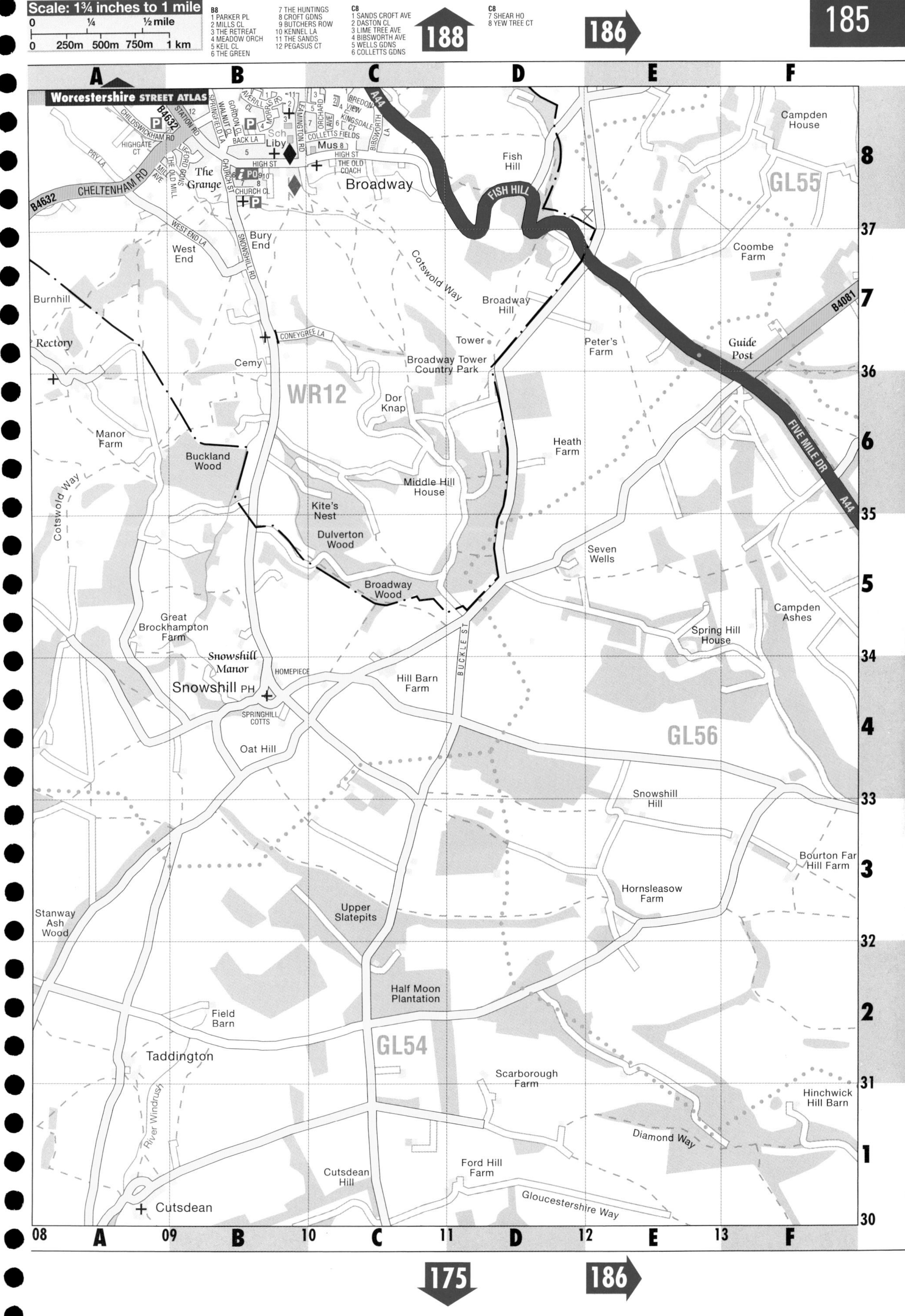

175
186

188 185 189

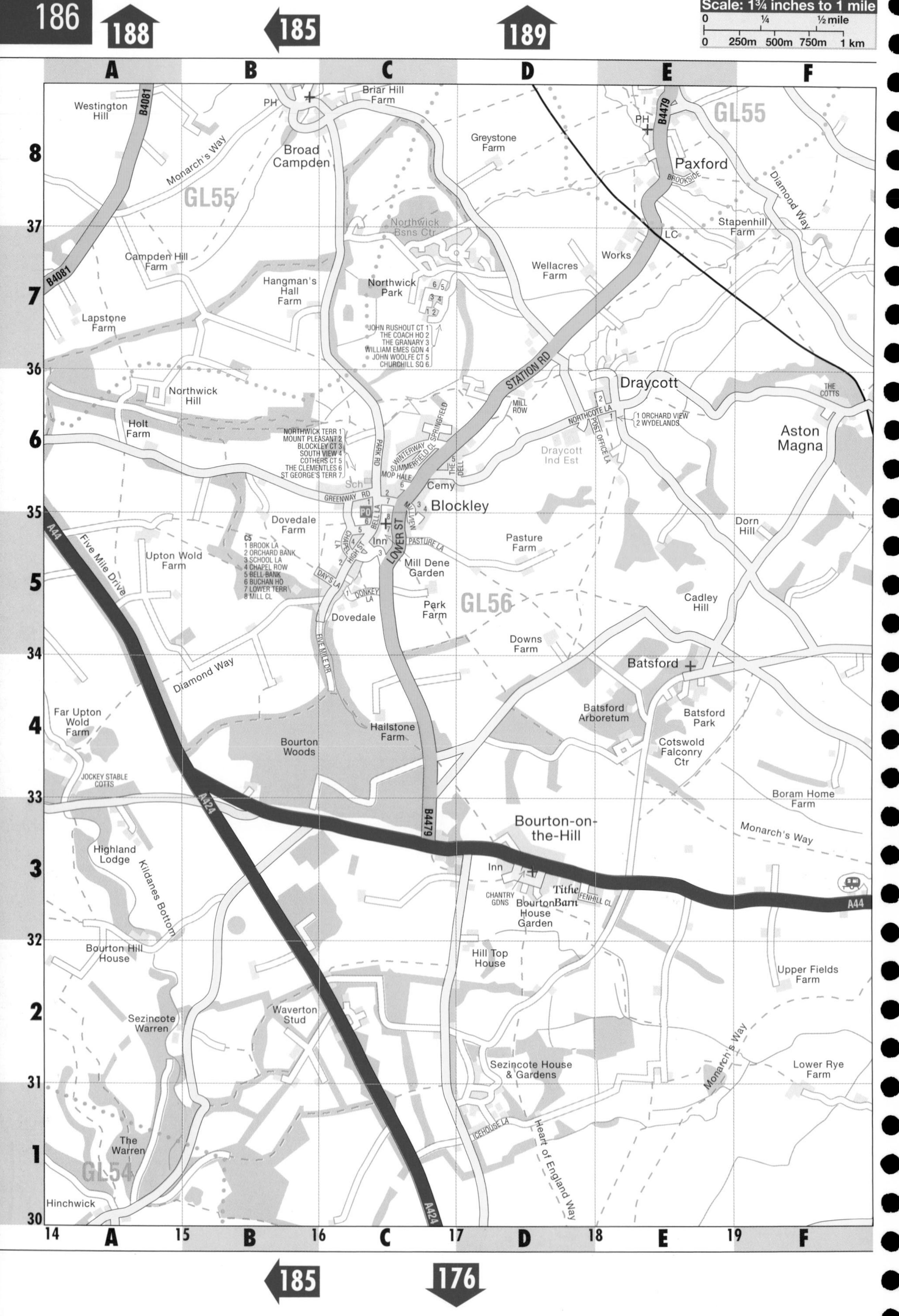
Scale: 1¾ inches to 1 mile
Westington Hill
Briar Hill Farm
Broad Campden
Greystone Farm
Paxford
Monarch's Way
GL55
Northwick Bsns Ctr
Stapenhill Farm
Diamond Way
Campden Hill Farm
Hangman's Hall Farm
Northwick Park
Wellacres Farm
Works
Lapstone Farm
JOHN RUSHOUT CT 1
THE COACH HO 2
THE GRANARY 3
WILLIAM EMES GDN 4
JOHN WOOLFE CT 5
CHURCHILL SQ 6
STATION RD
Draycott
Northwick Hill
Holt Farm
1 ORCHARD VIEW
2 WYDELANDS
Aston Magna
NORTHWICK TERR 1
MOUNT PLEASANT 2
BLOCKLEY CT 3
SOUTH VIEW 4
COTHERS CT 5
THE CLEMENTLES 6
ST GEORGE'S TERR 7
Draycott Ind Est
Blockley
Dovedale Farm
Pasture Farm
Dorn Hill
Upton Wold Farm
C5
1 BROOK LA
2 ORCHARD BANK
3 SCHOOL LA
4 CHAPEL ROW
5 BELL BANK
6 BUCHAN HO
7 LOWER TERR
8 MILL CL
Mill Dene Garden
GL56
Cadley Hill
Park Farm
Dovedale
Downs Farm
Diamond Way
Batsford
Far Upton Wold Farm
Hailstone Farm
Batsford Arboretum
Batsford Park
Bourton Woods
Cotswold Falconry Ctr
JOCKEY STABLE COTTS
Boram Home Farm
Bourton-on-the-Hill
Monarch's Way
Highland Lodge
Inn
Tithe Barn
Kildanes Bottom
CHANTRY GDNS
Bourton House Garden
Bourton Hill House
Hill Top House
Upper Fields Farm
Waverton Stud
Sezincote Warren
Sezincote House & Gardens
Lower Rye Farm
The Warren
Heart of England Way
GL54
Hinchwick
A44
A424
B4479
B4081

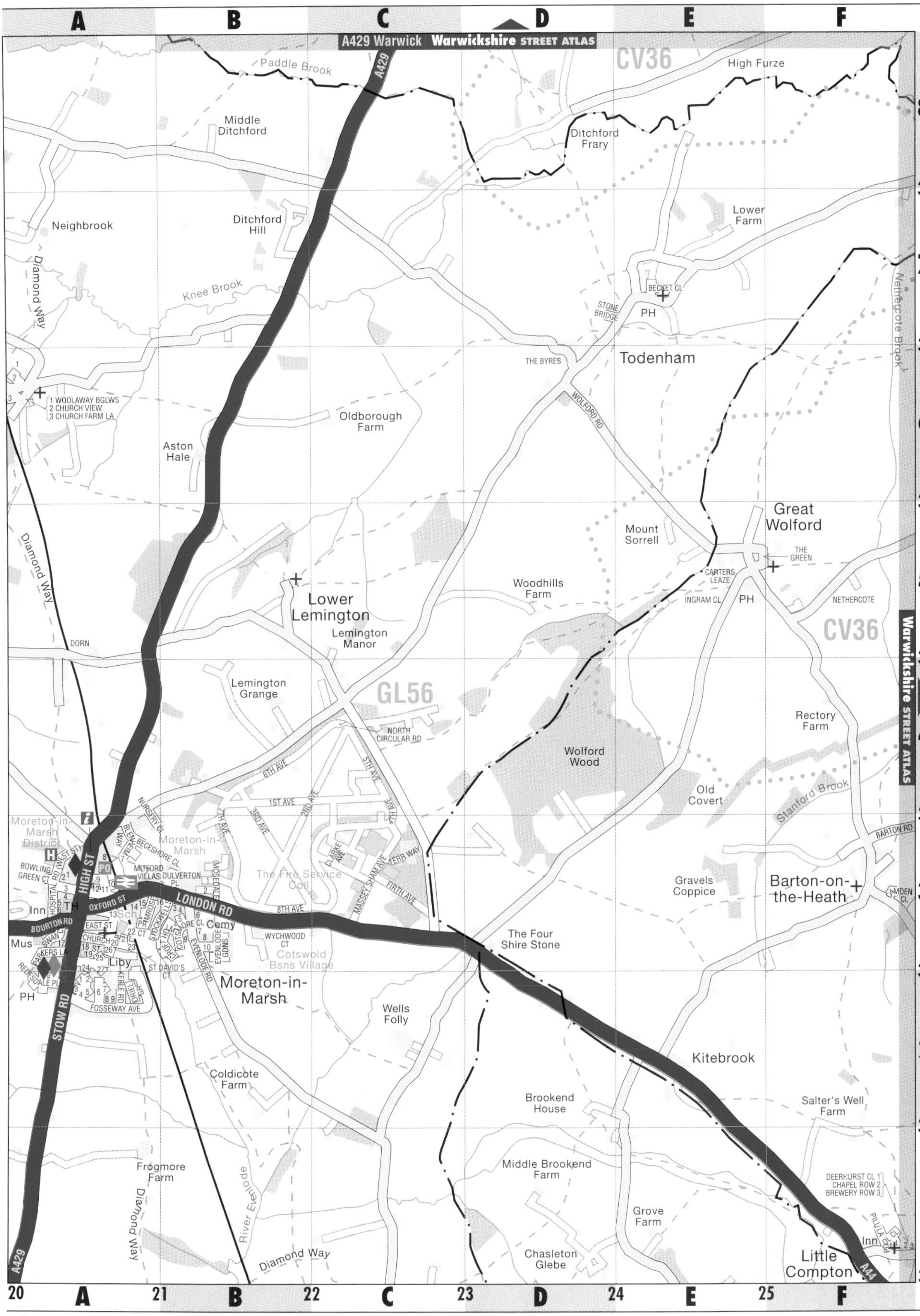

189

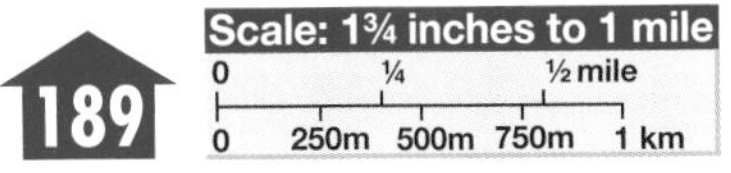

A429 Warwick Warwickshire STREET ATLAS

Paddle Brook
CV36
High Furze
Middle Ditchford
Ditchford Frary
Neighbrook
Ditchford Hill
Lower Farm
Diamond Way
Knee Brook
BECKET CL
STONE BRIDGE
PH
Nethercote Brook
THE BYRES
Todenham
1 WOOLAWAY BGLWS
2 CHURCH VIEW
3 CHURCH FARM LA
WOLFORD RD
Oldborough Farm
Aston Hale
Great Wolford
Mount Sorrell
THE GREEN
CARTERS LEAZE
Woodhills Farm
INGRAM CL
PH
NETHERCOTE
Lower Lemington
Lemington Manor
DORN
Lemington Grange
GL56
NORTH CIRCULAR RD
Rectory Farm
Wolford Wood
Old Covert
Stanford Brook
BARTON RD
6TH AVE
1ST AVE
Moreton-in-Marsh District
Moreton-in-Marsh
The Fire Service Coll
Gravels Coppice
Barton-on-the-Heath
LONDON RD
OXFORD ST
HIGH ST
BOURTON RD
8TH AVE
Cemy
Inn
Mus
Liby
Sch
The Four Shire Stone
WYCHWOOD CT
Cotswold Bsns Village
Moreton-in-Marsh
PH
STOW RD
FOSSEWAY AVE
Wells Folly
Kitebrook
Coldicote Farm
Brookend House
Salter's Well Farm
Frogmore Farm
Middle Brookend Farm
DEERHURST CL 1
CHAPEL ROW 2
BREWERY ROW 3
River Evenlode
Grove Farm
Diamond Way
Chasleton Glebe
Inn
Little Compton
A44
A429

Warwickshire STREET ATLAS

A2
1 ST JAMES CT
2 ST EDWARDS CT
3 ST PETERS CT
4 BOWES LYON CL
5 ST PAULS CT
6 FOSSEWAY DR
7 FOSSEWAY CL
8 ROLPH CT
9 SANKEY GR

A3
1 MARSH CT
2 DEVONSHIRE TERR
3 CORDER'S LA
4 MANCHESTER CT
5 CORDERS CL
6 REDESDALE MEWS
7 ROUNDHOUSE MEWS
8 THE GRANGE
9 NEW RD
10 THE GREEN
11 STATION RD
12 OLD MARKET WAY
13 OXFORD ST
14 ODDFELLOWS' TERR
15 TURNPIKE CL
16 CICESTER TERR
17 UNIVERSITY FARM
18 STONEFERN CT
19 DUNSTALL HO
20 GRAY'S LA
21 ST GEORGE'S CL
22 MEAD CL
23 WARNEFORD PL
24 JAMESON CT
25 COTSWOLD GDNS
26 OLD TOWN
27 TINKER'S CL

B3
1 DAVIES RD
2 ERRINGTON
3 HARVARD CL
4 RADBURN CL
5 THE GROVE
6 LONDON ROAD TERR
7 CHARLTON TERR
8 WELLINGTON TERR
9 CORNISH HOS
10 WELLINGTON RD

177

Scale: 1¾ inches to 1 mile
0 ¼ ½ mile
0 250m 500m 750m 1 km

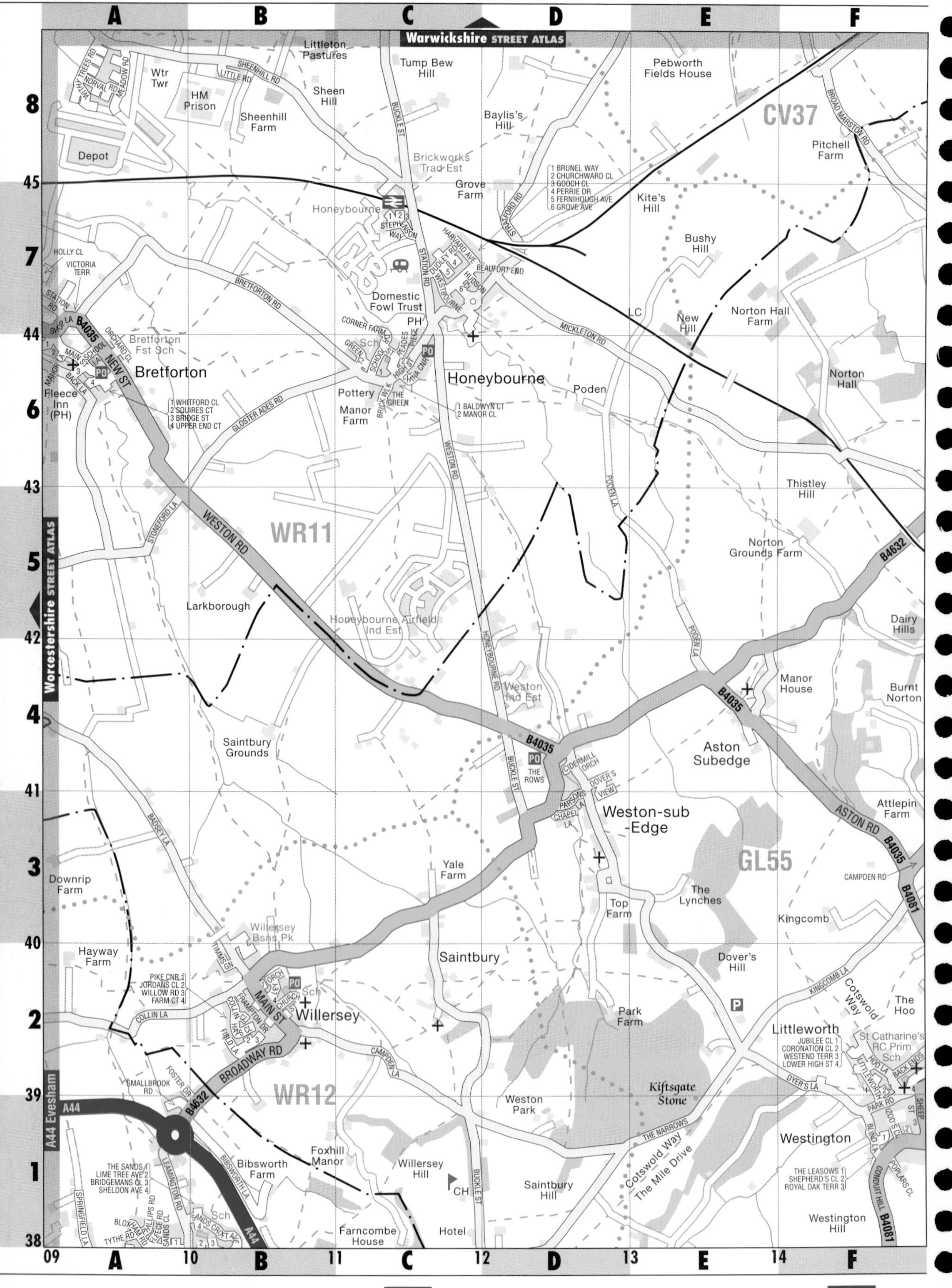

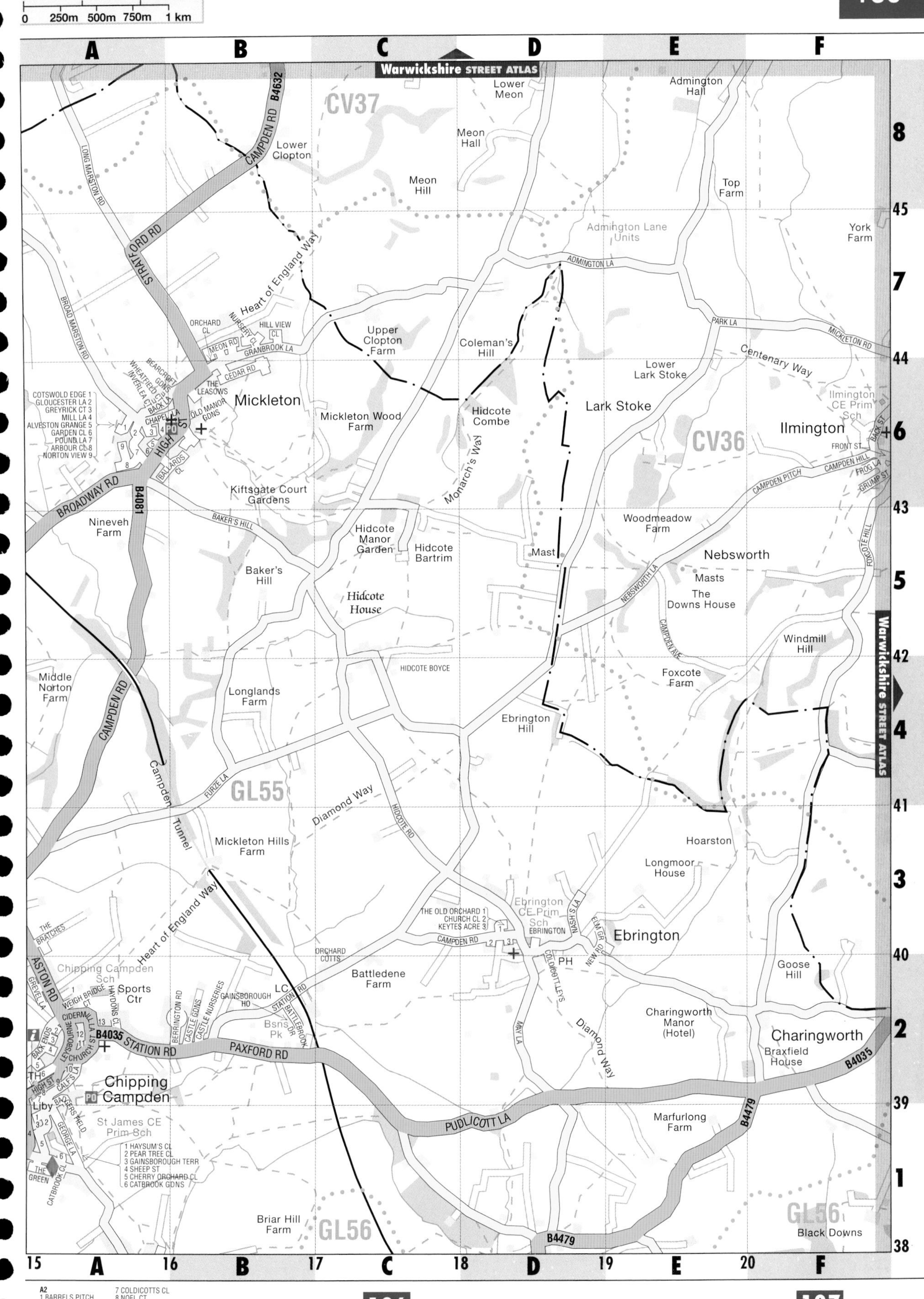

A2
1 BARRELS PITCH
2 WOLDS END CL
3 GRIGGS CL
4 ROLLING STONES
5 SEYMOUR GATE
6 THE SQUARE
7 COLDICOTTS CL
8 NOEL CT
9 THE OLD GRAMMAR SCHOOL MEWS
10 GLEBE FOLD
11 ALMSHOUSES
12 VICARAGE COTTS
13 CHURCH COTTS

186 187

150 150 150

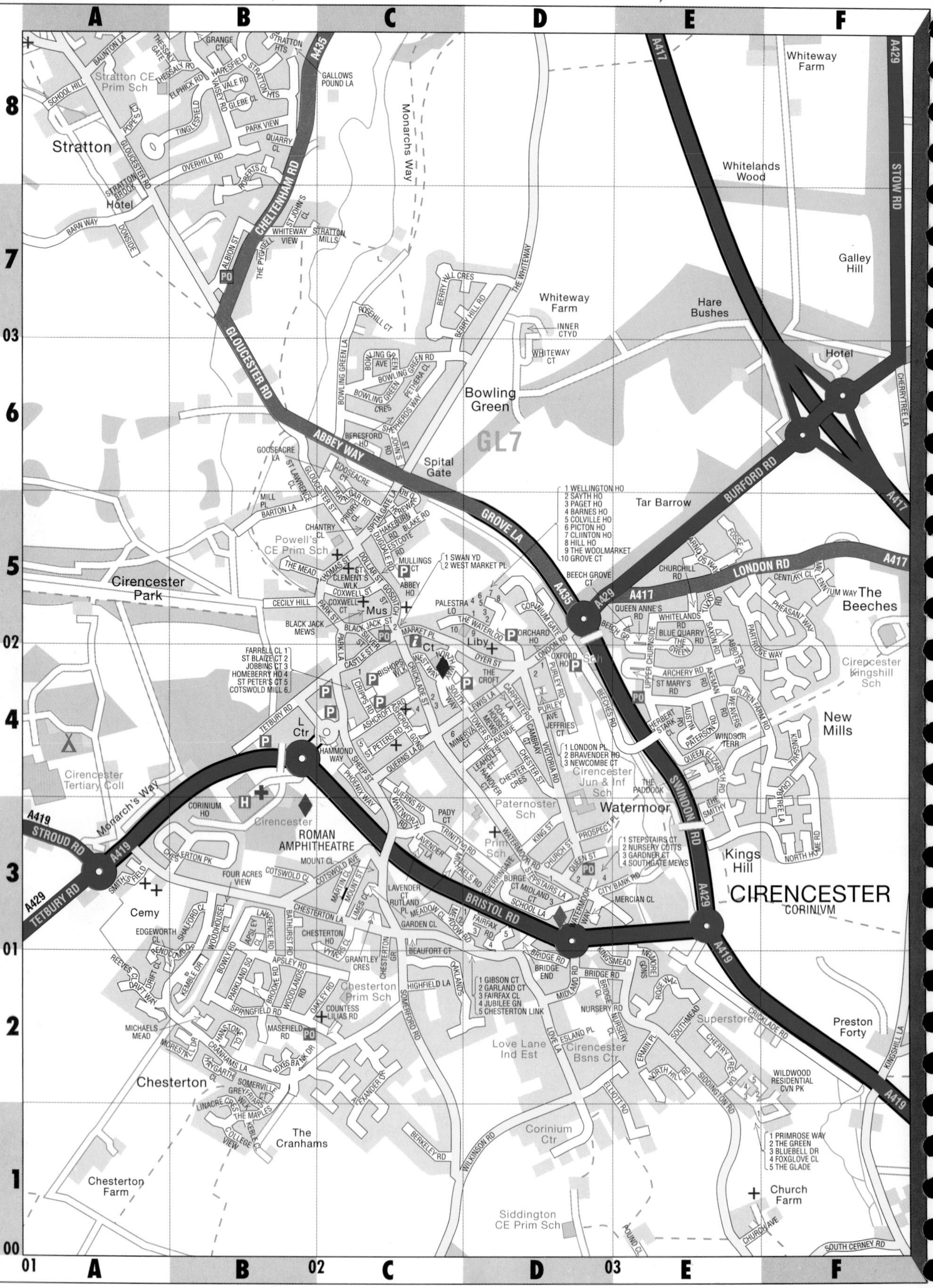

A B C D E F

Stratton
Stratton CE Prim Sch
Hotel
Whiteway Farm
Whitelands Wood
Galley Hill
Hare Bushes
Hotel
Whiteway Farm
Bowling Green
GL7
Spital Gate
Tar Barrow
Monarchs Way
Powell's CE Prim Sch
Cirencester Park
Mus
Liby
Ct
The Beeches
Cirencester Kingshill Sch
New Mills
Cirencester Tertiary Coll
Cirencester
ROMAN AMPHITHEATRE
Paternoster Sch
Cirencester Jun & Inf Sch
Watermoor
Kings Hill
CIRENCESTER
CORINIVM
Cemy
Chesterton Prim Sch
Love Lane Ind Est
Cirencester Bsns Ctr
Superstore
Preston Forty
Chesterton
The Cranhams
Corinium Ctr
Chesterton Farm
Siddington CE Prim Sch
Church Farm
WILDWOOD RESIDENTIAL CVN PK

A435 CHELTENHAM RD
GLOUCESTER RD
ABBEY WAY
GROVE LA
A417
A429
STOW RD
BURFORD RD
LONDON RD
A419 STROUD RD
A429 TETBURY RD
BRISTOL RD
SWINDON RD
CRICKLADE RD
THE WHITEWAY

1 WELLINGTON HO
2 SAYTH HO
3 PAGET HO
4 BARNES HO
5 COLVILLE HO
6 PICTON HO
7 CLINTON HO
8 HILL HO
9 THE WOOLMARKET
10 GROVE CT

1 SWAN YD
2 WEST MARKET PL

FARRELL CL 1
ST BLAIZE CT 2
JOBBINS CT 3
HOMEBERRY HO 4
ST PETER'S CT 5
COTSWOLD MILL 6

1 LONDON PL
2 BRAVENDER HO
3 NEWCOMBE CT

1 STEPSTAIRS CT
2 NURSERY COTTS
3 GARDNER CT
4 SOUTHGATE MEWS

1 GIBSON CT
2 GARLAND CT
3 FAIRFAX CL
4 JUBILEE GN
5 CHESTERTON LINK

1 PRIMROSE WAY
2 THE GREEN
3 BLUEBELL DR
4 FOXGLOVE CL
5 THE GLADE

8
7
03
6
5
02
4
3
01
2
1
00

01 A B 02 C D 03 E F

150 150 150

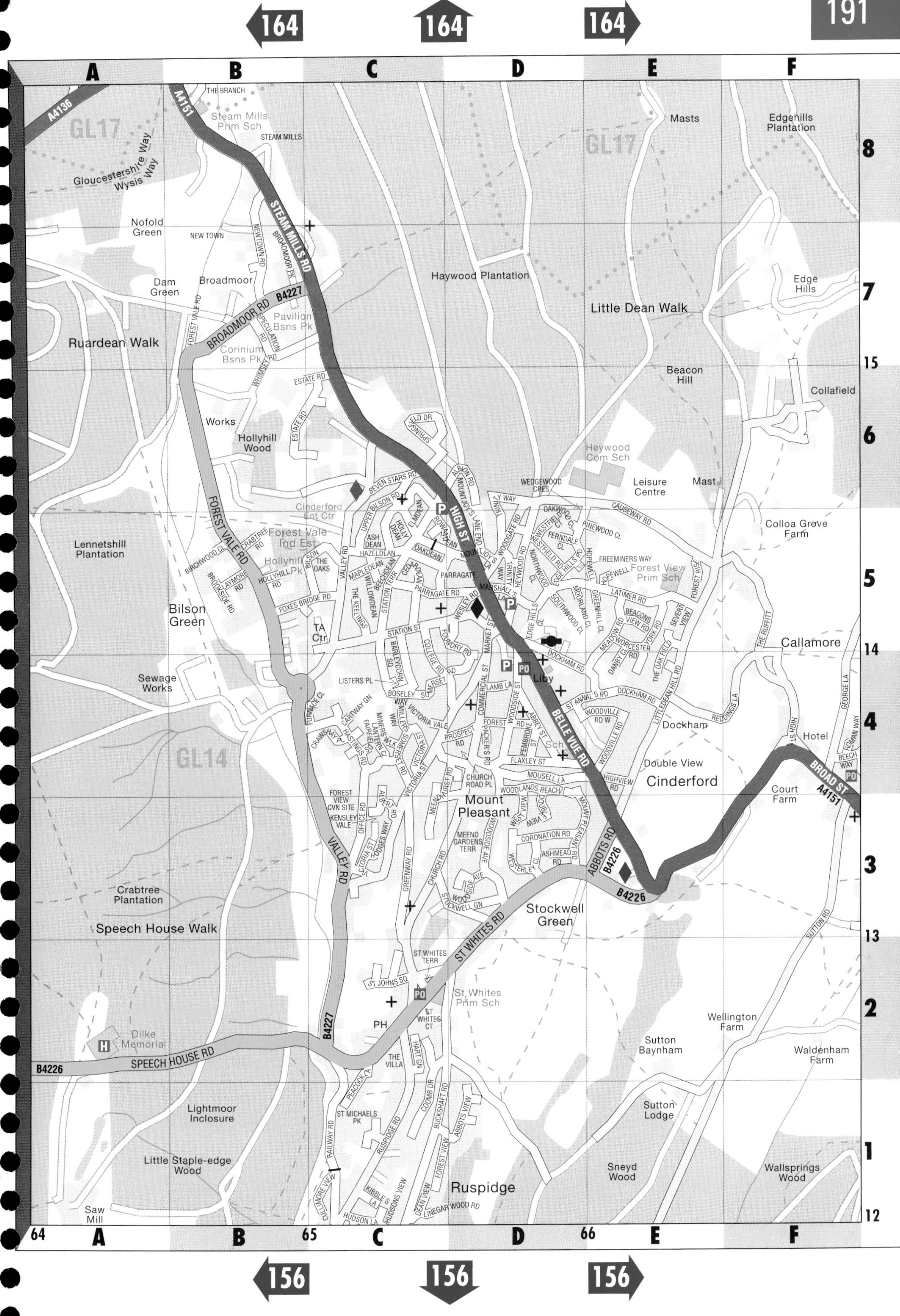
164
164
164
A
B
C
D
E
F
8
7
15
6
5
14
4
3
13
2
1
12
64
65
66
GL17
GL17
GL14
A4136
A4151
THE BRANCH
Steam Mills
Prim Sch
STEAM MILLS
Masts
Edgehills
Plantation
Gloucestershire Way
Wysis Way
Nofold
Green
NEW TOWN
NEWTOWN RD
BROADMOOR PK
STEAM MILLS RD
Haywood Plantation
Dam
Green
Broadmoor
B4227
BROADMOOR RD
FOREST VALE RD
Pavilion
Bsns Pk
Corinium
Bsns Pk
SPECULATION RD
WHIMSEY RD
Little Dean Walk
Edge
Hills
Ruardean Walk
Beacon
Hill
Collafield
ESTATE RD
Works
Hollyhill
Wood
SPRINGFIELD DR
Heywood
Com Sch
Leisure
Centre
Mast
WEDGEWOOD
CRES
SEVEN STARS RD
ALBION RD
MOUNTJOYS LANE END
HIGH ST
Cinderford
Ent Ctr
Forest Vale
Ind Est
Lennetshill
Plantation
CAUSEWAY RD
Colloa Grove
Farm
PINEWOOD CL
OAKWOOD CL
FERNDALE CL
FREEMINERS WAY
Forest View
Prim Sch
HOPEWELL
LATIMER RD
FOREST RISE
Hollyhill
Pk
BIRCHWOOD CL
CRABTREE RD
LAYMORE RD
HOLLYHILL RD
BROOKSIDE RD
FOXES BRIDGE RD
VALLEY RD
ASH DEAN
HAZELDEAN
HOLLY DEAN
ELMDEAN
OAKDEAN
MAPLEDEAN
BEECHDEAN
WILLOWDEAN
THE KEELINGS
STATION TERR
CEDAR DEAN
PARRAGATE
PARRAGATE RD
WESLEY RD
MARSHALL'S LA
MOUNTJOY'S LA
WOODGATE RD
TRINITY WAY
HEYWOOD RD
NORTHWOOD CL
WESTFIELD RD
EDGE HILLS RD
SOUTHWOOD CL
MOORLAND CL
GREENHILL CL
BEACONS VIEW RD
WORCESTER RD
SEVERN VIEW
YORK RD
MEADOW RD
DANBY CL
THE OAK FIELD
Bilson
Green
TA
Ctr
STATION ST
FOUNDRY RD
MARKET ST
EDGE HILLS CL
DOCKHAM RD
THE RUFFITT
Callamore
Sewage
Works
BARLEYCORN SQ
COLLEGE RD
LISTERS PL
BOSELEY WAY
SOMERSET RD
Liby
ST ANNAL'S RD
DOCKHAM RD
LITTLEDEAN HILL RD
COMMERCIAL ST
LAMB LA
WOODSIDE ST
REDDINGS LA
GEORGE LA
FURNACE CL
CARTWAY GN
MINERS WALK
MILLERS WAY
VICTORIA VALE
VICTORIA ST
FOREST RD
BELLE VUE RD
WOODVILLE RD W
WOODVILLE RD
Dockham
HIGH ST
ROMAN WAY
BEECH WAY
Hotel
CRAWSHAY PL
HASTINGS RD
LAKERN CL
FAIRFIELD CL
PROSPECT RD
PACKER'S RD
PEMBROKE ST
ABBEY ST
Sch
FLAXLEY ST
Double View
Cinderford
BROAD ST
A4151
MEENDHURST RD
CHURCH ROAD PL
MOUSELL LA
WOODLANDS REACH
HIGHVIEW RD
Court
Farm
FOREST VIEW CVN SITE
KENSLEY VALE
OFFICE RD
ALBERT RD
Mount
Pleasant
WEST VIEW
DOUBLE VIEW
MOUNT PLEASANT RD
VICTORIA ST
HODGES WAY
GREENWAY RD
MEEND GARDENS TERR
WOODSIDE AVE
CORONATION RD
ASHMEAD RD
WESTERLEY CL
ABBOTS RD
B4226
B4226
CHURCH RD
WOODSIDE AVE
STOCKWELL GN
Stockwell
Green
Crabtree
Plantation
VALLEY RD
Speech House Walk
ST WHITES RD
SUTTON RD
ST WHITES TERR
ST JOHNS SQ
PO
St Whites
Prim Sch
Wellington
Farm
B4227
ST WHITES CT
PH
Dilke
Memorial
H
SPEECH HOUSE RD
B4226
HART GN
THE VILLA
Sutton
Baynham
Waldenham
Farm
PEACOCK LA
Lightmoor
Inclosure
ST MICHAELS PK
COOMB DR
BUCKSHAFT RD
ABBOTS VIEW
Sutton
Lodge
RUSPIDGE RD
RAILWAY RD
FOREST VIEW
Little Staple-edge
Wood
Sneyd
Wood
Wallsprings
Wood
KIBBLE'S LA
HUDSONS VIEW
DEAN VIEW
Ruspidge
CULLIMORE VIEW
LINEGAR WOOD RD
HUDSON LA
Saw
Mill
156
156
156

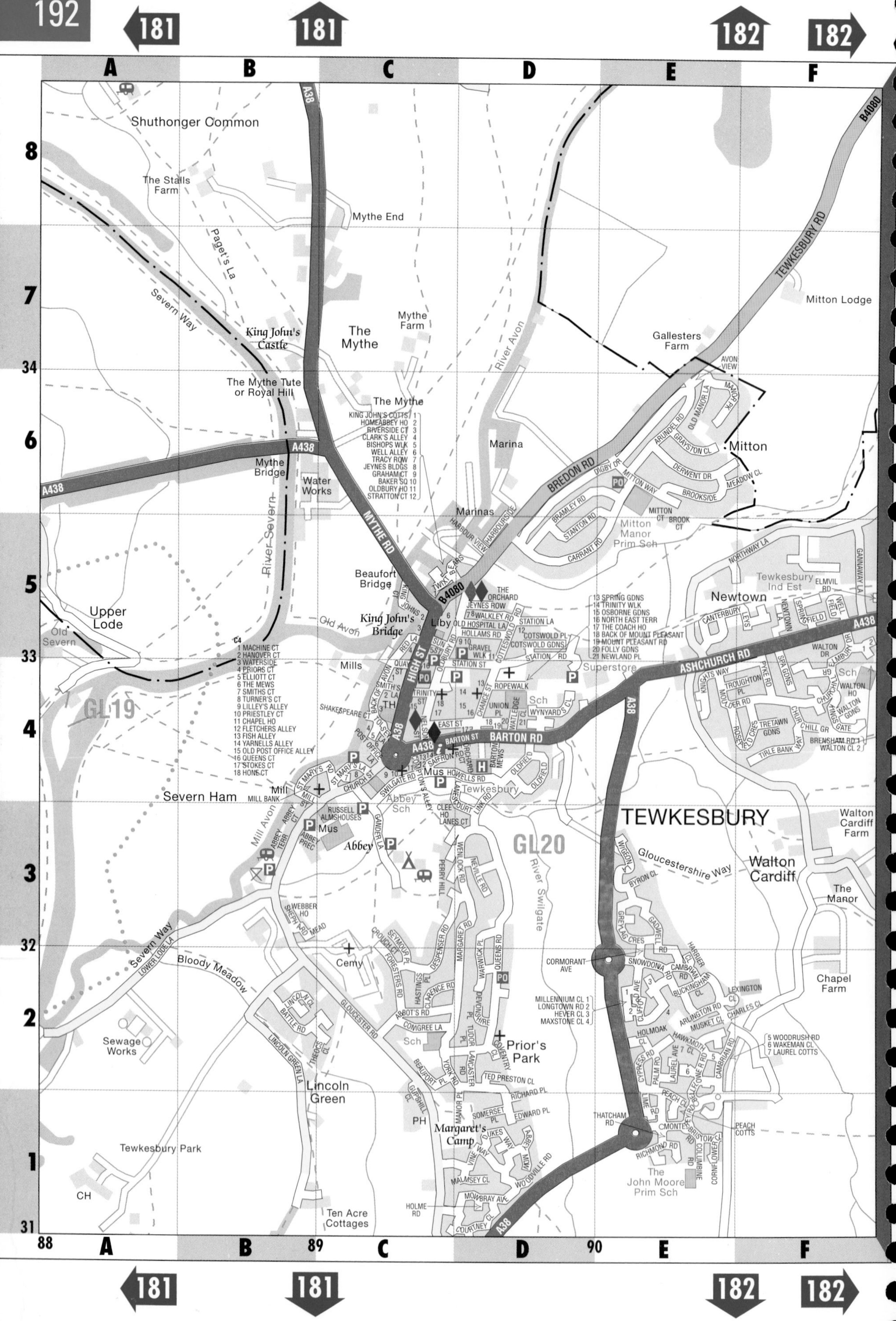
181
181
182
182
A
B
C
D
E
F
8
7
34
6
5
33
4
3
32
2
1
31
88
89
90
Shuthonger Common
The Stalls Farm
Mythe End
Paget's La
Severn Way
King John's Castle
The Mythe
Mythe Farm
The Mythe Tute or Royal Hill
The Mythe
KING JOHN'S COTTS 1
HOMEABBEY HO 2
RIVERSIDE CT 3
CLARK'S ALLEY 4
BISHOPS WLK 5
WELL ALLEY 6
TRACY ROW 7
JEYNES BLDGS 8
GRAHAM CT 9
BAKER SQ 10
OLDBURY HO 11
STRATTON CT 12
A438
Mythe Bridge
Water Works
MYTHE RD
River Avon
Marina
Marinas
HARBOUR VIEW
HARBOURSIDE
BREDON RD
B4080
TEWKESBURY RD
Mitton Lodge
Gallesters Farm
AVON VIEW
ARUNDEL RD
OLD MANOR LA
MANOR PK
GRAYSTON CL
Mitton
DERWENT DR
BROOKSIDE
MEADOW CL
DIGBY DR
MITTON WAY
MITTON CT
BROOK CT
Mitton Manor Prim Sch
BRAMLEY RD
STANTON RD
CARRANT RD
River Severn
Beaufort Bridge
Upper Lode
Old Severn
Old Avon
King John's Bridge
THE ORCHARD
JEYNES ROW
WALKLEY RD
OLD HOSPITAL LA
STATION LA
HOLLAMS RD
COTSWOLD PL
COTSWOLD GDNS
STATION RD
GRAVEL WLK
COTTESWOLD RD
STATION ST
ROPEWALK
13 SPRING GDNS
14 TRINITY WLK
15 OSBORNE GDNS
16 NORTH EAST TERR
17 THE COACH HO
18 BACK OF MOUNT PLEASANT RD
19 MOUNT PLEASANT RD
20 FOLLY GDNS
21 NEWLAND PL
Superstore
NORTHWAY LA
Tewkesbury Ind Est
ELMVIL RD
Newtown
CANTERBURY
LEWIS
NEWTOWN LA
SPRINGFIELD
WELL FIELD
GANNAWAY LA
A438
ASHCHURCH RD
WALTON DR
KNIGHTS WAY
TROUGHTON PL
PYKE RD
SPA GDNS
MULLER RD
TRETAWN GDNS
ROSEFIELD CRES
CHURCHILL GR
WALTON HO
WALTON GDNS
KINGS GATE
BRENSHAM RD 1
WALTON CL 2
TIRLE BANK WAY
Sch
C4
1 MACHINE CT
2 HANOVER CT
3 WATERSIDE
4 PRIORS CT
5 ELLIOTT CT
6 THE MEWS
7 SMITHS CT
8 TURNER'S CT
9 LILLEY'S ALLEY
10 PRIESTLEY CT
11 CHAPEL HO
12 FLETCHERS ALLEY
13 FISH ALLEY
14 YARNELLS ALLEY
15 OLD POST OFFICE ALLEY
16 QUEENS CT
17 STOKES CT
18 HONE CT
GL19
Mills
HIGH ST
QUAY ST
RED LA
SHAKESPEARE CT
BACK OF AVON
TRINITY ST
CHANCE ST
UNION PL
WATLEDGE CL
WYNYARDS CL
EAST ST
BARTON ST
BARTON RD
A38
A438
SAFFRON RD
ORCHARD CT
BARTON MEWS
OLDFIELD
POST OFFICE LA
TOLSEY LA
Severn Ham
Mill
MILL BANK
ST MARY'S RD
ST MARY'S LA
CHURCH ST
SWILGATE RD
HOWELLS RD
Mus
Tewkesbury
Abbey Sch
RUSSELL ALMSHOUSES
GANDER LA
CLEE HO
LANES CT
LINK RD
TEWKESBURY
GL20
River Swilgate
Mill Avon
ABBEY TERR
ABBEY CT
ABBEY PREC
Abbey
WENLOCK RD
NEVILLE RD
PERRY HILL
WIGGON
Gloucestershire Way
Walton Cardiff
Walton Cardiff Farm
The Manor
BYRON CL
GREYLAG CRES
GADWELL
HARRIER CL
SNOWDONIA RD
CAMBRAY RD
BUCKINGHAM CL
LEXINGTON
CHARLES CL
CORMORANT AVE
MILLENNIUM CL 1
LONGTOWN RD 2
HEVER CL 3
MAXSTONE CL 4
CLIFFORD AVE
ARLINGTON RD
MUSKET CL
HOLMOAK
HAWKMOTH CL
CYPRESS RD
PALM RD
LAUREL AVE
CAMBRIAN RD
5 WOODRUSH RD
6 WAKEMAN CL
7 LAUREL COTTS
Chapel Farm
WEBBER HO
SHEPHERD MEAD
Severn Way
LOWER LODE LA
Bloody Meadow
Cemy
CROUCH CT
SEYMOUR PL
DESPENSER RD
MARGARET RD
WARWICK PL
QUEENS RD
FORESTERS RD
HASTINGS
CLARENCE RD
DEVONSHIRE
ABBOT'S RD
COMGREE LA
TUDOR PL
Prior's Park
COVENTRY
LANCASTER
YORK RD
BEAUFORT PL
TED PRESTON CL
RICHARD PL
GLOUCESTER RD
LINCOLN CL
BATTLE RD
THEOCS CL
LINCOLN GREEN LA
Sewage Works
Lincoln Green
GUPSHILL CL
PH
MANOR PL
SOMERSET PL
EDWARD PL
Margaret's Camp
VINE WAY
DUKES WAY
ABBEY MDW
WOODVILLE RD
MALMSEY CL
MOWBRAY AV
HOLME RD
COURTNEY CL
Tewkesbury Park
CH
Ten Acre Cottages
LIME
PEACH CL
THATCHAM RD
MONTFORT
BRISTOW CL
COLUMBINE RD
CORNFLOWER
RICHMOND RD
PEACH COTTS
The John Moore Prim Sch

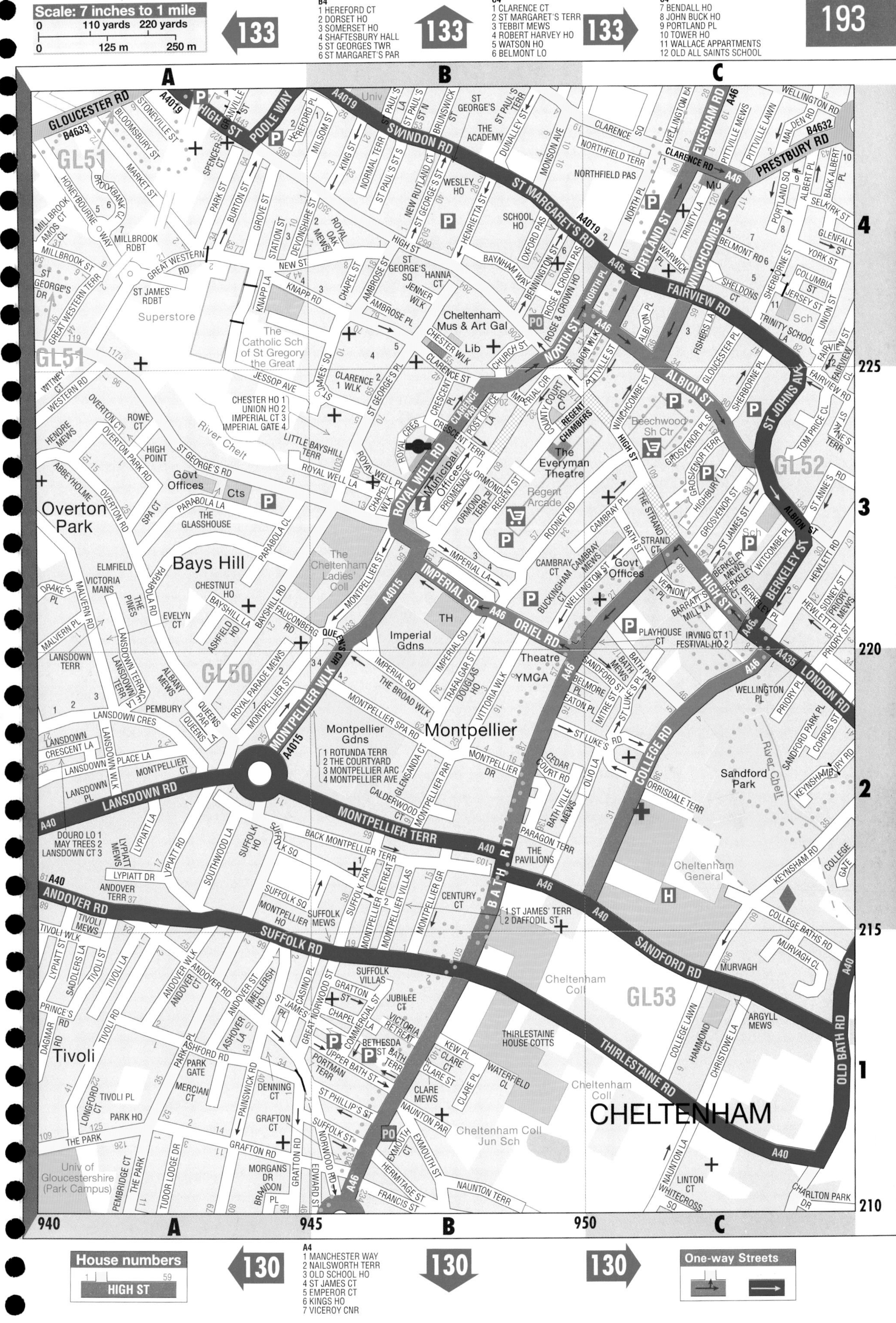

193
Scale: 7 inches to 1 mile
0 110 yards 220 yards
0 125 m 250 m
133
B4
1 HEREFORD CT
2 DORSET HO
3 SOMERSET HO
4 SHAFTESBURY HALL
5 ST GEORGES TWR
6 ST MARGARET'S PAR
133
C4
1 CLARENCE CT
2 ST MARGARET'S TERR
3 TEBBIT MEWS
4 ROBERT HARVEY HO
5 WATSON HO
6 BELMONT LO
133
C4
7 BENDALL HO
8 JOHN BUCK HO
9 PORTLAND PL
10 TOWER HO
11 WALLACE APPARTMENTS
12 OLD ALL SAINTS SCHOOL
A
B
C
4
3
2
1
225
220
215
210
940
945
950
GLOUCESTER RD
B4633
GL51
HIGH ST
POOLE WAY
SWINDON RD
ST MARGARET'S RD
A4019
CLARENCE SQ
NORTHFIELD TERR
NORTHFIELD PAS
EVESHAM RD
PITTVILLE MEWS
PITTVILLE LAWN
WELLINGTON RD
PRESTBURY RD
B4632
CLARENCE RD
PORTLAND ST
WINCHCOMBE ST
FAIRVIEW RD
MILLBROOK RDBT
GREAT WESTERN RD
ST JAMES' RDBT
Superstore
The Catholic Sch of St Gregory the Great
Cheltenham Mus & Art Gal
Lib
NORTH ST
ALBION ST
ST JOHNS AVE
GL52
Beechwood Sh Ctr
CHESTER HO 1
UNION HO 2
IMPERIAL CT 3
IMPERIAL GATE 4
River Chelt
ST GEORGE'S RD
Govt Offices
Cts
Overton Park
Bays Hill
The Cheltenham Ladies' Coll
ROYAL WELL RD
Municipal Offices
PROMENADE
Regent Arcade
The Everyman Theatre
REGENT CHAMBERS
HIGH ST
THE STRAND
IMPERIAL SQ
ORIEL RD
TH
Imperial Gdns
Theatre
YMCA
PLAYHOUSE CT
IRVING CT 1
FESTIVAL HO 2
LONDON RD
A435
GL50
MONTPELLIER WALK
A4015
Montpellier Gdns
1 ROTUNDA TERR
2 THE COURTYARD
3 MONTPELLIER ARC
4 MONTPELLIER AVE
Montpellier
COLLEGE RD
Sandford Park
LANSDOWN RD
A40
MONTPELLIER TERR
DOURO LO 1
MAY TREES 2
LANSDOWN CT 3
BATH RD
A46
THE PAVILIONS
Cheltenham General
H
1 ST JAMES' TERR
2 DAFFODIL ST
ANDOVER RD
SUFFOLK RD
SANDFORD RD
GL53
Cheltenham Coll
THIRLESTAINE HOUSE COTTS
THIRLESTAINE RD
OLD BATH RD
Tivoli
CHELTENHAM
Cheltenham Coll Jun Sch
Univ of Gloucestershire (Park Campus)
THE PARK
130
A4
1 MANCHESTER WAY
2 NAILSWORTH TERR
3 OLD SCHOOL HO
4 ST JAMES CT
5 EMPEROR CT
6 KINGS HO
7 VICEROY CNR
130
130
House numbers
HIGH ST
One-way Streets

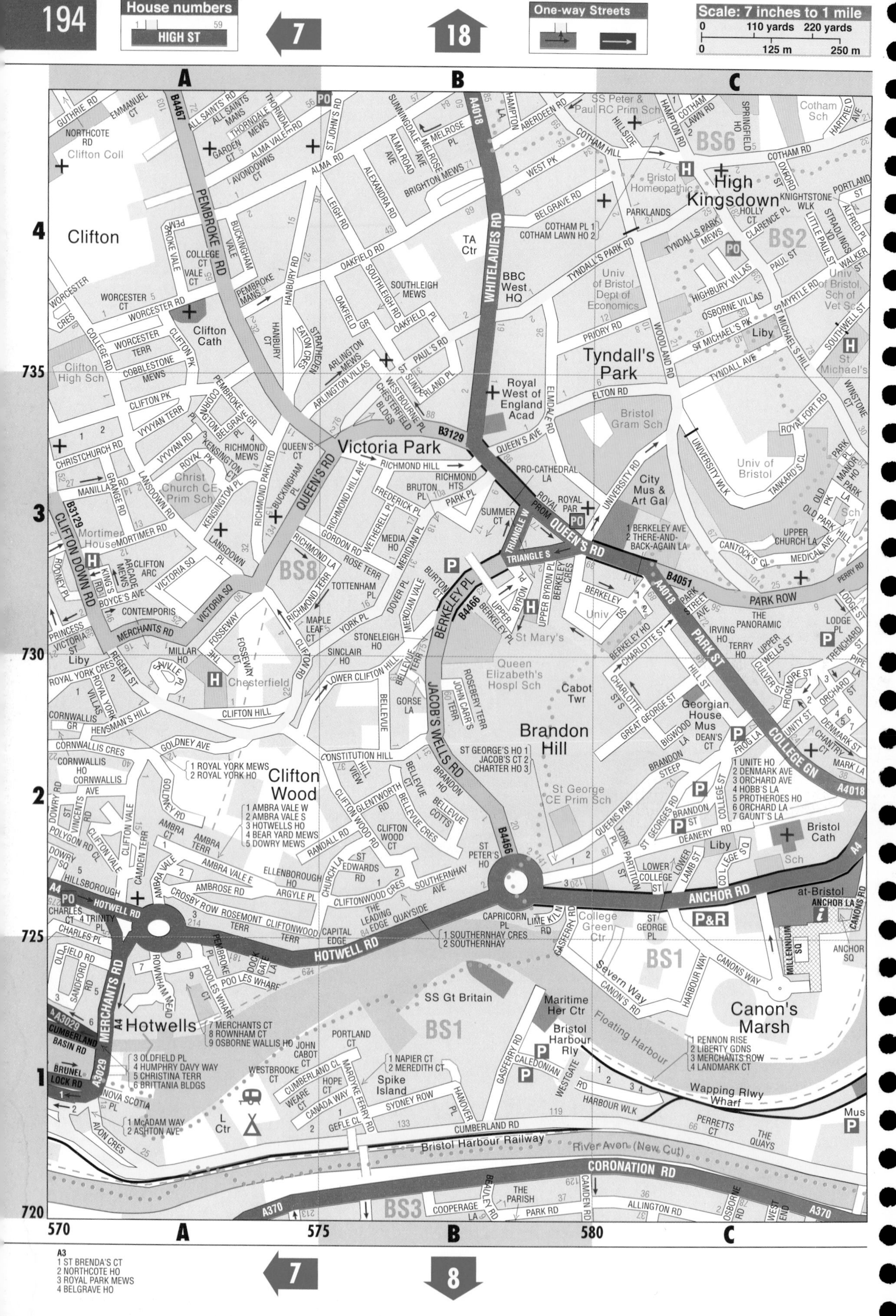
194
House numbers
HIGH ST
7
18
One-way Streets
Scale: 7 inches to 1 mile
0 110 yards 220 yards
0 125 m 250 m
A
B
C
4
3
2
1
735
730
725
720
570
575
580
Clifton
Clifton Coll
Clifton Cath
Clifton High Sch
Christ Church CE Prim Sch
Mortimer House
Victoria Park
Royal West of England Acad
Bristol Gram Sch
Univ of Bristol
City Mus & Art Gal
Tyndall's Park
High Kingsdown
Bristol Homeopathic
BBC West HQ
TA Ctr
Univ of Bristol Dept of Economics
Univ of Bristol, Sch of Vet Sc
St Michael's
Cotham Sch
SS Peter & Paul RC Prim Sch
BS6
BS2
BS8
BS1
BS3
Brandon Hill
Cabot Twr
Queen Elizabeth's Hospl Sch
Georgian House Mus
St George CE Prim Sch
St Mary's
Chesterfield
Clifton Wood
Bristol Cath
College Green Ctr
Canon's Marsh
Hotwells
SS Gt Britain
Maritime Her Ctr
Bristol Harbour Rly
Floating Harbour
Spike Island
Wapping Rlwy Wharf
Bristol Harbour Railway
River Avon (New Cut)
CORONATION RD
WHITELADIES RD
PEMBROKE RD
QUEEN'S RD
PARK ST
PARK ROW
COLLEGE GN
ANCHOR RD
HOTWELL RD
JACOB'S WELLS RD
CLIFTON DOWN RD
MERCHANTS RD
CUMBERLAND RD
TYNDALL'S PARK RD
COTHAM HILL
ALMA RD
OAKFIELD RD
QUEEN'S AVE
ELTON RD
UNIVERSITY RD
BERKELEY PL
A4018
B4467
B3129
B4466
B4051
A4
A3029
A370
1 ROYAL YORK MEWS
2 ROYAL YORK HO
1 AMBRA VALE W
2 AMBRA VALE S
3 HOTWELLS HO
4 BEAR YARD MEWS
5 DOWRY MEWS
1 UNITE HO
2 DENMARK AVE
3 ORCHARD AVE
4 HOBB'S LA
5 PROTHEROES HO
6 ORCHARD LA
7 GAUNT'S LA
1 PENNON RISE
2 LIBERTY GDNS
3 MERCHANTS ROW
4 LANDMARK CT
7 MERCHANTS CT
8 ROWNHAM CT
9 OSBORNE WALLIS HO
3 OLDFIELD PL
4 HUMPHRY DAVY WAY
5 CHRISTINA TERR
6 BRITTANIA BLDGS
1 McADAM WAY
2 ASHTON AVE
1 NAPIER CT
2 MEREDITH CT
1 SOUTHERNHAY CRES
2 SOUTHERNHAY
ST GEORGE'S HO 1
JACOB'S CT 2
CHARTER HO 3
1 BERKELEY AVE
2 THERE-AND-BACK-AGAIN LA
A3
1 ST BRENDA'S CT
2 NORTHCOTE HO
3 ROYAL PARK MEWS
4 BELGRAVE HO
7
8

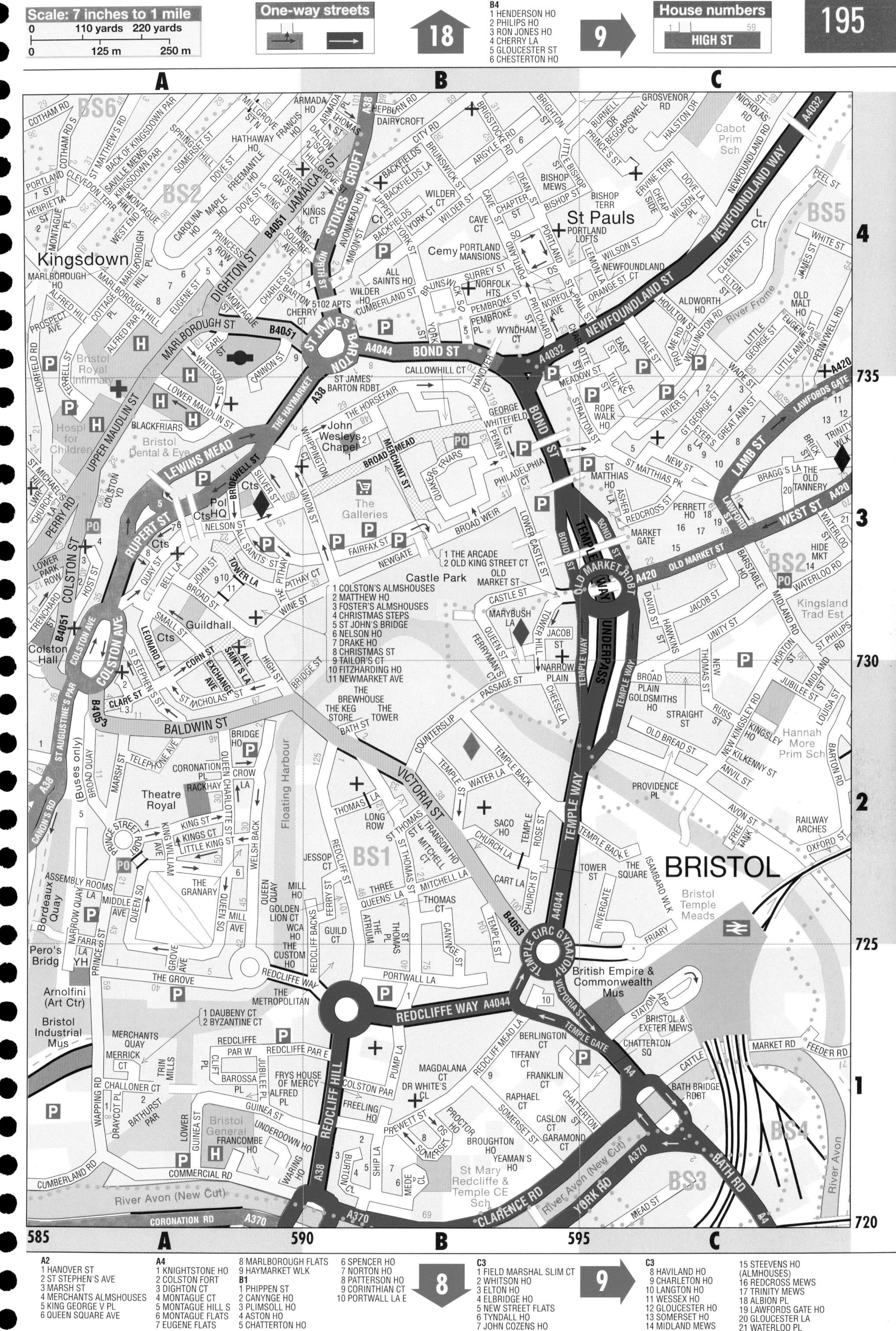
Scale: 7 inches to 1 mile
0 110 yards 220 yards
0 125 m 250 m
One-way streets
18
B4
1 HENDERSON HO
2 PHILIPS HO
3 RON JONES HO
4 CHERRY LA
5 GLOUCESTER ST
6 CHESTERTON HO
9
House numbers
1 59
HIGH ST
A
B
C
4
735
3
730
2
725
1
720
585
590
595
A2
1 HANOVER ST
2 ST STEPHEN'S AVE
3 MARSH ST
4 MERCHANTS ALMSHOUSES
5 KING GEORGE V PL
6 QUEEN SQUARE AVE
A4
1 KNIGHTSTONE HO
2 COLSTON FORT
3 DIGHTON CT
4 MONTAGUE CT
5 MONTAGUE HILL S
6 MONTAGUE FLATS
7 EUGENE FLATS
8 MARLBOROUGH FLATS
9 HAYMARKET WLK
B1
1 PHIPPEN ST
2 CANYNGE HO
3 PLIMSOLL HO
4 ASTON HO
5 CHATTERTON HO
6 SPENCER HO
7 NORTON HO
8 PATTERSON HO
9 CORINTHIAN CT
10 PORTWALL LA E
8
C3
1 FIELD MARSHAL SLIM CT
2 WHITSON HO
3 ELTON HO
4 ELBRIDGE HO
5 NEW STREET FLATS
6 TYNDALL HO
7 JOHN COZENS HO
9
C3
8 HAVILAND HO
9 CHARLETON HO
10 LANGTON HO
11 WESSEX HO
12 GLOUCESTER HO
13 SOMERSET HO
14 MIDLAND MEWS
15 STEEVENS HO (ALMSHOUSES)
16 REDCROSS MEWS
17 TRINITY MEWS
18 ALBION PL
19 LAWFORDS GATE HO
20 GLOUCESTER LA
21 WATERLOO PL

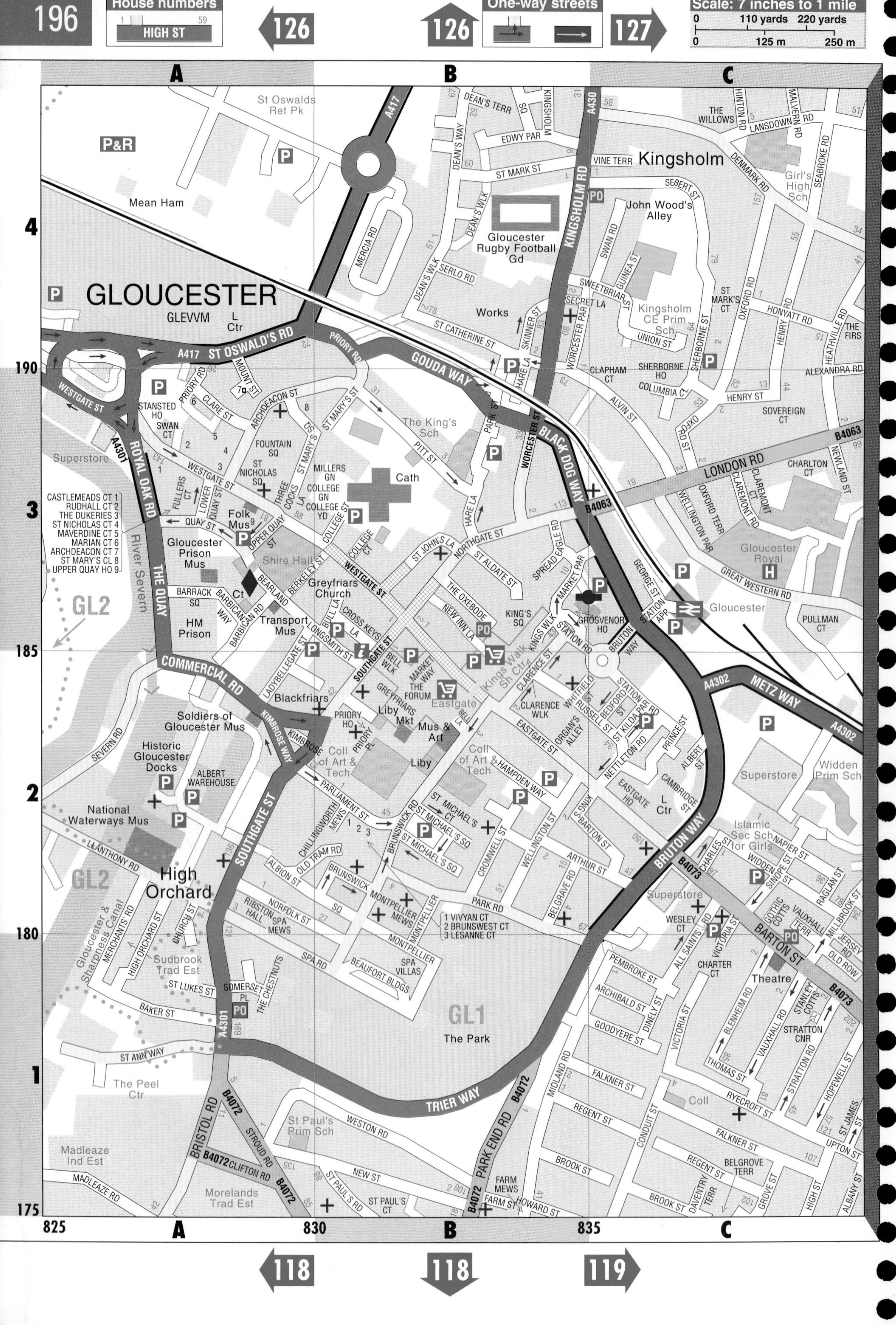
196
House numbers
HIGH ST
126
126
One-way streets
127
Scale: 7 inches to 1 mile
0
110 yards
220 yards
125 m
250 m
A
B
C
4
3
2
1
190
185
180
175
825
830
835
118
118
119
GLOUCESTER
GLEVVM
Kingsholm
St Oswalds Ret Pk
Mean Ham
Gloucester Rugby Football Gd
John Wood's Alley
Kingsholm CE Prim Sch
Girl's High Sch
The King's Sch
Cath
Folk Mus
Gloucester Prison Mus
Shire Hall
Greyfriars Church
HM Prison
Transport Mus
Blackfriars
Soldiers of Gloucester Mus
Historic Gloucester Docks
National Waterways Mus
High Orchard
Sudbrook Trad Est
The Peel Ctr
Madleaze Ind Est
Morelands Trad Est
St Paul's Prim Sch
The Park
GL1
GL2
River Severn
Gloucester & Sharpness Canal
Gloucester Royal
Gloucester
Superstore
Widden Prim Sch
Islamic Sec Sch for Girls
Theatre
Coll of Art & Tech
Liby
Mkt
Mus & Art
Kings Walk Sh Ctr
Eastgate
The Forum
Works
A417 ST OSWALD'S RD
GOUDA WAY
BLACK DOG WAY
KINGSHOLM RD
WESTGATE ST
ROYAL OAK RD
THE QUAY
COMMERCIAL RD
SOUTHGATE ST
TRIER WAY
BRUTON WAY
METZ WAY
LONDON RD
PARK END RD
BRISTOL RD
STROUD RD
CLIFTON RD
BARTON ST
EASTGATE ST
NORTHGATE ST
CASTLEMEADS CT 1
RUDHALL CT 2
THE DUKERIES 3
ST NICHOLAS CT 4
MAVERDINE CT 5
MARIAN CT 6
ARCHDEACON CT 7
ST MARY'S CL 8
UPPER QUAY HO 9
1 VIVYAN CT
2 BRUNSWEST CT
3 LESANNE CT

Index

Church Rd 6 Beckenham BR2..........53 C6

Place name
May be abbreviated on the map

Location number
Present when a number indicates the place's position in a crowded area of mapping

Locality, town or village
Shown when more than one place has the same name

Postcode district
District for the indexed place

Page and grid square
Page number and grid reference for the standard mapping

Public and commercial buildings are highlighted in magenta **Places of interest** are highlighted in blue with a star ★

Abbreviations used in the index

Acad	**Academy**	Comm	**Common**	Gd	**Ground**	L	**Leisure**	Prom	**Promenade**
App	**Approach**	Cott	**Cottage**	Gdn	**Garden**	La	**Lane**	Rd	**Road**
Arc	**Arcade**	Cres	**Crescent**	Gn	**Green**	Liby	**Library**	Recn	**Recreation**
Ave	**Avenue**	Cswy	**Causeway**	Gr	**Grove**	Mdw	**Meadow**	Ret	**Retail**
Bglw	**Bungalow**	Ct	**Court**	H	**Hall**	Meml	**Memorial**	Sh	**Shopping**
Bldg	**Building**	Ctr	**Centre**	Ho	**House**	Mkt	**Market**	Sq	**Square**
Bsns, Bus	**Business**	Ctry	**Country**	Hospl	**Hospital**	Mus	**Museum**	St	**Street**
Bvd	**Boulevard**	Cty	**County**	HQ	**Headquarters**	Orch	**Orchard**	Sta	**Station**
Cath	**Cathedral**	Dr	**Drive**	Hts	**Heights**	Pal	**Palace**	Terr	**Terrace**
Cir	**Circus**	Dro	**Drove**	Ind	**Industrial**	Par	**Parade**	TH	**Town Hall**
Cl	**Close**	Ed	**Education**	Inst	**Institute**	Pas	**Passage**	Univ	**University**
Cnr	**Corner**	Emb	**Embankment**	Int	**International**	Pk	**Park**	Wk, Wlk	**Walk**
Coll	**College**	Est	**Estate**	Intc	**Interchange**	Pl	**Place**	Wr	**Water**
Com	**Community**	Ex	**Exhibition**	Junc	**Junction**	Prec	**Precinct**	Yd	**Yard**

Index of localities, towns and villages

A

Abbeydale 119 D4
Abbeymead 119 E6
Abbotside 65 F2
Abbots Leigh 7 A8
Ablington 159 F3
Abwell 85 E6
Acton Turville 35 F6
Adlestrop 177 E5
Adsett 165 D1
Alderley 68 E2
Alderton
Luckington 47 F2
Tewkesbury 183 E4
Alderton Fields 183 E3
Aldsworth 160 E5
Alkerton 96 E7
Allaston 92 B6
Almondsbury 40 B5
Alstone
Cheltenham 133 B2
Tewkesbury 183 C3
Alveston 51 B4
Alveston Down 50 F5
Alvington 147 D3
Amberley 91 C7
Ampney Crucis 151 B5
Ampney St Mary 151 E5
Ampney St Peter 151 D4
Andoversford 166 C6
Apperley 173 C7
Arle 132 F4
Arlebrook 102 A5
Arlingham 157 B5
Arlington Pike 159 F1
Arno's Vale 9 B4
Ashbrook 151 E5
Ashchurch 182 C4
Ashleworth 172 C4
Ashley 141 A5
Ashley Down 18 F4
Ashmead Green 88 D4
Ashton Court Estate 7 C4
Ashton Gate 7 F4
Ashton Keynes 142 F5
Ashton under Hill 183 D8
Ashton Vale 7 F2
Aston Crews 170 A2
Aston Cross 182 E4
Aston Down 148 E4
Aston Ingham 170 C2
Aston Magna 186 F6
Aston on Carrant 182 E5
Aston Somerville 184 C8
Aston Subedge 188 E4
Aust 49 A6
Avening 140 A8
Avening Green 66 D8
Avonmouth 26 D2
Awkley 39 E8
Awre 157 B3
Aylburton 147 E4
Aylburton Common 147 D5
Aylton 178 A8

B

Badbrook 99 B8
Badgeworth 129 B3
Badminton 46 F2
Badminton Park 46 F4
Bafford 131 A5
Bagendon 158 C1
Bagpath
Stroud 99 C3
Wotton-under-Edge 81 F2
Bagstone 53 A3
Baker's Hill 155 B6
Baldwins 108 B1
Ball's Green 91 F4
Bamfurlong 128 F8
Baptist Mills 19 A2
Barnsley 151 C8
Barnwood 127 E1
Barrow 173 E3
Barrow Common 1 B4
Barrow Wake 122 A4
Bartlett's Green 102 A4
Barton
Cheltenham 175 C4
Gloucester 119 A8
Barton End 83 B8
Barton Hill 9 C6
Barton-on-the-Heath 187 F3
Batsford 186 E4
Battledown 131 B8
Baunton 150 C7
Bayfield 60 B8
Bays Hill 193 A3
Beach 12 C2
Beachley 61 C3
Beavan's Hill 170 B3
Beckford 183 B6
Bedminster 8 C3
Bedminster Down 2 B8
Beeches Green 99 A7
Beech Hill 32 B7
Beechknap 91 E8
Beechpike 115 B2
Bencombe 81 C8
Bengrove 183 B3
Benhall 129 D8
Bentham 121 C6
Berkeley 85 F3
Berkeley Heath 86 B3
Berkeley Road 86 F4
Berrow 180 B5
Berry Hill 155 A7
Berwick 27 D6
Betty's Grave 151 F4
Bevington 76 F6
Bibstone 66 C3
Bibury 160 B1
Bilson Green 191 B5
Bird in Hand 102 F5
Birdlip 121 F2
Birdwood 165 F5
Birts Street 180 A7
Bishop's Cleeve 137 E3
Bishop's North 173 A3
Bishopston 18 D3
Bishopsworth 2 A5
Bisley 105 B1
Bitton 5 E8
Blackhorse 21 A7
Blaisdon 165 B3
Blakeney 156 E2
Bledington 177 E1
Blockley 186 C6
Boddington 173 F4
Bondend 119 F3
Botloe's Green 170 F7
Boughspring 73 C7
Boulsdon 170 E3
Bournes Green 148 D7
Bournside 130 A7
Bournstream 79 F2
Bourton-on-the-Hill 186 D3
Bourton-on-the-Water 169 A7
Bowbridge 99 D5
Bower Ashton 7 E4
Bowling Green 190 D6
Box 91 E5
Boxbush 164 E7
Bradley 67 F8
Bradley Green 67 E7
Bradley Stoke 29 E8
Brand Green 171 C7
Brandon Hill 194 B2
Breadstone 86 D6
Bread Street 102 F2
Bream 147 D8
Bream's Meend 155 C1
Bredon 182 C8
Bredon's Hardwick 182 B6
Brelston Green 162 F7
Brentlands 111 A6
Brentry 28 B2
Bretforton 188 A6
Bridgend 97 F6
Bridgeyate 11 E7
Brierley 163 F2
Brimpsfield 114 C6
Brimps Hill 164 E5
Brimscombe 99 E2
Brislington 9 E2
Bristol 195 C2
Broad Blunsdon 144 D1
Broad Campden 186 B8
Broadoak 157 B7
Broadrock 73 A5
Broadway 185 C8
Broadwell
Coleford 155 C6
Stow-on-the-Wold 177 A6
Brockeridge Common ..180 E9
Brockhampton 174 B1
Brockweir 146 D3
Brockworth 120 F6
Bromesberrow 179 C4
Bromesberrow Heath ..179 B3
Bromley Heath 30 D1
Brookend
Berkeley 93 E1
Lydney 147 C2
Brookthorpe 110 F1
Broomhill 19 E6
Broom Hill 9 F3
Broom's Green 178 F3
Brownshill 148 B5
Buckbury 181 A5
Buckland 184 F6
Buckover 65 B1
Bullo 156 F4
Bull's Hill 163 C7
Bulwark 60 E6
Bunting Hill 90 F4
Burchells Green 20 B1
Burleigh 91 E7
Burton 36 B3
Bushley 181 D5

Bushley Green 181 C5
Bussage 148 B6
Butterrow 99 D4

C

Cadbury Heath 11 B5
Cainscross 98 F7
Calcot 159 E5
Calcott's Green 117 A6
Calcutt 144 A4
Callamore 191 F5
Cam 88 B4
Cambridge 95 F4
Camer's Green 179 F6
Cannop 155 D6
Canon's Marsh 194 C1
Cas-Gwent/Chepstow 60 D6
Cashes Green 98 C7
Cassey Compton 166 F2
Castle Eaton 144 E6
Castle End 111 F5
Castletump 170 F8
Catbrain 28 B6
Catbrook 146 A5
Caudle Green 114 C1
Cerney Wick 143 C7
Chaceley 181 B1
Chaceley Stock 173 C8
Chalford 148 D5
Chalford Hill 148 C6
Chapel Hill
St Arvans 146 B2
Lydney 147 E4
Charfield 67 B4
Charfield Green 67 B5
Charfield Hill 66 F5
Chargrove 129 F4
Charingworth 189 F2
Charlton Abbots 174 A3
Charlton Kings 131 C6
Charlton Park 130 F6
Chase End Street 179 E6
Chase Hill 54 D6
Chastleton 177 E8
Chaxhill 165 F1
Chedglow 141 A4
Chedworth 159 A6
Chedworth Laines 158 F6
Cheltenham 193 C1
Chelworth 141 E5
Chelworth Lower Green 143 D3
Chelworth Upper Green 143 D3
Chepstow/Cas-Gwent 60 D6
Cherington 148 D1
Chester Park 20 B2
Chesterton 190 B2
Chewton Keynsham 4 E2
Chipping Campden 189 A2
Chipping Sodbury 44 D1
Christchurch 154 F8
Churcham 124 D2
Churchdown 128 D6
Churchend
Charfield 66 F3
Stonehouse 97 A8
Church End
Frampton on Severn 157 F1
Tewkesbury 181 F7
Church Westcote 169 F7
Cinderford 191 E4
Cirencester 190 F3
Clapton-on-the-Hill 168 F4
Claycombe 91 E8
Clay Hill 19 E2
Claypits 100 D1
Clearwell 155 A2
Cleddon 146 A6
Cleeve Hill 138 E2
Cleevemount 133 F4
Clements End 155 B2
Clifford's Mesne 170 E1
Clifton 194 A4
Clifton Wood 194 A2
Cloatley End 142 A1
Coaley 88 E8
Coalpit Heath 31 D6
Coalway 155 C5
Coates 149 F4
Coberley 123 A5
Cockshoot
Bisley 104 C8
Stroud 102 D3
Codrington 33 C2
Cold Ashton 13 F6
Cold Aston 168 B6
Cold Elm 181 A3
Coldharbour 146 E6
Cold Slad 121 E5
Coleford 155 B5
Colerne 15 F6
Colesbourne 158 A8
Colethrop 110 C2
Collafield 164 E1
Coln Rogers 159 D4
Coln St Aldwyns 152 D8
Coln St Dennis 159 D5
Coltham Fields 130 F8
Colt's Green 33 E8
Compton Abdale 167 B3
Compton Green 171 B7
Compton Greenfield 27 F8
Conderton 183 A7
Condicote 176 A7
Coney Hill 119 C8
Conham 10 A5
Coombe 68 D8
Coombe Dingle 17 C8
Coomb's End 34 A6
Corse 172 A7
Corse Lawn 180 F1
Cotham 18 C1
Coughton 163 C8
Cowhill 63 B3
Cowley 123 A2
Cranham 112 F6
Cress Green 97 A6
Crew's Hole 9 F7
Cribbs Causeway 28 D6
Cricklade 143 E5
Crocker's Ash 162 D3
Crofts End 19 F1
Cromhall 66 A1
Cross Hill 73 D5
Crossway Green 72 D2
Crossways 64 F2
Crowell Brook 79 F6
Crudwell 141 C3
Cruse 163 A6
Culkerton 141 A7
Cutsdean 185 A1

D

Daglingworth 150 A8
Damery 78 E1
Dancing Green 164 A7
Daneway 149 B6
Daylesford 177 E4
Deerhurst 173 D8
Deerhurst Walton 173 E7
Derry Fields 142 F4
Didbrook 184 D2
Didmarton 57 C4
Dixton
Monmouth 154 A8
Winchcombe 183 C1
Dodington 34 A4
Donnington
Ledbury 178 E5
Stow-on-the-Wold 176 F7
Doughton 140 A2
Down Ampney 143 F8
Downend
Bristol 20 E8
Nailsworth 90 F1
Down Hatherley 173 C1
Doynton 23 A1
Draycott
Dursley 87 F8
Moreton-in-Marsh 186 E6
Driffield 151 C2
Drybrook 164 B4
Duckhole 64 C5
Dumbleton 183 F7
Dundry 1 D2
Dundry Hill 3 B3
Dunfield 144 D8
Duntisbourne Abbots 107 C4
Duntisbourne Leer 107 D3
Duntisbourne Rouse 107 E1
Dursley 88 B2
Dursley Cross 165 A7
Dyer's Common 38 C3
Dymock 178 D2
Dyrham 23 D4

E

Earthcott Green 41 E7
Eastcombe 148 C7
Eastcourt 141 E3
East Dean 164 C7
East Dundry 2 B1
East End
Cheltenham 131 C6
Fairford 152 F4
Marshfield 15 A8
Easter Compton 39 A2
Eastfield 18 B7
Eastington
Northleach 160 C8
Stonehouse 96 F8
Eastleach Martin 153 D8
Eastleach Turville 153 C8
Eastnor 179 B8
Easton Grey 59 C3
Easton-in-Gordano 16 A4
Easton Town 58 D1
Eastville 19 C3
Ebley 98 C6
Ebrington 189 E3
Edge 103 B8
Edge End 155 C8
Edgeworth 106 D1
Egypt 91 B5
Elberton 50 A6
Eldersfield 180 C2
Elkstone 115 B5
Ellwood 155 C2
Elmbridge 127 E3
Elmore 117 A3
Elmore Back 116 E6
Elmstone Hardwicke 136 E1
Elton 165 B1
Emerson's Green 21 C6
Engine Common 43 B5
English Bicknor 163 B2
Epney 108 C3
Etloe 93 C8
Evenlode 177 C8
Everlands 88 A4
Ewen 142 B8

F

Fairford 152 E3
Fairview 133 F1
Falfield 65 E7
Far End 112 E2
Far Green 88 F6
Farley's End 116 E3
Farmington 168 B2
Far Oakridge 148 F6
Far Thrupp 99 F3
Fiddington 182 C1
Fiddler's Green 132 C2
Filton 29 A3
Filwood Park 2 E8
Fishponds 20 A5
Fishpool 170 A8
Five Acres 155 B7
Flaxley 165 A2
Flaxpits 30 E5
Ford 175 B8
Forest Green 91 A5
Forthampton 181 B3
Forthay 79 E5
Forwood 91 F5
Foss Cross 159 B4
Fossebridge 159 D6
Four Oaks 170 D7
Foxcote 166 C5
Framilode 157 F5
Frampton Cotterell 31 B7
Frampton End 31 D8
Frampton Mansell 148 F5
Frampton on Severn 100 A5
France Lynch 148 D6
Frenchay 20 B8
Fretherne 157 E4
Frocester 97 B3
Frogmarsh 180 B3
Fromebridge 100 D3
Fyfield 153 D6

G

Gadfield Elm 180 A2
Ganarew 162 B3
Ganders Green 165 B7
Gatwick 157 F8
Gaunt's Earthcott 41 B5
Gee Moor 10 F6
Gloucester 196 A4
Golden Hill 18 D5
Golden Valley 132 A2
Goodrich 163 A5
Goose Green
Bristol 21 C1
Wotton-under-Edge 81 C1
Yate 43 E3
Gorsley 170 C4
Gorsley Common 170 A4
Gossington 95 C1
Gotherington 138 B8
Grafton 183 C8
Grange Village 156 E7
Great Barrington 161 E8
Great Doward 162 D3
Great Rissington 169 C4
Great Stoke 29 F5
Great Washbourne 183 C5
Great Witcombe 121 B2
Great Wolford 187 F5
Green Bottom 164 E2
Green Street 120 E3
Greenway 178 E4
Greet 184 A1
Gretton 183 E1
Gretton Fields 183 E2
Guiting Power 175 A3
Guller's End 181 B6

H

Hagloe 156 F1
Hailes 184 C1
Haines Green 103 D8
Hallen 27 C5
Hall End 53 E2
Hallwood Green 178 B4
Halmore 94 B2
Ham
Berkeley 85 D1
Cheltenham 131 C7
Hambrook 30 C2
Ham Butts 103 E8
Ham Green 16 E4
Hampnett 167 F2
Hampton 145 B3
Hamshill 88 E6
Hamwell Leaze 98 E7
Hanham 10 C4
Hanham Green 10 C3
Hankerton 141 D1
Hannington 145 A4
Hannington Wick 145 A6
Hardwick 60 F7
Hardwicke
Cheltenham 136 B4
Gloucester 109 E6
Hardwick Green 180 D3
Haresfield
Gloucester 110 B1
Highworth 145 D4
Harleywood 91 B2
Harnhill 151 C3
Harrow Hill 164 C3
Harry Stoke 29 E2
Hartcliffe 2 C4
Hartpury 172 B3
Hasfield 172 E6
Hasfield Ham 173 A5
Hatherley 129 E6
Hatherop 152 E8
Hawcross 179 D1
Hawkesbury 55 D2
Hawkesbury Upton 56 A3
Hawling 174 E2
Hayden 132 A3
Hayden Green 132 A3
Hayes Knoll 143 F1
Hazelton 167 D5
Headley Park 2 B7
Heath End 53 B8
Heathfield 86 C1
Heath Hill 181 A8
Hempsted 118 B7
Henbury 27 E2
Henfield 31 D3
Hengrove 3 B6
Henleaze 18 C6
Henley 121 A5
Hester's Way 132 E3
Hethelpit Cross 171 F8
Hewelsfield 146 F5
Hicks Gate 4 B8
High Botheridge 112 E8
Highfield
Lydney 92 C4
Stroud 98 F7
Highfields 80 D7
High Kingsdown 194 C4
Highleadon 171 F2
Highnam 125 E5
Highnam Green 125 C5
High Nash 155 B5
High Orchard 196 A2
Highridge 1 E5
High Woolaston 147 A2
Highworth 145 D4
Hilcot End 151 D5
Hill 76 D3
Hill End 182 A8
Hillend Green 170 E7
Hillesley 55 E8
Hillfields 20 B3
Hillhouse 21 A5
Hinton
Berkeley 93 E3
Bristol 23 C6
Holbrook Common 12 A8
Holdfast 181 B8
Hollybed Common 179 F8
Hollybush 179 E7
Holywell 68 C8
Homedowns 182 C3
Honeybourne 188 C6
Hook Street 85 C4
Hoop 154 A2
Hope Mansell 163 F6
Hopewell Hill 20 D1
Horcott 152 D3
Horfield 18 F6
Horsepools 111 B1
Horsley 90 F1
Horton 45 B6
Hotwells 194 A1
Houndscroft 99 C1
Howle Hill 163 D7
Howley 79 E1
Hucclecote 120 B7
Hudnalls 146 D6
Huntingford 66 F8
Huntley 165 D6
Hyde 148 B4
Hystfield 77 B5

I

Icomb 177 B1
Ilmington 189 F6
Inchbrook 91 A6
Inglesham 153 C1
Ingst 49 C4
Innsworth 127 D7
Iron Acton 42 D4
Itchington 51 F2

J

Jackaments Bottom 141 D8
Jack's Green 104 D8
Jefferies Hill 10 C5
Joyford 155 B8
Joy's Green 163 D3

K

Kelston 6 C3
Kemble 141 F8
Kemerton 182 E8
Kempley 170 B8
Kempley Green 170 B8
Kempsford 144 E8
Kendleshire 31 A4
Kensington Park 9 C3
Kent End 143 A5
Kenton Green 116 E2
Kent's Green 171 B2
Kerne Bridge 163 B6
Ketford 179 A1
Keynsham 4 E3
Kikenny 166 B5
Kilcot 170 D4
Kiln Green 163 D6
Kineton 175 B5
Kingham 177 F2
Kingrove Common 33 C7
Kingscote 82 B5
Kingscourt 99 B4
Kingsditch 133 A5
Kingsdown 195 A4
Kingshill 87 F2
Kings Hill 190 E3
Kingsholm 196 C4
King's Stanley 98 A4
Kingswood
Bristol 10 E8
Wotton-under-Edge 67 E4
Kington 63 E1
Kinsham 182 D6
Kitebrook 187 E2
Knightsbridge 173 F5
Knight's Green 178 F2
Knockdown 57 F5
Knowle 8 F3
Knowle Park 9 A1
Kymin 154 B7

L

Lane End 164 B6
Langley 139 C5
Lansdown 130 B8
Lark Stoke 189 E6
Lasborough 82 C1
Lassington 125 D7
Latteridge 42 A6
Latton 143 E6
Laverton 184 F6
Lawrence Weston 27 A1
Lea 164 C8
Lea Line 164 E8
Lechlade-on-Thames 153 D3
Leckhampton 130 D5
Ledbury 178 D8
Leddington 178 D5
Leigh 143 B3
Leighterton 70 D3
Leigh Woods 7 D6
Leonard Stanley 97 E4
Leyhill 66 B4
Leys Hill 163 C6
Lightpill 99 A4
Lincoln Green 192 C1
Linden 118 D6
Linkend 180 E2
Linton 170 A4
Linton Hill 170 A3
Little Badminton 46 E5
Little Barrington 161 D7
Little Beckford 183 B5
Little Bristol 67 B3
Little Compton 187 F1
Littledean 156 E8
Little Doward 162 C3
Little Drybrook 155 C2
Little Gorsley 170 C4
Little Haresfield 101 E7
Little Herbert's 131 B4
Little London 165 B5

Little Marcle 178 B7
Little Rissington 169 C6
Little Shurdington 121 D7
Little Sodbury 45 B3
Little Sodbury End 44 E4
Little Stoke 29 D7
Littleton Drew 36 E5
Littleton-upon-Severn 49 E8
Little Washbourne 183 D4
Little Witcombe 121 B4
Littleworth
Chipping Campden 188 F2
Nailsworth 91 C8
Llandogo 146 B7
Llangarron 162 B8
Llangrove 162 C6
Lockleaze 19 C7
Lodway 16 B5
Long Ashton 7 A1
Longborough 176 E8
Longdon 180 F7
Longford 126 F6
Long Green 181 A4
Longhope 164 F5
Longlevens 127 D4
Long Newton 140 E3
Longney 108 C6
Longridge 104 C7
Longwell Green 10 E3
Lowbands 179 F2
Lower Almondsbury 40 A6
Lower Apperley 173 C6
Lower Berry Hill 155 A6
Lower Cam 87 E6
Lower Chedworth 159 B5
Lower Cockleford 115 D8
Lower Dowdeswell 166 B6
Lower Easton 19 D2
Lower Hamswell 13 C3
Lower Hazel 50 F3
Lower Kilcott 56 A7
Lower Knowle 8 E1
Lower Lemington 187 B5
Lower Ley 165 F2
Lower Littleworth 99 B1
Lower Lydbrook 163 C3
Lower Meend 146 D7
Lower Moor 142 D2
Lower Morton 64 C4
Lower Oddington 177 D4
Lower Redbrook 154 D4
Lower Slaughter 176 C1
Lower Soudley 156 D5
Lower Soundwell 20 F2
Lower Stone 77 C1
Lower Swell 176 D4
Lower Tuffley 118 B2
Lower Westmancote 182 D8
Lower Wick 78 E6
Luckington 47 E4
Ludlow Green 102 F3
Ludstock 178 C6
Luxley 164 F8
Lyde Green 21 E8
Lydney 92 C3
Lynworth 134 B3
Lypiatt 106 B5

M

Maiden Head 1 F1
Maisemore 126 A7
Malswick 171 C4
Mangotsfield 20 F6
Maniards Green 76 C2
Marle Hill 133 D4
Marsh Common 38 E4
Marshfield 14 F8
Marsh Lane 155 B2
Marston Hill 152 B2
Marston Meysey 144 C8
Marstow 162 E6
Mathern/Merthyr Tewdrig 60 C3
Matson 119 C3
Matson North 119 B4
Maugersbury 177 A4
Mayfield Park 20 A2
May Hill 154 A8
Mayshill 42 E1
Merthyr Tewdrig/ Mathern 60 C3
Meysey Hampton 152 A2
Mickleton 189 B6
Middle Duntisbourne 107 F2
Middle Street 96 F6
Middle Wick 78 F5
Middleyard 98 C3
Mile End 155 C6
Milkwall 155 A4
Millbottom 91 B3
Millend
Easington 97 A7
Monmouth/Trefynwy 154 F4
Mill Hill 155 D1
Milton End 152 D3
Minchinhampton 91 E6
Minety 142 D1
Minsterworth 116 E7
Miserden 106 B7
Mitcheldean 164 E5
Mitton 192 F6
Monmouth/Trefynwy 154 B8
Montpelier 18 E2
Montpellier 193 B2
Moorend
Dursley 95 C2
Gloucester 111 F8
Winterbourne 30 E2
Moor End 130 F5
Moorfields 9 C8
Moorslade 77 D1
Moreton-in-Marsh 187 B2
Moreton Valence 101 A8
Morton 64 D3
Mountain Bower 25 E3
Mount Hill 10 E6
Mounton 60 A7
Mount Pleasant
Cinderford 191 D3
Stroud 99 E6
Much Marcle 178 B7
Murrell's End 172 B1

N

Naas 92 D1
Nailbridge 164 B3
Nailsworth 91 C3
Narth The 154 A1
Nastend 101 C1
Naunton
Stow-on-the-Wold 175 D2
Tewkesbury 180 D10
Naunton Downs 175 B1
Naunton Park 130 E6
Nebsworth 189 E5
Netham 9 D6
Netherend 147 C3
Netherton 152 E7
Nether Westcote 169 F7
Nettleton 114 C8
Nettleton Green 36 B1
New Cheltenham 20 F1
New England 21 B7
Newent 171 A4
Newerne 92 B3
Newington Bagpath 82 B2
Newland 154 E4
Newleaze 29 B2
Newmarket 90 F4
New Mills 190 F4
Newnham 157 A6
New Passage 48 A1
Newport 78 B8
Newton
Bristol 9 A7
Sharpness 85 D8
Thornbury 64 D6
Newton Green 60 B4
Newtown
Lea 164 A6
Stonehouse 97 C8
Tewkesbury 192 F5
New Town
Moreton-in-Marsh 177 F8
Winchcombe 184 C3
Nibley
Blakeney 156 E1
Yate 43 A1
Nibley Green 79 C5
Ninewells 155 B7
Norman Hill 87 F4
North Cerney 158 D2
North Common 11 D6
North Corner 41 F1
North End 142 F5
Northfield 140 D4
Northleach 168 A1
North Nibley 79 D4
North Stoke 6 C6
Northville 29 A1
Northway 182 C5
Northwick 48 E2
North Woodchester 98 F2
Northwood Green 165 C3
Norton 173 B3
Notgrove 167 F7
Novers Park 2 D8
Noverton 134 D4
Nupdown 76 A4
Nupend
Nailsworth 90 E1
Stonehouse 101 B2
Nuppend 147 C4
Nympsfield 89 E5

O

Oakle Street 116 B8
Oakley 134 B2
Oakridge Lynch 148 E6
Oaksey 141 F4
Oatfield 100 B6
Ocker Hill 102 E2
Okle Green 171 D4
Old Bishton 73 B3
Oldbury Naite 63 E7
Oldbury-on-Severn 63 C6
Oldbury on the Hill 57 C5
Oldcroft 92 E8
Old Down 50 D4
Oldends 101 D1
Oldland 11 A3
Oldland Common 11 D3
Old Passage 48 F6
Old Sodbury 34 B8
Old Wharf 178 D7
Olveston 50 B3
Orange End 55 C4
Oridge Street 172 A6
Over
Bristol 39 D2
Gloucester 126 A4
Overbury 182 F8
Overton 157 D5
Overton Park 193 A3
Owlpen 89 E1
Oxenhall 170 F5
Oxenton 182 F2
Oxlynch 102 C4
Ozleworth 69 D7

P

Paganhill 103 A1
Painswick 103 E8
Palmer's Flat 155 B4
Pamington 182 E3
Parkend
Coleford 155 E3
Gloucester 109 C2
Park End 98 F8
Parkfield 22 A7
Park Hill 146 F2
Patchway 40 B2
Paxford 186 E8
Penallt 154 B5
Pencraig 162 F7
Pendock 180 A3
Pendock Moor 180 D5
Pennsylvania 13 F7
Pen-twyn 154 B4
Petty France 46 B7
Picklenash 170 F5
Pile Marsh 9 D7
Pill 16 C4
Pilley 130 E4
Pillowell 155 F1
Pillows Green 172 B8
Pilning 38 D7
Pinfarthings 91 C6
Piper's End 181 A5
Pitchcombe 103 B5
Pitt Court 79 F5
Pittville 133 E3
Playley Green 179 E2
Plump Hill 164 D4
Plusterwine 147 C2
Podsmead 118 D4
Pontshill 164 B8
Poole Keynes 142 A6
Poolhill 171 B8
Pool Meadow 126 C3
Pope's Hill 164 F1
Postlip 139 D3
Poulton 151 F4
Prescott 138 E7
Prestbury 134 C5
Preston
Cirencester 150 F3
Ledbury 178 C5
Priding 157 E5
Prior's Norton 173 C3
Prior's Park 192 D2
Pucklechurch 22 B5
Puckshole 98 E8
Puddlebrook 164 B5
Pullens Green 63 C5
Purton 94 A5
Purton Stoke 143 E1
Putloe 101 B8
Pwllmeurig/Pwllmeyric 60 B5
Pwllmeyric/Pwllmeurig 60 B5
Pye Corner 30 D3

Q

Quedgeley 117 E1
Queen Charlton 4 B3
Queenhill 181 B7
Quenington 152 C7

R

Randwick 102 D2
Rangeworthy 43 B8
Readings 163 E3
Redfield 9 C7
Redland 18 C3
Redmarley D'Abitot 179 C2
Redwick 38 C8
Rendcomb 158 D4
Reyworth 131 B7
Ridgeway 19 F3
Ripple 181 D8
Robinswood 119 B5
Rockhampton 64 E7
Rockness 91 A2
Rockstowes 80 F8
Rodborough 99 A6
Rodford 32 B6
Rodley 157 F6
Rodmarton 149 B1
Rooksmoor 99 A3
Rose Green 19 E1
Rowanfield 133 A2
Rowland's Green 178 C7
Ruardean 163 F4
Ruardean Hill 164 A4
Ruardean Woodside 163 F3
Ruddle 156 F6
Rudford 124 F8
Rudgeway 50 F1
Ruscombe 102 E3
Ruspidge 191 D1
Russell Town 9 B7
Ryton 179 A2

S

St Anne's 9 E5
St Anne's Park 9 E6
St Arvans 72 B6
St Briavels 146 F7
Saintbridge 119 C6
Saintbury 188 C2
St Catherine 14 F1
St Chloe 91 B8
St George 10 A7
St Mark's 132 F1
St Pauls
Bristol 195 C4
Cheltenham 133 D3
Gloucester 118 D7
St Peter's 133 B3
St Philip's Marsh 9 B5
Salperton 167 C7
Salperton Park 167 C6
Salterley Grange 122 D7
Saltford 5 D2
Sandhurst 172 E2
Sandpits 87 F3
Sandy Lane 130 F4
Sapperton 149 C6
Saul 157 F3
Sawyers Hill 142 D1
Scowles 154 F5
Sea Mills 17 B6
Sedbury 61 B8
Selsley 98 E4
Selsley West 98 D3
Sevenhampton
Cheltenham 166 E8
Highworth 145 D1
Seven Springs 123 B6
Severn Beach 38 A6
Shakesfield 178 D2
Shapridge 164 E3
Sharpness 93 B2
Shaw Common 170 D6
Shaw Green 134 B5
Sheepscombe 112 F1
Shepherd's Patch 95 C5
Shepperdine 75 D3
Sherborne 169 A1
Sherston 58 C1
Sherston Parva or Pinkney 58 E2
Shipton 166 F5
Shipton Moyne 59 E8
Shirehampton 16 E7
Shorncote 142 D7
Shortstanding 155 A8
Shortwood
Kingswood 21 D4
Nailsworth 90 F3
Shurdington 129 E2
Shuthonger 181 E6
Siddington 150 E2
Silver Street 89 A7
Siston 21 F3
Slad 104 A3
Slades Green 181 B5
Sledge Green 180 D5
Slimbridge 95 D4
Sling 155 A3
Smart's Green 33 D8
Sneyd Park 17 D3
Snig's End 172 B7
Snowshill 185 B4
Somerdale 4 E7
Somerford Keynes 142 D6
Sopworth 57 D1
Southam 134 C8
South Cerney 143 A7
Southend 79 E3
Southmead 28 D1
Southrop 153 D6
Southville 8 C4
South Woodchester 98 F1
Speedwell 20 A2
Springbank 132 D3
Standish 101 E5
Stanfields 99 B4
Stanley 157 F8
Stanley Downton 97 E5
Stanley Pontlarge 183 E1
Stanton 184 F5
Stanton Fitzwarren 145 A1
Stantway 157 E8
Stanway 184 E3
Staple Hill 20 E4
Stapleton 19 D4
Starveall 56 D4
Staunton
Gloucester 172 A8
Monmouth/Trefynwy 154 E7
Staverton 173 F2
Stidcot 52 E6
Stinchcombe 87 C2
Stockend 103 A7
Stockwell Green 191 D3
Stockwood 3 E5
Stockwood Vale 4 C6
Stoke Bishop 17 E5
Stoke Gifford 29 F4
Stoke Orchard 136 D5
Stone 77 F3
Stone Hill 10 E4
Stonehouse 97 E7
Stowe 154 F1
Stowe Green 154 F1
Stowell 159 E8
Stowfield 163 C4
Stow-on-the-Wold 176 E4
Strand 157 C8
Stratford 180 E9
Stratton 190 A8
Stroat 74 A8
Stroud 99 B8
Stroud Green 101 F4
Stroud Hill 99 D7
Stump Cross 184 F1
Sudgrove 106 A5
Summerhayes 87 E5
Sundayshill 65 C8
Sunhill 152 A5
Swanborough 145 B2
Swanley 78 C5
Swellshill 99 E1
Swindon 133 A7
Swineford 6 A7
Swinley Green 180 F3
Syde 114 D2
Symonds Yat 162 E3
Synwell 68 D7
Syreford 166 E7

T

Taddington 185 A2
Tadwick 13 E1
Talbot's End 66 C1
Tarlton 149 C2
Taynton 165 E8
Teddington 183 A4
Temple Guiting 175 B7
Tetbury 140 C4
Tetbury Upton 140 B6
Tewkesbury 192 E3
The Beeches 190 F5
The Butts 99 B5
The Camp 105 D7
The College 102 B8
The Dings 9 A6
The Eaves 155 E1
The Gibb 36 F3
The Haw 173 A6
The Knapp 64 F3
The Leigh 173 C5
The Mythe 192 C7
The Park 130 C6
The Pludds 163 E2
The Pound 178 E2
The Quarry 87 D4
The Ramplings 181 B5
The Reddings 129 B7
Thornbury 51 B8
Threescombe 91 A6
Througham 105 E4
Thrupp 99 E4
Tibberton 124 C8
Tickmorend 90 E1
Tidenham 73 D4
Tidenham Chase 146 E1
Tiller's Green 178 D3
Tilsdown 87 F3
Tiltups End 83 A7
Tintern Parva 146 C3
Tirley 172 F7
Tirley Knowle 172 E8
Tivoli 193 A1
Tockington 50 C1
Toddington 184 B3
Todenham 187 E6
Tormarton 34 E2
Tortworth 66 C7
Tortworth Green 66 C5

Totterdown 9 B4
Totteroak 44 F5
Townsend 102 D1
Town Street 173 A8
Townwell 66 B2
Tredington 136 A7
Trefynwy/Monmouth ...154 B8
Tre-gagle 154 B2
Tresham 69 C3
Trow Green 155 B1
Tuffley 118 E3
Tunley 149 A7
Turkdean 167 F4
Tutnalls 92 B2
Tutshill 73 A2
Twigworth 173 B1
Two Mile Hill 20 C1
Twyning 181 F7
Twyning Green 182 A7
Tyndall's Park 194 C4
Tytherington 52 C5

U

Uckinghall 181 C8
Uckington 132 D6
Uley 89 B1
Ullenwood Court 122 B6
Up Hatherley 129 D5
Uplands 103 E1
Upleadon 171 D5
Upper Barton End 83 B8
Upper Cam 88 B4
Upper Dowdeswell 166 B6
Upper Easton 9 B8
Upper Eastville 19 E3
Upper Framilode 108 A1
Upper Hill 76 E5
Upper Inglesham 145 D7
Upper Kilcott 56 C5
Upper Knowle 9 B2
Upper Ley 165 D4
Upper Lode 192 A5
Upper Lydbrook 163 D2
Upper Minety 142 C2
Upper Morton 64 E4
Upper Oddington 177 C4
Upper Redbrook 154 C5
Upper Rissington 169 E6
Upper Siddington 150 D2
Upper Slaughter 176 B2
Upper Soudley 156 D5
Upper Soundwell 20 D3
Upper Strensham 180 F10
Upper Swell 176 D5
Upper Up 142 F8
Upper Wick 79 A6
Upper Wraxall 25 E2
Upthorpe 88 B6
Upton Cheyney 6 B8
Upton St Leonards 119 F2

V

Victoria Park 194 B3
Viney Hill 156 C1
Vinney Green 21 B7

W

Walford 163 B7
Walham 126 D5
Walkleywood 91 A3
Wallow Green 90 F2
Wallsworth 173 A2
Walton Cardiff 192 F3
Wanswell 85 E7
Wapley 32 E4
Warden Hill 130 A6
Warmley 11 B7
Warmley Hill 10 F8
Warmley Tower 11 B6
Washpool 91 A1
Waterend 116 B1
Waterhay 143 B4
Waterlane 148 F7
Watermead 120 E4
Watermoor 190 E3
Watledge 91 B5
Watley's End 30 F7
Webb's Heath 11 E8
Welsh Bicknor 163 B4
Welsh Newton
Common 162 A4
Westbury-on-Severn 165 C1
Westbury on Trym 17 F7
Westbury Park 18 A3
West Crudwell 141 C4
Westend
Oldbury-on-Severn 63 B6
Stonehouse 101 A2
West End 53 E5
Westerleigh 32 B4
Westerleigh Hill 32 D3
Westington 188 F1
West Kington 25 F7
West Littleton 24 C3
Westmancote 182 D8
Westonbirt 58 D8
Weston-sub-Edge 188 D3
Westrip 98 C8
Westwell 161 F4
Whaddon
Cheltenham 134 A2
Gloucester 110 F8
Wheatenhurst 100 C6
Whelford 153 A1
Whitchurch
Keynsham 3 C3
Monmouth/Trefynwy 162 D4
Whitebrook 154 C1
Whitecliff 154 F5
Whitecroft 155 F1
White End 180 A5
Whitehall 19 D1
Whiteleaved Oak 179 D6
Whitelye 146 A4
Whiteshill
Stroud 103 A3
Yate 30 D3
Whiteway
Bristol 20 A1
Gloucester 113 D1
Nailsworth 91 A1
Whitfield 65 C3
Whitminster 100 E5
Whittington 166 C8
Wibdon 73 F7
Wick 12 D6
Wickridge Street 172 C6
Wick Street 103 D4
Wickwar 54 B5
Willersey 188 B2
Willesley 58 C6
Willsbridge 11 A1
Winchcombe 174 B7
Windmill Hill 8 E3
Windrush 161 B8
Windsoredge 90 F6
Winson 159 D3
Winstone 107 A8
Winterbourne 30 F6
Wishanger 105 E8
Withington 166 F2
Withy Bridge 132 B6
Withywood 2 A4
Woodchester 98 F2
Woodcroft 73 B4
Woodfield 87 E5
Woodford 78 A4
Woodhouse Down 40 D7
Woodmancote
Cheltenham 138 D4
Cirencester 158 B3
Dursley 80 B7
Wood Stanway 184 E2
Woodstock 10 F7
Woolaston 147 C3
Woolaston Common 147 B4
Woolaston Slade 147 A3
Woolaston Woodside 147 B3
Woolcott Park 18 B1
Woolridge 172 C2
Woolstone 183 A1
Worley 91 A4
Wormington 184 C7
Worrall Hill 163 D1
Wortley 68 C4
Wotton 127 B2
Wotton-under-Edge 68 B6
Wyck Hill 176 F1
Wyck Rissington 169 C8
Wyegate Green 154 E1
Wyesham 154 B7
Wymans Brook 133 C6

Y

Yanley 1 C8
Yanworth 159 C8
Yate 43 C1
Yate Rocks 43 F6
Yorkley 156 A1
Yorkley Slade 156 B2

1

1st Ave GL56 187 B4

2

2nd Ave GL56 187 B4

3

3rd Ave GL56 187 B3

5

5th Ave GL56 187 C4

6

6th Ave GL56 187 B4

7

7th Ave GL56 187 B3

8

8th Ave GL56 187 B3

1

125 Bsns Pk GL2 126 C1

5

5102 Apts BS1 195 B4

A

A P Ellis Rd GL54 169 D6
Aaron Rd GL7 150 F2
Abbenesse GL6 148 C6
Abbey Cl BS31 4 F6
Abbey Ct Bristol BS4 9 F5
Tewkesbury GL20 192 B3
20 Winchcombe GL54 174 A7
Abbey Ho
Cirencester GL7 190 C5
5 Yate BS37 32 D7
Abbey La BS35 51 D6
Abbey Mdw GL20 192 D1
Abbey Mews GL12 67 F4
Abbey Pk BS31 4 F6
Abbey Prec GL20 192 B3
Abbey Rd Bristol BS9 17 F7
Gloucester GL2 118 C8
Abbey Sch GL20 192 C4
Abbey St Cinderford GL14 191 D4
Kingswood GL12 67 F5
Abbey Terr
Tewkesbury GL20 192 B3
23 Winchcombe GL54 174 A7
Abbey Tintern Furnace*
NP16 146 A3
Abbey View
6 Gloucester GL4 119 C4
15 Winchcombe GL54 174 A7
Abbey Way GL7 190 C6
Abbey Wood Ret Pk
BS34 29 C2
Abbeydale BS36 30 E6
Abbeydale Ct GL4 119 E4
Abbeyfield Ho
Chipping Sodbury BS37 44 C1
6 Stow-on-t-W GL54 176 F4
Abbeyholme GL50 193 A3
Abbeymead Ave GL4 119 E6
Abbeymead Prim Sch
GL4 119 F5
Abbeywood Dr BS9 17 C5
Abbeywood Pk BS34 29 C2
Abbot's Rd GL20 192 C2
Abbots Ave BS15 10 C4
Abbots Cl Bristol BS14 3 A3
Cheltenham GL51 130 B5
Abbots Court Dr GL20 181 F7
Abbots Leigh Rd BS8 7 C7
Abbots Leys Rd GL54 139 F5
Abbots Mews GL52 137 E2
Abbots Rd Bristol BS15 10 C2
Cinderford GL14 191 E3
Cirencester GL7 190 E4
Gloucester GL4 119 E6
Abbots View GL14 191 D1
Abbots Way Bristol BS9 18 E6
Stonehouse GL10 97 E6
Abbots Wlk GL7 153 E2
Abbotsford Rd BS6 18 B1
Abbotswood Bristol BS15 10 D7
Yate BS37 32 D7
Abbotswood Cl GL4 118 D3
Abbotswood Prim Sch
BS37 32 D6
Abbotswood Rd GL3 120 F4
Abbott Rd BS35 38 A5
Abbotts Way GL7 141 F8
Aberdeen Rd BS6 194 B4
Abingdon Court La SN6 143 F4
Abingdon Rd BS16 20 A3
Ableton Ct BS35 38 A6
Ableton La
Compton Greenfield BS10 38 A1
Severn Beach BS35 38 A5
Ableton Wlk BS9 17 C5
Abnash GL6 148 C6
Abon Ho BS9 17 C4
Abraham Cl BS5 9 B8
Abraham Fry Ho BS15 10 E7
Abson Rd
Pucklechurch BS16 22 C3
Wick BS30 12 C8
Acacia Ave BS16 20 D4
Acacia Cl 9 Bream GL15 147 D8
Bristol BS16 20 D3
Cheltenham GL52 134 A5
Newnham GL14 157 A7
Acacia Ct
Cheltenham GL51 132 C2
Keynsham BS31 4 C4
Acacia Dr GL11 88 A3
Acacia Mews 4 BS16 20 D4
Acacia Pk GL52 137 D4
Acacia Rd BS16 20 D4
Academy The GL50 193 B4
Acer Gr GL2 117 E2
Acid Rd BS11 26 C4
Acomb Cres GL52 131 B6
Acorn Ct 9 GL4 119 C4
Acorn Gr BS13 1 E6
Acraman's Rd 7 BS3 8 C4
Acre Pl GL6 102 E1
Acre St GL5 99 C7
Acresbush Cl BS13 2 A5
Acton Rd BS16 20 A3
Acton Turville Rd GL9 35 B4
Adams Ct 6 BS8 7 F6
Adams Hay 6 BS4 9 D1
Adams Land BS36 31 C7
Adams Way 7 GL16 155 A7
Adderly Gate BS16 21 B7
Addis Rd GL51 133 B3
Addiscombe Rd BS14 3 B5
Addison Rd BS3 8 E3
Addymore GL11 87 F5
Adelaide Gdns GL10 101 F1
Adelaide Pl
Bristol,Fishponds BS16 19 F4
12 Bristol,Upper Easton BS5 9 B8
Adelaide St GL1 119 A7
Adelaide Terr 1 BS16 20 A4
Adelante Cl BS34 30 A4
Adey's La GL12 68 B8
Admington La CV36 189 D7
Admington Lane Units
CV36 189 E7
Admiral Cl Bristol BS16 19 E7
Cheltenham GL51 132 D2
Admirals Cl 6 GL15 155 D1
Adryan Ct 6 BS5 9 C7
Aesops Orch GL52 138 C3
Agate St BS3 8 B3
Aggs Cl GL52 138 A8
Aggs Hill GL54 134 D1
Aggs La GL52 138 A8
Aiken St BS5 9 B6
Aintree Dr BS16 30 F1
Air Balloon Ct 1 BS5 10 A7
Air Balloon Hill Jun & Inf
Schs BS5 10 A7
Air Balloon Rd BS5 10 A7
Airport Rd BS14 3 A8
Airthrie Sch GL50 133 B1
Aisne Rd GL15 156 B1
Akeman Rd GL7 190 E4
Akeman Way BS11 16 C8
Akermans Orch GL18 170 F4
Akers Ct SN26 144 E1
Alanscourt BS30 11 B5
Alard Rd BS4 2 F7
Alaska Ave GL7 152 E1
Albany GL10 101 E1
Albany Gate BS34 29 E5
Albany Ho 7 GL50 130 B8
Albany Mews GL50 193 A2
Albany Rd Bristol BS6 18 F1
Cheltenham GL50 130 B7
Albany St Bristol BS15 10 C8
Gloucester GL1 118 F7
Albany Way BS30 11 C5
Albemarle Gate GL50 133 E4
Albemarle Rd GL3 128 D5
Albermarle Row 10 BS8 7 F6
Albermarle Terr 2 BS8 7 F6
Albert Cres BS2 9 B5
Albert Ct GL52 133 F3
Albert Dr GL52 133 F4
Albert Gr BS5 9 F8
Albert Gr S BS5 9 F8
Albert Par BS5 9 D8
Albert Park Pl BS6 18 F1
Albert Pk BS6 18 F1
Albert Pl
1 Bristol,Bedminster BS3 8 C3
Bristol,Eastfield BS9 18 A7
Cheltenham GL52 193 C4
Albert Rd Brimscombe GL5 99 F1
Bristol,Hanham BS15 10 D5
Bristol,St Philip's Marsh BS2 9 A4
Bristol,Staple Hill BS16 20 E4
Cheltenham GL52 133 F3
Cinderford GL14 191 C3
Coleford GL16 155 A5
Keynsham BS31 4 E5
Ledbury HR8 178 E8
Severn Beach BS35 38 A6
Albert St Bristol BS5 9 C8
Cheltenham GL50 133 D3
Albert St *continued*
Gloucester GL1 196 C2
Lydney GL15 92 B3
Albert Terr BS16 19 F4
Albert Warehouse GL1 196 A2
Alberton Rd BS16 19 F6
Albion Cl BS16 20 F5
Albion Ct GL10 97 F7
Albion Pl 18 Bristol BS2 195 C3
Cheltenham GL52 193 C4
Albion Rd Bristol BS5 19 B1
Cinderford GL14 191 D6
Albion Sq 1 NP16 60 E8
Albion St 6 Bristol BS5 9 C8
Cheltenham GL52 193 C3
Gloucester GL1 196 A2
Stratton GL7 190 B7
Albion Terr Bristol BS34 40 B1
Stonehouse GL10 97 E6
Albion Wlk GL50 193 C4
Albright La HR8 179 D4
Alcotts Gn GL2 172 F2
Alcove Rd BS16 19 F3
Alcove Wood/Coed Cilfach
NP16 60 C8
Alden Ho BS36 30 D4
Alder Cl Gloucester GL2 127 C4
Walford HR9 163 C8
Alder Ct Bristol BS14 3 B5
Cheltenham GL51 132 C2
Alder Dr BS5 19 E1
Alder Way 7 GL6 148 C6
Aldercombe Rd BS9 17 C8
Alderdale GL15 92 B4
Alderdown Cl BS11 17 A8
Aldergate St GL10 97 F7
Aldergate Terr 6 GL10 97 F7
Alderley Rd GL12 68 D1
Alderman Knight Sch
GL20 182 B4
Alderman Twr BS6 18 C3
Aldermoor Way BS30 10 E4
Alderney Ave BS4 9 F4
Alderney Flats 1 GL2 127 B2
Alders Gn GL2 127 B5
Alders The Bristol BS16 30 B1
Cheltenham GL53 130 B4
Aldershaw Cl GL51 129 D6
Alderton Cl GL4 119 E4
Alderton Rd Bristol BS7 18 E8
Burton SN14 36 D6
Cheltenham GL51 129 E8
Aldridge Cl GL50 133 C3
Aldsworth Cl GL7 152 F4
Aldsworth Road Est
GL7 160 B2
Aldwick Ave BS13 2 C3
Aldworth Ho BS2 195 C4
Alex Farm SN6 144 A6
Alexander Ct 4 BS3 8 A3
Alexander Dr GL7 190 C2
Alexander Gdns 10 GL8 140 B4
Alexander Hosea Prim Sch
GL12 54 B5
Alexandra Apartments
BS6 18 C3
Alexandra Cl BS16 20 D4
Alexandra Ct BS16 19 F4
Alexandra Gdns BS16 20 D4
Alexandra Pk
Bristol,Cotham BS6 18 C2
Bristol,Ridgeway BS16 19 F4
Alexandra Pl BS16 20 D4
Alexandra Rd
Bristol,Clifton BS8 194 B4
Bristol,Eastfield BS10 18 C8
Bristol,Hanham BS15 10 D5
Bristol,Highridge BS13 1 F7
Chepstow/Cas-Gwent NP16 60 F6
Coalpit Heath BS36 31 D7
Gloucester GL1 127 A3
Alexandra St GL50 130 B7
Alexandra Way
Northway GL20 182 B4
Thornbury BS35 64 B3
Alexandria Wlk GL52 134 B2
Alford Rd BS4 9 C2
Alfred Hill BS2 195 A4
Alfred Lovell Gdns 7
BS30 11 A4
Alfred Par BS2 195 A4
Alfred Pl Bristol BS1 195 A1
Bristol,Tyndall's Park
BS2 194 C4
Alfred Rd
Bristol,Westbury Park BS6 18 A4
Bristol,Windmill Hill BS3 8 D3
Alfred St
Bristol,Moorfields BS5 9 D8
Bristol,Newton BS2 9 A6
Gloucester GL1 119 A8
Algars Dr BS37 42 E3
Algiers St BS3 8 D3
Alice Cres NP16 61 A4
Alington Cl 7 GL1 127 A1
Alkerton Rd GL10 96 F7
Alkerton Terr GL10 96 F7
All Alone GL54 168 A1
All Hallows Ct 11 BS5 9 B8
All Hallows Rd BS5 9 B8
All Saint's Ct 19 GL52 133 F2
All Saint's La BS1 195 A2
All Saints Cl BS30 11 A3
All Saints Fields GL5 99 E7
All Saints Ho BS2 195 B4
All Saints Mans BS8 194 A4
All Saints Rd
Blakeney GL15 156 E2
All Saints Rd *continued*
Stroud GL5 99 D8
All Saints' Rd Bristol BS8 194 A4
Cheltenham GL52 133 F4
Gloucester GL1 196 C1
All Saints' St BS1 195 A3
All Saints' Terr GL52 133 F1
All Saints' Villas Rd
GL52 133 F2
Allanmead Rd BS14 3 B8
Allaston Rd GL15 92 B6
Allen Dr GL5 99 A8
Allen's Almhouses The 12
GL54 168 A1
Allendale Cl GL2 127 C4
Allenfield Rd GL53 130 C5
Allengrove La SN14 47 C3
Allerton Cres BS14 3 B4
Allerton Gdns BS14 3 B5
Allerton Rd BS14 3 B4
Allfoxton Rd BS7 19 A3
Allington Dr BS30 10 F4
Allington Rd BS3 194 C1
Allison Ave BS4 9 E4
Allison Rd BS4 9 E3
Allotment La GL7 151 C5
Allsopp Cl GL14 156 F6
Alma Cl Bristol BS15 10 E8
Cheltenham GL51 129 F7
Alma Ct BS8 18 B1
Alma Dr NP16 61 A4
Alma Pl GL1 118 D7
Alma Rd
Bristol,Clifton BS8 194 B4
Bristol,Kingswood BS15 20 E1
Cheltenham GL51 129 F7
Alma Road Ave BS8 194 B4
Alma St BS8 18 B1
Alma Terr
Gloucester GL1 118 D7
Stroud GL5 98 F8
Alma Vale Rd BS8 194 A4
Almeda Rd BS5 10 A6
Almhouses GL7 190 C4
Almond Cl GL4 119 D3
Almond Ct GL51 132 C2
Almond Way BS16 20 F5
Almond Wlk GL15 92 B4
Almondsbury Bsns Ctr
BS32 40 D3
Almondsbury CE Prim Sch
BS32 40 A4
Almondsbury Intc BS32 40 E4
Almorah Rd BS3 8 E3
Almshouses
11 Chipping Campden
GL55 189 A2
Marshfield SN14 14 E8
1 Wotton-u-E GL12 68 B7
Almshouses Rd GL16 154 E4
Almshouses The GL54 176 F4
Alney Terr GL1 126 C3
Alpha Cl GL20 182 B4
Alpha Ctr The BS37 43 C3
Alpha Rd Bristol BS3 8 D4
Chepstow/Cas-Gwent NP16 60 F6
Alpine Cl GL4 119 B6
Alpine Rd BS5 19 C1
Alsop Rd 4 BS15 20 D1
Alstone Ave GL51 133 B2
Alstone Croft GL51 133 B2
Alstone Ct 1 GL51 133 B2
Alstone La GL51 133 A2
Alstone Lane Trad Est
GL51 133 A1
Alstone Mews GL51 133 B2
Althorp Cl GL4 118 B2
Alton Court Rd HR8 178 A7
Alton Rd BS7 18 F5
Altringham Rd BS5 9 D8
Alverstoke BS14 2 F7
Alverton Dr GL52 137 E2
Alveston Grange GL55 189 A6
Alveston Hill BS35 51 A6
Alveston Rd BS32 50 D3
Alveston Wlk BS9 17 B7
Alvin St GL1 196 C3
Alwins Ct 2 BS30 10 F4
Amaranth Way 7 GL51 129 F5
Amazing Hedge Puzzle The*
HR9 162 E4
Amber Cl GL4 118 C3
Amberley Cl Bristol BS16 20 D7
Keynsham BS31 4 E4
Amberley Ct 10 GL51 132 E2
Amberley House Sch
BS8 18 A1
Amberley Parochial Sch
GL5 91 C7
Amberley Rd
Bristol,Kingswood BS16 20 D7
Bristol,Patchway BS34 29 B8
9 Cheltenham GL51 132 E2
Gloucester GL4 119 B5
Amberley Ridge Sch GL5 99 C1
Amberley Way GL12 54 B4
Amble Cl BS15 10 F7
Ambleside Ave BS10 28 B2
Ambra Ct BS8 194 A2
Ambra Terr BS8 194 A2
Ambra Vale BS8 194 A2
Ambra Vale E BS8 194 A2
Ambra Vale S BS8 194 A2
Ambra Vale W BS8 194 A2
Ambrose La 1 GL16 155 B5
Ambrose Pl GL50 193 B4
Ambrose Rd BS8 194 A2
Ambrose St GL50 193 B4
Amercombe Wlk BS14 3 D7
America Gdns GL18 171 A4
Amos Cl GL50 193 A4
Ampney Crucis CE Prim Sch
GL7 151 C5
Ampney La GL14 165 D3
Ampney Mill Cotts GL7 151 C4
Anapa Mews 15 GL51 132 E2
Anbrook Cres GL4 119 E7
Anchor Cl BS5 9 F6
Anchor Ho BS4 9 B2
Anchor La BS1 194 C2
Anchor Rd
Bristol,Canon's Marsh
BS1 194 C2
Bristol,Kingswood BS15 21 A2
Anchor Sq BS1 194 C2
Anchor Way BS20 16 D4
Anchorage The
Gloucester GL2 118 B6
Lower Lydbrook GL17 163 C3
Ancient Rd GL16 162 F1
Andereach Cl BS14 3 B8
Anderson Cl GL52 138 B3
Anderson Dr 3 GL10 97 F7
Andorra Way GL3 128 B6
Andover Ct GL50 193 A1
Andover Rd Bristol BS4 8 F2
Cheltenham GL50 193 A1
Andover St GL50 193 A1
Andover Terr GL50 193 A2
Andover Wlk GL50 193 A1
Andoversford Link
GL54 166 D6
Andoversford Prim Sch
GL54 166 D6
Andrew Millman Ct BS37 43 F1
Andrew's Cl GL4 110 F5
Andrew's Cnr GL15 146 E7
Andruss Dr BS41 1 D2
Angel Field GL16 155 A5
Angelica Way GL4 119 F5
Angels Gd BS4 9 F6
Angers Rd BS4 9 A4
Anglesea Pl 15 BS8 18 A2
Anlaby Ct GL52 133 E3
Ann Cam CE Prim Sch
GL18 178 D2
Ann Edwards CE Prim Sch
GL7 142 F7
Ann Goodrich Cl GL52 134 C4
Ann Wicks Rd GL2 100 A5
Anne Edwards Mews
GL4 119 D4
Anne Hathaway Dr GL3 128 E5
Annie Scott Cl 2 BS16 20 A4
Anns Wlk GL17 164 D4
Ansdell Dr GL3 120 E6
Ansell Cl GL51 129 F6
Anson Bsns Pk GL51 173 E1
Anson Cl BS31 5 D2
Anstey St BS5 19 B1
Anstey's Ct BS15 10 C5
Anstey's Rd BS15 10 C5
Ansteys Cl BS15 10 B5
Antelope Paddock 11
GL54 168 A1
Anthea Rd BS5 19 E2
Anthony Cl SN16 58 C1
Anthony Ct GL6 148 C5
Antona Ct BS11 16 D7
Antona Dr BS11 16 D7
Antrim Rd BS9 18 B6
Anvil Ct GL11 80 C8
Anvil St BS2 195 C2
Apex Ct BS32 40 D3
Apna Ghar Ct GL1 119 A8
Apperley Cl BS37 32 E8
Apperley Dr GL2 117 E1
Apperley Pk GL19 173 C7
Apple Cl GL52 134 A5
Apple Orch GL52 134 A5
Apple Orch The GL20 182 C5
Apple Orchard Cl GL54 183 E1
Apple Tree Cl
4 Churchdown GL3 128 A7
Gloucester GL4 119 E4
Woodmancote GL52 138 C2
Appleby Wlk BS4 2 D7
Appledore Cl BS14 3 B8
Applegate BS10 28 B3
Appleridge La GL13 77 C4
Appleton Ave GL51 129 B6
Appleton Way GL3 120 A6
Applin Gn BS16 21 C6
Apprentice Cl NP16 61 B4
Approach The GL54 160 E5
April Cl GL11 80 A8
Apseleys Mead BS32 40 C2
Apsley Cl GL7 190 B3
Apsley Garden Apartments
BS6 18 E2
Apsley Mews BS8 18 A2
Apsley Rd Bristol BS8 18 A1
Cirencester GL7 190 B2
Apsley St BS5 19 C3
Aragon Ho GL54 139 F5
Aragon Way GL3 127 F7
Arbour Cl GL55 189 A6
Arbour Elms GL19 181 C3
Arbutus Dr BS9 17 C8
Arcade Mews BS8 194 A3
Arcade The BS1 195 B3
Archdeacon Ct GL1 196 A3
Archdeacon St GL1 196 A3

Archer Ct BS30 .... 10 F3
Archer Wlk BS14 .... 3 E6
Archers La GL52 .... 136 D5
Archers The SN6 .... 145 C3
Archery Rd GL7 .... 190 E4
Arches The 1 BS5 .... 9 B7
Archfield Ct BS6 .... 18 C1
Archfield Rd BS6 .... 18 C1
Archibald St GL1 .... 196 C1
Archway Cl GL14 .... 156 C5
Archway Ct GL17 .... 164 D5
Archway Gdns GL5 ...... 99 A8
Archway Sch GL5 .... 98 F8
Ardagh Ct BS7 .... 18 F7
Ardea Cl GL2 .... 117 D1
Arden Cl BS32 .... 29 E6
Arden Ho GL2 .... 118 C4
Arden Rd GL53 .... 130 D5
Ardenton Wlk BS10 ..... 28 A3
Ardern Cl BS9 .... 17 B8
Ardmore BS8 .... 7 D7
Ardmore Cl GL4 .... 118 E2
Argus Ct BS3 .... 8 C2
Argus Rd BS3 .... 8 C3
Argyle Ave BS5 .... 19 C2
Argyle Dr BS37 .... 43 E4
Argyle Pl BS8 .... 194 A2
Argyle Rd
Bristol,Chester Park BS16 .. 20 B2
Bristol,St Pauls BS2 ..... 195 B4
Argyle St
5 Bristol,Eastville BS5 .... 19 C2
6 Bristol,Southville BS3 ... 8 C4
Argyll Mews GL53 ...... 193 C1
Argyll Pl GL2 .... 127 B2
Argyll Rd
Cheltenham GL53 .... 130 F8
Gloucester GL2 .... 127 B2
Ariel Lodge Rd GL52 ... 133 F2
Arkells Ct GL12 .... 54 A6
Arkendale Dr GL2 ...... 109 D8
Arkle Cl GL50 .... 133 C5
Arle Ave GL51 .... 133 B2
Arle Cl GL51 .... 133 B2
Arle Cotts GL51 .... 132 F4
Arle Dr GL51 .... 133 A3
Arle Gdns GL51 .... 133 A3
Arle Rd GL51 .... 133 A3
Arlebrook GL10 .... 102 A5
Arley Cotts 4 BS6 ...... 18 D1
Arley Hill BS6 .... 18 D1
Arley Pk BS6 .... 18 D1
Arley Terr BS5 .... 19 E1
Arlingdon Fields GL7 ... 142 D6
Arlingham 13 GL51 ..... 129 E5
Arlingham Rd GL4 ..... 118 D4
Arlingham Way BS34 .... 39 F1
Arlington Cnr GL7 ..... 160 A1
Arlington Ct NP16 ...... 61 B8
Arlington Mews BS8 ... 194 B4
Arlington Mill Mus*
GL7 .... 160 A1
Arlington Pike GL7 ..... 159 F1
Arlington Rd Bristol BS4 ... 9 D5
Tewkesbury GL20 .... 192 E2
Arlington Row* GL7 ... 160 A1
Arlington Villas BS8 .... 194 B3
Armada Cl GL3 .... 127 F7
Armada Ho BS2 .... 195 A4
Armada Pl BS1 .... 195 B4
Armada Rd BS14 .... 3 A6
Armidale Ave 4 BS6 ..... 18 E1
Armidale Cotts 5 BS6 .. 18 E1
Armoury Sq BS5 .... 9 A8
Armscroft Cres GL2 .... 127 B2
Armscroft Ct GL2 ...... 127 C1
Armscroft Gdns GL2 .... 127 B1
Armscroft Pl GL2 ...... 127 B1
Armscroft Rd GL2 ...... 127 C1
Armscroft Way GL2 .... 127 B1
Armstrong Cl BS35 ...... 51 D7
Armstrong Ct BS37 ..... 43 C3
Armstrong Dr BS30 ..... 11 B5
Armstrong Way BS37 ... 43 B3
Arnall Dr BS10 .... 27 F1
Arncliffe BS10 .... 18 C8
Arneside Rd BS10 .... 28 C1
Arno's St BS4 .... 9 A3
Arnold Ct BS37 .... 44 B1
Arnold's La GL6 .... 91 B3
Arnolds Field Trad Est
GL12 .... 54 A5
Arnolds Way GL7 ...... 190 E5
Arnolfini (Art Ctr)*
BS1 .... 195 A1
Arran Way SN6 .... 145 C4
Arreton Ave GL4 .... 119 C6
Arrowfield Cl BS14 ...... 3 A2
Arrowhead Cl GL4 ..... 119 B4
Arrowsmith Dr GL10 ... 101 F1
Arthur Bliss Gdns 3
GL50 .... 130 B6
Arthur Cooper Way
GL16 .... 155 A4
Arthur Dye Prim Sch
GL51 .... 132 D4
Arthur Skemp Cl BS5 ..... 9 B7
Arthur St
7 Bristol,Moorfields BS5 ... 9 C8
Bristol,St Philip's Marsh BS2 9 A5
Gloucester GL1 .... 196 B2
Arthurs Cl BS16 .... 21 C6
Arthurswood Rd BS13 .... 2 A4
Arundel Cl Bristol BS13 .... 2 B5
Gloucester GL4 .... 118 C1
Arundel Ct BS7 .... 18 D3
Arundel Dr GL5 .... 99 B6
Arundel Ho 12 GL51 .... 132 E2
Arundel Rd
Bristol BS7 .... 18 D3
Tewkesbury GL20 .... 192 E6
Arundel Wlk BS31 .... 4 D5
Arundell Mill La GL5 .... 99 D6
Ascot Cl BS16 .... 30 F1
Ascot Ct GL1 .... 119 A8
Ascot Rd BS10 .... 28 E2
Ash Cl
Bristol,Hillfields BS16 ..... 20 C3
Bristol,Little Stoke BS34 ... 29 D7
Charlton Kings GL53 ..... 131 C4
Chepstow/Cas-Gwent NP16 60 E5
Dursley GL11 .... 88 A4
Lydney GL15 .... 92 B4
Yate BS37 .... 43 D3
Ash Ct BS14 .... 3 A6
Ash Dene Rd GL17 ..... 163 E3
Ash Gr
Bristol BS16 .... 20 D3
Bussage GL6 .... 148 B6
Mitcheldean GL17 ...... 164 D6
Upton St Leonards GL4 ... 119 E3
Ash Grove Pl GL15 ..... 156 B1
Ash La
Down Hatherley GL2 .... 173 B1
Over BS32 .... 39 D2
Randwick GL6 .... 102 D1
Ash Path The GL4 ...... 119 E3
Ash Rd Bristol BS7 .... 18 E5
Northway GL20 .... 182 C4
Stroud GL5 .... 99 A4
Ash Ridge Rd BS32 ...... 40 B3
Ash The GL6 .... 102 C2
Ash Tree Cl 23 GL18 .... 171 A4
Ash Way GL15 .... 147 C3
Ash Wlk BS10 .... 28 B3
Ashbed Cl GL4 .... 119 E6
Ashbourne Cl 1 BS30 ... 11 C6
Ashbrook La GL7 .... 151 E4
Ashburton Rd BS10 ..... 28 C1
Ashchurch for Tewkesbury
Sta GL20 .... 182 C4
Ashchurch Ind Est GL20 182 C4
Ashchurch Prim Sch
GL20 .... 182 C4
Ashchurch Rd GL20 .... 192 E4
Ashcombe Cres BS30 .... 11 D6
Ashcot Mews 3 GL51 ... 129 E5
Ashcott BS14 .... 2 F7
Ashcroft Ave BS31 .... 4 D5
Ashcroft Cl GL4 .... 119 D2
Ashcroft Gdns GL7 ..... 190 C4
Ashcroft Ho GL5 .... 99 D5
Ashcroft Rd
Bristol BS9 .... 17 C7
Cirencester GL7 .... 190 C4
Wotton-u-E GL8,GL12 ..... 81 D3
Ashdale Cl GL54 .... 160 E5
Ashdean GL14 .... 191 C5
Ashdene Ave BS5 .... 19 D3
Ashdown Ct BS9 .... 17 F8
Asher La BS2 .... 195 C3
Ashes La HR9 .... 162 E4
Ashfield SN6 .... 143 A5
Ashfield Cl GL52 .... 138 A3
Ashfield Ho GL50 ...... 193 A3
Ashfield Pl BS6 .... 18 F1
Ashfield Rd Bristol BS3 .... 8 B3
Ruardean Hill GL17 ..... 164 A3
Ashfield Terr 8 BS3 ...... 8 B3
Ashford Rd
Bristol BS34 .... 29 A7
Cheltenham GL50 .... 193 A1
Ashford Way BS15 .... 11 A7
Ashgrove
Charlton Kings GL53 ..... 131 C4
Thornbury BS35 .... 64 C1
Ashgrove Ave
Abbots Leigh BS8 .... 7 B7
Bristol BS7 .... 18 F4
Gloucester GL4 .... 119 C6
Ashgrove Cl
Bristol BS7 .... 18 F4
Hardwicke GL2 .... 109 E7
Ashgrove Cotts GL6 .... 102 F4
Ashgrove Rd
Bristol,Ashley Down BS7 ... 18 F4
Bristol,Bedminster BS3 ..... 8 B3
Ashgrove Way GL4 ..... 119 C6
Ashland Rd BS13 .... 2 A4
Ashlands Cl GL51 ...... 132 E3
Ashlands Rd GL51 ...... 132 E3
Ashlea Mdws GL52 ..... 137 D4
Ashleigh La GL52 ...... 138 D1
Ashletts Rd GL6 .... 106 C1
Ashleworth CE Prim Sch
GL19 .... 172 D4
Ashleworth Gdns GL2 .. 109 E8
Ashleworth Tithe Barn*
GL19 .... 172 D4
Ashley BS15 .... 10 F8
Ashley Cl
Bristol BS7 .... 18 F4
Charlton Kings GL52 ..... 131 B7
Ashley Court Rd 2 BS7 .. 18 F2
Ashley Ct BS2 .... 18 F1
Ashley Down Jun & Inf Schs
BS7 .... 18 F5
Ashley Down Rd BS7 .... 18 F4
Ashley Dr 2 GL6 .... 148 B6
Ashley Grove Rd
7 Bristol BS2 .... 18 F2
1 Bristol BS2 .... 19 A1
Ashley Hill BS6,BS7 ...... 18 F2
Ashley Ho BS34 .... 39 F1
Ashley Lo GL53 .... 130 C6
Ashley Par BS2 .... 18 F2
Ashley Pk BS6 .... 18 F3
Ashley Rd
Bristol BS6 .... 18 E1
Cheltenham GL52 .... 131 B8
Ashley St BS2 .... 19 A1
Ashley Trad Est 6 BS2 .. 18 F2
Ashman Cl BS5 .... 9 A8
Ashman Cl 1 BS16 ...... 19 E3
Ashmead GL2 .... 127 B5
Ashmead Dr GL52 ...... 138 A8
Ashmead Ho 12 BS5 ...... 9 C7
Ashmead Pk BS31 .... 5 B5
Ashmead Rd
Cinderford GL14 .... 191 D3
Keynsham BS31 .... 5 B5
Ashmead Road Ind Est
BS31 .... 5 B5
Ashmead Way 8 BS1 ..... 7 F5
Ashmore Rd GL4 .... 118 F4
Ashover La GL50 ...... 193 A1
Ashton BS16 .... 30 C1
Ashton Ave BS1 .... 194 A1
Ashton Cl GL4 .... 119 E3
Ashton Court Est* BS41 .. 7 C4
Ashton Dr BS3 .... 7 F2
Ashton Gate Prim Sch
BS3 .... 8 A4
Ashton Gate Rd BS3 ...... 8 A4
Ashton Gate Stad(Bristol City
FC) BS3 .... 7 F3
Ashton Gate Terr 4 BS3 .. 8 A4
Ashton Gate Trad Est BS3 . 7 E3
Ashton Gate Underpass
BS3 .... 7 F3
Ashton Keynes CE Prim Sch
SN6 .... 142 F5
Ashton Park Sch BS3 ..... 7 E4
Ashton Rd
Ashton Keynes SN6 ..... 142 F3
Beckford GL20 .... 183 B6
Bristol,Ashton Gate BS3 .... 7 F4
Bristol,Bower Ashton BS3,
BS41 .... 7 D3
Siddington GL7 .... 150 E1
Ashton under Hill Fst Sch
WR11 .... 183 D8
Ashton Vale Prim Sch BS3 7 F2
Ashton Vale Rd BS3 ...... 7 E3
Ashton Vale Trad Est BS3 .. 7 F1
Ashton Way BS31 .... 4 E6
Ashville Bsns Pk GL2 ... 173 E1
Ashville Ind Est GL2 .... 118 C5
Ashville Rd Bristol BS3 .... 8 A4
Gloucester GL2 .... 118 C5
Ashville Trad Est GL51 .. 133 B6
Ashway 17 GL54 .... 168 A1
Ashway Ct GL5 .... 98 E7
Ashway Ho GL5 .... 98 E7
Ashwell GL6 .... 103 F8
Ashwell Cl BS14 .... 3 E6
Ashwicke BS14 .... 3 A6
Ashwicke Rd SN14 .... 15 B3
Ashwood Way GL3 ..... 119 F6
Askham Ct 8 GL52 ..... 133 F2
Askwith Rd GL4 .... 119 B6
Aspen Cl SN14 .... 15 F6
Aspen Dr GL2 .... 117 E2
Asquith Rd GL53 .... 130 E6
Assembly Rooms La
BS1 .... 195 A2
Aston Bank HR9 .... 170 C2
Aston Bridge Rd GL17 .. 163 E3
Aston Cl Berry Hill GL16 .. 155 A7
16 Ledbury HR8 .... 178 E8
Aston Farm Cotts GL8 .. 148 C1
Aston Gr
Cheltenham GL51 .... 132 D2
Cold Aston GL54 .... 168 B6
Aston Ho 4 BS1 .... 195 B1
Aston Rd GL55 .... 188 F3
Aston View GL6 .... 148 C6
Astor Cl GL3 .... 120 D6
Astridge Rd GL3 .... 121 A4
Astry Cl BS11 .... 27 A1
at-Bristol* BS1 .... 194 C2
Atchley St 18 BS5 .... 9 B7
Atcombe Rd GL5 .... 90 F8
Athelney Way 4 GL52 .. 130 F8
Athena Ct 3 BS7 .... 18 F4
Atherston BS30 .... 11 D5
Atherstone Cl GL51 .... 132 C3
Atherton Cl GL51 ...... 129 D2
Atherton Ho GL51 ..... 129 D2
Athlone Wlk BS4 .... 8 E1
Atkins Cl BS14 .... 3 E6
Atlantic Rd BS11 .... 16 C8
Atlas Cl BS5 .... 20 A2
Atlas Rd BS3 .... 8 E3
Atlas St BS2 .... 9 B5
Atrium The BS1 .... 195 B2
Attwood Cl GL51 ...... 132 F5
Attwoods Patch GL54 ... 175 B3
Atwell Dr BS32 .... 40 B1
Atwood Dr BS11 .... 27 B2
Atyeo Cl BS3 .... 7 E1
Aubrey Ho 9 BS3 .... 8 B3
Aubrey Meads BS30 ...... 5 E8
Aubrey Rd BS3 .... 8 B3
Auburn Ave BS30 .... 11 B3
Auburn Rd BS6 .... 18 B1
Auckland Ho 1 GL51 .... 132 F3
Audley Cl BS37 .... 43 A8
Audrey Wlk BS9 .... 18 D7
Augustine Way GL4 .... 119 F6
Augustus Ho BS15 ...... 10 B6
Augustus Way GL15 ..... 92 B4
Aust Cres NP16 .... 60 F5
Aust La BS9 .... 18 A8
Aust Rd Northwick BS35 ... 48 D3
Olveston BS35 .... 49 F5
Austen Gr BS7 .... 19 A8
Austen Ho BS7 .... 19 A8
Austen Pl BS11 .... 16 E7
Austin Dr GL2 .... 126 F6
Austin Rd
Ashchurch GL20 .... 182 D4
Cirencester GL7 .... 190 E4
Australia Ho GL51 ..... 132 E1
Avalon La BS5 .... 10 B6
Avalon Rd BS5 .... 10 B6
Avebury Cl GL4 .... 118 B1
Avebury Rd BS3 .... 7 F2
Avenall Ct 9 GL52 ..... 130 F8
Avenall Par GL53 ...... 130 F8
Avening Prim Sch GL8 .148 A1
Avening Rd Bristol BS15 .. 10 A8
Gloucester GL4 .... 118 F5
Nailsworth GL6 .... 91 E3
Avenue Terr GL10 .... 97 D7
Avenue The
Bourton-on-t-W GL54 ... 168 F8
Brimscombe GL6 .... 148 B5
Bristol BS34 .... 40 B2
Bristol,Ashley Down BS7 ... 18 E3
Bristol,Clifton BS8 .... 18 A1
Bristol,Crew's Hole BS5 ..... 9 F8
Bristol,Frenchay BS16 ..... 29 E1
Bristol,Little Stoke BS34 ... 29 C6
Bristol,Sneyd Park BS9 .... 17 E3
Cheltenham GL53 .... 130 F5
Churchdown GL3 .... 128 D5
Cirencester GL7 .... 190 D4
Dursley GL11 .... 87 D3
Gloucester GL2 .... 127 C4
Keynsham BS31 .... 4 E6
Stanton Fitzwarren SN6 .. 145 A1
Woodchester GL5 .... 99 A2
Yate BS37 .... 43 D1
Averay Rd BS16 .... 19 C4
Averill Cl WR12 .... 185 B8
Avon Bsns Pk BS16 ...... 20 A3
Avon Cl Bristol BS5 .... 9 F6
Keynsham BS31 .... 4 F6
Avon Cres Bristol BS1 ... 194 A1
Brockworth GL3 .... 120 F5
Wickwar GL12 .... 54 B6
Avon Ct Bristol,Clifton BS8 . 18 A1
Bristol,Fishponds BS16 .... 20 B5
Avon Gorge Ind Est BS11 16 C7
Avon Gorge Nature Reserve*
BS8 .... 7 E7
Avon Gr BS9 .... 17 D2
Avon Ho GL2 .... 118 C4
Avon La BS31 .... 5 F5
Avon Meads BS2 .... 9 C5
Avon Mill La BS31 .... 4 F6
Avon Pk BS5 .... 9 D7
Avon Prim Sch BS11 .... 16 D8
Avon Rd Bristol BS13 ...... 2 A6
Charfield GL12 .... 67 A4
Cheltenham GL52 ...... 134 A2
Keynsham BS31 .... 4 F5
Pill BS20 .... 16 C5
Avon Rise SN14 .... 47 E4
Avon Riverside Est BS11 . 16 C7
Avon Riverside Sta* BS31 5 E6
Avon St BS2 .... 195 C2
Avon Trad Est BS2 .... 9 A5
Avon Vale BS9 .... 17 D4
Avon Valley Bsns Pk BS4 .. 9 E6
Avon Valley Ctry Pk*
BS31 .... 5 D6
Avon Valley Farm BS31 ... 5 D5
Avon Valley Rly* BS30 ... 11 C3
Avon View Bristol BS15 ... 10 B3
Tewkesbury GL20 .... 192 E6
Avon Way
Bristol,Sneyd Park BS9 .... 17 C4
Bristol,Southmead BS10 ... 18 D7
Thornbury BS35 .... 51 D7
Avonbank Ind Est BS11 .. 16 B7
Avonbridge Trad Est
BS11 .... 16 C8
Avondale Bsns Ctr BS15 . 20 C2
Avondale Ct
Bristol,Oldland BS30 ...... 10 F3
Bristol,Sneyd Park BS9 .... 17 D3
Avondown Cl BS10 ...... 28 D2
Avondown Ct BS3 .... 8 C2
Avondowns Ct BS8 ..... 194 A4
Avonlea Bristol BS15 ..... 10 C5
Yate BS37 .... 32 D8
Avonlea Ct BS30 .... 11 A3
Avonleaze BS9 .... 17 B5
Avonleigh Ct 4 BS3 ...... 8 B2
Avonleigh Rd BS3 .... 8 B2
Avonmead Ho BS1 ..... 195 B4
Avonmouth CE Prim Sch
BS11 .... 16 C8
Avonmouth Rd
Avonmouth BS11 .... 16 C8
Avonmouth BS11 .... 26 B1
Avonmouth Sta BS11 .... 26 B1
Avonmouth Way
Avonmouth BS11 .... 26 D1
Bristol BS10 .... 27 E3
Avonmouth Way W BS11 . 26 B1
Avonside Ind Est BS2 ..... 9 C6
Avonside Rd BS2 .... 9 C6
Avonside Way BS4 .... 9 F6
Avonsmere Residential Pk
BS34 .... 29 C3
Avonvale Rd BS5 .... 9 C7
Avonwood Cl BS11 ...... 16 E6
Avro Rd GL54 .... 169 D7
Awdelett Cl BS11 .... 27 B1
Awdry Way GL4 .... 118 D2
Awebridge Way GL4 .... 119 C4
Awkward Hill GL7 ..... 160 A1
Awre Rd GL15 .... 156 E1
Axbridge Rd BS4 .... 8 F2
Axe Ct 4 BS35 .... 51 C8
Axis BS14 .... 2 D5
Aycote Cl GL4 .... 119 B5
Ayford La SN14,BA1 ..... 14 F4
Ayland Cl 29 GL18 ..... 171 A4
Ayland Gdns GL1 ...... 119 A8
Aylburton CE Prim Sch
GL15 .... 147 E5
Aylesbury Cres BS3 ...... 8 B1
Aylesbury Rd BS3 .... 8 B1
Aylmer Cres BS14 .... 3 B6
Aylminton Wlk BS11 ..... 27 B2
Aylton Cl GL51 .... 129 D6
Aysgarth Ave GL51 .... 129 E5
Azalea Dr GL51 .... 130 A5
Azalea Gdns GL2 ...... 117 E1
Aztec Ctr The BS32 ...... 40 A2
Aztec W BS32 .... 40 A2

B

Back Albert Pl GL52 .... 193 C4
Back Edge La GL6 ...... 103 B8
Back Ends GL55 .... 189 A2
Back La
Ashton under Hill WR11 .. 183 D8
Beckford GL20 .... 183 B6
Bisley GL6 .... 148 D8
Bredon GL20 .... 182 C8
Bretforton WR11 .... 188 A6
Broad Blunsdon SN26 .... 144 D2
Broadway WR12 .... 185 B8
Drybrook GL17 .... 164 B4
Fairford GL7 .... 152 E3
Keynsham BS31 .... 4 E6
Leighterton GL8 .... 70 C3
Marshfield SN14 .... 14 F8
Mickleton GL55 .... 189 A6
Pill BS20 .... 16 C5
Pucklechurch BS16 .... 22 C4
Upper Oddington GL56 ... 177 C4
Wickwar GL12 .... 54 A5
Winchcombe GL54 ...... 174 A7
Winstone GL7 .... 107 A8
Back Montpellier Terr
GL50 .... 193 B2
Back Of Avon GL20 .... 192 C4
Back Of Kingsdown Par
BS6 .... 195 A4
Back Of Mount Pleasant
GL20 .... 192 D4
Back Rd
Bristol BS3 .... 8 A4
Llandogo NP16 .... 146 A5
Back Row GL56 .... 177 E6
Back St
Ashton Keynes SN6 ..... 142 F5
Hawkesbury Upton GL9 ... 56 A3
Ilmington CV36 .... 189 F6
Newnham GL14 .... 157 A6
Back Stoke La BS9 .... 17 F6
Back The NP16 .... 72 F1
Back Walls GL54 .... 176 F4
Backfield Farm BS37 .... 42 F5
Backfields BS2 .... 195 B4
Backfields Ct BS2 ...... 195 B4
Backfields La BS2 ...... 195 B4
Backwell Wlk BS13 .... 1 F8
Baden Hill Rd GL12 ...... 52 C6
Baden Rd
Bristol,Kingswood BS15 ... 11 A7
Bristol,Redfield BS5 .... 9 C7
Badenham Gr BS11 ...... 16 F8
Bader Ave GL3 .... 128 C5
Bader Cl BS37 .... 43 D3
Badger Cl Bristol BS30 .... 10 F3
Gloucester GL4 .... 119 D3
Badger Sett BS5 .... 10 B7
Badger Vale Ct GL2 .... 118 C5
Badger's La BS32 .... 39 C3
Badgers Cl BS32 .... 40 D3
Badgers Dene
Chepstow/Cas-Gwent NP16 60 D8
North The NP25 .... 154 B1
Badgers Field GL55 .... 189 A2
Badgers Holt BS14 .... 3 C6
Badgers Mdw NP16 ...... 60 B6
Badgers Rise BS10 ...... 28 E4
Badgers Way
9 Bream GL15 .... 155 D1
Nailsworth GL6 .... 90 F5
Badgers Wlk BS4 .... 9 D2
Badgeworth BS37 .... 32 D6
Badgeworth La GL51 ... 129 B2
Badgeworth Rd GL51 ... 129 A7
Badhams The GL20 ..... 180 F7
Badminton BS16 .... 30 C1
Badminton Cl GL53 .... 130 D6
Badminton Ct BS37 ..... 43 C2
Badminton Ctr The BS37 . 43 C2
Badminton Rd
Bristol,Downend BS16 ..... 20 E7
Bristol,Montpelier BS2 ..... 18 F1
Chipping Sodbury BS37 ... 34 B7
Frampton Cotterell BS36,
BS37 .... 31 C6
Gloucester GL4 .... 119 B5
Badminton Road Trad Est
BS37 .... 43 B1

Badminton Sch BS9 . . . . .18 A5
Badminton Wlk BS16 . . . .20 E7
Badock's Wood Prim Sch
BS10 . . . . .28 B1
Badsey La WR12 . . . . . .188 A3
Bafford App GL53 . . . . . .131 A4
Bafford Gr GL53 . . . . . . .130 F4
Bafford La GL53 . . . . . . .131 A5
Baglyn Ave BS15 . . . . .20 F3
Bagnell Cl BS14 . . . . .3 E5
Bagnell Rd BS14 . . . . .3 E5
Bagpath La GL5 . . . . .99 D2
Bagshots Sq GL54 . . . . . .176 B2
Bagstone Rd BS37,GL12 . . .53 A2
Bagworth Dr BS30 . . . . . .10 F3
Bailey Cl 21 GL54 . . . . . .176 F4
Bailey Hill GL15 . . . . .156 B1
Bailey La NP16,GL15 . . . .146 D4
Bailey's Court Prim Sch
BS32 . . . . .29 F6
Bailey's Hay NP16 . . . . . . .60 B4
Baileys Court Rd BS32 . . .29 F6
Baileys Ct BS32 . . . . .29 F6
Baileys Mead Rd BS16 . . .19 C5
Bailiffe Piece SN6 . . . . .143 E5
Baines Cl 11 GL54 . . . . . .168 F7
Bakehouse La GL50 . . . . .130 B7
Baker Sq GL20 . . . . .192 D5
Baker St
Cheltenham GL51 . . . . . . .133 C3
Gloucester GL2 . . . . .196 A1
Baker's Hill GL55 . . . . . . .189 B5
Baker's La GL19 . . . . . . .172 B3
Bakers Ground BS34 . . . .30 A5
Bakers Hill GL16 . . . . . . .155 B6
Bakers Piece Rd GL17 . . .163 F3
Bakers Pk BS13 . . . . .2 B6
Bakersfield BS30 . . . . .11 B3
Bala Rd GL51 . . . . .129 F6
Balaclava Ind Est BS16 . .19 F3
Balaclava Rd BS16 . . . . . .19 F3
Balcarras GL53 . . . . .131 C5
Balcarras Gdns GL53 . . .131 C5
Balcarras Rd GL53 . . . . .131 C5
Balcarras Retreat GL53 .131 C5
Balcarras Sch GL53 . . . .131 C5
Baldwin Cl GL7 . . . . .149 B1
Baldwin St BS1 . . . . .195 A2
Baldwyn Ct WR11 . . . . . .188 C6
Balfour Rd Bristol BS3 . . . . .8 B3
Gloucester GL1 . . . . .118 D6
Ballards Cl GL55 . . . . . . .189 A6
Ballast La BS11 . . . . .26 E2
Ballinode Cl GL50 . . . . . .133 B5
Ballinska Mews GL2 . . .127 D5
Balmain St BS4 . . . . .9 A4
Balmoral Cl BS34 . . . . . . .29 D4
Balmoral Ct Bristol BS16 . .21 A5
Cheltenham GL53 . . . . . . .130 F6
Balmoral Mans 3 BS7 . . .18 F2
Balmoral Rd
Bristol,Longwell Green
BS30 . . . . .10 F2
Bristol,Montpelier BS7 . . . .18 F2
Keynsham BS31 . . . . .4 E4
Baltic Pl BS20 . . . . .16 D4
Bamfield BS14 . . . . .3 A6
Bamfurlong Ind Pk
GL51 . . . . .173 E1
Bamfurlong La
Bamfurlong GL51 . . . . . . .128 F8
Bamfurlong GL51 . . . . . . .129 A8
Cheltenham GL51 . . . . . . .173 F1
Bampton Cl
Bristol,Emerson's Green
BS16 . . . . .21 C6
Bristol,Headley Park BS13 . . .2 B7
Bampton Croft BS16 . . . .21 C6
Bampton Dr BS16 . . . . . . .30 D1
Banady La GL52 . . . . . . .136 E5
Baneberry Rd GL4 . . . . . .119 A4
Banfield Cl BS11 . . . . .17 A8
Bangor Gr BS4 . . . . .9 F5
Bangrove Wlk BS11 . . . . .16 E8
Bangup La GL54 . . . . . . .168 B6
Banister Gr BS4 . . . . .2 D7
Bank Cres 1 HR8 . . . . . .178 F8
Bank Leaze Prim Sch
BS11 . . . . .27 B2
Bank Pl BS20 . . . . .16 D4
Bank Rd Avonmouth BS11 . .26 D7
Bristol BS15 . . . . .10 D8
Pilning BS35 . . . . .38 E6
Bank Sq 6 NP16 . . . . .60 E8
Bank St
Chepstow/Cas-Gwent NP16 60 E8
Coleford GL16 . . . . .155 A5
Bank The Broadwell GL56 177 A6
Cheltenham GL52 . . . . . . .134 C4
Stroud GL6 . . . . .98 D8
Banks Fee La GL56 . . . .176 D8
Bankside Bristol BS16 . . . .20 F4
North Cerney GL7 . . . . . . .158 D3
Bankside Ind Est HR8 . . .178 E8
Bankside Rd BS4 . . . . .9 D3
Banner Rd BS6 . . . . .18 E1
Bannerleigh La BS8 . . . . . .7 E6
Bannerleigh Rd BS8 . . . . . .7 E6
Bannerman Rd BS5 . . . . . .9 B8
Bannerman Road Prim Sch
BS5 . . . . .19 B1
Bannetts Tree Cres BS35 .51 A5
Bantock Cl BS4 . . . . .2 D6
Bantry Rd BS4 . . . . .2 E8
Banwell Cl Bristol BS13 . . . .2 A8
Keynsham BS31 . . . . .5 A2
Banwell Rd BS3 . . . . .8 A3
Banyard Cl GL51 . . . . . . .132 D2
Baptist Cl GL4 . . . . .119 F6
Baptist St BS5 . . . . .19 A1
Baptist Way GL17 . . . . . .164 A3
Baranwheel Ct BS5 . . . . . . .9 F6
Barber La GL8 . . . . .140 A2
Barberry Cl GL50 . . . . . . .130 B6
Barbican Rd GL1 . . . . . . .196 A3
Barbican Way GL1 . . . . .196 A3
Barbour Gdns BS13 . . . . . . .2 D3
Barbour Rd BS13 . . . . .2 D3
Barbridge Rd GL51 . . . . .132 E3
Barcelona Dr GL6 . . . . . . .91 F6
Barcroft Cl BS15 . . . . .10 C8
Baregains La HR8 . . . . . .178 B8
Barker Ct 5 BS5 . . . . .9 C7
Barker Pl 1 GL7 . . . . . . .152 E4
Barker Wlk BS5 . . . . .19 A1
Barker's Leys GL52 . . . . .138 B4
Barkers Mead BS37 . . . . . .43 F4
Barkleys Hill BS16 . . . . . .19 C5
Barksdale GL54 . . . . . . .139 F5
Barlands Ho BS10 . . . . . . .27 F3
Barlands The GL52 . . . . .131 E4
Barley Cl Bristol BS16 . . . .21 A6
Cheltenham GL51 . . . . . . .132 D5
Frampton Cotterell BS36 . . .31 C8
Hardwicke GL2 . . . . .109 E6
Barley Close Com Prim Sch
BS16 . . . . .21 A6
Barley Croft BS9 . . . . .17 F5
Barleycorn Sq GL14 . . . .191 C4
Barleycroft Cl GL4 . . . . .119 D2
Barlow Cl GL10 . . . . .97 E7
Barlow Rd GL51 . . . . . . .132 F4
Barn Bsns Ctr The GL54 169 D4
Barn Cl Bristol BS16 . . . . .21 B6
Gloucester GL4 . . . . .119 E4
Gretton GL54 . . . . .183 E1
Nailsworth GL6 . . . . .91 B3
Barn Cotts The GL15 . . .146 F6
Barn End SN14 . . . . .15 A8
Barn Field 5 GL52 . . . . .134 A1
Barn Field Ave GL6 . . . . .91 A4
Barn Field Rd GL6 . . . . . .91 A4
Barn Field Terr GL6 . . . . .91 A4
Barn Ground GL2 . . . . . .125 D5
Barn Hill Rd GL16 . . . . .155 C6
Barn La GL17 . . . . .163 F3
Barn Owl Way BS34 . . . . .29 F5
Barn Way GL7 . . . . .190 A7
Barnabas St 9 BS2 . . . . .18 E1
Barnaby Cl GL1 . . . . .118 F7
Barnack Trad Est BS3 . . . .8 C1
Barnacre Dr GL3 . . . . . . .127 F1
Barnage La GL15 . . . . . .147 A4
Barnard Par 5 GL10 . . . .97 F7
Barnard Wlk BS31 . . . . .4 D4
Barnes Ho GL7 . . . . .190 D5
Barnes St BS5 . . . . .9 D8
Barnes Wallis Way GL3 .128 C5
Barnets Wood/Coed Barnet
NP16 . . . . .60 C8
Barnett Ave HR8 . . . . . .178 E8
Barnett Cl GL51 . . . . . . .132 E5
Barnett Way
Gloucester GL4 . . . . .127 D1
5 Northleach GL54 . . . . .168 A1
Barnetts Cl 4 HR8 . . . . .178 E8
Barnfields GL4 . . . . .118 F5
Barnhay GL3 . . . . .128 C4
Barnhill Cl BS37 . . . . .44 A4
Barnhill Rd BS37 . . . . .44 B1
Barnmeadow Rd 8
GL54 . . . . .174 A7
Barnsley House Gdn★
GL7 . . . . .151 C7
Barnstaple Ct BS4 . . . . . . .2 E8
Barnstaple Rd BS4 . . . . . . .2 E8
Barnstaple Wlk BS4 . . . . .2 F8
Barnwood Ave GL4 . . . . .119 D8
Barnwood CE Prim Sch
GL4 . . . . .127 D1
Barnwood Park High Sch for
Girls GL4 . . . . .119 D8
Barnwood Rd
Gloucester GL2 . . . . .127 C2
Yate BS37 . . . . .32 C7
Barons Cl BS3 . . . . .7 F3
Barossa Pl BS1 . . . . .195 A1
Barra Cl SN6 . . . . .145 C3
Barrack Sq GL1 . . . . .196 A3
Barrack's La BS11 . . . . . .16 D8
Barracks The GL15 . . . . .156 A4
Barratt Ind Pk GL1 . . . . .126 D4
Barratt St BS5 . . . . .19 C1
Barratt's Mill La GL53 . .193 C3
Barrel La GL17 . . . . .164 F8
Barrels Pitch 1 GL55 . . .189 A2
Barrington Ave GL51 . . .129 B7
Barrington Cl BS15 . . . . .20 F2
Barrington Ct
11 Bristol,Knowle BS2 . . . . . .8 F4
Bristol,New Cheltenham
BS15 . . . . .20 E1
Barrington Dr GL3 . . . . .119 F8
Barrington Mews GL51 . .129 B7
Barrow Cl GL2 . . . . .109 F8
Barrow Elm Barns GL7 .152 F7
Barrow Hill
Churchdown GL3 . . . . . . .128 D3
Wick BS30 . . . . .12 B5
Barrow Hill Cres BS11 . . .16 C7
Barrow Hill Rd BS11 . . . .16 D6
Barrow Hospl BS48 . . . . . .1 A6
Barrow Rd BS2 . . . . .9 A7
Barrowell La GL15 . . . . .146 F7
Barrowfield Rd GL5 . . . .103 A1
Barrowmead Dr BS11 . . .16 F7
Barrs Court Ave BS30 . . .11 A5
Barrs Court Prim Sch
BS30 . . . . .10 F5
Barrs Court Rd BS30 . . . .11 A5
Barrs La GL11 . . . . .79 E4
Barry Cl BS30 . . . . .11 C1
Barry Rd BS30 . . . . .11 C2
Barstable Ho BS2 . . . . . .195 C3
Bartholomew Cl GL19 . .172 D4
Bartholomew Sq BS7 . . . .18 F7
Bartlett's Rd BS3 . . . . .8 C2
Bartletts Pk GL54 . . . . . .176 F4
Bartley Croft 3 GL8 . . . .140 C4
Bartley Ct BS5 . . . . .9 D7
Bartley St BS3 . . . . .8 D4
Barton Cl Alveston BS35 . . .51 A5
1 Bristol BS4 . . . . .9 F6
Charlton Kings GL53 . . . . .131 A4
Winterbourne BS36 . . . . . . .30 E5
Barton Ct Bristol BS5 . . . . .9 C6
Highworth SN6 . . . . .145 D3
Barton Gn BS5 . . . . .9 B7
Barton Hill GL17 . . . . . . .164 E5
Barton Hill Prim Sch BS5 .9 B6
Barton Hill Rd BS5 . . . . . . .9 B7
Barton Hill Trad Est 10
BS5 .9 B6
Barton Ho BS5 . . . . .9 C6
Barton La GL7 . . . . .190 B5
Barton Manor BS2 . . . . . . .9 A6
Barton Mews GL20 . . . . .192 D4
Barton Rd
Barton-on-t-H GL56 . . . . . .187 F3
Bristol BS2 . . . . .195 C2
Tewkesbury GL20 . . . . . . .192 D4
Barton St Bristol BS1 . . . .195 A4
Gloucester GL1 . . . . .119 A8
Tewkesbury GL20 . . . . . . .192 C4
Barton The Bristol BS15 . . .10 C4
Hawkesbury Upton GL9 . . . .55 F3
Barton Vale 6 BS2 . . . . . . .9 A6
Barton Way GL51 . . . . . .129 E6
Bartonend La GL6 . . . . . . .91 A1
Bartonia Gr BS4 . . . . .9 D1
Bartwood La HR9 . . . . . .164 A8
Barwick Ho BS11 . . . . . . .16 E7
Barwick Rd 6 GL51 . . . . .129 F5
Barwood Cl BS15 . . . . . . .10 F8
Base La GL2 . . . . .172 F1
Basil Cl GL4 . . . . .119 D4
Bassett Cl 3 GL54 . . . . .174 A7
Bassett Rd GL54 . . . . . .168 A1
Bassetts The GL5 . . . . . .98 D8
Batch The BS31 . . . . .5 F3
Batches The BS3 . . . . .8 B2
Batchfield La BS16,BS37 .22 D8
Batchfields GL18 . . . . . .178 E2
Bateman Cl GL4 . . . . . . .118 D1
Bates Cl BS5 . . . . .9 A8
Bath Bldgs BS6 . . . . .18 E1
Bath Bridge Rdbt BS1 . .195 C1
Bath Cres GL15 . . . . .155 F1
Bath Hill BS31 . . . . .4 F5
Bath La GL9 . . . . .55 E2
Bath Mews GL53 . . . . . . .193 C2
Bath Par GL53 . . . . .193 C2
Bath Pl
11 Berry Hill GL16 . . . . . .155 A7
Lydney GL15 . . . . .92 B3
Bath Race Course★ BA1 . .6 F6
Bath Rd Bitton BS30,BA1 . . .5 F7
Bristol BS3 . . . . .195 C1
Bristol,Brislington BS4 . . . . . .9 F1
Bristol,Longwell Green
BS30 . . . . .10 F3
Bristol,North Common BS30 11 D6
Bristol,Totterdown BS4 . . . . .9 B4
Bristol,Upper Knowle BS4 . . . .9 D2
Bristol,Willsbridge BS30 . . .11 C1
Cheltenham GL50,GL53 . . .193 B2
Chipping Sodbury BS37,GL9 34 C4
Colerne SN14 . . . . .15 E2
Cricklade SN6 . . . . .143 E4
Eastington GL10 . . . . .96 F6
Hardwicke GL2 . . . . .109 E4
Leighterton GL8 . . . . .70 B2
Leonard Stanley GL10 . . . . .97 E4
Nailsworth GL6 . . . . .91 B2
Saltford BS31 . . . . .5 D3
Stonehouse GL10 . . . . .97 F7
Tetbury GL8 . . . . .140 B2
Thornbury BS35 . . . . .51 B8
Wick BS30 . . . . .12 E4
Woodchester GL5 . . . . .99 A3
Bath Road Trad Est GL5 . .98 F5
Bath St Bristol BS1 . . . . .195 B2
Bristol,Ashton Gate BS3 . . . .8 A4
Bristol,Staple Hill BS16 . . . .20 E4
Cheltenham GL50 . . . . . . .193 C3
Stroud GL5 . . . . .99 C7
Bath Terr GL53 . . . . .193 B1
Bath Ville Mews GL53 . .193 B2
Bathams Cl GL17 . . . . . .164 F5
Bathings The 1 BS35 . . . .51 C8
Bathleaze GL10 . . . . .98 A4
Bathurst Par BS1 . . . . . .195 A1
Bathurst Park Rd GL15 . .92 A3
Bathurst Rd
Cirencester GL7 . . . . .190 B3
Gloucester GL1 . . . . .118 F6
Bathurst Row GL7 . . . . .149 E3
Bathwell Rd BS4 . . . . .9 A3
Batley Ct BS30 . . . . .11 D4
Batsford Arboretum★
GL56 . . . . .186 E4
Batten Ct BS37 . . . . .44 C1
Batten's La BS5 . . . . . . .10 A6
Battenburg Rd BS5 . . . . .10 A8
Battens Rd BS5 . . . . .10 B7
Battersby Way BS10 . . . . .27 E2
Battersea Rd BS5 . . . . .9 C8
Battle Rd GL20 . . . . .192 B2
Battlebrook Dr GL55 . . . .189 B2
Battledown App GL52 . . .131 A8
Battledown Childrens Ctr
GL52 . . . . .134 A1
Battledown Cl GL52 . . . .134 A1
Battledown Dr GL52 . . . .131 A8
Battledown Grange
GL52 . . . . .131 A8
Battledown Mead GL52 .134 A1
Battledown Priors GL52 134 A1
Battledown Trad Est
GL52 . . . . .131 A8
Batts La GL17 . . . . .164 A4
Battson Rd BS14 . . . . .3 E4
Baugh Gdns BS16 . . . . . . .30 E1
Baugh Rd BS16 . . . . .30 E1
Baunton La GL7 . . . . . . .150 C7
Bavon Cotts GL20 . . . . . .181 F8
Baxter Cl BS15 . . . . .10 F8
Baxters Barns GL7 . . . . .153 D6
Bay Gdns BS5 . . . . .19 C2
Bay Tree Cl BS34 . . . . . . .28 F7
Bay Tree Ct GL52 . . . . . .134 C4
Bay Tree Rd GL4 . . . . . . .119 F5
Bayberry Pl Cvn Pk 10
GL16 . . . . .155 B5
Bayfield Gdns GL18 . . . .178 D2
Bayham Rd BS4 . . . . .9 A3
Bayham's Wlk GL16 . . . .155 C6
Baylands GL13 . . . . .85 D8
Bayleys Dr BS15 . . . . . . .10 C6
Bayliss Ho GL51 . . . . . . .132 E4
Bayliss Rd GL20 . . . . . . .182 E8
Baynham Ct 4 BS15 . . . . .10 B5
Baynham Rd GL17 . . . . .164 D5
Baynham Way GL50 . . . .193 B4
Baynham's Wlk GL16 . . .155 B6
Baynton Ho 2 BS5 . . . . . . .9 B7
Baynton Mdw BS16 . . . . .21 C6
Baynton Rd BS3 . . . . .8 A4
Bays Hill GL13 . . . . .85 D8
Bayshill La GL50 . . . . . .193 A3
Bayshill Rd GL50 . . . . . .193 A3
Bayswater Ave BS6 . . . . .18 B3
Bayswater Rd BS7 . . . . . .18 F7
Bazeley Rd GL4 . . . . . . .119 B2
Beach Ave BS35 . . . . .38 A7
Beach Hill BS30 . . . . .11 F3
Beach La BS30 . . . . .12 C2
Beach Rd BS35 . . . . .37 F7
Beachgrove Gdns BS16 . .20 C4
Beachgrove Rd BS16 . . . .20 B4
Beachley Rd
Beachley NP16 . . . . .61 B4
Tutshill NP16 . . . . .73 A1
Beachley Wlk BS11 . . . . .16 D7
Beacon Cl GL6 . . . . .112 A5
Beacon La BS16 . . . . .30 C6
Beacon Rd
Gloucester GL4 . . . . .119 B2
Llandogo NP25 . . . . .146 A8
Beacon Rise Prim Sch
BS15 . . . . .10 D6
Beaconlea BS15 . . . . .10 D6
Beacons View Rd GL14 .191 E5
Beaconsfield Cl 6 BS2 . . .9 B6
Beaconsfield Ct 1
GL50 . . . . .130 B8
Beaconsfield Rd
Bristol,Clifton BS8 . . . . . . .18 A1
Bristol,Crew's Hole BS5 . . . . .9 E7
Bristol,Kensington Park BS4 .9 B3
Beaconsfield St 7 BS5 . . . .9 B6
Beagles The GL5 . . . . . . .98 D7
Beale Cl Bristol BS14 . . . . . .3 E6
Bussage GL6 . . . . .148 B6
Beale Rd GL51 . . . . .132 D3
Beam St BS5 . . . . .9 C7
Bean Acre The BS11 . . . .16 D8
Bean Hill GL56 . . . . .176 E8
Bean St 11 BS5 . . . . .19 A1
Beanhill Cres BS35 . . . . .51 A5
Beanwood Pk (Cvn Site)
BS37 . . . . .32 E3
Bear Hill GL5 . . . . .99 B2
Bear La GL20 . . . . .180 F6
Bear St GL12 . . . . .68 B7
Bear Yard Mews BS8 . . .194 A2
Bearbridge Rd BS13 . . . . . .1 F4
Bearcroft Gdns GL55 . . .189 B6
Beard's La GL5 . . . . .99 A7
Bearland GL1 . . . . .196 A3
Bearlands GL12 . . . . .68 C6
Bearpacker Almshouses
GL12 . . . . .68 C8
Bearsfield GL6 . . . . .105 A1
Beauchamp Cl 2 GL7 . . .152 E4
Beauchamp Mdw GL15 . . .92 C4
Beauchamp Rd BS7 . . . . .18 D4
Beaudesert Park Sch
GL6 . . . . .91 C5
Beaufort BS16 . . . . .30 C1
Beaufort Ave BS37 . . . . . .43 D2
Beaufort Bldgs
8 Bristol BS8 . . . . .7 F7
Gloucester GL1 . . . . .196 B1
Beaufort Cl BS5 . . . . .9 D7
Beaufort Com Sch GL4 .118 B2
Beaufort Cres BS34 . . . . .29 E4
Beaufort Ct Bristol BS16 . .21 A8
Cirencester GL7 . . . . .190 C3
Beaufort Dr GL15 . . . . . . .92 B2
Beaufort End WR11 . . . .188 C7
Beaufort Ho 12 BS5 . . . . . .9 B7
Beaufort Hts BS5 . . . . .9 E7
Beaufort Mews
9 Bristol BS8 . . . . .7 F7
Chipping Sodbury BS37 . . . .44 B1
Beaufort Pl
Bristol,Frenchay BS16 . . . . .30 B1
Bristol,Upper Easton BS5 . . .9 A8
Chepstow/Cas-Gwent NP16 60 E8
Tewkesbury GL20 . . . . . . .192 C2
Beaufort Rd
Bristol,Clifton BS8 . . . . .18 A1
Bristol,Horfield BS7 . . . . . . .18 F6
Bristol,Kingswood BS15 . . . .20 C1
Bristol,Pile Marsh BS5 . . . . . .9 E7
Bristol,Staple Hill BS16 . . . .20 E5
Bristol,Vinney Green BS16 . .21 A8
Cheltenham GL52 . . . . . . .131 A7
Frampton Cotterell BS36 . . .31 A8
Gloucester GL4 . . . . .119 A5
Yate BS37 . . . . .43 D2
Beaufort Sq 5 NP16 . . . . .60 E8
Beaufort St
Bristol,Bedminster BS3 . . . . .8 C2
4 Bristol,Upper Easton BS5 .9 A8
Beaufort Trad Pk BS16 . . .22 B5
Beaufort Way BS10 . . . . .18 D8
Beauley Rd BS3 . . . . .8 B4
Beaumont Cl BS30 . . . . . .11 A3
Beaumont Dr GL51 . . . . .132 D4
Beaumont Pl GL15 . . . . . .92 A2
Beaumont Rd
Cheltenham GL51 . . . . . . .132 D3
Gloucester GL2 . . . . .127 C5
Beaumont Row 5 GL12 . . .68 B7
Beaumont Sq 4 GL12 . . . .68 B7
Beaumont St BS5 . . . . .9 A8
Beaumont Terr 6 BS5 . . . .9 A8
Beaumoor Pl GL7 . . . . . .152 E3
Beaver Cl BS36 . . . . .30 F7
Beazer Cl 5 BS16 . . . . . . .20 D3
Beceshore Cl GL56 . . . . .187 A3
Beck Cl BS16 . . . . .21 C7
Beck Ho BS34 . . . . .29 A8
Becket Cl GL56 . . . . .187 E7
Becket Ct BS16 . . . . .22 B5
Becketts La GL54 . . . . . .174 A8
Beckford Cl GL20 . . . . . .183 B6
Beckford Gdns BS14 . . . . . .3 A3
Beckford Rd
Alderton GL20 . . . . .183 D4
Ashton under Hill WR11 . .183 D8
Gloucester GL4 . . . . .119 E4
Beckford Silk★ GL20 . . . .183 B6
Beckington Rd BS3 . . . . . . .8 F2
Beckington Wlk BS3 . . . . . .8 F2
Beckside Ct 2 GL1 . . . . .127 A1
Beckspool Rd BS16 . . . . .30 C1
Becky Hill GL54 . . . . . . .176 B1
Beddome Way GL54 . . . .168 F8
Bedford Ave GL51 . . . . . .133 A2
Bedford Cres BS7 . . . . . . .18 F5
Bedford St
Gloucester GL1 . . . . .196 C2
8 Stroud GL5 . . . . .99 C7
Bedminster Down Rd BS3,
BS13 .8 B1
Bedminster Down Sch
BS13 .1 F7
Bedminster Par BS3 . . . . . .8 D4
Bedminster Pl 9 BS3 . . . . .8 D4
Bedminster Rd BS3 . . . . . .8 C2
Bedminster Sta BS3 . . . . . .8 D3
Beech Ave GL16 . . . . . . .155 B7
Beech Cl Alveston BS35 . . .51 A5
Bristol BS30 . . . . .11 A5
Cheltenham GL52 . . . . . . .134 C4
Hardwicke GL2 . . . . .109 E7
Highnam GL2 . . . . .125 D4
Beech Croft BS14 . . . . .3 B5
Beech Ct BS14 . . . . .3 A5
Beech Gr
Chepstow/Cas-Gwent NP16 60 D7
Cirencester GL7 . . . . .190 E5
Highworth SN6 . . . . .145 C3
Woodchester GL5 . . . . .99 A2
Beech Green Prim Sch
GL2 . . . . .117 F1
Beech Grove Ct GL7 . . . .190 E5
Beech Ho BS16 . . . . .19 C5
Beech La GL6 . . . . .104 B8
Beech Lea
Broad Blunsdon SN26 . . . .144 E1
Meysey Hampton GL7 . . . .152 B3
Beech Leaze BS35 . . . . . .51 A5
Beech Rd Bristol BS7 . . . . .18 E5
Saltford BS31 . . . . .5 E3
Yorkley GL15 . . . . .156 A2
Beech Tree Gdns 5
GL8 . . . . .140 C4
Beech Way Bream GL15 .147 D8
Littledean GL14 . . . . .156 E8
Beech Well La GL16 . . . .155 C8
Beechacres BS35 . . . . . . .64 C1
Beechcroft BS41 . . . . .1 D2
Beechcroft Rd GL2 . . . . .127 B5
Beechcroft Wlk BS7 . . . . .19 A8
Beechdean GL14 . . . . . . .191 C5
Beechen Dr BS16 . . . . . . .20 B3
Beechenhurst GL15 . . . .155 F1
Beechenhurst Lodge Visitor
Ctr★ GL16 . . . . .155 E7
Beeches Cl GL10 . . . . . . .98 A4
Beeches Gn GL5 . . . . .99 B8
Beeches Gr BS4 . . . . .9 D2
Beeches Ind Est BS37 . . .43 B2

Beeches Pk GL6 ...148 B2
Beeches Rd
Charlton Kings GL53 ...131 B4
Cirencester GL7 ...190 D4
6 Newnham GL14 ...157 A6
Beeches The
Bristol,Bradley Stoke BS32 .29 D8
Bristol,Frenchay BS16 ...30 B1
Bristol,Oldland Common BS30 ...11 C2
Bristol,St Anne's BS4 ...9 E5
King's Stanley GL10 ...98 A4
Beechfield Cl BS41 ...7 C2
Beechfield Gr BS9 ...17 C8
Beechmore Dr 10 GL51 .129 E5
Beechmount Ct BS14 ...3 B8
Beechmount Gr BS14 ...3 B8
Beechurst Ave GL52 ...133 F1
Beechurst Way GL52 ...137 D4
Beechwood Ave BS15 ...10 D5
Beechwood Cl Bristol BS14 3 C8
Cheltenham GL52 ...131 B8
Beechwood Dr 4 GL6 ..148 B6
Beechwood Gr
Gloucester GL4 ...118 E3
Wotton-u-E GL12 ...68 D8
Beechwood Rd
Bristol BS16 ...20 B4
Easton-in-G BS20 ...16 A4
Beechwood Rise GL11 ..87 F2
Beechwood Sh Ctr GL50 ...193 C3
Beehive Trad Est BS5 ...9 E7
Beek's La SN14,BA1 ...14 D5
Beesmoor Rd BS36 ...31 B6
Begbrook Dr BS16 ...19 F6
Begbrook La BS16 ...19 F6
Begbrook Pk BS16 ...20 A7
Begbrook Prim Sch BS16 19 F6
Beggar Bush La BS8 ...7 B6
Beggarswell Cl BS2 ...195 C4
Bekdale Cl GL2 ...109 D8
Belas Knap Long Barrow★ GL54 ...174 A4
Belfast Wlk BS4 ...2 E8
Belfry BS30 ...11 B6
Belfry Ave BS5 ...10 A8
Belfry Cl GL4 ...119 E8
Belfry The NP16 ...61 C8
Belgrave Hill 5 BS8 ...18 A2
Belgrave Ho 4 BS8 ...194 A3
Belgrave Pl BS8 ...194 A3
Belgrave Rd Bristol BS8 .194 B4
Gloucester GL1 ...196 B2
Belgrove Terr GL1 ...196 C1
Bell Bank 5 GL56 ...186 C5
Bell Barn Rd BS9 ...17 D6
Bell Cl BS10 ...18 E7
Bell Cotts GL2 ...95 F4
Bell Hill BS16 ...19 C4
Bell Hill Rd BS5 ...9 F8
Bell La Blockley GL56 ...186 C5
Bristol BS1 ...195 A3
Bromesberrow Heath GL18 ...179 B4
Gloucester GL1 ...196 B2
Lechlade on T GL7 ...153 E2
Minchinhampton GL6 ...148 A3
Poulton GL7 ...151 F4
Stroud GL5 ...98 E4
Westbury-on-S GL14 ...157 C8
Bell Orch GL2 ...157 B6
Bell Pitch GL6 ...102 F3
Bell Rd BS36 ...31 C6
Bell Sq SN14 ...15 A8
Bell Wlk GL1 ...196 B2
Bella Vista GL52 ...138 B3
Bellamy Ave BS13 ...2 C4
Bellamy Cl BS15 ...10 A5
Belland Dr Bristol BS14 ...2 F4
Charlton Kings GL53 ...131 A4
Belle Ct 7 BS2 ...8 F4
Belle Vue Cl GL5 ...99 C7
Belle Vue Rd Bristol BS5 ..19 C1
Cinderford GL14 ...191 D4
Ruardean GL17 ...163 F4
Stroud GL5 ...99 C7
Belle Vue Terr GL6 ...148 C5
Bellevue BS8 ...194 B2
Bellevue Cl BS15 ...10 E7
Bellevue Cotts
5 Bristol BS9 ...18 A7
Bristol,Clifton Wood BS8 ..194 B2
Bellevue Cres BS8 ...194 B2
Bellevue Ct BS8 ...194 B2
Bellevue Pk BS4 ...9 D2
Bellevue Rd
Bristol,Kingswood BS15 ...10 F7
Bristol,St George BS5 ...10 A8
6 Bristol,Windmill Hill BS2 ..8 F4
Bellevue Terr
Bristol,Brislington BS4 ...9 D2
Bristol,Clifton Wood BS8 ..194 B2
Bristol,Windmill Hill BS2 ...8 F4
Bellfields La BS16 ...30 C1
Bellflower Rd GL20 ...192 E2
Bellhouse Wlk BS11 ...27 B1
Bellingham La SN6 ...145 D1
Bells Pl Cinderford GL14 .156 C6
Coleford GL16 ...155 A5
Belluton Rd BS4 ...9 A3
Belmont Ave GL3 ...120 B7
Belmont Dr BS34 ...29 E5
Belmont La GL16 ...155 A8
Belmont Lo 6 GL52 ...193 C4
Belmont Pk BS7 ...28 F1
Belmont Rd
Bristol,Arno's Vale BS4 ...9 C3
Bristol,Montpelier BS6 ...18 E2
Cheltenham GL52 ...193 C4
Hewelsfield GL15 ...146 E5
Stroud GL5 ...99 E6
Belmont Sch GL51 ...130 A7
Belmont St BS5 ...19 B1
Belmont Terr GL17 ...164 D5
Belmore Pl GL53 ...193 B2
Beloe Rd BS7 ...18 E5
Belroyal Ave BS4 ...9 F3
Belsher Dr BS15 ...11 A6
Belstone Wlk BS4 ...2 C8
Belton Rd BS5 ...9 B8
Belvedere Mews GL6 ...148 C5
Belvedere Rd BS6 ...18 B3
Belvoir Rd BS6 ...18 E2
Belworth Ct 5 GL51 ...129 F7
Belworth Dr GL51 ...130 A7
Bence Ct 3 BS15 ...10 B5
Bences Cl SN14 ...14 F8
Bendall Ho 7 GL52 ...193 C4
Bendy Bow SN16 ...141 F4
Benford Cl BS16 ...20 C6
Benhall Ave GL51 ...129 E8
Benhall Gdns GL51 ...132 E1
Benhall Ho GL51 ...129 F8
Benhall Inf Sch GL51 ...129 D7
Bennett Rd BS5 ...9 E7
Bennett Way BS1,BS8 ...7 F5
Bennett's Ct BS37 ...44 A1
Bennington St GL50 ...193 B4
Bensaunt Gr BS10 ...28 D4
Benson Cl 3 GL4 ...119 E6
Bentley Cl Bristol BS14 ...2 F3
Quedgeley GL2 ...117 F2
Bentley La GL52 ...134 D7
Benton Ct GL10 ...89 E6
Benville Ave BS9 ...17 C8
Berchel Ho 4 BS3 ...8 D4
Berenda Dr BS30 ...11 B3
Beresford Cl BS31 ...5 E2
Beresford Ho GL7 ...190 C6
Berkeley Ave
Bristol,Bishopston BS7 ...18 D3
Bristol,Brandon Hill BS8 ..194 C3
Berkeley Castle & Butterfly Ho★ GL13 ...85 F2
Berkeley Cl Bristol BS16 ..21 A8
Charfield GL12 ...67 A5
Gloucester GL3 ...120 C6
South Cerney GL7 ...142 F7
Stroud GL5 ...98 D7
Berkeley Cres
Bristol BS8 ...194 B3
Lydney GL15 ...92 B5
Berkeley Ct
Bristol,Bishopston BS7 ...18 D3
Cheltenham GL52 ...193 C3
Slimbridge GL2 ...95 D3
Berkeley Ct Bsns Pk BS5 ..9 B7
Berkeley Gdns BS31 ...4 E4
Berkeley Gn BS16 ...30 B1
Berkeley Gn Rd BS5 ...19 D2
Berkeley Gr BS5 ...19 C2
Berkeley Ho
Bristol,Brandon Hill BS1 ..194 C3
7 Bristol,Staple Hill BS16 .20 D5
7 Cheltenham GL52 ...133 F2
4 Cheltenham,Hester's Way GL51 ...132 E3
Berkeley Hospl GL13 ...85 E3
Berkeley Mews GL52 ...193 C3
Berkeley Pl Bristol BS8 ..194 B3
Cheltenham GL52 ...193 C3
Berkeley Prim Sch GL13 .85 E3
Berkeley Rd
Bristol,Bishopston BS7 ...18 D3
Bristol,Kingswood BS15 ...10 D7
Bristol,Mayfield Park BS16 .20 B2
Bristol,Staple Hill BS16 ...20 D5
Bristol,Westbury Park BS6 .18 B4
Cirencester GL7 ...190 C1
Berkeley Sq BS8 ...194 C3
Berkeley St Bristol BS5 ..19 C3
Cheltenham GL52 ...193 C3
Gloucester GL1 ...196 A3
Berkeley Sta GL13 ...85 F5
Berkeley Vale Com Sch GL13 ...85 E7
Berkeley Vale Pk GL13 ..85 D4
Berkeley Way Bristol BS16 21 B7
7 Tetbury GL8 ...140 C5
Berkeleys Mead BS34 ...30 A6
Berkhampstead Sch GL52 ...134 A2
Berkley Pl BS3 ...8 D2
Berkshire Rd BS7 ...18 D3
Berlington Ct BS1 ...195 B1
Berners Cl BS4 ...2 D7
Berrells Rd GL8 ...140 B3
Berrells The GL8 ...140 B3
Berrington Rd GL55 ...189 B2
Berrow Wlk BS3 ...8 E2
Berrows Mead BS37 ...43 A8
Berry Cl GL6 ...103 F8
Berry Croft 5 BS3 ...8 D4
Berry Hill Cl BS10 ...28 D1
Berry Hill Cres GL7 ...190 C7
Berry Hill Prim Sch GL16 ...155 A7
Berry Hill Rd GL7 ...190 D7
Berry La BS7 ...18 F6
Berry Lawn GL4 ...119 D3
Berrycroft GL13 ...85 E4
Berryfield GL5 ...98 F2
Berryfield Glade GL3 ...128 A6
Berrymore Rd GL5 ...98 F2
Bertha's Field GL9 ...57 B4
Berton Cl SN26 ...144 E1
Berwick Cl BS10 ...27 E8
Berwick Ct BS10 ...27 B5
Berwick Dr BS10 ...27 E5
Berwick La BS10 ...27 D7
Berwick Rd
Bishop's Cleeve GL52 ...137 F5
Bristol BS5 ...19 B2
Beryl Gr BS14 ...3 C8
Beryl Rd BS3 ...8 B3
Besbury Pk GL6 ...148 A4
Besford Rd GL52 ...138 E3
Besom La BS37 ...32 D5
Bessemer Cl 22 GL16 ...155 A5
Beta Cl GL20 ...182 B4
Bethel Rd BS5 ...9 F8
Bethesda St GL50 ...193 B1
Betjeman Cl GL2 ...118 C4
Betjeman Ct 2 BS30 ...11 A5
Bettenson Rise 10 GL54 168 A1
Bettertons Cl GL7 ...152 D3
Bettridge Ct GL52 ...134 B3
Bettridge Sch GL51 ...130 A6
Betts Gn BS16 ...21 C7
Betworthy Est GL11 ...88 E8
Bevan Ct BS34 ...28 F2
Bevan Gdns GL20 ...182 C5
Bevans Hill GL13 ...85 D4
Beverley Ave BS16 ...30 F1
Beverley Cl BS5 ...10 B6
Beverley Croft GL51 ...132 C2
Beverley Gdns Bristol BS9 17 D7
Woodmancote GL52 ...138 C3
Beverley Rd BS7 ...18 F8
Beverly Ct 3 BS16 ...20 D3
Beverston Gdns BS11 ...27 B2
Beverstone BS15 ...10 C8
Beverstone Cl GL7 ...142 F7
Beverstone Rd GL7 ...142 F7
Bevington Cl BS34 ...39 E1
Bevington La GL11 ...76 F7
Bevington Wlk BS34 ...39 E1
Bewicks The GL2 ...95 D3
Bewley Way GL3 ...128 A6
Bexley Rd BS16 ...20 B3
Beyon Cl GL11 ...87 F6
Beyon Dr GL11 ...87 F6
Bibstone BS15 ...11 A8
Bibsworth Ave 4 WR12 185 C8
Bibsworth La
Broadway WR12 ...185 C8
Broadway WR12 ...188 B1
Bibury Ave BS34 ...29 B8
Bibury CE Prim Sch GL7 ...160 A1
Bibury Cl BS9 ...18 D7
Bibury Cres
Bristol,Hanham BS15 ...10 C5
Bristol,Henleaze BS9 ...18 D7
Bibury Farm Cotts GL7 .160 B2
Bibury Rd
Cheltenham GL51 ...129 E8
Gloucester GL4 ...119 A6
Bibury Trout Farm★ GL7 ...160 A1
Bickerton Cl BS10 ...27 F3
Bickford Cl BS30 ...11 A6
Bickley Cl BS15 ...10 C2
Bicknor St GL16 ...155 A8
Bicks La 30 GL54 ...174 A7
Biddel Springs SN6 ...145 D3
Biddestone Rd BS7 ...28 E1
Biddulph Way HR8 ...178 E7
Bideford Cres BS4 ...2 F8
Bidwell Cl BS10 ...28 B3
Bifield Cl BS14 ...3 F5
Bifield Gdns BS14 ...3 E5
Bifield Rd BS14 ...3 F5
Bigstone Cl NP16 ...73 A2
Bigstone Gr NP16 ...73 A2
Bigstone Mdw NP16 ...73 A2
Bigwood La BS1 ...194 C2
Bijou Ct GL1 ...126 F4
Bilberry Cl Bristol BS9 ..17 C8
5 Gloucester GL4 ...119 F5
Bilbie Cl BS10 ...18 E7
Billand Cl BS13 ...1 E3
Billbrook Rd GL3 ...120 A7
Billingham Cl GL4 ...119 B6
Billings Way GL50 ...130 B6
Bilsham La BS35 ...48 F2
Bilson GL14 ...191 C5
Bindon Dr BS10 ...28 D4
Binley Gr BS14 ...3 D5
Binmead Gdns BS13 ...2 B4
Binyon Rd GL54 ...139 F5
Birbeck Rd BS9 ...17 E5
Birch Ave GL4 ...119 C6
Birch Cl
Bishop's Cleeve GL52 ...138 B4
Bristol BS34 ...28 E7
Charlton Kings GL53 ...131 C4
Ledbury HR8 ...178 E8
Birch Croft BS14 ...3 A3
Birch Ct Keynsham BS31 ...4 C4
Yate BS37 ...43 D2
Birch Dr Alveston BS35 ...50 F4
Pucklechurch BS16 ...22 B5
Birch Glade 4 SN6 ...142 F4
Birch Ho BS16 ...20 B5
Birch Pk GL16 ...155 C5
Birch Rd
Bristol,Kingswood BS15 ...20 E3
Bristol,Southville BS3 ...8 B4
Dursley GL11 ...88 A4
Birch Rd *continued*
Mile End GL16 ...155 C6
Woodchester GL5 ...99 A3
Yate BS37 ...43 D2
Birchall Ave GL4 ...119 C3
Birchall Rd BS6 ...18 C4
Birchdale Rd BS14 ...3 A8
Birches Cl GL5 ...99 C8
Birches Dr GL5 ...99 C8
Birches La GL18 ...170 F7
Birches Rd NP25 ...154 B5
Birches The GL5 ...99 C8
Birchfield Rd GL52 ...138 A4
Birchills Trad Est BS4 ...9 F1
Birchley Rd GL52 ...131 B8
Birchmore Rd GL1 ...119 A8
Birchwood Cl GL14 ...191 B5
Birchwood Ct BS4 ...9 F6
Birchwood Fields GL4 ..118 E3
Birchwood Rd Bristol BS4 ..9 F4
Woolaston GL15 ...147 C3
Bird Rd GL3 ...120 B6
Birdale Cl BS10 ...27 E3
Birdland★ GL54 ...168 F7
Birdlip Fm GL4 ...121 F1
Birdlip Ho GL1 ...127 A2
Birdlip Prim Sch GL4 ..121 F1
Birds Bush La GL6 ...106 B5
Birdwell Prim Sch BS41 ...1 A8
Birdwood BS15 ...10 D6
Birdwood Cl GL4 ...119 E4
Birdwood Gdns NP16 ...60 C4
Birgage Rd GL9 ...55 F2
Birkdale Bristol BS30 ...11 B6
Yate BS37 ...32 E8
Birkin St 5 BS2 ...9 A6
Bishop Ct GL51 ...133 A2
Bishop La BS7 ...18 E8
Bishop Manor Rd BS10 ..18 D7
Bishop Mews BS2 ...195 B4
Bishop Rd
Bristol,Bishopston BS7 ...18 D4
Bristol,Emerson's Green BS16 ...21 C6
Shurdington GL51 ...129 E2
Bishop Road Prim Sch BS7 ...18 D4
Bishop St BS2 ...195 B4
Bishop Terr BS2 ...195 C4
Bishop's Castle Way GL1 ...119 A8
Bishop's Cl GL5 ...99 D6
Bishop's Cleeve Prim Sch GL52 ...137 F3
Bishop's Wlk GL19 ...181 C3
Bishop's Wood BS32 ...40 C6
Bishops Cl
Bishop's Cleeve GL52 ...138 A3
Bristol BS9 ...17 E3
Chepstow/Cas-Gwent NP16 60 F4
Bishops Cove BS13 ...1 F5
Bishops Ct BS9 ...17 C3
Bishops Dr GL52 ...137 F3
Bishops Gate GL15 ...92 A2
Bishops Knoll BS9 ...17 C3
Bishops Mdw GL52 ...137 E4
Bishops Mead NP16 ...60 B4
Bishops Rd GL4 ...119 E6
Bishops Wlk
Cirencester GL7 ...190 C4
Tewkesbury GL20 ...192 C5
Whiteshill GL6 ...102 F3
Bishopsfield 2 SN6 ...143 E4
Bishopstone Cl GL51 ...132 C1
Bishopstone Rd GL1 ...119 A8
Bishopsworth CE Jun Sch BS13 ...1 F6
Bishopsworth Rd BS13 ...2 A7
Bishopthorpe Rd BS10 ..18 E7
Bishport Ave BS13 ...2 C3
Bishport Cl BS13 ...2 B4
Bishport Gn BS13 ...2 C3
Bishton La NP16 ...73 B3
Bisley BS37 ...32 C7
Bisley Bluecoat CE Prim Sch GL6 ...148 D8
Bisley Old Rd GL5 ...99 E7
Bisley Rd Bisley GL6 ...104 E2
Cheltenham GL51 ...129 E8
Gloucester GL4 ...118 E1
Stroud GL5 ...99 E6
Bisley St GL6 ...103 F8
Bissex Mead BS16 ...21 B5
Bittern Ave GL4 ...119 D6
Bitterwell Cl BS36 ...31 D3
Bittlemead BS13 ...2 F4
Bitton Sta★ BS30 ...11 B1
Bixhead Wlk GL16 ...155 C5
Blaby Cl GL4 ...119 F5
Black Berry Field GL52 .134 C3
Black Dog Way GL1 ...196 B3
Black Horse Hill GL8 ...140 B3
Black Jack Mews GL7 ..190 C5
Black Jack St GL7 ...190 C5
Black Stone Kilns La HR9 ...162 D3
Black Wells GL11 ...80 B7
Blackacre BS14 ...3 C4
Blackberry Ave 5 BS16 ..19 E5
Blackberry Cl GL4 ...119 E4
Blackberry Dr BS36 ...31 C6
Blackberry Gr GL52 ...137 E4
Blackberry Hill BS16 ...19 E5
Blackberry Hill Hospl BS16 ...19 F5
Blackbird Ave GL3 ...127 D6
Blackbird Ct GL10 ...97 F8
Blackboy 18 GL5 ...99 C7
Blackboys GL11 ...88 A3
Blackburn Rd GL52 ...137 E1
Blackdown Ct BS14 ...3 B5
Blackford La GL7 ...144 E6
Blackfriars BS1 ...195 A3
Blackfriars Church★ GL1 ...196 A2
Blackhorse Ct BS15 ...10 C8
Blackhorse Hill BS35, BS10 ...28 B8
Blackhorse La BS16 ...21 A8
Blackhorse Pl BS16 ...21 A6
Blackhorse Prim Sch BS16 ...21 A8
Blackhorse Rd
Bristol,Kingswood BS15 ...10 D8
Bristol,Mangotsfield BS16 ..21 A7
Blacklow Cl GL5 ...98 F2
Blackmans Cl GL18 ...170 F4
Blackmoor Rd BS8 ...16 E2
Blackmoors La BS3 ...7 E4
Blackquarries Hill GL12 ..68 E7
Blackrock La BS14 ...3 D1
Blacksmith Cl GL20 ...183 B5
Blacksmith Hill GL12 ...69 C7
Blacksmith La
Churchdown GL3 ...128 D4
The Leigh GL19 ...173 D5
Blacksmith's La BA1 ...6 B3
Blacksmiths Ground GL2 ...125 D5
Blacksmiths La
Beckford GL20 ...183 B5
Cheltenham GL52 ...134 C4
Dumbleton WR11 ...183 F7
Highnam GL2 ...125 F7
Blacksmiths Rd GL20 ...183 E4
Blackswarth Ho 6 BS5 ...9 D7
Blackswarth Rd BS5 ...9 D7
Blackthorn Cl BS13 ...2 D5
Blackthorn Dr BS32 ...29 D7
Blackthorn End GL53 ...130 A4
Blackthorn Gdns GL2 ...117 F1
Blackthorn Rd BS13 ...2 D5
Blackthorn Wlk BS15 ...20 E2
Blackwater Way GL2 ...127 E5
Blackworth SN6 ...145 D4
Blackworth Ct SN6 ...145 D4
Blackworth Ind Est SN6 145 D4
Bladon Mews GL51 ...129 B7
Blagdon Cl BS3 ...8 E2
Blagrove Cl BS13 ...2 C3
Blagrove Cres BS13 ...2 C3
Blaisdon BS37 ...32 E7
Blaisdon Cl Bristol BS10 ..28 A1
Gloucester GL4 ...119 E4
Blaisdon La GL17 ...165 B4
Blaisdon Rd GL14 ...165 C1
Blaisdon Way GL51 ...132 E5
Blaise Castle Mus★ BS10 27 E2
Blaise Hamlet BS11 ...27 D2
Blaise Prim Sch BS10 ...27 F2
Blaise Wlk BS9 ...17 C6
Blake Croft GL51 ...132 E4
Blake Hill Way GL4 ...119 D7
Blake Rd Bristol BS7 ...19 B6
Cirencester GL7 ...190 C5
Blake St 13 NP25 ...154 A7
Blakeley Ct GL3 ...127 F6
Blakeney Cl GL4 ...118 D3
Blakeney Hill Rd GL15 ..156 D2
Blakeney Mills BS37 ...43 E1
Blakeney Prim Sch GL15 ...156 D1
Blakeney Rd Bristol BS34 .39 E1
Bristol,Horfield BS7 ...19 A7
Blakes Rd BS35 ...64 B1
Blakewell Mead GL6 ...103 E8
Blanchards BS37 ...33 D8
Blanchards Cotts BS37 ..33 D8
Blandford Alley SN6 ...145 D3
Blandford Cl 2 BS9 ...18 B6
Blands Row BS35 ...48 B1
Bleasby Gdns GL50 ...130 A8
Bledington Prim Sch OX7 ...177 E1
Blenheim Cl
Alderton GL20 ...183 D4
Upper Rissington GL54 ..169 D6
Blenheim Ct Bristol BS32 .40 D3
14 Winchcombe GL54 ...174 A7
Blenheim Dr
Bredon GL20 ...182 C7
Bristol BS34 ...29 B4
3 Ledbury HR8 ...178 F7
28 Newent GL18 ...171 A4
Yate BS37 ...43 D3
Blenheim Ho GL3 ...120 A7
Blenheim Orch GL51 ...129 E2
Blenheim Rd Bristol BS6 ..18 B3
Gloucester GL1 ...196 C1
Blenheim Sq GL51 ...132 E3
Blenheim St BS5 ...19 A1
Blenheim Way GL56 ...187 A3
Blenman Cl BS16 ...20 A7
Bleriot Rd GL54 ...169 D6
Blethwin Cl BS10 ...27 F1
Blimeshire GL15 ...155 F1
Blind La
Chipping Campden GL55 ..188 F1
Tetbury GL8 ...140 C5
Blinkhorns Bridge La GL2 ...127 B1
Block 2 Government Bldgs BS10 ...28 B1
Blockley CE Prim Sch GL56 ...186 C6
Blockley Ct GL56 ...186 C6

Bloomfield Rd Bristol BS4 .9 D4
Gloucester GL1 .118 D7
Bloomfield Road Link BS4 9 C4
Bloomfield Terr GL1 .118 D6
Bloomsbury St GL51 .193 A4
Bloxham Rd WR12 .188 A1
Bloxhams Orch GL19 .172 D4
Bloy Sq BS5 .19 C1
Bloy St BS5 .19 C1
Blue Boys' Pk GL6 .148 A4
Blue Coat CE Prim Sch GL12 .68 B6
Blue Falcon Rd BS15 .20 E1
Blue La GL18 .170 D4
Blue Quarry Rd GL7 .190 E5
Blue Rock Cres 5 GL15 155 D1
Bluebell Chase GL6 .148 C6
Bluebell Cl Bristol BS9 .17 B6
Gloucester GL4 .119 D5
Milkwall GL16 .155 B4
Thornbury BS35 .64 D2
Bluebell Dr
Chepstow/Cas-Gwent NP16 60 F5
Cirencester GL7 .190 E2
Bluebell Gr GL51 .130 A5
Bluebell Rise GL6 .148 C6
Bluebells The BS32 .29 F7
Blunsdon Hill SN26 .144 C2
Blunts Hay GL7 .153 C8
Boakes Dr GL10 .97 E6
Boat Ho The HR9 .162 E4
Bobble Ct GL54 .169 C6
Bockenem Cl BS35 .51 D7
Bodenham Field GL4 .119 E6
Bodey Cl BS30 .11 A5
Bodiam Ave GL4 .118 B1
Bodmin Wlk BS4 .2 F8
Bodnam Rd GL51 .132 E4
Bodyce Rd 4 BS35 .51 A5
Boiling Wells La BS2 .19 A3
Boleyn Cl GL3 .127 F7
Boleyn Cotts GL51 .133 B7
Boleyn Ho GL54 .139 F5
Bolton Rd BS7 .18 E3
Bond St BS1 .195 B3
Bond's La SN14 .24 E1
Bondend Rd GL4 .119 F2
Bonds Mill Est GL10 .97 C7
Bonnington Wlk BS7 .19 B7
Bonville Bsns Ctr BS4 .9 F2
Bonville Rd BS4 .9 F2
Book End GL17 .164 F5
Boot La BS3 .8 D4
Bootenhay Rd GL52 .138 A4
Booth Rd BS3 .8 C4
Borage Cl GL4 .119 F5
Bordesley Rd BS14 .3 A3
Borleyton Wlk BS13 .1 F4
Born Ct 10 HR8 .178 F8
Borough Cl GL10 .98 A3
Borver Gr BS13 .2 B4
Boscombe Cres BS16 .20 F7
Boscombe La GL6 .90 E1
Boseley Way GL14 .191 C4
Bospin La GL5 .98 F1
Boston Rd BS7 .18 F8
Boswell St 4 BS5 .19 C2
Botany SN6 .145 C3
Botham Dr BS4 .9 E1
Boucher Pl 2 BS2 .19 A2
Boulevard The GL5 .99 B5
Boulters Rd BS13 .2 C4
Boulton La GL11 .88 B1
Boulton Rd GL50 .133 D5
Boulton's La 6 BS15 .10 D8
Boulton's Rd 5 BS15 .10 D8
Bouncer's La GL52 .134 B3
Boundary Cotts GL3 .121 A4
Boundary Pl GL19 .172 A7
Boundary Rd
Avonmouth BS11 .26 D3
Coalpit Heath BS36 .31 D7
Bourchier Gdns BS13 .2 B3
Bourne Cl Bristol BS15 .10 B8
Winterbourne BS36 .30 E7
Bourne La
Brimscombe GL5,GL6 .148 A6
Bristol BS5 .19 B2
Bourne Lake Pk SN6 .143 C3
Bourne Rd BS15 .10 A8
Bourne The GL7 .153 D8
Bourneville Rd BS5 .9 D8
Bournside Cl GL51 .130 A7
Bournside Dr GL51 .130 A7
Bournside Rd GL51 .130 B7
Boursland Cl BS32 .40 D2
Bourton Ave BS34 .29 C8
Bourton Cl BS34 .29 C8
Bourton House Gdn* GL56 .186 D3
Bourton Ind Pk GL54 .169 A8
Bourton Link GL54 .169 A8
Bourton Mead BS41 .7 A1
Bourton Rd
Gloucester GL4 .118 E2
Moreton-in-M GL56 .187 A3
Bourton Wlk BS13 .2 A8
Bourton-on-the-Water Prim Sch GL54 .168 F8
Bouverie St BS5 .9 B8
Boverton Ave GL3 .120 E6
Boverton Dr GL3 .120 D6
Boverton Rd BS34 .29 B4
Bovone La GL2 .124 D8
Bow Cotts BS20 .16 C4
Bow La
5 Bourton-on-t-W GL54 .168 F7
Ripple GL20 .181 D8
Bow Wow GL7 .143 A8
Bowbridge La
Cheltenham GL52 .134 B5
Stroud GL5 .99 D6
Bowbridge Lock GL5 .99 D5
Bowden Cl BS9 .17 C8
Bowden Pl BS16 .20 F7
Bowden Rd BS5 .19 E1
Bowen Cl GL52 .134 A3
Bowen's Hill 16 GL16 .155 A5
Bowen's Hill Rd 15 GL16 .155 A5
Bower Ashton Terr BS3 .7 F4
Bower Ct BS3 .8 A2
Bower Rd BS3 .8 A3
Bower Wlk BS3 .8 E3
Bowerleaze BS9 .17 C5
Bowes Lyon Cl 4 GL56 .187 A2
Bowl Hill GL5 .99 A3
Bowland Ct BS32 .40 D1
Bowldown Cotts GL8 .71 A5
Bowldown Rd GL8 .71 C3
Bowler Rd GL20 .182 C5
Bowlers Lea GL11 .87 F5
Bowling Green Ave GL7 190 C6
Bowling Green Cres GL7 .190 C6
Bowling Green Ct GL56 .187 A3
Bowling Green La GL7 .190 C6
Bowling Green Rd GL7 .190 C6
Bowling Hill BS37 .44 A1
Bowling Hill Bsns Pk BS37 .44 A1
Bowling Rd BS37 .33 B8
Bowly Cres GL7 .150 E2
Bowly Rd Cirencester GL7 190 B2
Gloucester GL1 .118 D6
Bowmead 7 BS4 .9 D1
Bownham Mead GL5 .99 D2
Bownham Pk GL5 .99 D1
Bowood BS16 .30 C1
Bowring Cl BS13 .2 C3
Bowsland BS32 .40 E2
Bowsland Green Prim Sch BS32 .40 E2
Bowsland Way BS32 .40 D2
Bowson Rd GL15 .155 D1
Bowson Sq GL15 .155 D1
Bowstreet La BS35 .28 A8
Box Cres GL6 .91 F6
Box Gdns GL6 .91 F6
Box La GL6 .91 F5
Box Rd GL11 .88 A8
Box Road Ave GL11 .88 A8
Box Tree Cl GL17 .163 F4
Box Wlk BS31 .4 C4
Boxbush Cl GL7 .143 A8
Boxbush Rd
Coleford GL16 .155 A5
South Cerney GL7 .143 A8
Boxhedge Farm La BS36 .31 E3
Boxwell Rd GL8 .70 B4
Boxwood Cl GL8 .82 B5
Boyce Cl GL4 .119 E3
Boyce Dr BS2 .19 A2
Boyce's Ave BS8 .194 A3
Boyd Cl BS30 .12 B7
Boyd Rd BS31 .5 D3
Bozard La GL20 .136 B8
Brabazon Rd BS34 .29 B2
Bracelands GL6 .148 C7
Bracelands Dr 1 GL16 .155 A7
Bracewell Gdns BS10 .28 C4
Bracey Dr BS16 .20 C6
Bracken Cl GL15 .92 C3
Bracken Dr GL15 .92 B3
Brackenbury Dr BS34 .29 F5
Brackendene BS32 .40 C1
Bracton Dr BS14 .3 A5
Bradeston Gr BS16 .20 A7
Bradford Rd 5 GL2 .127 B2
Bradfords Cl GL18 .170 F4
Bradfords Ct GL18 .170 F4
Bradfords La GL18 .170 F4
Bradhurst St 8 BS5 .9 B6
Bradley Ave Bristol BS11 .16 E6
Winterbourne BS36 .30 E5
Bradley Cl GL2 .127 C4
Bradley Court Rd GL17 .164 D6
Bradley Cres BS11 .16 E6
Bradley Ct BS16 .20 C5
Bradley Pavilions BS32 .40 C2
Bradley Rd Bristol BS34 .39 F1
Charlton Kings GL53 .131 A4
Wotton-u-E GL12 .68 A8
Bradley Rise GL17 .164 D6
Bradley St GL12 .68 A7
Bradley Stoke Way BS32 .29 E7
Bradshaw Cl GL2 .127 E5
Bradstone Rd BS36 .30 D5
Bradwell Gr BS10 .18 C8
Brae Wlk GL4 .119 D4
Braeburn Cl
Cheltenham GL51 .132 E2
Gloucester GL2 .127 C2
Braemar Ave BS7 .28 F1
Braemar Cres BS7 .28 F1
Braemor Ct BS9 .18 A8
Bragg's La BS2 .195 C3
Braikenridge Rd BS4 .9 D4
Brainsfield BS9 .17 F6
Brake Cl
Bristol,Bradley Stoke BS32 .29 E7
Bristol,Warmley Hill BS15 .10 F7
Brake The
Coalpit Heath BS36 .31 C5
Yate BS37 .43 E5
Brakewell Gdns BS14 .3 A4
Bramble Chase GL52 .137 F4
Bramble Dr Bristol BS9 .17 D3
Dursley GL11 .88 A3
Bramble La Bristol BS9 .17 C3
Stonehouse GL10 .97 F8
Bramble Lawn GL4 .119 D3
Bramble Rd GL16 .155 B4
Bramble Rise GL52 .134 C3
Brambles The
Berkeley GL13 .85 E4
Bristol BS13 .2 C4
Keynsham BS31 .4 D3
Lea HR9 .164 C8
Brambling Wlk BS16 .19 F6
Bramery The GL51 .133 B2
Bramley Cl
Kingswood GL12 .67 F4
4 Ledbury HR8 .178 E7
Olveston BS35 .50 A3
Pill BS20 .16 C4
Bramley Ct 6 BS30 .10 F4
Bramley Dr GL19 .165 D6
Bramley Mews GL4 .120 A6
Bramley Rd
Cheltenham GL51 .132 F3
Tewkesbury GL20 .192 D6
Bramleys The GL17 .164 F5
Branch Hill Rise GL53 .131 A4
Branch Rd
Bamfurlong GL51 .129 A7
Cheltenham GL51 .129 B7
Branch The GL17 .164 B3
Branche Gr BS13 .2 D3
Brandash Rd BS37 .44 C1
Branders 17 SN6 .143 E4
Brandon Cl GL3 .128 A8
Brandon Ho BS8 .194 B2
Brandon Pl GL50 .193 A1
Brandon St BS1 .194 C2
Brandon Steep BS1 .194 C2
Brangwyn Gr BS7 .19 B6
Branksome Cres BS34 .29 B3
Branksome Dr
Bristol BS34 .29 B3
Winterbourne BS36 .30 E6
Branksome Rd BS6 .18 B3
Brannigan Ct GL20 .182 C5
Brans La GL56 .177 C4
Branscombe Ct BS3 .8 D2
Branscombe Rd BS9 .17 C4
Bransdown Hill SN16 .59 A3
Brantwood Rd GL6 .148 C6
Branwhite Cl BS7 .19 B7
Brasenose Rd GL20 .182 C7
Brassington Gdns GL54 .166 E2
Bratches The GL55 .189 A3
Bratton Rd BS4 .2 D7
Braunton Rd BS3 .8 C3
Bravender Ho GL7 .190 D4
Bray Ave HR8 .178 F8
Braybrooke Cl GL8 .140 C4
Braydon Ave BS32 .29 D7
Braydon La SN6 .143 D3
Braydon Rd SN6 .143 A1
Brayne Ct BS30 .10 F3
Breach Rd BS3 .8 A3
Breaches Gate BS32 .29 F6
Breaches The BS20 .16 B5
Bream Ave GL15 .155 B1
Bream CE Prim Sch GL15 .155 D1
Bream Rd Bream GL15 .147 E7
St Briavels GL15 .147 B7
Brean Down Ave BS9 .18 B5
Brean Gdns BS3 .8 E2
Brecknock Rd BS4 .9 A3
Brecon Cl Bristol BS9 .18 B6
Quedgeley GL2 .109 E8
Brecon Rd BS9 .18 B6
Brecon Way GL16 .155 C8
Bredon BS37 .32 D7
Bredon Cl BS15 .10 F7
Bredon Hancock's Endowed Fst Sch The GL20 .182 C8
Bredon Lodge GL20 .182 C7
Bredon Nook Rd BS10 .18 C7
Bredon Rd GL20 .192 D6
Bredon Sch GL20 .181 C7
Bredon Tythe Barn* GL20 .182 B7
Bredon View WR12 .185 C8
Bregawn Cl GL52 .137 E2
Breinton Way GL2 .127 D5
Brendon Cl BS30 .11 C4
Brendon Rd BS3 .8 D3
Brendon Wlk GL52 .134 B3
Brenner St BS5 .19 B2
Brensham Ct GL3 .120 A7
Brent Rd BS7 .18 F5
Brentry Ave 5 BS5 .9 B7
Brentry La BS10 .28 B3
Brentry Lo BS10 .28 A3
Brentry Prim Sch BS10 .28 B4
Brentry Rd BS16 .19 F3
Brereton Way BS30 .11 B4
Bretforton Fst Sch WR11 .188 A6
Bretforton Rd WR11 .188 B7
Brevel Terr GL53 .131 B5
Brewerton Cl BS10 .28 C3
Brewery Cotts NP25 .154 C5
Brewery Ct BS3 .8 A4
Brewery Hill BS30 .5 F7
Brewery La
Nailsworth GL6 .91 B3
Thrupp GL5 .99 E2
Brewery Row GL56 .187 F1
Brewery St SN6 .145 D3
Brewery Yd 25 GL54 .176 F4
Brewhouse The BS1 .195 B2
Briar Cl GL5 .103 D1
Briar Ct BS20 .16 C4
Briar Lawn GL4 .119 D3
Briar Way BS16 .20 C3
Briar Wlk Bristol BS16 .20 C3
Cheltenham GL52 .134 C3
Briarbank Rise GL52 .131 C7
Briarfield Ave BS15 .10 C5
Briarleaze BS35 .50 F2
Briars Cl GL3 .128 A6
Briarside Ho BS10 .28 D3
Briarside Rd BS10 .28 D3
Briarwood BS9 .17 F6
Briarwood Sch BS16 .20 B3
Briary Rd GL7 .153 E3
Briavels Gr BS6 .18 F2
Brick Cotts BS35 .62 E1
Brick St BS2 .195 C3
Brick Wlk WR11 .188 C6
Brickfield Terr GL5 .99 A6
Brickfields GL12 .68 B6
Bricknell Ave GL20 .182 C7
Brickrow GL5 .99 C7
Brickworks Trad Est WR11 .188 C8
Bridewell St BS1 .195 A3
Bridge Access Rd BS35 .49 A7
Bridge Cl
Cirencester GL7 .190 D2
Gloucester GL2 .118 B6
Lechlade on T GL7 .153 F2
Whitchurch BS14 .3 C4
Bridge End
Cirencester GL7 .190 D3
Staunton GL19 .180 C2
Bridge Farm GL2 .126 B7
Bridge Farm Cl BS14 .3 A3
Bridge Farm Inf Sch BS14 3 A4
Bridge Farm Jun Sch BS14 .3 A4
Bridge Ho Alveston BS35 .50 F5
Bristol BS1 .195 A2
Bridge Rd
Bristol,Eastville BS5 .19 B3
Bristol,Lower Soundwell BS15 .21 A3
Bristol,Shortwood BS16 .21 C4
Cirencester GL7 .190 D2
Frampton on Severn GL2 .157 F3
Harrow Hill GL17 .164 B3
Leigh Woods BS8 .7 E6
Sharpness GL13 .93 C1
Stroud GL5 .98 D6
Yate BS37 .43 A2
Bridge St Blakeney GL15 .156 D1
Bretforton WR11 .188 A6
Bristol BS1 .195 A2
Bristol,Eastville BS5 .19 D2
Cheltenham GL51 .133 B4
Chepstow/Cas-Gwent NP16 72 F1
Fairford GL7 .152 E4
Ledbury HR8 .178 E8
Nailsworth GL6 .91 C4
Newent GL18 .171 A5
Stroud GL5 .98 E6
Bridge Valley Rd BS8 .7 E8
Bridge Way BS36 .31 B8
Bridge Wlk BS7 .19 A8
Bridge-Side GL5 .98 F6
Bridgeleap Rd BS16 .20 F8
Bridgemans Cl WR12 .188 B1
Bridgend Ct GL10 .97 E6
Bridgend Rd GL51 .129 C7
Bridges Ct 2 BS16 .20 B4
Bridges Dr 3 BS16 .20 C6
Bridgeside GL54 .168 F8
Bridget Dr NP16 .61 A7
Bridgman Gr BS34 .29 B3
Bridgwater Rd BS41,BS13, BS48 .1 D6
Bridle The GL5 .98 D7
Bridle Way BS35 .50 F4
Briercliffe Rd BS9 .17 D7
Brierley Banks GL17 .163 F2
Brierley Cl GL4 .119 E5
Brierley Council Hos GL17 .163 F2
Brierley Rd GL17 .163 F3
Brierley Way GL15 .156 B1
Brierly Furlong BS34 .29 D3
Briery Leaze Rd BS14 .3 A4
Bright St
Bristol,Kingswood BS15 .10 D8
Bristol,Russell Town BS5 .9 B7
Brightlands 11 GL14 .157 A6
Brighton Cres BS3 .8 B2
Brighton Mews BS8 .194 B4
Brighton Pk 16 BS5 .9 B8
Brighton Pl BS15 .20 D1
Brighton Rd
Bristol,Patchway BS34 .28 F8
Bristol,Redland BS6 .18 C1
Cheltenham GL52 .133 F1
Brighton St 12 BS2 .18 E1
Brighton Terr 9 BS3 .8 B2
Brigstocke Rd BS2 .195 B4
Brimbles The BS7 .29 B2
Brimley GL10 .97 F4
Brimscombe CE Prim Sch GL5 .99 F1
Brimscombe Hill GL5 .91 E8
Brimscombe La GL5 .99 F2
Brimsham Green Sch BS37 .43 D4
Brimsham Park Sh Ctr BS37 .43 F4
Brimsome Mdw GL2 .125 D5
Brindle Cl GL4 .119 C4
Brinkmarsh La GL12 .65 D2
Brinkworthy Rd BS16 .19 E6
Brinmead Wlk BS13 .1 F3
Brins Cl BS34 .29 F4
Brinsham La BS37 .44 A6
Brinsmead Cres BS20 .16 D4
Brionne Way GL2 .127 B5
Brisbane GL10 .101 F1
Briscoes Ave BS13 .2 D4
Brislington Enterprise Coll BS4 .3 F8
Brislington Hill BS4 .9 E2
Brislington Ret Pk BS4 .9 E1
Brislington Trad Est BS4 .9 F2
Bristol & Anchor Ho BS5 .9 D8
Bristol & Exeter Mews BS1 .195 C1
Bristol Bsns Pk BS16 .29 E1
Bristol Cathedral* BS1 194 C2
Bristol Cathedral Sch BS1 .194 C2
Bristol Dental Hospl BS1 .195 A3
Bristol Eye Hospl BS1 .195 A3
Bristol Gate 1 BS8 .7 F5
Bristol Gateway Sch The BS2 .19 A2
Bristol General Hospl BS1 .195 A1
Bristol Gram Sch BS8 .194 C3
Bristol Harbour Rly* BS1 .194 B1
Bristol Hill BS4 .9 D2
Bristol Homeopathic Hospl BS6 .194 C4
Bristol Ind Mus* BS1 .195 A1
Bristol Old Vic Theatre Sch BS8 .18 A1
Bristol Parkway N BS34 .30 A5
Bristol Parkway Sta BS34 29 E4
Bristol Rd Bristol BS16 .30 C2
Cambridge GL2 .95 F3
Cirencester GL7 .190 D3
Cromhall GL12 .53 B7
Frampton Cotterell BS36 .42 B3
Gloucester GL1,GL2 .118 C6
Keynsham BS31 .4 E6
Luckington SN14 .47 E3
Stonehouse GL10 .97 E7
Thornbury BS35 .51 B8
Upper Rissington GL54 .169 D7
Whitchurch BS14 .3 D3
Winterbourne BS16 .30 D4
Bristol Royal Hospital for Children BS1 .195 A3
Bristol Royal Infmy BS2 195 A4
Bristol South End BS3 .8 D2
Bristol Steiner Waldorf Sch BS6 .18 B2
Bristol Vale Ctr For Ind BS3 .8 B1
Bristol Zoo Gdns* BS8 .17 F1
Bristow Broadway BS11 .26 C1
Bristow Rd GL20 .192 E1
Bristowe Ho BS16 .20 B5
Bristowe Lodge BS16 .20 C4
Britannia Cl 4 BS16 .30 F1
Britannia Cres BS34 .29 D5
Britannia Ct 1 BS16 .20 D5
Britannia Ho BS34 .28 F2
Britannia Rd
Bristol,Kingswood BS15 .10 C8
Bristol,Lower Easton BS5 .19 C1
Bristol,Patchway BS34 .28 E7
Britannia Way GL52 .138 B3
British Empire & Commonwealth Mus* BS1 .195 C1
British Rd BS3 .8 C3
British Sch The GL12 .68 C6
British The BS37 .43 B4
Briton Cl NP16 .61 A4
Brittania Bldgs BS8 .194 A1
Britten Ct 10 BS30 .10 F4
Britten Pl GL51 .132 E2
Britton Bottom GL9 .56 B1
Britton Gdns BS15 .20 C1
Britton Ho BS15 .11 B8
Brittons Pas SN14 .14 F8
Brixham Rd BS3 .8 C1
Brixton Rd BS5 .9 B8
Brixton Road Mews 22 BS5 .9 B8
Brizen La GL53 .130 B4
Broad Croft BS32 .40 C2
Broad La
Coalpit Heath BS36 .31 D5
Westerleigh BS37 .32 A4
Yate BS37 .43 C4
Broad Leys Rd GL4 .119 D7
Broad Marston Rd GL55 189 A7
Broad Oak Rd BS13 .1 F4
Broad Oak Way GL51 .129 F6
Broad Oaks BS8 .7 E6
Broad Plain BS2 .195 C2
Broad Quay BS1 .195 A2
Broad Rd BS15 .20 C1
Broad St Bristol BS1 .195 A3
Bristol,Staple Hill BS16 .20 F4
Chipping Sodbury BS37 .44 B1
Hartpury GL19 .172 C4
King's Stanley GL10 .98 A3
Littledean GL14 .191 F4

Broad St continued
13 Newent GL18 171 A4
Stroud GL5 98 D3
Broad Weir BS1 195 B3
Broad Wlk BS4 9 A2
Broad Wlk The GL50 193 B2
Broadacre Cl GL20 182 C7
Broadbury Rd BS4 2 E8
Broadclose Rd GL2 173 B2
Broadfield Ave BS15 20 C1
Broadfield Cotts GL54 160 C6
Broadfield Rd Bristol BS4 9 B1
Eastington GL10 96 F8
Broadlands Ave BS31 4 D6
Broadlands Ct GL54 168 F7
Broadlands Dr BS11 27 A1
Broadlands Sch BS31 4 D6
Broadleas BS13 2 C7
Broadleaze Bristol BS11 16 E7
Down Ampney GL7 143 F8
Broadleys Ave BS9 18 C7
Broadmead BS1 195 B3
Broadmead La BS31 5 A6
Broadmead Lane Ind Est BS31 5 B7
Broadmere GL11 87 E4
Broadmere Cl GL11 87 E3
Broadmoor La BA1 6 F4
Broadmoor Pk GL14 191 B7
Broadmoor Rd GL14 191 B7
Broadoak Hill BS41 1 F2
Broadoak Wlk BS16 20 B4
Broadstone Cl GL4 119 E8
Broadstone Wlk BS13 2 D5
Broadwalk Sh Ctr BS4 9 B2
Broadway Gloucester GL4 118 F5
Saltford BS31 5 D3
Yate BS37 43 F2
Broadway Ave BS9 18 D6
Broadway Bears & Dolls Mus★ WR12 185 C8
Broadway Cl
Cheltenham GL52 134 A5
Kempsford GL7 144 E8
Broadway Ct GL7 142 F7
Broadway Fst Sch WR12 188 B1
Broadway Inf Sch BS37 43 F2
Broadway La
Minsterworth GL2 116 A2
South Cerney GL7 143 A6
Broadway Rd
Bristol,Bishopston BS7 18 D3
Bristol,Bishopsworth BS13 1 F5
Mickleton GL55 189 A6
Toddington GL54 184 C3
Willersey WR12 188 B2
Winchcombe GL54 174 A7
Broadway The
Chalford GL6 148 E6
Dursley GL11 80 A8
North Nibley GL11 79 F8
Broadway Tower Ctry Pk★ WR12 185 D4
Broadway,St Mary's RC Prim Sch WR12 185 B8
Broadways Dr BS16 19 F7
Broadwell Bridge 7 GL16 155 B6
Broadwell Cl GL4 119 E5
Broadwell Rd GL56 177 C5
Broadwell Terr GL11 88 B1
Brock Cl GL51 129 B6
Brockeridge Cl GL2 117 E2
Brockeridge Inf Sch BS36 31 C7
Brockeridge Rd GL20 181 F7
Brockhampton La GL51 133 B7
Brockhampton Pk GL54 174 B1
Brockhollands GL15 147 E8
Brockhollands Rd GL15 147 D8
Brockhurst Gdns BS15 10 A8
Brockhurst Rd BS15 10 A8
Brockley Acres GL6 148 C7
Brockley Cl BS34 29 C7
Brockley Rd
Leonard Stanley GL10 97 F4
Saltford BS31 5 D3
Brockley Wlk BS13 2 A8
Brockmoor La HR9 170 C4
Brockridge La BS36 31 C7
Brocks 4 BS4 9 D1
Brocks Rd BS13 2 C3
Brockworth BS37 32 C6
Brockworth Cotts GL3 120 F4
Brockworth Cres BS16 19 F6
Brockworth Enterprise Sch GL3 120 F6
Brockworth Prim Sch GL3 120 E5
Brockworth Rd GL3 128 E2
Brome Rd GL4 119 F5
Bromesberrow Heath Bsns Pk HR8 179 B3
Bromfield Wlk BS16 21 B7
Bromley Dr BS16 20 D8
Bromley Heath Ave BS16 20 D8
Bromley Heath Jun & Inf Schs BS16 20 E8
Bromley Heath Rd BS16 20 D8
Bromley Rd Bristol BS7 18 F5
Ellwood GL16 155 C3
Brompton Cl BS15 11 A8
Broncksea Rd BS7 28 F1
Bronte Cl 2 GL51 129 F7
Bronte Dr 2 HR8 178 E8
Bronte Wlk BS7 19 A8
Brook Cl Long Ashton BS41 7 B1
15 Northleach GL54 168 A1
Winchcombe GL54 139 F4
Brook Ct
Cheltenham GL50 130 B6
Tewkesbury GL20 192 E5
Brook End SN14 47 F5
Brook Gate BS3 7 E1
Brook Hill BS6 18 F1
Brook Ho Bristol BS34 29 C8
8 Cheltenham GL51 129 F7
3 Thornbury BS35 51 C8
Brook La
1 Blockley GL56 186 C5
Bristol,Montpelier BS6 18 F1
Bristol,Stapleton BS16 19 E6
Down Hatherley GL2 173 B1
Brook Lintons BS4 9 D3
Brook Office Pk BS16 31 B2
Brook Rd
Bristol,Hillfields BS16 20 B4
Bristol,Mangotsfield BS16 20 F6
Bristol,Montpelier BS6 18 F1
Bristol,Southville BS3 8 D4
Bristol,Speedwell BS5 19 F1
Bristol,Warmley BS15 11 B8
Cheltenham GL51 133 A4
Brook St Bristol BS5 9 C7
Chipping Sodbury BS37 33 A8
Gloucester GL1 196 B1
Mitcheldean GL17 164 D5
Brook Vale GL52 131 A7
Brook Way BS32 29 D8
Brookbank Cl GL50 193 A4
Brookcote Dr BS34 29 D6
Brookdale Rd BS13 2 B6
Brooke Rd GL7 190 B2
Brookfield SN6 145 C3
Brookfield Ave BS7 18 D3
Brookfield Cl BS37 44 C2
Brookfield La
2 Bristol BS6 18 D2
Churchdown GL3 128 E5
Brookfield Rd
3 Bristol,Montpelier BS6 18 D2
Bristol,Patchway BS34 29 B8
Churchdown GL3 128 D5
Gloucester GL3 119 F7
Brookfield Wlk BS30 11 C3
Brookhouse Mill GL6 104 A7
Brookland Rd BS6 18 D5
Brooklands Pk GL2 127 D5
Brooklea BS30 11 B3
Brookleaze BS9 17 C5
Brooklet Rd GL15 147 B4
Brooklyn Cl 4 GL51 132 F3
Brooklyn Ct GL51 133 A4
Brooklyn Gdns GL51 133 A3
Brooklyn Rd Bristol BS13 2 B8
Cheltenham GL51 132 F2
Brookmead BS35 51 D7
Brookridge Ct 5 BS16 20 D4
Brookridge Ho BS10 27 F3
Brooksdale La GL53 130 C6
Brookside Alderton GL20 183 E4
Crudwell SN16 141 C3
4 Newent GL18 171 A4
Paxford GL55 186 E8
Pill BS20 16 D3
Tewkesbury GL20 192 E6
Tintern Parva NP16 146 B3
Brookside Cotts GL5 91 B5
Brookside Dr BS36 31 B8
Brookside Rd Bristol BS4 9 E2
Cinderford GL14 191 B5
Brookside Villas GL2 127 B2
Brookthorpe BS37 32 D8
Brookthorpe Ave BS11 27 A1
Brookthorpe Cl GL4 118 D3
Brookthorpe Ct BS37 32 D8
Brookview Wlk BS13 2 B7
Brookway Dr GL53 131 A6
Brookway Rd GL53 131 A6
Broom Bglws GL4 119 A5
Broom Hill Bristol BS16 19 E5
Coleford GL16 154 F7
Broom Hill Forest Trail★ GL16 154 F7
Broom Ho GL4 119 A5
Broomhill Inf Sch BS4 9 F3
Broomhill Jun Sch BS4 9 F3
Broomhill Rd BS4 10 A2
Brooms The BS16 31 A1
Brosnan Dr GL51 132 C1
Brotherswood Ct BS32 40 D4
Broughton Ho BS1 195 B1
Brown Cl GL51 132 E3
Brown's End Cotts HR8 179 C5
Brown's La GL10 98 A6
Brown's Piece GL12 68 B7
Browne Ct 5 BS8 7 F6
Browning Ct BS7 19 B8
Browning Mews GL51 129 F7
Browns Hill GL6 148 B5
Brownshill Rd GL6 148 B5
Broxholme Wlk BS11 16 F8
Bruce Ave BS5 19 C1
Bruce Rd BS5 19 C1
Brummels Dr GL16 155 A7
Brunel Cl BS30 11 C7
Brunel Ct BS37 43 C2
Brunel Lock Rd BS1 7 F5
Brunel Rd Bristol BS13 2 A8
Chepstow/Cas-Gwent NP16 60 E6
Brunel Way Bristol BS1,BS3 7 F4
Honeybourne WR11 188 C7
Brunel Way continued
Stonehouse GL10 101 C1
Thornbury BS35 51 B7
Brunswest Ct GL1 196 B2
Brunswick Pl 10 BS1 7 F5
Brunswick Rd GL1 196 B2
Brunswick Sq
Bristol BS2 195 B4
Gloucester GL1 196 B2
Brunswick St
Bristol,Redfield BS5 9 C7
Bristol,St Pauls BS2 195 B4
Cheltenham GL50 133 D3
Brush The GL5 98 D8
Bruton Cl BS5 9 F8
Bruton La GL12 67 F5
Bruton Pl BS8 194 B3
Bruton Way GL1 196 C3
Bryansons Cl BS16 19 D6
Bryant's Hill BS5 10 B6
Bryants Cl BS16 30 C1
Bryaston Cl GL51 133 A2
Bryerland Rd GL3 121 A4
Brymore Ave GL52 134 A5
Brymore Cl GL52 134 A5
Brynland Ave BS7 18 E4
Bryony Bank GL53 130 B4
Bryworth La GL7 153 C3
Buchan Ho 6 GL56 186 C5
Buchanan Ave GL16 155 A6
Buchanan Cl 2 GL16 155 A6
Buckholt Rd GL4 112 E8
Buckholt Way GL3 120 E5
Buckholt Wood Nature Reserve★ GL4 112 F7
Buckingham Ave GL51 132 F2
Buckingham Cl
Eastington GL10 96 E8
Tewkesbury GL20 192 E2
Buckingham Ct
Bristol BS32 40 D3
Cheltenham GL50 193 B3
Buckingham Dr
Bristol BS34 29 D5
2 Churchdown GL3 128 A7
Buckingham Gdns BS16 20 E6
Buckingham Ho BS34 28 F2
Buckingham Lodge BS31 4 F5
Buckingham Par BS35 64 B1
Buckingham Pl
Bristol,Mangotsfield BS16 20 E6
Bristol,Victoria Park BS8 194 A3
Buckingham Rd BS4 9 D5
Buckingham St BS3 8 C2
Buckingham Vale BS8 194 A4
Buckland Cl GL52 137 F3
Buckle St
Broadway WR12,GL54, GL56 185 D5
Honeybourne WR11 188 C8
Weston-s-E GL55 188 D4
Buckle Wood NP16 60 C8
Buckle's Row GL53 131 B5
Bucklehaven GL53 130 F5
Buckles Cl GL53 131 B5
Bucklewell Cl BS11 16 F6
Buckshaft Rd GL14 191 C1
Buckstone Cl GL16 155 B7
Budding Rd GL10 96 E8
Budding The GL5 103 E1
Buddleia Cl GL4 119 F4
Buddleia Ct 7 GL3 128 A7
Bude Ave BS5 10 A8
Bude Rd BS34 29 B4
Buildings The GL11 87 D3
Bull La Bristol BS5 9 F6
Gloucester GL1 196 B3
Pill BS20 16 C4
27 Winchcombe GL54 174 A7
Bull Pitch GL11 88 B1
Bull Ring The GL17 164 D5
Bullens Cl BS32 40 D2
Buller Rd BS4 9 C2
Bulley La Birdwood GL2 165 F6
Churcham GL2 124 C3
Bullfinch Rd GL4 119 C6
Bullfinch Way GL3 127 D7
Bullingham Ct GL51 133 C3
Bulls Cross GL6 104 B6
Bully La BS37 53 D1
Bulwark Ave NP16 60 F5
Bulwark Bsns Pk NP16 60 E6
Bulwark Rd NP16 60 E7
Bulwarks The GL6 148 A3
Bungalows The
Coleford GL16 155 B5
Lydney GL15 92 C2
Bunting Hill GL6 91 A4
Bunting Way GL6 90 F4
Burbank Cl BS30 11 A3
Burchells Ave BS15 20 B1
Burchells Green Cl BS15 20 B1
Burchells Green Rd BS15 20 B1
Burcombe GL7 158 B4
Burcombe Cl BS36 31 D6
Burcombe La GL7 158 A3
Burcombe Rd GL6 148 C6
Burcombe Way GL6 148 C6
Burcott Rd BS11 26 D5
Burden Cl BS32 29 F6
Burdett Cl GL10 97 F7
Burdett Ho 10 GL10 97 F7
Burdett Rd GL10 97 F7
Burfoot Rd BS14 3 E4
Burfoote Gdns BS14 3 E4
Burford Ave BS34 29 C8
Burford Dr GL5 99 A7
Burford Gr BS11 16 F5
Burford Mews GL1 119 A8
Burford St GL7 153 E2
Burgage 4 NP25 154 A8
Burgage Cl BS37 33 B8
Burgage The GL52 134 B5
Burge Ct GL7 190 D3
Burgess Green Cl BS4 9 E7
Burghill Rd BS10 28 A1
Burghley Ct BS36 30 E5
Burghley Rd BS6 18 E2
Burgis Rd BS14 3 D6
Burleigh Croft GL3 119 F8
Burleigh La GL5 91 F8
Burleigh Tor GL5 91 F7
Burleigh View 7 GL6 148 B6
Burleigh Way GL12 54 B5
Burley Ave BS16 20 F5
Burley Crest BS16 20 F5
Burley Gr BS16 20 F5
Burlington Ct 9 BS6 18 B2
Burlington Rd BS6 18 B2
Burltons The GL12 66 B2
Burma Ave GL52 134 B2
Burma Rd GL6 91 A4
Burnbush Cl BS14 3 E6
Burnbush Prim Sch BS14 3 D5
Burnell Dr BS2 195 C4
Burneside Cl BS10 28 C2
Burnet Cl GL4 119 A4
Burnett Bsns Pk BS31 5 B1
Burney Way BS30 11 A3
Burnham Cl BS15 20 F1
Burnham Dr BS15 20 F1
Burnham Rd BS11 16 D6
Burns Ave GL2 118 C4
Burnt Barn Rd NP16 60 F4
Burnt Oak GL11 88 A2
Burrington Wlk BS13 2 A8
Burrough Way BS36 30 E6
Burrups La HR9 170 B5
Burton Cl BS1 195 B1
Burton Ct
2 Bristol,Upper Eastville BS16 19 E3
Bristol,Victoria Park BS8 194 B3
Burton Farm Cl SN14 36 B3
Burton Rd GL9 35 F6
Burton St GL50 193 A4
Burtons Bank OX7 169 F7
Burwalls Rd BS8 7 E6
Bury Bar La GL18 171 A4
Bury Court Rd GL14 157 F6
Bury Hill BS36 30 F3
Bury Hill La BS37 44 A8
Bury Hill View BS16 30 E1
Bury La Doynton BS30 12 F7
Minsterworth GL2 116 E7
Burycourt Cl BS11 27 A1
Burytown La SN26 144 E1
Buscombe Gdns GL3 120 B7
Bush Ave BS34 29 D5
Bush Cl GL10 96 F8
Bush Ct Alveston BS32 50 F5
10 Bristol BS4 8 F4
Cheltenham GL52 134 B3
Bush Hay GL3 128 B5
Bush Ind Est BS5 9 D8
Bushcombe Cl GL52 138 C3
Bushcombe La GL52 138 D4
Bushes La BS37 45 A6
Bushy Beeches GL6 105 D7
Bushy Ho BS2 8 F3
Bushy Pk BS2 8 F3
Bushy Way GL51 132 D5
Business Park The BS13 2 E3
Bussage CE Prim Sch GL6 148 B6
Bussage Hill GL6 148 B6
Butcher Hill's La GL6 91 B3
Butcher Row Folk Mus★ HR8 178 F8
Butchers Row 9 WR12 185 B8
Butcombe Wlk BS14 3 B5
Bute Cl SN6 145 C4
Butler Ho BS5 9 F8
Butler's Field GL7 153 E3
Butlers Cl Bristol BS5 9 F7
Sherston SN16 58 C1
Butlers Mead GL15 156 E1
Butlers Wlk 3 BS5 9 F6
Butt Gn GL6 111 F1
Butt La BS35 64 C3
Butt St GL6 148 A3
Butt's La Dyrham SN14 24 B4
Woodmancote GL52 138 C4
Butt's Wlk GL51 129 C7
Buttercliffe Rise BS41 7 C3
Buttercross La GL52 134 D3
Buttercup Lawn GL4 119 D2
Butterfield Cl Bristol BS10 18 E7
Frampton Cotterell BS36 31 B6
Butterfield Rd BS10 18 E7
Buttermere Cl GL51 129 F6
Buttermilk La GL3 128 C6
Butterow W GL5 99 B5
Butterrow Hill GL5 99 C4
Butterrow La GL5 99 D4
Buttersend La GL19 171 F4
Butterworth Ct BS4 2 D7
Buttington GL4 119 F5
Buttington Hill NP16 61 B7
Buttington Rd NP16 61 A7
Buttington Terr NP16 61 B6
Button Cl BS14 3 A6
Button Mills Est GL10 97 E6
Butts Farm The★ GL7 151 B1
Butts La GL15 156 E2
Butts The Crudwell SN16 141 C3
Butts The continued
Gloucester GL4 119 A4
Newent GL18 171 A5
Poulton GL7 151 F3
Buxton Wlk BS7 19 A8
Byard Rd GL2 118 B5
Bybrook Gdns GL4 118 D1
Bybrook Rd GL4 118 D1
Bydemill Gdns SN6 145 C3
Bye Mead BS16 21 B8
Bye St HR8 178 E8
Byfield Cl GL52 138 C2
Byfords Cl GL19 165 D6
Byfords Rd GL19 165 D6
Byre Cl SN6 143 F4
Byres The GL56 187 D6
Byron Ave GL2 118 C4
Byron Cl GL20 192 E3
Byron Ct 17 GL52 133 F2
Byron Pl
Bristol,Brandon Hill BS8 194 B3
Bristol,Staple Hill BS16 20 E4
Byron Rd
Cheltenham GL51 132 F1
Dursley GL11 80 C7
Stroud GL5 99 A8
Byron St
Bristol,Moorfields BS5 9 C7
5 Bristol,St Pauls BS2 19 A1
Byzantine Ct BS1 195 A1

C

Cabot Cl Bristol BS15 10 C7
Saltford BS31 5 D2
Yate BS37 43 F1
Cabot Ct BS7 28 F1
Cabot Gn BS5 9 B7
Cabot Ho 6 BS35 51 C8
Cabot Pk BS11 26 E5
Cabot Prim Sch BS2 195 C4
Cabot Twr★ BS1 194 B2
Cabot Way Bristol BS8 7 F5
Pill BS20 16 D3
Cadbury Cl GL3 120 B6
Cadbury Heath Prim Sch BS30 11 B6
Cadbury Heath Rd BS30 11 B5
Cadbury Rd BS31 5 A2
Caddick Cl BS15 20 F2
Cade Cl
Bristol,Kingswood BS15 10 F6
Bristol,Stoke Gifford BS34 29 E5
Cadmium Rd BS11 26 C4
Cadogan Ho 18 GL52 133 F2
Cadogan Rd BS14 3 A8
Caen Rd BS3 8 D3
Caernarvon Cl GL51 129 E6
Caernarvon Ct GL51 129 D6
Caernarvon Rd
Cheltenham GL51 129 F6
Keynsham BS31 4 C4
Caerwent La NP16 60 F4
Caesar Rd GL2 118 C5
Caesars Cl GL15 92 C4
Caine Rd BS7 18 F7
Caine Sq GL51 132 C1
Cains Cl BS15 10 E6
Cainscross Rd GL5 98 F7
Cainscross Rdbt GL5 98 F7
Caird St NP16 60 E7
Cairn Gdns BS36 30 E4
Cairns Ct BS6 18 C4
Cairns Rd BS6 18 C4
Cairns' Cres 12 BS2 18 F1
Caitlin Ct BS14 3 D6
Cakebridge Pl GL52 133 F3
Cakebridge Rd GL52 133 F4
Cala Trad Est BS3 7 F3
Calcott Rd BS4 9 A3
Calcutt St SN6 143 F4
Caldbeck Cl BS10 28 D2
Calder Cl BS31 5 A4
Calderdale GL4 119 F5
Calderwood Ct GL50 193 B2
Caldicot Cl
Bristol,Lawrence Weston BS11 27 C2
Bristol,Willsbridge BS30 11 B2
Caledonia Mews BS8 7 F6
Caledonia Pl BS8 7 F7
Caledonian Rd
Bristol BS1 194 B1
Gloucester GL4 119 C2
Calf Way GL6 105 C5
Calf's La GL55 189 A2
California Rd BS30 11 B3
Callicroft Inf Sch BS34 28 F8
Callicroft Jun Sch BS34 28 F8
Callicroft Rd BS34 29 A7
Callington Rd BS4 9 D1
Callowell GL6 103 A1
Callowell Prim Sch GL5 103 A1
Callowhill Ct BS1 195 B3
Calspick Way GL2 127 D5
Calton Jun & Inf Schs GL1 118 E5
Calton Rd GL1 118 E6
Calverley Mews 1 GL51 129 E5
Cam & Dursley Sta GL10 96 A1
Cam Everlands Prim Sch GL11 88 A4
Cam Gn GL11 88 C5
Cam Hopton CE Prim Sch GL11 88 B4
Cam House Cotts GL11 88 C2

Cam House Sch GL11 ...88 C2
Cam Pitch GL11 ...87 F5
Cam Rd GL52 ...134 B3
Cam Woodfield Inf Sch GL11 ...87 E5
Cam Woodford Jun Sch GL11 ...87 E5
Camberley Cl GL3 ...120 A8
Camberley Dr BS36 ...30 F8
Camberley Rd BS4 ...2 D8
Camberwell Rd GL51 ...132 D2
Camborne Rd BS7 ...19 A7
Cambourne Pl GL15 ...92 B2
Cambray Ct
Cheltenham GL50 ...193 B3
Cirencester GL7 ...190 D4
Cambray Mews GL50 ...193 C3
Cambray Pl GL50 ...193 C3
Cambrian Dr BS37 ...43 E3
Cambrian Rd GL20 ...192 E2
Cambridge Ave
Cheltenham GL51 ...132 F1
Dursley GL11 ...80 B7
Cambridge Cres BS9 ...18 A7
Cambridge Pk BS6 ...18 B3
Cambridge Rd BS7 ...18 E4
Cambridge Sq GL20 ...183 E4
Cambridge St
8 Bristol,Redfield BS5 ...9 C7
Bristol,Windmill Hill BS3 ...8 F4
Gloucester GL1 ...196 C2
Cambridge Way GL6 ...91 F6
Camden Cl GL56 ...187 F3
Camden Rd BS3 ...194 B1
Camden Terr BS8 ...194 A2
Camelford Rd BS5 ...19 D1
Camellia Ct GL51 ...130 A5
Camellia Wlk GL2 ...117 E2
Cameron Ho GL50 ...130 A8
Cameron Wlk BS7 ...19 C6
Cameroons Cl BS31 ...4 E4
Camerton Cl BS31 ...5 E3
Camerton Rd BS5 ...19 D1
Camomile Cl 3 GL4 ...119 F5
Camomile Gn GL17 ...163 D2
Camp Gdns 1 GL54 ...176 F4
Camp La SN14 ...24 C4
Camp Rd Bristol BS8 ...7 F7
Cheltenham GL52 ...134 C1
Chepstow/Cas-Gwent NP16 60 F6
Oldbury-on-S BS35 ...63 B6
Camp View BS36 ...30 E4
Campbell Cl GL3 ...127 E7
Campbell Ct BS11 ...26 F1
Campbell Farm BS11 ...26 F1
Campbell Farm Dr BS11 .26 F1
Campbell Rd GL16 ...155 B6
Campbell St BS2 ...18 E1
Campden Ave CV36 ...189 E5
Campden Hill CV36 ...189 F6
Campden La
Hawling GL54 ...174 D5
Willersey WR12 ...188 C2
Campden Pitch CV36 ...189 F6
Campden Rd
Cheltenham GL51 ...129 E8
Chipping Campden GL55 .189 A4
Ebrington GL55 ...189 C3
Gloucester GL4 ...118 E3
Mickleton GL55 ...189 B8
Campian Wlk BS4 ...2 D6
Campion Cl
Gloucester GL4 ...119 B4
Thornbury BS35 ...64 D2
Campion Dr BS32 ...40 D2
Campion Pk GL51 ...130 A4
Cams Ground GL2 ...125 D6
Camwal Ind Est BS2 ...9 A5
Camwal Rd BS2 ...9 A5
Canada Way BS1 ...194 B1
Canal Ironworks GL5 ...99 E2
Canal Row GL2 ...108 A1
Canal Way GL2 ...126 B4
Canal Wlk HR8 ...178 E8
Canberra GL10 ...101 E1
Canberra Gr BS34 ...29 B4
Canberra Ho
Cheltenham GL51 ...132 E1
11 Coleford GL16 ...155 B5
Candy Ct BS4 ...9 D5
Canford La BS9 ...17 E8
Canford Rd BS9 ...17 F8
Cann La BS30 ...11 E6
Cannans Cl BS36 ...30 E7
Canning Rd GL2 ...127 E5
Cannon St
Bristol,Kingsdown BS1 ...195 A4
Bristol,Southville BS3 ...8 C4
Cannop Cotts GL16 ...155 D6
Cannop Rd GL15 ...155 E3
Cannop Valley Trail* GL16 ...155 E5
Cannop Villas GL16 ...155 D7
Canon Pk GL13 ...85 F4
Canon St BS5 ...9 C8
Canon's Rd BS1 ...194 C1
Canon's Wlk BS15 ...20 F2
Canonbury St GL13 ...85 F3
Canons Dr GL7 ...153 F2
Canons Rd BS1 ...194 C2
Canons Way BS1 ...194 C1
Canowie Rd BS6 ...18 B3
Cantell Gr BS14 ...3 F5
Canterbury Cl BS37 ...43 E3
Canterbury Ct BS16 ...19 E6
Canterbury Leys GL20 ...192 E5
Canterbury St 5 BS5 ...9 B6
Canterbury Wlk GL51 ...130 A6
Canters Leaze GL12 ...54 B4
Cantock's Cl BS8 ...194 C3
Canton Acre GL6 ...111 F1
Cantors Ct GL52 ...137 F2
Cantors Dr GL52 ...137 E2
Cantors Way SN16 ...142 E1
Canvey Cl BS10 ...18 E7
Canynge Ho 2 BS1 ...195 B1
Canynge Rd BS8 ...7 F8
Canynge Sq BS8 ...7 F8
Canynge St BS1 ...195 B2
Capel Cl BS15 ...11 B8
Capel Ct GL5 ...99 D8
Capel Rd Bristol BS11 ...27 B1
Gloucester GL4 ...119 C2
Capgrave Cl BS4 ...10 A3
Capgrave Cres BS4 ...10 A3
Capital Edge BS8 ...194 B2
Capital Pk GL2 ...118 B4
Capricorn Pl BS1 ...194 B2
Captain Barton Cl GL5 ...99 E8
Captains Green Rd GL15 ...156 A2
Caraway Gdns BS5 ...19 C2
Cardigan Mews BS9 ...18 B5
Cardigan Rd BS9 ...18 B6
Cardill Cl BS13 ...2 A8
Cares Cl GL52 ...138 A4
Carfax Ct BS6 ...18 A3
Carisbrook Rd GL17 ...164 D6
Carisbrooke Dr GL52 ...131 C6
Carisbrooke Lodge BS6 .18 A3
Carisbrooke Rd Bristol BS4 2 D7
Gloucester GL3 ...120 A7
Carlow Rd BS4 ...2 E8
Carlton Ct
1 Bristol,Ashley Down BS7 18 F4
3 Bristol,Eastfield BS9 ...18 A7
Carlton Gdns GL5 ...99 C6
Carlton Ho 2 BS9 ...18 A7
Carlton Pk BS5 ...9 C8
Carlton Pl GL50,GL51 ...133 C3
Carlton St GL52 ...133 F1
Carlyle Gr GL51 ...132 D4
Carlyle Rd BS5 ...19 C1
Carmarthen Cl BS37 ...43 F4
Carmarthen Gr BS30 ...11 B1
Carmarthen Rd
Bristol BS9 ...18 A5
Cheltenham GL51 ...129 E6
Carmarthen St 2 GL1 ...118 F7
Carnarvon Rd BS6 ...18 D2
Carne Pl GL4 ...127 C1
Carolina Ho BS2 ...195 A4
Caroline Cl
Chipping Sodbury BS37 ...44 B2
Keynsham BS31 ...4 C4
Carpenter Cotts GL16 ...154 F3
Carpenter's Shop La BS16 ...20 E6
Carpenters Cl SN16 ...58 D1
Carpenters La
Cirencester GL7 ...190 D4
Keynsham BS31 ...4 E5
Carr Ho 3 BS2 ...18 F1
Carrant Brook Jun Sch GL20 ...182 C5
Carrant Rd GL20 ...192 D5
Carriage Dr BS10 ...28 B2
Carrick Ho 8 BS8 ...7 F6
Carrington Rd BS3 ...8 A3
Carrol Gr GL51 ...132 D4
Carroll Ct BS16 ...29 E1
Carsons Rd BS16 ...21 B2
Cart La BS1 ...195 B2
Carter Rd GL51 ...132 F4
Carter Wlk BS32 ...29 D8
Carter's Bldgs 18 BS8 ...7 F7
Carters Leaze CV36 ...187 E5
Carters Orch GL2 ...117 F2
Carters Way GL6 ...90 F5
Cartledge Rd 6 BS5 ...19 C1
Cartway Gn GL14 ...191 C4
Carwardine Field GL4 ...119 E6
Cary Ct 2 BS2 ...18 F1
Casey Cl GL1 ...127 B1
Cash Hill GL17 ...163 E4
Cashes Green Prim Sch GL5 ...98 D8
Cashes Green Rd GL5 ...98 E7
Cashmore Ho 9 BS5 ...9 B7
Casino Pl GL50 ...193 A1
Caslon Ct BS1 ...195 B1
Cassell Rd BS16 ...20 C5
Cassey Bottom La BS5 ...10 A7
Cassey Compton GL54 ...166 F2
Cassin Dr GL51 ...132 E2
Casson Dr BS16 ...19 E8
Castle Cl Bristol BS10 ...27 E2
Painswick GL6 ...103 F7
Castle Coombe BS35 ...64 C1
Castle Cotts
Gloucester GL3 ...119 F8
Marshfield SN14 ...24 E2
Castle Cres GL15 ...146 F7
Castle Ct Bristol BS34 ...30 A4
Bristol,Arno's Vale BS4 ...9 C4
20 Stroud GL5 ...99 C7
Thornbury BS35 ...64 B1
Castle End GL6 ...111 E5
Castle Farm Cl GL8 ...70 C3
Castle Farm La BS41 ...1 B2
Castle Farm Rd BS15 ...10 C2
Castle Gdns
Chepstow/Cas-Gwent NP16 72 D1
Chipping Campden GL55 ..189 B2
Castle Hill Dr GL3 ...120 F4
Castle Hill Prim Sch GL3 ...120 E4
Castle La Goodrich HR9 ..163 A6
Marshfield SN14 ...24 E2
Moreton Valence GL2 ...108 E2
Castle Mead GL10 ...97 F3
Castle Nurseries GL55 ..189 B2
Castle Pitch GL5 ...99 C6
Castle Prim Sch BS31 ...4 D4
Castle Rd
Bristol,Kingswood BS15 ..20 D2
Bristol,Oldland Common BS30 ...11 D3
Pucklechurch BS16 ...22 C6
Castle Rise GL5 ...99 C6
Castle Sch Sixth Form Ctr The BS35 ...64 B1
Castle Sch The BS35 ...64 B2
Castle St Bristol BS1 ...195 B3
Cirencester GL7 ...190 C4
Dursley GL11 ...88 B1
King's Stanley GL10 ...98 A3
Stroud GL5 ...99 C6
Thornbury BS35 ...64 B1
Winchcombe GL54 ...174 A7
Castle The GL5 ...99 C6
Castle View NP16 ...73 A1
Castle Villas 19 GL5 ...99 C7
Castle Wood/Coed Castell NP16 ...60 C8
Castlefields Ave GL52 ..131 C6
Castlefields Dr GL52 ..131 C6
Castlefields Rd GL52 ..131 C6
Castleford Gdns NP16 ...72 F2
Castleford Hill NP16 ...72 E2
Castlegate Ho BS4 ...9 E3
Castlemaine Dr GL51 ..129 C8
Castlemead Rd GL5 ...99 B6
Castlemeads Ct GL1 ...196 A3
Castleton Rd GL4 ...119 D8
Castlett St GL54 ...175 B3
Caswell Ct GL11 ...80 D8
Caswell Mews GL11 ...80 D8
Catbrain Hill BS10 ...28 B6
Catbrain La BS10 ...28 B6
Catbrook Cl GL55 ...189 A1
Catbrook Gdns GL55 ...189 A1
Catchmays Ct NP16, NP25 ...146 C5
Catchpot La BS37 ...34 A6
Cater Rd BS13 ...2 B6
Cathedral Church of St Peter & the Holy Family* GL1 ...196 B3
Catherine Ct 14 BS6 ...18 E1
Catherine Hill BS35 ...49 F2
Catherine Mead St BS3 ...8 D4
Catherine St BS11 ...16 C8
Catherine's Cl GL5 ...99 E7
Catholic Sch of St Gregory the Great The GL50 ...193 A4
Catkin Cl GL2 ...109 E7
Catley Gr BS41 ...7 B2
Cato St BS5 ...19 B2
Catswood Ct GL5 ...103 E1
Catswood La GL6 ...104 D3
Cattistock Dr BS5 ...10 A6
Cattle Market Rd BS1 ..195 C1
Cattybrook Rd N BS16 ..21 D5
Cattybrook St
7 Bristol BS5 ...9 B7
23 Bristol BS5 ...9 B8
Caudle Cl GL17 ...163 E4
Caudle La GL17 ...163 E4
Causeway Rd GL14 ...191 E5
Causeway The
Coalpit Heath BS36 ...31 D7
3 Quedgeley GL2 ...117 D1
Redmarley D'Abitot GL19 .179 D2
Causley Dr BS30 ...11 A5
Cavan Wlk BS4 ...8 D1
Cave Cl BS16 ...20 D6
Cave Ct BS2 ...195 B4
Cave Dr BS16 ...20 D6
Cave Gr BS16 ...21 B7
Cave St BS2 ...195 B4
Cavendish Ave GL3 ...128 D5
Cavendish Bldgs 3 GL15 92 A3
Cavendish Cl Saltford BS31 5 D2
Tormarton GL9 ...34 E2
Cavendish Gdns BS9 ...17 C4
Cavendish Rd
Bristol,Henleaze BS9 ...18 A5
Bristol,Patchway BS34 ...28 F8
Caves Cotts BS16 ...20 E7
Cecil Ave BS5 ...19 F1
Cecil Rd Bristol,Clifton BS8 ..7 F8
Bristol,Kingswood BS15 ...10 D8
Gloucester GL1 ...118 D6
Cecily Ct GL6 ...148 A3
Cecily Hill GL7 ...190 B5
Cedar Cl
Bristol,Oldland BS30 ...11 B4
Bristol,Patchway BS34 ...28 F7
Charlton Kings GL53 ...131 B5
Chepstow/Cas-Gwent NP16 60 E5
Down Ampney GL7 ...143 E8
Stroud GL5 ...98 D6
Cedar Court Rd GL53 ...193 B2
Cedar Ct
Bristol,Coombe Dingle BS9 .17 D7
Bristol,Mangotsfield BS16 ..20 E6
Bristol,Sneyd Park BS9 ...17 C4
Bristol,Westbury on Trym BS9 ...17 F8
Ledbury HR8 ...178 F8
Cedar Dr Dursley GL11 ...88 A1
Keynsham BS31 ...4 D4
Cedar Gdns GL10 ...97 F8
Cedar Gr Bristol BS9 ...17 D5
Walford HR9 ...163 C8
4 Winchcombe GL54 ...174 A7
Cedar Hall BS16 ...20 C8
Cedar Pk BS9 ...17 D5
Cedar Rd
Brockworth GL3 ...120 D7
Mickleton GL55 ...189 B6
Northway GL20 ...182 C4
Cedar Row BS11 ...16 F6
Cedar Way Mile End GL16 155 B6
Pucklechurch BS16 ...22 C5
Winterbourne BS36 ...30 D5
Cedardean GL14 ...191 C5
Cedars The
Gloucester GL3 ...120 A8
Wotton-u-E GL12 ...68 C8
Cedarwood Dr GL4 ...118 E3
Celandine Bank GL52 ...138 B4
Celandine Cl BS35 ...64 D2
Celandine Ct NP16 ...60 F5
Celestine Rd BS37 ...43 C3
Celia Terr BS4 ...9 F6
Cemetery La Bibury GL7 .160 A1
Bourton-on-t-W GL54 ...169 A7
Cemetery Rd Bristol BS4 ..9 A3
Gloucester GL4 ...119 A6
Cennick Ave BS15 ...20 E1
Centaurus Rd BS34 ...28 D7
Central Ave Bristol BS15 ..10 C5
Mitcheldean GL17 ...164 D5
Severn Beach BS10 ...38 A3
Central Cross Dr GL50, GL52 ...133 E3
Central Pk BS14 ...3 B7
Central Rd
Gloucester GL1 ...118 E7
Stroud GL5 ...98 F7
Central Tech Coll GL4 ..119 B5
Central Trad Est BS4 ...9 B4
Central Way Bristol BS10 .18 E8
Cheltenham GL51 ...133 B3
Centre for Science & Art* GL5 ...99 C7
Centre The BS31 ...4 F5
Centurion Cl 1 GL4 ...119 E6
Centurion Rd GL15 ...92 B4
Centurions Wlk 20 GL16 155 A5
Century Cl GL7 ...190 F5
Century Ct GL50 ...193 B2
Ceres Cl BS30 ...10 F2
Cerimon Gate BS34 ...29 E5
Cerney House Gdns* GL7 ...158 C2
Cerney La BS11 ...16 E5
Cerney Wick La GL7 ...143 C7
Cesson Cl BS37 ...33 C8
Ceylon Ho GL51 ...132 F4
Chaceley Cl
Gloucester GL4 ...119 E5
Quedgeley GL2 ...109 E8
Chad Rd GL51 ...132 F1
Chadbournes GL3 ...128 B6
Chadleigh Gr BS4 ...2 D7
Chadwick Cl GL4 ...118 D2
Chaffinch Cl GL3 ...127 D7
Chaffinch Ct 5 GL10 ...97 F8
Chaingate La BS37 ...43 A6
Chakeshill Cl BS10 ...28 C3
Chakeshill Dr BS10 ...28 C4
Chalcombe Cl BS34 ...29 C8
Chalcroft Ho 2 BS3 ...8 A4
Chalcroft Wlk BS13 ...1 E4
Chalet The BS10 ...27 F3
Chalfield Cl BS31 ...5 A2
Chalford Ave GL51 ...129 B7
Chalford Cl BS37 ...32 D8
Chalford Hill Prim Sch GL6 ...148 C5
Chalford Ind Est GL6 ...148 C5
Chalford Rd GL4 ...118 E1
Chalks Rd BS5 ...9 D8
Challender Ave BS10 ...27 F2
Challoner Ct BS1 ...195 A1
Chamberlayne Cl 29 GL54 ...176 F4
Chamberlayne Ho 28 GL54 ...176 F4
Chambon Cl SN16 ...142 D1
Champion Rd BS15 ...21 A2
Champions Ct GL11 ...80 B8
Champneys Ave BS10 ...27 F3
Champs Sur Marne BS32 29 E8
Chamwells Ave GL2 ...127 B4
Chamwells Wlk GL2 ...127 B4
Chance St GL20 ...192 D4
Chancel Cl Bristol BS9 ...17 D3
Gloucester GL4 ...127 C1
Chancel Pk GL53 ...130 F6
Chancel Way
Charlton Kings GL53 ...131 A6
Lechlade on T GL7 ...153 E2
Chancery St BS5 ...9 B7
Chandag Inf Sch BS31 ...5 A4
Chandag Jun Sch BS31 ...5 A4
Chandag Rd BS31 ...5 A4
Chandler Rd GL52 ...137 F2
Chandos BS6 ...18 C2
Chandos Almshouses 22 GL54 ...174 A7
Chandos Dr GL3 ...120 E6
Chandos Rd Bristol BS6 ...18 C1
Keynsham BS31 ...4 E7
Stroud GL5 ...99 A4
Chandos St 26 GL54 ...174 A7
Chandos Trad Est BS2 ...9 A5
Change The GL6 ...102 D1
Channel View NP16 ...60 E5
Channell's Hill BS9 ...18 A8
Channon's Hill BS16 ...19 F4
Chantry Cl
Cirencester GL7 ...190 C5
Lydney GL15 ...92 A1
Chantry Ct Bristol BS1 ...194 C2
Tetbury GL8 ...140 C4
Chantry Gate GL52 ...137 E2
Chantry Gdns GL56 ...186 D3
Chantry Gr BS11 ...27 C2
Chantry La BS16 ...30 F1
Chantry Rd Bristol BS8 ...18 B1
Thornbury BS35 ...64 B2
Chapel Apartments 13 GL16 ...155 A5
Chapel Barton 7 BS3 ...8 B2
Chapel Bglws HR9 ...170 B4
Chapel Cl Bristol BS15 ...11 B8
Chepstow/Cas-Gwent NP16 60 B5
Kempsford GL7 ...144 E8
Monmouth/Trefynwy NP25 ...154 A7
Tarlton GL7 ...149 C2
Chapel Cotts GL54 ...174 B1
Chapel Ct
Bristol,Brentry BS10 ...28 D3
Bristol,St Philip's Marsh BS2 .9 A5
Dursley GL11 ...87 D4
Chapel Gdns Bristol BS10 .28 A1
Hardwicke GL2 ...109 F7
Chapel Green La BS6 ...18 B2
Chapel Hay Cl GL3 ...128 C4
Chapel Hay La GL3 ...128 D4
Chapel Hill
Aylburton GL15 ...147 E4
Broad Blunsdon SN26 ...144 D1
English Bicknor GL16 ...163 A1
Newport GL13 ...78 B7
Chapel Ho 11 GL20 ...192 C4
Chapel La
Acton Turville GL9 ...36 A6
Birdwood GL2 ...165 F5
Blockley GL56 ...186 C5
Bristol,Clay Hill BS5 ...19 E2
Bristol,Fishponds BS16 ...20 A4
Bristol,Frenchay BS16 ...20 C7
Bristol,Lawrence Weston BS11 ...27 C2
Bristol,Warmley BS15 ...11 B8
Cheltenham GL50 ...193 B1
Chepstow/Cas-Gwent NP16 60 B5
Chipping Sodbury BS37 ...34 A7
Cold Aston GL54 ...168 B6
Gorsley HR9 ...170 B4
Hankerton SN16 ...141 E1
Hillesley GL12 ...55 E8
Hinton SN14 ...23 C5
Kinsham GL20 ...182 D6
Longhope GL17 ...165 B5
Mickleton GL55 ...189 A6
Minchinhampton GL6 ...148 A3
Minety SN16 ...142 D1
North Cerney GL7 ...158 D3
Staunton GL19 ...171 E8
Stroud GL5 ...98 D6
Thornbury BS35 ...65 A1
Westmancote GL20 ...182 D8
Weston-s-E GL55 ...188 D3
Woodmancote GL52 ...138 C3
Chapel Orch BS37 ...43 C2
Chapel Pill La BS20 ...16 E4
Chapel Pitch GL18 ...170 D2
Chapel Rd
Berry Hill GL16 ...155 A7
Bristol,Bishopsworth BS13 ..2 A6
Bristol,Hanham BS15 ...10 C5
2 Bristol,Lower Easton BS5 ...19 B1
Kempsford GL7 ...144 E8
Oldbury-on-S BS35 ...63 C5
Viney Hill GL15 ...156 C1
Chapel Row
4 Blockley GL56 ...186 C5
Little Compton GL56 ...187 F1
Luckington SN14 ...47 E4
Pill BS20 ...16 C4
4 Stonehouse GL10 ...97 F7
Chapel St
Bledington OX7 ...177 E1
Bristol BS2 ...9 A5
Broadwell GL56 ...177 A6
Cheltenham GL50 ...193 B4
Dursley GL11 ...88 A5
5 Stow-on-t-W GL54 ...176 F4
Stroud GL5 ...99 D7
Thornbury BS35 ...51 B8
Chapel Way BS4 ...9 E6
Chapel Wlk
Cheltenham GL50 ...193 B3
Didmarton GL9 ...57 B3
Edge End GL16 ...155 C8
Chapelfields HR9 ...162 B6
Chaplin Rd BS5 ...19 B1
Chapman Way GL51 ...129 F7
Chapman's Cross GL6 ...149 A4
Chapter St BS2 ...195 B4
Chapter Wlk BS6 ...18 B3
Charbon Gate BS34 ...29 F5
Charborough Ct
Bristol BS34 ...28 F2
Bristol BS34 ...29 A2
Charborough Rd BS34 ...28 F2
Charborough Road Prim Sch BS34 ...28 F2

Charbury Wlk BS11 16 E5
Chard Ct BS14 3 B6
Chardstock Ave BS9 17 D8
Chardwar Gdns 7 GL54 168 F7
Charfield 4 BS15 11 A8
Charfield Prim Sch GL12 66 F5
Charfield Rd Bristol BS10 28 D1
Kingswood GL12 67 E5
Chargrove 2 Bristol BS30 11 C6
Yate BS37 32 D7
Chargrove La GL51 129 E4
Charis Ave BS10 18 C7
Charlecombe Ct BS9 17 F6
Charlecombe Rd BS9 17 F6
Charlecote Ave GL4 110 C8
Charlecote Cnr GL52 137 E3
Charles Ave BS34 29 E4
Charles Cl
Tewkesbury GL20 192 E2
Thornbury BS35 64 C3
Charles Ct BS8 194 A2
Charles England Ho
BS34 28 F7
Charles Pl BS8 194 A2
Charles Rd BS34 29 B3
Charles St Bristol BS1 195 A4
Cheltenham GL51 133 C3
Gloucester GL1 196 C2
Charles Wesley Cl BS5 10 A6
Charlesway GL56 176 E8
Charleswood Rd GL15 155 F1
Charleton Ho 9 BS2 195 C3
Charlham La GL7 143 E8
Charlham Way GL7 143 E8
Charlock Cl GL4 119 A4
Charlotte Rose Ho 3
GL50 133 B1
Charlotte St
Bristol,Brandon Hill BS1 194 C3
Bristol,St Pauls BS2 195 C4
Charlotte St S BS1 194 C2
Charlton Ave BS34 28 F2
Charlton Cl GL53 131 A5
Charlton Court Rd GL52 131 A7
Charlton Ct Bristol BS34 39 F1
Gloucester GL1 196 C3
Charlton Down Cotts
GL8 71 E4
Charlton Dr GL53 130 F7
Charlton Gdns BS10 28 D4
Charlton Kings Inf Sch
GL52 131 B6
Charlton Kings Jun Sch
GL53 131 B5
Charlton La Bristol BS10 28 A3
Cheltenham GL53 130 D5
Charlton Lane Ctr Hospl
GL53 130 E5
Charlton Lawn GL53 131 A7
Charlton Mead Ct BS10 28 D4
Charlton Mead Dr BS10 28 D3
Charlton Park Dr GL53 130 F7
Charlton Park Gate
GL53 130 F6
Charlton Pk BS31 4 D5
Charlton Pl BS10 28 D4
Charlton Rd
Bristol,Brentry BS10 28 C3
Bristol,Kingswood BS15 20 B1
Keynsham BS31,BS14 4 C3
Tetbury GL8 140 B4
Charlton St 17 BS5 9 B7
Charlton Terr 7 GL56 187 B3
Charlton Way GL2 127 C5
Charminster Rd BS16 20 B3
Charmouth Ct BS3 8 D1
Charnell Rd BS16 20 E4
Charnhill Brow BS16 21 A4
Charnhill Cres BS16 20 F4
Charnhill Dr BS16 20 F4
Charnhill Ridge BS16 21 A4
Charnhill Vale BS16 20 F4
Charnwood BS16 21 A4
Charnwood Cl GL53 130 D5
Charnwood Ct GL15 92 B5
Charnwood Rd Bristol BS14 3 B4
Cheltenham GL53 130 D5
Charter Ct GL1 196 C1
Charter Ho BS1 194 B2
Charter Wlk BS14 3 A6
Charterhouse Rd BS5 9 D8
Chartford Ho BS8 7 F8
Chartist La GL19 179 F2
Chartist Piece GL19 172 B8
Chartist Way GL19 172 A8
Chartists Way NP16 60 E5
Chartley BS9 17 D2
Chartwell Cl GL2 118 A6
Chase Ave GL52 131 C6
Chase La Gloucester GL4 119 B7
Wickwar GL12 54 C6
Chase Rd BS15 20 D2
Chase The Bristol BS16 20 C3
Churchdown GL3 128 D4
Gloucester GL4 119 D5
Stroud GL5 98 E7
Chasefield La 1 BS16 20 B4
Chasely Cres 6 GL51 129 E5
Chasewood Cnr 3 GL6 148 B6
Chatcombe BS37 32 E7
Chatcombe Cl GL53 131 B4
Chatcombe Ho GL4 119 B5
Chatcombe Rd GL4 119 B5
Chatsworth Ave GL4 118 C1
Chatsworth Dr GL53 130 D4
Chatsworth Pk BS35 64 C3
Chatsworth Rd
Bristol,Arno's Vale BS4 9 C4
Bristol,Hillfields BS16 20 B3
Chattenden Ho BS9 17 E3
Chatterton Gn BS14 2 F3
Chatterton Ho 5 BS1 195 B1
Chatterton Rd BS37 43 D1
Chatterton Sq BS1 195 C1
Chatterton St BS1 195 C1
Chaucer Cl GL1 118 D5
Chaucer Rd GL11 80 C7
Chaundey Gr BS13 2 B5
Chavenage BS15 21 A1
Chavenage Ho* GL8 140 A6
Chavenage La GL8 140 B4
Cheap St GL54 159 A6
Cheapside Bristol BS2 195 C4
Stroud GL5 99 B7
Cheapside St 8 BS3 8 F4
Cheddar Gr BS13 2 A8
Cheddar Grove Prim Sch
BS13 2 A8
Chedworth Bristol BS15 20 F3
19 Newent GL18 171 A4
Yate BS37 32 B7
Chedworth Rd Bristol BS7 19 A6
Gloucester GL4 118 E3
Chedworth Roman Villas
(rems of)* GL54 159 A8
Chedworth Way GL51 129 E8
Cheese La BS2 195 B2
Chelbury Mews 1 GL52 134 A3
Chelford Gr BS34 29 B8
Chelmer Gr BS31 4 F4
Chelmsford Ave GL51 130 A5
Chelmsford Wlk BS4 9 F5
Chelsea Cl
Cheltenham GL53 130 F7
Keynsham BS31 5 A5
Chelsea Pk BS5 9 C8
Chelsea Rd BS5 19 B1
Chelston Rd BS4 2 D7
Chelt Rd GL52 134 B3
Cheltenham & Gloucester
Nuffield Hospl The
GL51 129 C7
Cheltenham Bournside Sch &
Sixth Form Ctr GL51 130 A6
Cheltenham Coll GL53 193 B1
Cheltenham Coll Jun Sch
GL53 193 B1
Cheltenham Cres 2 BS6 18 D1
Cheltenham General Hospl
GL53 193 C2
Cheltenham Kingsmead
GL51 132 F4
Cheltenham La BS6 18 D2
Cheltenham Ladies' Coll The
GL50 193 B3
Cheltenham Mus & Art Gal*
GL50 193 B4
Cheltenham Race Course*
GL50,GL52 134 A6
Cheltenham Racecourse Hall
of Fame* GL50 133 F6
Cheltenham Racecourse
Sta* GL50 133 E7
Cheltenham Rd
Beckford GL20 183 B6
Bishop's Cleeve GL52 137 F3
Bisley GL6 105 A1
Bredon GL20 182 D7
Bristol BS6 18 E1
Broadway WR12 185 A8
Gloucester GL2 127 D3
Painswick GL6 112 A2
Pitchcombe GL6 103 C4
Stratton GL7 150 D7
Winchcombe GL54 139 F4
Cheltenham Rd E GL3 128 A7
Cheltenham Spa Sta
GL51 133 A1
Cheltenham Trade Pk
GL51 133 B3
Chelvy Cl BS13 2 D3
Chelwood Rd Bristol BS11 16 D7
Saltford BS31 5 E4
Chelworth Ind Est SN6 143 D3
Chelworth Rd SN6 143 E3
Chepstow Bulwark*
NP16 60 F6
Chepstow Castle* NP16 72 E1
Chepstow Com Hospl
NP16 60 D8
Chepstow Comp Sch
NP16 72 D2
Chepstow Ho 13 GL51 132 E2
Chepstow Mus* NP16 72 F1
Chepstow Pk BS16 30 F1
Chepstow Race Course*
NP16 72 C3
Chepstow Rd BS4 2 D8
Chepstow Sta NP16 60 F8
Chepstow Wlk BS31 4 D5
Chequers Cl BS30 11 C3
Chequers Ct BS34 30 A6
Chequers Rd GL4 119 B7
Cherington Bristol BS15 10 B5
Yate BS37 32 D6
Cherington Rd BS10 18 D7
Cheriton Cl GL51 129 F5
Cheriton Pl
Bristol,Eastfield BS9 18 B7
Bristol,Warmley BS30 11 C6
Cherrington Dr GL4 119 E5
Cherry Ave GL53 131 C4
Cherry Bank GL18 171 A4
Cherry Blossom Cl GL52 137 F5
Cherry Cl GL2 109 E7
Cherry Ct BS1 195 A4
Cherry Garden La BS30 11 B2
Cherry Garden Prim Sch
BS30 11 C2
Cherry Garden Rd BS30 11 C1
Cherry Gdns Bristol BS30 11 C1
Gloucester GL3 120 A8
Cherry Gr BS16 21 A6
Cherry La 4 BS1 195 B4
Cherry Orch
Bredon GL20 182 C7
Highworth SN6 145 D3
Wotton-u-E GL12 68 C7
Cherry Orch The GL51 173 F2
Cherry Orchard Cl GL55 189 A1
Cherry Orchard La
4 Bristol BS5 9 F8
Luckington SN14 47 C5
Twyning GL20 181 F7
Cherry Orchard Rd 6
GL8 140 C4
Cherry Rd BS37 44 A1
Cherry Tree Cl
Bristol BS16 20 C2
Churchdown GL3 128 A7
Keynsham BS31 4 C4
Nailsworth GL6 91 A4
Cherry Tree Ct 14 GL4 119 C4
Cherry Tree La GL16 155 C6
Cherry Tree Rd 12 SN6 143 E4
Cherry Wlk GL15 92 A4
Cherry Wood BS30 11 B2
Cherrytree Cres BS16 20 C2
Cherrytree Ct BS16 22 C5
Cherrytree La GL7 150 F5
Cherrytree Rd BS16 20 C2
Cherrywood Gdns GL4 118 E3
Cherston Ct GL4 119 E8
Chertsey Rd BS6 18 B1
Chervil Cl GL4 119 B4
Cherwell Cl BS35 51 C7
Cherwell Rd BS31 5 A4
Chesford Dr GL3 128 C6
Chesham Way BS15 20 D1
Cheshire Cl BS37 43 E3
Cheshire Rd GL3 127 E6
Chesils The GL54 174 A8
Chesley Hill BS30 11 F7
Chesmann Ct GL1 126 F4
Chessel Cl BS32 40 C2
Chessel Ct 6 BS3 8 B2
Chessel St BS3 8 B3
Chessell Ave BS35 38 C7
Chessgrove La GL17 164 F6
Chessington Ave BS14 3 B5
Chestal GL11 88 B1
Chester Cl GL19 173 C7
Chester Cres GL7 190 D4
Chester Ct 4 BS5 9 C7
Chester Ho GL50 193 B3
Chester Park Jun & Inf Schs
BS16 20 A3
Chester Park Rd BS16 20 B2
Chester Pk BS5 19 E1
Chester Rd Bristol BS5 19 E1
Gloucester GL4 119 C8
Chester St Bristol BS5 19 B2
Cirencester GL7 190 D4
Chester Wlk GL50 193 B4
Chesterfield Ave BS6 18 E2
Chesterfield Bldgs BS8 194 B3
Chesterfield Ho BS10 27 F1
Chesterfield Hospl BS8 194 A2
Chesterfield Rd
Bristol,Mangotsfield BS16 20 E5
Bristol,Montpelier BS6 18 E2
Chestermaster Cl BS32 40 A5
Chesters BS30 11 A4
Chesterton Ct GL2 126 F6
Chesterton Gr GL7 190 C3
Chesterton Ho
6 Bristol BS2 195 B4
Cirencester GL7 190 C3
Chesterton La GL7 190 C3
Chesterton Link GL7 190 D3
Chesterton Pk GL7 190 B4
Chesterton Prim Sch
GL7 190 C2
Chestnut Ave GL10 97 F8
Chestnut Cl
Acton Turville GL9 36 A6
Bristol BS14 3 F5
Down Ampney GL7 143 E8
Hardwicke GL2 109 E7
15 Ledbury HR8 178 E8
2 Mile End GL16 155 B6
Nailsworth GL6 91 B4
6 Tetbury GL8 140 B4
Chestnut Cnr WR12 184 E5
Chestnut Cotts GL2 125 D5
Chestnut Ct
Bristol,Bishopsworth BS13 2 A7
Bristol,Hillhouse BS16 21 A5
10 Monmouth/Trefynwy
NP25 154 A7
Chestnut Dr
Chipping Sodbury BS37 44 A1
Thornbury BS35 64 C1
Chestnut Hill GL6 91 B4
Chestnut Ho
Bristol,Hartcliffe BS13 2 D3
7 Bristol,Staple Hill BS16 20 D4
Cheltenham GL50 193 A3
Chestnut La GL5 98 F7
Chestnut Park Est GL12 67 F4
Chestnut Pl GL53 130 B4
Chestnut Rd
Bristol,Lower Soundwell
BS15 20 F3
Bristol,Mangotsfield BS16 20 D6
Gloucester GL4 119 E5
Long Ashton BS41 7 B2
Chestnut Terr
Charlton Kings GL53 131 A5
7 Monmouth/Trefynwy
NP25 154 A7
Chestnut Way BS15 20 F3
Chestnut Wlk Bristol BS13 2 A6
Saltford BS31 5 E3
Chestnuts The
Bussage GL6 148 B6
Gloucester GL1 196 A1
Chetwode Cl BS10 28 D3
Chetwood Ho BS5 9 C6
Chevening Cl BS34 29 D4
Cheviot Cl Quedgeley GL2 109 E8
1 Tetbury GL8 140 C5
Cheviot Dr BS35 51 E8
Cheviot Rd GL52 134 B4
Cheviot Way BS30 11 C5
Chew Cotts BS31 4 F5
Chewton Cl BS16 20 B3
Chewton Rd BS31 4 F2
Cheyne Rd BS9 17 D6
Cheyney Cl GL4 119 B6
Chichester Ho BS4 9 F6
Chichester Way BS37 43 D3
Chicknalls La GL15 156 F3
Childer Rd HR8 178 D8
Childswickham Rd
WR12 185 A8
Chillingworth Mews
GL1 196 B2
Chillwood Cl BS37 42 E3
Chiltern Ave GL52 137 E4
Chiltern Cl
Bristol,Warmley BS30 11 C5
Bristol,Whitchurch BS14 3 B4
Chiltern Pk BS35 51 E8
Chiltern Rd
Cheltenham GL52 134 B3
Quedgeley GL2 109 E8
Chilton Rd BS4 3 A8
Chilwood Cl BS37 42 E3
China Cnr WR11 188 C6
Chine The BS16 19 D5
Chine View BS16 20 F8
Chiphouse Rd BS15 20 F3
Chipmans Platt GL10 101 A1
Chippenham Rd SN14 15 A8
Chipperfield Dr BS15 20 F1
Chipping Campden Bsns Pk
GL55 189 B2
Chipping Campden Sch
GL55 189 A2
Chipping Cl GL12 68 B7
Chipping Ct 12 GL8 140 C4
Chipping Edge Est BS37 44 C1
Chipping Gdns 6 GL12 68 B7
Chipping Sodbury Sch
BS37 33 B8
Chipping St GL8 140 C4
Chipping The GL12 67 F4
Chippings The BS16 19 D5
Chisbury St BS5 19 C3
Chislet Way GL4 118 D1
Chittening Ind Est BS11 26 E8
Chittening Rd BS11 26 E7
Chock La BS9 18 A7
Choirs Cl GL4 119 E6
Chosen Dr GL3 128 B5
Chosen Hill Sch GL3 128 E5
Chosen View Rd GL51 133 B5
Chosen Way GL3 119 F8
Christ Church CE Inf Sch
BS16 20 D5
Christ Church CE Prim Sch
Bristol,Victoria Park BS8 194 A3
Chalford GL6 148 C5
Cheltenham GL50 133 B1
Christ Church Hanham CE
Prim Sch BS15 10 B4
Christ Church Jun Sch
BS16 20 D5
Christ Church Rd GL50 130 B8
Christ Church Terr 8
GL50 133 B1
Christ Church Villas 7
GL50 133 B1
Christ the King RC Prim Sch
Bristol BS4 2 E8
Thornbury BS35 64 D1
Christchurch Ave BS16 20 D5
Christchurch Ct 4
GL50 130 B8
Christchurch La BS16 20 D5
Christchurch Rd BS8 194 A3
Christina Terr BS8 194 A1
Christmas St BS1 195 A3
Christmas Stps BS1 195 A3
Christmas Tree BS34 28 D6
Christowe La GL53 193 C1
Chubb Cl BS30 10 F5
Chuch Wlk GL12 68 C7
Church Ave
Bristol,Sneyd Park BS9 17 E4
3 Bristol,Upper Easton
BS5 19 B1
Bristol,Warmley BS30 11 D7
Falfield GL12 65 E7
Siddington GL7 190 E1
Church Cl Bristol BS10 27 E2
Broadway WR12 185 B8
Cranham GL4 112 E5
Church Cl *continued*
Ebrington GL55 189 D3
Frampton Cotterell BS36 31 B8
Longborough GL56 176 D8
Church Cotts 13 GL55 189 A2
Church Ct 9 BS16 20 D3
Church Dr Bristol BS5 9 E8
Parkend GL15 155 E2
Quedgeley GL2 117 F1
Church Farm 2 NP25 154 A7
Church Farm Bsns Ctr
GL53 130 C3
Church Farm La GL56 187 A6
Church Farm Rd BS16 21 C6
Church Furlong GL54 176 C1
Church Gdns GL15 92 A2
Church Hill Bisley GL6 148 D8
Bristol BS4 9 E2
Burton SN14 36 B3
Oldbury-on-S BS35 63 B5
Olveston BS35 49 F3
Upper Lydbrook GL17 163 D2
Church Hill Cl GL16 163 B2
Church Hill Ho BS4 9 E2
Church Ho BS7 18 F8
Church La
Ashton Keynes SN6 142 F5
Badminton GL9 46 E5
Berkeley GL13 85 E3
Bitton BS30 5 E7
Bledington OX7 177 E1
Bristol BS1 195 B2
Bristol,Bromley Heath BS16 30 F1
Bristol,Clifton Wood BS8 194 B2
Bristol,Henbury BS10 27 E2
Bristol,Southville BS3 8 D3
Chipping Sodbury BS37 34 B8
Churcham GL2 124 D1
Coalpit Heath BS36 31 C6
Corse GL19 172 B5
5 Cricklade SN6 143 E4
Cromhall GL12 66 A1
Evenlode GL56 177 C7
Forthampton GL19 181 C3
Gloucester GL4 119 D8
Hambrook BS16 30 E2
Hankerton SN16 141 E1
Hardwicke GL2 109 D6
Harnhill GL7 151 B3
17 Ledbury HR8 178 F8
Long Ashton BS41 7 C2
Marshfield SN14 15 A8
Minsterworth GL2 116 F7
Moreton Valence GL2 101 A8
Northwood Green GL14 165 C2
Rangeworthy BS37 52 F1
Sapperton GL7 149 B6
Saul GL2 100 A7
Sevenhampton GL54 166 E8
Sharpness GL13 93 E1
Shurdington GL51 129 E2
Sopworth SN14 57 D1
South Cerney GL7 142 F8
St Arvans NP16 72 B6
Stanton WR12 184 E5
Stonehouse GL10 97 E7
The Leigh GL19 173 C4
Toddington GL54 184 B3
Whaddon GL4 110 E8
Whitchurch BS14 3 B3
Wickwar GL12 54 A6
Windrush OX18 161 C7
Winterbourne BS36 30 C6
Woolaston,Alvington GL15 147 D3
Woolaston,Plusterwine
GL15 147 B2
Church Leaze BS11 16 D6
Church Mdws
Toddington GL54 184 B3
Whitchurch BS14 3 C4
Church Par BS4 9 E2
Church Path Rd BS20 16 C4
Church Piece GL53 131 B5
Church Pl
Lower Oddington GL56 177 D4
Pill BS20 16 C4
Church Rd Abbots Leigh BS8 7 A8
Alderton GL20 183 E4
Almondsbury BS32 40 A5
Alveston BS35 51 A1
Arlingham GL2 157 B5
Aylburton GL15 147 E5
Bibury GL7 160 A1
Bishop's Cleeve GL52 137 F4
Bitton BS30 5 E7
Bristol,Bedminster BS3 8 C3
Bristol,Bishopsworth BS13 2 A6
Bristol,Filton BS34 29 A3
Bristol,Frenchay BS16 20 C7
Bristol,Hanham BS15 10 B5
Bristol,Horfield BS7 18 E5
Bristol,Kingswood BS15 10 E8
Bristol,Moorfields BS5 9 D8
Bristol,Sneyd Park BS9 17 D3
Bristol,Stoke Gifford BS34 29 E4
Bristol,Upper Soundwell
BS16 20 E3
Bristol,Westbury on Trym
BS9 18 A7
Cheltenham,Leckhampton
GL53 130 C3
Cheltenham,St Mark's
GL51 129 F8
Chepstow/Cas-Gwent NP16 72 F1
Churchdown GL3 128 C4
Cinderford GL14 191 C3
Doynton BS30 23 A1
Dundry BS41 1 D2

Church Rd *continued*
Dursley GL11 88 B3
Easter Compton BS35 39 A1
Easton-in-G BS20 16 A4
Frampton Cotterell BS36 31 C8
Gloucester GL2 127 C4
Guiting Power GL54 175 B3
Hewelsfield GL15 146 F5
Kemble GL7 141 F8
6 Ledbury HR8 178 F8
Leigh Woods BS8 7 D6
Leonard Stanley GL10 97 E3
Longhope GL17 164 F6
Lower Oddington GL56 177 D4
Luckington SN14 47 F4
Lydney GL15 92 A2
Maisemore GL2 126 A7
Nailsworth GL6 91 A6
5 Newnham GL14 157 A6
Oldbury-on-S BS35 63 B5
Pilning BS35 38 B7
Quenington GL7 152 D7
Severn Beach BS35 38 A6
Stanton WR12 184 C8
Stroud GL5 98 E6
Swindon GL51 133 B6
Thornbury BS35 64 B2
Tormarton GL9 34 D2
Upper Lydbrook GL17 163 D2
Upper Soudley GL14 156 C5
Whitchurch BS14 3 C4
Wick BS30 12 B6
Winterbourne BS36 30 E4
Woodchester GL5 98 F2
Yate BS37 43 E3
Yate BS37 43 F2
Church Rise GL2 126 A7
Church Road Pl GL14 191 D4
Church Row
Chedworth GL54 159 A7
Gretton GL54 183 E1
Nailsworth GL6 91 A6
Overbury GL20 182 F8
Poole Keynes GL7 142 A6
Shipton GL54 166 E5
Church Sq GL15 156 E2
Church St Avening GL8 148 A1
Bledington OX7 177 E1
Bredon GL20 182 C7
Bristol BS1 195 B2
Bristol,Lower Easton BS5 19 B1
Bristol,Russell Town BS5 9 B6
Broadway WR12 185 B8
Charlton Kings GL53 131 B5
Cheltenham GL50 193 B4
Chipping Campden GL55 189 A2
Cirencester GL7 190 D3
Clearwell GL16 155 A2
Gloucester GL2 196 A2
King's Stanley GL10 98 A4
Kingham OX7 177 F2
5 Ledbury HR8 178 F8
Littledean GL14 156 E8
Meysey Hampton GL7 152 A2
Moreton-in-M GL56 187 A3
Nailsworth GL6 91 C4
Newent GL18 171 A4
Nympsfield GL10 89 E5
Sherston SN16 58 C1
St Briavels GL15 146 E7
9 Stow-on-t-W GL54 176 F4
Stroud GL5 99 C7
Tetbury GL8 140 B3
Tewkesbury GL20 192 C4
Willersey WR12 188 B2
Wotton-u-E GL12 68 B7
Church View
Almondsbury BS32 39 F4
Aston Magna GL56 187 A6
Bristol,Filton BS34 29 A3
Bristol,Staple Hill BS16 20 D5
Castle Eaton SN6 144 D6
Churchdown GL3 128 D4
Condicote GL54 176 B7
Gorsley HR9 170 A4
Highworth SN6 145 C3
Hillesley GL12 55 D8
Leonard Stanley GL10 97 E3
Newport GL13 78 C8
Thornbury GL13 64 E7
Church Way
Blakeney GL15 156 E2
Gloucester GL4 119 C7
9 Newent GL18 171 A4
Church Wlk
Ashton Keynes SN6 142 F5
Charlton Kings GL52 131 B6
6 Coleford GL16 155 B6
Littledean GL14 156 E8
Parkend GL15 155 E2
Pill BS20 16 C4
8 Stow-on-t-W GL54 176 F4
Viney Hill GL15 156 C1
Churcham Prim Sch GL2 124 C2
Churchdown La GL3 120 C8
Churchdown Parton Manor Jun Sch GL3 128 B6
Churchdown Sch GL3 128 B5
Churchdown Village Inf Sch GL3 128 C5
Churchdown Village Jun Sch GL3 128 C4
Churchdown Wlk BS11 16 E5
Churchend GL2 95 D4
Churchend Cotts GL2 95 D4
Churchend La GL12 66 F3
Churches Mill GL5 99 A1
Churchfarm Cl BS37 43 F3
Churchfield Rd
Stroud GL5 99 D6
Upton St Leonards GL4 119 E3
Churchfields GL52 138 A4
Churchhill Rd GL5 148 A5
Churchill Ave SN26 144 E1
Churchill Cl Bristol BS30 11 A5
1 Nailsworth GL6 91 B4
Churchill Dr Bristol BS9 17 D7
Cheltenham GL52 131 A7
Churchill Gdns GL52 131 A7
Churchill Gr GL20 192 F4
Churchill Ind Est GL53 130 D6
Churchill Mdw HR8 178 E8
Churchill Pl 9 GL7 152 E4
Churchill Rd Bristol BS4 9 C4
Cheltenham GL53 130 E6
Cirencester GL7 190 E5
Gloucester GL1 118 E7
Nailsworth GL6 91 B4
Churchill Sq GL56 186 C7
Churchill Way
Mitcheldean GL17 164 D5
Painswick GL6 103 F8
Churchlands Flats GL54 174 A6
Churchlands Lawns GL54 139 F5
Churchlands Rd 8 BS3 8 B2
Churchside BS16 20 B7
Churchview Dr GL4 119 D8
Churchward Cl
Bristol BS15 10 B5
Honeybourne WR11 188 C7
Churchward Rd BS37 43 B3
Churchway SN26 144 E1
Churchways BS14 3 C4
Churchways Ave BS7 18 E6
Churchways Cres BS7 18 E6
Churn Ave GL52 134 A2
Churn Cl GL7 142 F8
Churn Hill GL7 158 D3
Churn The GL6 103 F8
Churnside GL7 158 D2
Churston Cl BS14 3 A3
Cicely Way GL15 119 F5
Cicester Terr 16 GL56 187 A3
Cicil Rd 1 BS15 10 D8
Cidermill Cl NP16 60 F4
Cidermill La GL55 189 A2
Cidermill Orch GL55 188 D4
Cilgant Defiw/Oak Cres 8 NP25 154 A7
Cinder Hill Coleford GL16 155 A5
St Briavels GL15 146 E7
Cinder La GL7 152 F4
Cinderford Ent Ctr GL14 191 C5
Cinderford Rd GL15 156 D2
Cinderhill Way GL17 163 E4
Circle The GL5 99 C8
Circuit 32 BS5 9 B8
Circular Rd BS9 17 E2
Cirencester Bsns Ctr GL7 190 D2
Cirencester Deer Park Sch GL7 150 B4
Cirencester Hospl GL7 190 B4
Cirencester Jun & Inf Sch GL7 190 D3
Cirencester Kingshill Sch GL7 190 F5
Cirencester Rd
Charlton Kings GL53 131 A4
Fairford GL7 152 C3
Latton SN6 143 D7
Little Witcombe GL3 121 A4
Minchinhampton,Burleigh GL5,GL6 91 E7
Minchinhampton,Hyde GL6 148 C4
South Cerney GL7 151 A2
Tetbury GL8 140 C4
Cirencester Tertiary Coll GL7 190 A4
City Academy Bristol The BS5 9 C8
City Bank Rd GL7 190 D3
City Bsns Pk BS5 9 A8
City Mus & Art Gal★ BS8 194 C3
City of Bristol Coll (Folly La Ctr) BS2 9 A6
City of Bristol Coll (Kingswood Ctr) BS15 10 E8
City of Bristol Coll Hartcliffe Ctr BS13 2 D4
City of Bristol Coll, Bedminster Ctr BS3 8 E2
City of Bristol Coll, College Green Ctr BS1 194 C2
City of Bristol Coll, Downend Ctr BS16 21 A8
City of Bristol Coll,Ashley Down Ctr BS7 18 F4
City of Bristol Coll,Soundwell Ctr BS16 20 E2
City of Bristol College Lawrence Weston Ctr BS11 27 B1
City of Bristol Parkway Transport Tech Ctr BS34 29 D3
City Rd BS2 195 B4
City View BS4 9 A3
Claire's Cl GL5 148 A5
Clamp The BS30 11 C3
Clanage Rd BS3 7 E4
Clanna Cty Pk GL15 147 C5
Clanna La GL15 147 C4
Clanna Rd GL15 147 D4
Clapham Ct GL1 196 C3
Clapton Row 8 GL54 168 F7
Clapton Wlk BS9 17 C5
Clare Ave BS7 18 C3
Clare Ct Cheltenham GL53 193 B1
Stroud GL5 99 E7
Clare Mews GL53 193 B1
Clare Pl GL53 193 B1
Clare Rd
Bristol,Cotham BS6 18 D1
Bristol,Kingswood BS15 20 C2
Bristol,Lower Easton BS5 19 B2
Clare St Bristol BS1 195 A2
Bristol,Moorfields BS5 9 C8
Cheltenham GL53 193 B1
Gloucester GL1 196 A3
Clare Wlk BS35 64 B2
Claremont 1 GL52 133 F2
Claremont Ave BS7 18 D3
Claremont Ct Bristol BS9 18 C5
Gloucester GL1 196 C3
Claremont Rd Bristol BS7 18 D3
Gloucester GL1 196 C3
Claremont Specl Sch BS9 18 C5
Claremont St BS5 19 A1
Claremont Terr 10 BS5 9 D7
Clarence Ave BS16 20 E5
Clarence Ct Bristol BS15 20 B1
1 Cheltenham GL52 193 C4
2 Wotton-u-E GL12 68 B7
Clarence Gdns BS16 20 E5
Clarence Ho BS15 20 B1
Clarence Par GL50 193 B3
Clarence Pl BS2 194 C4
Clarence Rd Bristol BS1 195 B1
Bristol,Kingswood BS15 20 B1
Bristol,Newton BS2 9 A7
Bristol,Staple Hill BS16 20 E5
Cheltenham GL52 193 C4
Tewkesbury GL20 192 C2
Wotton-u-E GL12 68 B7
Clarence Sq GL50 193 C4
Clarence St
Cheltenham GL50 193 B4
Gloucester GL1 196 B2
Clarence Wlk
Cheltenham GL50 193 B3
Gloucester GL1 196 B2
Clarendon Cl NP16 61 A4
Clarendon Ct 6 GL5 99 C7
Clarendon Rd Bristol BS6 18 C2
Winchcombe GL54 174 A8
Claridge Cl GL4 119 D4
Clarington Mews GL50 133 E3
Clark Dr BS16 19 F7
Clark St BS5 9 A8
Clark's Alley GL20 192 C5
Clark's Hay GL7 142 F8
Clark's La Blakeney GL15 156 D1
Siddington GL7 150 D2
Clarke Ave GL56 187 C3
Clarke St BS3 8 D4
Clarke Way GL50 133 D3
Clarken Coombe BS41 7 B3
Clarkes Field SN16 142 D1
Clarkia Cl GL3 127 F7
Clarrie Rd 1 GL8 140 C4
Clattergrove GL6 112 A2
Clatworthy Dr BS14 3 A7
Claudians Cl GL4 119 E7
Claudius Way GL15 92 B4
Clavell Rd BS10 27 F2
Claverham Rd BS16 20 A5
Claverton Rd BS31 5 E2
Claverton Rd W BS31 5 D3
Clay Bottom BS5 19 E2
Clay Hill BS5 19 E2
Clay La Bitton BS30 5 D8
Bristol,Little Stoke BS34 29 C7
Bristol,Willsbridge BS30 11 D1
Thornbury BS35 64 E1
Clay Pit Rd BS6 18 A3
Clay Pitch BS37 45 E3
Clay Rd GL16 155 B7
Clayburn Cl GL2 125 E5
Claydon Gn BS14 2 F3
Clayfield BS37 43 E5
Clayfield Rd BS4 9 E3
Clayfurlong Gr GL7 141 F8
Claymore Cres BS15 20 B1
Claypatch Rd 5 NP25 154 A7
Claypiece Rd BS13 2 A4
Claypit Hill BS37 33 B7
Claypits Hill GL2,GL10 100 D1
Claypits La GL6 99 F5
Claypool Rd BS15 10 E7
Clays Rd GL16 155 B2
Clayton St
Avonmouth BS11 26 A1
21 Bristol BS5 9 B8
Clearview NP25 154 B1
Clearwater Dr GL2 117 E1
Clearwell Caves★ GL16 155 A3
Clearwell CE Prim Sch GL16 155 A2
Cleave St BS2 19 A2
Clee Ho GL20 192 C3
Cleeve Ave BS16 20 E7
Cleeve Cloud La GL52 134 D3
Cleeve Ct
Bishop's Cleeve GL52 137 F3
Bristol BS16 20 D7
Cleeve Gdns BS16 20 D7
Cleeve Gr BS31 4 D5
Cleeve Hill BS16 20 D7
Cleeve Hill Extension BS16 20 E6
Cleeve Ho GL5 99 F1
Cleeve La BS30 22 D1
Cleeve Lake Ct GL52 137 E4
Cleeve Lawns BS16 20 D7
Cleeve Lodge Cl BS16 20 E6
Cleeve Lodge Rd BS16 20 E6
Cleeve Mill Bsns Pk GL18 171 A5
Cleeve Mill La GL18 171 A5
Cleeve Park Rd BS16 20 E7
Cleeve Rd Bristol BS4 9 B3
Bristol,Frenchay BS16 20 C8
Bristol,Mangotsfield BS16 20 E6
Gloucester GL4 119 B4
Gotherington GL52 138 A7
Yate BS37 43 E1
Cleeve Rise GL18 171 A4
Cleeve Sch GL52 138 A2
Cleeve View GL52 136 E5
Cleeve View Rd GL52 134 A2
Cleeve Wood Pk BS16 20 C8
Cleeve Wood Rd BS16 20 D7
Cleevecroft Ave GL52 138 A3
Cleeveland St GL51 133 C3
Cleevelands Ave GL50 133 E4
Cleevelands Cl GL50 133 E5
Cleevelands Dr GL50 133 E5
Cleevemont GL52 133 E5
Cleevemount Cl GL52 133 F3
Cleevemount Rd GL52 133 F4
Clegram Rd GL1 118 D7
Clematis Ct GL52 137 E3
Clement St Bristol BS2 195 C4
Gloucester GL1 119 A8
Clementies The GL56 186 C6
Clements End Rd GL16 155 B2
Clencher's Mill La HR8 179 B7
Clent Ct GL52 133 F1
Cleve Ct
4 Bristol,Clifton Wood BS8 7 F6
Bristol,Filton BS34 29 B4
Cleve House Sch BS4 9 B3
Cleve Rd BS34 29 A4
Clevedale BS16 20 D7
Clevedale Ct BS16 20 D7
Clevedon Rd Bristol BS7 18 D4
Gloucester GL1 118 F6
Clevedon Sq GL51 133 A2
Clevedon Terr BS6 195 A4
Cleveland Cl BS35 51 E8
Clevewood BS16 20 C7
Clewson Rise BS14 2 F3
Cliff Court Dr BS16 20 B7
Cliff View NP16 61 B7
Clifford Ave GL20 192 E2
Clifford Gdns BS11 16 E6
Clifford Rd BS16 20 C4
Cliffords 8 SN6 143 E4
Clift House Rd BS3 8 A4
Clift House Spur BS3 7 F4
Clift Pl BS1 195 A1
Clift Rd BS3 8 A4
Clifton Arc BS8 194 A3
Clifton Cath★ BS8 194 A4
Clifton Cl 1 Bristol BS8 7 F7
14 Stow-on-t-W GL54 176 F4
Clifton Coll BS8 194 A4
Clifton College Prep Sch BS8 17 F1
Clifton Down BS8 7 F7
Clifton Down Rd BS8 194 A3
Clifton Down Sh Ctr 11 BS8 18 B1
Clifton Down Sta BS8 18 B1
Clifton High Gr BS9 17 E5
Clifton High Sch BS8 194 A4
Clifton Hill BS8 194 A2
Clifton Metro 10 BS8 18 B1
Clifton Park Rd BS8 7 F8
Clifton Pk BS8 194 A3
Clifton Pl BS5 9 A8
Clifton Rd Bristol BS8 194 A2
Gloucester GL1 196 A1
Clifton St
Bristol,Bedminster BS3 8 C3
Bristol,Upper Easton BS5 9 A8
Clifton Suspension Bridge★ BS8 7 E7
Clifton Vale BS8 194 A2
Clifton Vale Cl BS8 194 A2
Clifton View 1 BS3 8 F4
Clifton Wood Ct BS8 194 B2
Clifton Wood Rd BS8 194 B2
Cliftonwood Cres BS8 194 B2
Cliftonwood Terr BS8 194 A2
Cliinton Ho GL7 190 D5
Clingre Down GL11 87 C4
Clingre La GL11 87 C4
Clinton Rd BS3 8 C2
Clissold Ct GL6 91 B3
Clive Rd BS14 3 C8
Cloatley Rd SN16 141 E1
Clock House Sq GL54 166 C6
Cloisters BS8 7 F8
Cloisters Rd BS36 30 F6
Cloisters The
Bishop's Cleeve GL52 137 E4
Chepstow/Cas-Gwent NP16 72 D2
Clomoney Way GL2 127 D5
Clonmel Rd BS4 8 D1
Close Field GL54 183 F1
Close Gdns
Condicote GL54 176 B7
14 Tetbury GL8 140 B4
Close The
Bristol,Henbury BS10 28 A5
Close The *continued*
Bristol,Little Stoke BS34 29 C6
Bristol,Patchway BS32 40 C1
Bristol,Upper Soundwell BS16 20 D3
Cheltenham GL53 130 D4
Coaley GL11 88 E7
Coalpit Heath BS36 31 C6
Coleford GL16 155 C6
Dursley GL11 87 E4
Lechlade on T GL7 153 E3
Siddington GL7 150 E2
Slimbridge GL2 95 E3
South Cerney GL7 143 A8
Southam GL52 134 C8
Thornbury BS35 51 B8
Whiteshill GL6 102 F3
Whitminster GL2 100 F5
Clothier Rd BS4 9 F2
Cloud The GL12 68 B7
Clouds Hill Ave BS5 9 E8
Clouds Hill Rd BS5 9 F8
Clovelly Cl BS5 9 F8
Clovelly Rd BS5 9 F8
Clover Cl
Cinderford GL14 156 C6
Milkwall GL16 155 B4
Clover Dr GL2 109 E6
Clover Ground BS9 18 B7
Clover Leaze BS32 29 D6
Clover Piece GL4 119 D6
Cloverdale Dr BS30 11 A3
Cloverlea Bsns Ctr BS36 31 C3
Cloverlea Rd BS30 11 C5
Clyde Ave BS31 4 F4
Clyde Cres GL52 134 A2
Clyde Ct 2 BS3 8 C3
Clyde Gdns BS5 10 B6
Clyde Gr BS34 28 F2
Clyde Ho 7 BS35 51 C8
Clyde La BS6 18 C2
Clyde Mews 3 BS6 18 C2
Clyde Rd
Bristol,Redland BS6 18 B2
Bristol,Totterdown BS4 9 A3
Brockworth GL3 120 F5
Frampton Cotterell BS36 31 B8
Clyde Terr
3 Bristol,Bedminster BS3 8 C3
Bristol,Totterdown BS4 9 A3
Clydesdale Cl BS14 3 A6
Co-operation Rd BS5 19 C1
Coach Cl GL13 85 E3
Coach Ho The
Blockley GL56 186 C7
Tewkesbury GL20 192 D4
Coach House Mews GL7 190 D4
Coach Rd HR9 164 D8
Coachworks The BS30 10 F4
Coaley CE Prim Sch GL11 88 E8
Coaley Rd BS11 16 D5
Coalsack La BS36 31 B3
Coalville Rd BS36 31 D7
Coalway Inf Sch GL16 155 B5
Coalway Jun Sch GL16 155 B5
Coalway Rd GL16 155 B5
Coape Rd BS14 3 F5
Coates Gdns GL10 97 F8
Coates Ho 11 GL51 132 E2
Coates La GL7 149 F4
Coates Mill Cotts GL54 139 F4
Coates The GL54 139 F4
Coates Wlk BS4 2 D6
Cobbler's Cl The GL52 138 A7
Cobblestone Mews BS8 194 A4
Cobden Ctr The BS16 31 B2
Cobden St BS5 9 C7
Coberley BS15 10 C6
Coberley CE Prim Sch GL53 123 A5
Coberley Rd
Cheltenham GL51 129 D8
Gloucester GL4 118 E3
Cobham Ct GL51 133 B3
Cobham Rd GL51 133 B3
Cobhorn Dr BS13 1 F4
Cobourg Rd BS6 18 F2
Coburn Gdns GL51 132 C1
Cochran Cl GL3 128 C5
Cock La SN14 23 D5
Cock Rd BS15 10 F6
Cockadilly GL10 89 D5
Cockatoos La HR9 170 B5
Cockshoot Hill GL15 146 E7
Codrington Pl BS8 194 A3
Codrington Rd BS7 18 D3
Cody Ct 2 BS15 10 B5
Coed Barnet/Barnets Wood NP16 60 C8
Coed Castell/Castle Wood NP16 60 C8
Coed Cilfach/Alcove Wood NP16 60 C8
Coed Fedw/Fedw Wood NP16 60 C8
Coed Ffwyth/Fryth Wood NP16 60 C8
Coed Hale/Hale Wood NP16 60 C8
Coed Maenor/Manor Wood NP16 60 C8
Coed Wallwern/Wallwern Wood NP16 72 C1

Coed Woolpitch/Woolpitch
Wood NP16 60 B8
Cogan Rd BS16 20 E3
Cogsall Rd BS14 3 F6
Colburn Ct BS7 18 F7
Colchester Cl
Mitcheldean GL17 164 D5
Westbury-on-S GL14 165 C1
Colchester Cres BS4 2 D7
Cold Pool La
Cheltenham,Up Hatherley
GL51 129 D6
CheltenhamBadgeworth
GL51 129 B5
Coldharbour La
Bristol BS16 19 E8
Newent GL18 170 F6
Coldharbour Rd
Bristol BS6 18 B4
St Briavels GL15 146 E6
Coldicott Leys GL55 189 D2
Coldicotts Cl 7 GL55 189 A2
Coldpark Gdns BS13 1 E5
Coldpark Rd BS13 1 E5
Coldray Cl GL1 127 B1
Coldrick Cl BS14 2 F3
Coldwell GL10 98 B3
Coldwell Cl GL10 98 B3
Coldwell La GL10 98 B3
Cole Ave GL2 118 C3
Cole Rd BS2 9 B6
Colebridge Ave GL2 127 C3
Colebrook Rd BS15 10 C8
Coleford Rd Bream GL15 147 C8
Bristol BS10 28 D1
Tutshill NP16 72 F2
Colemead BS13 2 B5
Coleridge Ho BS34 40 A1
Coleridge Rd BS5 19 C3
Colerne Dr GL3 120 B7
Colesborne Cl BS37 32 E8
Colesbourne Rd GL51 129 D8
Coleshill Dr BS13 2 B5
Colin Cl BS35 64 C1
Colin Rd GL4 127 D1
Collard Ho 2 BS16 19 F4
College Ave BS16 20 A5
College Baths Rd GL53 193 C2
College Ct
Bristol,Clifton BS8 194 A4
Bristol,Fishponds BS16 20 A5
Gloucester GL1 196 B3
College Farm Wkshps
GL7 150 B3
College Fields Bristol BS8 7 F8
Gloucester GL2 127 D4
College Gate GL53 193 C2
College Gn Bristol BS1 194 C2
Gloucester GL1 196 B3
College Lawn GL53 193 C1
College Mews BS9 18 A7
College Park Dr BS10 27 F1
College Rd Bredon GL20 182 B7
Bristol,Clifton BS8 7 F8
Bristol,Fishponds BS16 20 A5
Bristol,Westbury on Trym
BS9 18 A7
Cheltenham GL53 193 C2
Cinderford GL14 191 C4
Stroud GL5 99 A8
College Sq BS1 194 C2
College St Bristol BS1 194 C2
Gloucester GL1 196 B3
College View
Cirencester GL7 190 B1
9 Stonehouse GL10 97 F7
College Way BS34 29 A4
College Yd GL1 196 A3
Collett Cl BS15 10 B5
Collett Ho BS36 30 D4
Collett Pl SN6 143 E6
Collett Way BS37 43 C3
Colletts Ct 2 GL54 168 F7
Colletts Dr GL51 133 B3
Colletts Fields WR12 185 C8
Colletts Gdns 6 WR12 185 C8
Colliers Break BS16 21 B5
Colliers Pitch GL15 147 C5
Colliers Wood GL6 91 A5
Collin Cl WR12 188 B2
Collin La WR12 188 A2
Collin Rd BS4 9 D4
Collingbourne Rd GL4 119 A7
Collingwood Ave BS15 20 E1
Collingwood Cl
Chepstow NP16 61 A5
Saltford BS31 5 E2
Collingwood Rd 4 BS6 18 B1
Collins Ave BS34 29 C6
Collins Cl GL19 172 A8
Collins Dr BS35 38 C3
Collins St BS11 16 B8
Collinson Rd BS13 2 B5
Colliter Cres BS3 8 B2
Collum End Rise GL53 130 D4
Collyberry Rd GL52 138 B4
Coln House Sch GL7 152 D3
Coln Pk GL54 166 D6
Coln Rise GL54 166 D6
Coln Sq BS35 51 C8
Colne Ave GL52 134 A3
Colne Gn BS31 5 A4
Colston Ave BS1 195 A3
Colston Cl Bristol BS16 20 D3
Winterbourne BS36 30 E4
Colston Ct BS7 18 D3
Colston Dale BS16 19 E4
Colston Fort 2 BS2 195 A4
Colston Hall★ BS1 195 A3
Colston Hill BS16 19 D4
Colston Mews BS6 18 E1
Colston Par BS1 195 B1
Colston Rd BS5 19 C1
Colston St
Bristol,Kingsdown BS1 195 A3
Bristol,Upper Soundwell
BS16 20 D3
Colston Yd BS1 195 A3
Colston's Almshouses
BS2 195 A3
Colston's Lower Sch
BS16 19 D5
Colston's Prim Sch BS6 18 D1
Colston's Sch BS16 19 C4
Colstone Ct 3 BS16 19 E3
Colstons Girls' Sch BS6 18 E1
Colsty Mdw GL15 156 D1
Coltham Cl 7 GL52 130 F8
Coltham Fields GL52 130 F8
Coltham Rd GL52 130 F8
Colthurst Dr BS15 10 E5
Coltman Cl GL1 127 B1
Colts Gn BS37 33 E8
Columbia Cl GL1 196 C3
Columbia St GL52 193 C4
Columbine Rd GL20 192 E1
Colville Ho GL7 190 D5
Colwell Ave GL3 128 A1
Colwell School Cl GL1 127 A1
Colwyn Dr GL51 129 E6
Colwyn Rd 2 BS5 19 C1
Colyton Ct BS3 8 D1
Comb Paddock BS9 18 B7
Combe Ho GL8 140 B4
Combermere BS35 51 D8
Combfactory La 13 BS5 9 B8
Combrook Cl GL4 119 E4
Commerce Rd GL2 173 E1
Commercial Rd
Bristol BS1 195 A1
Chalford GL6 148 C5
Gloucester GL1 196 A2
Commercial St
Cheltenham GL50 193 B1
Cinderford GL14 191 D4
Common (East) The
BS32 40 C1
Common Hill SN6 143 E4
Common La BS20 16 B2
Common Mead La BS16 30 A1
Common Rd Bristol BS15 10 B3
Minchinhampton GL6 91 E6
Winterbourne BS36 30 F7
Common The
Berkeley Heath GL13 86 C3
Bristol,Frenchay BS16 20 B7
Bristol,Patchway BS32 40 C1
Minety SN16 142 E1
Olveston BS35 49 F3
Siddington GL7 150 E2
Commonfield Rd BS11 27 B1
Commonmead La BS37 33 F8
Compton Cl
Churchdown GL3 128 A8
Corse GL19 172 A7
Compton Dr BS9 17 C7
Compton Gn BS31 4 E4
Compton Lodge 3 BS6 18 B3
Compton Rd GL51 133 B4
Compton Rise GL54 166 E2
Compton St BS5 9 C7
Compton's Alley GL20 192 C4
Comyn Wlk BS16 20 A5
Concord GL6 91 A3
Concorde Dr BS10 28 B1
Concorde Ho BS34 28 F2
Concorde Rd BS34 28 E7
Concorde Way GL4 119 B7
Conderton Pottery★
GL20 183 A8
Condicote La GL54 176 B5
Condor Ho BS7 19 C7
Condover Rd BS4 10 A3
Conduit Hill GL55 188 F1
Conduit Pl 2 BS2 19 A1
Conduit Rd BS2 19 A1
Conduit St GL1 196 C1
Condurrow Ct 18 GL54 176 F4
Cone The BS10,BS34 28 C6
Coney Hill Com Prim Sch
GL4 119 C7
Coney Hill Par GL4 119 C7
Coney Hill Rd GL4 119 C7
Coneygar Rd GL7 152 C7
Coneygree BS13 1 F6
Coneygree La WR12 185 B7
Congleton Rd BS5 9 D8
Conham Hill BS15 10 A5
Conham Rd BS4,BS5,BS15 9 F5
Conifer Cl Bristol BS16 20 D6
Frampton Cotterell BS36 42 A1
Conifers The
2 Cheltenham GL52 134 A3
Gloucester GL1 119 A7
Minety SN16 142 D1
Conigree La GL20 192 C2
Coniston Ave BS9 17 E6
Coniston Cl BS30 11 D6
Coniston Prim Sch BS34 39 F1
Coniston Rd Bristol BS34 39 F1
Cheltenham GL51 129 E7
Gloucester GL2 127 C4
Connaught Prim Sch BS4 2 E8
Connaught Rd BS4 2 E8
Consell Gn GL54 184 C3
Constable Cl BS31 4 F6
Constable Rd BS7 19 B6
Constance Cl GL5 98 F5
Constantine Ave BS34 29 E5
Constitution Hill BS8 194 B2
Contemporis BS8 194 A3
Convent Cl BS10 27 D3
Convent La GL5 90 F7
Convent The OX7 169 E7
Conway Ct 4 GL16 155 A7
Conway Gn BS31 5 A3
Conway Rd Bristol BS4 9 C4
Gloucester GL3 120 A8
Conygar Rd GL8 140 C4
Conygre Gr BS34 29 C3
Conygre Rd BS34 29 B3
Cook Cl BS30 11 C4
Cook St BS11 16 C8
Cook's Folly Rd BS9 17 D3
Cook's Hill GL19 172 C4
Cook's La GL19 179 F4
Cooke's Dr BS35 39 A1
Cooks Cl BS32 40 D3
Cooks La BS36 31 D3
Cooks Orch GL1 127 A3
Cooksley Rd BS5 9 C8
Cookson Terr GL15 84 B8
Cookspool 2 GL8 140 C4
Cookworthy Cl 2 BS5 9 B6
Coomb Dr GL14 191 C1
Coomb Rocke BS9 17 D6
Coombe Ave BS35 64 B2
Coombe Bridge Ave BS9 17 D6
Coombe Cl BS10 27 D3
Coombe Dale BS9 17 C6
Coombe Gdns Bristol BS9 17 E6
Stinchcombe GL11 87 C3
Coombe Glen La GL51 129 D6
Coombe Ho BS15 10 E8
Coombe La Bristol BS9 17 E6
Easton-in-G BS8 16 A1
King's Stanley GL10 98 C2
Wotton-u-E GL12 68 D8
Coombe Lea NP16 146 A5
Coombe Mead GL52 138 B3
Coombe Rd Bristol BS5 19 C2
Wotton-u-E GL12 68 C8
Coombe Terr GL12 68 C8
Coombe Way BS10 27 F1
Coombes Way BS30 11 D4
Coombs Rd GL16 155 A6
Cooper Rd Bristol BS9 17 F7
Thornbury BS35 51 B7
Cooper's Ct
Brockworth GL3 120 E5
Charlton Kings GL53 131 B5
Cooper's Hill★ GL3 120 E2
Cooper's View GL3 120 E5
Cooperage La BS3 194 B1
Cooperage Rd BS5 9 D7
Coopers Dr BS37 43 F5
Coopers Elm GL2 117 F2
Coopers Mill GL5 91 A6
Coopers Rd GL16 155 A8
Coopers Way 27 GL18 171 A4
Coots The BS14 3 E6
Cope Pk BS32 40 C5
Copeland Dr BS14 3 B5
Copenacre SN16 142 B1
Copford La BS41 7 B1
Copley Ct BS15 10 E5
Copley Dr 10 GL16 155 A5
Copley Gdns BS7 19 B6
Copper Beech Gr GL2 117 E1
Copper Beeches SN6 145 C3
Copperfield Cl GL4 119 B4
Coppice Daw Pitch
GL19 165 D5
Coppice Gate GL51 132 F5
Coppice Hill GL6 148 D5
Coppice La SN16 141 F4
Coppice Rd GL17 163 D3
Coppice The
Bristol,Bradley Stoke BS32 29 E7
Bristol,Highridge BS13 1 E4
Copse Rd Bristol BS4 9 B3
Keynsham BS31 5 C4
Copse The
Broad Blunsdon SN26 144 D1
Gloucester GL4 119 E7
Copsehill Rd GL54 176 C1
Copt Elm Cl GL53 131 A6
Copt Elm Rd GL53 131 A6
Copthorne Cl BS14 3 B5
Coral Cl GL4 118 B3
Corbet Cl BS11 27 C2
Corbett Cl BS37 43 F4
Corbett Ho 11 BS5 9 C7
Corder's La 3 GL56 187 A3
Corders Cl 5 GL56 187 A3
Cordingley Cl GL3 128 C5
Cordwell Wlk BS10 18 D7
Corey Cl 6 BS2 18 F1
Corfe Cl GL52 134 C4
Corfe Cres BS31 4 E4
Corfe Pl BS30 11 B1
Corfe Rd BS4 2 D7
Coriander Dr Bristol BS34 30 A7
Innsworth GL3 127 F7
Coriander Wlk BS5 19 C2
Corinium Ave GL4 127 D2
Corinium Bsns Pk GL14 191 B7
Corinium Cntr GL7 190 D1
Corinium Gate GL7 190 D5
Corinium Ho GL7 190 B3
Corinium Mus★ GL7 190 C5
Corinthian Ct 9 BS1 195 B1
Corinum Cl BS16 21 C6
Corker's Hill 9 BS5 9 F6
Cormorant Ave GL20 192 E2
Corn St BS1 195 A3
Corncroft La GL4 119 D2
Corndean La GL54 174 A5
Corner Farm Dr WR11 188 C6
Corner Rd GL15 155 F1
Cornfield Cl BS32 40 C1
Cornfield Dr
Bishop's Cleeve GL52 137 E4
Hardwicke GL2 109 E7
Cornfields The GL52 137 E4
Cornflower Cl GL20 192 E1
Cornflower Rd GL4 119 E5
Cornhill GL5 99 C7
Cornhill Dr BS14 3 A7
Cornish Gr BS14 3 E6
Cornish Hos
Cinderford GL14 156 C6
9 Moreton-in-M GL56 187 B3
Cornish Rd BS14 3 E6
Cornish Wlk BS14 3 E6
Cornleaze BS13 2 A5
Cornmeadow Dr GL51 132 D5
Cornwall Ave GL51 133 A2
Cornwall Cres BS37 43 F3
Cornwall Rd BS7 18 D4
Cornwallis Ave BS8 194 A2
Cornwallis Cres BS8 7 F6
Cornwallis Gr BS8 194 A2
Cornwallis Ho BS8 194 A2
Corolin Rd GL2 118 B4
Coronation Ave
Bristol BS16 20 A4
Keynsham BS31 4 D4
Coronation Cl
Bristol BS30 11 A5
Chipping Campden GL55 188 F2
Coronation Flats GL52 131 A7
Coronation Gr GL2 127 B2
Coronation Pl BS1 195 A2
Coronation Rd
Bristol,Cadbury Heath BS30 11 B5
Bristol,Mangotsfield BS16 20 E5
Bristol,Southville BS3 194 C1
Bristol,Warmley BS15 11 A7
Cheltenham GL52 134 B4
Cinderford GL14 191 D3
Stroud GL5 99 B6
Tetbury GL8 140 B5
Coronation Sq GL51 132 E2
Coronation St GL7 152 D4
Corpus St GL52 193 C2
Corriett The GL11 88 A5
Corsend Rd GL19 172 B4
Corsley Wlk BS4 2 F8
Corston Wlk BS11 16 D7
Cossham Cl BS35 64 C2
Cossham Meml Hospl
BS16 20 C2
Cossham Rd BS5 9 D7
Cossham St BS16 21 B5
Cossham Wlk BS5 20 A1
Cossington Rd BS4 2 F8
Cossins Rd BS6 18 B3
Costers Cl BS35 51 A5
Costiland Dr BS13 1 F6
Cote Bank Ho BS9 18 B7
Cote Dr BS9 18 A4
Cote House La BS9 18 A5
Cote La BS9 18 A5
Cote Lea Pk BS9 18 B7
Cote Paddock BS9 17 F4
Cote Pk BS9 17 E6
Cote Rd BS9 18 A4
Cotham Brow BS6 18 D1
Cotham Gdns 15 BS6 18 B1
Cotham Gr BS6 18 D1
Cotham Gram Sch
(Charnwood Annex)
BS6 18 C1
Cotham Hill BS6 194 C4
Cotham Lawn Ho BS6 194 C4
Cotham Lawn Rd BS6 18 C1
Cotham Pk BS6 18 C1
Cotham Pk N BS6 18 C1
Cotham Pl BS6 194 C4
Cotham Rd BS6 194 C4
Cotham Rd S BS6 195 A4
Cotham Sch BS6 194 C4
Cotham Side BS6 18 D1
Cotham Vale BS6 18 C1
Cothar's Pitch HR9 170 A5
Cothers Ct GL56 186 C6
Cotman Wlk BS7 19 B6
Cotrith Gr BS10 27 E3
Cotsmore Cl GL56 187 B3
Cotswold Ave
Cirencester GL7 190 C3
Eastington GL10 96 F7
Cotswold Bsns Village
GL56 187 B3
Cotswold Chine Home Specl
Sch GL6 91 D5
Cotswold Cl
Bredon GL20 182 C7
Brimscombe GL5 148 A5
Cirencester GL7 190 B3
5 Tetbury GL8 140 C5
Cotswold Community
GL7 142 E6
Cotswold Cotts
Eastcombe GL6 148 C7
Nailsworth GL6 90 F3
Cotswold Court Pk
GL51 173 F1
Cotswold Ct BS37 44 B1
Cotswold Ed Ctr The
BS34 28 F2
Cotswold Edge GL55 189 A6
Cotswold Edge Bsns Pk
GL2 118 C8
Cotswold Falconry Ctr★
GL56 186 E4
Cotswold Farm Pk★
GL54 175 D5
Cotswold Gdns
Gloucester GL2 127 D5
25 Moreton-in-M GL56 187 A3
Tewkesbury GL20 192 D5
Wotton-u-E GL12 68 C7
Cotswold Gn GL10 98 A8
Cotswold La BS37 34 A8
Cotswold Lo 11 GL52 133 F2
Cotswold Mdws GL54 169 C4
Cotswold Mead GL6 103 E7
Cotswold Mill GL7 190 C4
Cotswold Pl GL20 192 D5
Cotswold Rd Bristol BS3 8 D3
Cheltenham GL52 134 B3
Chipping Sodbury BS37 33 B8
Stroud GL5 98 E8
Cotswold Sch The GL54 168 F8
Cotswold Terr GL10 89 D5
Cotswold View
Bristol,Filton BS34 29 A3
Bristol,Kingswood BS15 20 D2
Charfield GL12 67 B5
Tirley GL19 172 F7
Wickwar GL12 54 B6
Woodmancote GL52 138 B3
Cotswold Water Pk★
GL7 142 D5
Cotswold Way
Cold Ashton SN14 14 A6
Highworth SN6 145 C3
Cotswolds Countryside Mus★
GL54 167 F2
Cotswolds Motoring Mus &
Toy Collection The★
GL54 168 F7
Cotswolds Water Pk★
GL7 153 A2
Cottage Field GL2 125 D5
Cottage Gdns BS5 10 A7
Cottage Pitch GL18 171 A5
Cottage Pl BS2 195 A4
Cottage Rake Ave GL50 133 C5
Cottage The GL5 98 C7
Cotteswold Rd
Gloucester GL4 119 B5
Tewkesbury GL20 192 D5
Cotteswold Rise GL5 99 D7
Cottington Ct BS15 10 E5
Cottisford Rd BS5 19 B4
Cottle Gdns BS14 3 F6
Cottle Rd BS14 3 F6
Cotton Cl GL4 119 F5
Cotton's La GL8 140 B3
Cottonwood Dr BS30 11 A3
Cottrell Ave BS15 20 C2
Cottrell Rd BS5 19 C3
Cotts The GL56 186 F6
Coughton Pl HR9 163 C8
Coulson Ho 2 BS7 18 F4
Coulson Wlk BS15 20 C2
Coulson's Cl BS14 3 A3
Coulson's Rd BS14 3 A3
Council Hos
Cold Aston GL54 168 B6
Eastnor HR8 179 C7
Ledbury HR8 178 A8
Stow-on-t-W GL54 176 F5
Council Villas
Clearwell GL16 154 F3
Edge End GL16 155 C8
English Bicknor GL16 163 B1
Sling GL16 155 B3
Counterpool Rd BS15 10 C7
Counterslip BS1 195 B2
Counterslip Gdns BS14 3 C6
Countess Lilias Rd GL7 190 C2
Countess Wlk BS16 19 D6
Country Choice Cvn Pk
GL20 180 E9
County Court Rd GL50 193 B3
County Cres 5 GL1 127 A1
County St BS4 9 A4
County Way BS34 30 A4
Court Ave BS34 29 F5
Court Cl BS7 18 E7
Court Cotts BS37 45 D6
Court Dr GL19 173 B6
Court Farm Oaksey SN16 142 A4
Tibberton GL19 124 B8
Court Farm La
Beckford GL20 183 B6
Mitcheldean GL17 164 D5
Court Farm Mews GL10 97 D7
Court Farm Rd
Bristol,Longwell Green
BS30 10 E2
Bristol,Whitchurch BS14 2 F3
Court Field 11 GL8 140 B4
Court Gdn GL11 89 B1
Court Gdns
Gloucester GL2 118 B6
St Arvans NP16 72 B6
Westbury-on-S GL14 157 C8
Yate BS37 32 E8
Court Gdns The GL2 157 B5
Court Hay BS20 16 A4

Court La 8 Newent GL18 171 A4
Wick BS30 12 B6
Court La continued
Woolaston GL15 147 D3
Court Mdw Stone GL13 77 E3
Wotton-u-E GL12 68 C7
Court Mead GL13 77 E3
Court Mews GL52 131 A7
Court Orch Gretton GL54 183 E1
Wotton-u-E GL12 68 C7
Court Pl GL4 119 D7
Court Rd
Bristol,Horfield BS7 18 F6
Bristol,Kingswood BS15 10 D7
Bristol,Oldland Common BS30 11 C3
Brockworth GL3 120 E6
Cheltenham GL52 134 C4
Frampton Cotterell BS36 30 F8
Frocester GL10 97 B3
Lydney GL15 92 B5
Newent GL18 171 A5
Upper Strensham WR8 180 A10
Court St SN16 58 C1
Court View Chalford GL6 148 D6
Stonehouse GL10 97 D7
Wick BS30 12 C6
Court View Cl BS32 40 A5
Court Way GL5 99 A5
Courtbrook GL7 152 E3
Courtenay Cres BS4 2 D7
Courtenay Rd BS31 5 B2
Courtenay St GL50 133 D3
Courtfield Dr 6 GL52 131 B6
Courtfield Gr BS16 20 A4
Courtfield Rd GL2 109 F8
Courthouse Gdns GL11 87 F6
Courtiers Dr GL52 138 A3
Courtlands Bristol BS32 40 C1
Keynsham BS31 4 E5
Courtlands La BS3 7 E4
Courtlands Unit BS4 2 D8
Courtney Cl GL20 192 D1
Courtney Prim Sch BS15 10 F7
Courtney Rd BS15 10 E7
Courtney Way BS15 11 A7
Courtside Mews BS6 18 C1
Courtyard The
Bourton-on-t-W GL54 168 F8
Cheltenham GL50 193 A2
Gloucester GL1 127 A2
Stow-on-t-W GL54 176 F5
Tewkesbury GL20 182 B5
Courville Cl BS35 51 A4
Cousins Cl BS10 27 D3
Cousins La BS5 9 F8
Cousins Mews BS4 9 F6
Cousins Way BS16 21 B8
Cousley Cl GL3 120 A7
Couzens Cl BS37 44 B2
Couzens Pl BS34 29 F5
Cove House Gdns 3 SN6 142 F5
Coventry Cl GL20 192 D2
Coventry Wlk BS4 9 F6
Coverham Cl 10 GL16 155 A7
Coverham Rd GL16 155 A7
Cow La GL5 91 A6
Cow St SN5 143 D1
Cowcombe Hill GL6 148 C5
Cowdray Rd BS4 2 D7
Cowhorn Hill BS30 11 C4
Cowl La GL54 174 A7
Cowler Wlk BS13 1 F4
Cowley Cl GL51 129 E7
Cowley La HR9 170 C2
Cowley Rd GL4 118 E3
Cowling Dr BS14 3 C5
Cowling Rd BS14 3 D5
Cowlsmead GL51 129 E2
Cowper Rd Bristol BS6 18 C1
Cheltenham GL51 132 E1
Cowper St BS5 9 C7
Cowship La GL12 53 D6
Cowslip Mdw GL52 138 B3
Coxwell La GL6 148 B6
Cox Ct BS30 10 F4
Cox's Hill SN6 142 F5
Cox's Way Bream GL15 155 D1
Gloucester GL4 120 A6
Coxbury & Wyegate La GL15 154 D2
Coxgrove Hill BS16 21 F7
Coxmoor Cl OX7 177 F2
Coxmore Cl GL3 120 A7
Coxwell Ct GL7 190 C5
Coxwell St GL7 190 C5
Cozens La OX7 177 F2
Crab Tree Pl GL50 133 C3
Crabtree Cl BS41 1 D1
Crabtree La
Cirencester GL7 190 F3
Dundry BS41 1 D2
Duntisbourne Abbots GL7 107 B3
Crabtree Pk GL7 152 E4
Crabtree Rd GL14 191 B5
Crabtree Wlk BS5 19 D2
Craddock Ct GL6 90 F5
Craddock Rd 7 GL18 171 A4
Cradock Cl BS30 11 B4
Craftes Ct BS5 19 E1
Craig Yr Afon NP16 60 E7
Crail View GL54 168 A1
Cranberry Wlk BS9 17 C8
Cranbourne GL12 68 C7
Cranbourne Rd BS34 28 F7
Cranbrook Rd BS6 18 C3
Crandell Cl BS10 27 F4
Crane Cl BS15 11 B8
Crane Furlong SN6 145 D4
Cranford Cl GL52 138 C3
Cranford Ct 1 BS9 18 B6
Cranham BS37 32 C7
Cranham CE Prim Sch GL4 112 E6
Cranham Cl Bristol BS15 20 F2
6 Gloucester GL4 119 E5
Cranham Dr BS34 40 C1
Cranham La GL3 128 D3
Cranham Rd Bristol BS10 18 C8
Cheltenham GL52 133 F1
Cranhams La GL7 190 B2
Cranleigh Ct Inf Sch BS37 43 D3
Cranleigh Court Rd BS37 43 D2
Cranleigh Gdns BS9 17 E4
Cranleigh Rd BS14 3 B5
Cranley GL50 133 E3
Cranmoor Gn BS35 38 D6
Cranmore Ave BS31 4 E6
Cranmore Cres BS10 28 D1
Cranside Ave BS6 18 C4
Cransley Cres BS9 18 C7
Crantock Ave BS13 2 B8
Crantock Dr BS32 40 B5
Crantock Rd BS37 43 D1
Cranwell Cl GL4 119 C4
Cranwell Gr BS14 3 A5
Crapen The GL11 87 E4
Crashmore La GL20 182 F7
Crates Cl BS15 10 E8
Craven Cl BS30 10 F5
Craven Dr GL3 128 B6
Craven Way BS30 10 F5
Crawley Hill GL11 89 B3
Crawley La GL11 89 B2
Crawshay Pl GL14 191 C4
Craydon Gr BS14 3 D4
Craydon Rd BS14 3 D5
Craydon Wlk BS14 3 D5
Crease The 16 GL18 171 A4
Crediton Cres BS4 8 F1
Credon Rd GL3 127 E1
Crescent Cl
Coleford GL16 155 A6
Stonehouse GL10 97 E6
Crescent Pl GL50 193 B3
Crescent Rd Bristol BS16 20 C6
Stonehouse GL10 97 E6
Crescent Terr GL50 193 B3
Crescent The
8 Berry Hill GL16 155 A7
Bristol BS16 29 F1
Bristol,Frenchay BS16 29 F1
Bristol,Henleaze BS9 18 C6
Bristol,Sea Mills BS9 17 C6
Bristol,Upper Soundwell BS16 20 D3
Brockworth GL3 120 D6
Chalford GL6 148 E6
Coleford GL16 155 A5
Coleford,Baker's Hill GL16 155 A6
Dursley GL11 87 F4
Mitcheldean GL17 164 D6
Newton GL13 85 D8
Northwood Green GL14 165 D3
Olveston BS35 50 D4
Wick BS30 12 C7
Crescentdale GL2 127 A5
Crest The Bristol BS4 9 C2
West Kington SN14 25 F3
Crest Way GL4 127 F1
Creswicke Ave BS15 10 C5
Creswicke Rd BS4 2 E7
Crew's Hole Rd BS5 9 E7
Cribbs Causeway Ctr BS34 28 A6
Cribbs Cswy BS10 28 A6
Cricket La BS10 18 A8
Cricklade Mus* SN6 143 F4
Cricklade Rd Bristol BS7 18 E4
Cirencester GL7 190 E2
Highworth SN6 145 C3
Purton Stoke SN5 143 E1
Cricklade St
Cirencester GL7 190 C4
Poulton GL7 151 E3
Crickley Hill Ctry Pk GL4 122 A5
Crickley Hill Ctry Pk Visitor Ctr* GL4 121 F5
Criftycraft La GL3 128 C3
Crippetts La GL51 130 B3
Cripps Rd Bristol BS3 8 C3
Cirencester GL7 190 C4
Crispin Cl Gloucester GL2 127 C5
1 Winchcombe GL54 174 A7
Crispin La 4 BS35 64 B1
Crispin Rd GL54 174 A7
Crispin Way BS15 20 F2
Critchford La GL54 175 A5
Crock Mead GL4 119 E6
Crockerne CE Prim Sch BS20 16 C4
Crockerne Dr BS20 16 C3
Crockerne Ho BS20 16 D4
Croft Ave Bristol BS16 19 C4
Charlton Kings GL53 131 B5
Croft Cl Bitton BS30 5 D8
Churchdown GL3 128 D4
Latton SN6 143 E6
Newent GL18 171 A5
Croft Cotts GL7 142 C6
Croft Dr GL53 131 A5
Croft Farm Leisure & Water Pk* GL20 182 A6
Croft Gdns
8 Broadway WR12 185 B8
Charlton Kings GL53 131 B4
Croft Holm GL56 187 B3
Croft La 12 Fairford GL7 152 E4
Latton SN6 143 E6
Winstone GL7 107 A7
Croft Par GL53 131 B5
Croft Rd
Charlton Kings GL53 131 A5
Newent GL18 171 A5
Croft Sch The GL6 103 E8
Croft St GL53 130 D6
Croft The
Bristol,Mangotsfield BS16 20 F5
Bristol,Oldland Common BS30 11 C3
Cirencester GL7 190 D4
Dursley GL11 88 A4
14 Fairford GL7 152 E4
Painswick GL6 111 F1
Croft Thorne Cl GL51 129 F5
Croft View BS9 18 C6
Crofters Wlk BS32 29 D8
Croftlands The GL20 182 C7
Crofton Ave BS7 18 F6
Crofton Fields BS36 30 E6
Crofton Mews BS15 10 E7
Crofts End Ind Est BS5 19 E1
Crofts End Rd BS5 19 E1
Crofts Field GL20 181 D5
Crofts The GL18 171 A5
Crokeswood Wlk BS11 27 A1
Crome Rd BS7 19 B7
Cromer Rd BS5 19 C2
Cromers Cl GL20 182 C5
Cromhall La GL12 65 D1
Cromwell Ct BS15 10 E5
Cromwell Rd
Bristol,Montpelier BS6 18 E2
Bristol,St George BS5 10 A8
Cheltenham GL52 134 A3
Chepstow/Cas-Gwent NP16 60 E5
Cromwell St Bristol BS3 8 C3
Gloucester GL1 196 B2
Cromwell View BS6 18 E2
Cromwells Hide BS16 19 E5
Crooked End Pl GL17 163 F4
Crooks Ind Est GL53 130 D6
Croomes Hill BS16 20 D6
Cropthorne Rd BS7 29 A1
Cropthorne Road S BS7 19 A8
Crosby Cl GL3 120 B6
Crosby Row BS8 194 A2
Cross Barn GL16 163 B2
Cross Chambers GL15 147 F5
Cross Combe Dr BS13 2 C3
Cross Combe Wlk BS13 2 B3
Cross Cotts GL13 76 C3
Cross Elms La BS9 17 E5
Cross Farm Cl GL15 147 E4
Cross Hands GL15 92 C4
Cross Hands Rd BS35 38 D7
Cross Keys GL15 146 F7
Cross Keys La GL1 196 B3
Cross Keys Rdbt GL2 109 E4
Cross Lanes BS20 16 C4
Cross St Bristol BS15 20 D1
Keynsham BS31 4 F7
Cross The
Bromesberrow Heath HR8 179 B4
Horsley GL6 90 F1
Nympsfield GL10 89 E6
Ripple GL20 181 D8
Cross Tree Cres GL7 144 E8
Cross Tree Flats GL7 144 E7
Cross Tree Gr BS32 29 D8
Cross Vane NP25 154 B3
Cross Wlk BS14 3 A6
Crossfield Rd BS16 20 E3
Crossfields GL54 166 D6
Crossing La SN16 142 C2
Crossleaze Rd BS15 10 C3
Crossley Cl BS36 30 F7
Crossman Ave BS36 30 E5
Crossways Coleford GL16 154 F6
Lower Wick GL11 78 F8
Crossways Jun & Inf Schs BS35 64 D1
Crossways La BS35 64 E2
Crossways Rd Bristol BS4 9 A1
Thornbury BS35 64 D1
Crouch Ct GL20 192 C3
Crow Ash 9 GL16 155 A7
Crow Ash Rd GL16 155 A7
Crow La Bristol BS1 195 A2
Henbury BS10 27 F2
Crow Mdw GL12 67 F4
Crowfield GL52 138 B4
Crowfield La GL18 178 E2
Crowgate La GL14 157 F8
Crowley Way BS11 26 B1
Crown Cl
Bishop's Cleeve GL52 137 F3
Dymock GL18 178 D2
Crown Cotts GL5 98 F8
Crown Ct GL10 98 A3
Crown Dr GL52 137 F2
Crown Gdns BS30 11 B7
Crown Hill BS5 9 F8
Crown Hill Wlk BS5 19 F1
Crown Ind Est BS30 11 C7
Crown La Bristol BS16 20 D4
Parkend GL15 155 E2
St Briavels GL15 146 E7
Yorkley GL15 156 A1
Crown Mdw 13 GL16 155 B5
Crown Rd
Bristol,Upper Soundwell BS15 20 D2
Bristol,Warmley BS30 11 C6
Crown Way BS30 11 C7
Crowndale Rd BS4 9 A3
Crownleaze BS16 20 D3
Crows Gr BS32 40 D3
Crowther Pk BS7 19 A4
Crowther Rd BS7 19 A4
Crowther St 4 BS3 8 B3
Crowthers Ave BS37 43 E3
Croydon Ho 1 BS5 9 B8
Croydon St BS5 9 B8
Crucible Cl GL16 155 A5
Crucible Ct GL16 155 A5
Crudwell CE Prim Sch SN16 141 C3
Crudwell La GL8 140 F3
Crump Pl GL15 92 C2
Crumps Cotts GL20 183 B6
Crunnis The BS32 29 E6
Crusty La BS20 16 C5
Crypt Ct GL4 118 C3
Crypt Sch The GL2 118 D4
Crypt The GL18 178 D2
Crystal Way BS32 29 E8
Crythan Wlk 4 GL51 129 F5
Cuckoo Cl 4 GL6 148 C6
Cuckoo La BS36 30 F3
Cuckoo Row GL6 91 F6
Cud La GL6 103 B8
Cudnall St GL53 131 A7
Cuffington Ave BS4 9 D4
Culkerton GL8 140 F6
Cullerns The SN6 145 D3
Culleysgate La BS30 12 F6
Cullimore View GL14 191 C1
Cullingham Cl GL19 172 A8
Cullis La GL16 155 B6
Culls Mdw GL54 184 A4
Culross Cl GL50 133 E4
Culver Hill GL5 91 A8
Culver St Bristol BS1 194 C2
Newent GL18 171 A4
Culverhay
11 Cricklade SN6 143 E4
Wotton-u-E GL12 68 B7
Culverhill Rd BS37 44 A1
Culverhill Sch BS37 32 D7
Culvers Ct BS31 4 E6
Culvers Rd BS31 4 E6
Culvert Ave BS37 43 B1
Culvert The BS32 29 D8
Culverwell Rd BS13 2 A4
Cumberland Basin Rd BS8 7 F5
Cumberland Cl BS1 194 A1
Cumberland Cres GL51 133 A2
Cumberland Gr 5 BS6 18 F2
Cumberland Pl 7 BS8 7 F6
Cumberland Rd BS1 194 B1
Cumberland St BS2 195 B4
Cumbria Cl BS35 64 E1
Cumming Ct GL52 134 A4
Cunningham Gdns BS16 20 B5
Cunnington Cl BS30 11 B1
Cupola Cl GL16 155 A5
Curland Gr BS14 3 B5
Curlew Cl Bristol BS16 19 F6
Northway GL20 182 B5
Curlew Rd GL4 119 C6
Cursey La GL51 136 B5
Cursey Lane Cvn Site GL51 173 F7
Cursus The GL7 153 E3
Curtis Hayward Dr GL2 117 E1
Curtis La BS34 30 A4
Custom Cl BS14 3 A7
Custom Ho The BS1 195 A1
Cut & Fry Rd GL15 156 B1
Cut Throat La HR9 170 A2
Cutham La GL7 158 C1
Cuthwine Pl GL7 153 E3
Cutler Rd Bristol BS13 1 F6
Stroud GL5 99 D8
Cutsdean Cl GL52 137 D4
Cutsheath Rd GL12 52 C8
Cutters Row BS3 8 E4
Cutwell GL8 140 B3
Cylde Pk BS6 18 B2
Cynder Way BS16 31 A1
Cypress Ct BS9 17 D3
Cypress Gdns Bristol BS8 7 E6
Gloucester GL2 127 D5
Cypress Gr BS9 18 C6
Cypress Rd GL20 192 E2
Cypress Wlk SN14 15 F6
Cyrus Ct BS16 21 B7

D

Daffodil Cl GL4 119 E5
Daffodil Leaze GL10 98 B3
Daffodil St GL50 193 B2
Daffodils The GL10 98 B3
Daglingworth Path GL7 149 E6
Dagmar Rd GL50 193 A1
Daines Ct 4 BS16 19 E3
Dainty St GL1 118 F7
Dairy Farm SN6 142 F4
Dairy La WR11 183 F6
Dairycroft BS2 195 B4
Daisy Bank GL5 99 E6
Daisy Green La GL12 79 D2
Daisy Rd BS5 19 C2
Daisybank Rd GL53 130 E2
Dakin Cl BS4 8 E1
Dakota Dr BS14 3 A4
Dalby Ave BS3 8 D4
Daldry Gdns BS35 50 A3
Dale Cl GL4 118 F5
Dale St Bristol,St George BS5 9 F8
Bristol,St Pauls BS2 195 C4
Temple Guiting GL54 175 D2
Dale Wlk GL52 138 A3
Dalebrook HR9 170 B4
Dalkeith Ave BS15 20 C1
Dallaway GL5 99 E2
Dalrymple Rd 10 BS2 18 E1
Dalston Rd BS3 8 B4
Dalton Sq BS2 195 B4
Damery La Stone GL13 77 F3
Woodford GL13 78 A4
Damery Works GL13 78 B3
Dampier Rd BS3 8 A3
Damsells The 9 GL8 140 C4
Damson Cl GL4 119 E4
Danbury Cres BS10 28 C1
Danbury Wlk BS10 28 C1
Danby Cl Cinderford GL14 191 E4
Yorkley GL15 156 B2
Danby Ho BS7 19 A5
Danby Rd GL15 156 B2
Dancers Hill GL4 119 E6
Dancey Mead BS13 1 F6
Dancey Rd GL3 127 F6
Dancing Gn HR9 164 A7
Dane Cl GL2 127 C5
Dane La GL7 149 B6
Danes Cl NP16 60 D8
Danes Hill NP16 61 B7
Danford La GL19 172 B3
Danford Villas GL19 172 B3
Dangerfield Ave BS13 1 F6
Daniels Ind Est GL5 98 F5
Daniels Mdw GL4 118 A2
Daniels Rd GL5 99 F7
Danwood Ct GL1 118 D7
Dapps Hill BS31 4 F5
Dapwell La BS14,BS31 4 A1
Darell Cl GL2 109 F7
Darell Gdns GL2 157 F3
Dark La Chalford GL6 148 C5
Nailsworth GL6 91 A4
North Cerney GL7 158 E3
Stroud GL5 99 B5
Swindon GL51 133 A7
Dark Ride GL7 149 C8
Darken La GL15 147 E4
Darks Rd GL18 170 C3
Darley Cl BS10 27 D3
Darleydale Cl GL2 109 D8
Darnell's La HR9 170 B4
Darnley Ave BS7 18 F6
Darren Rd 13 GL16 155 A7
Dart Cl Quedgeley GL2 117 F2
Thornbury BS35 51 B8
Dart Rd GL52 134 B3
Darters Cl GL15 92 A2
Dartmoor St BS3 8 B3
Dartmouth Wlk BS31 4 D4
Darwin Cl GL51 129 C8
Darwin Rd GL4 119 A5
Daston Cl 2 WR12 185 C8
Daubeny Cl BS16 20 B5
Daubeny Ct BS1 195 A1
Davallia Dr GL51 129 F5
Daventry Rd BS4 8 F1
Daventry Terr GL1 196 C1
Davey Cl GL2 109 F6
Davey Rd GL20 182 C4
Davey St BS2 18 F1
Davey Terr 8 BS2 18 F1
David French Ct GL51 130 A5
David St BS2 195 C3
David Thomas Ho BS6 18 E2
David's La BS35 51 A4
David's Rd BS14 3 C6
Davids Cl BS35 51 A4
Davies Dr BS4 9 F5
Davies Rd 1 GL56 187 B3
Davillian Ct GL2 118 A3
Davin Cres BS20 16 C3
Davis Cl BS30 10 F5
Davis Ct BS35 64 C2
Davis St BS11 16 B8
Davron Ct BS3 8 E4
Dawes Cl
Meysey Hampton GL7 152 A3
Southrop GL7 153 C6
Dawes Ct 3 BS8 7 F6
Dawes The GL2 109 F8
Dawley Cl BS36 30 E7
Dawlish Rd BS3 8 D2
Dawn Rise BS15 21 A1
Dawneys The SN16 141 C3
Daws Ct BS16 20 B4
Day House La GL12 55 C8
Day's La GL56 186 C5
Day's Rd BS2 9 A6
Daylesford Cl GL51 129 D8
Days Ct SN16 141 C3
Days Road Commercial Ctr BS2 9 A7
De Clifford Rd BS11 27 C2
De Ferrieres Wlk 12 GL51 132 D2
De Havilland Rd GL54 169 D7
De La Warre Ct 11 BS4 9 F6
De Verose Ct BS15 10 E4
Deacon Cl
Cheltenham GL51 129 F7

Deacon Cl *continued*
Winterbourne BS36 30 E5
Deacons Pl GL52 137 E2
Deakin Cl GL51 133 B7
Deakin's Ho GL15 155 E2
Dean Ave BS35 64 C2
Dean Cl BS15 10 B4
Dean Close Prep Sch
GL51 130 A8
Dean Close Sch GL51 129 F8
Dean Cres 8 Bristol BS3 8 C4
1 Bristol BS3 8 D4
Littledean GL14 156 E8
Dean Ct Lydney GL15 92 B4
Yate BS37 43 C3
Dean Farm Cotts GL7 160 F2
Dean Forest Railway Mus*
GL15 147 F7
Dean Forest Rly* GL15 92 A2
Dean Hall Sch GL16 155 F6
Dean Heritage Mus*
GL14 156 D5
Dean La Bristol BS3 8 C4
Stoke Orchard GL52 136 E5
Dean Mdws GL17 164 D5
Dean Rd Avonmouth BS11 26 C5
Newnham GL14 156 F6
Yate BS37 43 C3
Dean Rise GL14 156 F6
Dean St
Bristol,Southville BS3 8 C4
Bristol,St Pauls BS2 195 B4
Dean Swift Cl HR9 162 F6
Dean The HR9 163 E6
Dean View GL14 191 C1
Dean's Ct BS1 194 C2
Dean's Dr BS5 20 A2
Dean's Quarry GL5 91 F7
Dean's Terr GL1 196 B4
Dean's Way GL1 196 B4
Dean's Wlk GL1 196 B4
Dean's Wlk GL17 164 B4
Deanery Cl BS15 11 B8
Deanery Rd
Bristol,Warmley BS15 11 B8
BristolBrandon Hill BS1 194 C2
Deanery Rd Rdbt BS15 11 B8
Deanhill La BA1 6 F2
Deanna Ct BS16 20 E6
Deans Ct 3 GL51 129 F7
Deans Gdns NP16 72 D1
Deans Hill NP16 60 D8
Deans Mead BS11 17 A8
Deans Row GL1 126 E4
Deans Way GL52 137 F3
Deansfield SN6 143 E4
Debecca's La BS20 16 B4
Deep Coombe Rd BS3 8 A2
Deep Pit Rd BS5 19 F2
Deep St GL52 134 B4
Deer Park Rd GL3 128 A1
Deer Pk GL15 156 A2
Deer's Wood Sch BS15 21 A2
Deerhurst Bristol BS15 20 E3
Yate BS37 32 C8
Deerhurst & Apperley CE
Prim Sch GL19 173 C7
Deerhurst Cl
Gloucester GL4 119 E4
Little Compton GL56 187 F1
Deerhurst Pl GL2 117 E1
Deering Cl BS11 27 B1
Deerswood BS15 21 A2
Dehaviland Rd GL52 137 E1
Delabere Ave BS16 20 B5
Delabere Rd GL52 138 A2
Delancey Hospl GL53 130 D4
Delavale Rd GL54 174 A7
Deleware Rd GL7 152 E2
Delius Gr BS4 2 D7
Delkin Rd GL11 87 F4
Delkin The GL11 87 F4
Dell Prim Sch The NP16 72 E1
Dell The Blockley GL56 186 C6
Bredon GL20 182 C8
Bristol,Bradley Stoke BS32 29 E7
Bristol,Oldland Common
BS30 11 C5
Bristol,Westbury on Trym
BS9 17 F5
Gloucester GL4 119 E7
Dell View NP16 60 E8
Delmont Gr GL5 99 C8
Delphinium Dr GL52 137 E3
Delta Dr GL20 182 B4
Delta Way GL3 120 C6
Delvin Rd BS10 18 C8
Denbigh Dr NP16 61 A5
Denbigh Rd GL51 129 E6
Denbigh St BS2 18 F1
Dene Cl BS31 4 F3
Dene Magna Sch GL17 164 D4
Dene Rd BS14 3 C4
Denehurst GL17 163 F3
Denfurlong Farm Trail*
GL54 159 B5
Denham Cl
Gloucester GL4 118 C1
Woodmancote GL52 138 C3
Denleigh Cl BS14 3 A4
Denley Cl GL52 137 F2
Denmark Ave BS1 194 C2
Denmark Ct GL1 127 A3
Denmark Dr NP16 61 B7
Denmark Pl BS7 18 E3
Denmark Rd GL1 196 C4
Denmark St BS1 194 C2
Denmark Villas GL14 165 F1
Denning Ct GL50 193 A1
Dennisworth BS16 22 B5
Dennor Pk BS14 3 B7
Denny Isle Dr BS35 38 A6
Denston Wlk BS13 2 A7
Dent's La GL19 172 B2
Dent's Terr 24 GL54 174 A7
Denton Patch BS16 21 B7
Dentwood Gr BS9 17 B8
Denvale Trad Pk BS4 2 E7
Denys Ct BS35 50 A3
Derby Ct GL1 127 A1
Derby Rd Bristol BS7 18 E3
Gloucester GL1 127 A1
Derby St BS5 9 D7
Derham Rd BS13 2 A5
Dermot St 11 BS2 18 F1
Derrick Rd BS15 10 D8
Derricke Rd BS14 3 F6
Derry Pk SN16 142 E1
Derry Rd BS3 8 B2
Derry The SN6 142 F4
Derwent Cl Bristol BS34 29 A8
Brockworth GL3 120 E5
Derwent Ct BS35 51 D8
Derwent Dr GL20 192 E6
Derwent Gr BS31 5 A5
Derwent Rd BS5 19 F1
Derwent Wlk 1 GL51 129 F7
Desford Cl GL4 119 F5
Despenser Rd GL20 192 C2
Detmore Cl GL53 131 D5
Devaney Cl BS4 9 F5
Devauden Rd NP16 72 B7
Devereaux Cres GL5 98 C7
Devereaux Rd GL5 98 C7
Deveron Gr BS31 5 A4
Devil's Chy* GL53 130 D1
Devil's Elbow The GL6 91 E4
Devil's La GL12 67 A2
Devon Ave GL51 133 A2
Devon Gr BS5 9 C8
Devon Rd BS5 19 C1
Devon Road Trad Est 1
BS5 19 C1
Devonshire Bldgs BS3 8 E4
Devonshire Pl GL20 192 D2
Devonshire Rd BS6 18 B4
Devonshire St GL50 193 A4
Devonshire Terr 2
GL56 187 A3
Dewey Cl GL52 138 B3
Dewfalls Dr BS32 40 D1
Dial La BS16 20 D6
Diamond Rd BS5 9 F7
Diamond St BS3 8 C3
Diamonite Ind Pk BS16 20 A3
Diana Gdns BS32 29 E8
Dianas Cl GL4 119 F6
Dibden Cl BS16 21 A8
Dibden La Alderton GL24 183 E4
Bristol BS16 21 B7
Dibden Rd BS16 21 A7
Dickens Cl Bristol BS7 19 A8
Gloucester GL4 118 F5
Dickens Mews GL4 118 F5
Didbrook Mews GL4 119 E4
Didbrook Prim Sch
GL54 184 D2
Didsbury Cl BS10 27 F1
Digbeth St 10 GL54 176 F4
Digby Dr GL20 192 E6
Dighton Ct 3 BS2 195 A4
Dighton Gate BS34 29 E5
Dighton St BS2 195 A4
Dikler Cl GL54 169 A6
Dilke Meml Hospl GL14 191 A2
Dill Ave GL51 132 E4
Dillon Ct 18 BS5 9 D7
Dimore Cl GL2 109 E7
Dinas Cl GL51 129 F6
Dinas Rd GL51 129 F6
Dinely St GL1 196 C1
Dingle Bglws GL53 158 A8
Dingle Cl BS9 17 C6
Dingle Ct BS13 1 F7
Dingle La GL20 182 A8
Dingle Rd BS9 17 D7
Dingle The Bristol BS9 17 D7
Winterbourne BS36 30 F3
Yate BS37 43 F4
Dingle View BS9 17 C7
Dinglewell GL3 119 F7
Dinglewell Inf Sch GL3 119 F7
Dinglewell Jun Sch GL3 119 F7
Dinglewood Cl BS9 17 D7
Dings Wlk 4 BS2 9 A6
Discovery Rd GL4 119 F6
Distel Cl GL50 133 C5
District Ctr BS32 29 E8
Ditch La GL7 159 E3
Dixon Bsns Ctr BS4 9 F2
Dixon Rd BS4 9 F2
Dixton Cl NP25 154 A8
Dixton Rd NP25 154 A8
Dock Gate La BS8 194 A1
Dock La GL20 182 C8
Dock Rd GL13 93 B1
Dockham Rd GL14 191 D4
Dockins Hill Way GL17 164 D4
Doctors La 20 GL54 168 A1
Dodington Ash BS37 34 B2
Dodington Cl GL4 119 D7
Dodington La BS37 33 D5
Dodington Rd BS37 33 B7
Dodisham Wlk BS16 20 B6
Dog La GL3 121 D5
Dog Trap La SN16 142 C1
Dollar St GL7 190 C5
Dolman Cl BS10 27 F3
Domby Cl 18 GL16 155 A5
Domestic Fowl Trust*
WR11 188 C7
Dominion Rd BS16 19 F3
Donald Rd BS13 1 F7
Doncaster Rd BS10 18 C8
Doncombe Hill SN14 15 F7
Doncombe La SN14 15 F7
Donegal Rd BS4 8 D1
Dongola Ave BS7 18 E4
Dongola Rd BS7 18 E4
Donkey Field The GL7 151 C5
Donkey La GL56 186 C5
Donnington Wlk BS31 4 D4
Donside GL7 190 A7
Doone Rd BS7 18 F8
Dora Wlk 6 GL1 118 F7
Dorcas Ave BS34 29 F5
Dorchester Ct GL50 130 C6
Dorchester Rd BS7 19 A7
Dorester Cl BS10 28 C4
Dorian Cl BS7 18 E7
Dorian Rd BS7 18 E7
Dorian Way BS7 18 E8
Dorington Ct 6 GL6 148 B6
Dorington Wlk 13 GL51 132 D2
Dormer Cl BS36 31 D6
Dormer Rd Bristol BS5 19 B3
Cheltenham GL51 132 F4
Dormers The SN6 145 D3
Dorn GL56 187 A5
Dorney Rd GL1 118 E7
Dorrit Cl GL1 118 F6
Dorset Ave GL51 133 A2
Dorset Gr 9 BS2 19 A2
Dorset Ho 2 GL50 193 B4
Dorset Rd
Bristol,Kingswood BS15 20 D1
Bristol,Westbury on Trym
BS9 18 B6
Dorset St 6 BS3 8 B3
Dorset Way BS37 44 A3
Double View GL14 191 D3
Doubledays 7 SN6 143 E4
Doudney Ct BS3 8 E4
Doughmeadow Cotts
WR12 184 F6
Douglas Ho GL50 193 B2
Douglas Rd
Bristol,Horfield BS7 18 F7
Bristol,Kingswood BS15 10 D7
Douglas Road Ind Pk
BS15 10 D7
Doulton Way BS14 3 B5
Douro Lo GL50 193 A2
Douro Rd GL50 133 B1
Dove La
Bristol,Russell Town BS5 9 C7
Bristol,St Pauls BS2 195 C4
Dove St BS2 195 A4
Dove St S BS2 195 A4
Dovecote BS37 32 E7
Dovedale BS35 51 D8
Dovedale Cl GL2 109 D8
Dover Hay GL51 129 F5
Dover Pl BS8 194 B3
Dover's View GL55 188 D4
Dovercourt Rd BS7 19 A6
Doverdale Dr GL2 127 D4
Doveswell Gr BS13 2 A4
Dovey Ct BS30 11 C5
Dowdeswell Cl BS10 27 F3
Dowding Cl BS37 44 C2
Dowding Way GL3 128 C5
Dowers' La GL7 150 A8
Dowland Gr BS4 2 D6
Dowling Rd BS13 2 D3
Down Ampney CE Prim Sch
GL7 143 F8
Down Ampney Rd GL7 143 D7
Down Farm Ho BS36 30 D6
Down Hatherley La GL2 173 C1
Down Leaze 2 BS35 51 A5
Down Rd Alveston BS35 51 A5
Marshfield SN14 25 C2
Winterbourne BS36 30 F4
Down The Alveston BS35 50 F5
Tockington BS32 50 D3
Down View Bristol BS7 18 F3
Chalford GL6 148 C6
Downend Park Rd BS16 20 D5
Downend Pk BS7 18 F5
Downend Rd
Bristol,Fishponds BS16 20 C5
Bristol,Horfield BS7 18 F5
Bristol,Kingswood BS15 20 D1
Downend Sch BS16 20 F7
Downfield Bristol BS9 17 C7
Keynsham BS31 4 D5
Stroud GL5 98 F7
Downfield Cl 1 BS35 51 A5
Downfield Dr BS36 31 B8
Downfield Ho GL51 129 D2
Downfield La GL20 182 A8
Downfield Lodge BS8 18 A1
Downfield Rd Bristol BS8 18 A1
Stroud GL5 98 F7
Downham Ct GL11 80 D8
Downham View GL11 80 D8
Downham Wlk GL11 80 D8
Downhams The 14
NP25 154 A7
Downleaze
Bristol,Downend BS16 20 D8
Bristol,Stoke Bishop BS9 17 F3
Downleaze Dr BS37 33 B8
Downman Rd BS7 19 A5
Downs Cl 3 BS35 51 A5
Downs Cote Ave BS9 17 F6
Downs Cote Dr BS9 17 F6
Downs Cote Gdns BS9 18 A6
Downs Cote Pk BS9 18 A6
Downs Cote View BS9 18 A6
Downs Ct BS9 18 B6
Downs Mill GL6 148 E4
Downs Pk E BS6 18 A4
Downs Pk W BS6 18 A4
Downs Rd Bristol BS9 18 A6
Dundry BS41 1 D2
Downs The GL12 53 F7
Downs View SN6 145 D3
Downs Way GL7 150 D7
Downside Cl BS30 10 F5
Downside Rd BS8 18 A1
Downsview Ct BS8 18 A1
Downton Rd Bristol BS4 8 D1
Stonehouse GL10 97 E6
Downy Cl GL2 117 E2
Dowry Mews BS8 194 A2
Dowry Pl 3 BS8 7 F5
Dowry Rd BS8 194 A2
Dowry Sq BS8 194 A2
Dowty Rd GL51 132 E2
Doynton La SN14,BS30 23 B3
Dozule Cl GL10 97 F3
Dr Brown's Cl GL6 91 F6
Dr Brown's Rd GL6 91 F7
Dr Crawfords Way GL6 91 F6
Dr Crouch's Rd GL6 148 B7
Dr Middletons Rd GL6 148 C5
Dr Newton's Way GL5 99 C6
Dr White's Cl BS1 195 B1
Drag Rd HR9 162 E3
Dragon Ct BS5 19 E1
Dragon Rd BS36 30 D5
Dragon Wlk BS5 19 F1
Dragons Hill Cl BS31 4 F5
Dragons Hill Ct BS31 4 F5
Dragons Hill Gdns BS31 4 F5
Dragonswell Rd BS10 28 A2
Drake Cl Innsworth GL3 127 F7
Saltford BS31 5 D2
Drake Ho BS1 195 A3
Drake La GL11 88 C2
Drake Rd BS3 8 A3
Drakes Pl GL50 193 A3
Dram La BS5 10 A6
Dramway Rdbt BS16 21 D6
Draper Ct 3 BS5 9 C7
Draper's La GL19 172 D6
Drapers Ct GL52 138 B3
Draycot Pl BS1 195 A1
Draycott GL11 87 F7
Draycott Bsns Pk GL11 87 F7
Draycott Cres GL11 87 F7
Draycott Ind Est GL56 186 D6
Draycott Rd BS7 18 F5
Draydon Rd BS4 2 D8
Drayton Cl Bristol BS14 3 B8
Cheltenham GL51 133 B6
1 Gloucester GL4 119 C4
Drayton Rd Bristol BS9 17 C8
Cheltenham GL51 129 E8
Drayton Way GL4 119 C5
Drews Cl GL3 128 C4
Drews Ct GL3 128 C4
Driffield Cross Rds GL7 151 B1
Driffield Rd GL15 92 C5
Drift Cl GL7 190 A2
Drift Way GL7 190 A2
Drifton Hill SN14 25 F7
Drive The
Bristol,Hengrove BS14 3 C6
Bristol,Henleaze BS9 18 B5
Dursley GL11 87 F4
Tetbury GL8 140 D2
Drivemoor GL4 119 D3
Druetts Cl BS10 18 E6
Drugger's End La WR13 180 C8
Druid Cl BS9 17 E5
Druid Hill BS9 17 E5
Druid Rd BS9 17 D4
Druid Stoke Ave BS9 17 D5
Druid Woods BS9 17 C5
Druids Cl GL4 119 C7
Druids La GL4 119 C7
Druids Oak GL2 109 F8
Drummond Ct BS30 10 F4
Drummond Rd
Bristol,Fishponds BS16 19 F3
Bristol,St Pauls BS2 18 E1
Drury La GL19 179 D2
Dry Meadow La GL3 127 C7
Drybrook Prim Sch
GL17 164 B4
Drybrook Rd GL17 164 B4
Dryland Mews GL3 120 B6
Dryleaze Keynsham BS31 4 E7
Wotton-u-E GL12 68 A7
Yate BS37 43 E5
Dryleaze Ct GL12 68 A7
Dryleaze Gdns GL12 68 A7
Dryleaze Ho GL12 68 A7
Dryleaze Rd BS16 19 F6
Dubbers La BS5 19 E2
Dublin Cres BS9 18 B6
Duchess Rd BS8 18 A1
Duchess Way BS16 19 D6
Ducie Cl GL12 66 B2
Ducie Ct BS16 20 E4
Ducie Rd
Bristol,Russell Town BS5 9 B7
Bristol,Staple Hill BS16 20 E5
Ducie Rd Bsns Pk 6 BS5 9 B7
Ducie St GL1 118 F7
Duck St GL12 52 C5
Duckmoor Rd BS3 8 A3
Duckmoor Road Ind Est
BS3 8 A4
Duckworth Cl GL53 130 D5
Dudbridge Hill GL5 98 F6
Dudbridge Mdw GL5 98 F5
Dudbridge Rd GL5 98 F5
Duderstadt Cl GL5 98 F8
Dudley Cl BS31 4 E4
Dudley Cnr GL7 151 C5
Dudley Ct 3 BS30 10 F4
Dudley Farm GL7 151 C5
Dudley Gr BS7 19 A8
Dudley Rd WR11 188 C7
Duffield's La NP25 154 C5
Dugar Wlk BS6 18 C3
Dugdale Rd GL7 190 C5
Duglynch La GL54 183 E1
Duke of Beaufort Ct
GL1 118 D5
Duke Of York Rd GL16 154 C7
Duke St GL52 133 F1
Dukeries The GL1 196 A3
Dukes Field GL7 143 F8
Dukes Way GL20 192 D1
Dulverton Cl GL51 132 D3
Dulverton Pl GL56 187 B3
Dulverton Rd BS7 18 D4
Dumaine Ave BS34 29 E5
Dumbleton Gr GL51 129 B6
Dunalley Par GL50 133 D3
Dunalley Prim Sch
GL50 133 E3
Dunalley St GL50 193 B4
Dunbar Cl GL51 132 D4
Duncombe La BS15 20 B2
Duncombe Rd BS15 20 B1
Duncroft Rd GL3 127 F1
Dundas Cl BS10 27 E2
Dundonald Rd BS6 18 B3
Dundridge Gdns BS5 10 A6
Dundridge La BS5 10 A6
Dundry CE Prim Sch BS41 1 D2
Dundry Cl BS15 10 D6
Dundry La BS41 1 C3
Dundry View BS4 9 A1
Dunford Rd BS3 8 D3
Dunkeld Ave BS34 28 F2
Dunkerry Rd BS3 8 D3
Dunkirk Cotts GL9 56 C1
Dunkirk Rd BS16 19 F3
Dunlin Cl GL2 117 D1
Dunmail Prim Sch BS10 28 C2
Dunmail Rd BS10 28 C2
Dunmore St 3 BS2 8 F4
Dunmurry BS9 17 D3
Dunns Copse 15 HR8 178 F8
Dunsdown La SN14 24 B5
Dunsmore Gn GL19 181 B3
Dunstall Ho 19 GL56 187 A3
Dunstan Glen GL3 128 D4
Dunster Cl
Cheltenham GL51 132 D3
Gloucester GL4 118 B1
Dunster Gdns Bristol BS30 11 B2
Cheltenham GL51 132 D3
Dunster Gr GL51 132 D3
Dunster Rd Bristol BS4 2 F8
Cheltenham GL51 132 D3
Keynsham BS31 4 E4
Dunstone Pl GL17 164 D5
Durand Cl GL2 127 C6
Durand Ct GL12 68 A7
Durban Ho 4 GL51 132 F4
Durban Rd BS34 28 F8
Durbin Wlk BS5 9 A8
Durbridge Rd GL19 179 C1
Durdham Ct BS6 18 A3
Durdham Pk BS6 18 A3
Durham Cl GL51 130 A5
Durham Gr BS31 4 D4
Durham Rd 10 Bristol BS2 19 A2
Charfield GL12 67 A5
Gloucester GL4 119 C8
Durleigh Cl BS13 2 A7
Durley Hill BS31 4 C7
Durley La BS31 4 D7
Durn's Rd GL12 68 C7
Durncourt Cotts GL7 151 C5
Durnford Ave BS3 8 A4
Durnford St BS3 8 A4
Dursley CE Prim Sch
GL11 80 C8
Dursley Cl BS37 43 E1
Dursley Ct GL11 88 A1
Dursley Rd Bristol BS11 16 E5
Dursley GL11 87 E3
Slimbridge GL2 95 F3
Durville Rd BS13 2 B6
Durweston Wlk BS14 3 C8
Dutton Cl BS14 3 D6
Dutton Leys GL54 168 A1
Dutton Rd BS14 3 D6
Dutton Wlk BS14 3 D6
Duttons La GL17 163 F3
Dye House Rd GL12 67 F5
Dyer St GL7 190 D4
Dyer's La
Chipping Campden GL55 188 F2
Yate BS37 43 A4
Dyers Cl BS13 2 D4
Dyersbrook GL12 68 B7

Dyke House La GL18 179 B4
Dylan Thomas Ct [4] BS30 11 A5
Dymock Rd Ledbury HR8 178 E7
Much Marcle HR8 178 A3
Dynevor St GL1 118 F7
Dynevor Terr GL7 152 D4
Dyrham BS16 30 C1
Dyrham Cl
Bristol,Henleaze BS9 18 D6
Bristol,Kingswood BS15 10 F8
Pucklechurch BS16 22 C4
Thornbury BS35 64 C3
Dyrham Par BS34 29 C8
Dyrham Park* SN14 23 F5
Dyrham Rd BS15 10 F8

E

Eagar Ho GL53 131 B4
Eagle Cl GL6 148 B6
Eagle Cres BS16 22 C5
Eagle Dr BS34 28 E8
Eagle Mill Cl GL5 99 D5
Eagle Rd BS4 9 D2
Eagle Way GL4 119 C5
Eagles Wood BS32 40 D3
Eagles Wood Bsns Pk BS32 40 C3
Ealy Hill GL7 107 C5
Eardisland Rd GL4 118 E2
Earl Russell Way BS5 9 B7
Earl St BS1 195 A4
Earls Cnr SN16 141 F4
Earlsmead BS16 19 E4
Earlstone Cl BS30 11 A4
Earlstone Cres BS30 11 A4
Early Way BS7 18 E8
Earthcott Rd BS35 51 F1
Easedale Cl BS10 28 D2
East Allcourt GL7 153 E2
East Approach Dr GL52 133 F4
East Court Mews GL52 131 C5
East Croft BS9 18 C7
East Ct BS3 7 F3
East Dr GL5 98 C7
East Dundry La BS41 2 A1
East Dundry Rd BS13,BS14 2 F2
East End GL54 168 A1
East End Flats GL53 131 C5
East End Rd GL52,GL53 131 C5
East Gable GL52 138 B3
East Gr BS6 18 F1
East Hill BS9 18 B7
East Link GL17 164 D5
East Par BS9 17 C6
East Park Dr BS5 19 C2
East Pk BS5 19 C2
East Priory Cl BS9 18 A7
East Ridge Dr BS13 1 F5
East Shrubbery [3] BS6 18 B2
East St Avonmouth BS11 26 A1
Bristol,Southville BS3 8 D4
Bristol,St Pauls BS2 195 C4
Moreton-in-M GL56 187 A3
St Briavels GL15 146 F7
Tewkesbury GL20 192 C4
East View Bristol BS16 20 F6
Newnham GL14 156 F7
East Wlk BS37 43 E1
Eastbourne Rd [9] BS5 9 B8
Eastbourne Terr GL7 152 E3
Eastbrook Rd GL4 119 C8
Eastbury Cl BS35 64 C1
Eastbury Rd Bristol BS16 20 A4
Thornbury BS35 64 C1
Eastcote Pk BS14 3 B5
Eastcott Way GL3 128 A6
Easter Ct BS37 43 B1
Eastern Ave
Gloucester GL4 119 B8
Mitcheldean GL17 164 D5
Eastern Way GL14 156 C6
Eastfield
Ashton Keynes SN6 142 F5
Bristol BS9 18 B7
Eastfield Dr BS37 43 E4
Eastfield Mews GL4 118 F5
Eastfield Rd
Bristol,Eastfield BS9 18 B7
Bristol,Montpelier BS6 18 D2
Bristol,Westbury on Trym BS9 18 A7
Minchinhampton GL6 148 A3
Eastfield Terr BS9 18 B6
Eastgate Ho GL1 196 C2
Eastgate Office Ctr BS5 19 B3
Eastgate Ret Pk BS5 19 B3
Eastgate Sh Ctr GL1 196 B2
Eastgate St GL1 196 B2
Eastholm Lawns GL3 128 C5
Eastington Prim Sch GL10 97 A8
Eastington Rd GL54 168 A1
Eastington Trad Est GL10 100 F1
Eastlake Cl BS7 19 B7
Eastland Ave BS35 64 C2
Eastland Rd BS35 64 C2
Eastleigh Cl BS16 20 E4
Eastleigh Rd
Bristol,Brentry BS10 28 D1
Bristol,Staple Hill BS16 20 E3
Eastley Cl GL12 65 E7
Eastlyn Rd BS13 2 B8
Eastmead Ct BS9 17 E4
Eastmead La BS9 17 E4
Eastnor Castle* HR8 179 B7
Eastnor CE Prim Sch HR8 179 B8
Eastnor Ho [14] GL51 132 E2
Eastnor Rd BS14 3 A3
Easton Bsns Ctr BS5 9 B8
Easton CE Prim Sch BS5 9 A8
Easton Hill Rd BS35 64 D1
Easton Rd
Bristol,Newton BS5 9 A7
Bristol,Upper Easton BS5 9 B8
Pill BS20 16 C4
Easton Sq SN16 58 D1
Easton Town SN16 58 D1
Easton Way BS5 9 A8
Eastover Cl BS9 18 A8
Eastpark Trad Est BS5 19 D1
Eastrop SN6 145 D3
Eastrop Inf Sch SN6 145 D3
Eastview Terr SN6 145 D3
Eastville Cl GL4 119 B8
Eastwood Cres BS4 9 F3
Eastwood Rd Bristol BS4 9 F4
Harrow Hill GL17 164 B3
Eaton Cl
Bristol,Fishponds BS16 20 B4
Bristol,Stockwood BS14 3 E5
Eaton Cres BS8 194 A4
Eaton Pl GL53 193 B2
Eaton St [15] BS3 8 C3
Ebenezer La BS9 17 E5
Ebenezer St BS5 9 D7
Ebley Ind Pk GL5 98 D6
Ebley Rd GL10 98 B6
Ebor Rd GL2 127 C1
Ebrington GL55 189 D3
Ebrington CE Prim Sch GL55 189 D3
Ebrington Cl GL4 119 D8
Eccles Ct [11] GL8 140 C4
Eccleston Ho [1] BS5 9 B6
Echo La GL11 87 B2
Eclipse Ct [1] BS16 20 C4
Eclipse Office Pk [2] BS16 20 C4
Eddys La GL17 163 E3
Eden Gr BS7 29 A1
Eden Office Pk BS20 16 E4
Eden's Hill GL18 171 D6
Edencroft SN6 145 D4
Edendale App GL51 129 C8
Edendale Rd GL51 132 C1
Edenwall GL16 155 B5
Edenwall Rd GL16 155 B4
Edge End Rd [1] GL16 155 B6
Edge Hills Cl GL14 191 D5
Edge Hills Rd GL14 191 D5
Edge La GL6 103 C8
Edge Rd GL6 103 E8
Edgecombe Cl BS15 20 F1
Edgecorner La SN14 36 A3
Edgecumbe Rd BS6 18 D2
Edgefield Cl BS14 2 F3
Edgefield Rd BS14 2 F3
Edgeware Rd
Bristol,Southville BS3 8 C4
Bristol,Staple Hill BS16 20 D4
Edgewood Cl
Bristol,Hengrove BS14 3 B8
Bristol,Longwell Green BS30 11 A3
Edgeworth BS37 32 C6
Edgeworth Cl
Cirencester GL7 190 B2
[5] Gloucester GL4 119 E5
Edinburgh Pl
Cheltenham GL51 132 E2
[3] Coleford GL16 155 B5
Edinburgh Rd BS31 4 E4
Edington Gr BS10 28 A2
Edmond Rd NP16 61 B8
Edmund Cl BS16 20 D6
Edmund Ct BS16 22 B6
Edna Ave BS4 9 E3
Edward Bird Ho BS7 19 B6
Edward Ct BS31 4 F4
Edward Jenner Mus* GL13 85 E3
Edward Massey Gdns GL4 119 C3
Edward Pl GL20 192 D1
Edward Rd
Bristol,Kingswood BS15 10 E8
Bristol,Totterdown BS4 9 B4
Edward St
Bristol,Eastville BS5 19 D2
Bristol,Moorfields BS5 9 C7
Cheltenham GL50 193 B1
Edward Wilson Ho [2] GL51 132 E3
Edward Wilson Villas [2] GL50 130 B6
Edwards Cl
Joy's Green GL17 163 D3
Poulton GL7 151 E3
Edwards Ct [17] BS5 9 D7
Edwards' Coll GL7 142 F8
Edwin Short Cl BS30 5 E8
Edwy Par GL1 196 B4
Effingham Rd BS6 18 E2
Egerton Brow BS7 18 D4
Egerton Rd BS7 18 D4
Eggshill La BS37 43 D1
Eglin Croft BS13 2 B4
Egypt Ho GL6 91 B4
Eighth Ave
Bristol,Filton BS7 29 B1
Bristol,Hengrove BS14 3 A7
Eirene Terr BS20 16 D4
Elberton BS15 11 A8
Elberton Rd Bristol BS9 17 B7
Elberton BS35 49 F5
Elbridge Ho [4] BS2 195 C3
Elbury Ave BS15 20 C2
Elbury View GL12 67 B5
Elcombe GL11 81 A7
Elderberry Mews GL3 127 F6
Elderberry Wlk BS10 28 C3
Eldersfield Cl
Quedgeley GL2 117 E2
Winchcombe GL54 174 A8
Eldersfield Lawn CE Prim Sch GL19 180 F1
Elderwood Dr BS30 11 A3
Elderwood Rd BS14 3 B7
Elderwood Way GL4 118 C2
Eldon Ave GL52 134 A1
Eldon Rd GL52 133 F1
Eldon Terr BS3 8 D3
Eldon Way BS4 9 C5
Eldonwall Trad Est BS4 9 C5
Eldorado Cres GL50 133 B1
Eldorado Rd GL50 133 B1
Eldred Cl BS9 17 D5
Eleventh Ave BS7 29 B1
Elf Mdw GL7 151 F4
Elfin Rd BS16 20 A5
Elgar Cl Bristol BS4 2 D6
Ledbury HR8 178 E8
Elgar Ho GL51 132 E2
Elgin Ave BS7 28 F1
Elgin Hall GL10 97 F7
Elgin Pk BS6 18 B2
Elgin Rd BS16 20 B2
Eliot Cl Bristol BS7 29 A1
Gloucester GL2 118 C4
Elizabeth Cl BS35 51 D8
Elizabeth Cres BS34 29 E4
Elizabeth Gdns
Meysey Hampton GL7 152 B3
[5] Tetbury GL8 140 B4
Elizabeth Way
Bristol BS16 21 B3
Siddington GL7 150 E2
Elizabeths Mews [12] BS4 9 F6
Elkstone Wlk BS30 11 C2
Ellacombe Rd BS30 10 F2
Ellan Hay Rd BS34 30 A6
Ellbridge Cl BS9 17 D5
Ellenborough Ho BS8 194 A2
Ellenborough Rd GL52 138 A2
Ellendene Dr GL20 182 E4
Ellenor Dr GL20 183 E4
Ellerncroft Rd
Kingswood GL12 67 F8
Wotton-u-E GL12 68 A8
Ellesmere BS35 51 C8
Ellesmere Cl GL3 119 F8
Ellesmere Gr [5] GL50 130 B6
Ellesmere Rd [1] BS4 9 D1
Ellfield Cl BS13 1 F6
Ellicks Cl BS32 40 E2
Ellicott Rd BS7 18 F5
Ellingham Ct GL52 133 E3
Ellinghurst Cl BS10 28 A2
Elliott Ave BS16 30 C1
Elliott Ct [5] GL20 192 C4
Elliott Ho BS7 19 A3
Elliott Pl GL51 129 F7
Elliott Rd GL7 190 E1
Ellis Ave BS13 2 A8
Ellison Cl GL4 120 A6
Ellison Rd GL51 132 E2
Elliston La BS6 18 C2
Elliston Rd BS6 18 C2
Ellsbridge Cl BS31 5 B5
Ellsbridge Ho Norton Radstock Coll BS31 5 B5
Ellsworth Rd BS10 27 F2
Ellwood Prim Sch GL16 155 B3
Ellwood Rd GL16 155 B3
Ellyott Ct [5] BS16 19 E3
Elm Cl Avonmouth BS11 26 F1
Bristol BS34 29 D7
Cheltenham,Prestbury GL52 134 A5
Cheltenham,St Peter's GL51 133 B3
Chipping Sodbury BS37 44 A1
King's Stanley GL10 98 A4
Tutshill NP16 73 A2
Elm Ct
Bristol,Hengrove BS14 3 A6
Bristol,Redland BS6 18 B2
Cheltenham GL52 133 F4
Keynsham BS31 4 C4
Woolaston GL15 147 C3
Elm Dr GL3 120 D7
Elm Farm Cl SN16 142 B1
Elm Garden Dr GL51 129 A7
Elm Gr Dursley GL11 87 F4
Ebrington GL55 189 D3
Huntley GL19 165 D6
Elm Hayes BS13 1 F6
Elm La BS6 18 B2
Elm Lodge GL11 88 B4
Elm Park Prim Sch BS36 30 E6
Elm Pk BS34 29 A2
Elm Rd Bristol,Horfield BS7 18 E5
Bristol,Kingswood BS15 10 E6
Northway GL20 182 C4
Stroud GL5 98 E8
Tutshill NP16 73 A2
Elm Side GL2 173 B3
Elm St GL51 133 B4
Elm Terr GL5 98 D6
Elm View GL7 142 C6
Elm Wood BS37 32 E8
Elmbridge Inf Sch GL2 127 C2
Elmbridge Jun Sch GL2 127 C2
Elmbridge Rd GL2 127 C3
Elmbury Dr GL20 192 F5
Elmcroft Cres BS7 19 A4
Elmdale NP16 72 E1
Elmdale Cotts NP16 72 E1
Elmdale Cres BS35 64 C1
Elmdale Gdns [4] BS16 20 A4
Elmdale Rd
Bristol,Bedminster BS3 8 B2
Bristol,Tyndall's Park BS8 194 B3
Elmdean GL14 191 C5
Elmfield Bristol BS15 10 E6
Cheltenham GL50 193 A3
Elmfield Ave GL51 133 C4
Elmfield Cl BS15 10 E6
Elmfield Rd Bristol BS9 18 A8
Cheltenham GL51 133 C4
Elmfield Sch for Deaf Children BS10 18 B8
Elmgrove Ave [10] BS5 9 B8
Elmgrove Dr BS37 43 F2
Elmgrove Est GL2 109 E7
Elmgrove Pk [1] BS6 18 D1
Elmgrove Rd
Bristol,Fishponds BS16 19 E3
Bristol,Redland BS6 18 D1
Gloucester GL3 120 A6
Elmgrove Rd E GL2 109 E7
Elmgrove Rd W GL2 109 D7
Elmhirst Gdns BS37 44 A2
Elmhurst Ave BS5 19 D3
Elming Down Cl BS32 29 D6
Elmira Rd GL4 118 F4
Elmlea Ave BS9 17 F5
Elmlea Jun & Inf Schs BS9 17 F5
Elmlea Rd GL10 98 A4
Elmleaze GL2 127 D3
Elmleigh Ave BS16 21 B5
Elmleigh Cl BS16 21 B5
Elmleigh Rd BS16 21 B5
Elmley Rd WR11 183 D8
Elmore Bristol BS15 20 F2
Yate BS37 32 D8
Elmore Lane E GL2 117 F3
Elmore Lane W GL2 117 D2
Elmore Rd Bristol BS34 39 F1
Bristol,Horfield BS7 19 A6
Elms Gr BS34 40 B1
Elms Rd GL10 97 E8
Elms The
Bristol,Frenchay BS16 30 C1
Bristol,Henbury BS10 27 F2
Highworth SN6 145 C3
Tockington BS32 50 B2
Elmsdale Rd [14] HR8 178 E8
Elmtree Ave BS16 21 A7
Elmtree Cl BS15 20 D1
Elmtree Cotts GL12 68 D3
Elmtree Dr BS13 1 F5
Elmtree Way BS15 20 D1
Elmvil Rd GL20 182 B4
Elphick Rd GL7 190 B8
Elsbert Dr BS13 1 E6
Elstree Rd BS5 19 E1
Elstub La GL11 87 E5
Eltham Lawn [5] GL50 130 B8
Elton Ho [3] Bristol BS2 195 C3
Huntley GL19 165 D7
Elton La BS7 18 D2
Elton Mans [5] BS7 18 D2
Elton Rd
Bristol,Bishopston BS7 18 D2
Bristol,Kingswood BS15 20 C1
Bristol,Tyndall's Park BS8 194 C3
Elton GL14 157 A8
Littledean GL14 156 E8
Elton St BS2 195 C4
Elvard Cl BS13 2 A4
Elvard Rd BS13 2 A4
Elvaston Rd BS3 8 E3
Elwell La BS40,BS41 1 A1
Ely Gr BS9 17 B7
Embassy Rd BS5 19 E1
Embassy Wlk BS5 19 E1
Embleton Prim Sch BS10 28 C2
Embleton Rd BS10 28 C2
Embrook GL56 177 C4
Emerald Cl GL4 118 C3
Emerson Sq BS7 19 A8
Emerson Way BS16 21 C7
Emersons Green La BS16 21 B6
Emersons Green Prim Sch BS16 21 B7
Emery Rd BS4 9 F1
Emet Gr BS16 21 B6
Emet La BS16 21 B6
Emlyn Rd BS5 19 C2
Emma-Chris Way BS34 29 C2
Emmanuel Ct BS8 194 A4
Emmanuel Gdns GL53 130 D6
Emmerson La GL6 149 A4
Emmett Wood BS14 3 B3
Emperor Cl [2] GL51 132 D2
Emperor Ct [5] GL50 193 A4
Empire Cres BS15 10 E4
Empire Way GL2 118 C5
Emra Cl BS5 19 F1
Emra Ho BS5 9 B8
Enborne Cl GL4 118 D1
Enfield Rd BS16 20 A3
Enfield Villas GL54 139 F5
Engine Common La BS37 43 C5
England's Cres BS36 30 E7
English Bicknor CE Prim Sch GL16 163 B2
Englishcombe Rd BS13 2 C3
Ennerdale Ave GL2 127 D5
Ennerdale Rd Bristol BS10 28 D2
Cheltenham GL51 129 E7
Enoch's Row GL54 176 F4
Enstone Cvn Pk GL51 129 C7
Enterprise Way GL51 133 B3
Epney Cl BS34 39 F1
Epney Rd GL4 118 C3
Epsom Cl BS16 30 F1
Epworth Rd BS10 28 A3
Equinox BS32 40 C3
Erin Pk GL5 99 A5
Erin Wlk BS4 2 D8
Ermin Pk GL3 120 D6
Ermin Pl GL7 190 E2
Ermin St
Broad Blunsdon SN26 144 D1
Brockworth GL3 120 E5
Ermine Par GL3 120 D6
Ermine Way BS11 16 C7
Erminster Dr GL3 120 A7
Ermleet Rd [1] BS6 18 C2
Ernest Barker Cl [15] BS5 9 B7
Ernestville Rd BS16 19 F3
Eros Cl GL5 99 A5
Errington [2] GL56 187 B3
Ervine Terr BS2 195 C4
Eskdale BS35 51 D7
Esland Pl GL7 190 D2
Essery Rd BS5 19 C2
Essex Ave GL51 133 A2
Essex Cl GL3 128 A8
Essex Pl GL54 168 F8
Esson Rd BS15 20 B1
Estate Rd GL14 191 B6
Estcote Rd GL7 190 C5
Estcourt Cl GL1 127 A4
Estcourt Gdns BS16 19 D5
Estcourt Rd GL1 127 A3
Estoril BS37 43 F1
Estune Wlk BS41 7 A2
Etheldene Rd GL5 98 D8
Etheridge Pl GL1 127 B1
Etloe Rd BS6 18 A4
Eton Rd BS4 9 D3
Ettington Cl GL51 132 C3
Ettricke Dr BS16 20 B5
Eugene Flats [7] BS2 195 A4
Eugene St
Bristol,Kingsdown BS2 195 A4
Bristol,St Pauls BS2,BS5 195 C4
Eunice Saunders Way HR9 164 A7
Evans Cl BS4 9 F5
Evans Rd BS6 18 B2
Eve Rd BS5 19 B1
Evelyn Cl GL53 130 F5
Evelyn Ct GL50 193 A3
Evelyn Rd BS10 18 C7
Evenlode Ave GL52 134 A2
Evenlode Gdns
Bristol BS11 16 F5
Moreton-in-M GL56 187 B3
Evenlode Rd
Gloucester GL4 118 D1
Moreton-in-M GL56 187 B3
Evenlode Way BS31 5 A3
Evercreech Rd BS14 3 B4
Everest Ave BS16 19 E4
Everest Cl GL6 91 E6
Everest Rd Bristol BS16 19 E4
Cheltenham GL53 130 E4
Evergreen Ind Pk GL7 142 F7
Evergreen Wlk GL2 127 D5
Everlands GL11 88 A4
Everside Cl GL11 87 F6
Everside La GL11 87 F6
Everyman Theatre The* GL50 193 B3
Evesham Rd
Bishop's Cleeve GL52 137 F5
Cheltenham GL50,GL52 133 E5
Greet GL54 184 A1
Stow-on-t-W GL54 176 E5
Evington Ct [7] GL51 132 E2
Evington Rd [8] GL51 132 E2
Ewell Rd BS14 3 B6
Ewens Rd GL52 131 A8
Ewlyn Rd GL53 130 D6
Ewlyn Terr GL53 130 D6
Exchange Ave BS1 195 A2
Exchange Ct [8] BS15 10 D8
Exemouth Pl [14] NP16 60 E8
Exeter Bldgs BS6 18 B2
Exeter Rd BS3 8 B4
Exley Cl BS30 11 D5
Exmoor St BS3 8 B3
Exmouth Ct GL53 193 B1
Exmouth Rd BS4 8 F1
Exmouth St GL53 193 B1
Exton Cl BS14 3 B5
Eyer's La BS2 195 C3
Eyford Cotts GL54 176 A3
Eynon Cl GL53 130 C5

F

Faber Gr BS13 2 C4
Fabian Dr BS34 29 E5
Factory Rd BS36 30 F7

Failand Cres BS9 … 17 C5
Failand La BS20 … 16 A1
Failand Wlk BS9 … 17 C6
Fair Furlong BS13 … 2 A4
Fair Furlong Prim Sch
BS13 … 2 B4
Fair Lawn BS30 … 11 B4
Fair View
Chepstow/Cas-Gwent NP16 60 D6
Highworth SN6 … 145 C3
Fair View Cl GL6 … 91 B5
Fair View Cvn Pk GL1 … 126 C3
Fair View Dr BS6 … 18 C2
Fairacre Cl BS7 … 19 B5
Fairacres Cl BS31 … 4 F5
Fairfax Cl GL7 … 190 D3
Fairfax Rd GL7 … 190 D3
Fairfax St BS1 … 195 B3
Fairfield 14 SN6 … 143 E4
Fairfield Ave GL53 … 130 D6
Fairfield Cl
21 Coleford GL16 … 155 A5
Marshfield SN14 … 15 A8
Fairfield Ct 15 GL4 … 119 C4
Fairfield High Sch BS6 … 18 F2
Fairfield Par GL53 … 130 D6
Fairfield Park Rd GL53 … 130 D6
Fairfield Pl BS3 … 8 B4
Fairfield Rd
Bristol,Montpelier BS6 … 18 F2
Bristol,Southville BS3 … 8 B4
Cheltenham GL53 … 130 D6
Chepstow/Cas-Gwent NP16 60 E6
Lydney GL15 … 92 B3
Fairfield St GL53 … 130 D6
Fairfield Wlk GL53 … 130 D6
Fairfields GL14 … 191 C4
Fairfields Rd 13 HR8 … 178 E8
Fairfoot Rd BS4 … 9 A3
Fairford CE Prim Sch
GL7 … 152 E4
Fairford Cl BS15 … 20 F2
Fairford Cres BS34 … 29 C8
Fairford Hospl GL7 … 152 E4
Fairford Rd Bristol BS11 … 16 D7
Quenington GL7 … 152 D7
Fairford Way GL4 … 119 B7
Fairhaven BS37 … 43 F1
Fairhaven Ave GL3 … 120 E6
Fairhaven Park Cvn Pk
GL51 … 129 B6
Fairhaven Rd Bristol BS6 … 18 C4
Cheltenham GL53 … 130 D6
Fairhaven St GL53 … 130 D6
Fairhavens Ct 9 GL52 … 133 F2
Fairlawn BS16 … 20 D4
Fairlawn Ave BS34 … 29 A3
Fairlawn Rd BS6 … 18 F2
Fairlyn Dr BS15 … 20 F3
Fairmead GL11 … 87 F5
Fairmile Gdns GL2 … 126 F5
Fairmoor Cl GL15 … 155 E2
Fairmount Rd GL51 … 132 F1
Fairoaks BS30 … 11 A3
Fairview SN6 … 143 F4
Fairview Cl
Cheltenham GL52 … 193 C3
Monmouth/Trefynwy
NP25 … 154 A7
Fairview Ct BS15 … 10 D6
Fairview Ho BS9 … 17 F8
Fairview Rd Bristol BS15 … 10 F8
Cheltenham GL52 … 193 C4
Fairview St GL52 … 193 C4
Fairwater Pk GL4 … 127 D1
Fairway Bristol BS4 … 9 D1
Northway GL20 … 182 C4
Fairway Cl BS30 … 11 B4
Fairway Ind Ctr BS34 … 28 F3
Fairways BS31 … 5 E2
Fairways Ave GL16 … 155 A5
Falcon Cl
Bristol,Patchway BS34 … 28 E8
Bristol,Westbury on Trym
BS9 … 17 F8
Innsworth GL3 … 127 C6
Quedgeley GL2 … 117 F3
Falcon Ct BS9 … 18 A7
Falcon Dr BS34 … 28 E8
Falcon La HR8 … 178 C8
Falcon Way BS35 … 64 D2
Falcon Wlk BS34 … 39 E1
Falcondale Rd BS9 … 17 F7
Falcondale Wlk BS9 … 18 A8
Falconride Prim Sch
BS15 … 20 F1
Falcons Gate BS37 … 43 C3
Faldo Cl GL4 … 119 F5
Falfield Rd Bristol BS4 … 9 C3
Gloucester GL4 … 118 D3
Falfield Wlk BS10 … 18 C8
Falkland Pl GL51 … 132 D3
Falkland Rd 4 BS6 … 18 F2
Falkner St GL1 … 196 C1
Fallodon Ct BS9 … 18 B5
Fallodon Way BS9 … 18 B5
Fallowfield BS30 … 11 D5
Fallows Rd GL54 … 168 A1
Falmouth Rd BS7 … 18 E4
Fancy Rd GL15 … 155 E3
Fane Cl BS10 … 28 A3
Fanshawe Rd BS14 … 3 A7
Far Handstones BS30 … 11 A4
Far Leazes GL5 … 99 D7
Far Sandfield GL3 … 128 C5
Far View Cotts 7 GL10 … 97 F7
Far Wells Rd GL6 … 148 D8
Far Westrip GL6 … 98 C8
Faraday Cl 4 GL1 … 118 F7
Faraday Rd 2 BS8 … 7 F5
Farendell Rd BS16 … 31 B1
Farfield La SN6 … 143 F2
Faringdon Rd GL51 … 129 D7
Farington Rd BS10 … 18 D7
Farlands BS16 … 22 B6
Farleigh Cl GL52 … 131 C6
Farleigh La GL12 … 66 C2
Farleigh Rd BS31 … 4 D4
Farleigh Wlk BS13 … 2 A8
Farley Cl BS34 … 29 C7
Farm Cl Bristol BS16 … 21 B6
Cheltenham GL51 … 132 E3
Northway GL20 … 182 C5
Farm Ct Bristol BS16 … 20 E7
Willersey WR12 … 188 B2
Woodchester GL5 … 90 F8
Farm Hill GL8 … 140 A8
Farm La Bredon GL20 … 182 C7
Cheltenham GL51,GL53 … 130 B4
Easter Compton BS35 … 38 E2
Leighterton GL8 … 70 C3
Llangrove HR9 … 162 B5
Shurdington GL51 … 129 E1
Westmancote GL20 … 182 E8
Farm Lees GL12 … 67 A6
Farm Mews GL1 … 196 B1
Farm Rd Bristol BS16 … 20 E7
Edgeworth GL6 … 106 C1
Ruardean Woodside GL17 … 163 F3
Farm St GL1 … 196 B1
Farman Cres GL54 … 169 D6
Farmcote GL12 … 55 D8
Farmcote Cl GL6 … 148 B6
Farmcote Gdns GL54 … 139 F5
Farmer Rd BS13 … 1 E4
Farmfield Rd GL51 … 130 A5
Farmhill Cres GL5 … 98 F8
Farmhill La GL5 … 102 F1
Farmhouse Mews NP25 146 B7
Farmington Cl 4 GL4 … 119 E5
Farmington Rd
Cheltenham GL51 … 129 E8
Northleach GL54 … 168 A1
Farmington Rise 13
GL54 … 168 A1
Farmor's Sch GL7 … 152 E4
Farmwell Cl BS13 … 2 B5
Farnaby Cl BS4 … 2 C7
Farndale BS5 … 10 A6
Farne Cl BS9 … 18 B5
Farr St BS11 … 16 B8
Farr's La Bristol BS1 … 195 A2
Stroud GL5 … 99 C7
Farrant Ave GL3 … 128 A6
Farrant Cl BS4 … 2 D6
Farrell Cl GL7 … 190 C4
Farriers Croft 9 GL6 … 148 C6
Farriers Ct 10 GL16 … 155 A6
Farriers End GL2 … 117 F1
Farriers Reach GL52 … 137 D4
Farriers The GL7 … 153 C6
Farringford Ho BS5 … 19 D2
Farthing Croft GL2 … 125 D4
Farthings WR13 … 180 C5
Farthings The GL54 … 166 E2
Fauconberg Rd GL50 … 193 A3
Faulkner's Cl GL7 … 152 E3
Fawkes Cl BS15 … 11 B8
Fawkes Pl 7 GL5 … 99 C7
Fawley Dr GL52 … 134 C4
Featherbed La BS35 … 63 B6
Featherstone Rd 4 BS16 19 F4
Fedw Wood/Coed Fedw
NP16 … 60 C8
Feeder Rd BS2 … 9 A5
Felix Rd BS5 … 9 B8
Felstead Rd BS10 … 28 E1
Feltham Ct BS34 … 28 F2
Feltham Rd BS16 … 22 C6
Felton Gr BS13 … 2 A8
Fenbrook Cl BS16 … 30 B1
Fenhill Cl GL56 … 186 D3
Fennel Cl GL4 … 119 D4
Fennel Dr BS34 … 30 A7
Fennell Gr BS10 … 28 A2
Fennell's View GL5 … 103 E1
Fenshurst Gdns BS41 … 1 A8
Fenton Cl BS31 … 5 D3
Fenton Ct BS7 … 18 D4
Fenton Rd BS7 … 18 D4
Fermaine Ave BS4 … 9 F3
Fern Cl BS10 … 28 B3
Fern Ct NP16 … 60 F5
Fern Gr BS32 … 29 D8
Fern Lawn GL4 … 119 D2
Fern Rd Bristol BS16 … 20 D5
Ellwood GL16 … 155 C3
Fern St BS2 … 18 F1
Fernbank Ct 2 BS6 … 18 C2
Fernbank Rd BS6 … 18 C2
Fernbrook Cl BS16 … 30 B1
Ferndale Ave BS30 … 11 A3
Ferndale Cl
Cinderford GL14 … 191 D5
Gloucester GL2 … 127 B5
Woodhouse Down BS32 … 40 D7
Ferndale Rd Bristol BS34 … 29 A2
Whiteshill GL6 … 103 A3
Ferndales Cl 2 GL51 … 129 F5
Ferndene BS32 … 40 C2
Ferndown BS37 … 43 E1
Ferndown Cl BS11 … 17 A7
Ferndown Grange BS9 … 18 B6
Ferndown Rd 7 HR8 … 178 E7
Ferney GL11 … 80 C8
Fernhill BS32 … 40 C7
Fernhill Ct Bristol BS11 … 27 B1
Tockington BS32 … 40 C7
Fernhill La BS11 … 27 B1
Fernhurst Rd BS5 … 19 F1
Fernihough Ave WR11 … 188 C7
Fernlea Gdns BS20 … 16 B4
Fernleaze BS36 … 31 C6
Fernleigh Cres GL51 … 129 E6
Fernleigh Ct 1 BS6 … 18 B2
Ferns The GL8 … 140 B4
Fernsteed Rd BS13 … 1 F6
Ferrie La HR9 … 162 E3
Ferris Court View 9
GL6 … 148 B6
Ferry Gdns GL2 … 117 D1
Ferry La GL20 … 181 C8
Ferry Rd BS15 … 10 D1
Ferry St BS1 … 195 B2
Ferry Steps Ind Est BS2 … 9 A4
Ferry Way NP16 … 61 B4
Ferryman's Ct BS2 … 195 B2
Festival Ho GL52 … 193 C3
Festival Rd GL10 … 97 E7
Fewster Rd GL6 … 91 B4
Fewster Sq GL6 … 91 B4
Fiddes Rd BS6 … 18 C4
Fiddle The SN6 … 143 E4
Fiddler's Green La GL51 132 C2
Fiddlers Wood La BS32 … 29 E8
Fidges La GL6 … 148 C7
Field Cl GL7 … 143 A8
Field Court CE Inf Sch
GL2 … 109 F8
Field Court Dr GL2 … 109 E7
Field Court Gdns GL2 … 109 E8
Field Court Jun Sch
GL2 … 109 F8
Field End GL3 … 128 A7
Field Farm Cl BS34 … 29 F4
Field La Bristol BS30 … 10 F3
Coaley GL11 … 88 E7
Dursley GL11 … 87 D5
Dyrham SN14 … 23 F6
Littleton-u-S BS35 … 50 A8
Tytherington BS35 … 51 E3
Field Marshal Slim Ct 1
BS2 … 195 C3
Field Pl GL5 … 98 F8
Field Rd Bristol BS15 … 20 C1
Kingham OX7 … 177 F2
Stroud,Bowbridge GL5 … 99 D6
Stroud,Rodborough GL5 … 99 B6
Whiteshill GL6 … 103 A3
Field View BS5 … 9 A8
Field View Dr BS16 … 20 C6
Fieldcote Dr GL3 … 120 A7
Fieldcourt Farmhouse
GL2 … 109 E8
Fielden GL4 … 119 D3
Fieldfare GL4 … 119 D5
Fieldgate Rd GL52 … 138 A4
Fields La WR12 … 188 B2
Fields Rd GL54 … 159 B5
Fieldview GL13 … 85 E4
Fieldways GL6 … 91 A4
Fiennes Cl BS16 … 20 E4
Fiery La GL11 … 89 C2
Fifth Ave Bristol,Filton BS7 29 A1
Bristol,Hengrove BS14 … 3 B7
Fifth Way BS11 … 26 E2
Filbert Cl GL4 … 119 D3
Filby Dr BS34 … 29 C8
Filton Abbey Wood Sta
BS34 … 29 B1
Filton Ave
Bristol,Filton BS34 … 29 B3
Bristol,Horfield BS7,BS34 … 19 A7
Filton Avenue Jun & Inf Schs
BS7 … 19 A7
Filton Coll N BS34 … 29 A4
Filton Coll S BS34 … 29 A4
Filton Gr BS7 … 18 F6
Filton High Sch BS34 … 29 D3
Filton Hill Prim Sch
BS34 … 29 B4
Filton La BS34 … 29 D2
Filton Rd
Bristol,Frenchay BS16 … 29 F2
Bristol,Harry Stoke BS34 … 29 D2
Bristol,Horfield BS7 … 18 F8
Filton Rdbt BS34 … 29 A2
Filton Way GL4 … 119 B7
Filwood Broadway BS4 … 2 E8
Filwood Ct BS16 … 20 B3
Filwood Dr BS15 … 10 F8
Filwood Ho BS15 … 10 F8
Filwood Rd BS16 … 20 A3
Finch Cl BS35 … 64 C2
Finch Rd
Chipping Sodbury BS37 … 33 A8
Innsworth GL3 … 127 D7
Finchcroft Ct GL52 … 134 D4
Finchcroft La GL52 … 134 C4
Finchmoor Mews GL2 … 126 F6
Finlay Com Sch GL4 … 119 A6
Finlay Pl GL4 … 118 F5
Finlay Rd GL4 … 118 F5
Finstock Cl GL51 … 129 F8
Fir Rd SN14 … 15 F6
Fir Tree Cl Bristol BS34 … 28 F7
Cheltenham GL52 … 134 A4
Fir Tree La BS5 … 10 A7
Fir View Rd GL14 … 156 C6
Fircroft Cl GL3 … 119 F8
Fircroft Rd GL2 … 126 F5
Fire Engine La BS36 … 31 D7
Fire Service Coll The
GL56 … 187 C3
Fire Station La BS11 … 26 B2
Firethorne Cl GL2 … 127 B5
Firework Cl BS15 … 11 B8
Firfield St BS4 … 9 A4
Firgrove Cres BS37 … 44 A2
Firgrove Wlk GL51 … 129 C7
Firs Cl OX7 … 177 E1
Firs Ct BS31 … 4 C4
Firs Rd GL5 … 91 C5
Firs The Bristol BS16 … 20 E6
Gloucester GL1 … 196 C4
Kemble GL7 … 141 D6
Swindon GL51 … 133 B7
First Ave
Bristol,Hengrove BS14 … 3 A7
Bristol,St Anne's BS4 … 9 E5
Dursley GL11 … 80 C8
First Way BS11 … 26 C1
Firth Ave GL56 … 187 C3
Firwood Dr GL4 … 118 E3
Fish Alley 18 GL20 … 192 C4
Fish Hill WR12 … 185 D8
Fisher Ave BS15 … 21 A1
Fisher Cl 30 GL54 … 176 F4
Fisher Rd BS15 … 21 A1
Fisherman's Wlk NP16 … 60 F5
Fishers La GL52 … 193 C4
Fishers Rd GL13 … 85 E4
Fishers Way GL5 … 99 A4
Fishponds Rd BS5 … 19 D3
Fishponds Trad Est BS5 … 19 E2
Fishpool Hill BS10 … 28 B4
Fitchett Wlk BS10 … 27 F3
Fitzgerald Rd BS3 … 8 F3
Fitzhamon Pk GL20 … 182 C4
Fitzharding Ho BS1 … 195 A3
Fitzharding Rd BS20 … 16 E3
Fitzhardinge Way GL13 … 85 E4
Fitzosborn Cl NP16 … 60 D7
Fitzroy Rd BS16 … 20 B2
Fitzroy St BS4 … 9 A4
Fitzroy Terr 7 BS6 … 18 B2
Five Acre Dr BS16 … 20 A7
Five Acres GL11 … 80 A8
Five Lanes SN16 … 141 B1
Five Mile Dr GL56 … 186 C5
Five Trees Cl 8 GL8 … 140 B4
Flaxley Ho GL1 … 127 A2
Flaxley Rd GL4 … 118 E3
Flaxley St GL14 … 191 D4
Flaxman Cl BS7 … 19 B6
Flaxpits La BS36 … 30 E5
Flecker's Dr GL51 … 129 F7
Fleece Alley 24 GL54 … 176 F4
Fleece Inn* WR11 … 188 A6
Fleece Rd WR12 … 188 A1
Fleet Close Cvn Site
GL20 … 182 A7
Fleet La GL20 … 182 A7
Fleet Rd GL20 … 182 A7
Fleming Cl GL2 … 127 C6
Fletchers Alley 12 GL20 … 192 C4
Flint Rd GL51 … 129 E6
Flisteridge Rd SN16 … 142 B2
Florence Brown Com Sch
The BS4 … 2 D8
Florence Pk
Almondsbury BS32 … 40 C5
Bristol BS6 … 18 B4
Florence Rd BS16 … 20 E3
Florence Terr SN16 … 142 E1
Florida Bvd GL7 … 152 E3
Florida Dr GL52 … 134 C4
Flower Way GL2 … 127 B4
Flowers Hill BS4 … 9 E1
Flowers Hill Cl BS4 … 9 E1
Flowers Hill Trad Est BS4 … 9 E1
Flowerwell Rd BS13 … 2 B5
Folders The GL15 … 92 B3
Foley Cl GL4 … 118 D3
Foley Rd GL18 … 171 A4
Foley Rise GL19 … 172 C4
Folk Mus* GL1 … 196 A3
Folland Ave GL3 … 120 B6
Folleigh Cl BS41 … 7 B2
Folleigh Dr BS41 … 7 B2
Folleigh La BS41 … 7 B2
Folliot Cl BS16 … 20 A7
Folly Bridge Cl BS37 … 43 D2
Folly Brook Rd BS16 … 31 B1
Folly Cl SN6 … 145 D4
Folly Cres SN6 … 145 D4
Folly Dr SN6 … 145 D4
Folly Field GL54 … 169 A8
Folly Gdns GL20 … 192 D4
Folly La Bristol BS2 … 9 A6
Cheltenham GL50 … 133 D3
English Bicknor GL16 … 163 A1
Huntley GL17 … 165 B7
Stroud GL5,GL6 … 103 E2
Folly Rd BS37 … 42 A5
Folly Rise GL5 … 103 D1
Folly The Bristol BS16 … 20 F7
Cold Ashton SN14 … 13 F6
Longborough GL56 … 176 E8
Saltford BS31 … 5 F2
Folly Way SN6 … 145 D4
Follyfield SN16 … 141 E1
Fontana Cl BS30 … 11 B3
Fonthill Prim Sch BS10 … 28 E2
Fonthill Rd BS10 … 28 D2
Fonthill Way BS30 … 11 C2
Fontmell Ct BS14 … 3 D7
Fontwell Dr BS16 … 30 F1
Footes La BS36 … 31 B7
Footshill Cl BS15 … 10 C6
Footshill Dr BS15 … 10 C7
Footshill Rd BS15 … 10 C6
Fop St GL11 … 89 A1
Forbes Cl GL4 … 119 F6
Ford House Rd GL18 … 171 B6
Ford La Bristol BS16 … 21 B6
Gorsley GL18 … 170 D4
Ford St BS5 … 9 C6
Forde Cl BS30 … 10 F5
Fordell Pl BS4 … 9 A3
Fordwich Cl NP16 … 72 B5
Fore St SN6 … 142 F5
Forest Ave BS16 … 20 B3
Forest Cl GL16 … 154 E7
Forest Dr BS10 … 28 C3
Forest Edge BS15 … 10 C4
Forest Hills BS32 … 40 B5
Forest of Dean Sculpture
Trail* GL16 … 155 E7
Forest Par 4 GL15 … 92 A3
Forest Park Camping Site
GL16 … 154 F7
Forest Patch 6 GL16 … 155 A7
Forest Rd Bream GL15 … 147 D8
Bristol,Fishponds BS16 … 20 B4
Bristol,Kingswood BS15 … 10 D7
Cinderford GL14 … 191 D4
Lydney GL15 … 92 A3
Mile End GL16 … 155 B7
Milkwall GL16 … 155 B4
Ruardean Woodside GL17 … 163 F3
Forest Rise
Cinderford GL14 … 191 E5
Nailsworth GL6 … 90 F4
Upper Lydbrook GL17 … 163 D2
Forest Vale Ind Est
GL14 … 191 B5
Forest Vale Rd GL14 … 191 B5
Forest View
Cinderford GL14 … 191 C1
Narth The NP25 … 154 B1
Forest View Cvn Site
GL14 … 191 C3
Forest View Prim Sch
GL14 … 191 E5
Forest View Rd
Berkeley GL13 … 85 E4
Gloucester GL4 … 118 E1
Forest Wlk
Bristol,Fishponds BS16 … 20 B2
Bristol,Kingswood BS15 … 10 C7
Foresters Rd GL20 … 192 C2
Forge Cotts GL18 … 171 D6
Forge Gdns NP16 … 72 B6
Forge Hill GL17 … 163 C3
Forge La GL18 … 171 D6
Forge The GL17 … 163 C3
Forsdene Wlk GL16 … 155 B5
Forsyte Way GL4 … 119 B7
Forsythia Cl 8 GL3 … 128 A7
Fort La GL11 … 80 B8
Fort View Terr GL5 … 98 E6
Fortey Rd GL54 … 168 A1
Fortfield Rd BS14 … 3 B5
Fortfields GL11 … 80 B8
Fortina Cl GL50 … 133 C5
Fortress The GL11 … 80 B8
Forty Acre La
Alveston BS35 … 51 B3
Stroud GL6 … 148 A8
Forty The SN6 … 143 E4
Forty's Pitch HR9 … 170 B5
Forum The GL1 … 196 B2
Foscombe La GL19 … 172 C5
Foss Ct 8 BS5 … 9 F8
Foss Field GL7 … 107 A8
Foss La BS35 … 63 E6
Fosscross La GL54,GL7 … 159 C3
Fosse Cl Cirencester GL7 … 190 E5
Gloucester GL4 … 119 E6
Fosse Folly GL54 … 176 F5
Fosse La GL54 … 176 F5
Fossedale Ave BS14 … 3 C6
Fosseway Ave GL56 … 187 A2
Fosseway Cl 7 GL56 … 187 A2
Fosseway Cl Bristol BS8 … 194 A2
Lechlade on T GL7 … 153 E3
Fosseway Dr 6 GL56 … 187 A2
Fosseway Ho GL54 … 176 F5
Fosseway The BS8 … 194 A3
Foster Cl GL52 … 138 A5
Foster Ct 3 GL52 … 134 A3
Foster Dr WR12 … 188 A2
Foster St BS5 … 19 B2
Foster's Almshouses
BS1 … 195 A3
Foundry La BS5 … 19 F2
Foundry Rd GL14 … 191 D5
Foundry Wood Forest
Trails* GL14 … 156 D5
Foundry Yd BS5 … 19 F2
Fountain Cres GL12 … 68 C6
Fountain Ct Bristol BS32 … 40 C3
2 Yate BS37 … 32 D7
Fountain Sq GL1 … 196 A3
Fountain St GL6 … 91 C4
Fountain Way NP16 … 60 F4
Fountaine Ct 3 BS5 … 19 C2
Fountains Dr BS30 … 10 F6
Four Acre Ave BS16 … 20 E8
Four Acre Cl SN6 … 143 A4
Four Acre Cres BS16 … 30 E1
Four Acre Rd BS16 … 20 E8
Four Acres BS13 … 1 E4
Four Acres Cl BS13 … 1 F4
Four Acres Prim Sch BS13 1 E4
Four Acres View GL7 … 190 B3

Four Seasons Sq BS37 43 E1
Fourth Ave
Bristol,Filton BS7 29 A1
Bristol,Hengrove BS14 3 B7
Dursley GL11 80 C8
Fourth Way BS11 26 E1
Fowbridge Gdns HR9 163 C8
Fowler's Hill GL7 152 D7
Fox & Hounds La BS31 4 F5
Fox Ave BS37 43 D2
Fox Cl Bristol BS4 9 F5
Gloucester GL4 119 F5
Hawkesbury Upton GL9 55 F3
Stroud GL5 98 C7
Fox Ct BS30 10 F3
Fox Den Rd BS34 29 D3
Fox Dr GL54 176 D4
Fox Elms Rd GL4 118 E2
Fox Hill GL8 140 C3
Fox Ho BS4 9 E3
Fox La 7 GL54 176 F4
Fox Rd BS5 19 B1
Fox Run GL2 118 A2
Fox's La GL16 155 B5
Foxborough Gdns BS32 40 D2
Foxcombe Rd BS14 3 B4
Foxcote Bristol BS15 10 F7
Gloucester GL2 127 B5
Foxcote Hill CV36 189 F5
Foxcote Rd BS3 8 A3
Foxcott SN6 143 E6
Foxcroft Cl BS32 29 F6
Foxcroft Rd BS5 9 D8
Foxe Rd BS36 31 B8
Foxes Bank Dr GL7 190 B2
Foxes Bridge Rd GL14 191 B5
Foxes Cl
3 Bourton-on-t-W GL54 168 F7
6 Chalford GL6 148 C6
Foxes Dell GL5 91 A5
Foxes Row GL56 177 A6
Foxfield Ave BS32 40 D3
Foxglove Cl Bristol BS16 19 E5
Cirencester GL7 190 E2
Gloucester GL4 119 E5
Thornbury BS35 64 D2
Foxglove Way GL16 155 B4
Foxgrove Dr GL52 134 A1
Foxholes La BS32 50 C4
Foxleaze SN6 143 E5
Foxleigh Cres GL2 127 E5
Foxmoor GL52 137 E4
Foxmoor La GL5 98 C7
Foxmoor Prim Sch GL5 98 D7
Foxtail Cl GL4 119 A5
Foxwell Dr GL3 120 A8
Foye Ho BS8 7 E6
Fraley Rd BS9 18 A7
Framlington Ct GL51 133 A1
Frampton Cotterell CE Prim Sch BS36 31 A8
Frampton Cotts GL20 183 E3
Frampton Cres BS16 20 C4
Frampton Ct
8 Bristol,Longwell Green BS30 10 F4
16 Bristol,Pile Marsh BS5 9 D7
Frampton Dr WR12 188 B2
Frampton End Rd BS37 42 D2
Frampton Mews GL51 129 B7
Frampton Rd GL1 118 D7
France La GL9 56 B2
Frances Ct GL52 133 F1
Frances Greeves Ct BS10 27 F1
Francis Ct BS5 9 F7
Francis Ho BS2 195 A4
Francis Pl BS30 10 F4
Francis Rd
Bristol,Bedminster BS3 8 C2
Bristol,Westbury on Trym BS10 18 C8
Francis St GL53 193 B1
Francis Way BS30 11 D6
Francis Woodcock Trad Est 5 GL1 119 A8
Francombe Gr BS10 18 E6
Francombe Ho BS1 195 A1
Frank Brookes Rd GL51 133 A4
Franklin Ct BS1 195 B1
Franklyn Ct
6 Bristol BS16 19 E3
6 Cheltenham GL51 132 E2
Franklyn La 10 BS2 18 F1
Franklyn St BS2 18 F1
Fraser St BS3 8 D3
Frayne Rd BS3 8 A4
Frazier's Folly GL7 150 E2
Freame Cl GL6 148 B6
Frederick Pl BS8 194 B3
Frederick Thomas Rd GL11 87 E4
Fredericks Way SN14 36 B3
Fredrick St BS4 9 A4
Free Tank BS2 195 C2
Freeland Bldgs 1 BS5 19 C2
Freeland Pl BS8 7 F6
Freeling Ho BS1 195 B1
Freemans Cl GL20 181 F8
Freemans Orch 30 GL18 171 A4
Freemantle Gdns BS5 19 C3
Freemantle Ho BS2 195 A4
Freemantle Rd BS5 19 C3
Freeminers Way GL14 191 D5
Freestone Rd BS2 9 A6
Freezinghill La BS30 13 B4
Fremantle La 8 BS6 18 D1
Fremantle Rd BS6 18 D1
Fremantle Sq BS6 18 D1
French La
Lower Redbrook NP25 154 C4
Newland GL16 154 D4
Frenchay CE Prim Sch BS16 20 B7
Frenchay Cl BS16 20 B7
Frenchay Hill BS16 20 C7
Frenchay Hospl BS16 20 B8
Frenchay Park Rd BS16 19 F6
Frenchay Rd BS16 20 C6
Freshland Way BS15 10 B8
Fretherne Rd GL4 118 D3
Frewin Cl GL51 132 D2
Frewins La GL14 165 D3
Friar's Wlk GL18 171 A5
Friars Cl GL51 130 B5
Friars Ho 4 BS37 32 D7
Friary BS1 195 C2
Friary Grange Pk BS36 30 E6
Friary Rd Bristol BS7 18 D4
Gloucester GL4 119 E6
Friday St Arlingham GL2 157 C6
Minchinhampton GL6 148 A3
Painswick GL6 103 F8
Fridays Ham La SN6 143 A5
Friendly Row BS20 16 C5
Friendship Rd BS4 9 A2
Friezewood Rd BS3 8 A4
Fripp Cl BS5 9 B6
Frith La GL12 53 F3
Frith The GL6 148 B6
Frithwood GL6 148 B6
Frithwood Cl GL6 148 B6
Frithwood Pk GL6 148 B6
Frobisher Mews GL3 127 F8
Frobisher Rd BS3 8 A3
Frocester Hill GL10 89 C8
Frog Furlong La GL2, GL3 127 E8
Frog La Bristol BS1 194 C2
Coalpit Heath BS36 31 E7
Frocester GL10 97 A3
Huntley GL19 165 D6
Ilmington CV36 189 F6
North Nibley GL11 79 C5
Frogmarsh La GL5 91 A8
Frogmore Rd GL19 165 D6
Frogmore St BS1 194 C2
Frome Ave GL5 99 A6
Frome Ct BS35 51 C8
Frome Gdns GL5 98 E6
Frome Glen BS36 30 E4
Frome Park Rd GL5 99 A6
Frome Pl 1 BS16 19 E5
Frome Rd Bristol BS2 195 C4
Chipping Sodbury BS37 44 C1
Frome Terr BS16 19 E5
Frome Valley Rd BS16 19 F6
Frome View BS36 31 B7
Frome Villas BS16 20 C7
Frome Way BS36 30 E5
Fromebank Jun Sch BS37 43 D3
Fromeside GL5 99 C6
Fromeside Dr GL5 98 D6
Fromeside Ind Est GL5 99 C6
Fromeside Pk BS16 20 B7
Front La SN26 144 D2
Front St Ilmington CV36 189 F6
Nympsfield GL10 89 E5
Froomshaw Rd BS16 20 A7
Frost & Reed Ho 3 BS5 9 F8
Frowens La HR9 170 B4
Fry Ct 2 BS3 8 C4
Fry's Cl BS16 19 D4
Fry's Hill BS4 9 D2
Frys Hill BS15 20 E2
Frys House of Mercy BS1 195 B1
Fryth Wood/Coed Ffwyth NP16 60 C8
Fulbrook Cl GL51 132 D5
Fulford Ctr BS13 2 C4
Fulford Rd BS13 2 C5
Fulford Wlk BS13 2 C5
Fuller's La GL19 172 B4
Fullers Ave 10 SN6 143 E4
Fullers Ct GL1 196 A3
Fulmar Cl BS35 64 D2
Furber Ct BS5 10 B6
Furber Rd BS5 10 B6
Furber Ridge BS5 10 B6
Furber Vale BS5 10 B6
Furlong Ct 3 HR8 178 E7
Furlong La GL52 137 F3
Furlong Rd GL1 118 E7
Furlong The BS6 18 D6
Furlongs The GL12 69 C3
Furnace Cl GL14 191 C4
Furnace La GL18 171 A5
Furnace Valley GL15 156 D1
Furnwood BS5 10 A6
Furze Croft GL2 109 F7
Furze La GL55 189 B4
Furze Rd BS16 20 C3
Furze The GL4 119 A4
Furzewood Rd BS15 10 F8
Fussell Ct BS15 10 F8
Fylton Croft BS14 3 B3

G

Gabb La GL19 173 B7
Gable Cl BS35 39 A2
Gable Cotts GL7 152 E3
Gable Point GL52 138 B3
Gable Rd 7 BS5 19 A1
Gable Row GL20 182 F8
Gadshill Dr BS34 29 E5
Gadshill Rd Bristol BS5 19 C2
Charlton Kings GL53 131 B3
Gadwell Rd GL20 192 E3
Gages Cl BS15 10 F7
Gages Rd BS15 10 F7
Gaineys Well GL5 99 D7
Gainsborough Dr GL4 118 C2
Gainsborough Ho GL55 189 B2
Gainsborough Mews BS10 28 B2
Gainsborough Rd BS31 4 F5
Gainsborough Sq BS7 19 B7
Gainsborough Terr GL55 189 A1
Gales Ct GL7 153 E2
Galileo Gdns GL51 132 C1
Gallagher Ret Pk
Bristol BS30 10 E4
Cheltenham GL51 132 F5
Galleries The BS1 195 B3
Galley Orch SN6 143 F4
Gallivan Cl BS34 29 B8
Gallops La GL52 134 D4
Gallops The GL2 118 B6
Gallows Pound La GL7 190 B8
Galway Rd BS4 8 E1
Gambier Parry Gdns GL2 126 F4
Gambles La GL52 138 D2
Gambril La GL12 65 F5
Ganborough Rd GL56 176 D8
Gander Cl BS13 2 B5
Gander La
Teddington GL20 183 A4
Tewkesbury GL20 192 C3
Gannaway La GL20 192 F5
Gannet Cl GL3 120 E5
Gannicox Rd GL5 99 A7
Ganzell La GL11 80 C7
Gara Cl GL51 132 F5
Garamond Ct BS1 195 B1
Garden City Way 12 NP16 60 E8
Garden Cl Bristol BS9 17 C5
Cirencester GL7 190 C3
Dumbleton WR11 183 F7
Mickleton GL55 189 A6
Garden Cotts GL19 172 A2
Garden Ct BS8 194 A4
Garden Rd GL53 131 B4
Garden Suburb GL11 88 A1
Garden The GL5 99 A2
Garden Way GL2 127 B4
Gardeners Way
King's Stanley GL10 98 A4
Newent GL18 170 F4
Gardeners Wlk BS41 7 B1
Gardenia Gr GL51 129 F5
Gardens The
Bristol,Frenchay BS16 29 F1
4 Bristol,Upper Soundwell BS16 20 D3
Cheltenham GL50 133 E4
Monmouth/Trefynwy NP25 154 A8
Gardiner Cl GL6 148 C6
Gardiners Cl GL3 128 A6
Gardner Ave BS13 1 F7
Gardner Ct GL7 190 D3
Gardner's La GL51 133 C4
Gardners Lane Prim Sch GL51 133 C4
Garfield Ct BS5 9 F8
Garfield Rd BS5 10 A8
Garland Ct GL7 190 C3
Garlands Rd GL15 147 D3
Garlandstone Wlk GL2 118 C6
Garnalls Rd GL4 119 C4
Garnet St BS3 8 B3
Garnett Pl BS16 20 F7
Garns Cl GL11 89 B1
Garren View HR9 162 C7
Garrett Dr BS32 29 D7
Garretts The GL7 152 D4
Garth Rd BS13 2 A8
Garton Ho 3 BS16 20 D5
Garvey Cl NP16 60 F4
Garvey Ho 14 BS5 9 C7
Gas La Bristol BS2 9 A6
Cricklade SN6 143 F4
Gasferry Rd BS1 194 B1
Gaskins The BS7 19 A5
Gassons Rd GL7 153 E3
Gassons Way GL7 153 E2
Gaston Ave BS31 4 F6
Gaston La SN16 58 D1
Gastons The BS11 17 A8
Gastrells Com Prim Sch GL5 99 A4
Gasworks La GL54 168 F7
Gasworks Villas GL2 118 B4
Gatcombe Cl GL52 137 E3
Gatcombe Dr BS34 29 E4
Gatcombe Rd BS13 2 B5
Gatehouse Ave BS13 2 A5
Gatehouse Cl BS13 2 A5
Gatehouse Ct BS13 2 B5
Gatehouse Ctr The BS13 2 B5
Gatehouse Way BS13 2 A5
Gatesby Mead BS34 29 E5
Gathorne Cres BS37 43 D2
Gathorne Rd BS3 8 B4
Gatmeres Rd GL4 119 C3
Gatton Rd BS2 19 A1
Gatton Way GL3 127 F1
Gatwick Cl GL14 157 E8
Gaunt's La BS1 194 C2
Gaunts Earthcott La BS32 41 B5
Gaunts Rd BS37 33 B8
Gay Elms Prim Sch BS13 2 A4
Gay Elms Rd BS13 2 A4
Gayner Rd BS7 29 A1
Gays Rd BS15 10 B4
Gaywood Ho 7 BS3 8 B3
Gazelle Cl GL2 117 F2
Gazzard Cl BS36 30 E7
Gazzard Rd BS36 30 E7
Gee Moors BS15 10 F7
Gefle Cl BS1 194 B1
Genista Way 3 GL51 129 F5
Geoffrey Cl BS13 1 E6
George & Dragon La 11 BS5 9 D7
George Ct 12 Bristol BS6 18 B1
Painswick GL6 103 F8
George Dowty Dr GL20 182 C5
George Jones Rd BS2 9 A6
George La
Chipping Campden GL55 189 A1
Cinderford GL14 164 E1
Littledean GL14 191 F4
Marshfield SN14 24 E1
George Naisey Ho 6 GL52 134 A3
George Pl 14 GL16 155 A7
George Rd GL15 156 A2
George Readings Way GL51 133 A4
George St Bisley GL6 105 A1
Bristol BS5 9 C8
Gloucester GL1 196 C3
Nailsworth GL6 91 C4
5 Stroud GL5 99 C7
George The GL54 174 A7
George Whitefield Cl 5 GL4 119 C4
George Whitefield Ct BS1 195 B3
Georgia Rd GL7 152 E2
Georgian Cl GL4 119 E3
Georgian House Mus* BS1 194 C2
Gerald Rd BS3 8 A3
Geralds Way GL6 148 C6
Gere Cl GL4 118 D2
Gerrard Cl BS4 2 D7
Gerrish Ave
Bristol,Moorfields BS5 9 C8
Bristol,Staple Hill BS16 20 F5
Gervase Rd GL54 174 A8
Gibbet La BS14 3 D1
Gibbs Ct 15 BS5 9 D7
Gibbsfold Rd BS13 2 C4
Gibraltar Way NP16 61 B4
Gibson Cl GL5 99 F7
Gibson Ct GL7 190 D3
Gibson Rd Bristol BS6 18 D1
Innsworth GL3 127 E7
Giffard Ho BS34 29 D6
Giffard Way GL53 130 D4
Gifford Cl Gloucester GL2 127 C5
Rangeworthy BS37 43 A8
Gifford Cres BS34 29 C6
Gifford Ct BS34 29 D2
Gifford Rd BS10 27 F4
Giffords Pl BS13 2 A7
Gilbert Hill GL13 85 E4
Gilbert Rd
Bristol,Kingswood BS15 20 D1
Bristol,Moorfields BS5 9 C8
Gloucester GL2 127 C5
Gilberts La GL4 110 F6
Gilda Cl BS14 3 C5
Gilda Cres BS14 3 B6
Gilda Par BS14 3 C5
Gilda Sq W BS14 3 B5
Gilder Rd GL52 138 A2
Gilders Paddock GL52 137 F4
Giles Ave SN6 143 E3
Giles Cox GL2 109 F8
Gill Ave BS16 20 B6
Gillard Cl BS15 10 B8
Gillard Rd BS15 10 B8
Gillebank Cl BS14 3 D5
Gillett Cl GL54 139 F5
Gillham Ho 4 BS7 18 D2
Gillingham Hill 7 BS15 10 B5
Gillingstool BS35 51 C8
Gillingstool Prim Sch BS35 51 B8
Gillray Cl BS7 19 B6
Gilpin Ave GL3 127 F1
Gilpin Cl BS15 20 F1
Gilroy Cl BS30 11 B3
Gilslake Ave BS10 28 B3
Gilton Ho BS4 9 E2
Gimson Cl GL4 118 D2
Gingell's Gn 4 BS5 10 A8
Gipsy La Chalford GL6 148 D4
Leonard Stanley GL10 97 E2
Gipsy Patch La BS34 29 C6
Glade The GL7 190 E2
Glades The BS5 19 E2
Gladfield Gdns GL5 98 E6
Gladfield Sq GL5 98 E6
Gladiator Cl GL3 120 E5
Gladstone Ct BS16 20 E4
Gladstone Dr BS16 20 E3
Gladstone La BS36 31 C7
Gladstone Rd
Bristol,Hengrove BS14 3 B6
2 Bristol,Kingswood BS15 20 D1
Charlton Kings GL53 131 A5
Gladstone Rd *continued*
Gloucester GL1 118 D6
Gladstone St
Bristol,Bedminster BS3 8 B3
Bristol,Kingswood BS16 20 D3
13 Bristol,Pile Marsh BS5 9 D7
Glaisdale Rd BS16 20 A5
Glamorgan Rd GL51 129 E6
Glanville Gdns BS15 10 E7
Glass House La BS2 9 B5
Glasshouse The GL50 193 A3
Glastonbury Cl BS30 10 F5
Glebe Cl
Frampton on Severn GL2 157 F1
Long Ashton BS41 7 C2
Mitcheldean GL17 164 D6
Newent GL18 170 F5
11 Stow-on-t-W GL54 176 F4
Stratton GL7 190 B8
Glebe Ct GL18 170 F5
Glebe Farm Ct GL51 129 F5
Glebe Field BS32 40 A5
Glebe Fold 10 GL55 189 A2
Glebe Inf Sch GL18 170 F5
Glebe La GL7 141 F8
Glebe Orch HR8 178 A3
Glebe Pl SN6 145 D3
Glebe Rd Bristol BS5 9 E8
Cheltenham GL52 134 B4
Long Ashton BS41 7 C2
Minchinhampton GL6 148 A3
Newent GL18 170 F4
Glebe The Pilning BS35 38 C7
Sapperton GL7 149 B6
Glebe View GL7 158 C4
Glebe Way GL18 170 F5
Glebe Wlk BS31 4 C4
Glebeland Dr GL20 182 C7
Glebelands GL11 87 F5
Glebelands Rd BS34 29 A3
Glebes The BS5 9 E8
Gledemoor Dr BS36 31 D7
Glen Ct GL10 97 F8
Glen Dr BS9 17 D5
Glen Hospl The BS6 18 A2
Glen La BS4 9 D2
Glen Park Cres GL5 99 A4
Glen Park Gdns BS5 10 A8
Glen Pk
Bristol,Eastville BS5 19 C2
Bristol,St George BS5 10 A8
Glen The
Bristol,Hanham BS15 10 B4
Bristol,Redland BS6 18 B3
Saltford BS31 5 F1
Yate BS37 43 E2
Glena Ave BS4 9 B2
Glenarm Rd BS4 9 E2
Glenarm Wlk BS4 9 E2
Glenavon Ct BS9 17 C4
Glenavon Pk BS9 17 C4
Glenburn Rd BS15 20 B1
Glencairn Ave GL4 118 C1
Glencairn Ct GL50 130 A8
Glencairn Park Rd GL50 130 A8
Glencarn Pl 15 GL16 155 A7
Glencoe La GL17 164 D4
Glencoyne Ct 1 BS10 28 C2
Glencoyne Sq BS10 28 C2
Glendale 17 Bristol BS8 7 F6
Bristol,Downend BS16 20 E8
Bristol,Hillfields BS16 20 C3
Glendare St BS5 9 C6
Glendevon Rd BS14 3 A3
Glendower Cl GL3 127 F8
Glendower Ho 5 BS8 7 F7
Gleneagles BS37 43 E1
Gleneagles Dr BS10 27 D3
Gleneagles Rd BS30 11 B6
Glenfall BS37 32 D7
Glenfall Com Prim Sch GL52 131 C6
Glenfall St GL52 133 F2
Glenfall Way GL52 131 B6
Glenfrome Prim Sch BS5 19 B4
Glenfrome Rd BS2 19 B3
Glenlea Gr GL51 129 F5
Glenroy Ave BS15 20 B1
Glensanda Ct GL50 193 B2
Glenside Cl BS16 20 C7
Glenside Hospl Mus* BS16 19 E5
Glenside Pk 3 BS16 19 E5
Glenthorne Cl GL10 101 F1
Glentworth Rd
Bristol,Clifton Wood BS8 194 B2
Bristol,Redland BS6 18 C2
Glenview Rd BS4 9 D2
Glenville Par GL3 120 A7
Glenwood BS16 20 C3
Glenwood Dr BS30 11 B4
Glenwood Rd BS10 18 C7
Glevum Cl Bristol BS16 21 C7
Gloucester GL2 127 B4
Glevum Ct 11 GL51 132 D2
Glevum Sh Ctr GL4 119 D4
Glevum Way GL4 119 E4
Glevum Works (Trad Est) GL1 119 A7
Glevum Works Trad Est GL1 118 F7
Gloster Ades Rd WR11 188 B6
Gloster Ave BS5 19 D3
Gloucester Bsns Pk GL3 120 B6
Gloucester Cl BS34 29 D5

Gloucester Coll of Arts & Tech GL1 196 B2
Gloucester Cotts 5 GL50 133 B2
Gloucester Ho 12 BS2 195 C3
Gloucester House Mews GL12 68 A8
Gloucester La
20 Bristol BS2 195 C3
Mickleton GL55 189 A6
Gloucester Mus & Art Gal★ GL1 196 B2
Gloucester Pl GL52 193 C4
Gloucester Prison Mus★ GL1 196 A3
Gloucester Rd
Almondsbury BS32,BS35 40 C6
Andoversford GL54 166 D6
Avonmouth BS11 26 A1
Bristol,Bishopston BS7 18 E4
Bristol,Patchway BS34 29 B7
Bristol,Staple Hill BS16 20 E3
Cheltenham GL51 132 D1
Cirencester GL7 190 B6
Coleford GL16 155 A5
Corse GL19 172 B8
Mitcheldean GL17 164 D5
Newton GL13 85 C8
Painswick GL6 111 F1
Stone GL13 77 F3
Stonehouse GL10 101 F1
Tadwick BA1 13 F2
Tewkesbury GL20 181 F1
Thornbury BS35 64 C3
Tutshill NP16 73 A2
Upleadon GL18 171 D5
Gloucester Rd N BS7, BS34 29 A4
Gloucester Retail Pk GL4 119 C8
Gloucester Road Prim Sch GL51 133 B2
Gloucester Row
7 Bristol BS8 7 F7
Kingswood GL12 67 F8
Gloucester Royal Hospl GL1 196 C3
Gloucester Rugby Football Gd GL1 196 B4
Gloucester Ski Ctr★ GL4 119 B3
Gloucester St
12 Bristol,Clifton BS8 7 F7
Bristol,Eastville BS5 19 D3
5 Bristol,St Pauls BS2 195 B4
Cirencester GL7 190 B6
Newent GL18 171 A4
Painswick GL6 103 F8
2 Stroud GL5 99 C7
Winchcombe GL54 174 A7
Wotton-u-E GL12 68 A7
Gloucester Sta GL1 196 C3
Gloucestershire & Warwickshire Rly★
Bishop's Cleeve GL52 138 B5
★ Toddington GL54 184 C1
★ Winchcombe GL54 174 B8
Gloucestershire Airport GL51 128 D8
Gloucestershire Coll of Art & Tech GL51 132 D2
Gloucestershire Cty Cricket Club★ BS7 18 F4
Gloucestershire Royal Hospl GL1 127 A2
Gloucestershire Warwickshire Rly★ GL54 183 D1
Glyn Terr GL5 99 E3
Glyn Vale BS3 8 E1
Glynbridge Ct 3 GL1 118 F7
Glynbridge Gdns GL51 132 F5
Glyndthorpe Gr 12 GL51 129 E5
Glynfield Rise GL5 98 C7
Glynrosa Rd GL53 131 B5
Goddard Way Bristol BS10 28 A1
Gloucester GL4 118 D2
Godfrey Cl GL51 130 A7
Godfrey Ct 7 BS30 10 F4
Godwin Cl 15 GL52 133 F2
Godwin Rd GL54 174 A8
Goffenton Dr BS16 20 B6
Goldcrest Ct 6 GL10 97 F8
Goldcrest Rd BS37 32 F7
Golden Cl GL4 118 C2
Golden Farm Rd GL7 190 E4
Golden Hay WR11 183 F7
Golden Hill BS6 18 C5
Golden Jubilee Way GL5 98 E6
Golden La GL12 67 F4
Golden Lion Ct BS1 195 B2
Golden Miller Rd GL50 133 C5
Golden Vale GL3 128 B6
Golden Valley
Brimscombe GL5 148 A5
Newent GL18 171 D4
Golden Valley La BS30 11 F2
Goldfinch Way BS16 22 C4
Goldfoot Ho GL51 132 F1
Goldney Ave
Bristol,Clifton Wood BS8 194 A2
Bristol,Warmley BS30 11 C7
Goldney Ct 7 BS16 19 E3
Goldney Rd BS8 194 A2
Goldsborough Cl GL4 119 B6
Goldsbury Wlk BS11 27 A1
Goldsmith Cl GL51 132 E2
Goldsmith Rd GL51 132 E2
Goldsmiths Ho BS2 195 C2
Golf Club La Saltford BS31 5 E2
Watermead GL3 120 C5
Golf Course La BS34 28 F3
Golf Course Rd GL6 111 F2
Gooch Cl WR11 188 C7
Gooch Ct BS30 11 C3
Good Neighbours La NP25 154 B7
Good Shepherd Cl BS7 18 C4
Goode Ct 2 GL15 92 A3
Goodeve Pk BS9 17 D3
Goodeve Rd BS9 17 D3
Goodhind St BS5 9 A8
Goodier's La GL20 182 A7
Goodmans Terr 5 GL7 152 E4
Goodmoor Cres GL3 128 A6
Goodneston Rd BS16 20 A3
Goodrich Castle★ HR9 163 A6
Goodrich CE Prim Sch HR9 163 A6
Goodrich Cl BS37 43 B1
Goodrich Hill GL19 172 D4
Goodridge Ave GL2 118 A3
Goodridge Trad Est GL2 118 A4
Goodring Hill BS11 27 A1
Goodwin Ct GL1 118 E7
Goodwin Dr BS14 2 F4
Goodwood Gdns BS16 30 F1
Goodyere St GL1 196 C1
Goolden St BS4 9 A3
Goose Acre BS32 29 F6
Goose Gn Bristol BS30 21 C1
Frampton Cotterell BS36 31 C8
Yate BS37 43 E3
Goose Green Way BS37 43 E4
Goose La GL14 157 F8
Gooseacre Ct GL7 190 C6
Gooseacre La GL7 190 C6
Gooseland Cl BS14 2 F3
Gooselands SN16 141 B3
Gopshill La GL54 183 E1
Gordano Gdns BS20 16 B4
Gordon Ave BS5 19 E1
Gordon Cl Bristol BS5 19 E1
Broadway WR12 185 B8
Highnam GL2 125 E5
Gordon Rd
14 Bristol,St Pauls BS2 18 F1
Bristol,Victoria Park BS8 194 B3
Bristol,Whitehall BS5 19 D1
Cheltenham GL53 130 C5
Gordon Terr
Brimscombe GL5 99 F1
Stroud GL5 99 D7
Gore Rd BS3 8 A3
Gore's Marsh Rd BS3 8 A2
Gorham Cl BS11 27 C2
Gorlands Rd BS37 44 C1
Gorlangton Cl BS14 3 A7
Gorse Bglws GL16 155 A6
Gorse Cl
Bourton-on-t-W GL54 169 A7
Gloucester GL4 119 F4
Gorse Cover Rd BS35 38 A7
Gorse Hill BS16 20 C3
Gorse La Bristol BS8 194 B2
Cold Ashton BS30,SN14 13 D7
Sling GL16 155 B3
Gorse Mdw GL54 169 A6
Gorse The GL54 169 A7
Gorsley Gdns HR9 170 B4
Gorsley Goff's Prim Sch HR9 170 B5
Gosditch
Ashton Keynes SN6 142 F4
Latton SN6 143 E6
Gosditch St GL7 190 C5
Gosforth Cl BS10 28 B1
Gosforth Rd BS10 28 B1
Goshawk Rd GL2 117 F3
Goslet Rd BS14 3 E5
Goss Wood Cnr GL2 109 E8
Gotherington Fields GL52 137 E8
Gotherington La GL52 138 A5
Gotherington Prim Sch GL52 138 B7
Gotherington Sta★ GL52 138 D8
Gothic Cotts GL1 196 C2
Gotley Rd BS4 9 D2
Gott Dr BS4 9 D5
Gouda Way GL1 196 B4
Gould Dr GL20 182 C5
Goulston Rd BS13 2 A5
Goulston Wlk BS13 2 A5
Goulter St BS5 9 B6
Gourney Cl BS11 27 B2
Gover Rd BS15 10 C3
Govier Way BS35 38 C4
Gower Cotts NP16 72 F2
Gowle Rd GL5 99 D6
Grace Cl BS37 44 C1
Grace Ct BS16 20 D6
Grace Dr Bristol BS15 11 A8
1 Northleach GL54 168 A1
Grace Gdns GL51 129 D7
Grace Park Rd BS4 9 D1
Grace Rd BS16 20 C5
Graces Pitch 15 GL18 171 A4
Graeme Cl BS16 20 A4
Grafton Ct GL50 193 B1
Grafton La GL19 180 B3
Grafton Rd
Cheltenham GL50 193 A1
Gloucester GL2 127 B3
Graham Ct GL20 192 D5
Graham Gdns GL2 127 B3
Graham Pl GL51 132 D3
Graham Rd
4 Bristol,Bedminster BS3 8 C3
Bristol,Downend BS16 20 F6
21 Bristol,Upper Easton BS5 19 B1
Grahamstown Gr NP16 61 B8
Grahamstown Rd NP16 61 B8
Grainger Ct BS11 16 E7
Grampian Cl BS30 11 C4
Granary The
Blockley GL56 186 C7
Bristol BS1 195 A2
Granbrook La GL55 189 B7
Granby Hill BS8 7 F6
Grandmother's Rock La BS30 12 D2
Grange Ave
Bristol,Hanham BS15 10 D5
Bristol,Little Stoke BS34 29 C6
Grange Cl
Bristol,Patchway BS32 40 C2
Bristol,Stoke Gifford BS34 30 A4
Highworth SN6 145 D3
Minchinhampton GL6 91 F6
Grange Cl N BS9 18 B6
Grange Cotts GL8 140 C3
Grange Court La GL19 165 D6
Grange Court Rd
Bristol BS9 18 A6
Westbury-on-S GL14 165 D2
Grange Ct Bristol BS15 10 D5
Bristol,Henleaze BS9 18 B6
Bristol,Westbury on Trym BS9 18 A8
Northway GL20 182 C5
Grange Dr
Bishop's Cleeve GL52 137 F3
Bristol BS16 20 C6
Grange Inf Sch GL4 118 C2
Grange Jun Sch GL4 118 C3
Grange La GL8 140 B3
Grange Pk
Bristol,Frenchay BS16 20 C8
Bristol,Westbury on Trym BS9 18 B6
St Arvans NP16 72 A6
Whitchurch HR9 162 D4
Grange Rd
Bristol,Bishopsworth BS13 2 A5
Bristol,Victoria Park BS8 194 A3
Gloucester GL4 118 D1
Northway GL20 182 C5
Saltford BS31 5 C3
St Arvans NP16 72 A6
Grange Sch & Sports Coll The BS30 11 B7
Grange The
Bristol,Coombe Dingle BS9 17 D7
Bristol,Sneyd Park BS9 17 F3
Cheltenham GL51 129 B6
Gloucester GL2 127 B2
8 Moreton-in-M GL56 187 A3
Grange View GL5 99 C8
Grange Wlk GL53 131 B5
Grangefield Prim Sch GL52 137 E3
Grangeville Cl BS30 11 B3
Grangewood Cl 4 BS16 20 C6
Granley Cl GL51 129 F8
Granley Ct GL1 118 D6
Granley Dr GL51 129 F8
Granley Gdns GL51 129 F8
Granley Rd GL51 129 F8
Granna La GL52 138 D8
Granny's La BS15 10 E6
Gransmoor Grange GL3 120 B7
Grantham Ct 1 BS15 10 C8
Grantham Ho BS15 20 C1
Grantham La BS15 10 C8
Grantham Rd BS15 20 C1
Grantley Cres GL7 190 C3
Grantson Cl BS4 9 E2
Granville Cl BS15 10 B3
Granville St Bristol BS5 9 C6
Cheltenham GL50 133 C3
Gloucester GL1 118 D6
21 Monmouth/Trefynwy NP25 154 A7
Grasby Cl GL4 119 E7
Grasmere Cl BS10 18 A8
Grasmere Rd
Cheltenham GL51 129 F7
Gloucester GL2 127 C4
Grasmere Way NP16 61 A4
Grass Meers Dr BS14 3 A4
Grassington Dr BS37 33 A8
Grassmere Gdns BS30 11 D6
Gratitude Rd BS5 19 C1
Gratton Rd GL50 193 A1
Gratton St GL50 193 B1
Gravel Hill Rd N BS37 44 A5
Gravel Pit Cotts GL52 131 C6
Gravel Pit La GL52 134 C5
Gravel Pits Cl GL20 182 C7
Gravel Wlk
Southam GL52 134 C8
Tewkesbury GL20 192 D5
Graveney Cl BS4 9 D1
Graveney Rd GL54 168 A1
Gravney Ct GL51 132 E4
Gray Cl Bristol BS10 27 E2
Innsworth GL3 127 E7
Gray Rd GL7 151 A2
Gray's La 20 GL56 187 A3
Grayle Rd BS10 28 A2
Grayling Cl 7 GL4 119 E5
Grayling Ho BS9 17 F7
Grayston Cl GL20 192 E6
Great Ann St BS2 195 C3
Great Brockeridge BS9 17 F6
Great Dowles BS30 11 A4
Great George St
Bristol,Brandon Hill BS1 194 C2
Bristol,St Pauls BS2 195 C3
Great Gr GL4 119 D7
Great Hayles Rd BS14 3 A6
Great Leaze BS30 11 A4
Great Mdw BS34 30 A6
Great Meadow Rd BS32 29 F6
Great Norwood St GL50 193 B1
Great Orch GL5 99 E3
Great Park Rd BS32 40 C3
Great Rissington Prim Sch GL54 169 D4
Great Rose La SN26 144 D3
Great Stoke BS34 30 A5
Great Stoke Way
Bristol,Great Stoke BS34 30 A5
Bristol,Harry Stoke BS34 29 D3
Great Western Bsns Pk BS37 43 B3
Great Western Ct
Bristol BS34 29 F4
3 Gloucester GL1 127 A1
Great Western La BS5 9 C6
Great Western Railway Mus★ GL16 155 A5
Great Western Rd
Cheltenham GL50 193 A4
Gloucester GL1 196 C3
Sharpness GL13 93 B1
Great Western Terr GL50 193 A4
Great Witcombe Roman Villa★ GL3 120 F1
Great Wood Cl BS13 2 C4
Greatfield Dr GL53 130 F5
Greatfield La
Cheltenham,Hatherley GL51 129 E5
Cheltenham,Warden Hill GL51 129 F5
Greatfield Park Prim Sch GL51 129 F5
Grebe Cl GL4 119 D5
Grebe Sq GL54 169 D6
Green Acre Bream GL15 147 D8
Watermead GL3 120 E5
Green Acre Rd BS14 3 A3
Green Bank GL3 120 E4
Green Cl
Honeybourne WR11 188 C6
Uley GL11 89 C2
Watermead GL3 120 E4
Green Colley Cl HR9 163 B6
Green Croft BS5 20 A1
Green Ct BS35 50 A2
Green Dell Cl BS10 27 D3
Green Dragon Rd BS36 30 D5
Green Gdns GL3 120 E4
Green Hayes BS37 33 C8
Green Hill BS35 51 A4
Green La Avonmouth BS11 26 B1
Chedworth GL54 159 B6
Churchdown GL3 128 C4
Easter Compton BS35 38 C1
Evenlode GL56 177 C7
Gloucester GL3 120 A6
Hardwicke GL2 109 E6
Little Witcombe GL3 121 C3
Marshfield SN14 14 E8
Moreton Valence GL2 101 A6
Naunton WR8 180 D10
Rangeworthy BS37,GL12 53 B2
Severn Beach BS35 38 B8
Sherston SN16 58 C1
Tewkesbury GL20 182 B4
Tytherington GL12 52 B8
Winterbourne BS36 30 C7
Green Lake Cl GL54 168 F8
Green Meadow Bank GL52 137 E3
Green Pastures NP25 154 A3
Green Pippin Cl GL2 127 C2
Green Pk GL2 109 E6
Green Side BS16 21 A6
Green St Bristol BS3 8 F4
Bushley GL19,GL20 181 B5
Chepstow/Cas-Gwent NP16 60 E8
Dursley GL11 88 C6
Watermead GL3 120 E3
Green The
Bishop's Cleeve GL52 137 F3
Bledington OX7 177 E1
Bristol,New Cheltenham BS15 20 E2
Bristol,Stoke Gifford BS34 29 E4
6 Broadway WR12 185 B8
Chepstow/Cas-Gwent NP16 60 B5
Chipping Campden GL55 189 A1
Chipping Sodbury BS37 34 A8
Churchdown GL3 128 C3
Cirencester,Siddington GL7 190 E2
Cirencester,The Beeches GL7 190 E5
Cromhall GL12 53 B8
Fairford GL7 152 D4
Frampton on Severn GL2 157 F2
Great Wolford CV36 187 E5
Green The *continued*
Highworth SN6 145 C3
Honeybourne WR11 188 C6
Iron Acton BS37 42 D4
Luckington SN14 47 E4
10 Moreton-in-M GL56 187 A3
Newnham GL14 156 F6
18 Northleach GL54 168 A1
Oaksey SN16 141 F4
Olveston BS35 50 A2
Pill BS20 16 D4
Tetbury GL8 140 C4
Uckington GL51 132 D6
Uley GL11 89 C2
Woodmancote GL52 138 C3
Green Way GL3 120 E5
Green Wlk BS4 9 A1
Green's Cl GL54 169 C4
Greenacres Bristol BS9 17 E7
Twyning GL20 181 F8
Greenacres Park Homes BS36 31 E5
Greenacres Pk GL7 152 A3
Greenaways GL18 170 F5
Greenbank Avenue E BS5 19 C1
Greenbank Avenue W BS5 19 C1
Greenbank Cl GL17 164 B3
Greenbank Rd
Bristol,Hanham BS15 10 D5
Bristol,Lower Easton BS5 19 D2
Bristol,Southville BS3 8 A4
Greenbank View BS5 19 D2
Greenbanks NP25 146 B7
Greendale Rd
Bristol,Lower Knowle BS3 8 E2
Bristol,Redland BS6 18 B3
Greenditch Ave BS13 2 C5
Greenditch St BS35 49 D1
Greendown BS5 10 A7
Greenfield Ave BS10 18 D8
Greenfield Cl GL17 163 D3
Greenfield Ct BS10 28 D1
Greenfield Rd
Bristol BS10 28 D1
Coleford GL16 155 A6
Joy's Green GL17 163 D3
Greenfinch Lodge BS16 19 E6
Greenhaven 5 BS5 19 C1
Greenhill BS35 51 A4
Greenhill Cl GL14 191 E5
Greenhill Ct GL4 118 B2
Greenhill Down BS35 51 A5
Greenhill Dr GL2 118 A3
Greenhill Flats GL5 99 E3
Greenhill Gdns BS35 51 A4
Greenhill Gr BS3 8 A2
Greenhill Ho GL52 137 F3
Greenhill La
Alveston BS35 50 F4
Bristol BS11 27 C1
Greenhill Par 5 BS35 51 A5
Greenhill Rd BS35 51 A5
Greenhills Cl GL53 130 E5
Greenhills Rd GL53 130 F5
Greenhouse La GL6 104 A7
Greenings The GL51 129 F5
Greenlands Cl 16 NP25 154 A7
Greenlands Way BS10 27 F4
Greenleaze Bristol BS4 9 B1
Marston Meysey SN6 144 B8
Greenleaze Ave BS16 30 D1
Greenleaze Cl BS16 30 D1
Greenmead Park Cvn Site GL51 129 D5
Greenmeadows Pk GL51 128 F8
Greenmore Rd BS4 9 B2
Greenore BS15 10 C7
Greenpark Rd BS10 28 E1
Greenridge Cl BS13 1 E4
Greenside Cl BS10 27 D3
Greensplott Rd BS11 26 E7
Greenstreet GL10 97 F8
Greenview Bristol BS30 11 A2
Quenington GL7 152 D7
Greenway GL52 138 B3
Greenway Bush La BS3 8 B4
Greenway Cl GL51 129 D1
Greenway Dr BS10 18 D8
Greenway Ho 10 BS6 18 B2
Greenway La
Charlton Kings GL52 131 C7
Cheltenham GL53 122 B7
Cold Ashton SN14 13 D5
Gretton GL54 183 F1
Little Shurdington GL51, GL53 121 E8
Llandogo NP25 146 A8
Shurdington GL51 129 D1
Greenway Pk BS10 18 D8
Greenway Rd
Blockley GL56 186 C6
Bristol BS6 18 B2
Cinderford GL14 191 C3
Greenway The
Bristol BS16 20 C3
Gloucester GL1 118 D6
Greenways Bristol BS15 21 A1
Lydney GL15 147 F5
Winchcombe GL54 174 A8
Greenways Dr GL16 155 B4
Greenways Rd BS37 43 E3
Greenwich Apartments BS6 18 C3
Greenwood Cl Bristol BS7 18 E7
Gloucester GL3 120 B6

Greenwood Dr BS35 50 F4
Greenwood Rd BS4 9 A1
Greet Rd GL54 174 A8
Gregory Ct BS30 11 A6
Grenadier Cl GL4 119 F6
Grenadier Rd GL51 132 E4
Grenville Chapel 5 BS8 7 F5
Grenville Cl Bristol BS5 9 F8
Innsworth GL3 127 F8
Grenville Pl 7 BS1 7 F5
Grenville Rd BS6 18 E3
Gresham Ct 5 GL51 132 E2
Gretton Prim Sch GL54 183 E1
Gretton Rd
Gotherington GL52 138 C8
Winchcombe GL54 174 A8
Gretton View GL20 183 E4
Greve Ct 5 BS30 10 F4
Grevel La GL55 189 A2
Grevil Rd 3 GL51 132 F4
Greville Cl GL2 126 E4
Greville Ct GL51 129 F8
Greville Rd BS3 8 B4
Greville St BS3 8 C4
Grey Gables BS35 50 A3
Greyfriars GL1 196 B2
Greyfriars Church★ GL1 196 B3
Greyfriars Wlk GL7 190 B2
Greyhound Gdns GL2 127 D5
Greylag Cres GL20 192 E3
Greylands Rd BS13 1 F7
Greyrick Ct GL55 189 A6
Greys Cl 5 GL6 148 B6
Greystoke Ave BS10 28 C1
Greystoke Gdns BS10 18 A8
Greystone Lodge GL3 120 B7
Greystones BS16 30 E1
Greystones La GL54 169 A7
Grierson Cl GL3 120 B6
Griffin Cl GL54 177 A4
Griffin Ct GL54 177 A4
Griffin Mill Est GL5 99 D4
Griffiths Ave GL51 132 F1
Griffon Cl GL2 117 F3
Griggfield Wlk BS14 3 A7
Griggs Cl 3 GL55 189 A2
Grimsbury Rd BS15 11 A7
Grimwade Cl GL51 132 F1
Grindell Rd BS5 9 D7
Grinfield Ave BS13 2 C4
Grinfield Ct BS13 2 C4
Grisedale Cl GL2 127 D5
Grist Mill Cl GL51 132 D5
Grittleton Rd BS7 18 E8
Groaten The WR11 183 D8
Grosvenor Ct 2 BS6 18 B1
Grosvenor Ho GL1 196 B3
Grosvenor Pl S GL52 193 C3
Grosvenor Rd Bristol BS2 18 F1
Gloucester GL2 127 B2
Stonehouse GL10 101 F1
Grosvenor St GL52 193 C3
Grosvenor Terr GL52 193 C3
Grove Ave Bristol BS1 195 A1
Bristol,Coombe Dingle BS9 17 C7
3 Bristol,Fishponds BS16 19 F4
Honeybourne WR11 188 C7
Grove Bank BS16 30 C1
Grove Cotts GL5 98 F8
Grove Cres
7 Coleford GL16 155 A6
Gloucester GL4 127 D1
Grove Ct BS9 17 E5
Grove Gdns GL8 140 B5
Grove Hall BS4 9 D2
Grove Hill SN6 145 C4
Grove Ind Est The BS34 29 B8
Grove La Cirencester GL7 190 D5
Hinton SN14 23 C6
Lydney GL15 92 B6
Whitminster GL2 100 F4
Grove Leaze BS11 16 D6
Grove Orch SN6 145 C4
Grove Park Ave BS4 9 D2
Grove Park Rd Bristol BS4 9 D2
Stroud GL5 99 C8
Grove Park Terr BS16 19 F4
Grove Pk
Bristol,Brislington BS4 9 D2
Bristol,Redland BS6 18 C2
Whitecroft GL15 155 F1
Grove Rd Berry Hill GL16 155 A7
Bristol,Coombe Dingle BS9 17 D8
Bristol,Fishponds BS16 19 F4
Bristol,Redland BS6 18 A2
Innsworth GL3 127 F6
Lydney GL15 147 F6
Whitecroft GL15 155 F1
Grove St
Cheltenham GL50 193 A4
Gloucester GL1 196 C1
Grove The Avening GL8 140 B8
Bristol,Canon's Marsh BS1 195 A1
Bristol,Oldland BS30 11 A4
Bristol,Patchway BS34 29 B7
Cheltenham,Battledown GL52 134 A1
Cheltenham,Lansdown GL50 130 B8
Chelworth SN16 141 E5
5 Moreton-in-M GL56 187 B3
Rangeworthy BS37 43 A8
Selsley GL5 98 E4
Stonehouse GL10 98 A6
Stroud GL5 98 D6
Grove View Bristol BS16 19 E6
Grove View *continued*
Greet GL54 184 A1
Grovefield GL19 180 A4
Grovefield Way GL51 129 B7
Grovelands GL4 127 E1
Grovelands Cl 1 GL53 131 B6
Groves Pl GL7 152 E3
Groves The BS13 2 D4
Grovesend Rd BS35 51 D8
Grump St CV36 189 F6
Gryphons The 16 GL52 133 F2
Guardian Ct 10 Bristol BS8 7 F7
Cheltenham GL53 130 F6
Guernsey Ave BS4 9 F4
Guest Ave BS16 21 B7
Guestriss Cotts GL50 133 C5
Guggle La 7 GL54 168 A1
Guild Ct BS1 195 B2
Guildford Rd BS4 9 E6
Guildings Way GL10 98 A4
Guinea La Bristol BS16 20 A4
Bristol BS16 20 A5
Guinea St Bristol BS1 195 A1
Gloucester GL1 196 C4
Guise Ave GL3 120 F4
Guise Cl GL2 109 F8
Gullimores Gdns BS13 2 B4
Gullivers Pl BS37 33 A8
Gullon Wlk BS13 1 F7
Gullons Cl BS13 2 A6
Gully La BS35 64 E7
Gully The BS36 30 F7
Gullybrook La 3 BS5 9 B6
Gumstool Hill 13 GL8 140 C4
Gunhouse La GL5 99 D5
Gunning Cl BS15 10 D6
Gunter's Hill BS5 10 A6
Gupshill Cl GL20 192 C2
Gurney Ave GL4 118 D2
Gustav Holst Birthplace Mus★ GL52 193 C4
Guthrie Rd BS8 194 A4
Gwentlands Cl NP16 60 E7
Gwernant Rd GL51 129 F6
Gwilliam St BS3 8 D3
Gwinnett Ct GL51 129 E2
Gwy Ct NP16 72 F1
Gwyn St BS2 18 E1
Gyde Ho GL6 111 F1
Gyde Rd GL6 111 F1
Gydynap La GL5 91 A7
Gypsy La Gorsley GL18 170 C3
Marshfield SN14 14 F7

H

Haberdashers Sch for Girls NP25 154 A8
Haberdashers' Agincourt Sch NP25 154 A8
Haberfield Hill BS8 16 E2
Haberfield Ho 1 BS8 7 F6
Hacket Hill BS35 51 F8
Hacket La BS35 51 F8
Haddrell Ct BS35 50 F5
Hadfield Cl GL19 172 A8
Hadley Ct BS30 11 B6
Hadley Rd GL11 87 E4
Hadnock Rd NP25 154 A8
Hadnock Road Ind Est 5 NP25 154 A8
Hadow Way GL2 109 F8
Hadrian Cl Bristol BS9 17 C4
Lydney GL15 92 B4
Hadrians Way GL4 119 F7
Hadrians Wlk BS16 21 C6
Hague Ave GL11 87 F4
Haig Cl BS9 17 B7
Hailes Abbey & Mus★ GL54 184 D1
Hailes Green Barns GL54 174 C8
Hailes Rd GL4 119 D7
Hailes St 28 GL54 174 A7
Hakeburn Rd GL7 190 C5
Halbrow Cres BS16 20 C5
Haldon Cl BS3 8 D1
Hale Cl BS15 10 D4
Hale La GL6 103 F8
Hale Wood/Coed Hale NP16 60 C8
Hale's Rd GL52 134 A1
Hales Cl GL52 134 A1
Hales Horn Cl BS32 29 D6
Halfacre Cl BS14 3 A3
Halfacre La BS14 3 B4
Halford Ho GL2 118 C4
Halfway Pitch GL6 103 B4
Halifax Rd BS37 43 D4
Hall End La BS37 53 D2
Hall La
Cold Ashton BA1,SN14 13 E2
Horton BS37 45 E5
Lower Hamswell BA1 13 B3
Hall Rd GL53 130 D4
Hall St BS3 8 C2
Halland Rd GL53 130 D5
Hallards Cl BS11 16 F8
Hallen Cl
Bristol,Emerson's Green BS16 21 C6
Bristol,Henbury BS10 27 D3
Hallen Dr BS9 17 C7
Hallen Ind Est BS10 27 A7
Hallen Rd BS10 27 D4
Hallmead Cl GL51 132 D5
Halls Gdns BS34 30 A4
Halls Rd BS15 10 D8
Hallsfield SN6 143 E5
Hallwood Dr HR8 178 D8
Halmore La GL13 86 A8
Halsbury Rd BS6 18 A4
Halstock Ave BS16 19 F3
Halston Dr BS2 195 C4
Halswell Gdns BS13 2 B4
Halt End BS14 3 C3
Halwyn Cl BS9 17 D5
Ham Cl GL52 131 C7
Ham Farm La BS16 21 B6
Ham Gn BS20 16 D3
Ham Green Hospl BS20 16 E4
Ham La Bristol BS16 19 E6
Charlton Kings GL52 131 D7
Doynton BS30 22 E1
Dundry BS41 1 D3
Kempsford GL7 144 F7
Oldbury-on-S BS35 63 C7
South Cerney GL7 142 F7
Ham Mill La GL5 99 E3
Ham Rd
Andoversford GL54 166 A8
Ashleworth GL19 172 E5
Charlton Kings GL52,GL54 131 E7
Ham Sq GL52 131 C7
Ham The GL11 89 A6
Hambidge La GL7 153 E3
Hamble Cl BS35 51 C8
Hambledon Cl GL7 150 F2
Hamblins Cotts GL53 123 A5
Hambrook La BS34 30 A3
Hambrook Prim Sch BS16 30 D3
Hambrook St GL52 131 B7
Hambutts Dr GL6 103 E8
Hambutts Mead GL6 103 E8
Hamer St GL1 127 B1
Hamfallow Ct GL13 85 D8
Hamfield La GL13 85 D3
Hamilton Croft GL7 152 A2
Hamilton Ct GL51 132 D3
Hamilton Rd
Bristol,Southville BS3 8 B4
Bristol,Upper Easton BS5 9 B8
Hamilton St GL53 131 B7
Hamlen Cl GL19 165 D6
Hamlet Cl GL51 132 E2
Hammersmith Bottom GL7 153 B7
Hammersmith Rd BS5 9 D8
Hammett Ct NP25 154 B7
Hammond Cl BS4 9 E1
Hammond Ct GL53 193 C1
Hammond Dr 3 GL54 168 A1
Hammond Gdns BS9 17 E7
Hammond Way
Cirencester GL7 190 C4
Gloucester GL4 127 D1
Hammonds SN6 143 F4
Hampden Cl BS37 43 D4
Hampden Rd BS4 9 B3
Hampden Way GL1 196 B2
Hampen Cotts GL54 167 A7
Hampshire Gdns GL16 155 A5
Hampshire Way BS37 43 F4
Hampstead Rd BS4 9 C3
Hampton Cl Bristol BS30 11 A5
Cheltenham GL51 130 A5
Gloucester GL3 120 B7
Hampton Cnr BS11 16 E6
Hampton Ct BS6 18 B1
Hampton Fields GL6 148 B2
Hampton Gr GL7 152 A3
Hampton Hill GL6,GL8 148 B1
Hampton La 17 BS6 18 B1
Hampton Mews GL15 92 B3
Hampton Pk BS6 18 B1
Hampton Pl GL3 128 A8
Hampton Rd BS6 18 B1
Hampton St Bristol BS15 20 D1
Tetbury GL8 140 B4
Hams Rd Keynsham BS31 4 F7
Lydney GL15 92 B3
Hamshill GL11 88 E6
Hanbury Cl BS15 10 D5
Hanbury Ct BS8 194 A4
Hanbury Ho NP16 60 C8
Hanbury Rd BS8 194 A4
Handel Ave 2 BS5 9 D7
Handel Cossham Ct 3 BS15 20 C1
Handel Rd BS31 4 E5
Handford Way BS30 11 B3
Handley La HR9 164 A8
Hanford Ct BS14 3 D7
Hang Hill Rd GL15 155 D1
Hangerberry New Rd GL17 163 D1
Hanham Abbots Jun Sch BS15 10 C4
Hanham Bsns Pk BS15 10 B5
Hanham Hall Hospl BS15 10 D4
Hanham High Sch BS15 10 C4
Hanham Lodge BS15 10 D7
Hanham Mills BS15 10 D1
Hanham Rd BS15 10 D7
Hankerton Rd SN16 142 B1
Hanley La NP16 73 E6
Hanman Rd GL1 118 F7
Hanman Villas GL2 124 C8
Hanna Ct GL50 193 B4
Hannah Boote Ho 8 GL52 134 A3
Hannah Cres
Siddington GL7 150 F2
South Cerney GL7 151 A2
Hannah More Prim Sch BS1 195 C2
Hannah Pl GL3 127 E7
Hannam Cl GL53 130 E4
Hanover Cl NP16 72 D1
Hanover Ct
Bristol,Filton BS34 29 A3
Bristol,St Pauls BS1 195 B3
14 Cheltenham GL51 130 B8
Cirencester GL7 190 D4
2 Tewkesbury GL20 192 C4
Tutshill NP16 61 A8
Hanover Gdns 2 GL6 91 B4
Hanover Ho Bristol BS2 9 A7
Highworth SN6 145 C3
Hanover Lodge GL5 98 D7
Hanover Pl BS1 194 B1
Hanover St
2 Bristol BS1 195 A2
Bristol,Russell Town BS5 9 C7
Cheltenham GL50 133 D3
Hanover Way 1 GL3 128 A7
Hanson Gdns GL52 137 D4
Hanstone Cl GL7 190 B2
Happerton La BS20 16 D2
Happy Land SN6 142 F4
Harbour Rd GL15 84 B8
Harbour View GL20 192 D5
Harbour Wall BS9 17 B4
Harbour Way BS1 194 C1
Harbour Wlk BS1 194 C1
Harbourside GL20 192 D5
Harbury Mews GL1 119 A8
Harbury Rd BS9 18 C7
Harcombe Hill BS36 30 E4
Harcombe Rd BS36 30 D5
Harcourt Ave BS5 10 A6
Harcourt Cl BS31 5 E2
Harcourt Hill BS6 18 C3
Harcourt Rd BS6 18 B3
Harden Rd BS14 3 E5
Hardenhuish Rd BS4 9 D5
Harding Pl BS31 5 B5
Harding's Dr GL11 88 A1
Hardings Cl GL11 88 A1
Hardington Dr BS31 5 A2
Hardwick Ave NP16 60 E7
Hardwick Bank Rd GL20 182 B5
Hardwick Cl
Bristol,Broom Hill BS4 9 E3
Bristol,North Common BS30 11 D5
Hardwick Hill NP16 60 E7
Hardwick Hill La NP16 60 E8
Hardwick Rd BS20 16 C5
Hardwicke BS37 32 C7
Hardwicke Prim Sch GL2 109 E6
Hardy Ave BS3 8 A4
Hardy Ct BS30 10 F5
Hardy La BS32 50 A1
Hardy Rd
Bishop's Cleeve GL52 138 A4
Bristol BS3 8 B2
Hare La GL1 196 B3
Harebell Pl GL4 119 E5
Hareclive Prim Sch BS13 2 C4
Hareclive Rd BS13 2 C4
Harefield Cl BS15 10 C2
Harefield Gr GL50 130 C6
Harescombe BS37 32 E7
Haresdown Hill GL7 141 C8
Haresfield GL7 190 B8
Haresfield CE Prim Sch GL10 110 B1
Haresfield Ct GL10 110 A1
Haresfield La GL2,GL10 109 F5
Haresfield Lodge GL4 119 B4
Harewood Cl GL4 118 C1
Harewood Ho BS16 18 A3
Harewood Jun & Inf Sch GL4 118 C1
Harewood Rd BS5 20 A1
Harford Cl BS9 17 C7
Harford Dr BS16 30 C1
Harlech Way BS30 11 B2
Harleston St 1 BS5 9 A8
Harley Ct 3 BS8 7 F7
Harley Mews 2 BS8 7 F7
Harley Pl 4 BS8 7 F7
Harleys Field GL4 119 D7
Harling Ct 12 HR8 178 E8
Harmer Cl BS10 27 F3
Harness Cl GL2 118 B6
Harnham La GL54 166 E2
Harnhill Cl BS13 2 B4
Harold Rd GL15 156 B2
Harolds Way BS15 10 C6
Harp Hill GL52 134 B1
Harper Rd GL5 98 E8
Harpfield Cl GL52 137 F3
Harpfield Rd GL52 137 F2
Harptree Ct 5 BS30 11 A4
Harptree Gr BS3 8 B2
Harptree Way GL17 164 D6
Harrier Cl GL20 192 E2
Harrington Ave BS14 3 E6
Harrington Cl BS30 5 E8
Harrington Dr GL51 129 F7
Harrington Gr BS14 3 E6
Harrington Rd BS14 3 E6
Harrington Wlk BS14 3 E6
Harris Barton BS36 31 B7
Harris Cl GL3 128 C5
Harris Ct BS30 10 F4
Harris Gdns GL54 169 D6
Harris Gr BS13 2 B3
Harris Rd SN6 143 A5
Harrison Cl Bristol BS16 21 B6
Harrison Cl *continued*
Newnham GL14 156 F6
Harrison Rd GL51 129 D2
Harrison Way GL15 92 C2
Harrow Rd BS4 9 D3
Harrowdene Rd BS4 9 B3
Harry Stoke Rd BS34 29 E2
Harry Yates Way GL51 132 D4
Hart Cl BS20 16 E4
Hart Gn GL14 191 C2
Hart La GL17 163 F4
Hartbury Cl GL51 132 C3
Hartcliffe Engineering Com Coll BS13 2 E4
Hartcliffe Rd BS4 2 E8
Hartcliffe Way BS3,BS4, BS13 2 C7
Hartcliffe Wlk BS4 2 F8
Hartfield Ave BS6 194 C4
Hartgill Cl BS13 2 B3
Harthurstfield Pk GL51 132 B1
Hartington Pk BS6 18 C2
Hartington Rd GL1 118 C6
Hartland Ho BS5 9 C6
Hartland Rd GL1 118 F6
Hartlands 22 GL18 171 A4
Hartlebury Way GL52 131 C6
Hartley Bridge Hill GL6 82 F8
Hartley Cl
Cheltenham GL53 130 F4
Chipping Sodbury BS37 44 C1
Hartley La GL53 122 E8
Hartpury CE Prim Sch GL19 172 C3
Hartpury Coll
Blaisdon GL17 165 A4
Hartpury GL19 172 A1
Harts Barn Flower & Craft Ctr★ GL17 164 E5
Harts Cotts GL2 157 F2
Harts Croft BS37 43 F4
Harvard Ave WR11 188 C7
Harvard Cl 3 GL56 187 B3
Harvest Cl BS32 40 D1
Harvest Gr GL51 132 D5
Harvest Way GL2 109 F7
Harvesters View GL52 137 D4
Harvey Cl GL2 118 C5
Harvey's La 6 Bristol BS5 9 F8
Winchcombe GL54 139 F5
Harveys La GL15 156 A2
Harwell Cl GL4 118 D1
Harwood Ho 14 BS5 9 B7
Haselbury Gr BS31 5 E2
Hasfield Cl GL2 117 E1
Hasfield Rd GL19 172 C6
Haskins Ct 4 BS30 11 A4
Haslemere Ct GL3 120 F5
Haslemere Ind Est BS11 26 C2
Haslette Way GL51 129 E5
Hasnett Rd HR8 178 E8
Hassell Dr BS2 9 A7
Hastings Cl BS3 8 C1
Hastings Pl GL20 192 C2
Hastings Rd Bristol BS3 8 C1
Cinderford GL14 191 C4
Hatcher's Cres SN26 144 D1
Hatchet La BS34 29 E4
Hatchet Rd BS34 29 E5
Hatchmere BS35 51 D8
Hatfield Rd GL1 119 A7
Hathaway Cl GL2 118 C4
Hathaway Ho BS2 195 A4
Hatherley BS37 32 E7
Hatherley Brake GL51 129 E7
Hatherley Court Rd GL51 130 B7
Hatherley Ct GL51 130 B7
Hatherley Gate GL51 130 B8
Hatherley Hall GL51 130 A7
Hatherley Ho 12 GL51 130 B8
Hatherley Inf Sch GL1 119 A7
Hatherley La GL51 129 D7
Hatherley Mews GL51 129 D7
Hatherley Rd Bristol BS7 18 E4
Cheltenham GL51 129 F7
Gloucester GL1 119 A7
Hatherley St GL50 130 B7
Hatherop Castle Sch GL7 152 E8
Hatherop CE Prim Sch GL7 152 E8
Hatherop Rd GL7 152 E4
Hathorn Rd GL3 120 B6
Hathway Wlk BS5 9 A8
Hatters' La BS37 44 C1
Hatton Cl GL17 163 D1
Havelock Rd GL3 120 A8
Haven Ave GL10 97 E6
Haven Ct GL2 127 C3
Haven Park Mobile Home Site GL51 129 C5
Haven The BS15 20 E1
Haverstock Rd BS4 9 A3
Haviland Ho 8 BS2 195 C3
Haw La BS35 50 B3
Haw Rd GL16 155 C8
Haw St Coaley GL11 88 F7
Wotton-u-E GL12 68 A7
Hawburn Cl BS4 9 D2
Hawcombe Mews 1 GL51 129 F5
Haweswater BS10 28 B2
Haweswater Cl BS30 11 D6
Haweswater Rd GL51 129 F6

Hawk Cl 5 Chalford GL6 .148 C6
Gloucester GL4 .119 D5
Hawker Hill GL17 .164 D5
Hawker Rd GL51 .133 E8
Hawker Sq GL54 .169 D6
Hawkers Hill GL7 .160 A1
Hawkesbury CE Prim Sch GL9 .55 F3
Hawkesbury Rd
Bristol BS16 .19 E3
Hillesley GL12 .55 D6
Hawkesley Dr BS34 .29 D6
Hawkesworth Rd BS37 .43 C3
Hawkfield Bsns Pk BS14 .2 D5
Hawkfield Cl BS14 .2 D5
Hawkfield Rd BS13 .2 D5
Hawkfield Way BS14 .2 D5
Hawkins Cl BS30 .11 C5
Hawkins Cres BS32 .29 E8
Hawkins La GL14 .157 A7
Hawkins St BS2 .195 C3
Hawkley Dr BS32 .40 D3
Hawkmoth Cl GL20 .192 E2
Hawkridge Dr BS16 .22 C5
Hawksmoor Cl BS14 .3 A6
Hawksmoor La BS16 .19 D5
Hawkswood Rd GL51 .130 B5
Hawksworth Dr BS15 .10 B5
Hawkwell Cotts GL17 .164 B3
Haworth Cl GL2 .117 F2
Hawthorn Ave BS15 .10 D5
Hawthorn Cl Bristol BS34 .28 E7
Charfield GL12 .67 A4
Chepstow/Cas-Gwent NP16 60 E4
Hawthorn Cres BS35 .64 C2
Hawthorn Ct GL15 .92 B3
Hawthorn Dr
Innsworth GL3 .127 F6
Sling GL16 .155 B2
Woodmancote GL52 .138 B3
Hawthorn Rd GL51 .132 E3
Hawthorn Ridge GL6 .90 F5
Hawthorn Rise GL5 .98 D8
Hawthorn Way
Bristol BS34 .29 E5
Northway GL20 .182 C5
Hawthorne Ave GL4 .119 C6
Hawthorne Cl BS16 .22 C5
Hawthorne Gdns BS16 .20 F4
Hawthorne Hill GL18 .170 D5
Hawthorne Rise BS10 .28 C3
Hawthorne St BS4 .9 A3
Hawthornes The
Bristol BS16 .20 F4
Cheltenham GL51 .129 D6
Hawthorns La BS31 .4 E5
Hawthorns Rd GL17 .164 B5
Hawthorns The
Bishop's Cleeve GL52 .137 E4
Bussage GL6 .148 B6
Dursley GL11 .87 F5
Lydney GL15 .92 B3
Hay La Ablington GL7 .159 E1
Horsley GL6 .83 A7
Hay Leaze BS37 .43 D4
Hay St SN14 .15 A8
Hay's Cotts GL53 .130 E6
Haycombe BS14 .2 F6
Haycroft Cl GL52 .137 E4
Haycroft Dr GL4 .119 D3
Haycroft La GL13 .78 C6
Haycroft Rd Bristol BS34 .29 A3
Northleach GL54 .168 F2
Haydale Gdns GL2 .127 C5
Hayden Court Cvn Pk GL51 .132 A1
Hayden Gn GL51 .132 A3
Hayden La GL51 .132 A3
Hayden Rd GL51 .132 F5
Haydock Cl BS16 .30 F1
Haydon Ct 12 BS8 .18 A2
Haydon Gdns BS7 .19 B5
Haydons Cl GL55 .189 A2
Haye's La GL9 .46 F2
Hayeley Dr BS32 .29 E6
Hayes Cl BS2 .9 A7
Hayes Ct Bristol BS34 .29 A7
Cheltenham GL52 .134 A2
Gloucester GL2 .126 F6
Hayes Knoll Sta* SN5 .143 F1
Hayes La GL7 .158 B4
Hayes Rd
Cheltenham GL52 .134 A2
Nailsworth GL6 .91 A5
Hayes The NP16 .61 B8
Hayfield SN14 .15 A8
Hayfield Way GL52 .137 E5
Haygarth Cl GL7 .190 B2
Hayhedge La GL6 .148 D8
Haylea Rd GL52 .137 D4
Hayleigh Ho BS13 .2 C4
Haymarket The BS1 .195 A3
Haymarket Wlk 9 BS1 .195 A4
Haymead La GL8 .70 D5
Haymes Dr GL52 .138 C1
Haymes Rd GL52 .138 C1
Haynes Ho 2 BS16 .20 D4
Haynes La BS16 .20 D5
Hays Cl WR12 .188 B2
Haysum's Cl GL55 .189 A1
Hayter Ct BS10 .28 D3
Haythorn Ct BS16 .20 F5
Haythorne Ct 8 BS16 .19 E3
Haytor Pk BS9 .17 D6
Hayward Cl GL4 .119 D7
Hayward Ind Est 1 BS16 20 D3
Hayward Rd
Bristol,Russell Town BS5 .9 C7
Bristol,Staple Hill BS16 .20 D3
Hayward's Rd GL52 .131 A8
Haywards GL7 .144 F7
Haywards La GL52 .131 A8
Haywood Pitch HR9 .170 C5
Hazebrouck Cl GL51 .129 E7
Hazel Ave BS6 .18 B2
Hazel Cl GL2 .127 B5
Hazel Cote Rd BS14 .3 B4
Hazel Cres BS35 .64 D1
Hazel Ct GL4 .127 D1
Hazel Field GL17 .164 B5
Hazel Gdns BS35 .51 A4
Hazel Gr BS7 .19 A8
Hazel La Alveston BS35 .50 F2
Tockington BS32 .50 E3
Hazel Rd GL17 .164 B4
Hazelbury Dr BS30 .11 C6
Hazelbury Rd BS14 .3 C7
Hazelcroft GL3 .128 B6
Hazeldean GL14 .191 C5
Hazeldene GL7 .153 E3
Hazeldene Rd BS34 .29 A7
Hazelgrove BS36 .30 E5
Hazelhurst Bglws HR9 .163 B5
Hazels The GL4 .119 E7
Hazelton Cl GL4 .118 F6
Hazelton Rd BS7 .18 D3
Hazelwood 1 GL10 .97 F7
Hazelwood Ct BS9 .17 D3
Hazelwood Rd BS9 .17 D3
Hazle Cl HR8 .178 E7
Hazlecote La GL6,GL8 .82 F6
Hazledean Rd GL51 .132 D4
Hazlewood Cl GL51 .130 B5
Hazlitt Croft GL51 .132 D4
Headford Ave BS5 .10 B7
Headford Rd BS4 .8 D1
Headington Cl BS15 .10 D4
Headlam Cl GL4 .118 D1
Headland The NP16 .61 A4
Headlands The GL5 .98 F2
Headley Ct BS13 .2 B6
Headley La BS13 .2 B7
Headley Park Ave BS13 .2 B7
Headley Park Prim Sch BS13 .2 B6
Headley Park Rd BS13 .2 A7
Headley Rd BS13 .2 A6
Headley Wlk BS13 .2 B7
Healey Dr SN14 .23 C6
Healey Mews GL1 .127 A2
Heapey Cl 8 GL51 .132 D2
Hearne Cl GL53 .131 B6
Hearne Rd GL53 .131 B6
Heart Meers BS14 .3 B5
Heath Cl BS36 .30 E6
Heath Ct Bristol BS16 .20 D7
Dursley GL11 .80 C8
Heath Gdns Bristol BS16 .20 D8
Coalpit Heath BS36 .31 C5
Heath House La BS7,BS16 19 C5
Heath House Priory Hospl BS16 .19 B4
Heath Lo 6 GL52 .133 F2
Heath Rd
Bristol,Downend BS16 .20 D8
Bristol,Eastville BS5 .19 B3
Bristol,Hanham BS15 .10 B4
Heath Ridge BS41 .7 A2
Heath Rise BS30 .11 B5
Heath St Bristol BS5 .19 C3
11 Monmouth/Trefynwy NP25 .154 A7
Heath The BS9 .17 E3
Heath Wlk BS16 .20 D7
Heathcote Dr BS36 .31 D7
Heathcote La BS36 .31 D7
Heathcote Rd
Bristol,Chester Park BS16 .20 B2
Bristol,Staple Hill BS16 .20 E5
Heathcote Wlk BS16 .20 C2
Heathdean Rd GL3 .127 F6
Heather Ave
Frampton Cotterell BS36 .31 B6
Gloucester GL4 .119 F4
Heather Cl Bristol BS15 .10 B8
Chepstow/Cas-Gwent NP16 60 F5
Stroud GL5 .99 A4
Heatherdene BS14 .2 F7
Heathfield Cl BS31 .4 C5
Heathfield Cres BS14 .3 B4
Heathfield Rd GL5 .103 A1
Heathfields BS16 .20 D8
Heathville Rd GL1 .127 A3
Heazle Pl GL5 .99 C8
Hebden Cl GL3 .120 F5
Heber St BS5 .9 C7
Heberden Ho 6 SN6 .143 E4
Hebron Ct BS3 .8 C3
Hebron Rd 10 BS3 .8 C3
Hedgeditch La GL8 .59 D7
Hedgemead Cl BS16 .19 D5
Hedgemead View BS16 .19 E5
Hedgerow The GL2 .127 B4
Hedwick Ave BS5 .9 E7
Hedwick St BS5 .9 E7
Heggard Cl BS13 .2 A5
Helens Cl GL51 .132 D3
Hellens* HR8 .178 A4
Hellier Wlk BS13 .2 C3
Hembury Cl GL2 .109 D7
Hemming Way GL52 .137 F3
Hemmings Par 4 BS5 .9 B7
Hemmingsdale Rd GL2 .126 C1
Hemplands The GL54 .159 B5
Hemplow Cl BS14 .3 D7
Hempsted CE Prim Sch GL2 .118 A7
Hempsted La GL2 .118 B7
Hempton La BS32 .40 B2
Henacre Rd BS11 .16 F8
Henbury Court Prim Sch BS10 .27 F3
Henbury Ct BS10 .27 E3
Henbury Gdns BS10 .27 E2
Henbury Hill BS9 .27 F1
Henbury Rd
Bristol,Hanham BS15 .10 B5
Bristol,Henbury BS10 .27 F2
Bristol,Westbury on Trym BS9 .18 A8
Henbury Road Henbury Hill BS9 .17 F8
Henbury Sch BS10 .27 E3
Hencliffe Rd BS14 .3 D7
Hencliffe Way BS15 .10 B3
Henderson Ho 1 BS2 .195 B4
Henderson Rd BS15 .10 B5
Hendingham Cl GL4 .118 B2
Hendre Mews GL50 .193 A3
Hendre Rd BS3 .8 A2
Hendrick Dr NP16 .61 A8
Heneage La GL12 .65 F8
Henfield Cres BS30 .11 B3
Henfield Rd BS36 .31 C4
Hengaston St BS3 .8 B2
Hengrove Ave BS14 .3 B8
Hengrove Com Arts Coll BS14 .3 B7
Hengrove La BS14 .3 B8
Hengrove Rd BS4 .9 A2
Hengrove Way BS14 .2 E6
Henleaze Ave BS9 .18 A5
Henleaze Gdns BS9 .18 A5
Henleaze Jun & Inf Schs BS9 .18 C5
Henleaze Park Dr BS9 .18 C6
Henleaze Pk BS9 .18 C5
Henleaze Rd BS9 .18 B6
Henleaze Terr BS9 .18 B7
Henley Dr SN6 .145 D4
Henley Gr BS9 .18 B5
Henley Grove Ct BS9 .18 B5
Henley Pl GL1 .118 D5
Henley Rd Bream GL15 .155 D1
Cheltenham GL51 .132 C3
Henley Villas GL5 .99 C8
Henlow Dr GL11 .80 B8
Hennessy Cl BS14 .2 F3
Henrietta St
Bristol,Kingsdown BS2 .195 A4
5 Bristol,Lower Easton BS5 .19 B1
Cheltenham GL50 .193 B4
Henry Rd GL1 .196 C4
Henry Ryder Cl GL4 .119 F6
Henry St Bristol BS3 .8 F4
Gloucester GL1 .196 C3
Henry Williamson Ct 1 BS30 .11 A5
Henry Withers Pl GL2 .100 F5
Henshaw Cl BS15 .20 C2
Henshaw Rd BS15 .20 C2
Henshaw Wlk BS15 .20 C2
Hensman's Hill BS8 .194 A2
Hentley Tor GL12 .68 C6
Heol Merthyr Tewdrig/Mathern Rd NP16 .60 D5
Hepburn Rd BS2 .195 B4
Herald Cl BS9 .17 D5
Herapath St BS5 .9 C6
Herbert Cres BS5 .19 D3
Herbert Howells Cl GL15 92 A2
Herbert St
Bristol,Moorfields BS5 .9 C8
Bristol,Southville BS3 .8 D4
Gloucester GL1 .119 A8
Herbert Stark Cl GL7 .190 E4
Herbert's Hill HR9 .162 B8
Herberts Way GL15 .156 B1
Hercules Cl BS34 .29 D6
Herd La GL8 .140 C4
Hereford Ct 1 GL50 .193 B4
Hereford Pl GL50 .193 A4
Hereford Rd BS2 .19 A2
Hereford St BS3 .8 D3
Hereward Rd GL7 .190 C5
Herkomer Cl BS7 .19 B7
Hermes Cl BS31 .5 D2
Hermitage Cl BS11 .16 E7
Hermitage Dr GL11 .80 B7
Hermitage Rd BS16 .20 E5
Hermitage St GL53 .193 B1
Heron Cl GL51 .129 E7
Heron Prim Sch GL4 .119 D5
Heron Rd BS5 .19 B1
Heron Way
Chipping Sodbury BS37 .33 A8
Gloucester GL4 .119 C5
Herrick Cl GL51 .173 F1
Herrick Way GL51 .173 F1
Herridge Cl BS13 .2 B4
Herridge Rd BS13 .2 B4
Hersey Gdns BS13 .1 E3
Hersta Cl GL7 .190 E4
Hertford Rd GL52 .138 A4
Hesding Cl BS15 .10 C3
Hester Wood BS37 .43 F4
Hester's Way La GL51 .132 D4
Hester's Way Prim Sch GL51 .132 E4
Hester's Way Rd GL51 .132 E3
Hestercombe Rd BS13 .2 B6
Hethersett Rd GL1 .119 A8
Hetton Gdns GL53 .131 A7
Hever Cl GL20 .192 E2
Hewelsfield La GL15 .146 F7
Hewelsfield Rd GL15 .147 A4
Hewland Ct BS11 .27 C2
Hewlett Pl GL52 .193 C3
Hewlett Rd GL52 .133 F1
Hewlett Way GL14 .156 C6
Hewlins La HR9 .162 D3
Heyford Ave BS5 .19 B4
Heyron Wlk BS13 .2 B4
Heywood Com Sch GL14 .191 E6
Heywood Rd
Cinderford GL14 .191 D5
Pill BS20 .16 C4
Heywood Terr BS20 .16 C4
Hiam's La GL19 .172 C2
Hiatt Rd GL6 .91 F7
Hibbs Cl SN14 .14 F8
Hicking Ct 8 BS15 .20 D1
Hickley Gdns GL3 .120 E6
Hicks Ave Bristol BS16 .21 B8
Dursley GL11 .87 F4
Hicks Beach Rd GL51 .132 D2
Hicks Common Rd BS36 .30 E5
Hicks Ct BS30 .10 F4
Hidcote Ave GL51 .130 A5
Hidcote Boyce GL55 .189 C4
Hidcote Cl GL6 .148 B6
Hidcote Manor Gdns* GL55 .189 C5
Hidcote Rd GL55 .189 C3
Hide Mkt BS2 .195 C3
High Beech Ave GL16 .155 C7
High Beech La/Lon Ffawyoden Uchel NP16 .60 D6
High Cnr BS10 .27 F1
High Cross GL53 .115 B7
High Delf Ct 9 GL16 .155 B5
High Delf Way GL15 .155 F1
High Elm BS15 .10 E6
High Furlong GL11 .87 F5
High Gr BS9 .17 B7
High Nash GL16 .155 A5
High Orchard St GL2 .196 A1
High Pk BS14 .9 B1
High Point GL50 .193 A3
High Point Ho 1 BS15 .20 C1
High Rd
Ashton Keynes SN6 .142 F4
Mitcheldean GL17 .164 D5
High Row GL17 .163 C3
High Sch for Girls GL1 .196 C4
High St Arlingham GL2 .157 B6
Avening GL8 .148 A1
Aylburton GL15 .147 E4
Badminton GL9 .46 E2
Berkeley GL13 .85 E3
Bisley GL6 .148 D8
Bitton BS30 .5 E8
Blakeney GL15 .156 E1
Blockley GL56 .186 C5
Bourton-on-t-W GL54 .168 F7
Bream GL15 .147 D8
Bredon GL20 .182 C7
Brierley GL17 .163 F2
Bristol BS1 .195 A2
Bristol,Clifton BS8 .18 A2
Bristol,Jefferies Hill BS15 .10 C5
Bristol,Kingswood BS15 .10 E8
Bristol,Lower Easton BS5 .19 B1
Bristol,Oldland Common BS30 .11 D4
Bristol,Shirehampton BS11 .16 E6
Bristol,Staple Hill BS16 .20 D4
Bristol,Warmley BS15 .11 B8
Bristol,Westbury on Trym BS9 .18 A7
Broad Blunsdon SN26 .144 D1
Broadway WR12 .185 B8
Chalford GL6 .148 C5
Cheltenham,Prestbury GL52 .134 C4
Cheltenham,St Paul's GL50,GL52 .193 B4
Chepstow/Cas-Gwent NP16 60 E8
Chipping Campden GL55 .189 A2
Chipping Sodbury BS37 .44 B1
Cinderford GL14 .191 D5
Clearwell GL16 .155 A3
11 Coleford GL16 .155 A5
Cricklade SN6 .143 F4
Doynton BS30 .22 F1
Drybrook GL17 .164 B4
Dursley GL11 .87 F6
Fairford GL7 .152 E4
Gloucester GL1 .118 F7
Hawkesbury Upton GL9 .55 F3
Highworth SN6 .145 D3
Hillesley GL12 .55 D8
Honeybourne WR11 .188 C6
Huntley GL19 .165 D6
Iron Acton BS37 .42 D4
Kempsford GL7 .144 E7
Keynsham BS31 .4 E6
King's Stanley GL10 .98 A3
Kingswood GL12 .67 F4
Lechlade on T GL7 .153 E2
Ledbury HR8 .178 F8
Littledean GL14 .191 F4
Longborough GL56 .176 D8
Lydney GL15 .92 A3
Marshfield SN14 .14 F8
Meysey Hampton GL7 .152 A2
High St *continued*
Mickleton GL55 .189 B6
Minchinhampton GL6 .148 A3
Mitcheldean GL17 .164 D5
Moreton-in-M GL56 .187 A3
Newent GL18 .171 A4
Newnham GL14 .157 A7
Northleach GL54 .168 A1
Ruardean GL17 .163 F4
Saltford BS31 .5 F3
Saul GL2 .157 F4
South Cerney GL7 .142 F7
St Briavels GL15 .146 E7
Stanton WR12 .184 F5
Stonehouse GL10 .97 F7
Stow-on-t-W GL54 .176 F5
Stroud GL5 .99 C7
Tewkesbury GL20 .192 C4
Thornbury BS35 .51 B8
Tormarton GL9 .34 D2
Upper Lydbrook GL17 .163 E3
Upton St Leonards GL4 .119 E1
Westbury-on-S GL14 .165 C1
Wick BS30 .12 D6
Wickwar GL12 .54 A5
Winchcombe GL54 .174 A7
Winterbourne BS36 .30 D6
Withington GL54 .166 D2
Woodchester GL5 .98 F1
Wotton-u-E GL12 .68 B7
High Vew Lodge 14 GL5 .99 C7
High View
Chepstow/Cas-Gwent NP16 60 E8
Gloucester GL2 .118 A6
Higham St 4 BS2 .8 F4
Highbank Pk GL2 .126 F5
Highbeech Rd
Bream GL15 .147 D8
Upper Lydbrook GL17 .163 E3
Highbury La GL52 .193 C3
Highbury Rd
Bream GL15 .147 D8
Bristol,Bedminster BS3 .8 C2
Bristol,Horfield BS7 .18 F7
Lower Redbrook NP25 .154 C4
Highbury Terr NP25 .154 C4
Highbury Villas BS2 .194 C4
Highclere Rd GL2 .117 E2
Highcroft 3 Bristol BS30 .11 C6
Minchinhampton GL6 .91 F7
Highcroft Jun Sch BS36 .31 C8
Highdale Cl BS14 .3 B4
Higher Newmarket Rd GL6 .90 F4
Highett Dr BS5 .19 A1
Highfield Blakeney GL15 .156 D1
Whiteshill GL6 .103 A3
Highfield Ave BS15 .10 D5
Highfield Bsns Pk GL19 .173 F7
Highfield Cl 4 GL15 .155 D1
Highfield Gdns BS30 .11 C2
Highfield Gr BS7 .18 D5
Highfield La
Cirencester GL7 .190 C2
Horton BS37 .45 E7
Lydney GL15 .92 C5
Highfield Pl
4 Coleford GL16 .155 B5
Gloucester GL4 .119 B7
Highfield Rd
Bream GL15 .155 D1
Chipping Sodbury BS37 .44 A1
Gloucester GL4 .119 B7
Keynsham BS31 .4 F2
Lydney GL15 .92 C4
Ruardean GL17 .163 F4
Stroud GL5 .99 E6
Tetbury GL8 .140 B5
Whiteshill GL6 .103 A3
Highfield Rise GL15 .92 B3
Highfield Villas GL14 .156 F6
Highfield Way GL6 .148 D6
Highfields
Frampton Mansell GL6 .148 F5
Hawkesbury Upton GL9 .55 F2
Highfields App GL11 .80 C8
Highfields Cl BS34 .29 F3
Highgate Ct WR12 .185 B8
Highgrove Cotts GL8 .140 A2
Highgrove St BS4 .9 A4
Highgrove The GL52 .137 E3
Highgrove Way GL3 .127 F8
Highland Cres 3 BS8 .18 A2
Highland Ho GL10 .89 E5
Highland Pl 13 BS8 .18 A2
Highland Rd GL53 .130 F4
Highland Sq 4 BS8 .18 A2
Highlands Dr GL11 .79 E4
Highlands Rd BS41 .7 A2
Highleaze Rd BS30 .11 C4
Highliffe Dr GL2 .118 A1
Highmead Gdns BS13 .1 E4
Highmeadow NP25 .154 A7
Highmore Ct BS7 .19 B7
Highmore Gdns BS7 .19 C7
Highnam Bsns Ctr GL2 .125 C5
Highnam CE Prim Sch GL2 .125 D5
Highnam Cl BS34 .40 B1
Highnam Gn GL2 .125 C5
Highnam Woods (Nature Reserve)* GL2 .124 F4
Highridge Cres BS13 .1 F5
Highridge Gn BS13 .1 E6
Highridge Inf Sch BS13 .1 F6
Highridge Pk BS13 .1 F6
Highridge Rd
Bristol,Bedminster BS3 .8 B2

Highridge Rd *continued*
Bristol,Withywood BS13,BS41 1 E4
Highridge Wlk BS13 1 E7
Highview Rd Bristol BS15 20 F2
Cinderford GL14 191 E4
Ruardean Hill GL17 164 A3
Yorkley GL15 156 A2
Highview Way GL15 147 D8
Highwall La BS14,BS31 3 F1
Highway BS37 43 F2
Highwood Ave GL53 130 C5
Highwood Bsns Pk BS34 28 E7
Highwood Ct GL6 90 F5
Highwood La BS10,BS34 28 D7
Highwood Pk Cvn Site BS34 28 E6
Highwood Rd BS34 28 F7
Highworth Cres BS37 32 D8
Highworth Rd Bristol BS4 9 D6
Gloucester GL1 118 F6
Highworth SN6 145 F1
Stanton Fitzwarren SN6 145 B1
Highworth Warneford Sch SN6 145 D3
Hilcote Dr GL54 169 A6
Hildyard Cl GL2 109 E7
Hilhouse BS9 17 C6
Hill Ash Mdw GL18 178 E3
Hill Ave BS3 8 E3
Hill Burn BS9 18 C6
Hill Cl Bristol BS16 21 B8
Dursley GL11 87 F4
Westmancote GL20 182 D8
Hill Court Rd GL52 133 E4
Hill Crest Bristol BS4 9 B1
Highnam GL2 125 E5
Hill Ct GL52 133 E4
Hill End Cl GL20 181 F7
Hill End Dr BS10 27 D3
Hill End Rd GL20 181 F8
Hill Gr BS9 18 C6
Hill Hay Rd GL4 119 C3
Hill Ho GL7 190 D5
Hill House Rd BS16 20 F5
Hill La
Chipping Sodbury BS37 34 B7
Thornbury BS35 76 A2
Hill Lawn BS4 9 D3
Hill Mead GL4 110 F5
Hill Paul GL5 99 B7
Hill Pk GL15 156 A2
Hill Rd Dundry BS41 1 D2
Dursley GL11 88 A1
Gloucester GL4 118 F4
Wotton-u-E GL12 68 C6
Hill Sq GL11 88 A3
Hill St
Bristol,Brandon Hill BS1 194 C2
Bristol,Kingswood BS15 10 F8
Bristol,St George BS5 9 F8
Bristol,Windmill Hill BS3 8 F4
Lydney GL15 92 A3
Hill The Almondsbury BS32 40 B4
Randwick GL6 102 E2
Stroud GL5 99 B7
Westwell OX18 161 F5
Hill Top BS16 60 D7
Hill Top Cl GL5 99 F7
Hill Top La GL18 171 B5
Hill Top Rd GL50 133 D5
Hill Top View GL6 148 B6
Hill View
Bristol,Blackhorse BS16 21 A8
Bristol,Clifton Wood BS8 194 B2
Bristol,Filton BS34 29 A3
Bristol,Henleaze BS9 18 C6
Bristol,Upper Soundwell BS16 20 D2
Elkstone GL53 115 B6
Lydney GL15 92 A3
Naunton GL54 175 E2
Sandhurst GL2 172 E1
Hill View Cl BS30 11 C4
Hill View Cotts GL4 118 E2
Hill View Ct BS16 20 C5
Hill View Ho 2 BS15 20 C1
Hill View La GL18 170 C4
Hill View Rd Bristol BS13 2 A8
Upper Strensham WR8 180 A10
Hill View Villas GL5 98 D6
Hill's Barton BS13 8 A1
Hillands Dr GL53 130 D4
Hillary Rd GL53 130 E4
Hillborough Rd GL4 118 E3
Hillbrook Rd 5 BS35 51 D8
Hillburn Rd BS5 10 A8
Hillclose Est GL5 99 A4
Hillcot Cl GL2 117 E1
Hillcrest Berkeley GL13 85 F4
Thornbury BS35 64 B1
Hillcrest Cl 15 NP25 154 A7
Hillcrest La GL16 155 B6
Hillcrest Prim Sch BS4 9 A3
Hillcrest Rd
Berry Hill GL16 155 A7
Monmouth/Trefynwy NP25 154 A7
Stroud GL5 98 E8
Hillcroft Cl BS15 10 E4
Hillersland La GL16 155 A8
Hillesley CE Prim Sch GL12 55 E8
Hillesley Rd GL12 67 F4
Hillfield Cheltenham GL51 132 F1
Stroud GL5 98 F7
Hillfield Court Rd GL1 127 A3
Hillfield Ct GL1 127 A3
Hillfields Ave BS16 20 C3
Hillfields Prim Sch BS16 20 C2
Hillgrove St BS2 195 B4
Hillier Cl GL5 103 D1
Hillier Dr 8 GL51 129 F5
Hillmill La GL12 69 B5
Hillrise GL15 155 D1
Hills Cl BS31 5 A5
Hills View 17 GL18 171 A4
Hillsborough BS8 194 A2
Hillsborough Rd BS4 9 C4
Hillsdon Rd BS9 17 F8
Hillside
Bristol,Mangotsfield BS16 21 A5
Bristol,Tyndall's Park BS6 194 C4
Burton SN14 36 A4
Chalford GL6 148 D6
Leigh SN6 143 B3
Hillside Ave BS15 10 C8
Hillside Cl
10 Bream GL15 155 D1
Cheltenham GL51 130 A7
Frampton Cotterell BS36 31 C7
Woodmancote GL52 138 C3
Hillside Ct Bristol BS5 10 B7
Dursley GL11 80 B8
Hillside Est 11 GL15 155 D1
Hillside Gdns GL52 138 C3
Hillside Ho 5 BS6 18 D1
Hillside La BS36 31 C7
Hillside Rd Bristol BS5 10 A7
Drybrook GL17 164 B5
Long Ashton BS41 7 B2
Mitcheldean GL17 164 D5
Hillside St BS4 9 A4
Hillside Terr GL17 163 D3
Hillside Villas GL5 99 D5
Hillside Way SN26 144 D1
Hilltop 8 GL15 147 D8
Hilltop Gdns
Bristol,St George BS5 10 A7
Bristol,Upper Soundwell BS16 20 D2
Hilltop Rd BS16 20 D2
Hilltop View Bristol BS5 10 A7
Dursley GL11 87 F4
Hillview GL7 158 D3
Hillview Ave GL3 120 D6
Hillview Dr GL3 120 A8
Hillview House Pk (Mobile Home Pk) 1 GL3 120 A8
Hillview La GL20 181 F8
Hillview Prim Sch GL3 120 A8
Hillview Rd
Cheltenham GL52 134 B2
Gloucester GL3 120 A8
Pucklechurch BS16 22 C5
Hillview Rise GL16 155 A7
Hillwell SN16 141 E1
Hilly Orch GL5 98 E6
Hillyfield Rd BS13 2 A6
Hilton Cl GL2 118 B6
Hilton Ct 5 BS5 9 B8
Hinders La GL17,GL19 165 B5
Hine Gdns GL52 133 F3
Hinton Cl BS31 5 E3
Hinton Ct GL13 85 C8
Hinton Dr BS30 11 C6
Hinton La 13 BS8 7 F6
Hinton Rd
Bristol,Fishponds BS16 20 A4
Bristol,Lower Easton BS5 19 C1
Gloucester GL1 126 F4
Hisnams Field GL52 137 F3
Historic Gloucester Docks* GL1 196 A2
Hitchen Cl SN14 14 F8
Hitchen Hollow NP16 61 B4
Hitchings GL15 156 D2
Hithe The GL5 99 C3
Hither Bath Bridge BS4 9 C1
Hither Mead BS36 31 B6
Hive The GL54 166 E5
Hobart Ho GL51 132 E2
Hobb's La BS1 194 C2
Hobbs La Bristol BS30 21 B1
Longhope GL17 165 A6
Woodmancote GL7 158 B4
Hobby Cl GL53 130 C5
Hobhouse Cl BS9 18 C7
Hobwell La BS41 7 C2
Hocker Hill St 4 NP16 60 E8
Hockeys La BS16 20 A4
Hoddon La BS16 22 D5
Hodges Way GL14 191 C3
Hodses Yd 7 HR8 178 E8
Hogarth Wlk BS7 19 C7
Hogues Wlk BS13 2 B4
Holbeach Way BS14 3 A2
Holbrook GL17 163 D2
Holbrook Cres BS13 2 D4
Holbrook La BS30 12 B7
Holbury Cres GL2 100 E5
Holcombe BS14 3 A5
Holcombe Gr BS31 4 D5
Holcot Cl 8 GL16 155 B5
Holcot Rd GL16 155 B5
Holdcroft Cl SN26 144 E1
Holdenhurst Rd BS15 20 C1
Holder Cl 13 GL8 140 B4
Holder Rd GL52 137 F2
Holders La GL18 170 E6
Holford Cres GL7 144 F7
Holford Ct BS14 3 B5
Hollams Rd GL20 192 D5
Holland Ct GL1 127 A3
Hollidge Gdns 3 BS3 8 D4
Hollies Hill GL6 91 C4
Hollies The BS15 10 E6
Hollingham La GL6 90 E1
Hollins Cl NP16 72 F1
Hollis Cl Long Ashton BS41 1 A8
Long Ashton BS41 7 A1
Hollis Gdns
Cheltenham GL51 129 D6
Luckington SN14 47 E4
Hollis Rd GL51 129 D6
Hollister's Dr BS13 2 D4
Hollow La GL5 99 D7
Hollow Rd
Almondsbury BS32 40 A4
Bristol BS15 10 E8
Hollow The GL17 164 A4
Holloway Hill SN14 25 F7
Holloway Rd Bisley GL6 148 D8
Severn Beach BS35 38 C4
Hollows The BS36 31 D2
Hollway Cl BS14 3 E5
Hollway Rd BS14 3 E5
Holly Cl Alveston BS35 50 F4
Bretforton WR11 188 A7
Bristol BS5 20 A2
Chepstow/Cas-Gwent NP16 60 E5
Pucklechurch BS16 22 C5
Holly Cres BS15 20 E1
Holly Ct BS2 194 C4
Holly Dr SN14 15 F6
Holly End GL2 109 F8
Holly Gn BS15 21 A1
Holly Gr BS16 20 C3
Holly Gr The GL2 109 F8
Holly Hill BS37 42 E3
Holly Hill Rd BS15 20 F1
Holly Ho BS11 27 C2
Holly La GL16 155 C3
Holly Lodge Cl BS5 20 A2
Holly Lodge Rd BS5 19 F2
Holly Tree Gdn GL5 98 D6
Holly Tree Pl GL15 156 B1
Holly Wlk BS31 4 D4
Hollybush Cl GL9 36 A6
Hollybush La Bristol BS9 17 E5
Bristol BS9 17 F4
Hollydean GL14 191 C5
Hollyguest Rd BS15 10 E6
Hollyhill Pk GL14 191 B5
Hollyhill Rd GL14 191 B5
Hollyhock La GL6 103 F8
Hollyleigh Ave BS34 28 F2
Hollymead La BS9 17 E4
Hollyridge BS14 3 C6
Hollywell Rd GL17 164 D6
Hollywood La BS10,BS35 28 A7
Hollywood Rd BS4 9 D2
Holm La BS35 49 B2
Holm-Mead La BS30 5 C7
Holmdale Rd BS34 29 C3
Holme Rd GL20 192 D1
Holmer Cres GL51 129 D6
Holmes Ct BS9 18 B5
Holmes Gr BS9 18 B5
Holmes Hill Rd BS5 9 F8
Holmes St BS5 9 B6
Holmesdale Rd BS3 8 E3
Holmfield Dr NP25 146 B7
Holmleigh Par GL4 118 C2
Holmleigh Rd GL4 118 C3
Holmoak Cl GL20 192 E2
Holmoak Rd BS31 4 C4
Holmwood BS15 10 C5
Holmwood Cl
Gloucester GL4 118 D2
Winterbourne BS36 30 D6
Holmwood Dr GL4 118 D2
Holmwood Gdns BS9 18 B8
Holroyd Ho BS3 8 D3
Holsom Cl BS14 3 F6
Holsom Rd BS14 3 F6
Holst Gdns BS4 2 D7
Holst Way GL4 118 D3
Holt The
Bishop's Cleeve GL52 137 E2
Gloucester GL4 119 E7
Holtham Ave GL3 128 B7
Holton Rd BS7 19 A6
Holts Rd GL18 170 F4
Holy Apostles CE Prim Sch GL52 131 A8
Holy Cross RC Prim Sch BS3 8 C4
Holy Family RC Prim Sch BS34 29 B8
Holy Trinity CE Prim Sch GL52 193 C4
Holy Trinity Prim Sch BS32 40 C2
Holy Well Cl BS4 9 E6
Holymead Inf Sch BS4 9 D2
Holymead Jun Sch BS4 9 D3
Holyrood Cl BS34 29 D4
Holywell Rd Dursley GL11 88 A4
Wotton-u-E GL12 68 C8
Home Cl Bristol BS10 28 E2
Cheltenham GL51 132 E3
Lower Oddington GL56 177 C5
Home Farm Ct GL52 131 A7
Home Farm Rd BS8 7 B8
Home Farm Way BS35 39 A1
Home Field Cl BS16 21 B6
Home Ground
Bristol,Eastfield BS9 18 B7
Bristol,Shirehampton BS11 16 D7
Cricklade SN6 143 E4
Home Mead BS4 2 E7
Home Orch Stroud GL5 98 D6
Yate BS37 43 D2
Home Piece GL7 149 E3
Homeabbey Ho GL20 192 C5
Homeapple Hill BS30 11 F6
Homeavon Ho BS31 4 F5
Homeberry Ho GL7 190 C4
Homecroft Dr GL51 132 E6
Homefarm SN6 145 C3
Homefield Nailsworth GL6 91 A3
Thornbury BS35 51 D8
Yate BS37 43 E3
Homefield Cl BS31 5 E3
Homefield Dr BS16 20 A5
Homefield Rd
Pucklechurch BS16 22 B5
Saltford BS31 5 F3
Homeground BS16 21 B6
Homeground La GL7 152 F4
Homeleaze Rd BS10 28 D3
Homemead BS30 11 A4
Homemead Dr BS4 9 D1
Homend Cres 2 HR8 178 F8
Homend The 16 HR8 178 F8
Homepiece WR12 185 B4
Homespa Ho 2 GL50 133 B1
Homespring Ho GL52 134 A2
Homestead Cl
Bredon GL20 182 C7
Frampton Cotterell BS36 31 D7
Homestead Ct GL4 119 F5
Homestead Gdns BS16 20 B8
Homestead Rd BS34 29 A3
Homestead The BS31 4 F2
Hone Ct 18 GL20 192 C4
Honey Garston Cl BS13 2 B4
Honey Garston Rd BS13 2 B4
Honey Hill Rd BS15 10 F8
Honey Suckle La BS16 19 E5
Honey Way BS15 10 F8
Honeyborne Way GL12 54 B5
Honeybourne Airfield Ind Est WR11 188 C5
Honeybourne Dr GL51 132 D4
Honeybourne Fst Sch WR11 188 C6
Honeybourne Pottery* WR11 188 C6
Honeybourne Rd WR11 188 D4
Honeybourne Sta WR11 188 C7
Honeybourne Way GL50 193 A4
Honeymead BS14 3 C6
Honeysuckle Cl
Bristol BS32 40 E2
Cheltenham GL52 134 C3
Honeysuckle Dr GL4 119 E5
Honeysuckle Way GL52 137 F5
Honeythorn Cl GL2 118 B7
Honeywick Cl BS3 8 C2
Honister Ho BS34 29 A8
Honiton Rd BS16 20 A3
Honyatt Rd GL1 196 C4
Hoo La
Chipping Campden GL55 188 F2
Tewkesbury GL20 173 E8
Hook's La GL18 171 D5
Hookshouse La
Doughton GL8 71 E4
Tetbury GL8 140 A3
Hooper Cl GL4 119 B6
Hooper Rd BS14 3 D5
Hoovers La HR9 164 B8
Hop Gdn The NP16 60 F4
Hope Brook CE Prim Sch GL17 164 F6
Hope Cotts GL5 99 D6
Hope Ct BS1 194 B1
Hope Mill La GL5 99 E2
Hope Mills Bsns Ctr GL5 99 E2
Hope Orch GL51 132 D4
Hope Rd Bristol BS3 8 C2
Yate BS37 43 A2
Hope Sq BS8 7 F6
Hope St GL51 133 B3
Hope Villas GL5 99 C8
Hopechapel Hill 11 BS8 7 F6
Hopes Cl GL15 92 C2
Hopetoun Rd BS2 18 F3
Hopewell GL14 191 E5
Hopewell Cl NP16 61 A4
Hopewell Colliery Mus* GL16 155 D6
Hopewell Gdns BS11 16 F7
Hopewell St GL1 196 C1
Hopkin Cl BS35 51 D7
Hopkins Ct 13 BS6 18 B1
Hopkins Orch 1 SN6 143 E4
Hopland Cl BS30 11 B3
Hopp's Rd BS15 10 D7
Hopton Rd GL11 88 B4
Hopwood Gr 1 GL52 134 A1
Hopyard La GL18 171 A5
Hopyard The GL20 182 B5
Horcott Ind Est GL7 152 D3
Horcott Rd GL7 152 D3
Horesham Gr BS13 2 C5
Horfield CE Prim Sch BS10 18 D7
Horfield Ct BS7 18 E4
Horfield Rd BS2 195 A4
Horley Rd BS2 19 A2
Horn La GL56 177 C7
Hornbeam Ho 5 BS16 20 C6
Hornbeam Mews GL2 127 B5
Hornbeam Wlk BS31 4 C3
Hornbeams The BS16 30 B1
Hornbury Cl SN16 142 D1
Hornbury Hill SN16 142 D1
Horns Rd GL5 99 D6
Horsbere Rd GL3 120 B8
Horse Fair La SN6 143 F4
Horse La BS35 64 D5
Horse Lane Orch HR8 178 F8
Horse Pool La HR9 162 E2
Horse St BS37 44 C1
Horsecroft Gdns BS30 11 A6
Horsefair Cl GL53 131 A5
Horsefair La GL18 170 F5
Horsefair St GL53 131 A5
Horsefair The BS1 195 B3
Horsemarling La GL10 101 F1
Horsepool La
Doynton BS30 12 F8
St Briavels GL15 146 E6
Horsepool Rd BS13 1 E3
Horsepool The 3 GL16 155 A7
Horseshoe Ct BS36 31 D7
Horseshoe Dr Bristol BS9 17 C4
Over GL2 126 B4
Horseshoe La BS37 44 B1
Horseshoe Way GL2 118 B6
Horsetrough Rdbt GL10 97 F6
Horsford Rd GL12 67 B5
Horslea GL17 163 D3
Horsley CE Prim Sch GL6 90 F1
Horsley Cl GL4 119 E5
Horsley Hill GL6 91 A1
Horsley Rd GL6 91 A2
Hortham La BS32 40 E5
Horton CE Prim Sch BS37 45 C5
Horton Ct* BS37 45 D7
Horton Hill BS37 45 C5
Horton Rd
Chipping Sodbury BS37 44 C2
Chipping Sodbury,Little Sodbury End BS37 44 D4
Gloucester GL1 127 A2
Horton St BS2 195 C3
Horwood Ct 3 BS30 11 A4
Horwood La GL12 54 B4
Hosey Wlk BS13 2 A5
Hospital Rd (West St) GL56 187 A3
Hossil La SN6 145 A1
Host St BS1 195 A3
Hot Water La BS15 21 A3
Hottom Gdns BS7 19 A7
Hotwell Rd BS8 194 B1
Hotwells Ho BS8 194 A2
Hotwells Prim Sch BS8 7 F6
Houlton St BS2 195 C4
Hounds Cl BS37 44 B1
Hounds Rd BS37 44 B1
Howard Ave BS5 9 E8
Howard Cl
Northway GL20 182 C4
Saltford BS31 5 D3
Howard Ho GL54 139 F5
Howard Pl GL3 120 A7
Howard Rd
Bristol,Southville BS3 8 C4
Bristol,Staple Hill BS16 20 D4
Bristol,Westbury Park BS6 18 B4
5 Coleford GL16 155 B6
Northway GL20 182 C4
Thornbury BS35 64 C2
Howard St Bristol BS5 19 E1
Gloucester GL1 118 F7
Howard Wlk BS30 11 D7
Howcroft GL3 128 C4
Howecroft Ct BS9 17 E4
Howecroft Gdns BS9 17 E4
Howell Rd
Cheltenham GL51 132 E4
Cheltenham GL51 132 F4
Howell's La GL15 156 E3
Howells Mead BS16 21 B7
Howells Rd GL20 192 D4
Howells Row NP16 72 F1
Howes Cl BS30 11 A6
Howett Rd 16 BS5 9 C7
Howgate Cl 1 GL4 119 F5
Howmead GL13 85 E4
Howsmoor La
Bristol,Lyde Green BS16 21 C8
Bristol,New England BS16 21 B8
Hoylake BS37 32 E8
Hoylake Dr BS30 11 B6
Hucclecote La GL3 128 D2
Hucclecote Mews GL3 119 F7
Hucclecote Rd GL3 120 B7
Huckford La BS36 31 A4
Huckford Rd BS36 30 E5
Huckley Way BS32 29 F6
Hudd's Hill Rd BS5 9 F8
Hudd's Vale Rd BS5 9 E8
Huddleston Rd GL54 174 A8
Hudman's Cl GL20 182 A7
Hudnalls View NP25 146 B7
Hudson Cl
Chipping Sodbury BS37 32 F8
Honeybourne WR11 188 C7
Hudson La GL14 191 C1
Hudson St GL50 133 D3
Hudsons View GL14 191 C1
Hughenden Rd
Bristol,Clifton BS8 18 A2
Bristol,Horfield BS7 18 E5
Hughes Cl GL20 182 C5
Hughes Cres NP16 60 E7
Hughes Gdn BS7 19 A8
Hughes Terr GL15 155 E3
Hulbert Cl Bristol BS4 10 A2
Swindon GL51 133 A7

Hulbert Cres GL51 129 F5
Hulse Rd BS4 9 D1
Humber Pl GL3 120 F5
Humber Rd GL52 134 A2
Humber Way BS11 26 D5
Humberstan Wlk BS11 16 E8
Humphreys Cl GL5 98 E8
Humphry Davy Way 6
BS8 7 F5
Humphrys Barton BS4 9 F5
Hung Rd BS11 16 E5
Hunger Hill GL11 80 A8
Hungerford Cl BS4 3 E8
Hungerford Cres BS4 9 E1
Hungerford Gdns BS4 3 E8
Hungerford Rd BS4 3 E8
Hungerford St GL50 133 D3
Hungerford Wlk BS4 9 E1
Hunter's Way
Andoversford GL54 166 C6
Bristol BS34 29 B3
Hunters Cl Bristol BS15 10 C5
Stroud GL5 98 D7
Hunters Dr BS15 20 F1
Hunters Gate GL4 119 D4
Hunters Mead GL9 56 A2
Hunters Rd
Bishop's Cleeve GL52 137 E4
Bristol BS15 10 C5
Hunters Rd E BS15 10 C4
Hunters Way GL5 98 D7
Huntfield Rd NP16 60 D8
Hunthill GL14 165 E1
Huntingdon Cl GL5 98 D6
Huntingham Rd BS13 1 F4
Huntings The 7 WR12 185 B8
Huntley CE Prim Sch
GL19 165 C6
Huntley Cl GL4 119 E5
Hunts Ground Rd BS34 29 F4
Hunts Grove View GL2 110 B7
Hunts Hill SN26 144 D1
Hunts La BS7 18 E6
Huntscote Rd GL51 133 A5
Huntsfield Cl GL50 133 E4
Huntsmans Cl GL52 138 A4
Huntsmans Meet GL54 166 D6
Hurcombe Way GL3 120 E6
Hurle Cres BS8 18 B1
Hurle Rd BS8 18 B1
Hurlingham Rd BS7 18 F2
Hurn La BS31 5 A3
Hurricane Rd GL3 120 C5
Hursley Hill BS14 3 D1
Hursley La BS14 3 E1
Hurst Cl GL2 127 D5
Hurst Rd BS4 2 F8
Hurst Wlk BS4 2 F8
Hurston Rd BS4 2 D7
Hurstwood Rd BS16 20 D5
Hutton Cl Bristol BS9 17 E7
Keynsham BS31 5 A2
Hutton Raufe GL51 132 F1
Huxley Ct GL7 143 A8
Huxley Rd GL1 118 F7
Huxley Way GL52 137 D4
Huyton Rd BS5 19 E3
Hyatts Way GL52 138 A3
Hyde Apartments BS6 18 C3
Hyde Ave BS35 64 B3
Hyde Bank GL14 156 F7
Hyde Cl GL1 127 A2
Hyde Cotts GL54 139 F4
Hyde La Gloucester GL1 127 A2
Newnham GL14 156 F7
Swindon GL50,GL51 133 D7
Whitminster GL2 100 F6
Hyde Park Cnr GL19 179 D2
Hyde The GL54 139 F5
Hyde View GL16 154 F3
Hyde's La SN14 14 A6
Hydes The BS31 4 F5
Hyett Cl GL6 103 F8
Hyett Orch GL6 103 F8
Hyett Rd GL5 98 E7
Hygrove La GL2 125 B1
Hyland Gr BS9 17 F8

I

Ibis Wlk GL2 117 D1
Icehouse La GL56 186 D1
Icombe Cl GL52 137 F3
Ida Rd 2 BS5 9 C8
Idaho St GL7 152 E2
Iddesleigh Rd BS6 18 B3
Idsall Dr GL52 134 C4
Idstone Rd BS16 20 B4
Iford Cl BS31 5 E3
Ilchester Cres BS13 8 B1
Ilchester Rd BS13 2 B8
Iles Cl BS15 10 D4
Ilex Cl BS13 1 F6
Ilmington CE Prim Sch
CV36 189 F6
Ilminster Ave BS4 2 F8
Ilminster Avenue Prim Sch
BS4 3 A8
Ilsom Cotts GL8 140 D5
Ilsyn Gr BS14 3 D7
Imber Court Cl BS14 3 B8
Imjin Rd GL52 134 B2
Imperial Arc 11 BS3 8 D4
Imperial Cir GL50 193 B3
Imperial Ct GL50 193 B3
Imperial Gate GL50 193 B3
Imperial Gate Bsns Pk
GL4 127 D2
Imperial La GL50 193 B3
Imperial Pk BS13 2 C6
Imperial Rd
8 Bristol,Clifton BS6 18 B1
Bristol,Knowle BS14 3 C8
Imperial Sq GL50 193 B2
Imperial Wlk BS14 9 B1
Ince Castle Way GL1 119 A8
Inchbrook Ct GL5 90 F6
Inchbrook Hill GL5,GL6 91 A6
Inchbrook Trad Est GL5 91 A7
Inchbrook Way GL5 90 F6
India Ho 2 GL51 132 E2
India Rd GL1 119 A8
Industrial Ctr BS15 10 D8
Inglecote Cl GL52 131 B6
Ingleside Rd BS15 20 C1
Ingleside Sch GL7 190 D4
Inglestone Rd GL12 54 B5
Ingmire Rd BS5 19 B3
Ingram Cl CV36 187 E5
Ingst Hill BS35 49 B3
Ingst Rd BS35 49 D4
Inkerman Cl BS7 18 E7
Inkerman La 16 GL50 130 B8
Inn Cotts BS11 17 A7
Inner Ctyd GL7 190 D7
Inner Down The BS12 50 D3
Inner Loop Rd NP16 61 B6
Innerstone La GL19 171 D8
Innocks Est GL11 79 D4
Innox Gdns BS13 2 A5
Inns Court Ave BS4 2 D7
Inns Court Dr BS4 2 D6
Inns Court Gn BS4 2 D7
Innsworth Jun Sch GL3 127 D6
Innsworth La GL3 127 D7
Innsworth Tech Pk GL3 127 C6
Insley Gdns GL3 119 F8
Instow Rd BS4 2 E8
Instow Wlk BS4 2 E8
International Sch of
Choueifat SN14 15 C4
International Trad Est
BS11 26 B2
Interplex 16 BS32 40 C3
Inverlea Ct GL55 189 A6
IO Ctr BS11 26 F5
Ipswich Dr BS4 9 E6
Irby Rd BS3 8 A3
Irena Rd BS16 19 F3
Ireton Rd BS3 8 B3
Iron Acton CE Prim Sch
BS37 42 E4
Iron Acton Way BS37 43 B3
Iron Hogg La GL12 65 C3
Iron Mills GL6 91 E3
Ironchurch Rd BS11 26 C5
Ironmonger's La GL13 86 B4
Ironmould La BS4 10 A1
Ironstone Cl 2 GL15 147 D8
Irving Cl BS16 20 E4
Irving Ct GL52 193 C3
Irving Ho Bristol BS1 194 C3
14 Cheltenham GL52 133 F2
Isambard Wlk BS1 195 C2
Isbourne Rd GL52 134 B2
Isbourne Way GL54 174 B8
ISF Rd BS11 26 C3
Islamic Sec Sch for Girls
GL1 196 C2
Island Gdns BS16 19 C4
Island Trad Pk BS11 26 C1
Islay Cres SN6 145 C4
Isle Of Rhé GL11 79 C5
Isleys Ct BS30 10 F3
Islington Rd BS3 8 C4
Ismay Rd GL51 132 F4
Ison Hill Rd BS10 27 D3
Itchington Rd
Alveston BS35 51 F4
Tytherington GL12 52 B4
Itlay GL7 150 A8
Itton Rd NP16 72 B2
Ivanhoe Ho GL2 118 C4
Ivor Rd BS5 9 C8
Ivory Cl GL4 118 C2
Ivy Bank GL52 134 C3
Ivy Cotts NP16 73 B1
Ivy House Est HR9 170 B5
Ivy House La HR9 170 B5
Ivy La Bristol BS16 20 A3
Broad Blunsdon SN26 144 D1
Ivy Lodge 4 BS9 18 A7
Ivy Lodge Barns GL4 121 F1
Ivy Mews GL1 118 F5
Ivy Terr BS37 32 B4
Ivywell Rd BS9 17 E3
Izod's Cl GL55 188 F1

J

Jack Knight Ho BS7 18 F5
Jack Price Cl BS13 2 C3
Jackbarrow Rd GL7 107 A8
Jackson Cl BS35 38 D7
Jackson Cres GL3 127 E6
Jackson Rd
Bledington OX7 177 E1
Siddington GL7 150 F2
Jacob St BS2 195 C3
Jacob's Ct BS1 194 B2
Jacob's Wells Rd BS8 194 B2
Jacobs Cl 4 GL8 140 C5
Jamaica St BS2 195 B4
James Ave 10 GL2 117 D1
James Cl Bristol BS16 20 E4
12 Quedgeley GL2 117 D1
James Ct
Cheltenham GL51 132 F1
Yorkley GL15 156 B1
James Donovan Ct
GL52 134 A2
James Dr 9 GL2 117 D1
James Grieve Rd GL4 119 F6
James Orch GL13 85 E3
James Pl 8 GL2 117 D1
James Rd BS16 20 E3
James Row 13 GL2 117 D1
James St
Bristol,Baptist Mills BS2 19 A2
Bristol,St Pauls BS5 195 C4
James Way
Gloucester GL3 120 C6
Quedgeley GL2 117 E1
James Wlk Pillowell GL15 155 F1
11 Quedgeley GL2 117 D1
Jameson Ct 24 GL56 187 A3
Jane St BS5 9 B7
Japonica Cl 5 GL3 128 A7
Japonica Dr GL51 130 A5
Jardine Dr GL52 137 E4
Jarvis St BS5 9 B6
Jasmin Way GL51 130 A5
Jasmine Cl GL4 119 D4
Jasmine Gr BS11 27 C2
Jasper St BS3 8 B3
Javelin Pk GL10 109 E1
Javelin Way GL3 120 F5
Jay's Gn HR9 170 A5
Jay's Mead GL12 68 C7
Jays The GL12 52 B6
Jaythorpe GL4 119 D3
Jean Rd BS4 9 E2
Jefferies Cl 7 GL7 152 E4
Jefferies Hill Bottom
BS15 10 B5
Jeffery Ct BS30 11 B6
Jeffreys Ct 9 BS16 19 E3
Jeffries Ct GL7 190 D4
Jellicoe Ave BS16 19 E8
Jena Ct BS31 5 D3
Jenkin's La GL6 103 C7
Jenner Cl
Chipping Sodbury BS37 33 D8
Gloucester GL3 119 F8
Jenner Ct GL13 85 E3
Jenner Wlk GL50 193 B4
Jennings Ct 1 BS3 8 A4
Jersey Ave Bristol BS4 9 F4
Cheltenham GL52 133 F2
Jersey Rd GL1 119 A8
Jersey St GL52 193 C4
Jesse Mary Chambers
Almshouses GL51 132 F1
Jesson Rd GL52 138 A3
Jessop Ave GL50 193 A3
Jessop Cres BS10 28 A1
Jessop Ct BS1 195 B2
Jessop Dr 2 GL54 168 A1
Jessop Underpass BS3 7 F4
Jet Age Air Mus* GL2 128 C8
Jewson Cl GL4 118 D2
Jeynes Bldgs GL20 192 D5
Jeynes Row GL20 192 D5
Jim O'Neil Ho BS11 16 D7
Joan Hawley Mews
GL52 131 A7
Job's La GL20 182 E8
Jobbins Ct GL7 190 C4
Jocelyn Rd BS7 18 F7
Jockey La BS5 10 A7
Jockey Stable Cotts
GL56 186 A4
John Bevan Cl GL5 99 D8
John Buck Ho 8 GL52 193 C4
John Cabot City Tech Coll
BS15 10 C7
John Cabot Ct BS1 194 A1
John Carr's Terr BS8 194 B2
John Cozens Ho 7 BS2 195 C3
John Daniels Way GL3 128 B4
John James Ct BS7 19 B7
John Lamb Ho GL51 129 D2
John Masefield High Sch
HR8 178 F8
John Moore Countryside
Mus* GL20 192 C4
John Moore Gdns 4
GL50 130 B6
John Moore Prim Sch The
GL20 192 E1
John of Gaunt Rd GL7 144 E8
John Repton Gdns BS10 28 B4
John Rushout Ct GL56 186 C7
John St Bristol BS1 195 A3
Bristol,Baptist Mills BS2 19 A2
Bristol,Two Mile Hill BS15 10 C8
Stroud GL5 99 C7
John Tame Cl 4 GL7 152 E4
John Wesley Ct 9 BS16 20 D5
John Wesley Rd BS5 10 B6
John Wesleys Chapel*
BS1 195 B3
John Woolfe Ct GL56 186 C7
Johnson Dr BS30 10 F5
Johnson Rd BS16 21 C5
Johnsons La BS5 19 D1
Johnsons Rd Bristol BS5 19 C8
1 Bristol,Moorfields BS5 9 C8
Johnsons Way GL15 156 B2
Johnstone Cl GL19 172 A7
Johnstone Rd 3 GL18 171 A4
Joiners La GL6 148 D8
Jones Ho 3 NP25 154 A8
Jordan Wlk BS32 29 D8
Jordans Cl WR12 188 B2
Jordans Way GL2 126 F5
Jorrocks Ind Est BS37 32 C4
Josend Cres GL19 172 F7
Joy Hill BS8 7 F6
Joyce Cl BS7 19 A8
Joyford Hill GL16 155 A8
Joyner Rd GL51 133 A4
Joys Green Prim Sch
GL17 163 D3
Joys Green Rd GL17 163 D2
Jubilee Ave GL11 87 F6
Jubilee Cl
Chipping Campden GL55 188 F2
Dursley GL11 87 F6
Ledbury HR8 178 F7
12 Stow-on-t-W GL54 176 F4
Jubilee Cotts GL6 148 B5
Jubilee Cres BS16 21 A6
Jubilee Ct Bristol BS4 9 D4
Cheltenham GL50 193 B1
Jubilee Dr Bredon GL20 182 C7
Thornbury BS35 64 D1
Jubilee Flats GL7 150 E2
Jubilee Gdns
South Cerney GL7 142 F7
Yate BS37 44 A2
Jubilee Gn GL7 190 D3
Jubilee Ho BS34 29 C8
Jubilee La Bream GL15 147 D8
Cromhall GL12 53 B7
Jubilee Pk* HR9 162 E4
Jubilee Pl Bristol BS1 195 A1
Bristol,Woodstock BS15 10 F7
Corse GL19 172 A7
Jubilee Rd
Bristol,Baptist Mills BS2 19 A1
Bristol,Crew's Hole BS5 9 F7
Bristol,Staple Hill BS15 20 E3
Bristol,Upper Knowle BS4 9 C2
Dursley GL11 88 A2
Lydney GL15 92 C3
Mitcheldean GL17 164 D3
Nailsworth GL6 91 A5
Jubilee St BS2 195 C2
Jubilee Way
Avonmouth BS11 26 B2
Newton GL13 85 D8
Judge's La
Longhope GL18 170 F1
Taynton GL18 171 A1
Julian Cl Bristol BS9 17 E3
Gloucester GL4 119 D8
Julian Ct BS9 17 E3
Julian Rd BS9 17 E3
Julius Cl BS16 21 C6
Julius Rd BS7 18 D3
Julius Way GL15 92 B4
Jumpers La GL13 85 E3
Junction Rd BS4 9 C4
Juniper Ave GL4 119 B4
Juniper Cotts GL6 103 F5
Juniper Ct 2 Bristol BS5 19 C2
Cheltenham GL51 132 C2
Juniper Way Bristol BS34 30 A7
Stonehouse GL10 97 F8
Juno Dr GL15 92 B5
Jupiter Rd BS34 28 E7
Jupiter Way GL4 119 F6
Justice Ave BS31 5 E3
Justice Rd BS16 20 A3
Justicia Way GL51 129 F5
Justin's Hill NP25 154 A7
Jutland Rd BS11 26 B1

K

Kansas Dr GL7 152 E2
Karelean Ct BS10 28 D3
Kaskelot Way GL2 118 C6
Katharine Ct GL51 130 A5
Katharine Lady Berkeley
Mews GL12 68 B7
Kathdene Gdns BS7 18 F3
Katherine Cl
Charfield GL12 67 A5
Innsworth GL3 127 F8
Katherine Lady Berkeley's
Sch GL12 67 F6
Katherine's Wlk
Lechlade on T GL7 153 E2
5 Ledbury HR8 178 E7
Kaybourne Cres GL3 128 D5
Kayte Cl GL52 137 F2
Kayte La GL52 138 A2
Keats Ave GL2 118 C4
Keats Ct BS7 19 A8
Keats Gdns GL5 103 A1
Keble Ave BS13 1 F5
Keble Cl Cirencester GL7 190 B1
Lechlade on T GL7 153 E3
Keble Lawns GL7 152 E3
Keble Rd Chalford GL6 148 D6
Moreton-in-M GL56 187 A2
Keel Cl BS5 9 F6
Keelings The GL14 191 C5
Keels SN6 143 E5
Keen's Gr BS35 38 C7
Keep The BS30 11 D5
Keepers La BS7 18 F3
Keepers Mill GL52 138 B3
Keg Store The BS1 195 B2
Keil Cl 5 WR12 185 B8
Keinton Wlk BS10 28 A2
Keirle Wlk GL51 133 A4
Kelbra Cres BS36 31 B6
Kellaway Ave BS7 18 D5
Kellaway Cres BS9 18 D6
Kellaway Ct BS6 18 D5
Kells Meend GL16 155 A7
Kells Rd GL16 155 A7
Kellys La NP16 146 F1
Kelston Cl Saltford BS31 5 D4
Yate BS37 32 D7
Kelston Gdns BS10 18 D8
Kelston Gr BS15 10 E6
Kelston Rd Bristol BS10 18 D8
Kelston BA1 6 E1
Keynsham BS31 4 D5
Kelston Wlk BS16 20 C4
Kemble Bsns Pk SN16 141 D6
Kemble Cl Bristol BS15 10 E6
Gloucester GL4 118 D2
Kemble Dr GL7 190 B2
Kemble Gdns BS11 16 F5
Kemble Gr GL51 129 B7
Kemble Ho BS34 39 F1
Kemble Pk GL7 141 F7
Kemble Prim Sch GL7 141 F8
Kemble Rd GL4 118 E2
Kemble Sta GL7 141 F8
Kemerton Rd
Bredon GL20 182 C7
Cheltenham GL50 130 B6
Westmancote GL20 182 D8
Kempe's Cl BS41 7 A2
Kemperleye Way BS32 29 D7
Kempley Rd GL18 178 C1
Kemps La GL6 103 F8
Kempsford Acre GL52 138 B3
Kempsford CE Prim Sch
GL7 144 E8
Kempton Cl
2 Bristol BS16 30 F1
Thornbury BS35 64 B3
Kempton Gr GL51 132 D2
Kencot Wlk BS13 2 B3
Kencourt Cl 2 GL2 127 B2
Kendal Rd Bristol BS7 19 A7
Gloucester GL2 127 C4
Kendall Gdns BS16 20 D4
Kendall Rd BS16 20 D4
Kendon Dr BS10 18 D7
Kendon Way BS10 18 D8
Kendrick La 11 GL5 99 C7
Kendrick St 9 GL5 99 C7
Kenelm Dr GL53 130 C6
Kenelm Gdns GL53 130 B6
Kenelm Rise GL54 174 A8
Kenilworth BS37 32 F8
Kenilworth Ave GL2 127 B3
Kenilworth Cl BS31 4 D4
Kenilworth Dr BS30 11 B2
Kenilworth Ho 3 GL51 132 E3
Kenilworth Rd BS6 18 C1
Kenmare Rd BS4 8 E1
Kenmore Cres BS7 28 E1
Kenmore Dr BS7 28 E1
Kenmore Gr BS7 28 E1
Kenn Court Bsns Pk BS4 2 E7
Kenn Rd BS5 10 A7
Kennard Cl BS15 10 C7
Kennard Rd BS15 10 C8
Kennard Rise BS15 10 C8
Kennedy Cl GL3 127 F1
Kennedy Ho BS37 43 F1
Kennedy Way BS37 43 F1
Kennel Dr GL9 46 E2
Kennel La
Broadwell GL56 177 A6
Watermead GL3 120 E4
10 Broadway WR12 185 B8
Kennel Lodge Rd BS3 7 E4
Kennerwell La GL12 68 E3
Kennet Cl GL20 182 B4
Kennet Rd BS31 5 A4
Kennet Way 4 BS35 51 D8
Kenneth Cl GL53 130 E4
Kenneth Rd BS4 9 D2
Kennett Gdns GL4 119 F4
Kennington Ave
Bristol,Bishopston BS7 18 F4
3 Bristol,Two Mile Hill
BS15 20 D1
Kennion Rd BS5 10 A7
Kennmoor Cl BS30 11 A6
Kensal Ave BS3 8 E3
Kensal Rd BS3 8 E3
Kensington Apartments
BS6 18 C3
Kensington Ave GL50 130 A8
Kensington Cl BS35 64 B2
Kensington Ct BS8 194 A3
Kensington Ho 5 BS5 10 A8
Kensington Park Rd BS4 9 C2
Kensington Pk 12 BS5 19 A1
Kensington Pl BS8 194 A3
Kensington Rd
Bristol,Redland BS6 18 C1
3 Bristol,St George BS5 10 A8
6 Bristol,Staple Hill BS16 20 D4
Kensley Vale GL14 191 C3
Kent Ave BS37 43 F3
Kent Cl Bristol BS34 29 D4
Churchdown GL3 128 D5
Kent End SN6 143 A5
Kent End Cl SN6 143 A5
Kent Mews BS16 19 E7
Kent Rd BS7 18 E4
Kent St BS3 8 C3

Kentmere Cl GL51 . . . . . .129 E7
Kenton Dr GL2 . . . . .127 C5
Kenton Ho BS34 . . . . .39 F1
Kenton Mews BS9 . . . . . . .18 C5
Kents Gn BS15 . . . . .20 E2
Kenulf Rd 20 GL54 . . . . .174 A7
Keppel Cl BS31 . . . . .5 D8
Keriston Ave GL3 . . . . . .128 A6
Kerr Way GL56 . . . . . . .187 C3
Kerrin La GL15 . . . . . . .147 C2
Kerris Ct 9 GL3 . . . . . .128 A7
Kerry Rd BS4 . . . . .8 E1
Kersteman Rd BS6 . . . . . .18 C3
Kerstin Cl GL50 . . . . . . .133 C5
Kestrel Cl Bristol BS34 . . . .28 E8
Cheltenham GL53 . . . . . . .130 C5
Chipping Sodbury BS37 . . . .32 F8
Thornbury BS35 . . . . .64 D2
Kestrel Ct 8 GL10 . . . . . .97 F8
Kestrel Dr BS16 . . . . .22 C4
Kestrel Gdns GL2 . . . . . .117 F3
Kestrel Par GL3 . . . . . . .127 D6
Kestrel Way GL20 . . . . . .182 B5
Keswick Cl GL2 . . . . .127 B3
Keswick Rd GL51 . . . . . .129 E7
Keswick Wlk BS10 . . . . . . .28 C2
Ketch Rd BS3 . . . . .8 F3
Kevin Cl GL4 . . . . .127 D1
Kew Pl GL53 . . . . .193 B1
Kew Wlk BS4 . . . . .3 C8
Kews La GL18 . . . . .170 D4
Kewstoke Rd BS9 . . . . . . .17 E4
Keynes Ctry Pk* GL7 . . .142 D7
Keynsham Bank GL52 . . .130 F8
Keynsham By-Pass BS31 . .4 E7
Keynsham Hospl BS31 . . . .4 F4
Keynsham La GL15 . . . . .147 B2
Keynsham Prim Sch BS31 .4 D5
Keynsham Rd
Bitton BS30,BS31 . . . . .5 A8
Cheltenham GL53 . . . . . . .193 C2
Keynsham St GL52 . . . . .130 F8
Keynsham Sta BS31 . . . . . .4 F6
Keynshambury Rd GL52 193 C2
Keys Ave BS7 . . . . .18 F7
Keytes Acre GL55 . . . . . .189 D3
Kibble's La GL14 . . . . . .191 C1
Kidnalls Rd GL15 . . . . . .155 F1
Kidnams Wlk GL2 . . . . . .100 F5
Kidnappers La GL53 . . . .130 B4
Kidney Hill BS37 . . . . .32 A3
Kiftsgate Court Gdns*
GL55 . . . . .189 C6
Kilbirnie Rd BS14 . . . . .3 A3
Kilburn Ct 17 BS5 . . . . .9 B8
Kilburn St 19 BS5 . . . . .9 B8
Kilda Rd SN6 . . . . .145 C4
Kildare Rd BS4 . . . . .8 D1
Kilham La GL54 . . . . . . .166 E5
Kilkenny St BS2 . . . . . . .195 C2
Killcott Rd GL12 . . . . .55 E8
Kilmersdon Rd BS13 . . . . . .2 B4
Kilminster Cl BS34 . . . . . .29 D7
Kilminster Ct 10 GL3 . . .128 A7
Kilminster Rd BS11 . . . . . .16 D7
Kilmore La GL20 . . . . . . .181 F7
Kiln Cl BS15 . . . . .20 B2
Kiln Ct BS5 . . . . .9 B8
Kilnhurst Cl BS30 . . . . . . .10 F2
Kilvert Cl BS4 . . . . .9 D5
Kimberland Way GL4 . . .119 E6
Kimberley Ave BS16 . . . . .20 C5
Kimberley Cl Bristol BS16 .20 F7
Gloucester GL2 . . . . .127 D4
Lydney GL15 . . . . .92 B3
Kimberley Cres BS16 . . . .20 C5
Kimberley Dr GL15 . . . . . .92 B3
Kimberley Rd
Bristol,Fishponds BS16 . . . .20 C5
Bristol,Kingswood BS15 . . .20 D1
Kimberley Wlk GL52 . . . .134 C2
Kimbrose GL1 . . . . .196 A2
Kimbrose Way GL1 . . . . .196 A2
Kimmins Rd GL10 . . . . . . .98 A8
Kinder Ho GL52 . . . . .134 B4
Kinema Ho BS4 . . . . .9 C4
King Alfred Way GL52 . . .130 F8
King Alfreds Rd NP16 . . . .61 A8
King Arthur Cl GL53 . . . .130 F7
King Dick's La 7 BS5 . . . . .9 F8
King Edmund Com Sch
BS37 . . . . .43 E1
King Edward Cl BS14 . . . . .3 A6
King Edward's Ave GL1 .118 E7
King George Cl GL53 . . .130 F6
King George V Pl 6
BS1 . . . . .195 A2
King George's Rd BS13 . . .1 F5
King Georges Field
GL54 . . . . .176 F4
King Henry Cl GL53 . . . .130 F6
King John's Cotts GL20 192 C5
King John's Rd BS15 . . . .20 B2
King Johns Ct GL20 . . . .192 C5
King La BS37 . . . . .45 A7
King Rd BS4 . . . . .9 C1
King Road Ave BS11 . . . . .26 B2
King Sq BS2 . . . . .195 A4
King Square Ave BS2 . . .195 A4
King St Avonmouth BS11 . . .26 A1
Bristol BS1 . . . . .195 A2
Bristol,Lower Easton BS5 . .19 C1
Bristol,St George BS15 . . . .10 B8
Cheltenham GL50 . . . . . . .193 B4
Cirencester GL7 . . . . .190 D3
Minchinhampton GL6 . . . . .148 A3
Stroud GL5 . . . . .99 C7
King Street Par 4 GL5 . . .99 C7
King William Ave BS1 . .195 A2
King William Dr GL53 . .130 F6
King William St BS3 . . . . . .8 B4
King's Ave BS6,BS7 . . . . . .18 C4
King's Barton St GL1 . . .196 C2
King's Dr BS7 . . . . .18 C4
King's Head La BS13 . . . . .1 F7
King's Mill La GL6 . . . . .103 E7
King's Parade Ave 1
BS8 . . . . .18 B1
King's Parade Mews BS8 18 A1
King's Rd
Bristol,Kensington Park BS4 .9 C3
Bristol,Victoria Park BS8 . .194 A3
Cheltenham GL52 . . . . . . .133 F1
Stonehouse GL10 . . . . .101 F1
Stroud GL5 . . . . .99 B6
King's Sch The GL1 . . . .196 B3
King's Sq GL1 . . . . .196 B3
King's Stanley CE Jun Sch
GL10 . . . . .98 A4
King's Stanley Inf Sch
GL10 . . . . .98 A3
Kingcomb La GL55 . . . . .188 F2
Kingfisher Bsns Pk GL5 . .99 E2
Kingfisher Cl Bristol BS32 .40 E2
Thornbury BS35 . . . . .64 D2
Kingfisher Ct GL51 . . . . .132 E5
Kingfisher Dr Bristol BS16 19 E6
Cheltenham GL51 . . . . . . .132 E5
Kingfisher Pl GL7 . . . . . .143 A8
Kingfisher Rd BS37 . . . . .33 A8
Kingfisher Rise 6 GL2 . .117 D1
Kingham Sta OX7 . . . . . .177 F1
Kingley Rd GL5 . . . . .98 E7
Kingrove Cres BS37 . . . . .33 C8
Kingrove La BS37 . . . . . . .33 C7
Kings Ave Bristol BS15 . . . .10 B4
Highworth SN6 . . . . .145 D3
Kings Chase BS15 . . . . . . .10 D8
Kings Court Prim Sch
BS37 . . . . .32 E8
Kings Ct Bristol BS13 . . . . . .1 F4
Bristol,Canon's Marsh
BS1 . . . . .195 A2
Bristol,Kingsdown BS1 . . .195 B4
Bristol,Little Stoke BS34 . . .29 C6
Kings Dr
Bristol,Hanham BS15 . . . . . .10 B4
Bristol,Stoke Gifford BS34 . .30 A4
Dursley GL11 . . . . .88 A2
Kings Elm GL2 . . . . .173 B3
Kings Gate GL20 . . . . . . .192 F4
Kings Head La GL54 . . . .166 F2
Kings Ho 6 GL50 . . . . . .193 A4
Kings Mdw
Bourton-on-t-W GL54 . . . . .168 F8
Crudwell SN16 . . . . .141 B3
Kings Mead GL14 . . . . . .156 F6
Kings Meade GL16 . . . . . .155 A5
Kings Park Ave BS2 . . . . . .9 C6
Kings Sq BS30 . . . . .5 D8
Kings Walk Sh Ctr GL1 .196 B2
Kings Well La GL54 . . . .176 C1
Kings Weston Ave BS11 . .16 E8
Kings Weston La
Avonmouth BS11 . . . . .26 E3
Bristol BS11 . . . . .17 A8
Kings Weston Rd BS11,
BS10 . . . . .27 C1
Kings Wlk Bristol BS13 . . . .1 E7
Gloucester GL1 . . . . .196 B3
Kingsbridge Mews
GL51 . . . . .132 D3
Kingsclere Dr GL52 . . . .137 E3
Kingscote BS37 . . . . .32 D6
Kingscote Ave GL51 . . . .129 D7
Kingscote Cl
Cheltenham GL51 . . . . . . .129 D7
Churchdown GL3 . . . . .128 D4
Kingscote Dr GL4 . . . . . .119 E5
Kingscote Gr GL51 . . . . .129 D7
Kingscote Pk BS5 . . . . . . .10 B6
Kingscote Rd E GL51 . . .129 D7
Kingscote Rd W GL51 . .129 D6
Kingscourt Cl BS14 . . . . . . .3 A4
Kingscourt La GL5 . . . . . .99 A4
Kingscroft Rd GL3 . . . . .120 A7
Kingsdale Ct WR12 . . . .185 C8
Kingsditch La GL51 . . . .133 A5
Kingsditch Ret Pk GL51 133 A5
Kingsdown GL11 . . . . .88 A3
Kingsdown Par BS6 . . . .195 A4
Kingsfield La
Bristol,Longwell Green
BS15 . . . . .10 E5
Bristol,Mount Hill BS30 . . .10 E4
Kingsfield Rdbt BS15 . . . .10 E5
Kingsfield Sch BS15 . . . . .11 A8
Kingsgate Ct BS37 . . . . . .32 E8
Kingshill GL7 . . . . .190 F4
Kingshill Ho BS4 . . . . .9 B1
Kingshill La
Cirencester GL7 . . . . .150 F4
Dursley GL11 . . . . .88 A2
Kingshill Pk GL11 . . . . . . .88 A3
Kingshill Rd Bristol BS4 . . .9 B1
Dursley GL11 . . . . .88 A2
Kingsholm CE Prim Sch
GL1 . . . . .196 C4
Kingsholm Ct GL1 . . . . .126 E4
Kingsholm Rd
Bristol BS10 . . . . .18 D8
Gloucester GL1 . . . . .196 B4
Kingsholm Sq GL1 . . . . .196 B4
Kingsholme Rd BS15 . . . .20 D1
Kingsland Cl 1 BS2 . . . . . .9 A6
Kingsland Rd BS2 . . . . .9 A6
Kingsland Road Bridge 3
BS2 . . . . .9 A6
Kingsland Trad Est BS2 . . .9 A7
Kingsleigh Ct BS15 . . . . . .10 F7
Kingsleigh Gdns BS15 . . .10 F7
Kingsleigh Pk BS15 . . . . .10 F7
Kingsley Gdns GL51 . . . .129 E8
Kingsley Ho Bristol BS2 .195 C2
Bristol,Westbury on Trym
BS9 . . . . .18 A8
Kingsley Pl 1 BS3 . . . . . . .8 C4
Kingsley Rd
Bristol,Lower Easton BS5 . .19 C1
Bristol,Montpelier BS6 . . . .18 D2
Gloucester GL4 . . . . .119 A5
Kingsmark La/Lon Cyn Farch
NP16 . . . . .72 D1
Kingsmarsh Ho 3 BS5 . . . .9 B7
Kingsmead
Cirencester GL7 . . . . .190 E2
Gloucester GL4 . . . . .119 F4
Lechlade on T GL7 . . . . . .153 E3
Painswick GL6 . . . . .103 E8
Kingsmead Ave GL51 . . .132 F4
Kingsmead Cl GL51 . . . .132 F4
Kingsmead Ind Est
GL51 . . . . .133 A4
Kingsmead Rd Bristol BS5 20 A1
Cheltenham GL51 . . . . . . .132 F4
Kingsmead Wlk BS5 . . . .20 A1
Kingsmill BS9 . . . . .17 D5
Kingston Ave BS31 . . . . . . .5 C3
Kingston Cl BS16 . . . . . . .21 A7
Kingston Dr Bristol BS16 .21 A7
Cheltenham GL51 . . . . . . .132 C1
Kingston Rd Bristol BS3 . . .8 C4
Northway GL20 . . . . .182 C4
Slimbridge GL2 . . . . .95 C4
Kingstone Ave GL3 . . . . .127 F1
Kingstree St BS4 . . . . .9 A4
Kingsville Rd GL51 . . . . .133 A5
Kingsway
Bristol,Little Stoke BS34 . . .29 C6
Bristol,St George BS5 . . . . .10 B7
Coleford GL16 . . . . .155 B6
Dursley GL11 . . . . .88 A3
Preston GL7 . . . . .150 F3
Kingsway Ave BS15 . . . . .10 B8
Kingsway Cres BS15 . . . .10 C8
Kingsway La GL17 . . . . .163 F4
Kingsway Pk BS30 . . . . . .11 B6
Kingsway Sh Prec BS5 . . .10 B7
Kingswear Rd BS3 . . . . . . .8 D2
Kingsweston Down Nature
Res* BS9,BS11 . . . . .27 C1
Kingsweston Sch BS11 . .17 A8
Kingswood Abbey
Gatehouse* GL12 . . . . . .67 F5
Kingswood Cl GL52 . . . .137 F3
Kingswood Foundation Est
BS15 . . . . .10 C7
Kingswood Heritage Mus*
BS30 . . . . .11 B6
Kingswood Hts BS15 . . . .20 D1
Kingswood Prim Sch
GL12 . . . . .67 F5
Kingswood Rd GL12 . . . . .55 D8
Kingswood Trad Est
BS15 . . . . .20 D1
Kington La BS35 . . . . .63 E1
Kington Rd BS35 . . . . .63 E3
Kinmoor GL4 . . . . .119 D3
Kinsale Rd BS14 . . . . .3 C7
Kinsale Wlk BS4 . . . . .8 E1
Kinsham La GL20 . . . . . .182 E7
Kinvara Rd BS4 . . . . .2 E8
Kipling Cl GL2 . . . . .118 C4
Kipling Rd Bristol BS7 . . . .29 B1
Cheltenham GL51 . . . . . . .132 E1
Dursley GL11 . . . . .80 C7
Kirby Rd GL54 . . . . .169 E6
Kirkby Rd BS11 . . . . .27 A1
Kirkstone Gdns BS10 . . . .28 C2
Kirkstone Ho BS34 . . . . . .29 A8
Kirtlington Rd BS5 . . . . . .19 B3
Kitchener Ave GL1 . . . . .118 E5
Kite Hay Cl BS16 . . . . . . .19 E5
Kitefield 15 SN6 . . . . . . .143 E4
Kites Cl BS32 . . . . .40 C2
Kitesnest La GL5 . . . . . . .99 A4
Klondyke Ave GL15 . . . . .92 B3
Knap La GL6 . . . . .103 F7
Knapp Cl HR9 . . . . .163 A6
Knapp Cotts GL18 . . . . . .179 B3
Knapp La
Brimscombe GL5 . . . . .148 A4
Cheltenham GL50 . . . . . . .193 A4
Coaley GL11 . . . . .89 B5
Cromhall GL12 . . . . .66 B3
Dursley GL11 . . . . .87 F6
Stroud GL6 . . . . .104 B2
Woolaston GL15 . . . . .147 D3
Knapp Rd
Cheltenham GL50 . . . . . . .193 A4
Thornbury BS35 . . . . .64 D1
Wotton-u-E GL12 . . . . .68 C7
Knapp The Dursley GL11 . .88 B1
Yate BS37 . . . . .43 F5
Knapps Cres GL52 . . . . .138 B4
Knapps La BS5 . . . . .19 E2
Kneller Cl BS11 . . . . .17 A8
Knighton Rd BS10 . . . . . .28 E1
Knights Cl BS9 . . . . .18 B6
Knights Cres GL18 . . . . .170 F4
Knights Way
Newent GL18 . . . . .170 F4
Tewkesbury GL20 . . . . . . .192 E4
Knightsbridge Bsns Ctr
GL51 . . . . .173 F5
Knightsbridge Cres
GL53 . . . . .130 F7
Knightsbridge Gn GL51 .173 F5
Knightsbridge Pk BS13 . . .2 E4
Knightshill HR9 . . . . . . .164 D8
Knightstone Ct BS5 . . . . .19 D2
Knightstone Gdns BS4 . . . .9 B2
Knightstone Ho 1 BS2 .195 A4
Knightstone Lodge BS6 .18 D1
Knightstone Mount BS5 .10 A6
Knightstone Rise 5 BS5 . .9 F8
Knightstone Sq BS14 . . . . .3 C5
Knightstone Wlk BS2 . . .194 C4
Knightwood Rd BS34 . . . .29 F5
Knockdown Rd SN16 . . . .58 C1
Knockley Patch GL15 . . .155 D1
Knole Cl BS32 . . . . .39 F4
Knole La BS10 . . . . .28 B3
Knole Pk BS32 . . . . .39 F3
Knoll Ct BS9 . . . . .17 D3
Knoll Hill BS9 . . . . .17 D3
Knoll The Kempsford GL7 144 E8
Stroud GL5 . . . . .99 D7
Uley GL11 . . . . .89 C1
Knollys End GL2 . . . . . . .109 F8
Knovill Cl BS11 . . . . .27 B2
Knowlands SN6 . . . . . . .145 D4
Knowle Park Jun & Inf Schs
BS4 .9 A1
Knowle Rd BS2 . . . . .8 F3
Knowles Rd GL1 . . . . . . .118 F7
Knowsley Rd BS16 . . . . . .19 E3
Knox Rd GL15 . . . . .147 E8
Kyderminster Rd GL54 . .174 A8
Kyght Cl BS15 . . . . .11 A8
Kylross Ave BS14 . . . . .3 B5
Kymin Lea NP25 . . . . . . .154 A7
Kymin Rd NP25 . . . . .154 B7
Kynges Mill Cl BS16 . . . .20 A7
Kyngstone Ct 10 BS16 . . .19 E3

L

La Maison BS5 . . . . .20 A2
Labbott The BS31 . . . . .4 E5
Laburnum Cres GL6 . . . . .102 F2
Laburnum Ct GL51 . . . . .132 C2
Laburnum Gdns GL2 . . .117 F2
Laburnum Gr BS16 . . . . . .20 B4
Laburnum Mews GL10 . . .97 E7
Laburnum Rd Bristol BS15 10 C5
Gloucester GL1 . . . . .118 D5
Laburnum Way NP16 . . . .60 E5
Laburnum Wlk
Keynsham BS31 . . . . .4 C3
Stonehouse GL10 . . . . .97 E7
Lacca Cl GL2 . . . . .127 D5
Lacey Rd BS14 . . . . .3 F6
Lacock Dr BS30 . . . . .10 F5
Lacy Cl GL2 . . . . .127 C6
Ladbarrow Cotts GL54 . .161 A4
Ladd Cl BS15 . . . . .10 F7
Ladden Ct BS35 . . . . .51 C8
Ladder The GL6 . . . . .91 C4
Ladies Mile BS8 . . . . .17 F1
Ladman Gr BS14 . . . . .3 E6
Ladman Rd BS14 . . . . .3 E5
Lady Chapel Rd GL4 . . .119 E6
Lady Downe Cl GL4 . . . .119 E3
Lady La SN25 . . . . .144 D1
Lady Margaret Ct NP16 . .60 F4
Lady Mead SN6 . . . . . . .143 E4
Ladybellegate St GL1 . .196 A2
Ladygrove Bsns Pk
GL17 . . . . .164 E5
Ladysmith Rd Bristol BS6 .18 B4
Cheltenham GL52 . . . . . . .134 B2
Gloucester GL1 . . . . .118 E6
Ladywell Cl GL2 . . . . . . .118 B7
Laggar La GL5 . . . . .98 F1
Laines Est The GL54 . . . .158 F6
Lake Cl GL2 . . . . .124 B3
Lake La Churcham GL2 . . .124 B3
Frampton on Severn GL2 . .157 F3
Lake Louise SN6 . . . . . . .143 E6
Lake Rd BS10 . . . . .18 C8
Lake Side GL18 . . . . . . .171 A5
Lake St Cheltenham GL52 .134 B5
Quedgeley GL2 . . . . .116 D4
Lake View BS16 . . . . .19 F3
Lake View Rd BS5 . . . . . . .9 D8
Lakefield CE Prim Sch
GL2 . . . . .100 A6
Lakemead Gdns BS13 . . . .1 F4
Lakemead Gr BS13 . . . . . . .1 F6
Lakers Rd GL16 . . . . . . .155 A7
Lakers Sch GL16 . . . . . . .155 B7
Lakeside Bristol BS16 . . . . .19 E3
Fairford GL7 . . . . .152 D3
South Cerney GL7 . . . . . .143 A8
Lakeside Ave GL15 . . . . . .92 C2
Lakeside Ct GL52 . . . . . .133 F4
Lakeside Dr GL15 . . . . . . .92 C2
Lakeside Gdns GL15 . . . . .92 B2
Lakeside Prim Sch
GL51 . . . . .129 E7
Lakewood Cres BS10 . . . .18 B8
Lakewood Rd BS10 . . . . . .18 B8
Lamb Hill BS5 . . . . .9 F7
Lamb La GL14 . . . . .191 D4
Lamb St BS2 . . . . .195 C3
Lambert Ave GL51 . . . . .129 D1
Lambert Cl GL51 . . . . . .129 D1
Lambert Dr GL51 . . . . . .129 D1
Lambert Gdns GL51 . . . .129 D1
Lambert Pl BS4 . . . . .2 D6
Lambert Terr GL51 . . . . .129 D2
Lamberts Field GL54 . . .169 A7
Lambley Rd BS5 . . . . .9 E8
Lambourn Cl Bristol BS3 . . .8 D3
Gloucester GL2 . . . . .127 E3
Lambourn Rd BS31 . . . . . . .5 A4
Lambourne Ave GL19 . . .165 D6
Lambourne Cl 14 HR8 . .178 F8
Lambrook Rd BS16 . . . . . .20 A4
Lambs Barn Pitch GL18 171 A5
Lambs Cross HR9 . . . . . .170 B4
Lambsdowne GL11 . . . . . .87 F3
Lambsquay Rd GL16 . . . .155 A3
Lamington Cl BS13 . . . . . . .1 F6
Lamord Gate BS34 . . . . . .29 E5
Lampern View GL11 . . . . .89 B1
Lampeter Rd BS9 . . . . . . .18 A7
Lampreys The GL4 . . . . .119 B6
Lampton Ave BS13 . . . . . . .2 E3
Lampton Gr BS13 . . . . .2 E3
Lampton Rd BS41 . . . . .7 A1
Lanaway Rd BS16 . . . . . . .20 B6
Lancashire Rd BS7 . . . . . .18 E3
Lancaster Cl BS34 . . . . . .29 D4
Lancaster Ct
2 Cheltenham GL50 . . . . .130 B8
Lydney GL15 . . . . .92 B5
Lancaster Dr Lydney GL15 .92 B5
Upper Rissington GL54 . . .169 D6
Lancaster Rd Bristol BS2 .19 A2
Kempsford GL7 . . . . .144 F7
Tewkesbury GL20 . . . . . . .192 D2
Yate BS37 . . . . .43 E3
Lancaster St 10 BS5 . . . . .9 C7
Lancaster Terr GL18 . . . .171 A5
Lancaster Way NP16 . . . .60 D8
Lancaut La NP16 . . . . . . .72 F6
Lancelot Ct GL2 . . . . .95 D4
Lancelot Rd BS16 . . . . . . .19 E8
Land The BS36 . . . . .31 C7
Landgate Yd 2 GL54 . . .176 F4
Landmark Ct BS1 . . . . . .194 C1
Landor Gdns 20 GL52 . . .133 F2
Landseer Ave BS7 . . . . . .19 B7
Lane End Fairford GL7 . . .152 F2
Great Rissington GL54 . . .169 C4
Lane The
Broadway WR12 . . . . .184 F7
Chastleton GL56 . . . . .177 E8
Easter Compton BS35 . . . . .38 F2
Randwick GL6 . . . . .102 D2
Lanercost Rd BS10 . . . . . .28 C2
Lanes Ct GL20 . . . . .192 C3
Lanes Dairy BS34 . . . . . . .29 A3
Lanes End BS4 . . . . .9 C1
Lanes The
Cheltenham GL53 . . . . . . .130 B4
Gorsley HR9 . . . . .170 B4
Lanesborough Rise BS14 .3 D7
Lanescourt GL20 . . . . . . .192 D3
Langdale Ct BS34 . . . . . . .29 A8
Langdale Gdns GL2 . . . .127 C5
Langdale Rd Bristol BS16 .19 F4
Cheltenham GL51 . . . . . . .129 F6
Langdon Rd GL53 . . . . .130 D6
Langdown Ct BS14 . . . . . . .3 E5
Langet GL7 . . . . .142 F7
Langetts Rd 4 GL16 . . . .155 A5
Langfield Cl BS10 . . . . . .27 E3
Langford Rd BS13 . . . . . . .1 F8
Langford Way BS15 . . . . .10 E7
Langham Ho NP16 . . . . . .60 F5
Langham Rd BS4 . . . . .9 B2
Langhill Ave BS4 . . . . .2 D7
Langley Cl GL54 . . . . . . .139 F5
Langley Cres BS3 . . . . .7 E1
Langley Mow BS16 . . . . . .21 B7
Langley Rd
Gloucester GL4 . . . . .119 B5
Winchcombe GL54 . . . . . . .139 D5
Langsdown Ho 7 BS2 . . .18 F1
Langston Priory Workshops
OX7 . . . . .177 F1
Langthorn Cl BS36 . . . . . .31 C7
Langtoft Rd GL5 . . . . .99 E7
Langton Cl GL4 . . . . . . .119 E8
Langton Court Rd BS4 . . . .9 D5
Langton Ct 11 BS16 . . . . .19 E3
Langton Grove Rd GL52 131 A7
Langton Ho 10 BS2 . . . .195 C3
Langton Pk BS3 . . . . .8 C4
Langton Pl GL53 . . . . . . .131 A7
Langton Rd BS4 . . . . .9 D5
Langton Way BS4 . . . . .9 F6
Lanham Gdns GL2 . . . . .109 F7
Lannett Rd GL1 . . . . .118 E6
Lansdown Stroud GL5 . . . .99 C7
Yate BS37 . . . . .32 E8
Lansdown Castle Dr
GL51 . . . . .129 F8
Lansdown Cl Bristol BS15 .20 D2
Cheltenham GL51 . . . . . . .130 A8
Lansdown Cotts GL54 . .168 F8
Lansdown Cres GL50 . . .193 A2
Lansdown Crescent La
GL50 . . . . .193 A2
Lansdown Ct GL50 . . . . .193 A2
Lansdown Ho BS15 . . . . .20 D2
Lansdown Ind Est GL51 .133 A1
Lansdown La BS30 . . . . . .12 C1
Lansdown Lodge Dr
GL51 . . . . .130 A8
Lansdown Par GL50 . . . .130 B8
Lansdown Pl Bristol BS8 194 A3

Lansdown Pl *continued*
Cheltenham GL50 193 A2
Lansdown Place La
GL50 193 A2
Lansdown Rd
Bristol,Kingswood BS15 20 D2
Bristol,Redland BS6 18 C1
6 Bristol,Upper Easton BS5 9 B8
Bristol,Victoria Park BS8 194 A3
Cheltenham GL51 130 A8
Gloucester GL1 127 A3
Pucklechurch BS16 22 C6
Saltford BS31 5 E3
Lansdown Terr
Bristol BS6 18 D5
Cheltenham GL50 193 A2
Lansdown Terrace La
GL50 193 A2
Lansdown View BS15 10 F8
Lansdown Wlk
11 Bream GL15 147 D8
Cheltenham GL50 193 A2
Lansdowne BS16 30 C1
Lansdowne Ct 2 BS5 9 B8
Lantern Cl Berkeley GL13 85 E3
Cinderford GL14 191 C4
Lapdown La GL9 34 D1
Laphams Ct 11 BS30 10 F4
Lapwing Cl Bristol BS32 40 D2
Northway GL20 182 B5
Lapwing Ct 10 GL6 148 C6
Lapwing Gdns BS16 19 F6
Larch Cl GL53 131 C5
Larch Rd Bristol BS15 20 E3
Colerne SN14 15 F6
Larch Rise GL53 130 B4
Larch Way BS34 28 E7
Larches The GL4 119 E6
Larchmere Gr 8 GL51 129 E5
Larchwood Dr GL4 118 E3
Lark Rise Chalford GL6 148 C6
Coleford GL16 155 A6
Yate BS37 43 F4
Lark's La BS37 42 B7
Larkfield BS36 31 D7
Larkfield Ave NP16 60 E7
Larkfield Gr NP16 60 D7
Larkfield Ho NP16 60 D7
Larkfield Inf Sch GL3 127 E6
Larkfield Pk NP16 60 D7
Larkham Cl GL4 119 B3
Larkham Pl GL4 119 B3
Larkhay Rd GL3 120 A8
Larkhill Cl NP16 60 E7
Larkrise GL11 87 F5
Larks Field BS16 19 E5
Larksfield Rd
Harrow Hill GL17 164 B4
Stroud GL5 99 A4
Larksleaze Rd BS30 10 F2
Larkspear Cl GL1 118 E5
Larkspur Cl BS35 64 D1
Larput Pl GL50 133 D3
Lasbury Gr BS13 2 C5
Lasne Cres GL3 120 F4
Lassington Gr GL2 125 C5
Lassington La GL2 125 D6
Lassington Wood (Nature
Reserve)* GL2 125 E5
Latchen GL17 164 F5
Latchen Orch GL17 164 F5
Latchmoor Ho BS13 2 A8
Latimer Cl Bristol BS4 9 E4
Minchinhampton GL6 148 A3
Latimer Ct GL54 175 B3
Latimer Rd
Cinderford GL14 191 E5
Stonehouse GL10 101 D1
Latteridge La
Latteridge BS37 42 A7
Tytherington BS35 51 F1
Latteridge Rd BS37 42 D4
Latton Rd BS7 18 F8
Latymer Croft GL3 128 B5
Launceston Ave BS15 10 B5
Launceston Rd BS15 20 B1
Laundry Cotts GL56 177 E5
Laundry Rd GL16 154 E4
Laura Cl GL2 127 B4
Laurel Ave GL20 192 E2
Laurel Cotts GL20 192 E2
Laurel Dr
Cheltenham GL52 134 B4
Colerne SN14 15 F6
Laurel Farm Cl GL4 118 F4
Laurel Gate GL4 119 F5
Laurel Pk NP16 72 B6
Laurel St BS15 10 D8
Laureldene GL16 155 B3
Laurels The
Bristol,Catbrain BS10 28 A6
Bristol,Mangotsfield BS16 21 A6
Castle Eaton SN6 144 D6
Gloucester GL1 118 F7
South Cerney GL7 142 F8
Laurence Cl GL51 129 D2
Laurie Cres BS9 18 D6
Laurie Lee Ct 3 BS30 11 A5
Lauriston Pk GL50 130 B6
Lavender Cl BS35 64 D1
Lavender Ct Bristol BS5 19 F1
Cirencester GL7 190 C3
Lavender La GL7 190 C3
Lavender Mews GL52 137 E3
Lavender Rd GL51 129 F5
Lavender View GL4 119 F4
Lavender Way BS32 29 F7
Lavenham Rd BS37 43 B2
Lavers Cl BS15 10 E6
Lavington Dr GL2 127 E4
Lavington Rd BS5 10 B6
Lawford Ave BS34 29 C6
Lawford St BS2 195 C3
Lawfords Gate BS2 195 C3
Lawfords Gate Ho 13
BS2 195 C3
Lawn Ave BS16 20 B5
Lawn Cres GL51 129 E2
Lawn Rd
Ashleworth GL19 172 D4
Bristol BS16 20 B5
Lawns Pk GL5 98 F2
Lawns Rd BS37 43 F2
Lawns The Bristol BS11 16 E7
Gloucester GL4 119 D3
Gotherington GL52 138 B7
Stonehouse GL10 97 E8
Lawnside GL6 91 A4
Lawnside Rd 6 HR8 178 E8
Lawnwood Ind Units 14
BS5 9 B8
Lawnwood Rd 15 BS5 9 B8
Lawrence Ave BS5 19 B1
Lawrence Cl Bristol BS15 21 A2
Charlton Kings GL52 131 B6
Lawrence Dr BS37 43 B2
Lawrence Gr Bristol BS9 18 B5
Dursley GL11 88 A2
Lawrence Hill BS5 9 B7
Lawrence Hill Ind Pk BS5 9 B8
Lawrence Hill Rdbt BS5 9 A7
Lawrence Hill Sta BS5 9 B7
Lawrence Rd
Avening GL8 148 B1
Cirencester GL7 190 B3
Lawrence Way N GL1 126 E4
Lawrence Weston Rd
Avonmouth BS11 26 F4
Bristol BS11 27 A2
Lawrence's Mdw GL52 138 A8
Lawson Cl BS31 5 C2
Lawson Glade GL53 131 A4
Laxey Rd BS7 18 F7
Laxton Cl BS35 50 A3
Laxton Dr GL12 67 F4
Laxton Rd
Cheltenham GL51 132 E2
Gloucester GL4 120 A6
Laymore Rd GL14 191 B5
Laynes Rd GL3 120 A7
Lays Dr BS31 4 C5
Lays Farm Bsns Ctr BS31 4 C4
Lays Farm Trad Est BS31 4 C4
Lazenby Ct GL51 132 C1
Lea CE Prim Sch HR9 164 C8
Lea Cres GL2 127 C5
Lea Croft BS13 2 A4
Lea Ct GL10 96 E7
Lea Rd GL3 120 F5
Leacey Ct GL3 128 A7
Leacey Mews GL3 128 A7
Leading Edge The BS8 194 B2
Leadon Cl GL3 120 F5
Leadon Pl 9 HR8 178 E7
Leadon Way HR8 178 E7
Leafield Rd GL7 152 E4
Leaholes Ct GL7 190 D4
Leaholme Gdns BS14 3 A3
Leaman Cl BS37 44 B1
Leamington Rd WR12 188 A1
Leap Vale BS16 21 A8
Leap Valley Cres BS16 21 A8
Leaping Stocks Rd HR9 162 D3
Lear Cl BS30 11 B5
Lears Dr GL52 138 A3
Leasbrook La/Lon Leasbrook
NP25 154 A8
Leaside Cl GL11 88 A4
Leasow La GL54 169 B5
Leasows The
Broadwell GL56 177 A6
Chipping Campden GL55 188 F1
Mickleton GL55 189 B6
Leaze Cl GL13 85 E3
Leaze Ct GL15 92 C2
Leaze The
2 Ashton Keynes SN6 142 F5
South Cerney GL7 142 F7
Yate BS37 43 D2
Lechlade Rd
Highworth SN6 145 D4
Lechlade on T GL7 153 F1
Southrop GL7 153 C6
Upper Inglesham SN6 145 D7
Lechmere Rd 1 GL51 132 E3
Leckhampton CE Prim Sch
GL53 130 D4
Leckhampton Farm Ct
GL51 130 B3
Leckhampton Gate
GL51 130 A4
Leckhampton Hill GL53 130 D2
Leckhampton La GL51,
GL53 130 A2
Leckhampton Pl GL53 130 D5
Leckhampton Rd GL53 130 D5
Leckhampton View
GL51 129 F2
Leda Ave BS14 3 A7
Ledbury Heritage Ctr*
HR8 178 F8
Ledbury Pk 9 HR8 178 F8
Ledbury Prim Sch HR8 178 E8
Ledbury Rd Bristol BS16 20 C4
Dymock GL18 178 E3
Eastnor HR8 179 B8
Ledbury Road Cres
GL19 172 A8
Leddington Ct HR8 178 D7
Ledmore Rd GL53 131 B6
Lee Cl Bristol BS34 28 F8
Cheltenham GL51 132 F3
Lee Rd GL20 182 C4
Lee Villa Cvn Pk HR9 164 D8
Leechpool Way BS37 43 E5
Leeming Way BS11 16 C8
Lees Ct BS15 20 E1
Lees Hill BS15 20 E2
Lees La BS30 11 D5
Lefroy Ct GL51 130 A8
Leicester Sq BS16 20 D3
Leicester St 6 BS3 8 D4
Leicester Wlk BS4 9 F5
Leigh CE Prim Sch SN6 143 B3
Leigh Court Bsns Ctr
BS8 17 A2
Leigh Ct BS9 17 D3
Leigh La Cold Ashton BA1 14 B3
Westerleigh BS37 32 B1
Leigh Rd BS8 194 B4
Leigh St BS3 8 A4
Leigh Woods Forest Walks*
BS8 17 C1
Leighterton Prim Sch
GL8 70 C3
Leighton Rd
Bristol,Southville BS3 8 B4
Bristol,Upper Knowle BS4 9 B2
Cheltenham GL52 133 F1
Leinster Ave BS4 2 D8
Leinster Cl GL51 132 D4
Leisure Rd BS15 10 E5
Lemon La BS2 195 C4
Lena Ave 3 BS5 19 C1
Lena St BS5 19 C1
Lennards The GL7 143 A8
Lennox Ho BS11 26 B1
Lenover Gdns BS13 2 B4
Lensbrook GL15 93 A8
Leonard La BS1 195 A3
Leonard Rd Bristol BS5 9 D7
Gloucester GL1 118 F6
Leonard Stanley CE Prim Sch
GL10 97 F4
Leonards Ave BS5 19 C1
Leopold Rd BS6 18 E2
Lesanne Ct GL1 196 B2
Lescren Way BS11 26 D1
Letch Hill Dr GL54 168 F7
Letch La 10 GL54 168 F7
Leven Cl GL2 127 D4
Lever's Hill GL11 89 B7
Lewin St 9 BS5 9 D7
Lewington Rd BS16 20 C4
Lewins Mead BS1 195 A3
Lewis Ave GL2 126 F6
Lewis Cl
Bristol,Emerson's Green
BS16 21 C5
Bristol,North Common BS30 11 D5
Lewis Glade 2 GL16 155 B5
Lewis La GL7 190 D4
Lewis Rd Bristol BS13 2 A8
Cheltenham GL51 132 D2
Lewis St BS2 9 B5
Lewis Way NP16 60 F4
Lewisham Rd GL1 118 E5
Lewisham Terr GL13 85 C8
Lewiston Cl GL5 148 A5
Lewiston Rd GL5 148 A5
Lewton La BS36 30 E7
Lexington Cl GL20 192 E2
Lexington Sq GL52 133 E5
Ley La BS35 49 F3
Ley Mary Farm OX18 161 C8
Ley Orch WR12 188 B2
Ley Rd GL2 116 A5
Leyland Wlk BS13 1 F4
Leys The GL13 85 E4
Leysbourne GL55 189 A2
Leyson Rd GL51 129 C6
Leyton Villas BS6 18 B2
Libby's Dr GL5 99 D8
Libertus Ct GL51 133 A1
Libertus Rd GL51 133 A1
Liberty Gdns BS1 194 C1
Liberty Ind Pk BS3 8 A1
Library Pl 2 NP16 60 E8
Lichfield Dr GL51 130 A5
Lichfield Rd Bristol BS4 9 E6
Gloucester GL4 119 D8
Lidderdale Rd GL54 169 D6
Liddington Cl GL53 130 D4
Liddington Rd
Cheltenham GL53 130 D4
Gloucester GL2 127 E3
Liddington Trad Est
GL53 130 D5
Lifford Gdns WR12 185 B8
Lightenbrook La GL2 95 C3
Lightfoot 21 GL18 171 A4
Lightpill Trad Est GL5 99 A6
Lightwood La GL6 102 E3
Lilac Cl Bristol BS10 28 C1
Cheltenham GL51 130 A5
Lilac Ct BS31 4 C4
Lilac Way Gloucester GL4 118 C3
Quedgeley GL2 117 F1
Lilley's Alley 9 GL20 192 C4
Lillian St 5 BS5 9 C8
Lilliesfield Ave GL3 119 F8
Lilliput Ave BS37 33 A8
Lilliput Ct BS37 33 B8
Lilly Hall La HR8 178 C7
Lilstock Ave BS7 18 F4
Lilton Wlk BS13 8 A1
Lilymead Ave BS4 9 A3
Limber Hill GL50 133 C5
Limbury Hostels GL19 172 A2
Lime Ave GL9 35 B8
Lime Cl Brentry BS10 28 B3
Cheltenham GL52 134 A5
Lime Croft BS37 43 F4
Lime Ct Innsworth GL3 127 F6
Keynsham BS31 4 C4
Lime Gr Alveston BS35 50 F4
Stroud GL5 99 C7
Lime Kiln Cl BS34 29 D3
Lime Kiln Gdns BS32 40 D2
Lime Kiln Rd BS1 194 B2
Lime Rd
Bristol,Hanham BS15 10 A5
Bristol,Southville BS3 8 B4
Tewkesbury GL20 192 E1
Lime St GL19 180 D1
Lime Tree Ave 3 WR12 185 C8
Lime Tree Cotts GL7 152 D7
Lime Tree Ct GL1 118 E5
Lime Tree Gr BS20 16 D3
Lime Trees Rd BS9 18 D6
Lime Way GL15 92 B4
Limekiln Gr GL2 125 D5
Limekiln La GL6 148 E8
Limekiln Rd BS37,GL12 53 C2
Limekilns Cl BS31 4 F5
Limerick Rd BS6 18 C2
Limes Cl GL7 190 C3
Limes Pl SN6 143 E6
Limes Rd GL7 141 F8
Limes The Badminton GL9 46 E2
Bristol BS16 30 B1
Gloucester,Barnwood GL4 127 C1
Gloucester,Kingsholm GL2 126 E5
South Cerney GL7 142 F7
Limetree Ave 9 NP25 154 A7
Linacre Cres GL7 190 B2
Lincoln Ave GL51 130 A5
Lincoln Cl Keynsham BS31 4 C4
Tewkesbury GL20 192 B2
Upper Rissington GL54 169 D6
Lincoln Ct BS16 19 D6
Lincoln Green La GL20 192 B2
Lincoln St BS5 9 B7
Lincombe Ave BS16 20 D6
Lincombe Rd BS16 20 C6
Linden Ave GL52 134 A5
Linden Cl
Bristol,Mayfield Park BS16 20 A2
Bristol,Stockwood BS14 3 E6
Cheltenham GL52 134 B5
Chepstow/Cas-Gwent NP16 60 E5
Colerne SN14 15 F6
Winterbourne BS36 30 E6
Linden Dr BS32 29 E8
Linden Grange BS6 18 C3
Linden Ho BS16 19 C5
Linden Lea GL7 143 F8
Linden Prim Sch GL1 118 D6
Linden Rd Bristol BS6 18 B4
Gloucester GL1 118 D6
Lindon Ct BS15 20 B1
Lindon Ho BS4 9 E3
Lindrea St 3 BS3 8 B3
Lindsay Rd BS7 19 A4
Line The HR9 170 A3
Linegar Wood Rd GL14 191 C1
Lines Way BS14 3 C3
Linfoot Rd GL8 140 B4
Lingfield Pk BS16 30 F2
Link Rd Bristol BS34 28 F3
Pillowell GL15 155 F1
Tewkesbury GL20 192 D4
Yate BS37 43 F1
Linkend Rd GL19 180 F2
Links The GL16 155 A5
Links View GL7 150 C7
Linley Rd SN26 144 E1
Linnell Cl BS7 19 B6
Linnet Cl Bristol BS34 28 E8
Gloucester GL4 119 C5
Linsley Way GL4 118 D1
Lintern Cres BS30 11 B6
Lintham Dr BS15 10 F6
Linton Ct GL53 193 C1
Linton Rd HR9 170 B4
Linton's Wlk BS14 3 A7
Linwell Cl GL50 133 B5
Linworth Rd GL52 138 A3
Lion Cl GL2 117 F2
Lipson Rd GL51 132 E4
Lipson Villas GL51 132 E4
Lisburn Rd BS4 8 E1
Lisle Pl GL12 68 A7
Lismore Rd SN6 145 C4
Listers Pl GL14 191 C4
Litfield Pl BS8 7 F7
Litfield Rd BS8 7 F8
Lithgow Rd GL54 169 D6
Little Acorns GL52 137 E5
Little Acre GL12 68 A8
Little Ann St BS2,BS5 195 C4
Little Bayshill Terr
GL50 193 B3
Little Birch Croft BS14 3 A3
Little Bishop St BS2 195 B4
Little Bristol Cl GL12 67 B4
Little Bristol La GL12 67 B4
Little Caroline Pl 4 BS8 7 F5
Little Cleevemount
GL52 133 F3
Little Compton Jun & Inf Sch
GL56 177 F8
Little Dowles BS30 11 A4
Little Elmbridge GL2 127 E3
Little Field GL4 119 D7
Little Fishers GL5 99 A4
Little George St BS2 195 C4
Little Gn GL19 179 D2
Little Green La BS35 38 A7
Little Hayes BS16 20 B6
Little Headley Cl BS13 2 B7
Little Herbert's Cl GL53 131 B5
Little Herbert's Rd GL53 131 B4
Little Holbury GL2 100 E5
Little Horcott La GL7 152 E3
Little King St BS1 195 A2
Little Lancarridge GL2 125 D4
Little Marcle Court Rd
HR8 178 A7
Little Marcle Rd HR8 178 E8
Little Mdw BS34 30 A6
Little Mead BS11 27 B1
Little Normans GL2 127 C5
Little Oaks GL18 179 B4
Little Orch GL52 137 E4
Little Paradise BS3 8 D3
Little Parr Cl BS16 19 C5
Little Paul St BS2 194 C4
Little Pheasants GL53 131 A5
Little Quillet Ct GL11 87 F4
Little Rd WR11 188 B8
Little Rose La SN26 144 C3
Little Stoke La BS34 29 D6
Little Stoke Prim Sch
BS34 29 D6
Little Stoke Rd BS9 17 E4
Little Trewen La HR9 162 C5
Little Witcombe Ct GL3 121 C3
Little Withey Mead BS9 17 F5
Little Wlk GL2 127 C5
Littlecote Cl GL52 137 E3
Littlecross Ho BS3 8 B4
Littledean BS37 32 E7
Littledean CE Prim Sch
GL14 156 E8
Littledean Hall* GL14 156 E8
Littledean Hill Rd GL14 191 E4
Littledown Rd GL53 130 F4
Littlefield GL2 117 E2
Littleton Ct BS34 39 F1
Littleton Drew La GL9 36 A6
Littleton La BS41 1 C1
Littleton Rd BS3 8 D2
Littleton St 4 BS5 19 C1
Littlewood Cl BS14 3 B3
Littleworth GL55 188 F2
Livia Way GL15 92 B4
Livingstone Mews BS3 8 C3
Llanarth Villas 3 BS6 18 D1
Llandilo St 1 GL1 118 F7
Llandogo Prim Sch
NP25 146 B7
Llangarron Bsns Ctr
HR9 162 B7
Llangrove CE Prim Sch
HR9 162 B6
Llanthony Cotts GL20 136 B7
Llanthony Ind Est GL2 126 C1
Llanthony Rd GL2 126 C1
Llanthony Secunda Priory*
GL2 126 C1
Llanwrithy HR9 162 C5
Llewellyn Ct BS9 18 A8
Lloyd Baker Ct GL2 109 E7
Lloyd Cl GL51 132 D2
Lobb Ct 4 GL1 127 A1
Lobleys Dr GL4 120 A5
Lock Gdns BS13 1 E7
Lock's La BS37 41 E4
Lockemor Rd BS13 2 F4
Locking Hill 3 GL5 99 C7
Lockingwell Rd BS31 4 D5
Lockleaze Rd BS7 19 A6
Locombe Hill GL7 153 D8
Locombe Pl GL12 68 C6
Lodersfield GL7 153 E2
Lodge Causeway Trad Ctr
BS16 19 F3
Lodge Cswy BS16 20 A3
Lodge Ct BS9 17 E4
Lodge Dr Bristol BS30 11 C2
Long Ashton BS41 7 B2
Lodge Gdns GL15 146 E7
Lodge Hill BS15 20 C2
Lodge La GL15 147 D6
Lodge Park & Sherborne
Est* GL54 160 D7
Lodge Pl BS1 194 C3
Lodge Rd Bristol BS15 20 C1
Wick BS30 22 B1
Yate BS37 43 A3
Lodge St BS1 194 C3
Lodge Wlk BS16 20 D6
Lodgemore Cl GL5 99 A7
Lodgemore La GL5 99 A7
Lodgeside Ave BS15 20 C1
Lodgeside Gdns BS15 20 C1
Lodore Rd BS16 19 F3
Lodway BS20 16 C4
Lodway Cl BS20 16 C5
Lodway Gdns BS20 16 C4
Lodway Rd BS4 9 C2
Logan Rd BS7 18 D3
Logus Ct 14 BS30 10 F4
Loiterpin GL15 156 D2
Lombard St BS3 8 D4

Lomond Rd BS7 28 F1
Lon Cyn Farch/Kingsmark La NP16 72 D1
Lon Ffawyoden Uchel/High Beech La NP16 60 D6
Lon Leasbrook/Leasbrook La NP25 154 A8
London La SN16 142 E1
London Pl GL7 190 D4
London Rd
Brimscombe GL5,GL6 148 B5
Bristol,St Pauls BS2 18 F1
Bristol,Warmley BS30 11 D7
Charlton Kings GL52,GL53 131 C5
Cheltenham GL52 130 F8
Fairford GL7 152 F4
Gloucester GL1,GL2 127 A2
Moreton-in-M GL56 187 B3
Stroud GL5 99 C6
10 Tetbury GL8 140 C4
Thrupp GL5 99 E3
Wick BS30 12 E6
London Road Terr 6 GL56 187 B3
London St Bristol BS15 10 D8
Fairford GL7 152 E3
Londonderry Farm BS30 5 A8
Lone La NP25 154 C4
Long Acre Rd BS14 3 A3
Long Acres 5 HR8 178 E8
Long Acres Cl BS9 17 D7
Long Ashton Rd BS41 7 B2
Long Beach Rd BS30 11 B3
Long Cl
Bristol,Fishponds BS16 20 C6
Bristol,Little Stoke BS32 29 E6
Long Croft BS37 43 D4
Long Cross BS11 27 B2
Long Dr GL16 155 B6
Long Eaton Dr BS14 3 B7
Long Eights GL20 182 C5
Long Field GL2 125 D6
Long Fox Manor BS4 10 A1
Long Furlong GL52 137 F7
Long Furlong La GL8 140 B3
Long Handstones BS30 11 A4
Long Lease SN14 36 C1
Long Marston Rd CV37, GL55 189 A8
Long Mdw BS16 19 D6
Long Mead BS37 43 E5
Long Mynd Ave GL51 129 E6
Long Rd BS16 21 A5
Long Row Bristol BS1 195 B2
Castle Eaton SN6 144 D6
Long St Dursley GL11 88 B1
Tetbury GL8 140 B4
Wotton-u-E GL12 68 B7
Longaston Cl GL2 95 D4
Longaston La GL2 95 D5
Longborough CE Prim Sch GL56 176 D8
Longborough Dr GL4 119 E4
Longcross GL12 66 B1
Longden Rd BS16 20 F6
Longdon St Mary's CE Prim Sch GL20 180 F7
Longfield GL2 117 E2
Longfield Rd BS7 18 E3
Longford BS37 32 C8
Longford Ave BS10 18 D8
Longford Ct GL50 193 A1
Longford La GL2 127 A5
Longford Mews GL2 126 F6
Longhill Rd GL7 149 E8
Longhope Cl 3 GL4 119 E5
Longhope Rd GL19 165 C6
Longland Ct GL2 127 B4
Longland Gdns GL2 127 B4
Longlands Cl GL52 138 B4
Longlands Ho 18 BS5 9 C7
Longlands Rd GL52 138 B4
Longleat GL53 131 A5
Longleat Ave GL4 118 C1
Longleat Cl BS9 18 C5
Longlength La GL6 83 C8
Longlevens Inf Sch GL2 127 D4
Longlevens Jun Sch GL2 127 C4
Longmead Ave BS7 18 D5
Longmead Croft BS13 1 F4
Longmead Rd BS16 31 B1
Longmeadow Rd BS31 4 C4
Longmoor Ct BS3 8 A2
Longmoor Rd BS3 8 A2
Longmore Ave GL54 169 D6
Longney CE Prim Sch GL2 108 C5
Longney Pl BS34 39 F1
Longney Rd GL4 118 D3
Longreach Gr BS14 3 D6
Longridge La GL19 172 C3
Longs Dr BS37 43 C2
Longs View GL12 67 A5
Longsmith St GL1 196 B3
Longtown Rd GL20 192 E2
Longtree Cl GL8 140 B5
Longville Cl GL4 119 F5
Longway Ave
Bristol BS13,BS14 2 F4
Charlton Kings GL53 131 A4
Longwell Green Prim Sch BS30 10 F3
Longwell Ho BS30 10 F3
Longwood BS4 10 A2
Lonk The GL16 155 A7
Lons Ct BS30 11 C1
Lonsdale Bsns Ctr BS15 20 C2
Lonsdale Cl SN26 144 E1
Lonsdale Rd GL2 127 C2
Loop Rd NP16 61 B5
Lorain Wlk BS10 27 F2
Lord Eldon Dr NP16 60 F4
Lord's Hill GL16 155 A5
Lord's Hill Cl 5 GL16 155 A5
Lords Gate GL16 155 A5
Lords Gn GL52 138 C3
Loriners Cl GL2 117 F2
Lorton Cl BS10 28 B1
Lorton Rd BS10 28 B1
Lotts The 6 SN6 142 F5
Loughman Cl BS15 10 E8
Louisa St BS2 195 C2
Louise Ave BS16 21 A5
Lovage Cl GL3 127 F6
Love La
Chipping Sodbury BS37 33 A8
Cirencester GL7 190 D2
Yate BS37 44 A4
Love Lane Ind Est GL7 190 D2
Lovedays Mead GL5 99 C8
Lovell Ave BS30 11 D4
Lovell's Hill BS15 10 B5
Lovells The BS20 16 B4
Loveridge Ct BS36 31 B7
Loveringe Cl BS10 27 F4
Lovers Wlk HR9 170 B4
Lovett Cl GL19 172 A8
Lowbourne BS14 2 F6
Lowdilow La GL51 136 E1
Lower Ashley Rd
Bristol,Baptist Mills BS2, BS5 19 A1
13 Bristol,St Pauls BS2 18 F1
Lower Berrycroft GL13 85 E3
Lower Castle St BS1 195 B3
Lower Chapel La BS36 31 C7
Lower Chapel Rd BS15 10 C5
Lower Cheltenham Pl BS6 18 F1
Lower Church La BS2 195 A3
Lower Church St NP16 72 F1
Lower Churchfield Rd GL5 99 D6
Lower Clifton Hill BS8 194 B2
Lower Cock Rd BS15 10 F7
Lower College St BS1 194 C2
Lower Comm GL15 147 D5
Lower Conham Vale BS15 10 A5
Lower Court Rd BS32 40 A5
Lower Croft GL7 152 E4
Lower Cross GL16 154 F3
Lower Fallow Cl BS14 2 F3
Lower Farm Cotts GL7 151 C3
Lower Gay St BS2 195 A4
Lower Grove Rd BS16 19 F4
Lower Guinea St BS1 195 A1
Lower Hanham Rd BS15 10 C6
Lower High St
Bristol BS11 16 D7
Chipping Campden GL55 189 A2
Lower House Cres BS34 29 B4
Lower Kitesnest La GL6 103 A3
Lower Knole La BS10 28 A3
Lower Lamb St BS1 194 C2
Lower Leazes GL5 99 D7
Lower Lode La GL20 192 A2
Lower Maudlin St BS1 195 A3
Lower Mdw GL2 109 F7
Lower Mill St GL51 133 B3
Lower Moor Rd BS37 43 E4
Lower Newmarket Rd GL6 90 F4
Lower Park Row BS1 195 A3
Lower Park St 27 GL54 176 F4
Lower Poole Rd GL11 80 B8
Lower Quay St GL1 196 A3
Lower Rd Berry Hill GL16 155 A7
Ledbury HR8 178 E8
St Briavels GL15 146 E7
Upper Soudley GL14 156 C5
Yorkley GL15 156 A2
Lower Redland Mews 2 BS6 18 B2
Lower Redland Rd BS6 18 B2
Lower Road Trad Est HR8 178 E8
Lower Sidney St BS3 8 A4
Lower Spillman's GL5 99 A6
Lower St Blockley GL56 186 C5
Dyrham SN14 23 D4
Stroud GL5 99 D6
Whiteshill GL6 102 F3
Lower Station Rd
6 Bristol,Ridgeway BS16 20 A4
Bristol,Staple Hill BS16 20 C4
Lower Stone Cl BS36 31 C7
Lower Terr 7 GL56 186 C5
Lower Thirlmere Rd BS34 29 A8
Lower Tockington Rd BS32 50 B1
Lower Tuffley La GL2 118 B4
Lower Washwell La GL6 104 A8
Lower Wharf Ind Est GL5 99 B7
Lower Wyndcliff Nature Trail* NP16 72 D7
Lowerhouse La GL11 79 D5
Loweswater Cl GL51 129 F7
Loweswater Rd GL51 129 F7
Lowfield Rd GL8 140 B5
Lowlis Cl BS10 27 F3
Lowther Rd BS10 28 C2
Loxton Sq BS14 3 A6
Lucas Cl BS4 9 D1
Luccombe Hill BS6 18 B2
Lucinia Mews GL51 132 F3
Luckington Com Sch SN14 47 E5
Luckington Court Gdns* SN14 47 F5
Luckington Rd BS7 18 E8
Luckley Ave BS13 2 C5
Luckwell Prim Sch BS3 8 A3
Luckwell Rd BS3 8 B3
Lucky La BS3 8 D4
Lucy Ct GL16 163 B2
Ludgate Hill GL12 68 B7
Ludlow Cl
Bristol,St Pauls BS2 18 F1
Bristol,Willsbridge BS30 11 B2
Keynsham BS31 4 D5
Ludlow Ct BS30 11 B1
Ludlow Gn GL6 102 F3
Ludlow Rd BS7 19 A7
Ludwell Cl BS36 30 D5
Luggs The GL10 98 A3
Luke La GL3 127 E6
Lullington Rd BS4 9 B2
Lulsgate Rd BS13 2 A8
Lulworth Cres BS16 20 F8
Lulworth Rd BS31 4 E4
Lurgan Wlk BS4 8 D1
Lurks La GL6 103 B4
Lushill Cotts SN6 144 E5
Luther Challis Bsns Ctr The GL4 127 D2
Lutyens Cl BS16 19 E8
Lux Furlong BS9 17 B7
Luxton St BS5 9 B8
Lych Gate Mews GL15 92 A2
Lych Vale Cvn Pk GL13 85 D4
Lydbrook Cl BS37 32 D8
Lydbrook Prim Sch GL17 163 D2
Lyddington Rd BS7 18 F8
Lyde Green Rdbt BS16 21 B8
Lydfield Rd GL15 92 B3
Lydford Wlk BS3 8 C2
Lydiard Croft BS15 10 C4
Lydney & District Hospl GL15 147 F6
Lydney CE Com Sch GL15 92 A3
Lydney Ind Est GL15 84 C8
Lydney Junc Sta* GL15 92 A1
Lydney Park Gdns* GL15 147 E5
Lydney Rd Bream GL15 147 D8
Bristol,Southmead BS10 28 D1
Bristol,Staple Hill BS16 20 E4
Lydney Sta GL15 84 A8
Lydney Town Sta* GL15 92 A3
Lydstep Terr BS3 8 C4
Lye La GL52 138 D1
Lyefield Cl GL52 131 B6
Lyefield Rd E GL53 131 B6
Lyefield Rd W GL53 131 A6
Lygon Ct GL7 152 E3
Lygon Wlk 3 GL51 132 F3
Lyley Ho GL12 68 A7
Lynch Ct BS30 10 F4
Lynch Rd Berkeley GL13 85 D3
Chalford GL6 148 D6
Lynch Road Ind Est GL13 85 C3
Lyncombe Wlk BS16 20 B2
Lyncroft GL2 116 F7
Lyncroft Farm Wkshps GL7 150 C8
Lyndale Ave BS9 17 D5
Lyndale Rd Bristol BS5 9 D8
Yate BS37 43 D1
Lyndale Terr
Cheltenham GL51 133 A2
Norton GL2 173 B3
Lynde Cl BS13 2 B4
Lyndhurst Cl GL52 138 B3
Lyndhurst Gdns GL51 132 D3
Lyndhurst Rd Bristol BS9 17 F7
Keynsham BS31 4 F3
Lyndley Chase GL52 137 D4
Lyng Cl GL4 119 E8
Lynmouth Rd
3 Bristol BS2 19 A2
Gloucester GL3 119 F7
Lynn Rd BS16 19 D5
Lynt Farm Cotts SN6 145 D7
Lynt Rd SN6 145 D7
Lynton 3 BS15 11 A8
Lynton Pl 9 BS5 9 C8
Lynton Rd Bristol BS3 8 D2
Gloucester GL3 119 F7
Lynton Way BS16 30 B1
Lynwood Rd Bristol BS3 8 B2
Lydney GL15 92 A5
Lynworth Ct 5 GL52 134 A3
Lynworth Exchange 9 GL52 134 A3
Lynworth La GL20 181 F8
Lynworth Orch GL20 181 F8
Lynworth Pl GL52 134 A3
Lynworth Prim Sch GL52 134 B3
Lynworth Terr GL52 134 B4
Lyons Court Rd BS14 3 D7
Lypiatt Dr GL50 193 A2
Lypiatt La GL50 193 A2
Lypiatt Mews GL50 193 A2
Lypiatt Rd GL50 193 A2
Lypiatt St GL50 193 A1
Lypiatt View GL6 148 B6
Lyppiatt Rd BS5 9 D8
Lyppincourt Rd BS10 28 A3
Lysander Ct GL3 128 C5
Lysander Rd BS10,BS34 28 C6
Lysander Wlk BS34 29 E5
Lysons Ave GL1 118 D7
Lytchet Dr BS16 20 F8
Lytes Cary Rd BS31 5 A3
Lytham Ho BS4 9 D1
Lytton Gr Bristol BS7 19 A8
Keynsham BS31 5 A5
Lyveden Gdns BS13 2 B5
Lyvedon Way BS41 7 B1

M

Mabberley Cl BS16 21 C5
Mabel's Furlong 12 HR8 178 F8
Macaroni Wood GL7 153 A7
Macarthur Rd GL54 168 A1
Macauley Rd BS7 19 A8
Macdonald Wlk 3 BS15 10 D8
Macey's Rd BS13 2 D3
Machen Rd GL16 155 B6
Machin Cl BS10 27 F3
Machin Gdns BS10 28 A3
Machin Rd BS10 28 A3
Machine Ct 1 GL20 192 C4
MacKenzie Way GL51 133 A5
Mackie Ave BS34 29 B2
Mackie Gr BS34 29 B2
Mackie Rd BS34 29 B2
Macrae Ct BS15 10 E8
Macrae Rd BS20 16 E4
Madeline Rd BS16 19 F2
Madison Cl BS37 43 D2
Madleaze Ind Est GL1 196 A1
Madleaze Rd GL1 196 A1
Madocke Rd NP16 61 A7
Maesbury BS15 10 E6
Maesbury Rd BS31 5 A2
Maesknoll La BS14 3 B1
Maesknoll Rd BS4 9 A2
Magdala Rd 1 GL1 127 A1
Magdalana Ct BS1 195 B1
Magdalen Rd GL8 140 B4
Magdalene Pl BS2 18 F1
Maggs Cl BS10 28 C3
Maggs La Bristol BS5 19 E2
Whitchurch BS14 3 C4
Magnolia Cl NP16 60 F5
Magnolia Ct 1 GL51 132 D2
Magnolia Wlk GL2 117 E1
Magpie Bottom La
Bristol BS15 10 C6
Bristol BS5 10 B6
Magpie Ct GL10 97 F8
Maida Vale Rd GL53 130 D6
Maiden Way BS11 16 C8
Maidencroft GL7 144 F7
Maidenhall GL2 125 D5
Maidenhead Rd BS13 2 D3
Maidenhill Sch GL10 101 F1
Maidstone St BS3 8 F3
Main Rd Bristol BS16 21 D5
Mile End GL16 155 B6
Pillowell GL15 155 F1
Tintern Parva NP16 146 B3
Whiteshill GL6 102 F3
Woolaston,Alvington GL15 147 D3
Woolaston,Brookend GL15 147 C2
Main St Adlestrop GL56 177 E6
Beckford GL20 183 B6
Bledington OX7 177 E1
Bretforton WR11 188 A6
Willersey WR12 188 B2
Main View BS36 31 D7
Mainard Sq GL2 127 C5
Maine St GL7 152 E2
Maisemore BS37 32 E6
Maisemore Ave BS34 40 B1
Maitlands GL4 110 F5
Makin Cl BS30 11 C5
Malago Rd BS3 8 D3
Malago Vale Est BS3 8 D3
Malago Wlk BS13 1 E4
Malden Mead BS14 3 A5
Malden Rd GL52 133 E3
Maldon Gdns GL1 118 F7
Maldowers La 2 BS5 10 A8
Malet Cl GL2 127 C5
Mall The Bristol,Clifton BS8 7 F7
Bristol,Cribbs Causeway BS34 28 D6
Mallard Cl Bristol BS32 40 D2
Bristol,Crofts End BS5 19 F1
Cheltenham GL51 132 E5
Chipping Sodbury BS37 33 A8
1 Quedgeley GL2 117 D1
Malleson Rd GL52 137 F8
Mallow Cl BS35 64 D2
Malmains Dr BS16 30 B1
Malmesbury Cl
Bristol,Bishopston BS6 18 C4
Bristol,Longwell Green BS30 10 F5
Malmesbury Rd
Cheltenham GL51 133 A5
Gloucester GL4 119 B7
Leigh SN6 143 C3
Malmsey Cl GL20 192 D1
Malt House Cl GL15 147 D3
Malthouse Cl SN26 144 E1
Malthouse La
Cheltenham GL50 133 D3
Lower Slaughter GL54 176 C1
17 Winchcombe GL54 174 A7
Malthouse Wlk 9 GL8 140 B4
Maltings The GL17 163 E4
Malvern Ct BS5 9 F7
Malvern Dr Bristol BS30 11 C5
Thornbury BS35 51 D8
Malvern Gdns GL5 98 E7
Malvern Pl GL50 193 A3
Malvern Rd
Bristol,Crew's Hole BS5 9 F7
Bristol,Kensington Park BS4 9 D3
Cheltenham GL50 133 B1
Corse GL19 172 B8
Gloucester GL1 126 F4
Malvern St GL51 133 B4
Malvern View Bsns Pk GL52 137 C4
Malvern Way GL16 155 C8
Malverns The GL4 119 D6
Manchester Ct 4 GL56 187 A3
Manchester Pk GL51 133 B4
Manchester Way 1 GL50 193 A4
Mancroft Ave BS11 16 F7
Mandalay Dr GL2 173 B3
Mandara Gr GL4 119 D4
Mandarin Way GL50 133 C5
Mandeville Cl GL2 127 C6
Mangotsfield CE Prim Sch BS16 21 B6
Mangotsfield Rd BS16 21 A5
Mangotsfield Sch BS16 21 B4
Manilla Rd BS8 194 A3
Mankley Rd GL10 97 F4
Manley Gdns GL2 127 C5
Mannings Rd GL17 164 B4
Manor Ave Dursley GL11 87 F5
Lechlade on T GL7 153 F2
Manor Barn GL53 122 C6
Manor Cl
Broad Blunsdon SN26 144 E1
Coalpit Heath BS36 31 C6
Dursley GL11 87 F6
Easton-in-G BS20 16 A4
8 Fairford GL7 152 E4
Honeybourne WR11 188 C6
Minchinhampton GL6 91 F6
Sherston SN16 58 C1
Stratton GL7 150 C7
Teddington GL20 183 A3
Tockington BS32 50 C1
Manor Cl The BS8 7 A8
Manor Coalpit Heath Prim Sch The BS36 31 D6
Manor Cott SN16 141 B4
Manor Cotts Pitt Ct GL11 79 F5
Sopworth SN14 57 D1
Manor Court Dr BS7 18 E7
Manor Ct
Bristol,Fishponds BS16 19 E4
9 Bristol,Upper Easton BS5 19 B1
15 Fairford GL7 152 E4
Gloucester GL4 119 B4
Lydney GL15 92 C3
Swindon GL51 133 A6
Whitminster GL2 100 F5
Manor Dr GL5 99 A1
Manor Farm Bristol BS32 29 D8
Little Rissington GL54 169 C6
Manor Farm Barns GL54 166 D6
Manor Farm Cl OX7 177 F3
Manor Farm Cotts GL8 141 A6
Manor Farm Cres BS32 40 D1
Manor Fields GL54 183 F1
Manor Gardens Ho BS16 19 F5
Manor Gdns
Gloucester GL4 119 E8
Lechlade on T GL7 153 E2
Newnham GL14 156 F6
Woodchester GL5 99 A2
Manor Gr Bristol BS34 40 B2
Bristol,Mangotsfield BS16 21 A4
Manor Ho 6 Bristol BS5 19 B1
Bristol,Kingsdown BS2 194 C3
Manor La
Bretforton WR11 188 A6
Charfield GL12 67 A4
Gotherington GL52 138 B7
Winterbourne BS36 30 F7
Wotton-u-E GL12 68 C7
Manor Orch SN6 143 F4
Manor Park Bsns Ctr GL51 133 A5
Manor Pk Bristol BS6 18 B3
Cheltenham GL51 129 D5
Gloucester GL2 127 E4
Tewkesbury GL20 192 E6
Tockington BS32 50 C1
Manor Pl
Bristol,Frenchay BS16 30 C1
Bristol,Stoke Gifford BS34 30 A4
Tewkesbury GL20 192 D1
Manor Rd Abbots Leigh BS8 7 A8
Bristol,Bishopston BS7 18 E4
Bristol,Bishopsworth BS13 2 A6
Bristol,Fishponds BS16 20 A5
Bristol,Mangotsfield BS16 21 A4
Cheltenham GL51 133 A6
Lydney GL15 92 C3
Rangeworthy BS37 43 A7
Saltford BS31 5 C2
Wick BS30 12 C5
Manor St GL6 105 A1
Manor The
Churchdown GL3 128 C4

Manor The *continued*
4 Newnham GL14 ... 157 A6
Manor View
St Arvans NP16 ... 72 B5
Stroud GL5 ... 98 E4
Manor Way BS37 ... 44 C2
Manor Wlk BS35 ... 64 B3
Manor Wood Forest Trail★ NP25 ... 146 B8
Manor Wood/Coed Maenor NP16 ... 60 C8
Manorbrook Prim Sch BS35 ... 64 C2
Manse Gdns 4 GL51 ... 129 F7
Manse La The HR9 ... 170 B5
Manse Rd GL17 ... 164 B4
Mansel Cl BS31 ... 5 C3
Mansell Cl GL2 ... 118 C5
Manser St GL50 ... 133 D3
Mansfield Mews GL2 ... 109 F7
Mansfield St BS3 ... 8 C2
Manson's La NP25 ... 162 A1
Manston Cl BS14 ... 3 C7
Manworthy Rd BS4 ... 9 D3
Manx Rd BS7 ... 18 F8
Maple Ave Bristol BS16 ... 20 C3
Chepstow/Cas-Gwent NP16 60 E5
Thornbury BS35 ... 64 C1
Maple Cl
Bristol,Little Stoke BS34 ... 29 C7
Bristol,Oldland BS30 ... 11 B4
Bristol,Stockwood BS14 ... 3 D5
Dursley GL11 ... 88 A3
Hardwicke GL2 ... 109 E8
Maple Ct Bristol BS9 ... 17 F8
Gloucester GL2 ... 127 E4
5 Bristol BS15 ... 20 D1
Maple Dr
Brockworth GL3 ... 120 D7
Charlton Kings GL53 ... 131 B5
Stroud GL5 ... 103 A1
Maple Ho BS2 ... 195 A4
Maple Leaf Ct BS8 ... 194 A3
Maple Rd
Bristol,Horfield BS7 ... 18 E5
Bristol,St Anne's BS4 ... 9 D5
Maple Wlk Keynsham BS31 .4 D4
Pucklechurch BS16 ... 22 C5
Mapledean GL14 ... 191 C5
Maplefield GL15 ... 147 E5
Mapleleaze BS4 ... 9 D3
Maplemeade BS7 ... 18 C4
Mapleridge La BS37 ... 44 D7
Maples The
Cirencester GL7 ... 190 B1
Gloucester GL4 ... 119 E6
Maplestone Rd BS14 ... 3 A3
Mapstone Cl BS16 ... 30 B3
Marbeck Rd BS10 ... 28 B1
Marchant Cl GL51 ... 132 F3
Mardale Cl BS10 ... 28 C2
Marden Rd BS31 ... 5 A4
Mardon Rd BS4 ... 9 D6
Mardyke Ferry Rd BS1 . 194 B1
Marefield Cl GL4 ... 119 E7
Marfells Way GL17 ... 163 F3
Margaret Rd Bristol BS13 ... 1 F4
3 Ledbury HR8 ... 178 E8
Tewkesbury GL20 ... 192 D3
Margate St BS3 ... 8 F3
Margery La GL15 ... 154 F2
Margrett Rd GL50 ... 133 D3
Marguerite Rd BS13 ... 1 F7
Marian Ct GL1 ... 196 A3
Marian La GL16 ... 155 A7
Marians Wlk GL16 ... 155 A7
Marigold Wlk BS3 ... 8 A2
Marina Gdns BS16 ... 19 E3
Marina The GL15 ... 84 B8
Marine Gdns GL16 ... 155 A5
Marine Par BS20 ... 16 C5
Mariner's Way BS20 ... 16 C5
Mariners Dr BS9 ... 17 D4
Mariners Reach NP16 ... 61 A4
Mariners' Path BS9 ... 17 E3
Marion Rd BS15 ... 10 B3
Marion Wlk BS5 ... 10 A7
Marissal Cl BS10 ... 27 E3
Marissal Rd BS10 ... 27 E3
Mariston Way BS30 ... 11 C6
Marjoram Cl 2 GL4 ... 119 F5
Marjoram Pl BS32 ... 29 F7
Mark La BS1 ... 194 C2
Market Cl GL54 ... 168 F8
Market Gate BS1 ... 195 C3
Market La GL54 ... 184 A1
Market Par GL1 ... 196 B3
Market Pl Berkeley GL13 ... 85 E3
Cirencester GL7 ... 190 C5
Coleford GL16 ... 155 A5
Dursley GL11 ... 88 B1
11 Fairford GL7 ... 152 E4
Lechlade on T GL7 ... 153 E2
Marshfield SN14 ... 15 A8
14 Tetbury GL8 ... 140 C4
Market Sq Bristol BS16 ... 20 C3
Minchinhampton GL6 ... 148 A3
14 Newent GL18 ... 171 A4
Stow-on-t-W GL54 ... 176 F4
Market St
Cheltenham GL50 ... 193 A4
Cinderford GL14 ... 191 D5
Ledbury HR8 ... 178 E8
Nailsworth GL6 ... 91 B3
Wotton-u-E GL12 ... 68 B7
Market Way GL1 ... 196 B2
Marketside BS2 ... 9 B4
Marklands BS9 ... 17 E3
Marksbury Rd BS3 ... 8 D2
Marlborough Ave 13 BS16 ... 19 E3
Marlborough Cl
Bishop's Cleeve GL52 ... 137 E3
Cheltenham GL53 ... 130 F6
Marlborough Cres GL4 . 119 A7
Marlborough Dr BS16 ... 30 B1
Marlborough Flats 8 BS2 ... 195 A4
Marlborough Hill BS2 ... 195 A4
Marlborough Hill Pl BS2 ... 195 A4
Marlborough Ho BS2 ... 195 A4
Marlborough Pl GL52 ... 133 F1
Marlborough Rd GL4 ... 119 A7
Marlborough St
Bristol,Eastville BS5 ... 19 E3
Bristol,Kingsdown BS2 ... 195 A4
Marle Hill GL6 ... 148 C5
Marle Hill Par GL50 ... 133 D3
Marle Hill Rd GL50 ... 133 D3
Marle Rise GL52 ... 133 E4
Marlepit Gr BS13 ... 1 F6
Marley La GL6 ... 148 D5
Marleyfield Cl 3 GL3 ... 128 A7
Marleyfield Way GL3 ... 128 A7
Marlfield Wlk BS13 ... 1 E7
Marling Cl GL5 ... 91 C8
Marling Cres GL5 ... 98 F7
Marling Rd BS5 ... 9 F8
Marling Sch GL5 ... 98 F7
Marlstone Rd GL11 ... 88 A4
Marlwood Dr BS10 ... 28 A3
Marlwood Sch BS32 ... 50 F5
Marmaduke St BS3 ... 8 F3
Marment Rd GL11 ... 87 E4
Marmion Cres BS10 ... 27 F3
Marne Cl BS14 ... 3 D5
Marram Cl GL4 ... 119 F5
Marsh Cl
Cheltenham GL51 ... 133 C3
Winterbourne BS36 ... 30 E5
Marsh Common Rd BS35 38 E3
Marsh Ct 1 GL56 ... 187 A3
Marsh Dr GL51 ... 133 C4
Marsh Gdns GL51 ... 133 C3
Marsh La
Bristol,Ashton Vale BS3 ... 8 B2
Bristol,Barton Hill BS5 ... 9 C6
Burton SN14,GL9 ... 36 C4
Cheltenham GL51 ... 133 C3
Easton-in-G BS20 ... 16 A4
Frampton on Severn GL2 ... 157 F1
Leonard Stanley GL10 ... 97 F3
Marsh Mews GL10 ... 97 F4
Marsh Rd Bristol BS3 ... 7 F3
Chepstow/Cas-Gwent NP16 60 F5
Leonard Stanley GL10 ... 97 E4
Marsh St Avonmouth BS11 .16 C8
4 Bristol BS1 ... 195 A2
Marsh Terr GL51 ... 129 D2
Marsh Way GL16 ... 155 B2
Marshacre La BS35 ... 49 F6
Marshall Ho 1 BS16 ... 19 F4
Marshall Wlk BS4 ... 2 D7
Marshall's La GL14 ... 191 D5
Marsham Way BS30 ... 10 F4
Marshfield CE Prim Sch SN14 ... 15 B8
Marshfield La BS30 ... 12 D1
Marshfield Pk BS16 ... 20 C8
Marshfield Rd
Bristol,Frenchay BS16 ... 20 C8
Bristol,Hillfields BS16 ... 20 C4
Tormarton GL9 ... 34 E1
Marshmouth La GL54 ... 169 A6
Marshwall La BS32 ... 39 E6
Marsland Rd GL51 ... 132 D2
Marston Hill GL7 ... 152 C2
Marston Rd Bristol BS4 ... 9 B3
Cheltenham GL52 ... 133 F4
Martcombe Rd BS20 ... 16 C2
Marten Cl GL4 ... 120 A5
Marten Rd NP16 ... 60 E6
Martha's Orch BS13 ... 1 E7
Martin Cl Bristol BS34 ... 28 E8
Cirencester GL7 ... 190 C3
Martin Ct 12 BS16 ... 19 E3
Martin St 2 BS3 ... 8 B3
Martin's Rd BS15 ... 10 C5
Martindale Rd GL3 ... 128 B6
Martingale Rd BS4 ... 9 D4
Martins Cl BS15 ... 10 C5
Martins The Stroud GL5 ... 98 D8
Tutshill NP16 ... 73 A1
Martins Way HR8 ... 178 E7
Martlock Cres BS3 ... 8 C1
Martock Cres BS3 ... 8 C1
Martock Rd Bristol BS3 ... 8 C2
Keynsham BS31 ... 5 A3
Martor Ind Est SN14 ... 25 A2
Marwood Rd BS4 ... 2 E8
Mary Carpenter Pl 15 BS2 ... 18 F1
Mary Ct BS5 ... 9 D8
Mary Godwin Ct GL51 ... 132 F4
Mary Gr GL2 ... 125 D5
Mary Rose Ave GL3 ... 127 F7
Mary St BS5 ... 9 D8
Mary's La GL16 ... 154 F6
Marybrook St GL13 ... 85 E3
Marybush La BS2 ... 195 B3
Marygold Leaze BS30 ... 11 A4
Mascot Rd BS3 ... 8 D3
Masefield Ave GL2 ... 118 C4
Masefield Cl 8 HR8 ... 178 E8
Masefield Rd GL7 ... 190 B2
Masefield Way BS7 ... 19 A6
Maskelyne Ave BS10 ... 18 D7
Mason Ct GL13 ... 85 E3
Mason Rd GL5 ... 99 F7
Masons View BS36 ... 30 F7
Massey Par 5 GL1 ... 118 F7
Massey Rd GL1 ... 119 A7
Massey Sham Ave GL56 187 C3
Matchells Cl BS4 ... 9 E6
Materman Rd BS14 ... 3 E5
Matford Cl Bristol BS10 ... 28 D4
Winterbourne BS36 ... 30 E5
Matford La GL13 ... 77 F4
Mathern Cres NP16 ... 60 B4
Mathern Rd/Heol Merthyr Tewdrig NP16 ... 60 D5
Mathern Way NP16 ... 60 E5
Mathews Way GL5 ... 99 A8
Matson Ave GL4 ... 119 C3
Matson La GL4 ... 119 B3
Matson Lodge 13 GL4 ... 119 C4
Matson Pl GL1 ... 119 A7
Matthew Ho BS1 ... 195 A3
Matthew's Rd 17 BS5 ... 9 C7
Matthews Cl BS14 ... 3 F6
Maud's Elm Ho GL51 ... 133 B4
Maugersbury Cl GL54 ... 176 F4
Maugersbury Pk GL54 ... 176 F4
Maules La BS16 ... 29 F2
Maunsell Rd BS11 ... 27 B2
Maurice Rd BS6 ... 18 E2
Mautravers Cl BS32 ... 29 D7
Maverdine Ct GL1 ... 196 A3
Mawdeley Ho 11 BS3 ... 8 C4
Mawley Rd GL7 ... 152 D7
Maxse Rd BS4 ... 9 B2
Maxstone Cl GL20 ... 192 E2
May Bush La HR9 ... 162 E2
May Evans Cl GL11 ... 87 F5
May Gr GL12 ... 67 B5
May La Dursley GL11 ... 88 A1
Ebrington GL55 ... 189 D2
May Meadow La GL17 ... 164 D5
May Park Prim Sch BS5 . 19 C2
May St BS15 ... 20 C1
May Tree Cl GL7 ... 149 E3
May Tree Sq GL4 ... 119 C7
May Tree Wlk BS31 ... 4 C3
May Trees GL50 ... 193 A2
May's Cres 6 GL54 ... 168 A1
Mayall Ct GL4 ... 119 C3
Mayalls Cl GL19 ... 172 F7
Mayalls The GL20 ... 182 A7
Maybank Rd BS37 ... 43 D1
Maybec Gdns BS5 ... 10 A6
Maybourne BS4 ... 10 A2
Maycliffe Pk BS6 ... 18 F2
Mayfair Cl GL2 ... 118 C8
Mayfield Ave BS16 ... 20 A2
Mayfield Cl GL52 ... 137 F2
Mayfield Ct BS16 ... 20 A3
Mayfield Dr GL3 ... 119 F8
Mayfield Ho 8 GL50 ... 130 B8
Mayfield Pk BS16 ... 20 A2
Mayfield Pk (Mobile Home Ctr) GL7 ... 150 C8
Mayfield Pk N BS16 ... 20 A2
Mayfield Pk S BS16 ... 20 A2
Mayfields BS31 ... 4 E5
Mayhill Ind Est 24 NP25 154 A7
Mayhill Way GL1 ... 127 A2
Maynard Cl BS13 ... 2 C5
Maynard Rd BS13 ... 2 C5
Mayors Bldgs BS16 ... 20 B5
Maypole Cl GL9 ... 56 A2
Maypole Ct 1 BS15 ... 10 B5
Maypole Gn 3 GL15 ... 147 D8
Maypole Rd GL15 ... 147 D8
Maypole Terr GL5 ... 98 F8
Mays Cl BS36 ... 31 D7
Mays La GL8 ... 140 B8
Maythorn Dr GL51 ... 132 D4
Maytree Ave BS13 ... 2 B7
Maytree Cl BS13 ... 2 B7
Maytrees BS5 ... 19 C2
Mayville Ave BS34 ... 29 A3
Maywood Ave 3 BS16 ... 20 B4
Maywood Cres BS16 ... 20 B4
Maywood Rd BS16 ... 20 C4
Maze St BS5 ... 9 B6
Maze Wlk GL16 ... 155 A7
McAdam Way BS1 ... 7 F5
McLaren Rd BS11 ... 26 B1
Mead Cl Bristol BS11 ... 16 E6
Cheltenham GL53 ... 130 E5
22 Moreton-in-M GL56 ... 187 A3
Mead Ct Bsns Pk BS35 ... 51 B8
Mead La Aylburton GL15 . 147 F4
Ingst BS35 ... 49 D2
Lydney GL15 ... 84 A8
Saltford BS31 ... 5 F4
Mead Lane Ind Est GL15 147 F4
Mead Rd Bristol BS34 ... 29 F5
Cheltenham GL53 ... 130 E5
Chipping Sodbury BS37 ... 44 C1
Gloucester GL4 ... 119 E5
Mead Rise BS3 ... 8 F4
Mead St BS3 ... 195 C1
Mead The Alveston BS35 ... 51 A5
3 Ashton Keynes SN6 ... 142 F4
Bristol BS34 ... 29 B4
Cirencester GL7 ... 190 B5
Dundry BS41 ... 1 D2
Mead Way BS35 ... 51 B7
Meade-King Gr GL52 ... 138 B3
Meadgate BS16 ... 21 B7
Meadow Cl Bristol BS16 ... 20 F7
Cheltenham GL51 ... 132 C1
Cirencester GL7 ... 190 C3
Tewkesbury GL20 ... 192 E6
Viney Hill GL15 ... 156 C1
Meadow Cotts WR12 ... 184 F6
Meadow Court Dr BS30 ... 11 C3
Meadow Ct 2 GL10 ... 97 F8
Meadow Gr BS11 ... 16 D7
Meadow La 9 GL51 ... 129 E5
Meadow La W GL5 ... 98 E6
Meadow Lea GL52 ... 137 E2
Meadow Mead
Frampton Cotterell BS36 ... 31 B8
Yate BS37 ... 43 E5
Meadow Orch 4 WR12 . 185 B8
Meadow Rd
Chipping Sodbury BS37 ... 44 A1
Cinderford GL14 ... 191 E5
Cirencester GL7 ... 190 C3
Honeybourne WR11 ... 188 A8
Leyhill GL12 ... 66 B4
Stonehouse GL10 ... 97 F8
Meadow Rise GL17 ... 164 F6
Meadow St
Avonmouth BS11 ... 26 A1
Bristol BS2 ... 195 C4
Meadow Vale Bristol BS5 . 20 A1
Dursley GL11 ... 87 F4
Meadow View
Baunton GL7 ... 150 D7
Frampton Cotterell BS36 ... 31 D7
Kempsford GL7 ... 144 E8
Meadow Way Bristol BS32 29 E7
Churchdown GL3 ... 128 B7
Kingham OX7 ... 177 F2
South Cerney GL7 ... 142 F8
Stroud GL5 ... 98 E6
Meadow Wlk
Chepstow/Cas-Gwent NP16 60 D8
Sling GL16 ... 155 B2
Meadoway GL52 ... 137 E2
Meadowbank GL15 ... 92 C3
Meadowbrook Prim Sch BS32 ... 29 E8
Meadowcroft Bristol BS16 21 A8
Gloucester GL4 ... 119 E5
Meadowland Rd BS10 ... 27 E4
Meadowleaze GL2 ... 127 D3
Meadows End GL17 ... 164 F6
Meadows Prim Sch The BS30 ... 5 D8
Meadows The
Bristol BS15 ... 10 D4
Luckington SN14 ... 47 F4
Minety SN16 ... 142 D1
Meadowside 2 BS35 ... 51 D8
Meadowside Dr BS14 ... 3 A3
Meadowside Prim Sch GL2 ... 117 F2
Meadowsweet Ave BS34 . 29 B3
Meadowview Cotts GL6 148 C5
Meads Cl
Bishop's Cleeve GL52 ... 138 A3
4 Coleford GL16 ... 155 A6
Meads Ct NP16 ... 60 E6
Meads The Bristol BS16 ... 20 F7
Burton SN14 ... 36 B3
Leighterton GL8 ... 70 C3
Meadvale Cl GL2 ... 126 F6
Meadway BS9 ... 17 C6
Meadway Rd GL10 ... 97 E6
Meardon Rd BS14 ... 3 E6
Mechanical Organ Mus★ GL17 ... 164 B5
Mede Cl BS1 ... 195 B1
Media Ho BS8 ... 194 B3
Medical Ave BS2,BS8 ... 194 C3
Medina Cl BS35 ... 51 C7
Medoc Cl GL50 ... 133 C5
Medway Cl BS31 ... 5 A3
Medway Cres GL3 ... 120 F5
Medway Ct
Cheltenham GL52 ... 134 A2
Thornbury BS35 ... 51 D8
Medway Dr
Frampton Cotterell BS36 ... 31 B7
Keynsham BS31 ... 5 A3
Meeks Hill NP25 ... 154 B1
Meeks Well La HR9 ... 162 E3
Meend Gardens Terr GL14 ... 191 D3
Meend La GL17 ... 163 F4
Meendhurst Rd GL14 ... 191 C4
Meerbrook Way GL2 ... 109 F7
Meere Bank BS11 ... 27 B1
Meerstone Way GL4 ... 119 D3
Meg Thatcher's Gdns BS5 ... 10 B7
Meg Thatchers Gn BS5 ... 10 B7
Melbourne Cl
Cheltenham GL53 ... 130 C6
Stonehouse GL10 ... 101 F1
Melbourne Dr
Chipping Sodbury BS37 ... 44 C1
Stonehouse GL10 ... 101 E1
Melbourne Rd BS7 ... 18 D4
Melbourne St E
Gloucester GL1 ... 118 F7
Gloucester GL1 ... 119 A7
Melbourne St W GL1 ... 118 F7
Melbury Rd BS4 ... 9 A2
Meldon Terr GL5 ... 99 B7
Melick Cl GL4 ... 119 A5
Melita Rd BS6 ... 18 E3
Mellent Ave BS13 ... 2 C3
Mellersh Ho GL50 ... 193 A1
Mells Cl BS31 ... 5 A2
Melmore Gdns GL7 ... 190 E2
Melody Way GL2 ... 127 E5
Melrose Ave Bristol BS8 . 194 B4
Yate BS37 ... 44 A2
Melrose Cl BS37 ... 44 A2
Melrose Pl BS8 ... 194 B4
Melton Cres BS7 ... 19 A7
Melville GL54 ... 168 F8
Melville Rd Bristol BS6 ... 18 B1
Churchdown GL3 ... 128 B5
Melville Terr BS3 ... 8 C3
Melvin Sq BS4 ... 8 E1
Memorial Cl BS15 ... 10 B4
Memorial Cotts
Coln St Aldwyns GL7 ... 152 D8
Tetbury GL8 ... 140 A2
Memorial Rd BS15 ... 10 B4
Memorial Stadium (Bristol Rovers FC)★ BS7 ... 18 F6
Mendip Cl
Cheltenham GL52 ... 134 A3
Keynsham BS31 ... 4 D5
Quedgeley GL2 ... 109 E8
Mendip Cres BS16 ... 21 A8
Mendip Ho 7 GL52 ... 134 A3
Mendip Rd Bristol BS3 ... 8 D3
Cheltenham GL52 ... 134 A3
Mendip View BS30 ... 12 C7
Mendip View Ave BS16 ... 20 A3
Menhyr Gr BS10 ... 28 B3
Meon Rd GL55 ... 189 B7
Mercer Ct BS14 ... 3 B8
Merchant St BS1 ... 195 B3
Merchants Almshouses 5 BS1 ... 195 A2
Merchants Ct BS8 ... 194 A1
Merchants Mead 5 GL2 ... 117 D1
Merchants Quay BS1 ... 195 A1
Merchants Rd
Bristol,Hotwells BS8 ... 194 A1
Bristol,Victoria Park BS8 ... 194 A3
Merchants Row BS1 ... 194 C1
Merchants The SN14 ... 47 E4
Merchants Trad Pk BS2 ... 9 C6
Merchants' Rd GL2 ... 196 A2
Mercia Dr BS2 ... 19 A2
Mercia Rd
Gloucester GL1 ... 196 B4
Winchcombe GL54 ... 139 F6
Mercian Cl GL7 ... 190 D3
Mercian Ct GL50 ... 193 A1
Mercian Way NP16 ... 61 A7
Mercier Cl BS37 ... 43 F2
Mercury Way GL4 ... 119 F6
Meredith Ct BS1 ... 194 A1
Meredith Ind Est GL17 . 163 C3
Merestones Cl GL50 ... 130 B6
Merestones Dr GL50 ... 130 B6
Merestones Rd GL50 ... 130 B6
Merevale Rd GL2 ... 127 C3
Merfield Rd BS4 ... 9 B2
Meridian Pl BS8 ... 194 B3
Meridian Rd BS6 ... 18 C1
Meridian Vale BS8 ... 194 B3
Meriet Ave BS13 ... 2 B4
Merioneth St BS3 ... 8 F3
Meriton St BS2 ... 9 B5
Merlin Cl Bristol BS9 ... 17 F8
Cheltenham GL53 ... 130 C5
Merlin Ct BS10 ... 18 B7
Merlin Dr GL2 ... 117 F2
Merlin Haven GL12 ... 68 A7
Merlin Rd BS10,BS34 ... 28 C6
Merlin Ridge BS16 ... 22 C4
Merlin Way
Cheltenham GL53 ... 130 C5
Chipping Sodbury BS37 ... 32 F8
Merret Cl GL20 ... 182 C5
Merrett Ct BS7 ... 19 B6
Merrett's Orch GL2 ... 95 D3
Merrick Ct BS1 ... 195 A1
Merricks La NP16 ... 146 D4
Merrimans Rd BS11 ... 16 D8
Merrin St GL17 ... 164 D5
Merriville Gdns GL51 ... 133 A3
Merriville Rd GL51 ... 133 A3
Merryfields GL10 ... 110 B1
Merrywalks GL5 ... 99 B7
Merrywalks Sh Ctr 1 GL5 ... 99 C7
Merryweather Cl BS32 ... 29 D8
Merryweathers BS4 ... 9 E2
Merrywood Cl 5 BS3 ... 8 C4
Merrywood Ct BS4 ... 9 B2
Merrywood Rd BS3 ... 8 C4
Mersey Rd GL52 ... 134 A2
Merstham Rd 12 BS2 ... 19 A2
Merthyr Terr GL17 ... 163 D2
Merton Cl GL10 ... 98 B6
Merton Cotts GL6 ... 90 F3
Merton Rd BS7 ... 18 E5
Mertons The GL14 ... 156 F6
Mervyn Rd BS7 ... 18 E4
Meryl Ct BS6 ... 18 B1
Meteor Way GL3 ... 120 E5
Metford Gr BS6 ... 18 B3
Metford Pl BS6 ... 18 C3
Metford Rd BS6 ... 18 C3
Metropolitan The BS1 ... 195 B1
Metz Way GL1,GL4 ... 119 B8
Mews Enterprise Workshops GL17 ... 164 D5
Mews The
Highworth SN6 ... 145 D3
6 Tewkesbury GL20 ... 192 C4
Meysey Cl GL7 ... 152 B3

Meysey Hampton CE Prim Sch GL7 .....152 A3
Michaelmas Ct GL1 .....127 A3
Michaels Mead GL7 .....190 B2
Michaels Way GL16 .....155 B2
Mickle Mead
Gloucester GL4 .....119 E6
Highnam GL2 .....125 D5
Mickleton Rd
Honeybourne WR11 .....188 D7
Ilmington CV36 .....189 F7
Middi Haines Ct SN6 .....145 D3
Middle Ave BS1 .....195 A2
Middle Croft GL4 .....119 D7
Middle Farm Ct GL7 .....144 E8
Middle Ground SN6 .....143 E4
Middle Hill Chalford GL6 .148 C6
Stroud GL5 .....99 E7
Middle Hill Cres GL6 .....148 C6
Middle Leazes GL5 .....99 D7
Middle Orch OX7 .....177 E1
Middle Rd Bristol BS15 .....20 F3
Little Barrington OX18 .....161 D7
Thrupp GL5 .....99 E3
Middle Spillman's GL5 .....99 A6
Middle Spring GL6 .....102 F3
Middle St
7 Chepstow/Cas-Gwent NP16 .....60 E8
Stroud,Bowbridge GL5 .....99 D7
Stroud,Uplands GL5 .....99 C8
Middle Tynings GL6 .....91 A4
Middle Way NP16 .....60 F5
Middlecroft GL10 .....96 F7
Middledown Rd SN14 .....24 C1
Middleford Ho BS13 .....2 C4
Middlehay Ct GL52 .....137 E3
Middlemoor Mill GL5 .....91 A6
Middleton Lawn GL3 .....127 E6
Middleton Rd BS11 .....16 F8
Midland Ct GL7 .....190 D3
Midland Mews 14 BS2 .....195 C3
Midland Rd
Bristol,Newton BS2 .....195 C3
Bristol,Staple Hill BS16 .....20 D4
Cirencester GL7 .....190 D2
Gloucester GL1 .....196 B1
Stonehouse GL10 .....97 E8
Midland Road Bsns Pk BS16 .....20 D4
Midland St BS2 .....195 C2
Midland Terr BS16 .....19 F3
Midland Way BS35 .....51 C7
Midsummer Wlk GL2 .....118 C6
Midway GL6 .....148 C6
Midwinter Ave GL51 .....133 C3
Midwinter Gdns GL50 .....133 C5
Midwinter Rd 4 GL54 .....168 A1
Mildred St BS5 .....9 C7
Mildred's Farm Barns GL7 .....150 F3
Mile End Rd GL16 .....155 B6
Mile Wlk BS14 .....3 A6
Miles Cl BS20 .....16 E3
Miles Cotts GL16 .....155 A3
Miles Ct
Bristol,Cadbury Heath BS30 10 F4
Bristol,Clifton BS8 .....18 A1
Miles Rd
Bishop's Cleeve GL52 .....137 E1
Bristol BS8 .....18 A1
Milestone Sch The GL2 .....127 B5
Milestone Wlk GL16 .....155 B2
Milford Ave BS30 .....12 B7
Milford Cl GL2 .....127 B5
Milford St BS3 .....8 C4
Mill Ave Bristol BS1 .....195 A2
Broadway WR12 .....185 A8
Mill Bank GL20 .....192 B4
Mill Cl 8 Blockley GL56 .....186 C5
Brimscombe GL5 .....99 F2
Frampton Cotterell BS36 .....31 C7
South Cerney GL7 .....143 A8
Wotton-u-E GL12 .....68 C6
Mill Cotts Saltford BS31 .....5 F2
Upper Redbrook NP25 .....154 C5
Mill Cres BS37 .....32 B4
Mill Ct 11 GL18 .....171 A4
Mill Dene Gdn* GL56 .....186 C5
Mill End GL17 .....164 D5
Mill Farm Dr GL5 .....98 E8
Mill Gr GL2 .....117 D1
Mill Hill NP16 .....146 D4
Mill Ho Bristol BS1 .....195 A2
10 Bristol,Baptist Mills BS5 19 A1
Mill La Avening GL8 .....140 B8
Bitton BS30 .....5 E8
Bristol,Southville BS3 .....8 D4
Bristol,Warmley BS30 .....11 C5
Brockworth GL3 .....120 F6
Castle Eaton SN6 .....144 D6
Charlton Kings GL54 .....131 D8
Cheltenham GL52 .....134 D4
Chipping Sodbury BS37 .....33 E6
Cranham GL4 .....112 D6
Doynton BS30 .....22 F1
Fairford GL7 .....152 D4
Falfield GL12 .....65 F7
Frampton Cotterell BS36 .....42 B1
Gorsley GL18 .....170 C3
Greet GL54 .....184 A1
Lechlade on T GL7 .....153 F2
Longhope GL17 .....165 A5
Lower Slaughter GL54 .....176 C1
Lower Swell GL54 .....176 D4
Mickleton GL55 .....189 A6
Redmarley D'Abitot GL19 .....179 F2
Stanton Fitzwarren SN6 .....145 A1
Mill La *continued*
Staunton GL19 .....179 F1
Stoke Orchard GL52 .....136 D5
Tockington BS32 .....50 B1
Upper Strensham WR8 .....180 B10
Upton Cheyney BS30 .....11 F1
Winchcombe GL54 .....174 A7
Mill Pl Cirencester GL7 .....190 B5
Gloucester GL1 .....119 A7
Mill Place Trad Est GL1 .....118 D7
Mill Rd BS36 .....30 D4
Mill Row Blockley GL56 .....186 D6
King's Stanley GL10 .....98 A5
Lower Lydbrook GL17 .....163 C3
Mill St Cheltenham GL52 .....134 C5
Gloucester GL1 .....127 A1
Tewkesbury GL20 .....192 B4
Mill Stps BS36 .....30 E4
Mill View Baunton GL7 .....150 D7
Northleach GL54 .....168 A1
Mill Way GL11 .....87 F4
Millar Ho BS8 .....194 A2
Millard Cl BS10 .....28 D2
Millbank GL11 .....88 A4
Millbank Cl BS4 .....9 E3
Millbook Ct 3 BS6 .....18 E1
Millbridge Rd GL3 .....120 A7
Millbrook GL5 .....148 A5
Millbrook Ave BS4 .....9 F3
Millbrook Cl Bristol BS30 .....11 C6
6 Gloucester GL1 .....127 A1
Millbrook Ct GL50 .....193 A4
Millbrook Gdns
Cheltenham GL50 .....133 B2
Lea HR9 .....164 D8
Millbrook Gn GL15 .....147 E5
Millbrook Ley GL56 .....177 A6
Millbrook Pl GL5 .....99 D7
Millbrook Rd BS37 .....43 B2
Millbrook Rdbt GL50 .....193 A4
Millbrook St
Cheltenham GL50 .....193 A4
Gloucester GL1 .....127 A1
Millbrook Wlk GL5 .....90 F6
Millend GL15 .....156 E1
Millend La GL10 .....97 A7
Millend Row GL10 .....97 A7
Millennium Cl
Frampton Cotterell BS36 .....31 D7
Tewkesbury GL20 .....192 E2
Millennium Cotts GL19 .....172 A7
Millennium Park Ctr* GL7 .....142 D6
Millennium Sq BS1 .....194 C1
Millennium Way GL7 .....190 F5
Miller Cl
Ashleworth GL19 .....172 D4
Gloucester GL2 .....127 D5
Miller Craddock Way 1 HR8 .....178 E7
Millers Cl BS20 .....16 C4
Millers Dr BS30 .....11 D5
Millers Dyke GL2 .....117 D1
Millers Gn
Drybrook GL17 .....164 A4
Gloucester GL1 .....196 B3
Millers Way GL14 .....191 C4
Millfield BS35 .....64 C2
Millfield Dr BS30 .....11 C6
Millfields GL3 .....120 A8
Millground Rd BS13 .....1 F5
Millgrove St N BS2 .....195 A4
Millham Rd GL52 .....138 A4
Millhill La GL16 .....154 F3
Millhouse Dr GL50 .....133 C5
Milliman Cl BS13 .....2 C5
Millin Ave GL4 .....118 D2
Milling Cl SN6 .....143 A5
Milling Cres GL15 .....147 E5
Millmead Ho BS13 .....2 C4
Millpill Cl BS9 .....17 D5
Millpond End GL5 .....99 A2
Millpond Prim Sch BS5 .....19 A1
Millpond St 9 BS5 .....19 A1
Millpool Ct BS9 .....18 B8
Mills Cl 2 WR12 .....185 B8
Millview GL56 .....186 C6
Millward Gr BS16 .....20 C4
Milne Pastures GL20 .....182 B4
Milne Wlk GL51 .....132 E4
Milner Gn BS30 .....11 A5
Milner Rd BS7 .....18 F5
Milo Pl GL1 .....118 E6
Milsom St Bristol BS5 .....9 A8
Cheltenham GL50 .....193 B4
Milton Ave
Cheltenham GL51 .....129 F8
Gloucester GL2 .....118 C5
Milton Cl BS37 .....43 D2
Milton Gr GL5 .....99 E7
Milton Pk 1 BS5 .....9 C7
Milton Pl GL7 .....152 D3
Milton Rd Bristol BS7 .....18 E6
Cheltenham GL51 .....132 F1
Yate BS37 .....43 D2
Milton St GL7 .....152 D3
Miltons Cl BS13 .....2 D4
Milverton Gdns BS6 .....18 F2
Milward Rd BS31 .....4 E6
Mimosa Ave GL51 .....130 A4
Mimosa Ct 6 GL3 .....128 A7
Mina Rd BS2 .....19 A2
Minchinhampton Sch GL6 .....148 A3
Mine Pitts La HR9 .....162 E3
Minehead Rd BS4 .....8 F1
Miners Wlk GL14 .....191 C4
Minerva Cl GL4 .....119 F6
Minerva Ct GL7 .....190 D4
Minerva Wlk GL15 .....92 B5
Minetts Ave GL52 .....138 A3
Minety CE Prim Sch SN16 .....142 D1
Minety Crossroads SN16 .....142 D1
Minety La SN16 .....142 A3
Minnow La OX18 .....161 D7
Minor's La BS10 .....27 A8
Minsmere Rd BS31 .....5 A4
Minster Cl GL52 .....137 E4
Minster Ct 1 BS37 .....32 D7
Minster Gdns GL4 .....119 F6
Minsterworth CE Prim Sch GL2 .....116 F7
Minstrel Way GL3 .....127 F8
Minto Rd BS2 .....19 A2
Minto Road Ind Ctr 8 BS2 .....19 A2
Minton Cl BS14 .....3 B5
Misarden Park Gdns* GL6 .....106 B6
Misarden Park Woodland Trail* GL6 .....106 B6
Miserden CE Prim Sch GL6 .....106 A6
Miserden Rd GL51 .....132 D1
Miss Grace's La NP16 .....146 E2
Mission Rd BS37 .....43 B4
Mistletoe Mews GL3 .....127 F6
Mitcheldean Endowed Prim Sch GL17 .....164 D5
Mitchell Ct BS1 .....195 B2
Mitchell La BS1 .....195 B2
Mitchell Wlk BS30 .....11 D7
Mitford Cotts OX18 .....161 F5
Mitford Villas GL56 .....187 A3
Mitre Pitch GL12 .....68 C7
Mitre St GL53 .....193 C2
Mitton Cl GL20 .....192 E6
Mitton Manor Prim Sch GL20 .....192 E6
Mitton Way GL20 .....192 E6
Mivart St BS5 .....19 B2
Moat Bank GL20 .....180 F7
Moat Ho GL4 .....119 B4
Moat La Corse GL19 .....172 A8
Huntley GL19 .....165 E8
Uckington GL51 .....132 D6
Moat Prim Sch GL4 .....119 B4
Moat The Kingham OX7 .....177 F3
Quedgeley GL2 .....117 F1
Mobley GL13 .....86 A3
Modecombe Gr BS10 .....27 F3
Model Village The* GL54 .....169 A7
Moffatt Rd GL6 .....91 A4
Mogg St BS2 .....19 A2
Mogridge Cl GL3 .....120 A7
Mohair Countryside Ctr* GL17 .....165 A5
Molesworth Cl BS13 .....2 A4
Molesworth Dr BS13 .....2 A4
Monarch Cl GL4 .....119 E4
Monarch Ct BS16 .....31 A1
Monica Dr GL50 .....133 E4
Monk Meadow Trad Est GL2 .....118 C7
Monk Rd BS7 .....18 D4
Monk's Park Ave BS7 .....18 E8
Monkey Mdw GL20 .....182 C5
Monkey Puzzle Cl GL5 .....98 E6
Monks Ave BS15 .....10 B8
Monks Croft GL51 .....132 E1
Monks Ho 3 BS37 .....32 D7
Monks La GL20 .....182 C2
Monks Park Sch BS7 .....18 F8
Monks Park Way BS7 .....18 E8
Monks Wlk GL7 .....153 F2
Monkscroft Com Prim Sch GL51 .....132 E1
Monkswell Cl 2 NP25 .....154 A8
Monkswell Rd 1 NP25 .....154 A8
Monkton Rd BS15 .....10 B5
Monmouth Comp Sch NP25 .....154 A8
Monmouth Ct BS20 .....16 C5
Monmouth Hill BS32 .....39 E4
Monmouth Rd Bristol BS7 18 D4
Edge End GL16 .....155 C8
Keynsham BS31 .....4 D5
Pill BS20 .....16 C5
Monmouth St BS3 .....8 F3
Monsdale Cl BS10 .....28 A3
Monsdale Dr BS10 .....28 A2
Monson Ave GL50 .....193 B4
Mont The 2 BS6 .....18 E1
Montague Cl BS34 .....29 E5
Montague Ct 4 BS2 .....195 A4
Montague Flats 6 BS2 .....195 A4
Montague Hill BS2 .....195 A4
Montague Hill S 5 BS2 195 A4
Montague Pl BS6 .....195 A4
Montague Rd BS31 .....5 D2
Montague St BS1 .....195 A4
Monterey Rd GL20 .....192 E1
Montfort Rd GL2 .....127 B5
Montgomery Cl GL3 .....120 B6
Montgomery Rd GL51 .....129 D6
Montgomery St BS3 .....8 F3
Montpelier Central 1 BS6 .....18 E1
Montpelier Ct BS6 .....18 E2
Montpelier Sta BS6 .....18 E2
Montpellier GL1 .....196 B1
Montpellier Arc GL50 .....193 B2
Montpellier Ave GL50 .....193 B2
Montpellier Ct GL50 .....193 A2
Montpellier Dr GL50 .....193 B2
Montpellier Gr GL50 .....193 B2
Montpellier Ho GL50 .....193 A2
Montpellier Mews GL1 .....196 B2
Montpellier Par GL50 .....193 B2
Montpellier Rd GL15 .....155 E1
Montpellier Retreat GL50 .....193 B2
Montpellier Spa Rd GL50 .....193 B2
Montpellier St GL50 .....193 B3
Montpellier Terr GL50 .....193 B2
Montpellier Villas GL50 .193 B2
Montpellier Wlk GL50 .....193 A2
Montreal Ave BS7 .....19 A8
Montreal Dr GL51 .....132 E3
Montreaux Ct 10 BS16 .....20 D3
Montreaux Ho 2 BS5 .....10 A7
Montrose Ave BS6 .....18 C1
Montrose Dr BS30 .....11 B6
Montrose Pk BS4 .....9 D2
Montroy Cl BS9 .....18 C6
Montserrat GL5 .....99 D3
Moon St BS2 .....195 B4
Moon's La GL6 .....148 E7
Moor Court Dr GL52 .....133 F2
Moor Croft Dr BS30 .....10 F3
Moor Gr BS11 .....17 A8
Moor Hall Pl GL5 .....98 E8
Moor House Cvn Pk BS10 .....27 A4
Moor La
Bourton-on-t-W GL54 .....169 A8
Fairford GL7 .....152 E3
Tockington BS32 .....40 A8
Moor Lane Ct GL7 .....152 E3
Moor St
Chepstow/Cas-Gwent NP16 60 E8
Gloucester GL1 .....118 F7
Saul GL2 .....157 F4
Moor The SN16 .....142 D2
Moor Wood Cotts GL7 .....158 B3
Moordell Cl BS37 .....43 D1
Moore Cottage Hospl GL54 .....168 F8
Moore Rd GL54 .....168 F7
Moorend Cres GL53 .....130 C6
Moorend Gdns BS11 .....16 F7
Moorend Glade GL53 .....130 F6
Moorend Gr GL53 .....130 C5
Moorend La GL2 .....95 C2
Moorend Park Rd GL53 .130 C6
Moorend Rd
Cheltenham,Charlton Park GL53 .....130 F6
Cheltenham,Leckhampton GL53 .....130 C5
Hambrook BS16 .....30 D3
Staunton GL19 .....180 C1
Moorend St GL53 .....130 C6
Moorend Terr GL53 .....130 C6
Moores Ground GL19 .....173 C6
Moorfield Ave GL15 .....156 D1
Moorfield Rd GL3 .....120 F5
Moorfields Ho BS5 .....9 C7
Moorgate GL7 .....153 D2
Moorgrove Ho BS9 .....17 C7
Moorhen Ct GL2 .....117 D1
Moorhill St 17 BS5 .....19 B1
Moorhouse La BS10 .....27 B4
Moorings The BS20 .....16 C4
Moorland Cl GL14 .....191 D5
Moorland Rd BS37 .....43 D1
Moorlands Rd
Bristol,Mayfield Park BS16 .20 A2
Bristol,Ridgeway BS16 .....19 F3
Moorpark Ave BS37 .....43 D1
Moors Ave GL51 .....133 A4
Moorslade La GL12 .....77 D1
Mop Hale GL56 .....186 C6
Mopla Rd NP16 .....72 F2
Moravian Ct 4 BS15 .....10 D8
Moravian Rd BS15 .....10 D8
Morcroft Pl GL15 .....155 F1
Morden Wlk BS14 .....3 D7
More Hall Pk GL5 .....102 D1
Morelands Gr GL1 .....118 E5
Morelands Trad Est GL1 .....196 A1
Morestall Dr GL7 .....190 B2
Moreton Cl
Bishop's Cleeve GL52 .....138 A2
Bristol BS14 .....3 A4
Moreton La GL20 .....182 C8
Moreton-in-Marsh District Hospl GL56 .....187 A3
Moreton-in-Marsh Sta GL56 .....187 A3
Morgan Cl BS31 .....5 D2
Morgan St BS2 .....18 F1
Morgan's Way GL14 .....156 C6
Morgans Dr GL50 .....193 A1
Morgans La GL17 .....164 A3
Morgans Terr GL7 .....142 F7
Mork La GL15 .....146 E7
Mork Rd GL15 .....146 E7
Morlands Dr GL53 .....131 B4
Morley Ave Bristol BS16 .....21 A4
Churchdown GL3 .....128 A6
Morley Cl
Bristol,Little Stoke BS34 .....29 C7
Bristol,Staple Hill BS16 .....20 D4
Morley Rd
Bristol,Southville BS3 .....8 C4
Bristol,Staple Hill BS16 .....20 D3
Morley Sq BS7 .....18 E4
Morley St
Bristol,Baptist Mills BS2 .....18 F1
Bristol,Russell Town BS5 .....9 B7
Morley Terr 1 BS15 .....20 D1
Morman Cl GL17 .....164 B4
Morningside Cl GL52 .....134 C4
Morningside Ctyd GL52 134 C4
Mornington Dr GL53 .....130 D6
Mornington Rd 14 BS8 .....18 A2
Mornington Terr 7 GL14 .....157 A6
Morpeth Rd BS4 .....2 D8
Morpeth St GL1 .....118 F7
Morris Cl GL15 .....156 B2
Morris Ct 7 GL51 .....129 F7
Morris Hill Cl GL51 .....133 B6
Morris Orch GL11 .....87 F6
Morris Rd Bristol BS7 .....19 A5
Broadway WR12 .....185 B8
Morse La GL17 .....164 A4
Morse Rd Bristol BS5 .....9 C7
Drybrook GL17 .....164 B4
Mortimer House Hospl BS8 .....194 A3
Mortimer Rd
Bristol,Filton BS34 .....29 B2
Bristol,Victoria Park BS8 .194 A3
Gloucester GL2 .....127 C5
Morton Mill BS35 .....64 C3
Morton St Bristol BS5 .....9 B7
Gloucester GL1 .....118 F7
Thornbury BS35 .....64 C4
Morton Way BS35 .....64 D1
Morwent Cl GL4 .....119 E6
Mosedale GL56 .....187 B3
Moselle Dr GL3 .....128 A6
Mosley Cres GL5 .....98 E7
Mosley Rd GL5 .....98 E7
Mostham Pl GL3 .....120 D6
Motor Mus (The Bugatti Trust)* GL52 .....138 E8
Motorway Distribution Ctr BS11 .....26 C2
Mottershead Dr GL3 .....127 E6
Mottershead Rd GL7 .....150 F2
Moulder Rd GL20 .....192 E4
Mount Cl Cirencester GL7 190 C3
Frampton Cotterell BS36 .....30 F8
Harrow Hill GL17 .....164 B4
Mount Craig Hall HR9 .....162 F8
Mount Cres BS36 .....30 E5
Mount Gdns BS15 .....10 D6
Mount Hill Rd BS15 .....10 D6
Mount Pleasant
Bisley GL6 .....148 D8
Blockley GL56 .....186 C6
Chepstow/Cas-Gwent NP16 60 E8
Fairford GL7 .....152 E4
Hallen BS10 .....27 C4
Lechlade on T GL7 .....153 E2
Lydney GL15 .....92 C2
Parkend GL15 .....155 E3
Pill BS20 .....16 D4
Stroud GL5 .....99 E7
Tirley GL19 .....172 F7
Wotton-u-E GL12 .....68 C7
Mount Pleasant Cl
Lydney GL15 .....92 C2
17 Stow-on-t-W GL54 .....176 F4
Mount Pleasant Rd
Cinderford GL14 .....191 D3
Tewkesbury GL20 .....192 D4
Mount Pleasant Terr BS3 .8 C4
Mount St Cirencester GL7 190 C3
Gloucester GL1 .....196 A3
Mount Way
Chepstow/Cas-Gwent NP16 60 D8
Chepstow/Cas-Gwent NP16 72 D1
Mountain Mews 5 BS5 .....10 A7
Mountain View GL17 .....163 F4
Mountbatten Cl BS37 .....43 D3
Mounteney's La GL12 .....54 D7
Mountjoy's La GL14 .....191 D5
Mountjoy's Lane End GL14 .....191 D5
Mounton Chambers NP16 .....60 D8
Mounton Cl NP16 .....60 D7
Mounton Dr NP16 .....60 D7
Mounton House Sch NP16 .....60 B7
Mounton Rd NP16 .....60 D8
Mousell La GL14 .....191 D4
Mousetrap La GL54 .....168 F8
Mow Barton Bristol BS13 .....1 F6
Yate BS37 .....43 D2
Mowberry Cl GL2 .....127 C5
Mowbray Ave GL20 .....192 D1
Mowbray Rd BS14 .....3 C7
Mowcroft Rd BS13 .....2 D4
Moxham Dr BS13 .....2 C4
Moyle Old School La NP16 .....73 A4
Muirfield Bristol BS30 .....11 A6
Yate BS37 .....32 E8
Mulberry Cl Bristol BS15 .....10 E8
Hardwicke GL2 .....109 E8
Mulberry Ct 2 GL51 .....132 D2
Mulberry Dr BS15 .....20 F1
Mulberry Gdns 11 BS16 .....20 D3
Mulberry Gn GL56 .....177 C4
Mulberry Wlk BS9 .....17 C8
Mule St GL13 .....78 B3
Muller Ave BS7 .....18 F4
Muller Rd BS5,BS7 .....19 B3

Mullings Ct GL7 190 C5
Mulready Cl BS7 19 C6
Mumbleys Hill BS35 50 E7
Mumbleys La
Thornbury,Alveston Down BS35 50 E6
Thornbury,Kington BS35 50 E8
Munday Cl 8 GL6 148 B6
Munsley Gr GL4 119 C3
Murdoch Sq BS7 18 F8
Murford Ave BS13 2 B4
Murford Wlk BS13 2 B4
Murray Cl GL52 137 F5
Murray St 9 BS3 8 C4
Murrells Rd GL16 163 A2
Murvagh GL53 193 C1
Murvagh Cl GL53 193 C1
Muscroft Rd GL52 134 D4
Musgrove Cl BS11 27 C2
Mushat Ind Pk GL16 155 B5
Mushet Pl GL16 155 A5
Musket Cl GL20 192 E2
Mutsilver Mews GL2 127 E5
Muzzle Patch GL2 124 C8
Myers Rd GL1 127 A1
Myrtle Cl GL4 119 A5
Myrtle Dr BS11 16 E5
Myrtle Hill BS20 16 C5
Myrtle Pl NP16 72 F1
Myrtle Rd BS2 194 C4
Myrtle St BS3 8 B3
Myrtles The NP16 73 A2
Mythe Rd GL20 192 C5
Mythe Terr 3 GL14 157 A6

N

Naas La Lydney GL15 92 D2
Quedgeley GL2,GL4 110 C6
Naas La Rdbt GL2 109 F7
Nags Head Hill BS5 10 A7
Nagshead Nature Reserve★ GL15 155 D4
Nagshead Nature Trails★ GL15 155 D3
Nailers La GL18 170 D3
Nailsea Cl BS13 2 A7
Nailsworth Ave BS37 43 E1
Nailsworth CE Prim Sch GL6 90 F5
Nailsworth Mills Est GL6 91 C4
Nailsworth Terr 2 GL50 193 A4
Naishcombe Hill BS30 12 C7
Naite The BS35 63 D6
Nanfan & Dobyn Pl GL18 171 A5
Napier Ct BS1 194 B1
Napier Ho BS6 18 B2
Napier Miles Rd BS11 17 A8
Napier Rd
Avonmouth BS11 26 B1
Bristol,Baptist Mills BS5 19 B2
Bristol,Redland BS6 18 B2
Napier Sq BS11 26 A1
Napier St Bristol BS5 9 B6
Gloucester GL1 196 C2
Napping La GL17 164 F6
Napping The GL17 164 F6
Narles Rd GL2 96 A3
Narrow La BS16 20 E4
Narrow Plain BS2 195 B2
Narrow Quay BS1 195 A2
Narroways Rd BS2 19 A3
Narrowcut La GL6 90 F1
Narrows The GL55 188 E1
Narth La NP25 154 B1
Naseby Ho 4 GL52 134 A3
Naseby Wlk BS5 19 F1
Nash Cl BS31 5 A5
Nash Dr BS7 19 C7
Nash Way 9 GL16 155 A5
Nash's La GL55 189 D3
Nasse Ct GL11 87 F5
Nastend La GL10 101 C1
National Birds of Prey Ctr★ GL18 170 E2
National Star Coll The GL53 122 C6
National Waterways Mus★ GL1 196 A2
Nature Cl GL3 120 E5
Naunton Cres GL53 130 D6
Naunton La GL53 130 D6
Naunton Par GL53 193 B1
Naunton Park Cl GL53 130 E6
Naunton Park Ind Est GL53 130 E6
Naunton Park Prim Sch GL53 130 E6
Naunton Park Rd GL53 130 E6
Naunton Rd GL4 119 D7
Naunton Terr GL53 193 B1
Naunton Way GL53 130 D6
Naval Temple★ NP25 154 B7
Neads Dr BS30 11 C5
Neale Way BS11 26 C1
Neata Farm GL54 184 A1
Neate Ct BS34 29 C8
Neath Rd BS5 9 D8
Nebraska Circ GL7 152 E1
Nebsworth La CV36 189 E5
Needham Ave GL2 110 B6
Neigh Bridge Ctry Pk★ GL7 142 C5
Nell Hill SN6 145 A4
Nelmes Row GL53 131 C5
Nelson Ho Bristol BS1 195 A3
8 Bristol,Staple Hill BS16 20 D5
Nelson Par 10 BS3 8 D4
Nelson Rd 3 Bristol BS16 20 D4
Bristol BS16 20 D5
Nelson St Bristol BS1 195 A3
Bristol,Ashton Vale BS3 8 A2
Chepstow/Cas-Gwent NP16 60 F8
Gloucester GL1 118 F6
Stroud GL5 99 C7
Tewkesbury GL20 192 C4
Nelsons Cl HR9 163 B7
Nene Cl GL2 117 E2
Neptune Cl GL4 119 F6
Nero Cl GL15 92 C4
Neston Wlk BS4 2 F8
Netham Gdns BS5 9 D7
Netham Park Ind Est BS5 9 D6
Netham Rd BS5 9 D6
Netham View Ind Pk BS5 9 D7
Nether-Swell Manor GL54 176 E3
Nethercote CV36 187 F5
Nethercote Dr GL54 169 A7
Nethercote Farm Dr GL54 169 A6
Netherend GL15 147 C3
Netherend Cres GL15 147 C3
Netherhope La NP16 73 B5
Netheridge Cl GL2 118 A4
Netherley La GL19 180 A4
Netherwood Cl GL51 133 A3
Netherwood Gdns GL51 133 A3
Netting La GL2 157 B6
Nettlestone Cl BS10 27 E4
Nettleton Rd Burton SN14 36 B2
Cheltenham GL51 129 E7
Gloucester GL1 196 C2
Nevalan Dr BS5 10 A6
Nevil Rd BS7 18 E4
Neville Rd Bristol BS15 20 E2
Tewkesbury GL20 192 D3
New Barn Ave GL52 134 A4
New Barn Cl GL52 134 A4
New Barn La GL52 134 A4
New Bldgs BS16 19 F4
New Brunswick Ave BS5 10 B7
New Charlotte St BS3 8 D4
New Cheltenham Rd BS15 20 E1
New Church St GL8 140 B4
New Cut GL11 89 B1
New Fancy View★ GL15 155 F4
New Fosseway Rd BS14 3 B6
New Fosseway Sch BS14 3 B6
New Inn La Avening GL8 140 B8
Gloucester GL1 196 B3
New John St 16 BS3 8 C3
New Kings Ct BS7 18 C4
New Kingsley Rd BS2 195 C2
New La BS35 51 C5
New Leaze BS32 40 C3
New Mdws BS14 3 B6
New Mills GL15 92 A6
New mills Ind Est HR8 178 E8
New Mills La GL12 55 E8
New Mills Trad Est GL5 99 D8
New Mills Way 1 HR8 178 E8
New Queen St
Bristol,St George BS15 10 B8
Bristol,Windmill Hill BS3 8 E4
New Rd Aylburton GL15 147 D5
Blakeney GL15 156 D1
Bledington OX7 177 E1
Bream GL15 147 D8
Bristol,Filton BS34 28 F3
Bristol,Harry Stoke BS34 29 D3
Coleford GL16 155 B5
Coleford,Cannop GL15, GL16 155 D6
Dursley GL11 87 E4
Ebrington GL55 189 D3
Kingham OX7 177 F2
Kingswood GL12 67 F6
Lydney GL15 147 F7
Minchinhampton GL6 91 F5
Mitcheldean GL17 164 D5
9 Moreton-in-M GL56 187 A3
North Nibley GL11 79 E4
Olveston BS35 50 A2
Parkend GL15 155 E2
Pendock WR13 180 A8
Pill BS20 16 C4
Rangeworthy BS37 43 A8
Rangeworthy,Hall End BS37 53 C1
Stroud GL5 98 E5
Tytherington GL12 52 C6
Woodmancote GL52 138 C2
Yorkley GL15 156 A1
New Row Aldsworth GL54 160 E5
Brockhampton GL54 174 B1
New Rutland Ct GL50 193 B4
New Siblands Sch BS35 64 D1
New St Bretforton WR11 188 A6
Bristol BS2 195 C3
Charfield GL12 67 A6
Charlton Kings GL53 131 B5
Cheltenham GL50 193 A4
Gloucester GL1 196 B1
King's Stanley GL10 98 A3
Ledbury HR8 178 E8
Mitcheldean GL17 164 D5
Newton GL13 85 C8
Painswick GL6 103 F8
New Stadium Rd BS5 19 B2
New Station Rd BS16 20 A6
New Station Way BS16 20 A4
New Street Flats 5 BS2 195 C3
New Thomas St BS2 195 C2
New Town
Cinderford GL14 191 B7
New Town GL54 184 C3
Toddington GL54 184 C3
New Tyning La BS37 45 C4
New Villa SN14 57 D1
New Walls BS41 8 F4
New Wlk BS15 10 B5
New Zealand Ho 2 GL51 132 F3
Newark Ho GL2 118 B7
Newark Pk★ GL12 69 A7
Newark Rd GL1 118 C6
Newbrick Rd BS34 30 A5
Newbridge Cl BS4 9 D5
Newbridge Farm Pk★ HR8 178 A8
Newbridge Ho BS9 17 C4
Newbridge Rd BS4 9 E6
Newbridge Trad Est BS4 9 D5
Newburgh Ho SN6 145 C3
Newburgh Pl SN6 145 C3
Newbury Rd BS7 19 A7
Newcombe GL4 114 B5
Newcombe Ct GL7 190 D4
Newcombe Dr BS9 17 C4
Newcombe Rd BS9 17 F7
Newcourt Pk GL53 131 A6
Newcourt Rd GL53 131 A5
Newent Ave BS15 10 B7
Newent Bsns Pk GL18 171 B4
Newent Comm Sch GL18 170 F4
Newent La GL19 165 C6
Newerne St GL15 92 B3
Newfoundland Ct BS2 195 C4
Newfoundland Rd
6 Bristol,Baptist Mills BS2 19 A1
Bristol,St Pauls BS2 195 C4
Newfoundland St BS2 195 C4
Newfoundland Way BS2 195 C4
Newgate BS1 195 B3
Newgrounds La GL2 95 B6
Newhouse Farm Ind Est NP16 60 F3
Newland Dr BS13 2 A4
Newland Pl GL20 192 D4
Newland Rd BS13 2 A3
Newland St
Coleford GL16 155 A5
Gloucester GL1 196 C3
Newland View GL51 132 F5
Newland Way 1 NP25 154 A7
Newland Wlk BS13 2 A3
Newlands Ave BS36 31 C7
Newlands Ct
20 Newent GL18 171 A4
Stow-on-t-W GL54 176 E5
Newlands Rd BS31 4 D4
Newlands The BS16 20 B7
Newleaze BS34 29 A2
Newleaze Gdns GL8 140 B4
Newleaze Ho BS34 29 B2
Newlyn Ave BS9 17 D5
Newlyn Way BS37 43 F2
Newlyn Wlk BS4 9 B1
Newman Cl BS37 32 B4
Newmarket Ave BS1 195 A3
Newmarket Rd GL6 91 A4
Newmills Hill HR9 162 F5
Newnham Cl BS14 3 D7
Newnham Pl BS34 39 F1
Newnham St Peter's CE Prim Sch GL14 157 A7
Newnton Hill GL8 140 D5
Newnton Rd GL8 140 C3
Newpit La BS30 11 F2
Newport Rd
Chepstow/Cas-Gwent NP16 60 D7
Pill BS20 16 C5
Newport St BS3 8 E3
Newquay Rd BS4 8 F1
Newry Wlk BS4 8 E1
Newsome Ave BS20 16 C4
Newstead Rd GL4 119 E8
Newth's La SN5 143 E1
Newton Ave GL4 119 C7
Newton Cl Bristol BS15 21 A1
Cheltenham GL51 132 E2
Huntley GL19 165 D6
2 Ledbury HR8 178 F7
Newton Court La NP25 162 B1
Newton Dr BS30 11 A5
Newton Rd Bristol BS30 11 A5
Cheltenham GL51 132 E2
Newton St BS5 9 A8
Newtown GL12 67 A5
Newtown La GL20 192 F5
Newtown Rd GL14 191 B7
Niblett Cl BS15 10 F6
Niblett's Hill BS5 10 A6
Nibley La BS37 42 F3
Nibley Rd BS11 16 E5
Nicholas La BS5 10 A6
Nicholas Rd BS5 19 B1
Nicholas St BS3 8 E4
Nicholettes BS30 11 D5
Nicholls Ct BS36 30 E7
Nicholls La BS36 30 E6
Nicolson Cl GL3 127 E6
Nigel Pk BS11 16 E7
Nightingale Cl Bristol BS4 9 E6
Frampton Cotterell BS36 31 A6
Thornbury BS35 64 D2
Nightingale Croft GL3 127 D6
Nightingale Ct BS4 9 D3
Nightingale Ho GL4 119 D4
Nightingale La BS36 31 A8
Nind La GL12 68 B4
Nine Elms Rd GL2 127 E4
Nine Tree Hill 16 BS1 18 E1
Nine Wells Cl 16 GL16 155 A7
Nine Wells Rd GL16 155 B7
Ninewells Forest Wlk★ NP25 146 B6
Ninth Ave BS7 29 B1
Niven Ctyd GL51 132 C1
Noake Rd GL3 120 A8
Noble Ave BS30 11 C4
Noden Dr HR9 164 C8
Nodens Way GL15 92 C4
Noel Ct 8 GL55 189 A2
Noel Lee Way GL11 87 F5
Norbury Ave GL4 119 B4
Norchard Sta★ GL15 147 F7
Nordown Cl GL11 87 F4
Nordown Rd GL11 87 F4
Norfolk Ave
Bristol,Montpelier BS6 18 E2
Bristol,St Pauls BS2 195 B4
Cheltenham GL51 132 F2
Norfolk Gr BS31 4 C4
Norfolk Hts BS2 195 B4
Norfolk Mews GL51 132 F2
Norfolk Pl BS3 8 C3
Norfolk St GL1 196 A2
Norland Rd BS8 7 F8
Norley La GL9 34 D2
Norley Rd BS7 18 F7
Normal Terr GL50 193 B4
Norman Ball Way GL1 127 B1
Norman Cl GL20 181 F7
Norman Gr BS15 20 D2
Norman Hill GL11 87 F4
Norman Rd
Bristol,Baptist Mills BS2 19 A2
Bristol,Warmley BS30 11 B8
Saltford BS31 5 E3
Norman Way GL17 163 F4
Norman's Cotts BS36 30 D7
Normanby Rd 20 BS5 19 B1
Normandy Way NP16 72 D1
Normanton Rd 16 BS8 18 A2
Norrisville Rd 8 BS6 18 E1
Norrland Pl HR9 163 C8
Norse Way NP16 61 B7
Nortenham Cl GL52 137 D4
North Ave
Ashchurch GL20 182 D4
Drybrook GL17 164 B4
North Cerney CE Prim Sch GL7 158 D3
North Circular Rd GL56 187 C4
North Croft BS30 11 D4
North Ct BS32 40 D3
North Devon Rd BS16 20 A5
North East Rd BS35 64 C2
North East Terr GL20 192 D4
North End SN14 47 E5
North End Gdns SN16 58 C1
North Farm Cotts GL8 141 A6
North Gr BS20 16 C4
North Green St 12 BS8 7 F6
North Hall Mews GL52 133 F2
North Hill Rd GL7 190 E2
North Home Rd GL7 190 F3
North Leaze BS41 7 B2
North Meadow (Nature Reserve)★ SN6 143 E5
North Meadow Rd SN6 143 E5
North Nibley CE Prim Sch GL11 79 D5
North Par BS37 43 E2
North Pk BS15 20 E1
North Pl GL50 193 C4
North Pole La HR9 170 C5
North Rd 7 Bristol BS3 8 A4
Bristol,Montpelier BS6 18 E2
Bristol,Stoke Gifford BS34 29 F4
Coleford GL16 155 B6
Engine Common BS37 43 B5
Gloucester GL1 126 F4
Huntley GL19 165 D6
Leigh Woods BS8 7 D7
Thornbury BS35 64 C2
Winterbourne BS36 30 F7
Yate BS37 43 B3
North Rd E GL51 129 C7
North Rd W GL51 129 B7
North Road Com Prim Sch BS37 43 B4
North Somerset Junc BS5 9 B6
North St
Bristol,Downend BS16 20 E5
Bristol,Oldland Common BS30 11 C4
Bristol,Southville BS3 8 B3
Bristol,St Pauls BS1 195 B4
Cheltenham GL50 193 B4
Wickwar GL12 54 A6
Winchcombe GL54 174 A7
North Stoke La BS30 6 B8
North Upton La GL4 119 E8
North View Bristol BS6 18 A4
Bristol,Mangotsfield BS16 20 E5
Bristol,Upper Soundwell BS16 20 D4
Highworth SN6 145 C3
North View Bglws GL7 151 F3
North Wall SN6 143 F4
North Way Bristol BS34 29 B4
Cirencester GL7 190 C4
North Wlk BS37 43 E1
Northavon Bsns Ctr BS37 43 C3
Northbank Cl GL51 129 B7
Northbrook Rd GL4 127 C1
Northcot La GL56 186 D6
Northcote Ho 2 BS8 194 A3
Northcote Rd
Bristol,Clifton BS8 17 F1
Bristol,Crew's Hole BS5 9 E7
Bristol,Mangotsfield BS16 20 F6
Northcote St 18 BS5 19 B1
Northcroft GL50 130 B7
Northen Cl GL7 144 F7
Northend Ave BS15 20 D2
Northend Gdns BS15 20 D2
Northend Rd BS15 20 E1
Northern Way GL17 164 D5
Northfield BS37 32 D8
Northfield Ave BS15 10 D5
Northfield Cl GL8 140 C4
Northfield Ho 10 BS3 8 C4
Northfield La SN14 24 F1
Northfield Pas GL50 193 C4
Northfield Rd Bristol BS5 10 B7
Gloucester GL4 118 F5
Tetbury GL8 140 C4
Northfield Sq GL4 118 F5
Northfield Terr GL50 193 C4
Northfields GL5 99 D8
Northfields Rd GL6 91 A5
Northgate St GL1 196 B3
Northington La GL14 157 B3
Northlands Way GL8 140 C5
Northleach CE Prim Sch GL54 168 A1
Northleach Wlk BS11 16 F5
Northleaze GL8 140 C4
Northleaze Prim Sch BS41 7 B2
Northmead La BS37 42 D6
Northmoor La GL7 151 A1
Northover Ct BS35 38 E6
Northover Rd BS9 28 A1
Northridge Bsns Ctr BS37 43 C2
Northumberland Rd BS6 18 D2
Northumbria Dr BS9 18 B4
Northview Prim Sch SN6 145 D4
Northville Rd BS7 29 A1
Northway Inf Sch GL20 182 C4
Northway La GL20 182 B4
Northway Trad Est GL20 182 C4
Northwick Bsns Ctr GL56 186 C8
Northwick Rd Bristol BS7 18 F8
Northwick BS35 48 E1
Northwick Terr GL56 186 C6
Northwood Cl GL14 191 D5
Northwoods Wlk BS10 28 D3
Norton CE Prim Sch GL2 173 B2
Norton Cl Bristol BS15 10 F7
Whitchurch HR9 162 D4
Winchcombe GL54 174 A8
Norton Ct GL6 90 F5
Norton Ho 7 Bristol BS1 195 B1
Bristol,Patchway BS34 39 F1
Cheltenham GL51 133 A2
Norton La BS14 3 C2
Norton Rd BS4 9 A3
Norton Ridge GL6 91 A5
Norton View GL55 189 A6
Nortonwood GL6 90 F5
Norval Rd WR11 188 A8
Norwich Dr Bristol BS4 9 E6
Cheltenham GL51 130 A6
Norwood Rd GL50 193 B1
Nostle Rd GL54 168 A1
Notch Rd GL7,GL53 107 C8
Notgrove Cl
Cheltenham GL51 129 E8
Gloucester GL4 118 C2
Notgrove Long Barrow★ GL54 167 E8
Notley Pl GL3 120 A7
Nottingham Rd
Bishop's Cleeve GL52 137 F5
Bristol BS7 18 E3
Nottingham St BS3 8 F3
Nouncells Cross GL5 99 D7
Nourse Cl GL53 130 B4
Nourse Pl GL17 164 D5
Nova Distribution Ctr BS11 26 B1
Nova Scotia Pl BS1 194 A1
Nova Way BS11 26 B1
Novers Cres BS4 2 C8
Novers Hill BS4 2 C8
Novers Hill Trad Est BS3 8 C1
Novers La BS4 2 D7
Novers Lane Inf Sch BS4 2 C7
Novers Lane Jun Sch BS4 2 C7
Novers Park Dr BS4 2 C8
Novers Park Rd BS4 2 D8
Novers Rd BS4 2 C8
Noverton Ave GL52 134 D4
Noverton La GL52 134 D4
Nugent Hill BS6 18 D1
Nunnery La GL11 80 B7
Nunney Cl BS31 5 A2
Nunny Cl GL51 132 C1
Nup End GL19 172 D4
Nup End La GL19 172 D4
Nupdown Rd BS35 75 E5

Nupend Gdns GL17 ...164 F5
Nupend La GL17 ...164 F5
Nurseries The
Bishop's Cleeve GL52 ...137 E2
Tytherington GL12 ...52 B5
Nursery Cl
Cirencester GL7 ...190 E2
Mickleton GL55 ...189 B7
Moreton-in-M GL56 ...187 A4
Stroud GL5 ...99 D6
Nursery Cott GL7 ...190 D3
Nursery Dr GL5 ...148 A5
Nursery Gdns BS10 ...28 A3
Nursery Rd GL7 ...190 E2
Nursery The Bristol BS3 ...8 B3
King's Stanley GL10 ...98 A4
Nursery View GL7 ...150 E2
Nut Croft GL4 ...119 B7
Nut Orchard La GL20 ...181 F8
Nutbridge Cotts GL52 ...138 C3
Nutfield Gr BS34 ...29 B2
Nutfield Ho BS34 ...29 B1
Nutgrove Ave BS3 ...8 E3
Nuthatch Dr BS16 ...19 F6
Nuthatch Gdns BS16 ...20 A6
Nuthill GL4 ...120 B2
Nutley Ave GL4 ...118 C2
Nutmeg Cl GL4 ...119 D4
Nympsfield BS15 ...20 E2
Nympsfield Long Barrow*
GL11 ...89 C7
Nympsfield Rd
Gloucester GL4 ...118 D3
Nailsworth GL6 ...90 E5

O

O'Brien Rd GL51 ...133 A4
Oak Ave GL52 ...131 A7
Oak Cl Bristol BS34 ...29 D7
Chepstow/Cas-Gwent NP16 60 E5
Yate BS37 ...43 D3
Oak Cres GL15 ...147 C3
Oak Cres/Cilgant Defiw 8
NP25 ...154 A7
Oak Ct Bristol BS14 ...3 A5
Cheltenham GL52 ...134 A1
Oak Dr Brockworth GL3 ...120 D6
Dursley GL11 ...88 A3
Highworth SN6 ...145 C3
Northway GL20 ...182 B4
Stroud GL5 ...99 B6
Oak Field The GL14 ...191 E5
Oak Gdns GL20 ...182 C7
Oak Gr BS20 ...16 C5
Oak Hill CE Prim Sch (Inf)
WR11 ...183 F7
Oak Hill CE Prim Sch (Jun)
GL20 ...183 E4
Oak Ho Bristol BS13 ...2 D4
Brockworth GL3 ...120 D6
Oak Inn GL1 ...119 A7
Oak La Bredon GL20 ...182 C7
Bristol BS5 ...19 F2
Oak Lodge BS37 ...32 D8
Oak Manor 3 GL52 ...134 A1
Oak Manor Dr GL52 ...134 A1
Oak Mdw GL15 ...92 B6
Oak Rd Bristol BS7 ...18 E5
Colerne SN14 ...15 F5
Down Ampney GL7 ...143 F7
Marston Meysey SN6 ...144 A6
Oak St GL7 ...153 E2
Oak The BS9 ...17 D3
Oak Tree Ave BS16 ...22 B4
Oak Tree Cl Bristol BS15 ...10 C3
Hardwicke GL2 ...109 E7
Oak Tree View GL4 ...119 C3
Oak Tree Wlk BS31 ...4 D3
Oak Way Huntley GL19 ...165 D6
Littledean GL14 ...156 E8
South Cerney GL7 ...142 F7
Stonehouse GL10 ...97 F7
Oakbank GL4 ...118 F4
Oakbrook Dr GL51 ...129 C7
Oakcroft Cl GL4 ...119 D3
Oakdale Ave BS16 ...20 D8
Oakdale Cl BS16 ...20 E8
Oakdale Ct BS16 ...20 D7
Oakdale Rd
Bristol,Downend BS16 ...20 E8
Bristol,Hengrove BS14 ...3 A8
Oakdean GL14 ...191 C5
Oakdene
11 Cheltenham,Lansdown
GL51 ...130 B8
2 Cheltenham,Whaddon
GL52 ...134 A1
Oakdene Ave BS5 ...19 D3
Oakenhill Rd BS4 ...9 E2
Oakenhill Wlk BS4 ...9 E2
Oakes La GL9 ...35 B5
Oakeys Cl 20 GL54 ...176 F4
Oakfield Ave NP16 ...72 D1
Oakfield Bsns Pk BS15 ...10 D7
Oakfield Gr BS8 ...194 B4
Oakfield Pl BS8 ...194 B4
Oakfield Rd
Bishop's Cleeve GL52 ...138 A4
Bristol,Kingswood BS15 ...10 D7
Bristol,Victoria Park BS8 ...194 B4
Keynsham BS31 ...4 F2
Oakfield St GL50 ...130 B7
Oakfield Way GL13 ...93 D1
Oakfields GL16 ...155 A6
Oakford La SN14 ...15 B2
Oakhanger Dr BS11 ...27 B1
Oakhill Ave BS30 ...11 C2
Oakhill La BS10 ...27 C4
Oakhill Pitch GL15 ...146 F3
Oakhill Rd GL17 ...164 D5
Oakhunger La GL13 ...85 C4
Oakhurst Cl GL3 ...128 A5
Oakhurst Rd BS9 ...17 F5
Oakhurst Rise GL52 ...131 A8
Oakland Ave GL52 ...133 F3
Oakland Bsns Pk BS37 ...43 A3
Oakland Dr HR8 ...178 E8
Oakland Rd
Bristol,Crew's Hole BS5 ...9 E8
6 Bristol,Redland BS6 ...18 B1
Harrow Hill GL17 ...164 B3
Oakland St GL53 ...131 A7
Oaklands Cirencester GL7 190 C2
Sling GL16 ...155 B2
Oaklands Cl BS16 ...21 B5
Oaklands Dr
Almondsbury BS32 ...40 A4
Bristol,Frenchay BS16 ...20 A7
Bristol,Oldland Common
BS30 ...11 C2
Oaklands Pk GL15 ...155 E1
Oaklands Rd BS16 ...21 A5
Oaklea Rd GL15 ...156 B2
Oakleaze
Coalpit Heath BS36 ...31 D7
Gloucester GL2 ...127 D3
Minety SN16 ...142 D1
Oakleaze Rd BS35 ...64 C1
Oakleigh Ave BS5 ...19 D1
Oakleigh Gdns BS30 ...11 C2
Oakley Flats GL7 ...144 E7
Oakley Rd Bristol BS7 ...18 F7
Cheltenham GL52 ...134 B1
Cirencester GL7 ...190 C2
Oakley Way 1 GL15 ...147 D8
Oakmeade Pk BS4 ...9 B2
Oakridge GL2 ...125 E5
Oakridge Cl Bristol BS15 ...11 A7
Gloucester GL4 ...119 E5
Oakridge Parochial Sch
GL6 ...148 E6
Oaks La GL18 ...170 D2
Oaks The Berry Hill GL16 ...155 A8
Bristol BS7 ...18 E4
Cheltenham GL51 ...129 D6
Cinderford GL14 ...191 C5
Gloucester GL4 ...119 E7
Kemble GL7 ...141 F8
Oaksey CE Prim Sch
SN16 ...141 F4
Oaksey Rd SN16 ...142 B2
Oaktree Cres BS32 ...40 C2
Oaktree Ct BS11 ...16 E7
Oaktree Gdn GL4 ...119 C3
Oaktree Gdns BS13 ...1 E5
Oakwood Ave BS9 ...18 C6
Oakwood Cl Bream GL15 155 D1
Cinderford GL14 ...191 D5
Oakwood Dr GL3 ...119 F6
Oakwood Gdns BS36 ...31 E7
Oakwood Pk BS16 ...20 A3
Oakwood Rd
Bream GL15 ...155 D1
Bristol BS9 ...18 B6
Sling GL16 ...155 B3
Oatfield GL2 ...117 E2
Oatfield Rd GL2 ...100 A6
Oatground GL12 ...68 C7
Oathill La GL7 ...141 A8
Oatlands Ave BS14 ...3 A6
Oatley Ho BS9 ...18 A5
Oatley Trad Est 6 BS15 ...20 D1
Oatleys Cres 11 HR8 ...178 E8
Oatleys Rd HR8 ...178 E8
Oatleys Terr 10 HR8 ...178 E8
Oberon Ave BS5 ...19 E2
Ocker Hill GL6 ...102 E2
Octagon The NP16 ...60 F5
Octavia Pl GL15 ...92 B4
Odda's Chapel* GL19 ...173 C8
Oddfellows Row 3
GL54 ...176 F4
Oddfellows Terr 18
GL54 ...174 A7
Oddfellows' Terr 14
GL56 ...187 A3
Oddington Rd GL54 ...176 F4
Odessa Pk GL20 ...173 F8
Offa's Mead Prim Sch
NP16 ...61 A8
Offas Cl NP16 ...61 A7
Office Rd GL14 ...191 C3
Ogbourne Cl GL2 ...127 E3
Ohio Ave GL7 ...152 E2
Okebourne Cl BS10 ...28 B4
Okebourne Rd BS10 ...28 B4
Okus Rd GL53 ...131 A5
Old Acre Rd BS14 ...3 A3
Old All Saints Sch 12
GL50 ...193 C4
Old Ashley Hill BS6 ...18 F2
Old Aust Rd BS32 ...40 C6
Old Barns The WR8 ...180 A10
Old Barrow Hill BS11 ...16 D7
Old Bath Rd GL53 ...130 E5
Old Bell Chambers 3
NP16 ...60 E8
Old Bread St BS2 ...195 C2
Old Brewery La 16 GL8 ...140 B4
Old Bristol Rd GL6 ...91 B3
Old Bulwark Rd NP16 ...60 E7
Old Burford Rd OX7 ...177 E1
Old Cheltenham Rd
GL2 ...127 D4
Old Co-op The GL15 ...156 A2
Old Coach Cl NP16 ...61 C2
Old Coach Rd NP16 ...61 C3
Old Coach The WR12 ...185 C8
Old Comm GL6 ...148 A4
Old Comm The GL6 ...148 C6
Old Common The GL6 ...148 B6
Old Court Dr GL19 ...171 D1
Old Dam Rd GL15 ...92 D7
Old Dean Rd GL17 ...164 D6
Old Dixton Rd NP25 ...154 A8
Old Down Hill BS32 ...50 B2
Old Down Rd GL9 ...35 C8
Old Elmore La GL2 ...117 F2
Old Farm Cl SN16 ...141 E1
Old Farm La BS5 ...10 B6
Old Forge Cl OX7 ...177 E1
Old Forge Cotts
Didbrook GL54 ...184 D2
Stoke Orchard GL52 ...136 E5
Old Forge The GL15 ...147 D3
Old Furnace Cl GL15 ...147 F5
Old George The GL6 ...91 C4
Old Gloucester Rd
Alveston BS35 ...51 B5
Bourton-on-t-W GL54 ...168 E7
Bristol,Hambrook BS16 ...30 B2
Bristol,Stoke Gifford BS16 ...30 B4
North Corner BS36 ...41 D3
Staverton GL51 ...173 F1
Thornbury BS35 ...65 B2
Uckington GL51 ...132 B5
Old Gram Sch Mews The
9 GL55 ...189 A2
Old Hill Avening GL8 ...148 B1
Longhope GL17 ...165 A5
Old Horsley Rd GL6 ...91 B3
Old Hospital La GL20 ...192 D5
Old Hundred La GL9 ...34 D2
Old King Street Ct BS1 ...195 B3
Old La BS16 ...21 C6
Old La (Simmonds La)
HR9,GL18 ...170 C4
Old Lodge Ct GL50 ...133 E3
Old London Rd GL12 ...80 C1
Old Malt Ho BS2 ...195 C4
Old Manor Cl GL12 ...67 A5
Old Manor Gdns GL55 ...189 B6
Old Manor La GL20 ...192 E6
Old Mansion The GL52 ...134 C4
Old Market GL6 ...91 B4
Old Market Rdbt BS2 ...195 C3
Old Market St BS2 ...195 C3
Old Market Way 12
GL56 ...187 A3
Old Mill Cl BS37 ...32 B4
Old Mill Mus The*
GL54 ...176 C1
Old Mill The WR12 ...185 B8
Old Millbrook Terr 4
GL50 ...133 B2
Old Moat Ctyd GL2 ...172 F1
Old Monmouth Rd GL17 165 A5
Old Neighbourhood
GL6 ...148 C6
Old Oak Cl NP16 ...60 F5
Old Orchard Ct GL7 ...152 D7
Old Orchard The GL55 ...189 D3
Old Painswick Cl GL4 ...119 B6
Old Painswick Rd GL4 ...119 B6
Old Park Hill BS2 ...194 C3
Old Park Rd BS11 ...16 D7
Old Pk BS2 ...194 C3
Old Police Sta The BS4 ...9 A3
Old Pooles Yd BS4 ...9 E2
Old Post Office Alley 15
GL20 ...192 C4
Old Priory Rd BS20 ...16 B4
Old Quarry Ind Units The
GL8 ...140 C3
Old Quarry Rd BS11 ...16 E7
Old Quarry Rise BS11 ...16 E7
Old Rd Coleford GL16 ...155 B5
Maisemore GL2 ...126 A8
Southam GL52 ...134 C8
Old Rd The/Yr Hen Heol 22
NP25 ...154 A7
Old Rectory Cl GL5 ...99 A5
Old Rectory Gdns GL56 ...176 D8
Old Rectory Rd GL12 ...67 F4
Old Rectory The
Longborough GL56 ...176 D8
Staunton GL16 ...154 E7
Old Reddings Cl GL51 ...129 C7
Old Reddings Rd GL51 ...129 C7
Old Row GL1 ...196 C1
Old School Cl
Bristol BS30 ...11 D7
Nailsworth GL6 ...91 B4
Old School Ct The 18
GL8 ...140 B4
Old School Ho Bristol BS4 ...9 B2
3 Cheltenham GL50 ...193 A4
Old School Mews The 4
GL53 ...131 B6
Old Silk Mill The GL6 ...148 B5
Old Sneed Ave BS9 ...17 D4
Old Sneed Cotts BS9 ...17 E4
Old Sneed Pk BS9 ...17 D4
Old Sneed Rd BS9 ...17 D4
Old Sodbury CE Prim Sch
BS37 ...34 B8
Old Station Dr GL53 ...130 D5
Old Station Rd GL18 ...171 A5
Old Station Way GL16 ...155 A5
Old Tannery The BS2 ...195 C3
Old Town
26 Moreton-in-M GL56 ...187 A3
Old Town *continued*
Wotton-u-E GL12 ...68 B7
Old Town Mews GL15 ...147 F5
Old Tram Rd GL1 ...196 A2
Old Vicarage Ct
6 Coleford GL16 ...155 A5
Whitchurch BS14 ...3 C4
Old Vicarage Gn BS31 ...4 E6
Old Vicarage La GL7 ...141 F7
Old Vicarage Pl BS8 ...18 A1
Old Vicarage The
Bristol,Highridge BS13 ...1 F6
Bristol,Montpelier BS6 ...18 E1
Old Wesleyan Chapel The
BS30 ...11 B5
Old Wharf Ind Est HR8 ...178 E7
Old Wharf La HR9 ...162 E4
Old White Hart GL13 ...85 E3
Old Winding Wheel The
GL15 ...147 C8
Oldacre Dr GL52 ...138 A4
Oldbridge Rd BS14 ...3 C3
Oldbury Chase BS30 ...11 A2
Oldbury Cl GL51 ...132 D3
Oldbury Court Dr BS16 ...20 B6
Oldbury Court Prim Sch
BS16 ...20 C7
Oldbury Court Rd BS16 ...20 A5
Oldbury Ho GL20 ...192 D5
Oldbury La
Thornbury BS35 ...64 B4
Wick BS30 ...12 D5
Oldbury Orch GL3 ...128 D4
Oldbury Power Station
Visitor Ctr* BS35 ...75 B1
Oldbury Rd
Cheltenham GL51 ...132 E3
Tewkesbury GL20 ...192 C5
Oldbury-on-Severn Prim Sch
BS35 ...63 B5
Oldcroft Rd GL15 ...156 B1
Olde La GL54 ...184 B3
Oldends La GL10 ...97 D8
Oldfield GL20 ...192 D4
Oldfield Cres GL51 ...129 F8
Oldfield Girls Sch BA1 ...6 F1
Oldfield Pl BS8 ...7 F5
Oldfield Rd BS8 ...194 A1
Oldfields La BS35 ...41 D7
Oldhill GL5 ...98 D8
Oldland Common Sta*
BS30 ...11 C3
Oldlands Ave BS36 ...31 C6
Oldmead Wlk BS13 ...1 E7
Oldminster Rd GL13 ...93 D1
Oldown Cty Pk* BS32 ...50 C4
Oldwood La BS37 ...43 B8
Olio La GL53 ...193 C2
Olive Gdns BS35 ...50 F4
Olive Gr GL11 ...88 A2
Oliver Cl GL4 ...118 D2
Ollney Rd GL6 ...91 F6
Olveston CE Prim Sch
BS35 ...50 A3
Olveston Rd BS7 ...18 E5
Olympus Cl BS34 ...29 D6
Olympus Pk GL2 ...118 A2
Olympus Rd BS34 ...28 D7
Onslow Rd GL18 ...171 A4
Oram Ct BS30 ...10 F4
Orange Cl SN6 ...145 D3
Orange St BS2 ...195 C4
Orangery The GL4 ...119 E7
Orchard Ave Bristol BS1 ...194 C2
Broadway WR12 ...185 C8
Cheltenham GL51 ...132 F2
Chepstow/Cas-Gwent NP16 60 E5
Thornbury BS35 ...64 D1
Orchard Bank
2 Blockley GL56 ...186 C5
Great Rissington GL54 ...169 C4
Orchard Bvd BS30 ...11 B4
Orchard Cl
Aylburton GL15 ...147 E4
Bredon GL20 ...182 D7
Bretforton WR11 ...188 A6
Bristol,Kingswood BS15 ...10 E8
Bristol,Westbury on Trym
BS9 ...17 F5
Charfield GL12 ...67 A5
Clearwell GL16 ...154 F3
Dursley GL11 ...87 F5
English Bicknor GL16 ...163 A2
Gloucester GL2 ...126 E5
Hardwicke GL2 ...109 D7
Kemble GL7 ...141 F8
Keynsham BS31 ...4 D6
King's Stanley GL10 ...98 B3
Lea HR9 ...164 C8
Lechlade on T GL7 ...153 D2
Leonard Stanley GL10 ...97 F4
Mickleton GL55 ...189 B7
Mitcheldean GL17 ...164 D5
Winterbourne BS36 ...30 E5
Woodcroft NP16 ...73 A4
Yate BS37 ...43 F2
Orchard Cotts
10 Bristol BS16 ...20 D5
Chipping Campden GL55 ...189 C2
Orchard Cres BS11 ...16 D7
Orchard Ct Bristol BS9 ...17 C3
Bristol,Filton BS34 ...29 A2
19 Bristol,Pile Marsh BS5 ...9 D7
3 Monmouth/Trefynwy
NP25 ...154 A7
Painswick GL6 ...103 F8
Stonehouse GL10 ...97 E7
Tewkesbury GL20 ...192 D4
Orchard Ct *continued*
Yate BS37 ...43 B3
Orchard Dr Aust BS35 ...49 A7
Bristol BS13 ...2 A6
Churchdown GL3 ...128 D4
Twyning GL20 ...182 A7
Orchard End
Apperley GL19 ...173 C7
Monmouth/Trefynwy
NP25 ...154 A7
Orchard Farm Cl NP16 ...61 B7
Orchard Field GL8 ...140 B8
Orchard Gate
Blakeney GL15 ...156 D2
Bristol BS32 ...40 C2
Orchard Gdns BS15 ...10 F8
Orchard Gr The GL51 ...129 D1
Orchard Grange BS35 ...64 B2
Orchard Ho 2 Bristol BS5 ...9 F8
Cirencester GL7 ...190 D5
Orchard Ind Est GL54 ...184 A3
Orchard La
Brimscombe GL5 ...99 F1
Bristol BS1 ...194 C2
Ledbury HR8 ...178 E8
Orchard Lea
6 Alveston BS35 ...51 A5
Pill BS20 ...16 D4
Orchard Leaze GL11 ...87 D4
Orchard Mead
Nailsworth GL6 ...91 B4
Painswick GL6 ...103 F7
Orchard Pk
Cheltenham GL51 ...132 F5
Gloucester GL3 ...120 A6
Twigworth GL2 ...173 A1
Orchard Pk The GL19 ...173 C6
Orchard Pl
4 Ledbury HR8 ...178 F7
Stonehouse GL10 ...97 E7
Orchard Rd
Alderton GL20 ...183 E4
Bishop's Cleeve GL52 ...137 F3
Bishop's Cleeve,Brockhampton
GL52 ...137 E1
Bristol,Ashley Down BS7 ...18 E4
Bristol,Crew's Hole BS5 ...9 F8
Bristol,Kingswood BS15 ...10 E8
Coalpit Heath BS36 ...31 D7
Coleford GL16 ...155 A6
Gloucester GL2 ...127 E4
Joy's Green GL17 ...163 D3
Lydney GL15 ...92 B2
Newent GL18 ...171 A7
Pucklechurch BS16 ...22 B5
Stroud GL5 ...98 C6
Winchcombe GL54 ...139 F6
Orchard Ridge GL20 ...180 F7
Orchard Rise
Chepstow/Cas-Gwent NP16 60 B5
Dursley GL11 ...87 F3
Longborough GL56 ...176 D8
Newnham GL14 ...156 F6
Olveston BS35 ...50 A3
Tibberton GL19 ...171 E1
Orchard Springs GL6 ...91 A4
Orchard Sq BS5 ...9 D7
Orchard St Bristol BS1 ...194 C2
Wotton-u-E GL12 ...68 B7
Orchard The Bristol BS34 ...29 F5
Clapton-on-t-H GL54 ...168 F4
13 Fairford GL7 ...152 E4
Frampton Cotterell BS36 ...31 C8
North Cerney GL7 ...158 D3
Oaksey SN16 ...141 F4
Pill BS20 ...16 C4
Tewkesbury GL20 ...192 D5
Tytherington GL12 ...52 B5
Uckington GL51 ...132 D7
Uley GL11 ...89 B1
Woolaston GL15 ...147 C3
Orchard Vale BS15 ...10 F7
Orchard View
Draycott GL56 ...186 E6
Stroud GL5 ...99 A4
Orchard Villas GL10 ...98 C3
Orchard Way
17 Berry Hill GL16 ...155 A7
Cheltenham GL51 ...132 F3
Churchdown GL3 ...128 B7
Huntley GL19 ...165 D6
Kingham OX7 ...177 F2
Maisemore GL2 ...126 A7
Orchard Wlk GL12 ...67 F4
Orchards The
Bristol,Kingswood BS15 ...10 F7
Bristol,Shirehampton BS11 ...16 E6
Charlton Kings GL52 ...131 C6
Gloucester GL3 ...120 A6
Longhope GL17 ...164 F6
Lydney GL15 ...92 A3
Orchid Mdw NP16 ...60 B5
Organ's Alley GL1 ...196 B2
Oridge St GL19 ...172 A6
Oriel Gr GL56 ...187 A2
Oriel Rd GL50 ...193 B3
Oriole Way GL4 ...119 D6
Orion Dr BS34 ...29 D6
Orland Way BS30 ...11 A3
Orlebar Gdns BS11 ...27 B2
Orlham La HR8 ...178 D6
Ormerod Rd Bristol BS9 ...17 E5
Sedbury NP16 ...61 B7
Ormond Pl GL50 ...193 B3
Ormond Terr GL50 ...193 B3

Ormonds Cl BS32 ....40 E1
Ormsley Cl BS34 ....28 C8
Orpen Gdns BS7 ....19 B5
Orpen Pk BS32 ....40 B3
Orpheus Ave BS34 ....29 D6
Orrisdale Terr GL53 ....193 C2
Orwell Dr BS31 ....5 A4
Orwell St BS3 ....8 E3
Osborne Ave Bristol BS7 ..18 F3
Gloucester GL4 ....118 C1
Osborne Cl BS34 ....29 D4
Osborne Gdns GL20 ....192 D4
Osborne Rd
Bristol,Clifton BS8 ....18 A1
Bristol,Southville BS3 ....8 C4
Severn Beach BS35 ....38 A7
Osborne Terr
10 Bristol BS3 ....8 B2
Thrupp GL5 ....99 E3
Osborne Villas BS2 ....194 C4
Osborne Wallis Ho BS8 .194 A1
Osbourne Ho 6 GL50 ....130 B8
Osier Cl GL4 ....119 A4
Osprey Cl GL4 ....119 D5
Osprey Ct BS14 ....2 D5
Osprey Dr GL10 ....97 F8
Osprey Pk BS35 ....64 D3
Osprey Rd 15 Bristol BS5 ...9 C7
Cheltenham GL53 ....130 C5
Osric Rd GL1 ....118 F6
Ossage GL54 ....166 C6
Othello Cl GL51 ....132 E2
Otter Rd GL4 ....120 A5
Otterburn Ho GL2 ....118 C4
Otterford Cl BS14 ....3 B5
Otters Field GL54 ....174 A8
Ottery Cl BS11 ....27 A1
Ottrells Mead BS32 ....40 C3
Our Lady of Lourdes RC Prim Sch BS15 ....10 E7
Our Lady of the Rosary CR Prim Sch BS11 ....17 A8
Our Lady of the Rosary Prim Sch BS11 ....27 A1
Oval App GL2 ....157 F3
Oval The
Frampton on Severn GL2 .100 A5
Gloucester GL1 ....118 D6
Over Bridge★ GL2 ....126 B4
Over Cswy GL1 ....126 C3
Over La BS35 ....39 D2
Over Old Rd GL19,GL2 ..172 C3
Overbrook Cl GL4 ....127 C1
Overbrook Dr GL52 ....133 F3
Overbrook Rd GL2 ....109 E7
Overbury CE Fst Sch GL20 ....182 F8
Overbury Rd GL1 ....119 A8
Overbury St GL53 ....131 A7
Overhill BS20 ....16 D4
Overhill Rd GL7 ....190 B8
Overley Rd GL7 ....149 E7
Overndale Rd BS16 ....20 C6
Overndale Sch BS37 ....34 A7
Overnhill Ct BS16 ....20 D5
Overnhill Rd BS16 ....20 D5
Overnhurst Ct 2 BS16 ..20 D5
Overton 5 BS4 ....9 D1
Overton Ct GL50 ....193 A3
Overton La GL2 ....157 E5
Overton Park Rd GL50 ..193 A3
Overton Rd Bristol BS6 ...18 E2
Cheltenham GL50 ....193 A3
Owen Gdns 1 GL16 ....155 A6
Owen Gr BS9 ....18 B5
Owen Henry Ho BS2 ....19 A1
Owen St 18 BS5 ....9 B8
Owl Cl GL4 ....119 D5
Owlpen Manor & Gdns★ GL11 ....89 E1
Owls End Rd GL52 ....138 A4
Owls Eye Cl 4 GL16 ....155 B6
Owls Head Rd BS15 ....10 E6
Ox Yd GL7 ....149 B1
Oxbarton BS34 ....29 F5
Oxbutts Cvn Pk GL52 ..138 B4
Oxbutts Ind Est GL52 ..138 B4
Oxebode The GL1 ....196 B3
Oxen Leaze BS32 ....40 E2
Oxford Cl 1 GL52 ....130 F8
Oxford Ho GL7 ....190 D4
Oxford Pas GL50 ....193 B4
Oxford Pl
19 Bristol,Clifton BS8 ....7 F6
14 Bristol,Upper Easton BS5 ....19 B1
Oxford Rd GL1 ....196 C4
Oxford St Bristol BS2 ...195 C2
7 Bristol,Redfield BS5 ....9 C7
Bristol,The Dings BS2 ....9 A6
Bristol,Tyndall's Park BS2 ....194 C4
Bristol,Windmill Hill BS3 ....8 F4
Cheltenham GL52 ....130 F8
10 Chepstow/Cas-Gwent NP16 ....60 E8
Gloucester GL1 ....196 C3
Lydney GL15 ....92 A2
Moreton-in-M GL56 ....187 A3
Oxford Terr
Gloucester GL1 ....196 C3
Stroud GL5 ....99 C8
Oxford Way GL51 ....130 A6
Oxford Wlk 2 GL52 ....130 F8
Oxhouse Gdns BS10 ....27 E3
Oxleaze BS13 ....2 D4
Oxleaze Cl 4 GL8 ....140 B4
Oxleaze La BS41 ....1 E3
Oxleaze Rd Culkerton GL8 140 F6
7 Tetbury GL8 ....140 B4
Oxmead Cl GL52 ....138 B4
Oxmoor GL4 ....119 E3
Oxpens GL54 ....167 D1
Oxstalls Com Sch GL1 ..127 A4
Oxstalls Dr GL2 ....127 A5
Oxstalls La GL2 ....127 B4
Oxstalls Way GL2 ....127 B4
Ozleworth BS15 ....11 A8

P

Packer's Rd GL14 ....191 D4
Packhorse La GL7 ....160 A1
Pacquet Ho BS20 ....16 D5
Paddock Cl Bristol BS32 ..40 E2
Bristol,Emerson's Green BS16 ....21 C6
Paddock Gdn BS14 ....2 F4
Paddock Gdns
Alveston BS35 ....51 A5
Gloucester GL2 ....127 D5
Paddock Rise GL10 ....97 F8
Paddock The
Chepstow/Cas-Gwent NP16 60 D6
Cirencester GL7 ....190 E4
Coleford GL16 ....155 B6
Highworth SN6 ....145 D3
17 Ledbury HR8 ....178 E8
South Cerney GL7 ....142 F7
Paddocks La GL50 ....133 D5
Paddocks The
Baunton GL7 ....150 D7
Bristol BS16 ....31 A1
Highnam GL2 ....125 D5
Thornbury BS35 ....64 D1
Paddocks The/Y Paddgau 6 NP25 ....154 A7
Padin Cl 3 GL6 ....148 C6
Padmore Ct 7 BS5 ....9 D7
Padstow Rd BS4 ....2 F8
Pady Ct GL7 ....190 C3
Paganhill Est GL5 ....98 F8
Paganhill La GL5 ....98 F7
Page Ct BS16 ....20 F4
Page Rd BS16 ....20 D4
Page's La GL20 ....181 F7
Pages Mead BS11 ....16 C8
Paget Ho GL7 ....190 D5
Pagets Rd GL52 ....138 A2
Painswick Ave BS34 ....29 B8
Painswick Dr BS37 ....43 E1
Painswick Hts GL6 ....104 A6
Painswick Lodge 2 GL4 ....119 C4
Painswick Old Rd GL6 ..103 C1
Painswick Rd
Cheltenham GL50 ....193 A1
Gloucester GL4 ....119 C4
Stroud GL6 ....103 B2
Watermead GL3 ....120 D3
Painswick Rococo Gdn★ GL6 ....111 E2
Pakistan Ho 1 GL51 ....132 E2
Palestra Lo GL7 ....190 C5
Palm Rd GL20 ....192 E2
Palmdale Cl BS30 ....11 A3
Palmer Ave
Gloucester GL4 ....119 F5
Severn Beach BS35 ....38 C3
Palmers Cl BS30 ....11 A6
Palmers Leaze BS34 ....30 A6
Palmerston Rd BS6 ....18 C4
Palmerston St 6 BS3 ....8 C3
Palmyra Rd BS3 ....8 B2
Pancake La GL19 ....173 E5
Panoramic The BS1 ....194 C3
Pantile The 8 BS3 ....8 C3
Paper Mill Cotts OX18 ..161 E7
Parabola Cl GL50 ....193 A3
Parabola La GL50 ....193 A3
Parabola Rd GL50 ....193 A3
Parade Ct BS5 ....19 F2
Parade The Bristol BS34 ..39 F1
Bristol,Bishopsworth BS13 ..2 A6
Bristol,Shirehampton BS11 .16 E6
Brockworth GL3 ....120 E5
Chipping Sodbury BS37 ....44 A1
Gloucester GL2 ....127 E4
Paradise Row GL54 ....167 E2
Paragon Terr GL53 ....193 B2
Paragon The BS8 ....7 F6
Parawell La GL15 ....147 C8
Parbrook Ct BS14 ....3 B5
Parfitt's Hill 8 BS5 ....9 F6
Parish The BS3 ....194 B1
Park Ave Bristol BS32 ....40 A2
Bristol,Eastville BS5 ....19 D3
Bristol,Rose Green BS5 ....9 E8
Bristol,Windmill Hill BS3 ....8 E3
Frampton Cotterell BS36 ...31 B6
Gloucester GL2 ....127 C5
Highworth SN6 ....145 D3
Winterbourne BS36 ....30 E7
Park Brake GL2 ....125 D4
Park Cl
Bristol,Cadbury Heath BS30 11 B5
Bristol,Kingswood BS15 ...10 E7
Fairford GL7 ....152 E4
Keynsham BS31 ....4 D5
Northway GL20 ....182 B5
St Briavels GL15 ....146 F7
8 Tetbury GL8 ....140 C4
Park Cres
Bristol,Cadbury Heath BS30 11 B5
Bristol,Frenchay BS16 ....30 C1
Bristol,Rose Green BS5 ....9 E8
Park Ct Lydney GL15 ....92 A3
Stroud GL5 ....99 D6
Park Dr GL2 ....117 F1
Park End 1 SN6 ....142 F4
Park End Rd GL1 ....196 B1
Park Farm GL54 ....168 F8
Park Farm Ct 13 BS30 ...10 F4
Park Farm Village Gn BS36 ....31 B6
Park Gate
Cheltenham GL50 ....193 A1
Redmarley D'Abitot GL19 .179 E2
Park Glade NP16 ....146 B4
Park Gr Bristol BS9 ....18 C5
Whitecroft GL15 ....155 E1
Park Hill Bristol BS11 ....16 F6
Whitecroft GL15 ....155 E1
Park Hill Comm GL15 ..147 A2
Park Hill La NP16,GL15 ..146 E2
Park Hill Rd
Tidenham Chase GL15 ....146 F2
Woolaston GL15 ....147 A2
Park Ho GL50 ....193 A1
Park Inf Sch The GL10 ...97 E7
Park Jun Sch GL10 ....97 E7
Park La Bristol BS2 ....194 C3
Brockhampton GL54 ....174 A1
Cheltenham GL52 ....134 B6
Cirencester GL7 ....190 C4
Frampton Cotterell BS36 ...31 B6
Ilmington CV36 ....189 E7
North Nibley GL11 ....79 E7
Woodchester GL5 ....90 F6
Wotton-u-E GL12 ....69 A8
Park Leaze BS34 ....39 E1
Park Mews GL50 ....130 C6
Park Par GL10 ....97 E8
Park Pl
5 Ashton Keynes SN6 ...142 F5
Bristol,Tyndall's Park BS2 ....194 C3
Bristol,Upper Eastville BS5 .19 E3
Bristol,Victoria Park BS8 ..194 B3
Cheltenham GL50 ....193 A1
Park Prim Sch The BS15 .10 E8
Park Rd Berry Hill GL16 ..155 A7
Blockley GL56 ....186 C6
Bristol,Brandon Hill BS3 ..194 B1
Bristol,Cadbury Heath BS30 11 B5
Bristol,Kingswood BS15 ...10 D8
Bristol,Northville BS7 ....29 A1
Bristol,Shirehampton BS11 .16 F6
Bristol,Staple Hill BS16 ....20 E5
Bristol,Stapleton BS16 ....19 D5
Chipping Campden GL55 ..188 F1
6 Coleford GL16 ....155 A6
Gloucester GL1 ....196 B2
Highleadon GL19 ....171 F2
Keynsham BS31 ....4 E4
Leyhill GL12 ....66 B4
Nailsworth GL6 ....91 C3
Stonehouse GL10 ....97 E8
Stroud GL5 ....99 D6
Thornbury BS35 ....64 B2
Park Road Cres GL6 ....91 C3
Park Row Aylburton GL15 147 D4
Bristol BS1 ....194 C3
Frampton Cotterell BS36 ...31 A8
Park St
Bristol,Brandon Hill BS1 ..194 C3
Bristol,Crew's Hole BS5 ....9 F8
Bristol,Totterdown BS4 ....9 A3
Cheltenham GL50 ....193 A4
Cirencester GL7 ....190 C5
Fairford GL7 ....152 E4
Gloucester GL1 ....196 B3
Hawkesbury Upton GL9 ....56 A2
Iron Acton BS37 ....42 D4
Stow-on-t-W GL54 ....176 F4
Park Street Ave BS1 ...194 C3
Park Terr GL6 ....91 F6
Park The Bristol BS32 ....40 C3
Bristol,Frenchay BS16 ....30 B1
Bristol,Kingswood BS15 ....10 E8
Bristol,Willsbridge BS30 ...11 B1
Cheltenham GL50 ....130 B6
Keynsham BS31 ....4 E6
Northway GL20 ....182 B5
Stow-on-t-W GL54 ....176 F4
Park View
Bristol,Kingswood BS15 ...10 E7
Bristol,Southville BS3 ....8 C4
Cheltenham GL51 ....132 E4
Chepstow/Cas-Gwent NP16 72 C1
4 Gloucester GL4 ....119 C4
Ruardean GL17 ....163 F4
Saul GL2 ....157 F4
Sedbury NP16 ....61 B8
Stratton GL7 ....190 B8
Yate BS37 ....32 E8
Park View Ave BS35 ....64 C2
Park View Ct BS16 ....20 E5
Park View Dr GL5 ....98 E8
Park View Rd GL13 ....85 D3
Park View Terr BS5 ....9 E8
Park Way BS30 ....11 B5
Park Wood Cl BS14 ....2 F4
Parkbury Cl GL51 ....133 A2
Parkend Prim Sch GL15 155 F2
Parkend Rd Bream GL15 .155 D1
Coleford GL16 ....155 B5
Yorkley GL15 ....156 A2
Parkend Sta★ GL15 ....155 E3
Parkend Wlk
Coleford GL16 ....155 B5
Sling GL16 ....155 B3
Parker Pl 1 WR12 ....185 B8
Parker St 5 BS3 ....8 B3
Parkers Ave BS30 ....12 C7
Parkers Barton BS5 ....9 B6
Parkers Cl BS10 ....28 E4
Parkers La GL56 ....187 A3
Parkfield Ave 3 BS5 ....9 D7
Parkfield Cotts GL6 ....112 A2
Parkfield Rank BS16 ....22 A7
Parkfield Rd BS16 ....22 A6
Parkhouse La BS31 ....4 C2
Parkhurst Ave 4 BS16 ...20 B4
Parkland Mews 26 GL54 176 F4
Parkland Rd
Cheltenham GL53 ....130 F4
Dursley GL11 ....87 F4
Parkland Sq GL7 ....190 B2
Parkland Way BS35 ....64 C3
Parklands
Bristol,High Kingsdown BS8 ....194 C4
Bristol,Kingswood BS15 ...10 E8
Churchdown GL3 ....128 A6
Quedgeley GL2 ....117 F1
Wotton-u-E GL12 ....68 B8
Quedgeley GL2 ....109 E8
Parklands Cl NP16 ....60 B4
Parklands Rd BS3 ....7 E4
Parkmill HR9 ....162 C7
Parks Rd GL17 ....164 D5
Parkside GL16 ....155 A5
Parkside Ave BS36 ....30 E6
Parkside Cl GL3 ....127 F6
Parkside Dr GL3 ....127 F6
Parkside Gdns BS5 ....19 B4
Parkstone Ave BS7 ....18 F6
Parkwall Cres BS30 ....10 F4
Parkwall Prim Sch BS30 .11 A4
Parkwall Rd BS30 ....11 A4
Parkway Bristol BS34 ....30 A4
Siddington GL7 ....150 D2
Parkway N BS34 ....30 A4
Parkway Trad Est 10 BS2 .18 F2
Parkwood Cres GL3 ....119 F6
Parkwood Gr GL53 ....131 A4
Parliament Cl GL5 ....99 C7
Parliament Prim Sch GL5 99 F7
Parliament St Bristol BS4 ..9 A4
Gloucester GL1 ....196 B2
Stroud GL5 ....99 D7
Parnall Cres BS37 ....43 C2
Parnall Rd BS16 ....20 A3
Parnall Road Ind Est BS16 ....20 A3
Parnell Rd BS16 ....19 E7
Parr Cl GL3 ....127 F7
Parr Ho GL54 ....139 F5
Parragate GL14 ....191 D5
Parragate Rd GL14 ....191 C5
Parry Rd GL1 ....118 F6
Parry's Cl BS9 ....17 E5
Parry's La BS9 ....17 F5
Parrys Gr BS9 ....17 E5
Parslow Barton 4 BS5 ..10 A7
Parson St BS3 ....8 B2
Parson Street Prim Sch BS3 ....8 C2
Parson Street Sta BS3 ....8 B2
Parson's Cnr GL54 ....176 F5
Parsonage Farm 8 SN6 143 E4
Parsonage Rd BS41 ....7 C2
Parsonage St GL11 ....88 A1
Parsons Ave BS34 ....29 F5
Parsons Ct GL6 ....148 A3
Parsons La
Redmarley D'Abitot GL19 .179 F2
Weston-s-E GL55 ....188 D3
Parsons Paddock BS14 ...3 A7
Parsons Wlk BS30 ....11 D7
Partition St BS1 ....194 C2
Parton Dr GL3 ....128 C5
Parton Manor Inf Sch GL3 ....128 B6
Parton Mews GL3 ....128 B6
Parton Rd GL3 ....128 C6
Partridge Cl
Gloucester GL2 ....118 C5
Stonehouse GL10 ....97 F8
Yate BS37 ....43 F4
Partridge Dr BS16 ....20 C6
Partridge Rd BS16 ....22 C4
Partridge Way GL7 ....190 E4
Parva Springs NP16 ....146 B4
Passage Leaze BS11 ....16 D6
Passage Rd
Arlingham GL2 ....157 B6
Aust BS35 ....48 F7
Bristol,Brentry BS10 ....27 F3
Bristol,Westbury on Trym BS9 ....18 A8
Saul GL2 ....157 F4
Passage Road Brentry Hill BS9,BS10 ....28 A2
Passage St BS2 ....195 B2
Pastor's Hill GL15 ....147 D8
Pasture La GL56 ....186 C5
Patch Ct BS16 ....21 A8
Patch Elm La BS37 ....42 F7
Patch La BS37 ....43 A8
Patches The GL17 ....163 F3
Patchway BS34 ....29 B8
Patchway Brook BS32 ...40 C2
Patchway CE Prim Sch BS34 ....40 C1
Patchway High Sch BS32 40 B1
Patchway Sta BS34 ....29 C6
Patchway Trad Est BS34 .28 E7
Paternoster Sch GL7 ...190 D3
Paterson Rd GL7 ....190 E4
Pates Ave GL51 ....133 B2
Pates Gram Sch GL51 ..132 E3
Patseamur Mews GL2 ..127 E5
Patterdale Cl GL51 ....132 F5
Patterson Ho 8 BS1 ...195 B1
Paul Mead GL6 ....111 B1
Paul St Bristol BS2 ....194 C4
Gloucester GL1 ....118 F7
Paul's Rise GL5 ....99 A2
Pauls Croft SN6 ....143 F4
Pauls Wlk GL19 ....165 D6
Paulton Dr BS7 ....18 C4
Paultow Ave BS3 ....8 E3
Paultow Rd BS3 ....8 E3
Pauntley CE Prim Sch GL18 ....171 B8
Pauntley Court Dr GL19 171 C7
Pavey Cl BS13 ....2 C4
Pavey Rd BS13 ....2 C4
Pavilion Bsns Pk GL14 ..191 B7
Pavilion Gdns GL50 ....130 C6
Pavilion Rd NP16 ....61 C2
Pavilions The Bristol BS4 ..9 C1
Cheltenham GL53 ....193 B2
Pawlett Rd BS13 ....2 C3
Pawlett Wlk BS13 ....2 C3
Paxford Rd GL55 ....189 B2
Paxhill La GL20 ....182 A8
Paxton BS16 ....19 E8
Paybridge Rd BS13 ....1 F4
Paygrove La GL2 ....127 D5
Payne Dr BS5 ....9 B7
Paynes Mdw GL2 ....100 F5
Paynes Orchard Pk BS10 28 D5
Paynes Pitch GL3 ....128 D4
Peach Cl GL20 ....192 E1
Peach Cotts GL20 ....192 E1
Peache Ct BS16 ....20 E6
Peache Rd BS16 ....20 F6
Peacock Cl
5 Cheltenham GL51 ....132 D2
Gloucester GL4 ....119 E5
5 Newent GL18 ....171 A4
Peacock Gdns 6 GL18 ..171 A4
Peacock La GL14 ....191 C1
Peacocks La BS15 ....10 C7
Peak La GL11 ....89 A7
Peakstile Piece GL52 ..138 B3
Pear Orch The GL20 ....182 C5
Pear Tree Cl
Chipping Campden GL55 ..189 A1
Hardwicke GL2 ....109 E7
Lower Swell GL54 ....176 D4
32 Winchcombe GL54 ....174 A7
Woodmancote GL52 ....138 C3
Pear Tree Hey BS37 ....43 E5
Pear Tree Rd BS32 ....40 C2
Pearce Way GL2 ....118 B4
Pearces Hill BS16 ....20 B7
Pearcroft Rd GL10 ....98 A6
Pearl St BS3 ....8 B3
Pearsall Rd BS30 ....10 E2
Peart Cl Bristol BS13 ....1 E5
Gloucester GL1 ....127 B1
Peart Dr BS13 ....1 E4
Peartree Cl BS13 ....2 B4
Peartree La
Bristol,Lower Soundwell BS15 ....20 F2
Bristol,St George BS5 ....10 B6
Pearwood Way GL4 ....118 C2
Peashill Cnr GL54 ....176 B2
Pecked La GL52 ....138 A3
Peel Cl GL53 ....131 C5
Peel Ctr The GL1 ....196 A1
Peel St BS5 ....195 C4
Peg Hill BS37 ....43 F4
Pegasus Bldg GL2 ....118 A2
Pegasus Ct
Bourton-on-t-W GL54 ....169 A8
12 Broadway WR12 ....185 B8
Cheltenham GL51 ....130 B7
Gloucester GL4 ....127 E1
Pegasus Gdns GL2 ....117 F2
Pegasus Pk BS34 ....29 C6
Pegasus Rd BS34 ....28 D7
Peggotty Bglws GL4 ....119 C7
Peghouse Cl GL5 ....103 D1
Peghouse Rise GL5 ....103 D1
Pelham Cres GL3 ....128 A6
Pemberton Ct BS16 ....20 C5
Pembery Rd BS3 ....8 B3
Pembridge Cl GL52 ....131 C6
Pembridge Ct GL50 ....193 A1
Pembroke Ave BS11 ....16 E6
Pembroke Gate BS8 ....18 A1
Pembroke Gr BS8 ....194 A3
Pembroke Mans BS8 ...194 A4
Pembroke Pl
Bristol,Hotwells BS8 ....194 A1
Bristol,St Pauls BS1 ....195 B4
Pembroke Prim Sch NP16 ....60 E6
Pembroke Rd
Bristol,Clifton BS8 ....194 A4
Bristol,Kingswood BS15 ...20 E2
Bristol,Shirehampton BS11 .16 E6
Bristol,Southville BS3 ....8 C4
Cheltenham GL51 ....129 E6
Chepstow/Cas-Gwent NP16 60 E6
Pembroke St Bristol BS2 195 B4
Cinderford GL14 ....191 D4
Gloucester GL1 ....196 C1
Pembroke Vale BS8 ...194 A4

Pembury GL50 ....193 A2
Pembury Rd GL4 ....118 E4
Pen Park Rd BS10 ......28 D2
Pen-Moel Cotts NP16 ...73 A4
Penard Way BS15 ....10 F7
Penby Lawn GL14 ......156 F6
Penda Pl NP16 ....61 A8
Pendennis Ave BS16 .....20 D4
Pendennis Ho 5 BS16 ...20 D5
Pendennis Pk BS4 ....9 D2
Pendennis Rd BS16 ......20 D5
Pendil Cl GL50 ....133 B6
Pendock CE Prim Sch
GL19 ....180 A4
Pendock Cl Bristol BS30 ..11 C1
Quedgeley GL2 ....117 E1
Pendock Cross GL19 ...180 A3
Pendock Ct BS16 ....21 B7
Pendock Rd Bristol BS16 .20 C6
Winterbourne BS36 ....30 E5
Penfield Ct BS2 ....19 A2
Penfield Rd BS2 ....19 A2
Penharva Cl GL51 ......133 A3
Penhill Ho GL4 ....119 B5
Penhill Rd GL4 ....119 B5
Penlea Ct BS11 ....16 D7
Penlea Ho BS11 ....16 D7
Penmoel La NP16 ....73 A3
Penmoyle Gdns NP16 ...73 A4
Penn Dr BS16 ....30 C1
Penn La GL10 ....98 B2
Penn St BS1 ....195 B3
Pennard Ct BS14 ....3 B5
Penngrove BS30 ....11 A3
Pennine Cl GL2 ....109 E8
Pennine Rd Bristol BS30 ..11 C4
Cheltenham GL52 ......134 B3
Pennington Ct GL51 ....132 E4
Pennlea BS13 ....2 C7
Pennon Rise BS1 ......194 C1
Pennsylvania Ave GL51 .132 F3
Pennsylvania Mews
GL51 ....132 F3
Penny Cl GL2 ....127 D4
Penny La GL2 ....95 B2
Pennyroyal Gr BS16 .....19 E4
Pennywell Ct 3 BS5 ......9 A8
Pennywell Rd BS5 ....9 A8
Penpole Ave BS11 ....16 E6
Penpole Cl BS11 ....16 D7
Penpole La BS11 ....16 E7
Penpole Pk BS11 ....16 E7
Penpole Pl BS11 ....16 E6
Penrith Cl GL51 ....129 F7
Penrith Gdns BS10 ......18 D8
Penrith Rd GL51 ....129 F7
Penrose BS14 ....2 F7
Penrose Cl GL6 ....102 E3
Penrose Dr BS32 ....29 D7
Penrose Rd GL3 ....127 D6
Pensfield Pk BS10 ......28 D4
Pensford Ct BS14 ....3 D5
Pensile Rd GL6 ....91 D4
Pentagon The BS9 ....17 B5
Pentathlon Way GL50 ..133 D5
Penterry La NP16 ....72 B7
Penterry Pk NP16 ....60 D8
Pentire Ave BS13 ....2 A6
Pentland Ave BS35 ......51 E8
Pentwyn Cl NP16 ....60 B6
Pentylands Cl SN6 .....145 C4
Peppercorn Alley GL20 .182 E8
Pepys Cl BS31 ....5 D2
Perch Dr GL16 ....155 C6
Percival Rd
Bishop's Cleeve GL52 ....137 E1
Bristol BS8 ....7 F8
Percy St 8 Bristol BS3 ....8 D4
Gloucester GL1 ....118 F7
Percy Walker Ct BS16 ...20 C6
Peregrine Cl GL2 ......117 F3
Peregrine Rd GL53 .....130 C5
Perrett Ho BS2 ....195 C3
Perrett Way BS20 ....16 E4
Perretts Ct BS1 ....194 C1
Perricks Cl GL14 ......165 D3
Perrie Dr WR11 ....188 C7
Perrinpit Rd BS36 ......41 E2
Perrinsfield GL7 ....153 E3
Perrott Rd BS15 ....21 A1
Perry Cl
Charlton Kings GL53 .....131 B5
28 Newent GL18 ....171 A4
Winterbourne BS36 ....30 D4
Perry Court Inf Sch BS14 .3 A6
Perry Court Jun Sch BS14 3 A6
Perry Ctr The GL2 .....109 F6
Perry Field GL15 ....147 C3
Perry Hill GL20 ....192 C3
Perry Orch Stroud GL5 ...98 D8
Upton St Leonards GL4 ...119 E2
Perry Rd BS1 ....195 A3
Perry St BS5 ....9 A8
Perry Way GL2 ....100 B3
Perry's Court La GL17 .163 E4
Perrycroft Ave BS13 ......2 A6
Perrycroft Rd BS13 ....2 A6
Perryfield Ct 1 GL54 ...168 F7
Perrygrove Rd GL16 ...155 A4
Perrygrove Rly★ GL16 .155 A4
Perrymans Cl BS16 ......20 A6
Perrys Lea BS32 ....40 D2
Persh La GL2 ....125 F6
Persh Way GL2 ....126 A7
Perth GL10 ....101 E1
Perwell Cl GL20 ....182 C8
Pesley Cl BS13 ....2 A4
Peter Pennell Cl GL51 ..132 E4
Peter's St GL10 ....96 E3
Peter's Terr BS5 ....9 B7
Petercole Dr BS13 ....2 A6
Peters Field GL12 ......125 E5
Peterson Sq BS13 ....2 C3
Petersway Gdns BS5 .....10 A6
Pethera Cl GL7 ....190 C6
Petherbridge Way BS7 ..19 A5
Petherton Cl BS15 ....10 E7
Petherton Gdns BS14 .....3 B7
Petherton Rd BS14 ....3 B7
Petherton Road Inf Sch
BS14 ....3 B7
Pethick Ho BS4 ....2 F8
Pettigrove Gdns BS15 ...10 E7
Pettigrove Rd BS15 ......10 E6
Petty La GL52 ....138 F3
Petty Marsh GL15 ......146 E6
Pettycroft GL17 ....163 F4
Petworth Cl GL4 ....110 C8
Pevelands GL11 ....87 F5
Pevensey Wlk BS4 ....2 D7
Peverell Cl BS10 ....27 F3
Peverell Dr BS10 ....27 F3
Peveril Ho GL2 ....118 C4
Peymans Terr GL7 .....142 F7
Pheasant La GL51 ......132 B1
Pheasant Mead GL10 ....97 F8
Pheasant Rise HR9 .....162 F7
Pheasant Way GL7 .....190 F5
Pheasantry The GL7 ....143 F8
Phelps Way GL19 ......171 E1
Philadelphia Ct BS1 ....195 B3
Philip St
Bristol,St Philip's Marsh BS2 .9 B5
Bristol,Windmill Hill BS3 ....8 D4
Gloucester GL1 ....118 D7
Philip's Cl GL15 ....156 B1
Philippa Cl BS14 ....3 A7
Philips Ho 2 BS2 ......195 B4
Phillimore Gdns GL2 ...100 A5
Phillimore Rd GL11 ......87 E4
Phillips La GL19 ....179 F2
Phillips Rd WR12 ......188 A1
Phippen St 1 BS1 ......195 B1
Phipps Barton BS15 .....10 B8
Phipps St BS3 ....8 B4
Phoenix Bsns Pk BS3 .....8 A2
Phoenix Cl GL16 ....155 A5
Phoenix Dr NP16 ....61 A4
Phoenix Gr BS6 ....18 C5
Phoenix Ho BS5 ....9 B6
Phoenix Trad Est GL5 ...99 E3
Phoenix Way GL7 ......190 C4
Piccadilly
Guiting Power GL54 .....175 B3
Stroud GL5 ....99 D7
Piccadilly Way GL52 ...134 D4
Picked Acre GL2 ....124 C2
Pickedmoor La BS35 ....63 E5
Pickering Cl GL53 ......130 C6
Pickering Rd GL53 .....130 C6
Picklenash Jun Sch
GL18 ....170 F5
Pickwick Cl GL2 ....127 D3
Picton Ho GL7 ....190 D5
Picton La BS6 ....18 E1
Picton Mews 6 BS6 .....18 E1
Picton St BS6 ....18 E1
Piece Hedge GL54 .....168 F8
Piece The
Churchdown GL3 ....128 D4
Hatherop GL7 ....152 E7
Piercefield Ave NP16 ...72 C1
Piercefield Terr NP16 ...72 B5
Piermont Dr NP16 ....73 A2
Pigeon House Dr BS13 ...2 D4
Pigeon La GL20 ....183 A8
Pigott Ave BS13 ....2 A4
Pigs Cross GL18 ....170 C3
Pike Cnr WR12 ....188 B2
Pike Hill Rise GL54 ....167 B3
Pike House Cl 13 SN6 ..143 E4
Pike La GL6 ....91 B3
Pike Rd 9 Coleford GL16 155 A6
Winstone GL7,GL53 .....115 A1
Pilemarsh BS5 ....9 D7
Pilford Ave GL53 ......130 E4
Pilford Cl GL53 ....130 E5
Pilford Ct GL53 ....130 E3
Pilford Rd GL53 ....130 E3
Pilgrim Cl 4 GL4 ....119 E6
Pilgrims Way
Avonmouth BS11 ....16 C7
Bristol BS16 ....20 D8
Pilgrims Wharf BS4 ......9 E7
Pilgrove Cl GL51 ....132 D4
Pilgrove Way GL51 .....132 E5
Pilkington Cl BS34 ......29 C2
Pill La GL56 ....187 F1
Pill Rd Abbots Leigh BS8 ..16 F1
Abbots Leigh BS8 ....7 A8
Pill BS20 ....16 E2
Pill St BS20 ....16 D4
Pillcroft Cl GL3 ....121 A4
Pillcroft Rd GL3 ....121 A4
Pilley Cres GL53 ....130 D4
Pilley La GL53 ....130 D4
Pillingers Gdns BS6 .....18 B2
Pillingers Rd BS15 ......10 C7
Pillowell Com Prim Sch
GL15 ....155 F1
Pillowell Dr GL1 ....127 A2
Pillowell Rd GL15 ......155 F1
Pillows Green Rd GL19 .172 B8
Pilning Prim Sch BS35 ..38 E6
Pilning St BS35 ....39 C8
Pilning Sta BS35 ....38 F5
Pimpernel Mead BS32 ...29 E7
Pincoate GL2 ....125 D6
Pincot La GL6 ....103 D5
Pincots La GL12 ....54 B3
Pine Bank GL52 ....138 B4
Pine Cl
Bishop's Cleeve GL52 ....138 B4
Cheltenham GL52 ....131 A8
Thornbury BS35 ....64 C1
Pine Crest Way 5 GL15 147 D8
Pine Ct BS31 ....4 C4
Pine Gr BS7 ....29 A1
Pine Grove Pl BS7 ....18 D3
Pine Halt GL54 ....166 C6
Pine Rd BS10 ....28 B3
Pine Ridge Cl BS9 ....17 C4
Pine Tree Dr GL4 ....119 E8
Pine Tree Way GL15 ....156 C1
Pinecroft BS14 ....2 F7
Pinedale GL15 ....147 B3
Pinefield BS9 ....18 B7
Pineholt Gate GL3 ......120 B7
Pinemount Rd GL3 .....120 A7
Pinery Rd GL4 ....119 E7
Pines La BS35 ....50 D3
Pines Rd BS30 ....11 C1
Pines The
Brimscombe GL6 ....148 B5
Cheltenham GL50 ....193 A3
Greet GL54 ....174 A8
Pinetrees GL53 ....130 F5
Pinetum Dr GL2 ....125 A3
Pineway GL4 ....119 B6
Pinewood BS15 ....20 F1
Pinewood Cl Bristol BS9 ..18 B7
Cinderford GL14 ....191 E5
Pinewood Rd GL2 ......109 E8
Pinewood Way SN14 ....15 F7
Pingry La GL16 ....155 A4
Pinhay Rd BS13 ....2 B6
Pinkers Mead BS16 .....21 C6
Pinkhams Twist BS14 ....3 A5
Pinlocks GL4 ....119 E3
Pinnell Gr BS16 ....21 C7
Pinnells End La GL11 ...88 D8
Pintail Cl GL2 ....117 D1
Pioneer Pk BS4 ....9 C5
Pipe La BS1 ....194 C2
Piper Rd BS37 ....43 E3
Pipers Gr GL2 ....125 D5
Pippin Cl Gloucester GL4 .120 A6
Newent GL18 ....171 A4
Pippin Ct 4 BS30 ....10 F4
Pippins Rd GL20 ....182 C7
Pirton Cres GL3 ....128 B5
Pirton La GL3 ....128 B5
Pirton Mdw GL3 ....128 B5
Pitch & Pay La BS9 .....17 E3
Pitch & Pay Pk BS9 .....17 E3
Pitch La BS6 ....18 D1
Pitch The GL6 ....148 B5
Pitchcombe BS37 ....32 C7
Pitchcombe Gdns BS9 ..17 D7
Pitching Gn GL15 ......156 C2
Pithay Ct BS1 ....195 A3
Pithay The BS1 ....195 A3
Pitlochry Cl BS7 ....28 F1
Pitman Pl GL12 ....68 C6
Pitman Rd GL51 ....132 E1
Pitt Ho GL52 ....133 F1
Pitt Mill Gdns GL3 ....120 A8
Pitt Rd BS7 ....18 E5
Pitt St GL1 ....196 B3
Pittsfield SN6 ....143 E4
Pittville Cir GL52 ......133 F2
Pittville Circus Rd GL52 133 F2
Pittville Cl BS35 ....64 C3
Pittville Cres GL52 .....133 F3
Pittville Crescent La
GL52 ....133 F3
Pittville Ct GL52 ....133 F4
Pittville Lawn GL52 ....133 E3
Pittville Mews GL52 ...193 C4
Pittville Pump Room & Mus★
GL52 ....133 E4
Pittville Sch GL52 ......133 F4
Pittville St GL52 ....193 C4
Pitville Pl 16 BS6 ....18 B1
Pixash Bsns Ctr BS31 ....5 B5
Pixash La BS31 ....5 C5
Place Hill GL18 ....170 C4
Plain The Stroud GL6 ...103 A2
Thornbury BS35 ....64 B1
Plantation Cres GL20 ..182 C7
Plantation The
Gloucester GL4 ....119 E6
Hardwicke GL2 ....109 D7
Platts Row GL17 ....164 D5
Players Cl BS16 ....30 B3
Playford Gdns BS11 .....16 E8
Playhouse Ct GL53 .....193 C3
Playhouse The★ GL50 ..193 B3
Pleasant Ho 4 BS16 ....20 D5
Pleasant Rd BS16 ....20 D5
Pleasant Stile GL14 ....156 E7
Pleydells 16 SN6 ....143 E4
Pleydells The GL7 ......151 B5
Plies The GL7 ....152 E3
Plimsoll Ho
3 Bristol BS1 ....195 B1
5 Bristol,Woolcott Park
BS6 ....18 B1
Plock Ct GL2 ....126 F5
Ploughmans Way GL2 ..109 E6
Plover Cl BS37 ....43 C2
Plowright Ho 8 BS15 ....10 B5
Pludds Court Rd GL17 .163 E3
Plum Tree Cl GL4 ......119 E4
Plummer's Hill BS5 ......9 E8
Plumpton Ct BS16 ....30 F1
Pochard Cl GL2 ....117 D1
Pockhill La GL54 ....168 F7
Poden La GL55 ....188 E4
Podsmead Pl GL1 ......118 D5
Podsmead Rd GL1 ......118 D5
Poets' Cl BS5 ....9 D8
Point Rd GL8 ....140 B8
Polar Gdns SN14 ....47 E4
Polden Ho BS3 ....8 D3
Polefield Gdns GL51 ...130 B8
Polefield Ho 13 GL51 ...130 B8
Pollards La GL15 ......156 D1
Polly Barnes Cl 6 BS15 .10 B5
Polly Barnes Hill BS15 ...10 B5
Polygon Rd BS8 ....194 A2
Polygon The
Avonmouth BS11 ....26 D1
16 Bristol BS8 ....7 F6
Pomfrett Gdns BS14 ......3 E5
Pomphrey Hill BS16 .....21 C4
Pond La SN5 ....143 D1
Ponsford Rd BS4 ....9 B1
Ponting Cl BS5 ....20 A1
Ponting's Cl SN26 ......144 E1
Pool Cl GL56 ....187 F1
Pool Cnr BS32 ....50 B2
Pool Ho BS34 ....29 A8
Pool La NP25 ....154 B1
Pool Meadow Cvn Pk
GL1 ....126 C3
Pool Rd BS15 ....20 E3
Poole Court Dr BS37 ....43 E2
Poole Ground GL2 .....125 D6
Poole St BS11 ....16 B8
Poole Way GL50 ....193 A4
Pooles La GL5 ....98 E4
Pooles Wharf BS8 ......194 A1
Pooles Wharf Ct BS8 ..194 A1
Poolhay Cl GL19 ....180 E1
Poolway Ct 1 GL16 ....155 A5
Poolway Pl GL16 ....155 A6
Poolway Rd GL16 ......155 B6
Poolway Rise 8 GL16 ..155 A6
Pope's Ct GL7 ....190 A8
Pope's Ct GL7 ....153 A1
Popes Cl GL50 ....133 D3
Popes Meade GL2 ......125 D5
Poplar Ave BS9 ....17 D6
Poplar Cl Bristol BS30 ...11 C6
Gloucester GL1 ....118 D5
Poplar Cres GL52 ......138 B4
Poplar Dr
Pucklechurch BS16 ....22 B5
Woodmancote GL52 .....138 C3
Poplar Fields BS30 ......11 D6
Poplar Gardens Ho BS15 10 E8
Poplar La GL12 ....54 B4
Poplar Pl BS16 ....20 A3
Poplar Rd
Bristol,Hanham BS15 .....10 A5
Bristol,Highridge BS13 .....1 F7
Bristol,North Common BS30 11 D6
Bristol,Speedwell BS5 .....19 F1
Poplar Rdbt BS11 ....26 E5
Poplar Terr BS15 ....10 F8
Poplar Way Colerne SN14 .15 F5
Hardwicke GL2 ....109 E7
Poplar Way E BS11 .....26 F5
Poplar Way W BS11 .....26 D6
Poplars Cl GL55 ....188 F1
Poplars Pk GL2 ....95 F3
Poplars The
Cheltenham GL51 ....129 E5
Easton-in-G BS20 ....16 B4
Poppy Field GL2 ....125 E6
Poppy Mead BS32 ....29 E7
Porchester Rd GL3 .....119 F7
Porlock Rd BS3 ....8 D3
Port Elizabeth Ho BS10 .28 B1
Port Ind Est GL5 ....99 F1
Port La GL5 ....99 F1
Port Side Cl 5 BS5 ....9 F6
Port Terr GL5 ....99 F1
Port View BS20 ....16 C5
Port Wall★ NP16 ....60 F8
Portbury Gr BS11 ....16 D6
Portbury Wlk BS11 .....16 D6
Portishead Way BS3 .....7 E3
Portland Ct Bristol BS1 .194 B1
Bristol,Upper Soundwell
BS16 ....20 D3
Portland Lofts BS2 .....195 B4
Portland Mans BS2 ....195 B4
Portland Pl Bristol BS16 ..20 D3
9 Cheltenham GL52 ....193 C4
Portland Sq Bristol BS2 .195 B4
Cheltenham GL52 ....193 C4
Portland St Bristol BS2 ..195 A4
Bristol,Clifton BS8 ....7 F7
Bristol,Staple Hill BS16 ...20 D3
Cheltenham GL52 ....193 C4
Portman Terr GL50 .....193 B1
Portmeirion Cl BS14 ......3 B5
Porturet Way 2 GL53 ...131 B6
Portview Rd BS11 ....16 B8
Portwall La BS1 ....195 B1
Portwall La E 10 BS1 ...195 B1
Portwall Rd NP16 ....60 E8
Portway
Bristol,Shirehampton BS11 .16 C6
Bristol,Sneyd Park BS8 ....17 C3
Upton St Leonards GL4 ...112 B7
Portway Com Sch BS11 ..16 E7
Portway La BS37 ....44 E2
Portway Rdbt BS11 .....16 C8
Portwell 4 SN6 ....143 E4
Post Office Cotts GL2 ..108 C6
Post Office La
Cheltenham GL50 ....193 B3
Cleeve Hill GL52 ....138 E3
Draycott GL56 ....186 D6
Tewkesbury GL20 ....192 C4
Post Office Row GL2 ...101 B2
Post Office Sq GL7 ....150 E2
Post Paddocks The
GL15 ....147 C3
Postlip Way GL51 ......129 D8
Potlicker's La
Ablington GL7 ....159 F2
Coln Rogers GL54,GL7 ...159 E4
Potters Croft NP16 ......61 B4
Potters Field Rd GL52 ..138 C3
Potters Pond GL12 ......68 C7
Pound Cl Ledbury HR8 ..178 E8
Siddington GL7 ....150 E2
Twyning GL20 ....181 F7
Watermead GL3 ....120 E4
Pound Dr BS16 ....19 F5
Pound Farm Ctyd GL3 ..120 E5
Pound Farm La HR9 ....170 B5
Pound Hill GL8 ....140 B8
Pound La Arlingham GL2 .157 B5
Bristol BS16 ....19 F4
Hardwicke GL2 ....109 D5
Little Rissington GL54 ....169 C6
Mickleton GL55 ....189 A6
Pound Mdw HR8 ....178 E8
Pound Rd Bristol BS15 ....20 F2
Highworth SN6 ....145 C4
Pound The
Almondsbury BS32 ....40 A5
Ampney Crucis GL7 ......151 B5
Little Rissington GL54 ....169 C6
Oldbury-on-S BS35 ....63 B6
Pountney Dr BS5 ....9 B8
Pow's Rd BS15 ....10 D7
Powell's CE Prim Sch
GL7 ....190 C5
Powells Way GL8 ......140 D3
Powis La GL8 ....148 B1
Poyntz Ct BS30 ....10 F3
Poyntz Rd BS4 ....2 F8
Pratten's La 1 BS16 ....20 D4
Preacher Cl BS5 ....10 B6
Preddy's La BS5 ....10 A6
Prescott BS37 ....32 D8
Prescott Ave GL4 ......119 B4
Prescott Wlk GL52 .....134 B4
Press Moor Dr BS30 .....10 F4
Prestbury BS37 ....32 D8
Prestbury Green Dr
GL52 ....134 C4
Prestbury Manor Ho
GL52 ....134 C5
Prestbury Rd GL52 .....134 A4
Prestbury St Mary's CE Jun
Sch GL52 ....134 B4
Preston Cl NP16 ....60 F4
Preston Cross HR8 ....178 B6
Preston Wlk BS4 ....9 A1
Prestwick Cl BS4 ....9 D1
Pretoria Rd BS34 ....28 F8
Prewett St BS1 ....195 B1
Price St GL1 ....118 D7
Prices Ground GL4 .....119 D6
Priddy Ct BS14 ....3 B5
Priddy Dr BS14 ....3 B5
Priestley Ct 10 GL20 ...192 C4
Priestwood Cl BS10 .....28 A3
Primrose Cl Bristol BS32 .40 D2
Bristol,St George BS15 ....10 C8
Gloucester GL4 ....119 A4
Primrose Ct GL56 ......187 A3
Primrose Dr
Milkwall GL16 ....155 B4
Thornbury BS35 ....64 D2
Primrose Hill CE Prim Sch
GL15 ....92 B5
Primrose Hill Rd GL15 ..92 A5
Primrose La BS15 ....20 C1
Primrose Terr BS15 .....20 C1
Primrose Way
Cirencester GL7 ....190 E1
Lydney GL15 ....92 B5
Prince Albert Ct GL3 ...120 C6
Prince Charles Rd 6
GL7 ....152 E4
Prince Cres GL19 ......172 A8
Prince Ct 12 GL8 ....140 B4
Prince Of Wales Row 17
GL8 ....140 B4
Prince St Bristol BS1 ...195 A1
Gloucester GL1 ....196 C2
Prince Street Rdbt BS1 195 A2
Prince's Bldgs BS8 ....7 F6
Prince's Rd GL50 ......130 B7
Prince's St Bristol BS2 ..195 C4
Cheltenham GL52 ....133 F1
Princes Ct BS30 ....10 F4
Princes Mews GL3 .....127 F7
Princes Rd GL5 ....98 E8
Princes' La BS8 ....7 F6
Princes' Pl BS7 ....18 E3
Princess Cl BS31 ....4 E4
Princess Elizabeth Way
GL51 ....132 E3
Princess Gdns BS16 .....19 D6
Princess Row BS2 ......195 A4
Princess Royal Ind Est
GL15 ....155 E1

Princess Royal Rd 7 GL15 ... 155 D1
Princess St
Bristol,Newton BS2 ... 9 A7
Bristol,Windmill Hill BS3 ... 8 E4
Princess Victoria St BS8 ... 7 F6
Prinknash Abbey* GL4 ... 112 B8
Prinknash Bird & Deer Pk* GL4 ... 112 B8
Prinknash Cl 7 GL4 ... 119 C4
Prinknash Ct 6 BS37 ... 32 D7
Prinknash Pottery* GL4 ... 112 C8
Prinknash Rd 8 GL4 ... 119 C4
Prior Park Prep Sch SN6 ... 143 F4
Prior's Hill 11 BS6 ... 18 D1
Priors Ct Baunton GL7 ... 150 D7
Cheltenham GL52 ... 134 B3
4 Tewkesbury GL20 ... 192 C4
Priors Lea BS37 ... 43 E1
Priors Lo 5 GL52 ... 133 F2
Priors Rd GL52 ... 134 B3
Priors Wlk GL7 ... 153 F2
Priory Ave BS9 ... 18 A7
Priory Cl
Chepstow/Cas-Gwent NP16 72 D1
Cirencester GL7 ... 190 C5
Priory Court Rd BS9 ... 18 A7
Priory Ct
Bristol,Hanham BS15 ... 10 C3
Bristol,Upper Knowle BS4 ... 9 B2
Churchdown GL3 ... 128 D5
Dursley GL11 ... 88 A3
Leonard Stanley GL10 ... 97 E3
Priory Dene BS9 ... 18 A7
Priory Fields GL6 ... 82 F8
Priory Gdns
Bristol,Horfield BS7 ... 18 F8
Bristol,Shirehampton BS11 . 16 D7
Easton-in-G BS20 ... 16 B4
Priory Gn SN6 ... 145 D3
Priory Ho GL1 ... 196 B2
Priory Ind Est GL8 ... 140 C4
Priory La
Bishop's Cleeve GL52 ... 138 A4
Monmouth NP25 ... 162 A1
Priory Lea HR9 ... 163 C8
Priory Lea Ho HR9 ... 163 C8
Priory Mews GL52 ... 193 C3
Priory Pl
Cheltenham GL52 ... 193 C2
Gloucester GL1 ... 196 B2
Priory Rd
Bristol,Shirehampton BS8 ... 16 D6
Bristol,Tyndall's Park BS8 ... 194 C4
Bristol,Upper Knowle BS4 ... 9 B2
Easton-in-G BS20 ... 16 B4
Gloucester GL1 ... 196 A3
Gloucester GL1 ... 196 B3
Keynsham BS31 ... 4 E7
Priory St GL52 ... 193 C3
Priory Terr GL52 ... 133 F1
Priory The SN6 ... 143 F5
Priory Way 7 GL8 ... 140 C4
Priory Wlk GL52 ... 133 F1
Pritchard St BS2 ... 195 B4
Private Rd GL5 ... 99 C2
Pro-Cathedral La BS8 ... 194 B3
Probertsbarn La GL17 ... 163 C3
Probyn Cl BS16 ... 20 A7
Proctor Cl BS4 ... 9 D1
Proctor Ho BS1 ... 195 B1
Promenade GL50 ... 193 B3
Promenade The BS7 ... 18 D2
Prospect Ave Bristol BS15 20 B1
Bristol,Kingsdown BS2 ... 195 A4
Prospect Cl
Coleford GL16 ... 155 A5
Easter Compton BS35 ... 39 A2
Frampton Cotterell BS36 ... 30 F8
Winterbourne BS36 ... 30 E4
Prospect Cres BS15 ... 20 F2
Prospect La
Frampton Cotterell BS36 ... 30 F8
Llangrove HR9 ... 162 B6
Prospect Pl
7 Bristol,Bedminster BS3 ... 8 C3
1 Bristol,Montpelier BS6 . 18 D2
Bristol,Moorfields BS5 ... 9 C8
Cirencester GL7 ... 190 D3
Dursley GL11 ... 88 A1
Prospect Rd
Cinderford GL14 ... 191 D4
Severn Beach BS35 ... 38 A5
Prospect Row HR9 ... 170 B4
Prospect Terr
Chalford GL6 ... 148 C5
21 Cheltenham GL52 ... 133 F2
Prosper La GL16 ... 155 B5
Protheroes Ho BS1 ... 194 C2
Providence La BS41 ... 7 A1
Providence Pl BS2 ... 195 C2
Providence View BS41 ... 7 A1
Prowse Cl BS35 ... 64 C1
Prudham St 7 BS5 ... 19 C1
Pry La WR12 ... 185 A8
Puck Pit La GL54 ... 174 A7
Pucklechurch CE Prim Sch BS16 ... 22 C6
Pucklechurch Trad Est BS16 ... 22 B4
Puckrup GL20 ... 181 E7
Puckrup La GL20 ... 181 E7
Pudlicott La GL55 ... 189 D1
Pullar Cl GL52 ... 137 F4
Pullar Ct GL52 ... 137 F4
Pullen Ct GL52 ... 138 A7
Pullens Rd GL6 ... 111 F1
Pullin Ct BS30 ... 11 D4
Pullins Gn 3 BS35 ... 64 B1
Pullman Ct GL1 ... 196 C3
Pullnoggin Pool La HR9 ... 162 D3
Pump La Bristol BS1 ... 195 B1
Tetbury GL8 ... 140 E3
Tockington BS32 ... 50 D4
Pump Row GL6 ... 91 C5
Pump Sq BS20 ... 16 D5
Pumphreys Ct GL53 ... 131 A5
Pumphreys Rd GL53 ... 131 A5
Purbeck Way GL52 ... 134 C4
Purcell Rd GL3 ... 128 A8
Purcell Wlk BS4 ... 2 D7
Purdown Rd BS7 ... 18 F5
Purdy Ct BS16 ... 20 A4
Purley Ave GL7 ... 190 D4
Purley Rd GL7 ... 190 D4
Pursey Dr BS32 ... 29 F6
Purslane Cl GL4 ... 119 B4
Purton Cl BS15 ... 10 E6
Purton Pl GL15 ... 92 C2
Purton Rd BS7 ... 18 D2
Puxley Cl BS14 ... 3 E6
Puzzle Cl 4 GL15 ... 147 D8
Puzzle Wood* GL16 ... 155 A4
Pwllmeyric Cl NP16 ... 60 B5
Pyart Ct GL16 ... 155 A5
Pye Croft BS32 ... 40 E3
Pyecroft Ave BS9 ... 18 C7
Pyghtell The
Luckington SN14 ... 47 E5
Stratton GL7 ... 190 B7
Pyke Rd GL20 ... 192 F4
Pylers Way GL15 ... 92 B2
Pylle Hill Cres BS3 ... 8 F4
Pynne Cl BS14 ... 3 F5
Pynne Rd BS14 ... 3 F5
Pyracantha Wlk BS14 ... 3 A6
Pyrton Mews 2 GL51 ... 129 E5
Pystol La GL15 ... 146 E7

Q

Quabbs Rd GL17 ... 164 B4
Quadrangle The
Naunton GL54 ... 175 D2
Westerleigh BS37 ... 32 C4
Quadrant BS32 ... 40 B3
Quadrant E BS16 ... 20 C3
Quadrant The
Bristol BS32 ... 40 A3
Bristol,Westbury Park BS6 . 18 B3
Quadrant W BS16 ... 20 C3
Quail Cl GL4 ... 119 E7
Quail Mdws GL8 ... 140 B4
Quaker Ct 1 BS35 ... 64 B1
Quaker La BS35 ... 64 B1
Quaker's Cl BS16 ... 20 D8
Quaker's Rd BS16 ... 20 E8
Quakers Row GL7 ... 149 E4
Quakers' Friars BS1 ... 195 B3
Quantock Cl BS30 ... 11 C5
Quantock Rd Bristol BS3 ... 8 D3
Quedgeley GL2 ... 109 E8
Quarhouse La GL5 ... 148 A5
Quarries The BS32 ... 40 C6
Quarrington Rd BS7 ... 18 E5
Quarry Barton BS16 ... 30 C4
Quarry Cl Hartpury GL19 . 172 C3
Stratton GL7 ... 190 B8
Quarry Cres SN6 ... 145 C3
Quarry Gdns GL11 ... 87 D4
Quarry La Bristol BS11 ... 27 C1
Gorsley HR9 ... 170 B4
Winterbourne BS36 ... 30 E4
Quarry Mead BS35 ... 50 F5
Quarry Rd Alveston BS35 ... 50 F5
Bristol BS8 ... 18 A2
Bristol,Frenchay BS16 ... 20 C7
Bristol,Kingswood BS15 ... 10 D6
Chipping Sodbury BS37 ... 44 A1
Quarry Stps 8 BS8 ... 18 A2
Quarry The Ablington GL7 159 F1
Bristol BS11 ... 27 C1
Dursley GL11 ... 87 D4
10 Fairford GL7 ... 152 E4
Quarry View GL7 ... 153 C6
Quarry Way
Bristol,Emerson's Green BS16 ... 31 A1
Bristol,Fishponds BS16 ... 19 E5
Quat Goose La GL51 ... 133 B7
Quay St Bristol BS1 ... 195 A3
Gloucester GL1 ... 196 A3
Tewkesbury GL20 ... 192 C4
Quay The GL1 ... 196 A3
Quays The BS1 ... 194 C1
Quayside Bristol BS8 ... 194 B2
Tintern Parva NP16 ... 146 C4
Quayside La 4 BS5 ... 9 F6
Quebec Dr GL51 ... 132 E3
Quedgeley BS37 ... 32 C8
Quedgeley Ent Ctr GL2 . 110 B8
Quedgeley Enterprise Ctr GL2 ... 118 A1
Quedgeley Trad Est E GL10 ... 109 F3
Quedgeley Trad Est W GL2 ... 109 D5
Queen Ann Rd BS5 ... 9 B6
Queen Anne's Rd GL7 ... 190 E5
Queen Charlotte St BS1 195 A2
Queen Charlton La BS14 ... 3 E2
Queen Elizabeth Rd GL7 ... 190 E4
Queen Elizabeth's Hospital Sch BS8 ... 194 B3
Queen Margaret Prim Sch GL20 ... 192 C2
Queen Quay BS1 ... 195 A2
Queen Sq Bristol BS1 ... 195 A2
Saltford BS31 ... 5 F3
Queen Square Ave 7 BS1 ... 195 A2
Queen St Avonmouth BS11 . 26 A1
Bristol BS2 ... 195 B3
Bristol,Eastville BS5 ... 19 D3
Bristol,St George BS15 ... 10 B8
Chedworth GL54 ... 159 A7
Cheltenham GL51 ... 133 C3
Cirencester GL7 ... 190 D3
Lydney GL15 ... 92 B4
Queen Victoria Rd BS6 ... 18 A4
Queen Victoria St BS2 ... 9 A6
Queen's Ave BS8 ... 194 B3
Queen's Cir GL50 ... 193 B2
Queen's Ct
Brimscombe GL5 ... 148 A5
Bristol BS8 ... 194 B3
Ledbury HR8 ... 178 E8
Queen's Dr Bristol BS7 ... 18 C5
Stroud GL5 ... 98 E8
Queen's Rd
Bristol,Ashley Down BS7 ... 18 F5
Bristol,Bishopsworth BS13, BS41 ... 1 F4
Bristol,Cadbury Heath BS30 11 B4
Bristol,Crew's Hole BS5 ... 9 F7
Bristol,Victoria Park BS8 ... 194 A3
Cheltenham GL50 ... 130 B8
Chepstow/Cas-Gwent NP16 60 E6
Pucklechurch BS16 ... 22 B5
Stonehouse GL10 ... 97 F7
Stroud GL5 ... 99 B6
Queen's Retreat GL51 ... 133 B2
Queen's Way HR8 ... 178 E8
Queens Acre GL14 ... 156 F6
Queens Ave SN6 ... 145 D3
Queens Cl GL3 ... 128 A1
Queens Ct
Cheltenham GL50 ... 130 A8
16 Tewkesbury GL20 ... 192 C4
Queens Down Ct BS4 ... 9 C3
Queens Down Gdns BS4 ... 9 C3
Queens Dr BS15 ... 10 B4
Queens Field GL7 ... 152 E4
Queens Gate BS9 ... 17 D5
Queens La GL50 ... 193 A2
Queens Par Bristol BS1 . 194 C2
Cheltenham GL50 ... 193 A2
Queens Rd Bristol BS4 ... 9 C2
Hannington SN6 ... 145 A4
Keynsham BS31 ... 4 D4
Tewkesbury GL20 ... 192 D2
Queens Sq Stroud GL5 ... 99 D7
21 Winchcombe GL54 ... 174 A7
Queens Way GL12 ... 68 B7
Queens Wlk BS35 ... 64 B3
Queens Wood Forest Trails* GL18 ... 170 B7
Queensdale Cres BS4 ... 9 A1
Queensdown Gdns BS4 ... 9 C2
Queenshill Rd BS4 ... 9 A1
Queensholm Ave BS16 ... 30 E1
Queensholm Cl BS16 ... 30 E1
Queensholm Cres BS16 ... 30 E1
Queensholm Dr BS16 ... 30 E1
Queensmead
Bredon GL20 ... 182 D7
Painswick GL6 ... 103 E7
Queensway Bristol BS34 ... 29 D6
Coleford GL16 ... 155 B5
Queenwood Gr GL52 ... 134 D5
Quenneys Cl GL4 ... 119 C3
Querns La GL7 ... 190 C4
Querns Rd GL7 ... 190 C3
Querns Westonbirt Sch GL8 ... 58 F8
Quickthorn Cl BS14 ... 3 A6
Quietways GL10 ... 97 E8
Quilter Gr BS4 ... 2 D7
Quinton Cl GL3 ... 128 B6

R

Rackham Cl BS7 ... 19 B6
Rackhay BS1 ... 195 A2
Radburn Cl 4 GL56 ... 187 B3
Radley Rd BS16 ... 20 B4
Radnor Bsns Ctr BS7 ... 18 E5
Radnor Rd
Bristol,Horfield BS7 ... 18 E5
Bristol,Westbury on Trym BS9 ... 18 B5
Cheltenham GL51 ... 129 E6
Raeburn Rd BS5 ... 10 B6
Rag La GL12 ... 53 D5
Raglan Gdns 1 GL15 ... 92 A3
Raglan La BS5 ... 10 A7
Raglan Pl Bristol BS7 ... 18 D3
Thornbury BS35 ... 51 B8
Raglan Rd BS7 ... 18 D3
Raglan St GL1 ... 196 C2
Raglan Way
Chepstow/Cas-Gwent NP16 60 F5
Uley GL11 ... 89 B1
Raglan Wlk BS31 ... 4 D4
Ragnal La GL6 ... 91 A3
Ragnall GL12 ... 68 D8
Raikes Rd GL1 ... 118 D6
Railton Jones Cl BS34 ... 29 E3
Railway Arches BS2 ... 195 C2
Railway Cotts BS37 ... 33 E8
Railway Dr 8 GL16 ... 155 A5
Railway Rd GL14 ... 191 C1
Railway Terr Bristol BS16 . 20 C4
Kemble GL7 ... 141 F8
Lechlade on T GL7 ... 153 E3
Lydney GL15 ... 84 A8
Railway View GL5 ... 148 A5
Rainbow Ct BS37 ... 43 B3
Raleigh Cl Innsworth GL3 127 F8
Saltford BS31 ... 5 D2
Raleigh Rd BS3 ... 8 B4
Ralph Rd BS7 ... 18 F4
Ram Hill BS36 ... 31 D4
Ram Hill Bsns Pk BS36 ... 31 D5
Ramsdale Rd GL2 ... 118 B4
Ramsey Rd BS7 ... 18 F7
Rance Pitch GL4 ... 119 E2
Randall Cl BS15 ... 20 F2
Randall Rd Bristol BS8 ... 194 B2
Upper Rissington GL54 ... 169 D6
Randalls Field GL6 ... 103 F7
Randalls Gn GL6 ... 148 C5
Randolph Ave Bristol BS13 . 2 B5
Yate BS37 ... 43 D4
Randolph Cl Bristol BS13 ... 2 B5
Cheltenham GL53 ... 130 F6
Randwick CE Prim Sch GL6 ... 102 D2
Randwick Rd GL4 ... 118 D3
Range The GL2 ... 125 D5
Rangers Ave GL11 ... 80 C7
Rangers The GL11 ... 80 C7
Rangers Wlk BS15 ... 10 C4
Rangeworthy CE Prim Sch BS37 ... 52 F1
Ranmoor GL4 ... 119 D3
Rannoch Rd BS7 ... 28 F1
Raphael Ct BS1 ... 195 B1
Ratcliff Lawns GL52 ... 134 B8
Ratcliffe Dr BS34 ... 29 E5
Rathbone Cl BS36 ... 31 C5
Rathmore Cl 2 GL54 ... 174 A7
Raven Ct BS9 ... 17 F8
Ravendale Dr BS30 ... 11 B2
Ravenglass Cres BS10 ... 28 D2
Ravenhead Dr BS14 ... 3 B8
Ravenhill Ave BS3 ... 8 F2
Ravenhill Rd BS3 ... 8 F3
Ravens Wood BS30 ... 11 B3
Ravenscourt Rd BS34 ... 29 B7
Ravensgate Rd GL53 ... 131 B4
Ravenswood Rd BS6 ... 18 C1
Ravis Cl GL4 ... 119 B6
Rawnsley Ho 18 BS5 ... 19 A1
Rayleigh Rd BS9 ... 17 E7
Raymend Rd BS3 ... 8 E3
Raymend Wlk BS3 ... 8 E2
Raymill BS4 ... 10 A2
Raymond Ho BS16 ... 20 F4
Raynes Rd BS3 ... 8 A3
Raysfield Inf Sch BS37 ... 32 F8
Raysfield Jun Sch BS37 ... 32 F8
Rea La GL2 ... 118 A6
Rea The GL2 ... 117 F5
Reaburn Cl 5 GL52 ... 131 B6
Read Way GL52 ... 137 F2
Reade St 12 NP25 ... 154 A7
Reades Piece WR11 ... 188 C6
Reading Ct BS15 ... 10 B8
Ready Token GL7 ... 151 F7
Rectory Barns GL54 ... 176 D4
Rectory Cl
Lower Swell GL54 ... 176 D4
Upton St Leonards GL4 ... 119 E2
Yate BS37 ... 43 F3
Rectory Cotts GL54 ... 176 D4
Rectory Ct GL52 ... 138 A4
Rectory La Avening GL8 ... 148 B1
Bristol BS34 ... 29 A3
Cricklade SN6 ... 143 F4
Cromhall GL12 ... 53 A8
Gloucester GL2 ... 118 A6
Rectory Mdw GL17 ... 164 F6
Rectory Rd
Easton-in-G BS20 ... 16 B3
Frampton Cotterell BS36 ... 31 A8
Gloucester GL4 ... 119 C4
Red Admiral Dr GL4 ... 119 E4
Red Ditch La GL19 ... 179 D1
Red House La
Almondsbury BS32 ... 40 B4
Bristol BS9 ... 17 E6
Red La GL20 ... 192 C5
Red Lion Ct 2 GL1 ... 119 A8
Red Lion La SN6 ... 143 F4
Red Maids Jun Sch The BS9 ... 18 A6
Red Maids Sch The BS9 . 18 A6
Red Rower Cl GL50 ... 133 C5
Red Well Rd GL4 ... 119 C3
Redbrook CE Prim Sch NP25 ... 154 C4
Redcar Ct BS16 ... 30 F1
Redcatch Rd BS4 ... 8 F2
Redcliff Backs BS1 ... 195 B2
Redcliff Cres BS3 ... 8 E4
Redcliff Hill BS1 ... 195 B1
Redcliff Mead La BS1 ... 195 B1
Redcliff St BS1 ... 195 B2
Redcliffe Coll GL1 ... 127 A2
Redcliffe Par E BS1 ... 195 A1
Redcliffe Par W BS1 ... 195 A1
Redcliffe Way BS1 ... 195 B1
Redcross Mews 16 BS2 . 195 C3
Redcross St BS2 ... 195 C3
Redding Cl GL2 ... 117 E1
Reddings Cl GL15 ... 147 C3
Reddings La GL14 ... 191 F4
Reddings Pk GL51 ... 129 D7
Reddings Rd GL51 ... 129 C7
Reddings The Bristol BS15 20 F2
Cheltenham GL51 ... 129 B6
Chepstow/Cas-Gwent NP16 60 F5
Pendock WR13 ... 180 A8
Redesdale Mews 6 GL56 ... 187 A3
Redesdale Pl GL56 ... 187 A2
Redfield Edge Prim Sch BS30 ... 11 D4
Redfield Hill BS30 ... 11 E3
Redfield Rd BS34 ... 29 B7
Redford Cres BS13 ... 1 F3
Redford La BS16 ... 22 D4
Redford Wlk BS13 ... 1 F3
Redgrove Cotts GL51 ... 129 C8
Redgrove Pk GL51 ... 129 D8
Redgrove Rd GL51 ... 132 F4
Redham La BS35 ... 38 F8
Redhill Cl BS16 ... 19 E3
Redhill Dr BS16 ... 19 E3
Redhill Farm Bsns Pk BS35 ... 49 F6
Redhill La BS35 ... 49 E6
Redhouse La
English Bicknor GL16 ... 163 A2
Stroud GL5,GL6 ... 98 D8
Redland Cl GL2 ... 127 B4
Redland Court Rd BS6 ... 18 C2
Redland Gr BS6 ... 18 C2
Redland Green Rd BS6 ... 18 B3
Redland High Sch BS6 ... 18 C2
Redland Hill BS6 ... 18 B2
Redland Pk BS6 ... 18 B2
Redland Rd BS6 ... 18 C2
Redland Sta BS6 ... 18 C2
Redland Terr 8 BS6 ... 18 B2
Redlands Cl SN6 ... 145 D2
Redlynch La BS31 ... 4 D2
Redmarley CE Prim Sch GL19 ... 179 D2
Redmarley Rd GL18 ... 171 A6
Rednock Dr GL11 ... 88 A2
Rednock Sch GL11 ... 88 A2
Redpoll Way GL4 ... 119 C6
Redshelf Wlk BS10 ... 28 C3
Redstart Way GL4 ... 119 C6
Redthorne Way GL51 ... 129 E5
Redwick & Northwick CE Prim Sch BS35 ... 48 D2
Redwick Cl BS11 ... 27 C2
Redwick Crossroads BS35 ... 38 C7
Redwick Gdns BS35 ... 38 C7
Redwick Rd Pilning BS35 . 38 C8
Redwick BS35 ... 38 B8
Redwind Way GL2 ... 127 D5
Redwing Gdns BS16 ... 19 E6
Redwood Cl Bristol BS30 . 11 A3
Chepstow/Cas-Gwent NP16 60 E5
Gloucester GL1 ... 118 D5
Redwood Ct
4 Cheltenham GL51 ... 132 D2
Northway GL20 ... 182 C5
Redwood Ho Bristol BS13 ... 2 D3
Brookthorpe GL4 ... 110 F5
Reed Cl BS10 ... 18 D6
Reed Ct BS30 ... 10 F3
Reed's Row GL12 ... 55 D7
Reedley Rd BS9 ... 17 F5
Reedling Cl BS16 ... 19 E6
Reeds SN6 ... 143 E4
Reema Hos The SN6 ... 145 D1
Reevers Rd 25 GL18 ... 171 A4
Reeves Cl GL7 ... 190 A2
Regency Dr BS4 ... 10 A2
Regent Apartments BS6 . 18 C3
Regent Arc GL50 ... 193 B3
Regent Chambers GL50 193 B3
Regent Ct GL51 ... 130 B8
Regent Ho 9 GL50 ... 130 B8
Regent Rd BS3 ... 8 D4
Regent St
Bristol,Clifton Wood BS8 . 194 A2
Bristol,Kingswood BS15 ... 10 D8
Cheltenham GL50 ... 193 B3
Gloucester GL1 ... 196 C1
Lydney GL15 ... 92 B3
Stonehouse GL10 ... 97 F7
Regent Way NP16 ... 60 E8
Regents Cl BS35 ... 64 B2
Regents The BS31 ... 4 F6
Regents Wlk 5 GL15 ... 92 A3
Regis Cl GL53 ... 131 A5
Reine Barnes Cl GL11 ... 80 B8
Remenham Dr BS9 ... 18 B5
Remenham Pk BS9 ... 18 B5
Remus Cl GL4 ... 119 F6
Rendcomb Cl GL4 ... 119 E4
Rendcomb Coll GL7 ... 158 C4
Rendcomb Dr GL7 ... 190 B2
Rendle Ho BS16 ... 20 F4
Rene Rd 12 BS5 ... 19 B1
Repton Hall BS10 ... 28 B2
Repton Rd BS4 ... 9 D3
Reservoir Cl GL5 ... 99 E7
Reservoir Rd
Gloucester GL4 ... 118 F4
Stroud GL5 ... 99 E7
Restway Wall 11 NP16 ... 60 E8
Retort Rd BS11 ... 26 C3

Retreat The
[3] Broadway WR12 185 B8
Gloucester GL4 118 D2
Highworth SN6 145 C3
[4] Tetbury GL8 140 C4
Reynold's Wlk BS7 19 A7
Reynolds Cl BS31 5 A5
Rhode Cl BS31 5 A3
Rhodesia Ho [1] GL51 132 F4
Rhodfa Wyesham/Wyesham Ave [4] NP25 154 A7
Ribble Cl GL3 120 F5
Ribblesdale BS35 51 D8
Ribston Hall GL1 196 A2
Ribston Hall High Sch GL1 118 E5
Ribston Mews GL1 118 E5
Ricardo Rd GL6 91 F7
Richard Pate Sch The GL53 130 E4
Richard Pl GL20 192 D1
Richards Rd GL51 133 B4
Richeson Cl BS10 27 F2
Richeson Wlk BS10 27 F2
Richmond Apartments BS6 18 C3
Richmond Ave
Bristol,Montpelier BS6 18 F2
Bristol,Stoke Gifford BS34 29 E5
Gloucester GL4 119 C6
Richmond Bldgs GL5 98 D6
Richmond Cl BS31 4 D4
Richmond Ct
[1] Ashton Keynes SN6 142 F5
Bristol BS34 39 F1
[7] Bristol,Clifton BS8 18 A2
[2] Bristol,Windmill Hill BS3 8 F4
Richmond Dale [6] BS8 18 A2
Richmond Dr [4] GL52 134 A1
Richmond Gdns GL2 127 D5
Richmond Hill BS8 194 B3
Richmond Hill Ave BS8 194 B3
Richmond Hts BS8 194 B3
Richmond La BS8 194 B3
Richmond Mews BS8 194 A3
Richmond Park Rd BS8 194 A3
Richmond Rd
Bristol,Mangotsfield BS16 21 A5
Bristol,Montpelier BS6 18 E1
Bristol,Pile Marsh BS5 9 E7
Tewkesbury GL20 192 E1
Richmond St BS3 8 F4
Richmond Terr
Avonmouth BS11 26 B1
Bristol BS8 194 A3
Richmonds The GL4 119 D4
Rickfield The NP25 162 A1
Rickyard Way GL2 100 E5
Riddle St GL13 94 B3
Ride The BS15 21 A2
Ridge Jun Sch The BS37 43 F2
Ridge Pl GL17 163 D1
Ridge The Bristol BS11 16 E7
Broad Blunsdon SN26 144 D1
Bussage GL6 148 B6
Coalpit Heath BS36 31 C7
Ridge Wlk GL17 164 A4
Ridge's La GL8 140 C7
Ridgehill BS9 18 C6
Ridgemeade BS14 3 B4
Ridgemont Rd GL5 99 E6
Ridgemount Cl GL3 120 E5
Ridgemount Gdns BS14 3 B5
Ridgeview BS41 7 B2
Ridgeway
Coalpit Heath BS36 31 D7
Eastnor HR8 179 B8
Monmouth/Trefynwy NP25 154 A7
Yate BS37 44 A2
Yorkley GL15 156 B2
Ridgeway Cres HR9 162 D4
Ridgeway Ct
Bristol,Henbury BS10 28 A1
Bristol,Hengrove BS14 3 C5
Ridgeway Gdns BS14 3 C5
Ridgeway Ind Ctr BS5 19 E2
Ridgeway La Bristol BS14 3 B5
Marston Meysey SN6 144 B6
Ridgeway Par BS5 19 E3
Ridgeway Rd Bristol BS16 19 F3
Long Ashton BS41 7 A2
Ridgeway The
Bristol BS10 28 A1
Bussage GL6 148 B6
Crudwell SN16 141 C3
Ridgeways GL56 177 C8
Ridgewood BS9 17 D3
Riding Barn Hill BS30 12 A6
Ridingleaze BS11 27 A1
Ridings Cl BS37 44 D1
Ridings High Sch The BS36 30 D6
Ridings Rd BS36 31 C6
Ridings The Bristol BS13 1 E4
Coalpit Heath BS36 31 C6
Maisemore GL2 126 A7
Nailsworth GL6 91 C3
Ridler Rd GL15 92 C2
Rigsby's La SN16 142 D3
Ring Fence GL15 147 B3
Ringer's Cl GL19 173 C7
Ringfield Cl GL6 91 C3
Ringspit La BS14 3 E1
Ringswell SN14 15 A7
Ringwood Cres BS10 28 D1
Ripley Rd BS5 20 A1
Ripon Ct BS16 30 F2
Ripon Rd BS4 9 E6
Rippledale Cl GL51 129 E7
Risdale Rd BS3 7 F1
Rise The GL54 166 E5
Risedale Ho BS15 10 D5
Rising Sun La GL52 138 E2
Rissington Cl GL51 129 E8
Rissington Rd
Bourton-on-t-W GL54 169 A6
Gloucester GL4 118 E3
Rivelands Rd GL51 133 B7
River Leys GL51 132 F5
River Mead BS37 43 C3
River Rd BS37 44 A1
River St BS2 195 C3
River Terr BS31 4 F5
River View Bristol BS16 19 E5
Chepstow/Cas-Gwent NP16 60 E8
River Way GL7 142 F8
Riverdale GL14 157 A6
Rivergate BS1 195 C2
Riverland Dr BS13 1 F5
Riverleaze BS9 17 C5
Rivermead Cl GL2 126 E4
Rivers Way SN6 145 C3
Riverside GL54 174 A7
Riverside Bsns Pk BS4 9 D6
Riverside Cl Bristol BS11 16 F5
Charlton Kings GL52 131 B6
Riverside Cotts
Bristol BS15 10 B1
Brockworth GL3 120 E5
Riverside Ct [2] Bristol BS4 9 F6
Tewkesbury GL20 192 C5
Riverside Dr BS16 20 C7
Riverside Mews BS4 9 F6
Riverside Pk
Eastington GL10 97 A8
[23] Monmouth/Trefynwy NP25 154 A7
Severn Beach BS35 37 F6
Riverside Stps BS4 9 E7
Riverside Way BS15 10 C3
Riverside Wlk [6] BS5 9 F6
Riversley Rd GL2 127 C2
Riversmeet GL3 120 F5
Riversmill GL11 80 D8
Riversmill Ct GL11 80 D8
Riversmill Wlk GL11 80 D8
Riverview Way GL51 133 A4
Riverwood Ho BS16 30 C1
Riverwood Rd BS16 30 C1
Riviera Cres BS16 20 E4
Riviera Way BS34 30 A4
Rixon Gate SN6 143 A5
Roach's La GL9 46 D2
Road Hill SN14 15 D1
Road Two BS10 38 A3
Robbers Rd GL6 102 C2
Robbins Cl Bristol BS32 29 F6
Marshfield SN14 14 F8
Stroud GL5 98 C6
Robbins Ct BS16 21 B6
Robel Ave BS36 31 A8
Robert Burns Ave GL51 129 D7
Robert Ct Bristol BS16 21 B7
Leigh Woods BS8 7 D7
Robert Franklin Way GL7 143 A8
Robert Harvey Ho [4] GL52 193 C4
Robert Raikes Ave
Gloucester GL4 118 D2
Gloucester GL4 118 E2
Robert St
Bristol,Baptist Mills BS5 19 B2
[16] Bristol,Russell Town BS5 9 B7
Roberts Cl
Bishop's Cleeve GL52 137 F4
Stratton GL7 190 B8
Roberts Rd
Cheltenham GL52 134 D3
Innsworth GL3 127 E7
Robertson Dr BS4 9 F6
Robertson Rd Bristol BS5 19 C2
Shurdington GL51 129 D2
Robin Cl
Bristol,Brentry BS10 28 B2
Bristol,Stockwood BS14 3 D6
[2] Chalford GL6 148 C6
Northway GL20 182 B5
Robin Ct GL10 97 F8
Robin Hood Junc GL16 154 F6
Robin Way BS37 33 A7
Robinhood St GL1 118 D7
Robinia Cl GL53 131 B5
Robinia Wlk BS14 3 A7
Robins Cl GL52 134 A2
Robins End GL3 127 D7
Robins Wood Hill Ctry Pk* GL4 119 A2
Robinson Cl GL18 171 A5
Robinson Dr BS5 9 A8
Robinson La
Upper Lydbrook GL17 163 D2
Woodmancote GL7 158 B4
Robinson Rd GL1 118 E7
Robinswood Gdns GL4 119 A4
Robinswood Hill Ctry Pk* GL4 118 F3
Robinswood Pl [11] GL4 119 C4
Robinswood Prim Sch GL4 119 C3
Rochester Cl GL51 130 A5
Rochester Rd BS4 9 F5
Rock & Fountain La GL14 157 E8
Rock Cl BS4 9 E2
Rock Cotts Pill BS20 16 E4
Stroud GL5 99 C8
Rock Ho BS10 28 C3
Rock La Bristol BS34 29 F4
Coleford GL16 155 A5
Elton GL14 157 E8
Northwood Green GL14 165 E1
Rock Rd Dursley GL11 87 D4
Keynsham BS31 4 E5
Wick BS30 12 D8
Rock St Chaceley GL19 181 B1
Thornbury BS35 51 B8
Rock The BS4 9 E3
Rock Villa La NP16 72 F1
Rockhill Est BS31 4 F4
Rockhill Ho BS31 4 F4
Rockingham Gdns BS11 17 A8
Rockingham Rdbt BS11 26 D6
Rockland Gr BS16 19 D5
Rockland Rd BS16 20 D7
Rockleaze Bristol BS9 17 E2
[9] Thornbury BS35 64 B1
Rockleaze Ave BS9 17 E3
Rockleaze Ct BS9 17 E3
Rockleaze Rd BS9 17 E3
Rockleigh Cl GL4 118 E3
Rockness Hill GL6 91 A2
Rocks Rd GL17 163 D3
Rocks The GL16 155 A3
Rockside Ave BS16 20 F8
Rockside Dr BS9 18 C6
Rockside Gdns
Bristol BS16 20 F8
Frampton Cotterell BS36 31 C8
Rockstowes Way BS10 28 D3
Rockwell Ave BS11 27 B1
Rockwood Ho BS37 44 A4
Rockwood Rd NP16 60 E7
Rodborough BS37 32 C7
Rodborough Ave GL5 99 B6
Rodborough Com Prim Sch GL5 99 B6
Rodborough Hill GL5 99 B6
Rodborough La GL5 99 C5
Rodborough Terr GL5 99 B5
Rodborough Way BS15 11 A7
Rodbourne Rd BS10 18 E6
Rodford Prim Sch BS37 32 D7
Rodford Way BS37 32 D7
Rodfords Mead BS14 3 A7
Rodley Rd GL15 92 C3
Rodley Sq GL15 92 C3
Rodmarton Sch GL7 149 B1
Rodmead Wlk BS13 2 A4
Rodney Ave BS15 10 A8
Rodney Cl GL2 127 B4
Rodney Cres BS34 29 A4
Rodney Pl BS8 194 A3
Rodney Rd Bristol BS15 10 A8
Cheltenham GL50 193 B3
Saltford BS31 5 E2
Rodney Wlk BS15 20 A1
Rodway Ct BS16 21 A5
Rodway Hill BS16 21 B3
Rodway Hill Rd BS16 21 A4
Rodway La GL19,GL2 172 E3
Rodway Rd Bristol BS34 29 A8
Bristol,Mangotsfield BS16 21 A5
Bristol,Patchway BS34 28 F7
Rodway View BS15 20 F3
Roebuck Mdws GL17 163 F3
Roegate Dr BS4 9 E6
Roegate Ho BS5 20 A1
Roel Gate GL54 174 D3
Rogers Cl BS30 11 B5
Rogers Ct BS37 44 C1
Rogers Wlk BS30 11 D7
Rokeby Ave BS6 18 C1
Rollers The GL6 91 B4
Rolleston Way GL51 129 F7
Rolling Stones [4] GL55 189 A2
Rolph Ct [8] GL56 187 A2
Roman Amphitheatre* GL7 190 B4
Roman Farm Ct BS11 27 C2
Roman Farm Rd BS4 2 E7
Roman Hackle Ave GL50 133 C5
Roman Rd Bristol BS5 19 B1
Cheltenham GL51 133 A1
Gloucester GL4 119 E6
Roman Way
Bourton-on-t-W GL54 169 A8
Bristol BS9 17 C4
Brockworth GL3 120 E6
Coleford GL16 155 A5
Highworth SN6 145 C3
Lechlade on T GL7 153 E3
Littledean GL14 191 F4
Roman Wlk
Bristol,Kensington Park BS4 9 C3
Bristol,Stoke Gifford BS34 29 E5
Romney Ave BS7 19 B6
Romney Avenue Jun & Inf Schs BS7 19 B6
Romney Cl GL1 118 E5
Romney Rd GL8 140 B4
Romo Ct BS16 20 C4
Ron Jones Ho [3] BS1 195 B4
Ronald Rd BS16 19 F6
Ronayne Wlk BS16 20 C6
Rookery La Newton GL13 85 E7
Pilning BS35 39 A6
Pucklechurch BS30,SN14 22 F4
St Briavels GL15 154 F2
Rookery Rd Bristol BS4 9 A3
Innsworth GL3 127 D6
Rookery The GL54 159 A6
Rookery Villas GL2 116 A3
Rookery Way BS14 2 F4
Rooksmoor Hill GL5 99 A3
Roosevelt Ave GL52 131 A8
Rope Walk Ho BS2 195 C3
Rope Wlk [3] GL12 68 B7
Rope Wlk The GL5 99 E3
Ropewalk GL20 192 D4
Rosary RC Prim Sch The GL5 99 B7
Rosary Rdbt The BS16 21 D7
Rosary The Bristol BS16 21 D7
Chepstow/Cas-Gwent NP16 72 D1
Rose & Crown Ho GL50 193 B4
Rose & Crown Pas GL50 193 B4
Rose Acre BS10 28 A3
Rose Cl BS36 30 E4
Rose Green Cl BS5 19 E2
Rose Green Rd BS5 19 D2
Rose Hill Sch GL12 68 D2
Rose La BS36 31 D6
Rose Mead BS7 19 A7
Rose Meare Gdns BS13 1 E7
Rose Oak Dr BS36 31 D7
Rose Oak Gdns BS36 31 D7
Rose Oak La BS36 31 D7
Rose Rd BS5 9 E7
Rose Row GL54 176 B2
Rose Terr BS8 194 B3
Rose Tree Ho BS16 20 F4
Rose Way GL7 190 E2
Rose Willis Ct [10] GL18 171 A4
Rose Wlk BS16 20 C3
Rosebank BS5 19 D2
Rosebay Gdns GL51 132 E5
Rosebay Mead BS16 19 E5
Roseberry Pk BS5 9 D8
Roseberry Rd BS5 9 C7
Roseberry Terr GL6 148 C5
Rosebery Ave Bristol BS2 19 A1
Gloucester GL1 118 E6
Rosebery Mount GL11 80 C8
Rosebery Pk GL11 80 C8
Rosebery Rd GL11 80 C8
Rosebery Terr BS8 194 B2
Rosedale Ave GL10 98 A7
Rosedale Cl GL2 109 D8
Rosedale Rd BS16 20 C3
Rosefield Cres GL20 192 F4
Rosehill Ct GL7 190 C7
Rosehill St GL52 130 F8
Rosehill Terr [6] GL52 130 F8
Rosehip Ct GL51 130 A4
Rosehip Way GL52 137 E4
Roselarge Gdns BS10 28 A2
Rosemary Cl Bristol BS32 29 F7
Gloucester GL4 119 D4
Rosemary La Bristol BS5 19 C2
Stroat NP16 146 F1
Rosemary Terr GL12 68 B7
Rosemont Terr BS8 194 A2
Rosemount Ct BS15 10 B8
Rosery Cl BS9 18 A8
Rosery The BS16 20 C3
Rosevear BS2 9 A7
Roseville Ave BS30 11 A2
Rosewood Ave BS35 50 F5
Rosewood Wlk GL52 138 B4
Roshni Gar E [16] BS5 19 B1
Roshni Gar W [15] BS5 19 B1
Rosling Rd BS7 18 E6
Roslyn Rd BS6 18 C1
Ross Cl BS37 44 B1
Ross Rd Berry Hill GL16 155 A8
Mitcheldean GL17 164 D6
Newent GL18 170 F5
Rossall Ave BS34 29 C6
Rossall Rd BS4 9 D3
Rossiter Wood Ct BS11 27 B2
Rossiter's La BS5 10 A6
Rosslyn Way BS35 64 C3
Rothermere Cl GL51 129 F5
Rothleigh GL51 129 E5
Rotunda Terr GL50 193 A2
Rougemont Gr NP16 60 F4
Rounceval St BS37 44 A1
Roundabouts The GL5 99 F1
Roundhills Mead SN6 145 D4
Roundhouse Mews [7] GL56 187 A3
Roundmoor Cl BS31 5 D3
Roundmoor Gdns BS14 3 D7
Roundways BS36 31 D6
Rousham Rd BS5 19 A3
Roves La SN6 145 D1
Row The Aust BS35 49 A7
Donnington GL56 176 F7
Lechlade on T GL7 153 F4
Southrop GL7 153 C6
St Arvans NP16 72 B6
Rowacres BS14 2 F6
Rowan Cl BS16 20 A2
Rowan Ct [10] Bristol BS5 9 B7
Yate BS37 43 C3
Rowan Dr NP16 60 E5
Rowan Gdns GL3 120 D6
Rowan Gr GL11 88 A3
Rowan Ho BS13 2 D4
Rowan Tree Ho BS16 20 F4
Rowan Way Bristol BS15 10 B3
[15] Cheltenham GL51 129 E5
Nailsworth GL6 90 F5
Rowan Wlk BS31 4 C4
Rowandean GL14 191 C5
Rowanfield Exchange GL51 133 A2
Rowanfield Inf & Jun Schs GL51 133 A2
Rowanfield Rd GL51 133 A1
Rowans The Bristol BS16 30 B1
Pontshill HR9 164 B8
Woodmancote GL52 138 B3
Rowberrow BS14 2 F7
Rowcroft GL5 99 B7
Rowcroft Retreat GL5 99 B7
Rowe Ct GL50 193 A3
Rowena Cade Ave GL50 130 B6
Rowland Ave BS16 19 D4
Rowlandson Gdns BS7 19 B6
Rowley GL11 88 A5
Rowley Mews GL11 88 A5
Rowley St BS3 8 C3
Rownham Cl BS3 7 E4
Rownham Ct BS8 194 A1
Rownham Hill BS8 7 E6
Rownham Mead BS8 194 A1
Rows The GL55 188 D4
Roxburgh BS8 7 F8
Roxton Dr GL51 129 C7
Roy King Gdns BS30 11 C6
Royal Agricultural Coll GL7 150 B4
Royal Albert Rd BS6 18 A4
Royal Cl BS10 27 D3
Royal Cres GL50 193 B3
Royal Ct [9] GL51 132 D2
Royal Forest of Dean Coll GL16 155 B7
Royal Fort Rd BS2,BS8 194 C3
Royal La GL1 127 A2
Royal Oak Mews GL50 193 B4
Royal Oak Rd
Gloucester GL1 196 A3
Upper Lydbrook GL17 163 E3
Royal Oak Terr GL55 188 F1
Royal Par BS8 194 B3
Royal Parade Mews GL50 193 A2
Royal Park Mews [3] BS8 194 A3
Royal Pk BS8 194 A3
Royal Prom BS8 194 B3
Royal Rd BS16 21 A6
Royal Spring GL17 165 A5
Royal Victoria Pk BS10 28 B2
Royal Well La GL50 193 B3
Royal Well Pl GL50 193 B3
Royal Well Rd GL50 193 B3
Royal West of England Acad* BS8 194 B3
Royal York Cres BS8 7 F6
Royal York Ho BS8 194 A2
Royal York Mews BS8 194 A2
Royal York Villas BS8 194 A2
Royate Hill BS5 19 D2
Roycroft Rd BS34 29 B2
Royston Wlk BS10 28 D2
Rozel Rd BS7 18 E5
Ruardean CE Prim Sch GL17 163 E4
Ruardean Garden Pottery* GL17 163 E4
Ruardean Rd GL17 163 F3
Rubens Cl BS31 5 A5
Ruby St BS3 8 B3
Rudford Cl BS34 40 B1
Rudge Cl BS15 20 F2
Rudge The GL2 126 B8
Rudgeway Pk BS35 50 F1
Rudgewood Cl BS13 2 D4
Rudgleigh Ave BS20 16 C4
Rudgleigh Rd BS20 16 C4
Rudhall Ct GL1 196 A3
Rudhall Gr BS10 18 E7
Rudhall View HR9 164 D8
Rudthorpe Rd BS7 18 E5
Ruffet Cl GL16 155 B4
Ruffet Rd BS36 31 B4
Ruffet's Cl NP16 60 D8
Ruffitt The GL14 191 F5
Rugby Rd BS4 9 D3
Rumsey Cl GL4 119 E4
Runnings Rd GL51 133 A5
Runnings The GL51 133 A6
Runnymead Ave BS4 9 D2
Runnymede Bristol BS15 20 E1
Cheltenham GL51 129 E5
Runswick Rd BS4 9 C3
Rupert St
Bristol,Kingsdown BS1 195 A3
Bristol,Redfield BS5 9 C7
Ruscombe Rd GL6 102 E2
Rush Cl BS32 40 D2
Rusham BS13 1 F4
Rushley La GL54 174 A7
Rushmead La SN14 24 F2
Rushton Dr BS36 31 D7
Rushworth Cl GL51 132 D2
Rushworth Ho GL51 132 D2
Rushy BS30 11 A4
Rushy Ho GL52 134 A4
Rushy Mews GL52 134 A4
Rushy Way BS16 31 A1
Rushyleaze GL15 92 B2
Ruskin Gr BS7 19 A8
Ruskin Ho BS34 29 A8
Ruspidge Cl GL4 119 E5
Ruspidge Rd GL14 156 C6
Russ St BS2 195 C2
Russell Almshouses GL20 192 C3
Russell Ave BS15 10 E7
Russell Cl GL9 57 B3

Russell Gr BS6 ...18 C5
Russell Pl GL51 ...133 C3
Russell Rd
Bristol,Chester Park BS16 ...20 B2
Bristol,Westbury Park BS6 ...18 B4
Russell St
Cheltenham GL51 ...133 C3
Gloucester GL1 ...196 B2
Stroud GL5 ...99 C7
Russell Town Ave BS5 ...9 B8
Russell Town Ind Pk 18
BS5 ...9 C7
Russet Ave GL7 ...153 F2
Russet Cl Bredon GL20 ...182 C7
Gloucester GL4 ...118 B3
2 Ledbury HR8 ...178 E7
Olveston BS35 ...50 A3
Russet Ct GL12 ...67 F4
Russet Rd GL51 ...132 F3
Russett Way 24 GL18 ...171 A4
Rustic Cl GL4 ...119 C4
Rustic Pk BS35 ...38 A6
Rutherford Cl BS30 ...11 A3
Rutherford Way GL51 ...133 A5
Ruthven Rd BS4 ...2 E8
Rutland Ave BS30 ...11 A2
Rutland Ct 4 GL50 ...133 B1
Rutland Pl GL7 ...190 C3
Rutland Rd BS7 ...18 E3
Ryalls La GL2 ...95 E5
Rydal Ho BS34 ...29 A8
Rydal Rd GL2 ...127 B4
Rydal Wlk GL51 ...129 E7
Ryde Rd BS4 ...9 B2
Ryder Cl GL11 ...88 A4
Ryder Row GL3 ...127 E6
Rye Ave GL51 ...132 D5
Rye Cl BS13 ...1 E6
Rye Close Bglws GL54 ...169 A7
Rye Cres GL54 ...169 A7
Rye St WR13 ...180 A6
Ryeclose GL54 ...169 A7
Ryecroft Ct BS36 ...31 C7
Ryecroft Rd BS36 ...31 C8
Ryecroft Rise BS41 ...7 B1
Ryecroft St GL1 ...196 C1
Ryedown La BS30 ...11 D2
Ryeford Ind Est GL10 ...98 A6
Ryelands GL4 ...118 C3
Ryelands Cl GL10 ...97 E8
Ryelands Rd
7 Bream GL15 ...147 D8
Stonehouse GL10 ...97 E8
Ryelands The GL6 ...102 D1
Ryeleaze Cl GL5 ...99 C7
Ryeleaze Rd GL5 ...99 C7
Ryeworth Dr GL52 ...131 B7
Ryeworth Rd GL52 ...131 B7
Ryland Cl GL8 ...140 C5
Ryland Pl 1 BS2 ...19 A2
Rylestone Cl BS36 ...30 F8
Rylestone Gr BS9 ...17 F5
Rysdale Rd BS9 ...17 F6

S

Sabre Cl GL2 ...118 A3
Sabrina Way Bristol BS9 ...17 C4
Lydney GL15 ...92 B4
Sackville App GL50 ...133 D4
Saco Ho BS1 ...195 B2
Saddlers La GL50 ...193 A1
Saddlers Rd GL2 ...117 F2
Sadlers Ct 8 GL52 ...130 F8
Sadlers Field 4 SN6 ...142 F5
Sadlier Cl BS11 ...17 A8
Saffron Cl GL4 ...119 A5
Saffron Rd GL20 ...192 C4
Sage Cl GL3 ...127 F6
Sages Mead BS32 ...29 E8
Saint Andrews Mews
BS6 ...18 E3
Saint Way BS34 ...30 A4
Saintbridge Cl GL4 ...119 B5
Saintbridge Pl GL4 ...119 B5
SS Gt Britain* BS1 ...194 B1
SS Peter & Paul RC Prim Sch
BS8 ...194 C4
St Agnes Ave BS4 ...8 F2
St Agnes Gdns BS4 ...8 F2
St Agnes Wlk BS4 ...8 F2
St Aidan's Cl BS5 ...10 B6
St Aidan's Rd BS5 ...10 B6
St Aidans Cl GL51 ...132 E2
St Alban's Rd BS6 ...18 B4
St Albans Cl GL51 ...130 A5
St Albans Rd GL2 ...118 C5
St Aldams Dr BS16 ...22 B5
St Aldate St GL1 ...196 B3
St Aldwyn Rd GL1 ...118 F6
St Aldwyn's Cl BS7 ...18 F8
St Andrew CE Prim Sch
SN26 ...144 E1
St Andrew's Ave NP16 ...60 E7
St Andrew's CE Prim Sch
GL54 ...159 A6
St Andrew's CE Prim Sch
GL12 ...66 A1
St Andrew's Rd
Avonmouth BS11 ...26 B1
Avonmouth BS11 ...26 B4
Bristol BS6 ...18 E2
St Andrews
Ashleworth GL19 ...172 D4
St Andrews *continued*
Bristol BS30 ...11 B6
Yate BS37 ...43 F1
St Andrews Cl GL20 ...182 C4
St Andrews Gate Rdbt
BS11 ...26 B2
St Andrews Gn GL3 ...128 B5
St Andrews Road Sta
BS11 ...26 B4
St Andrews Trad Est
BS11 ...26 C2
St Ann St NP16 ...72 F1
St Ann Way GL1 ...196 A1
St Ann's Cross 10 GL15 ...147 D8
St Annal's Rd GL14 ...191 E4
St Anne's 13 GL52 ...133 F2
St Anne's Ave BS31 ...4 D6
St Anne's CE Prim Sch
BS30 ...11 C3
St Anne's Cl Bristol BS30 ...11 B4
Cheltenham GL52 ...133 F2
St Anne's Ct BS31 ...4 D6
St Anne's Dr
Coalpit Heath BS36 ...31 C5
Wick BS30 ...12 B7
St Anne's Inf Sch BS4 ...9 D5
St Anne's Jun Sch BS4 ...9 D5
St Anne's Park Prim Sch
BS4 ...9 E5
St Anne's Park Rd BS4 ...9 E5
St Anne's Rd
Bristol,St Anne's Park BS4 ...9 D6
Bristol,St George BS5 ...10 B6
Cheltenham GL52 ...193 C3
St Anne's Terr Bristol BS4 ...9 E5
Cheltenham GL52 ...193 C3
St Annes Cl 7 Bristol BS5 ...9 F6
Brockworth GL3 ...120 E6
St Annes Ct BS4 ...9 D5
St Annes Dr BS30 ...11 C2
St Annes Way GL15 ...146 E7
St Anthony's Dr BS30 ...12 B7
St Anthony's Sch GL14 ...191 D4
St Arild's Rd GL9 ...57 B4
St Aubin's Ave BS4 ...9 F3
St Augustine's Par BS1 ...195 A2
St Augustine's Pl 1
BS1 ...195 A2
St Augustine's Working
Farm* GL2 ...157 B6
St Augustines of Canterbury
RC Sch BS16 ...20 F8
St Barbara's Cl GL20 ...182 D4
St Barnabas CE Prim Sch
Bristol,Mont Pelier BS6 ...18 F1
Bristol,North Common BS30 11 C6
St Barnabas Cl
Bristol,Lower Knowle BS4 ...8 F1
Bristol,Warmley BS30 ...11 C7
Gloucester GL1 ...118 E4
St Barnabas Ho BS30 ...11 C7
St Bartholomew's Rd
BS7 ...18 F3
St Bartholomews 12
GL18 ...171 A4
St Bartholomews Cl GL11 87 F5
St Bede's RC Coll BS11 ...27 B2
St Bede's Rd BS15 ...20 D2
St Benedict's RC Sch &
Sports Coll GL51 ...133 A3
St Bernadette RC Prim Sch
BS14 ...3 B6
St Bernadette RC Sec Sch
BS14 ...3 B6
St Bernard's RC Sch
BS11 ...16 E6
St Bernard's Rd BS11 ...16 E6
St Birinus Ct GL7 ...153 E3
St Blaize Ct GL7 ...190 C4
St Bonaventure's RC Prim
Sch BS7 ...18 D4
St Brelades Gr BS4 ...9 F5
St Brenda's Ct 1 BS8 ...194 A3
St Brendan's Rd GL5 ...99 E7
St Brendan's Sixth Form Coll
BS4 ...10 A1
St Brendan's Way BS11 ...26 B1
St Brendans Rdbt BS11 ...26 C1
St Briavels Castle*
GL15 ...146 E7
St Briavels Dr BS37 ...32 D8
St Briavels Parochial CE Prim
Sch GL15 ...146 E7
St Briavels Rd GL15 ...147 B2
St Bruel's Cl GL15 ...146 F7
St Cadoc Ho BS31 ...4 F5
St Catharine's RC Prim Sch
GL55 ...188 F2
St Catherine Ct GL1 ...118 E7
St Catherine St GL1 ...196 B4
St Catherine's Ind Est BS3 8 D3
St Catherine's Mead
BS20 ...16 D3
St Catherine's Terr BS3 ...8 D3
St Catherines Pl 7 BS3 ...8 D4
St Chloe Mead GL5 ...91 B8
St Christopher's Sch BS6 18 B4
St Clair Cotts GL51 ...173 F2
St Clement's Wlk GL7 ...190 C5
St Clements Ct
6 Bristol BS16 ...20 D3
Keynsham BS31 ...4 E4
St Clements Rd BS31 ...4 F4
St Cyril's Rd GL10 ...97 F7
St David's Ave BS30 ...11 B5
St David's Cl
Chepstow/Cas-Gwent NP16 60 E7
Gloucester GL4 ...118 D3
St David's Cres BS4 ...9 F6
St David's Ct GL56 ...187 A3
St David's Rd BS35 ...64 C1
St David's Sch GL56 ...187 A3
St Davids Cl GL51 ...130 A6
St Davids Rd GL20 ...182 C4
St Dominics RC Prim Sch
GL5 ...91 A7
St Dunstan's Rd BS3 ...8 C2
St Dunstans Cl BS31 ...4 E6
St Edward's Rd BS8 ...194 B2
St Edward's Sch GL52 ...131 A7
St Edwards Ct 2 GL56 ...187 A2
St Edwards Dr GL54 ...176 F4
St Edwards Jun Sch
GL52 ...131 B7
St Edwards Rd GL54 ...176 F4
St Edwards Wlk GL53 ...131 A6
St Edyth's Rd BS9 ...17 C6
St Ewens Rd NP16 ...60 E6
St Fagans Ct BS30 ...11 B2
St Francis Dr Wick BS30 ...12 B7
Winterbourne BS36 ...30 F6
St Francis Rd
6 Bristol BS3 ...8 A4
Keynsham BS31 ...4 D6
St Gabriel's Bsns Pk 24
BS5 ...9 B8
St Gabriel's Rd BS5 ...9 B8
St George CE Prim Sch
BS1 ...194 B2
St George Pl BS1 ...194 C2
St George Rd NP16 ...60 E7
St George's GL50 ...193 B4
St George's Ave GL10 ...98 A4
St George's Cl
2 Cheltenham GL51 ...133 B2
Dursley GL11 ...88 B3
Gloucester GL4 ...118 C3
21 Moreton-in-M GL56 ...187 A3
St George's Dr GL51 ...133 B2
St George's Hill BS20 ...16 A3
St George's Ho BS1 ...194 B2
St George's Hts 12 BS5 ...9 D7
St George's Pl GL50 ...193 B3
St George's Rd
Cheltenham GL50 ...193 A3
Dursley GL11 ...88 A3
Keynsham BS31 ...4 D6
St George's Sq GL50 ...193 B4
St George's St GL50 ...193 B4
St George's Terr GL56 ...186 C6
St Georges Ave 10 BS5 ...9 F6
St Georges Bsns Pk
GL51 ...133 A2
St Georges Cl GL10 ...97 F4
St Georges Ho BS5 ...9 E8
St Georges Ind Est BS11 ...26 B3
St Georges Rd
Ashchurch GL20 ...182 C4
Bristol BS1 ...194 C2
Watermead GL3 ...120 E5
St Georges Twr 5 GL50 ...193 B4
St Georges Way NP16 ...61 B4
St Giles Barton GL12 ...55 D8
St Giles's Rd GL20 ...182 C7
St Gregory's Rd BS7 ...18 F8
St Helen's Wlk BS5 ...20 A1
St Helena Rd BS6 ...18 B4
St Helens CE Prim Sch
BS35 ...51 A4
St Helens Dr Bristol BS30 ...11 C2
Wick BS30 ...12 C7
St Helier Ave BS4 ...9 F3
St Hilary Cl BS9 ...17 D5
St Ivel Way BS30 ...11 C6
St Ives Ct GL52 ...133 F4
St James CE Prim Sch
Cheltenham GL50 ...130 B6
Chipping Campden GL55 ...189 A1
St James Cl BS35 ...64 C3
St James Ct Bristol BS32 ...40 C3
4 Cheltenham GL50 ...193 A4
1 Moreton-in-M GL56 ...187 A2
St James Cvn Pk GL16 ...155 B3
St James Mews 3 GL1 ...119 A8
St James Pl BS16 ...21 A5
St James Sq GL15 ...147 D8
St James St
Cheltenham GL52 ...193 C3
Gloucester GL1 ...119 A8
St James Trad Est 4
GL1 ...119 A8
St James' GL2 ...117 F1
St James' Barton BS1 ...195 B4
St James' Barton Rdbt
BS1 ...195 B4
St James' CE Jun Sch
GL1 ...119 A8
St James' Cl GL2 ...117 F1
St James' Pl GL50 ...193 A1
St James' Rdbt GL50 ...193 A4
St James' Sq
Cheltenham GL50 ...193 B3
20 Monmouth/Trefynwy
NP25 ...154 A7
St James' St 18 NP25 ...154 A7
St James' Terr GL50 ...193 B2
St James's Ct BS8 ...18 B1
St James's St BS16 ...21 A5
St John St
Hawkesbury Upton GL9 ...56 A3
2 Thornbury BS35 ...64 B1
St John's Bridge BS1 ...195 A3
St John's CE Prim Sch
Bristol BS8 ...18 A2
Cheltenham GL52 ...193 C3
Coleford GL16 ...155 A5
St John's CE Prim Sch
BS31 ...4 E5
St John's Cl
Bishop's Cleeve GL52 ...137 F4
Stratton GL7 ...190 B7
St John's Cres BS3 ...8 E2
St John's Ct 3 GL50 ...133 B2
St John's Ct GL20 ...136 A8
St John's Gdns NP16 ...72 D1
St John's Ho BS5 ...9 D8
St John's La Bristol BS3 ...8 E2
Gloucester GL1 ...196 B3
St John's Mead CE Prim Sch
BS37 ...44 B1
St John's Rd Bristol BS8 ...18 A1
Bristol,Bedminster BS3 ...8 C3
Cirencester GL7 ...190 C6
Ruardean GL17 ...163 F4
Slimbridge GL2 ...95 E3
St John's St Bristol BS3 ...8 C3
12 Coleford GL16 ...155 A5
Lechlade on T GL7 ...153 E2
St John's-on-the-Hill Sch
NP16 ...72 F2
St Johns Ave
Cheltenham GL52 ...193 C3
Churchdown GL3 ...128 A6
St Johns Ct Bristol BS16 ...20 A3
Bristol,Bedminster BS3 ...8 D2
7 Coleford GL16 ...155 A5
Keynsham BS31 ...4 E6
St Johns Sq GL14 ...191 C2
St Johns Way BS37 ...44 C2
St Joseph's RC Prim Sch
BS16 ...20 B3
St Joseph's RC Prim Sch
GL10 ...89 E6
St Joseph's Rd BS10 ...28 B3
St Judes Wlk GL53 ...130 F6
St Katherine's Hospl The
Alms Houses 7 HR8 ...178 F8
St Katherine's Sch BS20 ...16 E3
St Kenya Ct BS31 ...4 F5
St Keyna Rd BS31 ...4 E5
St Kilda Par GL1 ...196 C2
St Kingsmark Ave NP16 ...72 D1
St Ladoc Rd BS31 ...4 D6
St Laud Cl BS9 ...17 D5
St Lawrence Cl
Cirencester GL7 ...190 B5
Sandhurst GL2 ...172 F2
St Lawrence La NP16 ...60 C7
St Lawrence Pk NP16 ...60 C8
St Lawrence Rd
Chepstow/Cas-Gwent NP16 60 C8
Gloucester GL4 ...119 D8
Lechlade on T GL7 ...153 E2
St Lawrence's CE Prim Sch
GL7 ...153 E2
St Leonard's Ct OX7 ...177 E1
St Leonard's Rd
Bristol,Horfield BS7 ...18 E5
Bristol,Lower Easton BS5 ...19 C2
St Leonard's Row SN16 ...142 B2
St Leonards Cl
Upper Minety SN16 ...142 B2
Upton St Leonards GL4 ...119 E2
St Loe Cl BS14 ...2 E3
St Loes Pitch GL5 ...91 A8
St Lucia Cl BS7 ...18 E7
St Lucia Cres BS7 ...18 E7
St Luke St 13 BS5 ...9 B7
St Luke's Cres BS3 ...8 F4
St Luke's Ct BS3 ...8 E4
St Luke's Gdns BS4 ...9 E2
St Luke's Mews BS4 ...9 E2
St Luke's Pl GL53 ...193 C2
St Luke's Rd Bristol BS3 ...8 E4
Cheltenham GL53 ...193 C2
St Lukes Cl BS16 ...21 C7
St Lukes St GL1 ...196 A1
St Margaret's Cl BS31 ...4 D6
St Margaret's Dr BS9 ...18 C5
St Margaret's Par 6
GL50 ...193 B4
St Margaret's Rd
Cheltenham GL50 ...193 B4
Ruardean GL17 ...163 F4
St Margaret's Terr 2
GL52 ...193 C4
St Margarets GL1 ...127 A2
St Margarets Dr GL20 ...183 E4
St Margarets Rd
Alderton GL20 ...183 E4
Gloucester GL3 ...119 F8
St Mark St GL1 ...196 B4
St Mark's Ave 1 BS5 ...19 B1
St Mark's CE Jun Sch
GL51 ...129 D7
St Mark's Ct GL1 ...196 C4
St Mark's Gr 8 BS5 ...19 B1
St Mark's Ho 13 BS5 ...19 B1
St Mark's Rd BS5 ...19 B1
St Mark's Terr 11 BS5 ...19 B1
St Marks Church Ho 4
BS5 ...19 B1
St Marks Cl BS31 ...4 E6
St Martin's Gdns BS4 ...9 B1
St Martin's La SN14 ...14 F8
St Martin's Pk SN14 ...14 F8
St Martin's Rd BS4 ...9 B2
St Martin's Wlk BS4 ...9 B1
St Martins Cl BS4 ...9 B1
St Martins Terr GL50 ...133 E3
St Mary Redcliffe & Temple
CE Sch BS1 ...195 B1
St Mary Redcliffe CE Prim
Sch BS3 ...8 E4
St Mary St
8 Chepstow/Cas-Gwent
NP16 ...60 E8
Thornbury BS35 ...51 B8
St Mary Street Arc 9
NP16 ...60 E8
St Mary's Abbey Church*
GL20 ...192 C3
St Mary's CE Inf Sch
GL52 ...134 B3
St Mary's CE Prim Sch
Bromesberrow Heath HR8 179 C5
Tetbury GL8 ...140 B4
Thornbury BS35 ...64 A2
St Mary's CE Prim Sch
BS37 ...43 E2
St Mary's Cl GL1 ...196 A3
St Mary's Cl
Kempsford GL7 ...144 F7
Lower Swell GL54 ...176 D4
St Mary's Halt* GL15 ...92 A2
St Mary's Hill GL5 ...91 A7
St Mary's Hospl BS8 ...194 B3
St Mary's La GL20 ...192 C4
St Mary's Mead GL6 ...103 E7
St Mary's RC Prim Sch
NP16 ...60 E7
St Mary's Rd Bristol BS11 ...16 D7
Cirencester GL7 ...190 E4
Leigh Woods BS8 ...7 D6
Tetbury GL8 ...140 B4
Tewkesbury GL20 ...192 B4
St Mary's Sq
Gloucester GL1 ...196 A3
Lydney GL15 ...92 C3
St Mary's St
Gloucester GL1 ...196 B3
Painswick GL6 ...103 F8
St Mary's Way BS37 ...43 F2
St Mary's Wlk BS11 ...16 D6
St Marys Cl Bristol BS30 ...11 B5
Dymock GL18 ...178 D2
St Marys Dr GL7 ...152 E4
St Marys Field GL7 ...152 A3
St Marys RC Prim Sch
Bristol BS34 ...30 A7
Innsworth GL3 ...127 F6
St Marys Way 6 BS35 ...64 B1
St Matthew's Ave 10 BS6 18 D1
St Matthew's CE Prim Sch
GL5 ...98 E7
St Matthew's Rd BS6 ...195 A4
St Matthews Ct GL5 ...98 E6
St Matthias & Dr Bell's CE
Prim Sch BS16 ...20 A4
St Matthias Ho BS2 ...195 C3
St Matthias Pk BS2 ...195 C3
St Maur Gdns NP16 ...72 D1
St Michael On The Mount CE
Prim Sch BS2 ...194 C3
St Michael's Ave SN6 ...145 C3
St Michael's CE Prim Sch
BS34 ...29 E5
St Michael's Cl GL17 ...165 B4
St Michael's Cl
Mitcheldean GL17 ...164 D5
Winterbourne BS36 ...30 E7
St Michael's Ct GL1 ...196 B2
St Michael's Hill BS2 ...194 C4
St Michael's Hospl BS2 194 C4
St Michael's Pk BS2 ...194 C4
St Michael's Pl GL5 ...98 D8
St Michael's Sq GL1 ...196 B2
St Michaels 3 HR8 ...178 F8
St Michaels Ave GL52 ...138 A3
St Michaels CE Prim Sch
BS36 ...30 E6
St Michaels Cl BS7 ...18 E4
St Michaels Ct BS15 ...10 B8
St Michaels Pk GL14 ...191 C1
St Michaels Rd
Cheltenham GL51 ...130 B5
Cirencester GL7 ...190 C3
St Monica Ct BS9 ...18 A5
St Nicholas Cl GL20 ...183 A3
St Nicholas Ct
Gloucester GL1 ...196 A3
Hardwicke GL2 ...109 E7
St Nicholas Dr GL50 ...133 D5
St Nicholas of Tolentine RC
Prim Sch BS5 ...9 A8
St Nicholas Pk 10 BS5 ...19 B1
St Nicholas Rd BS14 ...3 C4
St Nicholas Sq GL1 ...196 A3
St Nicholas St BS1 ...195 A2
St Nicholas' Rd BS2 ...18 F1
St Oswald's Ct BS13 ...2 A8
St Oswald's Ct BS6 ...18 B3
St Oswald's Rd Bristol BS6 18 B3
Gloucester GL1 ...196 A4
St Oswalds Ret Pk GL1 ...126 D4
St Patrick's Ct GL3 ...120 E5
St Patrick's RC Prim Sch
BS5 ...9 D7
St Patricks Ct BS31 ...4 E5
St Patricks Rd GL20 ...182 C4
St Paul St BS2 ...195 B4
St Paul's Ct GL1 ...118 E7
St Paul's La GL50 ...133 D3
St Paul's Par GL50 ...133 D3
St Paul's Prim Sch
GL1 ...196 A1
St Paul's RC Prim Sch
BS37 ...32 E8
St Paul's Rd
2 Bristol,Southville BS3 ...8 D4
Bristol,Victoria Park BS8 ...194 B4
Cheltenham GL50 ...133 D3

St Paul's Rd *continued*
Gloucester GL1 .118 E7
St Paul's St N GL50 .133 D3
St Paul's St S GL50 .193 B4
St Paul's Terr GL50 .193 B4
St Pauls Ct 5 GL56 .187 A2
St Peter's Cl 10 GL14 .157 A6
St Peter's Cres BS36 .31 B8
St Peter's Ct GL7 .190 C4
St Peter's Ho BS8 .194 B2
St Peter's RC High Sch & Sixth Form Ctr GL4 .118 E1
St Peter's RC Prim Sch GL1 .127 B2
St Peter's Rd GL4 .119 C3
St Peter's Rise BS13 .2 B7
St Peter's Sq GL51 .133 A4
St Peter's Wlk 3 BS9 .18 B6
St Peters Cl
Cheltenham GL51 .133 B4
Rodmarton GL7 .149 B1
St Peters Ct 3 GL56 .187 A2
St Peters Rd GL7 .190 C4
St Peters Way 12 GL54 .174 A7
St Philip's Cl GL3 .120 A8
St Philip's Ct GL1 .118 D7
St Philips Central BS2 .9 A5
St Philips Cswy BS2 .9 B5
St Philips Trad Pk BS2 .9 B4
St Phillip's St GL50 .193 B1
St Phillips Rd BS2 .9 A7
St Pierre Dr BS30 .11 B6
St Pius X RC Prim Sch BS13 .2 A5
St Ronan's Ave BS6 .18 C1
St Rose's Specl Sch GL5 .99 B7
St Sampson's CE Jun Sch SN6 .143 E4
St Sampson's Inf Sch SN6 .143 E4
St Saviour's Rise BS36 .31 B6
St Saviours Ho BS4 .8 F2
St Stephen's Ave 3 BS1 .195 A2
St Stephen's CE Jun Sch BS15 .20 D2
St Stephen's Ct GL1 .118 D7
St Stephen's Manor GL51 .130 B7
St Stephen's Rd
Bristol BS16 .20 D2
Cheltenham GL51 .130 B7
St Stephen's St BS1 .195 A2
St Stephens Bsns Ctr BS30 .11 C5
St Stephens Cl
2 Bristol,Brentry BS10 .28 C2
Bristol,Upper Soundwell BS16 .20 E3
Cheltenham GL50 .130 B7
St Swithin's Rd GL10 .97 E4
St Swithins Rd GL15 .156 B1
St Swithuns Rd GL2 .118 A6
St Tecla Rd NP16 .60 E6
St Teresa's RC Prim Sch BS7 .28 E1
St Tewdric Rd NP16 .60 E7
St Tewdrics Pl NP16 .60 B4
St Thomas More RC Prim Sch GL51 .132 D2
St Thomas More RC Sch BS7 .19 A3
St Thomas Pl BS1 .195 B2
St Thomas St BS1 .195 B2
St Thomas St E BS1 .195 B2
St Ursula's High Sch BS9 18 A6
St Vincent Way GL3 .128 A8
St Vincent's Hill 1 BS6 .18 A2
St Vincent's Rd BS8 .194 A2
St Vincents Trad Est BS2 .9 D6
St Werburgh's Pk BS2 .19 A2
St Werburgh's Prim Sch BS2 .19 A2
St Werburgh's Rd BS2 .18 F2
St Whites Ct GL14 .191 C2
St Whites Prim Sch GL14 .191 C2
St Whites Rd GL14 .191 D3
St Whites Terr GL14 .191 C2
St Whytes Rd BS4 .2 D8
St Wulfstans Ave BS10 .18 A8
Salamanca Rd GL52 .134 B2
Salcombe Rd BS4 .9 A1
Salem Rd BS36 .30 F7
Salisbury Ave Bristol BS15 10 B8
Cheltenham GL51 .130 A5
Salisbury Dr BS16 .20 E6
Salisbury Gdns BS16 .20 E5
Salisbury Ho 1 GL1 .119 A8
Salisbury Pk BS16 .20 E6
Salisbury Rd
Bristol,Mangotsfield BS16 .20 E6
Bristol,Redland BS6 .18 D2
Bristol,St Anne's BS4 .9 D5
Gloucester GL1 .119 A8
Salisbury St
Bristol,Pile Marsh BS5 .9 E7
Bristol,Russell Town BS5 .9 B6
Salix Ct GL51 .130 A4
Sallis Cl GL20 .182 B5
Sallybarn Cl BS30 .10 E2
Sallys Way BS36 .30 F7
Sallysmead Cl BS13 .2 B4
Salmon Cl BS35 .38 A6
Salmon's Spring Ind Est GL6 .103 B1
Salmons Way BS16 .21 B8
Salmonsbury Cotts GL54 .169 A8
Salt Way
Coln St Aldwyns GL7 .152 D8
Compton Abdale GL54 .167 D3
Salter St GL13 .85 E3
Salter's La GL54 .174 C8
Salterley Grange GL53 .122 D7
Saltford CE Prim Sch BS31 .5 E2
Saltford Ct BS31 .5 E3
Salthouse Farm Pk BS35 38 A7
Salthrop Rd BS7 .18 E4
Saltmarsh Dr BS11 .27 A1
Saltwell Ave BS14 .3 C5
Salvia Cl GL3 .127 F6
Sambourne La BS20 .16 C4
Sambourne Rd SN16 .142 E1
Samian Way BS34 .29 E5
Sampson House Bsns Pk BS10 .27 D7
Sampsons Rd BS13 .2 D4
Sams La SN26 .144 E1
Samuel St 3 BS5 .9 C8
Samuel White Rd BS15 .10 C4
Samuel White's Inf Sch BS15 .10 C4
Samuel Wright Cl BS30 .11 D5
San Andreas BS34 .28 E6
San Remo GL1 .118 E6
Sanctuary Gdns BS9 .17 D3
Sand Hill BS4 .9 C4
Sandalwood Dr GL2 .118 B7
Sandbach Rd BS4 .9 D4
Sandbed Rd BS2 .19 A2
Sandburrows Rd BS13 .1 F6
Sandburrows Wlk BS13 .1 F6
Sandcroft BS14 .2 F6
Sandfield Cres GL2 .100 A7
Sandfield Rd GL3 .128 D5
Sandfield The GL20 .182 C5
Sandfields GL18 .179 B3
Sandford Leaze GL8 .148 B1
Sandford Mill Cl GL53 .130 F7
Sandford Mill Rd GL53 .130 F7
Sandford Park Pl GL52 .193 C2
Sandford Rd
Aylburton GL15 .147 D4
Bristol BS8 .194 A1
Cheltenham GL53 .193 C1
Sandford Sch GL53 .123 B7
Sandford St GL53 .193 C2
Sandford Terr GL15 .147 D4
Sandford Way GL4 .118 B1
Sandgate Rd BS4 .9 D3
Sandgrove GL6 .82 F8
Sandholme Cl BS16 .20 E8
Sandholme Rd BS4 .9 D4
Sandhurst BS37 .32 D8
Sandhurst Cl BS34 .40 B1
Sandhurst La
Down Hatherley GL2 .173 A2
Gloucester GL2 .126 E5
Sandhurst Rd Bristol BS4 .9 D4
Charlton Kings GL52 .131 B6
Gloucester GL1 .126 E4
Sandiway La HR9 .162 D3
Sandling Ave BS7 .19 A7
Sandown Cl BS16 .30 F1
Sandown Rd
Bishop's Cleeve GL52 .137 F4
Bristol,Filton BS34 .29 C3
Bristol,Kensington Park BS4 .9 D4
Sandpiper Cl 2 GL2 .117 D1
Sandpits La
Hawkesbury Upton GL9 .56 A2
Randwick GL6 .102 C1
Sherston SN16 .58 C1
Stroud GL6 .98 C8
Sandpool La GL7 .149 C2
Sandringham Ave
Bristol BS16 .20 E8
Gloucester GL4 .118 C1
Sandringham Ct GL53 .130 F7
Sandringham Pk BS16 .20 E8
Sandringham Rd
Bristol,Kensington Park BS4 .9 D4
Bristol,Longwell Green BS30 .10 F2
Bristol,Stoke Gifford BS34 .29 D4
Sands Cl WR12 .188 A1
Sands Croft Ave WR12 .188 B1
Sands Hill SN14 .23 E3
Sands La BS36 .41 F1
Sands The 11 WR12 .185 B8
Sandstar Cl GL2 .127 D5
Sandstone Rise BS36 .30 E4
Sandtumps GL15 .147 B4
Sandwich Rd BS4 .9 D4
Sandy Cl BS32 .29 E6
Sandy La Aust BS35 .49 A7
Aust BS35 .49 A8
Bristol BS5 .19 C3
Cheltenham GL53 .130 F4
Easton-in-G BS20 .16 A1
Hewelsfield GL15 .146 E5
Upper Rissington GL54 .169 D6
Sandy Lane Ct GL54 .169 D6
Sandy Lane Rd GL53 .130 F5
Sandy Lodge BS37 .32 E8
Sandy Park Rd BS4 .9 C3
Sandy Pluck La GL51 .121 B8
Sandycroft Rd GL3 .128 A7
Sandyleaze Bristol BS9 .17 E7
Gloucester GL2 .127 D3
Sandywell Pk GL54 .166 C7
Saniger La Berkeley GL13 .85 D6
Newton GL13 .85 C7
Sankey Gr 9 GL56 .187 A2
Sappercombe La GL53 .131 B5
Sapperton CE Prim Sch GL7 .149 B6
Sapperton Rd GL4 .118 F5
Sapphire Cl GL4 .118 C2
Sarah Siddons Wlk 1 GL50 .130 B6
Sarah St BS5 .9 B7
Sargent St BS3 .8 E4
Sargent's La HR9,GL18 .170 B4
Sarn Hill Grange GL20 .181 C5
Sarnedy Rd 3 GL16 .155 A5
Sarum Cl BS16 .21 C6
Sarum Cres BS10 .28 C1
Sassoon Ct BS30 .10 F5
Satchfield Cl BS10 .27 F2
Satchfield Cres BS10 .27 F2
Satellite Bsns Pk BS5 .9 D6
Sates Way BS9 .18 C6
Saturn Cl GL4 .119 F6
Saunders Cl
Huntley GL17 .165 A7
Lea HR9 .164 D8
Saunders Rd BS16 .20 E4
Saunton Wlk BS4 .2 E8
Savage Hill GL16 .154 E4
Savages Wood BS32 .29 E8
Savages Wood Rd BS32 .29 D8
Savernake Rd GL4 .119 A7
Saville Cl GL50 .133 E4
Saville Gate Cl BS9 .17 F4
Saville Mews BS6 .195 A4
Saville Pl BS8 .194 A2
Saville Rd BS9 .17 F3
Savoy Rd BS4 .9 D4
Savoy The BS11 .16 E6
Saw Mill La 5 BS35 .64 B1
Saw Mills End GL4 .127 D1
Sawpit La GL19 .173 C7
Sawpits La GL56 .177 D5
Sawpitts La HR9 .162 E4
Sawyers Cl SN16 .142 D1
Sawyers Hill SN16 .142 D1
Sawyers Rise
Ashleworth GL19 .172 D4
Minety SN16 .142 D1
Saxon Cl Cricklade SN6 .143 E4
Gloucester GL2 .127 C5
Sherston SN16 .58 C1
Saxon Pl NP16 .61 A7
Saxon Rd Bristol BS2 .19 A2
Cirencester GL7 .190 E5
Saxon Way Bristol BS32 .40 C1
Cheltenham GL52 .131 A8
Fairford GL7 .152 D4
Say Wlk BS30 .11 D7
Sayers Cres GL3 .120 E5
Saylittle Mews GL2 .127 E5
Sayth Ho GL7 .190 D5
SBI Ctr BS15 .10 B5
Scandrett Cl BS10 .27 E2
Scantleberry Cl BS16 .20 D8
Scar Hill GL6 .91 D4
Scarr Rd GL18 .171 A7
Scarr The GL18 .171 A7
Scholars Ct GL51 .133 B2
School Cl
Bristol,Eastville BS5 .19 D2
Bristol,Patchway BS34 .29 C8
Bristol,Whitchurch BS14 .2 F4
5 Coleford GL16 .155 B5
Dursley GL11 .87 E4
Hillesley GL12 .55 E8
School Cres Corse GL19 .172 B7
Joy's Green GL17 .163 D3
Lydney GL15 .92 B5
School Ct BS34 .30 A5
School Hill
Bourton-on-t-W GL54 .168 F7
Chepstow/Cas-Gwent NP16 .60 E8
Stratton GL7 .190 A8
Winstone GL7 .107 A8
School Hill Ind Est 13 NP16 .60 E8
School Ho GL50 .193 B4
School La
Ampney Crucis GL7 .151 C5
Badminton GL9 .46 E2
Berkeley GL13 .85 E3
3 Blockley GL56 .186 C5
Bretforton WR11 .188 A6
2 Bristol BS16 .19 E5
Castle Eaton SN6 .144 D6
Cirencester GL7 .190 D3
Edgeworth GL6 .106 D1
Hardwicke GL2 .109 E8
Longhope GL17 .164 F6
Meysey Hampton GL7 .152 A2
Narth The NP25 .154 B1
Overbury GL20 .182 F8
Ruardean GL17 .163 F4
Shipton GL54 .166 E5
Shurdington GL51 .129 E2
South Cerney GL7 .142 F8
Southam GL52 .134 C8
Whitminster GL2 .100 E5
School Mead GL51 .133 A2
School Mews GL4 .119 B4
School Rd Alderton GL20 183 E4
Apperley GL19 .173 C6
Bishop's Cleeve GL52 .138 A4
Bisley GL6 .105 A1
Bristol BS15 .10 C8
Bristol,Broom Hill BS4 .9 E3
Bristol,Cadbury Heath BS30 11 A4
Bristol,Oldland Common BS30 .11 C3
School Rd *continued*
Bristol,Totterdown BS4 .9 A3
Charlton Kings GL53 .131 B6
Dursley GL11 .80 C8
Frampton Cotterell BS36 .31 A8
Joy's Green GL17 .163 D3
Kemble GL7 .141 F8
Minchinhampton GL6 .148 A3
Ruardean GL17 .163 F4
Upper Lydbrook GL17 .163 D2
Whitecroft GL15 .155 F1
Wotton-u-E GL12 .68 B7
School Road Flats 3 GL53 .131 B6
School Row GL7 .149 E3
School Sq GL5 .98 F5
School St WR11 .188 C6
School Terr GL5 .98 D6
School Way BS35 .38 A6
School Wlk Bristol BS5 .19 D1
Yate BS37 .43 E2
Schooler's La GL56 .177 E6
Scop The BS32 .40 B5
Scotland La BS4,BS14 .4 A7
Scott Ave GL2 .118 C4
Scott Ct BS30 .10 F5
Scott Ho GL51 .132 E3
Scott Lawrence Cl BS16 .20 A7
Scott Way BS37 .32 F8
Scott Wlk BS30 .11 D7
Scowles Rd GL16 .154 F6
Scrubbett's La GL8 .69 F8
Sea Mills Inf Sch BS9 .17 C7
Sea Mills Jun Sch BS9 .17 B5
Sea Mills La BS9 .17 C5
Sea Mills Sta BS9 .17 B4
Seabright Cl GL51 .132 E5
Seabroke Rd GL1 .196 C4
Seabrook Rd GL3 .120 E5
Seacome Rd GL51 .132 D2
Seagry Cl BS10 .28 E1
Searle Court Ave BS4 .9 E4
Seaton Ct BS3 .8 D1
Seaton Rd BS5 .19 C1
Seawalls BS9 .17 D2
Seawalls Rd BS9 .17 D2
Sebert St GL1 .196 C4
Second Ave Bristol BS14 .3 B7
Dursley GL11 .80 C8
Second Chance Touring Pk SN6 .144 C7
Second Way BS11 .26 D1
Secret La GL1 .196 B4
Secunda Way (Hempsted By-Pass) GL2 .118 C7
Sedbury Bsns Pk NP16 .61 B8
Sedbury Chase NP16 .73 A1
Sedbury La NP16 .73 A1
Seddon Rd 4 BS2 .19 A2
Sedgefield Gdns BS16 .30 F1
Sedgewick Gdns GL51 .129 D6
Sedgewick Ho BS11 .16 E7
Sedgley Cl GL4 .118 C2
Sedgley Rd GL52 .137 F4
Sedum Ho 1 GL50 .133 B1
Sefton Park Jun & Inf Schs BS7 .18 F3
Sefton Park Rd BS7 .18 F3
Sefton Wlk GL51 .129 D6
Selborne Rd
Bishop's Cleeve GL52 .137 F4
Bristol BS7 .18 F5
Selbrooke Cres BS16 .20 C6
Selby Rd BS5 .19 F1
Selden Rd BS14 .3 E5
Selkirk Cl GL52 .133 F2
Selkirk Ct 3 GL52 .133 F2
Selkirk Gdns GL52 .133 F2
Selkirk Rd BS15 .20 C1
Selkirk St GL52 .133 F2
Sellars Rd GL2 .109 D7
Selley Wlk BS13 .2 A5
Selsey Rd GL5 .98 F2
Selsley Hill GL5 .98 E4
Selworthy Bristol BS15 .10 E7
Cheltenham GL51 .129 E5
Selworthy Cl BS31 .4 D5
Selworthy Rd BS4 .9 B2
Selwyn Cl GL10 .98 A5
Selwyn Rd GL4 .118 F5
Seneca Pl 1 BS5 .9 D7
Seneca St BS5 .9 D7
Seneca Way GL50 .133 B5
Septimus Bldgs BS14 .2 D5
Serlo Rd GL1 .196 B4
Serridge La BS36 .31 D4
Setts Row GL7 .149 E4
Sevelm 11 GL51 .129 E5
Seven Acres GL4 .119 D7
Seven Bridges Cotts SN6 .144 B3
Seven Stars Rd GL14 .191 C6
Seven Waters GL10 .97 D4
Sevenacres Rd GL6 .91 A4
Sevenfields SN6 .145 D4
Sevenleaze La Edge GL6 111 B2
Gloucester GL4,GL6 .111 D5
Seventh Ave
Bristol,Filton BS7 .29 B1
Bristol,Hengrove BS14 .3 A7
Gloucester GL4 .118 D2
Severn Ave NP16 .73 A1
Severn Beach Prim Sch BS35 .38 A6
Severn Beach Sta BS35 .38 A6
Severn Bridge Pk NP16 .61 B5
Severn Cl Charfield GL12 .67 A4
Maisemore GL2 .126 B7
Severn Cres NP16 .60 F7
Severn Dr Berkeley GL13 .85 E4
Tewkesbury GL20 .182 B5
Thornbury BS35 .64 B2
Severn Grange BS10 .27 D3
Severn Ho BS10 .27 D3
Severn La Berkeley GL13 .84 E1
Bevington GL13 .76 F8
Severn Lodge 3 GL4 .119 C4
Severn Oaks GL2 .109 F7
Severn Rd
Avonmouth BS11 .26 C4
Bristol BS11 .16 D6
Cheltenham GL52 .134 A3
Dursley GL11 .87 E4
Gloucester GL1 .196 A2
Hallen BS10 .27 A7
Lydney GL15 .92 B2
Newton GL13 .85 B8
Pill BS20 .16 C5
Severn Beach BS35 .37 F3
Stonehouse GL10 .97 E8
Severn St 8 GL14 .157 A6
Severn Terr 9 GL14 .157 A6
Severn Vale Sch GL2 .109 E8
Severn View Bristol BS10 .27 C1
Cinderford GL14 .191 E5
Severn View Par GL13 .85 C8
Severn View Rd
Thornbury BS35 .64 C2
Woolaston GL15 .147 B3
Yorkley GL15 .156 B2
Severn Way
Apperley GL19 .173 C7
Bristol BS34 .39 F1
Keynsham BS31 .5 A5
Severnbank Ave GL15 .92 C3
Severnbanks Prim Sch GL15 .92 C3
Severnleigh Gdns BS9 .17 F3
Severnleigh Ho BS9 .17 F3
Severnside Trad Est
Avonmouth BS11 .26 C5
Gloucester GL2 .126 C1
Severnvale Dr GL2 .117 E2
Severnwood Gdns BS35 .38 A5
Sevier St BS2 .18 F2
Seymour Ave BS7 .18 E4
Seymour Cl 5 GL16 .155 A7
Seymour Gate 5 GL55 .189 A2
Seymour Pl
Tewkesbury GL20 .192 C3
10 Winchcombe GL54 .174 A7
Seymour Rd
Bristol,Ashley Down BS7 .18 E4
Bristol,Kingswood BS15 .20 C1
Bristol,Staple Hill BS16 .20 E4
Bristol,Upper Easton BS5 .19 A1
Gloucester GL1 .118 D7
Seyton Wlk BS34 .29 E5
Sezincote Cl GL6 .148 B6
Sezincote House & Gdns* GL56 .186 D2
Shackel Hendy Mews BS16 .21 B5
Shackleton Ave BS37 .32 F8
Shackleton Cl GL3 .128 C5
Shadwell GL11 .81 A8
Shadwell Rd BS7 .18 D3
Shaft Rd BS35 .38 A8
Shaftesbury Ave BS6 .18 E1
Shaftesbury Hall 4 GL50 .193 B4
Shaftesbury Ind Est GL51 .133 B6
Shaftesbury Pl 10 GL51 .132 D2
Shaftesbury Terr 8 BS5 .9 D7
Shakespeare Ave
Bristol BS7 .19 A8
Gloucester GL2 .118 C4
Shakespeare Cotts GL51 .129 B7
Shakespeare Ct GL20 .192 C4
Shakespeare Rd
Cheltenham GL51 .132 E1
Dursley GL11 .80 C7
Shaldon Rd BS7 .19 A4
Shalford Cl GL7 .190 B3
Shallowbrooks La SN14 .47 F8
Shallows The BS31 .5 F3
Shambles Mus The* GL18 .171 A4
Shambles The 12 GL5 .99 C7
Shamrock Cl GL3 .127 F6
Shamrock Rd BS5 .19 D3
Shanklin Dr BS34 .29 B3
Shannon Ct BS35 .51 D8
Shannon Pl GL20 .182 B5
Shannon Way GL20 .182 B4
Shapcott Cl BS4 .9 B1
Shaplands BS9 .17 F4
Shard The GL6 .102 F3
Sharland Cl BS9 .17 E3
Sharland Gr BS13 .2 C4
Sharman Pitch HR9 .163 C7
Sharpness Prim Sch GL13 .85 D8
Sharps Way NP16 .60 F5
Shaw Cl Bristol BS16 .21 B3
3 Bristol,Upper Easton BS5 .9 B8
Shaw Gdns BS14 .3 A8
Shaw Green La GL52 .134 C5
Shaymoor La BS35 .39 A4
Shear Ho 7 WR12 .185 C8
Shearmore Cl BS7 .19 A7

Shearwater Ct BS16 .....19 F6
Shearwater Gr GL3 .....127 E6
Sheene Ct 17 BS3 .....8 C3
Sheene La BS3 .....8 C3
Sheene Way BS3 .....8 C3
Sheenhill Rd WR11 .....188 B8
Sheens Mdw GL14 .....156 F7
Sheep St Cirencester GL7 190 C4
Highworth SN6 .....145 D3
Stow-on-t-W GL54 .....176 F4
Sheepfair La SN14 .....14 F8
Sheeps Croft BS13 .....2 A5
Sheepscombe Cl GL51 ..129 E8
Sheepscombe Prim Sch
GL6 .....112 E1
Sheepwash The BS35 .....63 D5
Sheepwood Cl BS10 .....28 A2
Sheepwood Rd BS10 .....28 A2
Sheevaun Cl GL2 .....127 D5
Sheiling Sch BS35 .....64 B2
Shelburne Rd GL51 .....129 F8
Sheldare Barton BS5 .....10 B7
Sheldon Ave WR12 .....188 B1
Sheldons Ct GL52 .....193 C4
Sheldrake Dr BS16 .....19 E6
Shelduck Rd GL2 .....117 D1
Shellard Rd BS34 .....29 A2
Shellards La BS35 .....51 E2
Shellards Rd BS30 .....10 F3
Shelley Ave
Cheltenham GL51 .....132 E1
Gloucester GL2 .....118 C4
Shelley Cl BS5 .....9 F8
Shelley Ho BS34 .....40 A1
Shelley Rd
Cheltenham GL51 .....132 E1
Dursley GL11 .....80 C7
Shelley Way BS7 .....19 A8
Shellmor Ave BS34 .....40 B1
Shellmor Cl BS32 .....40 D1
Shephard Mead GL20 .....192 B3
Shepherd Rd GL2 .....118 B3
Shepherd's Cl GL55 .....188 F1
Shepherd's Leaze GL12 ..68 C6
Shepherdine Cl GL15 .....92 C3
Shepherds Cl Bristol BS16 20 E5
Cheltenham GL51 .....132 D4
8 Ledbury HR8 .....178 E7
Stroud GL5 .....99 D8
Shepherds Croft GL5 .....99 D8
Shepherds Mead 3
GL8 .....140 C5
Shepherds Row 4 GL54 176 F4
Shepherds Way
Cirencester GL7 .....190 C6
Innsworth GL3 .....127 F7
Northleach GL54 .....167 F1
19 Stow-on-t-W GL54 .....176 F4
Shepherds Well GL5 .....99 D1
Shepherds Wlk GL12 .....68 C6
Sheppard Rd BS16 .....20 C6
Sheppard Way
Minchinhampton GL6 .....91 F7
Newent GL18 .....171 A4
Shepperdine Rd BS35 .....75 D2
Sheppey Cnr WR12 .....184 F5
Shepton Wlk BS3 .....8 C2
Sherborne CE Prim Sch
GL54 .....169 A1
Sherborne Cl GL10 .....97 F8
Sherborne Ho
Gloucester GL1 .....196 C3
1 Stonehouse GL10 .....97 F8
Sherborne La GL54 .....169 C3
Sherborne Park Nature
Trail★ GL54 .....168 E1
Sherborne Pl GL52 .....193 C3
Sherborne St
Bourton-on-t-W GL54 .....168 F7
Cheltenham GL52 .....193 C4
Gloucester GL1 .....196 C4
Lechlade on T GL7 .....153 E2
Sherborne Stables GL54 168 F1
Sherborne Terr 4 GL54 .168 F7
Sherbourne Ave BS32 .....29 E7
Sherbourne Cl BS15 .....20 F2
Sherbourne St BS5 .....9 E7
Sherbourne's Brake
BS32 .....29 E6
Shergar Cl GL4 .....119 D4
Sheridan Rd BS7 .....19 A8
Sheridan Way BS30 .....11 A2
Sherrin Way BS13 .....1 E3
Sherrings The BS34 .....29 B8
Sherry The GL54 .....175 B7
Sherston Cl BS16 .....20 B5
Sherston Rd Bristol BS7 ..18 E8
Luckington SN14 .....47 F5
Sherwell Rd BS4 .....9 E3
Sherwood Cl BS31 .....4 E5
Sherwood Gn GL2 .....126 F6
Sherwood Rd Bristol BS15 20 B1
Keynsham BS31 .....4 E5
Tetbury GL8 .....140 B4
Shetland Rd BS10 .....28 D1
Shield Ret Ctr BS34 .....29 A3
Shield Road Prim Sch
BS7 .....29 A1
Shields Ave BS7 .....29 A1
Shiels Dr BS32 .....29 D7
Shilton Cl BS15 .....10 F7
Shimsey Cl 2 BS16 .....20 C6
Ship La BS1 .....195 B1
Shipham Cl BS14 .....3 B5
Shipley Mow BS16 .....21 B6
Shipley Rd BS9 .....18 A8
Shipman Ct BS16 .....20 E4
Shipton's Grave La GL6 .91 C1
Shipway Ct GL52 .....137 F4
Shire Gdns BS11 .....16 D8
Shire Hill SN14 .....25 A7
Shire Way BS37 .....32 D6
Shirehampton Prim Sch
BS11 .....16 D6
Shirehampton Rd BS9 .....17 C6
Shirehampton Sta BS11 .16 D5
Shirreff Ct 14 BS6 .....18 B1
Shooters End GL5 .....99 C8
Shop La Badminton GL9 ..46 E2
Bretforton WR11 .....188 A7
Shophouse Rd GL15,
GL16 .....155 A2
Shorland Ho BS8 .....18 A1
Short Hedges Cl 16
GL54 .....168 A1
Short La BS41 .....7 A2
Short St Bristol BS2 .....9 A5
Cheltenham GL53 .....130 C6
Short Way BS35 .....51 B7
Shorthill Rd BS37 .....32 C4
Shortlands Rd BS11 .....27 A1
Shortwood Hill BS16 .....21 E4
Shortwood Rd Bristol BS13 2 E3
Nailsworth GL6 .....91 A3
Pucklechurch BS16 .....22 A4
Shortwood View BS15 .....10 F8
Shortwood Wlk BS13 .....2 E3
Shotts La GL18 .....170 C3
Showering Cl BS14 .....3 D5
Showering Rd BS14 .....3 D5
Shrivenham Rd SN6 .....145 D2
Shrubberies Sch The
GL10 .....97 E8
Shrubbery Cotts 4 BS6 .18 B2
Shrubbery Ct 6 BS16 .....20 D5
Shrubbery Rd BS16 .....20 D5
Shrublands GL53 .....130 F5
Shubbery The GL7 .....153 E2
Shurdington CE Prim Sch
GL51 .....129 D1
Shurdington Rd
Cheltenham GL50,GL51,
GL53 .....130 B5
Little Shurdington GL3,
GL51 .....121 B7
Shurdington GL51 .....129 E2
Shute St GL10 .....98 A3
Shutehay Dr GL11 .....87 F5
Shuter Rd BS13 .....1 E5
Shuthonger Manor
GL20 .....181 E6
Shutter La GL52 .....137 F8
Sibland BS35 .....51 D8
Sibland Cl 3 BS35 .....51 D8
Sibland Rd BS35 .....51 D8
Sibland Way BS35 .....51 D8
Sibree Cl GL6 .....148 B6
Sidcot BS4 .....10 A2
Siddington CE Prim Sch
GL7 .....190 D1
Siddington Hall GL7 .....150 E2
Sideland Cl BS14 .....3 E6
Sidelands Rd BS16 .....20 C6
Sidings The Bristol BS34 ..29 C2
Charfield GL12 .....67 B5
Sidmouth Ct BS3 .....8 D1
Sidmouth Gdns BS3 .....8 D2
Sidmouth Rd BS3 .....8 E2
Sidney St
Cheltenham GL52 .....193 C3
Gloucester GL1 .....127 A1
Signal Rd BS16 .....20 F4
Silbury Rd BS3 .....7 E2
Silbury Rise BS31 .....5 A2
Silcock Cl GL3 .....127 F7
Silcox Rd BS13 .....2 C4
Silk Mill Ct 31 GL54 .....174 A7
Silk Mill La GL54 .....174 A7
Silklands Gr BS9 .....17 C6
Silley's Cl NP16 .....72 F2
Silver Birch Cl
Bristol BS34 .....29 D7
Quedgeley GL2 .....117 E1
Silver Cl Gloucester GL4 .118 C3
Minety SN16 .....142 D1
Silver St Arlingham GL2 ..157 C6
Bristol BS1 .....195 A3
Cirencester GL7 .....190 C5
Coaley GL11 .....89 A7
Dursley GL11 .....88 B1
Littledean GL14 .....156 E8
Minety SN16 .....142 D1
Mitcheldean GL17 .....164 D5
South Cerney GL7 .....142 F8
15 Tetbury GL8 .....140 C4
7 Thornbury BS35 .....64 B1
Silverdale Par GL3 .....119 F8
Silverhill Brake BS35 .....50 E1
Silverhill Rd BS10 .....27 E4
Silverhill Sch BS36 .....30 E7
Silverthorne Cl GL53 .....130 B5
Silverthorne La BS2 .....9 A6
Silverthorne Wharf BS2 ..9 B6
Silverton Ct BS4 .....8 F1
Silvertree Gdns GL5 .....99 E3
Silverwood Way GL51 .....129 E5
Simmonds Ct GL6 .....148 A3
Simmonds Rd GL3 .....119 F6
Simmonds View BS34 .....29 F5
Simmons Bldgs BS16 .....30 C3
Simon Rd GL2 .....127 C5
Simplex Ind Est The
BS30 .....11 D4
Sims La GL2 .....117 F4
Sinclair Ho
Bristol,Clifton Wood BS8 ..194 A2
Bristol,Filton BS34 .....29 A2
Sinclair Rd GL51 .....129 D1
Sinderberry Dr GL20 .....182 C5
Sinope St GL1 .....196 C2
Sion Hill BS8 .....7 F7
Sion La BS8 .....7 F7
Sion Pl BS8 .....7 F7
Sion Rd 11 BS3 .....8 C3
Sir Bernard Lovell Sch
BS30 .....11 C4
Sir Bernard Lovell Sch
(annexe) BS30 .....11 D5
Sir Bevil Grenville's Mon★
BA1 .....13 A1
Sir John's La Bristol BS7 .19 B5
Bristol,Eastville BS5 .....19 B4
Sir Thomas Rich's Sch
GL2 .....127 D3
Sir Walter Montague
Almshouses NP16 .....72 E1
Sir William Romney's Sch
GL8 .....140 C5
Siskin Rd GL54 .....169 D7
Sissinghurst Gr GL51 .....130 A5
Sisson End GL2 .....127 D2
Sisson Rd GL2 .....127 C2
Siston Cl BS15 .....21 A2
Siston Comm Bristol BS15 21 A2
Bristol BS30 .....21 B1
Siston Ctr The BS15 .....21 A2
Siston Hill BS30 .....21 B1
Siston Hill Rdbt BS15 .....21 B2
Siston La BS30 .....21 F2
Siston Pk BS15 .....21 A2
Sivell Cl GL2 .....127 A6
Six Acres GL4 .....119 F3
Sixth Ave Bristol,Filton BS7 29 B1
Bristol,Hengrove BS14 .....3 A7
Skillicorne Mews GL50 .....130 B8
Skinner St GL1 .....196 B4
Skinner's Cl SN6 .....145 A4
Skippon Ct BS15 .....10 E5
Skye Cl SN6 .....145 C4
Skylark Way GL4 .....119 B6
Slad La GL5,GL6 .....99 F8
Slad Mill GL5 .....99 D8
Slad Rd GL5 .....99 D8
Slad The Longhope GL17 .165 B5
Popes Hill GL14 .....156 E8
Thornbury BS35 .....51 F6
Slade Brook GL5 .....99 E8
Slade Rd Woolaston GL15 147 A3
Yorkley GL15 .....156 B2
Slade The GL11 .....80 B8
Slaney St GL1 .....118 F7
Sleep La BS14 .....3 D3
Slimbridge Cl BS37 .....32 F7
Slimbridge La GL13 .....94 D2
Slimbridge Prim Sch
GL2 .....95 E2
Slimbridge Rd GL4 .....118 D3
Sloan St BS5 .....9 D8
Slough La SN14 .....13 F5
Slymbridge Ave BS10 .....28 A3
Small La BS16 .....19 E5
Small St Bristol BS1 .....195 A3
Bristol,St Philip's Marsh BS2 .9 A5
Smallbrook Rd WR12 .....188 A1
Smarts Gn BS37 .....33 C8
Smeaton Rd BS1 .....7 F5
Smith Barry Cir GL54 .....169 E6
Smith Barry Cres GL54 .169 D6
Smith Barry Rd GL54 .....169 D6
Smith's Field GL7 .....190 A3
Smith's La GL20 .....192 C4
Smithcourt Dr BS34 .....29 D6
Smithmead BS13 .....2 B5
Smiths Ct Bristol BS34 .....29 A8
7 Tewkesbury GL20 .....192 C4
Smiths Hill GL16 .....155 C3
Smithville Cl GL15 .....146 F7
Smithville Pl GL15 .....146 F7
Smithwood Gr GL53 .....131 A4
Smithy Cl GL16 .....163 A2
Smithy La GL54 .....184 A1
Smithy The
Blakeney GL15 .....156 E2
Cirencester GL7 .....190 E3
Smithyman Ct 1 GL14 .....157 A6
Smoke La BS11 .....26 D6
Smooth Stones NP16 .....60 A7
Smyth Ho BS8 .....7 E6
Smyth Rd BS3 .....8 A3
Smyth Terr 3 BS3 .....8 C4
Smythe Croft BS14 .....3 A3
Smythe Mdw GL6 .....148 B5
Smythe Rd GL51 .....133 B6
Smyths Cl BS11 .....26 B1
Snake Dr GL7 .....152 D7
Snead Pk GL4 .....119 F5
Sneedhams Rd GL4 .....119 B2
Sneyd Park Ho BS9 .....17 D3
Snipe Rd GL54 .....169 D6
Snowberry Cl BS32 .....29 E8
Snowberry Wlk BS5 .....19 E1
Snowden Ho BS16 .....19 F5
Snowdon Cl BS16 .....19 F4
Snowdon Gdns GL3 .....128 A7
Snowdon Rd BS16 .....19 F4
Snowdonia Rd GL20 .....192 E2
Snowdrop Cl 1 GL4 .....119 E5
Snowshill Cl GL4 .....119 D7
Snowshill Dr GL52 .....137 F3
Snowshill Manor★
WR12 .....185 B4
Snowshill Rd
Broadway WR12 .....185 B7
Gloucester GL4 .....119 E7
Snowswick La SN7 .....145 F8
Soapers La BS35 .....51 B8
Soaphouse Ind Est BS5 ...9 E8
Sochi Mews 17 GL51 .....132 E2
Sodbury Rd
Acton Turville GL9 .....35 F7
Wickwar GL12 .....54 A4
Soldiers of Gloucester Mus★
GL1 .....196 A2
Solent Way BS35 .....51 D7
Solon Ct BS13 .....1 F5
Solway Rd GL51 .....132 D4
Somerby Cl BS32 .....29 D7
Somerdale Ave BS4 .....9 A1
Somerdale Rd BS31 .....4 F7
Somerdale Rd N BS30,BS31 4 F8
Somerford Ct BS10 .....27 F1
Somerford Rd GL7 .....190 C2
Somergate Rd GL51 .....132 D4
Somermead BS3 .....8 C1
Somerset Ave
Cheltenham GL51 .....133 A2
Dursley GL11 .....80 C7
Yate BS37 .....43 F3
Somerset Cl GL12 .....67 F4
Somerset Cres BS34 .....29 F5
Somerset Ho
18 Bristol BS2 .....195 C3
3 Cheltenham GL50 .....193 B4
Somerset Pl
Gloucester GL1,GL2 .....196 A1
Tewkesbury GL20 .....192 D1
Somerset Rd Bristol BS4 ...9 B3
Cinderford GL14 .....191 C4
Somerset Sq BS1 .....195 B1
Somerset St Bristol BS1 .195 B1
Bristol,Kingsdown BS2 .....195 A4
Somerset Terr BS3 .....8 D3
Somerset Way NP16 .....60 F4
Somerton Cl BS15 .....10 E7
Somerton Rd BS7 .....18 E6
Somerville Cl BS31 .....5 E2
Somerville Ct GL7 .....190 B2
Somerville Ho BS10 .....18 A8
Somme Rd GL52 .....134 B2
Sommerville Rd BS7 .....18 E3
Sommerville Rd S 1 BS6 18 F2
Soper Gdns BS4 .....2 D7
Sopwith Rd GL54 .....169 D7
Sopworth Rd SN14 .....47 E5
Soren Larsen Way GL2 .118 C6
Sorrel Cl Gloucester GL4 .119 A4
Thornbury BS35 .....64 D2
Soudley Sch GL14 .....156 D5
Soundwell Rd BS15,BS16 .20 D2
South Africa Ho 2
GL51 .....132 F4
South Ave
Ashchurch GL20 .....182 D4
Yate BS37 .....43 B1
South Bank GL51 .....132 F3
South Bristol Ret Pk BS3 .8 A3
South Bristol Trad Pk BS3 .7 F3
South Cerney GL7 .....151 A2
South Cerney Rd GL7 .....150 E2
South Cl GL2 .....127 B4
South Croft BS9 .....18 C7
South Ct BS32 .....40 D3
South Dene BS9 .....17 E6
South Farm Cotts GL7 .....153 B5
South Gate Ct GL54 .....169 D6
South Gloucestershire
Central Teaching Unit
BS16 .....21 A5
South Gr Bristol BS6 .....18 C5
Pill BS20 .....16 C4
South Green St 9 BS8 .....7 F6
South Hayes BS5 .....19 B4
South Liberty La
2 Bristol BS13 .....8 B2
Bristol BS3 .....8 A1
South Mdw La SN5 .....143 F2
South Meadow La SN5 .144 A2
South Par
11 Ledbury HR8 .....178 F8
Yate BS37 .....43 E1
South Rd
12 Bristol,Bedminster BS3 ..8 C3
Bristol,Kingswood BS15 ...10 D8
Bristol,Redland BS6 .....18 C2
3 Coleford GL16 .....155 A6
Coleford,Broadwell GL16 .155 B5
Lydney GL15 .....92 A4
Woodhouse Down BS32 ...40 E6
South St Bristol BS3 .....8 B3
Uley GL11 .....89 C1
South Street Prim Sch
BS3 .....8 B3
South Terr 6 BS6 .....18 B2
South View
Blockley GL56 .....186 C6
Bristol BS16 .....20 E5
Frampton Cotterell BS36 ...31 B7
Ripple GL20 .....181 D8
Stroud GL5 .....98 C7
South View Bsns Pk
BS16 .....20 F5
South View Cotts GL5 .....98 E8
South View Cres BS36 ...31 D6
South View Rise BS36 ...31 D6
South View Way GL52 .....134 C4
South Way GL7 .....190 C4
South Wlk
Mitcheldean GL17 .....164 D5
Yate BS37 .....43 E1
Southall Terr GL18 .....170 E2
Southam La GL52 .....134 B8
Southampton Gdns BS7 .18 F5
Southampton Mews BS7 .18 F5
Southbank GL5 .....99 A2
Southbow Ho 2 BS3 .....8 A3
Southbrook Rd GL4 .....127 C1
Southcourt Cl GL53 .....130 D5
Southcourt Dr GL53 .....130 D5
Southdown Rd BS9 .....17 F8
Southend Ho GL12 .....54 A5
Southend La GL18 .....171 A4
Southend The HR8 .....178 F8
Southern Ave GL4 .....118 E4
Southern Rd GL53 .....130 E4
Southernhay
Bristol,Clifton Wood BS8 ..194 B2
Bristol,Staple Hill BS16 ....20 D4
Southernhay Ave BS8 .194 B2
Southernhay Cres BS8 .194 B2
Southey Ave BS15 .....20 E1
Southey Ct BS15 .....20 D1
Southey St BS2 .....18 F2
Southfield
Minchinhampton GL6 .....91 F6
Tetbury GL8 .....140 B3
Southfield App GL53 .....130 E4
Southfield Ave BS15 .....20 E1
Southfield Cl GL53 .....130 E4
Southfield Ct BS9 .....18 A7
Southfield Jun Sch SN6 145 D3
Southfield Manor Pk
GL53 .....130 F3
Southfield Rd
Bristol,Cotham BS6 .....18 D1
Bristol,Westbury on Trym
BS9 .....18 A7
5 Coleford GL16 .....155 A6
Gloucester GL4 .....118 F5
Woodchester GL5 .....99 A2
Southfield Rise GL53 .....130 E4
Southfield Way BS37 .....44 A4
Southgate Cres GL5 .....99 A5
Southgate Dr GL53 .....130 F7
Southgate Gdns GL5 .....99 A5
Southgate Mews GL7 .....190 D3
Southgate St GL1 .....196 A2
Southlands
Bristol,Clifton BS8 .....18 A1
Bristol,Knowle Park BS4 ....9 B1
Tytherington GL12 .....52 B4
Southleigh Mews BS8 .194 B4
Southleigh Rd BS8 .....194 B4
Southmead GL7 .....190 E2
Southmead Hospl BS10 ..18 E8
Southmead La GL6 .....105 B5
Southmead Rd BS10,BS34 28 E1
Southmead Way BS10 .....18 D8
Southover Cl BS9 .....18 A8
Southrop CE Prim Sch
GL7 .....153 D6
Southsea Rd BS34 .....29 A8
Southside GL8 .....59 E7
Southside Cl BS9 .....17 B8
Southville Pl BS3 .....8 D4
Southville Prim Sch BS3 ..8 C4
Southville Rd BS3 .....8 C4
Southway Dr BS15 .....11 D5
Southwell St BS2 .....194 C4
Southwood Ave BS9 .....17 C8
Southwood Cl GL14 .....191 D5
Southwood Dr BS9 .....17 B8
Southwood Dr E BS9 .....17 C8
Southwood La GL50 .....193 A2
Sovereign Chase GL19 .172 B8
Sovereign Ct GL1 .....196 C3
Spa Cl SN6 .....145 D4
Spa Ct GL50 .....193 A3
Spa Gdns GL20 .....192 F4
Spa Mews GL1 .....196 A2
Spa Rd GL1 .....196 B1
Spa Villas GL1 .....196 B1
Spalding Cl BS7 .....19 A3
Spaniorum View BS35 .....38 F2
Spar Rd Avonmouth BS11 ..26 D4
Yate BS37 .....43 D2
Spark Hill GL11 .....87 F6
Sparrow Cl 1 GL6 .....148 C6
Sparrow Hill GL16 .....155 A5
Sparrows La HR9,GL18 .170 B4
Spartan Cl 2 GL4 .....119 E6
Spartley Dr BS13 .....1 F6
Spartley Wlk BS13 .....1 F6
Speculation Rd GL14 .....191 B7
Speech House Rd
Cinderford GL14,GL16 ...156 A7
Coleford GL16 .....155 D6
Speedwell 3 GL16 .....155 B6
Speedwell Ave 5 BS5 ....9 D7
Speedwell Cl
Gloucester GL4 .....119 E5
Thornbury BS35 .....64 D2
Speedwell Rd BS5,BS15 ..20 A1
Speedwell Tech Coll
BS15 .....20 A1
Spencer Cl GL3 .....119 F7
Spencer Ct GL50 .....193 A4
Spencer Ho 6 BS1 .....195 B1
Spencer's Ct BS35 .....51 B5
Spenser Ave GL51 .....132 E1
Spenser Rd GL51 .....132 E1
Sperringate GL7 .....190 D3
Spey Cl Quedgeley GL2 ...117 F2
Thornbury BS35 .....51 C8
Spider La GL5 .....99 E6
Spillman's Pitch GL5 .....99 A6
Spillman's Rd GL5 .....99 A6
Spindles The GL53 .....130 A4

Spine Rd W GL7 142 D5
Spine Road E GL7 143 B7
Spinnaker Ho GL2 118 C8
Spinnaker Rd GL2 118 C8
Spinners Cotts GL6 91 F3
Spinners Ho 15 GL5 99 C7
Spinney Croft BS13 1 F5
Spinney Ct GL5 99 F1
Spinney Rd GL4 119 E7
Spinney The Bristol BS32 29 E7
Cheltenham GL52 133 E4
Frampton Cotterell BS36 31 B7
Lechlade on T GL7 153 E2
Stroud GL6 105 C7
Spinning Wheel Ct GL5 98 E7
Spire Way GL4 119 D8
Spires View 4 BS16 19 E5
Spital La SN6 143 F4
Spitalgate La GL7 190 C5
Spittle Leys 5 GL54 174 A7
Spoonbill Cl GL2 117 D1
Spout Hill GL15 147 C3
Spout La GL17 164 A4
Spouthouse La GL11 88 A5
Spratsgate La GL7 142 D6
Spread Eagle Rd GL1 196 B3
Spring Cotts
Stonehouse GL10 98 A6
Stroud GL6 104 A2
Spring Dale GL2 165 F5
Spring Field Terr GL5 99 A6
Spring Gdns Bristol BS4 9 A1
Lechlade on T GL7 153 E2
Quenington GL7 152 D7
Stow-on-t-W GL54 176 F4
Tewkesbury GL20 192 D4
Spring Gr 6 HR8 178 F7
Spring Hill
Bristol,Kingsdown BS2 195 A4
Bristol,Upper Soundwell
BS15 20 E2
Eastington GL10 97 A8
Nailsworth GL6 91 B4
Spring Ho 2 BS35 51 C8
Spring La
Cheltenham GL52 134 B6
Cleeve Hill GL52 138 E2
Dundry BS41 2 A1
Stroud GL5 99 D6
Thrupp GL5 99 E3
Spring Meadow Rd GL15 92 A4
Spring Mill Ind Est GL6 91 D3
Spring Pl GL17 163 E4
Spring St BS3 8 E4
Spring Street Pl BS3 8 E4
Springbank Cl GL51 132 D4
Springbank Dr GL51 132 C3
Springbank Gr GL51 132 C3
Springbank Rd GL51 132 C3
Springbank Way GL51 132 D4
Springdale HR9 170 B4
Springdale Cl GL2 109 D8
Springfield
Blockley GL56 186 C6
Bourton-on-t-W GL54 168 F7
Dursley GL11 87 E4
Hardwicke GL2 109 E7
Tewkesbury GL20 192 F5
1 Thornbury BS35 51 D8
Springfield Ave
Bristol,Horfield BS7 18 F5
Bristol,Mangotsfield BS16 21 A7
Bristol,Shirehampton BS11 16 D6
Springfield Bsns Ctr
GL10 97 C8
Springfield Cl
Bristol BS16 21 A7
Cheltenham GL51 129 C7
2 Coleford GL16 155 A5
Springfield Cotts BS30 6 A8
Springfield Dr GL14 191 C6
Springfield Gr BS6 18 C5
Springfield Ho
Bristol BS6 194 C4
Cheltenham GL51 132 E4
Springfield La WR12 185 B8
Springfield Lawns BS11 16 D6
Springfield Pl GL4 121 F1
Springfield Rd
Bristol,Cotham BS6 18 D1
Bristol,Mangotsfield BS16 21 A7
Cirencester GL7 190 B2
Lydney GL15 92 A4
Pill BS20 16 C4
Quenington GL7 152 D7
Stroud GL5 99 C8
Stroud,Westrip GL5 98 D8
Springfield Terr GL5 98 D6
Springfields Bristol BS34 29 A2
Tetbury GL8 140 C4
Springfields Ct GL11 87 E4
Springfort BS9 17 F3
Springhill Dursley GL11 88 C3
Sandhurst GL2 172 F2
Stroud GL5 99 C8
Springhill (Old Court)
GL11 88 B3
Springhill Cl GL6 91 B4
Springhill Cotts WR12 185 B4
Springhill Cres GL6 91 B4
Springhill Ct GL2 172 F1
Springleaze
Bristol,Knowle Park BS4 9 A1
Bristol,Mangotsfield BS16 21 A7
Springly Ct BS15 11 A8
Springs The GL15 92 A4
Springvale GL54 168 F8
Springville Cl BS30 11 A3
Springwater Cl GL20 182 C5
Springwater Pk Trad Est
BS5 9 E7
Springwell Gdns GL3 128 B6
Springwood Dr BS10 27 D3
Spruce Rd GL16 155 C6
Spruce Ride
Cinderford GL14,GL16 156 A5
Coleford GL16 155 F6
Spruce Way BS34 28 F7
Square The Alveston BS35 51 A4
Bibury GL7 160 A1
Bristol BS1 195 C2
Bristol,Knowle Park BS4 9 A2
Bristol,Staple Hill BS16 20 E4
6 Chipping Campden
GL55 189 A2
Goodrich HR9 163 A6
Guiting Power GL54 175 B3
Ruardean GL17 163 E4
St Briavels GL15 146 E7
3 Stonehouse GL10 97 F8
Stroud GL5 99 C8
Toddington GL54 184 B3
Wotton-u-E GL12 68 C6
Squires Cl GL6 148 B6
Squires Ct
Bretforton WR11 188 A6
Bristol BS30 10 F4
Squires Leaze BS35 64 D2
Squirrel Cl GL2 109 E7
Stable Cotts
Adlestrop GL56 177 E5
Bromesberrow Heath HR8 179 C5
Stable Yd GL5 99 C8
Stable Yd The GL9 46 B7
Stables The
Cheltenham GL52 134 C4
Lechlade on T GL7 153 E3
Stow-on-t-W GL54 176 F5
Stackpool Rd BS3 8 C4
Stadium Rd BS6 18 C5
Stafford Cl 8 GL16 155 B6
Stafford Cres BS35 64 B1
Stafford Rd BS2 19 A2
Stafford St BS3 8 D4
Staffords Ct BS30 11 A6
Stag Hill GL15 156 A2
Stainer Cl BS4 2 D7
Staites Orch GL4 119 E3
Stamage's La GL6 103 F7
Stambourne La GL13 85 E8
Stambourne Villas GL13 85 E8
Stamp's Mdw GL2 126 F5
Stanborough La GL54 167 F8
Stanbridge Cl BS16 20 F6
Stanbridge Prim Sch
BS16 20 F6
Stanbridge Rd BS16 20 F6
Stanbury Ave BS16 20 C5
Stanbury Mews GL3 120 B6
Stanbury Rd BS3 8 E3
Stancombe La
Bisley GL6 104 F2
Winchcombe GL54 174 B7
Stancombe View
North Nibley GL11 79 D5
25 Winchcombe GL54 174 A7
Standfast Rd BS10 27 F3
Standish Ave BS34 40 C1
Standish Cl BS10 27 F1
Standish Ct GL10 101 E5
Standish Hospl GL10 102 B2
Standish La GL2,GL10 101 C6
Standish Park Cotts
GL10 102 C4
Standle La GL11 87 A2
Standon Way BS10 28 C2
Stane Way BS11 16 C7
Stanfield Cl BS7 19 C6
Stanford Cl BS36 30 F8
Stanford Pl BS4 2 D7
Stanford Rd Lydney GL15 92 A3
Northway GL20 182 C4
Stanhope Rd BS30 10 F2
Stanhope St BS2 9 A5
Stank La GL2 109 C6
Stanleigh Terr GL2 126 A7
Stanley Ave
Bristol,Bishopston BS7 18 E3
Bristol,Filton BS34 29 B2
Stanley Chase BS5 19 E2
Stanley Cotts
Gloucester GL1 196 C1
Gretton GL54 183 E1
Stanley Cres BS34 29 B2
Stanley Gdns BS30 11 B4
Stanley Hill BS4 9 A4
Stanley Mead BS32 40 E2
Stanley Mills Cotts GL10 98 A5
Stanley Park Rd BS16 20 E3
Stanley Pk Bristol BS5 19 C1
Stroud GL5 98 E4
Stanley Pl GL51 132 D3
Stanley Rd
Bristol,Cotham BS6 18 C1
Bristol,Warmley BS15 11 B8
Cheltenham GL52 134 B1
Gloucester GL1 118 E6
Stanley St
5 Bristol,Bedminster BS3 8 C3
Bristol,Upper Easton BS5 9 A8
Stanley St N 13 BS3 8 C3
Stanley St S BS3 8 C2
Stanley Terr Bristol BS3 8 C2
Gloucester GL1 118 E7
Stanley The GL4 119 F2
Stanley View GL5 98 F5
Stanley Wlk GL4 119 F1
Stanmoor GL4 119 E3
Stansby Cres GL3 128 A6
Stansby Park Cvn Pk
GL51 129 B6
Stansby Touring Pk
GL51 129 B6
Stanshaw Cl BS16 20 A7
Stanshaw Rd BS16 20 A7
Stanshawe Cres BS37 43 E1
Stanshawes Court Dr
BS37 32 E8
Stanshawes Dr BS37 43 D1
Stanshaws Cl BS32 40 C2
Stansted Ho GL1 196 A3
Stanthill Dr GL11 80 C8
Stanton Cl BS15 20 F1
Stanton Rd Bristol BS10 28 E2
Stroud GL5 98 E8
Tewkesbury GL20 192 D5
Stanton Way GL51 129 E8
Stantons Dr GL51 133 A7
Stantway La GL14 157 E8
Stanway BS30 11 C1
Stanway House & Water
Gdns* GL54 184 E3
Stanway Rd
Cheltenham GL51 129 D8
Gloucester GL4 119 C7
Stanton WR12 184 E5
Stanway Wood Dr GL52 137 E3
Stanwick Cres GL51 133 B5
Stanwick Dr GL51 133 B5
Stanwick Gdns GL51 133 B4
Staple Gr BS31 4 D5
Staple Grove Cres BS5 10 A7
Staple Hill Prim Sch
BS16 20 D4
Staple Hill Rd BS16 20 B4
Staples Rd BS37 43 D2
Stapleton Cl Bristol BS16 19 D5
Highworth SN6 145 C3
Stapleton Rd
Bristol,Baptist Mills BS5 19 B1
Bristol,Eastville BS5 19 C3
Stapleton Road Sta BS5 19 B1
Star Ave BS34 30 A4
Star Barn Rd BS36 30 E7
Star Beech Hill GL17,
HR9 163 E6
Star Ct 10 GL52 133 F2
Star Hill GL6 91 A5
Star La Avening GL8 140 B8
Bristol BS16 19 F3
Pill BS20 16 D4
Starling Ct 7 GL10 97 F8
Stars Pitch GL17 164 D5
Station App Bristol BS1 195 C1
Gloucester GL1 196 C3
Minety SN16 142 E1
Station Ave 3 BS16 20 A4
Station Avenue S 5
BS16 20 A4
Station Cl Bristol BS15 11 C8
Chipping Sodbury BS37 33 D8
Churchdown GL3 128 D5
Station Cotts GL20 182 C7
Station Ct BS5 9 E8
Station Dr GL20 182 C7
Station Ind Est NP16 60 F8
Station La Bristol BS7 19 A4
Longhope GL17 164 F5
Tewkesbury GL20 192 D5
Station Mdw GL54 168 F8
Station Rd
Acton Turville GL9 35 F8
Andoversford GL54 166 D6
Ashton under Hill WR11 183 E8
Beckford GL20 183 B6
Berkeley GL13 85 E5
Bishop's Cleeve GL52 138 B4
Bledington OX7 177 F1
Blockley GL56 186 D6
Bourton-on-t-W GL54 168 F8
Bretforton WR11 188 A7
Bristol,Ashley Down BS7 18 F4
Bristol,Filton BS34 29 A3
Bristol,Fishponds BS16 20 A4
Bristol,Henbury BS10 27 F4
Bristol,Montpelier BS6 18 E2
Bristol,Newleaze BS34 29 B2
Bristol,Patchway BS34 29 C7
Bristol,Shirehampton BS11 16 D5
Bristol,Shirehampton BS11 16 E6
Bristol,Staple Hill BS15 20 F3
Bristol,Upper Knowle BS4 9 D2
Bristol,Warmley BS30 11 C7
Broadway WR12 185 B8
Charfield GL12 67 B5
Chepstow/Cas-Gwent NP16 60 F8
Chipping Campden GL55 189 A2
Churchdown GL3 128 C5
Coalpit Heath BS36 31 C5
Dursley GL11 88 A5
Gloucester GL1 196 C2
Highworth SN6 145 C3
Honeybourne WR11 188 C7
Iron Acton BS37 42 D3
Kemble GL7 141 F8
Keynsham BS31 4 E6
Kingham OX7 177 F2
Lechlade on T GL7 153 E3
Lydney GL15 84 A8
Milkwall GL16 155 B4
Minety SN16 142 E1
11 Moreton-in-M GL56 187 A3
Nailsworth GL6 91 C4
Newnham GL14 156 F7
Station Rd *continued*
Pill BS20 16 C4
Pilning BS35 38 F4
Ripple GL20 181 D8
Severn Beach BS35 38 A6
South Cerney GL7 143 A7
Stroud GL5 99 B7
Tewkesbury GL20 192 D5
Wickwar GL12 54 B7
Winterbourne BS36 30 E4
Woodchester GL5 99 A1
Woolaston GL15 147 C2
Yate BS37 43 C2
Station Road Bsns Ctr
BS15 21 A3
Station Road Link BS15 21 A2
Station Road Workshops
BS15 21 A3
Station St
Cheltenham GL50 193 A4
Cinderford GL14 191 C5
Tewkesbury GL20 192 D4
Station Terr
Cinderford GL14 191 C5
Dymock GL18 178 D2
Staunton & Corse CE Prim
Sch GL19 172 B8
Staunton Cl GL4 119 E4
Staunton Ct Bsns Pk
GL19 172 A8
Staunton Fields BS14 3 C4
Staunton Ho GL16 154 D7
Staunton La BS14 3 D3
Staunton Rd
Coleford GL16 154 F6
Monmouth/Trefynwy GL16,
NP25 154 C7
Staunton Way BS14 3 D4
Staveley Cres BS10 28 C2
Staverton Cl BS32 40 C1
Staverton Connection
GL51 173 F1
Staverton Pk GL51 173 F1
Staverton Tech Pk GL51 173 F1
Staverton Way BS15 11 A7
Stavordale Gr BS14 3 B6
Staynes Cres BS15 10 E8
Steadings Bsns Ctr The
GL2 126 A8
Steam Mills GL14 191 B8
Steam Mills Prim Sch
GL14 191 B8
Steam Mills Rd GL14 191 B7
Stean Bridge Rd BS32 29 E6
Steanbridge BS32 29 D6
Steel Ave GL15 92 B3
Steel Ct BS30 10 F3
Steel Mills BS31 4 F4
Steep St NP16 60 E8
Steeple Cl GL4 119 D8
Steeple View GL15 92 A2
Steevens Ho (almshouses) 15
BS2 195 C3
Stella Gr BS3 8 A2
Stella Way GL52 137 D4
Stenders Bsns Pk GL17 164 C5
Stenders Ct GL17 164 D5
Stenders Rd GL17 164 D5
Stenders The GL17 164 C5
Step's La GL6,GL8 148 B1
Stepaside NP16 60 C3
Stepbridge Rd GL16 155 B4
Stephen St BS5 9 C8
Stephens Dr BS30 10 F5
Stephens Pl GL16 155 B5
Stephenson Way WR11 188 C7
Stepney Rd BS5 19 C1
Stepney Wlk BS5 19 C1
Stepping Stone La GL6 103 E6
Stepping Stones The BS4 9 E6
Steps Cl GL11 87 F6
Stepstairs Ct GL7 190 D3
Stepstairs La GL7 190 D3
Sterling Cl GL54 176 F4
Sterling Ct GL51 133 B2
Sterncourt Rd BS16 20 A7
Sterrys Cnr HR9 170 C4
Sterrys Rd HR9 170 C4
Stevans Cl GL2 127 A5
Stevens Cres BS3 8 F4
Stevens Way GL6 90 F1
Stevens Wlk BS32 29 D8
Steward Rd GL20 182 C4
Stewarts Mill La GL4 119 E4
Stibbs Ct BS30 10 F4
Stibbs Hill BS5 10 A7
Sticky La GL2 109 E6
Stidcot La GL12 52 D5
Stidcote La GL12 52 E5
Stile Acres BS11 27 A1
Stillhouse La BS3 8 D4
Stillingfleet Rd BS13 2 C5
Stillman Cl BS13 1 E4
Stinchcombe BS37 43 E1
Stirling Cl BS37 43 D4
Stirling Rd BS4 9 C3
Stirling Way
Gloucester GL4 118 B2
Keynsham BS31 4 E4
Stirrup Cl GL2 118 B6
Stirrup The GL5 98 D7
Stock Hill BS35 63 C1
Stock La GL13 85 E3
Stockdale Cl GL2 109 D8
Stocken Cl GL3 120 B6
Stockham Cl SN6 143 F4
Stockholm Pl HR9 164 C8
Stockley Way GL4,GL6 111 D6
Stocks The GL6 102 D2
Stockton Cl
Bristol,Oldland BS30 11 B3
Bristol,Whitchurch BS14 2 F4
Cheltenham GL53 130 F4
Stockwell Ave BS16 21 A6
Stockwell Cl BS16 20 F7
Stockwell Dr BS16 21 A6
Stockwell Gn GL14 191 D3
Stockwell La
Aylburton GL15 147 E4
Woodmancote GL52 138 D3
Stockwells GL56 187 A3
Stockwood Chambers BS5 9 C7
Stockwood Cres BS4 8 F2
Stockwood Green Prim Sch
BS14 3 E4
Stockwood Hill BS31 4 C7
Stockwood La BS14 3 E5
Stockwood Mews BS4 9 F5
Stockwood Rd BS4 9 F1
Stoke Bishop CE Prim Sch
BS9 17 D5
Stoke Bridge Ave BS34 29 D6
Stoke Common La SN5 143 D1
Stoke Cotts BS9 17 E4
Stoke Gr BS9 17 E6
Stoke Hamlet BS9 17 F6
Stoke Hill BS9 17 E3
Stoke La
Bristol,Broomhill BS16 19 E7
Bristol,Patchway BS34 29 C8
Bristol,Westbury on Trym
BS9 17 F6
Stoke Lodge Prim Sch
BS34 29 C8
Stoke Mdws BS32 40 D1
Stoke Paddock Rd BS9 17 D6
Stoke Park Cl GL52 137 F4
Stoke Park Ct GL52 137 F4
Stoke Park Rd BS9 17 F4
Stoke Park Rd S BS9 17 E3
Stoke Rd
Bishop's Cleeve GL52 137 E4
Bristol BS8 18 A2
Stoke Orchard GL52 137 C4
Stoke View BS34 29 A3
Stoke View Bsns Pk 6
BS16 19 F4
Stoke View Rd BS16 19 F3
Stokefield Cl BS35 64 B1
Stokeleigh Wlk BS9 17 C5
Stokemead BS34 29 C8
Stokes Croft BS1 195 B4
Stokes Ct 1 Bristol BS30 11 A4
17 Tewkesbury GL20 192 C4
Stokes Rd GL20 181 D5
Stone Bridge GL56 187 D7
Stone Cl GL4 119 E7
Stone Cotts GL6 91 B3
Stone Cres GL51 132 F2
Stone House Mews BS37 44 B1
Stone La BS36 30 F3
Stone Manor GL5 99 E6
Stone Manor Ct GL5 99 E7
Stone Monolith BS34 28 E6
Stone Rd The GL19 172 A7
Stone with Woodford CE
Prim Sch GL13 77 E4
Stone's Cotts BS10 27 C4
Stoneberrow Pl GL18 178 D2
Stoneberry Rd BS14 3 B3
Stonebrack Piece GL4 119 E6
Stonebridge Pk BS5 19 E2
Stonechat Ave GL4 119 C5
Stonechat Gdns BS16 19 E6
Stonecote Ridge 8
GL6 148 C6
Stonecroft Cl GL52 137 E4
Stonedale Rd GL10 97 D8
Stonefern Ct 18 GL56 187 A3
Stonefield Dr SN6 145 D2
Stoneford La WR11 188 A5
Stonehenge Rd GL4 119 B7
Stonehill BS15 10 E4
Stonehill Ctr BS30 10 E4
Stonehill Farm BS15 10 E4
Stonehill La GL7 141 B7
Stonehouse Ct GL54 176 D4
Stonehouse Sta GL10 97 F7
Stonelea GL11 87 E4
Stoneleigh Cl GL53 130 D3
Stoneleigh Cres BS4 9 A2
Stoneleigh Dr BS30 10 F5
Stoneleigh Ho BS8 194 B3
Stoneleigh Rd BS4 9 A2
Stoneleigh Wlk BS4 9 A2
Stones Ct BS6 18 B2
Stones La SN6 143 D4
Stoneville St GL51 193 A4
Stoney Bridge GL4 119 E6
Stoney Field GL2 125 E5
Stoney Pool GL7 151 E3
Stoney Rd GL18 170 C4
Stoney Stile Rd BS35 51 A5
Stoneyfield Cl BS20 16 B5
Stoneyfields BS20 16 B4
Stoneyhills Ind Est HR9 162 D4
Stony Riding GL6 148 C5
Stores Rd BS11 26 C4
Storrington Pl 8 GL10 97 F7
Storrington Rd GL10 97 F7
Stothard Rd BS7 19 B7
Stottbury Rd BS7 19 A3
Stoulgrove La NP16 73 A4

Stoulton Gr BS10 28 A3
Stourden Cl BS16 20 A7
Stourton Dr BS30 10 F4
Stover Rd BS37 43 B2
Stover Trad Est BS37 43 B2
Stow Cl GL4 118 F6
Stow Ct GL51 133 A1
Stow Gn 15 GL54 176 F4
Stow Hill Rd GL12 52 B6
Stow Ho BS11 16 E5
Stow Rd Baunton GL7 150 E7
Bledington OX7 177 E1
Moreton-in-M GL56 187 A2
Stow-on-the-Wold Prim Sch
GL54 176 F4
Stowe La GL15 154 E1
Stowe Rd GL15 146 D8
Stowell Hill Rd GL12 52 B6
Stowell Mews GL4 119 D7
Stowell Pk GL54 159 D8
Stowfield Rd GL17 163 C4
Stowick Gdns BS11 27 C2
Strachans Cl GL5 99 A7
Stradbrook Ave BS5 10 B7
Stradling Rd BS11 27 C2
Stradlings Yd BS2 194 C4
Straight La GL19 172 B8
Straight St BS2 195 C2
Straits Par BS16 20 B5
Strand Ct GL53 193 C3
Strand La GL14 157 C8
Strand The GL50 193 C3
Stranks Cl SN6 145 D2
Stratford Bridge GL20 180 E9
Stratford Cl Bristol BS14 2 F3
Gloucester GL2 118 C4
Stratford Ct BS9 17 F8
Stratford Rd
Honeybourne WR11 188 D7
Mickleton GL55 189 A7
Stroud GL5 99 A8
Strathearn Dr BS10 28 B2
Stratheden BS8 194 A4
Strathmore Rd BS7 18 B8
Stratmore Est GL16 155 B3
Stratton Brook GL7 190 A7
Stratton CE Prim Sch
GL7 190 A8
Stratton Cl BS34 29 C7
Stratton Cnr GL1 196 C1
Stratton Ct GL20 192 D5
Stratton Hts GL7 190 B8
Stratton Mills GL7 190 C7
Stratton Rd
Gloucester GL1 196 C1
Saltford BS31 5 E3
Stratton St BS2 195 C3
Strawberry Field 2
GL16 155 A7
Strawberry Hill GL18 171 A6
Strawberry La Bristol BS5 9 E7
Dundry BS13,BS41 1 E3
Meysey Hampton GL7 152 B2
Strawbridge Rd 11 BS5 9 B7
Stream Cl BS10 28 D3
Stream La GL18 171 B5
Stream Side BS16 20 F6
Stream The BS16 30 B2
Streamfield GL12 68 B8
Streamleaze BS35 51 C8
Streamleaze Ct BS35 51 B8
Streamside
Bishop's Cleeve GL52 137 F4
Gloucester GL4 118 A2
Stroud GL5 99 C7
Streamside Rd BS37 44 A1
Streamside Wlk BS4 9 E3
Street Cotts SN16 142 A4
Street The
Acton Turville GL9 35 F6
Alveston BS35 51 B5
Burton SN14 36 B4
Castle Eaton SN6 144 D6
Coaley GL11 88 E8
Crudwell SN16 141 C3
Didmarton GL9 57 C3
Frampton on Severn GL2 157 F2
Horsley GL6 90 F1
Latton SN6 143 E6
Leighterton GL8 70 C3
Leonard Stanley GL10 97 E3
Luckington SN14 47 E4
Marston Meysey SN6 144 B8
North Nibley GL11 79 D4
Oaksey SN16 142 A4
Olveston BS35 50 A3
Shipton Moyne GL8 59 D8
Uley GL11 89 B1
Woodchester GL5 99 B3
Strensham Bsns Pk
WR8 180 A9
Strensham Court Mews
WR8 180 A10
Strensham Gate WR8 180 A10
Stretford Ave BS5 9 D8
Stretford Rd BS5 9 D8
Strickland Homes 5
GL52 130 F8
Strickland Rd GL52 130 F8
Stride Cl BS35 38 A6
Striguil Rd NP16 60 E6
Stringer's Cl GL5 99 A5
Stringer's Dr GL5 99 A5
Strode Comm BS35 50 F5
Strode Gdns BS35 50 F5
Stroma Way SN6 145 C4
Strongbow Rd NP16 60 E6
Stroud Coll GL5 99 A8
Stroud Ent Ctr GL5 98 F4
Stroud General Hospl
GL5 99 D6
Stroud Girls' High Sch
GL5 99 A7
Stroud Maternity Hospl
GL5 99 D6
Stroud Rd Bisley GL6 105 A1
Bristol,Patchway BS34 28 F8
Bristol,Shirehampton BS11 16 E5
Cirencester GL7 150 B4
Gloucester GL1,GL4 118 E6
Nailsworth GL6 91 B5
Painswick GL6 103 D6
Stroud Sta GL5 99 B7
Stroud Valley Com Prim Sch
Stroud GL5 99 C6
Stroud GL5 99 C7
Stuart Ave NP16 72 D1
Stuart St BS5 9 C7
Studland Ct BS9 18 B6
Studland Dr GL52 134 C4
Stump La GL3 120 B8
Stumpwell La GL12 79 E2
Sturden La BS16 30 C3
Sturdon Rd BS3 8 A3
Sturmer Cl BS37 43 E4
Sturmey Way BS20 16 E3
Sturminster Cl BS14 3 D6
Sturminster Rd BS14 3 D7
Sturmyes Rd GL6 148 D6
Sudbrook Trad Est GL2 196 A1
Sudbrook Way GL4 119 C5
Sudeley Castle & Gdns*
GL54 174 B6
Sudeley Dr GL7 142 F7
Sudeley Ho 5 GL51 132 E3
Sudeley View GL54 139 F5
Sudgrove Pk GL4 119 E5
Sudmeadow Rd GL2 126 C1
Suffolk Cl 2 GL8 140 C5
Suffolk Ho GL50 193 A2
Suffolk Mews GL50 193 B1
Suffolk Par GL50 193 B2
Suffolk Pl GL7 143 E8
Suffolk Rd GL50 193 A1
Suffolk Sq GL50 193 A2
Suffolk St GL50 193 B1
Suffolk Villas GL50 193 B1
Sugar Tump HR9 170 B4
Sugley La GL6 90 F2
Sulgrave Cl GL4 118 C1
Sullivan Cl BS4 2 D6
Summer Cl GL5 99 E7
Summer Cres GL5 99 E7
Summer Ct BS8 194 B3
Summer Hill BS4 9 A4
Summer House Way
BS30 11 B7
Summer La SN14 36 F3
Summer Mdw GL4 119 B4
Summer St 4 Bristol BS3 8 C4
Stroud GL5 99 E7
Summerfield Cl
Blockley GL56 186 C6
Cheltenham GL51 132 F5
Summerhayes BS30 11 D5
Summerhill Jun & Inf Schs
BS5 9 E8
Summerhill Rd BS5 9 F8
Summerhill Terr BS5 9 F7
Summerhouse La NP16 60 F4
Summerland Dr GL3 128 C5
Summerleaze
Bristol BS16 20 C3
Keynsham BS31 4 E7
Lydney GL15 92 B3
Summerleaze Rd GL15 92 B2
Summers Dr BS30 23 A1
Summers Mead BS37 43 E4
Summers Rd
4 Bristol BS2 19 A1
13 Winchcombe GL54 174 A7
Summers Terr 3 BS2 19 A1
Summersfield Cl GL6 148 A3
Summersfield Rd GL6 148 A4
Sun Green Cl 2 GL15 155 D1
Sun Green Rd 3 GL15 155 D1
Sun La GL16 155 B6
Sun Rise Rd 1 GL15 155 D1
Sun St Cheltenham GL51 133 C3
Tewkesbury GL20 192 C5
Sun Tump GL15 147 D8
Sundale HR9 170 B4
Sundays Hill BS32 40 A4
Sundayshill La GL12 65 D7
Sunderland Ct GL3 128 C5
Sunderland Pl BS8 194 B3
Sundridge Pk BS37 32 E8
Sunground The GL8 148 B1
Sunningdale Bristol BS8 194 B4
Yate BS37 32 E8
Sunningdale Dr BS30 11 B6
Sunny Bank Bristol BS15 20 B1
14 Coleford GL16 155 A5
Wick BS30 12 B7
Sunny Hill BS9 17 C7
Sunny View GL6 90 F4
Sunny Wlk BS15 20 B1
Sunnybank Bristol BS16 20 E6
Westerleigh BS37 32 A3
Sunnybank Rd GL16 155 A6
Sunnybrook Terr GL13 93 D2
Sunnycroft Cl GL52 138 A2
Sunnycroft Mews GL1 118 E5
Sunnydene BS4 9 D4
Sunnyfield La GL51 129 C5
Sunnyfield Rd GL2 109 D8
Sunnyhill GL5 98 E8
Sunnyhill Dr BS11 16 E6
Sunnyhill Ho E BS11 16 E6
Sunnyhill Ho W BS11 16 E6
Sunnymead Bristol BS30 11 D6
Keynsham BS31 4 F3
Sunnymead Cl GL17 164 B4
Sunnyside Bristol BS9 17 E5
Frampton Cotterell BS36 31 B8
Sunnyside Farm Trad Est
BS20 16 C2
Sunnyside La Bristol BS16 30 C2
Yate BS37 43 C1
Sunnyvale Dr BS30 11 B3
Sunridge BS16 20 D6
Sunrise Gr BS4 9 D4
Sunset La GL52 134 C8
Sunset Pl GL19 165 D6
Surrey Ave GL51 132 F2
Surrey Rd BS7 18 E3
Surrey St BS2 195 B4
Sussex Ave GL51 133 A2
Sussex Gdns GL3 120 B7
Sussex Pl BS2 18 F1
Sussex St BS2 9 A6
Sutherland Ave
Bristol BS16 20 E7
Yate BS37 43 D4
Sutherland Pl 9 BS8 18 A2
Sutton Ave BS4 9 D4
Sutton Cl GL11 80 B8
Sutton Pk SN26 144 E1
Sutton Pl GL5 99 D7
Sutton Rd
Littledean GL14 191 F3
Upper Soudley GL14 156 C5
Swagwater La HR9 170 C5
Swainswick BS14 2 F6
Swaish Dr 2 BS30 11 A4
Swallow Cres GL3 127 D6
Swallow Croft GL10 96 F7
Swallow Ct BS14 3 F6
Swallow Dr BS34 28 E8
Swallow Pk BS35 64 D3
Swallows Ct BS34 29 E4
Swallowtail Cl 6 GL51 132 D2
Swan Cl
Lechlade on T GL7 153 E2
Moreton-in-M GL56 187 A3
Swan Ct GL1 196 A3
Swan Field BS37 43 F2
Swan La Blakeney GL15 156 E2
Leigh SN6 143 A3
Stoke Orchard GL52 136 D5
13 Stroud GL5 99 C7
Winterbourne BS36 30 C8
Swan Rd Gloucester GL1 196 C4
Lydney GL15 92 A3
Swan Yd GL7 190 C5
Swane Rd BS14 3 F6
Swanley La GL13 78 B5
Swanmoor Cres BS10 28 A4
Swanscombe Pl 14
GL51 129 E5
Swansfield GL7 153 E3
Swanswell Dr GL51 129 E8
Sweden La GL20 183 B5
Sweetbriar Cl GL52 137 E4
Sweetbriar Ho GL3 128 D4
Sweetbriar St GL1 196 C4
Sweetmore Cl GL56 177 C5
Sweets Cl BS15 20 E2
Sweets Rd BS15 20 E2
Swell CE Prim Sch
GL54 176 D4
Swells Hill GL5 99 E1
Swift Rd GL4 119 D5
Swifts Hill View GL5 103 E1
Swilgate Rd GL20 192 C4
Swindon & Cricklade Rly*
SN5 143 F1
Swindon Cl GL51 133 C3
Swindon La GL50 133 D5
Swindon Manor GL51 133 A6
Swindon Rd
Cheltenham GL50 193 B4
Cheltenham,St Peter's
GL51 133 B4
Cirencester GL7 190 E3
Cricklade SN6 143 F4
Highworth SN6 145 C2
Swindon St
Cheltenham GL51 133 C3
Highworth SN6 145 D3
Swindon Village Prim Sch
GL51 133 B7
Swinhay La GL12 67 B8
Swish La GL17 164 A4
Swiss Dr BS3 7 F2
Swiss Rd BS3 7 F1
Swordfish Cl GL3 128 C5
Swynford Cl GL7 144 E7
Sybil Rd GL1 119 A6
Sycamore Ave NP16 60 E5
Sycamore Cl
Bristol,Hanham BS15 10 B3
Bristol,Whitehall BS5 19 E1
Gloucester GL1 118 D5
Sycamore Cres GL52 138 B4
Sycamore Ct Bristol BS7 18 E3
3 Cheltenham GL51 132 D2
St Arvans NP16 72 B5
Sycamore Dr Bristol BS34 28 F7
Stroud GL5 99 D8
Thornbury BS35 64 C1
Sycamore Ho 6 BS16 20 C6
Sycamore Rd
Harrow Hill GL17 164 B3
Northway GL20 182 C4
Sydenham Hill BS6 18 D1
Sydenham La BS6 18 E1
Sydenham Pl 15 BS6 18 E1
Sydenham Rd
Bristol,Cotham BS6 18 E1
Bristol,Totterdown BS4 9 A3
3 Cheltenham GL52 130 F8
Sydenham Rd S GL52 130 F8
Sydenham Terr GL1 118 E7
Sydenham Villas Rd
GL52 130 F8
Sydenham Way BS15 10 C3
Sydney GL10 101 E1
Sydney Row BS1 194 B1
Sylvan Cl 19 GL16 155 A5
Sylvan View NP16 146 B4
Sylvan Way BS9 17 B7
Sylvia Ave BS3 8 F3
Symes Ave BS13 2 C4
Symington Rd BS16 20 B5
Symn La GL12 68 B7
Synwell La GL12 68 C7
Syon Rd GL6 148 A3
Syston View BS15 11 A8
Syston Way BS15 20 D1

T

T T Trad Est BS37 44 C1
Tabernacle Pitch GL12 68 B7
Tabernacle Rd
Bristol BS15 10 C6
Wotton-u-E GL12 68 B8
Tabernacle Wlk GL5 99 B5
Tabrams Pitch GL6 91 C4
Tackley Rd BS5 19 B3
Tadwick La BA1 13 E1
Taena Pottery* GL4 120 B2
Tailor's Ct BS1 195 A3
Tainmor Cl GL2 127 E5
Tait's Hill GL11 87 C4
Tait's Hill Rd GL11 87 D4
Taits Hill Ind Est GL11 87 C4
Talbot Ave BS15 20 C1
Talbot Ct GL54 176 F4
Talbot Mews GL1 118 D6
Talbot Pl GL17 164 D5
Talbot Rd Bristol BS4 9 C2
Cheltenham GL51 130 A8
Talbot Sq GL54 176 E4
Talboy's Wlk 6 GL8 140 C5
Talgarth Rd BS7 18 F4
Tall Elms Cl GL3 128 B5
Tallard's Pl NP16 61 A8
Tallis Gr BS4 2 D6
Tallis Rd GL3 127 F8
Tally Ho La GL54 175 B3
Talybont La HR9 162 C3
Tamar Cl BS35 51 D7
Tamar Dr BS31 5 A4
Tamar Rd Bristol BS2 9 C6
Brockworth GL3 120 F5
Cheltenham GL52 134 A2
Tamarisk Cl GL51 130 A4
Tamesis Dr GL7 141 F8
Tamsin Ct BS31 4 F5
Tamworth Rd BS31 4 E4
Tandey Wlk GL3 127 E6
Tanglewood Way GL6 148 B6
Tanhouse La BS37 43 D7
Tankard's Cl BS8 194 C3
Tanner Cl BS30 10 F5
Tanner Ct BS30 10 F5
Tanner's La GL51 132 F3
Tanner's Piece GL6 91 C3
Tanner's Rd GL51 132 F3
Tanners Cl GL3 120 E6
Tanners Ct
Bristol,Frenchay BS16 30 B1
4 Bristol,Two Mile Hill
BS15 20 C1
Thornbury BS35 51 B8
Tanners La SN14 14 F8
Tanners Wlk SN14 14 F8
Tannery Cl GL10 97 E3
Tannery Gdns GL16 154 F3
Tannery La 19 GL54 168 A1
Tanorth Cl BS14 3 A3
Tanorth Rd BS14 2 F3
Tansy Cl GL4 119 F5
Tanyard The BS30 11 B2
Tapscott Ct GL12 68 A7
Tapsters BS30 11 A4
Tara Cl BS36 41 F1
Target Cl GL5 99 F7
Tarlton Cl GL4 119 E4
Tarn Ho BS34 29 A8
Tarnock Ave BS14 3 A7
Tarragon Pl BS32 29 F7
Tarrington Rd 7 GL1 118 F7
Tasmania Ho 4 GL51 132 E2
Tatchley La GL52 134 B4
Taunton Wlk BS7 19 A7
Taurus Cl GL2 126 F5
Taut The GL6 148 F6
Taverner Cl BS4 2 D7
Tavistock Rd BS4 8 F1
Tavistock Wlk BS4 8 F1
Tawny Cl GL20 182 B5
Tayberry Gr GL51 129 F4
Tayler Rd GL54 168 A1
Taylor Cl BS15 10 F8
Taylor Gdns BS13 1 F4
Taylors End GL50 130 B6
Taylors Ground GL2 117 F2
Taylors Row 23 GL54 176 F4
Tayman Cl BS10 18 E6
Tayman Ridge BS30 5 D8
Taynton Cl BS30 11 C2
Teal Cl Bristol BS32 40 D2
Quedgeley GL2 117 D1
Teasel Cl GL2 126 F5
Teasel Mead BS32 29 E7
Tebbit Mews 3 GL52 193 C4
Ted Preston Cl GL20 192 D2
Teddington Gdns GL4 119 B6
Teewell Ave BS16 20 E4
Teewell Cl BS16 20 E4
Teewell Ct BS16 20 E4
Teewell Hill BS16 20 E4
Teignmouth Rd BS4 8 F1
Telephone Ave BS1 195 A2
Telford Ho Bristol BS8 7 E7
Cheltenham GL51 132 F3
Telford Way GL2 109 F7
Telford Wlk BS5 20 A1
Tellings Orch SN16 142 B2
Teme Rd GL52 134 A2
Tempest Dr NP16 60 D8
Templar Rd BS37 43 E3
Temple Back BS1 195 B2
Temple Back E BS1 195 C2
Temple Circle Gyratory
BS1 195 B1
Temple Cl
Gloucester GL4 119 E8
Lydney GL15 147 F6
Temple Ct BS31 4 E5
Temple Gate BS1 195 B1
Temple Gate District Ctr
BS3 8 F4
Temple Guiting CE Prim Sch
GL54 175 A6
Temple Hill Inf Sch BS31 4 F5
Temple Jun Sch BS31 4 F6
Temple Meads Sta BS1 195 C2
Temple Rose St BS1 195 B2
Temple St Bristol BS1 195 B2
Bristol,Bedminster BS3 8 B2
Keynsham BS31 4 F5
Temple Trad Est BS2 9 C5
Temple Way BS2 195 B2
Temple Way Underpass
BS2 195 C3
Templefields GL54 166 C6
Templefields Cl GL54 166 C6
Templeland Rd BS13 1 F5
Templeway GL15 147 F6
Templeway W GL15 147 F6
Tenby Rd BS31 4 D4
Tenby St BS5 9 B7
Tennessee Gr BS6 18 C5
Tennis Rd BS4 9 A2
Tenniscourt Rd BS15 21 A1
Tennyson Ave GL2 118 C4
Tennyson Cl BS31 4 F6
Tennyson Rd Bristol BS7 18 E5
Cheltenham GL51 132 E1
Dursley GL11 80 C7
Tensing Rd GL53 130 E4
Tenth Ave BS7 29 B1
Tereslake Gn BS10 28 D4
Terhill 4 GL52 133 F2
Tern Cl GL4 119 C6
Terrace The
Nailsworth GL6 91 A2
Wotton-u-E GL12 68 D8
Terrell Gdns 14 BS5 9 D7
Terrell St BS2 195 A4
Terris Ct BS34 29 E4
Terry Ho BS1 194 C3
Terry Ruck Cl GL51 132 D2
Tesco Rdbt GL2 117 F1
Tetbury Cl BS34 29 C7
Tetbury Hill GL8 140 B8
Tetbury Hospl GL8 140 C3
Tetbury La
Crudwell SN16 141 B3
Leighterton GL8 70 C3
Nailsworth GL6 91 C2
Tetbury Police Mus*
GL8 140 B4
Tetbury Rd Bristol BS15 10 B8
Cirencester GL7 150 B3
Cirencester GL7 190 B4
Gloucester GL4 118 E1
Sherston SN16 58 D1
Tetbury St GL6 148 A3
Teviot Rd BS31 5 A4
Tewkesbury CE Prim Sch
GL20 192 D4
Tewkesbury Hospl
GL20 192 D4
Tewkesbury Ind Est
GL20 192 F5
Tewkesbury Mus*
GL20 192 C4
Tewkesbury Rd
11 Bristol BS2 19 A2
Cheltenham GL51 133 A4
Gloucester GL2 126 F5
Newent GL18 171 B5
Northway GL20 182 B6
Stow-on-t-W GL54 176 E5
Uckington GL51 132 E6
Tewkesbury Sch GL20 182 B4
Tewther Rd BS13 2 D3
Texas Cl GL7 152 E2
Teyfant Com Sch BS13 2 E4
Teyfant Rd BS13 2 E4
Teyfant Wlk BS13 2 E4

Thackeray BS7 19 A8
Thames Cl Charfield GL12 67 A4
Cricklade SN6 143 E4
Thames Ho 9 BS35 51 C8
Thames La SN6 143 F4
Thames Rd GL52 134 A2
Thames St GL7 153 E2
Thames View 2 SN6 142 F4
Thamesmead Cotts SN6 143 E4
Thanet Rd BS3 8 B2
Thatcham Rd GL20 192 E1
Thatchers Cl BS5 10 B7
Thatchers End GL52 138 B3
Theatre Royal* BS1 195 A2
Theescombe Hill GL5 91 B6
Theocs Cl GL20 192 C2
There-and-Back-Again La BS1 194 C3
Theresa Ave BS7 18 E4
Theresa St GL1 118 D7
Thessaly Gate GL7 190 A8
Thessaly Rd GL7 190 B8
Theyer Cl GL3 120 E5
Theynes Croft BS41 7 B1
Thicket Ave BS16 20 C3
Thicket Rd BS16 20 C4
Thicket Wlk BS35 64 C1
Thiery Rd BS4 9 C2
Thingwall Pk BS16 19 E3
Third Ave
Bristol,Filton BS7 29 A1
Bristol,Hengrove BS14 3 B7
Dursley GL11 80 C8
Third Way BS11 26 C2
Thirlebrook Cotts GL20 182 E4
Thirlestaine House Cotts GL53 193 B1
Thirlestaine Rd GL53 193 C1
Thirlmere Ct BS30 11 D6
Thirlmere Rd Bristol BS34 29 A8
Cheltenham GL51 129 E7
Thistle Downs GL20 182 C5
Thistle St 1 BS3 8 B3
Thistlebank GL2 127 B5
Thistledown Cl GL51 132 D4
Thomas Ave BS16 21 B8
Thomas Ct BS1 195 B2
Thomas Keble Sch GL6 148 C7
Thomas La BS1 195 B2
Thomas Moore Cl GL3 128 A8
Thomas Pring Wlk 1 BS5 20 A1
Thomas St
Bristol,Kingsdown BS2 195 B4
8 Bristol,Russell Town BS5 9 B7
Bristol,St Pauls BS2 18 F1
Chepstow/Cas-Gwent NP16 60 E8
Cirencester GL7 190 C5
Gloucester GL1 196 C1
Thomas St N 12 BS2 18 D1
Thomas Stock Gdns GL4 119 E6
Thomas Way BS16 19 E7
Thomond Cl GL51 133 C4
Thompson Dr GL53 130 D4
Thompson Rd Bristol BS14 3 E6
Siddington GL7 150 F2
Stroud GL5 99 D8
Thompson Way GL3 127 E6
Thomson Rd 7 BS5 9 B8
Thoresby GL52 133 E5
Thoresby Ave GL4 110 C8
Thorn Cl BS37 43 D1
Thorn Tree Dr NP16 60 F4
Thornbury Cl GL51 133 B2
Thornbury Hospl BS35 64 C1
Thornbury Ind Pk BS35 51 B7
Thornbury Mus* BS35 51 B8
Thornbury Rd BS35 51 A5
Thorncliffe 10 GL51 130 B8
Thorncliffe Dr GL51 130 B8
Thorndale BS8 194 A4
Thorndale Mews BS8 194 A4
Thornhaugh Mews 5 GL51 129 E5
Thornhayes Cl BS36 31 A8
Thornhill Cl GL1 118 D5
Thornhills The BS16 20 B6
Thornleigh Rd BS7 18 E5
Thornmead Gr BS10 28 A2
Thorns Farm BS37 43 E1
Thornwell Prim Sch NP16 60 F5
Thornwell Rd NP16 60 F5
Thornycroft Cl BS7 19 B7
Thorpe Lodge 9 BS6 18 D1
Threadneedle St 10 GL5 99 C7
Three Ashes La GL18 171 A6
Three Brooks La BS32 29 E8
Three Choirs Vineyard* GL18 170 F7
Three Cocks La GL1 196 A3
Three Counties Pk WR13 180 C5
Three Oaks Cl BS16 20 C4
Three Queens' La BS1 195 B2
Three Sisters La GL52 134 D3
Three Wells Rd BS13 1 F4
Thrissell St BS5 9 A8
Throat The GL6 102 F4
Throgmorton Rd BS4 2 F8
Thrupp La GL5 99 E3
Thrupp Sch GL5 99 E3
Thrush Cl GL4 119 D6
Thurlestone BS14 3 A6
Thurlow Rd BS5 19 C2
Thurston's Barton BS5 19 E1
Tibberton BS15 11 A8
Tibberton Com Prim Sch GL19 171 E1
Tibberton Gr GL51 129 B7
Tibberton La GL19 165 D6
Tibbiwell Gdns GL6 103 F8
Tibbiwell La GL6 103 F8
Tibbott Rd BS14 3 D5
Tibbott Wlk BS14 3 D5
Tiberius Ave GL15 92 B4
Tichborne Rd BS5 9 C7
Tide Gr BS11 17 A8
Tidenham Way BS34 39 F1
Tidling Cnr SN16 142 B3
Tidswell Cl GL2 109 F8
Tiffany Ct BS1 195 B1
Tilley Cl BS31 5 A2
Tilling Rd BS10 18 E7
Tilling Wlk BS10 18 E7
Tillis View GL16 154 D7
Tilney Rd GL50 133 D4
Tilnor Cres GL11 87 F4
Tilsdown GL11 87 F4
Tilsdown Cl GL11 87 F4
Tilting Rd BS35 64 B2
Timber Dene BS16 19 D4
Timbercombe La GL53 131 B3
Timbercombe Mews GL53 131 B4
Timberscombe Wlk BS14 3 C5
Timbrells Cl GL7 142 F8
Timbrells The GL7 142 B8
Timmis Cl GL4 119 C4
Timms Gn WR12 188 B2
Timperley Way GL51 129 E5
Timsbury Rd BS3 8 E2
Timsbury Wlk BS3 8 E2
Tindell Ct 12 BS30 10 F4
Tinglesfield GL7 190 B8
Tinker's Cl 27 GL56 187 A3
Tinkley La GL10 90 B5
Tinmans Gn NP25 154 C4
Tintagel Cl BS31 4 D4
Tintern Abbey* NP16 146 C2
Tintern Ave BS5 9 D8
Tintern Cl BS30 10 F6
Tintern Hts NP16 146 A5
Tintern Old Sta* NP16 146 C3
Tintern Rd GL4 118 E3
Tippetts Rd BS15 10 D6
Tirle Bank Way GL20 192 F4
Tirlebrook Grange GL20 182 D4
Tirlebrook Prim Sch GL20 192 F4
Tirley Cl GL2 117 E1
Tirley Ho BS34 39 F1
Tirley Knowle GL19 172 E8
Tirley St GL19 172 F7
Tithe Farm La GL19 165 E6
Tiverton Cl GL51 132 D3
Tiverton Wlk BS16 20 A2
Tivoli La GL50 193 A1
Tivoli Mews GL50 193 A2
Tivoli Pl GL50 193 A1
Tivoli Rd GL50 193 A1
Tivoli St GL50 193 A1
Tivoli Wlk 17 GL50 130 B8
Toadsmoor Rd GL5 148 A5
Tobacco Cl GL54 139 F4
Tobacconist Rd GL6 148 A3
Tobias Gdns BS37 43 D1
Tobyfield Cl GL52 138 A3
Tobyfield La GL52 138 A3
Tobyfield Rd GL52 138 A3
Tockington Gn BS32 50 B2
Tockington La BS32 40 A7
Tockington Manor Sch BS32 50 C2
Tockington Park La BS32 40 E8
Tocknell Ct GL11 87 F8
Toddington Cl BS37 32 D8
Toddington Prim Sch GL54 184 C3
Toddington Sta* GL54 184 D3
Toghill La BS30 13 A8
Toll Down Way SN14 36 A3
Toll House Ct 5 BS3 8 A4
Tolsey La GL20 192 C4
Tom Price Cl GL52 193 C3
Tomlin Pl GL15 156 B1
Tommy Taylor's La GL50 133 D4
Tone Dr GL3 120 F5
Tooke Rd GL6 91 E7
Top Rd Kempsford GL7 144 E8
Upper Soudley GL14 156 C5
Torchacre Rise GL11 88 A1
Tormarton Cres BS10 27 F4
Tormarton Intc BS37 34 B1
Tormarton Rd
Acton Turville GL9 35 E6
Marshfield SN14 25 A4
Marshfield,East End SN14 15 A8
Toronto Rd BS7 19 A8
Torpoint Rd BS3 8 D2
Torrance Cl BS30 11 D6
Torridge Rd BS31 5 A4
Torrington Ave BS4 2 F8
Tortworth Farming Mus* GL12 66 B6
Tortworth Prim Sch GL12 66 C7
Tortworth Rd BS7 18 E5
Torwood House Sch BS6 18 A3
Totshill Dr BS13 2 E4
Totshill Gr BS13 2 E4
Tottenham Pl BS8 194 B3
Totterdown Bridge Ind Est BS2 9 A4
Totterdown La GL7 152 E2
Touching End La SN14 14 F8
Touchstone Ave BS34 29 F5
Tower Cl GL4 119 D8
Tower Hill BS2 195 B3
Tower Ho
10 Cheltenham GL52 193 C4
Woodchester GL5 98 F1
Tower House Dr GL19 179 F2
Tower La Bristol BS1 195 A3
Bristol,Cadbury Heath BS30 11 B6
Tower Rd Bristol BS15 20 C1
Yorkley GL15 156 A2
Tower Rd N BS30 11 B7
Tower Rd S BS30 11 B5
Tower St Bristol BS1 195 B2
Cirencester GL7 190 D4
Tower The BS1 195 B2
Towerleaze BS9 17 D3
Town St GL19 173 A8
Townsend
Almondsbury BS32 39 F4
Mitcheldean GL17 164 D5
Ruardean GL17 163 E4
Townsend Cl Bristol BS14 3 F5
St Briavels GL15 146 F7
Townsend La BS32 40 A5
Townsend Rd BS14 3 F5
Townsend St GL51 133 C3
Townwell GL12 66 B2
Tozers Hill BS4 9 C2
Tracy Cl BS14 2 F7
Tracy Row GL20 192 D5
Trafalgar Dr GL3 127 F8
Trafalgar Rd GL7 190 C5
Trafalgar St GL50 193 B2
Trafalgar Terr 3 BS3 8 B2
Traherne Cl 5 HR8 178 F7
Trajan Cl GL4 119 F6
Tralee Wlk BS4 8 D1
Tram Rd The 17 GL16 155 A5
Tramway Rd Bristol BS4 9 C3
Cinderford GL14 156 C6
Upper Soudley GL14 156 C5
Tranmere Ave BS10 28 A4
Tranmere Gr BS10 28 A3
Transom Ho BS1 195 B2
Transport Mus* GL1 196 A3
Tranton La GL13 76 C4
Tratman Wlk BS10 27 F3
Travers Cl BS4 2 D6
Travers Wlk BS34 29 F5
Tredegar Rd BS16 20 B3
Tredington Com Prim Sch GL20 136 B6
Tredington Pk GL20 173 F8
Tredworth Jun & Inf Schs GL1 118 F7
Tredworth Rd GL1 118 F6
Tree Leaze BS37 43 F2
Treefield Pl 5 BS2 19 A2
Treelands Cl GL53 130 D5
Treelands Dr GL53 130 D5
Tregarth Rd BS3 7 F1
Trelawney Ave BS5 9 D8
Trelawney Pk BS4 9 D3
Trelawney Rd BS6 18 C1
Trelleck Rd NP16 146 B4
Trellick Wlk BS16 19 E8
Tremes Cl SN14 14 F8
Trench La BS32 40 E2
Trenchard Gdns GL7 150 F2
Trenchard Rd
6 Bream GL15 147 D8
Saltford BS31 5 D3
Stanton Fitzwarren SN6 145 A1
Trenchard St BS1 194 C3
Trendlewood Pk BS16 19 E5
Trenley Rd GL11 88 F7
Trent Dr BS35 51 D7
Trent Gr BS31 5 A4
Trent Rd GL3 120 F5
Trentham Cl 7 BS2 19 A2
Tresham Cl BS32 40 D2
Tresmore 2 GL52 133 F2
Tretawn Gdns GL20 192 F4
Trevanna Rd BS3 7 F1
Trevelyan Wlk
Bristol,Henbury BS10 27 F3
Bristol,Stoke Gifford BS34 30 A5
Treverdowe Wlk BS10 27 D3
Trevethin Cl BS15 10 D7
Trevisa Cres GL13 85 E3
Trevisa Gr BS10 28 C4
Trevor Rd GL3 119 F7
Trewint Gdns BS4 2 F8
Trewsbury Rd GL7 149 E3
Triangle S BS8 194 B3
Triangle The
Hewelsfield GL15 146 D4
Longlevens GL2 127 C3
Triangle W BS8 194 B3
Tribune Pl GL4 119 E6
Trident Cl BS16 31 A1
Trier Way GL1 196 B1
Trin Mills BS1 195 A1
Trinder Rd BS20 16 B4
Trinity CE Prim Sch GL9 36 A6
Trinity Coll BS9 17 E4
Trinity Dr GL6 148 A3
Trinity La GL52 193 C4
Trinity Mews 17 BS2 195 C3
Trinity Pl BS8 194 A2
Trinity Rd Bristol BS2 9 A7
Cirencester GL7 190 C3
Gloucester GL4 119 F6
Trinity Rd *continued*
Harrow Hill GL17 164 B3
Stroud GL5 99 D6
Trinity School La GL52 193 C4
Trinity St Bristol BS2 9 A7
Tewkesbury GL20 192 C4
Trinity Way GL14 191 D5
Trinity Wlk Bristol BS2 195 C3
Bristol,Newton BS2 9 A7
Tewkesbury GL20 192 D4
Tripps Row BS41 7 A1
Triscombe Way GL51 132 D3
Troon BS37 32 E8
Troon Dr BS30 11 B6
Troopers' Hill Rd BS5 10 A7
Trotman Ave GL11 87 F5
Troughton Pl GL20 192 E4
Trowbridge Rd BS10 28 C1
Trowbridge Wlk BS10 28 C1
Trowscoed Ave GL53 130 D6
Trubodys Yd BS30 11 E7
Trubshaw Ct GL3 128 C5
Trull Cotts GL8 140 F7
Truro Rd BS3 8 B3
Tryes Rd GL50 130 C6
Trygrove GL4 119 D6
Trym Bank BS9 17 D7
Trym Cross Rd BS9 17 C5
Trym Rd BS9 18 A7
Trym Side BS9 17 C5
Trymleaze BS9 17 C5
Trymwood Cl BS10 27 F2
Trymwood Par BS9 17 D6
Tubular Cotts NP16 73 A1
Tucker St BS2 195 C3
Tuckett Ho BS16 20 C7
Tuckett La BS16 20 C7
Tuckwell Rd GL7 144 F7
Tudor Cl Bristol BS30 11 C3
Innsworth GL3 127 F7
Tudor Ct Gloucester GL1 127 A3
Leonard Stanley GL10 97 E4
Tudor Dr NP16 72 C1
Tudor Lo GL50 130 C6
Tudor Lodge Dr GL50 193 A1
Tudor Lodge Rd GL50 130 C6
Tudor Pl GL20 192 D2
Tudor Rd
Bristol,Hanham BS15 10 C5
Bristol,Lower Easton BS5 19 C1
Bristol,St Pauls BS2 18 F1
Cirencester GL7 190 E5
Monmouth/Trefynwy NP25 154 B7
Tudor St GL1 118 C6
Tudor Wlk GL16 155 A7
Tuffley Ave GL1 118 D5
Tuffley Cres GL1 118 C5
Tuffley La GL4 118 C3
Tuffley Pk GL1 118 B4
Tuffley Prim Sch GL4 118 D1
Tuffley Rd BS10 18 C8
Tufthorn Ave GL16 155 A4
Tufthorn Cl GL16 155 B4
Tufthorn Ind Est GL16 155 B4
Tufthorn Rd GL16 155 B4
Tufton Ave BS11 17 A8
Tufts The GL15 147 C8
Tug Wilson Cl GL20 182 C5
Tugela Rd BS13 1 F7
Tulworths The GL2 127 B5
Tunacre GL2 125 D6
Tunbridge Way BS16 21 A8
Tuners La SN16 141 C3
Tunstall Cl BS9 17 E4
Turkdean Rd GL51 129 E8
Turley Rd BS5 19 D1
Turnberry Bristol BS30 11 B6
Yate BS37 32 E8
Turnberry Wlk 3 BS4 9 D1
Turnbridge Cl BS10 28 D4
Turnbridge Rd BS10 28 C3
Turner Cl BS31 5 A5
Turner Dr BS37 43 B1
Turner Gdns BS7 19 B6
Turner Rd GL11 87 E4
Turner Wlk BS30 11 D7
Turner's Ct 8 GL20 192 C4
Turners Cl GL2 125 D4
Turners Ct 9 BS30 10 F4
Turnpike Ave GL12 68 C6
Turnpike Cl
Chepstow/Cas-Gwent NP16 72 C1
15 Moreton-in-M GL56 187 A3
Yate BS37 43 E2
Turnpike End NP16 61 B4
Turnpike Gate GL12 54 B6
Turnpike Rd SN6 145 D3
Turnstone Dr GL2 117 D1
Turtlegate Ave BS13 1 E4
Turtlegate Wlk BS13 1 E4
Turville Barns GL7 153 C8
Turville Dr BS7 19 A6
Tuscany Ho BS6 18 A3
Tusculum Way GL17 164 D5
Tuthill Rise GL15 92 B3
Tutnalls St GL15 92 B3
Tutshill Gdns NP16 73 A1
Tweed Cl BS35 51 C8
Tweenbrook Ave GL1 118 E6
Tweeny La BS30 11 D6
Twenties The GL7 150 E2
Twenty Acres Rd BS10 28 B2
Twickenham Rd BS6 18 C5
Twigworth CE Prim Sch GL2 127 A8
Twigworth Ct GL2 173 A1
Twinberrow La GL11 80 B7
Twinnell Ho 5 BS5 9 A8
Twixtbears GL20 192 C5
Two Acres Rd BS14 3 A7
Two Hedges Rd GL52 138 A3
Two Mile Ct BS15 10 C8
Two Mile Hill Jun & Inf Schs BS15 10 C8
Two Mile La GL2 125 B4
Twomile Hill Rd BS15 10 B8
Twyning Manor GL20 181 F8
Twyning Rd WR8 180 A10
Twyning Sch GL20 182 A7
Twynings The BS15 20 E2
Twyver Bank GL4 119 F3
Twyver Cl GL4 119 F3
Tybalt Way BS34 29 E5
Tylea Cl GL51 129 C7
Tyler Cl BS15 10 E5
Tyler Ct 3 GL51 132 E2
Tyler St BS2 9 A6
Tyler's La BS16 20 D5
Tylers Farm BS37 43 F4
Tylers Way Chalford GL6 148 C6
Sedbury NP16 61 B8
Yate BS37 43 F5
Yorkley GL15 156 B2
Tyndale Ave Bristol BS16 20 A4
Yate BS37 43 D3
Tyndale Cl GL11 79 E4
Tyndale Ct 7 BS6 18 B1
Tyndale Mon The* GL11 79 E4
Tyndale Rd Bristol BS15 20 E2
Dursley GL11 87 E4
Gloucester GL3 120 A8
Slimbridge GL2 95 B1
Tyndale View BS35 51 B8
Tyndall Ave BS8 194 C4
Tyndall Ho 6 BS2 195 C3
Tyndall Rd BS5 9 B8
Tyndall's Park Rd BS8 194 C4
Tyndalls Park Mews BS2 194 C4
Tyndalls Way BS10 18 E8
Tyne Ho 8 BS35 51 C8
Tyne Rd BS7 18 D3
Tyne St BS2 19 A2
Tyning Cl Bristol BS14 3 A7
Yate BS37 43 E2
Tyning Cres GL2 95 E3
Tyning Hengrove Jun Sch BS14 3 A7
Tyning Rd Bristol BS3 8 F3
Saltford BS31 5 E2
Tynings Ct GL3 128 D5
Tynings Rd GL6 91 A4
Tynings Sch The BS16 20 E4
Tynings The GL6 148 A4
Tynte Ave BS13 2 E3
Tyntesfield Rd BS13 2 A8
Tyrone Wlk BS4 2 E8
Tyrrel Way BS34 29 E5
Tythe Ct Dursley GL11 87 F5
Marshfield SN14 15 A8
Tythe Rd WR12 188 A1
Tythe Terr 19 GL54 174 A7
Tytherington Rd BS35 52 A6
Tythings Cres GL18 170 F4
Tythings Mews GL18 170 F4
Tythings The GL18 170 F4

U

Uley CE Prim Sch GL11 89 C1
Uley Long Barrow (Hetty Pegler's Tump)* GL11 89 B5
Uley Rd GL11 80 E8
Ullenwood Court Bsns Pk GL53 122 B7
Ullenwood Rd GL4 119 D7
Ullswater Cl Bristol BS30 11 D6
Yate BS37 43 E3
Ullswater Rd Bristol BS10 28 C1
Cheltenham GL51 129 E7
Underbanks BS20 16 D4
Undercliff Ave GL53 130 D3
Undercliff Terr GL53 130 D3
Underdown Ho BS1 195 A1
Underhill NP16 146 C4
Underhill Ct 12 GL4 119 C4
Underhill Rd
Charfield GL12 67 A5
Gloucester GL4 119 C4
Underwood Cl BS35 51 A4
Underwood Est NP25 154 B7
Unicorn Bsns Pk BS4 9 D5
Unicorn Pk BS4 9 D5
Union Ho GL50 193 B3
Union Pl GL20 192 D4
Union Rd 2 Bristol BS2 9 A6
Coleford GL16 155 B6
Union St Bristol BS1 195 B3
Cheltenham GL52 193 C4
Dursley GL11 80 B8
Gloucester GL1 196 C4
Stow-on-t-W GL54 176 F4
Stroud GL5 99 C7
Unite Ho BS1 194 C2
Unity Ct BS31 5 A5
Unity Rd BS31 5 A6
Unity St Bristol BS2 195 C3
Bristol,Brandon Hill BS1 194 C2
Bristol,Kingswood BS15 10 C8
Univ of Bristol BS8 194 C3

Univ of Bristol Dept of Economics BS8 ....194 C4
Univ of Bristol Dept of Ed BS8 ....194 C3
Univ of Bristol Sch of Veterinary Science BS2 ....194 C4
Univ of Gloucestershire (Hardwick Campus) GL50,GL51 ....133 C3
Univ of Gloucestershire (Oxstalls Campus) GL2 127 B3
Univ of Gloucestershire (Park Campus) GL53 ....130 C6
Univ of Gloucestershire (Pittville Campus) GL52 ....133 F4
Univ of Gloucestershire(Francis Close Hall) GL50 ......133 D3
Univ of the West of England BS3 ....7 E4
Univ of the West of England Faculty of Health & Social Care BS16 ....19 E5
Univ of the West of England Frenchay Campus BS16 .29 E1
Univ of the West of England, St Matthias Campus BS16 ....20 A5
University Cl BS9 ....17 F4
University Farm 17 GL56 ....187 A3
University Rd BS8 .....194 C3
University Wlk BS8 .....194 C3
Unlawater Ho GL14 .....157 A7
Unlawater La GL14 .....157 A7
Unwin Cl GL51 ....129 C7
Unwin Rd GL51 ....129 C7
Up Hatherley Way GL51 129 E5
Upcott SN6 ....143 E6
Upfield Cl GL5 ....98 F8
Upfield Prep Sch GL5 ...98 F8
Uphill Pl GL1 ....118 D5
Uphill Rd Bristol BS7 .....18 F5
Upper Lydbrook GL17 ....163 D2
Upjohn Cres BS13 ....2 D3
Uplands Com Prim Sch GL5 ....99 D8
Uplands Dr BS31 ....5 F2
Uplands Rd Bristol BS16 ..20 D3
Saltford BS31 ....5 F2
Stroud GL5 ....99 D8
Uplands View Terr GL5 ..99 D7
Upper Bath Rd BS35 ....51 B8
Upper Bath St GL50 ....193 B1
Upper Belgrave Rd BS8 .18 A2
Upper Belmont Rd BS7 ..18 E3
Upper Berkeley Pl BS8 .194 B3
Upper Bilson Rd GL14 ..191 C6
Upper Byron Pl BS8 ....194 B3
Upper Chapel La BS36 ...31 C7
Upper Cheltenham Pl BS6 ....18 E1
Upper Church La BS2 ..194 C3
Upper Church Rd GL5 ...98 E7
Upper Church St NP16 ...60 F8
Upper Comm GL15 .....147 D5
Upper Conham Vale BS15 ....10 A5
Upper Cranbrook Rd BS6 18 B4
Upper Cross 8 HR8 ....178 F8
Upper Dorrington Terr GL5 ....99 D6
Upper End Ct WR11 ....188 A6
Upper Hayes Rd GL6 ....91 A4
Upper Horfield Prim Sch BS7 ....19 A8
Upper Kitesnest La GL6 102 F4
Upper Leazes GL5 ......99 D7
Upper Lynch Rd GL6 ...148 D6
Upper Maudlin St BS2 .195 A3
Upper Mill La GL52 ....134 E5
Upper Mills Ind Est GL10 97 F6
Upper Myrtle Hill BS20 ..16 C4
Upper Nelson St NP16 ...60 E8
Upper Norwood St GL53 ....130 C6
Upper Park Rd GL6 .....91 C3
Upper Park St GL52 ....130 F8
Upper Perry Hill BS3 .....8 C4
Upper Poole Rd GL11 ....80 B8
Upper Quay Ho GL1 ....196 A3
Upper Quay St GL1 ....196 A3
Upper Queen's Rd 2 GL10 ....97 F7
Upper Rd Eastnor HR8 ..179 B8
Pillowell GL15 ....155 F1
Upper Rissington Bsns Pk GL54 ....169 D6
Upper Rodley Rd GL14 .157 F8
Upper Sandhurst Rd BS4 .9 D4
Upper Springfield Rd GL5 ....99 C8
Upper St Bristol BS4 ......9 A4
Dyrham SN14 ....23 D4
Upper Station Rd BS16 ..20 D4
Upper Stone Cl BS36 ....31 C7
Upper Stowfield Rd GL17 ....163 C4
Upper Sydney St BS3 .....8 B3
Upper Terr BS11 ....27 B1
Upper Tockington Rd BS32 ....50 A2
Upper Tynings GL6 ......91 A4
Upper Tynings The GL5 ..98 D8
Upper Washwell GL6 ...111 F1
Upper Wells St BS1 ....194 C3
Upper York St BS2 .....195 B4
Upperfield Rd GL51 ....133 A5
Upperhall Cl 4 HR8 ....178 F8
Upthorpe GL11 ....88 B5
Upthorpe La GL11 ....88 B6
Upton Cl GL4 ....119 E7
Upton Gdns GL8 ....140 B5
Upton Hill GL4 ....119 D1
Upton La
Brookthorpe GL4 ....111 B6
Gloucester GL4 ....119 F4
Maiden Head BS41 ....1 F1
Upton Rd BS3 ....8 B4
Upton St GL1 ....119 A8
Upton St Leonards CE Prim Sch GL4 ....119 F3
Upton's Gdn GL2 ......100 E5
Urfords Dr 1 BS16 ......20 C6
Usk Ct 5 BS35 ....51 C8
Usk Way GL3 ....120 F5
Utah Dr GL7 ....152 E2

V

Vaisey Field GL2 ....100 F5
Vaisey Rd GL7 ....190 B8
Vale Bank GL2 ....157 B6
Vale Ct Bristol BS8 ......194 A4
9 Cricklade SN6 ....143 E4
Vale La BS3 ....2 C8
Vale Rd GL7 ....190 B8
Vale St BS4 ....9 A4
Vale The BS16 ....21 F6
Valentine Cl Bristol BS14 ...3 B5
Chepstow NP16 ....61 A4
Valerian Cl Bristol BS11 ...16 F6
Gloucester GL4 ....119 E7
Valiant Way GL3 ....120 C7
Vallenders Rd GL20 ....182 C7
Valley Cl GL5 ....148 A5
Valley Cotts GL51 ......173 F1
Valley Gdns BS16 ......20 F8
Valley La GL4 ....120 A1
Valley Pk GL2 ....128 F8
Valley Rd
Bristol,Bedminster Down BS13 ....2 A8
Bristol,Mangotsfield BS16 ..21 A5
Bristol,Warmley BS30 .....11 D6
Cinderford GL14 ....191 C3
Leigh Woods BS8 ....7 C7
Lydney GL15 ....92 C2
Upper Lydbrook GL17 ....163 D1
Wotton-u-E GL12 ....68 C8
Valley View
Chedworth GL54 ....159 A6
Dursley GL11 ....87 F4
Valley View Pk GL54 ...168 E7
Valley View Rd GL5 .....99 F6
Valls The BS32 ....29 F6
Valma Rocks BS5 ....10 A6
Van Der Breen St GL6 ..105 B1
Vanbrugh La BS16 ......19 E7
Vandyck Ave BS31 ....4 F6
Vantage Point Bsns Village GL17 ....164 D5
Varley Ave GL3 ....120 B6
Varnister La GL17 ......163 F4
Varnister Rd GL17 ......163 F4
Vassall Ct BS16 ....20 B5
Vassall Rd BS16 ....20 B5
Vatch La GL5 ....148 B7
Vatch View GL5 ....103 E1
Vattingstone Ho BS35 ...50 F5
Vattingstone La BS35 ...50 F5
Vaughan Cl BS10 ....27 F3
Vauxhall GL18 ....170 F4
Vauxhall La NP16 ....60 D8
Vauxhall Rd
Chepstow/Cas-Gwent NP16 60 D8
Gloucester GL1 ....196 C1
Vauxhall Terr
3 Bristol BS3 ....8 A4
Gloucester GL1 ....196 C1
Vayre Cl BS37 ....44 C1
Veldt House Barns HR8 .178 B5
Velhurst Dr 1 GL6 .....148 B6
Velthouse La GL17 .....165 A5
Vennings The GL11 .....87 F6
Venns Acre GL12 ....68 B6
Vensfield Rd GL2 ......117 E2
Vention La GL17 ....163 D3
Ventnor Ave 1 BS5 ......9 F8
Ventnor Rd
Bristol,Filton BS34 ....29 B3
Bristol,St George BS5 .....19 F1
Venton Ct 5 BS15 ......10 B5
Vera Rd BS16 ....19 F2
Verbena Cl 2 GL4 .....119 E5
Vernal Cl GL4 ....119 F5
Vernals La GL12 ....67 C8
Verney Cl GL53 ....130 E6
Verney Rd GL10 ....97 F7
Verneys The GL53 .....130 E6
Vernon Cl BS31 ....5 D3
Vernon Pl GL53 ....193 C3
Vernon St 5 BS2 ....8 F4
Verrier Rd BS5 ....9 C7
Vertican Rd GL3 ....127 D6
Vervain Cl GL3 ....128 A7
Verwood Dr BS30 ....11 C2
Vestry Gdns GL4 ......119 C7
Vetch Cl GL4 ....119 A4
Viburnum Cl 6 GL50 ...130 B6
Viburnum View 4 GL4 ..119 F5
Vicarage Cl
Churchdown GL3 ....128 C4
Lydney GL15 ....92 A2
Shurdington GL51 ....129 E2
Vicarage Cotts
11 Bristol BS16 ....20 D5
12 Chipping Campden GL55 ....189 A2
Vicarage Ct Bristol BS15 ..10 B5
Brockworth GL3 ....120 E5
Vicarage La
Arlingham GL2 ....157 B5
Brockworth GL3 ....120 E6
Frampton on Severn GL2 ..157 F1
Highworth SN6 ....145 D3
Hillesley GL12 ....55 D8
Olveston BS35 ....50 B3
Vicarage Rd
Bristol,Bishopsworth BS13 ..2 A6
Bristol,Hanham BS15 .....10 B5
Bristol,Moorfields BS5 ......9 C8
Bristol,Southville BS3 ......8 B4
Coalpit Heath BS36 ....31 C6
Gloucester GL1 ....119 A7
Leigh Woods BS8 ....7 D6
Pilning BS35 ....38 C7
Vicarage St GL6 ....104 A8
Vicars Cl BS16 ....20 B4
Viceroy Cnr 7 GL50 ....193 A4
Vickers Rd GL54 ....169 D7
Victor Ho BS34 ....29 C7
Victor Rd BS3 ....8 C3
Victor St
9 Bristol,Russell Town BS5 .9 B6
Bristol,St Philip's Marsh BS2 .9 A4
Victoria Ave BS5 ....9 C7
Victoria Cl BS35 ....64 B3
Victoria Cotts
Quedgeley GL2 ....117 E3
4 Stonehouse GL10 ....97 F8
Victoria Cres BS35 ......38 A6
Victoria Ct
6 Bristol,Cotham BS6 ....18 D1
Bristol,Redland BS6 ....18 A3
Gloucester GL2 ....126 F6
Victoria Dr GL10 ....97 F7
Victoria Gdns 7 BS6 ....18 D1
Victoria Gr BS3 ....8 E4
Victoria Ho BS31 ....4 F4
Victoria Mans GL50 ....193 A3
Victoria Par BS5 ....9 C8
Victoria Park Com Inf Sch BS3 ....8 E3
Victoria Park Com Jun Sch BS3 ....8 E3
Victoria Pk
Bristol,Fishponds BS16 ....20 A5
Bristol,Kingswood BS15 ...20 D1
Victoria Pl Bristol BS3 .....8 C3
Cheltenham GL52 ....133 F1
Victoria Rd
Avonmouth BS11 ....16 B7
Brimscombe GL5 ....99 F1
Bristol,Hanham BS15 .....10 C5
Bristol,St Philip's Marsh BS2 .9 A5
Bristol,Warmley BS30 .....11 D5
Chepstow/Cas-Gwent NP16 60 F5
Cirencester GL7 ....190 D4
Coleford GL16 ....155 A5
Gloucester GL2 ....126 F6
Ledbury HR8 ....178 E8
Lydney GL15 ....92 A3
Quenington GL7 ....152 D7
Saltford BS31 ....5 D3
Victoria Retreat GL50 ..193 B1
Victoria Sq BS8 ....194 A3
Victoria St
6 Bourton-on-t-W GL54 ..168 F7
Bristol BS1 ....195 B2
Bristol,Staple Hill BS16 ...20 D5
Cheltenham GL50 ....133 D3
Cinderford GL14 ....191 C3
Cinderford GL14 ....191 C4
Gloucester GL1 ....196 C1
Painswick GL6 ....103 F8
Victoria Terr
9 Bourton-on-t-W GL54 ..168 F7
Bretforton WR11 ....188 A7
15 Bristol,Clifton BS8 ....7 F6
Bristol,St Philip's Marsh BS2 .9 B5
Cheltenham GL52 ....133 F1
Victoria Vale GL14 .....191 C4
Victoria Wlk BS6 ....18 D1
Victory Cl GL3 ....128 A8
Victory Rd
Gloucester GL1 ....118 F7
Whiteshill GL6 ....103 A3
Victory Villas GL7 ......152 F4
Vigor Rd BS13 ....2 B5
Villa The GL14 ....191 C2
Villa Way HR8 ....178 E7
Village Ave GL54 ......175 D2
Village Cl BS37 ....43 D1
Village Farm
Elberton BS35 ....50 A6
Preston GL7 ....150 F3
Village Mews GL51 ....132 F4
Village Rd GL51 ....132 F4
Village The Bristol BS16 ..21 C7
Westbury-on-S GL14 .....165 C1
Villiers Rd BS5 ....19 B1
Vilner La BS35 ....51 B7
Vilverie Mead GL52 ...137 D4
Vimpany Cl BS10 ....27 F3
Vimpennys La BS35 .....38 E1
Vincent Ave GL4 ....118 D1
Vincent Cl BS11 ....27 C2
Vincent Ct 2 BS16 ......20 D3
Vine Cotts NP16 ....60 E8
Vine Ct GL50 ....133 C3
Vine Hall GL15 ....147 E4
Vine Terr GL1 ....196 C4
Vine Way GL20 ....192 D1
Vinecroft GL13 ....85 E8
Viner's La GL9 ....36 B5
Vineries Cl GL53 ....130 C4
Vines The GL3 ....120 B7
Vineyard La GL12 ....67 F5
Vineyard St GL54 ......174 A7
Vineyard The WR12 ....184 E5
Vineyards Cl GL53 .....131 B4
Vineyards The GL51 ....133 A1
Vining Wlk 4 BS5 ....9 B8
Vinney La BS37 ....44 F8
Vinny Ave BS16 ....21 A7
Vintery Leys BS9 ....18 B7
Virginia Ave GL7 ....152 E2
Virginia Cl BS37 ....44 A1
Virginia Rd GL20 ......182 C4
Vittoria Wlk GL50 .....193 B2
Vivian St BS3 ....8 D3
Vizard Cl GL11 ....80 B8
Vorda Rd SN6 ....145 D4
Vowell Cl BS13 ....2 B4
Voxwell La GL52 ....137 E3
Voyager Cl BS34 ....30 A4
Voyce Cl GL4 ....118 D2
Vulcan Way GL4 ....119 F6
Vyners Cl GL7 ....190 C2
Vyvian Ct GL1 ....196 B2
Vyvyan Rd BS8 ....194 A3
Vyvyan Terr BS8 ....194 A3

W

Wad La GL19 ....180 F2
Wade Ct GL51 ....129 C7
Wade Hill SN6 ....145 C3
Wade Rd BS37 ....43 A3
Wade St BS2 ....195 C3
Wadehurst Ind Pk BS2 ....9 A7
Wades La GL6 ....103 C3
Wades Rd BS34 ....29 B3
Wadham Cl GL7 ....153 C6
Wadham Dr BS16 ....30 B1
Wadham Gr BS16 ....21 B5
Waggons La GL19 .....172 C4
Wagtail Dr GL20 ....182 B5
Wainbridge Cres BS35 ..38 D7
Wainbrook Dr BS5 ......19 D2
Wainland Pl GL16 ......154 F3
Wainlode La GL2 ......173 A3
Wakefield Cl GL7 ......144 F7
Wakeford Rd 1 BS16 ....21 A7
Wakeford Way BS30 .....11 D7
Wakeman Cl GL20 .....192 E2
Walden Rd BS31 ....5 A4
Waldrist Cl GL51 ....132 F5
Walford Prim Sch HR9 .163 C7
Walham La GL1 ....126 E4
Walk Mill La GL12 ......67 F4
Walk The GL12 ....67 F5
Walker Cl
Bristol,Downend BS16 .....21 A7
Bristol,Upper Easton BS5 ...9 B8
Walker Ct BS16 ....20 F5
Walker St BS2 ....194 C4
Walker Way BS35 ....51 B7
Walker's La GL17 ......163 F4
Walkers Gdn 14 GL54 ...168 A1
Walkley Hill GL5 ....99 A5
Walkley Rd GL20 ......192 D5
Wallace Appartments 11 GL52 ....193 C4
Wallace Ho GL51 ....129 F6
Wallbank Ho GL1 ......127 A3
Wallbridge GL5 ....99 B7
Wallbridge Ind Est GL5 ..99 B6
Wallcroft Ho BS6 ....18 A3
Walled Gdn The
Kingscote GL8 ....82 B5
Ledbury HR8 ....178 F8
Wallingford Rd BS4 ......2 D7
Walliscote Ave BS9 .....18 C6
Walliscote Rd BS9 ......18 C6
Wallow Gn GL6 ....90 F2
Wallscourt Rd BS34 .....29 B2
Wallscourt Rd S BS34 ...29 B1
Wallsend La SN14 ....24 C5
Wallsworth Hall Nature in Art Mus* GL2 ....173 A1
Wallwern Wood/Coed Wallwern NP16 ....72 C1
Walmer's View GL14 ...156 B6
Walmore Hill Prim Sch GL2 ....165 F1
Walnut Ave BS37 ....44 A2
Walnut Bank Dr GL20 ..183 A4
Walnut Cl Bristol BS15 ...20 F1
Broadway WR12 ....185 B8
Cheltenham GL52 ....133 E4
12 Coleford GL16 ....155 B5
Easton-in-G BS20 ....16 A3
Frampton Cotterell BS36 ...31 C6
Gloucester GL4 ....119 D3
Keynsham BS31 ....4 C4
Thornbury BS35 ....64 D1
Winchcombe GL54 ....139 F5
Walnut Cres BS15 ....10 F8
Walnut Ct GL20 ....183 A4
Walnut Dr SN14 ....15 F6
Walnut La BS15 ....11 A8
Walnut Tree Cl BS32 ....40 A5
Walnut Wlk Bristol BS13 ...2 A6
Walnut Wlk *continued*
Keynsham BS31 ....4 C4
Walsh Ave BS14 ....3 A7
Walshe Ave BS37 ....44 C1
Walsingham Rd BS6 .....18 E2
Walter Preston Ct GL5 ...98 E7
Walter Reynold Homes GL54 ....176 E5
Walter St BS3 ....8 A4
Walton Ave BS4 ....9 D5
Walton Cl Bristol BS30 ...11 C1
Keynsham BS31 ....4 D4
Upton St Leonards GL4 ...119 E3
Walton Dr GL20 ....192 F5
Walton Gdns GL20 .....192 F4
Walton Heath BS37 ......43 F1
Walton Ho
Cheltenham GL51 ....132 E2
Tewkesbury GL20 ....192 F4
Walton House Bglws 8 GL54 ....168 A1
Walton House Ct 9 GL54 ....168 A1
Walton Rd BS11 ....16 D6
Walton Rise BS9 ....18 A7
Walton St BS5 ....19 B1
Walwyn Cl GL17 ....164 D5
Walwyn Gdns BS13 ......2 C3
Wandsdyke Prim Sch BS14 ....2 F4
Wansbeck Rd BS31 ....5 A4
Wanscow Wlk BS9 ......18 B6
Wansdyke Ct BS14 ....3 B5
Wansdyke Workshops BS31 ....5 A6
Wantridge GL18 ....170 B8
Wapley Bank BS37 ......32 D5
Wapley Hill BS37 ....32 E4
Wapley Rd BS37 ....33 B3
Wapping Rd BS1 ....195 A1
Ward Ave GL3 ....127 E6
Ward Cl GL52 ....138 A4
Ward Ind Est GL15 ......84 A8
Ward Rd GL54 ....168 A1
Warden Hill Cl GL51 ...129 F6
Warden Hill Prim Sch GL51 ....130 A5
Warden Hill Rd GL51 ..130 A6
Warden Rd BS3 ....8 C4
Wardour Rd BS4 ....2 D8
Wards Rd GL51 ....129 D6
Ware Ct BS36 ....30 D5
Warend Hill Dursley GL11 .80 A6
North Nibley GL11 ....79 F6
Waring Ho BS1 ....195 A1
Warman Cl BS14 ....3 F6
Warman Rd BS14 ....3 F6
Warmington Rd BS14 .....3 C8
Warminster Rd BS2 .....19 A2
Warmley Park Sch BS30 .11 B7
Warneford Pl 23 GL56 ..187 A3
Warner Cl BS15 ....10 F6
Warns Ct 15 GL8 ....140 B4
Warns The BS30 ....11 A4
Warren Cl Bristol BS32 ...40 D3
Cheltenham GL51 ....129 F6
Churchdown GL3 ....128 A7
Warren Croft GL11 ......79 E4
Warren Dr 13 HR8 .....178 F8
Warren Gdns BS14 ....3 F5
Warren La HR9 ....170 A1
Warren Rd Bristol BS34 ...29 B3
Northway GL20 ....182 B4
Warren Slade NP16 .....60 F5
Warren Way BS37 ....43 E3
Warrens Gorse Cotts GL7 ....150 B8
Warrington Rd BS4 ....9 D2
Warth La Arlingham GL2 .157 C6
Northwick BS35 ....48 D3
Warwick Ave
7 Bristol BS5 ....19 B1
Gloucester GL4 ....118 C1
Warwick Cl Bristol BS30 ..11 B2
Chepstow/Cas-Gwent NP16 60 D6
3 Fairford GL7 ....152 E4
Stroud GL5 ....99 A4
Warwick Cres GL52 ....131 B6
Warwick Pl
Cheltenham GL52 ....193 C4
Tewkesbury GL20 ....192 D3
Thornbury BS35 ....64 A1
Warwick Rd
Bristol,Baptist Mills BS5 ...19 B1
Bristol,Redland BS6 ....18 B1
Keynsham BS31 ....4 D4
Washing Pound La BS14 ..3 B4
Washing's La NP25 ....154 C5
Washingpool Hill BS35 ..50 E1
Washingpool Hill Rd BS32 ....50 D2
Washingpool La BS11 ...26 F7
Washington Ave BS5 ....19 C1
Washpool La
Fairford GL7 ....152 F1
Kempsford GL7 ....144 F8
Wasley Rd GL51 ....132 E1
Watch Elm Cl BS32 ......29 E6
Watch House Rd BS20 ..16 D4
Watchill Ave BS13 ....1 F6
Watchill Cl BS13 ....1 F6
Water Furlongs SN6 ...143 E4
Water La Brimscombe GL5 .99 E1
Bristol BS1 ....195 B2
Bristol,Hanham Green BS15 10 B2
Bristol,Upper Knowle BS4 ...9 D2
Bristol,Windmill Hill BS3 ....8 F3
Charlton Kings GL52 .....131 B6

Water La *continued*
Pill BS20 16 C4
Woodchester GL5 98 F3
Wotton-u-E GL12 68 B6
Water Mdw GL2 109 E7
Water St GL11 88 B1
Water Wheel Cl 7 GL2 117 D1
Water's La BS9 18 A7
Waterbridge Rd BS13 1 F4
Watercress Rd BS2 18 F3
Waterdale Cl Bristol BS9 18 C7
Hardwicke GL2 109 D8
Waterdale Gdns BS9 18 C7
Waterfield Cl GL53 193 B1
Waterford Cl BS35 51 D8
Waterford Ct GL53 130 C6
Waterford Rd BS9 18 B6
Watergrip La GL20 183 A8
Waterloo Bsns Pk GL17 163 D2
Waterloo Cl GL20 182 D7
Waterloo Ho BS20 16 D5
Waterloo La GL7 152 E3
Waterloo Pl 21 BS2 195 C3
Waterloo Rd BS2 195 C3
Waterloo St Bristol BS2 195 C3
11 Bristol,Clifton BS8 7 F7
Cheltenham GL51 133 B3
Waterloo The GL7 190 D5
Waterloo Way GL20 182 D7
Watermans Ct 4 GL2 117 D1
Watermead GL15 92 A3
Watermill Cl GL12 65 E7
Watermoor CE Prim Sch GL7 190 D3
Watermoor Cl GL51 132 D4
Watermoor Ct GL3 128 B5
Watermoor Rd GL7 190 D3
Watermoor Way GL7 190 D3
Watermore Cl BS36 31 C7
Waters Rd BS15 10 C8
Waters Reach GL2 118 B6
Waters Way NP16 60 E7
Watershoot Cl GL52 134 A5
Waterside 3 GL20 192 C4
Waterside Cl
Andoversford GL54 166 D6
Quedgeley GL2 117 D1
Waterside Dr BS32 40 A1
Waterton Cl GL3 120 B6
Waterwells Dr GL2 110 A6
Watery La Doynton BS30 13 A8
Frampton on Severn GL2 157 F2
Gloucester GL4 111 F8
Kinsham GL20 182 D6
Lea HR9 164 C8
Lydney GL15 147 F5
Minsterworth GL2 117 B7
Newent GL18 170 F4
Wathen Rd BS6 18 F3
Watkins Cnr SN5 143 E1
Watkins Terr GL11 88 E8
Watkins Yd BS9 18 A8
Watledge Bank GL6 91 B5
Watledge Cl GL20 192 D4
Watledge Rd GL6 91 B5
Watley's End Rd BS36 30 F7
Watling Way BS11 16 D7
Watson Ave BS4 9 D4
Watson Gr GL4 119 F5
Watson Ho 5 GL52 193 C4
Watson's Rd BS30 10 F3
Watters Cl BS36 31 D6
Watts Cl Berkeley GL13 85 E4
Gloucester GL3 120 B7
Wavell Cl BS37 43 D3
Waveney Rd BS31 5 A3
Waverley Rd
Bristol,Cotham BS6 18 C1
Bristol,Shirehampton BS11 16 E6
Gloucester GL2 127 C2
Yate BS37 43 B2
Waverley St 8 BS5 19 A1
Waycroft Prim Sch BS14 3 E5
Wayend St HR8 179 C7
Wayford Cl BS31 5 A3
Wayland Ct 7 BS16 20 A4
Waylands SN6 143 F4
Wayleaze
Coalpit Heath BS36 31 D7
Wapley BS37 32 F3
Wayridge The GL4 119 D4
Wayside Cl BS36 31 B7
WCA Ho BS1 195 A2
Weald Cl GL4 119 C5
Weare Ct BS1 194 A1
Weavers Cl Dursley GL11 80 B8
Kingswood GL12 67 F4
Weavers Dr GL11 89 B1
Weavers Ho 17 GL5 99 C7
Weavers Rd
Cirencester GL7 190 E4
Quedgeley GL2 117 F2
Weavers Row GL5 99 F1
Webb Rd GL8 140 B5
Webb St BS5 9 A8
Webber Ho GL20 192 B3
Webbs Heath BS30 11 E8
Webbs Wood BS32 29 F7
Webbs Wood Rd BS32 29 F7
Webley Rd GL17 163 F3
Wedgewood Cotts WR12 184 E5
Wedgewood Cres GL14 191 D6
Wedgewood Rd BS16 30 D1
Wedgwood Cl BS14 3 B5
Wedgwood Dr GL2 127 C4
Wedlock Way BS3 7 F3
Wedmore Cl BS15 10 F7
Wedmore Rd BS31 5 D4
Wedmore Vale BS3 8 E2
Weedon Cl 6 BS2 19 A2
Weigh Bridge Ct GL55 189 A2
Weight Rd 2 BS5 9 C7
Weir Bridge Cl GL4 119 E8
Weir La SN14 14 F8
Welch Ho GL51 129 D2
Welch Rd GL51 132 E4
Welcomyn 11 GL6 148 C6
Well Alley GL20 192 C5
Well Cl
Chepstow/Cas-Gwent NP16 60 F4
Long Ashton BS41 7 B1
Northway GL20 182 C5
Well Cross Rd GL4 119 A4
Well End GL5 99 E8
Well Hill GL6 148 A3
Well House Cl BS9 17 E3
Well La Badminton GL9 46 E5
Drybrook GL17 164 A4
Guiting Power GL54 175 B3
Stow-on-t-W GL54 176 F4
Well Pl GL50 133 B1
Well Vale La HR9 162 D3
Welland Ct GL52 134 A4
Welland Dr GL52 134 A4
Welland Lodge Rd GL52 134 A4
Welland Rd Keynsham BS31 4 F4
Quedgeley GL2 117 F2
Wellbrook Rd GL52 137 F5
Weller Bglws GL2 118 C4
Wellesley Prim Sch BS37 32 D6
Wellesley Rd GL50 133 E3
Wellesley St GL1 118 F6
Wellfield GL20 192 F5
Wellgarth Ct BS4 9 A2
Wellgarth Rd BS4 9 A2
Wellgarth Wlk BS4 9 A2
Welling Cl GL11 80 C7
Wellington Ave BS6 18 E1
Wellington Aviation Mus* GL56 187 A3
Wellington Cres BS7 18 E6
Wellington Ct 11 BS6 18 E1
Wellington Dr Bristol BS9 18 D6
Yate BS37 43 B2
Wellington Hill BS7 18 E6
Wellington Hill W BS9 18 D7
Wellington Ho GL7 190 D5
Wellington La Bristol BS6 18 E1
Cheltenham GL52 133 E3
Wellington Lodge Cl GL20 182 D7
Wellington Mews BS11 16 D5
Wellington Par GL1 196 C3
Wellington Pk BS8 18 A2
Wellington Pl Bristol BS16 30 B1
Cheltenham GL52 193 C2
Wellington Rd
Bristol BS2 195 C4
Bristol,Kingswood BS15 20 D2
Cheltenham GL52 133 E3
10 Moreton-in-M GL56 187 B3
Upper Rissington GL54 169 D6
Yate BS37 43 E3
Wellington Sq GL50 133 E3
Wellington St
Cheltenham GL50 193 C3
Gloucester GL1 196 B2
Wellington Terr
18 Bristol BS8 7 F6
8 Moreton-in-M GL56 187 B3
Newnham GL14 156 F6
Wellington Wlk BS10 18 C7
Wellmeadow GL16 154 D7
Wellmeadow La GL16 155 A8
Wells Cl Bristol BS14 3 C5
Cheltenham GL51 129 F5
Wells Gdns 5 WR12 185 C8
Wells Rd Bisley GL6 148 D8
Bristol BS4 9 B2
Gloucester GL4 119 C8
Maiden Head BS41 1 E1
Wells St BS3 8 A4
Wellsprings Ho GL2 127 C3
Wellsprings Rd GL2 127 C3
Wellstead Ave BS37 43 D1
Wellsway BS31 4 F3
Wellsway Sec Sch BS31 5 A5
Welsford Ave BS16 19 D4
Welsford Rd BS16 19 C4
Welsh Back BS1 195 A2
Welsh House La GL18 170 F8
Welsh St NP16 72 D1
Welsh Way
Bagendon GL7 158 D1
Fairford GL7 152 B5
Sunhill GL7 151 F7
Welton Wlk BS15 20 C2
Welveland La GL4 127 E1
Welwyn Mews 4 GL51 129 E5
Wenchford Forest Trail* GL15 156 C2
Wend The GL17 164 F5
Wendover Gdns GL50 133 B1
Wenlock Rd GL20 192 D3
Wenmore Cl BS16 30 D1
Wentforth Dr 2 BS15 20 C2
Wentsfield GL10 96 F7
Wentworth Bristol BS30 11 A6
Yate BS37 43 E1
Wentworth Cl
Cheltenham GL51 132 D3
Gloucester GL2 127 B5
Wentworth Rd Bristol BS7 18 D3
Cheltenham GL51 132 D3
Werth La GL19 181 B1
Wescott Gr BS11 27 C2
Wesley Ave BS15 10 D5
Wesley Cl Aylburton GL15 147 E4
7 Bristol,Upper Soundwell BS16 20 D3
Bristol,Whitehall BS5 19 D1
Wesley Ct
Gloucester GL1 196 C2
16 Stroud GL5 99 C7
Wesley Hill BS15 20 D1
Wesley Ho GL50 193 B4
Wesley La BS30 11 B5
Wesley Pl BS8 18 A2
Wesley Rd Bristol BS7 18 E4
Cinderford GL14 191 D5
Leonard Stanley GL10 97 E3
Whitecroft GL15 155 F1
Wesley St BS3 8 C3
Wesley Theological Coll BS10 27 F1
Wessex Ave BS7 18 F7
Wessex Ct BS7 18 F7
Wessex Dr GL52 134 B2
Wessex Ho 11 BS2 195 C3
Wessex Way SN6 145 D4
West Allcourt GL7 153 E2
West Approach Dr GL52 133 E4
West Ave GL17 164 B4
West Broadway BS9 18 D6
West Coombe BS9 17 D6
West Country Water Pk* BS36 40 F2
West Croft BS9 18 C7
West Dene BS9 17 E6
West Dr GL50 133 E3
West Dundry La BS41 1 E2
West End Avening GL8 140 A8
Bristol,Kingsdown BS2 195 A4
Bristol,Southville BS3 194 C1
Coaley GL11 96 D1
Kingham OX7 177 F2
Minchinhampton GL6 148 A3
Northleach GL54 168 A1
Oldbury-on-S BS35 63 C6
Ruardean GL17 163 E4
West End Gdns GL7 152 D4
West End La
Broadway WR12 185 B7
Gloucester GL3 120 B6
West Field GL2 125 D5
West Gr BS6 18 F1
West Grange Ct GL5 99 B8
West Hay Gr GL7 141 F8
West Hill SN26 144 D2
West La GL7 141 F8
West Leaze Pl BS32 29 E6
West Littleton Rd SN14 24 E2
West Lodge Dr GL4 119 D6
West Mall BS8 7 F7
West Market Pl GL7 190 C5
West Mill La SN6 143 E4
West Par BS9 17 C7
West Park Rd BS16 20 E5
West Pk BS8 194 B4
West Point Row BS32 40 C3
West Priory Cl BS9 18 A7
West Ridge BS36 31 C7
West Rocke Ave BS9 17 D6
West Shrubbery 5 BS6 18 B2
West St Bristol BS2 195 C3
Bristol,Bedminster BS3 8 C3
2 Bristol,Kingswood BS15 10 D8
Bristol,Oldland Common BS30 11 C4
Kingham OX7 177 F3
Tetbury GL8 140 B4
Tytherington GL12 52 B5
West Town Ave BS4 9 D1
West Town Dr 2 BS4 9 D1
West Town Gr BS4 3 D8
West Town La BS4 9 D1
West Town Lane Inf Sch BS4 9 C1
West Town Lane Jun Sch BS4 9 C1
West Town Pk BS4 9 D1
West Town Rd BS11 16 C7
West Tynings GL6 91 A4
West View Alveston BS35 50 F4
Bristol BS16 21 A6
Cinderford GL14 191 D3
Joy's Green GL17 163 D3
Newent GL18 170 F4
Newnham GL14 156 F7
Poulton GL7 151 F3
Wotton-u-E GL12 68 C7
West View Rd Bristol BS3 8 B3
Keynsham BS31 4 E5
West Way
Bristol BS10,BS34 28 E4
Cirencester GL7 190 C4
Lechlade on T GL7 153 E3
West Wlk BS37 43 E1
Westacre Cl BS10 28 A2
Westal Gn 15 GL50 130 B8
Westal Pk GL51 130 B7
Westbourne WR11 188 C7
Westbourne Ave BS31 4 E5
Westbourne Cl 2 BS16 21 A7
Westbourne Ct BS5 9 B8
Westbourne Dr
Cheltenham GL52 133 F2
Hardwicke GL2 109 E7
Westbourne Gr 9 BS3 8 C3
Westbourne Ho 12 GL52 133 F2
Westbourne Pl BS8 194 B3
Westbourne Rd
Bristol,Downend BS16 20 F8
Westbourne Rd *continued*
8 Bristol,Upper Easton BS5 9 B8
Westbourne Terr BS16 20 B7
Westbrook Rd BS4 3 D8
Westbrooke Ct BS1 194 A1
Westbury Court Gdns* GL14 157 C8
Westbury Court Rd BS9 18 A7
Westbury Ct BS9 18 A7
Westbury Hill BS9 18 A7
Westbury La BS9 17 C7
Westbury Mews 6 BS9 18 A7
Westbury Park Prim Sch BS6 18 B3
Westbury Pk BS6 18 A4
Westbury Rd Bristol BS6 18 A4
Cheltenham GL53 130 E4
Gloucester GL4 118 D3
Westbury-on-Severn CE Prim Sch GL14 165 C1
Westbury-on-Trym CE Prim Sch BS9 18 A8
Westcote Rd GL4 118 E1
Westcourt Dr BS30 11 B4
Westdown Gdns GL52 133 F1
Westend GL11 87 D4
Westend Cross GL10 101 A2
Westend La BS35 63 B6
Westend Par GL1 126 C3
Westend Rd GL12 53 E5
Westend Terr
Chipping Campden GL55 188 F2
Gloucester GL1 126 C3
Westering Cl BS16 21 A5
Westerleigh Bsns Pk BS37 43 B1
Westerleigh Cl BS16 20 F7
Westerleigh Rd
Bristol BS16 20 F6
Coalpit Heath BS36 31 D2
Pucklechurch BS16 22 C7
Westerleigh BS36,BS37 32 B5
Yate BS37 32 C8
Westerley Cl GL14 191 D3
Western Approach Distribution Pk BS35 38 C4
Western Ave
Chepstow/Cas-Gwent NP16 60 F5
Frampton Cotterell BS36 42 A1
Mitcheldean GL17 164 D5
Western Ct Bristol BS34 30 A4
6 Cheltenham GL50 133 B1
Western Dr BS14 2 E6
Western Grange BS34 29 A3
Western Hill Rd GL20 183 B5
Western Rd Bristol BS7 18 E6
Cheltenham GL50 193 A3
Western Way GL18 178 D2
Westfield Dursley GL11 88 A2
Llangrove HR9 162 B6
Westfield Ave
Brockworth GL3 120 D6
Northway GL20 182 C4
Westfield Cl Bristol BS15 10 D5
Keynsham BS31 4 C5
Westfield Cotts GL51 136 B3
Westfield Ct GL14 191 D5
Westfield Gn GL7 152 A3
Westfield Ho BS9 17 F5
Westfield La BS34 29 E3
Westfield Pk BS6 18 B1
Westfield Pl BS8 7 F7
Westfield Rd Bristol BS9 18 A8
Brockworth GL3 120 D6
Cinderford GL14 191 D5
Westfield Terr GL2 126 E5
Westfield Way BS32 40 D2
Westfields GL12 68 A7
Westgate BS1 194 B1
Westgate St GL1 196 A3
Westhill Cl SN6 145 C3
Westland Ave BS30 11 C4
Westland Rd GL2 109 D7
Westleigh Cl Bristol BS10 28 D1
Yate BS37 43 C1
Westleigh Ct BS37 43 C1
Westleigh Pk BS14 3 B8
Westleigh Rd BS10 28 D1
Westmarsh BS35 63 B5
Westmarsh La BS35 63 B5
Westmead Rd Bristol BS5 10 B7
Gloucester GL2 127 D5
Westminster Cl
1 Bristol BS9 18 A7
Cheltenham GL53 130 F7
Westminster Ct 3 GL2 127 B2
Westminster Rd BS5 9 D8
Westmoreland Rd BS6 18 B3
Westmorland Ho BS6 18 A3
Westmorland Terr BS37 34 D7
Weston Ave 4 BS5 9 D7
Weston Cl BS9 17 C7
Weston Cotts SN7 145 E8
Weston Cres BS7 18 E6
Weston Ind Est WR11 188 D4
Weston Park Prim Sch BS11 16 F8
Weston Rd
Bretforton WR11 188 B5
Gloucester GL1 196 B1
Honeybourne WR11 188 C6
Long Ashton BS41 7 A1
Westonbirt Arboretum* GL8 58 B8
Westonbirt Sch GL8 58 E8
Westonian Ct BS9 17 C4
Westons Brake BS16 31 A1
Westons Hill Dr BS16 31 A1
Westons Way BS15 10 F7
Westover Cl BS9 27 F1
Westover Ct GL3 128 B7
Westover Dr BS9 28 A1
Westover Gdns BS9 17 F8
Westover Rd BS9 28 A1
Westover Rise BS9 28 A1
Westpoint Trad Est BS15 10 D7
Westridge Rd GL12 68 A8
Westrip Pl GL5 98 D8
Westrop SN6 145 D3
Westrop Prim Sch SN6 145 C3
Westview GL19 173 C7
Westward BS41 7 B2
Westward Ct GL5 98 D6
Westward Dr BS20 16 C4
Westward Gdns BS41 7 B2
Westward Rd Bristol BS13 1 F7
Stroud GL5 98 D6
Westwick Rd GL19 165 D6
Westwood Cres BS4 9 D5
Westwood La GL52 134 D3
Westwood Rd BS4 3 D8
Wetherby Ct BS16 30 F1
Wetherby Gr 1 BS16 30 F1
Wetherell Pl BS8 194 B3
Wetherleigh Dr GL2 125 E5
Wexford Rd BS4 2 D8
Weyhouse Cl GL5 99 D5
Weymouth Rd BS3 8 D2
Whaddon Ave GL52 134 A2
Whaddon Dr GL52 133 F2
Whaddon Prim Sch GL52 134 B2
Whaddon Rd GL52 134 A2
Whaddon Road (Cheltenham Town FC) GL52 133 F3
Whaddon Way GL4 118 D1
Wharf La Kempsford GL7 144 E7
Lechlade on T GL7 153 E2
Wharf Rd 5 BS16 19 F4
Wharf The GL19 173 E6
Wharfdale Sq GL51 132 F3
Wharfdale Way
Hardwicke GL2 109 D8
Stonehouse GL10 97 E6
Wharfedale BS35 51 D8
Wharfings The GL7 144 E7
Wharncliffe Cl BS14 3 B5
Wharncliffe Gdns BS14 3 B5
Whartons 8 BS4 9 D1
Whatley Ct 9 BS8 18 B1
Whatley Rd BS8 18 B1
Wheal Cl GL20 182 C4
Wheal Rd GL20 182 C4
Wheat Cl GL56 177 A6
Wheat Hill 2 GL8 140 B4
Wheatfield Ct GL55 189 A6
Wheatfield Dr BS32 40 D1
Wheatfield Prim Sch BS32 40 D1
Wheathill Cl BS31 4 D5
Wheatland Dr GL51 132 D4
Wheatridge E The GL4 119 E4
Wheatridge The GL4 119 D4
Wheatsheaf Dr GL52 137 D4
Wheatsheaf La SN16 142 A4
Wheatstone Cl GL20 182 C5
Wheatstone Rd GL1 118 F7
Wheatway GL4 119 D3
Wheelers Patch BS16 21 B5
Wheelers Rise GL5 98 F8
Wheelers Wlk GL5 98 F8
Wheelwrights Cnr 3 GL6 91 B4
Whelford Rd GL7 144 E8
Whetstones GL14 157 A7
Whimbrel Rd GL2 117 D1
Whimsey Rd GL14 191 B6
Whinchat Gdns BS16 19 F6
Whip La GL6 91 B5
Whippington Ct BS1 195 B3
Whippington's Cnr GL16 154 E7
Whitby Rd BS4 9 C4
Whitchurch CE Prim Sch HR9 162 E4
Whitchurch District Ctr BS14 3 A5
Whitchurch La
Bristol,Bishopsworth BS13 2 B5
Bristol,Hartcliffe BS13 2 C5
Bristol,Whitchurch BS14 2 E5
Dundry BS41 2 C1
Whitchurch Rd BS13 2 A6
Whitchurch Under Fives BS14 3 C4
White Cotts GL5 98 E6
White Cross Rd GL15 92 A2
White End GL19 172 D4
White Hart Ct GL7 152 E3
White Hart La 18 GL54 176 F4
White Hart St GL51 133 C3
White Horse La GL6 103 F8
White Horse Rd SN6 143 E4
White House Bsns Ctr The BS15 10 D7
White Lodge Rd BS16 20 F4
White St BS5 195 C4
White Tree Rbdt BS6 18 A4
White Tree Rd BS9 18 B4
Whitebeam Cl GL2 127 B5
Whitebeam Ct BS5 9 E8
Whitebeam Ho 7 BS16 20 C6

Whitechapel Rd 8 GL15 155 D1
Whitecourt GL11 89 A1
Whitecroft GL6 91 B4
Whitecroft Rd GL15 155 E1
Whitecroft Sta★ GL15 155 F1
Whitecroft Way BS15 11 A7
Whitecross Ave BS14 3 C6
Whitecross Sch GL15 92 A2
Whitecross Sq GL53 193 C1
Whitecross St 19 NP25 154 A7
Whitefield Ave
Bristol,Hanham BS15 10 D5
Bristol,Speedwell BS5 20 A1
Whitefield Cl
8 Bristol BS16 20 D3
Stonehouse GL10 97 F6
Whitefield Fishponds Com Sch BS16 19 F4
Whitefield Rd BS5 20 A2
Whitefields BS37 44 C1
Whitefields Rd GL52 137 D4
Whitefriars La SN6 142 F6
Whitegates BS36 30 D6
Whitehall GL5 99 D7
Whitehall Ave BS5 19 E1
Whitehall Gdns BS5 19 D1
Whitehall La GL2 124 E6
Whitehall Prim Sch BS5 19 D1
Whitehall Rd BS5 9 C8
Whitehall Trad Est 4 BS5 9 C8
Whitehart Ho GL51 133 C3
Whitehill La GL17 164 B4
Whitehouse Ctr BS13 2 C5
Whitehouse Farm GL14 165 D1
Whitehouse La Bristol BS3 8 D4
Gorsley HR9,GL18 170 C5
Pilning BS35 38 C7
Tetbury GL8 140 C1
Whitehouse Pk GL5 98 E7
Whitehouse Pl BS3 8 E4
Whitehouse St BS3 8 E4
Whitehouse Way GL52 138 B3
Whiteladies Rd BS8 194 B4
Whitelands La
Little Shurdington GL51 121 C8
Little Shurdington GL51 121 D8
Whitelands Rd GL7 190 E5
Whiteleaze BS10 18 C8
Whitemarsh Cl GL51 132 D4
Whitemead Ho 3 BS3 8 A3
Whites Hill BS5 10 A6
Whiteshill BS16 30 D3
Whiteshill Prim Sch GL6 102 F3
Whitethorn Cotts GL51 133 A7
Whitethorn Dr GL52 134 C3
Whitewall La BS35 64 F1
Whitewater Rd GL8 70 C4
Whiteway GL11 80 C6
Whiteway Cl
Bristol,St Anne's Park BS4 9 E6
Bristol,St George BS5 10 A8
Dursley GL11 80 C7
Whiteway Ct
1 Bristol BS5 10 A8
Cirencester GL7 190 D6
Whiteway Mews BS5 10 A8
Whiteway Rd
Bristol BS5,BS15 20 A1
Gloucester GL4 119 B5
Whiteway View GL7 190 B7
Whitewell Cl GL4 119 E7
Whitewood Rd BS5 19 F1
Whitfield Ho 7 BS15 10 D8
Whitfield Rd BS35 64 C2
Whitfield St GL1 196 B2
Whitford Cl WR11 188 A6
Whiting Rd BS13 2 A4
Whitland Ave BS13 2 B5
Whitland Rd BS13 2 B5
Whitley Cl BS37 43 C3
Whitley Mead BS34 29 E3
Whitlow La GL19 165 E5
Whitmead Gdns BS13 2 C4
Whitminster CE Prim Sch GL2 100 E5
Whitminster La GL2 100 A6
Whitmore Ave BS4 10 A3
Whitmore Rd GL54 174 A8
Whitmores The GL54 176 C1
Whitson Ho 2 BS2 195 C3
Whitson St BS1 195 A4
Whittingham Hall GL14 156 E5
Whittington Ct★ GL54 166 C7
Whittington Ho GL5 99 A7
Whittington Rd
Bristol BS16 20 C6
Cheltenham GL51 129 D8
Whittington Way GL15 147 D8
Whittington Wlk 18 GL18 171 A4
Whittle Ave GL4 118 D2
Whittle Cl GL51 129 C8
Whittles La GL2 157 F2
Whittlestone Cl GL54 176 D4
Whittlestone Hollow GL54 176 D4
Whittock Rd BS14 3 D6
Whittock Sq BS14 3 D7
Whittucks Cl BS15 10 D4
Whittucks Rd BS15 10 C4
Whitwell Rd BS14 3 B8
Whitworth Mews GL3 120 C6
Whitworth Rd GL7 190 C3
Whornes Orch GL4 119 F3
Whytes Cl BS9 18 A8
Wick CE Prim Sch BS30 12 B6
Wick Cres BS4 9 D3
Wick House Cl BS31 5 D3
Wick La
Lower Apperley GL19 173 C6
Upton Cheyney BS30 12 A2
Wick Rd Bristol BS4 9 D4
Oaksey SN16 142 A4
Pilning BS35 38 C7
Wick St GL6 103 E4
Wick Wick Cl BS16,BS36 31 A2
Wickets The
Bristol,Filton BS7 28 F1
Bristol,Upper Soundwell BS15 20 D2
Wicketts The BS7 28 F2
Wickfield La GL52 138 F4
Wickham Cl BS37 33 D8
Wickham Ct BS16 19 D5
Wickham Glen BS16 19 D5
Wickham Hill BS16 19 D5
Wickham View BS16 19 D4
Wicklow Rd BS4 2 E8
Wickridge Cl GL5 99 C8
Wickwar Rd
Kingswood GL12 67 E4
Rangeworthy BS37 53 B1
Yate BS37 44 B5
Wickwater La GL7 143 B6
Widcombe BS14 3 A6
Widcombe Cl 3 BS5 10 A7
Widden Prim Sch GL1 196 C2
Widden St GL1 196 C2
Widhill La SN26 144 D1
Widmore Gr BS13 2 B5
Wigeon La GL20 192 E3
Wigmore Cl 5 GL4 119 E6
Wigton Cres BS10 28 C2
Wilbye Gr BS4 2 D7
Wilcox Cl BS15 10 C6
Wildcroft Ho BS9 18 B4
Wildcroft Rd BS9 18 B4
Wilder Ct BS2 195 B4
Wilder Ho BS2 195 B4
Wilder St BS2 195 B4
Wildfowl & Wetlands Trust Slimbridge★ GL2 95 A6
Wildlife Wlk GL3 120 E4
Wildmoorway La GL7 143 A8
Wildwood Residential Cvn Pk GL7 190 F2
Wilkes Ave GL3 120 A8
Wilkes Mdw GL16 155 B6
Wilkinson Rd GL7 190 D1
Willada Cl BS3 8 B2
Willcox Dr GL52 138 B3
Willersey Bsns Pk WR12 188 B3
Willersey CE Prim Sch WR12 188 B2
Willersey Rd GL51 129 E8
William Emes Gdn GL56 186 C7
William Gough Cl GL51 132 D5
William Mason Cl 19 BS5 9 B7
William St
Bristol,Fishponds BS16 20 B3
8 Bristol,Moorfields BS5 9 C8
Bristol,Newton BS2 9 A6
Bristol,St Pauls BS2 18 F1
Bristol,Windmill Hill BS3 8 E4
Williams Cl BS30 10 F3
Williams Orch GL2 125 D5
Williamson Rd BS7 18 F3
Williamstrip Farm Cotts GL7 160 F1
Willinton Rd BS4 2 F8
Willis Est BS2 18 F3
Willis Rd BS15 20 F2
Willis Wlk GL20 182 C5
Willment Way BS11 26 D1
Willmott Cl BS14 2 F3
Willoughby Cl
Alveston BS35 51 A4
Bristol BS13 2 B7
Willoughby Rd BS7 18 E5
Willow Ave GL4 119 B7
Willow Bank BS10 18 C7
Willow Bank Rd GL20 183 D4
Willow Bed Cl BS16 20 B6
Willow Cl
Ashton under Hill WR11 183 D8
Bristol,Patchway BS34 28 E7
Bristol,Warmley BS30 11 D6
Charfield GL12 67 A4
Chepstow/Cas-Gwent NP16 60 D6
Dursley GL11 88 A3
Wick BS30 12 B6
Woodmancote GL52 138 B3
Willow Ct BS7 19 A7
Willow Cvn Site GL2 126 D5
Willow Dr GL52 138 B4
Willow Gr 1 Bristol BS16 20 C2
South Cerney GL7 143 A8
Willow Ho BS13 2 D4
Willow Hts GL15 92 B5
Willow Park Dr GL52 137 F4
Willow Rd Bristol BS15 10 C3
Charlton Kings GL53 131 C5
King's Stanley GL10 98 A4
Stonehouse GL10 97 E7
Willersey WR12 188 B2
Willow Sh Ctr The BS16 20 E6
Willow Way
Coalpit Heath BS36 31 C6
Gloucester GL4 119 B7
Willow Wlk Bristol BS10 28 B3
Willow Wlk *continued*
Keynsham BS31 4 D4
Willowbrook Dr GL51 132 D4
Willowcroft Cl GL4 119 D3
Willowdean GL14 191 C5
Willowherb Cl GL52 134 C3
Willowleaze GL2 127 D3
Willows The Bristol BS16 20 E4
Bristol,Bradley Stoke BS32 29 D8
Bristol,Frenchay BS16 30 B1
Coalpit Heath BS36 31 F7
Dymock GL18 178 D2
Gloucester GL1 196 C4
Highworth SN6 145 D3
Longhope GL17 164 F5
Quedgeley GL2 117 E1
Yate BS37 43 D2
Wills Dr BS5 9 A8
Wills Way BS13 2 D6
Willsbridge Hill BS30 11 A2
Willsbridge Mill★ BS30 11 A2
Willway St BS3 8 D4
Wilmot Ct BS30 11 A6
Wilmots Way BS20 16 D4
Wilshire Ave BS15 10 D5
Wilson Pl BS2 195 C4
Wilson Rd GL51 129 D1
Wilson St BS2 195 C4
Wilton Cl Bristol BS10 28 C2
Gloucester GL1 118 D6
Wilton Rd GL1 118 D6
Wiltshire Ave BS37 44 A3
Wiltshire Pl BS15 20 E3
Wilverley Ind Est BS4 9 E1
Wimbledon Rd BS6 18 C5
Wimborne Cl GL51 129 E6
Wimborne Rd BS3 8 C1
Winash Cl BS14 3 D7
Wincanton Cl BS16 30 F1
Wincel Rd GL54 174 A7
Winchcombe Abbey CE Prim Sch GL54 174 A7
Winchcombe Folk & Police Mus★ GL54 174 A7
Winchcombe Gr BS11 16 F5
Winchcombe Hospl GL54 139 F4
Winchcombe Railway Mus★ GL54 174 A7
Winchcombe Rd
Dumbleton WR11 184 A8
Frampton Cotterell BS36 31 B8
Gloucester GL4 118 E2
Winchcombe Sch GL54 174 A8
Winchcombe St GL52 193 C4
Winchcombe Sta GL54 174 A8
Winchester Ave BS4 9 D3
Winchester Ct BS16 19 E6
Winchester Dr GL4 118 E3
Winchester Ho 5 GL50 133 B1
Winchester Rd BS4 9 D3
Winchester Way GL51 129 F6
Wincombe Trad Est BS2 9 A4
Wincroft BS30 11 C4
Windcliff Cres BS11 16 E7
Windermere Cl GL51 129 E7
Windermere Rd
Bristol BS34 29 A8
Cheltenham GL51 129 E7
Gloucester GL2 127 C4
Windermere Way BS30 11 D6
Windfall Way GL2 127 C2
Windmill Cl BS3 8 E4
Windmill Cotts GL8 82 A6
Windmill Farm Bsns Ctr BS3 8 D4
Windmill Field GL4 119 D7
Windmill Hill BS3 8 D3
Windmill La Bristol BS10 27 D3
Kingscote GL8 82 A6
Windmill Rd Kemble GL7 141 F8
Minchinhampton GL6 91 E6
Windrush SN6 145 C3
Windrush Ct
Temple Guiting GL54 175 A8
Thornbury BS35 51 C8
Windrush Gn BS31 5 A4
Windrush Rd
Cheltenham GL52 134 A2
Gloucester GL4 118 E2
Keynsham BS31 5 A4
Windrush View GL54 175 D2
Windscreens Ave BS2 9 A7
Windsor Ave Bristol BS5 10 B6
Keynsham BS31 4 E4
Windsor Cl BS34 29 E4
Windsor Cres BS10 27 C4
Windsor Ct
14 Bristol,Clifton BS8 7 F6
Bristol,Downend BS16 20 E7
Wick BS30 12 C7
Windsor Dr Lydney GL15 92 B6
Yate BS37 43 D2
Windsor Gr 20 BS5 9 B8
Windsor La GL11 81 A8
Windsor Pl
Bristol,Clifton BS8 7 F6
Bristol,Mangotsfield BS16 21 A5
Stroud GL6 103 B1
Windsor Rd
Bristol,Longwell Green BS30 10 F2
Bristol,Montpelier BS6 18 E2
Dursley GL11 88 B1
3 Tetbury GL8 140 B4
Windsor St GL52 133 F3
Windsor Terr
Bristol,Clifton BS8 7 F6
Windsor Terr *continued*
Bristol,Windmill Hill BS3 8 F4
Cirencester GL7 190 E4
Windsoredge La GL6 91 A6
Windyridge GL6 105 A1
Windyridge Gdns GL50 133 C5
Windyridge Rd GL50 133 C5
Wine St BS1 195 A3
Wineberry Cl BS5 19 D1
Winfield GL18 170 F4
Winfield Rd BS30 11 C7
Winford Ct BS6 18 A5
Winford Gr BS13 2 A8
Winford La BS41 1 C1
Winford Terr BS41 1 C5
Wing La GL20 182 E8
Wingfield Rd BS3 8 E2
Winkworth Pl 4 BS2 18 F1
Winniecroft Cotts GL4 119 D2
Winnycroft La GL4 119 C1
Winsbury Way BS32 40 D1
Winscombe Cl BS31 4 D6
Winsdor Dr GL4 118 C2
Winsford St 2 BS5 9 A8
Winsham Cl BS14 3 B5
Winsley Ct 10 GL4 119 C4
Winsley Rd Bristol BS6 18 D1
Gloucester GL4 119 C4
Winstanley Ho 4 BS5 9 B6
Winston Cl 1 HR8 178 F7
Winston Rd GL3 128 B5
Winstone Ct BS2 194 C3
Winstonian Rd GL52 133 F2
Winterbotham Rd
Cheltenham GL51 132 D2
Dursley GL11 87 F4
Winterbourne Hill BS36 30 D5
Winterbourne Rd BS34 29 E6
Wintersfield GL7 144 F8
Winterspring La GL12 68 F3
Winterstoke Cl 5 BS3 8 B2
Winterstoke Ctr 1 BS3 8 B2
Winterstoke Ho 1 BS3 8 A3
Winterstoke Rd BS3 8 A2
Winterstoke Underpass BS3 7 F4
Winterway GL56 186 C6
Wintle's Hill GL14 157 D8
Wintles Cl GL17 164 D5
Wintles La GL14 165 C3
Winton Cl GL51 130 A7
Winton Rd GL51 130 A7
Winton St BS2 8 F4
Wintour Cl NP16 72 D1
Wirewood Cl NP16 73 A2
Wirewood Cres NP16 73 A2
Wishford Cl GL2 127 E4
Wisloe Rd GL2 95 F2
Wistaria Ave BS37 44 A1
Wistaria Rd 1 GL8 140 B4
Wisteria Ct GL51 130 A4
Wisteria Way GL3 128 A7
Wistley Rd GL53 131 B4
Witch Hazel Rd BS13 2 E3
Witchell Rd BS5 9 C7
Witcombe BS37 32 C7
Witcombe Cl BS15 20 F1
Witcombe Pl GL52 193 C3
Witham Rd BS31 5 A3
Witherlies Rd BS16 19 F6
Withers The GL52 137 F4
Withey Cl W BS9 17 F5
Witheys The BS14 3 C4
Withington CE Prim Sch GL54 166 E2
Withington Cl BS30 11 C2
Withleigh Rd BS4 9 B2
Withy Cl E BS9 17 F6
Withy Mews GL4 119 B5
Withy Trees Rd WR11 188 A8
Withy Way GL11 87 F5
Withybridge Gdns GL51 132 B7
Withybridge La GL51 132 A6
Withyfield Rd GL52 138 A4
Withyholt Ct GL53 130 F5
Withyholt Pk GL53 130 F5
Withymead Rd SN14 15 A8
Withypool 7 GL51 129 E5
Withypool Gdns BS14 3 B5
Withys The BS20 16 D4
Withywood Com Sch BS13 2 A5
Withywood Gdns BS13 1 F4
Withywood Rd BS13 1 F4
Witley Lodge Cl GL51 129 D6
Witney Cl BS31 5 D3
Witney Ct GL50 193 A3
Witney Mead BS36 31 B8
Witpit La GL7 150 F4
Woburn Ave GL4 118 C1
Woburn Cl BS30 10 F5
Woburn Rd BS5 19 B3
Woefuldane Bottom GL6 148 A3
Wolds End Cl 2 GL55 189 A2
Wolferton Rd BS7 18 F2
Wolford Rd GL56 187 D6
Wolfridge Gdns BS10 28 A4
Wolfridge La BS35 50 F4
Wolfridge Ride BS35 50 F4
Wolseley Lodge GL2 127 B2
Wolseley Rd Bristol BS7 18 D3
Gloucester GL2 127 C2
Wood Edge Rd GL16 155 B3
Wood End St GL18 179 B4
Wood End Wlk BS9 17 C6
Wood La
Down Hatherley GL2 173 D1
Gorsley GL18 170 D4
Wood La *continued*
Horton BS37 55 A1
Nailsworth GL6 91 C3
Wood Mews GL2 126 A4
Wood Rd Bristol BS15 10 D8
Mile End GL16 155 B6
Wood St Bristol BS5 19 B2
Bushley GL20 181 C5
Stroud GL5 99 D7
Woodbine Cl GL4 119 E5
Woodbine Rd BS5 9 D8
Woodbines Park Mobile Home Pk GL51 129 C6
Woodborough Cl GL6 103 F7
Woodborough St BS5 19 B1
Woodbridge La GL54 166 E1
Woodbridge Rd BS4 9 A2
Woodbury La BS8 18 A2
Woodchester Bristol BS15 20 E3
Yate BS37 32 E7
Woodchester CE Prim Sch GL5 99 A2
Woodchester Mansion★ GL10 89 F7
Woodchester Park Walks★ GL10 89 D7
Woodchester Pk★ GL10 90 B7
Woodchester Rd BS10 18 C7
Woodcock Cl
Gloucester GL4 119 D5
Stonehouse GL10 101 F1
Woodcock La GL10 97 F8
Woodcote Bristol BS15 10 D6
Gloucester GL2 127 B5
Woodcote Rd BS16 20 B3
Woodcote Wlk BS16 20 B2
Woodcroft Ave BS5 19 D1
Woodcroft Cl Bristol BS4 9 E4
Woodcroft NP16 73 A4
Woodcroft La NP16 73 A4
Woodcroft Rd BS4 9 E4
Woodcroft Terr NP16 73 B4
Woodend BS15 10 D6
Woodend Cl GL4 119 E8
Woodend La Awre GL14 157 B2
Dursley GL11 87 D7
Dursley GL11 87 F6
Gorsley HR9 170 A4
Rockhampton BS35 76 E1
Woodend Rd
Frampton Cotterell BS36 31 C7
Harrow Hill GL17 164 B3
Woodfield Rd Bristol BS6 18 B2
Dursley GL11 87 E4
6 Ledbury HR8 178 E7
Woodford Ct GL4 119 B7
Woodgate Cl
Charlton Kings GL52 131 C5
Gloucester GL4 119 E8
Woodgate Rd
Cinderford GL14 191 D5
Mile End GL16 155 B7
Woodgrove Rd BS10 27 D2
Woodhall Cl BS16 20 F6
Woodhouse Ave BS32 40 D7
Woodhouse Cl
Cirencester GL7 190 B3
Woodhouse Down BS32 40 D6
Woodhouse Dr GL5 99 B6
Woodhouse Gr BS7 18 E6
Woodington Ct 1 BS30 10 F4
Woodland Ave
Bristol BS15 20 D2
Dursley GL11 88 A2
Woodland Cl BS15 20 C2
Woodland Ct BS9 17 C3
Woodland Dr GL11 88 A2
Woodland Gn GL4 119 E3
Woodland Gr BS9 17 D6
Woodland Pl GL15 156 B2
Woodland Rd
Berry Hill GL16 155 A7
Bream GL15 155 D1
Bristol BS8 194 C4
Coleford GL16 154 F8
Drybrook GL17 164 B4
Leyhill GL12 66 B4
Parkend GL15 155 E3
Woodland Rise
Lydney GL15 92 B4
Parkend GL15 155 E3
Woodland Terr
Bristol,Kingswood BS15 10 E7
Bristol,Redland BS6 18 B2
Woodland View
Joy's Green GL17 163 D3
Leonard Stanley GL10 97 F3
Monmouth/Trefynwy NP25 154 A7
Ruspidge GL14 156 C6
Woodmancote GL7 158 B4
Woodland Way BS15 20 C2
Woodlands
Bristol,Downend BS16 20 E6
Bristol,Patchway BS32 40 D3
Bristol,Sneyd Park BS9 17 E3
Leonard Stanley GL10 97 E3
North The NP25 154 B1
Tytherington GL12 52 B6
Woodlands Cl
St Arvans NP16 72 B6
Whitecroft GL15 155 E1
Woodlands Ct BS32 40 B3
Woodlands Dr GL5 99 E8
Woodlands La
Berkeley GL13 85 A1
Bristol BS32 40 C3
Woodhouse Down BS32 40 E5

Woodlands Park Cvn Pk
GL50 ....133 D5
Woodlands Pk
Bristol BS32 ....40 C3
Quedgeley GL2 ....117 D1
Woodlands Rd
Charfield GL12 ....67 A4
Cheltenham GL51 ....130 B5
Cirencester GL7 ....190 B2
Tytherington GL12 ....52 B6
Woodlands Reach
GL14 ....191 D4
Woodlands Rise BS16 ..20 D6
Woodlands The
Llandogo NP25 ....146 B7
Stroud GL5 ....99 D8
Woodleaze BS9 ....17 B6
Woodleigh BS35 ....64 C1
Woodleigh Cl 9 HR8 ..178 E8
Woodleigh Field GL2 ..125 E6
Woodleigh Gdns BS14 ....3 C6
Woodleigh Rd HR8 .....178 E8
Woodmancote
Dursley GL11 ....80 B7
Yate BS37 ....32 D8
Woodmancote Rd 7 BS6 18 E1
Woodmancote Sch
GL52 ....138 B4
Woodmancote Vale
GL52 ....138 B3
Woodmans Cl BS37 .....33 B8
Woodmans Rd BS37 .....33 C8
Woodmans Vale BS37 ...33 C8
Woodmans Way GL52 ..137 F3
Woodmarsh Cl BS14 ......3 A4
Woodmead Gdns BS13 ...2 C4
Woodmead La BS30 .....23 A1
Woodnook The BS10 ....28 C2
Woodpecker Cres BS16 ..22 C4
Woodpecker Rd GL2 ...118 C5
Woodpecker Wlk GL6 ...90 F5
Woodpeckers Cl GL19 ..172 D5
Woodrow Way GL2 .....118 A3
Woodruff Cl GL4 ....119 B4
Woodrush Rd GL20 .....192 E2
Woods Cl SN16 ....58 C1
Woods Orch GL4 ......118 F2
Woods Orchard Rd GL4 .118 E2
Woodside Bristol BS9 ....17 D3
Stroud GL5 ....99 F8
Turkdean GL54 ....167 F4
Woolaston GL15 ....147 B3
Woodside Ave GL14 .....191 D3
Woodside Gr BS10 ......27 D3
Woodside La GL10 ......97 F2
Woodside Prim Sch
GL17 ....163 F3
Woodside Rd
Bristol,Downend BS16 .....20 C7
Bristol,Kingswood BS15 ...10 C7
Bristol,St Anne's Park BS4 ...9 E6
Coalpit Heath BS36 ....31 E6
Woolaston GL15 ....147 B3
Woodside St GL14 ......191 D4
Woodside Terr GL6 .....102 F3
Woodstock Ave BS6 .....18 C1
Woodstock Cl
Avening GL8 ....148 A1
Bristol BS15 ....10 F8
Woodstock La GL8 .....148 A1
Woodstock Rd
Bristol,Kingswood BS15 ....10 F7
Bristol,Redland BS6 ......18 C2
Woodstock Sch BS10 ....27 E2
Woodstock Terr GL11 ....89 C1
Woodview
Four Oaks GL18 ....170 D7
Frampton Mansell GL6 ...148 E5
Woodview Cl BS11 ......16 E7
Woodview Rd GL11 .....88 A4
Woodville Ave GL16 ....155 C6
Woodville Rd
Cinderford GL14 ....191 E4
Tewkesbury GL20 ....192 D1
Woodville Rd W GL14 ..191 E4
Woodward Ave BS37 ....43 B1
Woodward Cl GL8 ......140 B5
Woodward Dr BS30 ......10 F4
Woodwell Rd BS11 ......16 E5
Woodyleaze Dr BS15 ....10 D6
Woolaston Comm GL15 .147 C3
Woolaston Prim Sch
GL15 ....147 C3
Woolaway Bglws GL56 .187 A6
Woolcot St BS6 ....18 B2
Woollard La BS14 ....3 E1
Woolley Rd BS14 ....3 E5
Woolmarket The GL7 ...190 D5
Woolpitch Wood/Coed
Woolpitch NP16 ....60 C8
Woolridge Hill GL19 ...172 C2
Woolstone La GL52 .....137 F8
Woolstrop Way GL2 ....118 A3
Woolthorpe La GL2 ....157 C6
Wootton Cres BS4 ....9 E6
Wootton Pk BS14,BS4 .....9 B1
Wootton Rd BS4 ....9 F6
Worcester Cl BS16 ......20 B2
Worcester Cres BS8 ....194 A4
Worcester Ct BS8 ......194 A4
Worcester Par GL1 .....196 B4
Worcester Rd
Bristol,Clifton BS8 ......194 A4
Bristol,Kingswood BS15 ...20 D1
Cinderford GL14 ....191 E5
Corse GL19 ....172 B6
Ledbury HR8 ....178 F8
Worcester St GL1 ......196 B3
Worcester Terr BS8 ....194 A4
Worcester Wlk GL16 ...155 C6
Wordens The GL5 ....98 D8
Wordings Mount GL6 ...104 E8
Wordsworth Ave GL51 ..132 E1
Wordsworth Ho BS34 ....29 A8
Wordsworth Rd
Bristol BS7 ....19 B7
Dursley GL11 ....80 C7
Working La GL54 ......183 E1
Workshop Rd BS11 ......26 C4
World of Mechanical Music
Mus★ GL54 ....168 A1
World's End La BS31 .....5 C5
Worlds End La GL12 .....68 C7
Worldsend La GL13 .....76 E7
Worley Ridge GL6 ....91 A4
Wormwood Hill GL6 .....91 A1
Worrall Mews 10 BS8 ....18 A2
Worrall Pl 11 BS8 ....18 A2
Worrall Rd BS8 ....18 A2
Worrel's La BS16 ....30 D3
Worsley St BS5 ....9 D7
Worthing Rd BS34 ....28 F8
Worthy Cl BS15 ....10 F6
Worthy Rd BS11 ....26 D7
Worthys The BS34 ....30 A6
Wortley Rd GL12 ....68 C6
Wortley Terr GL12 ....68 C6
Wotton Cres GL12 ....68 C6
Wotton Ct GL4 ....127 D1
Wotton Elms Ct 4 GL2 .127 B2
Wotton Heritage Ctr★
GL12 ....68 B7
Wotton Lawn Hospl
GL1 ....127 A2
Wotton Rd Charfield GL12 .67 B5
Iron Acton BS37 ....42 F5
Kingswood GL12 ....67 F5
Wragg Castle La GL6 ...103 C6
Wragg Ct GL11 ....88 A5
Wraggs Row 22 GL54 ...176 F4
Wraxall Gr BS13 ....2 A8
Wraxall Rd BS30 ....11 A6
Wren Cl Bristol BS16 .....19 E7
Gloucester GL4 ....119 B6
Wren Dr BS16 ....20 A6
Wren Terr GL3 ....127 D6
Wrenbert Rd BS16 ......20 D5
Wright Cl GL54 ....169 D7
Wright Rd GL54 ....169 D7
Wright Way BS16 ....19 E8
Wrington Cl BS34 ....29 C7
Wrington Cres BS13 ......2 A7
Wroughton Dr BS13 ......2 D4
Wroughton Gdns BS13 ...2 D4
Wroxham Dr BS34 ......29 C8
Wyatt Ave BS13 ....1 F5
Wyatt Cl BS13 ....1 F5
Wyatt Ct GL54 ....166 E5
Wyatts View BS4 ....9 E6
Wychbury Cl GL53 .....130 D5
Wychwood BS15 ....10 E6
Wychwood Ct GL56 ....187 B3
Wyck Beck Rd BS10 .....28 A3
Wyck Rissington GL54 ..169 C8
Wycliffe Coll GL10 ......97 F6
Wycliffe Prep Sch GL10 .98 A6
Wycliffe Rd BS9 ....18 B7
Wycliffe Row 9 BS3 ......8 F4
Wycombe Gr BS4 ....9 D2
Wydelands GL56 ....186 E6
Wye Cres NP16 ....60 E7
Wye Croft Cl BS10 ......28 D3
Wye Ct BS35 ....51 C8
Wye Rapids Cotts HR9 .162 E2
Wye Rd GL3 ....120 F5
Wye Valley Link Rd NP16 .60 E5
Wye View Ho NP16 ......61 A7
Wye View La HR9 ......162 E3
Wye View Terr NP25 ....154 C4
Wye's Gn NP25 ....154 C4
Wyebank Ave NP16 ......73 A1
Wyebank Cl NP16 ....61 A8
Wyebank Cres NP16 .....61 A8
Wyebank Dr NP16 ....73 A1
Wyebank Pl NP16 ....61 A8
Wyebank Rd NP16 ....61 A8
Wyebank Rise NP16 .....61 A8
Wyebank View NP16 .....61 A8
Wyebank Way NP16 .....61 A7
Wyebridge St 17 NP25 ..154 A7
Wyedale Ave BS9 ....17 C7
Wyedean Cl GL15 ....92 C2
Wyedean Sch NP16 ......61 A8
Wyelands Pk GL17 .....163 D4
Wyelands View NP16 ....60 B4
Wyesham Ave/Rhodfa
Wyesham 4 NP25 ....154 A7
Wyesham Inf Sch NP25 .154 A7
Wyesham Jun Sch
NP25 ....154 A7
Wyesham La (Sky Farm La)
NP25 ....154 B7
Wyesham Rd NP25 .....154 B7
Wyeside Commercial Ctr 25
NP25 ....154 A7
Wyeside Pk HR9 ....163 C5
Wykis Ct BS15 ....10 E5
Wyman's La GL51 ......133 B6
Wyman's Rd GL52 ......134 A3
Wymans Ct GL50 ....133 C5
Wymbush Cres BS13 .....2 C5
Wymbush Gdns BS13 .....2 C5
Wyndbrook La GL19 ....179 F4
Wyndcliffe View NP16 ...72 B5
Wyndecliffe Ho NP16 ....61 A7
Wyndham Cres
Bristol BS4 ....10 A3
Easton-in-G BS20 ....16 B4
Wyndham Ct BS2 ......195 B4
Wynford Villas GL19 ....171 C1
Wynols Cl 6 GL16 .....155 B5
Wynols Ct 7 GL16 .....155 B5
Wynols Hill La GL16 ....155 B5
Wynols Rd GL16 ....155 B5
Wynstones Dr GL4 .....110 F5
Wynstones Sch GL4 ....110 E8
Wynstones The BS15 ....10 C7
Wyntour Ho NP16 ....61 A8
Wyntour's Par GL15 .....92 A2
Wynyards Cl GL20 .....192 D4
Wyvern Rd NP16 ....61 B1
Wyvern Villas BS9 ....18 A8

Y

Y Paddgau/The Paddocks 6
NP25 ....154 A7
Yalta Cl 16 GL51 ....132 E2
Yanleigh Cl BS13 ....1 D6
Yanley La BS41,BS13 ......1 C7
Yard The BS2 ....19 A3
Yarlington Cl GL52 .....137 E4
Yarnells Alley 14 GL20 ..192 C4
Yarnold Terr GL51 ......133 A4
Yarnolds GL51 ....129 E1
Yarrow Cl GL4 ....119 A4
Yartleton La GL17 .....165 A7
Yate Her Ctr★ BS37 .....43 E2
Yate Rd BS37 ....42 F3
Yate Rocks BS37 ....43 F7
Yate Sta BS37 ....43 C2
Yatton Cl BS13 ....1 F8
Yeaman's Ho BS1 ......195 B1
Yeldham Mews GL52 ...133 F4
Yellow Hundred Cl GL11 .80 C8
Yelverton Rd BS4 ....9 E1
Yeomans Cl BS9 ....17 D5
Yeomanside Cl BS14 .....3 C5
Yeomeads BS41 ....7 A1
Yetts The NP16 ....61 B8
Yew Tree Cl
Cheltenham GL50 ....133 C5
Shipton GL54 ....166 E5
Whitchurch HR9 ....162 D4
Yew Tree Cott 10 GL6 ...148 B6
Yew Tree Cotts 16 GL54 .176 F4
Yew Tree Ct Bristol BS14 ...3 B5
8 Broadway WR12 .....185 C8
Yew Tree Dr Bristol BS15 ..20 F3
Gotherington GL52 ....138 A8
Yew Tree Gdns BS20 .....16 C4
Yew Tree Way
Churchdown GL3 ....128 A5
Thrupp GL5 ....99 E3
Yew Tree Wood NP16 ....60 B8
Yewcroft Cl BS14 ....3 A4
Yewtree Cl GL11 ....87 D3
Yokehouse La GL6 .....104 A6
York Ave BS7 ....18 F4
York Bldgs BS3 ....8 E4
York Cl
Bristol,Bromley Heath BS16 30 F1
Bristol,Stoke Gifford BS34 .29 D4
Yate BS37 ....43 E4
York Ct BS2 ....195 B4
York Gdns Bristol BS8 .....7 F6
Winterbourne BS36 ....30 F8
York Pl
Bristol,Brandon Hill BS1 ..194 C2
Bristol,Victoria Park BS8 ..194 B3
York Rd
Bristol,Lower Easton BS5 ..19 C1
Bristol,Montpelier BS6 ....18 E1
Bristol,Staple Hill BS16 ....20 E4
Bristol,Windmill Hill BS3 ....8 E4
Cinderford GL14 ....191 E5
Gloucester GL4 ....119 C8
Tewkesbury GL20 ....192 C2
York Row GL52 ....134 A4
York St
Bristol,Baptist Mills BS2 ...19 A2
2 Bristol,Clifton BS8 .....18 A2
9 Bristol,Redfield BS5 .....9 C7
Bristol,St Pauls BS2 .....195 B4
Cheltenham GL52 ....193 C4
Yorkley La GL15 ....156 A1
Yorkley Prim Sch GL15 .156 A1
Yorkley Wood Rd GL15 .156 A1
Youngs Cotts GL6 .....148 B4
Youngs Ct BS16 ....21 B8
Youngs Orch
Brimscombe GL5 ....148 A5
Gloucester GL4 ....119 D6
Yr Hen Heol/The Old Rd 22
NP25 ....154 A7

Z

Zetland Rd BS6 ....18 D2
Zinc Rd BS11 ....26 C3
Zinnia Cl GL3 ....127 F7
Zion Apartments 12
GL16 ....155 A7
Zion Hill GL6 ....102 F3
Zoons Rd GL3 ....120 A8

Notes

Name and Address	Telephone	Page	Grid reference